*Human Development
Across the Life Span*

Human Development Across the Life Span

Fergus P. Hughes
Lloyd D. Noppe

University of Wisconsin–
Green Bay

with contributions from
Illene C. Noppe
University of Wisconsin–
Green Bay

Merrill, an imprint of
Macmillan Publishing Company
New York

Collier Macmillan Canada, Inc.
Toronto

Maxwell Macmillan International Publishing Group
New York   Oxford   Singapore   Sydney

Cover Image: Jasper Johns, *0 through 9*, © Jasper Johns/VAGA New York 1990
Title Page Photo: Gale Zucker

Administrative Editor: Linda A. Sullivan
Developmental Editor: Linda Kauffman Peterson
Production Editor: Peg Connelly Gluntz
Art Coordinator: Mark D. Garrett
Photo Editor: Gail Meese
Cover Designer: Brian Deep
Production Buyer: Janice E. Wagner

This book was set in Usherwood.

Macmillan Publishing Company
866 Third Avenue, New York, NY 10022

Collier Macmillan Canada, Inc.

Library of Congress Catalog Card Number: 90-61449
International Standard Book Number: 0-675-21241-3

Printing: 1 2 3 4 5 6 7 8 9
Year: 1 2 3 4

To my wife, Bonnie,
and to my children,
Peter and Jonathan,
with love
—F. P. H.

For Illene, Alex, and Laura
my beautiful family
—L. D. N.

About the Authors

Fergus Hughes is a Professor of Human Development at the University of Wisconsin–Green Bay, where he has been teaching courses on child, adolescent, and adult development since 1972. A native of Dublin, Ireland, he was raised there, in Toronto, and in the New York City area. He earned his B.A. degree from St. John's University, New York, and his M.A. and Ph.D. degrees from Syracuse University.

Professor Hughes is an active scholar and writer. In addition to co-authoring this book, he has written other development texts. His scholarly articles have appeared in such journals as *Developmental Psychology, Journal of Genetic Psychology,* and *Academic Psychology Bulletin*. In 1987 he was the co-author of a chapter in *The Annual Review of Psychology*. He maintains a strong commitment to undergraduate teaching, with classes ranging in size from 20 to 300, and he has been honored by his faculty colleagues for teaching excellence.

Lloyd D. Noppe is Chairperson of the Human Development Program at the University of Wisconsin–Green Bay, with which he has been affiliated since 1980. Born in Forest Hills, New York, he earned his B.A. degree from Lake Forest College and his Ph.D. degree from Temple University. He has taught courses ranging from life span and child and adolescent development, to tests and measurements and educational psychology.

In addition to this book, Professor Noppe co-authored another textbook on child development. He has also published articles in the *Journal of Personality Assessment,* the *Journal of Creative Behavior,* and the *Journal of Genetic Psychology,* and has contributed to other books and professional symposia. In addition to his teaching and scholarly activities, he has consulted on a variety of educational evaluation programs and frequently presents workshops for teachers and other school personnel. He is currently studying the longitudinal sequelae of high-risk neonates during the infancy, early childhood, and school-age years.

Preface

One of the most intriguing questions about human development has no easy answer: "If I had my life to live over again, how would I do it differently?" Speculation about lost dreams, missed opportunities, and "roads not taken" are common when people assess the quality of their lives. But the answers are found only in the realm of the theoretical, because, as far as we know, the process of human development happens only once to each of us. Fortunately, however, this is not the case for human development textbooks. A new edition is, in a sense, a second life—one in which a writer hopes to improve significantly upon the first one.

In this edition, we have given much thought to how we have presented the content of human development and have remained true to our original purpose—to present a topical approach, with an interdisciplinary emphasis that blends the theoretical and the applied. Our philosophy also reflects the respect we have for our readers and is represented in a writing style that is readable, but also challenging. So let us look at the content and features of the text to give you a sense of what *Human Development: Across the Life Span* entails and how our purpose and philosophy have been translated in the text.

ORIENTATION OF THE TEXT

A Topical Approach

We have chosen to present a topical approach to the study of human development because it offers the student a richer feel for the interrelatedness of the developmental process. At the same time, this approach underscores the fact that the human life span is a product of many influences; to divide it into arbitrary age segments denies the multiplicity of our lives. In short, we believe that this book's topical approach most closely approximates the actual continuous nature of human development.

Interdisciplinary Emphasis

Though human development is not the equivalent of developmental psychology, it does encompass the areas of biology, sociology, and cultural anthropology, and so we have also chosen to emphasize the interdisciplinary nature of human development. Many of the contributions to the field of human development come from these disciplines, as will be evident throughout the text. You will also see in Chapter 1 that many of our current ideas are rooted in the works of philosophers. This emphasis remains at the core of human development, as well as at the core of our book. Since it also remains at the core of our experience in the university, we continue to present this perspective here.

A Balance of Theory and Research

Another feature of this is the in-depth coverage of the topics. Though we reject the encyclopedic concept of textbook writing, in which many topics are covered but a few in depth, we do provide extensive coverage of theory and research in our field. Instead of putting the major theoretical perspectives in a single chapter on developmental theory, though, we carry them throughout the book, so the ideas of Freud, Erikson, and Piaget are discussed in a number of chapters. We have presented comprehensive reviews of the classic and current research in our field and often have discussed specific studies in some detail. This coverage of research and theory, however, should not intimidate you, because it is research and theory that move this field of study forward. We apply these presentations to human development in tangible and understandable ways that will help you make the connections between theory and its application.

Readability

Human development is an inherently appealing field of study for college students, but its appeal is enhanced considerably if the material is presented in an interesting way. We hope that we have done so and that our enthusiasm for the subject is both obvious and infectious; we hope you will be challenged by unanswered questions rather than frustrated. We want you to do more than learn a set of facts about human development; we want you to think about what you have learned and perhaps someday be motivated enough to seek the answers on your own. And to foster this curiosity and transfer of knowledge, we have written the text with you in mind. You should find the chapters both interesting and readable, and hopefully this will encourage and facilitate your learning.

Real-World Applications

We are unwilling to accept the view that the college student of today is unable to deal with abstractions and responds only to the most concrete presentations of material. In fact, we have included many interesting real-world applications of theory and research, but much to be learned in our field is more theoretical than applied. Similarly, contradictions and complexities in human development cannot and should not be simplified, even for

students at the introductory level, so sometimes we will challenge you as we remain true to the integrity of the field and its foundations in theory.

PEDAGOGICAL AIDS

Chapter Outlines

Each of our 15 chapters opens with an outline of the material that is included in that chapter. These outlines serve as a guide for organizing what we cover and are also a good tool for reviewing chapter contents as you study.

Margin Notes and Key Terms

To make the meanings of key terms and concepts more accessible for you as you read and review, we provide definitions of the terms in the margins throughout every chapter. In addition, the terms are in boldface type in the text and are again referenced at the end of each chapter with a page number. (A glossary at the end of the book provides concise definitions of all the terms highlighted in the text.)

Special Features

Each chapter contains pedagogical features designed to enrich the learning experience by focusing on examples of developmental research, pressing issues in the field, or applications of human development principles in real-world situations. These special features appear in the text under the following designations:

 Research Close-up describes a particular study in some detail and is designed to show how individual studies attempt to answer general questions about the developmental process, as well as illustrate many of the research strategies discussed in Chapter 2.

 Issues in Human Development focuses on controversies or unanswered questions, such as "Who Is the Hyperactive Child?"

(Chapter 6), "Is There a Cultural Bias in IQ Testing?" (Chapter 8), and "What Happens When Mother Goes to Work?" (Chapter 11).

 Applying Our Knowledge illustrates practical applications of developmental principles to assist students in recognizing that theory and research can often be directly relevant to problem solving in the everyday world.

Summary

A numbered list of important concepts and content appears at the close of each chapter. This information and the concepts also serve as an excellent review tool and can be a check to make sure you remember the chapter emphasis.

Review Questions

Review questions at the end of every chapter serve to extend and reinforce your knowledge and expand the application of the chapter's contents. These also serve as another tool by which you can monitor your comprehension of the chapter.

Suggested Readings

An annotated list of suggested readings encourages your investigation of and curiosity about subjects contained within each chapter. You may want to refer to these as sources for class assignments or simply for your own personal and professional development.

Glossary

A glossary at the end of the text with definitions of the terms highlighted in the text can refresh your memory of terms used in previous chapters.

References

A complete list of references at the end of the book provides complete bibliographic information for all the sources we cite.

WHAT'S NEW IN THIS EDITION?

Updated References

It goes without saying that one of the major purposes of a new edition is to present the student with the most recent information in the field—a task of particular importance in the social sciences, where changes in the state of our knowledge occur almost continuously. We have made extensive efforts to update our material since the previous edition, adding more than 1,000 new research references.

Structural Improvements

In addition to updating our research base, we have incorporated a number of organizational changes:

- Chapter 1, "Concepts and Theories," includes an introduction to human development, a history of developmental theory, and major theoretical perspectives.
- Chapter 3, "Physical Growth and Development," now includes material on prenatal development and birth, and Chapter 4, "Sexuality," explores the nature of human sexuality, which parallels our physical growth and development.
- A new chapter, Chapter 6, "Information Processing: Attention, Learning, and Memory," emphasizes recent research in learning. It and Chapter 7, "Cognitive Development," present two of the most current areas of present-day research focus in human development., Chapter 8, "Intelligence and Creativity," then builds upon the knowledge bases of the two previous chapters.
- "Morality" now stands on its own as Chapter 13 to allow a greater focus and depth of study.

Expanded Emphasis

Some changes in the new edition reflect current thought in the focus and emphasis of topics. Expanded coverage of adult development throughout the text and of infancy is evident. A conscientious effort to recognize the contributions of women, to focus greater attention on the development of the family as a system throughout the life span, and to include additional material on variations from the traditional family resulted in a text that truly reflects the complexity of human development.

All of these elements make this edition a more realistic reflection of human development in the 1990s, as well as a text that is attentive to variations from typical (and stereotypical) patterns of human development.

ACKNOWLEDGMENTS

A textbook reflects the work of many people in addition to the authors, and we would like to acknowledge the contributions of several who helped make this book possible. First we would like to offer a special thanks to Illene C. Noppe for writing the chapters on "Gender Roles" and "Death and Dying," areas in which she has a particular expertise. Illene did a wonderful job for us because she is a painstaking and methodical researcher, an excellent writer, and, perhaps most important, a dedicated and widely respected teacher.

We would also like to acknowledge the special assistance and encouragement provided by three of our editors at Merrill: Dave Faherty, a longtime friend, was one of the first people to see merit in this project, and worked energetically in his role as Acquisitions Editor to bring us and Merrill together. Linda Peterson, our Developmental Editor, then assumed the responsibility for directing the project. She digested the reviews for us, made numerous helpful suggestions, listened to and respected our concerns, and provided much encouragement along the way. Finally, Peg Gluntz, our Production Editor, worked closely with us in the final phase of the project, cheerfully attending to numerous details and making the production process as pleasant and stress-free as possible.

In addition, we would like to acknowledge the assistance of reviewers from colleges and universities throughout the country who helped us refine our manuscript and assisted us with our goal of producing the finest text possible. Their constructive comments helped shape the book in many positive ways. For their participation, we offer our thanks to Lynne Baker-Ward, North Carolina State University; Nancy S. Elman, University of Pittsburgh; Megan P. Goodwin, Central Michigan University; Jaqueline V. Lerner, Pennsylvania State University; Becky White Loewy, San Francisco State University; Sharyl Bender Peterson, St. Norbert College; Mary Ellen Ross, St. Olaf College; and M. Virginia Wyly, Buffalo State College.

Finally, we would like to acknowledge the invaluable contributions of our student research assistants, Susan Jacquet and June Smet. Susan and June spent many hours in the library reading journals, assembling annotated bibliographies, and tracking down elusive references. They also put a considerable amount of time into entering references into our computer, and we could not have completed this project without them.

Contents in Brief

Chapter One
Introduction: Concepts and Theories   3

Chapter Two
Methodological Approaches   37

Chapter Three
Physical Growth and Development   69

Chapter Four
Sexuality   125

Chapter Five
Perceptual Development   167

Chapter Six
Information Processing: Attention,
Learning, and Memory   207

Chapter Seven
Cognitive Development   255

Chapter Eight
Intelligence and Creativity   295

Chapter Nine
Language   339

Chapter Ten
Personality and the Self   383

Chapter Eleven
Family Development   437

Chapter Twelve
Social Interaction   495

Chapter Thirteen
Morality   547

Chapter Fourteen
Gender Roles and Gender Differences   579

Chapter Fifteen
Death and Dying   625

Glossary   G–1

References   R–1

Index   I–1

Contents

Chapter One
Introduction: Concepts and Theories — 3

Characteristics of Human Development — 4

An Individual Experience 4 | A Life-Span Process 6 | An Interdisciplinary Study 8

Issues in Human Development — 10

Heredity and Environment 11 | Development and Change 12 | Ages, Stages, and Continuity 14

Theoretical Perspectives — 15

Meaning and Purpose of Theory 15 | History of Developmental Theory 16 | Issues in Human Development: Do We Really Value Children? 20 | Modern Perspectives on Development 23

Chapter Two
Methodological Approaches — 37

The Scientific Method — 38

Establishing the Problem 38 | Methodology for the Study 39 | Research Close-up: Prematurity and the Scientific Method 40 | Analysis of the Results 41 | Interpretation of the Research 44

Research Strategies — 44

Experimental Approach 45 | Nonexperimental Methods 46 | Studying Individuals 47 | Issues in Human Development: The Ethics of Research 48 | The Laboratory or the Field? 50 | Problems in Doing Research 51

Procedures for Collecting Data — 52

Survey Method 52 | Observational Method 53 | Testing Method 56

Developmental Designs — 58

Cross-sectional Research 59 | Longitudinal Research 60 | Time Lag Research 62 | Sequential Research 63 | Applying Our Knowledge: The Use of Developmental Theory and Research 65

Chapter Three
Physical Growth and Development — 69

Determiners of Growth — 70

Genetic Plan 70 | Message of the Hormones 71

Prenatal Development and Birth — 73

Stages of Prenatal Development 74 | Applying Our Knowledge: Testing for Genetic Disorders in the Fetus 78 | Influences on Fetal Development 81 | The Birth Process 86 | The Newborn Child 88

Patterns of Growth: Birth to Old Age — 93

Brain Development 94 | Body Development 96 | Issues in Human Development: Are Children Growing Up Faster Than Their Parents Did? 98

Individual Variations in Growth — 107

Early and Late Maturation at Puberty 107 | Individual Variations in Aging 112

Psychological Issues in Physical Development — 113

Ideal Physique and Body Satisfaction 113 | Body Image, Self-Esteem, and Social Interaction 116 | Physical Attractiveness and Social Desirability 118 | Research Close-Up: The Stereotyping of Attractiveness Among the Elderly 120

Chapter Four
Sexuality   *125*

Sexual Anatomy and Function   126

Prenatal Development 127 | Female Reproductive
System 129 | Male Reproductive System 132

Sexual Behavior and Development   134

Infant Experiences 135 | Childhood Interests and
Activities 137 | Issues in Human Development: Child
Sexual Abuse 138 | Adolescent Attitudes and Behaviors
140 | Adult Practices and Values 145 | Research Close-
up: The Gap Between Adolescent Sexual Attitudes and
Behaviors 146 | Applying Our Knowledge: Sexual
Behavior and AIDS 152 | Characteristics of the Elderly
155

Gender Roles and Sexuality   160

Chapter Five
Perceptual Development   *167*

Sensory Processes   168

Vision 168 | Issues in Human Development: How Can
Infant Perception Be Studied? 170 | Research Close-up:
The Visual Cliff 178 | Audition 182 | Research Close-
up: Sensory Impairment and Intellectual Functioning in
Middle Age 188 | Taste 190 | Smell 193 | Touch 195 |
Integration of the Senses 196

Cognitive Aspects of Perception   197

Environmental Influences on Perception 198 | Applying
Our Knowledge: Learning to Read 200 | Theories of
Perceptual Development 202

Chapter Six
Information Processing: Attention,
Learning, and Memory   *207*

Attention   208

Infancy 209 | Later Childhood 210 | Issues in Human
Development: Who Is the Hyperactive Child? 212 |
Adulthood and Old Age 214

Learning   215

Conditioning 216 | Applying Our Knowledge:
Conditioning as Therapy: Behavior Modification 222 |
Social Learning 225 | The Adult Learner 234 |

Research Close-up: The Elderly Need Supportive
Learning Environments 238

Memory   239

Types of Memory 240 | Factors Influencing Memory
241 | Memory Development in Childhood 243 |
Memory Development in Adulthood 245 |
Metamemory 250

Chapter Seven
Cognitive Development   *255*

The Theory of Jean Piaget   256

Content of Intelligence 257 | Structure of Intelligence
257 | Function of Intelligence 258 | Motivation for
Growth 258

Piaget's Stages of Development   259

Sensorimotor Development 259 | Pre-operational
Development 265 | Research Close-up: Lucienne and
the Silver Watch Chain: An Early Mental Solution to a
Problem 266 | Issues in Human Development: Did
Piaget Underestimate the Preschool Mind? 270 |
Concrete Operations Stage 272 | Formal Operations
Stage 278

Cognitive Development in the Adult Years   281

Operational Task Performance During Adulthood 281 |
Beyond Formal Operations? 283 | Applying Our
Knowledge: Piaget's Theory and Education 284 |
Instead of Formal Operations: Beyond Piaget 284

Environmental Influences
on Cognitive Development   286

Cross-cultural Perspectives 286 | Influence of
Education 288 | Family Factors 289 | Nutritional
Factors 290

Chapter Eight
Intelligence and Creativity   *295*

Nature of Intelligence   296

Definitions of Intelligence 296 | Intelligence Testing
299 | Applying Our Knowledge: Interpreting an IQ
Score 304 | What IQ Scores Really Predict 305 | Issues
in Human Development: Defining Mental Retardation
306 | Issues in Human Development: Is There a
Cultural Bias in IQ Testing? 310

Development of Intelligence   310

Childhood 311 | Adulthood 311

Genetic Influences of Intelligence   318

Heredity-Environment Interaction 319 | Meaning of
Heritability 322

Environmental Influences of Intelligence   323

Child-rearing Patterns 324 | Nutrition 325 | Birth Order
and Family Size 325 | Gender Roles 326

Construct of Creativity   326

Creative Personality 327 | Creative Process 327 |
Creative Product 329

Development of Creativity   330

Theories of Creative Development 330 | Developmental
Patterns 330

Chapter Nine
Language   339

Nature of Communication   340

Issues in Language Development 341 | Research Close-
up: Can Chimpanzees Use Language? 342 | Five
Components of Language Study 344

Infant Antecedents of Language   347

Early Sounds 348 | From Words to Sentences 349 |
Applying Our Knowledge: Language Acquisition in the
Deaf 350 | Understanding and Communicating 352

Early Childhood and the
Linguistic Explosion   354

Improving Speech 354 | Emergence of Grammar 355 |
Semantics and Pragmatics 357

Language Refinements of Later
Childhood and Adolescence   358

Words and Sentences Revisited 359 | Meanings and
Conversations 360 | Issues in Human Development:
Learning a Second Language 362

Course of Language During
Adulthood and Old Age   363

Adult Skills and Patterns 364 | Are There Deficits
Among the Elderly? 365

Theories of Language Development   366

Behavioral Approach 367 | Nativist Approach 369 |
Interactionist Approach 371

Variations in Language Development   373

Communication and Socioeconomic Status 374 |
Dialect Differences 376

Chapter Ten
Personality and the Self   383

Freud's Psychoanalytic Revolution   385

Basic Principles 386 | Personality Structures 388 |
Stages of Development 389 | Psychoanalytic
Controversy 393

Erikson's Psychosocial Modifications   393

Basic Principles 393 | Issues in Human Development:
Neoanalytic Critiques of Freud's Theory 394 | Stages of
Development 395 | Psychosocial Evaluation 402

Development of the Self   403

Research Close-up: James Marcia and the Identity Sta-
tus Interview 404 | Maslow's Hierarchy of Needs 406 |
What Is the Self? 408 | Development of the
Self-Concept 410 | Self-Esteem and Life Satisfaction
414 | Applying Our Knowledge: A Positive Note on the
Institutionalization of the Elderly 416

Issues in Personality Development   417

Does Personality Have Biological Origins? 418 | How
Does Culture Affect Personality? 421 | Does Personality
Change Across the Life Span? 423 | How Does
Personality Development Deviate from "Normality"? 427

Chapter Eleven
Family Development   437

The Family System   438

The Family Life Cycle   438

Marriage 439 | Becoming a Parent: The Childbearing
Years 443 | The Childhood Years of the Family 455 |
Issues in Human Development: What Happens When
Mother Goes to Work? 460 | The Adult Family 469 |
Research Close-up: Behavioral Expectations of
Grandparenthood 476

The Disrupted Family   477

Divorce: The Adult's Point of View 478 | Issues in
Human Development: Divorce After 60: Too Old to
Start Over? 480 | Divorce: The Child's Point of View
481 | Stepparents and Stepchildren 487

Chapter Twelve
Social Interaction   *495*

Development of Social Awareness   496

Childhood and Adolescence 496 | Research Close-up:
Concern for the Victim 502 | Social Cognition in
Adulthood 504

Patterns of Social Interaction   506

Infant Peer Interaction 507 | The Childhood Peer Group
509 | Issues in Human Development: What are the
Origins of Shyness 510 | Adolescent Groups and Dating
511 | Characteristics of Popularity 513 | Applying Our
Knowledge: Helping the Unpopular Child 514 |
Adulthood Socialization Patterns 517 | Disengagement
or Continued Activity in Later Life? 521

Play and Socialization   522

What Is Play? 523 | Theories of Play 523 |
Developmental Patterns in Play 528

Work in the Life Cycle   536

Early Basis for Adult Work 537 | Occupational Choice
and Personality 538 | Women in the Work Force 538 |
Developmental Patterns in Work 541 | Retirement from
Work 542

Chapter Thirteen
Morality   *547*

Theories of Moral Development   548

Social Learning Approach 548 | Applying Our
Knowledge: Coping with an Aggressive Child 550 |
Psychoanalytic Approach 551 | Cognitive Approaches
550

Moral Judgment and Behavior   559

Developmental Changes 561 | Research Close-up:
Moral Judgment and Behavior in High School and
College Students 562 | Motivation for Growth and Moral
Education 566

Alternative Moral Perspectives   568

Gender Differences in Morality 568 | Issues in Human
Development: Morality: Female Lawyers and Physicians
570 | Cross-Cultural Research 571 | Synthesis 574

Chapter Fourteen
Gender Roles and Gender Differences   *579*

Development of Gender Roles   583

Infancy 584 | Childhood 586 | Applying Our
Knowledge: The Boy Scouts and Male Gender Role
588 | Adolescence 591 | Early Adulthood and Middle
Age 594 | Later Life 597 | A Model of the Life Span
Gender Approach 599

Theories of Gender Role Development   600

Psychoanalytic Theory 600 | Learning Theories 601 |
Issues in Human Development: The Significance of the
Couvade 602 | Issues in Human Development: The
Effects of Paternal Absence 604 | Cognitive
Developmental Theory 608 | A Contemporary Cognitive
View: Information Processing Theory 612 | A Synthesis
613

Current Issues in Gender Development   614

Conducting Bias-Free Research 614 | Androgyny 615 |
Gender Roles and Schooling 617

Chapter Fifteen
Death and Dying   *625*

Study of Death and Dying   627

Biological Definitions of Death 627 | Social and
Psychological Definitions of Death 629 | Research on
Death and Dying 631 | Research Close-up: A
Naturalistic Study of Death Attitudes 632

Biological Perspective   633

Genetic Theories of Aging and Death 634 | Error
Accumulation Theories of Aging and Death 635

Sociological and Anthropological
Perspectives   636

Demography of Death and Dying 637 | Issues in
Human Development: Funerals 638 | Sociological
Explanations of Suicide 639 | Sociological Explanation

of Death Denial 640 | Anthropological Perspective
642 | Issues in Human Development: How the Hmong
in the United States Cope with Death 644

Psychological Perspective   644

Psychoanalysis 644 | Psychological Explanation of the
Process of Dying 646

Developmental Perspective   648

Infancy 650 | Early and Middle Childhood 650 |
Adolescence and Early Adulthood 654 | Middle Age
655 | Old Age 656 | Conclusions About the Life Span
Approach 657

Special Topics in Death and Dying   657

Bereavement, Grief, and Mourning 657 | Hospice
Movement 660 | Death and Dying in the Future 661 |
Applying Our Knowledge: The Living Will and
Euthanasia 662

Glossary   *G–1*

References   *R–1*

Index   *I–1*

Issues in Human Development

Do We Really Value Children?   20
The Ethics of Research   48
Are Children Growing Up Faster
Than Their Parents Did?   98
Child Sexual Abuse   138
How Can Infant Perception Be Studied?   170
Who Is the Hyperactive Child?   212
Did Piaget Underestimate
the Preschool Mind?   270
Defining Mental Retardation   306
Is There a Cultural Bias in IQ Testing?   310
Learning a Second Language   362
Neoanalytic Critiques of Freud's Theory   394
What Happens When
Mother Goes to Work?   460
Divorce After 60: Too Old to Start Over?   480
What Are the Origins of Shyness?   510
Morality: Female Lawyers and Physicians   570
The Significance of the Couvade   602
The Effects of Peternal Absence   604
Funerals   638
How the Hmong in the United
States Cope with Death   644

Research Close-up

Prematurity and the Scientific Method   40
The Stereotyping of Attractiveness
Among the Elderly   120
The Gap Between Adolescent
Sexual Attitudes and Behavior   146

The Visual Cliff   178
Sensory Impairment and Intellectual
Functioning in Middle Age   188
The Elderly Need Supportive
Learning Environments   238
Lucienne and the Silver Watch Chain: An
Early Mental Solution to a Problem   266
Can Chimpanzees Use Language?   342
James Marcia and the Identity
Status Interview   404
Behavioral Expectations of
Grandparenthood   476
Concern for the Victim   502
Moral Judgment and Behavior in
High School and College Students   562
A Naturalistic Study of Death Attitudes   632

Applying Our Knowledge

The Use of Developmental
Theory and Research   65
Testing for Genetic Disorders in the Fetus   78
Sexual Behavior and AIDS   152
Learning to Read   200
Conditioning as Therapy:
Behavior Modification   222
Piaget's Theory and Education   284
Interpreting an IQ Score   304
Language Acquisition in the Deaf   350
A Positive Note on the Institutionalization
of the Elderly   416
Helping the Unpopular Child   514
Coping with an Aggressive Child   550
The Boy Scouts and Male Gender Role   588

*Human Development
Across the Life Span*

Chapter One

Introduction: Concepts and Theories

Characteristics of Human Development
An Individual Experience
A Life-Span Process
An Interdisciplinary Study

Issues in Human Development
Heredity and Environment
Development and Change
Ages, Stages, and Continuity

Theoretical Perspectives
Meaning and Purpose of Theory
History of Developmental Theory
Modern Perspectives on Development

 Everyone knows that if a crying baby is attended to promptly by its mother, it is being rewarded for crying, and so will grow into a spoiled and dependent toddler. Children from large families, because they are spoken to so often, are superior in language skills to children from smaller families. Because of our preference for nuclear rather than extended family units, elderly people in the United States are typically not involved in the lives of their children and grandchildren. Children without brothers and sisters grow up to be fiercely independent and self-centered adults.

All of these statements are widely believed "common sense" notions about human development. None of them is true. In fact, a substantial amount of scientific evidence contradicts each of these often-heard opinions.

The existence of these and so many other widely circulated but inaccurate bits of folk wisdom makes an important point about the study of human development: Familiarity with a subject can be a disadvantage as well as an advantage. Unlike students who are beginning a course in neurophysiology, ancient history, or nuclear physics, beginning human development students often feel that they are already well informed about the area they have chosen to study. Most feel they at least know what is meant by human development, as well as a good deal about the developmental process itself. And why not? All of us are aware of our own development, and we have all observed at close range the development of others. Everyone has heard about, seen films about, and read much in the popular literature about the norms and abnormalities of human functioning at various points in the life span.

Our goal in this chapter is to introduce the concept of human development and, in doing so, to challenge students to question some of their "common sense" beliefs about the process. We open with a discussion of the essential characteristics of human development—its unique and personal nature, its interdisciplinary nature, and its continuity across the life span. Then we turn to some of the issues that complicate our efforts to define human development—questions about the relative influences of heredity and environment, the difference between development and simple change, the relationship between development and chronological age, and the characteristics of developmental stages. This is followed by a section on the nature and usefulness of developmental theory. We shall discuss what a theory is and what it is not, how developmental theory is used, and how such theories have evolved throughout the centuries from the time of Plato and Aristotle to the present day.

Examining the origins of modern theories will show the diversity of views that make up our understanding of human development, the magnitude of change across the centuries, and the relationship between philosophical positions and the kinds of theories formulated. The questions we ask today about the nature of human beings have been asked before, and many have been asked for hundreds and even thousands of years. We like to think, however, that we are closer now to providing answers, because in this century we have added the techniques of careful scientific research to what has been a very long history of philosophical speculation.

CHARACTERISTICS OF HUMAN DEVELOPMENT

Human development is the study of an individual's development from conception to death from an interdisciplinary perspective. Let us examine separately the three key elements of this definition. Human development is (1) an individual experience, (2) a continuous process across the life span, and (3) an interdisciplinary study.

An Individual Experience

Kate Wilson, an energetic, talkative, and witty woman in her middle 70s, owned a large home that she had divided into several apartments. In addition to providing her with a much-needed source of income, her job as a landlady gave her a chance to interact with a variety of interesting tenants. Wilson enjoyed socializing with all her tenants except one—a socially reclusive woman named Martha Weiss who was approximately the same age and who was habitually late in paying her rent.

One afternoon, Wilson was conversing with another tenant about her frustration in trying to collect the monthly rent from Weiss on the day it was due. She ended the conversation by throwing her hands up in disgust and remarking as she walked away, "Well, you know how these old people are. I just can't get along with them."

Although she didn't realize it, Wilson had just made a perceptive comment about a fundamental characteristic of human development: Development is an individual process. When people are asked how it feels to be 21, 40, or 75, for example, they usually answer that they feel like *themselves,* and much the same as they felt the year before. What they mean, and what the landlady meant, is that no one ever feels like a typical 21-year-old, a typical 40-year-old, or a typical 70-year-old. In fact, there is no such thing as a typical person of any age. People always feel only like themselves. They feel unique, and in a real sense they are. Human development is an individual process that defies the stereotypes of age or stage.

Despite its individual nature, human development can be studied scientifically. Scientific research studies individual instances of a particular physical or psychological phenomenon and then generalizes from those instances to related phenomena. For example, a physicist discovers that when solid objects are released and allowed to fall freely to the ground, their falling speed accelerates at a consistent and predictable rate. The physicist then makes a generalization by applying the newfound information to the acceleration rate of all falling bodies in the atmosphere, even though only a small number of instances of the phenomenon have actually been observed.

The same approach—generalization from a small but representative number of examples—is used in the social sciences as well. Because of the complexity of human nature, however, the social scientist generalizes with a lesser degree of confidence than the physicist does. The rate of falling bodies may be highly predictable, but human beings provide numerous exceptions to every rule. Because every person's development is a unique experience, behavioral norms do not apply to everyone. To be sure, similarities occur in our developmental patterns. We are all members of the same species, and most of us are raised in roughly similar social settings. Nevertheless, the infinite complexity of the individual, the complexity of the environments in which we develop, and the complexity of our interaction with those environments virtually guarantee that no two human beings will develop in precisely the same way.

According to the social clock, these first-time parents were "late" in starting their family—a phenomenon that is becoming more and more common.

Students of human development must constantly keep in mind individual differences within populations, although in fact most of the information in this or any other textbook is derived from behavioral norms. Although we have no choice but to rely on norms for our information, psychologist Bernice Neugarten (Neugarten, 1973; Neugarten, Moore, & Lowe, 1965; Troll, 1985) warned that norms have a way of turning into constraints. That is, people often try to force their own lives, and those of others, into what they perceive as "normal" patterns of development.

Neugarten was particularly interested in an overreliance on norms associated with chronological age. The normal age of first marriage in the United States is now approximately 24 or 25. Not only did the majority of those interviewed by Neugarten and her associates correctly identify the age norm for first marriage, but they also believed that early adulthood is the "best" time to marry. In other words, what is usually done was seen as what *should* be done, converting a simple age norm into an age constraint (see Table 1.1).

Social clock

The tendency of people to measure their developmental progress in terms of adherence to established norms.

A belief that there is a "right" time to marry, to have a first child, to finish school, to begin a career, or to retire may cause people to limit their own possibilities for development. They may become obsessed with society's right times instead of looking for right times of their own. They may find themselves living according to a **social clock,** constantly evaluating their progress in completing major life activities and determining whether they are early, late, or on time (Neugarten, 1973).

Of course, valid reasons exist for many age constraints. An obstetrician may have a real basis for suggesting to a woman patient that she should not consider a first pregnancy at the age of 43. Similarly, few would argue that the average 12-year-old in the United States is mature enough to marry, or even to drive an automobile. However, many age constraints have no validity at all, except that they are based on norms to which society has become accustomed. We must guard against this latter set of constraints to maintain an appreciation of the individual nature of human development.

A Life-Span Process

The development of an individual is a process of continuous integration of current experience into previously formed structures. It is a continuous unfolding, beginning at conception and ending at the moment of death. For that reason, human development is a life-span study. To examine only isolated segments of the life span is equivalent to studying isolated scenes from a film or play. Imagine the difficulty of understanding the story line of a play or in following the development of its characters if the viewer was present only for the second of three acts! Similarly, how can we understand the development of an individual human being if we observe that person only during infancy, adolescence, or old age? Just as the second act of a play

Table 1.1
Age Norms Agreed to by a Sample of Middle-Aged, Middle-Class Adults

	Age Range Designated as Appropriate or Expected
Best age for a man to marry	20–25
Best age for a woman to marry	19–24
When most people should become grandparents	45–50
Best age for most people to finish school and go to work	20–22
When most men should be settled on a career	24–26
When most men hold their top jobs	45–50
When most people should be ready to retire	60–65
A young man	18–22
A young woman	18–24
A middle-aged man	40–50
A middle-aged woman	40–50
An old man	65–75
An old woman	60–75
When a man has the most responsibilities	35–50
When a man accomplishes most	40–50
The prime of life for a man	35–50
When a woman has the most responsibilities	25–40
When a woman accomplishes most	30–45
A good-looking woman	20–35

Source: "Age Norms, Age Constraints and Adult Socialization" by B. L. Neugarten, J. W. Moore, and J. C. Lowe, 1965, *American Journal of Sociology, 70,* p. 712. Copyright © 1965 by the University of Chicago Press. Adapted by permission.

evolves from and builds on the first, while at the same time forming the basis for the third act, a person's adolescence evolves from and builds on the experience of childhood and forms the basis for all later life experiences.

Anthropologist Margaret Mead (1972) commented on the necessity of the life-span approach to human development when she discussed the importance of the relationship between children and their grandparents. She suggested that children and their grandparents learn from one another about the continuity of life. The grandparent offers the child a link with the past, and the child gives the grandparent an appreciation for the future of humanity. In the relationship between the grandparent and the child, the

Grandparents offer children a link to the past, and children give grandparents a feeling for the future of humanity.

past and future come together in the present. Perhaps the same can be said of the value of the life-span approach to the study of human development: It is the merging of our own individual pasts and futures that leads us to a present awareness of the continuity of life.

An Interdisciplinary Study

No single discipline is broad enough to describe all the biological, social, intellectual, and emotional changes that people experience as they journey across the life span. How, for example, can we discuss the physical changes of puberty without at the same time discussing the psychological effects of physical maturation? How can we examine the psychological effects of divorce on a young child without also examining recent changes in one of our major social institutions, the family unit? Can we paint an accurate picture of the experience of growing old if we study only our own culture and no others? Clearly, the perspectives of scholars from many disciplines must be considered, not in isolation from one another but in an integrated fashion (Charlesworth, 1972).

The major contributions to human development come from the social science disciplines of anthropology, sociology, and psychology, as well as from the natural science discipline of biology. The contributions have not been of equal weight, however. The vast majority of scholars in the field of human development are psychologists, and most of the research discussed in this text is psychological research. The contributions of the specific disciplines will be introduced only when such references are appropriate. For example, in some areas, such as sensory, physical, and reproductive development, most of the work has been contributed by biologists. In other areas, such as learning, cognition, intelligence, and perception, psychologists have contributed the greatest amount. Finally, although much may be learned from cross-cultural comparisons about virtually any aspect of human development, this text will focus primarily on development in U.S. society. Cross-cultural references will be made only when a comparison of cultures illustrates a point about our culture or when such comparisons provide a test of the universality of developmental principles.

The field of anthropology focuses on the study of human culture and examines cultural variations throughout the world. The value of an anthropological perspective on human development becomes apparent when we realize that most of what we know about development across the life span comes from the work of researchers studying development in the United States and Western Europe (Munroe, Munroe, & Whiting, 1981). Therefore, what we consider "normal" development may be normal only in these cultures, whereas totally different developmental progressions might be observed in other parts of the world. Only by making cross-cultural comparisons can we avoid the serious error of generalizing too freely from data collected in our own society. Furthermore, if we fail to make cross-cultural comparisons, we may never know which human qualities are primarily of biological origin (nature) and which are learned (nurture). For this reason, anthropology is an essential component of the interdisciplinary study of human development.

Sociology is the branch of social science that analyzes group relationships and social institutions (Goodman & Marx, 1982). Human development cannot be studied in a vacuum. We must constantly be attuned to the social forces impinging on our lives—to the changes in values as well as institutions. For example, a sociologist might study how the U.S. family unit has been changing in recent generations, differences in reactions to unemployment among the various socioeconomic classes in our country today, the implications of recent population shifts from industrial northern states to what is known as the Sun Belt, or the tendency of the U.S. population to "age" as the birth rate declines and longevity increases.

In each example, the sociologist emphasizes the social unit or institution rather than the specific life experiences of individuals within these groups. However, we cannot study social systems without reference to the individuals within them. And it seems equally obvious that we cannot completely understand the development and behavior of individuals if we fail to take into account the broader social context. For this reason, sociology is an essential component in the study of human development.

Psychology may broadly be defined as the study of individual consciousness and behavior (Gleitman, 1986). The field is divided into at least a dozen areas of specialization exploring emotions, thoughts, body language, sensations, learning, memory, perceptions, morals, the diagnosis and treatment of behavioral problems, complex organizations, small group functioning, gender roles and differences, and numerous other functions of the mind and its resulting activities.

Developmental psychologists, in particular, are heavily identified with the field of human development. They are interested in the intellectual, social, and emotional changes that occur over time and the underlying mechanisms responsible for such developments. In addition, their concern with physical growth, neurophysiology, genetics, or endocrinology is an attempt to make a connection between biology and psychology.

Although developmental psychology provides the core of the interdisciplinary study of human development, the field of human biology offers an equally extensive tradition of describing the processes of life. Human beings are obviously biological organisms who are influenced to some extent by heredity. The interaction of psychology and biology has often been incorporated into models of development, including those of G. Stanley Hall, Arnold Gesell, Sigmund Freud, Jean Piaget, and Erik Erikson.

Many behavioral scientists believe, however, that the biological components in human development have been either totally ignored or at least underestimated for far too long. Psychologist David Lykken, director of a project involving hundreds of pairs of twins at the Minnesota Center for Twin and Adoption Research, believes that an astonishing number of intellectual and personality characteristics may have biological rather than psychological origins. These include extroversion, conformity, a tendency to worry, creativity, optimism, and cautiousness. As Lykken (Wellborn, 1987) pointed out, "The evidence is so compelling that it is hard to understand how people could not believe in the strong influence of genetics on behavior" (p. 59).

The extent to which biological factors influence the process of human development has yet to be determined, but explanations of behavior that focus on the biological rather than the environmental seem to be increasingly in evidence in recent years (Wellborn, 1987). For now, we can only conclude that excluding biological components from our search for a complete understanding of human development is unreasonable.

ISSUES IN HUMAN DEVELOPMENT

The study of human development has been characterized by a number of controversial questions—some have been satisfactorily resolved, but others continue to trouble developmental researchers. Three major areas of controversy have centered on (1) the relative influences of heredity and environment on individual growth, (2) the difference between qualitative development and quantitative change, and (3) the relationship of development to chronological age and the meaningfulness of developmental stages.

Heredity and Environment

One of the oldest controversies in the history of philosophy, and eventually in human development as well, is the nature-nurture controversy: Is behavior primarily determined by biological or genetic factors within the organism (nature) or by experience in the external world (nurture)? As far as can be determined, the heredity-environment issue can be traced to the arguments of ancient Greek philosophers, such as Plato and Aristotle, over whether ideas were innate in human beings or were acquired through experience (Miller, 1989). As will be seen in the section of this chapter on the history of developmental theory, the debate continued on and off throughout the centuries.

The modern extreme of the nature side of the question was represented by the maturation theorists at the turn of the century, while the extreme advocates of the opposite stress on nurture were the early behaviorists; both theories will be discussed later in this chapter. The argument between the

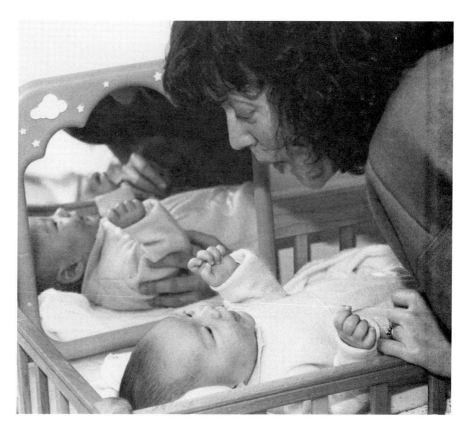

Is this baby smiling because the adult appears to be happy, or is the adult happy because the child is smiling? In a human interaction, the direction of influence is often difficult to determine.

behaviorists and the maturation theorists was never really resolved. Instead, by the 1950s psychologists came to realize that "either-or" explanations of human development and behavior would not suffice; neither side could offer a complete explanation of human behavior (Anastasi, 1958).

Interactionist approach

The belief that human development is a dynamic, multidirectional process in which heredity and environment continuously influence each other in such a way that determining the relative contributions of each to the developmental process is difficult.

The approach to the nature-nurture question most often taken today is the *interactionist approach:* Behavior is the product of the interaction of *both* heredity and environment. This interaction is not a simple additive process; heredity and environment do not merely combine as the ingredients in a recipe are combined so that the percentage contributed by each to the overall process of development can be easily determined. Instead, interaction is multiplicative, with the contributions of each element continuously influencing and being influenced by the contributions of the other.

Interaction is a dynamic, two-directional process, as illustrated by the following example. Many adults have had the experience of trying to calm a crying baby and finding that the more the baby cries, the more tense the person holding it becomes, and the more tense the adult becomes, the more the baby cries. Can we determine how much of the infant's distress was caused by the adult and how much by the baby? Of course not. The additive approach is unworkable in an interactive situation. All we can reasonably conclude is that both infant and adult simultaneously influenced each other in a back-and-forth fashion.

Despite the difficulty of accounting precisely for all hereditary and environmental factors in human behavior, the nature-nurture question remains extremely important. The interaction concept should not be considered an easy solution to the question because it seems to cover all possibilities. Efforts to separate hereditary from environmental factors continue in human development today, many of them employing imaginative research strategies and some of them raising fascinating questions.

In reading this text, remember that a person's characteristics may never be determined totally by hereditary factors or totally by environmental influences. Both elements combine in an interactive fashion, and separating them for purposes of study is difficult, but at least theoretically possible.

Development and Change

All development involves change, but not every change represents a genuine development. To develop means to grow out of, to evolve from. In the literal sense of the word, to develop is to unwrap, and, indeed, the developmental process exhibits a definite sense of unwrapping—a sense of one state of affairs not only following but emerging directly from that which preceded it. Nondevelopmental change, in contrast, is a transition requiring no evolution, no unwrapping. A woman, for example, might change her clothing, the arrangement of the furniture in her apartment, or the oil in her automobile engine. In each of these instances, one situation merely follows another without the necessity of any connection between the current state of events and the preceding state. It would be absurd to suggest that the oil in an automobile engine last year *developed* into what is there at present, when in fact no relationship exists between the oil currently being used and what was used in the past.

Human development, then, is an orderly process dealing with the emergence of one state from another, and those who investigate this process engage in little analysis of nondevelopmental change. For this reason, the study of human development involves much more than a mere cataloguing of events occurring in children's lives as they grow older. Listing all the changes observed in an individual over the span of a lifetime, or even over the span of a single year, would be difficult and pointless.

As a practical example of the difference between a developmental and a nondevelopmental change, consider the case of Keith, a high school sophomore preparing for a psychology exam by memorizing the definitions at the end of each chapter in his textbook. Knowing that he would not be able to memorize all the definitions in one sitting, he begins his studying early and sets a goal of memorizing only five terms a day. What Keith is studying certainly will change from day to day, and the total number of definitions he has learned will gradually increase. However, these are nondevelopmental changes. Why? Because what Keith studies on any given day is unrelated to what he studied the day before.

However, Keith's situation might illustrate a developmental as well as a nondevelopmental change. Let us suppose that Keith discovers that each day he learns new lists of words more quickly and efficiently than he did the day before. He finds that he is becoming skilled at absorbing new information; he notices changes in the quality of his approach to the material, as well as quantitative changes in the total amount of material learned. Now the changes in his study habits and his approach to learning are truly developmental changes. Each day's activity builds on and emerges from the previous day's activity. The experience of studying the first chapter definitely affected the experience of studying the second, and so on. In summary, whereas the changes in the content of Keith's knowledge—the sum total of what he knows—may be nondevelopmental changes, the changes in the way he learns are genuine developments.

Developmental psychologists are interested in the patterns created when people integrate new experiences into their already existing reservoir of experiences while simultaneously drawing on that reservoir to interpret the experience at hand. The life experiences themselves are not of interest, but how the person interacts with them and how the interactions lead to increasingly more sophisticated interactions. To use the concrete terms of the earlier example, it is not what the student has learned that is of interest, but how his approach to learning has changed because of exposure to the learning process, and how the changes in his approach will allow him to function more effectively when he encounters a new learning situation.

Ages, Stages, and Continuity

The development of an individual human being is a process of constant integration of current experiences into previously formed structures—a continuous unfolding, beginning at conception and ending at the moment of death. The developmental process is often described in terms of ages ("You're old enough to pick up after yourself") or stages ("Mid-life is a time for reviewing your accomplishments and determining new directions"). However, ages or stages often tell us little about the developmental level of a particular human being, as parents know from observing differences between their children. Jane may be able to pick up after herself at 4, but 6-year-old Katie never seems to remember to clean up her room. Steve may have had major difficulties adjusting to the changes in his body at puberty, while Michael's life hardly changed at all when he became a teenager.

Age and Development

What is the relationship between chronological age and human development? Yale psychologist William Kessen (1960) proposed that a characteristic may be considered development if it can be related to age in an orderly way. He argued that age in itself is not the equivalent of development, however, because many factors besides age affect development and because wide individual variations appear in the rate of human growth. In other words, human development occurs over a definite period of time, but time alone is not a sufficient condition for development.

Age is a convenient reference point for development, and we frequently generalize from age norms, as when we say that children begin to use logic at age 6 or that the "mid-life crisis" occurs when people are in their 40s. However, we should always remember that we are not describing age but the developmental process; we should not expect all human beings to develop at the same rate, even though we all measure our chronological ages in the same units of time.

Developmental Stages

Developmental stage
A period within the life span characterized by a cohesive cluster of physical, emotional, intellectual, or social characteristics.

For explanatory purposes, the span of life is often divided into developmental stages: infancy, early childhood, middle childhood, adolescence, early adulthood, middle adulthood, and old age. A *developmental stage* can be thought of as a time period within the life cycle that is defined by a particular cluster of physical, emotional, intellectual, or social characteristics. In other words, some coherence within stages should mark the characteristic that is studied, as when we say that the infant's ways of solving problems, of expressing needs, or of interacting with peers differ from the ways of the preschool child.

Convenient as the stage concept is for academic purposes, it may foster serious misconceptions, one of which is that stages of development are discrete and separate entities. In reality, they are not separate at all but evolve from one another continuously. The stage concept may also lead to the false impression that stages of development are static—but stages are anything but static, because they all include continuous development within them. For example, we do not simply remain suspended in the stage of infancy until we are ready to spring forward into early childhood; constant changes occur within the phase of infancy, as within all life stages. Similarly, adolescence not only follows middle childhood but gradually evolves from it. People do not wake up one morning to discover that they are not young adults anymore, but are now middle-aged.

Much of who we are during any life stage is an outgrowth of who we were during the preceding stages. Although developmental stages or phases and their associated chronological ages are valuable reference points, individual variation is the predominant characteristic of human development.

THEORETICAL PERSPECTIVES

When Professor Walsh returned to her office after teaching her human development class, she found one of her students waiting to see her. Jeff was disappointed about Professor Walsh's statement in class that although no one knows for certain how human thinking develops, she would be discussing some of the most widely accepted theories of cognition. "I want to learn how people think," Jeff complained. "I don't want to learn how Jean Piaget *thinks* that people think."

The professor tried to explain that no absolute certainty exists about the workings of the human mind, but, as in any science, several theoretical positions hope to approximate truth. This explanation went unappreciated, however, and the professor soon realized that her student had no understanding of the role, or the value, of theory in human development. Jeff needed to learn what a theory is and what it is intended to do. In fact, among undergraduate students, Jeff is probably not alone.

Meaning and Purpose of Theory

A theory is a model designed to help scientists, as well as members of the general public, to interpret observable data in their field of study, to make predictions based on those data, and to formulate further research questions. It does not offer absolute truth, but perhaps it provides a framework through which truth can be more closely approximated.

A viable theory has four characteristics, according to developmental psychologist Patricia Miller (1989). First, a theory must be *internally consistent.* That is, it must have no internal contradictions. Second, it must be *empirically sound,* meaning that it is not contradicted by scientific evidence. Third, it must be *testable;* a theory of any sort that lacked the possibility for testing its basic assumptions would have little value. Finally, a theory should be capable of *integrating previous research findings* and making sense of them.

Why work from a theoretical base instead of merely storing independently all the information one can remember from a field of study? Information will be better understood and remembered if it is organized, and a theoretical framework imposes organization and meaning on the facts at hand. In addition, the existence of a theory serves to raise research questions for the future; these research questions, incidentally, are not raised only by advocates of a particular theory, but often by its detractors. As an example, we shall observe later in this chapter that some contributions of cultural anthropologists to the study of human development were stimulated by efforts to disprove the universality of psychoanalytic theory.

History of Developmental Theory

Human beings themselves may have changed little throughout the centuries, but interest in development and attitudes toward children, adolescents, and the elderly have certainly changed. Let us take a brief look now at the history of developmental theory. In doing so, we should keep in mind that some of these theoretical views were so sketchy that they hardly qualify as theories at all, according to Miller's (1989) definition. Others were considerably more elaborate. The main focus of this section, therefore, will be to examine historical changes in society's general views, however well articulated, of the developmental process. We shall begin with the writings of early Greek philosophers and continue to the present day.

Early Greek Conceptions

One of the earliest stage theories of human development was outlined by the Greek philosopher Plato (427–347 B.C.), who suggested that the human soul is made up of three elements: appetites, spirit, and reason. The appetites, which appeared at birth and dominated the infant and early childhood years, were the basic physical and emotional needs of a child. The spirit developed during later childhood and early adolescence, representing assertiveness, courage, and convictions. Finally, with adult maturity, the rational and intelligent component of the soul might become the most influential.

Idealism
The philosophical view that reality cannot be known independently from the mind that is perceiving it.

According to Plato's philosophy of *idealism,* human beings never come to know reality as it is but only acquire images that are filtered through and possibly distorted by their senses. Thus, any two people might have different perceptions of the real world because the world is filtered through their individual thought processes. As you will discover in Chapter 5, such ancient ideas are remarkably similar to those of modern psychologists who advocate "enrichment" theories of perception.

In contrast to Plato, Aristotle (384–322 B.C.) did not believe that the fundamental meaning of the world could be discovered in images or predetermined ideals in the mind. Instead, he felt that people could learn to understand reality by critically examining their sensory impressions to discover universal patterns in the environment. He felt that experiences (especially careful observations) could help to clarify reality rather than introduce distortions or misrepresentations of truth, as Plato had contended. Thus, reality can be known directly, and in this philosophy, known as *realism,* the truth of any knowledge can be demonstrated to the mutual consent of critical thinkers everywhere.

Realism
The philosophical position that reality has an existence independent of the perceiver's consciousness of it.

Middle Ages

The Middle Ages (the eleventh to the fourteenth centuries) can be characterized as a period of basic neglect of issues concerning the process of human development. Life was dominated by an adherence to narrowly defined religious dogma, a need to survive war and disease, and the chaos resulting from trying to cope with a feudal political system. These focuses were reflected in preoccupation with death, vast illiteracy and minimal education, lack of respect for elders and their wisdom, frequent abandonment of infants, and little recognition of the special needs of children or adolescents (Watson, 1978).

The pessimism of medieval Europe was partly grounded in the theological doctrine of original sin, and many related ideas about human development were similarly derived from literal interpretations of the Bible. Development, therefore, was to follow a strict path of religious education to counteract original sin and to permit the revelation of God's universal laws to all children (Muuss, 1988). Unquestioning obedience was expected from children, with stern disciplinary measures following any sign of misbehavior. Children were required to work at an early age, and toys, fairy tales, and make-believe were unknown. In paintings, children resembled miniature adults; their clothing was merely a smaller version of adult garments.

In summary, much of the special treatment of children that is taken for granted today was not in evidence during the Middle Ages in Europe (Aries, 1962) and little attention was paid to the developmental changes of adult life. In fact, until the middle of the twentieth century, most of the interest in human development was in the development of children (Brim & Kagan, 1980; Whitbourne, 1986).

Reawakening of Humanity

Between the Middle Ages and the eighteenth century, the early Greek concerns about philosophical ideas and their consequences for human development gradually returned. The period known as the Renaissance (the fifteenth and sixteenth centuries) was a time of increasing literacy and cultural advance for much of the European world, and it set the stage for the renewed study of human development (Watson, 1978).

In sharp contrast to the uniformity and insensitivity of the medieval period, the 1600s were characterized by an emphasis on individual differences as well as on developmental stages. John Amos Comenius

Throughout most of Western history, children were seen as miniature adults. It was not until the eighteenth century that the idea of childhood innocence emerged.

(1592–1670), for example, proposed four 6-year stages with corresponding educational goals. These stages focused on perception (0–6 years), imagination (6–12 years), rationality (12–18 years), and ambition (18–24 years) (Muuss, 1988).

Enlightenment

The eighteenth-century period known as the Enlightenment brought a new and more optimistic view of human freedom and potential. The Enlightenment was a time of greater interest in children by society, with parents shifting from a belief that children were amoral little beings to a belief in childhood innocence (Kessen, 1965). Children were not incomplete adults but special creatures worthy of attention and study. Thus, toward the close of the eighteenth century in Europe, a number of philosophers, educators, and scientists turned their attention to describing the course of children's development, with a clear implication that development in general was a process worthy of examination.

The first careful, systematic observations of children were presented in published diaries at this time. Dietrich Tiedemann's (1748–1803) biography of his infant son described motor skills, language, thinking capacities, and socioemotional behaviors. Heinrich Pestalozzi's (1746–1827) data are based on his 4-year-old son's learning, but he also contributed numerous suggestions to assist parents and teachers in their observations of children.

Age of Science

As the nineteenth century approached, increasing access to education helped to promote a technological revolution that ultimately altered views about childhood and affected the structure of the family. Although philosophers' writings on the nature of thought continued to influence educational theory and other practical areas, the principle impetus for understanding human development shifted to the realm of science.

Charles Darwin (1809–82), the leading advocate of the theory of evolution, maintained that the human being should be viewed as a part of nature, the highest of a long chain of life forms beginning with one-celled organisms. His concepts of natural selection and survival of the fittest were major influences on our understanding of the developmental process: Individuals of any species who are better equipped to adapt to their changing environment—for social, emotional, physical, or intellectual reasons—will survive to reproduce. Therefore, adaptability might be thought of as one of the most valuable characteristics a person can have.

Perhaps Darwin's most developmentally oriented contribution was to suggest a relationship between the evolution of the species and the growth of the child. This speculation made respectable the value of studying individual change. Indeed, the notion of seeking the origins of adult behaviors and attributes in childhood experiences is still widely accepted. The diary Darwin published about his infant son's activities demonstrated his commitment to the importance of individual development for under-standing human evolution. Darwin's ***baby biography*** was not the first published account of early development, but it was among the most influential because of his substantial scientific reputation (Kessen, 1965; Watson, 1978).

Baby biography
The informal and personal diary that certain educated middle-class parents keep regarding the develop-ment of their children.

The nineteenth century saw a virtual revolution in the conceptualization of human development. Philosophical discussion and religious dogma were gradually replaced by the scientific method. As an example, the require-ments of developing children were documented and distributed to parents in the form of child-rearing manuals. Books were written specifically for children, clothing was designed for their activities, discipline became less severe, restrictions were placed on the ages and hours of child workers, and compulsory public education was introduced. A major effort was under way to seek effective ways to understand the complex patterns of change in

Issues in Human Development
Do We Really Value Children?

 As a society we cherish, protect, and value our children. Television series have been developed especially for children. Restaurants have special menus for them. New toys and electronic gadgets are manufactured every year just to keep them entertained. Amusement parks exist to indulge childhood fantasies.

Disturbing signs, exist, however, that children are increasingly seen as an undesirable element in U.S. society. Reported incidents of child abuse are on the rise, child pornography has become a thriving enterprise, family size is decreasing, and owners of apartment complexes freely practice age discrimination by refusing to rent to people with children.

Cross-cultural psychologist Richard Logan (1977) suggested that children are increasingly seen as burdens in our society. In simpler, preindustrial cultures—those with a rich continuing tradition—children were seen as continuers of the cultural values. Furthermore, they were actually needed by their parents to perform the tasks necessary for their society's subsistence. They worked alongside their elders and felt responsible for themselves as well as for others. They had a strong sense of belonging to, and being committed to, their cultural group.

In the United States today, according to Logan, cultural change is so rapid that parents no longer see their children as continuing a cultural tradition.

They expect the future to be different from (and probably better than) what they have known. In addition, modern U.S. families do not rely on their children's economic contributions. The result is that children are seen as qualitatively different from adults, are rarely expected to work or to assume any meaningful responsibility, and are consumers rather than producers in the economy. The children themselves no longer experience a feeling of being needed by, or being committed to, the cultural group.

Few Americans would want their children to be forced into the world of work, and most parents encourage individual initiative and achievement in their offspring rather than group loyalty and dependence. However, Logan observed that many adults may unconsciously resent the privileged status of children and may see them as irresponsible, lazy time wasters with little else to do than spend their parents' hard-earned money. In other words, the same society that extends the privileges of affluence to its children may secretly resent them for accepting those privileges.

Ironically, even as the pressures of contemporary life lead adults to envy the freedom that children seem to have, parents may be unknowingly inflicting their own forms of stress on children (Elkind, 1981; Postman, 1982). For example, increasing competition is apparent in our schools and on our

children. The scientific study of the complex patterns of change during the span of *adult* life would have to wait until the twentieth century.

Twentieth Century

With the nineteenth century drawing to a close, a field of study specifically concerned with the ways in which human beings developed started to come together, although the primary emphasis at the beginning was on childhood and adolescent development. From the mid-1880s to the early 1920s, theorists in the United States were developing a legitimate scientific tradition, and developmental researchers began to be recognized as legitimate scientists. Somehow it seemed possible that with a great enough effort, the process of rearing children might be fully understood and

playing fields, and the rising divorce rate has resulted in major alterations in how the concept of family is defined. We may, in fact, be raising a generation of excessively pressured children, whose worries about their future in the nuclear age are comparable to the stresses experienced by adults. And the pressures of growing up in the 1990s may begin at a very early age. Consider the following example, provided by Zigler and Lang (1986):

> Nine-month-old Eric is typical of a phenomenon that has come to be known in the popular media as the "gourmet baby." He has two educated, professional parents who have delayed childrearing until their early thirties. He has all the best equipment that money can buy—the right furniture, the right stroller, and a genuine shearling cover for his car seat. Eric has swimming lessons, looks at flash cards of famous paintings and simple words, plays with the best "developmentally engineered" toys and will begin the study of the violin in a year or two. He also has enough stimulation in the course of a day to make even a college student want to take a nap and shut it all out—which is just what Eric does. (p. 8)

Whether or not it is correct to assert that children are less valued today than we may realize, the observations of Elkind, Logan, Postman, Zigler, and Lang make a significant point about the influence of culture, and of cultural change, on the process of human development.

Psychologists suggest that children today are often expected to grow up too fast and that they are hurried into adulthood before childhood is over.

perfected, and the study of child development was no longer regarded as a set of philosophical problems but rather as a part of the scientific enterprise.

After the end of World War I, a great deal of interest was shown in accumulating the details of children's healthy learning and growth, particularly in the United States—perhaps because viewing children as the hope of the future coincided with the spirit of optimism in the United States. This position was furthered by government actions (the passage of strict legislation to protect and promote children's welfare, along with the establishment and funding of institutes for child study), private philanthropy (the creation of charitable organizations and the support of extensive longitudinal research), and the universities. Furthermore, U.S. researchers developed an interest in comparing the child-rearing practices in our country to those of other cultures as the work of anthropologists became known.

As the twentieth century progressed, several trends in the study of human development became apparent. First, a major difference between earlier and more modern attitudes about development centered on the need to go beyond simple descriptions of age norms. Rather than concentrating only on *what* people are like at particular ages, developmentalists have become concerned with explaining the mechanisms of *how* or *why* changes take place.

A second twentieth-century trend was a greater emphasis on *all* the different phases of the human life span. By the 1960s, the earlier emphasis on child development was gradually balanced with new attention to prenatal development, infancy, and adolescence on one end of the life span and to later adulthood on the other. At last there was recognition in the middle of the twentieth century that growth and change, as opposed to stability and then deterioration, are characteristic of adult life (Brim & Kagan, 1980).

The new interest in adult development was initially confined to the period of old age, but later was expanded to include the years from 18 to 65. Indeed, the study of adulthood may have been stimulated by the increasing visibility of the elderly in U.S. society. Whereas in 1900 only 3 million Americans were over the age of 65, there were 20 million elderly in 1970, and the projected figure for the year 2000 is 35 million (Atchley, 1977).

An increase has occurred not only in the absolute number of elderly people but also in their proportion of the population. Four percent of the U.S. population was over the age of 65 in 1900, compared with a projected 11 percent in the year 2000. In other words, the elderly population is increasing faster than the population at large, apparently because our average life expectancy is increasing while our birth rate is declining.

Gerontology
The study of the human aging process from an interdisciplinary perspective.

Perhaps related to the aging of the American population is the emergence of the field of *gerontology,* the study of the aging process from biological, sociological, psychological, and anthropological perspectives. Although the first scientific journal devoted entirely to the study of aging appeared in 1947, gerontological research did not begin to make a significant impact on the published literature in psychology until the early 1960s (Elias, Elias, & Elias, 1977).

Finally, the mid-twentieth century has seen a growing recognition of the need for interdisciplinarity—the bringing together of a variety of disciplinary perspectives to obtain a balanced picture of human functioning at various points in the life span. A related trend has been an increasing realization that the sociocultural context of development cannot be ignored. Human beings do not develop in a vacuum, after all.

This recognition has been a major emphasis of so-called contextual approaches to human development, such as those expressed by Urie Bronfenbrenner (1977; Bronfenbrenner & Crouter, 1983), Richard M. Lerner and M. B. Kauffman (1985), and Klaus Riegel (1975; 1976). Contextual approaches try to identify the multiple influences (e.g., social, historical, cultural, and biological) that affect the developing human organism, the ways in which change occurs within each of these contexts, and the complex interactions among them.

Modern Perspectives on Development

Sometimes individual theories of human development seem too numerous to make sense of, but, in fact, they are considerably more cohesive than they often appear. A frequently used division of theories is the one that we shall employ here. We shall examine three general perspectives that differ in their assessments of the relative importance of hereditary and environmental factors, of nature and nurture, on human development. They differ also in another way: The first two perspectives, environmentalist and organismic theories, view the human being as essentially rational, while the third, the psychoanalytic theory, sees us as creatures of appetite and emotion rather than of reason (see Table 1.2).

Environmentalism

The first major perspective on human development will be referred to as **environmentalism,** emphasizing the view that people grow to be what they are made to be by their environments (Langer, 1969). Rejecting inborn tendencies and the concept of freedom of choice, environmentalist theorists see the human organism as being almost completely determined by external forces, much as a piece of clay is molded in a sculptor's hands.

British Empiricism. The origins of modern environmentalist perspectives can be traced to the ideas of John Locke (1632–1704), whose philosophy of British **empiricism** illustrated a new conception of human nature that was to change the direction of scientific thought forever.

Locke believed that the human mind is a "blank slate" at birth, and that all knowledge of the world comes to us through our senses. "Empty" at birth, the growing human organism is basically passive and simply receives and responds to elementary sense impressions. Complex ideas are nothing more than combinations of simple ideas that have become associated, or connected, in the mind, just as a mosaic is a picture formed from hundreds of individually meaningless bits of colored tile. The ultimate extension of Locke's theory is that children are uncivilized creatures who need the strong hand of adults to shape them into everything they are eventually to become. They are incomplete versions of adult human beings, and society's role is to civilize them.

Behaviorism. The twentieth-century equivalent of Locke's ideas can be found in the writings of John B. Watson (1878–1958), who believed that the

Environmentalism

The belief that human beings grow to be what the environments in which they find themselves make them.

Empiricism

The philosophical position that the only source of knowledge is sensory information.

Table 1.2
Perspectives in Human Development

Perspective	Representative Theories	Basic Beliefs About Human Development
Environmentalist	British empiricism (John Locke); Behaviorism (John Watson, B. F. Skinner, A. Bandura, H. and T. Kendler); Cultural anthropology (M. Mead, R. Benedict).	The human being is an empty organism at birth. The human being is passive, and its development is determined totally by experience with the environment. The adult's role is to shape the child according to socially accepted standards of behavior.
Organismic	Naturalism (Jean-Jacques Rousseau); Maturationism (G. S. Hall, A. Gesell); Cognitive-developmental theory (J. Piaget); Humanism (C. Rogers, A. Maslow, C. Buhler); Ethology (J. Bowlby)	The human being is active in determining its own course of development. An interaction occurs between organism and environment so that both are involved in varying degrees in the process of development.
Psychoanalytic	Psychoanalytic (S. Freud, A. Freud, M. Klein, E. Erikson)	The human being is not rational but is governed by emotion, or appetite. Development is a process of continual compromise between the individual's needs and society's expectations.

only way to understand the human organism was through the objective observation of behaviors. He rejected the methods of subjective introspection or analysis of the unconscious as well as explanations that relied on instincts or other interpretations that could not be scientifically proven.

Behaviorism

The theoretical view that environmental factors are largely responsible for influencing the observable changes of human development.

Watson's *behaviorism* was inspired not only by Locke's empiricist philosophy but also by the animal learning experiments that were taking place in the late 1800s and early 1900s. He agreed with Locke that the human mind is a blank slate at birth and that the human being is molded by environmental experience, but, for Watson, the new technology of learning researchers explained how environmental experience imposes itself on the person: through principles of conditioning and reinforcement. A prominent example of such principles, which will be discussed at length in Chapter 6, is the view that rewarded behaviors are more likely to appear in the future while punished behaviors are likely to diminish. Thus, Watson believed that the only behavior worth studying is learned behavior. Psychology's goal was not the understanding of the mind but the prediction and control of behavior.

Because a person's pattern of development is determined by what he or she learns and not by any instinctive or inherited tendencies, parents play a crucial role in shaping their children into the kinds of adults they will become. Indeed, Watson believed that children could be formed into virtually anything adults wanted them to be. "Give me a dozen healthy infants," he said, "and my own specified world to bring them up in and I'll guarantee to take any one at random and train him to become any type of specialist I might select—doctor, lawyer, artist, merchant, chief, and yes, even beggarman and thief, regardless of his talents, penchants, tendencies, abilities, vocations, and race of his ancestors. There is no such thing as an inheritance of capacity, talent, temperament, mental constitution, and behavioral characteristics" (Watson, 1925, p. 82).

A complete acceptance of Watson's point of view certainly makes parenting sound like an awesome and frightening responsibility. Behaviorists today, however, are not nearly so extreme in believing that inborn tendencies are of no consequence in the process of child development, that principles of animal learning can be applied unthinkingly to human beings, or that human learning can be so completely attributed to the experiences of reward and punishment. In fact, behaviorism has been continually expanded and modified throughout the twentieth century.

One modification of Watson's behaviorism involved the further extension of learning principles from the animal laboratory out to the real world. Although the work of conditioning researchers such as B. F. Skinner (1904–   ) was based on the responses of rats and pigeons to schedules of material reinforcements (such as food), generalizing these concepts to human behavior was fairly easy. Skinner himself started this process by describing an ideal society designed to ensure healthy human development by adherence to reinforcement principles. In time, conditioning techniques

According to social learning theory, much of what a child learns from a parent occurs without any direct reinforcement. Children spontaneously imitate the behaviors of adults who are important in their lives.

would be applied to everything from programmed instruction in the classroom to the modification of undesirable behaviors in schizophrenics, retardates, and delinquents.

A second variation on behaviorism was stimulated by the work of Albert Bandura (1925–   ) beginning in the 1960s. This perspective is known as *social learning,* and the key concept is that development is guided by the imitation or avoidance of behavior that is modeled by other people (see Chapter 6). By observing the consequences of someone else's actions, people could learn how to brush their teeth, how to ride a bicycle, how to solve a puzzle, or how to discipline a child. The major significance of the social learning approach is that it described learning as taking place without the presence of any obvious reward or punishment. For example, children use adults as models and imitate their behaviors without ever being rewarded for doing so. In fact, they often pick up parental behaviors, mannerisms, and speech patterns that parents actively try to discourage.

Social learning

The belief that development is heavily influenced by imitation or avoidance of behavior that is modeled by other people.

A third variation on Watson's behaviorism was inspired by the work of Howard and Tracey Kendler in the 1950s and 1960s. The Kendlers discovered developmental differences in the ways children and adults learn and solve problems in laboratory settings. Young children seem to respond to a learning task exactly as Watson predicted, and as animals do: They repeat rewarded behaviors and delete behaviors that are not rewarded. Older children and adults, perhaps as a result of their greater verbal skills, seem to develop mental strategies when solving problems and to verbalize these strategies to themselves. Simply stated, older children and adults do not always repeat rewarded behaviors and often repeat those that are punished or ignored as part of a long-range strategy for maximizing reward.

Cultural Anthropology. Watson's behaviorism, with its emphasis on principles of learning and conditioning, was not the only type of theory to stress the overwhelming significance of the environment (nurture instead of nature) in human development. Cultural anthropologists such as Margaret Mead (1901–1978) and Ruth Benedict (1887–1948) also emphasized the experiential factors in development and were eager to demonstrate that the different patterns of child rearing that reflected diverse cultural values would result in considerable variety in adult characteristics. Such theorists questioned the universality of developmental stages such as those advocated by psychoanalytic theorists, and they minimized the significance of hereditary mechanisms in the developmental process.

Ruth Benedict (1938) was a cultural anthropologist who provided major insights into the process of human development by differentiating between what she called a **continuous culture** and a **discontinuous culture**. In a continuous culture, children never learn anything that they will have to "unlearn" as adults. Development follows a gradual, continuous line from infancy through old age. Independence, responsibility, and status are acquired gradually, in such a way that people are, in a sense, preparing for adult roles from the days of early childhood.

In a discontinuous culture—and many anthropologists believe that contemporary U.S. society could be so characterized—the life span is usually segmented into discrete stages, the world of children is decidedly different from that of adults, and children are often intentionally shielded from adult concerns. As a result, children may learn little about what it means to be responsible; they may know virtually nothing about such adult concerns as work, the assumption of leadership roles, human sexuality, childbirth and child rearing, and even death. The approach of adulthood in such a culture involves a major, and very discontinuous, status transition, whereas no such adjustment is required in continuous cultures.

Needless to say, Benedict's ideas, and those of other cultural anthropologists such as Margaret Mead and Bronislaw Malinowski (1884–1942), both of whom discovered cultures in which growing up was a smooth and uneventful process, called into question some of the basic Western assumptions about human development. Specifically, such research sug-

Continuous culture

A culture in which development is a smooth and gradual process, in that children are never taught anything that they will have to relearn as adults.

Discontinuous culture

A culture characterized by age segregation and clearly defined differences in the roles and responsibilities of people at different points in the life span.

gested that, since cultural variation is so widespread, human development must be influenced not only by inner biological mechanisms but also by environmental factors.

Organismic Theories

The organismic perspective on human development puts considerably less emphasis on the role of experience than environmentalism does. Instead, organismically oriented theorists stress the importance of factors within the organism itself. Thus, people grow to be what they make themselves to be rather than what the environment makes them (Langer, 1969).

Some organismic theorists almost totally ignored environmental influences, believing that the entire plan for development is innate. Advocates of this extreme and no longer fashionable position were maturation theorists G. Stanley Hall and Arnold Gesell. The prevailing trend in **organismic theory** today is to stress the organism-environment interaction, with each side simultaneously and continuously influencing the other.

Naturalism. The philosophical viewpoint that best exemplifies the organismic perspective was the one expressed by the eighteenth-century philosopher Jean-Jacques Rousseau (1712–78). According to Rousseau's philosophy of **naturalism,** children are innately good unless corrupted by the evils of society. They come into the world equipped by God with a plan for their development, and no harm will come to them if they are allowed to grow with a minimum of supervision. Development, from Rousseau's perspective, consisted of five stages that correspond to the evolution of human culture: animal feelings of pleasure and pain (0–5 years), savage sensory awareness (5–12 years), rational functioning and exploration (12–15 years), emotional and social interests (15–20 years), and spiritual maturity during adulthood.

Maturationism. Early in the twentieth century, Rousseau's ideas about nature's plan for human development surfaced again in the writings of those who advocated the perspective of **maturationism.** A variety of maturational theories all shared a belief that the plan of development is innate, and the environment is a distant secondary influence. As an example, G. Stanley Hall (1844–1924) believed that the individual development of the child repeats, in brief, the phases of human evolution. Thus, a 6-year-old child playing cops and robbers might actually be reliving a period in human history in which we were primarily hunters and gatherers, living in caves. Hall described adolescence as a period of "storm and stress" corresponding to a turbulent state of Western civilization before the modern era. The extreme positions that Hall adopted, as might be supposed, were quickly challenged by cross-culturally and environmentally oriented theorists (Muuss, 1988).

Another prominent maturation theorist was Arnold Gesell (1880–1961), a student of G. Stanley Hall. Like his famous teacher, Gesell regarded behaviorism with suspicion and emphasized internal biological factors in

Organismic theory
A type of theory that stresses the importance in human development of factors within the organism itself over those that are found in the environment.

Naturalism
The philosophical view that nature provides the child with a plan for development, and no harm will result if the child is allowed to develop with little adult supervision.

Maturationism
The theoretical view that hereditary mechanisms are largely responsible for influencing the path of development.

development while virtually ignoring the role of the environment. Gesell, an extremely careful observer of child development who depended on extensive data collection, devoted his career to counteracting the environmental trend that was sweeping the social sciences throughout the middle of the twentieth century (Senn, 1975).

Normative tradition

The research approach that attempts to establish the natural timing and sequence of developmental change through the use of developmental norms.

Gesell advocated the **normative tradition** of developmental data analysis, an approach that was widely used from the 1920s until the 1950s. This involved the establishment of developmental norms for behavior, often with little interest in the analysis of deviations from those norms. For example, the notion of the "terrible 2s" suggests that parents should expect problems during their child's second or third year of life. In reality, of course, 2-year-olds vary greatly, and many parents report that 2 was a delightful age for their children, while 3 was an absolute nightmare. Nevertheless, Gesell's belief in typical behaviors for every age during childhood and adolescence became very popular with the general public in the 1920s and is still widely circulated today.

Cognitive-Developmental Theory.   Undoubtedly, the most significant of all organismic perspectives to emerge in the last half century has been cognitive-developmental theory. As opposed to focusing on learned behaviors, cognitive developmentalists attempt to explain how the individual thinks and how human thought processes vary. The perspective is organismic in that it emphasizes internal mental processes and their interactions with the environment rather than the influence of the environment itself. Intellectual development is seen as an active, dynamic, constructive process.

The most influential cognitive-developmental theorist was Jean Piaget (1896–1980), who believed that intellectual development is not merely a quantitative accumulation and association of learned events but a universal sequence of qualitatively different stages of interpreting the world. He suggested that we do not simply react to our environments; we each construct our own understanding of the world around us, which is based on an interaction of experience and inherent human characteristics (Flavell, 1985; Lerner, 1986; Miller, 1989; Senn, 1975).

As will be pointed out in Chapter 7, many of Piaget's specific conclusions about intellectual development are questioned today. Furthermore, his theory has been criticized for failing to account for intellectual change during adult life. However, Piaget's influence has been considerable, and many of his basic assumptions are still widely accepted. For example, today we take for granted that any point in a particular person's cognitive development represents more than, or at least something different from, the sum of accumulated bits of learning.

Humanism

The philosophical perspective that maintains that freedom, subjectivity, and creativity are essential for understanding the process of development.

Humanism.   Rather than being a particular theory, the perspective of **humanism** focuses on the dignity and freedom of all individuals in response to political, religious, or scientific authority that has become narrow and repressive. Humanists such as Abraham Maslow (1890–1970), Charlotte Buhler (1893–1974), and Carl Rogers (1902–88) rejected the view of human nature that emphasizes environmental control and observable action. Instead, they stressed internal factors and self-perceptions. Although they did not believe that scientific standards of objectivity are useless, they pointed out that the phenomenological perspective (an immediate, personal intuition) of the individual must be considered as well. Similarly, humanists feel that people should choose their own destinies and achieve their creative potentials by their own actions. Thus, the humanists share with other organismic theorists an interest in the internal workings of the human organism and a belief in the active role of the individual in determining its own path of development.

Ethology.   The study of animal behavior in its natural contexts is the basis of **ethology,** and ethologists generally maintain that much of animal behavior is genetically linked—the result of a long evolutionary process (Gould, 1982). As but one example, the newborn offspring of animals that constantly move about (e.g., cattle, sheep, chickens), must quickly recognize and learn to follow their parents to survive. The newborn offspring will therefore imprint on the parent, automatically following when the parent moves away while emitting a species-specific call.

Ethology

The naturalistic study of animal behavior and its underlying mechanisms.

The contribution of ethology to the study of human development centers on the suggestion that human as well as lower animal behavior may have biological origins. For example, John Bowlby (1907–   ) suggested that biological mechanisms are responsible for parent-child attachment in human beings, similar to those that occur in lower animals. When the infant is threatened or fears separation from its mother, an automatic attachment system is activated. The child displays behavior such as calling, crying, reaching, and following that trigger maternal reactions, such as approaching, smiling, touching, and so on.

The merits of Bowlby's point of view will be discussed further in Chapter 12. For now, we note only that the ethological perspective that certain behaviors are "wired into" the organism by virtue of its being human presents a challenge to the environmentalist view that the human being is "empty" at birth and is gradually shaped by its cultural experiences.

Psychoanalytic Perspective

Environmentalists and organismic theorists differed in their perceptions about the roles of nature and nurture in human development. Both shared a common assumption, however, that people are basically rational, and that human development proceeds by a set of orderly principles. In marked contrast is the third major perspective on development—*psychoanalytic theory,* represented by such figures as Sigmund Freud (1856–1939), Anna Freud (1895–1982), Karen Horney (1885–1952), and Erik Erikson (1902–   ).

Psychoanalytic theory

The view that stresses the importance of unconscious mechanisms in development and sees the human organism as a creature of appetite rather than reason.

Sigmund Freud (1856–1939) suggested that human beings are creatures of appetite rather than reason.

Sigmund Freud, the founder of psychoanalysis, was originally trained as a medical doctor specializing in nervous conditions. Perhaps as a result of this training, he arrived at the revolutionary belief that some physical disorders were caused by emotional problems. He combined an energy model from nineteenth-century physics, a concept of instinctual drives from evolutionary biology, and various literary and philosophical references to the unconscious and to sexuality with a variety of techniques (e.g., free association to verbal suggestions, dream interpretation, hypnosis, discussion of childhood memories) intended to bring to the surface the underlying dynamics of personality functioning. As a result, he produced what has been called "the most influential psychological theory in history" (Miller, 1989, p. 165).

Psychoanalytic theory resembles organismic theories in many of its features—the emphasis on internal psychological processes rather than external behaviors, the belief that human development proceeds through a series of qualitatively different stages, the view that human nature is constructed from a dynamic interaction between the individual and the environment. The major difference between the two is found in their assumptions about human rationality. According to the psychoanalytic perspective, rationality and conscious understanding of behavior played only a secondary role in motivation and development. The human being is a creature of appetite rather than reason, and development is a process whereby people try to resolve the inner conflicts that result from attempting to reach a compromise between their own needs and society's expectations (Langer, 1969).

Unconscious motivation

The psychoanalytic principle that people are usually unaware of the processes and factors that motivate their behavior and mental activity.

Psychic determinism

The psychoanalytic principle that past events continue to influence present psychological reality.

The irrationality of human nature becomes evident from an examination of two of the major assumptions of psychoanalytic theory—the significance of *unconscious motivation* and *psychic determinism* (Miller, 1989). That there were forces in the unconscious mind that shape and guide human behavior was a truly revolutionary belief and is one of the major contributions of psychoanalytic theory to modern conceptualizations of human nature. Psychic determinism, on the other hand, refers to the belief that early childhood experience plays a major role in determining adult personality. If human behavior is heavily influenced by psychological forces beneath the level of consciousness, many of which had their origins at an early point in development, it is meaningless to suggest that humans are rational organisms!

Sigmund Freud is often pictured as probing deeply into the early life experiences of his patients, and, in fact, as will be seen in Chapter 10, his theory of human development assumes that children progress through a series of psychosexual stages. Freud was not most interested in childhood, however, but in adult psychological functioning, and he formulated the developmental stages of childhood primarily to explain adulthood neuroses. But during the 1920s and 1930s, psychoanalysis was broadened to explore patterns of childhood growth for their own sake instead of merely as foundations of adult neurosis. Anna Freud and Melanie Klein (1882–1960) provided the most developmentally oriented modifications.

Anna Freud helped psychoanalysis to move from being primarily an adult therapy to one that was effective with children as well. She wrote extensively about the special characteristics of childhood psychoanalysis, and she made clear in her writings and in her own clinical casework that, with certain modifications, the therapy could be used effectively even with young children (Freud, 1946). Anna Freud also stimulated an interest in research involving children and adolescents. Her writings are especially detailed about the process of adolescent development; she indicated how the balanced personality of later childhood was upset by the changes of puberty and described the ways in which adolescents often react to the resulting anxiety.

Although Hermine Hug-Hellmuth (d. 1924) initially saw the possibilities of play as an aid to children's psychoanalysis, psychotherapist Melanie Klein was the first to incorporate play extensively into psychoanalytic therapy. Klein saw play as the childhood equivalent of adult free association, and she believed that in play children reveal all their secrets—their feelings about significant people in their lives, their likes and dislikes, their joys and fears, and the underlying causes of their hostilities (Schaefer, 1985). Klein's pioneering work not only emphasized the importance of an understanding of childhood as an end in itself, but also called attention to the significant role of play in early human development.

Perhaps the most influential psychoanalytic theorist of the mid- to late-twentieth century has been Erik Erikson. Before his psychoanalytic training in Germany, where he had studied with Anna Freud, Erikson had been an artist and a teacher. He later worked in the United States with children as well as with adult patients, studied both normal and deviant development, worked with lower- as well as upper-class individuals, and experienced a variety of ethnic settings. These interactions led Erikson away from the sexual orientation that characterized early psychoanalytic theory and toward a greater balance between biological and social factors. These very social, cultural, and historical variables that Erikson insisted on recognizing had typically been overlooked by researchers in the field of human development, who often appeared to be studying individuals in a state of virtual isolation (Miller, 1989).

Erikson suggested a universal life-span sequence of eight stages, each represented by a special conflict between the needs of the self (the ego) and society's demands. In doing so, he created a psychosocial approach to the study of personality development that has stimulated further theorizing and empirical research, particularly in the area of adolescent development (Miller, 1989; Muuss, 1988).

The three major developmental perspectives—the environmentalist, the organismic, and the psychoanalytic—will be referred to repeatedly throughout this book. Many of the areas to be covered are discussed by theorists within each of the perspectives. We will consider, for example, an environmentalist view of morality emphasizing the role of reinforcement and punishment in teaching a child appropriate behaviors, an organismic view focusing on the active role of the individual in constructing a set of moral values, and a psychoanalytic view linking moral development to the unconscious process of identification with the same-sex parent.

Remember that the appropriateness of the various perspectives in explaining human development depends on the particular aspect of development we are considering. For example, the organismic view of language acquisition is the most widely accepted today, the environmentalist view has lost favor since the 1950s, and the psychoanalytic view is virtually nonexistent.

Finally, remember that in most cases no one theory can provide complete answers to the complex question of how a person develops. In many situations, the best answer we can arrive at involves a synthesis of all three points of view.

Summary

1. Human development is a process both individual and continuous, influenced by a complex interaction of heredity and environment.
2. The study of human development is interdisciplinary and includes contributions from psychologists, sociologists, biologists, and anthropologists, as well as from professionals in other fields.
3. A major controversy has existed in the field of human development over the relative importance of heredity and environment. Today, researchers generally agree that neither he-

redity or environment can fully explain the developmental process but that both elements interact.

4. Those who study human development are primarily interested in qualitative change over time that results when one state of affairs evolves from what has come before. Quantitative change, on the other hand, is less likely to be of interest to developmentalists.

5. A developmental stage is a period within the life span that is defined by a particular cluster of physical, emotional, intellectual, or social characteristics.

6. A theory of human development is an explanatory model that is internally consistent, empirically valid, testable, and capable of integrating previous research.

7. The early Greek philosophers Plato and Aristotle offered perceptive ideas about the nature of development. Their disagreements sparked different ways of knowing that are reflected in more modern theoretical positions.

8. Little consideration for the individual or the study of human development was found during the Middle Ages. Rigid theological doctrine provided the only guidance for interpreting behavior.

9. Between the Middle Ages and the eighteenth century, concern about philosophical ideas

and their consequences for human development gradually returned.

10. By the late nineteenth century, the optimism of U.S. scholars led to the formation of the developmental field. Theories of development and the scientific method did not always work smoothly together, although valuable insights continued to emerge.

11. The early twentieth century was characterized by a strong belief in the importance of environmental influences on human development, a trend typified by the work of John Watson, the founder of behaviorism.

12. Early twentieth-century contrasts to Watson's behaviorism were Freud's psychoanalytic theory, with its emphasis on underlying emotional forces, and the maturationism of Hall and Gesell, with its suggestion that developmental patterns are innate.

13. The middle of the twentieth century has seen an emphasis on the *how* and *why* rather than on the *what* of human development; a greater concentration of emphasis on infant development, adolescence, and later adulthood; and a growing effort to blend a variety of theories and disciplines into a more integrated study of the human being.

Key Terms

baby biography (p. 19)
behaviorism (p. 25)
continuous culture (p. 27)
developmental stage (p. 14)
discontinuous culture (p. 27)
empiricism (p. 23)

environmentalism (p. 23)
ethology (p. 30)
gerontology (p. 22)
humanism (p. 29)
idealism (p. 16)
interactionist approach (p. 12)
maturationism (p. 28)

naturalism (p. 28)
normative tradition (p. 29)
organismic theory (p. 28)
psychic determinism (p. 32)
psychoanalytic theory (p. 30)

realism (p. 17)
social clock (p. 6)
social learning (p. 26)
unconscious motivation (p. 32)

Review Questions

1. Explain the difference between an age norm and an age constraint. Describe the ways in which age constraints may destroy the individuality of the process of human development.
2. How was the nature-nurture controversy eventually resolved? In what sense does the interaction approach represent a compromise between the two extremes in the nature-nurture argument?
3. Explain the relationship between genuine development and simple change. Provide examples of genuine developments and contrast them with examples of nondevelopmental change.
4. What is meant by a continuous culture and a discontinuous culture regarding the process of human development? In which type of culture does development appear to be an easier process? Why?
5. The study of human development in modern times has focused on explaining the mechanisms of change rather than merely describing them. For each of the dominant theoretical positions today (i.e., behavioristic, psychoanalytic, cognitive, humanistic, ethological), describe the strengths of the approach in terms of its ability to explain, rather than simply to describe, developmental change.
6. Why are theories of human development necessary? What are the characteristics of a good theory, and why do developmental psychologists believe that theories in their field of study often fail to possess all these characteristics?

Suggested Readings

Borstelmann, L. J. (1983). Children before psychology: Ideas about children from antiquity to the late 1800s. In P. H. Mussen (Ed.), *Handbook of child psychology* (4th ed.). New York: Wiley.

An excellent chapter that culls diverse information from a variety of sources. The historical data, spanning a period from biblical times to the present day, are fascinating, and the accompanying analysis is both insightful and helpful to the reader.

Cairns, R. B. (1983). The emergence of developmental psychology. In P. H. Mussen (Ed.), *Handbook of child psychology* (4th ed.). New York: Wiley.

This chapter provides a detailed and illuminating review of developmental psychology within the past century or so, outlining both the specific contributions of various child development experts and the general trends that have emerged.

Kessen, W. (1965). *The child.* New York: Wiley.

A classic collection of extensive excerpts and perceptive commentary on the nature of infants and children during the past few centuries. Included are selections from the writings of Plato, Locke, Rousseau, and Watson.

Lerner, R. M. (1986). *Concepts and theories of human development* (2nd ed.). New York: Random House.

A well-written, exhaustive text on the nature of theory in the field of human development. The author explores the most significant issues that developmentalists have wrestled with since the field of study was first conceptualized, and he analyzes in depth the various theories, and types of theories, that have emerged throughout the years.

Miller, P. H. (1989). *Theories of developmental psychology* (2nd ed.). New York: W. H. Freeman.

The second edition of what is becoming a classic work on the nature of developmental theory. Included are chapters on the definition and value of theory and on the various theories (e.g., cognitive-developmental, psychoanalytic, social learning, ethological) that have shaped the direction of the field of developmental psychology.

Chapter Two

Methodological Approaches

The Scientific Method

Establishing the Problem

Methodology for the Study

Analysis of the Results

Interpretation of the Research

Research Strategies

Experimental Approach

Nonexperimental Methods

Studying Individuals

The Laboratory or the Field?

Problems in Doing Research

Procedures for Collecting Data

Survey Method

Observational Method

Testing Method

Developmental Designs

Cross-sectional Research

Longitudinal Research

Time Lag Research

Sequential Research

 John is reading his local newspaper one Monday morning before leaving for his office. He comes across a headline that proclaims "Freud's Theory of Development Disproved." Recalling his undergraduate course in introductory psychology, John is intrigued and somewhat confused. His psychology professor did point out flaws in Freud's approach to development, but the value of the theory was clearly stated. In reading the brief newspaper article, John learns that the researchers could not find any evidence to support the connection between oral behaviors in adults and the weaning process in babies.

Perhaps John would be able to interpret the validity of the dramatic headline more effectively if he knew some of the details about how the researchers carried out their study. Did they work in a laboratory or in a natural setting? Were the participants in the research aware of the investigators' purposes? How was the information about infant weaning and adult behavior obtained? Research on development is often based on a theoretical framework about the problem—for instance, were the researchers sympathetic to Freud's theory or another view of development? John could not expect to evaluate the research properly without knowing what methods were selected for the study and why they were chosen.

This chapter discusses the scientific method, various research strategies, procedures for data collection, and developmental designs. As you read, ask yourself how each approach offers another small window into a very complex structure. How do we know if a theory about development is useful for understanding change across some portion of the life span? Where do we get information concerning perceptions in infants, adolescent sexual attitudes, or friendship among the elderly? To answer such questions, the developmental researcher follows a loosely organized set of principles that guide the research process from problem formation to final report.

THE SCIENTIFIC METHOD

Most professionals who study human development follow the steps in the basic scientific method. Not all knowledge of development has been obtained in this manner. However, because the scientific approach is more systematic and permits broader verification than do limited personal experience or unchallenged faith, the majority of research reported in this textbook has followed the scientific method. Table 2.1 summarizes this process.

Establishing the Problem

Scientific research begins with extensive consideration of a significant problem yet to be fully resolved. Then researchers narrow the issues to a manageable few by selecting certain variables that can be practically defined and examined. A *variable* is a concept that varies in at least two ways—in other words, it can be categorized or measured. Sex, for instance, can be categorized as male or female. It is a *dichotomous,* or two-part, *variable.* Intelligence can be measured by the number of intelligence quotient (IQ) points attained on a continuous scale of, for example, 0 to 200. Therefore, intelligence is a *continuous-scale variable.* Developmental researchers study problems that essentially establish relationships among variables of conse-

Variable

A concept with a property that varies in at least two ways. An independent variable is presumed to cause or influence a dependent variable.

Table 2.1
Structure of the Scientific Method

I.   Establishing the problem
     A. Significance and overview of the topic
     B. Theoretical background and past research
     C. Hypotheses and research questions
     D. Operational definition of variables
II. Methodology for the study
     A. Characteristics of the sample
     B. Research strategies
     C. Procedures for data collection
     D. Developmental designs
III. Analysis of the results
     A. Descriptive and inferential statistics
     B. Correlational and group differences statistics
     C. Univariate and multivariate statistics
IV. Interpretation of the research
     A. Relating results to hypotheses
     B. Limitations of the findings
     C. Implications of the study
     D. Suggestions for the future

quence to human change. They must also be careful to frame the problem within the context of appropriate theory and previous research on the topic.

Based on this knowledge, researchers often attempt to predict the outcome of their investigations before collecting data. This "educated guess" about how two or more variables are related is known as a *hypothesis.* Sometimes no hypotheses are formulated; instead, the researcher offers one or several questions derived from the research problem. This is usually the case in exploratory studies in which the relationships among the variables have yet to be clearly defined. Holmes and Nagy, in the *Research Close-up,* "Prematurity and the Scientific Method," did not state a formal hypothesis in their report, although the tone of their introduction implies that they did not expect to find that gestational age was the major factor in the behavioral problems of newborns.

Hypothesis
The formal statement of a researcher's educated guess about how two or more variables are related.

One of the variables Holmes and Nagy employed was the status of the newborn infants: preterm, sick full-term, healthy full-term with prolonged hospitalization because of maternal postnatal complications, and healthy full-term. Frequently, researchers distinguish between *independent* (causal) and *dependent* (resultant) variables. The infants' status was classified as an independent variable because it was presumed to be a potential cause of their problem behaviors. Note that some independent variables—such as neonatal status, sex, or gestational age—cannot be readily manipulated by researchers. Other independent variables, such as the type of therapeutic intervention or the amount of praise provided by a teacher, can be controlled by the researcher. This distinction is crucial for establishing genuine cause-and-effect relationships.

Operational definition
The specific meaning, in quantitative or categorical terms, assigned to the use of a variable.

The various scores Holmes and Nagy used for evaluating the infants' behaviors are classified as dependent variables, because they are presumed to be the result of variations in the independent variable. The researcher's task is to provide an *operational definition* for each variable studied. The operational definition assigns specific meaning in quantitative or categorical terms to the use of a variable. For Holmes and Nagy, the independent variable was operationally defined by classifying the infants into the four categories previously stated on the basis of gestational age, infant health, and maternal health. The dependent variables, which might be affected by the health and gestational status of the infant, were operationally defined by the scores on the Brazelton Neonatal Behavioral Assessment Scale.

Methodology for the Study

Sample
The persons, or subjects, who participate in a research project. They are generally chosen to reflect the characteristics of a larger similar group, or population, that the sample represents.

In addition to establishing the problem, some of the most important decisions facing the researcher are the various aspects of methodology. Selecting an appropriate *sample* is often the first step in the method for conducting research. The sample consists of those individuals, or subjects, who participate in the research project and are assumed generally to reflect the characteristics of similar people of concern to the researcher.

Research Close-up
Prematurity and the
Scientific Method

 A practical issue that has received much recent and deserved attention concerns the negative effects of prematurity on infant development. Much evidence has been obtained that indicates significant differences between full-term and preterm babies with respect to physical, social, and emotional characteristics. Researchers interested in examining this problem have several important steps to climb before collecting data. First, they must read past research relating to the topic to explore the nature of the problem, the exact procedures used to study it, the results of the investigations, and the limitations of any conclusions presented.

Deborah Holmes and Jill Nagy (1982) and their associates at Loyola University and the Evanston Hospital apparently were concerned that findings on the subject of prematurity were not clear. In particular, they noted (1) previous studies often failed to examine infants from the first days of life, (2) comparisons between healthy full-term and all preterm infants were inappropriate, and (3) there was a lack of sensitive assessment techniques for documenting conditions during the neonatal (newborn) period. Therefore, Holmes and Nagy were prepared to undertake the next step in planning their own work. They decided to attempt to clarify the confusion in the literature by examining infants thoroughly during the early weeks after birth and by sampling from the following four groups: (1) 11 preterms who were in the intensive care unit, (2) 12 sick full-terms who were in the intensive care unit, (3) 8 healthy full-terms who were in the neonatal nursery for prolonged periods because their mothers had postnatal complications, and (4) 13 healthy full-terms who were in the neonatal nursery for the usual 3 or 4 days.

According to the researchers, the infants were all from two-parent, middle-class families; received good prenatal care; were of birthweights that corresponded to gestational age; and did not evidence central nervous system damage. The infants were evaluated 48 hours before hospital discharge for qualities such as alertness, social responsivity, and motoric activity using the Brazelton Neonatal Behavioral Assessment Scale—Kansas modification. In addi-

The larger group from which the sample is drawn is known as the *population*. Because the researcher is rarely able to investigate a total population, the researcher attempts to obtain a representative sample to generalize the results beyond the sample to that larger population (large samples are usually more representative than small ones).

If researchers choose limited or inadequate samples, the results cannot be validly generalized to other samples. For example, Holmes and Nagy had difficulty obtaining an equal number of infants, balanced for males and females, in each of the four status groups. In addition, because equating infants for severity of illness, extent of hospital stay, and maternal complications was beyond their control, they expressed caution in the interpretation of their study.

tion, birthweights and gestational ages were recorded for each infant, and they were administered the Obstetrical Complications Scale and the Postnatal Complications Scale developed by Littman and Parmelee.

After collecting their data, Holmes and Nagy statistically analyzed the information to compare the effects of prematurity, illness, and extended hospitalization. The statistical techniques used were varied to effectively disentangle the influences of the different factors on the infant's development. In the Holmes and Nagy sample, results did confirm that preterm infants exhibit more immaturity and less optimal behaviors than their full-term counterparts. However, the researchers were led to conclude "that these deficits in early behavior may not be due to preterm birth per se but to other factors associated with preterm birth" (Holmes, Nagy, Slaymaker, Sosnowski, Prinz, & Pasternak, 1982, p. 748).

Indeed, the groups most similar in tested performance patterns were the preterm infants and the full-terms who were also in the intensive care unit. These full-term infants were, on the average, normal gestational age and birthweight and had mothers with no major obstetrical problems, but they did spend a prolonged period of time in the hospital (2 weeks compared with 3 weeks for the preterm infants). Neither illness nor hospitalization may be entirely responsible for behavioral differences in newborn babies, however, because on some measures the full-terms with sick mothers performed similarly to the preterms, while the sick full-terms with normal mothers had patterns similar to those of the healthy full-terms. The researchers suggest that perhaps perinatal (around the time of birth) stress, evidenced by the Obstetrical Complications Scale, might explain some of the difficulties. In sum, Holmes and Nagy claim that preterm delivery may lead to problems for infant development only when complicated by some combination of severe postnatal illness, the environment of an extended hospital stay, and the amount of stress during labor, rather than simply being due to immaturity itself.

Other aspects of methodology facing the developmental researcher are the overall strategy, procedures, and design of the study. These features must be explicit and unambiguous so that others can attempt to confirm the results independently. Subsequent sections of this chapter, therefore, will describe in greater detail research strategies, data collection procedures, and designs of particular interest for the study of development.

Analysis of the Results

Analysis of research results need not provoke fear among students new to the study of human development. Statistics are merely efficient numerical tools designed to simplify the researcher's task of drawing conclusions from the data obtained. The methods for analyzing data can be classified according to three questions that reflect the formulation and design of the research problem:

1. Does the researcher wish to summarize data or to estimate the likelihood of chance findings?
2. Does the researcher wish to focus on differences between groups or on the relationship among variables?
3. Does the researcher wish to examine only one dependent variable or more than one simultaneously?

Descriptive and Inferential Statistics

Summarizing data succinctly involves the use of familiar concepts, such as percentages and averages (mean, median, mode). These procedures and other related ones are known as *descriptive statistics.* In contrast, statistics that determine the probability of obtaining similar results with a different sample from the same population are called *inferential statistics.* The results of inferential analysis are always reported in terms of probability, because the researcher, without studying every member of the population, never can be completely certain that chance factors have been eliminated.

Furthermore, a statistically significant finding (a result that the researcher is fairly confident does not involve chance) does not necessarily imply practical or important results. These findings are probably not a fluke, but their meaning may be open to various interpretations. For example, Holmes and Nagy, by providing the average scores for each of the independent and dependent variables and by calculating a statistic for determining the likelihood of finding differences among the groups again, used both descriptive and inferential statistics, respectively.

Descriptive statistics
Mathematical procedures that simplify and succinctly summarize data (e.g., averages and percentages).

Inferential statistics
Mathematical procedures that estimate the probability of obtaining similar data with a different sample from the same population.

Statistical analysis, which helps reduce the complexity of data collected, takes many forms. Computers have greatly increased the efficiency with which researchers can process statistical information.

Correlational and Group Differences Statistics

Because Holmes and Nagy were primarily interested in comparing the behavioral characteristics of infants in the four neonatal statuses, their research first employed the group differences approach. When an investigation deals with attributes or performances of two or more groups, the data will be analyzed with *group differences statistics* (these usually are also inferential statistics).

Group differences statistics
Mathematical procedures that organize data in a manner to permit comparisons between two or more groups within a sample.

However, Holmes and Nagy were also interested in the relative contribution made by each independent variable used to create the four groups. It was possible, therefore, to focus on the degree of relationship among variables instead of on the differences between groups. For example, what is the relationship between gestational age or birthweight or length of hospital stay or maternal complication level and the behavioral characteristics of the infants? The analysis of data relating the degree and direction of relationship among two or more variables requires the use of *correlational statistics.*

Correlational statistics (positive and negative correlations)
Mathematical procedures that organize data to show the strength and direction of relationship between two or more variables.

Correlations may vary in strength from low (indicating little relationship) to high (indicating a strong relationship). In a sample of adults, for instance, the correlation between their height and weight is likely to be high (.79), but the correlation between their height and their IQ scores is likely to be low (.13). Correlation statistics may be both descriptive and inferential. The higher the correlation between variables, the better is our ability to predict one by knowing the other. If the amount of infant babbling correlates highly with verbal skill at age 3, for example, we might expect a vocal infant to be a talkative toddler. This type of relationship, known as a *positive correlation,* occurs when scoring high on one variable suggests scoring high on the second variable. However, the direction of a relationship can also be reversed. For example, suppose research demonstrated that the more time adolescents spend studying, the fewer juvenile delinquent acts they would commit. A relationship in which scores on one variable increase while scores on the other one decrease is called a *negative correlation.*

Even high positive or negative correlations cannot provide perfectly accurate predictions for a given individual, however. Statistics are usually procedures for describing general tendencies exhibited by a total sample. Correlation statistics, therefore, are expressed in terms of both strength and direction, and they describe the nature of relationships, as well as the probability of their existence in similar samples from the same population. Furthermore, correlations do not imply that one variable causes changes in another, merely that the two are somehow related. The interpretation of correlation statistics requires the utmost caution and a continued search for causal factors, as the Holmes and Nagy research demonstrates.

Univariate and Multivariate Statistics

In the Holmes and Nagy study, the combined influence of the independent variables was examined with respect to the scores on the Brazelton Scale

Multivariate statistics
Mathematical procedures that are
used to analyze the data of multiple
dependent variables simultaneously.

Univariate statistics
Mathematical procedures that are
used to analyze the data of only one
dependent variable at a time.

(the dependent variable) for the infants. Statistics that are used to analyze
more than one dependent and independent variable at a time are known as
multivariate statistics. A substantial increase in multivariate analyses in
recent years reflects the recognition by development theorists that human
behavior is difficult to understand without considering the simultaneous
effects of several variables.

Univariate statistics involve the analysis of only one dependent variable
at a time. Although easier to calculate as well as to interpret, they may not
accurately reflect developmental complexity. Holmes and Nagy also used
univariate statistics to analyze the overall differences among the four
neonatal groups.

Interpretation of the Research

The researcher who has subjected data to statistical analysis is ready to
begin the concluding phase of the project. This may take the form of a report
to professional colleagues (and possibly to the public as well), if the
researcher feels the contribution would be valuable. Research reports
describe the type of information outlined thus far in this chapter, including
a discussion of the value of the results. The discussion entails a review of all
findings with respect to the researcher's hypotheses, other relevant research
and theory, limitations of the methodology, potential applications of the
results, and appropriate directives for additional investigations. Several
points concerning Holmes and Nagy's discussion of their results have been
mentioned briefly. Perhaps, to the consumer of research, this final phase of
the project is the most exciting, because it links the past with the future of
the problem. It permits the researcher to offer some interesting speculation
that creatively may extend the original ideas and details presented.

RESEARCH STRATEGIES

Three nonstatistical questions, determined partly by the purposes of the
study and partly by practical considerations, also confront the researcher:

1. Can or should the researcher actively manipulate one or more variables
   of interest?
2. Can or should the researcher examine a single individual or a group?
3. Can or should the research be conducted in a natural or a laboratory
   setting?

The answers to these questions guide the overall methodology of the
investigation. Most of the following discussion, however, deals with aspects
of the first question.

Experimental Approach

Experimental strategy
A type of research in which one or more variables are manipulated and isolated to determine cause-and-effect relationships.

The primary goal of an ***experimental strategy*** is to isolate a particular variable hypothesized to affect development and to manipulate its influence within part of the sample. Ultimately, the researcher compares the effects of the manipulation and its absence among different groups in the sample to determine if that variable causes developmental change.

A recurring controversy in developmental methodology involves the significance of the experimental strategy for illuminating the nature of change. Borrowed from the physical sciences, the method of experimental research, according to Appelbaum and McCall (1983) and other critics, has become excessively worshipped. The problems of the experimental strategy will be discussed after the strategy is explained more fully. The research of Steuer, Applefield, and Smith (1971) will be used as an example.

Key factors in experimental research are (1) identifying a causal, or independent, variable that can be manipulated and (2) applying the manipulation or treatment to one part of a sample (experimental group), but not to another (control group) for comparative purposes. Steuer and her colleagues were interested in the effects of aggressive television programming on preschool children. They hypothesized that exposure to such hostile behaviors (independent variable) causes increased interpersonal aggression (dependent variable). Two small groups of 4- to 5-year-old children were shown approximately 2 hours of either aggressive (experimental group) or nonaggressive (control group) programming over a period of 11 days.

These groups of children previously had been matched on their typical amount of aggression displayed and frequency of television watching. The matching procedure was used to be certain that both groups were similar before application of the treatment. Sometimes the equivalence of groups in large samples can be assumed if the subjects are randomly assigned to the experimental or the control condition. Another possibility would be for the researcher to use only one group to compare the amount of interpersonal aggression before and after the treatment (watching aggressive programming) began. However, this strategy has several statistical flaws that need not concern us here.

In the Steuer, Applefield, and Smith study, several observers behind one-way mirrors were trained to record the amount of aggression displayed during free play by each child in both the experimental and control groups. The results of these observations clearly indicated that those children who viewed aggressive television programming (experimental group) displayed significantly more aggressive acts toward others in free play than did the children who viewed nonaggressive programs (control group). Therefore, the researchers suggested that watching televised hostility caused the children to behave more aggressively, because they appeared to behave similarly before viewing the programs.

If this conclusion appears reasonable, why do some developmental researchers question the value of the experimental strategy? Every study has its limitations. Research evidence should be accepted only after analyzing the results of many investigations of the same problem that used different approaches. In the experiment just discussed, the authors themselves point out a possible weakness: "that one or two subjects were influenced directly by the television manipulation and that other subjects began to display more hostility in retaliation, independently of the televised stimuli" (Steuer et al., 1971, p. 447). Although experimenters try to control for such difficulties by careful planning, being able to predict every potential confounding factor is rare.

The experimental strategy has other weaknesses, too. As mentioned, developmental change may be influenced simultaneously by several variables. However, a researcher is not likely to be able to manipulate more than one or two variables in any given experiment. In addition, many factors that concern human development are either impractical or unethical for a researcher to manipulate. Holmes and Nagy's research on prematurity provides an example. Although determining if infants are negatively affected by limited gestational age may be important, no experimenter would seriously consider research that deliberately induces premature labor and delivery. Therefore, Holmes and Nagy's research had to be nonexperimental. Even Steuer's study borders on the violation of ethical research principles (see *Issues in Human Development,* "The Ethics of Research"), because children were asked to view television programs that had a potentially negative impact on behavior. However, the treatment was of short duration (2 hours) and included programs the children would have viewed at home on Saturday mornings anyway.

Nonexperimental Methods

Wohlwill (1973), among others, has suggested that nonexperimental methods, especially if designed from a multivariate perspective, are most appropriate for developmental research. The nonexperimental strategy largely consists of (1) comparisons of group differences in which no researcher manipulations occur (such as the study by Holmes and Nagy), and (2) correlational approaches in which relationships between nonmanipulated factors are evaluated (also found in the Holmes and Nagy study). Common variables in nonexperimental group comparisons—which are significant to human development researchers but cannot be manipulated—include sex, age, race, and socioeconomic status. Correlational research (analyzed using correlation statistics, as described previously) focuses on the apparent influence of any one measurable variable on another.

The major flaw of nonexperimental research, however, concerns the apparent relationship between variables or the apparent relationship between variables or the apparent differences between groups. Because the researcher has not actually manipulated any of the variables, it is impossible to draw causal conclusions. Consider, for example, a study of elderly men that demonstrates a positive relationship between the number of good friends one has and a lack of concern about death. Does having many friends cause an elderly man to think about other things besides death? Or does the fact that the man does not talk constantly about dying cause others to be his friend? Perhaps high self-esteem causes him to think positively about life as well as to relate honestly and cheerfully to other people. Caution is necessary regarding the nature and direction of cause-and-effect relationships despite variables that seem to "go together." Complex correlation procedures, which indicate more effectively the likelihood of causal links in nonexperimental research, are increasingly being used, but this is beyond the scope of this chapter.

Studying Individuals

As Chapter 1 mentioned, most of the research in human development is based on the analysis of groups of individuals. Generalizations about how these findings can be applied to a particular person entail some degree of uncertainty. The difficulties of translating group data to the individual level occasionally have encouraged researchers to study only one subject or family in greater detail. Intensive examinations of a single person also point out questions or topics that should be more widely investigated through group research. In other words, the process of alternating between group and individual research strategies provides the study of human development with an appropriate balance.

Because many elements of group research have already been considered, this section will briefly describe a few variations of the individual strategy. The earliest type is merely an extension of the baby biography discussed previously. This strategy was elevated to a new plateau of respect by Jean Piaget's exhaustive studies of the cognitive development of his own three infants (1963). Piaget's observations—originally termed the *clinical method*—were largely nonexperimental. However, he frequently intervened to demonstrate developmental change convincingly. For example, consider the following excerpt from *The Origins of Intelligence in Children* in which Piaget (1963) discusses the behavior of his daughter Lucienne (4½ months old), who

> looks at a rattle with desire, but without extending her hand. I place the rattle near her right hand. As soon as Lucienne sees rattle and hand together, she moves her hand closer to the rattle and finally grasps it. A moment later she is engaged in looking at her hand. I then put the rattle aside; Lucienne looks at it, then directs her eyes to her hand, then to the rattle again, after which she slowly moves her hand toward the rattle. As soon as she touches it, there is an attempt to grasp it and finally, success. (p. 111)

Perhaps more common than Piaget's approach is the ***case-study method***. This strategy, primarily derived from the psychoanalytic perspective,

Clinical method
An individual research strategy in which the child is provided with certain materials and problems to solve within a flexible format and then observed closely, one on one.

Case-study method
An individual research strategy, derived from the methods of psychoanalysis, in which the details of a person's life are carefully documented and discussed within a flexible format.

Issues in Human Development
The Ethics of Research

 The aspects of methodology considered in this chapter pose issues of secondary importance in contrast to the rights of participants in human development research. Neither statistics nor research strategy is relevant if the dignity of the subject is not protected. However, determining where to draw the line between research that is ethical and research that violates human dignity is often quite difficult. Developmental research is not morally neutral. Researchers must accept responsibility for articulating ethical hypotheses, conducting safe investigations, alleviating the concerns of participants, reaching justifiable conclusions, and properly disseminating the information of colleagues and the public.

Although few formal restrictions are placed on the research process, a widely recognized set of guidelines is described in the American Psychological Association's booklet *Ethical Principles in the Conduct of Research with Human Participants* (1982). While thinking about some of the basic principles and controversial decisions the booklet raises, the researcher should also consider whether it is unethical *not* to do research that may ultimately contribute to the improvement of human welfare (Achenbach, 1978). Once the choice has been made to pursue the research, however, attention should be devoted to the details of the study that balance the rights of participants with the legitimate goals of the researcher.

Several principles appear to be so simple and straightforward that no honest researcher would hesitate to comply:

- Participants should be fully informed about the nature of the research.
- Subjects must volunteer without any coercion (consent should be obtained from participating children, as well as their parents).
- No treatment should be physically or mentally harmful.
- Confidentiality of the data must be preserved.
- Subject withdrawal at any time should not be restricted.
- Participants should be entitled to knowledge about the results.

There may be more to these ideals than meets the eye. For example, how can a researcher obtain the informed consent of a subject if the goal of a study is to compare the effects of cognitive development on racial prejudice? Most participants would attempt to behave according to socially acceptable standards unless the researcher disguised the true purpose of the investigation. In this case, after collecting the data, subjects could be debriefed (the entire process could be carefully explained). Although this is clearly not informed consent, is it an unethical procedure? Baumrind (1985), for instance, does not think so.

A researcher observing certain behaviors in a nursing home notices one of the residents stealing an expensive watch. Should the action be quietly coded and then ignored? If so, is the researcher accountable for assisting in a crime? Must the confidentiality and privacy of the participants be respected? Perhaps a casual warning to the thief would suffice. Or perhaps the incident should be reported to the nursing home director.

The establishment of a program to improve the memory skills of high school students may involve a different dilemma. If a control group is not also

carefully follows and documents the therapeutic progress of an individual. Excerpts from case studies may be used to highlight patterns of change, as well as developmental problems. The major advantages of case studies are that they permit a great deal of flexibility in procedure, require no sophisticated statistical analyses, and yield rich and often fascinating accounts of individual development. What the case study lacks in represen-

given the opportunity to learn from the treatment, is the researcher indirectly discriminating against this group? Does the researcher have an obligation to make potential benefits of the study available to all participants as compensation for their time and effort?

The reactions of participants to the mere presence of the researcher may itself be a surprising and important phenomenon. This was the case, for example, in Milgram's (1963) use of a phony electric-shocking device that subjects were operating to encourage learners (actually research assistants) in the next room. The subjects were clearly upset by the nature of their task. However, despite volunteering and knowing they could leave at any time, few of the adult subjects disobeyed the instruction to "shock" the "learners" or decided to withdraw from the anxiety-provoking situation. The status or implied authority of a researcher must be wielded very cautiously, especially for participants who may be less able to make "free" choices (infants and young children, the mentally retarded, the mentally ill, incarcerated juveniles, and even animals).

As we continue to work toward understanding socially sensitive issues in human development, what constitutes ethically defensible research will become increasingly difficult to define. There can be no easy, step-by-step cookbook of ethical guidelines that will enable researchers to eliminate all risks from their investigations. Each plan must be evaluated on its own merits and modified or abandoned if necessary so that the gains in knowledge are perceived to far outweigh the likelihood of problems. Researchers must design valuable studies that will inspire the confidence of participants in a joint venture to explore human development.

Research in human development is often nonexperimental because manipulation of critical variables by a scientist might be unethical. Would these young girls behave naturally if studied in a controlled setting?

tativeness and comparability, it makes up for in vivid details that may suggest the course of future developmental research.

As a final example of the individual strategy, consider the single-subject experimental design. In this research strategy, the behavior of only one person, or a few people, is manipulated over time. Single-subject experimental design is used to demonstrate the principles forwarded by the behaviorist perspective. When these principles are discussed in Chapter 6, bear in mind that they often are based on one person rather than on a group. In general, such mini-experiments show the processes of behavioral learning under relatively controlled conditions and the ways in which they may alleviate certain problems. A middle-aged woman who is afraid of dogs, for instance, might be systematically rewarded for behaving in a relaxed manner. Overall, single-subject experiments share with clinical, or case, studies the narrow focus on individual change. They do, however, emphasize observable behaviors and more controlled conditions instead of underlying cognitive or personality structures.

The Laboratory or the Field?

A major criticism of methodology in human development has been the tendency to avoid the natural settings of behavior in favor of the laboratory environment (McCall, 1977a). Although investigations in a highly controlled and standardized setting have made valuable contributions, the artificiality of laboratory research has limited a more complete understanding of change. The trend in recent years, therefore, has been a revival of the role of naturalistic research that was once the prevalent developmental methodology. Impetus for this shift in perspective has been provided by such diverse disciplines as ethology, cultural anthropology, and environmental psychology. A provocative synthesis by Bronfenbrenner (1979), *The Ecology of Human Development,* suggests the need for developmentalists to address the interaction of people within their natural settings.

The laboratory versus naturalistic setting should not be confused with the experimental versus the nonexperimental strategy controversy. Even though laboratory research has typically been experimental and naturalistic research usually has been nonexperimental, either strategy can be used in either setting. Bronfenbrenner (1979) stressed the importance of the "ecological validity" of the setting; that is, the experiment should be conducted in a setting that seems natural to participants. Day care centers, hospitals, restaurants, homes, schools, offices, shopping malls, parks and playgrounds, factories, skating rinks, senior citizens centers, and libraries are just a few of the locations that offer researchers an opportunity to examine behavior in a natural context. Furthermore, unobtrusive manipulation can be introduced into natural settings; this strategy is termed a *field experiment* (e.g., a small change in a classroom teaching technique).

Researchers who worry that important variables cannot be manipulated easily in settings outside the laboratory also must wonder how results obtained in strange situations can be generalized to the real world. Of course, the laboratory can be a most useful setting for examining how people behave in unfamiliar environments.

Sometimes a researcher may be able to take advantage of a *natural experiment*—one in which crucial changes may be investigated without deliberate intervention—by simply being in the right place at the right time. For example, if a business was planning to make some changes in working

Field experiment
A type of experimental strategy in which the research is conducted relatively unobtrusively in a natural setting rather than in a laboratory.

Natural experiment
A type of nonexperimental strategy in which the researcher is able to take advantage of a naturally occurring manipulation instead of deliberately intervening.

conditions, researchers could observe certain employee behaviors before the changes and again after the changes had been instituted. Thus, the researchers would be able to take advantage of a naturally occurring treatment without distorting the reality of the surroundings or events.

Problems in Doing Research

Regardless of the research strategy selected, there are several other problems beyond those previously mentioned. The details of the research design may produce biases that severely influence the data collected.

Demand characteristics
The cues about the nature of a research project to which the subjects unknowingly may react, thereby biasing the results.

Some of these biases are referred to as *demand characteristics,* or the cues about the research to which subjects may unknowingly react. For instance, participation in the research itself may stimulate some people to improve their performance or to change their attitudes. This is quite similar to the concept of a placebo: People think taking a pill (really only sugar) will make them better, and it does. Subjects may try to please the researcher, purposely resist the research, or attempt to figure out exactly what the researcher wants to explore. These behaviors may be a function of the attractiveness of the materials, where the research is conducted, the nature of the instructions or procedures, or the characteristics of the researchers themselves (such as age, sex, race, physical qualities, and personality).

Response set
The tendency of research subjects to react in a constantly similar manner despite variations in stimulation, thereby biasing the results of an experiment.

Another type of bias is known as a *response set,* or the tendency to respond continually in a similar manner despite any variation in the source of stimulation. Subjects, for example, often try to do what they believe will be considered socially good or conventionally correct, despite what the researcher says or does. Researchers, however, are also likely to be guilty of reacting according to response sets. One tendency of observers, for example, is to rate the present behavior of a subject according to previous ratings. When researchers allow their judgment to be affected by the past behavior of the subjects, the halo effect is said to be operating. A final instance of researcher bias is the expectancy effect, in which subjects pick up subtle clues as to what the researcher hopes will occur.

Researchers must take all possible precautions to minimize these different sources of bias. For example, they may choose procedures that do not create extreme reactions or hire assistants unfamiliar with the goals of the research to interact with their subjects.

This survey of research strategies clearly indicates the diversity of choices available to the investigator of human development. Figure 2.1 summarizes these principal research strategies according to the questions formulated earlier. This chapter has pointed out the limitations, as well as the benefits, of the various strategies. Unfortunately, because researchers can employ no more than a few of these approaches in any given study, the acquisition of useful data is a gradual, time-consuming process. As the following sections will show, researchers, having determined their basic strategy, then must select an appropriate data collection procedure and choose a suitable developmental design.

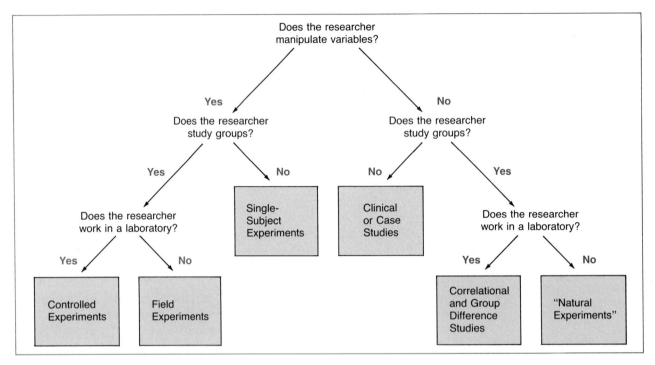

Figure 2.1
Flowchart of Basic Research Strategies

PROCEDURES FOR COLLECTING DATA

Whatever strategy researchers select for testing hypotheses or answering research questions, another critical decision they face is precisely how to operationalize the variables that are to be manipulated or measured. Thousands of somewhat different methods have been used for collecting data throughout the history of developmental research. However, these variations can be summarized in three basic ways: (1) surveying subjects directly, (2) obviously or unobtrusively observing subjects' behavior, and (3) providing subjects with certain tasks or tests to complete. Although each of these methods will be described separately, remember that researchers do not necessarily employ any one of them exclusively, even within the same investigation.

Survey Method

Survey approach
Data collection procedures that use the direct techniques of interviewing and questionnaires to obtain results.

Perhaps the most obvious method of obtaining information from people is to request it in a straightforward manner. This ***survey approach*** can take several forms. *Interviews* (often called interview schedules) are personal surveys administered face-to-face or, occasionally, by telephone. *Question-naires,* in contrast, are self-administered surveys that may be distributed individually or initiated through the mail. Surveys by mail or by telephone are plagued by lack of cooperation and have not been found to be cost-effective for gathering detailed and sensitive types of data (Kerlinger, 1973).

The personal interview and, to a lesser extent, the carefully constructed questionnaire can be useful methods to study human development. Respondents may be asked two extreme types of questions: structured and unstructured. If the interview is structured, the question sequence will be rigidly prepared and provoke fairly simple responses. Although structured questions may make interpretation easier, the unstructured interview offers the opportunity for the respondent to provide more detailed information. Furthermore, the interviewer is able to introduce follow-up questions for clarification and generally to establish greater rapport with the respondent.

A potential danger of the interview method is that questions of interest to the researcher may be too delicate for the respondent to react to comfortably. This may lead to resistance, dishonesty, or a general tendency to respond in a fashion presumed by the respondent to be socially desirable. In such cases, a self-administered questionnaire—especially if returned anonymously—would provide a more advantageous approach.

Why is the face-to-face interview used, considering the weaknesses suggested (not to mention the time and expense involved)? The answer lies in the weaknesses of the self-administered questionnaire. The self-administered questionnaire is based on possibly erroneous assumptions: that questions are interpreted the same way by all respondents and that all people are equally capable of expressing their ideas in writing. These assumptions are particularly doubtful for research with young children. Different survey methods, as well as various observational or testing approaches, are chosen according to the kind of information desired and the developmental level of the sample.

In sum, the survey method can be an important tool for the developmental researcher. Although a fairly costly procedure (except for relatively small samples), the flexibility of a personal interview is an attractive feature. The most difficult aspect of using an interview approach is being certain the interviewers are carefully trained and sensitive to the feelings of respondents.

Observational Method

Instead of directly confronting people, researchers often decide simply to observe them and draw conclusions from their behavior. Sometimes researchers elect to use observations made for them by others who are familiar with the subjects in their study (e.g., parents, friends, supervisors).

Observational research

Data collection procedures that use checklists, rating scales, narrative methods, or behavioral samples to obtain results. Researchers or their appointees usually try to obtain the data relatively unobtrusively in natural settings.

Unlike survey methods, ***observational research*** is appropriate for infants and young children, who are less likely to be as self-conscious as adolescents or adults. Of course, some types of observation may be unnoticed by the subjects because they occur after the fact (such as evaluating artwork) or involve disguised observers (disguised as passengers on a crowded bus, for example). Sometimes subjects will simply ignore observers after sufficient time has elapsed. The use of observational methods, however, places the entire burden of interpretive responsibility on the researchers' observations rather than on the subjects' own responses.

Just as survey methods vary in degree of structure, both open-ended and relatively restricted forms of observation may be used. Among the open, or narrative, forms are the subject's personal diaries, anecdotal accounts, and records of continuous behavioral sequences. Although rarely available, diaries are relatively regular, retrospective descriptions that provide developmentally interesting documentation of change. Anecdotal records offer more sporadic, yet disinterested, accounts of unusual or characteristic behaviors. Continuous narrative methods, called running records or specimen descriptions, involve richly detailed notes of behavior as it occurs. Specimen descriptions are the more extensive and formal variation of the running records that have been used frequently by teachers since the turn of the century to evaluate classroom interactions (Irwin & Bushnell, 1980).

The use of unstructured observational methods need not be restricted to studying behavior in school settings. Many kinds of research reports offer illustrative anecdotes, and others would benefit from incorporating narrative methods. A primary advantage of these techniques is the permanent availability of extensive descriptions of behavior in a natural context. Unfortunately, on-the-spot narrative methods require expensive and time-consuming recording, in contrast to diaries and anecdotes, which can be examined after the event. The researcher thus is asked to compromise between detailed sequences and an informal flexibility. It would be a serious mistake, however, to dismiss the value of casual observation methods. Piaget's descriptions, for instance, changed the course of research in infant development.

Structured observational approaches are typically less detailed samples of behavior that provide the dual benefits of efficiency and reliability. These techniques include time and event sampling, checklists, and rating scales. The time-sampling method is used to examine the frequency of predetermined categories of behavior (e.g., physically aggressive acts) for a specific interval (e.g., 30 minutes) at a selected period of the day (e.g., as 2–2:30 P.M.). In event sampling, the observer waits for an anticipated behavior to occur and then notes the duration and other details relevant to that behavior. For instance, the observer watches 4 minutes of consecutive physical aggression between Roger and Jim over a toy truck. The scuffle began when Roger started punching Jim to obtain the truck.

Checklists are carefully planned observation forms that allow little variation or elaboration from the fairly simple target behaviors selected in advance. Although such descriptions provide no time reference, they are extremely simple to use for many kinds of observations (see Figure 2.2). The rating scale is similarly efficient but requires the rater to judge the quantitative extent of the subject's behavior. An observer, for example, might be asked to rate the aggressiveness of Roger's behavior on a scale from 1 to 10, or to indicate how frequently Roger engages in aggressive behavior (often, occasionally, seldom, never).

Most observational research in human development has used structured techniques rather than unstructured ones. Several reasons for this

CHILD ___WALTER LEONARD___ DATE __9/24/79__

TASK	YES	NO	IF "NO," DATE FIRST SEEN
1. Can pick out the following shapes as they are named			
circle	✓		
square	✓		
triangle	✓		
rectangle	✓		
2. Can count from 1 to 10	✓		
3. Can name properly the following shapes			
circle	✓		
square	✓		
triangle	✓		
rectangle		✓	10/2
4. Demonstrates understanding of the following relational concepts			
bigger	✓		
smaller	✓		
longer		✓	10/19
shorter		✓	10/26
5. Can do one-to-one correspondence for			
two objects	✓		
three objects	✓		
five objects	✓		
ten objects		✓	11/9
more than ten objects		✓	11/9
6. Can follow directions involving the following concepts			
first	✓		
middle		✓	11/16
last		✓	12/13
7. Demonstrates understanding of			
more than		✓	3/7
less than		✓	4/2

Figure 2.2
A Sample Observation Checklist

Source: Observational checklist from *Observational Strategies for Child Study* by D. Michelle Irwin and Margaret M. Bushnell, copyright © 1980 by Holt, Rinehart and Winston, Inc., reprinted by permission of the publisher.

pattern are ease of recording or coding behaviors, greater efficiency in terms of time and money, more control over behavior to be observed, ability to obtain larger samples, and simplicity of scoring and statistical analysis. Even structured methods, however, are not without certain important weaknesses. Time sampling may miss the continuity of behavior; event sampling may miss the behavior altogether; checklists can be superficial; and rating scales are easily affected by observer bias (such as the halo effect described earlier).

Any type of observational data collection has the advantage of obtaining information in a relatively natural manner, especially if the observer makes an effort to remain in the background. The main weakness of this approach, however, is that the inferences the observer makes about a subject's behavior are colored by the observer's perspective. To minimize this difficulty, it is essential to compare the independent ratings of at least two observers. Agreement among observers tends to ensure the value of conclusions drawn from the observations. In recent years, observational methods have become more reliable tools for understanding human development because of technological advances in portable videotape equipment, electronic event recorders, and sophisticated computer programs. These improvements permit researchers to place increasing confidence in the use of observational techniques.

Testing Method

Standardized tests or tasks

Systematic methods for obtaining samples of categorical or numerical information that are inferred to represent a person's characteristics.

The data collection technique most widely used in developmental research is the presentation of **standardized tests** or **tasks** to subjects. These methods are more challenging to the subject than surveys and more intrusive than observation. However, they are able to provide large amounts of reliable (consistent) data that help researchers avoid the effects of their own biases and possibly those of the subjects in the study. Interpretations of the data are usually carefully defined by having all subjects respond to an identical set of stimuli or directions; researchers then score the responses according to a predetermined set of criteria. Because the subjects are not informed in advance of the "correct" responses, they are presumably less likely to be aware of the researcher's hypotheses.

Standardized tests or tasks can be defined as systematic methods for obtaining samples of categorical or numerical information. The samples are inferred to represent a person's characteristics. An individual's responses typically are compared with those of an appropriate representative sample (called a norm group) for interpretation.

Hundreds of commercially distributed tests and innumerable unpublished ones are available. They may be divided into tests that attempt to measure:

- achievement (mastery of specifically learned kinds of information)
- intelligence (several types, depending on the definition of intelligence accepted)

- special aptitudes (for example, motoric, linguistic, or musical)
- personality (attributes such as depression, femininity, and dominance)
- attitudes and values (religious, political, and aesthetic)
- interest or vocational orientations (career leanings such as artistic, social, or practical)

Clearly, this list is not exhaustive, and other reasonable ways may be used to classify the multitude of tasks and tests.

Despite the popularity of standardized tests in human development research, certain disadvantages accompany this method. These weaknesses

This young girl is being administered one of the many items from the Stanford Binet test. Standardized tests like this may provide valuable information to both researchers and clinicians.

should be considered above and beyond factors such as the qualifications of the test interpreter, rapport between test taker and test administrator, and any distracting conditions during the testing session. Tests, for example, can be considered artificial and limited samples of behaviors, thoughts, and feelings. Particularly in the realm of personality assessment, tests are not immune to deliberate distortions by subjects who wish to appear socially "normal" or who fear being labeled as somehow maladjusted. Also, some aspects of development may not be amenable to contrived measurement techniques and would be better assessed through surveys or observational methods. Furthermore, many tests cannot be interpreted any more objectively than other methods to draw inferences about development. The underlying question for test users, then, concerns the validity of a test for its intended purpose.

Testing, however, has been unfairly portrayed as a villainous approach for assessing human behavior. Certainly, abuses of the testing process in both research and actual practice have occurred. For instance, it can be unfair or misleading to label permanently a person's intelligence according to the results of one imperfect testing procedure. But such individually disturbing situations should not be permitted to diminish the contributions of tests. When carefully constructed and employed, they are efficient tools in such diverse areas as evaluation of academic performances, selection for employment opportunities, and counseling of troubled individuals. Optimism concerning the future of testing is warranted because of improved technical training, recent statistical advances, and an increasing awareness of the complex relationships between developmental theory and test construction.

This discussion of data collection methods has only begun to suggest the variety of resources from which the inventive researcher can either select or modify. These examples indicate the basis for most of the conclusions discussed in later chapters. Most of the important biological types of data frequently used in developmental research have not yet been mentioned. Many of these procedures may be familiar: measuring height and weight, heart rate, respiration rate, galvanic skin response, reaction time, brain wave patterns, visual acuity, auditory discrimination, and others. Exciting new biofeedback techniques demonstrating voluntary control over bodily processes also offer the possibility of integrating psychological and physiological data for a broader understanding of human development.

DEVELOPMENTAL DESIGNS

The strategies and procedures discussed up to this point would be familiar to all researchers in the social sciences and education. Additional considerations confront researchers in human development because they are primarily interested in examining patterns of change or stability across the life span. Important variables in developmental research, therefore, are time and the factors with which it interacts to produce developmental change.

Time, an elusive concept, presents special difficulties for the researcher, depending on how it is defined. In other words, time could refer to the interval between birth and the present (chronological age), to the period when an individual was born (generation or age cohort), or to the particular occasion when the research was conducted (time of measurement).

This section explores some of the designs and issues that relate to the meaning of time for the study of human development. Remember, however, that not every study is directly concerned with time itself. Much research, such as the Holmes and Nagy study, is only peripherally concerned with time (gestational age and future development). Other investigations use events that have occurred in the past but do not measure changes. Such retrospective, or historical, designs are actually quite common in developmental research.

Cross-sectional Research

Cross-sectional design

A developmental research method that compares the data from different chronological age groups simultaneously.

The *cross-sectional design* focuses on the simultaneous comparison of individuals of different chronological ages (see Figure 2.3). Developmental change and chronological age are not synonymous, as was pointed out earlier; therefore, such research provides specific details of age differences, from which we tend to infer developmental change. Researchers need to exercise caution in making inferences based on cross-sectional data, because they have not manipulated their subjects' age, cohort (year of birth), or development history. In other words, are age differences found due to universal processes of development or to the different experiences to which subjects of particular cohorts have been exposed?

Consider, for example, a study to examine the gender role development of female adults. Suppose the sample consisted of 20-year-olds, 30-year-olds, and 40-year-olds. Each female was interviewed during June 1988

Figure 2.3
Comparison of the Classic Developmental Designs (ages of the children circled within the figure)

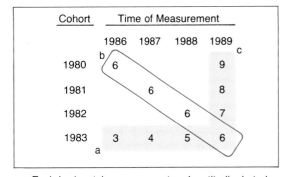

a - Each horizontal row represents a longtitudinal study.
b - Each diagonal row represents a cross-sectional study.
c - Each vertical row represents a time-lag study.

concerning her personal conceptions of masculinity and femininity. If the results indicated that 40-year-olds express the most feminine characteristics and 20-year-olds the most masculine characteristics, would a researcher be able to justify the conclusion that women become more feminine as they develop? Because the subjects were not followed continuously from the age of 20 to the age of 40, the only way we could confidently assume such a developmental pattern is if each cohort studied was quite similar. This assumption, however, might be seriously questioned. The experiences that influenced the gender role conception of females born in the 1968, 1958, and 1948 cohorts were probably vastly different. Miller (1987) suggests that the more biological the variable, the less susceptible to cohort effects the research will be. In the case of gender roles, however, cultural factors must be regarded highly.

Cross-sectional research is not without some significant advantages, particularly if relevant cultural variables appear to be minimal. It can be conducted in a short period of time; therefore, funding is not a major problem, nor is extensive cooperation required from either subjects or research associates. Many investigations of children's intellectual development have compared the abilities of one age to another. The value of this research for establishing challenging educational curricula, creating appropriate television programs or reading materials, designing interesting toys and games, and provoking further study of continuous individual development has been unparalleled. Nevertheless, interpretations of cross-sectional data should be evaluated cautiously in light of the possible confusion between age differences due to particular environmental variations and age differences due to genuine developmental processes.

Longitudinal Research

Longitudinal design

A developmental research method that compares the data from one sample at different chronological age intervals.

In contrast to the flaws of cross-sectional research, the **longitudinal design,** at first glance, may appear to be far more useful. This approach allows the researcher to study the same group of people over an extended period of months, years, or even longer (see Figure 2.3). Using a longitudinal design eliminates the two basic weaknesses of cross-sectional research: lack of comparability between different age groups and the absence of continuity in individual development. Although the longitudinal approach truly addresses age changes from one point in time to another, it has numerous practical disadvantages as well as one major conceptual dilemma. That is, because only one group is being evaluated, the findings at different ages may be a function of cultural conditions *when* the data were collected rather than the *age* of the sample. In other words, the time of measurement is a very critical variable that could be confused with developmental change. Research on vocational development in young adults during an economic recession, for instance, would be strongly influenced by a time-of-measurement component.

Longitudinal designs enable researchers to follow the same people across different stages of development. However, cultural changes over time and numerous practical problems can compromise this type of research.

Because time of measurement often may be reasonably ruled out as a problem, however, why are longitudinal studies employed relatively infrequently in developmental research? Unfortunately, they are costly ventures that require the long-term cooperation of subjects and researchers. The longitudinal approach also demands careful and foresighted planning to avoid the obsolescence of research strategy or data collection procedures. For example, if a researcher discovers in 1989 that an intelligence test used at the start of the investigation in 1978 is no longer valid, how can the results of comparisons with a revised form of the test be meaningful? Once the methodology has been established and the early data collected, the researchers are constricted by the original theory and procedures of the study.

In addition to the financial, intellectual, and practical problems of maintaining extended commitments by researchers to the project, the difficulties of retaining and continually relocating a representative sample are considerable. Our mobile society leads to the "disappearance" of subjects; some become ill or even die, and others merely lose interest in the research. How can the researcher be sure that what remains of the sample near the conclusion of the study is comparable on relevant characteristics to the original sample? For example, a longitudinal study of achievement motivation in college students could be conducted over a 4-year period. What could we conclude about the development of achievement motivation by comparing the senior class with themselves as freshmen? Those students lacking high-achievement motivation would likely have dropped out, transferred to an easier school, or taken some time off from college. In any event, the seniors are clearly not the same sample they were 4 years earlier. Not only are there fewer of them, but they possess different characteristics.

Terminal drop

A sharp and dramatic intellectual decline that occurs in many elderly people shortly before death.

A similar problem, identified by Riegel and Riegel (1972), plagues longitudinal research with the elderly. The controversial phenomenon known as **terminal drop**—defined by Miller (1987) as "a fairly sharp and abrupt decline in mental abilities in the months or years immediately preceding death" (p. 217)—can influence the interpretation of cognitive development over time. Although not all researchers believe that terminal drop occurs (at least for every person), declines in later adult intelligence could be attributed to imminent death rather than to a pattern of slow decline with age. Recent research by Cooney, Schaie, and Willis (1988) confirms the potential significance of the terminal drop phenomenon.

Furthermore, researchers must consider what effects participating in the study itself will have on the sample. Would adolescents tested on aspects of physical development react to the measurement process by intensively trying to improve their skills and coordination before retesting the following year? Similarly, researchers cannot control the individual experiences of subjects over the course of the investigation. How would we evaluate the results of a study on the personality development of adult males between the ages of 40 and 45 who may encounter varied life situations that will influence personality development (e.g., losing a spouse or parent, moving to another part of the country, getting a new job, having a serious illness or accident, winning a million-dollar lottery)? Lastly, the longitudinal approach involves only one cohort. Cultural factors that may affect patterns of development, therefore, are ignored. In other words, can the results of longitudinal research be attributed to universal developmental change or to the history of a particular cohort?

Time Lag Research

The discussion of both cross-sectional and longitudinal designs has commented on the issue of untangling age and the influences of cohort or

Time lag design
A research method that compares the data from different groups at different times while keeping chronological age constant.

time of measurement. The *time lag design,* which compares different groups at different times while keeping age constant, can be used to evaluate the effects of culture (see Figure 2.3). Because developmentalists typically have been concerned with patterns of individual change, the time lag design is quite rare in the research literature. Furthermore, because the time lag approach involves groups born in several years (cohorts), as well as measurements of them on successive occasions, the researcher cannot be sure whether the cultural effects are due to the year of birth or the year of measurement.

Although the time lag approach is not directly useful in understanding patterns of developmental change, this design can help clarify what environmental factors may be important to follow up on or which to ignore. As an example, we might consider political belief development in the elderly. If we were to evaluate the political beliefs of 70-year-olds in 1985, 1990, and 1995 and determine that they were similar for all three age cohorts, we could proceed to examine cross-sectional differences between 70-year-olds, 75-year-olds, and 80-year-olds in 1995 or longitudinal patterns in 70-year-olds to 80-year-olds from 1995 to 2005. We then would have more confidence that the results were due to developmental, rather than cultural, changes. Of course, if the time lag results indicated different political beliefs among the cohorts, our case for understanding political belief development using age differences or age changes would be considerably weakened.

Sequential Research

One approach to resolving the dilemmas posed by the previously discussed developmental designs involves a complex convergence of methods. Although the concept is not new, relatively little attention had been paid to the use of *sequential design* until the past decade. Sequential designs have been proposed in a variety of forms; however, the basic task is to link modifications of cross-sectional and longitudinal designs within a more comprehensive investigation. Sequential designs retain the advantages of the simpler designs while reducing their disadvantages. Thus, descriptions of developmental change can more accurately reflect the intricacies of the human being.

Sequential design
A developmental research method that blends elements of cross-sectional, longitudinal, and time lag designs to maximize the advantages and minimize the disadvantages of these simpler methods.

Perhaps the most effective means of illustrating the value of sequential designs is to discuss part of the work by Nesselroade and Baltes (1974) with adolescents. Their research focused on personality and ability changes over a 2-year period among four cohorts who ranged in age from 13 to 16 initially and from 15 to 18 at the conclusion of the study (see Figure 2.4). One of their findings, derived from nearly 3,000 subjects tested on 40 variables, concerned a decrease in socioemotional anxiety between 1970 and 1972. If only one cohort had been studied in a simple longitudinal design—say those born in 1956—Nesselroade and Baltes might have assumed that

Figure 2.4
Sequential Design of Nesselroade
and Baltes (1974) (years of measurement circled within the figure)

Source: From J. R. Nesselroade
and P. B. F. Baltes (1974) Adolescent personality development
and historical change: 1970–
1972. Monographs of the Society
for Research in Child Development 39 (1, Serial No. 154).
Copyright 1974 by the Society for
Research in Child Development,
Inc.

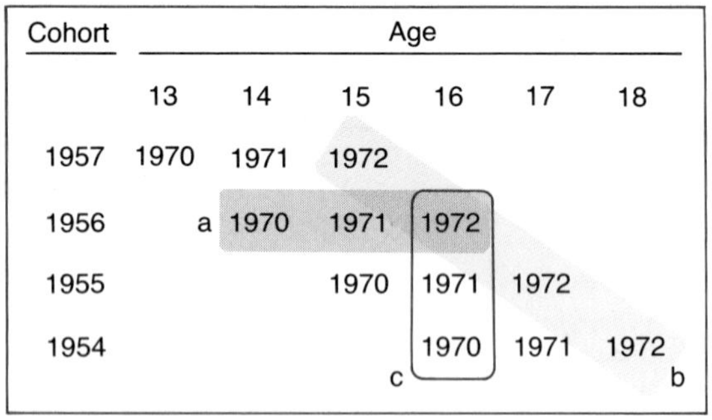

Cohort		Age				
	13	14	15	16	17	18
1957	1970	1971	1972			
1956		a 1970	1971	1972		
1955			1970	1971	1972	
1954				1970	1971	1972
				c		b

a - Each horizontal row represents a longtitudinal study.
b - Each diagonal row represents a cross-sectional study.
c - Each vertical row represents a time-lag study.

between the ages of of 14 and 16, adolescents become less anxious.
However, they noted that anxiety similarly decreased for the 1954, 1955, and
1957 cohorts (three additional longitudinal studies), suggesting instead that
cultural influences during the research interval were responsible for the
change. Any single cross-sectional study (in 1970, 1971, or 1972) would have
resulted in age differences in anxiety without indicating a possible source
for the apparent developmental change.

Therefore, sequential designs may be employed to limit the confusion
regarding the relative importance of cultural versus developmental factors
in age differences. These designs also provide the researcher with a
compromise between the desire to examine individual continuity over an
extended period and the practical aspects of more abbreviated research. For
example, Nesselroade and Baltes (1974) spent only 2 years obtaining data on
a 5-year interval (ages 13 through 18) of adolescent development. In
addition to saving time and money, ensuring the cooperation of subjects,
and eliminating the obsolescence of procedures, they were able to lessen the
effects of repeated testing and unusual personal experiences during the
study. Sequential designs, in sum, may well be worth the additional
planning and sophisticated statistical analyses they require.

The discussion of alternative designs demonstrates the avenues available to further the understanding of human development. No one approach
is best for developmental research. Each question or hypothesis presents its
own special set of circumstances that must be individually evaluated.
Despite the relatively recent improvement in developmental design principles, we are increasingly planning our investigations by fruitfully integrating
long-established canons of the scientific method with research strategies
and data collection procedures appropriate for exploring the nature of
development (see Applying Our Knowledge, "The Use of Developmental
Theory and Research" for a related note of caution).

Applying Our Knowledge
The Use of Developmental Theory and Research

 From ancient philosophers to contemporary developmentalists, the path to a fulfilling and successful life has long been sought. The public appetite for consuming unending quantities of information, advice, and support concerning nearly every aspect of development has reached staggering proportions in recent years. Books, magazines, tapes, newsletters, organizations, workshops, pamphlets, college courses, and a host of other resources are available dealing with caring for our babies, extending an adolescent's creativity, coping with retirement, maximizing our child's learning, pulling our family together after a divorce, and so on. This quest does not seem likely to be a passing fad, because the trend has been accelerating for decades. Our interest in advice on improvement reflects the history of attempts to share such knowledge, as well as the current status of developmental theory and research evidence.

Consider the following suggestions from a 1930 government pamphlet on how to train a child to be happy:

> Begin when he is born.
> Feed him at exactly the same hours every day.
> Do not feed him just because he cries.
> Let him wait until the right time.
> If you make him wait, his stomach will learn to wait.
> His mind will learn that he cannot get things by crying.
> You do two things for your baby at the same time. You teach his body good habits and you teach his mind good habits. (Weill, 1930, p. 1)

The spirit of these remarks was stimulated by J. B. Watson's ideas on the crucial role of the parent in controlling the infant's environment. Watson staunchly believed that establishing an early, "scientific" routine for child care would promote the development of a well-adjusted and self-disciplined adult. Despite the fact that little, if any research has been able to demonstrate the type of relationship that Watson hypothesized would exist, many parents have continued to practice rigid methods of infant caretaking. Ironically, the results of Bell and Ainsworth's (1972) research on coping with crying infants, for example, indicates that immediate attention to their needs is the most effective approach for having a baby that cries less frequently.

Many similar instances could be cited whereby premature recommendations were publicly adopted, conclusions drawn by developmentalists were widely misinterpreted, or generalizations from limited evidence were grossly exaggerated. These all-too-frequent distortions do not, and should not, diminish the importance of deriving practical applications from developmental theory and research. Instead, they should caution both professional and layperson alike about the need to examine carefully the implications of developmental work. Bear in mind that definitive conclusions are not based on a single investigation; that every piece of research or strand of theory has limitations; that each individual's development is an extremely complex interaction of many factors; and that our observations may be biased by the values of our culture, our training, and our personal histories.

Although we may never be in the position to offer perfect predictability about the course of life-span development, the techniques and knowledge of the present and the future offer an invaluable, practical awareness of the issues involved in understanding human change.

Summary

1. Most developmental research is conducted in accord with the traditional scientific method. This organizes the process into a series of logical steps—from clarifying the problem to interpreting results.

2. The initial task of the researcher is to define a problem carefully by focusing on a limited number of variables that can be provided with specific meanings.

3. Hypotheses or research questions about the relationships among the selected variables are developed. A sample, or representative group of research participants, is chosen to be studied.

4. After the data have been collected, researchers analyze the results using statistical techniques. The various statistics available are quantitative tools for organizing information.

5. Research findings are then summarized and communicated to other interested people.

6. The experimental approach manipulates and controls variables to provide comparisons for establishing the causes of developmental change.

7. Because not all variables in human development can be manipulated realistically or ethically, nonexperimental strategies are employed to suggest the reasons for group differences or relationships among variables.

8. Some researchers use clinical or case studies and single-subject experiments to obtain detailed assessments of individuals rather than broad generalizations about groups.

9. There has been a resurgence of interest in moving from extensive laboratory research toward developmental studies conducted in their natural settings.

10. Any research strategy has limitations—particularly demand characteristics and response sets—that must be considered seriously in designing a study.

11. Survey methods such as interviews and written questionnaires yield important data when carefully constructed and sensitively administered.

12. A wide variety of observational methods affords the researcher a more unobtrusive approach. However, the observer, rather than the subjects, may exhibit a biased perspective.

13. Testing, which offers considerable advantages and disadvantages to the developmental researcher, probably has been the most widespread data collection procedure.

14. Cross-sectional research frequently is used to compare groups of different chronological ages at the same time.

15. Longitudinal research allows one sample to be followed over an extended time period to trace the patterns of development.

16. Time lag designs occasionally are employed to evaluate the effects of cultural change.

17. In response to the weaknesses of classic developmental research, sequential designs are becoming accepted as the best method for studying complex developmental processes.

Key Terms

case-study method (p. 47)

clinical method (p. 47)

correlational statistics (p. 43)

cross-sectional design (p. 59)

demand characteristics (p. 51)

descriptive statistics (p. 42)

experimental strategy (p. 45)

field experiment (p. 50)

group differences statistics (p. 43)

hypothesis (p. 39)

inferential statistics (p. 42)

longitudinal design (p. 60)

multivariate statistics (p. 44)

natural experiment (p. 50)

observational research (p. 54)

operational definition (p. 39)

response set (p. 51)

sample (p. 39)

sequential design (p. 63)

standardized tests or tasks (p. 56)

survey approach (p. 52)

terminal drop (p. 62)

time lag design (p. 63)

univariate statistics (p. 44)

variable (p. 38)

Review Questions

1. Outline the basic steps of the scientific method and propose an illustrative problem to help you describe each step. Be sure to provide as much detail as possible about your specific plan.
2. Contrast experimental and nonexperimental strategies for conducting developmental research. Point out the strengths and weaknesses of each approach and include a brief discussion of laboratory versus natural settings for these strategies.
3. Human development researchers cannot avoid confronting ethical issues in their work. Explain some of the problems implied in this statement and discuss the relevant principles for researchers to acknowledge. Provide examples.
4. The three basic procedures for collecting data on human development are surveys, observations, and tests. Select any two of these methods and describe the advantages and disadvantages associated with each.
5. Discuss the concept of time in relation to developmental research. Explain the basic designs that enable us to explore change over time as well as their accompanying methodological problems.

Suggested Readings

Achenbach, T. M. (1978). *Research in developmental psychology: Concepts, strategies, methods.* New York: Free Press.

> An excellent integration of various aspects of research methodology presented with style, insight, and frequent examples.

Appelbaum, M. I. & McCall, R. B. (1983). Design and analysis in developmental psychology. In P. H. Mussen (Ed.), *Handbook of child psychology* (4th ed., Vol. 1). New York: Wiley.

> A very authoritative, contemporary, and concise overview of research methods and statistical analysis relevant to child development.

Baltes, P. B., Reese, H. W., & Nesselroade, J. R. (1988). *Lifespan developmental psychology: Introduction to research methods.* Hillsdale, NJ: Lawrence Erlbaum.

> Another volume that offers a good deal of information on research methods. However, it is not quite as interesting as Achenbach's presentation.

Bronfenbrenner, U. (1979). *The ecology of human development: Experiments by nature and design.* Cambridge, MA: Harvard University Press.

> A thoughtful discussion combined with a plea for developmental researchers to devote more attention to studying behavior in natural settings.

Miller, S. A. (1987). *Developmental research methods.* Englewood Cliffs, NJ: Prentice-Hall.

> The best recent undergraduate source devoted to developmental methodology across the life span. It is concise but thorough and generally well written.

Wolman, B. B. (Ed). (1982). *Handbook of developmental psychology.* Englewood Cliffs, NJ: Prentice-Hall.

> A massive book with several chapters dealing with cross-cultural research, longitudinal methods, and ethical issues.

Chapter Three

Physical Growth and Development

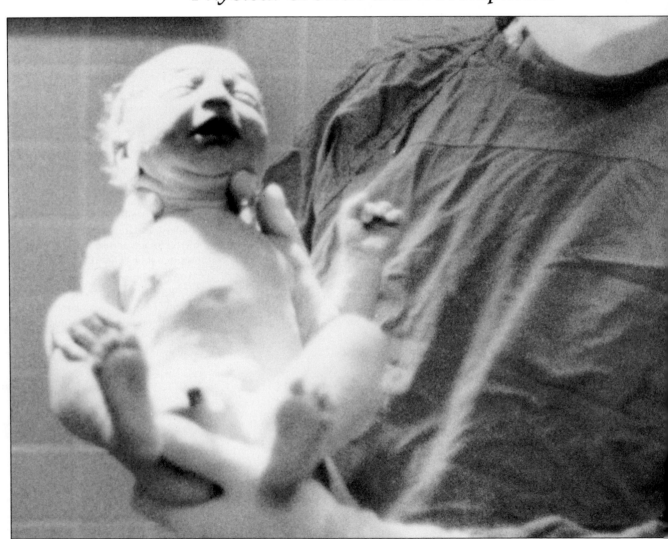

Determiners of Growth
Genetic Plan
Message of the Hormones

Prenatal Development and Birth
Stages of Prenatal Development
Influences on Fetal Development
The Birth Process
The Newborn Child

Patterns of Growth: Birth to Old Age
Brain Development
Body Development

Individual Variations in Growth
Early and Late Maturation at Puberty
Individual Variations in Aging

Psychological Issues in Physical Development
Ideal Physique and Body Satisfaction
Body Image, Self-Esteem, and Social Interaction
Physical Attractiveness and Social Desirability

 Certainly the most noticeable aspect of human development is the development of the body. We see our bodies every day. We observe every detail and note the changes, sometimes proudly and sometimes with a sense of foreboding. We notice, too, the bodies of those around us. We comment on how big the neighbor's children are getting, how much older Aunt Mary has been looking lately, or how much weight Uncle John has gained or lost. When we see our children growing up, we are reminded that we, too, are physically changing every day of our lives.

Physical development is in itself an important aspect of the process of human development, but it also affects psychological development. The self-image and the body image are inevitably correlated. Our bodies, after all, are not just shells that we inhabit. To a large extent, our bodies also define who we are.

In this chapter, we shall discuss the processes of physical development from conception to old age. We shall consider genetic and hormonal influences on human growth, normal growth patterns, individual differences within the population, and the psychological impact of physical development at various points in the life span.

DETERMINERS OF GROWTH

Genetic factors heavily influence the process of physical growth. A person's growth rate during childhood and adolescence, physical appearance throughout the life span, and rate of aging are largely determined at the moment of conception. We begin our discussion of human physical development by examining the genetic plan for growth and the hormonal mechanisms by which that plan is carried out.

Genetic Plan

The entire plan for physical growth and development is encoded in the *genes,* materials composed of the chemical substance deoxyribonucleic acid (DNA). Genes carry information that influences such hereditary characteristics as eye color, hair color, height, and skin pigmentation. These genes are contained in microscopic, threadlike structures known as *chromosomes* that are found in the nuclei of all cells in the human body (Mader, 1988).

Most cells contain 46 chromosomes, arranged in 23 pairs. Twenty-two of these pairs are referred to as *autosomes;* the remaining pair are the *sex chromosomes.* Each pair of autosomes is identical in size and shape in all human beings. The sex chromosomes are identical only in the female, who has 2 X chromosomes, but clearly different in the male, who has an X chromosome and a Y chromosome.

Unlike the other cells in the body, the sex cells—the sperm and the egg—each contain only 23 chromosomes, or half the usual number. An egg cell has 22 autosomes and 1 sex chromosome, which is always an X, and a sperm cell has 22 autosomes and 1 sex chromosome, which may be either an X or a Y. When egg and sperm unite at the moment of conception, they each contribute their 23 chromosomes to form a new 46-chromosome cell. If the fertilizing sperm contains an X sex chromosome, the fertilized egg has 2 X chromosomes and will be genetically female; if the sperm contains a Y sex chromosome, the new cell has an X and a Y sex chromosome, and the result will be a male child.

Genotype and Phenotype

Before discussing what happens to the new cell created when an egg and a sperm unite, we should point out that each parent contributes equally to the child's genetic makeup. Nevertheless, children often resemble one parent more than they do the other. This leads us to a discussion of the concepts of genotype and phenotype. The *genotype* is the total genetic inheritance of the organism. The *phenotype,* on the other hand, describes the physical appearance of the organism with regard to its hereditary characteristics (Mader, 1988).

Each parent contributes equally to the child's genotype, but the phenotype may be influenced more by one parent than by the other,

Gene

Hereditary material in the chromosomes that carries coded information that influences the physical characteristics of the organism.

Chromosome

A microscopic, threadlike structure, found in the nucleus of every human cell, which contains hereditary materials in the form of genes.

Genotype

The total genetic inheritance of a living organism.

Phenotype

The manifestation of genetic information as evidenced in the physical appearance of the organism.

depending on the particular genes contained in the sex cells that unite at conception. For convenience, we speak of *dominant* or *recessive* genes, although individual genes do not dominate over one another. However, certain traits are more likely to occur than others. For example, brown eyes is a trait that dominates over blue eyes in human beings, as does dark skin over light skin, dark hair over light hair, "free" rather than attached earlobes, short fingers rather than long fingers, and the presence rather than the absence of freckles (Mader, 1988). The actual manifestation of genetic inheritance, therefore, differs from one individual to the next, depending on the composition of the specific sex cells involved in fertilization and the dominance or recessiveness of the traits that are transmitted.

Cell Division

Human growth from the fertilized egg—a single cell containing hereditary information from the mother's and the father's sex cells—depends on the processes of cell division. There are two different types of cell division, the first occurring in the body cells and the second in the sex cells of the organism.

Body cells reproduce through a process known as ***mitosis***. During mitosis, the DNA replicates itself, enabling the chromosomes to make identical copies of themselves. Half the duplicated chromosomes migrate to one side of the dividing cell, and the other half to the opposite side. When the cell divides, two cells with exactly the same genetic material result from the original cell (see Figure 3.1).

Mitosis, however, does not account for the production of sex cells, which, as mentioned earlier, contain only 23 chromosomes each. How can we start at conception with a 46-chromosome cell and eventually develop sex cells containing only half that number of chromosomes? The answer is that sex cells reproduce through a second type of cell division process, known as ***meiosis***. Although similar to mitosis, meiosis differs in the arrangement of chromosomes before cell division (see Step 2 in Figure 3.1). In addition, meiosis involves a second division (Step 6), and this results in the formation of sex cells with only 23 chromosomes from the parent body cell.

Message of the Hormones

Human beings end up at different final points in their growth and grow at different rates because their genes transmit different messages. However, the mechanisms for translating these messages into growth patterns are the same for everyone: the endocrine glands, located in various parts of the body. Those that are most important in the process of physical growth are the ***pituitary gland,*** located at the base of the brain; the thyroid gland, with two lobes located on opposite sides of the windpipe; the cortex of the adrenal gland, located on the kidneys; and the gonads, or sex glands, located in the ovaries of a woman and the testicles of a man (Mader, 1988; Tanner, 1978; Tortora & Anagnostakos, 1990).

Mitosis
A process of cell division by which two identical new cells are formed from a parent cell.

Meiosis
The process of cell division by which sex cells are produced, in which two new cells are formed, each containing half the number of chromosomes found in its parent cell.

Pituitary gland
A pea-sized gland connected to the hypothalamus by a stalk of nerve fibers and responsible for stimulating and controlling all other glands in the endocrine system.

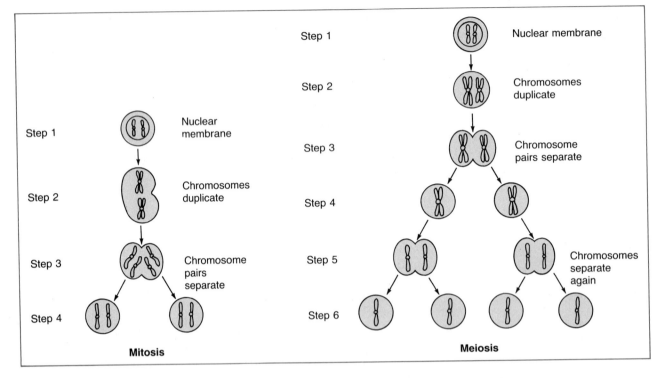

Figure 3.1
Mitosis and Meiosis

Hormone
A chemical substance secreted into the bloodstream by one of the various glands in the human body, whose function is to direct the course of growth or regulate the body's metabolism.

Hypothalamus
The area of the brain that regulates body temperature, blood pressure, and blood flow to the brain, and controls the endocrine system.

Trophins
Hormones secreted by the pituitary gland that stimulate one of the other glands in the endocrine system to secrete its particular hormone.

Each of these glands is capable of secreting into the bloodstream a chemical substance known as a *hormone,* which stimulates the body to grow and develop in prescribed ways. The control mechanism that informs the glands when and how much of their hormones to secrete is the *hypothalamus,* located in the lower central portion of the brain, which regulates the body's internal environment. The hypothalamus controls body temperature, blood pressure, and blood distribution to the brain and regulates the endocrine system.

The hypothalamus transmits its messages to the pituitary gland, located directly beneath it, to which it is connected by a stalk of nerve fibers. In turn, the pituitary gland stimulates and controls all the other glands in the endocrine system. For this reason, the pituitary is often referred to as the master gland of the body.

The pituitary controls the endocrine system by secreting into the bloodstream certain hormones, called *trophins,* whose sole function is to stimulate the other glands to secrete their own particular hormones. As an example, the pituitary secretes thyroid-stimulating hormone (TSH), which stimulates the thyroid gland to secrete thyroid hormone (thyroxine). In a sense, the pituitary sends out TSH to tell the thyroid when and how much thyroxine to secrete.

A number of hormones directly affect the growth process in human beings. *Human growth hormone* (HGH), secreted by the pituitary itself, is responsible for overall body growth, synthesis of protein, and carbohydrate and fat metabolism. *Thyroxine,* secreted by the thyroid gland, regulates the body's metabolism and the development of the brain and nervous system. Thyroxine also controls body size and skeletal proportion and is responsible for the conversion of cartilage to bone tissue and the development of teeth. The *adrenal hormones,* secreted by the adrenal cortex, include (1) cortisol, which affects cellular metabolism; (2) aldosterone, which maintains sodium in tissue fluids, and (3) adrenal androgens, which are male sex hormones responsible in part for the sex-related changes of puberty in both sexes. Cortisol and aldosterone levels are fairly constant throughout life, but adrenal androgen secretion increases dramatically at puberty, and this higher level gradually declines throughout adulthood.

Finally, growth is affected by the *sex hormones.* The most important male sex hormone is **testosterone,** produced by sex glands located in the testicles. Testosterone can be found in the blood of children, but the level increases dramatically at puberty and then declines gradually throughout adulthood. Its major effect is to masculinize the body; testosterone brings about such pubertal changes as broadening the shoulders, deepening the voice, and developing facial and body hair (Jones, 1984).

The major female sex hormone is *estrogen,* secreted by sex glands located in the ovaries and responsible for the development of such feminine attributes as wide hips, smooth skin, breasts, and a relatively hairless body. Estrogen, like testosterone, is present in young children, but the hormone level dramatically increases at puberty. Another major female sex hormone is **progesterone,** which is secreted from the ovaries in the middle and later part of the menstrual cycle. Its primary responsibility is to prepare the uterus for possible pregnancy.

Both male and female hormones are present in both sexes, although the proportions are obviously different. However, both masculine and feminine physical characteristics can be found to some extent in persons of either sex (Gilman, Goodman, Rall, & Murad, 1985; Jones, 1984; Katchadourian, 1989).

All the hormones mentioned, individually or in combination, directly influence every aspect of physical growth as predetermined by the genes. Thus, the body has a very sensitive and sophisticated system for regulating its own development, which proceeds in an orderly fashion under instructions from the hypothalamus. The end result, of course, depends on a person's genetic endowment.

Testosterone
The male sex hormone secreted by the testicles that masculinizes the body during and after puberty.

Estrogen
The major female sex hormone, secreted from a woman's ovaries and responsible for feminizing a woman's body.

Progesterone
The female sex hormone that prepares the wall of the uterus to receive a fertilized egg cell.

PRENATAL DEVELOPMENT AND BIRTH

At the point of orgasm, a man ejaculates a small amount of fluid that contains between 50 and 100 million sperm cells per cubic centimeter of semen. Each of these microscopic cells is composed of an oval-shaped head and a long, whiplike tail that propels the cell forward as it "swims" in the seminal fluid (Katchadourian, 1989; Mader, 1988).

When these sperm cells are deposited in a woman's vagina during sexual intercourse, they embark on a journey of about 6 inches up through the cervix into the uterus, and from the uterus into the fallopian tube, or oviduct, which is the pathway leading from the ovary to the uterus. Fewer than 1,000 sperm cells ever reach the oviduct, however. Only about 50 make contact with the egg, and only a single sperm will actually penetrate the egg cell (Katchadourian, 1989).

Conception, or fertilization, typically occurs in the oviduct—if an egg cell is available to be fertilized, of course. In actuality, fertilization is an improbable occurrence. Only one mature egg cell is released from a woman's ovary every month, a process known as *ovulation*. Optimally, the egg cell must be fertilized within 24 to 48 hours after ovulation, because beyond that point it is already beginning to deteriorate. Sperm cells ordinarily maintain their ability to fertilize an egg for only 72 hours after ejaculation. Therefore, fertilization is possible, although by no means inevitable, only if insemination occurs within a period beginning 72 hours before ovulation and ending 24 to 48 hours afterward. Exceptions occur, however; sperm cells have been known to have remarkably long lives (Jones, 1984).

The egg cell is surrounded by several layers of follicle cells through which the sperm must pass. Once the nucleus of one sperm cell has penetrated these barriers, a chemical reaction occurs in the egg cell wall that prevents penetration by any of the other sperm cells in the oviduct. Fertilization has now taken place, and the newly fertilized egg cell is referred to as a *zygote*.

Zygote
A newly fertilized egg cell.

Stages of Prenatal Development

The average length of a pregnancy is 38 weeks from ovulation, with variations of 2 weeks before and 2 weeks after for a full-term baby. During this period of *gestation,* a single-celled organism becomes a fully formed baby, with all major organ systems established and functional.

Germinal Stage (0–2 Weeks)
After fertilization, the zygote continues its journey down the oviduct to the uterus. The 12-hour-old zygote divides into two cells through mitosis. Cell division continues to occur approximately every 12 hours. By the time the developing organism reaches the uterus—on the fourth or fifth day after fertilization—it has become a cluster of about 500 cells and is referred to as a *blastocyst.*

Blastocyst
A cluster of about 500 cells that the fertilized egg has become by the time it has moved from the oviduct to the uterus.

Although the blastocyst resembles a solid ball, it actually consists of a fluid-filled center (blastocoel), a layer of cells that forms its outer wall, and a cluster of cells attached to the inner wall (the inner cell mass). The inner

Embryo

The developing human organism in the womb from the second to the eighth week after conception.

cell mass eventually will become the *embryo,* the name given to the developing organism from the second to the eighth week after conception. The outer cell wall, referred to as the chorion, will eventually become the placenta, amniotic sac, and other structures that support the pregnancy (see Figure 3.2).

On approximately the eighth day after fertilization, the blastocyst adheres to the uterine wall and begins to implant itself by digesting the surface cells of the uterine lining. After approximately 12 days, the egg is firmly implanted; and, by the end of the second week after fertilization, the uterine tissue completely surrounds the newly developing organism in a cozy nest. When implantation is complete, the organism is referred to as an embryo.

Embryonic Stage (2–8 Weeks)

The embryonic stage is often referred to as the critical period of prenatal development. The risk of spontaneous abortion due to genetic abnormalities

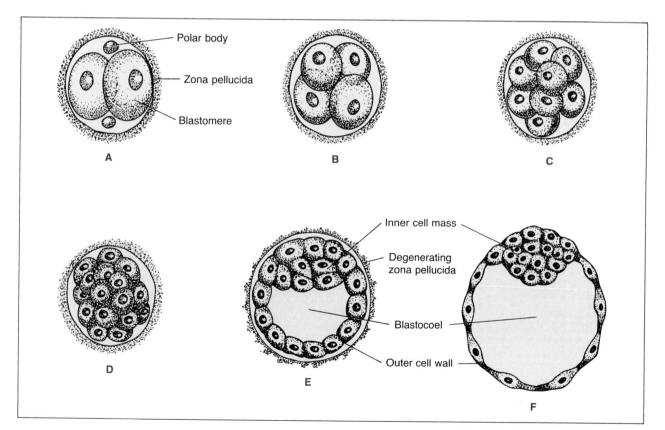

Figure 3.2
Early Stages of Cell Division in the Fertilized Egg

is high. Because all the major organ systems are forming (organogenesis), an injury to the rapidly differentiating tissue may cause defects in the heart, eyes, brain, and other organs. At the beginning of this stage, the embryo is simply a two-layered organism; by the end, it is 1¼ inches long and has the appearance of a human baby.

After implantation, tiny, threadlike projections of cells—the chorionic villi—begin to extend from the outer wall of the blastocyst (or chorion) into the surrounding uterine tissue. In a sense, the organism is beginning to tap the mother's blood vessels as a means of feeding itself, and it does so by absorbing vitamins, minerals, carbohydrates, fats, and proteins through the chorionic villi.

Placenta

The vascular disklike membrane that serves as an exchange filter between the mother's bloodstream and that of the developing fetus.

The area in which the chorion is attached to the uterine wall becomes the *placenta,* a disklike membrane that eventually covers over half the inner surface of the uterus. The placenta is a highly vascular membrane, meaning that it is rich in blood vessels; toward the end of the pregnancy, 75 gallons of blood will come in contact with the placenta every day. The blood volume is significant, because from the mother's bloodstream the child will draw needed nutrients, including oxygen; and into the mother's bloodstream the child will discharge waste products, such as carbon dioxide. Thus, the placenta serves as the exchange filter between mother and unborn child, although the circulatory systems of both remain independent.

Amniotic sac

The fluid-filled sac in which the embryo and fetus develop throughout the pregnancy.

While the outer cell wall (chorion) is busy transforming itself into structures related to the nurturing of the growing organism, the inner cell mass becomes the embryo and a membrane referred to as the *amnion*. The amnion grows over the embryo and later becomes the fluid-filled *amniotic sac*. This sac will be the organism's home for the duration of the pregnancy. Initially, the amniotic sac is quite distinct from the chorion. However, as the sac enlarges, the amnion and chorion eventually fuse.

The embryo is directly connected to the chorion wall and the placenta by the umbilical cord, which contains two arteries to transport the embryo's deoxygenated blood to the placenta and one vein to bring oxygen-rich blood back to the embryo.

Ectoderm

The outer layer of the embryo from which develop such structures as the skin, sensory organs, brain, and spinal cord.

Mesoderm

The middle layer of the embryo, which develops into such structures as the circulatory system, the muscles, and the blood.

Endoderm

The inner layer of the embryo from which develop such structures as the digestive system, respiratory system, and the linings of the internal organs.

A good deal occurs during the embryonic period of development. Early in this stage, the embryo itself has differentiated into three layers: the *ectoderm* (outer layer), which will give rise to the skin, sensory organs, brain, and spinal cord; the *mesoderm* (middle layer), which will form the muscles, blood, and circulatory system; and the *endoderm* (inner layer), which will give rise to the digestive system, respiratory system, and lining of the internal organs.

By the end of the third week after conception, the foundations for the brain, spinal column, and nervous system have been established, and a primitive heart has been formed that already beats. The neural tube, forming the spinal column, closes during the fourth week. If it does not, a serious abnormality—spina bifida—could result. Infants born with an open spine have impaired functioning of the legs, poor bowel and bladder control, and possible brain damage. The top of the neural tube forms three swellings that become the early structures of the brain. Also by the fourth week, the head is forming, and small buds appear that will later develop into arms and legs. By the time the embryonic period ends, arms and legs are well formed, and the blood vessels and all major internal organs are also formed. Bone cells begin to appear, which marks the end of the embryonic period.

The 8-week-old embryo is a top-heavy creature. The size of the head looks rather disproportionate to the rest of the body because of the rapid development of the brain (see Figure 3.3).

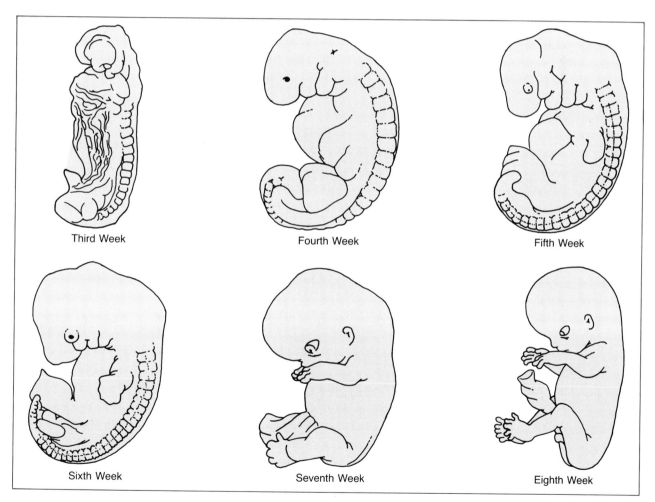

Third Week   Fourth Week   Fifth Week

Sixth Week   Seventh Week   Eighth Week

Figure 3.3
Development of the Human Embryo from the Third Week Through the Eighth Week After Conception

Applying Our Knowledge
Testing for Genetic Disorders in the Fetus

One of the most prevalent fears of expectant parents is that their child will be born with a tragic or even fatal disease, such as cystic fibrosis, Down's syndrome, hemophilia, Tay-Sachs disease, sickle-cell anemia, or a defect in the neural tube. Each of these so-called genetic disorders is extremely rare in the general population, and their probability of occurrence can be estimated by a genetic counselor who extensively examines the family history of the prospective parents.

Many of these genetic disorders can now be detected in the fetus by the middle of the pregnancy. For example, women routinely undergo blood tests early in their pregnancy to measure the maternal blood level of alpha-fetoprotein, or AFP. This substance is manufactured in the liver of the fetus; when the fetus urinates, it enters the amniotic fluid and eventually crosses into the mother's bloodstream. If a blood test indicates that the pregnant woman has abnormally high AFP levels, her fetus may have a neural tube disorder known as spina bifida—an "exposed" spinal cord not covered by the backbone. Such a condition can result in only minor physical impairment, but it also can lead to paralysis of the lower body and, in its extreme form, can result in death within the first 2 years of life. High AFP levels also may indicate severe underdevelopment of the fetal brain. However—and this is a crucial point to remember—high AFP levels may mean nothing at all as far as the health of the fetus is concerned (Chedd, 1981). For this reason, no decision is made about the future of the pregnancy based on a high AFP level until follow-up tests are performed.

Ultrasound involves analysis of high-frequency sound waves that are bounced off the fetus and then analyzed by a computer. It can be used to view fetal behaviors, as well as the physical development of the fetus. Ultrasound is a commonly used technique, although the procedure may have some side effects that are difficult to detect and may show up later in the child's life (Bases, 1985).

Another method of detecting genetic disorders in a fetus is amniocentesis. A 3-inch-long needle is inserted through the mother's abdominal wall during week 14 or 15 of pregnancy, and less than an ounce of fluid is withdrawn from the amniotic sac. Fetal cells contained in the fluid then can be tested to diagnose the presence of genetic disorders such as Down's syndrome or Tay-Sachs disease (a nervous system disorder). The procedure also is used as a follow-up when high AFP levels indicate the possibility of neural tube defects. Finally, amniocentesis is successful in ruling out the presence of genetic disorders in 95 to 98 percent of all cases (Fuchs, 1980).

A more recently developed genetic screening test is chorion villi sampling, which involves the removal of a small piece of the chorion for testing. The advantage of this procedure is that it can be done during the first trimester of pregnancy (which is earlier than amniocentesis). It is also relatively painless, because the tissue is removed through the vagina and the puncturing of the abdominal wall is not required (Fogel, 1984).

The possibility of screening for genetic disorders is a dramatic advance in medical technology, yet it raises a number of troublesome legal and moral issues. Few would argue against genetic screening if the disorder were treatable in utero; the screening then would be seen as preventive medicine. However, if disorders cannot be treated, awesome dilemmas arise. Should a child be brought into the world who may be physically handicapped, mentally handicapped, or both; who may have a limited life expectancy in any case; or who may place severe emotional or economic hardships on the parents? Which pregnancies should come to term and which should be terminated? Who should make the decision?

Fetal Stage (8 Weeks—Birth)

When bone cells make their appearance in X rays, the developing organism is referred to as a *fetus,* and it is called this until birth. The basic human structure now has been formed; the mechanisms by which it receives the nurturing necessary for development have been well established. During the

Fetus
The human organism in the womb from 8 weeks after conception to delivery.

fetal stage, routine blood tests may detect certain genetic disorders. (See *Applying Our Knowledge,* "Testing for Genetic Disorders in the Fetus.")

Cell differentiation slows down, but the fetal period still involves quite a few refinements in organs and systems. For example, during the third prenatal month, the unique patterns on toes, fingers, and palms are fairly developed; the veins develop and begin to nourish cells; and a complex network of muscles evolves. During the fetal period, many of the physiological systems link up with one another, leading to a more integrated organism. For example, during the fourth month, the brain becomes more compact, and the beginnings of interconnections between the brain, spinal column, and limbs are evident. Because of these links, behaviors such as swallowing, sucking, squinting, and frowning appear early in the fetal period. Also by the fourth month, the fetus is moving its limbs and body in utero, actions that are felt by the mother and may bring home the reality of the pregnancy. At 5 months, sleep and wake cycles are observable. A 6-month-old fetus is capable of breathing movements and crying; fetal respiration involves the taking in of amniotic fluid and exhaling it through the mouth.

Seven weeks after conception, most of the organs and appendages of the human embryo have been formed (top). By the fifth month, the sleep and wake cycles of the human fetus are observable (bottom).

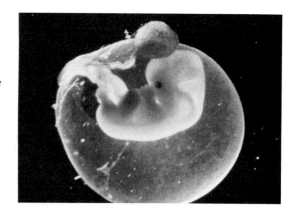

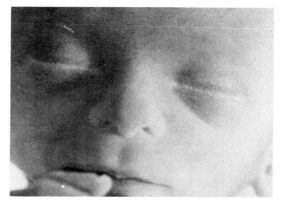

The respiratory system is not sufficiently developed to sustain life outside the uterus until the seventh month of pregnancy. Week 28, therefore, is often referred to as the *age of viability.* Medical support systems are able to help infants born earlier than week 28. However, before week 24, the lungs do not have any air sacs, and heroic acts to save the baby are at this time probably futile.

The last trimester is a time of rapid growth in height and weight. The fetus gains about 5½ pounds through the deposit of subcutaneous fat, which helps nourish and insulate the infant's body. The brain's structure more closely resembles that of an adult, with its distinctive layers, convolutions, and indentations. Additionally, the brain shows evidence that rudimentary sensory and motoric systems are in place. Table 3.1 summa-

Table 3.1
Characteristics of Prenatal Development

End of Month	Approximate Size and Weight	Representative Changes
1	0.6 cm (³⁄₁₈ in.)	Eyes, nose, and ears not yet visible. Backbone and vertebral canal form. Small buds that will develop into arms and legs form. Heart forms and starts beating. Body systems begin to form.
2	3 cm (1¼ in.) 1 g (¹⁄₃₈ oz)	Eyes far apart, eyelids fused, nose flat. Ossification begins. Limbs become distinct as arms and legs. Digits are well formed. Major blood vessels form. Many internal organs continue to develop.
3	7.5 cm (3 in.) 28 g (1 oz)	Eyes almost fully developed but eyelids still fused, nose develops bridge, and external ears are present. Ossification continues. Appendages are fully formed, and nails develop. Heartbeat can be detected. Body systems continue to develop.
4	18 cm (6½–7 in.) 113 g (4 oz)	Head large in proportion to rest of body. Face takes on human features, and hair appears on head. Many bones ossified, and joints begin to form. Continued development of body systems.
5	25–30 cm (10–12 in.) 227–454 g (½–1 lb)	Head is less disproportionate to rest of body. Fine hair (lanugo hair) covers body. Rapid development of body systems.
6	27–35 cm (11–14 in.) 567–681 g (1¼–1½ lb)	Head becomes less disproportionate to rest of body. Eyelids separate and eyelashes form. Skin wrinkled.
7	325–425 cm (13–17 in.) 1,135–1,362 g (2½–3 lb)	Head and body become more proportionate. Skin wrinkled. Seven-month fetus (premature baby) is capable of survival.
8	40–45 cm (16½–18 in.) 2,043–2,270 g (4½–5½ lb)	Subcutaneous fat deposited. Skin less wrinkled. Testes descend into scrotum of male fetus. Bones of head are soft. Chances of survival much greater at end of eighth month.
9	50 cm (20 in.) 3,178–3,405 g (7–7½ lb)	Additional subcutaneous fat accumulates. Lanugo hair shed. Nails extend to tips of fingers and maybe even beyond.

rizes the major changes that occur throughout fetal development and lists the approximate size of the fetus at the end of each month of prenatal life.

Influences on Fetal Development

Throughout the years, a number of factors have been identified that can have an impact on the developing fetus. Let us look first at the influence of the age of the parents at the time the child is conceived, and then at a variety of what might be called environmental factors that affect the developing organism.

Maternal and Paternal Age

The ideal biological age for a woman to conceive and give birth is within the range of 18 to 35. Mothers under the age of 18 are considerably more likely to deliver prematurely. This age effect is due in part to the immaturity of adolescent girls' reproductive systems and in part to the fact that teenage mothers are less likely to receive adequate prenatal care. On the other hand, mothers past the age of 35 have a greater chance of giving birth to children with chromosomal abnormalities, such as Down's syndrome. In addition, the rate of neonatal mortality increases significantly when mothers are 40 years of age or older (Smith, 1978). The typical age range of first-time mothers in the United States is between 20 and 24.

The father's age at the time of conception is less influential than the mother's age. Nevertheless, the likelihood of genetic disorders in the child increases tenfold from the time a new father is 30 to the time he is 60, although such paternally linked disorders are relatively rare.

Environmental Factors

Teratogens
Environmental factors that can affect the development of the fetus.

A number of environmental factors, referred to collectively as **teratogens,** can affect fetal development. Included in this classification are drugs, chemicals, maternal diseases, maternal chronic conditions, malnutrition, radiation, oxygen deprivation, and maternal stress.

As we discuss the various teratogens, keep in mind that environmental agents may account for a rather small percentage of birth defects. Approximately 60 percent of birth defects are due to unknown causes (Kalter & Warkany, 1983). With early detection and appropriate treatment, or with careful supervision of the pregnancy, the actual risk to the developing organism can be minimized.

Maternal Nutrition. A pregnant woman needs additional protein, calcium, iron, folic acid, and vitamin B_6 in her diet. Protein deficiencies in pregnant rats have resulted in smaller offspring, increased infant mortality, and lowered intelligence, as evidenced in maze-learning ability; some evidence indicates that maternal protein deficiencies produce similar effects in the human newborn. In particular, malnutrition may be related to a decrease in the number of cells in children's brains (Winick & Russo, 1969).

Research examining individuals who were conceived during a Nazi-imposed famine in western Holland during World War II has revealed that when malnutrition is temporary, as opposed to chronic, the effects on subsequent development are minimal. However, the rate of infertility, spontaneous abortions, and miscarriages was exceptionally high during the Dutch famine (Stein, Susser, Saenger, & Marolla, 1975).

A pregnant woman typically is advised to gain about 25 pounds, 11 pounds of which is additional body fat, 2 pounds for the placenta, 3 pounds for the increase in breast and uterine size, 1 pound each of amniotic fluid and increased maternal blood volume, and 7 pounds for the fetus itself (Jones, 1984).

Maternal Sensitization.   Approximately 90 percent of people living in the United States have in their bloodstreams an inherited substance known as the *Rh factor,* so named because an identical element had earlier been found in the blood of Rhesus monkeys. People who have this substance are referred to as Rh-positive, while those who lack it are called Rh-negative.

Maternal sensitization

A condition that occurs when an Rh-negative mother becomes "sensitized" to the Rh factor as a result of pregnancy and produces antibodies that will attack the red blood cells of an Rh-positive child she may carry at some future time.

If an Rh-negative woman is pregnant with an Rh-positive baby, a condition known as **maternal sensitization** could occur if the child's Rh-positive blood enters the mother's bloodstream. This is most likely to happen during delivery when the placenta tears free from the uterine wall. The mother's body responds by rejecting the Rh-factor as a foreign substance and creating chemical substances called *antibodies* to attack and destroy blood cells containing the Rh factor. Thus, the mother is "sensitized" by the pregnancy to the Rh factor, and in subsequent pregnancies the antibodies in her bloodstream may destroy the red blood cells of an Rh-positive fetus. In rare cases, the result is that the fetus will die, but more typically the child will be born suffering from anemia, a condition that is curable by means of blood transfusions (Guttmacher, 1973).

Maternal sensitization has become less of a troublesome concern, however, since the 1960's when Rhogam injections were first used. The current practice is that Rh-negative women are injected with Rhogam within 72 hours after the birth of their first child, and this prevents the buildup of Rh-positive antibodies and reduces the risk of Rh incompatibility in subsequent births. If Rhogam injections are not given, however, the antibodies in the woman's bloodstream cannot be neutralized at a later point. If a subsequent pregnancy should occur, her antibody level must be determined and the degree of destruction to the fetal red blood cells continually monitored. In some cases, an intrauterine transfusion may be required to save the baby's life.

Maternal Diseases.   Infectious diseases such as syphilis, gonorrhea, or rubella (German measles) can seriously affect the developing organism. Untreated venereal diseases in the mother will result in the child's being born with the same diseases or may result in the death of the fetus. Rubella is a viral infection that, if contracted by the mother during the first trimester of pregnancy, may result in miscarriage, stillbirth, or various forms of damage to the child's sensory and internal organs.

Some diseases, such as those of the herpes simplex virus family, are transmitted when the infant passes through the cervix during delivery. Another serious disease is toxoplasmosis, caused by a parasite that lives in uncooked meat and in cat feces. If a pregnant woman ate some raw or improperly cooked meat in which the parasite was found, or if she failed to wash her hands properly after cleaning a cat's litter box, the disease might be transmitted to her fetus. And although symptoms of toxoplasmosis are barely noticeable in an adult, the disease can cause damage to the brain, eyes, lungs, or liver of the developing child.

Of greater concern is the finding that the virus that causes acquired immune deficiency syndrome (AIDS) can be transmitted in utero, and has, in fact, been identified in fetuses as young as 15 weeks of age (Blanche, 1989; Di Maria, 1986; Marion, Wiznia, Hutcheon, & Rubenstein, 1986). At this time, however, the specific mechanisms of fetal transmission are unknown (Katz & Wilfert, 1989). For example, only about one-third of infants born to mothers infected with the virus will themselves be infected (Blanche, 1989), and in one study, researchers examining 18-month-old identical twins were surprised to discover that one twin tested positive for the AIDS virus while the other tested negative (Menez-Bautista, Fikrig, Pahwa, Sarangadharan, & Stoneburner, 1986).

There is also disagreement at this time on the question of whether exposure in utero to the AIDS-causing virus will result in specific physical abnormalities. For example, Marion et al. (1986) found that children suspected of contracting the AIDS virus prenatally failed to grow properly and developed small heads and facial abnormalities; other researchers found no such growth disturbances in similarly infected infants (Blanche, 1989).

Maternal exposure to the AIDS virus *can* affect the fetus, but much is still to be learned about the reasons for these effects and the specific mechanisms involved. The issue is becoming more pressing, because an increasingly large number of women of childbearing age are becoming infected with the virus through heterosexual contact or intravenous drug use (Katz & Wilfert, 1989).

Chronic noninfectious diseases in the mother also may affect the developing fetus. For example, for reasons that are not fully understood, diabetes may result in fetal death within a few weeks before the delivery. Hypertension (high blood pressure) may result in a maternal condition known as *toxemia,* characterized by excessive water in the tissues and protein in the urine. Toxemia can result in the spontaneous abortion of the fetus and is one of the major causes of maternal death.

Maternal Stress. A number of studies have demonstrated a relationship between high levels of maternal stress and pregnancy and labor complications (Ferreira, 1960), low birthweight in infants, infant irritability (Ottinger

& Simmons, 1964), and even behavioral problems of later childhood (Stott & Latchford, 1976). When a pregnant woman is under stress, the blood flow in her body is temporarily diverted from the uterus to various other organs; the result is a temporary oxygen deficiency in the fetus (Stechler & Halton, 1982). In many of these cases with poor developmental outcomes, the stress was long-term and accompanied by low socioeconomic conditions or an unfavorable environment (Rosenblith & Sims-Knight, 1985).

However, remember that a relationship between maternal stress and birth complications, infant irritability, and so on does not demonstrate that stress actually causes pregnancy problems. In fact, stress may be the result rather than the cause of such difficulties. Perhaps a woman is more likely to feel stress if she is carrying a very active fetus or if she is experiencing a particularly difficult pregnancy. In any case, no link exists between minor everyday stress levels and the condition of the fetus.

Smoking.   Although smoking is typically included under drugs in discussions of teratogens, it is unclear whether the observed effects are due to the drug nicotine or to other potentially harmful substances such as carcinogens, lead, arsenic, and cyanide. The major known effect of smoking on the fetus is oxygen deprivation (Stechler & Halton, 1982). This occurs in two ways: (1) nicotine causes the blood vessels to constrict, reducing the flow of oxygen from mother to fetus; and (2) the increased levels of carbon monoxide from the cigarette smoke reduce the capacity of the fetal blood to carry oxygen to cells of the body (Stevens, 1979).

Studies have commonly found that the incidence of prematurity, low birthweight, spontaneous abortion, and death rate during the perinatal period is higher for those infants whose mothers smoked during their pregnancy than for those infants whose mothers did not smoke (Naeye, 1978). The magnitude of the effects seems to increase directly with the number of cigarettes smoked. Even more frightening is the finding that the risk of an infant's dying from **sudden infant death syndrome** (SIDS, commonly known as crib death) is increased by 52 percent for those infants whose mothers smoked habitually during the pregnancy (Naeye, Ladis, & Drage, 1976).

Sudden infant death syndrome
The unexplained death of an apparently healthy infant.

Alcohol.   As a result of extensive research on the effects of alcohol on the developing fetus, alcohol is now widely recognized as a teratogen. The combined effects, which have been labeled *fetal alcohol syndrome* (FAS), produce four basic congenital problems (Clarren & Smith, 1978):

Fetal alcohol syndrome
A set of congenital problems in a child resulting from alcohol ingestion by a pregnant woman, which may include mental retardation, facial anomalies, and delayed growth.

1. Defects of the central nervous system leading to mental retardation, a small head, or irritability in infancy.
2. Low birthweight and overall poor postnatal growth in height and weight.
3. Distinctive facial appearance, including a narrow forehead, small nose and midface, and a wide space between the upper lip and nose.

4. A variety of other congenital defects, such as cardiac murmurs, malformations of the eyes and ears, and problems with joints in the skeleton.

How the alcohol produces the characteristics of FAS is unclear at present. Evidence derived from experiments with mice suggests that the facial anomalies are caused by early exposure to alcohol, corresponding to the third week of a human pregnancy (Sulik, Johnston, & Webb, 1981). Apparently, exposure to alcohol late in the pregnancy also has harmful effects on the fetus. The fetal brain is believed to be particularly susceptible to alcohol in the second and third trimester.

Finally it is unclear what, if any, are safe amounts of alcohol to consume during pregnancy. Any amount of alcohol may be harmful to the embryo and the fetus, but the effects may not be readily observable. Much of the research on FAS has focused on babies born to chronic alcoholics or heavy drinkers. Some evidence suggests that moderate drinking is related to low birthweight (Streissguth, Martin, Martin, & Barr, 1981) or milder versions of FAS (Hanson, Streissguth, & Smith, 1978). In all probability, some fetuses will be more sensitive to the teratogenic effects of alcohol than others. But, research has also found that 4-year-old children who had been exposed to alcohol in utero but who did not manifest any overt signs of FAS, had poorer scores in a task designed to assess ability to attend to visual stimulation, and poorer reaction times (Streissguth, Martin, Barr, & Sandman, 1984).

Other Drugs.   Narcotics such as heroin will cross the placenta and result in fetal addiction. Marijuana smoking has been linked to spontaneous abortion of the fetus, and hallucinogenic drugs such as lysergic acid diethylamide (LSD) may damage fetal chromosomes (Jones, 1984). Cocaine use has been related to a significantly higher rate of spontaneous abortions and infant death (Chasnoff, Burns, Schnoll, & Burns, 1985).

Obstetric medications of any sort will cross the placenta and influence the fetus in a variety of ways. For example, anesthetics and analgesics administered to a woman during the birth process have been known to depress the neonate and cause respiratory difficulty. Some researchers in this area (e.g., Steinschneider, 1970) have concluded that before any drug is considered safe, it must be studied carefully in terms of both its immediate and long-term effects on the child. For example, diethylstilbestrol (DES), a synthetic form of estrogen, was taken by women between 1945 and 1970 to prevent miscarriage. The harmful effects of this hormone were not noticeable until the offspring reached reproductive maturity: The risk of cervical cancer and problem pregnancies in females and deformities in the reproductive organs of males are statistically greater for those exposed prenatally to DES (Stechler & Halton, 1982).

Environmental Toxins.   Several chemicals commonly found in the environment have been linked to developmental problems. For example, women who ate large quantities of fish contaminated with polychlorinated biphenyls (PCBs)—as found in Lake Michigan salmon and trout—had infants who exhibited weak reflexes, were motorically immature, and showed disorganized behavior (Jacobson, Fein, Jacobson, Schwartz, & Dowler, 1985). PCB-exposed infants also had poor visual recognition memory (Jacobson et al., 1985). Depending on when it was ingested, lead may be related to children's poorer performance on language and visual spatial tasks (Shaheen, 1984). Organic mercury (methyl mercury), found in contaminated fish, has been clearly implicated in abnormal neurological development (Kalter & Warkany, 1983). Finally, radiation exposure to the ovum, embryo, or fetus has clearly been demonstrated to be teratogenic. Most of the effects involve the central nervous system, resulting in increased risks of microencephaly (small head), brain and skull malformations, and Down's syndrome. Such birth defects were made painfully apparent in studies of women who were pregnant when exposed to the radiation from the atomic bombs dropped on Hiroshima and Nagasaki during World War II (Blot & Miller, 1973).

The Birth Process

In the human being, the term of pregnancy is 266 days after conception, or 280 days after the mother's last menstrual period. The overwhelming majority of pregnancies come to term within 2 weeks in either direction from the due date.

The birth process occurs in three stages. The first is the opening, or *labor,* stage, which is also the longest of the three. The average labor time for a first pregnancy is 13 hours and just over 8 hours for later pregnancies (Guttmacher, 1973). Averages may mean little, however, because the duration of labor varies considerably, depending on the particular woman and the particular pregnancy.

Labor
The first and longest stage of the birth process, during which the cervix is gradually opened to permit the passage of the child through the birth canal.

Labor is defined by hormonally triggered contractions of the long muscles in the uterine wall, which eventually propel the fetus downward from the uterus through the cervix (the area connecting the uterus and vagina) and into the birth canal. Although many variations occur in the timing of labor, the general parameters are as follows: At the beginning of labor, the contractions come at intervals between 5 and 20 minutes apart, they last for less than a minute, and they are minor in their intensity; women in early labor can move about freely and continue their everyday activities. Gradually, however, the contractions increase in frequency, duration, and intensity. Toward the end of the labor stage there may be 1 minute between contractions; they may last for a minute to a minute and a half and cause great pain. Furthermore, toward the end of labor, many women experience nausea, chills, hyperventilation, loss of feeling in their hands and feet, and great emotional turmoil. It is little wonder that Lamaze instructors refer to the end of labor as the "hurricane phase."

During labor, the contractions cause the normally closed cervix to open to a diameter of 10 centimeters (4 inches). The cervix is first stretched as the fetal head presses downward and the uterine wall thins out, a process known as *effacement* of the cervix. Gradually, the opening enlarges to permit the child to pass through the birth canal. When the cervical opening is sufficiently wide, the labor stage is said to come to an end.

The second stage of childbirth is the delivery, or expulsion, stage, which can last from a half hour to 2 hours. The contractions now serve to expel the child from the uterus rather than to dilate the cervix. The appearance of the head is known as *crowning*. The head normally emerges in the face-down position. Then the infant rotates so that the shoulders are on a vertical axis

In the delivery of a child, after the cervix has completely dilated, the woman is encouraged to push (top left). The head typically appears first (top right), then the torso appears (lower left). Finally, the baby is given to the mother (lower right) so that the bonding process may begin.

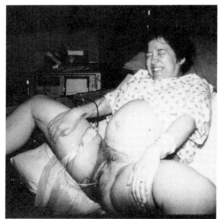
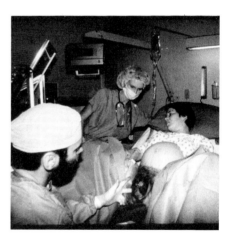
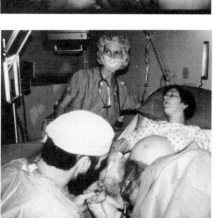
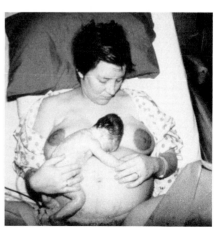

(i.e., on a line perpendicular to the floor if the woman is lying on her back) to permit easy passage through the birth canal.

In 96 percent of the cases, the fetus is positioned for delivery with the head downward. In the other 4 percent, the fetus presents buttocks first a (a breech presentation) or, very rarely, the fetus is positioned sideways on a horizontal plane (a transverse presentation) (Guttmacher, 1973). The latter presentations often necessitate a cesarean delivery, in which an incision is made in the lower abdomen and the fetus is removed surgically.

Cesarean deliveries have been increasing in recent years, from a nationwide average of only 5 percent in the 1960s to approximately 25 percent in 1988 (Goyert, Bottoms, Treadwell, & Nehra, 1989; Queenan, 1988; Notzon, Placek, & Taffel, 1987). The actual figure may be higher or lower, of course, in any specific locale. A surgical delivery is required in the case of many breech positions, in the presence of fetal distress, or when the fetus is simply too large to pass through the birth canal (National Institute of Child Health, 1980). Concern over anoxia, a lack of oxygen, may also account for the increased frequency of cesarean births. Oxygen deprivation can occur during a particularly hard or fast labor and may also result from premature separation of the placenta from the uterine wall or from the umbilical cord's being wrapped around the infant's neck during delivery. When oxygen deprivation continues for a few minutes, permanent loss of brain cells and bleeding within the skull may lead to cerebral palsy and poor motor and cognitive development.

After the child has been expelled, the third stage of birth begins. Known as the **afterbirth,** it consists of the expulsion of the placenta and amniotic sac by means of uterine contractions. The afterbirth lasts 30 minutes and is by far the easiest stage of birth, because the delivery passage already has been widened during the expulsion stage. The uterus contracts after birth, and the placenta tears away from the uterine wall. Some bleeding is to be expected as the placenta tears free, but as the uterus shrinks, the blood flow is stemmed. The placenta and fetal membranes then are expelled from the uterus by means of the contractions and perhaps a gentle tugging on the umbilical cord by those assisting at the birth.

Afterbirth
The third and last phase of the birth process, during which the amniotic sac and placenta are expelled from the uterus by the uterine contractions.

The Newborn Child

The average newborn is about 20 inches in length and weighs about 7½ pounds, with males slightly longer and heavier than females. Typically, the eyes of the neonate are smoky blue, the head is disproportionately large, and the infant has practically no voluntary control over the head or legs. The newborn's legs may be bowed, the neck is short, and the baby may have no chin and a flattened nose. Sometimes the head is misshapen because of the passage through the narrow birth canal.

Most newborns are given the Apgar Screening Test (Apgar, 1953) at 1 minute—and possibly, 3, 5, and 10 minutes—after birth. The Apgar is a quick assessment of the status of the newborn. The Apgar score, ranging

Table 3.2
Criteria and Scoring of the Apgar Test

Score	A Appearance (color)	P Pulse (heart rate)	G Grimace (reflex irritability)	A Activity (muscle tone)	R Respiration (respiratory effort)
0	Blue, pale, ashen	Absent	No response	Limp	Absent
1	Body normal, extremities blue or ashen	Slow (below 100)	Grimace	Some flexion of extremities	Slow, irregular
2	Completely normal	Rapid (over 100)	Cry	Active motion	Good, strong cry

from 0 to 10, is based on five signs: heart rate, respiratory effort, reflex irritability (determined by stimulation of the soles of the feet), muscle tone, and color. Each of these signs can be given a score of 0, 1, or 2, with a score of 2 being the best possible condition. Generally, newborns with low Apgar scores (0 to 3) must be closely monitored; Apgars of 7 to 10 are signs of a robust infant (see Table 3.2).

Another neonatal assessment that is becoming increasingly popular is the Dubowitz Scoring System (Dubowitz, Dubowitz, & Goldberg, 1970). This scoring system measures the neurological and physical characteristics of the newborn and is useful in determining the gestational age of a newborn. It is particularly helpful in assessing the condition of small-for-gestational-age and preterm infants.

A test that has become increasingly popular in neonatal assessment is the Brazelton Neonatal Behavioral Assessment Scale, or NBAS (Brazelton, 1984). The NBAS contains 20 neurological items that measure reflexes and movements such as grasping, sucking, and crawling. In addition, 27 items measure behaviors such as levels of wakefulness, sleeping, and crying; responses to a variety of stimuli; sociability; and irritability. The NBAS is designed to be used with the normal newborn; it has been useful in investigations on a variety of factors that can influence neonatal behavior. For example, a popular use of the NBAS involves relating infant scores to mother-infant interactions. The scale may be useful in determining how easily parents can adapt to the needs of their infant (Linn & Horowitz, 1983). Some researchers have even trained new mothers to give the Brazelton to their infants during their hospital stay, in an effort to sensitize the women to the behavioral capabilities of their newborn babies.

Reflexes

Much of the preceding discussion on neonatal assessment involved an examination of the newborn's reflexes. When infants come into the world, they are already equipped with a large number of automatic behavioral reactions, or reflexes. Some of these reflexes, such as sucking and rooting, are clearly related to the survival of the newborn, whereas others are not. All are significant because they reflect the maturation and development of the nervous system (Taft & Cohen, 1967). Reflex testing in infants, therefore, is helpful in localizing abnormalities in the central nervous system and determining the integrity of the peripheral nerves.

Reflexes actually develop in utero: The sucking reflex develops between 2 and 3 fetal months; the stepping reflex between 8 and 9 fetal months. Many reflexes do not persist indefinitely but disappear within the first 6 months of life, as they are replaced by more complex adaptations to the environment. Grasping, for example, is an involuntary response to an object placed in the hand and is replaced by deliberate grasping at about 4 months of age (see Table 3.3).

In the psychological sense, reflexes are significant because they indicate that the human baby is by no means an "empty organism" but has at its disposal a number of wired-in responses to the environment. They are significant, too, because they appear to form the foundations for later, more complex, learned behaviors. As will be discussed at length in Chapter 7, Jean

Table 3.3
Neonatal Reflexes and the Ages at Which They Disappear

Reflex	Behavior	Age at Which Reflex Disappears
Rooting	When their cheeks are stroked, infants open their mouths, begin sucking, and turn their heads in the direction of the stimulation.	9 months
Moro	When infants are startled or when they lose support from their heads and necks (as when the people holding them remove their hands), they throw their arms and legs outward, then bring them back toward the center of their bodies.	3 months
Tonic neck	When infants are laid on their backs, they assume a "fencing" position. One arm is extended outward, and the other is held close to the body and bent at the elbow.	3 months
Swimming	When placed into water, infants engage in rhythmic swimming movements.	4 months
Grasp	When their palms are stimulated, infants close their fists on the stimulating objects and grasp firmly.	2–3 months
Plantar	When the soles of the feet are stroked, infants spread their toes and twist their feet inward.	6 months

Piaget, the author of our most elaborate theory of children's intellectual development, thought of neonatal reflexes as the roots of sensorimotor intelligence during the period of infancy.

Infant States

For harried parents of newborn babies, the ideal newborn would immediately adjust to the adult day-night cycle of wakefulness and sleep. However, this sort of pattern is many weeks (or months) away. Rather, it often seems as if the infant's behaviors are random and disorganized; the baby appears to sleep and wake up, sometimes moving quite actively while asleep, sometimes lying still, sometimes fussing or looking about—with no apparent pattern to the behavior.

Neonatal behavior is organized around different levels of sleep and wakefulness, called states. These states are presumed to reflect the maturity of the central nervous system. By painstakingly observing neonatal behavior for hours, researchers have been able to categorize different types of sleep and wakefulness in infants. A number of such classification systems exist, but Wolff's (1966) is one of the most widely accepted. Table 3.4 provides Wolff's definitions of seven infant states.

Young infants spend about 16 to 17 hours per day asleep, with the rest of the time in various states of wakefulness (Parmelee, Wenner, & Schulz, 1964). However, the actual percentage of time in each state can vary greatly from one child to the next. These periods of sleep and wakefulness alternate during the day and night until about the age of 1 month, when the time spent in stretches of being asleep or awake increases.

Infant states provide an important window on both neurological organization and responsiveness of infants. For example, the slow, regular, or nonrapid eye movement (NREM) sleep seems to demand the most organization of the infant's central nervous system (Beckwith & Parmelee, 1986). A particular brain wave pattern during this form of sleep has predicted scores on intelligence tests up to 8 years of age for children who were born prematurely (Beckwith & Parmelee, 1986).

The rapid eye movements (REM) and diffuse motor activity associated with irregular sleep may actually serve as stimulation for the central nervous system as the baby sleeps; we do not know for certain if young babies dream as do adults. Interestingly, the amount of REM sleep declines as the infant ages and spends more time awake. Also, newborns tend to go immediately into REM sleep, whereas adults first go through a series of NREM stages before reaching the REM sleep state. The changeover to the adult pattern occurs during the first 6 months of life.

Another significant state is alert inactivity. Although newborns spend little time in this state, at this time they are the most responsive to the environment. They actively scan their visual world, and their behavior seems to encourage parents to interact with them. Byrne and Horowitz (1979) found that placing a crying infant on an adult's shoulder and intermittently

Table 3.4

Wolff's Classification of Infant States

Regular Sleep or Nonrapid Eye Movement Sleep (NREM Sleep)	Full rest; low muscle tone and motor activity; eyelids closed and eyes still; regular breathing (about 36 times per minute)
Irregular Sleep or Rapid Eye Movement Sleep (REM Sleep)	Increased muscle tone and motor activity; facial grimaces and smiles; occasional eye movements; irregular breathing (about 48 times per minute)
Periodic Sleep	Intermediate between REM and NREM sleep—bursts of deep, slow breathing alternating with bouts of rapid, shallow breathing
Drowsiness	More active than NREM sleep but less active than REM or periodic sleep; eyes open and close; eyes glazed when open; breathing variable but more rapid than in NREM sleep
Alert Inactivity	Slight activity; face relaxed; eyes open and bright; breathing regular and more rapid than in NREM sleep, eyes moving together
Active Alert	Frequent diffuse motor activity; vocalizations; skin flushed; irregular breathing
Distress	Vigorous diffuse motor activity; facial grimaces; red skin; crying

Source: Adapted from *Psychological Issues,* 5(1) by Peter H. Wolff by permission of International Universities Press, Inc. Copyright 1966 by International Universities Press, Inc.

rocking it can calm and soothe the infant. This procedure can bring the child to a state of alert inactivity and can also afford opportunities for enriched visual and social experiences.

PATTERNS OF GROWTH: BIRTH TO OLD AGE

Although we often tend to think of growth as an overall process, the growth rates for the various parts of the body are not the same (see Figure 3.4). Most development in the area of the brain and nervous system takes place prenatally or during early infancy. General body growth, including the growth of bones, musculature, and internal organs, is relatively rapid during the first 2 years, slows down during the preschool and elementary school

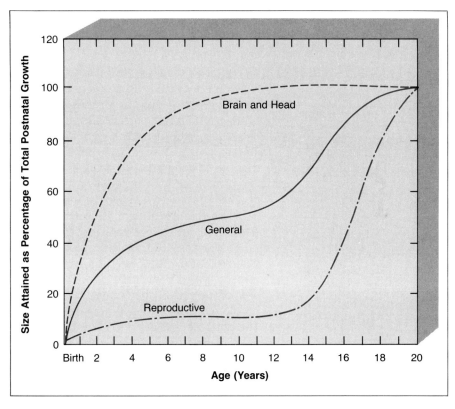

Figure 3.4
Growth Curves of Different Parts of the Human Body
Source: Redrawn from R. E. Scammon. In J. A. Harris, C. M. Jackson, D. G. Patterson, & R. E. Scammon (Eds.), *The measurement of man.* Minneapolis: University of Minnesota Press, 1930.

years, and then spurts again at puberty before it levels off. Finally reproductive growth, including growth of the internal sex organs and the emergence of reproductive capacity, is an uneventful process until puberty.

Brain Development

Cerebral cortex

The outer surface of the human brain, which is responsible for the sophisticated psychological functioning of the human organism.

The outer surface of the human brain is the **cerebral cortex,** which is responsible for the sophisticated psychological functioning that distinguishes human beings from lower animals, and which, in an adult, is divided into several areas with specialized functions. Certain cortical areas are concerned with motor activity, others are sensory areas, and still others are known as association areas, in which mental activity is integrated (Tanner, 1978).

Childhood and Adolescence

By the end of the second month of pregnancy, the cerebral cortex can be identified. The earliest development takes place in the primary motor area, with the areas for control of trunk and arms developing faster than the area for control of the legs. Next comes development in the primary sensory area, which is concerned with the sense of touch in various parts of the body, then development of the primary visual area, followed by development of the primary auditory area. The association areas, which involve the integration of primary impulses, lag behind the primary areas. This means that an infant's basic sensory and motor skills are developed before the baby is capable of integrating these skills into patterns. To use an example, infants are capable of moving their hands and seeing before they are capable of organizing these two activities into the pattern of visually guided reaching.

By 3 months of age, the primary areas of the cortex are fairly mature, particularly the motor area. Development continues to spread out from the primary areas until the cell structures are well developed throughout the cerebral cortex. Although an infant's ability to move the arms is clearly and directly linked to the development of a specific portion of the primary motor area of the cortex, the connection between a child's ability to solve a mental problem and the development of a specific area of the cortex is not so clear. The older people get, the more difficult it becomes to make direct connections between cortical structure and psychological functions. This does not mean, however, that such connections do not exist.

In addition to the increase in "association" fibers connecting the various areas of the cortex and laying the groundwork for higher-order thinking, brain development in infancy and childhood is characterized by an increase in the number of nerve cell fibers in the cerebral cortex and an increase in the number of nerve fibers connecting the cortex to the lower portions of the brain. These latter fibers conduct sensory impulses to the brain and motor impulses from the brain to the rest of the body. The most revealing evidence on brain development in childhood and adolescence comes from studies on the process of *myelination*. To understand this process, we must first discuss the structure and function of the nerve cell itself.

Neuron
A nerve cell.

The nerve cell, or **neuron,** consists of a cell body, which is the main portion, and a number of fine threadlike projections extending from it. These projections, which resemble the branches of a tree, are called dendrites; the dendrites in the cerebral cortex increase in number as people mature. In addition to the dendrites, each neuron has one extremely long projection, called an axon. The axon and the dendrites are referred to as the nerve fibers of the cell. When a neuron is stimulated, a nerve impulse is conducted electrically. The speed of the impulse actually can be measured and depends on the thickness of the axon. The thicker the axon, the faster the impulse is conducted. An increase in the speed of nerve impulse transmission indicates an increase in the efficiency of the system. Presumably, organisms with thicker nerve fibers would be more responsive to stimulation from the environment and more efficient in their overall functioning. Interestingly enough, human beings have relatively thin nerve fibers compared to many other organisms. How, then, can we explain our advanced and complex nervous system? The efficiency of our nerve fibers does not depend on thickness alone.

As we develop, most nerve fibers are increasingly surrounded by a fatty layer called a *myelin sheath*. This sheath, or cover, insulates the nerve fiber, protects it, and allows the fiber to conduct a nerve impulse much more rapidly than if the sheath were not present. In a sense, the myelin compensates for the relative thinness of our nerve fibers.

From a developmental standpoint, the level of brain and nervous system maturity is linked to the level of myelination of nerve fibers. The process is by no means complete at the time of birth, and it occurs at different times for different nerves. For example, the optic nerve is myelinated very shortly after birth, whereas the nerve fibers linking the cerebral cortex to the cerebellum and necessary for small muscle control are not myelinated until about the age of 4 years. Obviously, a child has some small muscle control before the age of 4, because nerve fibers can function before they are myelinated; the most efficient functioning, however, does not appear until myelination is complete. Some of the favorite play activities of 4- and 5-year-olds—drawing, painting, working with a pair of scissors, cutting, and pasting—illustrate the effects of myelination of nerve fibers on the activities children are capable of. Two- and 3-year-olds are not ready for such games.

Myelination in some areas is not complete until adolescence or beyond. Is there a relationship during adolescence between neural maturation and specific forms of complex thinking? This is extremely difficult to determine. In fact, considering the magnitude of the intellectual growth that occurs around the time of puberty, it is almost surprising that the brain does not show a corresponding significant growth at that time. Figure 3.4 showed that most growth in brain size takes place in early infancy and that brain changes during development are apparently changes in complexity. The increasing myelination and the increasing number of dendrites in the cerebral cortex are probably responsible for the vast cognitive changes that can be observed. The complex associations among the various nerve cells may be necessary for abstract thinking.

Adulthood and Aging

The most significant change in the adult brain is a progressive loss over time in the actual number of nerve cells and an increasing likelihood that remaining nerve cells will be damaged (Buell & Coleman, 1979; Spence, 1989). This loss of nerve cells is largely responsible for the loss of brain mass associated with the aging process. By the time a person is 30 years old, the brain has achieved its full adult weight of approximately 3 pounds, and it contains about 14 billion nerve cells. After age 30, a gradual decrease in the size and weight of the brain begins; the brain of a 90-year-old is about 20 percent smaller and 10 percent lighter than that of a 20-year-old (Huyck & Hoyer, 1982; Spence, 1989).

In addition to the loss of nerve cells, the rate of conduction by the neurons decreases, and this decline in speed and efficiency may be the result of a mild loss of myelin from the sheaths that surround the neurons (Spence, 1989). As a result, elderly people do not react as readily as they once did to visual, auditory, or tactile cues from the environment, and they are at least slightly impaired in their motor skills. Observed sensory and motor impairments among old people should not be attributed only to neurological factors, however. As always, the link between brain structure and behavior is a tenuous one. For example, impairment of the sense organs themselves may be largely responsible for many sensory deficits of later life, and the diminished motor functioning of the elderly may be influenced by such psychological variables as lowered motivation, increased anxiety, or simple caution when attempting motor tasks.

Body Development

When we speak of body development, we are referring to changes in the overall size and shape of the body. Included are changes in height and weight, in the size, shape, and composition of the bones, in the size and trainability of the muscles, and in the internal organs.

Height and Weight

A summary of height and weight changes across the life span is contained in Table 3.5. As the table indicates, growth in both areas is extremely rapid during prenatal development, gradually slows down throughout the years of childhood, and spurts during early adolescence. A gradual weight increase occurs from early to middle adulthood, and both weight and height decrease after the age of 65—the latter attributable to a tendency of the spine to curve slightly with advancing age.

Table 3.5
Growth in Height and Weight from Conception to Adulthood

Type of Growth	Prenatal	Infancy (birth–1 year)	Early Childhood (1–4 years)	Middle Childhood (5–12 years)	Adolescence (12–18 years)	Adulthood (18 years and up)
Height	One month after conception, 1 in. in length; 3 months, 3 in.; 4 months, 6 in.; 5 months, 12 in.; 6 months, 14 in.; 7 months, 16 in.; 8 months, 18 in.	Birth, 21 in.; increase by 10 in. in first year	Increase by 5 in. in second year; 2½ in. in third year, etc.	Increase by 5 to 6 percent per year	Increase by 10 to 12 percent per year during early adolescence. Males complete 98 percent of growth in height by age 16; females, by age 14	Maximum height attained by age 20; slight decrease in height ½ to 1 in. in late 50s and 60s
Weight	3 months, 1 oz; 4 months, 4 oz; 5 months, 1 lb; 6 months, 2 lb; 7 months, 3 lb; 8 months, 4½–5 lb	Birth, 7½ lb; weight doubles by 5 months; triples by end of first year	Second year, 7- to 8-lb increase; third year, 3- to 4-lb increase	Increase by 10 percent per year	Increase by 20 percent per year during early adolescence	Weight gain slows down in early adulthood; slight but steady increase from age 18 to 65, followed by a gradual decrease

Sources: From Bischof, L. J. *Adult psychology.* New York: Harper & Row, 1976, p. 90; Hamill, P. V., Drizd, T. A., Johnson, C. L., Reed, R. B., & Roche, A. F. *NCHS growth curves for children, birth to 18 years.* (Vital and Health Statistics: Series 11. National Health Survey, No. 154.) Washington, DC: U.S. Government Printing Office, 1977; Kent, S. How do we age? *Geriatrics,* vol. 31, 1976, pp. 128–34; Tanner, J. M. Physical growth. In P. H. Mussen (Ed.), *Carmichael's manual of child psychology* (p. 84). New York: Wiley, 1970; Tanner, J. M. *Fetus into man: Physical growth from conception to maturity.* Cambridge, MA: Harvard University Press, 1978, pp. 14–15; Tortora, G. J., & Anagnostakos, N. P. *Principles of anatomy and physiology* (4th ed.). New York: Harper & Row, 1984, p. 746; and Troll, L. E. *Continuations: Adult development and aging.* Monterey, CA: Brooks/Cole, 1982, pp. 68–70.

In addition to developmental height and weight changes, the proportions of the various parts of the body change from infancy to adulthood. The infant's head is proportionately about twice as large as that of an adult, while the arms and legs are shorter and more curved than those of adults.

Proportional changes are particularly noticeable between the ages of 2 and 6: the legs and arms grow longer, the abdomen flattens, the shoulders go from rounded to square, and the baby fat seems to disappear. More than does the toddler, the 6-year-old truly resembles a small adult, but changes in proportion continue to occur throughout the growing years.

The male's shoulders broaden after puberty, and the female's hips widen disproportionately. The adolescent's jawbone is longer, thicker, and

Issues in Human Development
Are Children Growing Up Faster Than Their Parents Did?

 A U.S. female born in 1985 will probably have her first menstrual period when she is between the ages of 12½ and 13. A U.S. female born in 1910 first experienced menstruation at age 14, and data from several European countries indicated that girls in the nineteenth century did not begin to menstruate until they were 15½ to 17½ (Malina, 1979; Tanner, 1962). A similar pattern has been observed in the timing of puberty among boys.

Not only do children grow up faster than they did 150 years ago, but each generation has tended to be taller by approximately an inch and heavier than the generation that preceded it. This phenomenon of advanced development is known as the *secular trend* (Roche, 1979; Tanner, 1962, 1978).

Two observations should be made about the secular trend. First, it has not been occurring throughout recorded history; as far as we can determine, children from ancient times up through the Middle Ages matured at the same rate as we do today and reached the same adult stature; puberty appears to have been delayed only in the nineteenth century (Malina, 1979). Second, the trend appears to be slowing in recent generations, or even coming to a complete stop. We are not getting indefinitely taller and reaching puberty indefinitely earlier.

What are the reasons for the secular trend across the last 150 years? A number of reasons have been cited: improved nutrition, improved environmental circumstances, reduced family size, urbanization, and the fact that genes for height seem to be dominant over genes for shortness. When a person from a tall family marries a person from a short one, the children tend slightly toward the taller side rather than being halfway in between (Malina, 1979; Tanner, 1978).

more prominent than it was during childhood; the chin also grows more prominent, the nose proportionately larger, and the profile straighter (Conger & Petersen, 1984; Lowrey, 1973; Smart & Smart, 1982).

Skeletal Structure

Skeletal development across the life span involves a number of processes. *Ossification* is a process by which cartilage, a gristly substance that cannot be detected by X rays, is transformed by the gradual accumulation of calcium into bone. In addition, development brings an increase in the size of the bones and a change in their shape. Finally, a gradual fusion occurs between the long bones and their epiphyses—the ossification centers between the long bones (Tanner, 1978).

Ossification occurs throughout childhood. The bones of a child consist mostly of water and proteinlike materials and do not have the mineral content of adult bones. A slight, not dramatic, increase in the rate of ossification occurs at puberty; during adolescence, the process is completed. Also during adolescence, the final fusion of the long bones of the body with the epiphyses occurs, so there are actually fewer bones in the body after puberty than before it—a reduction in number from 350 to 206 (Tanner, 1970, 1978).

During childhood, skeletal structure shows few gender differences, but at puberty the male sex hormone testosterone causes the cartilage in the shoulder area to expand rapidly, whereas the female hormone estrogen has a similar influence on the hips. The result is that a pubescent boy's shoulders expand noticeably compared with other areas of his torso, and he acquires a more or less V-shaped physique, with broad shoulders and narrower hips. The girl's hips develop more rapidly than other areas, so she acquires the typical female shape, with hips wider than shoulders (Tanner, 1978).

Osteoporosis
A condition of middle and old age in which the bones become lighter, less dense, and more brittle.

The density and weight of the bones is at its maximum point around the age of 35. No noticeable changes occur in either density or weight until after the age of 45 or so. Then the size and weight of the bones throughout the body gradually decrease. In this bone loss, called **osteoporosis,** the bones become lighter and more brittle. This condition, which is found in 15 to 20 million Americans, occurs more often in women than in men. It can result in the slight loss in height that was discussed earlier, in backache, in a tendency to slouch when standing or walking, and in the increased likelihood of bone fractures (London & Hammond, 1986).

What are the causes of osteoporosis? No one factor has been found to explain this degenerative process, although a number have been suggested, some dealing with nutrition, some with exercise, and some with hormonal changes in the body—specifically with the loss of estrogen that occurs during menopause (Kart & Metress, 1988). Suggested remedies for osteoporosis include maintaining a physically active lifestyle; avoiding tobacco, alcohol, and caffeine; consuming a diet rich in calcium; and replacing estrogen that a woman's body is no longer producing (Katchadourian, 1989).

Muscle Development and Strength

The size and number of muscle cells in the body from birth to young adulthood continuously increase, and muscle tissue enlarges as a result of diet, exercise, and hormone secretion. These changes bring with them a corresponding increase in strength. Males are more muscular and stronger than females at all ages. The differences are hardly noticeable before puberty, however, because the male sex hormone testosterone is responsible for the development of the musculature, and the levels of sex hormone are low until puberty (Conger & Peterson, 1984; Tanner, 1970). Thus, the adolescent spurt in muscle development is more dramatic for boys than for girls. Puberty brings with it not only an increase in muscle size but also an increase in trainability; the muscles of an adolescent or adult have a greater capacity to be developed through exercise than they did during childhood.

We are at our strongest between the ages of 25 and 30. After that, there is a gradual but steady decline until age 60 and then a more rapid decline in strength. We lose about 10 percent of our strength between the ages of 30 and 60, and most of this is in the muscles of the back and legs rather than the arms. Even though the muscle tissue actually deteriorates with increasing age, another reason for the decline in strength and loss of muscle efficiency is lack of exercise. Regular exercise can prevent a premature

*With adolescence comes an in-
crease in the trainability of the
muscles. Lifting weights can dramatically affect muscle size and
strength after puberty.*

decline in muscle tone during mid-life (Troll, 1985; Kart, Metress, & Metress, 1988).

Body Fat

Directly beneath the skin and covering the musculoskeletal inner structure is an uneven layer of subcutaneous body fat. This layer increases in thickness during the last 2 months of prenatal development and then gradually thins out from the time of birth to the age of 5 or 6 years (Smart & Smart, 1982). By the time most children are ready for school, they have lost the "baby fat" of infancy and have developed leaner, more angular physiques. After the age of 6, the thickness of the fat layer gradually increases, particularly in the trunk, but also in the limbs. Then, as puberty approaches, a spurt in fat growth occurs approximately a year after the beginning of the height spurt.

Noticeable gender differences in body fat begin to occur as children enter adolescence. The fat layer in girls of all ages is slightly thicker than the layer in boys; at puberty, however, because of the influence of the female sex hormone estrogen, the fat layer continues to grow rapidly in girls but not in boys. In fact, adolescent boys actually show a decrease in thickness of the fat layer as measured by skinfold calipers; their muscles and bones are growing rapidly, and as they do so, the ring of fat that surrounds them is stretched thinner (Tanner, 1970).

During adulthood, the fat layer continues to increase in thickness, and the percentage of body weight consisting of fat will double from adolescence to middle age. Fat deposits tend to accumulate in the trunk rather than the extremities, so with increasing age, the amount of fat in the trunk accounts for a greater and greater percentage of overall body fat (Troll, 1975, 1985).

Breast Development

The earliest sign of approaching puberty in the adolescent girl is the development of the breasts, which may occur as early as 8 years of age and is due to an increase of the female hormone estrogen in the bloodstream. Tanner (1962) described the stages of breast development in the typical adolescent girl. First, the papillae (the tips of the nipples) enlarge, causing them to protrude slightly from the chest. Then the areas surrounding the nipples enlarge so that the breasts protrude from the body as small mounds. At this stage the nipples also increase in diameter. The breasts continue to enlarge, and the nipples extend from them as secondary mounds. Finally, the nipples recede slightly so that they no longer stand out as projections from the breasts. In the adult stage, only the papillae continue to project from the breasts.

Gynecomastia
Temporary breast enlargement that occurs in approximately one in three boys at the onset of puberty.

Approximately one out of three boys experiences breast enlargement at puberty, a condition known as *gynecomastia* (Conger & Petersen, 1984; Tanner, 1962). This condition usually lasts for less than a year, but it is acutely embarrassing to many boys, who see it as reflecting their lack of masculinity.

Internal Organs

In addition to the external changes in the body, a number of internal changes occur during the process of human development. Let us now examine some of these internal changes.

Circulatory System. The average heart rate for a newborn baby is approximately 140 beats per minute. This rate declines gradually throughout the growing period until it reaches its adult level of roughly 70 to 80 beats per minute.

A gradual and regular increase in blood volume per unit of body weight occurs throughout childhood, with a spurt at adolescence for boys; this is due primarily to an increase in the number of red blood cells in the system. The blood volume increase has practical significance, because within the red blood cells the pigment hemoglobin carries oxygen from the lungs to the muscles. As the red blood cell count increases, the hemoglobin level also increases, and more oxygen is supplied to the muscles. Therefore, the adolescent or adult is much more efficient than the child in meeting physical challenges such as those involved in athletics or manual labor (Tanner, 1962, 1970).

The heart grows slowly during childhood compared with overall body growth. By puberty, it is approximately seven times larger than it was at birth, and during the adolescent years, it doubles again in size. In young adulthood, the circulatory system is at its peak of efficiency. The resting heart rate has reached its lowest point; blood pressure is stable, because the veins and arteries, which lagged behind the heart in their growth during adolescence, have now fully developed; and the blood volume is at its maximum.

After the age of 30, however, the efficiency of the system gradually decreases. The most noticeable change during adulthood is in what is referred to as the cardiac output—the amount of blood pumped by the heart per unit of time. This declines by about 20 percent between the ages of 30 and 60 and by about 30 percent between 30 and 80. The result is a loss of stamina with increasing age and a greater likelihood of fatigue.

Some researchers have suggested that the decrease in blood supply to the extremities may cause the drying of the skin associated with aging. About one-third of the blood that circulates in the body is used to nourish the skin and to help it rejuvenate itself. When the blood supply decreases, the rejuvenation process may be impaired. In addition, decreased blood circulation to the scalp may be partially responsible for the thinning, drying out, and graying of the hair (Kart et al, 1988).

The Respiratory System.   The lungs are functionally developed at birth but are filled with fluid, most of which is squeezed out through the mouth and nose during the birth process itself or drained out when the infant is suspended by its feet immediately after birth. With the first cry, air is taken into the lungs, and breathing begins. The newborn baby, when awake, has a respiratory rate of approximately 80 breaths per minute (Eichorn, 1970). With development, respiration becomes deeper, slower, and more efficient; the normal respiratory rate for an adult at rest is approximately 15 breaths per minute.

Increase in lung size and vital capacity (the amount of air exhaled from the lungs after a person has taken the deepest breath possible) are age-related. In girls, the increase follows the regular pattern of body growth: relatively rapid growth in early childhood, slower growth in middle childhood, and a slight increase in the growth rate at puberty. In boys, however, there is a noticeable spurt at puberty in both lung size and vital capacity, such that male-female differences are slight during childhood but considerable during adolescence and adulthood. The increased lung capacity results in increased stamina and a definite advantage in athletics.

After young adulthood, a regular decline occurs in vital capacity of the lungs. The maximum vital capacity is reached at the age of 30, and there is a decline of 20 percent by age 50 and a decline of 30 percent by age 60. In old age, the decline is even more rapid. In addition, increasing age brings an increasing likelihood of respiratory ailments, the most common one among elderly in the United States being chronic bronchitis (Kart et al., 1988).

Digestive System. At birth, the digestive tract is completely functional (Eichorn, 1970; Tortora & Anagnostakos, 1984). After growing at a relatively fast rate from birth through the preschool years, the digestive system grows more slowly during the years of elementary school, a period of life marked by increasing digestive stability: cases of upset stomach become less frequent, and children need to make fewer trips to the bathroom during the day.

At puberty, the stomach increases in size and capacity for food. Tanner (1970) observed that an average girl's need for calories increases by about 25 percent between the ages of 10 and 15, whereas a boy's needs increase by an incredible 90 percent between the ages of 10 and 19. The average male between the ages of 16 and 19 requires 3,600 calories a day—more than he ever will again during his lifetime—whereas a girl aged 13 to 15 requires 2,600 calories a day (Smart & Smart, 1982).

With each decade of life, the caloric need continues to decline. Moreover, after the age of 30, the amount and acidity content of the gastric juices secreted by the stomach for digesting food declines. Foods that are difficult to digest become more difficult to digest with each passing decade. This means that middle-aged adults who eat the same amount of food or the same types of food they ate during adolescence may be plagued by weight problems and digestive disorders such as gastritis and peptic ulcers (Kart et al., 1988; Spence, 1989).

The elderly may have special dietary problems, not only because of changes in the digestive system itself, but because (1) they may have difficulty chewing foods thoroughly; (2) they may not be able to afford an adequate diet; (3) they may tend toward obesity because they consume more than the approximately 1,500 calories a day they need; and (4) they may not want to or be able to prepare meals and thus may eat packaged foods, which are probably lower in nutritional value.

Locomotor Development

Locomotor development, the development of the ability to move the body, is not a random process. In fact, it is highly directional. Control over the

Cephalocaudal growth
Physical growth that proceeds in a pattern from the head to the trunk of the body.

Proximodistal growth
The pattern of human growth that proceeds from the center of the body out to the extremities.

muscles of the body that facilitate movement proceeds in two directions simultaneously, the first being *cephalocaudal growth* (literally meaning "from the head to the tail") and the second being *proximodistal growth* (from the area nearest the center of the body out to the extremities).

Cephalocaudal development is exemplified by the way in which an infant can control the muscles of the head and neck before it can control the muscles of the trunk. For example, a typical infant held at the shoulder can only lift the head intermittently at 3 days after birth but will hold the head erect and unsupported for increasingly longer periods during the first 3 months of life. By 4 months, the average baby can hold the head erect with no difficulty at all.

Proximodistal growth can be seen in the way in which prehension develops. A newborn infant moves both arms and both legs when stimulated, but gradually the movements become more localized: The forearm moves independently; then the wrist is rotated; and, eventually, the individual fingers are separately controlled. By the age of just under 4 months, on the average, an infant can grasp an object by "clamping" it between the palm and the four fingers, which seem to function as one unit (the thumb is not yet used effectively). By 7 months, there is complete opposition between the thumb and the other fingers (when the infant grasps), and by 9 months, the fingers seem to operate independently, as when the infant uses the thumb and forefinger (the pincer grasp) to pick up small objects (Bayley, 1969). The progression from gross to increasingly finer muscle control continues during childhood. Manual dexterity, such as that required for typing, playing the piano, or tying a knot, is not maximized until adolescence.

The proximodistal direction of growth also can be seen in the development of walking. The earliest stepping movements occurs at 7.4 months; children who are held under the arms and supported on a firm surface attempt to propel themselves forward by stepping. Children walk by holding an adult's hand or furniture by 9.6 months, stand alone at 11 months, and can take at least three steps without support at 11.7 months. Walking sideways and backward begins at 14.5 months, and walking upstairs with help, by the age of 16 months (Bayley, 1969). The average 2-year-old, therefore, can walk sideways and backward, and 3-year-olds also can walk on their tiptoes and walk a straight line.

Motor development in children from the ages of 6 to 12 has been described by Cratty (1970), who observed that children in the elementary school years regularly increase in their ability to perform most motor tasks. Boys are superior to girls in forceful acts of the hands and arms (such as throwing a ball) and in acts of the legs (such as running or jumping). Girls, in contrast, are superior to boys in motor activities requiring rhythm and accuracy, such as hopscotch and ball-bouncing games. Selected behaviors described by Cratty can be found in Table 3.6.

Table 3.6
Selected Locomotor Behaviors in School-Aged Children

Age	Motor Behaviors
6	Gallops
	Skips
	Balances on one foot (eyes open)
	Broad jumps
7	Performs jumping-jack exercise
	Balances on one foot (eyes closed)
	Jumps diagonally from one square to another
	Throws a ball with the proper step forward
8	Hops from one foot to the other without a break in rhythm
	Can achieve a grip strength of 12-lb pressure
9	Can throw a ball 40 ft
	Can jump 9–10 in. over standing height plus reach
	Can describe the left-right movements of other people when watching them
10	Throws a ball 70 ft
	Runs 16–17 ft per second

Sources: Cratty, B. J. (1970) *Perceptual and Motor Development in Infants and Children* (1st ed.) N.Y.: Macmillan; Cratty, B. J. & Martin, M. M. (1969) *Perceptual-motor Efficiency in Children,* Philadelphia: Lea and Febiger.

Adolescence brings with it an increase in speed of body movement, as well as an increase in motor coordination. Gradual improvement occurs in balance and agility and in motor skills such as running and jumping. Reaction time (the time required to respond to unexpected stimuli) improves until approximately the ages of 18 to 20. Because of a combination of biological and cultural factors, boys are superior to girls in motor coordination. Evidence of a gender difference in reaction time is mixed; some researchers have found that men in their late teens are faster than women of the same age at reacting to unexpected stimuli, while others report no difference at all (Katchadourian, 1977; Tanner, 1962).

Adults in their early 20s are at their peak in terms of motor skills, motor coordination, and reaction time. After the early 20s, there is a gradual decline in all three areas, and this decline continues throughout life. When people of different ages are asked to respond quickly to a sudden stimulus with a predetermined hand movement, the time needed to react and perform the movement decreases until early adulthood and then gradually increases (Wilkinson & Allison, 1989).

The typical laboratory situation used to measure movement and reaction time, in which a person must press a button as soon as a light next to it comes on, may seem a bit contrived. However, the loss of reaction speed is reflected all too clearly in real-life situations as well. Driving is a skill that

A baby usually can walk at about 10 months of age by holding an adult's hand and generally can take a few steps unassisted before the first birthday.

often requires the ability to respond quickly to unexpected situations, and the data would seem to suggest that as reaction time decreases in old age, poor driving becomes increasingly common (Aiken, 1982).

Loss of speed, loss of strength, increased likelihood of fatigue, and an increasing stiffness in the joints all combine to make movement more difficult for the elderly than for younger adults. However, about 80 percent of persons over the age of 65 still manage to get around satisfactorily (Aiken, 1982). The completely immobile older adult is the exception, fortunately, rather than the rule.

INDIVIDUAL VARIATIONS IN GROWTH

The major focus of this chapter has been the regularities of physical development, such as those observed in the endocrine functioning of the normal human being and the typical patterns of growth. However, dramatic individual differences occur in both the rate of growth and overall physical appearance—differences that are accounted for by heredity and environmental variations (Tanner, 1978). Here we will examine differences in the rate of human growth and the psychological impact of these differences, which is particularly apparent during adolescence. In the following section, we will look at body satisfaction and body image—the reaction of individuals to the recognition that their bodies are different from those of other people.

Early and Late Maturation at Puberty

Nowhere are the differences in the rate of human growth more evident than in a junior high school classroom. A group of 12- and 13-year-olds will contain some children who have already reached puberty and look like full-grown adults as well as some who are small and childlike in every respect. As is illustrated in Figure 3.5, some children complete the changes of puberty before many of their classmates have even begun.

Advantages and disadvantages are associated with the extremes of early and late maturation, and the psychological effects of the timing of puberty depend on the sex of the child in question. For this reason, we shall discuss separately the findings pertaining to female and male pubertal development.

Early and Late Maturing Girls

The girl who matures early may begin to notice breast development at the age of 8 or 9. She may experience her height spurt at the age of 9 or 10, and her first menstrual flow when she is 10 or 11. Thus, she will be taller, heavier, and more womanly in appearance than her age-mates (Petersen, 1988). As a result, the early developing girl may have a stronger sense of her femininity than does the girl who is slow to mature (Rierdan & Koff, 1980), and because of her size, strength, and stamina, she will undoubtedly have an athletic advantage over the other girls in her class.

Because she looks older than her peers and her figure is more attractive than theirs, she is more likely to be approached by boys interested in dates (Crockett & Dorn, 1987), although she may not actually begin dating ahead of her classmates, because chronological age is a better predictor of the onset of dating than sexual maturation (Dornbusch et al., 1981). However, the key point is that the early-developing girl will receive a greater amount of male attention and have more dating opportunities than will other girls (Steinberg, 1989). In addition, she is often popular among her female peers

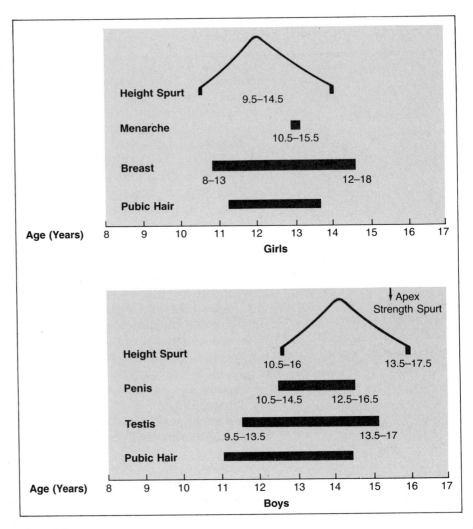

Figure 3.5
Sequence of Events at Puberty for the Average Boy and Girl
Source: "Growing Up" by J. M. Tanner. Copyright 1973 by SCIENTIFIC AMERICAN, INC. All rights reserved.

because of her elevated social status (Brooks-Gunn, Warren, Samuelson, & Fox, 1986; Simmons, Blyth, & McKinney, 1983).

Despite the potential advantages of early maturation for a girl, there appear to be a number of drawbacks as well. In the first place, the characteristics of womanhood that appear so early in her body may make her feel conspicuous, which of course she is. She may feel proud but may also be self-conscious about her physical changes. Self-image problems are common among early-developing girls (Aro & Taipale, 1987; Simmons &

Blyth, 1987; Tobin-Richards, Boxer, & Peterson, 1983). After all, no young adolescent wants to be noticeably different from her peer group. What is more, she may come to see her full womanly physique as less than desirable in a society that reveres the thin, leggy figure of a fashion model as the standard of feminine beauty (Katchadourian, 1989; Steinberg, 1989).

The considerable variation in the rate of physical growth is very obvious in early adolescence. Some junior high school students look like young adults while others of the same age still resemble children.

Because they take on a "grown-up" appearance at a very young age, early-developing girls often find themselves in the company of older adolescents. Perhaps as a result of this socialization, they are more likely than later developers to engage in what might be called deviant behaviors, such as truancy and other school-related problems, rebelliousness against parents, abuse of alcohol and other drugs, and juvenile delinquency (Adams & Gullotta, 1989; Duncan, Ritter, Dornbusch, Gross, & Carlsmith, 1985; Magnussen, Stattin, & Allen, 1986; Petersen & Crockett, 1985; Steinberg, 1989).

Finally, the sexual maturity that results in ego-boosting male attention for a young girl may also cause her problems. She is likely to become sexually active at an earlier age than will her later-developing peers, and she may not be emotionally mature enough to handle sexual relationships (Magnusson et al., 1986). In addition, early sexual activity may elevate an adolescent boy in the esteem of his male peers but may only tarnish a girl's reputation in a society that is uncertain about the value of female sexuality (Faunce & Phipps-Yonas, 1979).

The late-developing adolescent girl may not notice signs of breast development until she is 13 or 14. She may be 14 or 15 before she experiences her adolescent height spurt, and she may have to wait until she is nearly 16 for her first menstrual flow. She may feel as if she will have to wait an eternity to see her body take on a womanly appearance. As a result, she is likely to suffer some anxiety about her appearance, particularly when she compares her body with those of other girls her age.

Boys will not swarm around the late developer as they do her early-developing classmates, and she may worry that she is not feminine enough. She is generally less mature in her heterosexual interests. Dating, dancing, wearing makeup, and dressing to attract boys may appeal to her less than these activities appeal to her age-mates. Indeed, the late-maturing girl may still be playing children's games and cherishing her dolls while many of her classmates are preparing for their first dates.

The late-developing adolescent girl is more likely than the early developer to acquire the tall, slender figure that is so much admired by adolescents today. In addition, she may avoid many of the social problems faced by the early developer. She will not be drawn too early into heterosexual relationships. She will not associate with friends who are too emotionally mature for her. She will be less likely to engage in rebellious and antisocial behaviors. In fact, in much of the research on early and late maturity, the girl who is slow to develop is described as being more likable, more socially outgoing, and higher in leadership ability than is the early developer (Adams & Gullotta, 1989; Steinberg, 1989).

It is difficult to say, when comparing early- and late-maturing girls, which is in the advantaged position. Many women looking back on their adolescent years are grateful for their lack of sex appeal and popularity, because, instead of early dating, they developed other interests. Many early-developing adolescents grow into women who feel that their physical charms did them more harm than good when they were young. Indeed, the girl in the ideal position may be neither the early nor the late developer, but the one who is right "on time." In a recent study, the girl whose development was in step with her age-mates had the most positive self-concept; the late developer was second; and the early developer, last (Tobin-Richards et al., 1983).

Early and Late Maturing Boys

As is true of girls, both extremes of maturity in adolescent boys will have positive and negative consequences. However, for a male the advantages of early maturity far outweigh the disadvantages, and late maturity is a decided handicap.

The early-maturing boy may notice testicular development at the age of 9½ or 10, and penis development within a year after that. His height spurt may occur when he is 10 or 11 years old, and by the time he is 13, he may resemble a young adult.

As his body develops, the early-maturing boy will acquire a significant athletic advantage over his peers, because of the dramatic nature of the pubertal change in size, strength, and stamina. Not only is he bigger and stronger than he was before, but he can run faster, jump higher, and play longer and harder. This type of athletic advantage may carry well beyond the playing fields, because male high school athletes have been found to have higher self-esteem than nonathletes (Schumaker, Small, & Wood, 1986).

Social maturity and self-confidence quickly follow physical maturity in an early-developing boy. Like the early-developing girl, he will probably be quite attractive to the opposite sex. As a result, he may have more dating opportunities and earlier sexual experience with a larger number of partners than the late maturer; such heterosexual contacts may serve to reinforce his masculinity and boost his self-confidence (Crockett & Dorn, 1987). In addition, because he looks older than his peers, he may find himself entrusted by adults with major responsibilities, he may be regarded as competent—as a natural leader—by his peers, he is likely to be popular, and he may, therefore, become more assertive in social situations (Petersen, 1985; Steinberg, 1989).

Does the early-developing boy have any disadvantages? Apparently, there are some. For example, like an early-developing girl, he may often find himself in the company of adolescents who are much older than he, and he may become involved in the same sorts of deviant behaviors as his female counterpart: truancy, juvenile delinquency, alcohol and other drug abuse, and problems with teachers and parents (Duncan, Ritter, Dornbusch, Gross, & Carlsmith, 1985).

The late-maturing boy, whose body only begins to take on the first appearance of manhood when he is in his mid- to late teens, is the last one of his age-mates to develop. At least the late-developing girl is in step with her male peers, because girls reach puberty approximately 2 years before boys. The late-maturing boy, however, is at the end of the line.

Boys who are slow to develop are seen by peers and by adults as less physically attractive than other boys, less well-groomed, less athletic, and less likely to be leaders. They express a great need for the attention and the approval of other people and may try to get attention in socially unacceptable ways, such as by being disruptive in the classroom or by being the class clown. In addition, such boys may have difficulty dealing with authority figures, including parents and teachers, any may appear to be rebellious and hostile (Jones, 1957; Jones & Mussen, 1958).

In some sense, however, the late-developing boy may have certain advantages that appear only later in life, since rebelliousness can also have a positive side. When compared to late developers as they approach the age of 40, early developers tend to be more assertive, confident, self-controlled, and responsible, but they are also more conventional, humorless, and willing to conform. Late developers at middle age may be less assertive and less likely to be found in leadership positions, but they are also less likely to conform without question to society's standards, and less likely to prefer rules and routines. In addition, they display a greater amount of intellectual curiosity, exploratory behavior, and playful creativity (Livson & Peskin, 1980). Characteristics of this sort may make a late-developing boy a better adult problem solver than his early-developing counterpart. Perhaps the delayed onset of puberty gave him a longer time to prepare psychologically for the arrival of adulthood (Steinberg, 1989).

Nevertheless, from his own limited perspective during adolescence, the late developer may not think of himself as privileged. That delayed puberty will lead to better coping skills as an adult may offer little consolation to a boy who sees his age-mates surpassing him in athletic skills, leadership roles, and dating opportunities. It is hardly surprising that the feelings of inadequacy and need for attention and approval that characterize the late-developing American boy can still be found in early and even middle adulthood (Jones, 1957; Weatherly, 1964).

Individual Variations in Aging

Individual differences in growth rate are found at both ends of the life span. Although everyone ages, people do so at different rates (Spence, 1989). Men age faster than women, blacks faster than whites, and rural dwellers faster than people who live in cities (Troll, 1985).

It is important to be cautious in discussing what the body looks like at any given age during the span of adult life. Some people appear to be approaching "old age" when they are in their 40s; others may not be physically "old" until they are in their 80s or 90s. When does the hair turn gray? When do wrinkles first appear? No simple answers are possible, because much depends on the genetic makeup of the individual. People whose parents lived to an advanced age are likely to do so as well, and people who look old or young for their age probably have relatives who also did so.

In addition to genetic factors in aging, the influence of the environment must always be remembered. Adequate nutrition and an appropriate program of exercise may not prolong life, but they can counteract those factors that may bring an untimely death, and they can keep people healthier than they might otherwise have been (Kart et al., 1988).

PSYCHOLOGICAL ISSUES IN PHYSICAL DEVELOPMENT

As has probably already become clear, discussing physical growth and development is difficult without also examining its psychological correlates. We turn now to a more detailed analysis of the psychological aspects of growth.

Ideal Physique and Body Satisfaction

Human bodies vary considerably in almost every physical attribute, and yet most cultures have, or have had, certain ideas about what the "ideal" body is. What is an ideal physique in the United States today?

The average U.S. male wants to be tall (about 6 feet in height), with a sturdy frame, well-developed muscles, and a desired weight of about 180 to 200 pounds, and he would like to have hair on his face—even if he decides to shave it off—and some hair on his body as well (Adams & Gullotta, 1989; Dwyer & Mayer, 1968–1969; Gunderson, 1965).

In a sense, the ideal male body seems to be defined more in terms of function than appearance. The male is certainly not indifferent to his own physical appearance, but he seems to allow functional considerations to overshadow aesthetic ones. For example, males are less concerned than females about having an attractive face (Adams & Crossman, 1978; Adams & Gullotta, 1989), and they typically define the ideal body according to a global concept of fitness. Men are happy with their bodies if they see themselves as being "in shape" and if they exercise regularly; being handsome is not a prerequisite for body satisfaction (Cash, Winstead, & Janda, 1986). In addition, the self-esteem of a young male depends on his perception of his body as active, potent, and competent, whereas the female self-concept is correlated with a view of her body as physically attractive (Lerner, Orlos, & Knapp, 1976; Rodin, Silberstein, & Striegel-Moore, 1984).

The emphasis on function over aesthetics in the evaluation of the male body may reflect, and indeed may be influenced by, the male preoccupation with sports in U.S. society. Sports involvement is inextricably associated with masculinity in the United States (Sabo & Runfola, 1980), and athletic participation is a major predictor of social success among adolescent males (Snyder, 1972; Eitzen, 1975). A person needs a well-functioning body to be successful in sports, but physical beauty will not be particularly helpful on the playing field.

Perhaps because of the male pre-occupation with sports in U.S. society, men define body satisfaction in terms of physical fitness more than in terms of physical attractiveness.

Females in the United States place facial attractiveness higher on their list of desired physical characteristics than males do (Cash, Winstead, & Janda, 1986; Tobin-Richards et al., 1983). This finding is hardly surprising because, beginning even in the preschool years, facial attractiveness is highly correlated with peer group status and acceptance for females, although not for males (Maccoby & Jacklin, 1974; Rodin et al., 1984; Vaughn & Langlois, 1983). In adolescent dating situations, for example, the most beautiful girls attract the boys whose status in the peer group is highest, whereas the most powerful, high-status boys, if even reasonably good-looking, attract the prettiest girls; in other words, physical beauty is a major social asset for girls, but boys apparently acquire social status in different ways (Maccoby & Jacklin, 1974; Rodin et al., 1984).

Girls and women in the United States would like to have breasts that are average in size, and they particularly do not want them to be small. During adolescence, girls see their breasts as their most sexualized body parts, and the preteen girl is often preoccupied with breast development (Rosenbaum, 1979; Tobin-Richards et al., 1983). The psychological impact of breast development is suggested by the fact that the degree of development that has occurred in this area is related to adolescent girls' psychological adjustment, body image, and satisfaction with peer relationships (Brooks-Gunn, 1987).

Females also want to be relatively free of facial and body hair, and often view hair on their faces or bodies as masculine-looking and even as abnormal, which of course it is not (Brownmiller, 1984; Dwyer & Mayer, 1968–1969).

Finally, the U.S. female wants to have a relatively small frame. She does not want to be large-boned, or large in any sense. In fact, concern about being overweight is widespread among girls and women in our society. Research on adolescents (Davies & Furnham, 1986; Forehand, Faust, & Baum, 1985; Frazier & Lisonbee, 1950; Katchadourian, 1989; Stuart & Jacobson, 1979) and on adults (Berscheid, Walster, & Bohrnstedt, 1973; Cash, Winstead, & Janda, 1986; Fodor & Thal, 1984; Rodin & Stoddard, 1981) indicates that females worry more about being overweight than males do and are more likely than males to be dissatisfied with the size of their abdomen, hips, buttocks, and thighs. In fact, as girls mature physically, their tendency to be unhappy with their weight increases dramatically (Richards & Petersen, 1987). Stuart and Jacobson (1979) discovered that by late adolescence, three out of every four females were troubled by what they perceived as a need to lose weight.

An intriguing and often tragic feature of the weight preoccupation of the U.S. female is that her weight concerns are so often unnecessary. Many girls and women who are not overweight are still preoccupied with fears of weight gain, and many falsely believe that they need to shed "excess" pounds (Forehand, Faust, & Baum, 1985; Rodin, Silberstein, & Striegel-Moore, 1984; Rodin & Stoddard, 1981). This group, sometimes referred to as "thin-fat" people (Bruch, 1980), have been found to make up approximately 20 percent of the self-referred clients in overweight treatment groups (Fodor & Thal, 1984; Wooley and Wooley, 1980). In a recently published survey of 326 girls aged 13 to 18, the researchers found that half the girls who were categorized as *under*weight were "extremely fearful" of becoming overweight, and a third of the underweight girls were "preoccupied with body fat" (Moses, Banilivy, & Lifshitz, 1989). Furthermore, disturbed eating patterns (e.g., eating binges, self-induced vomiting) were found in one in four girls in *all* weight categories.

Why are U.S. girls and women today so preoccupied with body weight? Why, when asked in a magazine survey to choose the alternative that would make them happiest, did 42 percent of the female respondents say it would be to lose weight (Wooley & Wooley, 1980)? (Only 22 percent said success at work would make them happiest!)

Brownmiller (1984) suggested that a key reason for the female obsession with thinness is that a svelte physique allows women to compete more effectively with one another for male attention. However, although women identify the lean physique as the one to which they aspire and the one they think is most attractive to men, men have other ideas. When asked to identify the female figure they find the most attractive, men choose a physique that is considerably heavier than the one women *think* they will be drawn to—just as men erroneously identify the heavily muscled male body as the one that women prefer, even though women actually find a leaner physique more attractive in a man (Fallon & Rozin, 1984).

Rodin et al. (1984) argued that U.S. women do not view weight loss simply as an avenue to heterosexual opportunities. Instead, thinness has become a goal in itself. Thinness has become synonymous with attractiveness, and attractiveness is seen as the equivalent of success. The ability to control one's weight is for many women a demonstration of their ability to achieve while maintaining an attractive and "feminine" appearance. Indeed, dissatisfaction with body weight and a need to "achieve" thinness is most often found among professional women, who do not play traditional female roles, who value and seek out a variety of options, and who have high expectations and standards for themselves (Rodin & Striegel-Moore, 1984).

Body Image, Self-Esteem, and Social Interaction

Body image

The view people have of their bodies, which may or may not correspond to objective reality.

What do you like about yourself? What do you dislike? What would you like to change? A typical person responding to these questions will not immediately think about intellectual or personality characteristics; he or she will think about the body (Conger & Peterson, 1984). In fact, a definite relationship exists between the perception people have of their bodies—the *body image*—and the perception they have of themselves as a whole. People with positive body images are more likely than those with average or poor body images to see themselves as above average in likability, intelligence, and assertiveness (Berscheid et al., 1973; Jourard & Secord, 1955). Consider the comment made by one respondent to a body image survey: "If I had been plain instead of pretty, I would be a much weaker and sadder person," or the remark that "my body gets more and more pleasing as I grow more self-assured and begin to like myself more" (Berscheid et al., 1973, p. 126).

Other indications of a link between body image and self-esteem can be found in the previously mentioned studies of early- and late-maturing adolescents. Recall that adolescent boys, who generally are lower in body satisfaction than their earlier-maturing peers, also have been found to be less emotionally and heterosexually mature, more restless, more anxious, higher in need of attention and approval from others, lower in self-confidence, less likely to be assertive or take leadership positions, more dependent, and more rebellious (Dwyer & Mayer, 1968–1969; Mussen & Boutourline-Young, 1964; Weatherly, 1964).

The link between body image and overall self-concept is correlational and not necessarily causal. That is, although we know a relationship exists between body image and self-esteem, we do not know which one causes the other. Does having an attractive body raise a person's self-esteem and self-confidence? Or does having a self-confident outlook on life cause a

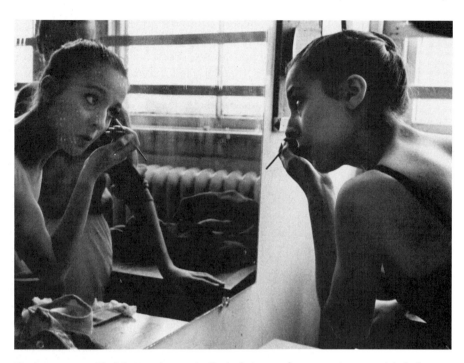

The importance of facial attractiveness to the body image of a woman in our society is illustrated by the careful attention paid to the application of makeup.

person to feel that his or her body is attractive, no matter what it really looks like? Clearly, forming a truly objective opinion about our physical appearance is difficult, and our opinion is probably influenced to some extent by our overall self-esteem.

In addition to the research on the connection between body image and self-concept, a number of studies have linked body image with such variables as perceived employment potential, athletic participation, and heterosexual functioning. For example, King and Manaster (1977) found a relationship between body image satisfaction and expectations of success in a job interview among college women. In other words, women who were most satisfied with their physical appearance were more likely to believe they would do well in a job interview. In a study of the relationship between athletic skill and psychological well-being. Snyder and Kivlin (1975) found that adult female athletes had more positive body images than nonathletic women and were higher in psychological well-being.

Along similar lines, Young and Semail (1976) found that a group of men who were in good physical condition were more intellectually inclined, emotionally stable, self-confident, and ambitious than a group of men who were not physically fit. Again, however, we must be careful not to conclude that physical exercise actually causes psychological well-being.

Mitchell and Orr (1976) found that self-ratings of physical attractiveness are related to heterosexual success. From their study of close to 1,000 college students, they observed that students who consider themselves physically unattractive are also likely to have difficulty in relating to the opposite sex. Berscheid et al. (1973) discussed a similar finding. Men and women who felt that they were physically attractive tended to have sex more often, have more sexual partners, and enjoy sex more than those who felt unattractive. Many of those with poor body images even felt that certain aspects of their bodies made them unsatisfactory sexual partners.

Physical Attractiveness and Social Desirability

"Beauty is only skin deep." "Beauty is in the eye of the beholder." Phrases of this type suggest that physical appearance is of little importance in human relationships because, after all, a person's inner self is what really matters. Physical attractiveness is superficial and fleeting, and certainly no basis for judging anyone's social desirability. These are admirable sentiments to be sure, but many researchers (e.g., Dion, 1986; Dion, Berscheid, & Walster, 1972; Dion & Dion, 1987) suggest a more appropriate phrase to describe the relationship between physical and social attractiveness: "What is beautiful is good."

Nearly 20 years ago, Dion et al. (1972) asked college students to rate people on a number of personality characteristics based *only* on their yearbook photographs. The most attractive people were judged to be the most likable, the best adjusted, and the most likely to succeed in life. In other words, there appeared what the authors described as a pervasive bias in favor of physically attractive people. Since that time, the results of a number of studies (Adams & Huston, 1975; Dion, 1986; Dion & Dion, 1987; Gross & Crafton, 1977; Johnson & Pittenger, 1984; Powell & Dobbs, 1976; Smits & Cherhoniak, 1976) have indicated that Americans tend to link physical attractiveness to social desirability.

Many researchers have used the evaluation of photographs technique employed by Dion et al. (1972). For example, Smits and Cherhoniak (1976) presented male college students with photographs of women, whom they were asked to evaluate in terms of their personalities, their looks, and their social desirability. The more physically attractive the woman was, the more likely she was to be rated as pleasant and friendly. Gross and Crafton (1977) found similar results using raters of both sexes, as did Adams and Huston (1975) when the photographs were of middle-aged people and the raters were of various ages. And Johnson and Pittenger (1984) found that, on the basis of photographs alone, both young and old adults rated attractive elderly people as both more likable and more accomplished.

A slightly different approach to the question of attractiveness and social desirability was taken by Powell and Dobbs (1976). They assigned students the task of interviewing more than 100 pedestrians on a city street and then secretly observed the interactions during the interviews. When the person being interviewed was physically attractive, the interviewers stood closer to them than they did to unattractive interviewees. The effect was particularly noticeable when the interviewer and the subject were of the opposite sex.

The physical attractiveness bias found in experimental studies also comes into play in real-world situations. A consistent finding in research on characteristics of popularity is that good looks and social success are highly correlated. At all age levels—in childhood (Cavior & Dokecki, 1969, 1970; Dion, 1977, 1986; Kleck, Richardson, & Ronald, 1974; Krantz, 1987; Krieger & Wells, 1969; Vaughn & Langlois, 1983; Zakin, 1983), adolescence (Cavior & Dokecki, 1973; Coleman, 1961; Crockett, Losoff, & Petersen, 1984), and adulthood (Byrne, Ervin, & Lamberth, 1970; Goldman & Lewis, 1977; Smits & Cherhoniak, 1976)–physically attractive people stand a better chance of being popular than do unattractive people.

If good-looking people are *perceived* as being more pleasant, more approachable, more desirable to have as friends, more achievement-oriented, and more likely to succeed in life, does this mean that they really possess these characteristics? As a matter of fact, the attractiveness bias discussed by Dion and Dion (1987) may be an expectation that fulfills itself. Consider the findings of Goldman and Lewis (1977), who asked participants in their study to rate the social skills and general likability of more than 100 college students solely on the basis of telephone conversations. When the students were independently evaluated in terms of physical attractiveness, the better-looking students were judged higher in likability by the raters, who had never actually seen them face to face.

If attractive people really *are* more socially skilled, perhaps it is because they grow up with more attention from other people and greater opportunities for social interaction. Many researchers have reported that from infancy onward, adults give attractive children special treatment: they smile at them more often, offer them more help, make more frequent positive remarks to them, and are more physically affectionate with them (Byrnes, 1987; Hildebrandt & Fitzgerald, 1983; Smith, 1985).

In addition to being more socially skilled, physically attractive people seem to be more successful than unattractive ones in other areas of life. For example, good-looking children are significantly higher in school achievement, as indicated by report card grades (Salvia, Algozyne, & Sheare, 1977) and by teacher ratings (Clifford, 1975). One researcher (Rich, 1975) found that teachers saw nice-looking pupils as having more desirable personality traits than did unattractive ones, and more often criticized less attractive children for misbehavior of various sorts.

What little research there is on the life success of good-looking adults indicates that the attractiveness continues into the adult years. Good-looking adults have been found to be higher in psychological well-being, character-ized by positive affect, satisfaction with life, and the relative absence of stress, than less attractive ones. Attractive adults have also been found to be more accomplished in life, as indicated by their family income, level of education attained, and occupational prestige (Umberson & Hughes, 1987),

Research Close-Up
The Stereotyping of
Attractiveness Among the
Elderly

We live in a society in which youth is often seen as a prerequisite for beauty, and we know that a bias toward attractive people has been demonstrated in numerous studies involving young adult participants. Are elderly Americans, whom many would see as beyond the age range in which beauty is emphasized, attentive to variations in the attractiveness of their age-mates? Are the elderly susceptible to the attractiveness bias that is found among the young?

To answer these questions, psychologists Douglas Johnson and John Pittenger of the University of Arkansas carried out an interesting experiment. They recruited a group of 36 women (aged 60 to 93) and 36 men (aged 60 to 89) from various nursing homes and senior centers and showed them sets of photographs of three elderly people, who had previously been judged as high, moderate, and low in physical attractiveness.

First, the researchers asked the participants to evaluate the people in the photographs on 27 personality traits. For example: Which of the three is the most and which the least exciting? Which is the most and which the least warm? Which is the most and which the least strong? Next, the participants were asked to judge who was the most and who the least likely to have certain life experiences, in the areas of marital happiness (e.g., "most likely to have an understanding spouse"), parental happiness (e.g., "least likely to have been a good parent"), and social happiness (e.g., "most likely to have led an interesting, exciting life"). Finally, the participants determined which person was the most and which the least likely to have worked in various occupations preselected as being of high status (e.g., physician), medium status (e.g., electrician) or low status (e.g., janitor).

Johnson and Pittenger discovered that, consistent with findings from research on young adults, elderly people were definitely susceptible to an attractiveness bias. Elderly adults rated their physically attractive age-mates as having more socially desirable personality characteristics (e.g., stronger, more exciting, warmer), and more positive life experiences (e.g., happier marriages, better relationships with their children, more eventful lives), and as more likely to have engaged in high-status careers. They concluded that the attractiveness stereotype is truly a life-span phenomenon in the United States.

We began this chapter by suggesting that the physical self cannot be separated from the psychological self—that the body is not simply a shell that we inhabit, but is a key ingredient in the formation of a person's identity, at least in our society. Research on the psychological impact of physical appearance certainly supports this contention. Research also points to a bias in our society in favor of physically attractive people. We may like to believe that people should be judged on the basis of their character instead of on their looks. Some writers (e.g., Byrnes, 1987; Lakoff and Scherr, 1984) suggest, however, that if we deny the importance that is placed on physical beauty we are ignoring a very real form of discrimination, and one that is very painful to many people.

Summary

1. The plan of human physical growth is laid down in microscopic structures containing hereditary material in the form of genes. The hormones—chemical substances secreted into the bloodstream by the glands of the body—carry out the genetic message.

2. Pregnancy is divided into three stages. The germinal stage includes the first 2 weeks after fertilization; the embryonic stage begins at 2 weeks and lasts until the end of 8 weeks; and the fetal stage goes from 8 weeks until the moment of birth.

3. Teratogens are environmental factors that can cause developmental malformations. They have their highest impact upon the developing organism during periods in which cell division is most rapid.

4. Birth is a three-stage process consisting of the opening stage (labor), the expulsion stage (delivery), and the afterbirth stage.

5. The brain and nervous system are the areas of the body that develop the fastest and are well developed earliest in life.

6. Growth in height and weight proceeds at a rapid pace during infancy and early childhood, slows down during middle childhood, and accelerates again during early adolescence.

7. Children in our society tend to be both taller and heavier than the generation that preceded them, a phenomenon known as the secular trend.

8. The internal organs grow rapidly during the prenatal, infant, and early childhood periods, more slowly during middle childhood, and more rapidly again during adolescence. Maximum efficiency of the internal organs is not reached until late adolescence or early adulthood.

9. In general, growth proceeds in two directions; the cephalocaudal direction (from the head downward into the trunk) and the proximodistal direction (from the center of the body to the extremities).

10. Puberty is initiated when a hormonal signal from the pituitary gland stimulates the sex glands (ovaries or testes) to secrete sex hormones. These sex hormones are responsible for the development of primary and secondary sex characteristics.

11. Wide individual variations occur in the rate of growth, with some adolescents reaching puberty significantly earlier than, and some significantly later than, their peers. Similarly, individual variations occur in the timing of the physiological events associated with aging.

12. There is a strong positive relationship between body image and self-esteem. Physically attractive people have been found to be more popular and more socially desirable than physically unattractive people at all age levels studied.

Key Terms

afterbirth (p. 88)
amniotic sac (p. 76)
blastocyst (p. 74)
body image (p. 116)
cephalocaudal growth (p. 104)
cerebral cortex (p. 94)

chromosomes (p. 70)
ectoderm (p. 76)
embryo (p. 75)
endoderm (p. 76)
estrogen (p. 73)
fetal alcohol syndrome (p. 84)

fetus (p. 78)
genes (p. 70)
genotype (p. 70)
gynecomastia (p. 101)
hormone (p. 72)
hypothalamus (p. 72)
labor (p. 86)

maternal sensitization (p. 82)
meiosis (p. 71)
mesoderm (p. 76)
mitosis (p. 71)
neuron (p. 95)
osteoporosis (p. 99)

phenotype (p. 70)   proximodistal growth   sudden infant death syn-   testosterone (p. 73)
pituitary gland (p. 71)   (p. 104)   drome (p. 84)   trophins (p. 72)
placenta (p. 76)   secular trend (p. 98)   teratogens (p. 81)   zygote (p. 74)
progesterone (p. 73)

Review Questions

1. What are the differences between meiosis and mitosis as forms of cell division? What type of cell division is mitosis unable to account for?

2. Describe the functions of the pituitary gland in regulating human growth. What is the relationship between the pituitary gland and the other glands that are also responsible for different aspects of growth?

3. List and discuss the various drugs that have been found to affect the developing embryo and fetus. What specific effects have been found for each one?

4. Explain the significance of the process of myelination in the development of the human brain and nervous system. Can aspects of myelination account for some of the neurophysiological changes associated with the aging process?

5. What is the secular trend in physical development? When did it begin? Are there possible implications of the secular trend for explaining some of the conflict between parents and their children?

6. Discuss the personality characteristics of the typical early- and late-developing male and the typical early- and late-developing female. Which of the four groups appears to have the greatest overall advantages?

7. What is the "ideal" body type for a male and for a female in U.S. society? How do men and women differ in the ways in which they define body satisfaction?

8. What evidence suggests a bias in U.S. society toward physically attractive people? What are some of the advantages of being physically attractive during childhood, adolescence, and adulthood?

Suggested Readings

Bruch, H. (1978). *The golden cage.* New York: Vintage Books.
    A fascinating and readable discussion of 70 case histories of adolescent girls who are victims of anorexia nervosa, in which the author discusses possible causes of the condition as well as successful treatments.

Kart, C. S., Metress, E. K., & Metress, S. P. (1988). *Aging, health, and society.* Boston: Jones and Bartlett.
    An in-depth treatment of the basic changes that are associated with the aging process in U.S. society, with an emphasis on the biomedical aspects and on health-related issues among the elderly. Included are chapters on the effects of aging on the major systems of the body, the nutritional needs of the elderly, drug use in later life, the importance of exercise, and institutionalization and its alternatives.

Katchadourian, H. (1989). *Fundamentals of human sexuality* (5th ed.). New York: Holt, Rinehart, & Winston.
    One of the most thorough treatments of the sexual changes in the human body across the life span. Included are chapters on sexual structure and function, the processes of reproduction, and issues related to sexuality and to gender in childhood, adolescence, and adulthood.

Tanner, J. M. (1978). *Fetus into man: Physical growth from conception to maturity.* Cambridge, MA: Harvard University Press.

A well-written summary of Tanner's work on physical development during childhood and adolescence. It includes a discussion of growth patterns, gender differences, standards of normal growth, growth disorders, and psychological consequences of growth variations.

Chapter Four

Sexuality

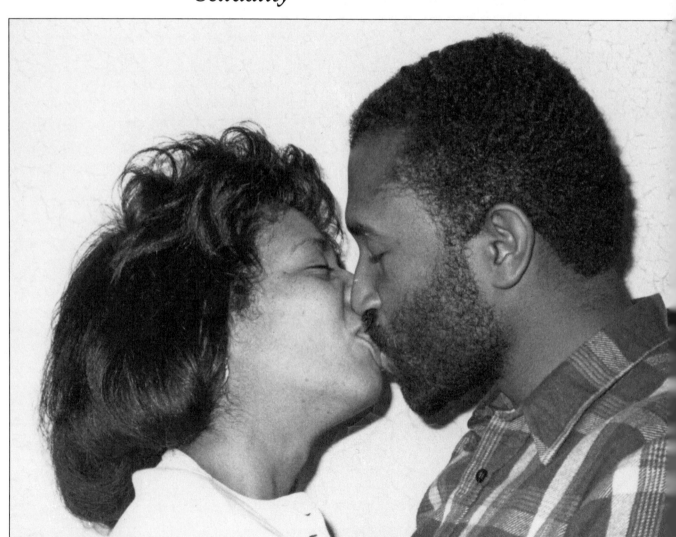

Sexual Anatomy and Function
Prenatal Development
Female Reproductive System
Male Reproductive System

Sexual Behavior and Development
Infant Experiences
Childhood Interests and Activities
Adolescent Attitudes and Behaviors
Adult Practices and Values
Characteristics of the Elderly

Gender Roles and Sexuality

 Artichokes, dried salamanders, bananas, oysters, crocodile eggs, and prunes. At some time in the past, all these items were thought to increase the human sexual appetite. Indeed, the notion that certain chemical substances, referred to as ***aphrodisiacs,*** can increase the human sex drive has been a part of our folklore throughout recorded history (Stark, 1982). At the same time, the rational side of modern human nature tells us that sexual needs and preferences must be culturally learned; they are, in a sense, an acquired taste.

Can human sexual behavior really be influenced by factors other than learning? Evidence in support of the effectiveness of aphrodisiacs is lacking, but a growing body of evidence suggests that sexual behavior is influenced by chemical substances in the bloodstream, namely the sex hormones. The relationship between hormone levels and sexual functioning has been demonstrated most dramatically in males. For example, testosterone levels in boys increase significantly from the ages of 12 to 16, and so does the incidence of masturbation, nocturnal emissions, and spontaneous erections (Udry, Billy, Morris, Groff, & Raj, 1985). Furthermore, men who are undergoing considerable stress show decreased levels of male sex hormone, as well as decreases in sexual interest (Kreuz, Rose, & Jennings, 1972). Viewing pornography has been found not only to cause sexual arousal in men, but also to raise their testosterone levels, although the hormone increase does not peak until an hour later (Luria & Rose, 1979).

Researchers have suggested that a woman's sex drive is highest in the middle of the menstrual cycle, when estrogen levels in the bloodstream reach a peak (Harvey, 1987), and certainly this is the case in lower animals. However, the evidence for an estrogen-linked peak of sexual arousal is quite inconsistent in human beings; in fact, women may be sexually responsive at all times during the menstrual cycle—even at the time of the menstrual flow, when estrogen levels are down (Katchadourian, 1989). In addition, menopause does not bring about a loss of interest in sex, as it might if a hormonal explanation of female sexual responsiveness were accurate.

Leaving aside the correlational evidence, chemical castration and the resulting loss of testosterone production apparently diminish a man's sex

Aphrodisiacs
Any substances, from bananas to dried salamanders, that have erroneously been thought to increase sexual drive.

drive. Several studies in which sexual offenders were administered hormone suppressant drugs—for example, Cooper (1986)—found that men's sexual arousal and interest were clearly reduced. In contrast, the injection of additional testosterone into healthy men does not increase their sex drives (Persky, 1983), although similar injections may enhance the sex drive in women by causing increased sensitivity in the genital area and increased orgasmic intensity (Gray & Gorzalka, 1980).

What, then, are the influences of hormones on human sexual functioning? A relationship of some sort exists. Nevertheless, the inconsistencies in the findings suggest that human sexual behavior is far too complex to be explained by a simple biological model. Sexuality is, after all, an integral component of the lives of human beings, and in its complexity it is truly representative of the entire process of development and behavior.

Our discussion of human sexuality will begin with the development of reproductive anatomy and function in the womb, when gender is determined and the genitals are formed. We will then turn to the pubertal years during which reproductive system functioning matures. Changes in the biological basis of sexuality for the adulthood years will be highlighted next.

Human sexual behavior, from infancy through old age, will be the focus of most of this chapter. Although such behavior is characterized by a large degree of variety, we will emphasize the activities that are most frequently practiced and that have received the greatest amount of attention from life-span sex researchers: masturbation, homosexuality, and heterosexuality.

Gender roles
The behaviors that society recognizes as appropriate for males and females.

Finally, this chapter will briefly explore the relationship between sexuality and *gender roles,* the behaviors society recognizes as appropriate for males and females. The material on gender role development will be treated more extensively in Chapter 14, but here we will preview the connections among various notions of masculinity and femininity and the sexual attitudes and interests of males and females as they develop physically, socially, and emotionally.

SEXUAL ANATOMY AND FUNCTION

The development of sexual anatomy and function from birth until puberty is a rather uneventful process. The genitals grow slowly, and the sex glands in the ovaries or testicles of even a young child are already producing low levels of sex hormones. However, the dramatic changes in reproductive anatomy, the beginnings of reproductive functioning, and the production of substantial amounts of male and female sex hormones will not occur until the early adolescent years. The reproductive system of a child is in a quiescent state, awaiting a signal from the hypothalamus to the pituitary gland to begin the process of sexual maturation. Before discussing these major events, however, we must elaborate on the significant developments of the prenatal months that were introduced in Chapter 3.

Prenatal Development

Each egg cell in a woman's body contains an X chromosome, whereas the man's sperm cells contain either an X or a Y chromosome. If an X-bearing sperm fertilizes an egg, the resulting sex chromosome combination will be XX, and a genetically female child will be produced. If the fertilizing sperm bears a Y chromosome, a genetically male child will be produced with the XY sex chromosome pattern. Therefore, the father determines the gender of the child.

The process of sex differentiation does not end with the meeting of the two sex chromosomes. Throughout prenatal development, several significant turning points, or "gates," influence the future maleness or femaleness of the organism (Money & Ehrhardt, 1972). Once a particular genetic or hormonal event has occurred, the choice cannot be redirected—the gate has closed. Gate 1 occurs at conception, when the genetic sex of the organism is determined.

Regardless of genetic sex, during the first 6 weeks after conception the unborn child has the potential to develop into either a male or a female, because the organs of reproduction, or gonads, are undifferentiated (see Figure 4.1). After 6 to 8 weeks of gestation, the Y chromosome of genetic males will direct the formation of testes, which, in turn, begin secreting two male hormones *(androgens)*. Testosterone stimulates tissues to differentiate into male internal organs, and ***Müllerian-inhibiting substance*** inhibits the development of female internal organs. If androgens are not produced, the gonadal organs will differentiate into ovaries by the sixth month of gestation. Thus, Gate 2 has closed (Money & Ehrhardt, 1972).

Gate 3 closes at around 3 to 4 months after conception, when the external genitals of the fetus are differentiated. The hormone testosterone influences the formation of male external genitalia (i.e., the formation of a penis). If the male's tissues are not responsive to testosterone at this point, female external genitalia will develop. Likewise, a female exposed to the male hormone at this point may develop male external genitalia (see Figure 4.1).

Gate 4 leads from the genitals to the brain. At this point, testosterone affects the midportions of the brain (the hypothalamus), rendering the brain sensitive to male hormones and insensitive to female hormones (estrogen). The hypothalamus controls the pituitary gland, which stimulates the production of testosterone in the testes and suppresses the female hormonal cycle in male adults. For female adults, the pituitary gland stimulates estrogen production in the ovaries and controls the menstrual cycle.

Gate 5 occurs during birth, when parents and medical staff look at the external genitalia of the newborn; exclaim triumphantly, "It's a boy!" or "It's a girl!" and initiate the complex socialization process that usually results in a correspondence between sex and gender (see Figure 4.1).

Several important conclusions should be drawn from this "relay race." First, at each of the turning points, the fetus will develop into a female

Androgens
Male sex hormones.

Müllerian-inhibiting substance
A male hormone, secreted by the newly formed testes after 6 to 8 weeks of prenatal development, which prevents the formation of female internal organs.

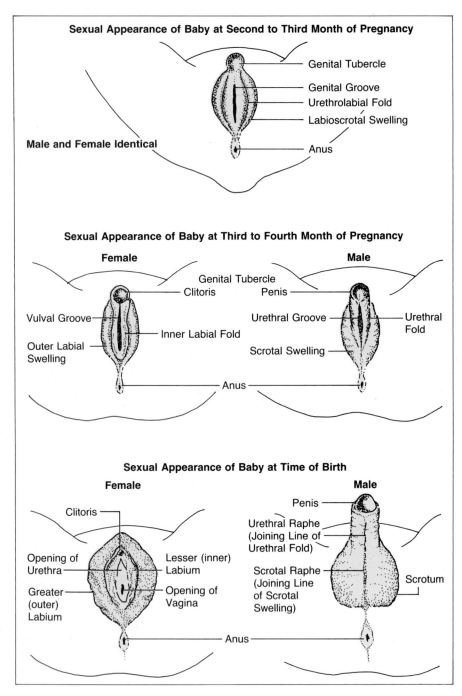

Figure 4.1
Prenatal Differentiation of the External Genitals

Source: Adapted with permission from J. Money & A. A. Ehrhardt. *Man and woman, boy and girl: The differentiation and dimorphism of gender identity from conception to maturity.* Baltimore: Johns Hopkins, 1972, p. 44.

unless a Y chromosome or androgen is introduced. Estrogen, however, is not necessary for the feminization of gonadal tissue. Second, there must be a correspondence among genes, hormonal secretion, and tissue receptivity for the proclamation of sex at gate 5 to match the preceding in utereo events. Third, the prenatal process of sex differentiation has an impact on the entire life span of the individual, not only in terms of the match (or mismatch) between sex and gender, but also in the programming of the portion of the brain that controls the cyclical production of hormones during adult life.

Female Reproductive System

The pituitary signal that initiates sexual maturation in an adolescent girl is the secretion into her bloodstream of a large amount of a trophic hormone known as *follicle-stimulating hormone* (FSH). Each dormant egg cell in her ovaries is surrounded by a capsule of cells (a follicle), and an egg cell will ripen only if the follicle surrounding it also develops. The FSH stimulates follicles to develop and become fluid-filled sacs with ripening egg cells within them. Thus begins a process that will recur monthly, on the average, for the next forty years of a woman's life—the menstrual cycle.

Usually only one follicle with an egg cell inside it reaches maturity each month. As it develops, the hormone estrogen is secreted from the follicle wall. About 2 weeks after the follicle has begun to ripen, the pituitary sends out luteinizing hormone (LH), causing the follicle to burst and release the egg cell. This process is known as *ovulation*. Then, as the newly released egg cell begins to make its way into the Fallopian tube, the follicle shrivels up and becomes a corpus luteum, which secretes both estrogen and progesterone (a hormone whose major function is to prepare the uterus to support a pregnancy). In a sense, the body expects that the egg will be fertilized in the Fallopian tube by a sperm cell, and progesterone prepares the uterine wall to receive a fertilized egg. The uterine lining becomes thicker, and increased blood flow nourishes it. If the egg is not fertilized, however, the corpus luteum eventually ceases to function, and the unused tissue is shed with the menstrual bleeding. The first episode of such bleeding, which can occur anywhere from age 10 to age 16, is referred to as the **menarche**.

Menarche
The first episode of menstrual bleeding, which can occur at any time from age 10 to age 16 in the developing adolescent girl.

The onset of menstruation has long been regarded as a major developmental milestone; however, empirical research on how girls react psychologically to this event has occurred primarily during the 1980s. Brooks-Gunn (1987) suggested that the negative reactions toward menstruation that prevailed in our culture for a long time are being replaced by more informed and less fearful attitudes. A study by Ruble and Brooks-Gunn (1982) indicated largely neutral to mixed to even positive feelings about menarche among their sample of adolescent females. Although they found some inital disruption in the lives of these girls, for the most part the process of menstruation appeared to be a symbol of maturity. Negative reactions to menarche were likely to be expressed only by those girls who were unprepared for the experience; that is, they did not expect the possibility of painful symptoms, they did not know how to use sanitary napkins or tampons, or they were unaware of any hormonal effects on mood.

Early menstrual cycles are somewhat irregular. Often they are anovulatory; that is, no egg actually is released from the mature follicle, although in every other respect the cycle is normal. Not until her late teens does a female reach full reproductive functioning (Katchadourian, 1989). At puberty, the uterine wall becomes thicker, and the uterus changes in shape. Whereas in a child it is somewhat tubular, in an adolescent it takes on the shape (and size) of an inverted pear (see Figure 4.2). In other words, the upper portion expands in size more than the lower portion. Second, the vagina enlarges, becoming wider and longer, and the vaginal walls become considerably thicker as a result of the estrogen secretions at puberty. Also, the vagina becomes capable of secreting a lubricating fluid at times of sexual excitation. Third, the contractile muscles in the walls of the uterus and vagina increase in strength; these muscles help expel the child from the uterus at childbirth. Fourth, the external sex organs enlarge at puberty.

A woman's menstrual cycles continue throughout her childbearing years. Then, at some time between the ages of 45 and 55, she arrives at *menopause,* when the monthly cycles cease. Of the half a million egg cells contained in her ovaries at birth, only about 10,000 remain. What became of the others? A small percentage (1 in 1,000) matured and were released into the oviducts; the vast majority disintegrated and were reabsorbed by the body. The remaining eggs do not mature because FSH appears to elicit no response from the follicles remaining in the ovaries, and as was noted earlier, if the follicles do not mature, neither do the egg cells within them. In that sense, the woman is no longer capable of childbearing.

The developing follicles, of course, are not only the containers of the egg cells; they are also the sources of estrogen production. Because follicles no longer develop beyond the time of menopause, estrogen levels in the woman's bloodstream drop precipitously, and a number of physical changes result: There is a loss of muscle tone, redistribution of fat tissue such that breasts may lose their fullness and sag, deepening of the voice, and possibly increased facial and body hair. Such "masculinization" occurs because a woman no longer has estrogen to counteract the effects of the androgens produced by her adrenal glands.

Changes also occur in physical characteristics related to sexual functioning. The vaginal canal decreases in length and elasticity, and the vaginal walls become thinner. The glands that lubricate the vagina during sexual arousal decrease in number and diminish in level of activity. As a result, sexual intercourse may become uncomfortable or even painful. Despite these changes, however, no physiological reason prevents sexual functioning into old age. The effects of estrogen loss can be counteracted by estrogen replacement therapy, the use of an artificial lubricant during intercourse, and increased awareness and sensitivity on the part of the woman's sexual partner. In addition, some sexual changes are minimized if a constant level

Menopause

The cessation of the menstrual cycles, which occurs between the ages of 45 and 55. The remaining egg cells in a woman's uterus will not mature, because the follicle cells surrounding them are no longer responsive to follicle-stimulating hormone.

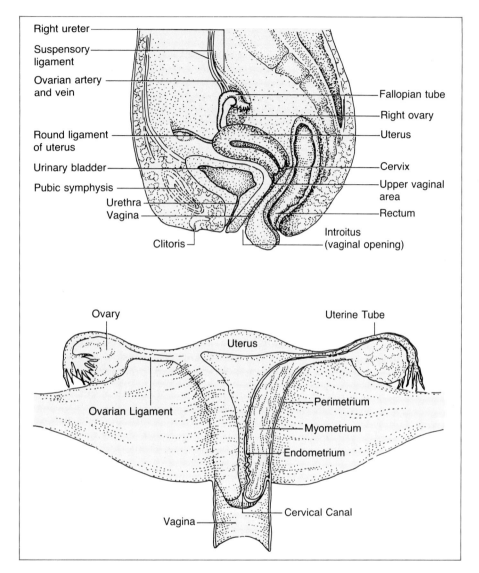

Figure 4.2
Female Reproductive System

of sexual activity has been maintained; regular activity—either masturbation or sex with a partner—can prevent a decrease in the amount of vaginal secretion during sexual arousal (Weg, 1983). Not only can sexual activity after menopause continue to be satisfying, but many older women find intercourse more enjoyable than ever, because they no longer worry about the possibility of conception (Neugarten, 1967).

Menopause can also bring a host of physiological and psychological complaints: anxiety, irritability, headaches, loss of appetite, insomnia, depression, and what has become known as the "hot flash"—a feeling of hotness that begins in the chest and extends to the face and neck and is accompanied by profuse sweating (Katchadourian, 1989). No one knows for certain the specific causes of these symptoms; generally they are thought to be related to the hormone imbalance as FSH levels increase while estrogen levels fall (Weg, 1983). However, to complicate the issue, the symptoms themselves are highly variable from one woman to another. Many women never register any of these complaints, and for most women, the experience of menopause is not nearly as negative as popular opinion would lead us to believe (Neugarten, 1967).

Male Reproductive System

In the male, at puberty the pituitary gland sends a message to the testes by way of the trophic hormones interstitial cell–stimulating hormone (ICSH) and FSH to begin secreting testosterone in larger quantities. The interstitial cells, or Leydig cells, are the sites of testosterone production, and these increase in number and size at puberty as testosterone production increases. There is also an increase in the size of the 300 to 600 seminiferous (or semen-bearing) tubules in the testes. Sperm production begins at puberty in these threadlike tubes (see Figure 4.3). The specific age at which sperm production begins is highly variable and difficult to determine. One study estimated that by the time they reach 15, roughly half the boys examined had begun to produce sperm cells (Richardson & Short, 1978). Sperm production is a continuous process, and the adult male produces approximately 200 million sperm cells every day (Jones, 1984).

Because of the increase in the size and number of the interstitial cells and the enlargement of the seminiferous tubules, the oval-shaped testes themselves enlarge, and the scrotal sac containing them hangs lower from the body. This is usually the first sign that the changes of puberty have begun, and it occurs somewhere between the ages of 10 and 13 (Katchadourian, 1989).

About a year after the testes have begun to enlarge, the penis enlarges, first in length and then in width. The skin of the scrotum takes on a darker, more reddish color, and the scrotum and testes continue to enlarge. These changes in genital appearance in the male do not occur suddenly. In fact, Tanner (1962) observed that from the time of initial enlargement of testes and scrotum to the time at which the mature adult appearance has been attained, there is a span of approximately 4 years.

Although a boy is capable of erection and orgasm during childhood, and even during infancy, the first ejaculation of seminal fluid at orgasm does not occur until puberty, usually at about the age of 12 or 13 (Katchadourian, 1989). This event, sometimes referred to as the *spermarche* (Shipman,

Spermarche
The first ejaculation of a seminal fluid at orgasm, which occurs as a boy reaches puberty.

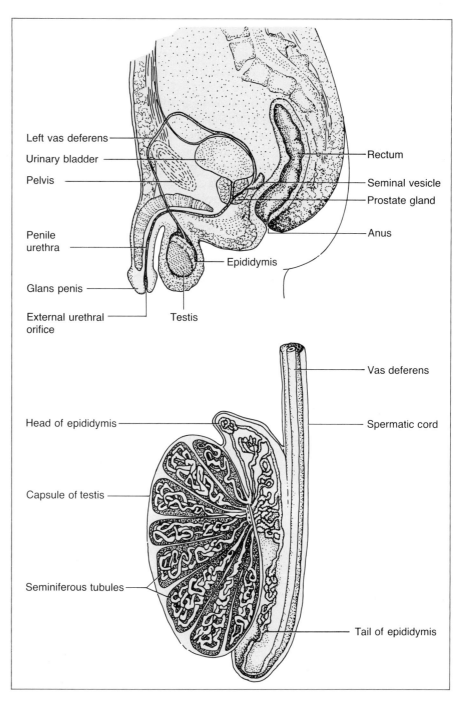

Figure 4.3
Male Reproductive System (Above) and the Testis and Epididymis (Below)

1968), can be thought of as a significant transition into adulthood—the equivalent of menarche in adolescent girls (Brooks-Gunn, 1987). Little is known about boys' psychological reactions to the first ejaculation. However, it appears that (1) boys know a little, but not much, about spermarche before it occurs; (2) boys' reactions to the event are generally positive, although one in three reported being a little bit frightened by it; and (3) boys are unwilling to discuss this marker event of puberty with either their parents or their peers (Gaddis & Brooks-Gunn, 1985).

Changes in the male reproductive system during adulthood are not nearly as dramatic as those that occur in the female. Men do not experience a sharp decline in sex hormone production at any point in life, although a gradual decline begins at about the age of 30, and this continues throughout life (Katchadourian, 1989). In addition, men never completely lose their ability to father children as they age, although the sperm count will decrease throughout adult life.

On the other hand, the aging process does bring about a number of changes in male sexual functioning. Compared to a young man, a man at middle age and beyond takes two to three times longer to attain an erection when sexually aroused (Katchadourian, 1989; Spence, 1989). The older man, however, will maintain his erection for a longer time, because he will take longer to achieve orgasm once erect; this age change may be attributable to physiological factors or to a greater amount of control based on sexual experience (Katchadourian, 1989). In addition, as men age, they take longer to achieve a second erection after orgasm.

With advancing age, many men, perhaps 40 percent, completely lose the ability to have an erection at all. However, most men in their 60s can still have erections, and a sizable minority can still do so in their 70s and 80s (Broderick, 1982). To what extent these sexual changes are influenced by physiological factors and to what extent cultural factors are involved are not known. Cross-cultural research tells us, for example, that in societies in which sexuality among the elderly is fully accepted, sexual activity remains an important part of the lives of approximately 70 percent of men and 85 percent of the women (Winn & Newton, 1982). In our own society, Masters and Johnson (1970) observed that many men who report sexual dysfunction in middle and old age have no specific physical problem that would account for their sexual difficulties. Sexual dysfunction often resulted from boredom with one's partner, anxiety, overeating or drinking, ill health, or simply fear that sexual dysfunction would be a problem!

SEXUAL BEHAVIOR AND DEVELOPMENT

Human sexual behavior is considerably more difficult to discuss than the developmental changes in reproductive anatomy and function that we just explored. Because sexuality is a sensitive area and because most data were obtained from interviews and questionnaires, our knowledge of the subject is probably far from complete. Some questionnaire respondents may not answer questions honestly, and those willing to discuss their sex lives may constitute a biased sample to begin with. To illustrate this point, one frequently cited sex research project (Hunt, 1974) was based on a large sample, but only one in five of the people initially contacted was willing to participate. Another major study analyzed the responses of female readers to *Redbook* (Levin & Levin, 1975), who may or may not represent a cross section of U.S. women. One of the best studies, conducted by Blumstein and Schwartz (1983), surveyed nearly 6,000 couples but significantly underrepresented minority, elderly, and working-class people. Thus, even carefully designed sexual behavior studies using sophisticated information-gathering techniques may be limited in their applicability because of sampling difficulties.

Another limitation of research in human sexuality is that sexual contact often is defined very narrowly. We speak in terms of specific sexual activities such as masturbation to the point of orgasm, oral-genital contact, and genital contact between a man and a woman. We determine the frequencies of erections and orgasms. What we often forget, however, is that sexuality is not restricted to specific physical activities or specific areas of the body, but can incorporate all the senses in a wide variety of pleasurable activities: looking at each other, formulating fantasies, holding hands, kissing, caressing, and so on. A loving embrace can be a sexual experience, even though no erections or orgasms are involved.

We will follow the standard procedure of describing sexuality in terms of specific activities, because such activities are easiest to document and because most of the research has focused on them. However, the data described provide only the most general picture of human sexual functioning, even when those data are scientifically obtained.

Infant Experiences

Little can be said about sexual behavior during the first 2 years of life, except that infants are sexual beings by virtue of their being human. As Chapter 10 describes, Freud horrified the Victorian world with his notion that oral stimulation may satisfy an infant's "sexual" needs. Said Freud, "He who sees a satiated child sink back from the mother's breast and fall asleep with reddened cheeks and blissful smile will have to admit that this picture remains as typical of the expression of sexual gratification in later life" (Freud, 1962).

As a matter of fact, infants and toddlers of both sexes have been found to masturbate. Infant boys frequently have erections, and some are even born with them. One in every three infants may be capable of experiencing a sexual orgasm (Jones, 1984). Ultrasound studies have also demonstrated male erections in utero (Calderone, 1983), and clitoral erections have been observed in newborn girls (Langfeldt, 1981).

Sexual expression during infancy, as in other life phases, may not always take an oral or genital form. Holding, cuddling, and bathing are

Toddlers may not understand the purposes of their anatomy, but they are curious about and derive pleasure from self-exploration.

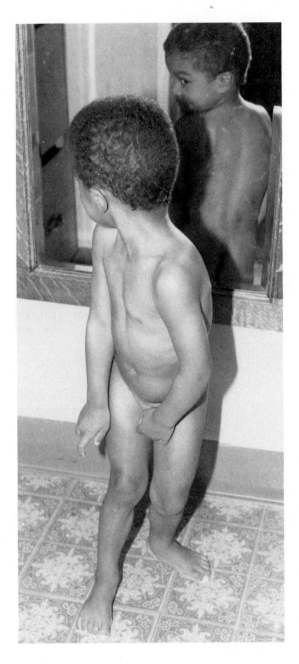

physically enjoyable sensations that promote parent-infant attachment and comfortable feelings about one's body. Parents should be neither surprised nor distressed by their infant's sensual responses or activities. Healthy adult sexuality may be promoted by calm and affectionate parent-child physical intimacy.

Childhood Interests and Activities

Sexual curiosity increases during the years from 2 to 5. Four- and 5-year-olds may develop an interest in inspecting the genitals of other children ("playing doctor") and exhibiting their genitals to others. A not-unrelated development is the growing interest in excretory functions and what many parents find to be an embarrassing tendency to discuss such functions publicly.

The number of young children who masturbate may be surprising to many adults. In one study, the estimate was a high as 60 percent, although, unlike the infant, the child between 3 and 5 years old rarely masturbates in public (Jones, 1984). Clearly in Western cultures there is a recognition at an early age that overt masturbation is an unacceptable activity. In addition, nearly 60 percent of the children in the 2-to-5 age range are capable of achieving orgasm (Kinsey, Pomeroy, & Martin, 1948; Kirkendall, 1978).

Freud referred to the period of childhood from the age of 5 to puberty as the latency period, a time when children's sexual energies were redirected

Young teenagers are concerned with human sexuality and are interested in the sexual features of the adult body.

Issues in Human Development
Child Sexual Abuse

 The subject of child sexual abuse was rarely discussed outside legal and clinical circles before the 1980s. Increasingly, media attention, autobiographical accounts, and the renewed interest of researchers has revealed a more extensive and varied world in which children are the victims of adult paraphilia, which involves unusual acts (exhibiting genitalia to a stranger or inflicting pain on a sexual partner), objects (intercourse with animals or children), or situations (overt sexual activity for public view or voyeurism) (Masters, Johnson, & Kolodny, 1988). Although we must recognize that sexual relations between children and adults are not always considered deviant, in contemporary Western cultures pedophiles, or child molesters, are usually treated both as criminals and as psychologically disturbed. (See Sandfort, 1984, for an alternate perspective.)

Several myths about the sexual abuse of children require immediate debunking (Lanyon, 1986). For instance, the belief that only a small number of children are sexually abused has been disproven. Apparently at least 10 to 15 percent of all children and adolescents suffer from one or more incidents of sexual abuse by an adult, which may range from fondling to actual intercourse. Furthermore, the abusers are typically not strangers to the child or otherwise violators of the law. In fact, most sexual abuse of children is perpetrated by relatives or neighbors and the incidents tend to occur in the child's or the molester's home. Girls are approximately twice as likely as boys to be the victims of sexual abuse, with the ages of between 8 and 12 as the most likely period of an inital incident. The offenders overwhelmingly tend to be males, but the intent of the abuse is rarely to harm the victim physically. Finally, the experiences of sexual abuse reported by children are almost never found to be fabrications, although Schetky (1986) discusses some important concerns in this regard.

The types of activities that might qualify as child sexual abuse vary greatly. Incestuous behavior, sexual relations between close family members, especially father/stepfather–daughter, is a common form of sexual abuse of children. Finkelhor (1984) has determined that the single most significant factor in predicting child sexual abuse is the presence in the home of a stepfather. Child molesters often do not engage in actual sexual intercourse with their victims, but simply engage in mutual fondling, "dirty"

toward a variety of more positive creative activities. In a sense, the latency period was a time in which sexual development was temporarily diverted.

As a matter of fact, there appears to be no major decline in sexual interest or sexual behavior during the latency period (Goldman & Goldman, 1982). Even by the age of 8, girls already are asking questions about menstruation and breast development, and 10- and 11-year-olds of both sexes are definitely curious about physical development in the opposite sex (Thornburg, 1978). As Table 4.1 shows, much information about human sexuality is initially obtained during the preadolescent years. This seems to indicate that elementary school children are not in a latency period at all, but have definite sexual interests.

Apparently, the sexual curiosity of children often finds some sort of behavioral expression; sexual activity is common during later childhood. (See *Issues in Human Development,* "Child Sexual Abuse" for a more tragic aspect of childhood sexuality.) As noted earlier, masturbation occurs frequently even during the preschool years, and it seems to continue. Bell Weinberg, and Hammersmith (1981) found that by the age of 13, some 63

talking, or just viewing the child or displaying their genitalia to the child (Elvik, Reikowitz, & Greenburg, 1986). A more recent form of sexual abuse involves the inclusion of children in pornographic films or in a network of other children to be sexually exploited by adults for profit. Burgess (1984) has reported on the details of 11 so-called sex rings, controlled by 14 adults, that included 66 children between the ages of 6 and 16.

Profiles of child molesters are somewhat difficult to compile because a single pattern of activity or even the origins of the behavior may have different sources (Travin, Bluestone, Coleman, Cullen, & Melella, 1986). Perhaps the most typical characteristic of adults who sexually abuse children is that they themselves were sexually abused as children (Groth, 1979). A classification system proposed by Finkelhor and Araji (1986) outlines four types of pedophiles: (1) emotionally immature with low self-esteem and poor interpersonal skills, (2) sexually misdirected with poor role models and previous childhood trauma, (3) sexually blocked with a history of stress and frustration and inadequate coping skills, and (4) sexually disinhibited with compounding problems such as substance abuse or senility. In sum, the sexually abusive behavior directed toward a child may be the result of one of a number of causes.

Sexual relations with children are generally considered harmful to them because children are too immature to understand fully such activities and may not feel safe in refusing the molester. Because more than 20,000 incidents of child sexual abuse are reported annually, a clearer picture of its long-term consequences than is currently available is needed (Alter-Reid, Gibbs, Lachenmeyer, Sigal, & Massoth, 1986). Future research should consider factors that might impact on the child's development, including the age of the first experience, the frequency of the activity, the degree of resistance the child feels about the activity, the extent of violence associated with the activity, the prevalence of the child's fear of the molester, and the aspects of the child's counseling or treatment. (How soon after? How supportive? How long-lasting?) At present, the negative outcomes of child sexual abuse in the realms of adult sexuality, family and marital relations, or self-esteem and depression remain controversial and inconclusive (Kilpatrick, 1986, 1987; Runyan, 1986).

percent of boys and 32 percent of girls already had begun masturbating. Boys also seem to masturbate sooner and more frequently than girls.

Precise statistics on children's homosexual behaviors are difficult to obtain. However, sex researchers suggest that homosexual experimentation occurs frequently during later childhood, particularly among males. There has even been speculation about a "homosexual stage" of development that precedes heterosexual functioning, although the evidence for a genuine stage of this type is not impressive (Kirkendall, 1978). Nevertheless, as far as can be determined, approximately half of the preadolescent boys in our society, and a third of the girls, engage in some forms of homosexual play (Jones, 1984). Because boys and girls tend to play separately during most of the childhood years, it is not unusual to find that their sexual curiosity may be stimulated by same-sex play. No support exists, however, for the notion that homosexual behavior during childhood is predictive of adult sexual orientation.

Heterosexual activity also occurs during childhood. Table 4.2 shows that most children in one study had engaged in some form of heterosexual

Table 4.1
Age at Which Sexual Terms Were First Learned

Terms	Age 9–11 (%)	Age 12–13 (%)	Age 14+ (%)
Abortion	36	48	16
Conception	69	25	6
Contraception	27	41	32
Ejaculation	26	36	38
Homosexuality	47	43	10
Intercourse	54	32	14
Masturbation	30	41	29
Menstruation	50	34	16
Petting	31	45	24
Prostitution	46	45	9
Seminal emissions	17	50	33
VD	22	61	17
Percentage of total	38	42	20

Source: H. D. Thornburg. *The bubblegum years.* Tucson, AZ: H.E.L.P., 1978, p. 113. Reprinted by permission.

behavior by the age of 13. A majority of them had at least held hands or kissed, and 1 boy in 4 and 1 girl in 10 has experienced coitus (Vener & Stewart, 1974). For the most part, however, heterosexual activity during childhood is fairly innocent and provides more titillation of the mind than of the body.

Thus, it would be naive to assume that human beings discover their sexual natures only when they reach puberty. Children are aware of sex, they are curious about it, and many engage in sexual activity. To be sure, there is less to report about childhood sexual behavior in our culture than there is concerning sexual behavior during adolescence or adulthood. Nevertheless, an honest discussion of life-span human sexuality must begin with infancy. Other cultures may be more tolerant of childhood sexual expression (Currier, 1981) than our own, but the activities and interests persist away from adult view.

Adolescent Attitudes and Behaviors

Unlike the situation for childhood sexuality, postpubertal sexuality presents parents with more realistic concerns. Adolescent sexual activity is complicated by greater personal and cultural awareness, critical physical changes, the possibility of pregnancy and sexually transmitted diseases, and general

Table 4.2

Levels of Sexual Activity of Adolescent Boys and Girls in One Community in 1973 (by Percent)

Levels of Sexual Activity	13 and Younger		14		15		16		17 and Older	
	F	M	F	M	F	M	F	M	F	M
Held hands	84	80	87	87	89	93	91	90	97	92
Held arm around other or been held	72	67	81	78	87	87	90	87	96	90
Kissed or been kissed	68	65	75	78	82	84	89	85	96	87
Necked (prolonged hugging and kissing)	43	48	56	56	65	70	77	69	84	78
Did light petting (feeling above the waist)	31	40	40	55	55	66	65	65	71	71
Did heavy petting (feeling below the waist)	17	34	28	42	40	56	49	55	59	62
Went all the way (coitus)	10	28	17	32	24	38	31	38	35	34
Had coitus with two or more partners	4	17	5	15	10	21	13	23	1	23
Number in sample	222	180	218	220	220	191	190	176	185	173

Source: A. Vener & C. Stewart. Adolescent sexual behavior in middle America revisited: 1970–1973. *Journal of Marriage and the Family,* 1974, 36, 728–735. Copyrighted 1974 by the National Council on Family Relations, 3989 Central Avenue N.E., Suite #550, Minneapolis, MN 55421. Reprinted by permission.

expectations for maturity and identity consolidation. Although this phase of development offers much hope for achieving independence and sexual fulfillment, most adolescents lack the knowledge, sensitivity, and security needed for the kinds of sexual encounters in which they sometimes find themselves involved.

Masturbation

Masturbation is a widespread practice during adolescence, particularly among males. Approximately 70 percent of boys in our culture have masturbated by the age of 15, as well as 30 percent of girls. Between the ages of 16 and 19, two-thirds of the male population and half of the female population masturbate at least once a week (Hass, 1979).

Masturbation is undoubtedly the most frequent sexual practice of adolescents, yet it is one of the least frequently studied (Dreyer, 1982). As an outlet for sexual tension as well as a means for exploring individual satisfaction, masturbation is no longer considered an unhealthy sexual activity. Perhaps as societal restrictions against masturbation are lessened, adolescents will become more open in discussing the practice, and more meaningful research can be conducted. The two passages that follow illustrate the contradictory feelings of pleasure versus guilt that researchers, such as Sorenson (1973), have found among adolescents. The first was written by a woman remembering her experiences with masturbation; the second by a man.

> Masturbation was always orgasmic. I can remember masturbating as far back as my childhood memories go. I was never chastised for it, and my sister and I gave it a pet name, the "wiggly-squirm!" My mother told me years later that she didn't even know how to masturbate until she saw us. Somehow, I became socialized and reserved masturbating for the privacy of my bedroom. Mom never told me to stop masturbating in the living room—I really don't remember where I got the idea that this was something that wasn't done in public. (Goethals & Klos, 1976, p. 154)

> I masturbated frequently and worried a great deal about it. I knew it was wrong, not from anything my parents had told me or what I had learned in school (there was no sex education at that time) but from the jokes about jerking off and the obvious resemblance to bedwetting. During my adolescence both of them would be cause for shame . . . I fought to control them [ejaculations] during junior high school years. I am not sure what I felt would happen if I did it too often, but I didn't want to risk finding out too late. I set goals for myself for reducing the number of times I would jerk off. I am sorry I was so guilt-ridden about it. Luckily I was never caught masturbating in the park or at camp. I knew that it was wrong, that I should be discreet, but I would not have known how to handle discovery or ridicule. No one prepared me for the changes that took place during my adolescence. Like most of my friends, I guess, I survived. That's about the most I could say. (Sommer, 1978, pp. 166–67)

Homosexual Activity

Based on an exhaustive review of the subject, psychologist Philip Dreyer (1982) listed three major conclusions about adolescent homosexual behavior in the United States. First, when homosexual experiences occur during adolescence, they are most likely to occur before age 15, and they are more frequent among boys than girls. Second, adolescents are extremely tolerant in their attitudes toward homosexuality. In one questionnaire, approximately two-thirds of a group of 16- to 19-year-olds believed that homosexual behaviors are acceptable (Hass, 1979). Third, in spite of their openmindedness, fewer than 15 percent of adolescent boys and fewer than 10 percent of adolescent girls admit to having had a homosexual experience. Furthermore, only 2 to 3 percent are involved in an ongoing homosexual relationship.

Homosexual behavior, then, is no more frequently observed among adolescents than it is within the adult population; in fact, there has been no increase in homosexuality from the previous to the current generation of adolescents (DeLamater & MacCorquodale, 1979). Although the factors responsible for a homosexual orientation are not yet clear it is unlikely that adolescent homosexual encounters result from adult seductions. Sorenson (1973) reports that of the teens who had homosexual experiences, 24 percent were with someone younger, 39 percent with their peers, 29 percent with older adolescents, and only 8 percent with adults.

In a study of the development of sexual preference, Bell, Weinberg, and Hammersmith (1981) indicated that adolescence was a critical period for the adoption of sexual identity. For both males and females, they found that the combination of arousal by same-sex peers and extensive participation in sexual activity with them was the best predictor of an adult homosexual orientation. Because most mental health professionals do not regard sexual preference to be related to psychopathology, we need to find ways to help adolescent homosexuals who wish to retain that orientation to deal more effectively with their sexual identity. Sadly, the socialization of gay or lesbian teenagers involves a process of learning to cover up for their perceived inadequacies or abnormality. Martin (1982), for instance, describes the unfairness of a social reality that forces homosexual adolescents to cope with even greater demands than heterosexual adolescents to resolve their sexual identities.

Heterosexual Activity

A hopeful but erroneous belief about adolescent heterosexual behavior is that today's teenagers are more openminded about sexuality than their parents were in their youth, but that no actual behavioral changes have occurred across the generations. Young people of today are indeed more likely to approve of various forms of sexual activity than their parents did (Reiss, 1986). However, some dramatic changes in behavior also have occurred in recent years—changes that might be described as startling.

Summarizing the research literature on adolescent heterosexual behavior (see Table 4.3), Dreyer (1982) observed that males always have been more sexually active than females, and the increases for males of college

Table 4.3

Percentage of White High School and College Students Reporting Premarital Sexual Intercourse at Three Historical Periods.

Period	High School		College	
	Boys	*Girls*	*Boys*	*Girls*
1925 to 1965	25	10	55	25
1966 to 1973	35	35	85	65
1974 to 1979	56	44	74	74

Source: P. H. Dreyer. Sexuality during adolescence. In B. B. Wolman (Ed.), *Handbook of developmental psychology.* Englewood Cliffs, NJ: Prentice-Hall, 1982, p. 575. Reprinted by permission.

Although adolescents may be more sexually permissive today than in earlier generations, they are normally not promiscuous.

age have been less dramatic since 1925 than the increases for females. In 1925, only one in four college women reported having engaged in premarital sexual intercourse; in 1973, two out of every three college women had done so. Recent data on adolescents suggest that by the age of 19, more than 85 percent of males have experienced coitus (Sonnerstein, Pleck, & Ku, 1989).

Of even greater significance, sexual behavior among adolescent females again increased dramatically from the early to the late 1970s. Some evidence of this trend appears in Table 4.3, but it is illustrated much more clearly by the research of Zelnik and Kantner (1980), who conducted surveys of adolescent sexual behavior in 1971, 1976, and 1979. Some of their findings are presented in Table 4.4. At all ages studied, there is a regular increase from 1971 to 1979 in the percentage of unmarried females having had intercourse. Similar percentages are reported in a more recent survey (Hofferth, Kahn, & Baldwin, 1987).

Table 4.4

Percentage of U.S. Women Aged 15 to 19 Who Had Intercourse Before Marriage (1979, 1976, and 1971) and Mean Age at First Intercourse for All U.S. Women (Married and Unmarried).

Age	1979	1976	1971
15–19	46.0	39.2	27.6
15	22.5	18.6	14.4
16	37.8	28.9	20.9
17	48.5	42.9	26.1
18	56.9	51.4	39.7
19	69.0	59.5	46.4
	Age at first intercourse		
Mean	16.2	16.1	16.4
N	933	726	936

Source: M. Zelnik & J. F. Kantner. Sexual activity, contraceptive use, and pregnancy among metropolitan-area teenagers: 1971–1979. *Family Planning Perspectives,* 1980, 12(5), 231. Copyright © The Alan Guttmacher Institute.

Zelnik and Kantner (1977, 1980) also observed two other changes in patterns of female sexual behavior since the early 1970s. First, the average age at first intercourse for girls declined slightly from 1971 to 1976 (16.4 years versus 16.1 years) but remained stable from 1976 to 1979. Second, there was a slight increase from 1971 to 1976 in the number of partners with whom a girl reported having sexual intercourse.

Clearly, adolescents and college students of the 1970s and 1980s were both more sexually tolerant and more likely to be sexually active than the members of their parents' generation. More recent studies have confirmed these patterns (Ostrov, Offer, Howard, Kaufman, & Meyer, 1985; Gordon & Gilgun, 1987), including the practice of oral sex (Newcomer & Udry, 1985). Despite increased rates of adolescent pregnancy and sexually transmitted diseases, contraceptive use is sporadic and sex education programs are far from universal or complete. An encouraging note was provided in the new study by Sonnenstein, Pleck, and Ku (1989), who report an increase from 21 to 58 percent in condom use among 17- to 19-year-old males residing in metropolitan areas. However, despite apparently responsible attitudes toward sexuality, teens often exhibit behaviors that are somewhat inconsistent with these beliefs (see *Research Close-up,* "The Gap Between Adolescent Sexual Attitudes and Behaviors").

Adult Practices and Values

Adult sexuality is commonly used as the standard by which sexual activity either earlier or later in life is judged. Although, as Broderick (1982) maintained, sexuality is an important component of adult lifestyles and

Zabin, Hirsch, Smith, and Hardy (1984) conducted a survey of 3,534 male and female students in grades 9 through 12 from four different schools. These surveys were self-administered in the students' homeroom classes, and a return rate of 98 percent was obtained. Questions on the survey pertained to the adolescents' beliefs and experiences regarding premarital sexual intercourse as well as related issues of contraceptive use and the nature of the emotional relationship with the partner. The results of the study by Zabin and her colleagues indicated that at least a moderate degree of inconsistency existed between the stated sexual attitudes of these adolescents and their reported sexual behavior.

Perhaps the most significant finding of this study was that 83 percent of the teenagers who experienced sexual intercourse felt that the best age for first coitus was older than the age at which they became sexually active. Additionally, 43 percent of those adolescents believed that the appropriate age for a first sexual intercourse was older than their current age. Most of the female adolescents who had given birth to an infant (88 percent) felt similarly that the best age to have a baby was older than they were when they experienced this event. Among the virgin adolescent respondents, the reported best ages for first coitus were 2 or 3 years later than those recommended by their sexually experienced peers.

Although more than one-third of all the teenagers surveyed stated that premarital sexual intercourse was wrong, the percentages of virgins agreeing with this idea was approximately 58 percent for females and 56 percent for males. However, more than 25 percent of the females and nearly 27 percent of the males who were not virgins reported that premarital sexual intercourse was wrong. Some degree of consistency exists in the pattern of these results, but a substantial number of adolescents were apparently engaging in behavior that

satisfaction, two reasons exist for not comparing adult behaviors to the practices at other age levels. First of all, using the values and behaviors of one phase of the life span as a definition of appropriateness violates the integrity and logic of what might be more reasonable for other phases of the life span. Secondly, again as Broderick (1982) pointed out, the variation in adult sexual behaviors and attitudes is extremely broad, prohibiting an effective typology for describing typical sexual patterns. Furthermore, Rykken (1987) cautions that differences between older and younger adults may be as much a function of cohort differences as of age patterns of sexuality. The sexual revolution may emerge in later life as we enter the twenty-first century.

Masturbation

In terms of frequency, masturbation reaches a peak for males during their early teenage years and then gradually declines throughout life; for females the peak comes somewhat later (Luria & Rose, 1979). As was mentioned earlier, relatively little is known about masturbation as compared with other

they did not consider acceptable. Views on premarital coitus appeared to be mitigated by the strength of the emotional ties between the partners. Zabin et al. (1984) pointed out that "women are much more likely than men to want a strong relationship before having sex" (p. 183).

The teenagers in this study typically assigned contraceptive responsibility to both male and female sexual participants, and such individuals were most likely actually to use some method of birth control. Those adolescents who desired the other partner to take contraceptive responsibility were somewhat less likely actually to use contraceptives, and the sexually active teens who attributed birth control efforts to neither partner were the least likely to use contraceptives. Even among the first group—joint contraceptive responsibility adolescents—however, more than one-third reported that they failed to use any birth control measures when last experiencing sexual intercourse. In addition, nearly one-quarter of the adolescents who claimed that they would have sex only if protected said they had used no contraceptive method during their most recent sexual experience.

Zabin et al. (1984) interpreted the divergence between sexual behaviors and attitudes "as a product of normative responses to the influences of peers, family, community and media" (p. 185). They attributed inconsistencies to these competing pressures, to possible changes in attitude over time, and to a lack of awareness of the contradictions in their lives. Although their findings revealed somewhat greater consistency for young women than for young men, the researchers suggested that this may reflect the young women's stronger need to think that their behaviors closely matched idealized beliefs. Finally, the authors recommended that limiting adolescent pregnancy requires programs to help both males and females translate their more responsible sexual attitudes into congruent behavioral practices.

forms of sexual activity, because adolescents and even adults are ashamed to admit that they masturbate. It is not unusual for respondents to sexual surveys simply to ignore questions about masturbation while readily providing details about their heterosexual activity. In one major survey, more young men admitted to having intercourse with women than admitted to having practiced solitary sex—a very unlikely possibility (Luria & Rose, 1979).

Adults may consider masturbation an adolescent form of sexuality that should be outgrown during adulthood and replaced by more mature forms of sexual contact. Adults may feel guilty when they masturbate. Nevertheless, adults of all ages masturbate—with men more likely to do so than women. One major study found that 72 percent of young married men masturbate an average of twice per month, and 18 percent of young married women masturbate once per month (Hunt, 1974).

Masturbation frequently is viewed as a poor substitute for heterosexual activity used only by those who have no sexual partner available to them (e.g., adolescents). This is clearly not the case. A more realistic view is that masturbation plays an integral role in the sex lives of adults, although its specific role may vary along gender lines. For men, masturbation is the first sexual experience in that it usually precedes sexual contact with another person. It also retains something of a "substitute" status during adulthood. Single men are more likely than married men to masturbate, and married men are most likely to masturbate when their wives are sexually unavailable to them. Nevertheless, men continue to masturbate even when they have other sexual outlets (Luria & Rose, 1979).

Masturbation is integrated somewhat differently into the sex lives of adult women. In the first place, as already mentioned, women are less likely than men to masturbate, and they do so less frequently. Virtually every man masturbates, but only two-thirds of women ever report doing so (Simon & Gagnon, 1969). However, Hite (1976) discovered that many women found masturbation to be more sexually satisfying than heterosexual intercourse, as well as a more effective means of achieving orgasm. In fact, a number of women had never had an orgasm during intercourse and only began to do so after they started to masturbate.

Simon and Gagnon (1969) suggested that the sexual behavior of women follows a different developmental path than that of men because of the different roles assigned to the act of masturbation. For women, social sex precedes solitary sex because they have not been socialized to be able to separate sexual pleasure from "making love" with another; for men, solitary sex comes first. As a result, women learn to see sexual behavior primarily in a social context, whereas men become proficient at "detached" sex engaged in purely for the physical pleasure of doing so. For women, sex becomes a means of relating to another person; for men, sex is defined by pleasurable genital contact. Such gender differences are both oversimplified and exaggerated, of course, yet they raise interesting questions about the role of masturbation in sexual development and about implications of gender differences in sexual needs in an adult love relationship.

Homosexual Activity

Homosexual activity is a *statistically* deviant behavior only because it is less likely than heterosexual activity to occur in the general population. Millions of adults in the United States regularly engage in sexual activity with partners of their own gender, and millions more do so at least occasionally or have done so in the past. Any discussion of adult sexual behavior that ignores homosexuality clearly is incomplete.

One of the most pervasive stereotypes about human sexual behavior is that a person is either heterosexual or homosexual in sexual preference. In fact, it seems to be more appropriate to think of exclusive homosexuality and exclusive heterosexuality as opposite ends of a continuum that encompasses a broad range of sexual activity. Based on extensive research on sexual behavior, Kinsey et al. (1948) placed the heterosexual-homosexual continuum on a scale from 0 to 6, as illustrated in Table 4.5. As the table

Table 4.5
Sexual Preferences in the United States

	Category	Percentage of Population Male	Female
0	Exclusively heterosexual	63	68–87*
1	Predominantly heterosexual, but with occasional homosexual experience	2–4	4–9
2	Predominantly heterosexual, but with a substantial amount of homosexual experience	3–7	1–4
3	Similar amounts of heterosexual and homosexual experience	2–4	0–3
4	Predominantly homosexual, but with a substantial amount of heterosexual experience	2–3	1–3
5	Predominantly homosexual, but with occasional heterosexual experience	1–3	1–3
6	Exclusively homosexual	2–5	1–3

*The range in numbers reflects difference by marital status and age. Also, 1–19 percent of females are rated *X*, not having any sociosexual experience on which to base a rating. Eighty-seven percent of females have not had any homosexual experience, but this percentage includes the *X* women.
Source: Data from A. C. Kinsey. W. B. Pomeroy, & C. E. Martin. *Sexual behavior in the human male.* Philadelphia: W. B. Saunders Company, 1948, and A. C. Kinsey, W. B. Pomeroy, C. E. Martin, & P. H. Gebhard. *Sexual Behavior in the human female.* Philadelphia: W. B. Saunders Company, 1953.

shows, although the majority of the U.S. population expressed a clearly heterosexual preference, a substantial minority reported at least occasional homosexual experience, with males more likely to do so than females. In fact, Kinsey et al. (1948) reported that approximately half the men they interviewed admitted to having been sexually aroused by another male at some time in their lives.

The Kinsey data illustrate the futility of trying to define sexual preferences in an either-or fashion. They also suggest a need to distinguish between homosexual identity and homosexual experience. Is it accurate to conclude, for example, that one in three U.S. males is homosexual because he admits to having had at least one homosexual experience?

In fact, participation in a homosexual act does not indicate that the participants are homosexual at all. Homosexual acts occur in many gender-segregated groups in our society (for example, in boarding schools, military service, and prisons), but the participants do not identify themselves as homosexuals. Homosexual acts have even been encouraged in many cultures as a means of preparing adolescents for adulthood. Luria and Rose

(1979) described a Pacific island culture in which adolescent boys were expected to develop a long-standing homosexual relationship with an adult man before they were ready for a heterosexual relationship. Nevertheless, the boys did not regard themselves as homosexuals, nor were they regarded as such by others in their society; homosexual liaisons between adults were frowned upon.

When people are referred to as homosexuals, it typically means that they have a homosexual identity. That is, they define themselves as homosexual in their orientation in much the same way as people define themselves as members of religious or ethnic groups (Luria & Rose, 1979). Self-defined homosexuals are thought to make up approximately 10 percent

Ten percent of the adults in our society identify themselves as homosexual. People with homosexual identities have lived in virtually every culture, past and present, throughout the world.

of the adult population. As has been noted, the percentage of people in the United States who have engaged in homosexual acts is significantly higher.

Homosexual behavior has been found in most civilizations, past and present, throughout the world. Homosexuality has been valued in some cultures, begrudgingly accepted in most, and solemnly condemned in the rest (Luria & Rose, 1979). Reasons for engaging in specific homosexual acts are numerous and depend on situational factors, such as sexual curiosity in children and adolescents, ready availability of partners, and cultural expectations. However, to date there has been no universally accepted explanation of why some people adopt a homosexual, versus a heterosexual, identity. Most of the available explanations focus on the parent-child interaction during early childhood and view a homosexual orientation as evidence of a failure in the process of gender identification. For example, Freud believed that a boy identifies with his father (and with maleness in general) because he can symbolically possess his mother and at the same time reduce his unconscious fear of his father—his powerful rival for his mother's hand (see Chapter 14 for a thorough discussion of this process). The homosexual male had a close relationship with his mother but was distant from his father. In a sense, he already possessed his mother, and because his father was neither a rival nor a serious threat to him, the boy had no reason to identify with him.

Other theories of homosexuality have emphasized learning: Homosexuals were rewarded as children for inappropriate gender role behaviors, such as dressing like or imitating the mannerisms of persons of the opposite gender, and eventually came to identify as members of that gender rather than their own (Green, 1974). A similar view is that homosexuals have been conditioned to associate pleasurable sexual feelings with same-sex contacts because as children they fantasized about same-sex people when they masturbated (Luria & Rose, 1979).

Finally, biological theories attribute homosexuality to a hormone imbalance or to other unknown genetic factors. The evidence for hormonal factors (for example, low levels of sex hormones in the bloodstream) has been mixed; some research indicates that homosexual males have low testosterone levels and homosexual females have low estrogen levels, but other research indicates an opposite conclusion (Jones, 1984).

The difficulty with all current theories of homosexuality is not that they are obviously incorrect, but that the findings are too often contradictory and are based on limited samples. Most research on homosexuality has focused only on homosexuals who are in therapy. Millions of homosexuals never seek therapy and apparently do not consider their homosexuality an illness requiring treatment. Well-adjusted and happy homosexuals rarely find their way into the samples on which theories are based, and for that reason the theories must be seen as somewhat limited in their applicability.

When the sexual behavior of self-defined homosexuals is examined, a number of patterns emerge. First, the specific sexual activities (for example,

Applying Our Knowledge
Sexual Behavior and AIDS

 Acquired immune deficiency syndrome (AIDS) is a serious disease, consisting of multiple symptoms, that nearly always ultimately results in death. Estimates, which change rapidly, are that approximately 2 million Americans are infected with the human immunodeficiency virus (HIV) that causes AIDS (Backer, Batchelor, Jones, & Mays, 1988). The virus is spread largely by sexual contact (although contaminated hypodermic needles and infected blood supplies are also responsible for transmission), and at least 75,000 of those with the virus have manifested AIDS. There is no known cure at present.

One of the primary difficulties in slowing the spread of AIDS is our lack of knowledge about sexual behavior patterns (Baum & Nesselhoff, 1988). Although the exact biological mechanisms of HIV transmission are not yet established, enough information is available to help people limit the risk of infection. Unfortunately, widespread ignorance regarding AIDS protection is enmeshed with general sexual mythology and sensitivity. For example, many individuals believe that they are safe from HIV infection if they are not homosexuals. Although AIDS rates are considerably higher in homosexual communities, hetereosexuals are not at all immune.

The only way to remain truly protected from the sexual transmission of AIDS is abstinence or intercourse only with a noninfected monogamous partner. Pelosi (1988) claims that prevention efforts to ensure less risky sexual behavior through education, counseling, and testing offer the best hope for limiting a potentially disastrous epidemic. Some first steps include reducing the number of sexual partners, finding out more about the past sexual history of the partner, using a condom and spermicides, and resisting sexual activity. Baum and Nesselhoff (1988) recommend the study of how the perception of AIDS varies among people at different age levels to determine appropriate ways to target prevention efforts.

Another realm of difficulty concerns the psychological reactions of AIDS victims, people who are uncertain about their HIV status, and the rest of the population. For example, AIDS victims can suffer from depression, guilt, anger, anxiety, and alienation (McKusick, 1988). Individuals who are not sure if they are infected may be fearful, preoccupied, paranoid, or very distrustful (McKusick, 1988). Others who do not have AIDS may be homophobic, repressed, unnaturally elated, and condescending. An atmosphere of support and hope, not one of blame and stigmatization, should be created.

As the most recent and deadly form of sexually transmitted disease, AIDS may affect the sexual attitudes and behaviors of children, adolescents, adults, and the elderly. If a cure is developed quickly, perhaps long-term impact will be limited. If prevention efforts are not successful, the specter of millions of AIDS victims may drastically change the nature of sexual activity. If AIDS becomes reasonably controllable through medical interventions coupled with generally effective prevention strategies, contemporary sexual values and practices may only be minimally altered.

fondling, mutual masturbation, oral-genital contact, and anal intercourse) are quite similar to those found in heterosexual coitus (Luria & Rose, 1979). Second, the lifestyles of homosexual women closely approximate the lifestyles of heterosexual women in terms of frequency of sexual activity, number of sexual partners, and attitudes toward sexual fidelity (Broderick, 1982). Third—and here is the major contrast between heterosexual and homosexual behavior—homosexual males are considerably more promiscuous than heterosexual males. One study found that one in four homosexual males had as many as 1,000 sexual partners, and 70 percent indicated that most of their sexual experiences were one-time encounters with strangers (Lief, 1978). The promiscuity of male homosexuals may reflect the fact that their sexual activities lack the constraining influence of women's more conservative patterns of sexual behavior (Broderick, 1982). Perhaps the recent impact of AIDS in the homosexual community might alter the promiscuous patterns of gay males over the long term (see *Applying Our Knowledge,* "Sexual Behavior and AIDS"). In one study, Martin (1987) found a 78 percent decline among gay men in reported sexual encounters with other men.

Heterosexual Activity

The data most often referred to when describing heterosexual activity during adult life concern frequency of intercourse between husbands and wives. Of course, these data do not describe all heterosexual behavior for several reasons. First, many adults are not married; rarely have researchers attempted to study separately the heterosexual behavior of single adults beyond traditional college age. Second, a couple's overall sexual activity may not be limited to specific acts involving genital contact, although sexual intercourse has been estimated to constitute 85 to 90 percent of sexual activity in U.S. marriages (Martin, 1977). Finally, some heterosexual activity of married people occurs outside the marriage relationship, so statistics concerning marital coitus hardly begin to describe the sex lives of some men and women.

The data on sexual intercourse between husband and wife form a consistent pattern. Married couples today, in general, are more sexually active than were those of the previous generation. The frequency of intercourse typically is greatest during the early years of marriage and appears to decline regularly throughout the span of the couple's life together. The median frequency of sexual contact per week is two to three times in early adulthood but only once a week or less among persons over the age of 55 (Hunt, 1974).

Not only is there an age-related difference in frequency of intercourse, there is also a difference in reported satisfaction. Mancini and Orthner (1978) asked married couples to choose their five favorite leisure activities from among a group of possible categories. "Sexual and affectional activity" was less and less likely to appear in the list of five with every passing decade of marriage. For example, 68 percent of the husbands and 41 percent of the wives who had been married 5 years or less selected "sexual activity" as one of their favorites; only 21 percent of the husbands and 8 percent of the wives who had been married for more than 30 years made a similar selection.

The reasons for age differences in frequency of and satisfaction with marital sex are elusive. Remember, first of all, that the existence of such differences does not mean that an age decline in sexual satisfaction is inevitable. The research on sexual behavior is cross-sectional rather than longitudinal; the fact that young couples are more sexually active and more sexually satisfied than older people may simply reflect the fact that the world in which today's young adults were raised regarded human sexuality more positively than did the world in which their parents grew up. As has been mentioned, young couples today are more sexually active than were young marrieds of the previous generation. Along similar lines, a 1929 study (Hamilton) suggested that half the adult female population had not experienced orgasm; in the 1970s only 7 percent of women interviewed said they never had orgasms (DeLora & Warren, 1977; Hunt, 1974).

Other reasons for age differences in sexual activity have been suggested. Perhaps the differences are related to physiological changes in the

Although many studies show a decline over time in sexual satisfaction within marriage, such a decline is by no means inevitable.

reproductive system, for example. Of course, such an explanation might apply to sexual functioning among the elderly but hardly could be used to account for differences between people in their 20s and people in their 30s. Perhaps the age differences could be attributed to increased anxieties brought on by changing life circumstances (for example, expenses incurred in raising children or greater job demands).

Lastly, a major difficulty in interpreting trends in the data on marital coitus is that age differences in sexual activity could mean a general loss of interest in sex, but they might reflect instead a loss of interest only in sex with the spouse. Perhaps the data say as much about changes in marriage across the life span as they do about changes in sexual appetite. Not surprisingly, couples who consider their marriages very close are also likely to be highly satisfied with their sex lives together; couples in distant relationships are less likely to take pleasure from marital sex (Hunt, 1974).

A somewhat ironic finding emerges when couples are questioned about their sexual appetites. At all ages, men express the greater interest in sex; however, men are most frequently responsible for changes in a couple's level of sexual activity. Older wives generally report that they stopped having coitus not because they themselves wanted to, but because their husbands were ill, had become impotent, or seemed to lose interest entirely. Men also blame themselves rather than their wives for the reduced level of activity (DeLora & Warren, 1977; Pfeiffer, 1969).

Characteristics of the Elderly

We pointed out earlier that certain physiological changes in the reproductive system can affect sexual functioning in later life: Older women experience a thinning of the vaginal wall and a decrease in the secretions that lubricate the vagina during sexual arousal. Some older men lose their ability to have an erection, whereas others simply take longer to achieve erection and orgasm than when they were younger. Such changes certainly will affect a person's sexual functioning, but an active sex life can be maintained until advanced old age.

In point of fact, however, most elderly people do not maintain as active a sex life as they did when they were younger. Although their sexual potential is only somewhat diminished, older people are further from realizing their potential than are younger adults. For example, in one study, half the women and one-quarter of the men over the age of 60, both married and unmarried, had not had sexual intercourse at all within the 6 months prior to the interview. This finding was in marked contrast to the pattern observed in younger respondents, as can be seen in Table 4.6 (Wilson, 1975).

To understand why elderly people in the United States become less sexually active, we must go beyond explanations based on anatomical and physiological changes. We must recognize that human sexuality occurs within a social context and that the major barriers to the maintenance of an active sex life after 60 may not be biological ones at all; they may be social.

Table 4.6

Frequency of Intercourse by Gender, Present Age, and Education* (Percentage Reporting a Given Frequency Category)

| Frequency of Intercourse | **Males (N = 911)** | | | | | | |
| | **Age** | | | | **Education** | | |
	Total	21–29	30–59	60+	College	High School	Elementary
Not at all	8	8	3	25	8	6	17
Some, but less than one per month	16	10	12	34	14	14	21
One or two times per month	17	8	20	18	17	16	16
One or two times per week	35	34	45	6	35	39	25
More than two times per week	16	35	14	3	20	18	8
No answer	8	5	6	14	6	7	13
	100	100	100	100	100	100	100

| Frequency of Intercourse | **Females (N = 1370)** | | | | | | |
| | **Age** | | | | **Education** | | |
	Total	21–29	30–59	60+	College	High School	Elementary
Not at all	20	12	13	50	21	14	38
Some, but less than one per month	11	4	11	15	9	10	16
One or two times per month	12	10	15	6	13	13	8
One or two times per week	30	34	37	5	29	34	17
More than two times per week	13	30	12	1	16	14	6
No answer	14	10	12	23	12	15	15
	100	100	100	100	100	100	100

*The exact wording of the item is, "In the past six months how often, on the average, did you engage in sexual intercourse?

Source: W. C. Wilson. The distribution of selected sexual attitudes and behaviors among the adult population of the United States. *Journal of Sex Research,* vol. 11, 1975, p. 52. Published by permission of the *Journal of Sex Research,* a publication of The Society for the Scientific Study of Sex.

Heterosexual Constraints

Sociologist Pauline K. Robinson (1983) has described a number of social constraints on sexuality in later life. In the first place, stigmas attached to old age suggest that elderly people are unattractive and unacceptable sexual partners. Sexual activity among the elderly is often seen as humorous or even ridiculous. Consider the number of jokes or cartoons in popular magazines portraying the foolishness of "dirty old men" or "dirty old women," who apparently have not gotten the message that they should have outgrown their sexual needs years ago. Consider also how rare it is to see passionate physical affection between older people in films and television programs; after viewing a fairly modest lovemaking scene in a film involving a middle-aged couple, one critic wrote that the audience could have been spared the sight of the embarrassing lovemaking scene. If older people themselves accept the view that sexual expression is for them shameful, ridiculous, bizarre, or disgusting, a genuine constraint against sexual activity has been established.

A second constraint described by Robinson against sexual functioning in later life is resistance from adult children. She pointed out that even sexually openminded adults may reject the view that their aging parents have sexual needs. Some may find the notion of sexual behavior among all older persons to be repugnant. Others with single parents may fear that their mother or father will find a new lover who will rob them of some of their inheritance. Finally, some adults may criticize their parents' sexuality as a way of getting even with them for the controls the parents once placed on their children during adolescence.

Sexual behavior also may be limited by institutional barriers during old age. For example, those in nursing homes or other long-term care facilities may find their privacy limited. They even may be separated from their spouses; some nursing homes follow a policy of separating men and women by floor or by building wing, and even married couples may not be allowed to share a room. A general lack of attention on the part of staff workers to the privacy needs of the elderly may be traced to the attitude that old people have no need for locked bedroom doors, because "what would they be doing in there anyway?"

Social constraints against sex among the elderly appear to be greater for women than for men. Robinson noted a number of particular disadvantages women face, including the following:

1. *The sex ratio.* Because women outlive men, there are relatively few elderly men in our society for women to seek as sexual partners, and this situation worsens as women get older. For example, in 1985 there were 128 women for every 100 men in the range of 65 to 74 and about twice as many women as men over the age of 75 (Atchley, 1988).
2. *Marital status.* Another way of saying that women outlive men in our society is to say that wives outlive husbands. Most men over the age of 65

(about three-fourths of them) are still married, but most elderly women (about two-thirds) are single. Therefore, men are more likely to have a spouse to serve as a sex partner. Single elderly men are also more likely to find a sex partner than are single elderly women because of the sex ratio. Also, because sex outside marriage is considered more acceptable in our society for men of all ages than for women, elderly women today are much more likely to be bound by a sexual double standard than are their daughters or granddaughters. Many would never even consider the possibility of sexual contact with a man to whom they were not married.

3. *Availability of younger partners.* We typically expect husbands to be the same age as or older than their wives. Therefore, an elderly single man has a larger age range of partners available to him than an elderly woman. Hardly an eyebrow is raised if a man of 70 marries a woman of 50, but if the ages were reversed, quite a bit of shock might be generated.

4. *Gender roles during courtship.* The man is expected to take the initiative in courtship, and traditionally the woman must wait to be asked. These patterns may be changing among today's high school and college women, but elderly women of today are keenly aware of their traditionally assigned roles. Asking a man for a date might be extremely threatening to their sense of femininity, and perhaps also to the masculinity of the man in question.

5. *The double standard of aging.* Older men are seen as more sexually attractive than older women. Silver-haired actors play leading men and make love to women young enough to be their daughters; silver-haired actresses portray sexless grandmothers, if they can find work at all. A *Playboy* pictorial from the mid-1970s featured "older women" ranging in age from 25 to 30!

Women may face particular sexual constraints as they age, but Robinson pointed out that men, too, have particular difficulties. For example, as was noted earlier, men have more physiological problems than women do, and these difficulties are aggravated by social pressures. Furthermore, men suffer greater anxiety about sexual performance, because they have always found themselves in the active sexual role. Sexual dysfunction is simply more threatening for men than for women and may result in a major loss in a man's self-esteem.

Despite the constraints associated with sexual activity during later adulthood, it is entirely inappropriate to consider old age as a sexless phase of life. In fact, according to Starr (1987), the best predictor of sexual activity for the elderly is the frequency of such behavior during the earlier years of their lives. For the elderly individual who is relatively healthy and has an available sexual partner, sex may be an active and fulfilling component of life. The nature of sexual activity during later adulthood, however, can assume any form that is pleasurable rather than attempting to emulate a model of vigorous heterosexual intercourse. Starr (1987) suggested that if

Human sexual love may continue throughout the life span. The barriers to an active sex life among older people appear to be social rather than physiological.

pleasure was adopted as the standard of sexual activity, instead of intercourse, the elderly would feel less threatened about successful sexual interaction.

Masturbation and Homosexuality

One approach to decoupling sexuality from intercourse is to reexamine the value of masturbatory activities. Masturbation continues throughout adult life, although it occurs less and less frequently with advancing age. Not surprisingly, individual differences are found, with those who masturbated most regularly during early adulthood most likely to do so during old age (Masters & Johnson, 1966). Especially for those elderly people who have no sexual partner, this is a healthy and increasingly acceptable form of sexual release (Brecher, 1984). A most difficult issue for some of the elderly to face is overcoming old-fashioned notions linking masturbation with guilt and shame.

Approximately half the single women between the ages of 50 and 70 masturbate (Meyners & Wooster, 1979), and one in four women over the age of 70 (Christenson & Gagnon, 1965). One in four men over the age of 65 regularly practices masturbation (Meyners & Wooster, 1979). In a sense, the gender pattern of earlier adulthood is reversed in later life, primarily because older men are more likely than older women to have sexual partners and thus may desire to masturbate less. It is not so much that women masturbate more as they age as it is that men masturbate less.

A few words are also in order about homosexual behavior in later life. Relatively little is known about aging homosexuals, because few researchers have been interested in studying them (Kimmel, 1978). However, the picture that emerges from the available findings is a generally positive one, in marked contrast to the stereotypical image of the lonely, aging homosexual cut off from family and too old to attract young lovers anymore. In the first place, older homosexuals are likely to seek out contact with people who are relatively close to them in age; they are not hopelessly youth oriented, as is commonly believed (Kelly, 1977; Harry & DeVall, 1978). Furthermore, although older homosexuals may not have the family ties that heterosexuals do, their social support systems are actually quite strong (Kimmel, 1979–1980; Wolf, 1978).

As Chapter 11 will show, *family* can be defined in a variety of ways, and supportive relationships go beyond the boundaries of kinship. Older homosexual females may even have advantages over elderly heterosexual women when it comes to social support networks, because more female than male partners are available (Laner, 1979; Livson, 1983b). A study of older male homosexuals also found them to be generally well adjusted, socially and sexually, partly because of their long struggle to resolve their sexual identities (Berger, 1982).

GENDER ROLES AND SEXUALITY

Although the development of masculine and feminine orientations will be the focus of Chapter 14, as an appropriate prelude to that material, we will consider here how gender roles interact with sexual behaviors and attitudes. The primary focus of this section, therefore, is on the similarities and differences in male and female interpretations of various sexual situations, activities, or interests.

DeLamater (1987) has argued that the narrowing of the previous gap between males and females on, for instance, the acceptability of premarital sex or the average age of first sexual experience has obscured the fact that significant sex differences still exist with regard to sexuality. Beyond obvious anatomical and physiological sex differences, and aside from the previously mentioned variations concerning masturbation, males and females have different values, perceptions, expectations, attitudes, and experiences in the sexual realm.

From the marker events of puberty—menstruation for girls and ejaculation for boys—to the adult "change of life"—menopause for women and the lessening of sexual drive for men—sexuality for females relates to reproduction, whereas sexuality for males connotes arousal and intercourse. In addition, girls tend to learn about sexuality from their mothers, while the primary source of information for boys is the peer group. Finally, sexual intimacy for women is linked closely to emotional intimacy, but for men sexuality is a more purely physical activity (DeLamater, 1987).

Needless to say, these generalizations are gender role stereotypes that do not apply to all individuals—and may be changing. However, contemporary sexual practices are at least partly shaped by the culturally imposed scenarios of acceptable male and female behavior. For example, in the study of adults by Bell et al. (1981), males report more positive reactions to, and less guilt feelings from, their first sexual encounters. Clark and Hatfield's (1982) research with college students found that 75 percent of the males approached by a female stranger accepted an invitation to have sexual relations but none of the females approached by a male stranger accepted such an invitation.

Much additional research needs to be conducted on gender differences with respect to what influences sexual arousal, aggressive versus passive roles in sexual encounters, emotional closeness in sexual intimacy, the responsibility for and use of contraceptives, acceptability of extramarital or

Gender roles with regard to sexuality are practiced in social situations where males and females interact.

group sex, attitudes toward homosexuality and bisexuality, and equality of participation in sexual control and expression. Although D'Emilio and Freedman (1988) state that we have attained an era of sexual relations in which "personal identity and individual happiness" (p. xii) are expected, gender role stereotypes have not sufficiently diminished to eliminate somewhat contrasting sets of sexual values.

Sexuality is a highly significant and complex aspect of human nature involving biological, psychological, and social factors. Sexual behavior is difficult to study, but it appears that human beings behave sexually from the time of birth and continue to do so until advanced old age. Developmental differences in sexual behavior are evident; genuine developmental changes are harder to identify, however, because there has been virtually no longitudinal research in the area. To this date, apparently we have many more questions than we do answers about the development of human sexual functioning.

Summary

1. In human beings, the genitals are differentiated by the third month of prenatal development. From infancy until early adolescence, however, the reproductive system's structure and function remain relatively unchanged.
2. Puberty is initiated when hormonal signals from the brain stimulate the sex glands (ovaries or testes) to secrete sex hormones. The consequences of these secretions are the primary and secondary sexual characteristics.
3. In the female, reproductive functioning ceases somewhere between the ages of 45 and 55, whereas in the male, fertility continues throughout life. Similarly, the level of sex hormones falls off sharply in women, but the male hormone level declines gradually in men.
4. Age-related changes in the genitals may interfere to some extent with the sexual activity of elderly people, but no physical reason prevents sexual functioning from continuing throughout the life span.
5. Sexual behavior occurs during the infant and early childhood years. Masturbation, same-sex play, cuddling, kissing, exhibitionism, and even sexual orgasm are not uncommon activities throughout preadolescent development. Although Western cultures tend to be more restrictive about childhood sexuality, such behavior is both tolerated and encouraged in other parts of the world.
6. A variety of sexual activity is a cornerstone of the adolescent years. Masturbation, homosexual experimentation, and heterosexual intercourse all increase in frequency. Masturbation is practiced by most adolescent males and by at least half of adolescent females, whereas homosexual activity is a decidedly minority preference. The heterosexual behaviors of adolescents during the 1970s and 1980s were more varied and more frequent and began earlier than in previous generations, particularly among females.
7. Adult sexual activity is a valued and diverse component of life. Masturbation continues to be widely practiced in adulthood, with males more likely to masturbate during early and middle adulthood. A homosexual orientation

is adopted by about 10 percent of the population, but specific homosexual acts occur in a considerably larger segment of our society. The reasons for sexual preference are not clearly understood.

8. Research on hetereosexual intercourse during adulthood is based largely on marital coitus, with little known about extramarital sex or sexual activity among single adults. The frequency of sexual intercourse apparently declines gradually during adulthood, as does sexual satisfaction.

9. Sexual activity, including masturbation and homosexuality, often continues among the elderly, but with considerably less frequency than among young people and middle-aged adults. The reasons for the sexual decline in old age are social and psychological, as well as physiological.

10. The relationship between gender roles and sexuality was explored briefly. Variations in socialization between males and females may be responsible for the complex set of attitudes and behaviors that continue to distinguish the approaches to sexuality by men and women.

Key Terms

androgens (p. 127)
aphrodisiacs (p. 126)
gender roles (p. 126)

menarche (p. 129)
menopause (p. 130)

Müllerian-inhibiting substance (p. 127)

spermarche (p. 132)

Review Questions

1. Describe the major biological aspects of sexual development from the prenatal months to the older adult years. Include the terminology appropriate to the differences in male and female reproductive anatomy and functioning.

2. Human sexual awakening is often thought to begin at puberty, but some evidence shows that children, and even infants, are sexual beings in a legitimate sense. Using your knowledge of infant and childhood sexuality, present an argument that supports the notion that human sexuality precedes reproductive maturity.

3. Adolescent sexual behavior provides a series of contradictions between responsible and tolerant attitudes and risky, immature activities. Referring to available evidence in the areas of masturbation, homosexuality, and heterosexual practices, present your position on the need for adolescent sex education.

4. Some observers have stated that the past couple of decades have seen the development of a sexual revolution in the United States. Compare and contrast the masturbatory and heterosexual behaviors of adults in our culture with those of their teenage offspring. Do you agree or disagree that contemporary sexual attitudes and practices differ significantly from those of previous generations? Explain how.

5. Identify and briefly describe three theories of the development of a homosexual identity. Why is research on homosexual activity limited? Why must the research findings be interpreted with caution?

6. List and describe the social constraints against sexual behavior among the elderly, focusing on any gender differences in social constraints as well as on how masturbatory and homosexual activities are related to sexuality in old age.

7. Analyze the differences and similarities between male and female sexual attitudes and behaviors. How does gender role socialization affect the formation of a sexual identity? Is such socialization likely to change as a result of newer models of gender roles? (You may wish to read Chapter 14 before answering this question.)

Suggested Readings

Hayes C. (Ed.). (1987). *Risking the future: Adolescent sexuality, pregnancy, and childbearing.* Washington, D.C.: National Academy Press.

> A detailed analysis and statistical tabulation by the National Academy of Sciences of some of the critical issues affecting sexually active teenagers and the consequences of their behavior.

Kelly, K. (Ed.). (1987). *Females, males, and sexuality: Theories and research.* Albany, N.Y.: State University of New York Press.

> A series of eight articles emphasizing both biological and sociological influences on gender role and sexual development. This short collection provides an interesting set of readings.

Olds, S. W. (1985). *The eternal garden: Seasons of our sexuality.* New York: Times Books.

> A highly readable treatment of sexuality across the life span. Organized chronologically, the chapters are liberally sprinkled with a variety of pertinent examples.

Sarrel, L. J. & Sarrel, P. M. (1984). *Sexual turning points: The seven stages of adult sexuality.* New York: D. C. Heath.

> Another easy-to-read discussion of sexuality, focusing on the adult years of life. The authors are sex counselors and provide a clinical perspective on adult sexual dysfunctions and critical issues.

Weg, R. B. (1983). *Sexuality in the later years.* New York: Academic Press.

> Sexuality in old age viewed from the perspectives of the psychologist, physiologist, and sociologist. This collection contains some empirically based readings and some theoretical readings.

Chapter Five

Perceptual Development

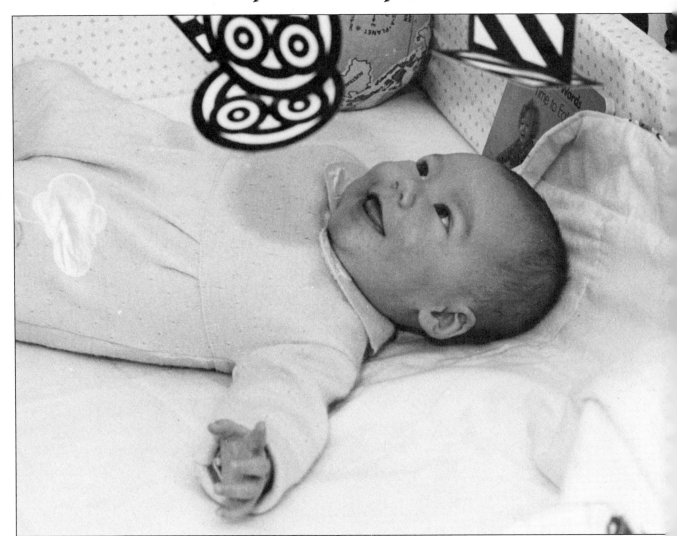

Sensory Processes
Vision
Audition
Taste
Smell
Touch
Integration of the Senses

Cognitive Aspects of Perception
Environmental Influences on Perception

Theories of Perceptual Development

 In this chapter, we examine the five major senses—vision, audition, taste, smell, and touch—and trace their development from infancy through old age. The senses will not be given equal coverage, however, nor will equal attention be given to sensory development at all points in the life span. The greatest emphasis will be placed on vision; more research has been done on vision than on the other senses. We shall also have more to say about audition than about the remaining three senses, because research on touch, taste, and smell has been limited both in quantity and scope.

The major emphasis of the chapter will be on the initial development of the senses during infancy and the sensory changes of later life. This, too, reflects the trend in research on sensation and perception, but, more importantly, it reflects the fact that the most significant changes in sensory and perceptual functioning occur during the earliest and latest stages of the life span, while the middle years are characterized by relative stability.

We shall also discuss factors that direct and focus human sensation and limit or elaborate on sensory input. The first topic will be the influence of culture on perception. The recognition that cultural differences exist in perceptual areas, such as the ability to perceive depth in pictures, leads psychologists to believe that a person's perception of the world can be heavily influenced by life experiences. We will then examine two major theoretical perspectives on perceptual learning and development and their implications for human development.

SENSORY PROCESSES

The five human senses are the channels through which we acquire information about the world. If these channels, or even any one of them, are not working to capacity, our ability to gather information is significantly reduced, and physical, intellectual, social, and emotional functioning is impaired.

This section details the development of the five senses, with particular attention to infancy, when the child begins to interact with the outside world, and to the sensory changes in the latter half of the adult life span. Three points will be emphasized. First, the senses are all well developed at birth or soon thereafter. Second, the sensory capacities of the young infant facilitate the parent-child attachment process and form the basis for later cognitive functioning. Third, although the adult years are characterized by an overall loss of sensory efficiency, the rates of decline are highly variable, and separating sensory functioning from general cognitive functioning is often difficult.

Vision

Familiarity with the structure of the human eye is necessary for an understanding of developmental changes in the sense of vision. A schematic diagram of the eye is shown in Figure 5.1.

Cornea
The curved transparent outer surface at the front of the eye.

Iris
The colored surface of the eye located behind the cornea that adjusts to control the amount of light admitted through the opening at its center.

Pupil
The opening at the center of the iris through which light enters the eye.

Lens
The structure of the eye located behind the iris that bulges or flattens to focus a visual image on the retina.

Retina
The grainy inner rear surface of the eye, made up of light-sensitive nerve cells, on which visual images are projected.

The *cornea* is the curved transparent outer surface at the front of the eye, through which light is admitted. The *iris* is the colored surface behind the cornea, which, like the lens of a camera, adjusts to control the amount of light admitted through the opening at its center. The opening itself is known as the *pupil.* Behind the iris is the curved *lens,* which focuses images that enter the eye. If the object of vision is close to the face, the lens bulges at the center; if the object is distant, the lens flattens out. The muscles in the eye that cause the lens to bulge or to flatten out are called the accommodatory muscles, or ciliary muscles.

The inner-rear surface of the eye upon which the visual image is focused is known as the *retina.* The grainy surface of the retina is made up of a mosaic of light-sensitive nerve cells. Among these receptor cells are rods, which are sensitive only to dim light, and cones, which are stimulated by brighter light and are sensitive to color. Finally, the center of the retina, the point at which an image is focused, is known as the fovea.

Visual Development During Childhood

The human visual apparatus is remarkably well developed at birth. In fact, even by the seventh month after conception, the eyes are anatomically complete and functional. Rods and cones can be found in the retina of a 6-month-old fetus, and by the time of birth the structure of the light receptors is fairly similar to that in an adult (Mauer, 1975). Myelination of the optic nerve fibers has taken place by the time of birth, although the

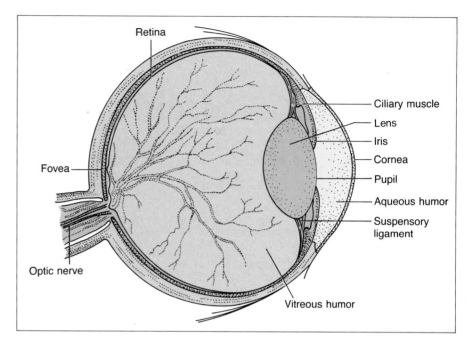

Figure 5.1
The Human Eye

myelin sheath of a newborn is thinner than that found in an adult (Kessen, Haith, & Salapatek, 1970). By the age of 2½ months, however, myelination of the optic nerve is complete. (As Chapter 3 explained, myelination increases the speed and efficiency with which a nerve fiber conducts an impulse to the brain).

The eye of a newborn infant is about half the size of an adult's eye. However, the individual structures of the eye do not develop at the same rate. For example, the lens, cornea, and retina are relatively large in a newborn, and little growth occurs in these structures after birth. Considerably more growth must be completed in the iris, the ciliary muscles, and the front-to-rear depth of the eye. A side view of an infant's eyeball would show that it is less rounded than that of an adult and more flattened toward the back—the condition described as a *short eyeball.*

Visual Acuity.   The ability to recognize all the individual components in a visual display is called ***visual acuity***. If a slide projected on a screen is out of focus, the viewer sees only a blur; the individual elements in the picture appear to run together. As the picture is brought into focus, however, the individual elements become increasingly distinct. The viewer reports seeing the picture more clearly. Visual acuity is this clarity of vision.

Visual acuity

The ability of the perceiver to recognize all the components in a visual display.

Issues in Human Development
How Can Infant Perception Be Studied?

 Because babies are unable to tell us about their sensory experience of the world, we must rely on nonverbal measures to study infant perceptual development. Of course, we could simply observe their everyday physical reactions (e.g., crying, blinking their eyes, pulling back their feet) to environmental stimulation, but, as Rosenblith and Sims-Knight (1985) pointed out, such naturalistic observations are not very scientific. Why? Because observers watching the same infant often disagree in their descriptions of the child's behavior, because naturalistic observations are difficult to quantify in terms of the intensity of the child's reaction, and because in a natural setting it is difficult to know exactly what the baby is reacting to. If infants turn their heads when offered a musical toy, is the reaction caused by the shape, color, smell, sound, or feel of the object, or even by the presence of the adult who approaches with the toy in hand?

Physical and physiological reactions are indeed used to gather data in research on infant perception. However, they are used in laboratory settings where guidelines for observation are established in advance, infant behaviors are carefully quantified, and efforts are made to determine exactly what features of the stimuli the infant is reacting to. The techniques most often used in research of this type are *habituation* and *paired comparisons*.

HABITUATION

A novel stimulus, such as a sudden loud noise or bright light, will cause a person to react physiologically (e.g., changes in brain wave patterns, slowing of heart rate) and possibly also physically (e.g., head turning, jumping up from a chair). This reaction is called an orienting reflex. After a while, however, the person gets used to the stimulus, so that it is no longer novel, and it no longer triggers the orienting reflex. The person is now said to have habituated to the stimulus.

The habituation technique is often used to test the ability of infants to discriminate among various stimuli. The child is first exposed to one stimulus (e.g., a tone, an odor, a colored light) until habituation has occurred and this first stimulus no longer produces an orienting reflex. Then a second stimulus is presented, similar but not identical to the first. If an orienting response occurs—a physiological reaction such as a change in heart rate or a physical reaction such as turning the head—the infant is responding to the second stimulus as if it were completely new. Thus, the infant can discriminate between the two tones, odors, or colors. If no orienting response occurs to the second stimulus, then the infant does not perceive a difference between the new stimulus and the habituated stimulus.

PAIRED COMPARISONS

Used primarily to assess infant visual perception, the paired comparisons technique involves presenting two stimuli side by side and observing the child's preference for one or the other. For example, the child might be placed in an infant seat and shown two visual displays on adjacent screens. A schematic drawing of a human face might appear on one screen and a bull's-eye pattern on the other (as in the research discussed in the section "Pattern Preferences").

Using sophisticated photographic techniques, researchers can determine exactly what the infant is looking at at any given moment. Thus, if infants spend considerably more time looking at one of the two slides, researchers can conclude that (1) they recognize the difference between them, and (2) they appear to prefer some stimuli over others.

The newborn infant does not see the world as clearly as the adult does—for a variety of reasons. For one thing, because of the "short eyeball" phenomenon, the visual image projected on the infant retina is less clearly focused. In addition, the retina itself is immature at birth. Rods and cones are functional in the newborn, but the cones are not as densely packed in the foveal area as occurs in the adult eye. The retina matures rapidly during infancy but is structurally unlike an adult retina until approximately 11 months of age (Banks & Salapatek, 1983). What is more, the ciliary muscles are immature at birth, although they will mature rapidly during the first 2 months of life. During the first month of life, infants attempt to accommodate to the distance of objects when they focus on them, but their efforts are often unsuccessful (Banks, 1980). Particularly during that first month, and even up until 3 months of age, infants misjudge distances and often over- or underaccommodate (Banks & Salapatek, 1983).

Finally, visual acuity is also influenced by the contrast between the object being viewed and the background against which it is presented. Most tests of visual acuity use a high degree of contrast between object and background, as when a child is asked to identify a row of black letters on a white chart in a doctor's office. In reality, however, the world consists of visual stimuli that vary considerably in their contrast levels. Consider the difficulty a person might have in reading an eye chart if both letters and background were presented in different shades of gray!

Contrast sensitivity
The sensitivity of the viewer to contrast between object and background in a visual display.

The range of contrast to which infants are sensitive is quite limited during the first 6 months of life, and adultlike *contrast sensitivity* will not be attained until late in the first year. However, the limits on their contrast sensitivity do not put young infants totally at a loss when they view the world. Many objects in their everyday environments are well within their contrast sensitivity range (e.g., the contrast between skin and hair at the hairline of a human face), and contrasts become easier to detect as objects are brought closer to the face and thus take up a larger portion of the visual field. The young infant derives the greatest amount of visual information, therefore, from high-contrast stimuli presented at close range (Banks & Salapatek, 1981, 1983).

Estimates of infant visual acuity for high-contrast stimuli are approximately 20/450 at 1 to 2 months and 20/150 at 3 to 4 months. This means that an infant can see an object at a distance of 20 feet as well as an adult with perfect vision can see it at 450 and 150 feet, respectively. Visual acuity of 20/20 is attained by the age of 6 months or shortly thereafter.

In summary, even a very young infant already sees the world with reasonable clarity, and current estimates of infant visual acuity are probably conservative (Banks & Salapatek, 1983). The infant definitely sees more than light and shadow. Many adults could instantly experience the visual acuity of a newborn infant by simply removing their glasses.

Form Perception.   When human infants enter the world from the darkness of the womb, they are already able to see an environment of various shapes and contours. In fact, even newborns will notice the contours of a form and will move their eyes to fixate the contour in the center of their fields of vision (Banks & Salapatek, 1983). According to Haith (1979), human beings appear to come into the world equipped with a number of looking "rules" that they use to find the interesting visual features of the environment:

• If you are awake and alert, and the light is not too bright, open your eyes.
• If opening your eyes reveals darkness, scan the environment intensively.
• If opening your eyes reveals light, scan the environment broadly.
• If you find an edge, stop scanning broadly and continue scanning around the edge.
• When scanning near an edge, reduce the range of fixations perpendicular to the edge if there are many contours in the area.

As infants mature, their visual-scanning strategies change considerably in two ways. First, the breadth of their scans across the visual field increases (Banks & Salapatek, 1983). Second, they exhibit an increasing tendency to go from scanning just the outer edges of forms to examining the internal features as well. Consider the difference between the ways in which 1- and 2-month-olds scan a human face (see Figure 5.2). The 1-month-old looks primarily at the contours of the face and spends little time examining the internal features, whereas the 2-month-old seems particularly drawn to the eyes and mouth while almost ignoring the external contours. In addition, the younger infant engages in repeated short-range fixations in areas of interest, while the scanning pattern of the older child shows a greater sweep across the visual display (Haith, Bergman, & Moore, 1977; Salapatek, 1975).

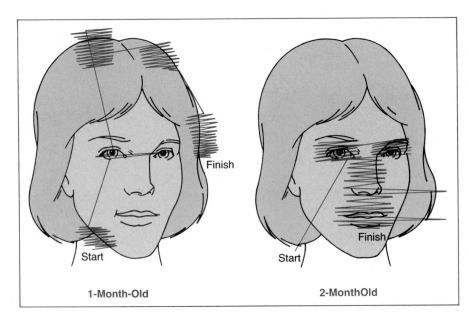

Figure 5.2
Scanning Patterns of a Human Face by 1- and 2-Month-Olds

Focusing on the edges rather than the internal features of perceived forms may actually cause the very young infant to miss much visual information (Siegler, 1986). As an illustration of what may be missed, consider the results of studies by Milewski (1976, 1978). Milewski first familiarized 1- to 4-month-old babies with a compound figure (a circle within a square) and then altered the figure in one or more ways to see if the babies would notice the difference. The alterations consisted of a change in the internal figure only, a change in the external figure only, or a change in both figures; a control group saw the original figure again with no alterations. Four-month-olds were likely to notice all the alterations equally. One-month-olds, on the other hand, noticed that something was different only if the external figure had been changed from a square to a circle or a triangle. Changes only in the internal figure were not apparent to them, presumably because they confined their visual scanning to the outer contours of the compound figure.

Reasons for the very young infant's tendency to scan the edges rather than the internal features of forms are not entirely clear. One possibility is the larger forms have more appeal than smaller ones, and the outer form is always larger than those contained within it (Milewski, 1978). Another explanation centers not on the size of the form itself, but on its innate appeal for the infant; if the internal features of an object are not especially interesting, then the outer contours will be scanned. However, if the internal features are particularly appealing to them, they will notice these features instead of looking primarily at the contours (Banks & Salapatek, 1983). Ganon and Swartz (1980) demonstrated this phenomenon, using Milewski's (1978) research design but substituting high-interest patterns (checker-boards, bull's-eyes) for simple geometric shapes as the internal figures in the display; now even the 1-month-old infants noticed internal changes in the figures as readily as they attended to external changes. Similarly, in the Salapatek (1975) study of infants' scanning of human faces, the 1-month-olds did in fact spend some time looking at the eyes and mouth, although they concentrated on the outer edges of the display.

To sum up, human beings perceive forms in their environments at a very young age, initially they are more taken with the edges of forms than with their internal features—unless the internal features are particularly stimulating—and between 1 and 2 months of age they become quite capable of and especially interested in exploring internal features as well as contours.

Pattern Preferences. In light of the sophistication of their visual acuities and their tendencies at an early age to scan their environments selectively, even young infants are able to see a world rich in varied patterns. A good deal of research on infant visual perception has focused on the question of what kinds of patterns the young infant prefers to look at. Newborns seem to prefer patterns that are neither too simple nor too complex, perhaps because of sensory limitations that make it difficult for them to appreciate complexity (Banks & Salapatek, 1983; Olson & Sherman, 1983). As infants develop, however, they increasingly appreciate complexity in patterns. Robert Fantz, a pioneer in pattern perception research, found that infants beyond the age of 1½ months typically prefer to look at bull's-eye patterns rather than stripes, at checkerboard patterns rather than simple squares, and at facelike patterns rather than anything else (Fantz, 1958, 1961, 1963; Fantz, Fagan, & Miranda, 1975; Fantz & Nevis, 1967). Some of these preferences are illustrated in Figure 5.3.

In addition to complexity, young infants prefer to look at curved rather than straight lines, at irregular rather than regular patterns, at concentric rather than nonconcentric patterns, and at symmetrical rather than asymmetrical stimuli. They also prefer patterns of high-contour density—contour

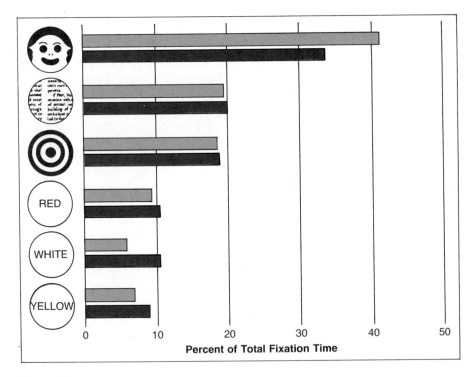

Figure 5.3
Pattern Preferences in Young Infants
Importance of pattern rather than color or brightness was illustrated by the response of infants to a face, a piece of printed matter, a bull's eye, and plain red, white, and yellow disks. Even the youngest infants preferred patterns. Black bars show the results for infants from 2 to 3 months old; gray bars for infants more than 3 months old.
Source: From "The Origin of Form Perception" by R. L. Fantz (p. 72). Copyright © 1961 by *SCIENTIFIC AMERICAN,* Inc. All rights reserved.

density is determined by dividing the total length of the stimulus edge by the surface area of the stimulus (Olson & Sherman, 1983).

Although even newborn babies show pattern preferences and preferences change with age, pattern preferences cannot be said to improve with age because, as Banks and Salapatek (1983) pointed out, the stimuli used in the various studies have differed considerably, and researchers have been unable to agree on developing specific guidelines. For example, what does it mean to say that infants prefer complex stimuli over simple stimuli without a clear, easily understood definition of complexity in a pattern? Does complexity refer to the number of elements in a display, the number of angles, the arrangement of elements, or some other variable? Until this and other such questions can be answered, little more can be said about the developmental aspects of pattern perception.

Perception of Faces.   The work of Robert Fantz and his associates indicated that young infants have a particular preference for the pattern of a human face. What is the reason for this fascination with faces or facelike patterns? Although a 1-month-old infant typically scans the external contours of a face, the gaze of the 2-month-old is drawn to the internal features, such as the eyes and mouth (Haith, Bergman, & Moore, 1977). The 2-month-old is

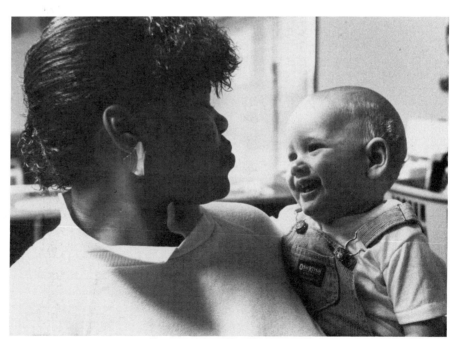

Whether the young infant sees it as a socially significant stimulus or merely as an interesting pattern, the human face is particularly appealing.

also able to differentiate between normally arranged facial displays and those that are scrambled—that is, schematic drawings containing the correct facial features but in the wrong places (Maurer & Barrera, 1981; Olson, 1981; Olson & Sherman, 1983). By the age of 3 months, infants' eyes are sensitive enough to distinguish between photographs of two different faces. Infants can also tell the difference between a smile and a frown (Barrera & Maurer, 1981). The 5-month-old seems to perceive a face as an overall pattern rather than as a collection of individual features; infants of this age are quick to notice when a feature is missing or misplaced in a schematic face they have become accustomed to looking at (Caron, Caron, Caldwell, & Weiss, 1973). At 6 months, the infant prefers real to schematic faces, familiar to unfamiliar ones, correctly drawn to scrambled ones, and moving ones to immobile ones (Sherrod, 1981). And by 7 months of age, the role of facial perception in parent-child communication becomes particularly clear because now the infant can generalize facial expressions, such as happiness and fear, from one face to another (Nelson & Dolgin, 1985).

The special appeal of faces for an infant has never been completely explained. On the one hand, sensitivity to faces could have adaptive significance for a child, and by the middle of the first year, this sensitivity probably has an important role in preverbal communication (Nelson & Dolgin, 1985). However, for the infant younger than 4 months, the face may be appealing only because it is an interesting and complex pattern and not because of its particular social significance (Siegler, 1986).

Depth Perception.   Human beings see the world in three, rather than two, dimensions. **Depth perception** involves a number of cues that indicate that objects in our visual fields vary in their distance from us. Two general categories of depth cues have been identified. *Monocular cues* need only one eye. This category can be further divided into *static cues* and *kinetic cues,* or cues that depend on movement. Because artists use static monocular cues to create the illusion of depth in a painting, such cues are often referred to as pictorial cues. These include partial overlap, shadow, relative and familiar size, blurring of background objects, and linear perspective. Kinetic monocular cues are provided when there is a change over time in the retinal image, as when the image enlarges as the object approaches the face. *Binocular cues* to depth require the use of two eyes. Such cues result from the fact that each eye sees a slightly different image, a characteristic of vision known as **binocular disparity**. The depth perception that results is known as **stereopsis;** it involves the convergence of the eyes on a single target and the fusion of the two slightly different visual images into one.

As can be seen in Table 5.1, young infants are sensitive to all three types of information about depth. However, the information becomes available in a developmental sequence: kinetic monocular cues appear first, then binocular cues, and finally static monocular cues. (For an interesting

Depth perception
The ability to perceive the world in three rather than two dimensions.

Binocular disparity
The tendency of each eye to view a visual display from a slightly different vantage point.

Stereopsis
Depth perception resulting from binocular disparity and involving the convergence of the eyes on a single target and the fusion of the different visual images perceived by each eye.

Table 5.1
Development of Depth Cues in the Human Infant

Type of Cue	Description	Development
Monocular		
Static	*Pictorial cues* such as those used by artists to create the illusion of depth in a painting. They include partial overlap, shadow, relative and familiar size, blurring of background objects, linear perspective.	5–7 months*
Kinetic	Cues produced by changes over time in the retinal image. When an object draws closer, it is gradually enlarged.	1 month**
Binocular		
Stereopsis	Cues resulting from *binocular disparity,* meaning that the eyes see slightly different images since they view the world from different vantage points. Stereopsis involves (1) the convergence inward of the two eyes as they fixate on the same point and (2) the fusion of the slightly different images seen by the two eyes.	2–4 months***

Data Sources:
*Kaufmann, Maland, & Yonas, 1981; Yonas, Cleaves, & Pettersen, 1978; Yonas, Pettersen, & Granrud, 1982.
**Carroll & Gibson, 1981; Yonas et al., 1977; Yonas et al., 1980.
***Bechtold & Hutz, 1979; Gordon & Yonas, 1976; Yonas et al., 1978.

experiment in infant depth perception, see *Research Close-Up,* "The Visual Cliff.")

Is the ability to perceive depth innate in human beings, or is it acquired? Little attention has been given to the role of experience in infant depth perception (Banks & Salapatek, 1983). The role of experience may vary depending on the depth cue under discussion. A later section of this chapter discusses sociocultural influences on perception and at that point cultural variations in the use of pictorial cues will be examined.

Size and Shape Constancy. A person stands near a railroad track and watches a train approach from a distance, pass by, and disappear across the horizon in the opposite direction. Throughout this experience, the visual image of the train projected on the viewer's retina changes constantly. The image increases in size and then decreases, and the shape of the image changes as the train is viewed from different angles. Nevertheless, the viewer knows that, despite the changing size and shape of the retinal image, the train itself does not change in size or shape, because the viewer possesses what are known as perceptual constancies.

Size constancy

The realization that the size of an object remains the same even when the actual visual image of the object changes when it is viewed from a different distance.

Size constancy is the realization that the actual size of an object stays the same despite changes in the size of the visual image. In a sense, the viewer compensates for differences in size by figuring the element of distance into

Research Close-Up
The Visual Cliff

 One of the more interesting classic techniques devised to study depth perception in infancy was the *visual cliff* (Gibson & Walk, 1960). The visual cliff consisted of a board located at the center of and spanning the width of a piece of heavy glass. The glass was raised a foot or more above the floor. On one side of the board, a checkerboard-patterned material lined the underside of the glass, while on the other side, the checkerboard-patterned material lined the floor some distance below. In other words, there was a "deep" and a "shallow" side of the cliff on opposite sides of the center board.

In the Gibson and Walk experiment, 36 babies, ranging in age from 6 to 14 months, were placed on the center board and called by their mothers to come across either the deep or the shallow side. A preference for the shallow, or safer, side was thought to indicate that the subject could perceive depth. Most of the babies were willing to cross the shallow side; only a few would venture out across the deep side of the cliff. Many of the infants sat on the board, crying and reaching for their mothers, but they would not approach on the deep side, and some even crawled away from their mothers onto the shallow side. Therefore, Gibson and Walk succeeded in demonstrating that babies as young as 6 months can perceive depth.

In a later study, Campos, Langer, and Crowitz (1970) found that 2-month-olds placed on the deep side showed consistently greater heart rate deceleration than 2-month-olds placed on the shallow side. Heart rate deceleration is an indicator of attention. Thus, even very young infants can differentiate between the deep and the shallow side.

Shape constancy
The realization that the actual shape of an object remains the same even when the object is viewed from a different angle.

the equation. *Shape constancy* is the realization that the shape of an object remains the same regardless of the angle from which it is viewed. A clock on the wall is seen as round by a person standing directly in front of it. As seen from underneath, the retinal image of the clock is not round at all, but elliptical; however, the viewer takes account of the viewing angle and still knows the clock is round.

As far as can be determined, size and shape constancy are not present at birth but are acquired during the first year of life. Size constancy is definitely present by the age of 6 months; whether it can be found earlier is open to debate. Some research indicates that even 4-month-olds show evidence of size constancy while other research indicates that they do not (Banks & Salapatek, 1983; Day & McKenzie, 1981; McKenzie, Tootell, & Day, 1980). In one early study, size constancy was found even in infants between 1 and 2 months of age, but no one has been able to replicate that finding (Bower, 1964). Banks and Salapatek (1983) suggested that size constancy may indeed be present at 4 months of age or even earlier, but its presence is difficult to demonstrate. They noted also that considerable development may occur in size constancy between 4 and 6 months of age, perhaps because during this time the infant begins to engage in visually guided reaching. Infants reach for what they look at, picking up objects within reach and moving them closer to their faces. This type of hands-on experience may be important for the development of perceptual constancies.

Shape constancy can be demonstrated at an earlier age than size constancy and is definitely found even as early as 3 months of age (Banks & Salapatek, 1983; Caron, Caron, & Carlson, 1979). The specific experiences that bring about the development of shape constancy, or size constancy for that matter, are not known. Most likely, the experience of the world need not be extensive, however, because 3-month-olds are not yet able to get around by themselves or to coordinate the activities of looking or reaching.

Color Vision.   Human beings, as well as many lower animals, see the world in color. As anyone knows who replaces a black-and-white television set with a color television set, color not only makes the world more attractive but also aids in visual perception. Color heightens the contrast among the elements in a visual display, making individual elements stand out more clearly against the background (Bornstein, 1978; Siegler, 1986).

Color is perceived because the light waves reflected off objects in the environment are of different lengths, ranging approximately from 400 to 700 nanometers. The colors of the spectrum—red, orange, yellow, green, blue, and violet—are arranged in order from the longest to the shortest wavelength. Thus, a person perceives an object as green instead of blue because the light waves reflected off that object are longer than those reflected off an object seen as blue.

Despite the popular belief that infants see the world only in fuzzy shades of gray, even very young infants respond differently to light waves of different lengths (Banks & Salapatek, 1983; Siegler, 1986). Three-month-old infants who have habituated to a particular light wave do dishabituate when presented with substantially longer or shorter waves. That is, they react to different wavelengths as novel stimuli and thus can be said to perceive the differences. Does this mean that infants psychologically perceive color just as adults do? Apparently they do, as indicated by the work of Bornstein (1976).

Bornstein first habituated 3- and 4-month-olds to a particular light wave and then exposed them to two other waves equally different in length from the first but in opposite directions. Most importantly, one of the new waves crossed a color boundary while the other one did not. For example, if the original wave were 510 nanometers in length, it would be seen as green; a light wave that is 30 nanometers shorter is clearly seen as blue while a wave that is 30 nanometers longer is still seen as green, but of a different shade than the original stimulus. If the infant can discriminate between wavelengths but does not actually perceive color as adults do, then each of the new light waves would be equally novel and would produce equal responses in the infant. What actually happened, however, was that the reaction to the blue light was considerably different from the response to the different shade of green. Although equally different in length from the first wave, the new stimuli were not equally novel to the infants, meaning that they were not only responding to wavelength differences. Infants really do react to color differences; indeed, such reactions have been found as early as the first week after birth (Adams & Maurer, 1984; Adams, Maurer, & Davis, 1986), indicating that color vision is well established very early in life.

Visual Changes of Adulthood

A number of structural changes in the visual system occur during the years of adulthood—changes that have a pronounced effect on human visual functioning, particularly after the age of 50. The cornea decreases in thickness from age 25 to 65. Because of a decrease in the amount of fluid that keeps it moist, the cornea appears to lose some of its luster from young adulthood to old age: Older adults seem to lose some of the sparkle from their eyes. The iris (the pigmented portion of the eye) loses some of its color, and the pupil, which had grown in size between the age of 1 year and adolescence, continually decreases in size after age 20.

The lens continues to grow throughout life, and as it does so, it becomes more compact. That is, it becomes increasingly denser at its center as new layers are formed on its surface. The increased thickness brings a gradual decrease in elasticity, which can be detected even after the age of 10 years. The lens not only thickens but tends to become increasingly yellow with age, a phenomenon that has never been adequately explained (Fozard, Wolf, Bell, McFarland, & Podolsky, 1977). Many elderly people develop cataracts, a condition described by the clouding up of the lens. Most cataract sufferers—approximately 90 percent of them—are elderly, but most elderly people do not develop cataracts. Only about 10 percent of people in their 60s develop cataracts, about 20 percent of people in their 70s, and approximately 33 percent of people in their 80s (Paton & Craig, 1974).

The ciliary muscles, whose function is to adjust the shape of the lens in the process of focusing on an image, increase in volume until the middle 30s. Afterward, their volume decreases gradually, with some of the muscle tissue being replaced by connective tissue. Finally, evidence suggests an age decline, particularly after the age of 60, in the sensitivity of the retina. Specifically, an age-related decrease in size of the retina's light-sensitive area seems to occur.

These structural changes combine to affect significantly the visual functioning of the average adult. The most noticeable functional changes are as follows. Visual acuity, which peaks at mid-adolescence, remains fairly stable until the age of 50 and markedly declines thereafter. The acuity decline results from a combination of the thickening, yellowing, and loss of elasticity of the lens; the decreased efficiency of the ciliary muscles; and the reduction of light entering the eye because of the decrease in pupil size. Contrast sensitivity is also negatively affected by the structural changes characteristic of the adult years (Owsley, Sekuler, & Siemsen, 1983).

The age-related changes in the ability of the lens to accommodate are most obvious in a person's near point, the closest point to the eye at which an object can be kept in focus. If you hold your hand out in front of your face and gradually bring it close, you will notice that the image of your hand will eventually blur. As soon as it does so, you have passed your near point.

At the near point, the eye's ability to accommodate is pushed to its limit. As visual accommodation worsens with each passing decade, the near point is located farther and farther away from the face. This decline begins in childhood and is particularly sharp during the 40s and 50s (Fozard et al., 1977; Pitts, 1982). The reading glasses that middle-aged and elderly people often wear become necessary when the near point is farther away from the face than the distance at which they ordinarily would hold a printed page.

As the lens thickens and the pupil size decreases, less and less light enters the eye (Carter, 1982). As was already mentioned, the light decrease impairs visual acuity somewhat, but it has another effect as well: The eye becomes less sensitive to low levels of illumination, and the effect is similar to that produced by wearing sunglasses. The ability of the eye to adapt quickly as a person goes from a bright to a dark area gradually worsens with each decade after the age of 20, and it takes increasingly longer to accommodate to sudden changes in illumination. In addition, the thickened lens tends to scatter the light as it enters the eye. Thus, the older people get,

Because visual accommodation worsens with age and declines sharply when people are in their 40s and 50s, many middle-aged adults need to wear reading glasses.

the more they are susceptible to the effects of glare (Kosnik, Winslow, Kline, Rasinski, & Sekuler, 1988).

Changes in depth perception during adulthood have received little attention from researchers, but what research there is clearly indicates a loss in depth perception after the age of 50 (Bell, Wolf, & Bernholtz, 1972; Jani, 1966). The specific reasons for the loss in depth perception are not completely understood, and determining which depth cues are most susceptible to loss is difficult. As noted earlier, however, accommodative ability declines rather noticeably between the ages of 40 and 50. In addition, visual acuity declines in later life, and susceptibility to glare increases. The loss of acuity, the increased glare, and the reduction of the eye's accommodative ability all contribute to the age-related decline in depth perception (Fozard et al., 1977).

With increasing age, the speed with which visual information is processed gradually declines; this is perhaps better thought of as a cognitive rather than a sensory deficit (Kline & Schieber, 1982; Kosnik et al., 1988; Walsh, 1982). For example, an older adult might need more time than a younger one to make sense of written material or to recognize an object presented visually. Perhaps we are ordinarily unaware of the speed of our visual processing because in our daily lives we are unlikely to have this dimension tested. However, such tests occasionally occur in natural settings, as when a driver attempts to read directional signals while traveling at 55 miles an hour on a busy highway.

In summary, little doubt exists that human vision worsens with age. Furthermore, age-related declines occur in a number of specific functions (e.g., light sensitivity, acuity, visual processing speed, ability to see in conditions of reduced light), although the declines do not appear to be uniform. Kosnik et al. (1988) found that, depending on the task, the proportion of adults reporting visual problems increased twofold to sixfold across the adult life span.

The visual changes of adulthood can undoubtedly affect a person's lifestyle. Consider, for example, the difficulty experienced by an elderly person doing something that for most young people is a routine and relatively simple task—driving an automobile at night. Corrective lenses will not compensate for the older driver's difficulty in adapting to extreme shifts in illumination level or to the glare of streetlights or oncoming headlights. If nighttime driving should become a problem, the elderly driver may simply stay home.

Audition

The human ear is a remarkably sensitive and highly efficient organ. It is capable of detecting the slightest whisper of a sound, even in atmospheres not particularly conducive to effective hearing. Consider the case of a parent who, in the midst of a busy, noisy party, suddenly hears the cries of a troubled infant coming from an upstairs bedroom. And who has not had the experience of standing in a crowd and listening simultaneously to two separate conversations? The same sensitive organ that can hear a baby's slightest whimper in another part of the house and can attend simultaneously to different conversations also can tolerate the overwhelming roar of jet engines, city traffic, and rock music. These often are referred to as ear-splitting sounds, but in fact the ear holds up extremely well under such assaults, provided they are only occasional.

The next section will briefly examine the structure and function of the human ear. Then the development of auditory capabilities in the infant and auditory changes throughout the life span will be discussed, with particular emphasis on the hearing difficulties of the elderly.

Structure and Function of the Ear

The human ear can be thought of as consisting of three parts: the outer ear, the middle ear, and the inner ear (see Figure 5.4). The outer ear consists of the external surface of the ear and the auditory canal (the passageway leading from the outside to the tympanic membrane, or eardrum). Sounds from the environment are transmitted through the auditory canal. When the sound waves strike the eardrum, they cause it to vibrate.

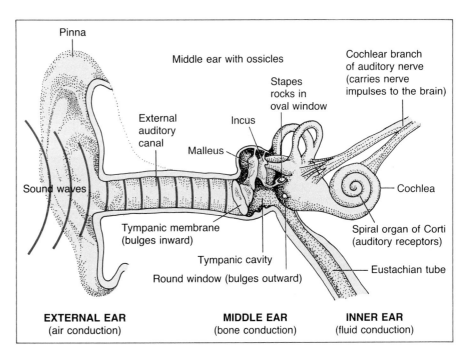

Figure 5.4
The Human Ear

The middle ear is a cavity filled with air; it is connected to the upper throat by the eustachian tube. The middle ear contains three tiny bones called ossicles, which because of their shapes are known as the hammer (malleus), and anvil (incus), and the stirrups (stapes). As Figure 5.4 shows, the ossicles of the middle ear serve as connectors between the outer and the inner ear. The malleus presses against the eardrum, and the stapes press against a membrane known as the oval window, which separates the middle from the inner ear. The function of the ossicles is to transmit sound vibration from the eardrum to the oval window. In a sense, the middle ear acts as a hydraulic press, a mechanical transformer of large-amplitude sound waves striking the eardrum. The sound is focused and condensed in a highly efficient manner by the ossicles.

The inner ear consists of fluid-filled spaces and the cochlea, or organ of Corti, which contains the auditory receptor cells. These receptor cells are connected to the auditory nerve, which carries the messages received by the receptor cells to the central nervous system.

Sound vibrations transmitted from the eardrum to the oval window via the ossicles cause the fluid in the inner ear to vibrate. The fluid vibrations are transduced, or converted, into an electric field by the receptor cells. The electric field stimulates the nerve endings, and a nerve impulse is carried to the brain.

Auditory Characteristics of Infancy and Childhood

From a structural standpoint, the ear is almost completely developed by the time of birth and is free of mucus and amniotic fluid within a few hours after birth (Keith, 1975). Thus, the newborn infant is already quite capable of hearing; in fact, as will be pointed out later in this section, the sense of hearing is well developed even before birth.

Intensity and Frequency. Studies of the hearing ability of newborns typically have used either physiological measures—such as heart rate (which accelerates when a newborn hears something)—or behavioral measures—such as blinking, a startle response, or the cessation of sucking (Acredolo & Hake, 1982). Results of these studies indicate that the newborn's hearing is actually quite well developed in relation to that of an adult, but a few minor deficiencies in newborn hearing should be mentioned.

Intensity
The characteristic of sound waves perceived by humans as variations in the loudness of sound.

Differences in *intensity* of sound waves are perceived by human beings as differences in loudness of sound; intensity is calculated according to units of sound referred to as *decibels* (db). The louder the perceived sound, the higher is the number of decibels. The *auditory threshold* is the number of decibels at which sound becomes audible. Below this threshold, sound will not be heard.

Newborn infants can hear sounds, but their auditory thresholds are approximately 20 db higher than those of adults (Aslin, Pisoni, & Jusczyk, 1983; Trehub & Schneider, 1985); thus, an infant might have trouble hearing a soft whisper but can easily hear sounds within the normal range of human

Frequency
A characteristic of sound waves perceived by human beings as the pitch of sound.

conversation. The amount of difference between an infant's and an adult's auditory threshold depends on the technique used to assess neonatal hearing (electroencephalogram [EEG] data indicate lower thresholds than data on heart rate), on the characteristics of the particular infant being tested (individual variation appears to be considerable), and on the *frequency* of the sound presented. Frequency is the characteristic of sound waves experienced by the perceiver as *pitch,* and the measure of frequency is a unit known as the *hertz* (Hz).

Pitch as well as loudness is involved in determining auditory thresholds because, although able to hear sounds within a broad frequency range of 20 to 20,000 Hz, human beings are most sensitive to sounds within a more limited range of 100 to 4,000 Hz. The greater the deviation in pitch from the maximum sensitivity range, the louder the sound must be to be heard.

Infants are able to hear sounds throughout the normal frequency range, but they are more sensitive to those at the higher than at the lower end (Lamb & Bornstein, 1987; Olsho, 1984). For low-frequency sounds, an infant's auditory threshold is higher than that of an adult; in other words, sounds that an average adult can hear will not be loud enough to be heard by an infant. At high frequencies, however, little difference exists between the auditory threshold or an adult and that of a young infant (Schneider, Trehub, & Bull, 1980; Trehub, Schneider, & Endman, 1980).

The greater responsiveness of infants to higher-pitched tones can be demonstrated by their behavior when exposed to several tones that vary in pitch. Newborns are more likely to turn their heads toward the source of sound when they are presented with a higher-frequency tone than when they are exposed to a lower one (Morrongiello & Clifton, 1984; Morrongiello, Clifton, & Kulig, 1982).

Research on the ability to detect minor frequency differences during infancy is rare. When infants in the first 6 months of life are studied, frequency discrimination has been found in some cases (Spears & Hohle, 1967; Wormith, Pankhurst, & Moffitt, 1975), but not in others (Leventhal & Lipsitt, 1964; Trehub, 1973); for now the only safe conclusion to draw about this age period is that more research is needed (Aslin et al., 1983). On the other hand, evidence of frequency discrimination after 6 months of age is more impressive. The older infant can discriminate among tones of different frequency nearly as well as an adult can (Olsho, 1984; Olsho, Schoon, Sakai, Turpin, & Sperduto, 1982).

Speech Perception.   In real life, of course, infants are rarely exposed to pure tones. What they hear instead are complex sounds consisting of tones of various frequencies—usually ranging between 100 and 4,000 Hz. They are most likely to hear the sounds they are especially responsive to—the sounds of human speech!

The fact that newborn infants respond more readily to sounds at higher than at lower frequencies does not mean that they prefer high-pitched sounds. In fact, they are easily distressed by sounds in the higher-frequency range (above 4,000 Hz), whereas complex sounds of lower frequencies (between 200 and 2,000 Hz) are soothing and relaxing to them. Perhaps it is more than coincidence that this preferred range is precisely the range in which normal human speech occurs (Rosenblith & Sims-Knight, 1985). Thus, human infants seem particularly keyed into the vocalizations of members of their own species, a finding that, in theory at least, could have adaptive significance for the survival of the offspring.

Even within their preferred frequency range of 200 to 2,000 Hz, infants are still more responsive to higher- than to lower-pitched sounds. Perhaps this is why adults automatically raise the pitch of their voices when speaking to a baby (Fogel, 1984). Indeed, adults may find it difficult *not* to raise the pitch of their voices when addressing an infant! This higher-pitched way of speaking to infants, accompanied by exaggerated intonations, has been referred to as **motherese** (Siegler, 1986). Almost 80 percent of the vocalizations of mothers to infants in the first 6 months of life fall into this category of speech (Stern, Spieker, & MacKain, 1982), although individual differences do come into play. For example, Bettes (1988) noted that mothers who were clinically depressed during the first 3 months after birth were significantly less likely to speak in motherese, a finding that has troublesome implications because motherese not only stimulates a baby but aids in the formation of the parent-infant bond.

Even by the time they are 1 or 2 months of age, infants can perceive differences between similar speech sounds: *pah* and *bah, ma* and *na, s* and *z* (Eimas, Siqueland, Jusczyk, & Vigorito, 1971; Siegler, 1986). By 4 months of age, they can readily distinguish among the various consonant and vowel sounds of their language (Aslin et al., 1983; Fogel, 1984; Kuhl & Miller, 1982; Trehub, 1973). Considering their preference for sounds in the frequency range of human speech and their early sophistication at discriminating between similar speech sounds, infants seem to come into the world with a natural predisposition for attending to, and later understanding, human speech (Eimas, 1985).

Not only is general speech perception apparent quite early in life, but very young infants can recognize specific adult voices—most typically the voices of their mothers (DeCasper & Fifer, 1980; Mehler, Bertoncini, Barriere, & Jassick-Gerschenfeld, 1978; Mills & Melhuish, 1974). DeCasper and Fifer (1980) found that 3-day-old infants would regularly vary their normal patterns of sucking to be rewarded by the sound of their mothers' voices reading a story; the same babies would not alter their sucking patterns to hear the voice of another woman reading the same story. Considering how young the babies were at the time of testing, it is unlikely that they had thoroughly familiarized themselves with their mothers' voices in the short time since birth; therefore, this study is thought to provide evidence that even a fetus can hear and distinguish sounds from the outside world (Aslin et al., 1983). Apparently, there may be some truth in the popular wisdom

Motherese

A pattern of speech, characterized by high pitch and exaggerated intonations, that is typically used by adults when speaking to infants.

that a mother's voice is more soothing to a crying newborn than the voice of a stranger. Interestingly enough, newborn infants show no preference for their fathers' voices over that of a male stranger (DeCasper & Prescott, 1984).

In summary, the sense of hearing is remarkably well developed in human infants. They hear particularly well at higher frequencies, and they can differentiate between one human voice and another. Little can be said about further development during childhood and adolescence, except that hearing continues to improve slightly as a child grows up.

Auditory Changes in Adulthood

The auditory system operates at maximum efficiency throughout the adolescent and early adulthood years. However, the middle and later years of adulthood are characterized by a number of structural changes in the ear, many of which can result in gradual hearing losses.

A slight increase in size and a decrease in flexibility of the outer ear, as well as a gradual accumulation of wax in the auditory canal, occurs as we age. In the middle ear, increased accumulation of fluid because of blockage of the eustachian tube is more likely attributable to age-related increases in the number of common colds than to the aging process itself. Elasticity of the eardrum decreases, and arthritic change occurs in the joints between the tiny ossicles of the middle ear (Belal, 1975; Corso, 1977; Olsho, Harkins, & Lenhart, 1985).

Structural changes in the inner ear include (1) degeneration of the sensory receptor cells in the cochlea; (2) loss of auditory nerve cells, which transmit impulses from the receptor cells to the central nervous system; (3) loss in the inner ear's ability to convert fluid vibrations into electrical fields; and (4) decrease of flexibility in the cochlear partition, which separates the upper from the lower chamber of the inner ear and which must retain its flexibility to transmit vibrations from one chamber to the other (Corso, 1977; Schuknecht & Igarashi, 1964).

The major functional change in human hearing during later adulthood is a progressive inability to hear high-frequency tones. Even after the age of 40, the ability to discriminate among sounds of different pitch begins to diminish, particularly when the range of pitches tested is at the higher frequencies.

Losses also occur in the absolute threshold of sound, but these may not cause serious difficulty for the older person unless the sounds are at a high frequency. For example, a normal conversation produces sound within a relatively low frequency range (200 to 800 Hz). The intensity threshold at such frequencies is between 5 and 10 db for young adults, between 15 and 20 db by age 55, and approximately 30 db by age 75. An increase in the intensity threshold by 25 db—meaning that sound must be 25 db higher to be heard—seems quite substantial. However, the average conversation is carried on at an intensity level of between 60 and 80 db, which means that

*Research Close-Up
Sensory Impairment and
Intellectual Functioning in
Middle Age*

 Frequently throughout this chapter, we have mentioned the sensory impairments of middle and later life and the impact of these impairments on the day-to-day functioning of adults. Sometimes the sensory changes experienced by mature adults have an impact beyond what is typically expected. For example, even minor hearing changes can affect performance on standardized intelligence tests.

Psychologists Laura Sands and William Meredith (1989) investigated the relationship between sensory and intellectual functioning in two groups of adults (a combined total of nearly 250 people) on two separate occasions roughly 15 years apart. At the time of the first testing, the average age of the groups was 39 and 48, respectively, and their ages were 54 and 61 at the time of the follow-up. Each participant was given the Wechsler Adult Intelligence Scale, a well-known individual intelligence test (see Chapter 8) on both occasions, and information on their visual and auditory functioning was obtained from physical examinations and from questionnaires completed by the participants themselves.

Although visual impairments had little or no effect on intelligence test performance, hearing impairments definitely did. Those people who reported, or were discovered to have, hearing losses either declined in their performance on certain subsections of the intelligence test or stayed at the same level. However, the group as a whole showed improvement from the first to the second testing, a typical developmental pattern on the subtests in question, which dealt with general information about culture and "social" intelligence. In other words, hearing losses were associated with adult intelligence changes that would ordinarily not be anticipated.

The findings indicate the significant role that sensory changes may play in human intellectual development and highlight the need to distinguish between cognitive ability and actual performance. People may display apparent signs of intellectual decline when no real decline has occurred at all! Based on their results, Sands and Meredith (1989) suggested that studies of developmental change in adult intelligence should *always* include information about the hearing abilities of the participants.

it is still well within the hearing capacity of most elderly people. In contrast, for high-pitched sounds, such as the highest note produced by a piano, the intensity threshold rises from 5 db in young adulthood, to 25 db by age 50, to 55 db by age 75 (Spoor, 1967).

If an average conversation is apparently loud enough for an elderly person to hear, why do older adults so often complain of hearing difficulties? Indeed, a consistently reported research finding is that speech intelligibility, the ability to hear and make sense of human speech, declines with age. Older people are less accurate than younger ones in reporting back words or sentences they have just heard, and this effect is particularly noticeable under less-than-ideal listening conditions, such as those with a lot of background noise (Bergman, 1971; Olsho et al., 1985; Plomp & Mimpen, 1979). Needless to say, speech perception problems can make conversation difficult to sustain, cause embarrassment for the person with the hearing loss, and lead the person to question his or her social competence (Corso, 1977).

Age-related difficulties in the perception of speech have more to do with the frequency than the intensity of sound, because such hearing losses are selective. That is, they are more likely to occur at the upper than at the lower end of the frequency scale, and some high-frequency sounds *(z, s, f, t)* seem to cause particular difficulty for the older listener. Perhaps the easiest way to conceptualize the hearing loss of many older persons is to turn up the bass control on the radio and turn down the treble. The sound will be somewhat muffled; raising the volume will do little to clarify the sound, because the muffled sound results not from a loss of volume but from a loss

Although structural changes in the ear contribute to the worsening of hearing with age, such declines may not be significant enough to cause serious difficulty for the older person.

of high-frequency tones. Similarly, raising voice volume when speaking to an elderly person with a hearing loss generally does little good. If anything, it only increases the listener's frustration.

A final point may be made here not only about the processes of hearing, but about all changes in adult sensation and perception. Many supposed sensory deficits may actually be more cognitive than sensory. For example, if older listeners are less able than younger ones to repeat sentences they have just heard, perhaps it is not because the older person did not hear the sentence as well. Perhaps, instead, the older adult does not process the information as quickly, or has more difficulty remembering what was heard. (You will see in Chapter 6 that age-related declines occur in information processing skills and in memory.) Perhaps, also, older listeners realize that they sometimes perceive speech incorrectly and are therefore more cautious in responding. Out of fear of being incorrect, the older person might prefer to say nothing at all. Those who study adult perception have become increasingly sensitive to the fact that cognitive influences on perceptual tasks must not be overlooked as contributors to the "sensory" deficits of later life (Olsho, Harkins, & Lenhardt, 1985; Poon, 1981).

Taste

An extremely sensitive area of the human body, the mouth is highly receptive to pressure, pain, temperature, and, uniquely, taste. *Taste buds*—tiny cells located on small raised surfaces known as *papillae*—are found throughout the mouth, but particularly on the upper surface of the tongue. They allow human beings to distinguish among the four primary taste qualities of sweetness, sourness, saltiness, and bitterness.

Infancy and Childhood

The taste buds are present and apparently capable of functioning in the fourth intrauterine month (Bradley & Stearn, 1967). In fact, they are distributed throughout a larger area of the mouth of a fetus or an infant than they are in the mouth of an adult. Whether the taste buds actually function, however, depends on the stimulation they receive. Because the fetus opens its mouth by 9½ weeks after conception and begins to swallow amniotic fluid soon thereafter (Humphrey, 1978), and because the fluid undergoes continual chemical changes throughout pregnancy, the taste buds may be stimulated prenatally; thus, the sense of taste is present even before birth (Acredolo & Hake, 1982).

The most frequently used measures of a new baby's taste discrimination have been sucking frequency and the amount of liquid swallowed. Infants ranging from 1 day old to 4 months old suck faster and swallow more when presented with sweet solutions than with any others (Desor, Maller, & Green, 1977; Desor, Maller, & Turner, 1973; Engen, Lipsitt, & Peck, 1974). Engen et al. (1974) even found a preference in newborns for a slightly sweeter sucrose

Taste preferences are influenced by experience, but a decided preference for sweetness seems to exist from birth.

solution over a glucose solution. Apparently, the first "tooth" to make its appearance in the human infant is the sweet tooth—and, for some unknown reason, the preference for sweetness is more noticeable in heavier newborns than in lighter ones and in girls than in boys (Nisbett & Gurwitz, 1970).

Newborns babies clearly do not like sour or bitter solutions. Steiner (1979) observed facial reactions of infants to a variety of different-tasting liquids and noted that sour and bitter solutions caused grimacing and pursing of the lips even in the youngest children, whereas sweet solutions resulted in facial relaxation and what resembled a look of contentment. Rosenstein and Oster (1988) observed that newborns would purse their lips at the taste of a sour solution and would respond to a bitter solution by grimacing and elevating their tongues in the backs of their mouths—actions that are components of the gag reflex and that prevent swallowing. The researchers suggested that such reactions could be highly adaptive, because bitter solutions encountered in the real world are often poisonous.

Interestingly enough, newborn babies seem to be fairly indifferent to the taste of salt and are equally likely to drink water salted or unsalted (Desor, Maller, & Andrews, 1975). By the time they are 4 months of age, however, they actually show a preference for salted over unsalted water, and this preference continues until they are approximately 2 years old (Beauchamp, Cowart, & Moran, 1986).

Even the newborn, then, is a discriminating taster, but do tastes change as children get older? Eating patterns certainly do. As Walk (1981) pointed out, children's preference for sweetness is usually outgrown by adolescence or adulthood. What is more, as children develop, taste preferences are increasingly affected by the context in which they are experienced. For example, children beyond the age of 2 will reject sweetened or salted water, but they will accept sweetness or saltiness in appropriate foods; salt adds to the flavor of soup but makes water undrinkable (Beauchamp & Moran, 1985; Cowart & Beauchamp, 1986).

A reasonable interpretation of these findings is that, while the basic sensory apparatus for taste is present from birth, actual taste preferences are heavily influenced by experience, even at a very young age. Although most 2-year-olds will not drink sweetened water, some will do so, and these are children whose mothers routinely fed them sweetened water during infancy (Beauchamp & Moran, 1985).

Taste Sensitivity in Adulthood

In reviewing the literature on developmental changes in taste, Engen (1977) noted that adults can differentiate among similar tasting solutions with greater accuracy than children can. Why are these age differences found? Does some physiological change in the organism bring about a greater refinement in taste discrimination, or do changes occur because of experience? Walk (1981) argued in support of the experiential explanation: The experience they have with eating allows people to discriminate more accurately between one food and another and to educate their taste buds by exposing them to a wider variety of foods. By tasting only a spoonful of soup, an experienced chef should be able to determine precisely what its ingredients are and in what proportions they were added.

Beyond the age of 50, taste sensitivity declines gradually (Engen, 1977). More specifically, the thresholds for the primary taste qualities of sourness, saltiness, and bitterness increase; age-related increases in the sweetness threshold have been found in some studies but not in others (Bartoshuk, Rifkin, Marks, & Bars, 1986; Moore, Nielsen, & Mistretta, 1982; Spitzer, 1988; Weiffenbach, Baum, & Burghauser, 1982). This means that taste concentrations must be increased to be identifiable as a person grows older, and the implications of such changes are significant. In the first place, the feeling of well-being that results from the enjoyment of a good meal may be increasingly harder to achieve in the later years of adulthood—a particularly painful blow to someone who has come to think of eating as one of life's greatest pleasures. Second, the nutritional deficiencies often observed among elderly in the United States may be attributable in part to age changes in taste sensitivity (Spitzer, 1988). Nutritious foods may be less exciting to the palate than nonnutritious junk foods at any age, and this difference will be enhanced as taste sensitivity declines. Often, the elderly may seek out heavily flavored and less nutritious substitutes. Finally, a decline in taste sensitivity may lead even more directly to serious health problems. For example, as sensitivity to saltiness declines, people may add increasing amounts of salt to their food, and, in some individuals at least, an elevated intake of salt has been related to the life-threatening disease of hypertension (Tobian, 1983; Spitzer, 1988).

Smell

About the seventh month after conception, the nostrils open. The human fetus should, theoretically at least, begin to respond to odors (Acredolo & Hake, 1982). The question is theoretical, of course, because testing the sense of smell in a fetus is not possible, although Sarnat (1978) found that even premature infants as young as 28 weeks gestational age respond to strong odors.

The research on olfaction—the sense of smell—during infancy has been somewhat limited, especially in comparison with studies of vision and audition. Existing research does indicate that infants are capable of detecting odors, and that olfactory sensitivity increases considerably even during the first week of life (Acredolo & Hake, 1982; Lamb & Bornstein, 1987).

Evidence of the increasing sensitivity of the olfactory system has been demonstrated in a number of studies of young infants' sensitivity to the odors of nursing mothers (Cernoch & Porter, 1985; MacFarlane, 1975; Makin & Porter, 1989; Porter, Balogh, & Makin, 1988; Schaal et al., 1980). Makin and Porter (1989) discovered, for example, that even bottle-fed infants, within the first few days of life, will turn their heads more consistently toward a breast pad worn by a nursing mother than toward a pad worn by a nonlactating female. Infants apparently are particularly responsive to chemical signals emitted by nursing women.

In addition, the young infant who is being nursed will quickly develop a preference for one lactating female—its own mother—over all others. This tendency was demonstrated by MacFarlane (1975), who tested infants' head-turning reactions to their mothers' breast pads. At 2 days of age, infants were no more likely to turn toward a breast pad used by their own mothers than they were to turn toward one used by a stranger. However, by 6 days a definite preference began to emerge, and the preference became stronger with each passing day. Young infants clearly favored the breast pad that gave off an odor characteristic of their own mothers.

In a study by Cernoch and Porter (1985), 2-week-old infants were more likely to turn their heads toward a pad that had been worn under their mothers' arms than toward a similar pad worn by a stranger. Interestingly enough, this effect was demonstrated only for breast-fed infants; bottle-fed infants did not show similar signs of odor recognition. Neither group of infants displayed any recognition of their fathers' underarm pads. Reasons for the greater olfactory sensitivity of breast-fed infants are unclear. Among the possibilities suggested by Cernoch and Porter (1985) are that the process

An infant is highly sensitive to smells. A young infant who is nursed quickly develops a preference for the scent of its own mother.

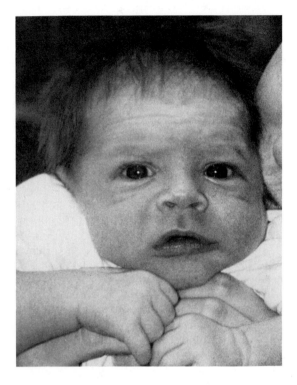

of nursing causes a mother's body to produce chemical substances whose odors are particularly appealing to a nursing child, or that a nursing infant simply has more prolonged contact with mother's skin than does a bottle-fed baby, and so her odor becomes more familiar. Whatever the reason, it seems that human olfaction is well developed in early infancy, and also that the sense of smell may play a role in early mother-child socialization. Not only do infants recognize and respond to their mothers' odors, but mothers can recognize their own 2-day-old infants by their characteristic odors alone (Porter, Cernoch, & McLaughlin, 1983; Russell, Mendelson & Peeke, 1983)!

As additional support for the view that olfaction is well developed early in life, Steiner (1979) found that infants on the day they were born made positive or negative facial responses to a variety of odors—despite the fact that they could have had no previous experience with the odors in question. Apparently, as in the case of the sense of taste, the sense of smell is present at a very early point in a child's development. Little can be reported about the development of olfaction throughout the childhood years, other than to say that the sense of smell seems to reach a peak of sophistication by the age of 10 (Rovee, Cohen, & Shlapack, 1975).

Research on life span changes in olfactory functioning has produced mixed results. Some studies of human sensitivity to smell indicate no age decline at all. As an example, Rovee et al. tested 120 people ranging in age from 6 to 94 years. The stimulus used was a form of alcohol, n-propanol, presented in seven different concentrations. Participants were asked to sniff the contents of a test tube and to estimate the relative strength of each presentation. Rovee and her associates reported no age differences in the ability to judge the subjective intensity of the solutions. By the age of 10, children were already quite sophisticated in their olfactory discrimination.

By way of contrast, other researchers (e.g., Stevens, Plantinga, & Cain, 1982; Stevens, Bartoshuk, & Cain, 1984) have found a definite loss of olfactory sensitivity in the later years of adulthood and have observed that this decline is greater than the decline in sensitivity to taste.

Perhaps sensitivity to smell may decline with age, but it does not follow the more steeply declining courses of the senses of vision and hearing. As Rovee et al. (1975) concluded, the senses that develop the earliest may endure the longest as we move across the span of life.

Touch

The sense of touch is mediated by nerve endings in the skin that serve as touch receptors. These are spread unevenly over the entire body, so some areas are more sensitive than others. The tips of the fingers, for example, are more sensitive than the backs of the hands.

The actual physical sensation of touch occurs when an external stimulus either deforms the skin or causes body hairs to move. If we touch a forefinger to the back of the opposite hand, we see the skin in the area touched change shape, and if we touch our hair even gently without actually touching our head, we definitely can feel the sensation.

The sense of touch is already well developed in newborn infants, and even in fetuses a few months before birth (Spears & Hohle, 1967; Acredolo & Hake, 1982). The early sophistication of the tactile system is evident in the newborn's reflexive responses. For example, pressing slightly on the palm will cause the infant to grasp the pressure stimulus and to begin sucking, and stroking the infant's cheek will also produce a sucking and rooting response.

As infants develop, the sense of touch is used more frequently and more efficiently as a means of exploring the environment. Illustrating these trends are findings by Ruff (1984), who studied the techniques used by 6- to 12-month-old infants in manipulating and exploring objects. Seated on their mothers' laps, the babies were given objects one at a time to handle, and their behaviors were recorded on tape. Ruff discovered that mouthing objects decreased with age, as did simply looking at them and transferring them between hand and mouth. Fingering objects increased significantly with age from 6 to 12 months; older infants were more likely than younger ones to move their fingertips across the surfaces of objects. Thus, the sense of touch was used increasingly as a means of exploring the world. In addition, touch was used more efficiently with increasing age. When objects differed in texture, fingering increased; when they varied in shape, infants were more likely to rotate them and to pass them from one hand to the other. Fingering objects seems to provide the most information about texture, while rotating objects and looking at them from different angles seem to tell more about shape. The infant, therefore, touches and handles materials in ways that are increasingly appropriate for getting as much information as possible from the environment.

Tactile sensitivity changes little throughout the childhood years, or for that matter throughout the remainder of the life span. Although some studies indicate a decrease in tactile stimulation after age 50, others do not. This leads to the conclusion that age decreases in tactile sensitivity are certainly not inevitable; such changes occur in a minority of individuals (Kenshalo, 1977).

Integration of the Senses

Up to this point, the various senses have been discussed separately, almost as if they function in isolation from one another—but, of course, this is not the case at all. Each of the senses can be thought of as a subsystem within the overall human perceptual system. Each subsystem is integrated with, or coordinated with, all the others (Mendelson & Haith, 1976). Six-month-old infants will turn their heads to see a ringing bell, will reach to touch it, and—if possible—will bring it immediately to their mouths to taste it. The ability of a person of any age to enjoy a meal depends not only on the taste, but also on the food's appearance, aroma, and texture. More generally, perception of the world depends on the coordination of information simultaneously processed by the various sensory subsystems.

Little disagreement exists on the necessity of sensory integration, but how and when this integration first occurs is controversial. One view is that the sensory systems first develop independently, and, as a result of interaction with the environment, slowly become coordinated during the first year of life. Jean Piaget, for example, spoke of action sequences such as looking, listening, sucking, and grasping as developing individually at first and gradually becoming coordinated; thus, looking and listening become coordinated between the ages of 2 and 4 months (e.g., the child turns head and eyes in the direction of a sound), as do looking and grasping, and grasping and sucking (Flavell, 1985).

The opposite side of the argument, and the one more widely accepted today, maintains that the sensory systems do not develop individually, but that some degree of sensory integration is present even from birth. A number of studies within the past 15 years point to evidence of sensory integration at a very young age (Gibson & Spelke, 1983; Siegler, 1986; Spelke, 1979, 1981, 1985). For example, babies within the first month of life seem to turn their heads toward a variety of sounds, such as a click, a rattle, or a human voice saying "baby" (Alegria & Noirot, 1978; Crassini & Broerse, 1980; Field, Muir, Pilon, Sinclair, & Dodwell, 1980; Wertheimer, 1961). Even newborn babies display a primitive form of eye-hand coordination! That is, they recognize a relationship between looking and touching. Von Hofsten (1982) found that newborns will extend their arms slightly forward when they look at a slowly moving object, as if aiming their hands at the object. Reaching and hearing also seem to be coordinated in early infancy; young babies who hear a noisemaking toy in a dark room seem to extend their arms in the general direction of the toy (Wishart, Bower, & Dunkeld, 1978).

Slightly older babies display signs of even more sophisticated sensory integration. For example, Spelke (1985) reported that 5-month-olds prefer to look at a film with a visually appropriate sound track rather than at one with an inappropriate sound track. The infants in her study saw films of a stuffed animal—a yellow kangaroo—bouncing up and down on a grassy surface. In one film they heard a *thump* each time the kangaroo landed on the grass; in another film the *thump* and the landings were not coordinated. The babies actually preferred to look at the film in which action and sound were matched. Even at this young age, their perception of events involved a blending of auditory and visual information, and the mismatch between the two was clearly noticeable to them—although they perhaps were not as annoyed as adults watching a film with a sound track out of sync!

A similar preference for coordinated information from the different senses was found by Schiff, Benasich, and Bornstein (1986), who studied infants' perceptions of approach and recession. When a sound-producing object comes closer, it looks larger and sounds louder; when it moves away from the viewer, it appears smaller and sounds softer. If auditory information and visual information are being coordinated, a person would naturally expect the pattern of larger-louder during approach and smaller-softer during recession. In fact, even 5-month-old infants display adequate auditory-visual coordination to expect such a pattern, and they appear confused when the pattern is altered. That is, if an approaching object becomes quieter instead of louder, they seem to have more difficulty making sense out of the experience.

In summary, not only are the individual senses quite well developed at birth or soon thereafter, but the young human infant is already skilled at coordinating input from the various senses into meaningful perceptions. This is not to say that experience is unimportant in sensory development, but only that infants begin life with an innate capacity to organize their sensory input (Lamb & Bornstein, 1987).

COGNITIVE ASPECTS OF PERCEPTION

Thus far, this chapter has emphasized the basic sensory channels through which information from the outside world is relayed to the human organism. But human beings are also capable of the active cognitive process that directs and translates sensory input. The adequate functioning of the sense organs determines what *can* be seen, heard, smelled, touched, or tasted, but what is actually perceived at any particular time is influenced by a host of psychological and sociocultural factors: attitudes, expectations, interests, needs, and prior experiences.

Environmental Influences on Perception

Although all human beings are equipped with the same sensory equipment, marked differences are evident in the ways in which we perceive our world, and these differences can usually be attributed to variations in life experiences. Applying Our Knowledge, "Learning to Read," discusses a major perceptual task in our culture.

Some of the most striking examples of the influence of the environment on perception are found when cultural variations in perception are studied. Consider as an example the effect of culture on a person's tendency to perceive three dimensions in a two-dimensional display. Human beings perceive in three dimensions, and some depth cues (e.g., kinetic cues, stereopsis) appear either to be innate or to depend on physiological maturation. Other depth cues such as size, shadowing, and the partial overlapping of figures appears to be learned, and these "pictorial" cues are susceptible to the influence of culture.

Pictorial depth cues allow us to perceive depth where none actually exists—on a two-dimensional surface such as a painting or a photograph. An artist suggests depth in a painting by making figures in the foreground larger than those in the background, by making "closer" figures overlap those "farther away," by using shadow, by blurring the figures in the background, and by using perspective (as when the buildings on two sides of a street seem to come closer to one another when viewed from an increasing distance). When looking at a painting or a photograph, people perceive depth only because they have learned to associate certain cues with depth. The sensory information provided by binocular cues clearly indicates that no depth really exists. In a sense, people learn to perceive depth in pictures despite sensory evidence to the contrary.

Pictorial depth perception is found in U.S. children as young as 5 months of age (Yonas, Cleaves, & Pettersen, 1978; Yonas & Granrud, 1985), and a relationship exists between the age of the child and sophistication in using pictorial depth cues. The performance of older children is more accurate and more consistent than that of younger ones (Gibson & Spelke, 1983). It is difficult to know, however, whether the age differences result from the maturing of the sense organs or from children's experience in looking at pictures, because age and experience can never be completely separated. The prevailing belief among psychologists is that learning is significantly involved in pictorial depth perception; people develop habits of attending selectively to certain types of information, such as pictorial depth cues, and ignoring others (Gibson, 1969). Such perceptual habits seem to depend on the characteristics of the culture in which the child is raised.

Hudson (1960) carried out one of the better-known studies of cultural differences in three-dimensional perception. In this study, South African children—and some adults—were tested. Some subjects were black, some white, some educated, and some uneducated. All were shown a group of line drawings containing a variety of depth cues (see Figure 5.5). The drawings contained depth cues of size (e.g., the man and the antelope are larger than the elephant and the tree), partial overlap (e.g., the overlapping hills, the antelope overlapping the elephant), and perspective (e.g., the sides of the road come together in the upper half of P4).

Hudson questioned the participants in his study about the relative nearness of the figures. An answer indicating that the man and the antelope were nearer than the elephant was characteristic of a three-dimensional perceiver, whereas a two-dimensional perceiver saw no difference in the nearness of the figures. Hudson discovered that three-dimensional perception was related to the degree of schooling the child had experienced, and to the degree of exposure to pictures in books and magazines. Unschooled children, who apparently had little opportunity to view drawings and photographs, were more likely to miss the depth cues in the stimulus drawings than were school-educated children and teachers.

Hagen and Johnson (1977) found further evidence of the influence of experience on depth perception in pictures. They tested U.S. children and adults using Hudson's materials and an Americanized version of his test. In the Americanized version, familiar-looking drawings of children were used instead of drawings of a hunter and wild animals. Hagen and Johnson found

Figure 5.5
Line Drawings Used to Study Cultural Differences in Depth Perception

Source: *Journal of Social Psychology, 52,* p. 186, 1960. Reprinted with permission of the Helen Dwight Reid Educational Foundation. Published by Heldref Publications, 4000 Albemarle St., N.W., Washington, D.C. 20016. Copyright © 1960.

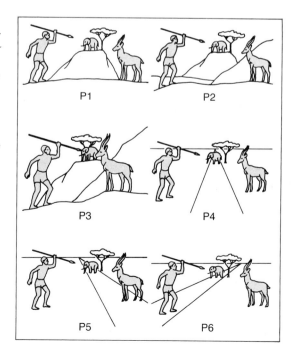

Applying Our Knowledge
Learning to Read

One of the most dramatic illustrations of perceptual development in the young child is the emergence of the ability to read. Ultimately, the sophistication of a child's reading skills is influenced by a variety of psychological and social factors, such as motivation, interest, the presence of direct reinforcement, and exposure to adult models who enjoy reading. However, the basic ability to make sense of the written word initially depends on a number of underlying perceptual processes.

What does a child need to do to derive meaning from written symbols? According to Gibson and Levin (1975; Gibson, 1969), reading occurs in three different phases. First is *the ability to differentiate among written symbols.* The child must recognize differences among the letters of the alphabet by attending to the distinctive features of each letter, and noticing how a particular letter differs from others. For example, the features of a capital *A* include a horizontal line (—), a diagonal line (/), a diagonal line in the reverse direction (\), an intersection of lines, and symmetry between the right and left halves of the letter. Unlike a *B,* an *A* contains no vertical line (|), and no curved lines of any sort. An *A* and a *B,* therefore, are relatively easy to differentiate. A *P* and an *R,* however, share a number of common features (e.g., vertical lines, closed curves, intersections) and differ only on the diagonal line contained in the *R.* Letters that contain similar features are harder to differentiate than letters with radically different features. What is more, some differences are easier to detect than others (Gibson, Gibson, Pick, & Osser, 1962). Letters that differ only in the fact that one is a closed figure and the other is an open figure *(O* and *U)* are easier to differentiate than letters differing only in rotation or reversal *(b* and *d).*

A second phase in the reading process according to Gibson (1969; Gibson & Levin, 1975) is *the ability to decode letters to sounds.* This is not, however, a simple one-to-one association process. Simple association can explain how a child learns to name the letters of the alphabet, but it does not explain how a child learns to read. In the English language, there is often little resemblance between the sound of a word and the sounds of the individual letters contained within it; for example, the spoken word *brought* does not include the sounds of the letters *o, u, g,* or *h.* A knowledge of the sounds of the individual letters will not always prepare a child to pronounce the entire word correctly.

What, then, does a child do when decoding letters to sounds? Gibson (1969) described the child's gradual recognition of "spelling patterns"—clusters of letters pronounced the same way in all words in which they appear. In a sense, the child acquires invariant rules for pronunciation that may be used when letters are combined in certain ways. As an illustration of the use of spelling pattern rules, consider the letter combinations *CABE* and *CIPE.* Although these are not real words, anyone who can read English can pronounce them correctly. The reader knows, first of all, that a *C* followed by an *A* is pronounced as a *K,* but a *C* followed by an *I* is pronounced as an *S.* The reader also knows that the *E* at the end of each word gives the initial vowel a long rather than a short sound. If the *E* were not present, as in *CIP,* the word would have a different sound. The ability to pronounce correctly such patterns in nonsense words improves with age from early elementary school to adulthood, and children characterized as good readers are better able to pronounce nonsense words than are poor readers (Calfee, Venezky, & Chapman, 1969).

Invariant spelling patterns can be entire one-syllable words (e.g., *cat, bed*) or merely letter combinations, such as *BL, SH,* or *CK,* that can be combined into words. The child who knows how to pronounce *BL* and *CK,* as well as the letter *A,* can pronounce the word *black.* In time, the child can pronounce words of any length as he or she recognizes the patterns contained within them.

A final stage in learning to read is *the ability to use higher-order units.* As Gibson and Levin (1975) pointed out, an effective reader goes beyond the word to derive meaning from sentences or para-

The ability to read involves differentiating among written symbols, decoding letters to sounds, and using higher-order units of meaning.

graphs. Indeed, some children are able to read words very well but treat the words as single units and therefore have little understanding of what they are reading (Cromer, 1970). To help children go beyond mere word recognition to meaningful reading, Gibson and Levin concluded that written material presented to children should be of high intrinsic interest and should contain sentences that vary in length and complexity. Many children's books contain short and overly simplified sentences, perhaps in the belief that complexity will confuse a beginning reader. However, a number of studies have found that comprehension is best when written material most closely resembles the child's own manner of speaking (Gammon, 1970). Even a kindergartner uses sentences that are lengthy and contain a rich variety of parts of speech, phrases, and clauses (Gibson & Levin, 1975). Underestimating a child's ability to handle complexity and variety on the printed page may actually inhibit the child's reading progress. A sentence such as *See Spot run* is rarely found in human speech, even during early childhood!

that adults performed better than children when the original Hudson stimulus materials were used, and that adults and children performed equally well when the American version was used. In other words, developmental differences in the ability to perceive pictorial depth disappeared when the stimulus materials were made more familiar, making it clear that prior experience is highly significant in studies of this type.

Theories of Perceptual Development

Having established that the changes in the ways human beings perceive the world as they develop are influenced by the particular experiences, attitudes, values, and biases of the cultures they live in, let us now turn to the question of how these experiences are acquired. In an attempt to answer that question, we present two major theories of perceptual development. The first theory emphasizes the child's developing ability to differentiate among the distinctive features of objects in the environment. The second theory stresses the child's tendency to enrich sensory input by bringing to it a set of prior experiences, attitudes, and values.

Differentiation Theory

Differentiation theory
The theory of perception that states that as people develop they attend more and more closely to the distinctive features of the environment.

According to *differentiation theory* (Gibson, 1979; Gibson & Spelke, 1983) perception is an *active, purposeful,* and *meaningful* process of seeking out the invariant abstract properties of events, objects, and places. The sense organs pick up stimulation from the environment, but it is not the stimulation that we perceive; instead, we perceive events and objects in an organized, unified way.

Affordances
According to differentiation theory, things that the environment provides to the perceiver that yield possibilities for action.

To illustrate the active and meaningful nature of perception, Gibson (1979) spoke of *affordances,* those things that the environment offers or provides to the perceiver: The sun affords warmth; a roof affords shelter from the rain. Affordances are possibilities for action. Thus, perception must be thought of as an active process rather than as a mere receiving of environmental stimulation. The meaningfulness of perception is illustrated by the fact that from the constant flow of available information, people select what is most meaningful to them. They perceive that which has the most important affordances for them. This principle was illustrated earlier in this chapter when we noted that newborn infants are particularly attentive to their mothers' voices and odors. The mother is an object that offers more important affordances, or possibilities for action, than are offered by various other objects in the environment.

Advocates of differentiation theory argue that five general trends in perceptual development occur:

1. Exploration of the world becomes more systematic and orderly.
2. The child continues to discover new affordances as he or she grows.

3. Perception increases in specificity, and more subtle invariants and affordances are discovered.
4. Perception becomes more efficient.
5. Perceived affordances become less narrowly focused and are easier to generalize to new situations.

Enrichment Theory

Enrichment theory

The belief that, as people develop, their perception is increasingly influenced by what they themselves bring to the process of perceiving.

Differentiation theory says that perceptual development means perceiving the world with increasing accuracy. *Enrichment theory* represents an opposite view. This theory argues that as people develop, their perception is increasingly influenced by what they bring of themselves to the act of perceiving. Illustrating this point of view, cognitive psychologist Jerome Bruner (1973) discussed the concept of going "beyond the information given" in the act of knowing, meaning that people bring to any cognitive act a good deal of their own previous cognitive history. Two individuals with different experiences of life, different theoretical biases, and different mental categories may view an identical object or event but have totally different perceptions of it. For example, some spectators at a basketball game never see the fouls committed by the home team but constantly see imagined fouls committed by the opponents.

Much of Bruner's early perceptual research dealt with the effects of values, needs, and personality factors in the process of perception. He found, for example, that poor children consistently overestimated the size of coins while richer children did not—presumably because the coins were more significant for those who needed them more (Bruner & Goodman, 1947). He observed that people recognize certain words more easily than others from a rapidly presented word list, and that people recognize most easily the words that have particular positive significance in their lives (Postman, Bruner, & McGinnies, 1948). In contrast, certain threatening words are specifically not seen in a visual display—a phenomenon described as perceptual defense (McGinnies, 1949). Bruner remarked that such findings resemble what occurs in the case of lovers who "either for defense or enhancement, see only the good and beautiful in their chosen ones" (1973, p. 97).

Summary

1. Human visual acuity develops rapidly during the first 6 months of life. The young infant's acuity is limited for a variety of reasons.
2. Even newborn infants are sensitive to the contours of forms; the earliest scanning strategies focus on the edges of forms, while later strategies emphasize the internal features.
3. Young infants show definite preferences for complex patterns over simple ones, and they seem to have a particular interest in the patterns of the human face.
4. Depth is perceived through the use of various cues. Monocular kinetic cues develop first, followed by binocular cues, and then monoc-

ular static cues. All three types of cues are present by the age of 7 months.

5. Size constancy is definitely present by the age of 4 to 6 months; shape constancy is found as early as 3 months.

6. Human infants see the world in color, and the current evidence indicates that color vision is present from birth.

7. As a result of a combination of structural changes in the human eye in later life, visual impairment may occur, and this can seriously restrict the social mobility of older adults.

8. Newborns' hearing is well developed, but their intensity thresholds are higher and their frequency discrimination is less developed than for the adult. In other words, infants have more difficulty than adults in hearing soft noises and distinguishing between tones of similar pitch.

9. Infants are particularly tuned in to human speech and can distinguish among various speech sounds by the time they are 1 to 2 months old.

10. The auditory system of a person beyond the age of 50 becomes somewhat less efficient than it was during young and middle adulthood. The elderly are most likely to experience hearing difficulty in the higher frequency range.

11. The senses of taste, smell, and touch are well developed at and even before birth, and little evidence supports an age decline in any of these senses. The senses that develop the earliest apparently are also the ones most likely to remain intact for the longest time.

12. The senses can be thought of as systems that do not develop in isolation but are integrated with one another early in life.

13. Noticeable cross-cultural differences affect visual perception, and even within cultures differences in perception are related to amount of schooling received. These differences, often observed in studies on three-dimensional perception of pictures, strongly suggest that perception has a significant experiential component.

14. The differentiation theory of perceptual development suggests that as people develop, they become increasingly attuned to the distinctive features of their environment.

15. The enrichment theory of perception holds that perceivers bring more of themselves to the act of perception as they develop, and it becomes increasingly difficult to distinguish between the mental state of the perceiver and the reality that he or she is perceiving.

Key Terms

affordances (p. 202)
binocular disparity (p. 176)
contrast sensitivity (p. 171)
cornea (p. 168)
depth perception (p. 176)

differentiation theory (p. 202)
enrichment theory (p. 203)
frequency (p. 185)
habituation (p. 170)
intensity (p. 184)

iris (p. 168)
lens (p. 168)
motherese (p. 186)
paired comparisons (p. 170)
pupil (p. 168)
retina (p. 168)

shape constancy (p. 178)
size constancy (p. 177)
stereopsis (p. 176)
visual acuity (p. 169)
visual cliff (p. 178)

Review Questions

1. Because infants are obviously unable to tell us what they perceive, how do psychologists study the processes of infant perception? Describe the techniques used and the advantages of each of them.
2. What are the reasons for the limitations on visual acuity in the first 6 months of life? Compared to an adult, how well does the young infant actually see?
3. Some researchers have suggested that the sensory capacities of the young infant are designed to facilitate the process of attachment between parent and child. Referring to the various senses discussed in the chapter, provide examples of the ways in which the senses may encourage parent-infant bonding.
4. Describe the visual changes that occur in later adulthood and their impact on the everyday functioning of elderly people.
5. Developmental changes in the sense of taste that occur in later life have been blamed for nutritional deficiencies among many elderly people. Explain the connection between taste impairment and diet in later adulthood.
6. Discuss the evidence that suggests that cultural factors significantly influence human perception. What does the cross-cultural research tell us about the ways in which we perceive the world?
7. Compare Gibson's differentiation theory of perceptual development with the enrichment theory suggested by Bruner. How specifically do they contradict each other?

Suggested Readings

Gibson, E. J. (1969). *Principles of perceptual learning and development.* New York: Appleton-Century-Crofts.
    The most concise and comprehensive overview of the work of James and Eleanor Gibson, pioneers in the study of human perception. This volume provides a thorough discussion of differentiation theory and compares and contrasts the theory with cognitive and "response-oriented" theories.

Perception: Mechanisms and Models: Readings from Scientific American. (1972). San Francisco: W. H. Freeman.
    A collection of *Scientific American* reprints spanning approximately 30 years. Many of the readings have already become classic articles in the field. Areas covered include the sensory systems, illusions, and development of specific perceptual functions. Many excellent illustrations appear throughout.

Walk, R. D. (1981). *Perceptual development.* Monterey, CA: Brooks/Cole.
    A relatively short but concise summary of theory and research in the area of perceptual development across the life span. Written with enthusiasm and humor, the book covers sensory development, attention, the effects of sensory deprivation, perception in special populations (e.g., the elderly, the blind, the deaf) and a number of theoretical issues related to human perception.

Chapter Six

Information Processing: Attention, Learning, and Memory

Attention
Infancy
Later Childhood
Adulthood and Old Age

Learning
Conditioning
Social Learning
The Adult Learner

Memory
Types of Memory
Factors Influencing Memory
Memory Development in Childhood
Memory Development in Adulthood
Metamemory

 Larry is a sixth grader who failed a history exam. Why, his teacher wondered, did Larry fail the test? Was it because he never learned the material adequately in the first place? Is it possible that, although he learned the material quite well, he was simply unable to remember it? Or does learning always imply the ability to remember, so that Larry's memory failure could only be interpreted as a failure to learn the material properly?

As a matter of fact, where the failing student experienced a breakdown in his system of processing information is not at all clear. The breakdown could have occurred at any point in the process from the minute the information first registered on Larry's senses to the minute when he tried, and failed, to retrieve the information from memory.

Psychologists who attempt to trace the sequence of mental operations needed for a person to perform a particular intellectual task use an information processing approach (Anderson, 1985), which involves first identifying the stages in the process, then analyzing success or failure in dealing with information at each stage. If Larry cannot remember an answer to an exam question, the information was lost somewhere on its journey through his information processing system. Perhaps Larry failed to hear the information when it was first presented in class. If he did hear the teacher presenting the material, did he attend to it, or was he distracted by something else at the time? If he attended to it, did he use strategies to make it memorable while it was still fresh in his mind—in what psychologists refer to as his short-term, working memory? For example, did he mentally repeat it, a process known as rehearsal? Did he organize the material into meaningful "chunks" of information? If he was effective in his use of such strategies while the information was still in short-term memory, then the material was entered into "storage" in Larry's long-term memory. If not, the material was probably lost. Finally, if the information was successfully stored in long-term memory but Larry was still unable to remember it on an exam, the failure in the system probably occurred in the process of the retrieval of information from long-term storage.

A certain air of mystery surrounds the ways in which people process information in their minds. We see what is available to them as input and we see the output in their behaviors, but we cannot see the processes by which information is registered, interpreted, stored, and retrieved at a later time. For convenience, psychologists discuss attention, learning, and memory separately, but all are aspects of the cognitive processing of information, which is the topic of this chapter.

We begin with a discussion of attention, the cognitive activity that specifies which information the person will enter into the information processing system. Then we shall deal with basic principles of several varieties of human learning and review the literature on learning from infancy through old age. Finally, we shall turn to the topic of memory, the process by which information that is taken into the system is stored and retrieved when needed.

ATTENTION

Attention

The screening mechanism by which an individual selects certain features of the environment to be processed while ignoring other features.

Attention is the screening mechanism by which certain features of the environment are selected to be processed and other features are ignored. In a very real sense, attention is the gateway to the information processing system.

The model of attention most widely accepted today is the *capacity limitations model,* which views attention as the capacity, or energy, needed to support cognitive processing. Because only a limited amount of cognitive energy is available for information processing, people must selectively allocate this energy to function efficiently (Plude & Hoyer, 1985; Rybash, Hoyer, & Roodin, 1986). To illustrate capacity limitations, a parent may devote full attention to preparing dinner *or* to supervising the children as they do their homework, but attending completely to both activities at once is hard.

Activities will vary, of course, in terms of the attention they require. Some are automatic and effortless, requiring little attentional capacity; these include skills that have been refined by experience, such as typing or driving a car. Because little attentional capacity is needed, the supply of remaining cognitive energy is considerable, and it may be possible, therefore, to engage in several "automatic" activities at once. On the other hand, less familiar activities require effortful rather than automatic processing; they call for active, conscious, controlled attention, and they use up much of a person's attentional capacity. An experienced driver can operate a clutch and shift gears and still attend carefully to a conversation with a passenger; a new driver uses so much attentional capacity on the motions of driving that little attention may be left for a serious conversation.

We will discuss the development of attention, looking first at the attentional limitations of the infant and young child. We will then examine research detailing the increasing efficiency of attentional processes as the child matures. Finally, we will look at attentional changes during adult life, when the distinction between automatic and effortful attention becomes particularly relevant.

Infancy

In Chapter 5, we discussed pattern perception and preferences in young infants. The existence of preferences indicates that infants are capable of selectively attending to features of their environments. That is, they are able to perceive as well as to sense the world around them. Attentional processes are limited during infancy, however, for several reasons. In the first place, the actual amount of time available for attending is initially somewhat restricted; a newborn infant sleeps a good deal, and the average length of nonfeeding alert periods is only 5 minutes, with more than 90 percent of the nonfeeding alert periods lasting for 10 minutes or less (Clifton & Nelson, 1976). By 3 months of age, the average alert period lasts for about 90 minutes.

A second attentional restriction during infancy is that, even in the second half of the first year, infants have limited knowledge about the world. As Olson and Sherman (1983) pointed out, a person's knowledge base affects the ability to attend selectively. For example, compare the careful attention to detail displayed by a shopper who really knows the merchandise with the relative inattention to the product's features that is typical of less knowledgeable buyers. The fact that increasing familiarity with the world leads to increasingly selective attention can be demonstrated in the social behavior of infants; as other people become more familiar to them, they increase selective smiling and devote greater and greater attention to the mother, or primary caretaker, as they mature (Olson & Sherman, 1983).

A third constraint on an infant's ability to attend is related to the boundaries on human attention at any age. People can attend to only limited amounts of environmental information at any one time. A person cannot be an attentive driver and at the same time worry about an upcoming final exam! Infants seem to be even more limited than adults in their ability to share their attention with two or more environmental stimuli (Olson & Sherman, 1983). Consider how quickly a first toy is "forgotten" by an infant who has just been offered a second one.

Adults can directly influence the attentional processes of infants by providing them with certain experiences. Tamis-LeMonda and Bornstein (1986) observed that some mothers call attention to themselves when they interact with their babies, while others direct their children's attention to objects in the environment. Mothers who call attention to themselves are likely to have infants who attend more to them than to the environment. Mothers who direct their infants' attention toward the environment have infants who explore objects more and mother less, and these effects are found early in the first year—between 2 and 5 months of age.

Later Childhood

As children mature, they attend with increasing efficiency to the world around them. They become more and more likely to attend to information that is useful, meaningful, and relevant, and to ignore irrelevant information (Maccoby, 1969; Walk, 1981). One way to illustrate this increasing efficiency of attention is to photograph children's eye movements as they attempt to solve a perceptual problem. Typical of this research on what is known as *visual scanning* is a study by Vurpillot (1968), who presented a perceptual problem to children aged 3 to 10. She showed them pairs of houses in silhouette (see Figure 6.1) and asked them to determine whether the members of each pair were identical or different.

Figure 6.1
Sample Pairs of Silhouettes of Houses
The top pair is a "different" pair, because three of the windows are not the same. The bottom pair is a "same" pair, with all windows identical.

Source: From E. Vurpillot. The development of scanning strategies and their relation to visual differentiation. *Journal of Experimental Psychology, 6,* 1968, p. 634. Orlando, FL: Academic Press. Reprinted by permission of the publisher.

Vurpillot (1968) photographed the children's eye movements to determine which features of the houses they attended to. Three-, 4- and 5-year-olds performed poorly on the task, perhaps because their eye movements were unsystematic; they often looked at irrelevant features of the displays while ignoring useful information. For example, these young children gave answers before they had even looked at all the windows. Older children compared pairs of windows one at a time and stopped as soon as they had found a pair that differed. Thus, the visual scanning of older children was designed to produce the greatest amount of information in the shortest possible time.

Other studies of developmental changes in attention have involved a technique known as *dichotic listening.* In studies of this type, the child wears a headphone, and a different message is presented to each ear. For example, Maccoby and Konrad (1966) had children ranging from kindergarten age to fourth grade listen to a male voice saying words into one ear and a female voice saying different words into the other. The children were then asked to report as many words as they could remember.

Kindergartners remembered significantly fewer words than fourth graders. In addition, the younger children displayed the effects of attentional interference in another rather amusing way. They combined sounds from the two words played simultaneously to construct nonsense words. "Squirrel" and "turtle" were reported as "squirtle" (Walk, 1981). Fourth graders rarely did this.

The ability to direct one's attention is by no means perfected by the age of 10; studies of visual scanning and dichotic listening indicate continued improvement through the years of childhood and adolescence, with maximum efficiency of attention reached by the time of early adulthood (Walk, 1981). Frustrated parents and teachers would do well to remember that if a child, and especially a young child, fails to "pay attention" when directed to do so, the problem may not be one of motivation. The child may be unable to tune out distractions and attend to the relevant information at hand—in this case, the directives provided by the adult.

Television and Attention

Not all studies of children's attentional processes have used such exotic procedures as eye photography or dichotic listening. Some of the "equipment" for research on this topic is found much closer to home; many recent studies of attention have relied on the most often used entertainment and information source in U.S. society—the television set (Comstock, Chaffee, Katzman, McCombs, & Roberts, 1978).

Studies of preschool children's visual attention to television programs have yielded a consistent pattern of findings; from the age of 1 to the age of

Issues in Human Development
Who Is the Hyperactive Child?

 As children grow up, improvement can be expected in their span of attention, resistance to distraction, and ability to attend selectively to the world around them. However, some children—between 3 and 5 percent of the population—do not show developmental improvement in these areas. These children, about 90 percent of whom are boys, suffer from what is known as *attention-deficit hyperactivity disorder* (Diagnostic and Statistical Manual of Mental Disorders, III-R, 1987).

Attention-deficit hyperactivity disorder (ADHD) is said to be present when a child gives signs of (1) developmentally immature forms of *inattention* (e.g., doesn't listen well, is easily distracted, is unable to concentrate on schoolwork, doesn't finish projects); (2) *impulsivity* (e.g., acts before thinking, is unable to wait for a turn in group games, needs much supervision, disrupts the class); (3) *hyperactivity* (e.g., cannot sit still, runs about excessively, moves excessively during sleep). Furthermore, for a diagnosis of ADHD, these conditions must be present for at least 6 months and must not be attributable to any specific known mental disorder or to mental retardation (American Psychiatric Association, 1980).

Perhaps it is not surprising that the presence of such attentional problems has a significant impact on the social environment in which a child operates. ADHD children often are rejected by their peers (Klein & Young, 1979; Mainville & Friedman, 1976). They are more likely than the average child to experience conflict with siblings (Mash & Johnston, 1980) and to have stricter controls placed on them by their parents (Cunningham & Barkley, 1979). Teachers are more intense and more controlling when dealing with an ADHD child, as well as with other children in a classroom in which an ADHD child is present (Whalen, Henker, & Dotemoto, 1980).

The actual causes of attention-deficit hyperactivity disorder are difficult to determine (Kohn, 1989; Routh, 1986). Some evidence indicates that genetic factors may be involved. For example, identical twins seem to resemble each other in level of distractibility (Torgersen & Kringlen, 1978), and adopted children of hyperactive parents are often hyperactive too, even if the adoptive parents are not (Cunningham, Cadoret, Loftus, & Edwards, 1975). Brain damage has been offered as a possible explanation of ADHD, but the relationship between the disorder and any specific brain damage is unclear,

5, attention to television increases dramatically (Alwitt, Anderson, Lorch, & Levin, 1980; Anderson & Levin, 1976; Anderson, Lorch, Field, Collins, & Nathan, 1986). Typical of such research is a study by Anderson and Levin (1976) of children's attention to a "Sesame Street" program. Each child was observed with his or her parent in a room containing a television set as well as refreshments and interesting toys. The "Sesame Street" videotape was played, and the child was free to watch or not as desired. Spontaneous attention to the program increased with age; for example, the 1-year-olds spent only 15–20 percent of the time in the room looking at the television set, while the 4-year-olds watched the program for about 55 percent of the total time they were in the room. The authors also found that this pattern closely matched the children's television viewing patterns at home, as indicated on questionnaires completed by the parents. Children were most attentive, incidentally, when program segments were short rather than prolonged, when animation and lively music were used, and when women rather than men were on the screen.

and many brain-damaged children do not show evidence of ADHD (Routh, 1986).

Diet has been studied extensively as a possible influence on the kind of hyperactive behavior found in ADHD children. For example, Feingold (1975) suggested that hyperactivity results from allergic reactions to artificial flavors and colors in foods, and, in fact, parents are often convinced that dietary factors are responsible for their children's behavior disorders (Crook, 1980). Although the evidence is far from complete, some studies point to links between food dyes and hyperactivity (Weiss et al., 1980) and between sugar and hyperactivity (Prinz, Roberts, & Hartman, 1980).

Finally, some psychologists believe that the quality of early parent-child interaction plays a role in the appearance of hyperactive behavior. For example, Sroufe and Jacobvitz (1989) followed a group of children from birth to age 8 and found that children later diagnosed as hyperactive had been handled differently during infancy than other children were: Their caretakers were unable to regulate the arousal levels of these infants, and often overstimulated them at precisely the times when they were excited and needed to be calmed down. The researchers suggested that hyperactive children do not learn, as other children do, to bring themselves back to a normal state when their behaviors border on the "out of control."

Whatever the causes of attention-deficit hyperactivity disorder, the problem is a serious one, not only because of the negative social consequences, but because the condition seems to carry over into adolescence and adulthood (Routh, 1986). Among adolescents and adults, ADHD has been associated with lowered self-esteem, difficulties in academic achievement, and even alcohol abuse (Routh, 1986).

To illustrate the seriousness of the problem, approximately 80 percent of hyperactive children in the United States are being treated with medication—typically the drug Ritalin—with the result that estimates suggest that in the year 1990 nearly 1 million children in this country were using such a drug (Kohn, 1989; Sroufe, 1989).

The developmental increase in preschoolers' attention to television has usually been attributed to cognitive changes in the children themselves. That is, as children develop, they are better able to understand what they are watching, and because the material is increasingly comprehensible, they are increasingly likely to attend to it (Anderson & Lorch, 1983; Anderson et al., 1986). A person's knowledge base and degree of familiarity with what is perceived certainly influence the efficiency of attentional processes (Olson & Sherman, 1983).

Developmental changes in visual attention to television during the school years have rarely been examined, and when studies have been done, the results are inconsistent. In one of the most extensive studies of this type, Anderson et al. (1986) observed television viewing patterns in the homes of 99 families, with an age range of family members from infancy to 62 years. The actual number of hours of television watching each week increased up to the age of 10 (an average of 13 hours) and then declined gradually through adolescence and into adulthood. However, the percentage of visual

From the time children are 1 year old until they reach age 5, they dramatically increase their attention to television viewing.

attention—the amount of time a child actually attended to television out of the total time spent in a room with the television set on—increased only throughout the preschool years and then leveled off after the age of 6, indicating again the improvement in the efficiency of attention throughout the preschool years. What the authors observed is what irritates so many parents—the television set is often playing when nobody is actually attending to it. In fact, about 15 percent of the time the set was on, no one was even present in the room (Anderson et al., 1986)!

Adulthood and Old Age

Studies of age differences in attention during adulthood have yielded a number of consistent findings. In the first place, young adults are superior to those beyond the age of 60 on tasks requiring *selective attention* to the environment, a pattern illustrated by a selective search task devised by Rabbitt (1965). Adults of different ages were shown "target" letters and then asked to sort cards according to whether a target letter did or did not appear on them. The amount of irrelevant information was varied by the appearance on the cards of different numbers of nontarget distractor letters; some cards had no distractor letters, some had one, some two, and some eight. An increase in the number of distractor letters meant an increase in the amount of irrelevant information that had to be ignored when solving the problem, and people of all ages were slower at sorting the cards that had many rather than few distractors. However, the increase in the number of distractors slowed the performance of the elderly more than that of the young, leading Rabbitt (1965) to conclude that older adults are not as efficient at attending selectively as young adults are.

Young adults also seem to have a greater overall attentional capacity, as indicated in research on divided attention, such as the dichotic listening experiments described earlier (Hoyer & Plude, 1980). If challenged to attend simultaneously to two unfamiliar sources of information, young adults are better able to do so than older ones. Apparently, the attentional capacity of older adults is more easily depleted. A key point to remember, however, is that we are speaking here of effortful rather than automatic processing; automatic processing does not so easily overload a person's attentional capacity. Age differences in automatic processing, involving practiced skills that demand little conscious attention, are minimal if they exist at all (Hoyer & Plude, 1980; Plude & Hoyer, 1985).

How significant are the attentional changes of adulthood in a person's everyday life? Probably not at all. On the one hand, with advancing age the effortful components of attention consume an increasingly larger proportion of an individual's declining attentional capacity. But the automatic components, which are less taxing on attentional capacity, depend on experience, and experience increases with age. The result is that even though older adults may have diminished attentional capacity, they have accumulated a wealth of life and work experiences, so many of what were initially attention-demanding activities eventually become habitual or automatic. Thus, the limits of attentional capacity may be lower as people age, but the increasing familiarity of the routines of everyday life may actually make those limits less likely to be reached.

LEARNING

If Larry, the sixth grader whose story opened this chapter, had received an A on his history exam instead of a failing grade, could his teacher be certain that he had learned the course material well? Perhaps, but perhaps not! Learning, which is said to occur when certain experiences bring about a change in behavior, is a mental *process,* a component of what we have been describing as an overall system of processing information. Because it is a process, learning itself is not directly observable.

Larry's experiences were certainly observable: He attended his history class, read his book, did his homework, and studied for the exam. His behavior—his performance on the test—was also observable. But for learning to have taken place, the experiences would have to have *caused* the behavior. Larry's teacher assumes that they did, and that he learned his history. But the boy might have learned nothing and cheated on the exam, or maybe he simply was a lucky guesser! The point is that learning cannot be seen but must always be assumed, and a person's actual performance may or may not provide an accurate measure of what has been learned.

We turn now to a discussion of the basic principles of several forms of learning and of the research dealing with these types of learning at various points in the span of human life.

Conditioning

The simplest form of learning is conditioning. In fact, conditioning studies comprised much of the early research on the processes of learning, and the "participants" in these studies were usually lower animals rather than human beings. Nevertheless, the conditioning literature, and particularly the literature on operant conditioning, offers useful information for understanding the acquisition of behaviors in the developing human being.

Principles of Conditioning

Classical conditioning

A basic form of learning involving reflexive behavior, in which two stimuli become associated when presented at the same point in time.

The technique of **classical conditioning** was first investigated by the Russian physiologist Ivan Pavlov (1849–1936), who placed dogs in a harness and trained them to salivate each time they heard a tone produced by a tuning fork. The training was accomplished by presenting the sound of the tuning fork at approximately the same time that food powder was inserted into the dogs' mouths. Salivation in response to the food powder is an automatic response, whereas salivation to the sound of a tuning fork obviously is not. After the food powder and the tuning fork were presented simultaneously for a consecutive number of trials, the dogs came to associate the two stimuli, so the sound of the tuning fork alone produced salivation.

Pavlov referred to the food powder in his experiment as the *unconditioned stimulus* (UCS), and the salivation to the food powder as the *unconditioned response* (UCR). This is an unconditioned, or unlearned, stimulus-response connection because it occurs reflexively without the necessity of learning. The sound of the tuning fork in Pavlov's experiment was referred to as the *conditioned stimulus* (CS), and the salivation response to the sound was called the *conditioned response* (CR). The CS-CR connection obviously is learned, because it simply would not occur naturally. The actual learning in the classical conditioning procedure involves the association of the UCS with the CS (the food powder and the tone in this case) so that both eventually elicit similar responses (see Figure 6.2).

The conditioned behavior will not continue indefinitely. The conditioned dogs would not salivate every time they heard a certain tone on a tuning fork for the rest of their lives. In fact, if the CS is presented alone, without the

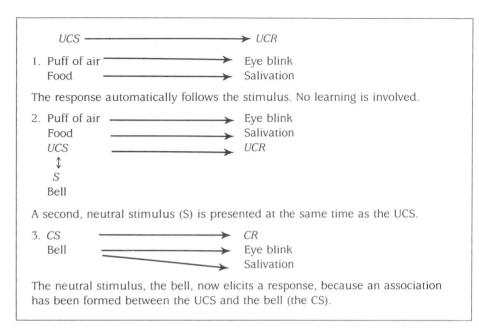

The neutral stimulus, the bell, now elicits a response, because an association has been formed between the UCS and the bell (the CS).

Figure 6.2
Classical Conditioning

reinforcement of the UCS, the CS soon will lose its effectiveness as an elicitor of a CR. This wearing away of the CS-UCS connection is referred to as *extinction.*

As will be seen in the discussion of learning in childhood, human beings are susceptible to classical conditioning. Consider for now the illustrative case of Albert in the classic experiment by Watson and Rayner (1920). Albert was a contented infant who showed very little fear. He exhibited no fear when a laboratory rat was introduced into the room in which he was playing. However, Albert soon was conditioned to respond with great distress to the rat. An extremely jarring and unpleasant sound (UCS) was produced each time the rat appeared. The sound elicited a distress response in Albert (UCR), and eventually the rat itself became a CS that produced a similar distress response in the child. The very sight of the rat, which was formerly a neutral stimulus, was enough to make Albert cry with fright.

Although Albert is a famous case in the annals of psychology, classical conditioning generally is thought to be of little significance to a study of human learning, because it is a somewhat mechanical procedure that relies on involuntary responses. Of greater significance is the concept of operant conditioning.

Operant conditioning, also referred to as instrumental conditioning, developed from the research of Edward L. Thorndike (1874–1949), one of

Chapter Six

the pioneers of American psychology. In 1905, Thorndike produced a doctoral dissertation that dealt with the behavior of hungry cats as they attempted to free themselves from a puzzle box to reach a supply of food on the outside. Each cat was placed alone in the box, and the only way it could escape was to press a latch that would open the door. The cat would make a number of responses, and eventually would manage to strike the latch. When it did so, the door would open, and the cat would receive its earned reward of food. The cat then was placed back in the box for another trial until it had fully learned the task.

Thorndike maintained that the cats learned to press the latch because a connection gradually was established between a stimulus, which might be the animal's hunger or the sight of the food, and the response of pressing the latch. Why was this particular stimulus-response bond established while other bonds (e.g., between the stimulus of food and the response of scratching the floor) were not? Thorndike maintained that what bonded the stimulus with the correct response was the reinforcement of being rewarded. The bonding occurred because of what he described as the *law of effect*—the basic tenet of operant conditioning—which states that responses followed by reinforcement are increasingly likely to be repeated.

Positive and Negative Reinforcement.   What follows an action and increases the likelihood that the action will be repeated is termed *reinforcement.* We speak of reinforcement as either positive or negative. Positive reinforcement is synonymous with reward—something of value (e.g., a piece of food, candy, or praise) is given to the learner. Negative reinforcement involves the removal of an unpleasant stimulus, as when a rat is exposed to an electric shock until it makes a desired response, after which the electricity is turned off. In a sense, positive and negative reinforcement are simply different ways of looking at the same behavioral outcome. Whether a pleasant stimulus is given or an unpleasant one is taken away, the net result is the same: The future likelihood of the behavior's being emitted has been increased.

Punishment.   Another behavioral outcome that a learner may experience is *punishment,* which must not be confused with negative reinforcement. The intent of punishment is to *decrease* the likelihood of a future occurrence of a behavior, and not to increase it, as either type of reinforcement is intended to do.

Punishment can certainly put a stop to unwanted behaviors. However, it generally is seen as less effective than reinforcement for a number of reasons. First, punishment may raise the learner's anxiety level to such a point that learning is actually inhibited. Second, punishment may teach the learner what not to do while failing to teach appropriate behavior. People can learn from their mistakes, but they can learn much more efficiently from their successes. Third, the threat of punishment often encourages the learner to make an avoidance response, a move designed to avoid the

---

Law of effect
The principle of learning that states that behaviors followed by reinforcement are likely to be maintained or increased.

Reinforcement
An outcome that follows a behavior and increases the likelihood that the behavior will occur in the future.

Punishment
An outcome that follows a behavior and decreases the likelihood that the behavior will occur in the future.

punishing authority. Parents who try to instill virtue in children merely by punishing instances of the opposite vice may raise a child who, instead of being virtuous, is skilled at avoiding the parents' notice while practicing the vice.

Timing of Reinforcement or Punishment. To be effective, reinforcement must be administered as soon as possible after the behavior is emitted; the longer the delay, the poorer will be the performance of the learned response (Logan, 1976). If Thorndike's cats had been rewarded with food for pressing the latch even a few minutes after the action was taken, the stimulus-response connection would not have been made. A similar pattern applies to the use of punishment as a means of influencing behavior. Consider the case of a woman who arrives home from work to discover that her dog chewed a hole in the sofa sometime during the day. She finds the dog in the kitchen innocently drinking from a pan of water, and she proceeds to slap the dog for its unacceptable sofa-chewing behavior. What has the dog learned from the punishment? Perhaps it has learned not to drink water when its mistress comes home.

Schedules of Reinforcement. A second consideration for those who use the operant conditioning technique concerns the reinforcement schedule. Reinforcement may be given after every response (continuous reinforcement) or only occasionally (intermittent, or partial, reinforcement).

Schedules of reinforcement, and particularly the intermittent schedule, are of much interest to those engaged in animal research. However, some useful applications for human development are apparent as well. Learning occurs more rapidly if a continuous schedule of reinforcement is used, but extinction occurs more slowly if an intermittent schedule is used—the latter phenomenon is known as the partial reinforcement effect (Gleitman, 1986). Therefore, the fastest and most durable learning apparently occurs when reinforcement is continuous at first but gradually decreases in frequency once the task has been mastered. A child should not expect to be rewarded for desired behaviors every time those behaviors are emitted; such expectation may result in dependence on reward and the fairly rapid extinction of the behavior when the rewards are not forthcoming.

Defining Reward and Punishment. In addition to questions about timing and schedules of reinforcement, many questions may be asked about the nature of reward and punishment themselves. An experimental psychologist may be fairly certain that an animal deprived of food for a period of time will see food as an extremely satisfying reward. Human beings, however, are not so predictable. What is rewarding to one may not be rewarding to another; in fact, what is intended as punishment often may be seen as a reward, and vice versa. Many an adult will never forget the painful embarrassment of being publicly singled out by an elementary school teacher as a positive example to the rest of the children in the class. Praise was the teacher's intended reward, but in fact the child may have been punished by the public recognition and by later teasing from classmates. The reverse may occur in the case of the child who views verbal or even physical punishment from a parent or teacher as rewarding because it provides needed attention.

Classical Versus Operant Conditioning.   Operant conditioning differs from classical conditioning in two major ways. First, classical conditioning involves primarily reflexive behavior, whereas operant conditioning deals with voluntary behavior. Second, as noted earlier, operant conditioning depends on the law of effect; the learner must emit a response, the future occurrence of which is influenced by the consequences of that response. In other words, the learner must act to receive the reward or punishment. Classical conditioning relies primarily on the **law of contiguity,** in that the learning occurs because of the simple association of the CS and UCS. In a sense, the reinforcer in classical conditioning is the UCS, but the learner's involuntary response does not lead to any reinforcement.

Classical and operant conditioning are neither easily comparable (because they involve essentially different forms of learning) nor easily separable. Frequently, classical conditioning takes place during the course of operant conditioning (Ellis, Bennett, Daniel, & Rickert, 1979); an example of this confusion will be considered in the discussion of conditioning during infancy.

Developmental Research on Conditioning

The vast majority of the studies of classical conditioning in humans have involved either infants or college students (Reese, 1976). In fact, most of the infant conditioning research has focused on the very young infant; few studies have included infants over the age of 5 months (Hirschman, Melamed, & Oliver, 1982).

Classical conditioning appears to be possible with the newborn infant, but it has been difficult to demonstrate. As an example, Lipsitt, Kaye, and Bosack (1966) inserted a rubber tube into the mouth of infants ranging from 1½ to 4 days old and presented sweetened water through the tube, which caused the infants to begin sucking. The sweetened water was the UCS and the sucking was the UCR. Eventually, the tube itself elicited the sucking response, even though no water was fed through it. Thus, the tube became a CS producing a CR (sucking).

On the surface, one might readily conclude that Lipsitt, Kaye, and Bosack were able to demonstrate classical conditioning in infants, but did they in fact do so? Sameroff (1971) later pointed out that the sucking response to the rubber tube would have occurred even without the association with sweetened water, and therefore the rubber tube is not a pure CS in the classical sense. In other words, the connection between the

Law of contiguity
The principle that learning occurs because two stimuli presented at the same time become associated in the mind of the learner.

tube and the sweet liquid may have made the tube a more powerful inducer of the sucking response, but the tube was never a completely neutral stimulus, as the CS should have been to demonstrate that classical conditioning had taken place.

In a further comment on the Lipsitt, Kaye, and Bosack study, Reese (1976) noted that the findings are interesting from a technical standpoint but have little practical value. They simply offer a scientific demonstration of what most parents already know: Infants usually become conditioned to the sight of a bottle or to the sounds made by the caretaker in preparing the bottle, evidenced by the fact that they engage in anticipatory sucking responses. In other words, particular sights or sounds become CSs when associated with food (a powerful UCS for a hungry infant).

Other studies of conditioning in the newborn have used heart rate (for example, Clifton, 1974a, 1974b), reflexive head turning (Papousek, 1967), and reflexive motor activity (Polikanina, 1961) as the CRs. Results from such studies have been mixed, with greater conditioning success demonstrated in studies of 3- to 4-week-old infants than in studies of newborns (Sameroff, 1971). However, classical conditioning of young infants has been successful often enough to indicate that it can be demonstrated if the circumstances are appropriate (Hirschman et al., 1982).

Although classical conditioning appears to be possible with young infants, operant conditioning is considerably easier to demonstrate (Hirschman et al., 1982; Sameroff & Cavanaugh, 1979). For example, the design of the Lipsitt, Kaye, and Bosack (1966) study referred to earlier included an operant as well as a classical conditioning aspect. Classical conditioning

Would this child sucking reflexively (UCR) when presented with milk (UCS) also suck (CR) when presented with the nipple alone (CS)? If so, classical conditioning may have been demonstrated. On the other hand, no conditioning can be said to have occurred unless the nipple was truly a neutral stimulus.

Applying Our Knowledge
Conditioning as Therapy: Behavior Modification

 Operant conditioning principles have been used extensively with both normal and disturbed people of all ages to bring about desired behavioral changes. The application of these principles of "therapeutic" purposes has been referred to as behavior modification. As an example of this procedure, consider the case of Danny, a 6-year-old who had been brought by his parents to a child development clinic because he was bossy and manipulative. He ate when he wanted to, went to bed when he wanted to, and generally ran the household to his own liking. Whenever his parents confronted him, he would scream until they relented. The psychologists at the child development clinic attempted to train Danny's mother in the effective use of behavior modification—the application of operant conditioning procedures to the solution of behavioral problems. Danny's mother was told to ignore completely every instance of what was described as commanding behavior, for example, when Danny said, "You go over there, and I'll stay here!" and to respond only to Danny's cooperative behavior. In other words, she was taught to reward the behavior she wished to see continue and to ignore that which she wished to eliminate. The results of the behavior therapy with Danny were precisely as

would be predicted from a knowledge of operant conditioning principles. Danny's cooperative behavior (the rewarded behavior) increased noticeably, and his commanding behavior decreased. Furthermore, Danny's mother reported that as the offensive behavior diminished, she felt increasingly comfortable in her interactions with her son. Danny's case illustrates two important concepts. First, operant conditioning principles can be effective in solving common behavioral problems. Second, operant conditioning occurs even when we are unaware of using it. Danny's mother changed her reinforcement patterns after she was taught to do so. Obviously, she had been reinforcing Danny all along, but for the wrong behaviors. She had been responding to him when he made manipulative demands and thus had rewarded unacceptable behavior. The training session forced her to realize that she had been responding inappropriately to her son by rewarding him for his bossiness.

Source: R. G. Wahler, G. H. Winkel, R. L. Peterson, & D. C. Morrison. Mothers as behavior therapists for their own children. In H. C. Quay (Ed.), *Children's behavior disorders.* New York: Van Nostrand Reinhold, 1968, pp. 92–95.

would have been demonstrated if the UCR of sucking elicited by the UCS of sweetened water later could have been elicited by a previously neutral stimulus because of its association with the sweetened water. Because the tube may not have been a previously neutral stimulus, pure classical conditioning was difficult to demonstrate. Nevertheless, operant conditioning clearly occurred in this study: The infants increased their rate of sucking to the rubber tube after the sweetened water was introduced. In other words, because sucking was rewarded with sweetened water, the incidence of sucking increased.

Siqueland and DeLucia (1969) also conditioned young infants to increase their sucking rates by rewarding them not with food, but with the chance to look at an interesting visual display. They found that 4-month-old infants will suck more vigorously on a nipple if their sucking seems to produce an interesting visual display (e.g., cartoon figures, human faces) on a screen positioned directly in front of them. The Siqueland and DeLucia study seems to demonstrate not only that infants are susceptible to operant conditioning, but also that they seem to enjoy a stimulating visual display.

Other studies of infant operant conditioning have demonstrated successful conditioning of smiling (Brackbill, 1958), vocalization (Rheingold, Gewirtz, & Ross, 1959; Smith & Smith, 1962; Weisberg, 1963), and motor responses such as eye movements and head turning (Siqueland, 1964).

Clearly, a variety of human behaviors can be conditioned, even during the first year of life. However, because conditioning principles are age irrelevant (that is, the age of the learner, in theory at least, should have no effect on the learning process), we will not attempt a developmental analysis of human conditioning, other than to set a lower limit in infancy and to say a few words now about research on conditioning among elderly adults. Keep in mind, however, that human adult conditioning studies are somewhat limited in usefulness and scope because (1) relatively little research has been done in this area, and (2) the applicability of research on the conditioned reflex to real-life situations is unclear. However, some studies are worthy of mention because they may shed light on the loss of reactivity in later life.

In one of the earlier studies on conditioning with adults of different ages, Braun and Geiselhart (1959) conditioned a young group (18 to 25 years) and an older group (62 to 84 years) on the blink response. Not only was it easier to condition the younger subjects, but it was also easier to extinguish the behavior. The older persons took longer to associate the increasing brightness of a disk (CS) with a puff of air delivered to the eye (UCS), and it took them longer to forget the association once it had been made.

Similar results were obtained in later studies (for example, Botwinick & Kornetsky, 1960; Kimble & Pennypacker, 1963; Shmavonian, Miller, & Cohen, 1970; Solyom & Barik, 1965) with human subjects. Summarizing these data, Botwinick (1978) and, later, Perlmutter and List (1982) suggested that older persons are less reactive than younger ones. Whether this is a result of increased susceptibility to adaptation of reflexes, as suggested by Kimble and Pennypacker (1963); lessened awareness of sensory cues, as suggested by Solyom and Barik (1965); or a general lowered arousal level is unclear. It is clear, however, that elderly human beings cannot be conditioned as easily as younger ones.

Mediation Theory: Beyond Conditioning

Conditioning principles may indeed be age irrelevant; human beings of all ages may readily form associations between UCSs and CSs, and work diligently to earn rewards and avoid punishments. However, a major developmental change occurs in susceptibility to conditioning—a change first described by psychologists Howard and Tracey Kendler (1963) more than a quarter of a century ago. Comprehending the significance of the Kendlers' work requires an understanding of the reversal learning experi-

Chapter Six

ments they carried out. Consider the shapes in Figure 6.3. They differ in the dimensions of size and color. Imagine that a child is presented with various pairs of these figures (large white, small black; large black, small white; large black, small black; etc.) over a series of trials and told that he or she must learn which member of the pair the experimenter has designated as the correct one. The experimenter will indicate each time a correct choice is made.

Because the experimenter has decided that the smaller figure will always be correct, regardless of color, the child will soon learn only to respond to the small ones, because such responses are the only ones that will be rewarded. However, to complicate the issue, after the child has learned to choose correctly, the experimenter changes the rules. Now only the large figures will be rewarded. This condition is what the Kendlers called a ***reversal shift,*** because the experimenter now is rewarding the opposite figure, but in the same dimension (see Figure 6.4). In contrast, if the new rule were to change from rewarding small figures to rewarding black figures,

Reversal shift

A form of discrimination learning in which the learner is initially rewarded for responding to one example of a particular dimension and is later rewarded for responding to an opposite example of the same dimension.

Figure 6.3
Stimuli Used in the Kendler Reversal Learning Task

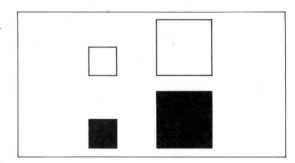

Figure 6.4
Schematic Representation of Reversal Shift and Nonreversal Shift Problems

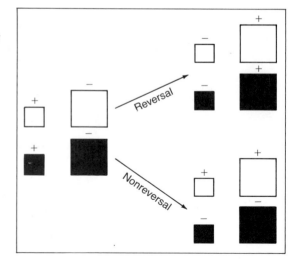

it would constitute a nonreversal shift in learning, because a new dimension (color) would be rewarded rather than simply the reverse figure in the previously rewarded dimension (size).

Which of the two—the reversal shift or the nonreversal shift—is easier to learn? According to basic operant conditioning principles, the nonreversal shift should be easier, because the learner already has been conditioned to respond positively to half of the new stimuli (the small black squares) designated as correct in the nonreversal condition. The learner needs only to unlearn the response to small white squares and learn to respond to large black squares instead.

In fact, rats and young children behave precisely as conditioning principles would predict. They find nonreversal shifts easier to learn than reversal shifts. However, human beings over the age of 5 or 6 typically find the reversal shift the easier to learn of the two. This is because the older child or adult, rather than blindly responding to the rewarded stimuli as a rat or a young child might do, first responds internally to the dimension of size; the internal response (size) must be changed in the case of a nonreversal shift, but not in the case of the simple reversal. This internal response is a mediating response, which comes between the presentation of the stimulus and the external response to it. Thus the Kendler's theory became known as ***mediation theory.***

Mediation theory
A theory that attempts to explain developmental differences in human learning by suggesting that internal "mediating" responses come between an external stimulus and an external response.

The ability to use mediating response radically alters the nature of the learning situation and sharply distinguishes between the human and animal response in a learning situation. The Kendlers' work highlighted the need to develop more sophisticated measures of human learning than are used with pigeons or rats because something occurs in the human thought process that rats are not capable of—whether this activity is referred to as internal responding, mediation, or concept formation. The Kendlers also emphasized the developmental aspect of human learning by discovering the age-related change in reversal learning. Finally, the Kendlers' work has generated a large amount of supporting data over the past 20 years—so much so that the classical stimulus-response explanations of human learning are no longer seen as totally adequate (Diamond, 1982). Simply put, in some situations human beings do not continuously repeat previously rewarded behavior, but instead use mental strategies to determine which behavior will be appropriate in the future. An adult who tells a joke at a party and is rewarded by laughter is unlikely to repeat the joke immediately again. Young children might; in fact, they often do.

Social Learning

Parents are often disconcerted to see their children engaging in behaviors that the parents definitely did not—or did not intend to—teach them. Of course, much learning occurs not by direct reinforcement at all, but as a result of observing other people's behavior, as well as by observing the

Observational learning
Learning that results from the observation of the behavior of others and its consequences.

Cognitive social learning
Learning characterized by imitation of, or identification with, observed models.

consequences of that behavior. Learning that occurs in this manner has been referred to as *observational learning;* the broader term used to describe any type of learning from a model, whether reinforcement is evident or not, is *cognitive social learning* (Bandura, 1969, 1977, 1986).

Basic Principles

In its simplest sense, social learning involves the application of operant conditioning procedures to the social arena. The early social learning studies (for example, Bandura, 1965; Bandura, Ross, & Ross, 1963a, 1963b, 1963c), some of which will be discussed later in this chapter, focused on the effects on the learner of watching a model receive reinforcement for specific behaviors. As will be shown, observers are more likely to imitate the rewarded behaviors of models than the unrewarded ones. However, observational learning has been found to go far beyond learning based on vicarious reinforcement (that is, the reinforcement received by the model.) As Bandura (1986) noted, children often imitate a model's behaviors when no reinforcement of any kind is evident. They often fail to imitate a model immediately, but later can be found at play engaged in a variety of imitative behaviors. To complicate the issue even further, imitation of a model does not guarantee that any learning has taken place. As the later discussion of the effects of television on children's aggressive behavior will show, imitation may not indicate learning, but rather may result from social facilitation. Previously learned behaviors are freely exhibited because the model has shown the observer that such behaviors are permissible.

Bandura (1986) outlined the social learning view of observational learning by dividing the actual learning into four necessary subprocesses: attentional, retention, motor reproduction, and motivational processes (see Figure 6.5). Attentional processes must be involved in observational learning, because even though the learner is exposed to a variety of experiences, only some features of observed behavior are modeled. The features that tend to be modeled most often are those that are distinctive enough to be easily recognized, those that occur frequently, those that are exhibited by a highly valued model, those that have been reinforced in the past, and so on.

It would be inappropriate here to try to describe all the characteristics of the model and of the observer that cause certain modeled behaviors to be singled out for imitation. However, an example of this attentional subprocess will be given later in this chapter in the discussion of the effects of status and perceived power of an adult model on children's imitative behavior.

The second subprocess of observational learning is the process of retention. As noted earlier, learners often exhibit the behaviors of models not immediately after seeing them, but considerably later. Memory processes, therefore, are involved in observational learning. The learner must be able to encode the model's behavior and store it for later retrieval by some sort of rehearsal process.

The third type of subprocess involved in observational learning is the motor reproduction process—the physical capability of the learner to reproduce a model's behavior and the self-monitoring of such processes. For example, a child might watch a talented gymnast perform a routine on the high bar, but even if the activity was particularly fascinating to the child and even if the child could mentally remember the details of the exercise, learning would not be said to have taken place if the child was physically unable to reproduce the routine.

Finally, the motivational process is involved in observational learning. Here Bandura (1986) was speaking of reinforcement, whether direct, vicarious, or self-administered. Bandura noted that even after a modeled behavior has been carefully attended to, remembered, and reproduced, the learning hardly ever may be activated if it is not reinforced. A child or adult may learn a variety of behaviors from a model but may not dare to exhibit those behaviors for fear of social disapproval.

Developmental Research on Social Learning

Even an infant is capable of learning by observing the behavior of other people. Jean Piaget (1896–1980), the Swiss biologist-philosopher whose extensive work on children's cognitive development will be described at

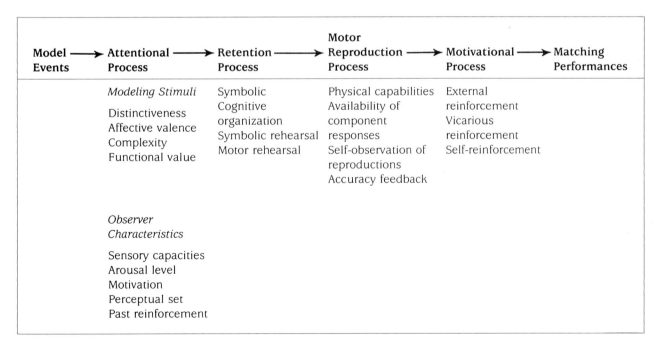

Model Events	→	Attentional Process	→	Retention Process	→	Motor Reproduction Process	→	Motivational Process	→	Matching Performances
		Modeling Stimuli Distinctiveness Affective valence Complexity Functional value		Symbolic Cognitive organization Symbolic rehearsal Motor rehearsal		Physical capabilities Availability of component responses Self-observation of reproductions Accuracy feedback		External reinforcement Vicarious reinforcement Self-reinforcement		
		Observer Characteristics Sensory capacities Arousal level Motivation Perceptual set Past reinforcement								

Figure 6.5

Subprocesses in the Social Learning View of Observational Learning

Source: From A. Bandura (Ed.). *Psychological Modeling: Conflicting Theories.* Reprinted by permission of the Publishers Lieber-Atherton Inc., Copyright 1971. All rights reserved.

length in Chapter 7, noted that his son Laurent engaged in imitative behavior at 2½ months. Piaget (1962) wrote that Laurent

> imitated me as soon as I uttered sounds identical with his own, or even when it was merely my intonation which recalled his. He again imitated me even when he had not been crooning himself immediately before. He began by smiling, then made an effort with his mouth open (remaining silent for a moment) and only then produced a sound. Such a behavior clearly indicates the existence of a definite attempt at imitation. (Piaget, 1962, p. 9)

Even though Piaget described his son's behavior as imitative, he clearly did not consider it a genuine example of social learning. Instead, he argued that it was a "pre-imitative" behavior—a forerunner of true imitation—because the child could imitate the adult only insofar as the adult first imitated the child's behavior. Piaget made sounds identical to those Laurent had made previously, and only then did Laurent "imitate" his father's sounds. In a sense, the child did not distinguish between his own sounds and those made by his father (Flavell, 1963; Piaget, 1962).

The question of when genuine imitations first occur in the human infant has become controversial in recent years. Piaget (1962) did not see genuine imitation as occurring before 7 or 8 months of age, but not all psychologists agree with Piaget's assessment. Meltzoff and Moore (1977, 1983) argued that even a newborn baby will spontaneously imitate such adult behaviors as sticking out the tongue or opening and closing the mouth. To demonstrate this phenomenon, they placed newborn babies in a semireclining position in an infant seat in a darkened room. The babies were then presented with a spotlighted adult face about 10 inches away from their own. The adult's mouth would slowly open and close four times during a 20-second period, then the adult would remain passive, then slowly extend and withdraw the tongue four times, then remain passive, and so on. The infants' facial gestures were recorded on videotape, and analysis of the tapes showed that the babies opened their mouths most often during the experimenter's mouth-opening periods and stuck out their tongues most often during the tongue protrusion periods. Meltzoff and Moore (1983) interpreted their findings as indicating true imitation at a very early age.

Although their actual findings are not in question, controversy continues over whether genuine imitation occurred in the Meltzoff and Moore (1977, 1983) studies. Critics argue that what occurred was in reality a reflexive rather than an imitative act. For example, Jacobson (1979) found that the 6- to 14-week-old infants she tested do in fact stick out their tongues when an adult first demonstrates this behavior, but they also stick out their tongues when presented with such objects as a moving pen or a dangling ring. She suggested that perhaps the mouth and tongue movements are not selective imitation at all but are adaptive feeding responses to any object that resembles a nipple.

In a later study, Abranavel and Sigafoos (1984) found that some 4- to 6-week-old infants did stick out their tongues following identical behaviors by the experimenter, but most did not. Furthermore, the tendency to engage in imitative tongue movements did not improve with age, as might be expected if genuine selective imitation were really occurring. Tongue protrusion actually decreased with age from 4 to 21 weeks, leading the authors to echo Jacobson's (1979) conclusion that reflex mechanisms of a sort may have been in operation in the case of the younger infants.

Answers to the question of whether very young infants selectively and intentionally imitate the behaviors of adult models are still undetermined; perhaps, as Flavell (1985) suggested, a definitive answer is impossible. On the other hand, by 5 to 6 months of age, genuine imitation of adult models does occur, and this imitation is intentional, selective, and nonreflexive (Kaye, 1982; Kaye & Marcus, 1978). The mutual imitation that occurs throughout infancy, with parents and babies producing similar patterns of sounds and facial gestures (leaving aside the question of which one initiates the pattern), has significant social value. Uzgiris (1984) described mutual imitation, which increases throughout the first year of life, as a meaningful shared experience that enhances the bonds of attachment between infant and parent. Furthermore, when parents imitate their infants' behaviors, the likelihood increases that the infants will attempt to imitate them in turn (Bandura, 1986; Kauffman, Gordon, & Baker, 1978).

As children develop, they are capable of increasingly sophisticated imitations. McCall, Parke, and Kavanaugh (1977) placed infants aged 12, 15, 18, and 24 months in a playroom with a variety of toys (rattles, bells, a toy telephone, a stuffed animal, a toy car, etc.). The infants first were observed playing spontaneously and then after they had watched an adult modeling certain prescribed behaviors with the toys. Imitation of adult behavior was found at all ages tested, although perfect imitation was never seen earlier

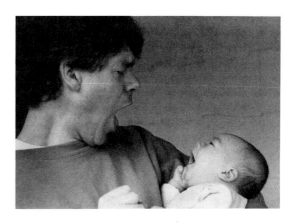

Contrary to what people once believed, even young infants can imitate adult behavior. This 6-month-old imitates his father's facial gestures quite well.

than 18 months of age. In general, imitative ability increased regularly from the youngest to the oldest group of children in the study.

Noting that even 1-year-olds are exposed to the influence of television, McCall, Parke, and Kavanaugh (1977) extended their investigation to examine the influence of televised models on the imitative behavior of young children. Children aged 18, 24, and 36 months either watched a videotape of an adult model playing with toys in a particular manner or watched a live adult model engaged in the identical activity. They then were observed playing with toys by themselves to determine whether social learning had occurred. Live models were more effective in "teaching" the younger children, but by the age of 3, the differences between the conditions had virtually disappeared. The authors suggested that by the time a child is between 3 and 4 years of age, television models become potentially as effective in inducing social learning as live models.

In reality, of course, all models are not equally likely to be imitated by children. In an examination of the characteristics possessed by the most-imitated models, Bandura et al. (1963a) studied children ranging in age from 3 to 5 years who watched two adults in a playroom. One adult, designated as the controller, had the most attractive toys to play with, dispensed the snacks, and was clearly in charge of the situation. The other adult, the consumer, played a more passive role. The children later were asked to play a guessing game, which consisted of determining in which of two boxes the experimenter—in some cases the controller and in some cases the consumer—had hidden a picture sticker. The real object of the game, however, was to see if the children were more likely to imitate spontaneously the activities of an adult perceived as powerful than those of one who was dependent. As they demonstrated the guessing game for the children, the controller and the consumer engaged in different activities, used different words to verbalize the instructions, and even wore thinking caps of different colors to "help" them guess which box contained the sticker.

Bandura et al. (1963) found that children usually were more likely to imitate the behaviors of the controller and obviously identified with the source of rewarding power. Apparently, some models have a greater influence on children than others do. Extending these findings from the laboratory to the world at large, parents—who are the ultimate dispensers of rewards to children, the ultimate sources of status and control—should have a greater influence than any other models available.

A positive relationship between dominance and the likelihood of being imitated has been found in other studies as well. For example, in studies of peer imitation in nursery school children at play, children who most often attract the attention of other children are also the children most likely to be imitated (Abramovitch & Grusec, 1978; Grusec & Abramovitch, 1982; Hold, 1976). Grusec and Abramovitch (1982) also noted that the amount of imitation in preschool groups declined from age 3 to age 5. Furthermore,

Like mother, like daughter. A parent is a highly significant model in a child's life—a source of affection and a symbol of power.

they suggested that peer imitation serves as more than just a means of learning new behavior; it is also a powerful means of facilitating social interaction with peers. Models generally responded positively to being imitated, and by doing so, they rewarded their imitators. Apparently, even for preschool children, imitation is the sincerest form of flattery, and flattery may bring about friendly social interaction.

Television and Social Learning

A number of social learning studies have dealt with the effects of televised models on children's behavior (e.g., Bandura, 1965; Bandura et al., 1963a, 1963b; Friedrich & Stein, 1973; Hicks, 1965). In some of these studies, children observed a televised model's behavior and then witnessed the consequences of that behavior to the model (e.g., punishment for aggression). In other studies, no behavior consequences were shown. The findings from the television studies were fairly consistent: Children can learn by watching the televised behavior of others, and observing the consequence of a model's behavior has much the same effect as experiencing the consequences of one's own behavior (Stevenson, 1970).

The question of the influence of television models becomes controversial when the modeled behavior is aggressive. Since the early days of television, when a House of Representatives committee dealt with the issue in 1952, questions have been asked about the possible effects on children of watching televised violence. Commercial television continues to have a high level of violence, and much of this violence can be found in Saturday morning cartoons (see Table 6.1).

Studies investigating the effects of viewing televised violence have been fairly consistent: Children display higher levels of aggression after watching

Table 6.1
Incidents of Violence Per Hour in Saturday Morning Children's Programs on Network Television (September 18, 1989–January 20, 1990)

Program	Acts of Violence* Per Hour
Very High Violence	
Dungeons and Dragons (CBS)	122
Bugs Bunny and Tweety (ABC)	49
Slimer! and the Real Ghostbusters (ABC)	40
Captain N: The Game Master (NBC)	39
Adventures of Raggedy Ann and Andy (CBS)	36
Smurfs (NBC)	27
Alf (NBC)	23
Garfield and Friends (CBS)	21
High Violence	
Kissyfur (NBC)	20
Alf-Tales (NBC)	19
Gummi Bears/Winnie the Pooh (ABC)	19
Beetlejuice (ABC)	17
Karate Kid (NBC)	15
Low Violence	
Rude Dog and the Dweebs (CBS)	8
Pup Named Scooby Doo (ABC)	8
Jim Henson's Muppet Babies (CBS)	5
Camp Candy (NBC)	5
Weekend Special (ABC)	4
Saved by the Bell (NBC)	2
California Raisins (CBS)	2
Chipmunks (NBC)	1
Pee-Wee's Playhouse (CBS)	1
Storybreak (CBS)	0
Animal Crack-ups (ABC)	0

*Acts of violence are defined as hostile acts committed with the intention of hurting another person, or character.

Source: National Coalition on Television Violence, Champaign, IL.

live adult models engaged in aggression—particularly if those models are rewarded for their behavior (Bandura, 1965; Bandura et al., 1963b; Hicks, 1965). Children who watch much violence on television are most likely to approve of it (Dominick & Greenberg, 1972). Finally, children who watch a good deal of violent television programming are also likely to be quite aggressive in real life (Lefkowitz, Walder, & Eron, 1963), and their high level of aggression apparently stays with them into early adulthood (Lefkowitz, Eron, Walder, & Huesmann, 1972).

The available research does not support the conclusion that watching televised models of aggression actually *causes* children or adults to be aggressive. Children who witness acts of violence and then behave more aggressively may not have actually learned any new behaviors. They instead may have learned only that their previously learned aggressive behaviors are acceptable to display. When studies find that aggressive children are more likely than nonaggressive children to watch violence on television, might this not be an example of self-selection? Perhaps, instead of deciding that the television viewing brought about the aggression, one should ask whether the aggressive children simply sought out televised material that appealed to them.

It is probably more accurate to say that viewing televised aggression may facilitate real-life aggression rather than actually teach it. Friedrich and Stein (1973), for example, found that 3- to 5-year-old children exposed to 9 weeks of violent segments of the television cartoon shows "Batman" and "Superman" showed a definite reduction in self-control; they showed a loss in their tolerance for delay, as well as a decline in their willingness to obey rules. As might be expected, a loss of tolerance for frustration could increase the likelihood of aggressive episodes. Friedrich and Stein suggested that researchers should explore a variety of personality factors when they study the effects of aggressive models on children. They also reported a finding from their research that calls into question any simple casual connection between aggression and television viewing: Interpersonal aggression did not increase for all children exposed to violent programming, but only for those who were above average in aggression in the first place.

This section on the effects of television models on children's social learning will end on an optimistic note. Children also can learn much that is positive from watching television. In the Friedrich and Stein study just mentioned, one group of children watched not "Batman" but "Mister Rogers' Neighborhood" for 9 weeks. The latter program generally is recognized as one that promotes the values of friendship, sharing, cooperation, rule acceptance, understanding of others, and so on. The children who watched "Mister Rogers' Neighborhood" improved in such prosocial qualities as self-regulation, tolerance for delay, task persistence, and rule obedience—a pattern exactly opposite to what was found among the "Batman" group.

Studies of the influence of television on children's development have far-reaching social implications. Even though violent television programming has not been found to "teach" violence to children, such programming may create an atmosphere in which aggressive solutions to problems will dominate. Furthermore, television has a remarkable (and relatively unexplored) potential for bringing about positive change.

The Adult Learner

The effects of conditioning have been examined extensively in populations of infants and very young children, and much of the research on social learning has also involved children of preschool age or younger. Adult learning research has taken different directions, however, and has encompassed a broad range from the highly theoretical to the applied. On the theoretical extreme is the extensive body of "laboratory" research on verbal learning. In the middle range is the research on problem solving, some of which has dealt with abstract problems but much, especially in recent years, with problems of a practical nature. Finally, growing interest in adult learning in applied settings, such as the classroom, reflects the realities of the changing educational needs of the American population.

Verbal Learning

Until the early 1970s, a considerable amount of research on developmental differences in adult learning involved verbal learning ability and employed what is known as a *paired-associate design* (Huyck & Hoyer, 1982). This means that the participant is shown a list of word pairs one at a time (e.g., *child—match*) and then shown in sequence the first word of each pair by itself (e.g., *child—?*). The learning that is expected to occur involves the association between words in each pair, so when the single words are presented later, the other half of the pair should be recalled.

The research on paired-associate learning has yielded consistent and unambiguous findings: young people perform better than older people (Arenberg, 1965; Canestrari, 1963, 1968; Gilbert, 1941; Monge, 1969; Monge & Hultsch, 1971). Typically, these studies compared a young and an elderly sample, a design characteristic of much of the gerontological research. However, two of the studies also included middle-aged people. Canestrari (1968) found linear age differences in performance when he compared people in their 30s, 40s, 50s, and 60s. Monge and Hultsch (1971) compared a group of 20- to 39-year-olds (mean age, 28.4 years) with a group of 40- to 66-year-olds (mean age, 49.4 years) and also found age differences in performance.

In attempting to explain the superior performance of younger over older adults on verbal learning tasks, researchers have taken a number of different approaches, as demonstrated in a review by Perlmutter and List (1982). Some have argued that the decline is a direct result of loss of speed among older adults in retrieving learned material from memory (for example, Arenberg, 1965; Canestrari, 1963, 1968; Monge & Hultsch, 1971). They note that age differences in verbal learning are considerably reduced, although not eliminated, when learners are given a generous amount of time to recall associate words when only the stimulus words are presented. In short, elderly people initially learn as well as young ones do, but need more time to remember what they have learned.

Other researchers maintain that older adults do not use memory aids when learning, or at least do not use them as efficiently as young adults do (e.g., Canestrari, 1968; Hulicka, 1965, 1966; Hulicka & Grossman, 1967). Most young learners have been found to use verbal mediators spontaneously (e.g., *child—match* is encoded as *The child lit a match*) in a verbal learning task, whereas most older adults do not (Hulicka & Grossman, 1967). In later adulthood there appears to be what Canestrari (1968) described as an associative impoverishment, and this is particularly true when the words to be remembered are abstract rather than concrete (Rowe & Schnore, 1971).

A third explanation of age-related deficits in verbal learning is that some older adults have not used the skills required for verbal learning in a number of years, so they have lost the "set," or mental predisposition, to learn (Hultsch, 1969, 1971a, 1971b; Monge, 1969; Monge & Gardner, 1972; Monge & Hultsch, 1971).

Finally, noncognitive factors must be considered in any meaningful discussion of age changes in verbal learning. Such factors include the anxiety level of the learner, motivation, and willingness to cooperate—all of which are related to the meaningfulness of the task to be learned. It often has been noted in laboratory settings that older adults may be more influenced by task meaningfulness than younger ones. For example, Hulicka (1967) observed that many of the older participants in her verbal learning study simply refused to learn paired-associate lists and referred to them as "nonsense." Older adults also may find a learning situation more threatening than young people do, or they may assume they are poor learners and then perform according to their own low expectations of themselves.

Problem Solving

Problem-solving ability can manifest itself in many ways, and, in fact, the concept of problem solving has been defined differently by different researchers. What is meant here by problem solving is a combination of processes involved in (1) the formation of ideas, (2) the testing of these ideas for adequacy, and (3) the acceptance or rejection of ideas on the basis of the results of the tests (Botwinick, 1978).

Consider as a measure of adult problem-solving ability the study conducted by Denney and Palmer (1981), in which participants ranging in age from their 20s to their 70s were challenged with a series of practical problems. What should you do if the inside of the refrigerator feels warm instead of cold? What should you do if, 2 weeks after purchasing a vacuum cleaner from a door-to-door salesperson, you discover that it no longer works?

The result of this particular study were quite clear and were consistent with findings from other studies of this type. Even in the solution of practical problems—the type people might deal with on an everyday basis—older people did not perform as well as younger ones. The best practical problem solvers were the people in their 40s and 50s, and with each decade the older groups were progressively worse. This does not suggest, of course, that people's experience with problems is unrelated to the effectiveness with which they solve them, but only that age-related differences in problem-solving ability cannot be totally explained by the experience factor.

Students might be surprised to discover that many of the measures used in psychological research are not at all exotic or abstract. Researchers studying adult problem solving, for example, have often used the familiar game of Twenty Questions, in which the player is asked to discover a word that the questioner is thinking of by asking no more than 20 questions that can be answered only yes or no. The game is appropriate for use in problem-solving studies because it is familiar and presumably nonthreatening, and it provides a good measure of reasoning strategies. The most effective strategy, of course, is to ask constraint-seeking questions—questions that gradually narrow the range of possibilities (Is it a living thing? Is it an animal? Does it walk on four legs?). A less effective strategy, if it can even be referred to as a strategy, is to ask a series of too-specific questions (Is it a mouse? Is it a bird? Is it a dog?).

The typical pattern in studies of problem solving that use the Twenty Questions game is that young and middle-aged adults ask more constraint-seeking questions than do the elderly, and therefore the younger players solve the problems more efficiently (Denney 1980; Denney & Denney, 1973; Denney & Palmer, 1981).

Why would elderly people be less effective game players than younger ones? No one knows for sure, but Denney (1980) suggested that elderly people may not be putting everything they are capable of into the solution of the problem. Arguing that old people can be encouraged to solve problems more efficiently than they ordinarily do and that increasing the difficulty of problems actually may force older players to use more efficient strategies, Denney devised several games of Twenty Questions that varied in difficulty.

Denney found that when the problems presented were so difficult that a solution was almost impossible, elderly people actually used more efficient strategies than they would use in a standard Twenty Questions game. Middle-aged people appeared to use their best strategies in both conditions. Her conclusion was that the elderly are often better problem solvers than they are likely to indicate on a test. No obvious reason explains this discrepancy between ability and performance; in fact, the discrepancy has not been found in other studies. Hartley and Anderson (1983a, 1983b) found that varying the complexity of a task similar to the one used by Denney had no effect on the strategies older people used. Nevertheless, we should remember that a person's performance in an experiment is not automatically a reflection of the person's true ability, particularly if the person tested is elderly and unused to being evaluated.

Learning for Life

One in every four Americans today is undergoing career transition, and mid-career change is increasingly common as economic and social circumstances restrict career mobility (Cross, 1981; Meadors, 1984). To plan for career advancement, to make a change in mid-life, or to gain entry into the job market as a mature adult, nearly two-thirds of the people involved in career transition say that they plan to seek additional education (Cross, 1981; Datan, Rodeheaver, & Hughes, 1987).

Various educational programs, whether in private industry, technical institutes, or colleges and universities, will likely see an influx of adult learners. Even now, older college students already outnumber those in the traditional 18 to 22 age group, and this trend is expected to continue through the 1990s (Chickering, 1981; Cross, 1985; Meadors, 1984). More and more, the classroom is becoming the social context, the real-life situation, in which adult learning takes place, and the research on conditioning and verbal learning may offer little information that is relevant to applied learning settings (Datan et al., 1987; Hughes, 1980; Wass & Olejnik, 1983).

As more and more older adults return to the college classroom, research on adult learning, problem solving, and memory becomes increasingly relevant.

Many factors other than basic intellectual ability can influence the way we learn. One of these is the degree to which we see a learning situation as supportive or threatening. What is most intriguing is that old people are more easily threatened in a learning environment than younger ones.

In a clever study of the relationship of a supportive environment to our ability to learn, Ross (1968) presented young (18- to 26-year-old) and elderly (65- to 75-year-old) adults with a paired-associate learning task. The instructions for the task varied. In the supportive condition, the learners were told that the study was designed to analyze the characteristics of words, and that their actual performance on the task did not concern the experimenter. In the challenging condition, the learners were told that they were taking an intelligence test and that it was very important that they do the best they could. Finally, in the neutral condition, standard instructions for a paired-associated learning task were provided.

Ross found that the young people learned equally well, regardless of the instructions provided. Older people, however, were heavily influenced by the instructions. Those in the challenging condition took significantly longer to learn than did those in the supportive condition, whereas those in the neutral condition were midway between the other two. Although the older participants in the Ross study were of advanced age and therefore not typical of the adult college student, it is interesting to speculate on the effect on learning of a threatening versus a nonthreatening perception of a learning environment such as a classroom. Particularly interesting, the young were not intimidated by the challenge, whereas the elderly apparently were. Clearly, age differences in learning ability may be the result of noncognitive, as well as specifically cognitive, factors.

Much of what is known about applied adult learning has emerged from the research of educators (e.g., Apps, 1981; Cross, 1971, 1981; Kidd, 1973; Knowles, 1978; Smith, 1982) interested in the special needs and problems of older learners, both within the classroom and outside it. Mature adult learners have been found to be more highly motivated than traditional college-age students, more accustomed to recognizing that learning occurs in informal as well as formal settings, and more capable of bringing a rich variety of past experience to a new learning situation. On the other hand, adult learners have been found to be more anxious, more likely to be deficient in specific skills required for classroom success, and lower in their self-confidence in formal learning settings. They are also more likely to face a number of practical obstacles, such as conflicting job or home responsibilities, absence of child care facilities, lack of social support, and difficulty in accommodating to the course schedules of formal learning institutions.

We mentioned earlier that noncognitive variables, such as motivation, interest, and anxiety level, can influence performance on verbal learning tasks. The study of adult learners in applied settings has done much to highlight the role of such variables. The extent to which a person's place in the life cycle, self-concept, interests, needs, and values can influence the learning process is becoming increasingly clear. Recognizing the importance of incorporating developmental principles into the study of adult learning, psychologist K. Warner Schaie (1982) proposed the following phases of intellectual development.

Acquisition phase: childhood and adolescence. The basic question for the child and adolescent learner is "What should I know?" The assumption is that authority figures, such as teachers and parents, realize what are the learner's needs, and it is the learner's role to absorb material without questioning its importance and its relevance for his or her own life.

Achieving stage: early adulthood. Young adults have a pressing need to achieve self-sufficiency and to acquire skills that will help them do so. They may have passed the age of peak performance for educational experiences that are task-specific and not clearly related to their broader personal and social goals (e.g., starting their families, entering the world of work). In learning situations, the question now becomes "How can I use what I know?" More specifically, the emphasis is on using what is learned to achieve one's personal goals.

Responsible stage: middle adulthood. Between the late 30s and early 60s, a person feels that independence has been attained and that a satisfactory identity has been established. Now the major motivator in learning comes from biological and social pressures to care for other people, such as one's spouse, children, or elderly parents, or to care in a broader sense by assuming leadership on the job or in the community. The question remains "How can I use what I know?" but now the value of learning is in the solution of practical problems involving long-term goals pertaining to the social units for which a person is responsible.

Reintegrative stage: old age. The elderly person has less responsibility for others than the younger adult, and the elderly person's attentional capacity has become more limited. Now the person attends selectively to only the most meaningful information. Motivational and attitudinal variables are more involved in learning than at any other time in life, and the question in a learning situation becomes "Why should I know?" The failure of an older adult to learn, therefore, may be heavily influenced by motivational variables instead of, or as well as, specific cognitive deficits.

MEMORY

All measures of learning, whether in the classroom or the laboratory, invariably include a memory component, and many studies discussed in the previous sections tested memory as well as initial learning. In much the same way, many studies examined here focus on the process of encoding incoming material, as well as retrieving it.

Obtaining "pure" measures of memory is difficult. After all, we cannot describe simple age changes in memory without referring to changes in other cognitive processes as well. For example, if young children cannot remember material as well as older children can, we must question whether the initial learning process was identical for the two groups. If young children have not learned as well as older ones, we could hardly expect them to remember as well, either.

Types of Memory

We have already referred to different types, or stages, of human memory; we will explain these stages in greater detail before discussing developmental changes during childhood. A frequently used distinction is between short-term and long-term memory. **Short-term memory,** also referred to as primary memory, active memory, or working memory, involves the retrieval of material still at the level of consciousness because it has recently been presented and is in the process of being rehearsed. Information in short-term memory will be held for only a short time, 1 minute or less, and will be lost unless efforts are made to transfer it to long-term storage. Consider as an example of short-term memory the experience of locating a telephone number in the directory and keeping it in mind while closing the book, picking up the phone, and dialing. You may repeat the number several times to keep it in mind until you make the call—the process of rehearsal—but probably do not feel the need to "memorize" the number—that is, to transfer it to permanent storage. If you are interrupted before you can make the call, the number fades from short-term memory, and if no efforts had been made to transfer the information to the more permanent long-term memory, you will have to go back again to the telephone directory.

How much information can be held in short-term memory at one time? The answer is difficult to determine because the capacity of short-term memory seems to depend on the meaningfulness of the material taken in (Anderson, 1985). Consider what happens when a list of words or syllables is presented and the listener is asked to repeat it immediately. A person can hold in short-term memory and repeat back four nonsense syllables (e.g., *GIB, BOF, DEX, WOB*) but not six; the short-term memory capacity for meaningful one-syllable words is six (e.g., *coat, dog, run, hand, cat, shoe*), but nine such words ordinarily will not be remembered. Finally, if a person is presented not with a list of words but with a meaningful sentence, the capacity of short-term memory goes up to 19 words (Anderson, 1985)! As the material increases in meaningfulness, the listener is better able to remember it immediately and better able to process it into long-term memory storage.

Learned material that is not at a person's immediate level of consciousness is said to have been transferred from short-term memory to relatively

Short-term memory

Memory for material still at the level of consciousness because it has recently been presented and is in the process of being rehearsed.

Long-term memory

Memory for information that is no longer held at the level of consciousness but must be retrieved from permanent storage.

permanent storage in **long-term memory**. Referring to the telephone caller example again, most people store in long-term memory several frequently called telephone numbers. A friend's telephone number may have been encoded but will not be brought to consciousness unless it is needed. When the need to call a particular friend arises, that number will be activated and brought from long-term to short-term memory—a process known as *retrieval*.

Factors Influencing Memory

A number of approaches can be used to help learners remember information better. Much opportunity for practice should be allowed so that the initial learning is firmly entrenched. The time between learning and retrieval should be minimized so that decay and interference are least likely to occur. The material should be presented in a form that is meaningful to the learner. Finally, mnemonic strategies, including rehearsal, organization, and elaboration, can be taught to a learner who does not spontaneously use them—and this group is more likely to include children than adults—with the result that memory can be improved considerably.

Quality of Initial Learning

Stated simply, the more completely a piece of information is learned in the first place, the easier it will be to remember. In a study by Anderson (1983), participants were involved in various numbers of practice sessions to memorize the sentences until they knew them by heart; they were later asked to select the memorized sentences from a list containing those sentences and others that had not been learned. The time required to identify a previously learned sentence was related to the number and days of practice. That is, the learners who had more time to practice were better able to retrieve the information from memory. Such findings were consistent with those of numerous other studies indicating that practice increases the memorability of learned material.

Interval Between Learning and Retrieval

As any student knows, the longer the delay between initial learning and the effort to remember what is learned, the more difficult it is to retrieve such information from storage. Two factors are involved in such memory loss. The first is decay, meaning that memory traces appear to fade with the passing of time (Anderson & Paulson, 1977). Reasons for this decay of the memory trace are unclear, but underlying physiological causes may be possible (Anderson, 1985). The second factor in memory loss is interference. Earlier or later learnings can interfere with efforts to remember what is learned. As an illustration of this point, students who study French in their first year of high school and Spanish the following year may find that familiarity with one language interferes with their ability to remember the other. When asked to recall the French word for *horse,* which they learned as "cheval" in their freshman year, some of them may remember only the Spanish word "caballo." Needless to say, the greater the time interval between learning and retrieval, the greater the likelihood of interference that can result in forgetting.

Meaningfulness of Material

As was discussed earlier, material that is meaningful is easier to remember than material that has little or no meaning for the learner—perhaps because the learner can organize meaningful information into "chunks" and can relate new learnings to what has previously been learned, whereas no framework can accommodate meaningless information.

The meaningfulness of material as an influence on memory has been demonstrated in a number of studies of children's interests. Children are most likely to pay attention to what interests them and are more likely to remember things that interest them than things that do not (Langsdorf, Izard, Rayias, & Hembree, 1983; Renninger & Wozniak, 1985; Wozniak, 1986). To illustrate this principle, Renninger and Wozniak (1985) had 3- and 4-year-olds look at nine toys, one at a time, which were then placed in a box. The children were asked, "What toys are in the box?" One of the toys had been identified previously as a toy the child particularly liked, and this high-interest toy was consistently the best remembered. The researchers concluded that interests and values definitely influence the cognitive performance of young children. Objects and experiences that have special meaning for a child are the easiest to remember later on.

Use of Mnemonic Strategies

As material is being learned, a number of strategies can be used to make that material more memorable. For example, learners may engage in spontaneous rehearsal, repeating the material to themselves, or, if the material is presented visually, naming or labeling the items to be remembered. Another approach involves organization of the material into meaningful patterns. For example, the list of numbers 278147349 might be easier to remember if it is broken into segments 278 147 349. Many a grade school child remembers the names of the Great Lakes only because the first letters of each name can be arranged to spell the word *HOMES*. A third mnemonic strategy is elaboration, in which the material to be learned is expanded upon in the mind of the learner. The larger the number of mental associations to the material, the easier it becomes to remember. Someone who has difficulty remembering people's names at a party might associate names with the colors of clothing worn by the guests: Jane-red, Mike-blue, and so on. Elaboration is illustrated also by strategy of making meaningful sentences out of lists of words (e.g., *child, hat, green, wall* becomes *The child threw her hat over the green wall*) or forming a visual image of the action described by such a sentence.

Mnemonic strategies may be used effectively to aid in memorization.

Memory Development in Childhood

The findings from studies of children's memory development—an extensive and rapidly growing body of research in the past 20 years—have led to the conclusion that no age differences exist in short-term memory. In contrast, children's long-term memory improves significantly with age (Hagen, 1971; Kail & Hagen, 1982; Kunzinger, 1985; Ornstein, Medlin, Stone, & Naus, 1985; Ornstein & Naus, 1978, 1983). Illustrating this pattern of findings were the results reported by Hagen (1971), who found no age differences in the ability of children to remember objects they had seen on a screen if they were asked to remember those objects immediately after viewing them. However, if a delay were allowed to occur between the stimulus presentation and the recall trial, preschoolers seemed to forget more than older children and adults did. Apparently, information gets into the system with equal ease in young and older children, but once it has reached the short-term memory stage, young children are less able to process it into long-term memory storage.

Most explanations of developmental improvements in long-term memory emphasize improvements in the use of mnemonic strategies. That is, older children are thought to be more capable than younger ones of using sophisticated strategies to place learned material in storage so that it will be easily retrieved.

In a classic study of the strategies used by children to enhance the memorability of stimulus material, Flavell, Beach, and Chinsky (1966) showed seven pictures to 5-, 7-, and 10-year-olds. The children were told that the pictures would later have to be remembered, and the researchers then observed the children's spontaneous verbalizations. Ten percent of the 5-year-olds, 60 percent of the 7-year-olds, and 85 percent of the 10-year-olds spontaneously spoke the names of the pictures to themselves as they studied them—presumably as a rehearsal strategy that would later aid their memory of the pictures. The strategy appeared to work, because the older children remembered the stimuli significantly better than the younger ones.

In a later study, Flavell, Friedrichs, and Hoyt (1970) tested children ranging from nursery school to fourth grade on a simple memory task. The children were exposed to a series of objects in a horizontal row of windows, each of which could be lit up for viewing by pressing a button underneath the window. They were told to study the objects until they were ready to remember them in the order in which they were displayed. The researchers noticed that the older children used more efficient rehearsal strategies— testing themselves, rehearsing the names of the objects, and pointing at the objects in turn—than did the younger ones. Not surprisingly, the older children were better able to remember the objects than were the pre- schoolers.

Using a type of stimulus material familiar to every college student, Brown and Smiley (1978) examined the strategies used by children and adults as they studied textbooks with the intent of learning material to be remembered. In analyzing the study strategies of fifth graders, seventh/ eighth graders, eleventh/twelfth graders, and college students, the research- ers found striking differences in study patterns. The older children and the adults were more capable of ignoring irrelevant material and focusing on the most important material than were the younger ones. As a result of this increased organizational ability, the older learner did not waste time studying trivia, but used instead a considerably more time-efficient study strategy. The older students were also much more likely to underline the textbook material and to take notes on it.

The finding that memorization strategies improve in efficiency as children mature does not mean, of course, that infants and young children cannot remember past experiences. Even by the age of 3 months, infants display evidence of fairly sophisticated long-term memory (Enright, Rovee- Collier, Fagen, & Caniglia, 1981; Olson & Sherman, 1983; Rovee-Collier, 1984). An often-used procedure in studies of infant memory is the following: As a 3-month old baby is lying in a crib, a ribbon connected to an overhead mobile is placed on the baby's ankle so that a kick causes the mobile to move. The average number of kicks per minute is found to increase considerably when the kicks produced such stimulating results—an example of operant conditioning. More relevant to the discussion of memory, however, is the finding that when the babies are "reminded" of the experience 2 weeks later by being shown the mobile, the kick rate again increases. Clearly, memory of past experience is apparent even at so young an age. Interestingly enough, such evidence of long-term memory does not appear when 2-month-old infants are tested in the same way (Vander Linde, Morrongiello, & Rovee-Collier, 1985).

Efficient strategies for transferring information from short- to long-term memory may indeed be lacking in the young child, but as any parent knows, preschoolers often display remarkable powers of memory. A child will point out, for example, that when he visited the doctor's office 6 months previously, the nurse gave him a red lollipop—a fact that the accompanying parent had completely forgotten. And yet the same child may fail to remember simple household rules that the parent has tried repeatedly to teach. Sometimes preschoolers appear to remember the "wrong" things; they often forget what they intentionally *try* to remember but remember incidental events that apparently had special meaning for them. This inability to control their powers of memory indicates the inefficiency of their memory processes.

That mnemonic strategies improve in efficiency with age does not mean that young children use no strategies at all. Even by the age of 18 months, primitive strategies have been observed (De Loache, Cassidy, & Brown, 1985), and Weissberg and Paris (1986) noticed spontaneous rehearsal in almost half of the 3- and 4-year-olds who were given lists of words and told they would have to remember them. The tendency in recent years is to see mnemonic strategies not as an all-or-nothing phenomenon but as being present in varying degrees from the years of early childhood and gradually improving with age (Ornstein & Naus, 1978, 1983).

Summarizing the literature on the use of efficient rehearsal strategies as an aid to memorization, Kail and Hagen (1982) noted that such strategies are rarely used spontaneously by children under 6 years of age. They are occasionally used by children 7 to 10 years old, depending on the nature of the learning situation, and mature strategies begin to appear consistently in children aged 10 or older. For these reasons, the effectiveness of providing mnemonic strategies to children and training them to develop their own will depend on the age of the children in question. The results of such training will be more dramatic in young children than in older children or adolescents, who are probably already using efficient mnemonic strategies of their own.

Memory Development in Adulthood

"What did you have for breakfast yesterday morning?" "What was your kindergarten classroom like?" "Can you list and describe the six substages of Piaget's sensorimotor stage of development?" All these questions call on a person's ability to remember. They also illustrate that memory is a complex element in the information processing system, and one that can be measured in a variety of ways. Recalling what you ate for breakfast yesterday, what your kindergarten classroom looked like, or what the names of Piaget's substages are each emphasizes a different aspect of human memory. Thus, memory can include visual memory, memory for meaningful discourse, and memory for lists. Furthermore, the process of committing information to memory can be intentional, as when a student memorizes Piaget's stages to prepare for an exam, or incidental, as in the case of remembering yesterday's breakfast.

The diversity of memory is important to consider as we discuss memory changes in adulthood, because until recently adulthood memory research was characterized by a very narrow focus (Kausler, 1985). In the first place, most studies of adult memory have been cross-sectional, and therefore yielded information about age differences rather than genuine age changes. Second, most memory research has been carried out in controlled laboratory settings, and the findings may have little applicability in the outside world. Finally, most adult memory research has emphasized only intentional verbal memory, as when people are asked to memorize a list of words on which they will later be tested; the ability to rehearse and remember lists of words bears little resemblance to many of the other ways in which we rely on our powers of memory in everyday life (Kausler, 1985).

Recent years have seen a dramatic expansion of memory research—away from the laboratory and away from procedures that emphasize only intentional memory for lists. We turn now to an examination of the findings of the traditional as well as the newer types of research on memory development during the span of adult life.

Intentional Memory for Lists

Research on the ability of adults to remember lists intentionally has typically involved either studies of dichotic listening or studies of memory span. In the dichotic listening experiment, two lists of items such as words or letters are presented simultaneously, one list in each ear. The listener is asked first to report all the material heard in one ear and then all the material heard in the other, and the usual finding is of no age differences in the amount of information remembered from the first ear, but significant age differences in what is remembered from the second (Clark & Knowles, 1973; Inglis, Ankus & Sykes, 1968; Inglis & Caird, 1963; Mackay & Inglis, 1963). This decline in ability to recall the second "half set" begins after the age of 30 and continues throughout life.

Apparently, therefore, when learned material has to be put on hold for even a short period of time before being recalled, older learners suffer a greater disadvantage than younger ones. In contrast, when immediate recall is demanded, no age differences are found. In other words, the difficulty of older adults occurs not in short-term, or primary, memory, but at the level of long-term, or secondary, memory.

Studies of memory span involve the presentation of a list of words, letters, or numbers with the requirement that the list be reproduced immediately after presentation. Memory span requires both short- and long-term memory, however, because only a few words at a time can be handled in short-term memory (Watkins, 1974), and therefore the remaining items must be processed into long-term memory. The memory span research has produced results that can also be interpreted in terms of differences in the efficiency of short- and long-term memory. For example, when Craik (1968) compared young adults (23–35 years old) and older adults (60–72 years old) on their ability to recall a list of meaningless syllables, no age differences appeared. However, when the same people were tested using meaningful words, the young were superior to the old. Why? Craik suggested that familiar items can be coded, or chunked, and this helped the young more than the elderly. In other words, if no mnemonic strategy is readily available, the young are penalized as much as the old. If it *is* possible to use a coding strategy, the young adults are more likely to do so.

Craik (1968) suggested that the meaningless items were held in short-term memory and acoustically encoded, while the meaningful stimuli were coded into long-term memory. Retrieval from short-term memory involves a simple "readout" of coded traces, but retrieval from long-term memory requires a more complex decoding of material that relates back to the strategies originally used in encoding. Therefore, as was true of the dichotic listening research, this memory span experiment provided evidence of age differences in long-term memory but not in short-term memory.

In summary, the research on intentional memory for lists typically indicates little or no age decline in short-term, or primary, memory, but a definite decline with age in long-term, or secondary, memory (Craik, 1977; Parkinson, Lindholm, & Inman, 1982; Poon, 1985). Adults of all ages are equally able to remember a list of items immediately after presentation, because the list is still at the level of short-term memory. If, however, the list is allowed to leave the immediate level of consciousness, and therefore must be systematically encoded into long-term storage, older adults are at a disadvantage when compared to the young. How can this disadvantage be explained? Either older adults do not encode material in the organized fashion of young adults, or they have more difficulty in retrieving the information from storage, or both (Hultsch, 1971a; Schonfield & Robertson, 1966). Interestingly enough, suggesting a mnemonic strategy to young adults does little to improve their long-term memory for lists, but suggesting such a strategy to the elderly helps them considerably. Perhaps this is because, unlike the elderly, young adults are already using effective encoding strategies of their own and need no assistance from the experimenter (Treat, Poon, & Fozard, 1981).

Memory for Meaningful Discourse

An aspect of verbal memory that is more relevant than memory for lists to everyday life experience is the ability to remember the content of inherently meaningful discourse. For example, a student who has missed a class often asks a classmate, "What did the professor talk about?" The classmate responds not with a word-by-word reconstruction of the lecture but with a summary of its contents, much as someone would respond if asked to recall a conversation, a television program, or a selection of written material. In everyday life, such memories are usually incidental, although researchers typically study the ability of adults to remember intentionally the "gist" of meaningful discourse (Kausler, 1985).

The findings from research on prose recall have been inconsistent, although a number of patterns have emerged. First, when adults of all ages are asked to recall a selection of prose verbatim, the elderly do not perform as well as the young (Craik & Masani, 1967; Poon, 1985). Second, when summary rather than verbatim recall is asked for, age differences favoring the young have been found by some researchers (e.g., Dixon, Simon, Nowak, & Hultsch, 1982; Cohen, 1979) but not by others (e.g., Labouvie-Vief, Campbell, Weaver, & Tannenhaus, 1979; Meyer & Rice, 1981; Meyer, Rice, Knight, & Jensen, 1979). How can this inconsistency be explained? Research on prose recall is still a relatively new area of study, and so a number of questions are still unanswered.

In addition, variables other than age can affect level of prose recall, and many such variables have yet to be identified. For example, Hultsch and Dixon (1983) discovered that the appearance of age differences in prose recall depends on the familiarity of the content of the prose. Wingfield, Lahar, and Stine (1989) found that age differences in memory for spoken prose depend on whether the speaker uses normal intonation patterns and variations in word stress. When a passage was read in an expressionless manner, as if the speaker were reciting words from a list, elderly listeners (mean age, 70 years) recalled significantly less of the passage than young ones (mean age, 19 years); with a "normal" prose reading, the age differences virtually disappeared. Finally, other researchers have found that verbal ability and level of education are better predictors of prose recall than age (Meyer & Rice, 1983; Rice & Meyer, 1985, 1986; Taub, 1979). Thus, if the participants in a study are highly verbal, well educated, and somewhat familiar with the content of the passages to be remembered, adult age differences in prose recall should not be found.

Visual and Spatial Memory

Visual and spatial memory involves memory for visual images or for the locations of objects in space—the arrangement of furniture in a room, for example, or the locations of the various stores in a shopping mall. When the intentional visual/spatial memory of adults of different ages is tested, the typical finding is that memory for visual information declines with age (Cherry & Park, 1989; Light & Zelinski, 1983, 1988; Moore, Richards, & Hood, 1984). Clues to reasons for such an age difference may be found in the research on the variables that influence visual and spatial memory, including (1) familiarity with the conditions of testing, (2) distinctiveness of the elements in a visual display, and (3) tendency of the perceiver to use encoding strategies spontaneously.

The *familiarity* component is illustrated in a study by Sharps and Gollin (1987), who employed two conditions of testing. In the "map" condition, the participants' attention was directed to 40 objects on a schematic map; later, with the objects removed, they were asked to identify the locations of as many objects as they could. A second condition, the "room" condition, more closely approximated the natural environment: Participants were shown 40 common objects in various locations in a room, and later, with the objects removed, were asked to identify where each of the 40 had previously been placed. Adults of all ages performed better in the "room" condition. More importantly, age differences favored the young adults in the "map" condition, but no age differences were found in the more familiar "room" condition. Thus, although familiarity benefited everyone, it particularly helped the elderly participants.

The existence of age differences in spatial memory also depends on the *distinctiveness of elements* in a visual display. Sharps and Gollin (1988) found that young adults surpassed the elderly in spatial memory for the location of objects on a two-dimensional black-and-white map, but when colored maps and three-dimensional models were used, the age differences disappeared. A similar finding was reported by Bruce and Herman (1986), who used as visual displays model towns containing buildings that were either highly differentiated (i.e., clearly identifiable as a house, barn, gas station, etc.) or undifferentiated (i.e., cubelike structures that varied in color and shape). The distinctiveness-of-elements variable came into play in that participants in both age groups remembered the realistic buildings better than the geometric structures.

However, another finding of this study indicated the existence of an additional performance variable: the young adults (mean age, 25 years) outperformed the older group (mean age, 65 years) in remembering the locations of the distinctive buildings, but no differences were found in memory for the cubelike structures. The authors suggested that if visual stimuli can be easily categorized and encoded, as is true of the distinctive

This woman seems somewhat disoriented on a busy city street, a result of the fact that intentional visual/spatial memory declines with increasing age.

buildings, young adults are more likely to do so spontaneously than older people are. In contrast, less structured stimuli such as the undifferentiated buildings are difficult for a person of any age to encode, and so the young adults lose their "encoding advantage" in that condition.

Therefore, the visual-spatial memory deficits of the elderly may be related in part to the unfamiliarity of the testing situation, in part to the distinctiveness of objects in a visual display, and in part to the fact that old people are less likely automatically to use mnemonic strategies. A reasonable assumption, therefore, is that the visual memory of the elderly might be improved by (1) using familiar materials and settings in testing, (2) increasing the distinctiveness of objects in a visual display, and (3) suggesting and encouraging the use of encoding strategies. In fact, a growing body of evidence indicates that visual memory in later adulthood *can* be enhanced by such approaches (Park, Puglisi, & Smith, 1986; Puglisi & Park, 1987).

Metamemory

Metamemory
The understanding people have of their own memory processes.

One of the more interesting recent approaches to the subject of memory is the research on what is known as **metamemory,** the knowledge people have about their own memory processes (Flavell & Wellman, 1977). Instead of viewing memory in isolation from other cognitive processes, advocates of the metamemory concept maintain that how well we remember is a function of how well we understand our own memory functions. People who remember best are those who best know the limits of their memory capacity, who best understand how to employ memory strategies, and who best realize how much effort will be needed to commit various materials to memory. College professors routinely encounter students who believe they have prepared adequately for an examination but who fail it nevertheless because they underestimated the amount of study time needed to remember the material. What is responsible for their poor grades—a memory failure or a lack of understanding of their own memory processes?

In studies dealing with metamemory, older children are typically more knowledgeable about their own memory processes than younger ones—a finding that may partly account for the long-term memory limitations of the younger child (Flavell, 1985; Flavell et al., 1970; Yussen & Levy, 1975). However, as is the case with other aspects of memory development, the ability to monitor one's own memory is not an all-or-nothing phenomenon. Even preschool children display some signs of metamemory (Cultice, Somerville, & Wellman, 1983). Perhaps this should not be surprising, because 3- and 4-year-olds, and particularly those who attend nursery schools, are often expected to please adults by memorizing songs, poems, stories, or parts in a school play. They are already capable of voluntary memory, and thus are conscious of their own memory processes and skills (Weissberg & Paris, 1986).

The findings from the adulthood metamemory studies are somewhat inconclusive. For example, Murphy, Sanders, Gabriesheski, and Schmitt (1981) presented a group of young adults (average age, 20 years) and a group of elderly adults (average age, 69 years) with cards containing line drawings of familiar objects. They asked the participants to estimate how many figures they could remember and then allowed them to take as much time as needed to study the cards so that they later could remember them. No age differences were found in the accuracy of the estimates of how many figures could be remembered, but young adults actually remembered more items that older adults. Young adults also studied for a longer time before they felt ready to be tested, leading the authors to conclude that the elderly were less able to monitor their own readiness.

Bruce, Coyne, and Botwinick (1982) found that young and old people differed in their estimates of how many words they could remember, with the older participants overestimating their skills. As was found in the Murphy, Sanders, Gabriesheski, and Schmitt study, young people actually remembered items better than the elderly did. Finally, in contrast to study of Murphy and his associates, the older participants in the Bruce, Coyne, and Botwinick study did not differ from the younger ones in the amount of preparation time they felt they needed. Bruce and her associates concluded that young people do indeed have a more accurate knowledge of their memory processes than older adults. They essentially agreed with Murphy and his associates, but for different reasons.

A final point about adult metamemory indicates much about the significance of memory changes in old age. In one recent study (Sunderland, Watts, Baddeley, & Harris, 1986), people in their 60s and 70s were asked to assess their memory skills subjectively. Most respondents said that their memory had declined markedly over the years, and indeed objective tests did indicate a degree of memory impairment. However, most also said that their memory deficits had little or no impact on their everyday lives. Again we see what is a common theme in the study of adult memory development:. The memory deficits found in the laboratory are real enough, but they may have little practical significance in the day-to-day lives of elderly people (Kausler, 1985; Neisser, 1982).

Summary

1. The efficiency of attention increases during childhood. As children mature, they are better able to attend to meaningful information from the environment and to ignore what is irrelevant.

2. Young adults are better than older ones on tasks requiring selective attention. The young adult is more skilled at dividing attention among different stimuli and at ignoring what is irrelevant. However, these age differences

may have little practical significance for everyday life.

3. Learning results in a relatively permanent change in behavior that is brought about by environmental experience. The process of learning itself is not directly observable.

4. Classical conditioning, first investigated by Pavlov, involves reflexive behavior and depends on an association between a neutral stimulus and an unconditioned stimulus. The association is formed by the law of contiguity.

5. Operant conditioning depends on the law of effect, which states that behaviors followed by reward are likely to be repeated, whereas those followed by punishment or by no consequences are likely to be discontinued. Operant conditioning deals with voluntary behavior.

6. Both classical and operant conditioning have been demonstrated successfully with human beings, even with young human infants.

7. Operant-conditioning principles have been less effective in explaining complex forms of human thinking than in explaining simple behaviors. Mediation theory was developed to explain the developmental shift from the straightforward operant response of a young child in a problem-solving task to the more complex strategies employed by older children and adults.

8. Social learning is the application of conditioning principles to the socialization process. Observational learning, the basic mechanism described by social-learning theorists, is a complex form of learning that depends on attentional, retention, motor-reproduction, and motivational factors.

9. Observational learning includes the phenomenon of modeling, in which the learner imitates and identifies with a significant model, often in the absence of apparent reinforcement for doing so. Modeling is recognized as one of the most powerful means for transmitting values, attitudes, behavioral patterns, and patterns of thought.

10. Research on adult learning has ranged from laboratory experiments on verbal learning, to practical problem solving, to studies of the conditions of adult learning in applied settings such as the college classroom.

11. Little developmental change in short-term memory occurs during childhood, but long-term memory improves significantly, probably because children's mnemonic strategies improve with age.

12. Memory of all types, at least as measured in laboratory settings, shows an age-related decline throughout adulthood, possibly because older adults are less likely than the young to use encoding strategies.

13. Metamemory is the knowledge people have about their own memory processes. Such knowledge increases throughout the childhood years, and then declines during the years of later adulthood.

Key Terms

attention (p. 208)
classical conditioning (p. 216)
cognitive social learning (p. 226)
extinction (p. 217)

law of contiguity (p. 220)
law of effect (p. 218)
long-term memory (p. 241)
mediation theory (p. 225)

metamemory (p. 250)
observational learning (p. 226)
operant conditioning (p. 217)

punishment (p. 218)
reinforcement (p. 218)
reversal shift (p. 224)
short-term memory (p. 240)

Review Questions

1. Describe the various components of the human information processing system. Why are these components better viewed as parts of a system than as isolated cognitive activities?
2. What is the capacity limitations model of attention, and how does it explain the attentional changes that occur in the later years of adulthood?
3. What are the similarities and differences between classical conditioning and operant conditioning? Name and describe the laws, or principles, on which each type of conditioning is based.
4. Why is reward more effective than punishment in the operant conditioning paradigm?
5. Does watching violent television programs make children more violent? What does the research tell us? Can television-aggression correlations be interpreted in more than one way? Explain.
6. Laboratory research on adult learning may have limited applicability to real-life learning situations. Why?
7. What reasons have been suggested for the poor performance of elderly people on measures of verbal learning?
8. What are the two major types of human memory? What developmental changes have been observed in each type of memory throughout the life span?
9. What is metamemory, and how does it change with age? How might the concept of metamemory be important in explaining differences in classroom performance of adults at various points in the life span?

Suggested Readings

Bandura, A. (1986) *Social foundations of thought and action: A social cognitive theory.* Englewood Cliffs, NJ: Prentice Hall.

A book ultimately about human learning that goes far beyond the scope of other works on the subject. Written by the originator of the social learning view of psychological modeling, it deals with a wide range of issues involving human thinking, motivation, and behavior.

Cross, K. P. (1981). *Adults as learners.* San Francisco: Jossey-Bass.

A detailed analysis of the recent changes in adult education in the United States, including discussion of the reasons for the changes and the characteristics of adult learners.

Reese, H. W. (1976). *Basic learning processes in childhood.* New York: Holt, Rinehart and Winston.

Written for nonpsychology students and lacking the technical jargon found in many books on learning. The author clearly describes children's learning in a variety of areas: conditioning, discrimination learning, verbal learning, and higher conceptual processing.

Chapter Seven

Cognitive Development

The Theory of Jean Piaget

Content of Intelligence

Structure of Intelligence

Function of Intelligence

Motivation for Growth

Piaget's Stages of Development

Sensorimotor Development

Pre-operational Development

Concrete Operations Stage

Formal Operations Stage

Cognitive Development in the Adult Years

Operational Task Performance During Adulthood

Beyond Formal Operations?

Instead of Formal Operations: Beyond Piaget

Environmental Influences on Cognitive Development

Cross-cultural Perspectives

Influence of Education

Family Factors

Nutritional Factors

What makes a sailboat move? Jane, 3½ years old, answers that it moves because the sky is blue. Obviously, Jane does not understand the principles of sailing. But what are we to think if we ask 20 preschool children the same question and receive 20 remarkably similar but incorrect answers? What if seven or eight of the children respond that the color of the sky is what makes a sailboat move? That the children give wrong answers obviously means they are less knowledgeable than we are; that they give similar or even identical wrong answers seems to indicate that they are not thinking the way adults do. In the case of the sailboat, they may be interpreting the question in a different way than it was intended, or their understanding of cause and effect relationships may not be the same as that of an adult.

In this chapter, we shall ask a number of questions about how human beings think: Do developmental changes occur in thinking processes from infancy through old age? At what point in development do children begin to analyze their own thought processes? What is the highest level of human intellectual functioning? When is this level reached, and is it reached by everyone? Can models of cognition originally based on research with children explain the complexity of adult intellectual functioning? All these are questions about the nature of human cognition, and although none has a simple answer, researchers in the field of cognitive psychology have been able to provide a number of interesting insights.

The purpose of this chapter is to discuss theory and research in the area of human cognition and to provide an understanding of the issues, and at least a partial answer to some of the major questions. More importantly, the focus of the chapter will be on cognitive development—the *differences* in problem-solving abilities that occur as the person progresses from infancy through old age. The emphasis will not be on the mere accumulation of knowledge, and instead of focusing on *what* is known, we shall deal more often with the *how* and the *why*—the process rather than the product.

The emphasis in this chapter will be on the work of Jean Piaget (1896–1980). This is neither because Piaget was completely correct in his assertions nor because his views are accepted unanimously. In fact, they are continuously challenged by researchers in the field of human cognition (e.g., Gelman & Baillargeon, 1983). What Piaget did was offer a model that psychologists and educators can use to attempt to understand cognitive development. Few would argue that it is the most comprehensive model available, that it has generated the greatest amount of research, and that it has been the model most widely applied in recent years, particularly in the field of education. Few would deny that Piaget's descriptions of children's behaviors were remarkable accurate, although serious questions have arisen in recent years about his interpretations of those behaviors. Specifically, some researchers have suggested that Piaget may have underestimated the cognitive capacities of young children. In addition, Piaget has been criticized for failing to recognize the developmental differences that occur beyond the adolescent years.

The final section of the chapter will be devoted to a discussion of environmental influences on human cognition. The influence of culture will be examined in a section on cross-cultural comparisons. Also included will be an analysis of educational and child-rearing influences and, recognizing that biological factors can affect human thought processes, a section on the significance of nutrition in cognitive growth.

THE THEORY OF JEAN PIAGET

The most comprehensive of all theories of human intellectual development is the one developed by the Swiss biologist-philosopher Jean Piaget. Piaget, originally trained in biology, began his career studying shellfish. He published his first paper at the age of 11, a remarkable accomplishment that marked the beginning of a long career spanning nearly three-quarters of a century.

Piaget's theory of intellectual growth is based on the belief that there are strong parallels between biological and psychological functioning. Intelligence is a particular instance of biological adaptation to the environment. Human beings do not have furry coats to protect them from the cold; they do not have the speed to outrun most predatory animals, or the skill in climbing trees to avoid them. They do, however, have the intelligence to produce clothing and vehicles of transportation. As you read this page, you are probably seated in an environment that has been carefully designed for your comfort and protection. The air temperature, humidity, and lighting may all be regulated. It is a natural environment only in the sense that it is an indication of natural human adaptation—intelligence.

Intelligence can be considered from three different perspectives: content, structure, and function (Piaget, 1983). All are important, but Piaget placed the greatest emphasis on the latter two. We will now discuss each in turn.

Content of Intelligence

The content of intelligence is the raw material; put simply, it is what is known. For example, a group of people asked to explain the working of an automobile engine might give different answers. One person might describe the four-stage operation of each cylinder in the engine block. Another might discuss the little horses under the hood of the car that produce the horsepower to make the wheels turn. Each of these answers has very different content.

What would lead a person to believe in the existence of horses under the hood? This is precisely the sort of thing that engaged Piaget's interest. He felt that to understand the nature of human intelligence, he needed to know more than whether people gave right or wrong answers to a question. He needed to know *why* they gave the answers they gave. What in the process of human thinking leads a person to put forth a certain product? To describe the underlying processes of human thinking, Piaget introduced the concept of the structure of intelligence.

Structure of Intelligence

Intellectual or cognitive structures are constructed because of the interaction between the human being and the environment. These structures determine how people can deal with ideas or issues. They provide an outlook on life (Flavell, 1982, 1985). A cognitive structure is not a tangible object; it cannot be seen or touched. Therefore, the concept may be difficult to understand at first unless illustrated by a concrete example: A child and an adolescent watch an identical film on television, and yet their cognitive experiences while viewing the film are different. The child sees a story filled with action and adventure, with several boring scenes in between, in which the characters speak to one another but do little else. The adolescent sees a story about the nature of human love or ambition or greed that uses many action scenes to convey the filmmaker's message. The child is not less intelligent than the adolescent but simply has a different worldview because the child's cognitive structures are not as well developed as those of the adolescent.

Cognitive structures originate in early infancy; they begin to develop as soon as the child begins to have environmental experiences. But what of the newborn, who has not yet had any environmental experiences? According to Piaget, even completely inexperienced infants have built-in structures that program them to interact with the environment. These are the *physical structures*, such as the human brain and nervous system and the specific sensory organs, and the reflexes, or, as Piaget referred to them, the automatic behavioral reactions. The infant exercises these structures in interacting with the environment, and by doing so, begins immediately to develop cognitive structures.

Cognitive structures
The ways in which human beings organize their knowledge to determine their intellectual view of the world.

Function of Intelligence

All living organisms, in interacting with their environments, function by the twofold process of *organization* and *adaptation*. Organization involves the tendency to integrate the self and the world into meaningful patterns of parts within a whole to reduce complexity. Thus, Piaget described the increasing organization of the developing embryo and fetus, and the impressive organization of the reproductive system. The same tendency toward increasing organization can be found in the realm of thought.

Adaptation to the environment is the second aspect of functioning in the organism. The living organism adapts to the demands of the environment in two ways. On the one hand, it manipulates the outside world to make it more similar to the organism itself. On the other hand, it modifies itself so that it becomes more like the environment. The first of these tendencies is referred to as *assimilation,* and the second as *accommodation* (Piaget, 1983).

To assimilate something means literally to make it similar to oneself. It involves taking something from the outside world and fitting it into a structure that already exists. Human beings assimilate food by breaking it down into its nutritional components; the food they eat in that sense becomes a part of themselves.

When people accommodate to something, they change themselves in some way to meet external demands. To continue with the food example, the body not only assimilates food but also accommodates to it by the secretion of gastric juices to break it down and by involuntary stomach contractions to digest it. Similar physical adaptations occur when the body accommodates to heat by perspiring and to cold by shivering.

Piaget maintained that the processes of assimilation and accommodation apply to intellectual processes as well as to physical processes. The child assimilates new ideas, new "food for thought," by fitting them into existing cognitive structures, and accommodates to these ideas by changing cognitive structures in response to them. If an idea is new, and the cognitive structures necessary to make sense of it are present, children will make it a part of their thought processes and will change their ways of thinking in response to it. Intellectual development will not occur, of course, if the ideas to which the child is exposed are familiar (i.e., have already been assimilated), or if they are too advanced for the structures to assimiliate.

Motivation for Growth

Intellectual structures organize the environment and adapt to it, but why do they do so? As discussed earlier, the organism seeks order and organization. It seeks balance, or equilibrium between itself and external reality. Therefore, the motivation for intellectual growth comes from an internal need for order, harmony, or balance, because people need to feel that their way of thinking about the world is consistent with perceived reality.

Assimilation

The aspect of the adaptive functioning of human intelligence that involves fitting new intellectual material into already existing cognitive structures.

Accommodation

The adjusting of the cognitive structures to adapt to new information from the environment.

The internal motivation for intellectual development is a highly significant concept in Piaget's theory. Theoretically, at least, children should not need to be coaxed or tricked into wanting to know about the world. They need only be exposed to it in a manner they are capable of appreciating. They seek knowledge because they have an inner drive toward that knowledge, and when some new intellectual "food" comes their way, they reach out for it spontaneously.

PIAGET'S STAGES OF DEVELOPMENT

Piaget believed that intellectual development passes through a series of qualitatively different stages, each building on and evolving from those that preceded it (Piaget, 1983). Let us now examine the stages through which individuals pass as they move from infancy to adulthood, beginning with the sensorimotor stage, which extends from birth to approximately 1½ years of age.

Sensorimotor Development

Sensorimotor intelligence
The action-oriented form of intelligence and problem solving that is typically engaged in by infants.

A key concept in Piaget's theory is that thought begins in activity, and thus *sensorimotor intelligence* is the earliest form of thinking and problem solving. Piaget stressed that intelligence can be sensory and physical as well as mental, as can be seen in his observations of his own daughter Lucienne. When Lucienne was approximately a year old, her father showed her the chain of his watch, and then placed it into a matchbox. He then partially closed the box so that the chain could be seen through an open slit that was too small to admit the child's fingers.

Lucienne approached the problem of recovering the chain on a physical, or sensorimotor, level. She shook the box, struck it with her hand, and banged it against the edge of her crib until finally the chain slipped out. Lucienne had solved her problem, but she had done so physically rather than mentally; the solution was the motor activity.

Schemes

If cognitive structures develop because of their interaction with the environment through organization and adaptation, what can be said of the neonate who has had little or no chance for environmental interaction? The newborn baby possesses only physical structures, including the human nervous system, the sense organs, and the reflexes. However, during the sensorimotor stage, basic physical structures are modified as a result of environmental interaction, and the infant is capable of increasingly sophisticated interactions with the world. For example, the newborn infant will suck indiscriminately on anything that is placed against its mouth. Gradually, however, the baby becomes more selective, and sucking becomes increasingly limited to the times when it is appropriate, as when

Schemes
The sensorimotor equivalent of concepts; consistent action sequences made up of classes of acts that have regular, common features.

the nipple is presented. This selectivity indicates the tendency on the part of the infant to organize the world: Some things are to be sucked on, but others are not. It also indicates adaptation to the environment: The child assimilates new experiences, and future behavior is accommodated accordingly.

Emerging from the basic physical structures during the sensorimotor period are what Piaget described as consistent action sequences—classes of acts that have regular common features. He called these action sequences *schemes,* which are the sensorimotor equivalent of concepts. Included among the infant's schemes are sucking, grasping, vocalizing, and looking—action patterns exercised by the infant on a variety of objects.

Substages of Sensorimotor Intelligence

In describing the development of schemes and, more generally, the transition from a primarily reflexive interaction with the world to a more sophisticated sensorimotor intelligence, Piaget divided his first stage into six substages.

Substage 1 (Birth–1 Month). The primary activity in the first substage is the exercise of reflexes. Minor variations in reflexive behavior may occur because of environmental interaction, such as the slight increase in the selectivity of sucking that has been mentioned.

Substage 2 (1–4 Months). Individual schemes continue to develop, but toward the end of the second substage, coordination of schemes is evident. As an example of this coordination, sucking-grasping is one of the most well-established schemes in Substage 2. Parents often notice that everything their baby grasps is brought to its mouth for sucking, and the baby will attempt to grasp whatever is placed in its mouth.

A key feature of Substage 2 is the *primary circular reaction:* The infant accidentally discovers an interesting sensory or motor experience related to its own body and continues to repeat it. Consider the behavior of Piaget's own son at 2 months of age:

> [Laurent] scratches and tries to grasp, lets go, scratches and grasps again, etc. [At first] . . . this can only be observed during the feeding. Laurent gently scratches his mother's bare shoulder. [The next day] . . . Laurent scratches the sheet which is folded over the blankets, then grasps and holds it a moment, then lets it go, scratches it again, and recommences without interruption.[1]

Substage 3 (4–8 Months). Coordination of schemes continues, and the circular reaction seen at Substage 2 takes on a new dimension. Up through

---

[1]Reprinted from *The Origins of Intelligence in Children* (p. 191) by Jean Piaget by permission of International Universities Press, Inc. Copyright © 1952, 1963 by International Universities Press, Inc.

the second substage, the activities repeated as ends in themselves were somewhat oriented toward the infant's own body. As young infants exercise their sensorimotor schemes, they appear more interested in their own actions than in the materials on which the actions are performed; thus, they are more interested in the experience of grasping than in the object grasped.

In Substage 3, infants are definitely interested in the effects of their actions on the outside world. In an effort to prolong interesting experiences resulting from their own action, infants perform *secondary circular reactions,* repeated behaviors with pleasing effects on the environment. Again, consider the behavior of Laurent Piaget at 4 months old. He is lying in his bassinet looking up at some rattles attached to the hood with a string. His father attaches a watch chain to the rattles.

> [Laurent] pulls . . . the chain or the string in order to shake the rattle and make it sound: the intention is clear. I now attach a paper knife to the string. The same day I attach a new toy half as high as the string . . . Laurent begins by shaking himself while looking at it, then waves his arms in the air and finally takes hold of the rubber doll which he shakes while looking at the toy.[2]

Substage 4 (8–12 Months). In the previous substage, Laurent definitely intended to pull the string, bringing about the result of shaking the rattle. However, Piaget was unwilling to see his son's actions as clearly goal-directed. Instead, he suggested that Laurent did not differentiate between his own actions and their results. In other words, he did not pull the string to shake the rattle, but he saw the pulling of the string and the shaking of the rattle as contained within the same activity.

Substage 4, however, is characterized by definite purposeful goal-directed activity. In fact, infants will activate one scheme for the specific purpose of producing another, as when they push aside an object to grasp what is behind it. In a sense, Substage 4 involves the deliberate bringing together or coordination of secondary circular reactions.

Substage 5 (12–18 Months). In the second year of life, the child goes a step beyond clearly intentional behavior and the deliberate coordination of unrelated schemes. Now the child intentionally varies interesting events. The Substage 3 infant repeats an action in an attempt to prolong an interesting environmental result. By Substage 5, the child employs repetition but also attempts to vary the activity instead of simply repeating it precisely. This behavior is referred to as a *tertiary circular reaction.* Furthermore, the child seems to enjoy novelty and looks for new ways of producing interesting

---

[2]Reprinted from *The Origins of Intelligence in Children* (p. 164) by Jean Piaget by permission of International Universities Press, Inc. Copyright © 1952, 1963 by International Universities Press, Inc.

experiences. Consider the experimental approach of Piaget's 13-month-old daughter Jacqueline in her bath:

> Jacqueline engages in many experiments with celluloid toys floating on the water . . . Not only does she drop her toys from a height to see the water splash or displace them with her hand in order to make them swim, but she pushes them halfway down in order to see them rise to the surface. Between the ages of a year and a year and a half, she amuses herself by filling with water pails, flasks, watering cans, etc. . . . by filling her sponge with water and pressing it against her chest, by running water from the faucet . . . along her arm, etc.[3]

Substage 6 (18–24 Months).　In some ways, Substage 5 marks the end of the sensorimotor stage because beyond the age of 1½ years, children begin to engage in representational thinking (Flavell, 1985: Ginsburg & Opper, 1988). That is, they become capable of using symbols, of letting one thing stand for another, and they are no longer limited in intelligence to sensorimotor activity on the world. Substage 6, then, can be thought of as a transitional period between sensorimotor and pre-operational intelligence, which will be discussed later in this chapter.

Object Concept

One of the most significant developments of the sensorimotor stage is the acquisition of the *object concept,* which involves the realization that objects exist independently of our awareness of them or interaction with them (Flavell, 1985). A person reading a book knows, for example, that the book has an existence independent of the reader; its existence is equally obvious whether it is being read or whether it sits on the back shelf of a library.

Piaget (1964) maintained that young infants do not have the object concept and must gradually acquire it through experience with the world. Although parents rarely define it as such, they often notice the lack of an object concept in their babies: A 4-month-old drops a spoon while seated in a highchair, but instead of looking for it, the baby ignores it. Being out of sight, the spoon no longer exists in the baby's mind.

Piaget believed that the object concept is acquired gradually during the sensorimotor stage. From birth to 4 monhs (sensorimotor Substages 1 and 2) the infant does not recognize that objects exist independently of the infant's sensory and motor knowledge of them. Out of sight means out of mind. Thus, if the infant is tracking a moving object with its eyes and the object disappears behind a screen, the infant will almost immediately lose interest in it (Flavell, 1985).

Between the ages of 4 and 8 months (Substage 3), however, infants begin to differentiate between object and self. Now infants will attempt to

---

[3]Reprinted from *The Origins of Intelligence in Children* (p. 273) by Jean Piaget by permisison of International Universities Press, Inc. Copyright © 1952, 1963 by International Universities Press, Inc.

look for the dropped spoon. If they watch an electric train disappearing into a tunnel, they will turn their attention to the other end of the tunnel in anticipation of the train's return (Nelson, 1971; Flavell, 1985). They will also attempt to uncover an object that is partly covered, apparently realizing that the hidden part of the object still exists although it can't be seen. On the other hand, 4- to 8-month-olds will not search for something that has been completely covered even as they watch; if the child is shown a toy and begins to reach for it, and the toy is then covered by a cloth, the child will stop in mid-reach, as if the toy has magically ceased to exist!

Between 8 and 12 months (Substage 4) infants will remove a cover to find an object that they have seen being covered, indicating that they recognize the object exists although they cannot directly perceive it. The object concept is still immature at this point, however, and babies can be easily tricked. If the baby has become accustomed to retrieving an object hidden under Cover A, and the adult then moves the object from Cover A to adjacent Cover B, the child will continue to seek the hidden object under Cover A. The child is unable to form a mental representation of the movement of the object from A to B and is dominated by the sensorimotor

Now you see it, now you don't. A key feature of the sensorimotor stage is the development of the object concept—the realization that objects exist even when we are unable to perceive them.

habit of going to Cover A, even though such an action is no longer appropriate. This behavior is referred to as the AB or Substage 4 error.

From 12 to 18 months (Substage 5), the concept of the object existing independently of the child's actions becomes more firmly established. Now the child will look for an object in the last place it was seen. Thus, if a toy is first placed under Cover A and then moved under Cover B, the child will go directly to Cover B to look for it. In Piaget's terminology, the child in Substage 5 can cope with *visible displacements* of objects. Not until Substage 6, however, from 18 to 24 months, is the object concept firmly established as the child learns to cope with *invisible displacements*.

Although able to handle visible displacements successfully, the Substage 5 child cannot deal with displacements that are not seen but must be imagined. For example, a toy is placed in a cup, and the cup is placed first under Cover A and then under Cover B, where the toy is dropped out; the empty cup is then set aside and the child is asked to find the toy. Because the cup was empty when removed from Cover B, a reasonable assumption is that the toy was deposited under Cover B, even though this displacement was not seen. Unable to deal with such an invisible displacement, the Substage 5 child looks for the toy where it was last seen—in the cup. The Substage 6 child, by contrast, notices that the cup is empty, mentally represents the displacement of the toy from cup to Cover B, and quickly locates the hidden object.

For Piaget, the development of the object concept illustrated movement from action-oriented sensory and motor intelligence to the more mature representational intelligence of the toddler. It also illustrated a decreasing egocentrism as the child slowly learned to separate self from the external world. In illustrating these points about infant development, the value of Piaget's object concept research is unchallenged. Furthermore, general agreement exists today that Piaget's actual descriptions of infant behavior were quite accurate. However, valid criticisms have been made of the object concept research, and we will now examine these criticisms.

Questions have recently arisen about Piaget's interpretations of infants' difficulties with displacement problems. In particular, much controversy surrounds the AB error. In the first place, many 8- to 12-month-olds do not commit the error of looking only under Cover A when a hidden object is moved from A to B. In addition, many children well into the second year of life do commit the AB error, making it difficult to argue that commission of the AB error illustrates a genuine substage of development (Flavell, 1985). Finally, does committing the AB error necessarily mean that infants are locked into sensorimotor habits and unable mentally to represent the movement of objects from A to B?

Critics of Piaget's interpretation suggest that the infant's deficiency may be one of memory rather than representational skill. Perhaps the infant who sees an object moved from one hiding place to another becomes confused and simply can't remember where the object was last seen. In fact, the longer the delay between hiding time and search, the greater the likelihood of AB errors (Fox, Kagan, & Weiskopf, 1979), and, in general, 8-to 10-month-old infants perform less well on delayed search tasks than 14- to 16-month-olds (Schacter & Moscovitch, 1984).

In one of the more intriguing studies of the AB error, Schacter, Moscovitch, Tulving, McLachlan, & Freedman (1986) found that adults with organic memory disorders are likely to perform like 8- to 12-month-old infants on a hidden object task. The participants in the Schacter study developed the habit of finding an object (e.g., a paper clip, a rubber band) in one of four drawers of a plastic container; when a new object was hidden in a different drawer, most of the amnesic adults were unable to find it and returned to their earlier habit of looking in the drawer that was intially used as a hiding place. The authors concluded that memory deficiencies should be considered as possible contributors to AB errors, and, in fact, a study by Baillargeon, Spelke, and Wasserman (1985) indicated that when the memory component is removed from measures of the object concept, even 5-month-old children display evidence of knowing that out of sight does not mean out of mind.

In summary, the sensorimotor stage involves intelligent activity on a sensory and motor level and provides the basis for all future intellectual development. It involves the modification of the physical structures through the infant's interaction with the environment. The sensorimotor stage is marked by the development of behavioral sequences called schemes, which the infant exercises on the materials in the environment, and by the eventual coordination of these schemes with one another, leading to increasingly complex forms of behavior. Finally, this stage involves the development of the object concept, the recognition that the world has an existence independent of a child's psychological contact with it.

Pre-operational Development

The end of the sensorimotor stage of development is marked by the emergence of an ability to represent experiences mentally without direct physical interaction. It is the ability to let one thing stand for another and to think about things without physically acting on them. This representational ability marks the appearance of **pre-operational intelligence**.

Representation occurs in many forms. A mental image is a representation of reality; an image of an isolated beach on a sunny day, with blue water, white sand, and swaying palm trees in a sense makes those objects present in the mind of the knower without the actual physical experience of the scene. Representation is also found in symbolic play. The child pretends that a cardboard box is a car, that an empty plate has food on it, or that a broom handle is a gun. Perhaps the most obvious indication of the emergence of the ability to use symbols is the child's use of language in the

Pre-operational intelligence
The mental activity of preschool children, who are capable of mental representation but do not yet have a system to organize their thinking.

*Research Close-up
Lucienne and the Silver
Watch Chain: An Early
Mental Solution to a
Problem*

"I put the chain . . . into the box and reduce the opening to three millimeters. Lucienne (aged 1 year, 4 months) is not aware of the functioning of the opening and closing of the matchbox and has not seen me prepare the experiment . . . She puts her finger inside and gropes to reach the chain, but fails completely. A pause follows during which Lucienne manifests a very curious reaction bearing witness not only to the fact that she tries to think out the situation and to represent to herself through mental combination the operations to be performed, but also to the role played by imitation in the genesis of representations. Lucienne mimics the widening of the slit. She looks at the slit with great attention, then several times in succession she opens and shuts her mouth, at first slightly, then wider and wider! [She] thus expresses, or even reflects her desire to change the opening of the box . . . Lucienne unhesitatingly puts her finger in the slit and . . . pulls so as to enlarge the opening. She succeeds and grasps the chain."

Reprinted from *The origins of intelligence in children* by Jean Piaget by permission of International Universities Press, Inc. Copyright © 1952, 1963 by International Universities Press, Inc.

second and third years of life. Clearly, the newfound ability to use language, to let a word stand for an object or person, indicates a dramatic change in the child's intellectual functioning.

To illustrate the emergence of representational ability, Piaget again presented Lucienne with the chain-in-the-matchbox problem when she was about 1½ years old—at the beginning of the pre-operational stage. This time she looked at the box, silently opened and closed her mouth several times, then reached over directly, slid the box open, and removed the chain. Apparently, she was able to represent the activity to herself mentally, and then proceed to solve the problem directly. Actually, the problem had been solved in her mind before she even touched the box, whereas when she was younger she didn't begin the problem-solving procedure until she took the box in her hands.

Pre-operational children share with adults the ability to represent reality to themselves by means of signs and symbols; like those of the adult, the young child's thought processes are internal. Nevertheless, compared to the older child and adult, the young child is still at a great disadvantage cognitively because pre-operational thought is unsystematic, inconsistent, and illogical. A look at some of the characteristics of pre-operational thought will illustrate its unsystematic nature.

A major characteristic of pre-operational thought is ***transductive reasoning***. The logical reasoning of the adult may be inductive, as when general rules are induced based on a series of particular observations: The sun always rises in the east. Adults also use deductive reasoning, which involves making a judgment about a particular instance based on a general rule:

Transductive reasoning
An illogical form of reasoning that is typical of children under the age of 6.

For children, something as simple as a row of portable chairs may become a train. The ability to represent reality to oneself and to engage in make-believe play appears during the pre-operational stage of development.

Because cows in general give milk, any particular cow will give milk. Transductive reasoning, on the other hand, is reasoning neither from the particular to the general nor from the general to the particular, but from particular instance to particular instance. For example, a child might reason that because dogs have four legs and horses have four legs, dogs are horses, a conclusion both illogical and incorrect. What the child has done is to relate two particular instances of the general class of four-legged animals. This is transductive reasoning.

Another characteristic of pre-operational thought is confusion about *cause and effect relationships*. The young child will often see a cause-effect relationship where none exists, while failing to see a true cause-effect relationship. For example, a child who falls and hurts himself while playing indoors during a thunderstorm may blame the thunderstorm and develop a fear of such weather. Or, more sadly, a child may not be able to understand that she did not cause her father to leave home after a divorce settlement.

A pre-operational child exhibits **animism** in thinking: Because the child has life, thoughts, and feelings, the child sees all things as having life. Rock gardens exist because the rocks like each other, chairs are hurt when big

Animism
The belief of pre-operational children that, because they themselves have life, all things are alive.

people sit on them, and dolls get lonely if you don't play with them often enough.

Pre-operational thought demonstrates **artificialism**. Everything that happens must have a psychological reason, just as children have psychological reasons for the things they do. Leaves fall off trees because they want to keep the ground warm, the moon shines to give us light at night, and flowers grow to make us happy. Young children are not capable of understanding things in terms of physical reasons, and, therefore, when they ask why the sky is blue, they are not asking for a discussion of refracted sunlight in the atmosphere. They may want to know why the person who painted the sky chose the color blue!

Pre-operational thought is *perceptually bound*. That is, children judge the world by the way it looks to them. Nickels must be more valuable than dimes because nickels are bigger. Two halves of a cookie look like more than a whole cookie, so the child prefers the halves to the whole. The child groups geometric shapes together not according to categories of size and shape, but according to pattern; they are arranged so they look nice.

Pre-operational thought is inflexible and irreversible. In what Piaget called a *mental experiment,* young children run off thoughts in their heads in the sequence in which they might act them out. It is as if the child's thinking resembles a film in a projector that cannot be stopped, rewound, reversed, or edited. The ability to reconstruct one's thought processes and the ability to reverse them mentally are essential in the development of logical thought.

Pre-operational thought possesses the characteristic of **centration**. The child centers on the features of the environment that are most noticeable and ignores other features. For example, a young child may believe that the taller of two glasses always contains more water than the shorter one regardless of the width of the glasses in question. In actuality, a shorter glass might contain more water than a taller one if the shorter glass is wider. However, the young child may center on height and fail to attend to the width of the glasses at all.

Finally, pre-operational thought is extremely *egocentric*. Children see the world from their own points of view. Piaget and his longtime colleague Barbel Inhelder (Piaget & Inhelder, 1956) presented children with a task in which they were required to point to a picture that represented the view of a landscape seen not by them, but by a doll placed opposite them. Most young children chose the scene they saw rather than what the doll might see, apparently unaware that viewpoints other than their own exist.

Piaget certainly described the thinking of young children as limited in its effectiveness and, as any adult knows who has tried to reason with a preschooler, a vast difference certainly exists between children's and adults' reasoning abilities. Nevertheless, a number of psychologists in recent years have challenged Piaget's analyses of young children's thinking, suggesting that he was too harsh in his estimate of their limitations. (See *Issues in Human Development,* "Did Piaget Underestimate the Preschool Mind?")

Artificialism
The belief that everything that exists, even natural phenomena, has a psychological reason for existence.

Centration
A characteristic of pre-operational thought whereby a child centers on the most noticeable features of the environment while ignoring others.

This little girl interrupting her mother's telephone conversation displays the egocentrism typical of toddlers. She is unable to see the world from any point of view other than her own.

The characteristics of pre-operational thought gradually disappear as children move from toddlerhood through early childhood. By the time children are ready to enter middle childhood, at about the age of 6 or 7, the first signs of operational thinking are beginning to emerge, and they are poised to enter a new and different stage of thought.

Issues in Human Development
Did Piaget Underestimate the Preschool Mind?

 In Piaget's theory, the mind of the pre-school child is characterized less by what the child can do than by what the child is not yet able to do. *Pre*-operational thinking is thinking without benefit of mental operations. The preschooler's mind is disorganized, confused, and devoid of an understanding of cause and effect, logical groupings, relationships, and the concept of quantity. Thus, the world they perceive lacks stability, consistency, and order. What is more, Piaget saw little value in trying to teach operational skills to young children. "It would be completely useless," he said. "The child must discover the method for himself through his own creativity" (Hall, 1970, p. 30).

However, a considerable amount of criticism has been directed at Piaget's unflattering assessment of young children's thinking (Brainerd, 1978, 1979, 1983; Flavell, 1985; Gelman, 1972, 1980, 1982; Gelman & Baillargeon, 1983; Mandler, 1983). The basis for criticism varies, but a recurring theme is that the mind of the preschooler is considerably more sophisticated than Piaget realized.

Most of the evidence used to challenge Piaget's description of the young child's thinking is found in the results of training studies, designed to induce operational skills in supposedly pre-operational children. The point of such studies is to demonstrate that operational skills do not depend on a particular underlying cognitive organization, as Piaget believed, but on the possession of specific information or a specific frame of reference needed to solve the problem. For example, Gelman (1982) suggested that nonconserving children may simply not be attending to the important features of the conservation problem, and can be taught to do so. Their performance improves significantly once they understand what is being asked of them. Other advocates of training argued that children who fail to conserve may not understand the psychologist's instructions, or may not understand how to use equipment such as the scale used in conservation of weight experiments.

Most training studies focused on conservation problems (Gelman & Baillargeon, 1983), and typical of such research is the extensive work of Rochel Gelman on children's understanding of number. Whereas Piaget maintained that number conservation (the realization that the number of items in a display remains constant regardless of the arrangement of items) is not characteristic of pre-operational thinkers, Gelman (1982) found that 3- and 4-year-olds can indeed conserve number. To induce conservation, she first showed children two rows of three and four objects and asked them to count aloud the objects in each row. After counting each row, the children had to tell her how many objects each row contained. Then she presented a standard conservation of number task.

Gelman (1982) found that, contrary to predictions based on Piaget's theory, the pre-operational children in her study could conserve number, presumably because they were influenced by the training phase of the experiment. Gelman did not suggest that the children actually learned to conserve during the training phase, but only that training may have given them a clearer understanding of what was being asked of them.

Positive effects of prior training have also been demonstrated in studies of classification. For example, Smiley and Brown (1979) found that, when given a group of objects to classify, preschoolers do indeed fail to use logical categories; they group instead according to overall themes or patterns, exactly as Piaget suggested. However, the researchers then demonstrated logical categorization of the objects for the children and asked them to sort the objects exactly as they had been shown to do. The children proceeded to do so, leading Smiley and Brown (1979) to suggest that young children apparently prefer to use perceptual and intuitive sorting strategies, which Piaget regarded as less mature than logical groupings, but, if directed to do so, can classify logically at an earlier age than Piaget (Inhelder & Piaget, 1964) indicated.

Other critics of Piaget's assessment of preschool cognition have argued that even without training, young children are better able to organize their perceived environments than Piaget realized. Rather than indicating a deficiency in the young child's ability to see the world as rational and orderly, failure on Piaget's operational tasks might indicate only that the task methodology is inappropriate for young children. Supporting this argument is the finding of Ross (1980) that even in the second year of life, children see the world in terms of categories rather than as a disorganized jumble of stimulation.

Ross (1980) did not follow Piaget's approach of asking children to sort objects into groups. Instead, she measured the attention paid by 12-, 18-, and 24-month-olds to a variety of objects. Seated on a parent's lap, each child was shown a number of objects in succession that belonged to the same category (e.g., men, animals, food, furniture). Then the child was shown a pair of objects, each new, but one of them belonging to a category the child had become used to seeing and the other belonging to a totally different category. The children displayed more interest in the different category object than in the familiar category object. On the basis of that finding, Ross (1980) concluded that very young children do perceive their worlds in terms of categories, even though they are obviously unable to actively sort objects into categories by themselves. In other words, by using what she considered a more appropriate methodology for preschoolers, Ross obtained results that directly contradicted those of Piaget (Inhelder & Piaget, 1964).

Did Piaget underestimate the intellectual abilities of preschool children? Apparently, he did. Not only can preschoolers conserve and classify under certain conditions, but they also have a more sophisticated understanding of cause and effect than Piaget imagined (Bullock & Gelman, 1979; Bullock, Gelman, & Baillargeon, 1982), and an easier time distinguishing between animate and inanimate objects (Gelman & Spelke, 1981). The mind of the preschooler appears to be less confused and better organized than was intially believed (Flavell, 1985).

Findings of elementary forms of categorization, classification, and causal reasoning in young pre-schoolers raise questions about Piaget's belief that cognitive structures gradually emerge as a result of environmental interaction. Modern cognitive psychologists suggest that Piaget erred in failing to realize that some structures that underlie human cognition may be innate (Gelman & Baillargeon, 1983). Human beings may have built-in mechanisms for organizing and making sense of the world, and these basic mechanisms may differ little from childhood to adulthood. However, until the age of 5 or 6 years, children lack the ability to reflect upon and to talk about their approaches to problem-solving (Flavell, 1985). Significantly, Piaget (1964) insisted that before a child could be credited with adequately solving an operational problem, the child had to provide a verbal explanation of how the problem was solved.

Preschoolers are also easily distractable and often unable to attend to relevant aspects of a problem while ignoring the irrelevant. They are too easily influenced by appearances rather than substance, and they can indeed be egocentric. Such characteristics could certainly be responsible for their failure to solve concrete operational problems, even though, as critics of Piaget suggest, the underlying cognitive structures that organize the world may actually be present in young children.

Few psychologists deny that significant cognitive development occurs during the preschool years, and few deny that Piaget was perhaps the greatest contributor thus far to current knowledge about children's cognitive development. His views that children are active rather than passive in the process of their own learning and that their cognitive structures influence their perceptions and their understanding of the world have gained widespread acceptance among psychologists and educators (Gelman & Baillargeon, 1983). However, although Piaget's descriptions of preschoolers' behavior were accurate, the prevailing view today is that his interpretations placed too strict a limit on the young child's cognitive capacities.

Concrete Operations Stage

Thinking in the concrete operational stage of development no longer consists of disjointed representational acts. Now these acts, which previously lacked order and consistency, become parts of whole systems of related acts. They become *concrete operations.* Operations may be logical, such as those dealing with principles of formal logic or those dealing with mathematical concepts. They may also be what Piaget termed "sublogical," and these deal with concepts of space and time.

A course in mathematics or in formal logic provides a student with a fairly good idea of what using a mental operation means. For example, the principles of algebra are the same regardless of the numbers entered into the algebraic formulas. Similarly, formal logic does not seek to determine whether statements are true or false, but whether they derive from a logically consistent system. For example, the statements that "All Irishmen have red hair" and "John is an Irishman" lead to the logically correct conclusion that "John has red hair." Logically correct as it is, the conclusion may not be true, of course, because the major premise is false. All Irishmen do not have red hair.

The development of concrete operations allows the child to deal with the concepts of classes, relations, and quantity, each of which we will examine in turn.

Classification

To understand the concepts involved in *classification,* the child must perceive the logical similarity among a group of objects and be able to sort them according to their common features. Pre-operational children tend to rely on perception when they classify; they make judgments on the basis of what things look like. When shown a group of objects and asked to put together the ones that go together, they frequently construct what Inhelder and Piaget (1964) referred to as graphic collections—interesting arrangements of the figures. For example, when given a group of circles, triangles, and squares and asked to sort them according to their defining properties, young children might place the triangle on top of the square and say they have made a house (see Figure 7.1).

By the age of 5 or 6, when they are moving into the stage of concrete operations, children begin to sort objects by their logical defining properties. Thus, in the example of the geometric shapes, they are now likely to group the objects according to shape, or to size or color, rather than to make an interesting pattern.

A mature notion of classification begins to appear after the age of 7, and in some children considerably later (Winer, 1980). Piaget termed this class inclusion: the relationship between classes and subclasses. An adult can readily understand that classes can be contained within classes. However, the young child's appreciation of class inclusion is somewhat limited.

Concrete operations

A stage of thinking, extending from the age of 6 to adolescence, in which a child can reason logically about concrete situations or events.

Classification

The ability to perceive logical similarity among a group of objects and to sort them according to their common features.

Figure 7.1

Graphic collections

Graphic collections are arrangements of figures into perceptually pleasing patterns rather than arrangements of figures by logically defining properties.

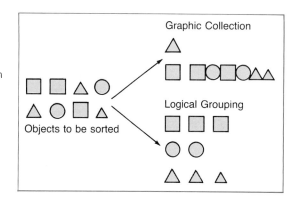

Consider what happens when a 6-year-old is shown a group of dogs, six of which are collies and two of which are poodles, and asked "Are there more dogs or more collies?" Because the child has trouble understanding the concept of class inclusion, he or she relies on a less sophisticated perceptual solution to the problem. The child sees more collies than poodles, and so responds that there are more collies than dogs. Instead of seeing the subclasses (collie and poodle) in relation to the supra-ordinate class (dog), the child compares the subclasses to each other and therefore fails to solve the problem (Ahr & Youniss, 1970).

By the age of 8 or 9, the child understands multiple classification and can classify on two dimensions at once. Piaget (1964) presented children with a picture of a row of green objects (e.g., a pear, a hat, a tree) that intersected with a column of different-colored leaves. At the point of intersection was a blank space, and the child was asked to determine what should appear in the space. The correct answer is a figure that shares the common feature of the row (green) and the column (leaf), and so the child should choose a green leaf. Multiple classification appears only after simple classification and class inclusion have been mastered.

Seriation

A second major development indicating the transition to operational thought is the development of a mature understanding of relations. This understanding will allow the child to see the world in an orderly manner, to detect and understand consistencies and patterns as the adult does.

The understanding of relations is illustrated by the following example: Suppose a child were asked to choose 10 people at random and order them according to height, a relatively simple task for an adult. A pre-operational child could not complete the ordering successfully. Young children do have a basic understanding of concepts such as "greater than" and "less than," but in an ordering task, the child is required to know not only that John is taller than Mary, but also that John is, at the same time, shorter than Jim. Thus the

A pre-operational child would have trouble arranging these blocks according to size, because it is necessary to keep in mind that the same block is simultaneously bigger than some blocks and smaller than others.

task becomes more difficult because it requires the ability to decenter, to attend simultaneously to more than one feature of the situation. As was noted in the previous section, pre-operational thought is characterized by centration, the tendency to focus on one dimension and to ignore others. The young child focuses on the fact that John is taller than Mary but cannot hold in mind at the same time the thought that John is shorter than Jim.

The task used to test the child's skill at ordinal relations is referred to as *seriation.* Typically, Piaget would present children with a group of sticks of different sizes and ask them to order the sticks from the smallest to the biggest. Pre-operational children do not seem to be capable of seriating because seriation involves the ability to view the world as an orderly place with systematic rules for relating objects or events. Seriation requires the use of concrete operations.

Seriation
A task designed to measure a child's understanding of ordinal relations.

Conservation

An understanding of quantity involves an awareness that, regardless of changes in physical appearance, quantity remains the same unless material is added or subtracted. A cookie that is broken in half looks different as two pieces than it did as one, but because nothing was added or subtracted, the actual quantity must still be the same. A young child, however, may decide that now there is more cookie to eat than before, because two pieces look like more than one piece. In contrast, the older child and the adult make judgments on the basis of a genuine understanding of quantity; the appearance may be different, but because nothing was added or subtracted, the total amount has not changed.

A person who uses logical operations is said to conserve the amount— to recognize that the amount does not change regardless of changes in the physical appearance of the material. Thus, the task used to determine understanding of quantity is referred to as *conservation.*

Conservation experiments have been carried out using a variety of materials. Piaget maintained that conservation does not occur suddenly but appears gradually, and that different forms of conservation emerge at different times in the child's life.

Conservation of Number (5–6 Years).   The child is presented with two rows of objects, one containing five objects and one containing four. Then the row containing the four objects is spread out, as the child watches, so that the objects at the ends of the row are farther apart from one another than the end objects in the row of five. The child is asked which row has more. The nonconserver will say that the spread-out row has more, because it looks longer. The older child and the adult would answer correctly; the row with five objects still has more, regardless of how the objects are arranged, because the number hasn't changed.

Conservation of Liquid (7–8 Years).   The child is shown two identical glasses of liquid. In the child's presence, the liquid from one glass is poured into a much taller but thinner glass, and the child is asked if the amount of liquid in the glasses is still equal (see Figure 7.2). The nonconserver will say the tall one has more, because it looks bigger. The conserving older child and adult will say that the amount of liquid is still the same because nothing has been added or subtracted; the new glass is taller, but it is also narrower.

Conservation of Length (7–8 Years).   The realization that the length of an object remains the same regardless of how the segments of the object are arranged involves conservation of length. For example, if two identical "roads" are made of long blocks, and one of the roads is subsequently arranged in a zigzag rather than a linear fashion, are the two roads still the same length? The conserver will answer correctly that they are.

Conservation of Mass (7–8 Years).   If two balls of clay are identical, and one of them is then flattened out, is the amount of clay in each ball still the same, regardless of the shape (see Figure 7.3)? The conserver says yes; the nonconserver says no.

Conservation of Weight (7–8 Years).   If two balls of clay are identical in weight, will they still weigh the same if one is flattened out, or will one weigh more than the other? The conserver will say they are still the same because nothing has been added to or subtracted from either one. The nonconserving child will say that they are now different, because they look different.

Conservation

A task requiring the ability to recognize that variations in the physical appearance of a substance do not alter the amount of the substance in question.

Figure 7.2
Conservation of liquid
The nonconserver answers that C now contains more liquid than A because the appearance of the liquid in the glasses is different. The conserver answers that A and C are the same because no liquid has been added to or taken away from the original amount in B.

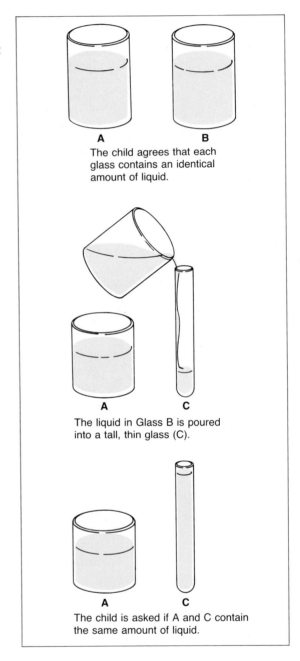

The child agrees that each glass contains an identical amount of liquid.

The liquid in Glass B is poured into a tall, thin glass (C).

The child is asked if A and C contain the same amount of liquid.

Conservation of Area (7–8 Years). A number of blocks, representing houses, are placed on a flat surface representing a field. If the houses are rearranged, spread all over the field instead of lined up along the edge, do they still cover the same area? The conserver says yes. The perceptually bound nonconserver says no; they look as if they cover more space.

Figure 7.3

Conservation of mass

The nonconserver answers that the amount of clay in the balls is now different because the balls no longer resemble each other. The conserver answers that the amount of clay in each ball is still the same because no clay was added to or subtracted from either side.

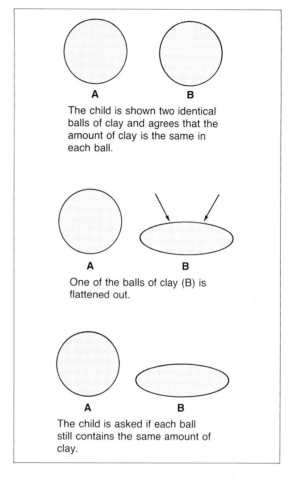

A   B

The child is shown two identical balls of clay and agrees that the amount of clay is the same in each ball.

A   B

One of the balls of clay (B) is flattened out.

A   B

The child is asked if each ball still contains the same amount of clay.

Conservation of Volume (11–12 Years).   A child might be presented with a tower that is two cubes long, two cubes wide, and three cubes high, so that each of the three layers has four cubes. Then the top layer is removed, and two of its cubes are added to each of the other two layers so that the structure is now three cubes long, two cubes wide, and two cubes high. The child is asked if the structure still takes up the same amount of space as before, or, putting the question another way, is the volume the same as it was originally? To conserve volume, the child must pay attention simultaneously to length, width, and height, and conservation of volume is the last of the conservation skills to appear, usually not before early adolescence.

Cognitive Conceit

In addition to changes in understanding of classes, relations, and quantity, Piaget described a huge number of changes in thinking that occur with the emergence of concrete operations. A mature understanding of the concepts of time, space, and causality appears, as well as the emergence of inductive reasoning, to replace the transductive reasoning of the pre-operational child.

Furthermore, as might be expected, these dramatic changes in the quality of children's thinking are reflected in their personalities. Elkind (1980) described the phenomenon of **cognitive conceit,** a form of egocentrism that characterizes the early elementary school years. Children, delighting in their newfound logical cognitive structures, develop too much faith in them. They believe that if they reason that something is correct, it *must* be correct, because they cannot distinguish between reality and their intellectual analysis of it. Only later will they learn that even flawless reasoning may not provide them with absolute "truth" if the information they are processing in their cognitive structures is flawed.

Children who display cognitive conceit are overwhelmed by their own cleverness, and, realizing that adults do not know everything, they sometimes decide that adults don't know anything. Such children find pleasure in attempting to trap adults in their own logical inconsistencies, and parents find themselves pressured to give logical reasons for all of their house rules. Hapless parents may be faced with statements like "The other night you let me stay up until 9:30. Why can't I say up tonight?" and they may be forced into an awareness of their inconsistent or illogical disciplinary practices.

Formal Operations Stage

The final stage in the development of thought in Piaget's theory is the stage of *formal operations*. As has been shown, the child develops from reliance on a sensorimotor form of intelligence to a stage of unsystematic mental representation to a stage of systematic mental representation. However, the child's thinking is still considerably more limited than that of the adolescent or adult, because the child lacks essential characteristics of formal operational thought.

Hypothetico-Deductive Cognitive Strategy
Formal operational thinkers deal with a problem by first considering all possible solutions and mentally examining the outcome of each solution. They set up hypotheses—if-then statements—and systematically test them, and they are able to speculate in advance on which of their hypotheses is the most likely to be correct. The concrete operational thinker, on the other hand, does not employ a planful approach to problem solving but usually resorts to a more time-consuming trial-and-error technique.

Combinatorial Analysis
Related to the hypothetico-deductive strategy is the ability to generate all possible combinations of a set of elements, an ability lacking in concrete thinkers but characteristic of formal reasoning. The best example of such differences in reasoning is found in the experiment in which children and

Cognitive conceit
A phenomenon whereby children new to the stage of concrete operations develop too much faith in their reasoning ability.

Formal operations
A stage of thinking during adolescence and adulthood in which people can deal with abstract, hypothetical, and contrary-to-fact propositions.

adolescents were given five flasks of colorless liquids and asked to combine them to produce a yellow liquid (Inhelder & Piaget, 1958). Adolescents usually consider all 26 possible ways in which the liquids can be combined before they begin to solve the problem, including combinations of three, four, and five as well as two. Children tend to combine the liquids two at a time, and often need prompting even to consider other possibilities. Their approach to the problem is unsystematic and disorganized.

Abstract Reasoning

The reasoning of concrete operational children is limited to the concrete. They have difficulty dealing with abstract concepts such as "democracy," "charity," "religion," and so on, and typically define them concretely. If asked for an explanation of democracy, they may say only that it means that all people can vote. Religion may mean attending church services and nothing more. The formal operational thinker, on the other hand, may define religion as a state of mind, or as an attitude toward the self or others, or as an abstract feeling.

Abstract reasoning allows adolescents to contemplate the meaning of their own lives, to question their social and moral values and those of others, to analyze human relationships, to try to understand the symbolism contained in art and literature, and to see beneath their own superficial

The adolescent who first acquires formal operational skills often spends much time lost in thought, concerned more with the realm of possibility than with current reality.

behavior and that of other people. One of the most significant features of adolescents' ability to reason about abstract issues is that for the first time they are capable of thinking about their own thought processes. They can, in a sense, perform operations on their own operations; they can deal with their thought processes as objects of thought, and, needless to say, this greatly enhances their cognitive flexibility.

Contrary-to-Fact Reasoning

The child can reason about situations that have happened or are happening, but not about those that might happen, or have never happened. But the adolescent and the adult can also reason about the hypothetical and the contrary-to-fact. For example, what might be the current status of United States–Soviet arms limitation talks if Michael Dukakis had been elected president in 1988 instead of George Bush?

Adolescent Egocentrism

We noted earlier that pre-operational children are egocentric in that they are unable to see the world from the perspectives of others, and that the school-age child's egocentrism appears in the form of cognitive conceit. Actually, Piaget believed that egocentrism of some sort accompanies the emergence of *all* stages of intellectual development, and the young formal operational thinker is not immune from such self-centeredness.

Adolescent egocentrism is characterized by a failure to distinguish between one's own thought processes and those of other people. Teenagers often believe, therefore, that if something is important in their lives, *everyone* must see it as equally important. The blemish that John sees on his face when he looks in the mirror may not be noticeable to anyone else, but because it is highly visible to him, John is convinced that everyone he encounters that day is staring at him. Likewise, Maura's work on the school newspaper is a central focus of her life, and she cannot understand why so many students do not even bother to read it.

Psychologist David Elkind (1981) described two major forms of egocentrism during adolescence: the imaginary audience and the personal fable. The *imaginary audience* involves the belief of young adolescents that they are "on stage," that their actions are highly visible to others, and that, in a sense, they are constantly performing. Some adolescents thrive on this imagined attention and strive to be noticed by others—by showing off, driving noisy cars, wearing outrageous clothes, and so on. Others do not enjoy their imagined visibility and become extremely self-conscious.

The *personal fable* involves a belief that one's thoughts, feelings, and experiences are completely different from those of others, and that one is special to the point of being safe from life's ordinary dangers. Young adolescents often believe that no one else has ever thought the way they do, and that no one could possibly understand their innermost feelings. The tragic side of the personal fable is that some adolescents take risks that would be unthinkable to most adults—reckless driving, drug abuse, sex without birth control, and so on—in the belief that nothing terrible will happen to them because they are so special.

Egocentrism eventually disappears, to some extent at least, as adolescents mature, and particularly as they form intimate relationships with others. Intimate knowledge of other people, and the feedback on the self that an intimate friend can provide, make the adolescent realize that he or she is not so different after all. This realization, which can be disappointing for some and a source of relief for others, makes clear that all human beings share common thoughts, feelings, hopes, and fears. Perhaps such a realization is a necessary ingredient in a definition of maturity.

In summary, the use of formal operations includes the ability to reason about the hypothetical and the contrary-to-fact, to understand abstract concepts, and to consider a wide range of possibilities instead of only a few. When adolescents first acquire these abilities, they become absorbed in them. In many ways, their minds are dominated by possibility instead of reality, and they may spend more time in a world that might have been rather than in the world that is. As a consequence, the adolescent is often seen as an idealist, a nonconformist, a daydreamer, and, in the minds of some people, a troublemaker. Adults who feel threatened by the questioning attitudes of adolescents should realize that such questioning is often a sign of healthy intellectual growth.

COGNITIVE DEVELOPMENT IN THE ADULT YEARS

According to Piaget, formal operations represented the final qualitatively different stage of intellectual development—the "final level of equilibrium" (Inhelder & Piaget, 1958, p. 331). Although Piaget was quick to point out that formal thinking continues to develop throughout adulthood, he stressed that development occurs *within* the formal operational stage and does not extend beyond it. Adult thought indeed may differ from that of the young adolescent, but only in the sense that the adult becomes more accustomed to using formal operations and uses them in an ever-expanding range of situations.

Although the overwhelming majority of the research based on Piaget's theory has examined the thinking of children, a number of Piagetian studies of adult cognition have been undertaken. Let us first look at the results typically obtained from such studies and then explore whether the Piagetian model can adequately explain the thinking of adults.

Operational Task Performance During Adulthood

Some surprising results have arisen from studies of the performance of adults on concrete operational tasks such as conservation, classification, and seriation, as well as on a variety of formal operational tasks. Adults do not

According to Piaget, formal think-ing continues throughout adult-hood, and the adult uses formal operations in more and more sit-uations.

perform nearly as well as they might be expected to. For example, in a review of the literature on cognitive functioning in adulthood, Papalia and Del Vento Bielby (1974) reported that (1) most adults perform well on concrete operational tasks, (2) performance by adults on formal operational tasks is highly variable, and (3) elderly people do not perform as well as younger adults on either concrete or formal operational tasks.

The first set of findings—that most adults can classify, seriate, and conserve—should not be surprising, because such skills are thought to emerge during the elementary school years. The second set of findings— that many adults fail tests of formal operational reasoning—has been widely observed in the literature. Some studies indicate that as many as 50 percent of high school and college students are unable to use formal operations in problem solving (Joyce, 1977; Kolody, 1977; Renner, 1977; Sayre & Ball, 1975)!

How can the failure of adults to use formal operations be explained? Remember that Piaget never claimed that all adolescents and adults actually use formal operations, but only that they are theoretically capable of doing so. Many people have little need for abstract formal reasoning, because for most of their daily routines, concrete operational thinking will suffice. It is surprising, nevertheless, that a person might graduate from college without acquiring the formal reasoning skills necessary to solve abstract problems in such areas as mathematics, philosophy, or the natural sciences. Also surprising is the failure of older adults to demonstrate what appear to be basic logical skills. How can this finding be interpreted?

Early explanations seemed to suggest that the difficulty lay in the intellectual functioning of the person performing the task. For example, Papalia and Del Vento Bielby (1974) expressed the view that older adults fail to demonstrate operational skills because of (1) possible neurological decrements associated with aging, or (2) isolation from social, educational, and job-related experiences that may aid people in their reasoning ability.

By way of contrast to such earlier interpretations, the trend in recent years is to suggest that the "failure" of many adults to provide strictly logical solutions to problems does not indicate a deficiency in adult cognition at all. Instead, it indicates the inadequacy of a model that describes formal reasoning as the highest form of human thinking.

Beyond Formal Operations?

Dissatisfaction with Piaget's explanations of adult cognition in terms of formal reasoning has taken many forms. Some cognitive psychologists, such as Patricia Arlin (1975, 1984), believe that a level of intellectual functioning may exist that is even more advanced than formal operations. Arlin pointed out that formal operational thought is characterized by a convergent problem-solving process. That is, people use formal reasoning skills to discover correct solutions to problems. They discover, for instance, the correct way to combine flasks of colorless liquids to produce the color yellow. In fact, many standard tests of formal reasoning do resemble scientific experiments—techniques of discovery or convergence upon truth about the world.

In contrast to the problem-solving approach, in which there is convergence upon correct answers, Arlin suggested a higher form of reasoning called the *problem-finding*, or divergent, approach, which includes "creative thoughts . . . , the formulation of generic problems, the raising of general questions from ill-defined problems, and the slow cognitive growth represented in the development of significant scientific thought" (Arlin, 1975, p. 603).

To measure problem-finding ability, Arlin showed a group of unrelated objects (e.g., scissors, a wooden cube, candles, thumbtacks) to a group of college seniors and asked them to make a list of questions about the objects. She then rated the questions in terms of their sophistication and determined the extent to which the students showed signs of problem finding.

When the same college students were also tested on Piaget's formal operational (problem-solving) tasks, Arlin found that a person has to be a problem solver to be a problem finder, but that being a problem solver is no guarantee that one will also be a problem finder. In other words, the creative problem-finding approach seemed to be a step beyond mere problem solving, leading Arlin to conclude that a fifth stage of cognitive development goes beyond Piaget's formal operations.

Arlin's work has been criticized on the grounds that problem finding may not be qualitatively different from problem solving (Fakouri, 1976). That is,

Applying Our Knowledge
Piaget's Theory and Education

 Although Piaget himself had little to say about the educational process, a theory of children's cognitive development would reasonably be expected to have implications for classroom teaching. A person's educational philosophy would certainly be affected by acceptance of the view that cognitive structures underlie a child's thought processes, that thinking progresses through a series of qualitatively different stages, and that the motivation for intellectual growth is internal. Ginsburg and Opper (1988) summarized a number of classroom implications of Piaget's theory, including the following:

- *The language and thought of the child differ from that of the adult.* When teachers present material to children, they must realize that the children may be viewing the material from a perspective that differs from that of the adult. Many college professors are disappointed to learn that what they see as the exciting issues in their field are rather uninteresting to their students. In the case of the elementary school child, the misperception can be more serious because the child may be unable to appreciate the issues the teacher is trying to discuss.
- *Children learn best when they can manipulate their environments.* Activity should be an important aspect of learning. Verbal instruction may be effective for a college student, but a child learns best when the method of presentation is concrete. Allowing a child to carry out a physics experiment or to take a nature hike is more effective than discussing principles of physics or ecology.
- *The material to be learned should be "moderately" new to the child.* The most interesting food for thought is unfamiliar but not too alien to the child's cognitive structures. The child has already adapted to the familiar, leading to boredom in the learner, but something that is far above the child's level cannot be adapted to, and the learner will be confused.
- *Because the appropriate level of presentation for one child may be different from that for another, children should be allowed to work at their own pace.* Because the child's thinking progresses through stages, a child should not be forced to learn material until ready for it. If such forced learning occurs, the pupil becomes frustrated, the teacher becomes frustrated, and the child may develop negative attitudes about schooling.
- *Children should be allowed to talk to one another, to argue, and to debate in the classroom.* Intellectual growth is stimulated by social interaction, as any college student knows who has experienced the benefit of an informed discussion of issues in a dorm or a cafeteria. Much knowledge comes from student interaction both inside and outside the classroom.

perhaps the two are related skills, and perhaps problem finding is merely a refinement of problem solving instead of a totally different way of thinking. Piaget never suggested that intellectual growth ends at adulthood, but only that continued growth occurs within the stage of formal operations. Perhaps the process of problem finding is still a feature of formal operational thought instead of a completely new stage of intellectual development.

Instead of Formal Operations: Beyond Piaget

Instead of trying to identify more sophisticated stages as Arlin (1975, 1984) did, some psychologists deal differently with the question of whether formal operations represents the high point of human thinking; they argue that in describing formal reasoning as the final stage, Piaget exposed a serious weakness in his whole theoretical model (Datan, Rodeheaver, & Hughes, 1987). As an illustration of this type of criticism, Labouvie-Vief (1984, 1985, 1986a, 1986b) challenged Piaget's view that a pure state of logical reasoning is developmentally superior to, and therefore inherently better than, the subjective and intuitive thinking processes of the child. She suggested instead that in an adolescent or adult, pure, objective reasoning exists side by side with personal, subjective forms of thinking and that the two continuously balance and enrich each other.

Young children are indeed limited because their thought processes cannot go beyond the egocentric, the perceptual, and the intuitive. Adolescents begin to use formal reasoning, but often neglect, or temporarily "forget," their powers of intuition. Adults are more successful at blending the two ways of knowing, and therefore a type of thinking exists that is beyond formal operations: a blend of rational/objective and intuitive/subjective elements of thought.

To understand the benefits of the rational-intuitive balance in thinking, consider the following question asked of adolescents and adults by Labouvie-Vief (1986b): A woman tells her husband that if he ever comes home drunk again she will leave him. Several days later he comes home drunk. What does the woman do?

Using the strictly logical hypothetico-deductive strategy characteristic of formal operations, the answer is clear: The woman will leave her husband. Adolescents and young adults typically gave this undeniably logical answer.

Sometimes logic alone is not enough; the human dimension must be considered. Older adults are better able to blend rational and intuitive thought and engage in complex social reasoning.

The older respondents in the study usually said, however, that logic alone will not provide an answer; the human dimension must also be considered. How much does the woman love her husband? Why was he drunk? How drunk was he? Is the wife usually a forgiving person? Is she prone to make idle threats? What are the consequences for her, and for him, if she leaves?

Many of the older adults spontaneously referred to their own life experiences and their intuitive feelings about what would happen. In that sense, they attempted to blend the rational and intuitive sides of thought and probably came up with more realistic answers to the question than the younger respondents. Labouvie-Vief (1986b) suggests that complex social reasoning, requiring both propositional logic and intuition, is actually a step beyond formal reasoning, not because it is a qualitatively different stage but because social reasoning incorporates more aspects of the human thinking process.

Is the formal operational model appropriate to describe the complexity of adult cognition? No final answers are available at this time. Perhaps it is wise to remember, however, that Piaget's stages represent but one theoretical model of cognitive development. This model may not reveal the complete truth about human cognition, but as a theory it is successful in the sense that it generates questions that are likely to engage cognitive researchers for years to come.

ENVIRONMENTAL INFLUENCES ON COGNITIVE DEVELOPMENT

Piaget's theory, like most organismic theories, is an interaction model. That is, development results when the organism and the environment interact in increasingly sophisticated ways. The environment is important, obviously, because it provides intellectual material for the cognitive structures to adapt to. Nevertheless, Piaget had little to say about the features of specific environments in which children are raised. For example, he never attempted to describe ideal environments for intellectual growth, nor did he write about environmental deficiencies.

In this section, we deal with specific environmental factors that influence cognitive development. We look first at cultural differences in the emergence of Piaget's stages and what the differences might mean. Then we look at the influence of education, child-rearing practices, and diet on intellectual growth.

Cross-cultural Perspectives

Cultural anthropologists repeatedly maintain that what are considered "normal" human characteristics may be normal only within a specific cultural context. In the area of intellectual development, what is described as the normal developmental pattern may not be universally observed. For that reason, cross-cultural research is essential. Most cross-cultural research on cognition has been carried out within the framework of Piaget's theory, and numerous attempts have been made to determine whether Piaget's stages of development can be found beyond the mainstream European and U.S. culture.

Turning now to the findings obtained in cross-cultural research on cognition, a fairly consistent pattern emerges: The stages of development appear to be universal, but the rate of development varies from culture to culture.

Comparative research on the sensorimotor stage is rare, and what there is has been undertaken only within the past 15 years. Some scholars suggested that the scarcity of this research is attributable to the lack of standardized testing procedures (Dasen & Heron, 1981). Whatever the reason, the few studies that have been done strongly support the view that the characteristics of sensorimotor development are universal. Whether the infants were American, French, Indian, English, or African, they performed in much the same way on sensorimotor tasks.

Dasen and Heron (1981) commented on how the similarity is sometimes unbelievable, citing as an example the behavior of 1-year-old infants when given a plastic tube and a chain of paper clips. Typically, the infant tries to pass the chain through the tube, and this behavior is equally likely occur in European countries, where the infants have seen the objects before, and in African countries, where the objects are completely unfamiliar.

Comparative research on the concrete operational stage of development has yielded similar findings. That is, evidence exists that children from a variety of different cultures all acquire the logical thought processes of concrete operations, although the ages at which these are acquired are quite variable. For example, children in the African nation of Kenya have been found to conserve mass, weight, and volume in precisely the same sequence as Piaget observed in European children (Kiminyo, 1977). Thai children have been shown to perform in much the same way as Piaget's Swiss children on a variety of cognitive tasks, including seriation, class inclusion, and various forms of conservation (Opper, 1977). Similar results have been found in studies of children in England, Australia, New Zealand, Holland, Poland, and Uganda (Goldschmid et al., 1973).

Finally, cross-cultural research on the formal operational stage of development has been somewhat disappointing because, as Dasen and Heron (1981) pointed out, the few studies that have been done in this area found little or no evidence of formal operational reasoning. For example, M. Kelly (1977) noted that performance on a formal operational task in Papua and New Guinea was so poor that he decided not to administer the test to all the children in his sample. Perhaps the failure on formal reasoning tasks should not be terribly surprising, because a large percentage of U.S. high school and college students fail on these tasks as well (Joyce, 1977; Kolody, 1977; Renner, 1977; Sayre & Ball, 1975).

Although the sequence of stages appears to be universal, the rate of progression through the stages is highly variable (Dasen & Heron, 1981; Price-Williams, 1981). Why are children in some cultures slower to progress through the stages of development than others? Explanations usually focus on variables such as urbanization, schooling, and task relevance (Dasen & Heron, 1981). Perhaps the tests themselves measure skills necessary for survival in some cultures but not in others. For example, Dasen (1975) observed more advanced spatial skills in Eskimo children who belonged to a wandering hunting-and-gathering society than in West African children who belonged to a sedentary, agricultural tribe. Presumably, the Eskimos need better spatial ability to survive. In contrast, the West African children outpaced the Eskimos in the development of various forms of conservation—possibly because the Africans needed a sophisticated understanding of quantity to exchange their foodstuffs in the markets while the Eskimos did not.

Finally, the "cultural differences" explanations of differences in the rate of Piagetian cognitive development have been challenged. Cross-cultural psychologist Raphael Nyiti (1982) suggested that the quantitative differences among cultures occur because (1) the researchers were usually outsiders who had insufficient knowledge of the children's language and culture, and (2) the researchers tried to use standardized rather than "open" interviews. Nyiti noted that cultural differences in the rate of development disappeared when an open interview approach was used and when the questions were asked by an examiner from the child's own culture.

In summary, few qualitative differences in the developmental process occur among widely diverse cultures throughout the world. However, the rate of progression through the stages varies considerably, and the explanations of this variance focus on cultural opportunities and necessities for advancement, and factors related to the data-gathering process itself.

Influence of Education

An extensive amount of research has examined the effects of schooling on cognition, and the findings can be summarized as follows:

1. Formally educated people are better than uneducated people at abstracting general rules and applying them to specific problems (Scribner & Cole, 1973).
2. Formally educated people are better able than uneducated people to verbalize their behavior (Scribner & Cole, 1973).
3. Formally educated people are more likely than uneducated people to apply previously learned cognitive skills to totally new situations (Nerlove & Snipper, 1981).
4. Formally educated people do better than uneducated people on memory tasks (Rogoff, 1981).

5. The findings based on performance on Piagetian tasks are inconsistent. Some studies indicate that schooling can improve a child's concrete operational skills, such as conservation, while others show no differences at all between the schooled and the unschooled (Rogoff, 1981; Nerlove & Snipper, 1981).

Actually, it is not surprising that formal schooling has little effect on operational skills. After all, Piaget believed that a child developed by interacting with the world, and the classroom is only one arena of that interaction. Everyday experiences can stimulate intellectual growth, and as was mentioned earlier in this chapter, formal training is often of little help in the child's acquisition of operational skills.

Even though a relationship may exist between formal schooling and certain intellectual abilities, we are unable to conclude that schooling itself enhances cognitive growth. As Rogoff (1981) observed, parents who send their children to school may be wealthier, may have more progressive attitudes, or may have a higher motivation to achieve and set higher goals for their children than those whose children do not attend school. In other words, a variety of factors may account for cognitive differences between schooled and unschooled children when these differences occur.

Family Factors

Although the findings from studies of family factors in cognitive development are too numerous and diverse to summarize, an overall pattern appears: Children who are overly dominated, overly controlled by their parents, seem to be slower in their cognitive development. For example, Munroe and Munroe (1977) discovered that children of mothers who used harsh punishment performed less well on a conservation of mass study than children of more lenient parents. Children who were more self-directed were found in another study to score higher on a memory test than more controlled children (Munroe & Munroe, 1978).

In a study of Japanese children (Hatano, Miyake, & Tajima, 1980), maternal directiveness was related to a child's ability to conserve number. Highly directive mothers were identified as those who, when playing with their children, selected tasks for the children, paid close attention to what the children did, pressured them to do well, and allowed them only a slight degree of freedom. The children were then given a basic conservation of number task, similar to the one described earlier in this chapter. The children first agreed that two parallel rows contained equal numbers of marbles; then the marbles in one row were spread out and the children were asked if the number was still the same. Children of directive mothers were less likely to conserve number than children of nondirective mothers, and the authors concluded that the directive parent actually inhibits a child's interaction with the world.

Because the cognitive structures develop through a child's interaction with the world, a family's child-rearing patterns, and even the family structure itself (i.e., intact versus single parent family) could influence that interaction. A small but interesting body of research suggests that cognitive development is, in fact, influenced by variables such as family size, father absence, or child care arrangements (Nerlove & Snipper, 1981).

Nutritional Factors

The area in which the most is known about biological influences on intellectual functioning is human nutrition. Unfortunately, however, much of what we know has been based on extensions of findings from animal research or on research with hospitalized children. In other words, little is known about the effects of chronic malnutrition on intellectual development in a "normal" human population (Townsend et al., 1982).

Another difficulty with nutrition studies is the number of confounding factors other than nutritional ones. For instance, if children from malnourished segments of society are found to be slow to develop intellectually, does their retardation result from the inadequacy of their diets, or from other factors often correlated with malnutrition: poverty, illness, lack of intellectual stimulation?

Keeping in mind the limitations, let us look at one of the most extensive studies of the effects of nutrition on preschool mental development. Townsend et al. (1982) carried out a longitudinal study of nutrition and mental development in four Guatemalan villages: a pair of small ones and a pair of large ones matched on a number of characteristics. Children and nursing mothers in one member of each pair were then provided with a nutritional supplement. The children were later tested, using a battery of preschool tests. For example, the researchers tested the children's reasoning skills, verbal ability, perceptual skills, learning ability, and memory. With careful control for the possibility of confounding variables (e.g., intellectual stimulation at home, illness), the researchers found that the nutritional supplement significantly improved the children's mental performance for most groups. Furthermore, they reported that some follow-up research suggested that the intellectual advantages attributed to an improved diet carry over into adolescence and perhaps into adulthood! Such findings were consistent with those of previous research on the relationship of diet to intellectual functioning.

Researchers in future years may discover that mental development is linked specifically to certain aspects of brain maturation, hormonal factors, and even physical growth. However, for now psychologists must be content with a certain amount of speculation and with theoretical models of intellectual functioning, such as that suggested by Piaget, that appear to have predictive and explanatory value.

Summary

1. Organismic theories of cognitive development, such as Piaget's, maintain that development is a process by which individuals progress through a series of qualitatively different stages of thought, each of which builds on those that preceded it.

2. Piaget viewed intelligence as a form of biological adaptation, and he separated intelligence into its content, structure, and function.

3. Intellectual growth for Piaget involved the growth of the cognitive structures, and this occurred because of the constant interaction between structures and external experience.

4. Piaget considered the functioning of intelligence to consist of the twofold process of organization and adaptation, with adaptation being further divided into assimilation and accommodation.

5. Piaget believed that children progress through four stages of thought: the sensorimotor stage (birth–1½ years), the pre-operational stage (1½–6 years), the concrete operational stage (6–12 years), and the formal operations stage (12 years–adulthood).

6. Much debate in recent years has questioned the appropriateness of the formal operational model for describing the cognitive functioning of mature adults. Specifically, discussion has centered on the effectiveness of pure logic in solving complex social problems.

7. Cross-cultural research on cognitive development indicates that the stages of development described by Piaget are universal, but the rate of progression through the stages varies from culture to culture.

8. Amount of formal education is related to performance on tests of abstract reasoning and memory and to verbal ability. A link between education and success on Piagetian measures of cognitive development has been difficult to establish.

9. A child's cognitive development is related to parental disciplinary techniques and to degree of parental control.

10. Most of the research on biological influences on cognitive development has emphasized nutritional factors. An inadequate diet appears to have an adverse effect on children's reasoning ability, verbal ability, learning, and memory.

Key Terms

accommodation (p. 258)
animism (p. 267)
artificialism (p. 268)
assimilation (p. 258)
centration (p. 268)
classification (p. 272)

cognitive conceit (p. 278)
cognitive structures (p. 257)
concrete operations (p. 272)

conservation (p. 275)
formal operations (p. 278)
pre-operational intelligence (p. 265)
schemes (p. 260)

sensorimotor intelligence (p. 259)
seriation (p. 274)
transductive reasoning (p. 266)

Review Questions

1. Distinguish among the three concepts of content, structure, and function of human intelligence in Piaget's theory. Which did Piaget view as the least important, and why?

2. Define assimilation and accommodation and give an example of each from the realm of physical development and from the realm of intellectual development.

3. Explain what Piaget meant by describing a scheme as the sensorimotor equivalent of a concept.

4. Define the object concept. How does it develop over the first 2 years of life? Discuss the argument that memory may be a factor that explains the young child's difficulty with the object concept.

5. Define the following characteristics of pre-operational development: centration, animism, artificialism, mental experiment, and egocentrism.

6. What is the significance of the research on conservation in the framework of Piaget's theory? Why did he see this research as important in identifying the limits of pre-operational thought? What do critics of Piaget's theory suggest as alternative explanations for young children's failure to conserve?

7. Discuss the evidence supporting the argument that Piaget underestimated the intellectual abilities of preschool children.

8. Describe the differences between traditional views of why adults often fail to solve formal operational problems and the interpretations of such "failures" that have emerged in recent years. What are the limitations of Piaget's theory in explaining adult cognition?

9. Does the cross-cultural research on Piaget's theory support or disprove his arguments? Explain your answer.

10. List and discuss six classroom implications of Piaget's theory.

Suggested Readings

Elkind, D. (1981). *Childhood and adolescence: Interpretative essays on Jean Piaget.* New York: Oxford.

> A collection of 11 well-written essays on various aspects of Piaget's theory. This book clearly illustrates the numerous practical applications of cognitive-developmental theory. Included are essays on children's questions, egocentrism, reading instruction, conceptions of time, educational applications of Piaget's theory, and a comparison of Piaget's educational views with those of Maria Montessori.

Flavell, J. H. (1985). *Cognitive development* (2nd ed.). Englewood Cliffs, NJ: Prentice-Hall.

> An infancy-through-adolescence coverage of various aspects of cognitive development, written by one of the nation's foremost cognitive psychologists. Topics include intelligence, problem solving, language, perception, memory, social cognition, and personality factors in cognition.

Furth, H. G., & Wachs, H. (1974). *Thinking goes to school: Piaget's theory in practice.* New York: Oxford.

> A clear and readable discussion of Piaget's theory followed by a well-defined educational curriculum based on the theory. One of the most effective presentations of the educational implications of Piaget's work.

Ginsburg, H., & Opper, S. (1988). *Piaget's theory of intellectual development* (3rd ed.). Englewood Cliffs, NJ: Prentice-Hall.

> One of the most thorough, accurate, and readable treatments of Piaget's theory, suited for undergraduate students. Many examples are used to illustrate major Piagetian concepts, and the practical implications of the theory are discussed.

Piaget, J., & Inhelder, B. (1969). *The psychology of the child.* New York: Basic Books.

> A brief, clear summary of Piaget and Inhelder's work in the area of child development. Much of Piaget's work is spread out across a number of different volumes, many of which are difficult for an introductory-level student to read. Highly readable, the book is an excellent introduction for the student interested in reading Piaget and Inhelder in the original.

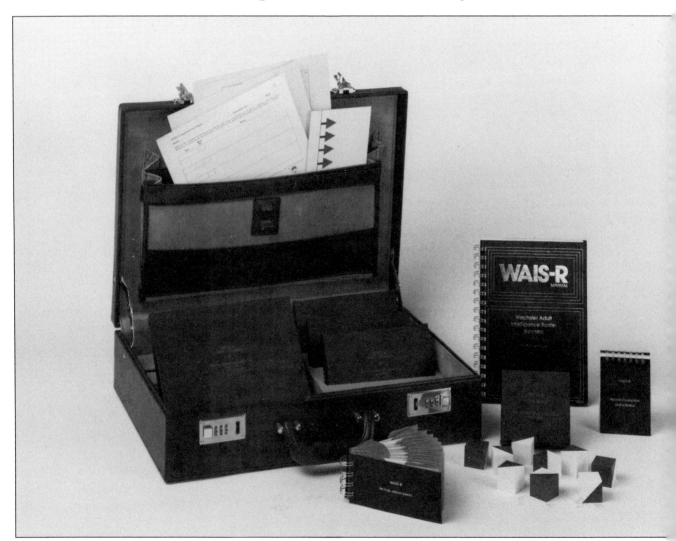

Chapter Eight

Intelligence and Creativity

Nature of Intelligence
Definitions of Intelligence
Intelligence Testing
What IQ Scores Really Predict

Development of Intelligence
Childhood
Adulthood

Genetic Influences on
Intelligence
Heredity-Environment Interaction
Meaning of Heritability

Environmental Influences on
Intelligence
Child-rearing Patterns
Nutrition
Birth Order and Family Size
Gender Roles

Construct of Creativity
Creative Personality
Creative Process
Creative Product

Development of Creativity
Theories of Creative Development
Developmental Patterns

 Randy was a high school junior whose entire scholastic career had been characterized by academic success. Then, for no apparent reason, his grades began to take a downward turn. His parents were surprised at first, and eventually became alarmed. What would cause an excellent student to undergo such a radical transformation? All the obvious possible explanations—physical illness, emotional stress, and even difficulties with particular teachers—were ruled out. Then one day Randy mentioned to his parents that, in the school guidance counselor's office several months before, he had accidentally seen in his file that his IQ score was 90, toward the lower end of the average range. Randy admitted that since that time he saw little point in pushing himself beyond what he now saw as his limited intellectual potential!

Randy's story had a happy ending: It turned out that the 90 he had seen was not his IQ score at all, but his percentile ranking in class! It was an indication of high academic standing and not low-average intelligence. Shortly after the mistake had been explained to him, Randy began to earn his customary A's and B's again, much to the relief of his worried parents.

Randy's story illustrates that intelligence, and particularly the IQ score, is frequently misunderstood; even if Randy's information about her score had been accurate, the IQ is not a fixed entity that sets limits on academic achievement. The second and more disturbing point of Randy's story is that IQ can have a frightening impact on a person's self-esteem—an impact so great that the belief one has about his or her own intelligence can significantly affect intellectual performance—despite the fact that most people, like Randy, have only a vague notion of what intelligence really means, or how intelligence can be measured, or what intelligence test scores indicate.

In this chapter, we will deal with a variety of issues related to individual differences in human intelligence, as well as with creativity, an aspect of human cognition that, like intelligence, is highly valued in our society. The intellectual processes involved in creativity are similar to those found in intelligence, but important differences exist as well.

We shall first attempt to define intelligence in the quantitative sense in which the term is commonly used, to illustrate the difficulties psychologists have had in formulating adequate definitions. We then discuss the controversies surrounding the effectiveness of, or even the desirability of, attempts to measure intelligence, and we will describe some of the better-known intelligence tests.

Questions about the relative contributions of heredity and environment in human intelligence are among the most controversial issues in the study of human development. Therefore, we shall examine the meaning and implications of current research suggesting inherited elements in intelligence, as well as the research on specific environmental contributions to intelligence during childhood.

Finally, we turn to a discussion of creativity. Creativity can be defined as an intellectual process or a personality characteristic, or in terms of a particular product, such as an invention or a work of art. We shall look at the three ways of defining creativity, and at what encourages the development of creativity across the life span.

NATURE OF INTELLIGENCE

The concept of intelligence is often misunderstood, perhaps because of a tendency to think of it as a "thing" that a person possesses. A more accurate view is that intelligence is an abstract concept based on, or abstracted from, human behavior. In other words, we never see intelligence; we see examples of behavior that can be described as more or less intelligent. Saying that a person has a certain amount of intelligence is incorrect, but one can say that the person behaved intelligently in a certain situation: He read a map correctly and found his destination; she helped resolve a family crisis by acting calmly; he answered questions properly on an intelligence test. In fact, the capacity for intelligent behavior varies within the same person, depending on the particular conditions under which the behavior occurs. The real danger in what anthropologist Stephen Jay Gould (1981) called the "reification" of intelligence—the assumption that intelligence is a thing rather than an abstraction—is that when people think of intelligence as a possession, they often become needlessly concerned about "How much of it do I have?" or "Do I have as much intelligence as other people do?"

Definitions of Intelligence

Many different approaches have been taken to the definition of intelligence. Jean Piaget, for example, saw it as a form of biological adaptation to the environment—the mechanism that allows us to interact successfully with our surroundings (see Chapter 7). Lewis Terman, the developer of the Stanford-Binet Intelligence Scale, viewed intelligence as the ability to engage in abstract thinking. Alfred Binet, who constructed the first widely used intelligence test, believed that intelligence involved "judgment, practical sense, initiative, and the ability to adapt . . . to circumstances" (Sattler, 1982). Perhaps the most comprehensive definition of intelligence came from David Wechsler, who developed two of the most widely used individual intelligence tests: Intelligence is the ability to think rationally, act purposefully, and deal effectively with the environment.

One area of disagreement concerning the intelligence concept centers on the question of the number of cognitive components, or factors, that underlie a person's intelligence. For example, Spearman (1927) believed that intelligence involved two factors: a general reasoning factor (*g*) and a factor specific to the type of test taken. Therefore, each section of an intelligence test would call upon the factor specific to that section (e.g., memory, spatial awareness) and would also call upon the *g* factor of general reasoning, which is required in every intellectual task. Thurstone (1938) rejected the concept of a single *g* factor and argued that seven basic abilities are involved in intelligence. The "primary mental abilities" are verbal meaning, inductive reasoning, perceptual speed, number facility, spatial relations, memory, and verbal fluency.

Perhaps the most complex analysis of what is involved in intelligence was proposed by Guilford (1967), who developed a three-dimensional model of intellectual functioning (see Figure 8.1). Guilford believed that five types of mental operations can be performed (cognition, memory, divergent thinking, convergent thinking, and evaluation), that these can be performed on four types of content (figural, symbolic, semantic, and behavioral) and that six different products might result (units, classes, relations, systems, transformation, and implications). As an illustration, cognition (i.e., recognition or simple interpretation) of symbolic (i.e., dealing with letters,

Figure 8.1

Guilford's Model of the Structure of Intelligence

Source: By permission from *The nature of human intelligence* by J. P. Guilford. Copyright © 1976. McGraw-Hill.

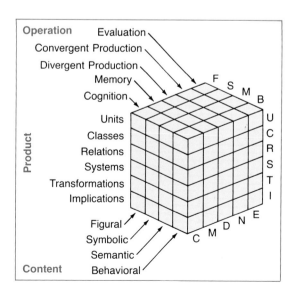

numbers, or other symbols) systems might be tested by a number series: What number is missing in the following series? 1 4 8 __ 19? (The answer is 13.)

Guilford hoped to identify components of intelligence in each of the 120 cells produced by the $4 \times 5 \times 6$ matrix and to develop tests for each component. Unfortunately, he was never able to reach his ambitious goal, and one critic remarked that such fragmenting of human intelligence gave the impression that people were "scatterbrained" (Cronbach, 1984).

In an interesting recent approach to the issue of the various cognitive components of human intelligence, Sternberg (1985, 1986) suggested that three different aspects of intelligence must be examined. The *componential aspect* closely resembles the concepts of intelligence described by the theorists already mentioned. It deals with internal mental processes, found in people of all cultures, that underlie intelligent behavior. A person high in componential intelligence would perform well on tests requiring analytical reasoning, including most traditional intelligence tests as well as most school examinations.

The *experiential aspect* of intelligence involves the ability to deal with new situations and to display a degree of insight and creativity in deciding how to solve unfamiliar problems. A person high in experiential intelligence would approach a novel situation by easily deciding which information is relevant and which to ignore, establishing an overall picture of the situation, and relating new information to what has already been experienced.

Finally, the *contextual aspect* of intelligence involves adapting oneself to a specific environment (e.g., adjusting to the routine of a new job), deciding when adaptation is no longer desirable (e.g., choosing to leave a job that no longer satisfies one's needs), and attempting to change an unsatisfactory environment (e.g., trying to improve conditions in a job one cannot leave).

Although the componential aspect of intelligence is universal, the experiential and contextual aspects differ from culture to culture. As an example, a person might be insightful in problem solving (experiential) and capable of adapting to the environment (contextual) of a small town, but might display considerably less intelligent behavior if relocated to a large metropolitan area. Additionally, a person could be highly proficient in one or more aspects of intelligence but only average or even deficient in others, as in the case of someone who is adept at analytical reasoning but lacks insight when confronted with unfamiliar situations.

On first glance, little agreement seems to exist about what constitutes human intelligence, but in fact the definitions share many similarities. Most psychologists agree that intelligence requires a general ability to reason. Most agree that a number of more specific cognitive abilities (e.g., verbal skills, quantitative skills, spatial awareness, intuition, memory, speed) are involved, and that these are correlated with rather than isolated from one another. Finally, most theorists agree that intelligence involves the ability to deal effectively with, or adapt to, the particular environment in which one

Solving a practical problem, such as reading or operating a computer, requires intelligence, which includes the ability to deal effectively with the environment.

lives. In other words, instead of viewing it only as an abstract mental ability, psychologists see intelligence as a problem-solving behavior, or class of behaviors, that occurs in a particular time and place and depends on the presence of certain mental abilities. The mental abilities in question, however, vary to some extent depending on the nature of the problem to be solved and are not easy to specify in every situation requiring intelligent behavior.

Intelligence Testing

Can intelligence be measured? Measuring human physical characteristics is a relatively simple task. Measuring psychological characteristics is considerably more difficult, particularly when, as in the case of intelligence, a clear and simple definition of the concept is not available.

Few psychologists deny that the concept of intelligence is a legitimate one, and few deny that human beings vary considerably in the effectiveness of their problem solving. Disagreement arises, however, over the effectiveness, and desirability, of attempts to measure human intelligence and to quantify individual differences in intelligent behavior.

In this section, we will discuss a number of intelligence tests that were developed by advocates of the measurement, or psychometric, approach to intelligence. Those mentioned are by no means the only tests of their kind, but they are among the best.

A good test of any kind has two essential characteristics. First, it must be reliable; if the same person is tested on two different occasions, the test scores should be highly similar. *Reliability* therefore refers to the consistency of scores yielded by a test (Anastasi, 1988). A good test must also be valid; it must measure what it claims to measure, so that test results provide clear and meaningful information about a person's performance in a particular area. *Validity* is established with reference to some outside criterion, such as another well-established test, or performance in a real-life situation (Anastasi, 1988). Thus, a reliable intelligence test should provide consistent scores over time, and a valid intelligence test should yield scores similar to those obtained on other valid tests, and the scores should bear some relationship to observed intelligent behavior in the outside world.

Critics of intelligence testing do not attack the reliability of the better-known tests such as those that will be described in the following section. Instead, they question the validity. They argue that the testing situation offers too artificial and too limited a sample of human behavior, and a person who performs poorly on a test might still exhibit highly intelligent behaviors in the everyday world. To use Sternberg's (1986) terminology, critics argue that most intelligence tests measure the componential aspects but not the experiential or contextual aspects of intelligence. Testing advocates respond that the tests do in fact measure a number of factors related to human intellectual functioning in a variety of situations; they point to the relationship between intelligence test performance and school success, occupational choice, and overall lifetime accomplishments as an indication that adaptive skills are indeed measured by the tests. Both perspectives should be kept in mind as we turn now to a discussion of some of the tests themselves.

Binet Tests

In 1904, the minister of public instruction in Paris appointed a committee to determine the levels of mental ability of children in the school system and thereby separate the normal from the subnormal. As members of the committee, Alfred Binet, a well-known psychologist, and Theodore Simon, a physician, developed in 1905 what was to be the first widely used intelligence scale. The 1905 Binet Scale included 30 tests arranged according to difficulty level. The test developers expected that the number of tests passed would be determined by the age of the child. Among other abilities, the tests measured sensory and motor skills, vocabulary, spatial awareness, memory, and the ability to tell time. Critics argued that the scale

Reliability
The consistency of the scores yielded by a particular psychological test.

Validity
The accuracy with which a psychological test actually measures what it is intended to measure.

relied too heavily on verbal ability and memory, maintaining that a child who had a facility with words would have a decided advantage over less verbal peers. Nevertheless, the scale represented a breakthrough in intelligence testing, and a number of U.S. researchers introduced translations and variations of it into this country.

The *Stanford-Binet Intelligence Scale,* the most successful U.S. version of the Binet tests, was produced by Lewis M. Terman (1877–1956) and several of his colleagues at Stanford University in 1916. Terman and his associates used the Binet Scale for more than half of their test items, and to these they added 40 additional items of their own. Test items were standardized; that is, they were tried out on about 1,000 children and 400 adults so that the questions could be placed at the appropriate age levels. (See Chapter 2 for a discussion of sampling procedures.)

The other major innovation of the 1916 scale was the initial use of the concept of IQ, or intelligence quotient. A person's IQ was determined by dividing mental age by chronological age and multiplying the results by 100 to eliminate the decimal—the ratio IQ formula.

The 1916 Stanford-Binet Scale was not a good measure of adult mental capacity, it was too heavily weighted with verbal as opposed to nonverbal items (a ratio of about two to one), and the instructions for scoring and administering it were not always adequate. In addition, although Terman attempted to standardize his test carefully, the standardization sample was relatively small and contained too few cases at the upper and lower extremes of intelligence. As such, the sample was not representative of the general population. The Stanford-Binet Intelligence Scale is still widely used today, although not in its original version. It was restandardized and updated in 1937 by Terman and Maud Merrill (1888–1978), and again in 1960, 1972, and most recently in 1985.

Wechsler Tests

Many individual intelligence tests appeared in the 1930s and 1940s. The most noteworthy of these was developed by David Wechsler (1896–1981), who carefully analyzed the standardized intelligence tests available at the time and experimented with them for 2 years using various populations of known intelligence, as determined by performance on other intelligence tests. Then, in 1939, he produced the *Wechsler-Bellevue Intelligence Scale,* which contained 11 of the most useful subtests taken from a variety of other tests. Included were tests of general information, arithmetical reasoning, memory, vocabulary, and spatial reasoning skills.

The Wechsler-Bellevue Intelligence Scale has undergone much revision and restandardization since 1939. Form II was modified and published as the Wechsler Intelligence Scale for Children (WISC) in 1949. Form I was revised into the Wechsler Adult Intelligence Scale (WAIS) in 1955, and these were replaced, respectively, by the WISC-R in 1974 and the WAIS-R in 1981. In 1963, Wechsler developed the Wechsler Preschool and Primary Scale of

*The Wechsler Intelligence Scale
for Children–Revised includes 12
verbal and performance tests that
determine IQ scores for children
aged 6 to 16.*

Intelligence (WPPSI), similar in basic form and content to the WISC but designed for use with children aged 4 through 6½ years. A 1989 revision of this test, WPPSI-R, expanded the age range to include ages 3 to 7. The WISC-R can be administered to children aged 6 to 16 and the WAIS-R to adults 16 years to 74 years old.

The 12 subtests of all three Wechsler tests are divided into verbal tests and performance tests. Wechsler saw the "verbal" subtests as relying heavily on a factor called verbal comprehension, which is, roughly speaking, the ability to derive meaning from words. The performance tests seem to rely on a factor of nonverbal organization that Wechsler described as "the capacity to organize discrete spatially perceived units into larger wholes or configurations" (Wechsler, 1958, p. 125). Other factors involved in intelligence, including a general reasoning factor and a memory factor, are found in both sections of the test.

Wechsler (1958) maintained that there are not different types of intelligence, but that intelligence shows itself in different ways. In fact, people who take a Wechsler test usually show a good deal of consistency across subtests. In other words, a person who scores well on the verbal subtests will probably score well on the performance subtests also—and vice versa.

Finally, Wechsler rejected as confusing the mental age concept of the IQ that Terman had used, and used instead the deviation IQ, determined by averaging the raw scores on the scales for each age group and arbitrarily equating average performance with an IQ score of 100. Virtually every IQ test used today employs the same procedure, including the updated Stanford-Binet. What people discover about themselves, therefore, when they take an IQ test, is not their mental age but the relationship of their performance to that of the "average" person who takes the test. (See *Applying Our Knowledge,* "Interpreting an IQ Score" for more information of the meaning of IQ scores.)

Infant Intelligence Testing

Infant "intelligence" tests are more accurately called tests of infant development because they emphasize physical, problem solving, basic motor skills, and indicators of social and emotional maturity. Needless to say, they do not contain the verbal emphasis so typical of IQ tests for older children and adults. Perhaps because the infant test examines different manifestations of human intelligence than the standard IQ test, scores earned on infant tests show little relationship to later IQ scores (Bloom, 1964; Ebel & Frisbie, 1986).

One of the more widely used infant intelligence tests is the *Bayley Scales of Infant Development,* developed by psychologist Nancy Bayley in 1969. The Bayley Scales are intended to provide a measure of an infant's progress from birth to age 2½, in three different developmental areas. The mental scale is a measure of memory, learning, and problem-solving ability; infant vocalizations, attempts at communication, and later understanding of speech; and ability to generalize and make simple classifications, which Bayley (1969) saw as the basis for later abstract thinking. The motor scale assesses motor coordination and manipulatory skills. For example, items deal with levels of proficiency in sitting, walking, and grasping objects of various sizes. Finally, the infant behavior record examines a child's emotions, activity level, energy, social tendencies, attitudes, and interests. For example, the examiner would look at an infant's fearfulness, cooperativeness, goal directedness, and responsiveness to mother and to persons in general.

The mental and motor scales produce scores referred to as the mental development index and the psychomotor development index, respectively. As with other intelligence tests, results are expressed in standard scores with a mean value of 100, and each infant's score is expressed in terms of its relationship to the mean. The range is from 50 to 150 on each scale.

Performance on the Bayley Scales of Infant Development, or on any other test of its kind, does not predict later intelligence but indicates how a particular infant is developing in comparison to the average infant of the same age. Bayley (1969) suggested that a value of the test is that

Applying Our Knowledge
Interpreting an IQ Score

 You have been informed that your child's score on the Wechsler Intelligence Scale for Children (WISC-R) is 116. Do you know what this means? Even an awareness that modern IQ tests produce *deviation IQ* rather than *ratio IQ* scores and that a score of 100 indicates average performance does not equip you to understand the meaning of your child's score. You know, of course, that your child's performance is better than the mean, or average, attained by children taking the WISC-R, but how much better is it? To answer this question, you need to know about the concept of the normal distribution and about the standard deviation of the test in question.

The *normal distribution* is a mathematical concept used to describe the way in which test scores distribute themselves around a mean. As Figure A shows, it is represented in the form of a graph known as a bell curve.

The bell curve indicates that in a representative sample of a population, the closer a person comes to the numerical average score on any particular test, the larger the number of scores that will be found there. Put another way, considerably more people are "average" on any measured characteristic than are exceptionally high or exceptionally low. In terminology more familiar to college students, if a class is distributed normally, more C's than A's or F's are earned on any examination.

The normal curve is segmented into percentages of the population defined by standard deviations above or below the mean. But what is a *standard deviation*? It is a numerical indication of the variance of the individual scores from the mean. To understand this concept, turn to a classroom example that may arise when a teacher grades on a curve.

Sue discovers that her score on an exam was 79, while the average score in the class was 72. Her score is obviously better than the numerical average, but is a 79 a grade of A or is it still a C? The answer depends on how the other students' scores clustered around the mean. If the range of scores was limited, and most students earned scores between 67 and 75 (that is, the standard deviation was low), Sue's 79 is quite impressive and may correspond to a grade of

A. If the majority of the class had scores between 62 and 82 and the range was considerably greater (that is, the standard deviation was high), Sue's 79 is less praiseworthy; it might now result in her getting a letter grade of C+ instead of A. It is obvious, therefore, that comparing Sue's score to the mean does not give her enough information; she also needs to know how the scores in the class were grouped around that mean.

A numerical standard deviation can be computed for any group of scores. If the distribution is normal, 34 percent of the population will fall within one standard deviation in either direction from the mean, 14 percent between one and two standard deviations from the mean, and so on. Turn back now to the original question about the meaning of your child's score of 116 on the WISC-R. The standard deviation on the WISC-R is 15 points (Wechsler, 1974). Thus, 68 percent of children taking the test earn scores between 85 and 115, 14 percent fall between 70 and 84 and 14 percent fall between 116 and 130, and 2 percent fall above 130 and 2 percent below 70. This is graphically depicted in Figure A. You now know that your child's score of 116 is above the normal range; your child performed better than approximately 85 percent of the children who take the test and would be considered "high average (bright)" according to the intelligence classifications provided in the WISC-R manual.

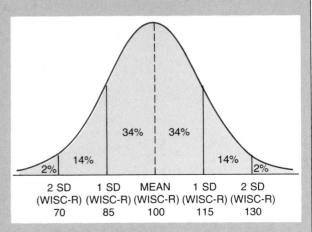

Figure A

developmental problems can be recognized early, and corrective treatment can begin. Poor performance on the Bayley Scales will not identify the cause of an infant's developmental problem (e.g., sensory deficits, neurological defects, emotional disturbances, difficulties in the home environment), but will alert a physician or psychologist that a problem exists, and that a search for its causes is warranted.

Group Intelligence Testing

Individual intelligence tests
Intelligence tests administered by a trained psychologist to one person at a time.

Group intelligence tests
Intelligence tests that can be administered to groups of people at a time.

The Stanford-Binet and the Wechsler tests are *individual intelligence tests*. That is, they are administered by a professional psychologist to one person at a time and are costly and time-consuming to administer on a large-scale basis. Most people who take intelligence tests take *group intelligence tests*.

The earliest group intelligence test was developed by a committee of psychologists during World War I as a service to the U.S. Army. Called the Army Alpha Test, it contained eight subtests, including measures of arithmetical skills, practical judgment, vocabulary, general information, and ability to follow directions. For those recruits who could not read or write, a nonverbal group test, the Army Beta, was also developed. More than a million men were tested during World War I, and by the end of 1918, when the war came to a close, group intelligence testing was fairly well established.

The 1920s witnessed a surge of interest in intelligence testing. Psychologists were so pleased by the successful use of the army tests that they pushed for the development of group tests for civilian use; in fact, the Army Alpha Test itself was used in schools and private industry as a predictor of future success (Haney, 1981). Numerous other group intelligence tests appeared as the United States became increasingly IQ conscious. Unfortunately, some of the early group tests were crude instruments administered indiscriminately to people of all ages and types, and for every conceivable reason (Anastasi, 1988).

The ease of administration and scoring (no psychology degree is required), and the possibility of mass testing for research purposes made group tests particularly attractive and probably contributed to the growing IQ consciousness, as well as to the eventual negative image of the intelligence testing movement. Many group intelligence tests were and are well standardized and sensitive instruments, but their indiscriminate use created a backlash in the early years; the result was suspicion and hostility directed toward all forms of psychological testing (Anastasi, 1988). In fact, the controversy surrounding the appropriate uses of group intelligence tests still continues today.

What IQ Scores Really Predict

A test of intellectual ability would have little value if the results were in no way related to performance in the real world. Because people presumably use their intelligence in their everyday functioning, one would expect a

Issues in Human Development
Defining Mental Retardation

 Approximately 6 million Americans, or 3 percent of the population, could be classified as mentally retarded, but what does this label mean? According to the American Association of Mental Deficiency (AAMD), mental retardation has three essential characteristics: (1) it is indicated by a score of 70 or lower on an intelligence test, (2) it involves an impairment in a child's ability to adapt to the environment, and (3) it first appears during childhood or adolescence (Goldstein, Baker, & Jamison, 1986).

A low IQ score *alone* is not an adequate indicator of mental retardation, primarily because a child may perform poorly on an IQ test for many reasons other than actual mental impairment (e.g., visual or speech problems, motor coordination problems, high anxiety, low motivation). Nevertheless, in a diagnosis of retardation based on a variety of relevant determining factors, IQ scores are used by the AAMD to define levels of impairment as shown in Table A. For a diagnosis of mental retardation to be made, the criterion of a low IQ score must be accompanied by the criterion of poor adaptive behavior. Adaptation problems are defined differently by the AAMD, depending on the age of the child in question (Grossman, 1983). Adaptation problems in infancy and early childhood include:

- problems in sensory and motor skill development
- problems in the development of communication skills
- difficulty in taking care of self needs (in the second year of life and beyond)
- inability to interact socially with other children or adults.

In later childhood and adolescence, adaptation problems include:

- problems in sensory and motor skill development
- inability to interact socially with other individuals or to participate in group activities
- inability to apply basic academic skills to everyday life
- inability to use appropriate judgment in everyday activities.

The experience of mental retardation may be particularly trying for children if the people in their environments do not understand their problems. Mildly retarded children, who are aware of their limitations, do not perform as well in learning situations and, as a result, may be less motivated to perform new tasks; they are often more anxious than the average child, more likely to feel frustrated by their limitations, and more likely to have lowered self-esteem (Goldstein et al., 1986). Adults who work with children in any capacity need to understand the concept of mental retardation and how a diagnosis of retardation is reached; they also need to be sensitive to the dangers of applying negative labels to any child, because the psychological impact of intellectual limitations can vary depending on a child's social circumstances.

degree of relationship between IQ scores and success in meeting life's daily challenges. In fact, such relationships do exist.

Before discussing the predictable power of IQ tests, a few words about the meaning of prediction are advisable. We are discussing prediction here in the statistical sense; one variable is said to predict another if even a modest degree of relationship has been established between the two.

Table A
AAMD Levels of Impairment

IQ SCORE	CATEGORY	DESCRIPTION
50–55 to 70	Mild mental retardation	Children in this category, comprising three-quarters of all those diagnosed as retarded, are considered "educable." They are often placed in special classrooms that teach academic skills up to a sixth-grade level, and increasingly such children are mainstreamed into regular classrooms.
35–40 to 50–55	Moderate mental retardation	Between 10 and 20 percent of all retarded children fit into this category. They are usually said to be "trainable" and are taught basic skills (e.g., housekeeping, counting money) that will allow them to function independently as adults.
20–25 to 35–40	Severe mental retardation; profound mental retardation	Because their mental impairment is so great and because they often have physical handicaps as well, children in these categories are often institutionalized. However, in recent years increasing attempts have been made to train these children in basic skills, either in trainable classrooms or in special centers.

Statistical prediction involves no guarantee of future performance and is based on group rather than individual data. This means that a finding of a positive relationship between IQ and classroom performance may lead us to assert that IQ scores predict school grades. It does not mean, however, that Jane will definitely be successful in school because she earns a high IQ score or that Tim has little chance of succeeding in the classroom because his IQ score is low. In reality, a number of factors (e.g., gender, motivational level, self-image) other than the intellectual processes measured by IQ tests are related to school success, and parents concerned about a child's academic potential would receive more meaningful information from a sensitive teacher than from an IQ score.

IQ and School Performance

Throughout years of research, a consistent pattern has emerged concerning the relationship between IQ and school performance. Modest but significant correlations exist at various grade levels between IQ and school grades (Matarazzo, 1972; Minton & Schneider, 1980), between IQ and rank in class (Conry & Plant, 1965; Willerman, 1979), between IQ and tests of general academic achievement (Bossard & Galusha, 1979), and between IQ and the ultimate educational attainment (years of schooling completed) of adults (Matarazzo, 1972; McCall, 1977). In addition, positive correlations exist between IQ and success in specific academic subject areas, such as mathematics, science, social studies, language arts, and reading (Bloom, Wagner, Bergman, Altshuler, & Raskin, 1981; Kavrell & Petersen, 1986). Finally, low IQ scores and the tendency to drop out of high school are linked (Brody & Brody, 1976), although the decision to drop out of high school is related to many social, cultural, and personality factors as well as to intellectual ability.

In summary, a relationship exists between IQ test performance and many aspects of school performance in children, adolescents, and adults. In fact, it would be surprising if intelligence were not related to academic achievement in some way, if only because classroom performance and IQ test performance may require similar cognitive and verbal skills. Nevertheless, IQ scores themselves are thought to have little predictive value for teachers because of the many variables involved in classroom performance; in fact, the best predictor of future academic achievement is not a standardized test score at all, but the student's current level of academic achievement (Antonak, King, & Lowy, 1982; Ebel & Frisbie, 1986).

IQ and the World of Work

An examination of the link between IQ and performance in the job world produces a mix of findings. A relationship definitely exists between IQ and occupational status (Matarazzo, 1972; McCall, 1977b; Willerman, 1979). That is, people in high-status professional-level careers (e.g., accountants, engineers, teachers) tend on the average to have higher IQs than people in lower-status nonprofessional careers (e.g., skilled laborers, truck drivers, miners).

We can look at the relationship between IQ and success in the work world in another way, however. We might look within particular careers at the relationship of IQ and job success. That is, we might ask if teachers with higher IQs are more successful than teachers with lower IQs, rather than comparing a group of teachers to a group of skilled laborers. Such within-career analyses do not yield significant findings; IQ scores may predict occupational status but they are considerably less effective in predicting success on the job (Matarazzo, 1972; Willerman, 1979). The reasons are similar to the reasons discussed earlier for not using IQ scores to predict school achievement; again, many factors are involved in job success, and these include motivation, interest, and overall emotional well-being in the workplace.

IQ and Success in Life

To what extent does a relationship exist between performance on an IQ test and life success as measured by conventional standards of wealth, fame, and educational attainment? To answer this question, Terman in 1921 identified a group of more than 1,500 children and adolescents (aged 3–19) whose IQ scores placed them in the top 2 percent of the population. These children were tested and interviewed repeatedly over almost 60 years, most recently in 1977; most of those who were still living were retired. The goal of this massive longitudinal study was to determine whether highly intelligent people live their lives any differently than the general population.

According to psychologists Pauline and Robert Sears (Goleman, 1980), the majority of Terman's highly intelligent people have done remarkably well for themselves. In terms of educational attainment, they were considerably ahead of the national average. Two-thirds of them were college graduates, and nearly 30 percent eventually earned advanced degrees (57 medical degrees, 92 law degrees, 92 Ph.D.s, 177 master's degrees). Great diversity of career choice was apparent among the highly intelligent group; they were writers, lawyers, business executives, film directors, bankers, scientists, and mail carriers, and they seemed to be highly successful in whatever career they chose. Many were nationally known figures by the time they reached middle age. For example, one was an Academy Award–winning film director, another a highly popular writer of science fiction. As a whole, the group had produced nearly 3,000 books, monographs, and scientific articles. Perhaps unsurprisingly, the income level of Terman's sample at middle age was remarkably high—four times the national average!

We cannot conclude, of course, that the lives of highly intelligent people are better in an absolute sense than those of people of lower intelligence, nor can we conclude that a high degree of intelligence is in itself a guarantee of accomplishment. However, by many standards of success (educational attainment, wealth, fame) the participants in Terman's study had certainly distinguished themselves. Performance on IQ tests clearly bears some relationship to performance in the real world.

Issues in Human Development
Is There a Cultural Bias in IQ Testing?

 One of the most frequently heard criticisms of the IQ concept is that IQ tests themselves are biased in favor of people who grow up in the white middle-class culture. Members of minority groups, such as blacks, Puerto Ricans, and Mexican-Americans, are at a distinct disadvantage when taking such tests for two reasons: (1) the questions themselves tap knowledge pertaining to the white middle-class culture, which is less accessible to members of minority cultures (e.g., "Which word does not belong? *cello, drum, viola, guitar, violin*"); and (2) the tests are presented in and responses must be given in the language of the white middle-class culture; many minority group members speak a foreign language or a variation of "street English" that differs considerably from standard English. Therefore, minority group test takers are being tested in their second language.

In opposition to the cultural bias argument, advocates of intelligence testing suggest that the most widely used intelligence tests have taken into account any cultural differences that may exist in our society by including a broad cross-section of the American public in the standardization sample and by carefully avoiding a sample that would give an advantage to any particular subculture. Furthermore, they argue that subcultural linguistic differences are greatly exaggerated; virtually everyone in our society is exposed via the media to standard English, regardless of the dialect they choose to speak at home.

The cultural bias argument appears to be one that nobody can win, because neither position can be proven conclusively. However, a truly "culture-free" test would be extremely difficult, if not impos-sible, to develop; because we all function within a cultural framework, how can a test developer ever be completely separated from that framework? In addition, no intelligence test is a perfect instrument, and test inadequacies contribute to some extent to observed racial/cultural IQ differences.

An interesting solution to the cultural bias problem in IQ testing was offered by sociologist Jane Mercer of the University of California (in Rice, 1979). Mercer developed an instrument known as the System of Multicultural Pluralistic Assessment (SOMPA). The SOMPA consists of (1) a Wechsler IQ test to measure the child's mental ability within the dominant culture; (2) a 1-hour interview with a parent to obtain the child's health history, a picture of the child's home life and family background, and a measure of the child's adaptive ability to function effectively in the everyday environment; and (3) a complete physical examination.

Mercer then combines all the information gathered and adjusts the Wechsler IQ score accordingly. For example, a child who does poorly on the WISC, but comes from an impoverished home environment and handles everyday problems quite effectively, would have the WISC score adjusted upward.

The merits of the particular SOMPA battery have been hotly debated, but Mercer's approach illustrates an important point about intelligence testing: The more information we have about a child's ability and performance, the better able we are to make meaningful decisions about that child's future. The IQ score should not be considered in isolation, but as only one piece of information in a complicated pattern of human intellectual functioning.

DEVELOPMENT OF INTELLIGENCE

Now that we have discussed the nature of intelligence and issues related to its measurement, we turn to questions about the development of intelligence across the life span. Do some aspects of intelligence change throughout the years of childhood and adulthood? Do some aspects remain the same? If changes do occur, how can those changes be explained?

Childhood

What changes in intelligence test performance occur as an individual moves through childhood? If we look at performance on two of the more widely used intelligence tests, the WISC-R and WAIS-R, we observe a pattern that is typical: Performance on each of the subtests improves gradually and continuously throughout childhood and adolescence until a peak is reached somewhere between the ages of 18 and 25.

Two points should be remembered when we consider age increases in the abilities involved in intelligence. First, although improvement occurs in the various abilities, this is not always reflected in improvement in the IQ score because the test norms change as we age so that expected improvements in performance are built into the tests themselves. As an example, a 9-year-old is expected to have a larger vocabulary than a 7-year-old and will outscore the younger child on the WISC vocabulary subtest. A 7-year-old who knows the meaning of 9 words will be awarded four scale points, whereas a 9-year-old would have to define at least 13 words correctly to get four scale points. However, when scale points are converted to IQ scores, the older child's IQ will not be higher than that of the younger child; the older child is expected to answer more questions than the younger one, and if improvement does *not* occur, the IQ score will actually decrease.

A second point to remember about intelligence changes in childhood is that the group stability of the IQ does not suggest the absence of individual variation. Researchers have generally recognized that the IQ is stable throughout childhood, at least after the preschool years. Bayley (1949) found correlations ranging from .80 and .96 between childhood and young adulthood and adolescent and young adulthood scores, respectively. However, this stability is based on group data and does not mean that a particular child's IQ will not change with age. The high correlations between childhood and young adult IQ tell us only that scores change very little relative to one another within the group: The high scorers on the first test are the high scorers on the second test, and the low scorers on the first test are the low scorers on the second. However, the average scores for the group may have changed in either direction.

Much of the research literature (e.g., Bayley, 1949; Honzik, Mcfarlane, & Allen, 1948; Moore, 1967; Sontag, Baker, & Nelson, 1958) suggests improvement across the childhood and adolescent years in IQ scores and significant differences for individual children, with some improving markedly and some showing test-retest decline. All this means that consistency can be present within the group despite changes in the group average, and even despite dramatic IQ changes for some individuals within the group.

Adulthood

Intelligence increases throughout childhood, but what happens to the IQ when people reach adulthood? Does it remain stable throughout life, does it continue to increase, or does it begin to decline? Unfortunately, no simple answers to these questions are possible. In fact, some evidence supports each of the three developmental patterns—decline, stability, and improvement—throughout adulthood. The particular pattern depends on many elements, including the type of research design used, the "type" of intelligence being examined, and the characteristics of the person in question. As we discuss adult changes in intelligence, keep in mind that we are referring to group norms, but intelligence is actually characterized by a high degree of individual variability.

Differences in Research Design

Let us look first at the influence of the research design on the findings relating age and intelligence during adulthood. The earliest research (e.g., Jones & Conrad, 1933; Miles & Miles, 1932) consisted of cross-sectional studies, comparing two age groups at the same point in time, and young adults typically scored higher than elderly adults on IQ tests. In marked contrast, however, were the later findings from longitudinal studies, in which the same group of people was tested at different points in time: IQ appeared to be stable, or even to improve, at least until the later years of adult life (Bayley, 1955, 1957, 1966; Cunningham & Owens, 1983; Owens, 1953). Using Schaie's (1970) description of the information yielded by the two types of research design, we might conclude that *age differences* in intelligence favor the young, but *age changes* across the life span are not significant.

Why should a researcher's results be so heavily influenced by the research design used? For several reasons. First, although the intent of the cross-sectional studies was to report on intelligence differences caused by age, they may also have described differences that were only accidentally related to age. To illustrate this distinction, a group of young adults and a group of elderly adults in 1990 are certainly different in age, but they are probably also different in level of education, health, speed of response, and experience with and attitude toward psychological testing. If the two age groups differ in intelligence scores, how do we know that the difference is caused by age alone and not by any or all of the other variables? In fact, all these other variables have been found to influence IQ test performance (Botwinick, 1978).

Level of education is related to intelligence in that better-educated people score higher on IQ tests, either because schooling provides them with knowledge or skills that are useful in answering test questions, or because more intelligent people are more likely than less intelligent ones to seek out advanced education. Older people in our society are not as well educated as those in their grandchildren's generation. However, in developmental studies that eliminate the education factor, the IQ differences virtually disappear (Green, 1969; Schaie & Strother, 1968). In other words, when young and elderly adults are matched in terms of educational attainment—

a situation that will not occur randomly—we can see the extent to which education contributes to an IQ score. As Green (1969) concluded, the declines that usually are found in intelligence can be attributed to the fact that higher levels of formal education are achieved with each succeeding generation.

Even minor *health problems* have been found to depress the performance of the elderly on the WAIS (Botwinick, 1978; Botwinick & Birren, 1963; Correll, Rokosz, & Blanchard, 1966), as well as on other forms of problem solving such as many of the Piagetian tasks described in Chapter 7 (LaRue & Waldbaum, 1980). More significant chronic health problems can obviously affect a person's intellectual functioning as well. For example, although high blood pressure is not an inevitable consequence of aging, among elderly adults suffering from this condition, a relationship exists between blood pressure level and intelligence test performance (Labouvie-Vief, 1985). A more intriguing argument in support of the view that intelligence and physical well-being are related is the phenomenon referred to as terminal drop: A sharp and dramatic intellectual decline occurs in many elderly people within a few years before death (Kastenbaum, 1985; Palmore & Cleveland, 1980). This death-related decline, a sort of cognitive disorganization, has never been fully explained, although it has been observed repeatedly in longitudinal research. Thus, uncharacteristically poor performance by an older adult on an IQ test may say more about the nearness of death than about the process of aging itself.

The loss of *speed* that typifies later adulthood (see Chapter 3) can definitely affect performance on intelligence tests, many of which have time limits on certain questions. When these limits are removed, the test performance of elderly people improves somewhat (Doppelt & Wallace, 1955). In a slightly different approach to the problem, L. W. Hoyer, W. J. Hoyer, Treat, and Baltes (1978–1979) retained the time limits but trained older people to make very fast responses, and some improvement in test performance resulted. Neither study, however, totally eliminated the age difference by negating the speed factor. What this means is that the elderly may be penalized by time restrictions on testing, but loss of speed alone does not account for age differences in IQ test performance.

Finally, *motivation, anxiety,* and *willingness to cooperate* can influence performance on an IQ test. If people of any age see little value in a test and refuse to cooperate, obviously they will not perform well. Younger people may be more familiar with the concept of intelligence testing and may be more willing than the elderly to take such tests. Older people may see test taking as a frivolous exercise or as a means of proving that they are not as smart as they used to be. They may also be frightened by such a test, and uncertain about what to expect from it, and fear may inhibit their performance (Botwinick, 1978).

For a cross-sectional study to demonstrate that age alone is responsible for observed age differences in intelligence, researchers must control for all other variables. For example, suppose a group of older people could be found who closely resemble young adults in terms of health, social class, educational attainment, financial condition, and academic interests. Schaie and Strother (1968) found just a group; 70 older people were identified who were extremely healthy, financially comfortable, living at home and satisfied with their living arrangements, and involved in a variety of social, educational, and creative activities. In other words, this was not an average sample of elderly Americans.

The performance of this superior elderly population closely resembled that of a group of average 17-year-olds on a variety of intellectual tasks. These findings do not prove, of course, that no intellectual decline occurs with age. They do demonstrate, however, that age alone does not bring about an inevitable intellectual decline and that the cognitive deficits of the elderly may have more to do with variables related to physical and psychological well-being than with age itself.

Thus, cross-sectional research that fails to isolate the age variable while holding other variables constant may give the wrong impression that age alone is responsible for IQ differences. This failure to account for the influence of other variables is partly responsible for the generally pessimistic picture that is drawn by cross-sectional research and for the contrast between these and the optimistic findings of longitudinal studies. However, the longitudinal studies may contain a bias, too, but in the opposite direction. Longitudinal studies of any kind usually suffer from a high rate of attrition. Over the years, participants may move away, die, or simply lose interest in the research project. A small drop in the number of participants would not present a major problem if the dropouts were equally distributed across all ability levels. What usually happens, however, is that the initially least able people are the most likely to drop out (Cooney et al., 1988; Riegel, Riegel, & Meyer, 1967). Therefore, the group average may improve with each testing in part because those with the lowest scores are no longer participating.

Longitudinal research is also affected by cultural change. If a group of people knew more about microcomputers in 1985 than they did in 1975, we would hardly conclude that microcomputer knowledge increases with age. The more logical explanation is that as a culture we have become increasingly familiar with computer technology.

Finally, the longitudinal design is susceptible to a test-retest practice effect. The very act of taking the same test repeatedly over time may make a person more comfortable in the testing situation and more familiar with the actual test items.

Current research on adult intellectual change often uses a sequential design, in which different age groups are tested at different points in time. The strength of the sequential design, which combines the best features of cross-sectional and longitudinal designs, is that it allows the researcher to analyze separately in the same study the effects of culture and the effects of age, and to determine the relative contributions of each factor. (See Chapter

2 for a discussion of the various research designs used in developmental research.)

Sequential studies of adult intelligence typically find that, although younger age groups perform better than older ones, relative stability remains over time *within* each age cohort (Labouvie-Vief, 1985; Nesselroade, Schaie, & Baltes, 1972; Schaie & Labouvie-Vief, 1974; Schaie & Parham, 1977). Intelligence declines that can be attributed only to age itself are not seen until the late 60s or early 70s. More importantly, the sequential research indicates that cultural/educational factors are largely responsible for age-related intelligence differences, and that what were once thought of as the normal intellectual "deficits" of later life are not inevitable at all. The implications of these findings are considerable. If age differences in intelligence have environmental origins, such differences might be reduced by appropriate environmental treatments. In fact, much recent research in adult cognition is devoted to exploring just such a possibility (Baltes & Baltes, 1980; Denney, 1981; Labouvie-Vief, 1977, 1985).

Differential Developmental Patterns in Abilities

Beyond the struggle to find appropriate research methodologies, another reason contributes to the difficulty in finding out whether intelligence stabilizes, declines, or continues to grow throughout the life span: Intelligence consists of many factors and is manifested in many different ways. Certain aspects of intelligence appear to decline with age; others do not. A convenient framework to use in discussing the different patterns of IQ change is found in the WAIS-R, which, as mentioned earlier in the chapter, contains a variety of subtests. Many studies have pointed to a typical pattern in performance on the WAIS: Verbal abilities show little or no decline with age and may even show improvement, whereas psychomotor skills and perceptual-integrative skills always decline. Scores on the WAIS verbal subtests, including information, comprehension, arithmetic, vocabulary, and similarities, maintain themselves very well across the life span. Scores on the performance subtests, such as picture completion, object assembly, block design, picture arrangement, and digit symbol, decline noticeably throughout middle age and beyond.

Some researchers (Horn, 1982; Horn & Cattell, 1966) maintain that the WAIS verbal and performance subtests measure different forms of intelligence. The verbal subtests measure *crystallized intelligence,* or the ability to use previously acquired skills and information to solve a problem, whereas the performance subtests measure *fluid intelligence,* which is formless and does not depend on previous experience (Matarazzo, 1972).

Crystallized intelligence
Intelligence that is based on previously acquired skills or information.

Fluid intelligence
A formless, intuitive type of intelligence that is unrelated to education or experience.

Crystallized Intelligence. Crystallized intelligence includes vocabulary and general information. It also includes formal reasoning, or the ability to reason deductively; social skills, or the ability to behave intelligently in a social situation; and arithmetic skills. All these skills are developed and refined through experiences with the culture in which people live. In fact, Horn (1982) described crystallized intelligence as "the extent to which an individual has incorporated the knowledge and sophistication that constitutes the intelligence of a culture" (p. 850).

If the skills involved in crystallized intelligence are acquired and refined through contact with our culture, as we grow older and have increasing amounts of such contact, we can be expected to increase in crystallized intelligence. This increase is precisely what Horn and Cattell (1966) predict, and, in fact, such an increase generally occurs.

Fluid Intelligence.   Fluid intelligence includes inductive reasoning, discrimination, figural relations, memory, and speed in solving mental problems. Inductive reasoning allows us to discover a general rule by observing a number of particular instances. For example, a U.S. tourist in London notices that on several walks through the city, he collided head-on with other pedestrians, which never happens at home. Putting together his observations about pedestrian collisions and his observation that the English drive on the left side of the road rather than on the right, he induces a general rule: English pedestrians keep to the left on a sidewalk, whereas people in the United States keep to the right. On his next walking tour, the visitor walks on the left and discovers that the collisions no longer occur.

Figural relations is the component of fluid intelligence that allows us to perceive spatial relationships, to use maps effectively, and to develop a sense of direction. It allows us to see patterns and detect relationships among objects.

The memory component of fluid intelligence involves association, as well as span of apprehension. An example of associative memory would be a paired-associate learning task. A list containing words paired with nonsense syllables (e.g., *house-dak, man-feb*) is presented. The test taker then sees one member of the pair by itself and is asked to remember the other member of the pair. Span of apprehension tests involve recognition and retention of the features of the immediate environment, as when people are asked to recite a list of words or numbers immediately after hearing them.

Crystallized intelligence increases with age, but Horn and Cattell (1967) found age decrements in fluid intelligence, even after the decade of the 20s. The curves for the development of crystallized and fluid intelligence are presented in Figure 8.2. The authors suggested that as people age, they substitute certain components of intelligence for others. The older person does not pick up new information as quickly and does not remember as well. The older person shows increasing distractibility, confusion, inattention to the form of an argument, abandonment of difficult problems, willingness to accept inconsistent solutions to a problem, and difficulties with classification (Horn, 1978). However, older persons are increasingly more knowledgeable about their own culture. Acquired skills are more

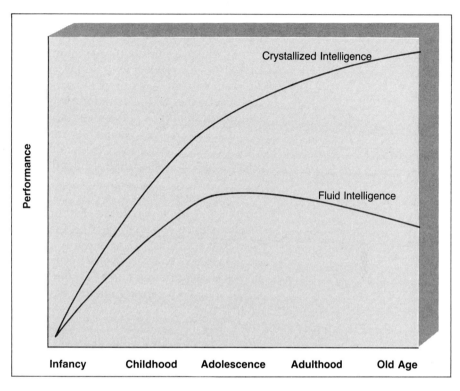

Figure 8.2

Development of Fluid Intelligence and Crystallized Intelligence across the Life Span.

Source: Adapted from J. L. Horn. Organization of data on life-span development of human abilities. In L. R. Goulet & P. B. Baltes (Eds.), *Life-span developmental psychology: Research and theory.* New York: Academic Press, 1970, pp. 423–66.

practiced, and an increase in common sense is apparent. In short, there is a tendency to substitute accumulated wisdom for brilliance.

Why does fluid intelligence decrease with age, whereas crystallized intelligence does not? Neurological change has been suggested as one contributing factor (Horn, 1970, 1981; Horn & Donaldson, 1980). Age-related injuries to the brain and central nervous system may affect fluid intelligence more than they affect crystallized intelligence. Psychological factors such as rigidity (Horn, 1978) and experiential factors such as lack of practice also must be considered in explaining the fluid intelligence decline. For example, Green (1971) rejected the neurological argument, maintaining instead that the abilities involved in crystallized intelligence are more likely to be practiced than those involved in fluid intelligence. The difference is in the use. How often do average older people encounter new problem-solving challenges? How often are they called upon to use inductive reasoning or to test their span of apprehension? In contrast, older people constantly use their vocabulary skills, their information about their world, and their social intelligence.

A similar point about age changes in fluid intelligence was raised by Rybash et al. (1986), who suggested that measures of fluid intelligence simply fail to take account of the context in which adults usually think. Thus, the observed decline in fluid intelligence may be more apparent than real. In support of such an argument, a growing body of evidence indicates that training procedures can significantly improve the performance of older adults on tasks requiring fluid intelligence (Baltes, Dittman-Kohli, & Dixon, 1984; Baltes & Willis, 1982; Hofland, Willis, & Baltes, 1980).

What, then, should we conclude about changes in intelligence during adulthood? At the very least, the outlook seems considerably more positive than was once believed. Poor performance on IQ tests may be increasingly typical across the span of adult life, but age alone has never been demonstrated as the cause of an intelligence decline, at least not before a person's late 60s or early 70s. Furthermore, intelligence is a complex construct. The pattern of intellectual change in adulthood seems to depend on the type of intelligence under discussion, with crystallized abilities more likely than fluid intelligence to remain stable or to improve with age. Even here, researchers disagree about whether the aging process itself accounts for the fluid intelligence decline, or whether we simply have fewer opportunities as we age to practice our fluid abilities. Finally, the entire direction of research on adult intellectual development has changed in recent years. Instead of following past practice of establishing young adult standards of performance, comparing older adults to those norms—often without recognizing differences in the sociocultural contexts in which young and old people function—and concluding that adulthood is characterized by increasing intellectual "deficits," researchers today are more likely to look at aging from a "differential" perspective (Baltes, 1982; Labouvie-Vief, 1985). That is, they maintain that older adults may function differently from the young when they solve problems, but such differences may reflect the real-world experiences of the problem solver rather than a loss of ability associated with age. (See Chapter 7 for a discussion of this issue in relation to Piaget's cognitive-developmental theory.)

GENETIC INFLUENCES ON INTELLIGENCE

Perhaps the most controversial aspect of any discussion of human intelligence involves how intelligence differences originate. Do these differences have biological origins, are they totally determined by environmental conditions, or does the answer to the question lie somewhere in between? In this section, we shall examine the evidence in support of genetic influences on the development of human intelligence, but, clearly, heredity versus environment questions rarely have simple answers.

Heredity-Environment Interaction

Heredity and environment interact so extensively in determining behavioral characteristics that separating them is virtually impossible. Attempts to do so typically focus on situations in which one of the two factors is held constant while the other is allowed to vary. In other words, researchers look for individuals whose genetic characteristics are similar or identical, but whose environments differ considerably, and for individuals whose genetic makeup is quite different, but whose environments are similar or identical. Finding genetically similar individuals is considerably easier, however, than finding individuals whose environments are identical because the concept of environment is difficult to define. Are two children raised in the same family raised in the same environment? The physical environment is certainly the same, but the social and psychological environment might be markedly different.

To locate genetically similar people is not difficult at all. One simply looks at kinship patterns. Identical, or monozygotic, twins are genetically identical; siblings are genetically similar, as are parents and children. Kinship correlations in IQ are found by forming two groups, each containing one member of a kinship pair (e.g., a group made up of husbands and a

Identical twins show virtually identical performance on intelligence tests. Such kinship correlations form the basis of the hereditarian view that intelligence is genetically transmitted.

group made up of their wives), by determining the IQ scores of the entire sample, and by examining the degree of relationship between the two groups.

Figure 8.3 summarizes the findings of 51 kinship correlation studies containing more than 30,000 pairs. The closest family relationships are found at the top of the figure, and the most distant at the bottom. The numbers are correlation coefficients, and the higher the number, the higher the degree of relationship in IQ. When a large number of cases is studied, a number below .40 is generally regarded as low, a number from .40 to .60 as moderate, and a number above .60 as a high correlation.

As can be seen from Figure 8.3, the most genetically similar group, monozygotic (MZ) twins, had the highest IQ correlations. That is, knowing the IQ score of one MZ twin would allow one to predict fairly well the IQ score of the other. For unrelated children, however, little or no IQ relationship existed between the groups, and this was true even if these children were raised in the same environment. In the middle of the chart with moderate correlations in IQ were the fraternal, or dizygotic (DZ) twins,

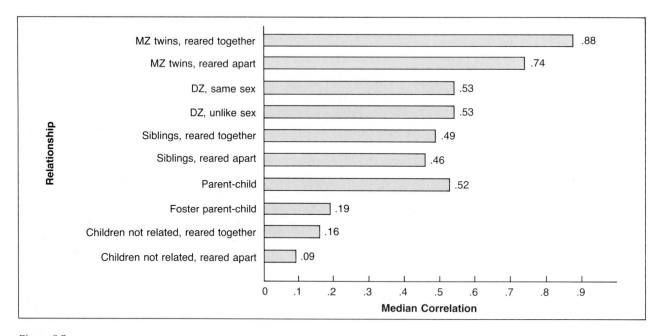

Figure 8.3

IQ Correlations for Various Degrees of Kinship

Source: From THE PSYCHOLOGY OF INDIVIDUAL AND GROUP DIFFERENCES. By Lee Willerman. Copyright © 1979 by W. H. Freeman and Company. Reprinted with permission.

the siblings, and the parent-child pairs, all of whom are genetically more similar than are unrelated children. What seems to be occurring, therefore, is that the correlations of the IQ scores increase as the individuals increase in genetic similarity, and this is precisely what would be expected if intelligence is genetically linked.

What does Figure 8.3 suggest about the influence of the environment on intelligence? The correlations for the groups, MZ twins, siblings, and unrelated persons differ very little from one another in the "reared together" and "reared apart" conditions. Furthermore, the IQs of MZ twins reared apart are more similar than the IQs of siblings reared in the same environment, and siblings reared apart resemble each other more than unrelated persons reared together. If intelligence were influenced completely or even largely by the environment, why would unrelated children raised in the same family not be more similar in IQ than MZ twins reared in different families?

Environmentalists respond to the findings of kinship correlation studies by arguing that even when siblings are raised separately, they are usually raised in very similar environments. As Kamin (Eysenck & Kamin, 1981) observed, in many studies of "separated" twins, the children were hardly separated at all. For example, in one study (Shields, 1962), three-quarters of the twins raised separately were raised by relatives, who in all likelihood provided the children with environments similar to what they would have experienced at home. Twins were considered separated if at any time during childhood (birth–18 years) they had lived apart for a period of 5 years or more. Many of them lived in the same houses during most of their childhood, went to school together, or at least saw each other frequently. Furthermore, Kamin (Eysenck & Kamin, 1981) noted that when children are made available for adoption, social service agencies usually attempt to place them in homes that closely resemble those of their natural parents (e.g., in race, religion, and even in the IQs of the parents). Lastly, among identical twins raised separately, the pairs whose adoptive environments were most similar were also most similar in intelligence while those from radically different adoptive environments differed most in adult intellectual ability (Cronbach, 1984).

Kamin (Eysenck & Kamin, 1981) also observed that identical twins are more similar in intelligence than fraternal twins or siblings because identical twins have more similar environments. That is, they are often dressed alike, usually spend a good deal of time together, sleep in the same room, and so on. On the surface, identical twins do seem to have more similar home environments than other siblings. However, whether similarity of rearing patterns within a home affects the similarity of children's intelligence has never been answered satisfactorily, in part because we have never used sophisticated measures of child-rearing similarity. Simply asking parents if they rear their twins in the same way, as has often been the methodological approach in studies of this type, is not enough (Loehlin & Nichols, 1976).

Meaning of Heritability

Modern researchers in the area of human intelligence rarely view the heredity-environment question as an either-or proposition. Instead, the focus of their inquiry is on the extent of the roles played by genetics and environment in determining IQ. Estimates of the percentage of the genetic contribution to intelligence have been set as low as 40 percent (Scarr, 1981), in the middle of the range at 50–60 percent (Vernon, 1979), and as high as 80 percent (Eysenck & Kamin, 1981; Herrnstein, 1971; Jensen, 1981). These percentages are estimates of *heritability,* the degree to which certain characteristics vary in a given population because of genetic factors. To illustrate the concept of heritability, consider the following example. In a physical education class, 25 children are learning how to play basketball. On the first day of class, each child attempts 12 foul shots, and the teacher keeps individual records of successes and failures. The teacher finds a good deal of variation among the children in the ability to throw a basketball through a hoop from a specific distance. Assuming that the variation is probably an interaction of heredity (e.g., body size, body proportion, motor coordination, rate of physical development) and environment (e.g., previous experience, motivation, attitude toward sports), the teacher attempts to determine the relative influence of heredity and environment and to assign a rough percentage to each.

The teacher works with the children for a month, drills them, encourages them, motivates them, then repeats the initial test. This time the average performance is better, but, more importantly, the variation is considerably reduced. Perhaps the range of scores, which earlier had been 0–10, is now 8–11. The teacher concludes that the major reason for the initial variation among the children was the variation in their experience with basketball (an environmental factor). On the other hand, if, despite practice and encouragement, the variation in the group had been reduced hardly at all, the teacher might have concluded that ability to make foul shots is influenced greatly by innate characteristics rather than by experience.

When we discuss heritability, we speak of variation within a group and the factors responsible for it. If most of the group variation in any human characteristic is due to heredity, then most of the variation should be eliminated if genetic variation in the group is reduced (e.g., by studying family groupings), but little variation would be eliminated if the environments of group members are equalized. On the other hand, if environmental factors account for most of the group variation, as in the case of our young basketball players, then reducing environmental variation (e.g., by training procedures) will significantly reduce the variation in the children's performance.

Heritability must always be thought of as a population characteristic rather than an individual one. For example, the teacher might conclude that environmental factors account for perhaps 80 percent of the variation in basketball skills of the physical education class, but that does not mean that 80 percent of the skill of any particular child is determined by experience. One can generalize from the population, of course, and say that environment is probably more important than heredity in the athletic skills of any one child, but any generalization from group to individual characteristics contains the possibility of error.

Advocates of the so-called hereditarian approach to the IQ controversy, including Arthur Jensen, Hans Eysenck, and Richard J. Herrnstein, suggest that heredity is more important in determining intelligence variation within a population than are the effects of the environment—approximately twice as important, to be specific. They do not set percentages on the hereditary and environmental factors in the intelligence of an individual, nor do they argue that intelligence is fixed in an absolute sense. To quote from Hans Eysenck, a well-known hereditarian:

> All that is said applies to conditions at a given time in a given place. Current environmental conditions in Western countries produce the results we have discussed. It is possible that new discoveries, either in physiology or in education, may alter conditions, and that in the new environment the population may achieve a different mean IQ, or a different distribution, or a different heritability. (Eysenck, 1981, p. 60)

In summary, the heredity-environment question is not an either-or issue. No one denies that a person's environment can influence intelligence. Similarly, few psychologists deny all genetic influence on intelligence. The question is one of the degree of influence of the two factors. Estimates of the heritability of intelligence range from 40 to 80 percent, but the heritability data apply to particular populations and not to individuals. Heredity may play a significant role in determining differences within a population, but no one can estimate the size of the genetic contribution to any one person's intelligence. Finally, the data on the heritability of intelligence apply only to the populations that have been studied in certain Western societies living in the world today. They cannot be applied to the past, nor should they be used to predict future intelligence patterns.

ENVIRONMENTAL INFLUENCES ON INTELLIGENCE

When we discussed developmental changes in intelligence, we pointed out that changes in intelligence across the life span are typically expressed in terms of averages. Some people have significant IQ gains, some have little or no gains, and some show IQ declines during childhood or adulthood. What are the reasons for these individual differences? Answers to this question typically point in the direction of environmental influences on intelligence. In this section, we examine some of the ways a person's cultural surroundings may influence intellectual growth.

Child-rearing Patterns

IQ gainers tend to come from families characterized by parental warmth, attentiveness, and generally positive attitudes toward the children (Bayley & Schaefer, 1964; Skeels & Dye, 1939). Overly strict or punitive parents tend to raise children whose IQs are less likely to increase (Bayley & Schaefer, 1964). Furthermore, the parents of IQ gainers encourage academic achievement in their children and provide accelerated educational experiences (McCall, Applebaum, & Hogarty, 1973), whereas children from intellectually impoverished home environments have actually shown IQ declines with age (Gordon, 1923; Roberts, Crump, Dickerson, & Horton, 1965; Sherman & Key, 1932).

When interpreting studies of child-rearing patterns in the homes of IQ gainers or decliners, a certain amount of caution should be used for two reasons. First, the evidence provided by such studies is correlational rather than causal. For example, parents who stress academic achievement may not actually be causing IQ gains in their children. Perhaps some parents perceive in their children an advanced level of intellectual functioning and respond by stressing academic achievement. Thus, a child's intellectual level could influence parents' child-rearing patterns as easily as the reverse.

A second reason for caution in interpreting the results of such studies is that it may not be the child-rearing approach but the parents' IQs that

Some children exhibit IQ gains as they grow up. Such children generally have parents who encourage academic achievement and provide accelerated educational experiences.

influence the intellectual growth of children. In other words, the parents who provide the most intellectually stimulating home environment might be the most intelligent parents to begin with, and therefore the children's intellectual gains could be attributable to genetic rather than environmental factors. In fact, the mother's IQ alone predicts a child's intelligence very well, but only until the child is 2 years old; after that, maternal IQ alone is not a good predictor of a child's IQ—the intellectual stimulation of the home environment must also be considered (Yeates, MacPhee, Campbell, & Ramey, 1983). In other words, the quality of the home environment becomes increasingly influential on the child's IQ as the child gets older.

Nutrition

The relationship between nutrition and intellectual development in childhood has long been recognized. More specifically, severe malnutrition in the first few years of life is correlated with a lowered IQ in later childhood or adolescence (DeLicardie & Cravioto, 1974; Galler, Ramsey, & Solimano, 1985; Puri, Chawla, Sharma, & Pershad, 1984; Ricciuti, 1981; Richardson, 1976; Winick, Meyer, & Harris, 1975). But a direct causal link between malnutrition and intellectual impairment, and the degree to which diet alone affects the intellect, have not been established. Researchers face difficulty in this area because malnutrition among infants is related to a variety of negative factors in the home environment. Malnourished children often come from homes that exhibit little social, emotional, or intellectual stimulation, and as a result, nutritional factors are not easy to isolate as influences on intellectual growth.

Attempts have been made to separate the effects of malnutrition from adverse psychological effects in the home (e.g., Richardson, 1976), but the relative contribution of nutritional factors varies from study to study (Ricciuti, 1981). However, the possible negative effects on a child's intellect of even severe early malnutrition apparently can be minimized or prevented by a positive home atmosphere; nutritional supplements for malnourished children have been found to reverse the negative effects on the intellect of an inadequate diet, but only if the overall home environment supports emotional, social, and intellectual growth (Ricciuti, 1981; Winick et al., 1975).

Birth Order and Family Size

Because a child's level of intelligence is influenced by parents' child-rearing patterns as well as by within-family genetic similarity, we would expect siblings to be similar to one another in intelligence. Indeed, as we noted earlier in our discussion of kinship correlations, siblings are more similar in IQ than unrelated children, but within-family variations still exist. To explain these variations, the factors of birth order and family size have been cited. For example, Belmont and Marolla (1973) examined military records of nearly 400,000 men living in Holland and found relationships between level of intelligence and both family size and birth order: Firstborn children performed better on IQ tests than did second-borns, and second-born children did better than third-borns, and so on.

To explain this birth order difference, which appeared in later studies as well, Zajonc and Markus (1975) developed what is known as the *confluence theory:* The intelligence of each family member is influenced by the average intellectual ability of the other family members. Thus, the firstborn child is influenced by the average intellectual ability of the parents, while later-born children are influenced by the average ability of the parents and the older siblings. The hypothetical average ability of the family decreases as family size increases, because children are intellectually less capable than their parents.

Intriguing as the theory is, support for it has not been impressive. A number of studies (e.g., Galbraith, 1982; Price, Walsh, & Vilberg, 1984; Rodgers, 1984; Rodgers & Rowe, 1985) have called into question the notion that each additional child in a family is less intelligent than those who came before. In examining children's IQs in 1,173 families, Rodgers and Rowe (1985) found no evidence that family size or position within the family influenced the intelligence of the individual child. As a further illustration that no simple birth order model can explain IQ variation among siblings, and as a challenge to the notion that the firstborn is the most advantaged, McCall (1984) observed that IQ performance of an older child actually dropped 10 points after a new sibling was born; fortunately, the drop was a temporary one!

Gender Roles

When we examine IQs during childhood, we typically discover that males are more likely to experience gains than females (Bayley, 1968; Moore, 1967; Roberts et al., 1965; Sontag et al., 1958), with the difference usually attributed to cultural rather than biological factors. Some have even suggested that girls who are the most accepting of the traditional feminine gender roles are least likely to experience IQ gains and most likely to show a pattern of actual decline during adolescence (Campbell, 1976). The IQ difference between males and females is increasingly evident during early adolescence, when gender roles become more and more inflexible; this might be seen as further evidence that the difference is culturally determined (Lamb & Urberg, 1978), because the female gender role in our culture frequently involves a denial of intellectual potential (Datan & Hughes, 1985; Troll, 1984).

Confluence theory

The theory that the intelligence of any particular family member is influenced by the average intellectual ability of other members of the family.

CONSTRUCT OF CREATIVITY

Defining, evaluating, and predicting creativity generate much interest but little agreement among psychologists. There is agreement, however, that the study of creativity somehow deals with the essence of development. As Kogan (1983) pointed out, creativity is a major value in practically every literate society ever known.

Creativity is difficult to define because it is a complex construct, or concept, containing three related elements. It is a *personality characteristic* and an *intellectual process,* and it results in a type of *product.* In the first sense, creativity is a way of being, an attitude toward the world and the self that reflects the personality characteristics of flexibility, spontaneity, curiosity, and persistence. In the second sense, it is a way of thinking, an intellectual approach to solving problems. Finally, a creative product can be defined as any original contribution to the appreciation, understanding, or improvement of the human condition. (In this last sense of creativity as a product, it is generally more accurate to describe children and adolescents as having the potential for being creative rather than as actually producing creative works.)

Creative Personality

A common belief about the personalities of creative people is that they are highly neurotic, at least bizarre, and possibly even frightening. Actually, this is not the case at all. Although some well-known creative individuals, such as Vincent van Gogh and Edgar Allan Poe, seem to have developed little emotional control, most children or adults designated as creative are psychologically quite healthy (Gough, 1979; Kubie, 1958; Maslow, 1964). Creative individuals who are emotionally disturbed are creative despite their personality handicaps, not because of them.

A number of personality characteristics differentiate the creative from the less creative child during the elementary and high school years. These include persistence, high-energy levels, self-confidence, independence of judgment, flexibility and openness to new experiences, tolerance of ambiguity, and a good sense of humor. Also, creative children seem to be aware and accepting of their feelings, playfully curious about their world, and less attached to conventional sex-role stereotypes (Barron & Harrington, 1981; Janos & Robinson, 1985). Such characteristics may not describe the typical child, but they can hardly be labeled unhealthy. This creative outlook on life seems to be fostered by parents who are not overly strict, who encourage the child's independence, and who are not excessively concerned with neatness, obedience, or emotional control (Nichols, 1964; Schaefer, 1961).

Creative Process

Besides personality characteristics, certain mental processes bring about the production of new ideas and material creations. A popular belief is that a creative person waits around for a brilliant solution to occur instantly. For example, Sir Isaac Newton supposedly discovered the principle of gravity while he was sitting under an apple tree. Blind luck, however, can play only

Although a child's artwork may demonstrate imagination and a creative personality, true creativity requires a creative product — an original contribution to the appreciation, understanding, or improvement of the human condition.

a small role in creativity. Austin (1978) proposed that both chance and creativity depend on an exploratory style, a highly prepared mind, and persistent activity. To illustrate this point, Mozart's brilliant musical compositions were not due to a flash of insight, but instead were the result of a long process of developing an incredible grasp of symphonic structure, an accurate memory for melodic themes, and a great flexibility in perceiving tonal relationships (Gardner, 1982).

Thus, the processes of creativity sound like a variation of the definition of intelligence. In fact, much of the research on creative thinking has attempted to distinguish the concept of intelligence from that of creativity. How are creativity and intelligence related? There appears to be no more than a modest correlation between intelligence and creativity. Put simply, high levels of intelligence do not guarantee creativity, but at least average intelligence is necessary to be creative. Creativity is unlikely in a person of low intelligence (Barron & Harrington, 1981).

A major task for researchers interested in the creative process is to determine which cognitive skills are necessary for creativity. Guilford (1967),

Divergent thinking
An aspect of intelligence requiring the ability to branch out from a single starting point to reach a variety of possible problem solutions.

Convergent thinking
The bringing together of various pieces of information to formulate a single correct solution to a problem.

whose theory of intellectual functioning was discussed earlier, suggested that creativity involves *divergent thinking,* the ability to branch out from a starting point to reach a variety of possibilities. The opposite is *convergent thinking,* the ability to bring bits of information together to come up with a single correct solution. To illustrate these concepts, answering in what year George Washington crossed the Delaware River requires a person to use convergent thinking, because only one answer is correct. Creativity is not involved. Answering how Washington might have felt as he crossed the river requires the person to use divergent thinking; there is no correct answer, and the person can be quite creative in considering a variety of possibilities.

The convergent-divergent distinction in defining the creative process is appealing, but research on this model has produced mixed results (Kogan, 1983; Wallach, 1985). Because divergent thinking is itself composed of several subprocesses—quantity of free-flowing ideas, flexibility of alternative solutions, elaboration of the ideas generated, and novelty of the proposed solutions—it is not surprising that inconclusive results have been reported. Moreover, the tasks used to assess divergent thinking (e.g., "In addition to holding pieces of paper together, what other ways can you think of to use a paper clip?") frequently are not very motivating to the person being tested.

Convergent thinking, which is frequently related to traditional intelligence test results, has been incorrectly viewed as having little significance for creativity. Hudson (1966) claimed that divergent thinking may be characteristic of creativity in the arts, but convergent thinking is essential to creativity in the sciences. Actually, both divergent and convergent thinking seem to be required for all forms of creativity, although this may not always be apparent to the casual observer.

Beyond divergent thinking, other mental processes thought to be involved in creativity include the tendency to form unusual associations, to relax conscious thought to gain access to more primitive modes of cognition, to use analogical and metaphorical reasoning, to formulate visual images, and to ask original questions (Barron & Harrington, 1981).

Creative Product

A child can have a creative personality and can engage in creative mental processes, but whether children really produce creative products is doubtful. Their products may be skillful, cute, unusual, and imaginative, but they are never creative in the real-world sense of Michelangelo's sculpture, Dostoyevski's novels, or Einstein's theories. Even the musical compositions Mozart wrote before the age of 20 are regarded more for their historical interest than as examples of extraordinary creativity.

Kogan (1973) stated that "there is reason to doubt that a creativity criterion can be found at the elementary school level that is more 'real' than the performance on divergent-thinking tasks" (p. 155). Thus, the issue of creative potential versus creative production, which is also relevant to adolescents who have not yet expressed their potential, remains a problem. Gowan (1977) suggested that the potential to be creative as an adult may be found in the gifted child. However, not every gifted child will become a creative adult, and, likewise, all creative adults were not gifted children (Gruber, 1982). We can review the creative work of historical figures and judge the timeless quality of a painting or a poem; we can also judge the value of a biological or sociological theory. However, what products can we use to predict which childhood "creators" will be viewed as creative in the future? Perhaps our best hope at this point is to adopt the evolving-systems approach of Wallace (1985), who recommended a rich case-study analysis of creative persons to determine the developmental path of creativity. Therefore, the next section turns to a discussion of the changing flavor of creativity from infancy through adolescence.

DEVELOPMENT OF CREATIVITY

The elusive nature of human creativity becomes all the more obvious when psychologists try to explain how creativity develops. In this section, we first examine two-stage theories of creativity development, each of which attempts to distinguish between genuine adult creative endeavors and the spontaneous, flexible, and playful activities of childhood, which may or may not represent true creativity. Then we will examine the research on creativity at various points during childhood and adolescence in an attempt to determine what changes and what remains the same as the child grows up.

Theories of Creative Development

Only a few theorists have presented a continuous sequence that attempts to describe the changes in creativity from childhood to adulthood. I. A. Taylor (1974), for example, proposed a model of creative development that outlines the qualitative changes appearing at different points in life. After its initial appearance, each change can be found at any time in the life cycle. First is *spontaneity* in early childhood, as seen in the language, play, and drawings of children and in the work of adult creative artists. From late childhood through adolescence, *technical proficiency* appears as children take advantage of specific forms of training and refine their skills. *Inventive ingenuity,* appearing during adolescence or early adulthood, involves working with gadgets and tinkering with materials. The inventor Thomas Edison exemplified this type of creativity in his ability to combine many elements to solve old problems in new ways. *Innovative flexibility,* appearing in early to middle adulthood, involves changing ideas and systems for new purposes, as Erikson did when he modified Freud's theory. Finally, in middle and old age, comes *emergentive originality*—the development of totally new ideas such as those contained in the psychoanalytic theory of Freud.

A similar developmental approach to the study of creativity was suggested by David H. Feldman (1974). In his system, creativity is potentially developed over four stages:

1. The universal achievements of all human beings.
2. The cultural advances common to members of particular social groups.
3. The idiosyncratic accomplishments of specific persons within a given culture.
4. The unique creative developments which "may alter for all time a mode of expression or a domain of knowledge" (p. 68).

Universal creativity refers to the normal discoveries of infancy and childhood. Cultural creativity reflects the knowledge acquired from being raised in a specific society. Idiosyncratic creativity means the special achievements that accompany changes within a limited area of expertise. Finally, unique creativity implies the invention of something totally new and extraordinary.

A problem with theories of creative development such as Taylor's and Feldman's is that they fail to explain why some people reach the original and unique levels associated with genuine creativity while others do not. Furthermore, relying too heavily on age-related or developmental factors in creativity is probably not a good idea, because in doing so we might neglect important historical, generational, and cultural factors (Romaniuk & Romaniuk, 1981).

Developmental Patterns

We now address a number of questions pertaining to developmental changes in creativity throughout the life span. When can a child be thought of as creative? How may creativity be influenced by the various social pressures children deal with as they develop? Are there changes in creativity during the span of adult life?

Infancy and Early Childhood

The notion of infant creativity may seem ridiculous to some people and obvious to others. The discussion might even begin at an earlier point; Anderson (1959) asserted that creativity is "characteristic of development [and] a quality of protoplasm" (p. 124). Biologist Edmund Sinnott (1959) similarly concluded that life itself is a creative process in which organization and regulatory properties are inherent in living organisms. It was Piaget (1981), however, who alerted us to the infant's creativity by regarding the sensorimotor period as "incredible in its amount of invention and discovery" (p. 229). The infant's creativity does not introduce new products or ideas to the world, but it does lead to original constructions of time, space, and language for the infant (see Chapter 7). More significantly, the process of solving sensorimotor problems suggests an inclination toward originality (Noppe & Noppe, 1976). Also, some infants, by virtue of their basic temperaments, could be more curious and more inclined to seek novelty than others (Thomas, Chess, & Birch, 1970).

Early childhood elaborates on the creative development that began in infancy. The young child is extremely playful and open to new experiences. The preschool years are a golden age of fantasy and imagination as indicated by the rich, imaginative quality of children's symbolic play. It is not easy to tell, however, which of these young children will maintain their creative imaginations into the years of adolescence and adulthood, although a longitudinal study by Harrington, Block, and Block (1983) provided some encouraging evidence for the predictability of preadolescent creativity from preschool tests of divergent thinking. The researchers administered creativity and intelligence tests to 75 children between the ages of 4 and 5 years. When the children were 11 years old, their sixth-grade teachers were asked to evaluate these students' levels of creativity. Results indicated significant correlations between the various tests of creativity at different ages. Apparently, some common element of creative thinking was maintained over a 6- to 7-year span.

Middle Childhood and Adolescence

During the middle childhood and adolescent years, creative potential appears to reach a critical point. Because of advances in logical thought, elementary and high school students have a tremendous opportunity to expand the range of their imaginations. However, conformity to parental and cultural expectations, the imitative rather than imaginative techniques of much of our educational process, and the capacity to be harshly self-judgmental may severely limit the freedom and playfulness essential for creativity to flourish. Children of this age need a firm foundation of knowledge and a clear sense of reality, but they should not be permitted to give up the spontaneity and imagination of their earlier childhood. Older children must learn to combine the discipline and purpose of working with the flexibility and joy of play.

Although the orientation to concrete reality limits the potential for truly creative thought during middle childhood, teachers can strive to follow the five principles suggested by Klausmeier (1985) for promoting creativity:

1. Provide for variety in instructional materials and forms of student expression.
2. Develop favorable attitudes toward creative achievement.
3. Encourage continuing creative expression.
4. Foster productivity.
5. Provide assistance and feedback.

Teachers and parents must do more than simply hope that creative activity will occur spontaneously. They need to pose challenging questions,

Students in a chemistry class looking for new solutions to old problems exhibit inventive ingenuity, a form of creativity that emerges during adolescence or young adulthood.

accept a variety of solutions to problems, and suggest tasks that will allow children to develop new ways of perceiving their world.

If Piaget (1981) could describe childhood as the most creative time in the life of a human being, why is much of this creativity apparently lost by adolescence? Wolf and Larson (1981) proposed that younger children are not nearly as creative as we often suppose, because their creations are accidental and often the result of their own ignorance of the world around them. Furthermore, the apparent loss of creativity in some adolescents may reflect peer pressure to conform, because conformity is the enemy of creative expression. Noppe and Noppe (1976) pointed out, though, that the formal operations that may emerge during adolescence contain the seeds of true creativity—the flexible system of combinatorial reasoning, the reversal of reality and possibility, and the tolerance of incomplete solutions and contradictions. Finally, adolescent creativity apparently can be stimulated through the use of imaginative methods and materials, active involvement in trying new ideas, and the provision of a receptive, encouraging atmosphere (Davis, 1975).

Creativity in Adult Life

Much of the research on creativity during the adult years has focused on a comparison of creative abilities from early to later adulthood. Although some studies have examined process development, most have emphasized creative products. Two studies of divergent thinking, which yielded opposing findings, represent the process approach. Alpaugh and Birren (1977) found significant age-related declines in creativity test performance for people between their 20s and their 80s. In contrast, Jaquish and Ripple (1981), testing a similar sample, did not find any age decrements. Middle-aged adults actually scored highest on three divergent thinking tests (as well as on self-esteem), supporting the belief that the middle years of adulthood represent the creative peak of life.

Conflicting results can also be found in the product approaches to the study of creativity. For example, Lehman (1953) traced the quantity and quality of creative works of historical figures from a variety of areas and found that the greatest amount of creative productivity occurred when people were in their 30s. He also discovered variations among the different fields of activity, with scientists peaking earlier than artists. However, although some research supports Lehman's general findings (Eagly, 1974; Simonton, 1984), other researchers have reported different results. For example, Diamond (1986) studied the lifetime scholarly accomplishments of mathematicians, natural scientists, and economists at six major American universities and found substantial variation in the peak age of creativity, at least as indicated by the number of research citations per year. The peak age ranged from 39 in the physics department at the University of California–Berkeley to 89 in the mathematics department at the University of Illinois!

How can we reconcile Lehman's findings that creative output typically peaks in middle adulthood with the observation that some creative individuals make their greatest contributions in their advanced old age? Perhaps we need to keep in mind the warning by J. G. Romaniuk and M. Romaniuk (1981) that we must not confuse creative capacity with actual creative output. Many creativity theorists (e.g., Arieti, 1976; McLeish, 1976) believe that high levels of productivity are possible at any age if environmental conditions encourage creative potential to be realized. Certainly, the works of creative adults have provided support for this belief. Claude Monet's famous water lily paintings, Frank Lloyd Wright's Guggenheim Museum design, Benjamin Franklin's bifocal lens, and Sophocles' great tragedy *Oedipus Rex* were all produced by men beyond the age of 70. And, as in the case of the U.S. artist Grandma Moses, creativity may even flower for the first time in an older adult whose potential had never before been adequately tapped. Perhaps the danger of assuming that the peak of creativity is reached early in life is that such an assumption often becomes

The middle years of adulthood probably represent the creative peak, but some creative individuals make their greatest contributions in their advanced old age. When environmental conditions encourage creative potential, high levels of productivity may be possible at any age.

a self-fulfilling prophecy. As a result, older adults may not be challenged to achieve their creative potential and may not receive the support and encouragement necessary to do so.

Summary

1. Intelligence should be considered as a concept that describes a person's problem-solving behavior in a particular setting rather than as an entity that people possess.

2. Definitions of intelligence vary, with some theorists arguing that a single general reasoning ability is involved in all intelligent behav-

ior and others maintaining that many separate but related factors are involved.

3. Intelligence testing began in the early years of the twentieth century. The first widely used individual test was developed for the French minister of public instruction by Alfred Binet in 1905. Group tests were originally developed for the U.S. Army in 1917 and 1918.

4. A regular increase in intelligence occurs throughout childhood. Intellectual development reaches a peak in young adulthood.

5. Wide individual differences exist in intellectual development, with some persons growing or declining faster than others.

6. Older adults do not score as well on IQ tests as young ones, but a number of reasons other than age alone are thought to be responsible for declines in intelligence.

7. Crystallized intelligence, which depends on the accumulation of experience in one's culture, does not decline with age, but fluid intelligence does. The reasons for this have never been completely explained.

8. Heredity plays a significant role in explaining IQ variation within a given population. However, no one has been able to determine the relative contributions of heredity and environment to the intelligence of an individual.

9. The heredity-environment question in intelligence should not be viewed as an either-or proposition. Both factors likely interact in determining intellectual ability.

10. Child-rearing patterns are related to IQ development in the sense that children's IQs are most likely to increase when parents are warm, attentive, and supportive of intellectual accomplishment.

11. The influence of birth order or family size on a child's intelligence is limited, and studies favoring such a relationship have come under increasingly heavy criticism in recent years.

12. Males are more likely to show IQ gains during childhood than females, particularly when the female assumes a more traditional gender role.

13. Childhood IQ scores are related to educational achievement in childhood and adolescence, to ultimate educational attainment in adulthood, and to adult occupational status.

14. Creativity can be thought of as a personality characteristic, an intellectual process, and an activity resulting in an original and interesting product.

15. Infants display a personal form of creativity that has no cultural ramifications. Similarly, the fantasy of preschool children is an individual, not a societal, expression of imagination.

16. Individual differences in creativity during middle childhood and adolescence may be blunted by pressures to conform and the structure of the educational system. Nonetheless, creative expression is demonstrated and can be encouraged.

17. Although an average peak of creativity is reached in middle age in most professional areas, any particular individual is capable of generating creative products until the years of advanced old age.

Key Terms

confluence theory (p. 326)

convergent thinking (p. 329)

crystallized intelligence (p. 315)

divergent thinking (p. 329)

fluid intelligence (p. 315)

group intelligence tests (p. 305)

heritability (p. 322)

individual intelligence tests (p. 305)

reliability (p. 300)

standard deviation (p. 304)

validity (p. 300)

Review Questions

1. Describe the componential, experiential, and contextual aspects of human intelligence outlined by Sternberg. What are the advantages of Sternberg's approach in studying intelligence that were lacking in earlier models?

2. What does standardization mean in the development of IQ tests? Why is it a necessary procedure?

3. Discuss the evidence in favor of both the hereditarian and the environmentalist views of human intelligence.

4. What are the differences between individual and group intelligence tests? List the advantages and disadvantages of each type.

5. What is meant by the concept of statistical prediction? Referring to this concept, what does performance on intelligence tests predict in terms of school achievement, life success, and job performance?

6. List and discuss the various factors that influence the performance of adults of different ages on intelligence tests. Explain the concepts of age changes and age differences as related to the research findings on adult intelligence.

7. What are crystallized intelligence and fluid intelligence? What developmental patterns would you expect to find in each of these areas as a person crosses the span of adult life?

8. Does IQ testing have a cultural bias? Present the evidence in support of this argument and the evidence against, and describe how some researchers have attempted to counteract what they see as a cultural bias.

9. Creativity has been described as an intellectual process and a personality characteristic, and it has often been defined in terms of a creative product. Describe the distinctions in these three ways of looking at human creativity.

10. The authors of this text suggest that creativity is really a characteristic of adult life, and that what is seen as creativity in childhood may not be creativity at all. What is the basis of this argument?

Suggested Readings

Eysenck, H. J. & Kamin, L. (1981). *The intelligence controversy.* New York: Wiley.

> The hereditarian and the environmentalist views of intelligence as presented by the leading advocate of each position. The format is that of a debate; the two "sides" of the issue were written separately, but each author was then asked to comment in writing about the other's argument. The result is a stimulating, and often heated, discussion of one of the major controversies in the field of human development.

Kamin, L. (1974). *The science and politics of IQ.* Potomac, MD: Erlbaum.

> Sobering and important reading for human development or psychology students. Kamin, an impassioned advocate of the environmentalist position on intelligence, argues that the IQ concept has been destructive since its inception. For example, he describes how intelligence testing was used to restrict immigration to the United States of racial and ethnic minorities perceived to be undesirable.

Loehlin, J. C., Lindzey, G. & Spuhler, J. N. (1975). *Race differences in intelligence.* San Francisco: W. H. Freeman.

> A straightforward and comprehensive review of the literature dealing with racial and ethnic differences in IQ performance. The authors examine a number of complicated issues: the meaning of race, the concept of heritability, the difficulties in measuring intelligence, and the sociopolitical implications of research in this area. One-quarter of the book is devoted to a number of enlightening and useful appendices pertaining to the topic.

Sternberg, R.J. (1986). *Intelligence applied: Understanding and increasing your intellectual skills.* New York: Harcourt Brace Jovanovich.

> An engaging presentation of Sternberg's theory of human intelligence, including numerous examples of tests of componential, experiential, and contextual intelligence. Included also are exercises for developing the three aspects of intelligence and a fascinating summary chapter devoted to why intelligent people often fail.

Chapter Nine

Language

Nature of Communication
Issues in Language Development
Five Components of Language Study

Infant Antecedents of Language
Early Sounds
From Words to Sentences
Understanding and Communicating

Early Childhood and the
Linguistic Explosion
Improving Speech
Emergence of Grammar
Semantics and Pragmatics

Language Refinements of Later
Childhood and Adolescence
Words and Sentences Revisited
Meanings and Conversations

Course of Language During
Adulthood and Old Age
Adult Skills and Patterns
Are There Deficits Among the
Elderly?

Theories of Language
Development
Behavioral Approach
Nativist Approach
Interactionist Approach

Variations in Language
Development
Communication and Socioeconomic
Status
Dialect Differences

The Egyptians before the reign of Psammetichus used to think that of all races in the world they were the most ancient; Psammetichus, however, when he came to the throne, took it into his head to settle this question of priority, and ever since his time the Egyptians have believed that the Phrygians surpass them in antiquity and that they themselves come second. Psammetichus, finding that mere inquiry failed to reveal which was the original race of mankind, devised an ingenious method of determining the matter. He took at random, from an ordinary family, two newly born infants and gave them to a shepherd to be brought up among his flocks, under strict orders that no one should utter a word in their presence. They were to be kept by themselves in a lonely cottage, and the shepherd was to bring in goats from time to time, to see that the babies had enough milk to drink, and to look after them in any other way that was necessary. All these arrangements were made by Psammetichus because he wished to find out what word the children would first utter, once they had grown out of their meaningless baby-talk. The plan succeeded; two years later the shepherd, who during that time had done everything he had been told to do, happened one day to open the door of the cottage and go in, when both children running up to him with hands outstretched, pronounced the word "becos." The first time this occurred the shepherd made no mention of it; but later, when he found that every time he visited the children to attend to their needs the same word was constantly repeated by them, he informed the master. Psammetichus ordered the children to be brought to him, and when he himself heard them say "becos," he determined to find out to what language the word belonged. His inquiries revealed that it was the Phrygian word for "bread," and in consideration of this the Egyptians yielded their claims and admitted the superior antiquity of the Phrygians.[1]

---

[1]From *The Histories* by Herodotus, translated by Aubrey de Sélincourt and revised by A. R. Burn (Penguin Classics, 1954, 1972). Copyright by The Estate of Aubrey de Sélincourt, 1954; copyright by A. R. Burn, 1972. Reproduced by permission of Penguin Books, Ltd.

As the preceding story from the historian Herodotus (500 B.C.) illustrates, language is surely one of our most intriguing mysteries. Despite recent advances in describing linguistic growth, analyzing the various uses of language, and evaluating individual differences, to say nothing of improvements in research methods, the basic issue of how a person acquires this remarkable ability has not been satisfactorily resolved. Thousands of different languages and dialect variations have been identified. But essential similarities in the structure and functions of these languages, as well as in the process of their development, also have been observed.

As a complex system of sounds and symbols created to transmit meaning, language serves several crucial functions. First, language permits us to express our feelings, ideas, and demands. Second, we learn about and regulate our environment—including other people—through language. Finally, language allows us to clarify our thinking or to extend it imaginatively. Each of these functions may be applied to various cultures, to different ages, and across countless generations. Language, therefore, is a significant unifying characteristic of our species. Most of our knowledge about the history of the world and its different peoples—not to mention our accumulated wisdom or creative accomplishments—has been transmitted through oral, and ultimately written, language.

This chapter will explore both the universal sequences of language use and the influences that foster linguistic variations. Furthermore, we will discuss the major theories that attempt to explain the nature of language development. The first tasks, however, are to provide an overview of the controversial questions concerning human communication and to outline the formal aspects of language study.

NATURE OF COMMUNICATION

Perhaps the most amazing phenomenon that can be readily appreciated by anyone studying language development is the apparent ease and rapidity with which language is acquired. In only a few years a toddler who can say a couple of words becomes a preschooler with a vocabulary of several thousand words. The preschool child also knows how to arrange these words in unique sentence variations with grammatical accuracy. Furthermore, this accomplishment occurs in all normal individuals throughout the world without direct instruction from parents or teachers.

To explain this process, some language theorists have suggested that the human species is genetically programmed to develop a linguistic system. Theorists who adopt a more experiential view, however, point out the diversity of languages and dialects acquired, parental modifications when directing language toward children, differences in the rate of language learning among individuals within the same culture, and the levels of auditory stimulation required for language development. The role of heredity versus environment in development continues to be vigorously debated among language theorists (de Villiers & de Villiers, 1978).

Issues in Language Development

One question that developmentalists wish to answer is the extent to which language skills depend on intrinsic curiosity, intellectual capacity, and evolutionary learning patterns. A most extreme version of this position suggests that the child, rather than learning a language, actually creates one by using the particular language available in conjunction with a natural tendency to discover the patterns and irregularities of language use. The opposite perspective emphasizes that the development of language is similar to the acquisition of any other skill in which exposure to appropriate models, adequate levels of reinforcement, and simplifications for the benefit of the child are required. If further research permits a clearer resolution of this issue, the conclusions will offer practical implications. For instance, what role can parents really play in facilitating their children's language development? How much do parents have to trust in the effectiveness of a predetermined language program? Will such information allow us to acquire a second or third language more easily (de Villiers & de Villiers, 1978)?

Another question in language development concerns the unique expression of this ability in the human species. All cultures on our planet have evolved some form of linguistic communication that shares several basic properties that can be distinguished from the communication of other animals. Although children learn to use the language to which they are exposed, the essential similarities in the characteristics and developmental sequences of all human languages strongly support an innate foundation for language acquisition. These properties include linking an extensive variety of meanings and sounds (semanticity), transmitting information about different places and times (displacement), and formulating nearly unlimited combinations of new messages (productivity).

Although most animals, of course, do communicate with one another, do other species appear to demonstrate all the defining characteristics of language (Brown, 1973)? Animal communication seems to be limited to a relatively small number of instinctive, present-oriented, and basic messages or emotions. The songs of birds to attract a mate, the purring of a cat in response to contentment, and the "dance" of a honeybee to show the way to flowers do not match the complexity, creativity, and variety of language in an average 3-year-old child. We may discover increasing subtleties in the communications of other animals, however, when we arrive at a better understanding of the environments in which they live. For instance, whales and porpoises emit very intricate and beautiful patterns of sound. Our unfamiliarity with their aquatic world makes it difficult to reliably assess the meaning of such communication; however, these mammals do possess highly advanced brains. Research with our primate cousins (see *Research Close-Up,* "Can Chimpanzees Use Language?") also has begun to challenge

*Research Close-Up
Can Chimpanzees Use
Language?*

Chimpanzees are intelligent and communicative creatures, yet they have not evolved a formal system of language. Researchers have long been fascinated by the prospect of teaching apes to use language to demonstrate the relationship of human to ape intelligence and to learn more about the process of language acquisition. Unfortunately, this effort has been compromised by the variety of methodological approaches that have been used in different studies. For example, an early attempt to teach a chimp to talk ended in failure when Viki, raised as Catherine and Keith Hayes's own daughter, could produce only three poorly articulated words. Because the vocal apparatus of the chimpanzee is apparently not suited for making the sounds of human speech, another approach was necessary (Miller, 1981).

Allen and Beatrice Gardner decided to capitalize on the ability of apes to use their hands. They reared an infant chimpanzee named Washoe using American Sign Language, the system of communication taught to deaf persons. Washoe's progress was quite impressive compared with the efforts of Viki. By the age of 4 years, Washoe used 132 signs alone and in combinations (Gardner & Gardner, 1973). However, Edward Klima and Ursula Bellugi (Klima & Bellugi, 1973) pointed out that Washoe's development did not match the level of a child of comparable age in terms of proper word order, size of vocabulary, or flexibility of language use.

The encouraging work of the Gardners nevertheless stimulated Ann and David Premack to train another chimpanzee, Sarah, to use a set of plastic tokens instead of hand gestures. The tokens were backed with magnets so that they would adhere to a large board, and they varied in size, color, and shape. Sarah was able to show more sensitivity to language flexibility and productivity than Washoe (Premack, 1976). In spite of Sarah's accomplishments, however,

the notion of exclusive human language ability. Aside from these few species, however, evidence clearly establishes that nonhuman animals do not spontaneously employ, nor can they be effectively taught, the essential aspects of language use (Miller, 1981).

An additional physiological and cognitive dilemma is to clarify the actual organization of language itself. This problem is created because communication consists of two related processes—listening (or reading) and speaking (or writing). The first, a *receptive process*—whether hearing a friend's troubles, struggling with a textbook, or interpreting a sign language—involves attempting to receive and make sense of a message. The second, a *productive process*—whether speaking to a teacher, writing a letter to a lover, or formulating hand signals—implies creating and trying to transmit an idea effectively. We often regard these processes as simple opposites and take for granted our ability to employ them appropriately. However, the acquisition of receptive and productive skills appears to follow somewhat divergent patterns. Children and adults may not be equally adept

Receptive process

One of the two basic aspects of communication, which involves the attempts to receive and make sense of a message through listening or reading.

Productive process

One of the two basic aspects of communication, which involves the attempts to transmit effectively a message through speaking or writing.

critics such as Terrace, Pettito, Sanders, and Bever (1979), who used extensive videotaped analysis of training sessions, remained convinced that she had learned little more than to imitate her trainers and to pile up strings of signs or gestures.

A series of experiments conducted by Duane Rumbaugh (1977) involved a chimp who was taught to use a computer-based language. Lana learned to press keys on a keyboard representing various symbols; the symbols were then displayed on a video monitor. She made even more progress than Sarah, demonstrating an ability to ask questions, correct mistakes, and indicate the end of a sentence with a period. After further analysis, however, Rumbaugh and his colleagues contended that chimpanzees use symbols merely to replace their natural gestures so that they can obtain rewards (e.g., food, games, and reassurance) rather than to express ideas and opinions.

As present, it is difficult to determine how effectively chimpanzees can learn to use human language. The process of language acquisition in chimpanzees appears to be both similar to, and different from, that of a child. The apes studied certainly demonstrated a degree of novelty in using signs or symbols, an ability to comprehend some messages, and a limited knowledge of "word" order. Future research must answer important questions before we can be confident about apes' linguistic achievements, however. For instance, will they teach a sign language to their own offspring, will they be able to understand more complex forms of grammar, and will they modify their messages to match the needs of different listeners? Some recent work by Fouts and Fouts (1985) does suggest that one chimp can teach sign language to another. The use of a consistent teaching method across time would help clarify these behaviors.

at both processes, and aging and injury may affect them differently. The discrepancy between the two aspects of language is most appreciated when communication has failed (Menyuk, 1982).

Perhaps it is valuable to conceptualize language, as psycholinguist Noam Chomsky (1972) has, at two levels of organization. The particular sounds heard and their arrangement as words, phrases, or sentences make up the **surface structure**. The meaning of these sounds (which is inferred from, but not identical to, them) is the **deep structure**. An example of distinguishing between surface and deep structures is two people responding to the same sentence with different interpretations, as is shown in the section "Words and Sentences Revisited."

Just as translating from one language to another is complicated by subtlety and ambiguity, the process of going between the deep and surface structures of any one language also can be confusing. A speaker formulates a thought at a deep level based on a unique perspective about the world and then converts this meaning to a particular sequence of sounds. The listener

Surface structure
The particular language sounds heard or spoken and their arrangement as words, phrases, or sentences.

Deep structure
The meaning inferred from, or imparted to, the language that is heard or read.

To understand more about language development, researchers have tried to teach human language to chimpanzees in several ways. One notable effort involved the use of American Sign Language, as shown here.

reverses the process by converting the surface structure into a personal meaning. Along the pathways of these translations is ample room for misinterpretation in communication.

Five Components of Language Study

To communicate effectively with one another, speakers and listeners must be aware of and use the rules of their language (Menyuk, 1982). These interrelated sets of rules have been analyzed by linguists and developmentalists within the following five areas: phonology, morphology, syntax, sematics, and pragmatics (see Table 9.1). Defining each component will permit a clearer appreciation of the process of language acquisition. The five types of rules, however, are distinguished only for the sake of reducing complexity. Engaging in everyday discourse does not imply a conscious application of these rules, nor do they develop independently of one another.

At a basic level, we must be able to recognize and articulate sound patterns. The knowledge of *phonology* consists of being able to pronounce,

Phonology
The study of the patterns of sound in a language, including intonation, stress, pronunciation, and blending.

put together, and properly stress the sound system of a particular language. For example, anyone familiar with the English language could say the word *solt,* even if it were not found in a dictionary. However, the same person also would realize that reversing those letters to form *tlos* does not yield a word that could exist in our language. We are similarly attuned to small distinctions in sound that create wide variations in meaning, such as comparing *fig* with *fog.* Another illustration of phonological rules relates to how the speaker formulates a question. If English speakers proceed toward the end of a phrase or sentence with a steadily rising intonation, listeners will attempt to answer the question. This pattern of sound, however, would not be useful for communication in Finnish.

Morphology

The study of the basic word units of a language, including how they are constructed and how they are modified.

Syntax

The way in which a language's words are arranged in terms of phrases and sentences, as well as their variations.

Two other rules of language concern *morphology,* the formation of words, and *syntax,* the arrangement of words within sentences. Just as children are taught something about phonology during a phonics lesson, their study of grammar usually includes some analysis of language structure. Morphological rules relate to the basic word units for constructing a language and to the ways that modifying them transforms meaning. For instance, linking *with* and *drawn* creates a word that is not obviously related—*withdrawn.* Attaching an *-s* to *pot* indicates that we are referring to more than one. Adding an *un-* to *finished* suggests the opposite of the original word. A person who is fluent in morphological rules (which vary considerably from one language to the next) is able to change the tense of a verb from present to past (*go* to *went*) or to turn an adjective (*nude*) into a noun (*nudity*).

Syntactic rules govern the order of words in a phrase or a sentence. Arranging words in various sequences provides the opportunity for linguistic creativity and is equally important for accurate communication. Rephrasing *The hat is blue* into *Is the hat blue?* changes a statement into a question. A

Table 9.1
Five Types of Rules for Studying Language Development

Phonological	Rules related to the sound units used in a given language
Morphological	Rules for how to construct words and how to modify them
Syntactic	Rules for putting words into appropriate phrases or sentences
Semantic	Rules related to selecting words that express intended meaning
Pragmatic	Rules governing the behaviors for engaging in effective communication

Source: Paula Menyuk from *The Child* by Claire Kopp and Joanne Krakow, © 1982, Addison-Wesley Publishing Co., Inc., Reading, Massachusetts. Table 6.1. Reprinted with permission of the publisher.

very simple juxtaposition may reverse the intended meaning—*Mary teased Jack* versus *Jack teased Mary*. The improper arrangement of words can make even routine conversation difficult (*horse put the before cart the*). Learning a second language is a challenge because mastery of vocabulary and pronunciation is only a preliminary accomplishment to understanding the syntax. For example, Spanish speakers and writers commonly place a noun before an adjective (*a table round*), but English speakers follow the reverse procedure. Every language has syntactical rules to help avoid ambiguous discourse.

Semantics
The study of the meaning of the words and sentences of a language.

Another aspect of language study is **semantics**, which concerns the meaning of words and sentences. Semantics is a controversial area because semantic development cannot be described without a simultaneous attempt to understand how people think. The use of grammatical rules is intimately connected to the acquisition of semantic rules. Researchers interested in semantics study how an infant comes to differentiate between an automobile and other moving objects on wheels (e.g., trains and buses), at what

When people converse, their words and sentences do not provide the complete arena for communication. Gestures and facial expressions help language to be understood in context.

point a child achieves a knowledge of opposites (e.g., right and left, up and down), and in what ways the meanings of words change across the life span. Simply possessing a vocabulary cannot be equated with understanding; a parrot can be trained to say many words without understanding a single one.

Pragmatics
The study of the social and contextual factors that govern conversation, as well as the nonverbal aspects of language.

The last of the five components of language, *pragmatics,* has been seriously examined only since the 1970s. Pragmatic rules concern the social and contextual factors that govern conversation. For example, if a man says to his wife, "These scrambled eggs are dry," he could mean that he dislikes the eggs *or* that he is pleased with the consistency. The pragmatic approach to language involves interpreting meaning according to a knowledge of the situation and the people in it (e.g., gestures, facial expressions, tone of voice, personality, and life history). Pragmatics also refers to more general rules, such as knowing how to take turns in a conversation or being able to adjust speech for the benefit of younger children or foreigners. In other words, pragmatic rules imply the nonverbal accompaniments to expressing joy or anger, the appropriateness of slang versus polite speech, and the interaction of linguistic, cognitive, and social factors in the total context of language development.

The next sections will relate some of the specific findings in the areas of phonology, morphology, syntax, semantics, and pragmatics to each of the following phases: infancy, early childhood, later childhood, adolescence, and adulthood. Thus, the material will focus on developmental changes rather than on the validity of any one theory of language, for two reasons. First, little consensus exists that any one theory can explain the diverse aspects of language development much more effectively than another. Second, few of the researchers whose work will be cited here have indicated pure theoretical convictions. Tempering early environmental views of language development with the heredity perspective of the 1960s has appeared to result in a better balance within the past decade. Whitehurst (1982) has concluded:

> If the field of developmental psycholinguistics is now ready to shift toward a more social conception of language, we may be close to a point at which the interaction of biological preparation and social learning of language may be addressed productively. Paradoxically it is only a rigorous examination of the role of environmental variables that can clarify the contributions of biology to the acquisition of that most complex and intriguing of skills—human language. (p. 384)

INFANT ANTECEDENTS OF LANGUAGE

In light of the derivation of the word *infancy* from the Latin *infantia* (an inability to speak), it may be puzzling why we should devote attention to this period of development in a chapter on language. Although infants clearly are limited in their abilities to use an extensive vocabulary, to construct complex sentences, and to understand subtle abstractions, they are certainly not impossible to communicate with and are far more receptive to our speech than most people typically believe. Before examining the preliminary language of infants, especially in regard to the meaning and context of their words, we must see how infants respond to and manipulate basic sounds.

Early Sounds

The capacity of infants to perceive and attend to their environment from the first days of life was discussed in Chapter 5. This section will examine further the infant's response to the stimulus of human language. Condon and Sander's (1974) videotapes of neonatal movements have offered illuminating evidence in support of a biological readiness for language. They found that the apparently uncoordinated squirming and flexing of body parts are not merely random movements. When the videotapes were analyzed frame by frame, they discovered that infant movements were highly synchronized with the adult patterns of speech. Therefore, before the first spoken word, infants may be practicing the intonations of their native language with barely perceptible rhythms of their bodies. Using a variety of other procedures developed by researchers of infant perception (e.g., analyzing head turning, heart-rate changes, and sucking force), psycholinguists have demonstrated that "the infant early in life possesses many of the speech discrimination abilities that characterize an adult language user" (Molfese, Molfese, & Carrell, 1982, p. 307).

Just as infants learn to distinguish human from nonhuman sounds during the first weeks of life, and familiar from strange voices during the second or third month, they become increasingly adept at formulating sounds by the end of their first year (Kaplan & Kaplan, 1971). All infants proceed through four stages of preverbal vocalizations. During the first 6 months of infancy, much to the chagrin of new parents, sound production largely takes the form of crying. Whether or not parents can determine if their infant's cries refer to pain, anger, or hunger on the basis of the pitch, pattern, and intonation of the cry alone (Schaffer, 1971; Wolff, 1971) or if knowledge of the context is also required (Muller, Hollien, & Murry, 1974), crying provides a basis for communication and exercises the infant's vocal cords and breathing apparatus.

Some time between the second and fourth months of life, infants begin to articulate sounds more clearly and to coo (produce squealing and gurgling noises). As in any sequence of developmental transitions, phonological changes are subject to much individual variability, and the stages certainly overlap. This second prelinguistic stage includes other sounds such as grunts, sighs, and noises that depend on lip and tongue movements.

By around 6 months of age, the important third stage—babbling—dominates cooing and crying. Babbling consists of the repetition of actual speechlike sounds—simple combinations of vowels and consonants (such as *ga-ga-ga-ga*) that may strike the unaware listener as a foreign language.

In fact, adults tend to have much difficulty identifying the language background of babbling infants at this stage (Thevenin et al., 1985). Most babies, even those who are born deaf, enjoy producing babbling sounds. The babbling of hearing infants continues to evolve after 6 months; however, deaf infants gradually cease their spontaneous vocalizations. A more complete discussion of how the deaf develop language skills is provided in *Applying Our Knowledge,* "Language Acquisition in the Deaf." Thus, the sounds of language provide essential stimulation for continued development of that language.

Between 8 and 10 months after birth, infant babbling usually becomes modified to such a degree that an adult sitting in the next room might mistake the sounds being produced for the native language itself. Kaplan and Kaplan (1971) have termed this fourth stage one of patterned speech. At this point, babies babble in lengthy "strings" that accurately reproduce the sound combinations and intonation patterns of their own language. They no longer emit the sounds characteristic of other languages. Nevertheless, sounds common to several languages will be learned and properly articulated by all infants in the same approximate sequence (Jakobson, 1968). For example, the vowel and consonant combination required to produce *papa* (or *padre* in Spanish) is relatively easy for an infant. Perhaps this is why some parents feel sure that their infant's babbling has meaning even though understanding lags months behind the apparent "word" production.

From Words to Sentences

One of the major events of infant development is the appearance of true language—the first word. The timing of this milestone varies from the age of 10 to 15 months; however, many infants achieve the first word around their first birthday. Dodd (1980) has cautioned:

> Identifying the first word is difficult because pronunciation is crude and the meaning may be different from the adult meaning; in fact, what seems to be a word may be only babbling. But, given an approximation to the correct sounds of some word, produced voluntarily, and paired with the appropriate referent, proud parents and language researchers will call it a first word. (p. 60)

On the basis of her detailed analysis of 18 white middle-class infants during their second year of life, Nelson (1973) concluded that the age when 10 words have been acquired (about 15 months) offers a more stable index of this critical step in language development. Several dozen to several hundred additional words will become part of the infant's vocabulary by 2 years of age. Most observers have reported that the period between 18 and 24 months is one of significant vocabulary expansion.

Nelson's (1973) research was also concerned with the types of words first acquired. The most commonly spoken words at the 50-word stage (approximately 20 months of age), for instance, were general nominals (categorical

Applying Our Knowledge
Language Acquisition in the Deaf

 A primary concern of parents with deaf children is whether their child's language skills will be adequate for socioemotional and cognitive development to proceed successfully. Several methods have been used to help deaf children learn to communicate effectively: lipreading, fingerspelling, sign language, and many variations or combinations of these procedures. Evidence concerning the superiority of any one method is uncertain; however, multiple approaches, begun as early as possible, appear to be the best solution. Factors such as the degree of deafness, the age of onset, the intelligence of the child, and the existence of other disabilities also should be considered when language remediation is attempted. The prognosis for normal development has improved in recent years, but for most deaf children, their deficient communication skills will hamper their progress (Dale, 1976; Reich, 1986).

Nonetheless, language acquisition in the deaf provides an amazing display of the apparently very powerful mechanisms through which children learn to communicate. Research by Susan Goldin-Meadow and Carolyn Mylander (1984) with deaf children who did not receive any form of language tutoring revealed the spontaneous creation of a system of gestures that parallel the typical course of early language development in hearing children. The researchers found no evidence that these deaf children were learning their gestural languages through either imitation or reinforcement. They concluded "that exposure to a conventional linguistic input is not a necessary precondition for a child to acquire at least certain of the properties of language" (p. 105).

For deaf children to refine their communication skills, however, a self-taught gestural system needs to be augmented by other procedures. Because fingerspelling is relatively slow and lipreading alone is not entirely effective, nearly all deaf children are now also taught a sign language. American Sign Language (known also as Ameslan or ASL) is the most widely used sign language in the United States. Based on a version originally developed by a French priest in the eighteenth century, ASL relies essentially on a set of hand movements for each morpheme, or meaningful word part, in the English language (see Figure A for several examples of ASL words). Although ASL is a manual language and regular English is an oral language, the similarities between the two outweigh the differences. ASL, for example, has more than one dialect, allows for puns and slips of the tongue (hand?), and follows the same developmental course as spoken languages (Bellugi & Klima, 1982).

It is the last property mentioned that distinguishes ASL as a genuine language in which deaf children may develop at a rate similar to that of their hearing peers. In fact, some research has found accelerated initial language acquisition for users of ASL (Bonvillian, Orlansky, Novak, & Folven, 1983). This finding can probably be explained by the visual and motoric activities that have been practiced during the months of infancy. The vocal apparatus and speech centers of the brain, in contrast, are maturing slowly; however, after 2 years of age, the advantages of ASL disappear. Thus, ASL development may occur earlier and more rapidly than spoken English, but little else differentiates language acquisition in these two modes. As Dale (1976) contends:

> The really important aspects of language and the really important abilities the child brings to the problem of language learning are independent of the modality in which the linguistic system operates. Language is a central process, not a peripheral one. The abilities that children have are so general, and so powerful, that they proceed through the same milestones of development as hearing children. (p. 59)

nouns, especially if they involve some type of action such as *ball, snow,* or *car*). General and specific nominals (such as a particular person, animal, or object) accounted for nearly two-thirds of the total vocabulary. The remaining types of words, in descending order of frequency, included action

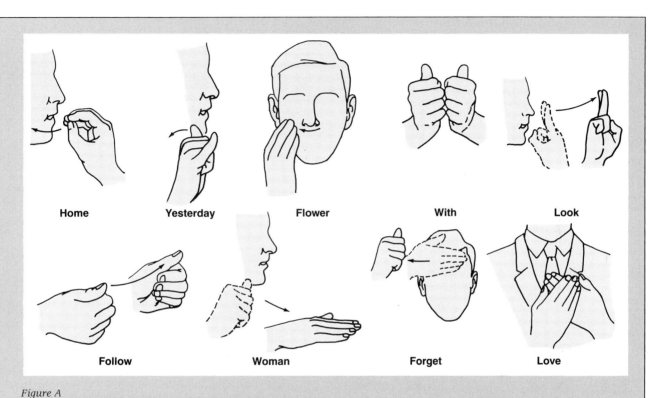

Figure A
Examples of Signs from American Sign Language (ASL)

Source: From L. L. Riekehof. *Talk to the deaf,* Springfield, MO.: Gospel Publishing House, 1978. Copyright 1978 by the Gospel Publishing House. Used by permission of the publisher.

words (*bye-bye, look,* and *up*), modifiers (*cold, blue,* and *nice*), personal/social words (*no, please,* and *ouch*), and function words (*where, to,* and *for*).

Whereas much research has emphasized the speaking aspects of early language, Gruendel's (1977) study evaluated the listening processes. She noted that in a child's attempt to understand the world "a word may be attached to a concept as soon as the functional core relations have been articulated" (p. 1575). This notion suggests that children are not likely to use words with notable consistency until they are able to integrate them within a conceptual scheme.

Once children have mastered the core vocabulary of 50 words or more, they begin to use two-word utterances in an inventive and unique form of grammar. Children's language at this stage, which usually begins at the age of 21 months, is a constructed version of adult speech, but it is not imitation. However, these two-word sentences do not seem to violate the appropriate rules for word sequence in the adult version of the language.

Because all children, including those who learn sign language, use the two-word utterance in similar ways at approximately the same time, it appears likely that a universal tendency to create and attend to language arises from the development of cognitive abilities, an innate mechanism for language acquisition, or both. Much controversy still exists over how to best describe the early grammatical rules children use to form the two-word utterance, as well as how to interpret the different meanings that underlie these "sentences."

Bloom, Lightbown, and Hood (1975) reported that not all children construct identical combinations of two words, and that, in fact, relatively few consistent patterns are used. Slobin (1971), in contrast, suggested seven functional relationships that effectively characterize the two-word utterances of children from different cultures. For example, the demands of the child may be stated *mehr milch* ("more milk" in German), and *mai pepe* ("give doll" in Samoan). Negative expressions are equally common at this stage: *no wash* and *ei susi* ("not wolf" in Finnish). Children are also eager to indicate ownership or possession, as in *Mama dress* or *pop moya* ("my navel" in Russian). Other functions include questions (*where ball*), modifiers (*piypiy kech,* or "hot pepper," in Luo), actions and objects (*hit ball* or *Bambi go*), and locations (*there book*).

Thus, infant grammar demonstrates a natural ability for abbreviating adult language. However, appreciating the meaning of a child's utterances requires an evaluation of the context within which they are spoken.

Understanding and Communicating

Communication during the months of infancy depends on strategies beyond the use of phonological and grammatical rules. Infants must attend to stress and intonation, to nonverbal signals such as hand gestures and facial expressions, and to cues associated with situations. The infant discovers such communication strategies even before producing recognizable words. Bates (1976) describes 1-year-old Carlotta's behavior:

> C. is sitting on her mother's lap, while mother shows her the telephone and pretends to talk. Mother tries to press the receiver against C.'s ear and have her

speak, but C. passes the receiver back and presses it against her mother's ear. This is repeated several times. When mother refuses to speak into the receiver, C. bats her hand against mother's knee, waits a moment longer, watches mother's face, and then, uttering a sharp, aspirated sound *ha,* touches her mother's mouth. (pp. 54–55)

Similarly, infants learn how to share their visual perspective with others by pointing accurately at objects (Leung & Rheingold, 1981). They are able to coordinate this activity with verbal labels by approximately 14 months (Murphy, 1978). Other researchers have demonstrated that infants can even grasp the rules for taking turns in having a conversation (Ninio & Bruner, 1978; Snow, 1977).

The emergence of the first words does not imply that infants attribute the same meanings to these words as adults do. In fact, such words are known as **holophrases** because "they appear to be attempts to express complex ideas, ideas that would be expressed in sentences by an adult" (Dale, 1976, p. 13). The infant pointing to the box of cookies on the table and saying "Cookie" may be labeling that object, expressing a desire to play with it, or indicating hunger. Greenfield and Smith's (1976) analysis of the holophrastic speech of two infant boys suggested that these early words may serve different functions according to the context.

Sometimes a word is used in a very restrictive manner referred to as *underextended.* For example, the infant may label the family pet *dog* but not use that word for other dogs. The opposite phenomenon is more common and is found in all languages. According to one report, between 20 and 34 percent of all words produced were *overextended* (Nelson, Rescorla,

Holophrases
The first words infants use, which tend to convey more meaning (i.e., the meaning of whole phrases) than the typical adult usage would imply.

Adults easily coordinate words with actions when they communicate, but young children acquire this skill gradually.

Gruendel, & Benedict, 1978). Many a father has been disappointed to hear his infant call another man "Daddy." Infants also may refer to any round object (for example, a rock, marble, or cherry) as a ball.

Although the two-word utterance provides additional clues to the meaning of infant language, these primitive "sentences" are also challenging for adults to interpret. The infant who says "Mama book," for instance, could be trying to communicate that the book belongs to Mother or that it would be nice of Mother to read this book aloud. Therefore, parents are forced to use similar strategies for understanding two-word expressions as they did in figuring out the meaning of holophrases.

Infants do offer some helpful hints in making themselves understood, however. In the expression *kitty food,* for example, stress on the first word could mean "This is the kitty's food," whereas stress on the latter word suggests "It is time to feed the kitty." These variations again demonstrate that infant communication can be quite complex and necessitates careful attention to the subtleties of the language context.

EARLY CHILDHOOD AND THE LINGUISTIC EXPLOSION

Beyond the infancy stage, language acquisition proceeds rapidly for the next 3 or 4 years. By the time a child is ready to begin receiving a formal education, pronunciation is usually accurate, a basic vocabulary has been established, the rules of grammar are intuitively applied, the meanings of language are considerably extended, and the use of words is related appropriately to their context. Although language production continues to lag behind the comprehension of speech throughout early childhood, advances in cognitive development ensure significantly easier communication than was possible for an infant. The following sections describe several ways in which the preschool period has been found to be exceptionally rich in language development.

Improving Speech

Young children react to the difficulties of acquiring the sounds of language in the same way they cope with grammar and meaning. That is, they reduce the complexity of what they hear from the speech environment. Dale (1976) has suggested that "the differences between the child's forms and those of the adult are not solely a matter of perceptual and articulation difficulties; rather, they reflect the workings of a rule-governed system that . . . appears to be quite similar in the early stages for children acquiring different languages" (p. 233). Most preschool children do not have persistent trouble in discriminating among the sounds of their native language. Eilers and Oller (1976) found that 2-year-olds could distinguish between *cow* and *pow,* had some problems with *rabbit* and *wabbit,* and were likely to confuse *monkey* with *mucky.* As children's short-term memory processes become more efficient, they pay greater attention to the finer distinctions in speech (including their own) and rely less on pragmatic clues to sound.

The ability of preschool children to produce sounds improves substantially between the ages of 2 and 6 years. Early attempts at pronunciation, such as *hefant* for *elephant* or *boon* for *spoon* (Ingram, 1974), result in common childish simplifications. These are gradually overcome by comprehension of the differences and by coordination of the lips and tongue, which allows better articulation of sounds. Through a spectrographic analysis (soundwave patterns) of certain words, Macken and Barton (1980) found distinctions in children's production of speech that were undetectable to the untrained ear. Other researchers (for example, Hodson, 1980; Ingram, 1981) have been able to identify the processes of phonological acquisition. Children, for instance, characteristically say *pay* before achieving the ability to say *play.* This cluster-reduction strategy involves simplifying the *pl* sound blend to only one of its component sounds.

The Emergence of Grammar

When speech has progressed to the point at which three or more words are combined into a single sentence, the child has grasped the essential elements of the language. For example, a preschooler who says "Daddy push truck" is expressing the relationships among a subject *(Daddy),* a verb or action *(push),* and an object *(truck).* Similar statements, such as "I go bye-bye," communicate messages in a syntactic form that has been called **telegraphic speech.** Because the cost of sending a telegram is based on the number of words in the message, we try to eliminate words that are not absolutely necessary for accurate communication. Young children's speech lacks the same type of words usually omitted from telegrams—articles, prepositions, conjunctions, and so on. Nevertheless, a preschooler almost always produces sentences with a word order consistent with adult language.

Psycholinguists have been studying children's language by using (1) naturalistic methods of transcribing spontaneous speech and (2) experimental studies that probe for specific abilities. Intensive efforts to understand the telegraphic grammar of children have been under way for more than two decades. According to Slobin (1973), the task of these analyses is to chart the sequence of grammatical development and to explain the cognitive strategies children apply to learning a language. Based on data from more than 40 different cultures, Slobin tentatively arrived at his seven principles that appear to guide language development. Similarly, Brown's (1973) longitudinal investigation of three children led him to conclude that "the order of progression in knowledge of the first language . . . will prove to be approximately invariant across children learning the same language and, at a higher level of abstraction, across children learning any language" (pp. 403–404).

Telegraphic speech
The first, abbreviated sentences that very young children create. They contain the minimum number of words needed to relate meaning but lack the auxiliary words that adults typically omit from telegram messages.

One aspect of morphology that has received careful study is the suffix. Suffixes are added to the ends of words to change their meaning. These markers, such as plural forms *-es* or *-s* and the past tense *-ed,* are also known as *inflections.* Two of Slobin's (1973) principles pertain to morphological development. Rather than learn language simply through imitation, children apparently try to abstract the rules of grammar by producing forms that do not exist but that are sensible, syntactic arrangements. This process of "regularizing" the language, called *overregularization,* demonstrates Slobin's principles of (1) avoiding exceptions and (2) attending to the ends of words.

In a classic study of the early awareness of plural forms, Berko (1958) presented young children with an illustration of a cartoonlike character labeled a *wug.* After showing them another illustration with two of these unfamiliar creatures, she said to the children, "Now there are two _____." Children almost always supplied the regular plural form *wugs.* Children often attempt to use the normal plural rule for irregular plurals *(gooses* and *foots)* or even as additions to the irregular forms themselves *(geeses* and *feets).* Clark and Clark (1977) pointed out that the overregularization of such rules can be found in a variety of languages.

The sequence of inflection development, however, is not what we might predict on the basis of a regularizing tendency. We might expect that

Although children often seem to listen carefully to adult speech, they tend to focus on the message rather than the actual words or sentences. Thus, their speech contains creative usage, such as wented, *that does not derive from imitation.*

regularizing would be the first stage, but Cazden (1968), for example, found it to be the third of the four stages in the acquisition of the past tense. At first, children do not use any past tense forms, such as *went* or *stopped.* Then they will use a few irregular forms *(went)* they have learned through imitation. In the third stage, children produce the regular form for both regular *(stopped)* and irregular verbs *(goed).* They even may extend the irregular forms to create novel words such as *wented* and *broked* (Kuczaj, 1978). Finally, toward the end of the preschool years, children eliminate virtually all of the overregularized forms. These patterns of use reveal the active role of children in constructing language.

Besides acquiring greater flexibility with the structure of words themselves, children quickly elaborate on the construction of their formerly short and crude sentences. The process through which children create sentence order is still a very controversial area. However, most researchers acknowledge that certain regular transformations must occur. These rules are not consciously applied by either children or adults attempting to formulate sentences, yet indirect evidence suggests that they are used. For instance, a person who is asked to transform the statement "The lors bliged the grint" into a question could easily complete the task: "Did the lors blig the grint?" Because these words or sentences were never heard before, the only way to transform the syntax is by following an appropriate set of rules. Comparisons between children of different ages demonstrate that transformational rules develop during early childhood for many grammatical forms including questions, negatives, passives, conjunctions, and embedded clauses (Elliot, 1981).

Semantics and Pragmatics

Although the growth of vocabulary itself during early childhood is an impressive feat—more than 20 words per day are added for a child of average intelligence (Miller, 1978)—the meanings of language develop gradually. The most significant constraint on improvement in semantic knowledge is likely to be the level of understanding the child brings in the speech arena. Factors that influence a child's understanding include the labeling of the environment by parents, the value of certain objects for the child, the context of word and sentence use, and the perceptual features of the child's world. J. G. de Villiers and P. A. de Villiers (1978) illustrate the profound nature of semantic acquisition for the child with a quote from Elizabeth, at age 3½: " 'You know what, Mommy? Yesterday today was tomorrow' " (p. 121).

One aspect of semantics that appears to give young children particular trouble is the use of relational and comparative terms (e.g., *big/little, now/later, right/left, more/less*). The evidence concerning the proper use of such words depends on the particular linguistic comparison, as well as the child's language environment. For example, a study by Clark and Sengul (1978) of 2- to 5-year-old children's comprehension of *here/there* and *this/that* yielded an interesting developmental pattern. The children were asked to give to the experimenter one of two identical animals placed at different distances from them, yet within reach. The 2- and 3-year-olds could not differentiate the opposing terms and always chose the animal either close to themselves or close to the experimenter. Only the 5-year-old children could always make the correct selection.

Today, preschoolers are viewed as effective and sensitive communicators, whereas in the past their linguistic deficiencies were emphasized. For example, Shatz and Gelman (1973) demonstrated that 4-year-old children are capable of adjusting their descriptions of a toy to suit the various language levels of 2-year-olds, other 4-year-olds, and adults. Even a child of 2½ years may be willing to engage in an active dialogue with an interested adult (Keenan, 1975). Nevertheless, Bacharach and Luszcz (1979) have shown that communicative competence still needs to improve during the early childhood years. They compared the abilities of 3- and 5-year-old children to use *implicit information* during conversations. Implicit information means attention to material newly introduced in a conversation or to action versus content or to beginnings and endings of a topic. The younger children failed to make appropriate remarks in light of the experimenter's comments. In contrast, the older children's responses were governed by the context that the experimenter had structured.

Implicit information

The skills that competent users of a language possess and take for granted in the process of having a conversation. For example, competent speakers are aware when the topic of conversation changes.

Bacharach and Luszcz's (1979) results suggest that younger preschool children have not yet acquired the competence to engage in a completely meaningful conversation because they lack a sense of implicit information. The researchers, however, were not certain about how to explain the children's deficiency or why the 5-year-olds were more responsive to the experimenter's remarks. Is it a matter of learning to identify and use implicit linguistic cues? Are younger children unable to process that much information? Perhaps preschoolers do not pay attention to such information? Or are these children biased to respond to objects rather than to actions? This last possibility is supported by the findings of Gentner (1978), who reported that preschoolers relied on perceptual features, not actions, to label an unfamiliar toy. In any event, the meanings of language during early childhood are again intimately related to both grammatical skills and contextual clues.

LANGUAGE REFINEMENTS OF LATER CHILDHOOD AND ADOLESCENCE

Later childhood and adolescence are highlighted by the capacity not only to use the rules of language, but also consciously to create and interpret subtle distinctions. After the age of 5 or 6 years, children develop a fuller appreciation of the sounds making up language. They expand their knowledge of word meanings and relationships; they refine their use of grammatical irregularities and minor syntactic rules; they become more attuned to linguistic ambiguities; and they achieve greater ability in perceiving the needs of those with whom they wish to communicate. Although preschoolers have begun these processes, the skills have not yet emerged in a consistent fashion at the complex levels that characterize later development. For instance, we might ask a youngster above the age of 6, "Do you know the time?" The child might reply, "Yes." Our immediate reaction may be that the child has a sense of humor, but, in fact, the simple reply shows how sensitive the child is to distinctions in language.

Words and Sentences Revisited

A study conducted by Shultz and Pilon (1973) demonstrated the grammatical confusion that obstructs the path of children's language development. They evaluated the skills of first, fourth, seventh, and tenth graders in detecting four types of linguistic ambiguities:

> Phonological:
>> "The doctor is out of patience (patients)."
>> "He saw three pears (pairs)."
> Lexical:
>> "No one liked the plant (factory)."
>> "He did not have enough dough (money)."
> Surface-Structure:
>> "He sent her kids story books." (emphasis on her *or* kids)
>> "He saw a man eating fish." (emphasis on man *or* eating)
> Deep-Structure:
>> "The duck is ready to eat." (duck could eat *or* be eaten)
>> "They are visiting sailors." (they could be going *or* here) (p. 730)

After the researchers explained and illustrated that sentences may have more than one meaning, the children were asked to listen to and interpret a random selection of sentences of the four ambiguous types or their unambiguous versions. For example, "The doctor has lost his temper" is the unambiguous version of "The doctor is out of patience." Similarly, "He saw a ferocious fish" is the unambiguous version of "He saw a man eating fish."

Schultz and Pilon found that the particular type of ambiguity determined the children's detection ability. Improvement in explaining phonological types occurred earliest (between the ages of 6 and 9 years). The lexical ambiguities showed a gradual, steady improvement with age. Finally, deep- and surface-structure ambiguities were not detected until at least age 12. We can conclude that grammatical constructions of our language require various levels of transformation to be accurately interpreted.

Not only do children have to learn that the surface structure of their language may not always provide unambiguous clues to sentence meaning; they also have to grasp elaborations of previously acquired morphological and syntactic forms. Such sentences include complications, similar to this one, that embed secondary clauses within the main point (e.g., the research of Huang, 1983). Word forms that are mastered during later childhood include stress shifts to distinguish a *greenhouse* from a *green house* and stem changes that alter *reproduce* to *reproduction*. Children continue to improve their articulation of language sounds, enlarge their vocabularies many times over, and further refine relational terms (e.g., *follow* versus *lead*). However, the most frustrating challenge for the later years of childhood is learning the exceptions to many of the rules that have so recently been acquired. For example, the irregular past tense form of many verbs *(bled, flew, and sent)* is but one aspect of this problem (de Villiers & de Villiers, 1978).

Meanings and Conversations

Communication with school-age children rapidly becomes easier as they develop the linguistic skills needed to convey intended meanings and to interpret speech subtleties. Semantic and pragmatic progress can be seen in the construction and comprehension of jokes, in the recognition that the form of address depends on the person to whom they are speaking (e.g., a parent as opposed to a playmate), and in their ability to tell an effective lie. By the time they are in the first grade, children have a fairly sophisticated understanding of commonly used words; in fact, such children are sensitive enough to subtleties in word usage that they can tell from the speaker's tone of voice and the context when someone is speaking sarcastically to them (Ackerman, 1982). However, many of these same children make errors in speech when using words that are quite familiar to them, and consistently fail to correct those errors.

Consider the words of 6-year-old Mindy, a child interviewed by Bowerman (1978): "You said what I was going to say . . . you *put* the words right out of my mouth" (p. 986). Why would Mindy make such a mistake? Certainly she had never heard an adult substitute *put* for *took* in the preceding expression. Bowerman explained the error by noting that a child who is trying to construct such a sentence must select from among semantically similar words, thus overloading mental limitations. In addition, children make rapid substitutions—either upon request or spontaneously—and never replace a correct word with an incorrect one. In sum, a child's semantic development proceeds as a consequence of information processing advances in attending to his or her own speech, as well as to the linguistic environment.

Thus far, this section has reviewed language accomplishments with respect to sounds, words, and sentences. However, the area of pragmatics offers the most interesting changes in the child's linguistic development. The social context of communication—from the perspective of the speaker or the listener—demands new skills from the older child.

Research on the increasing sensitivity of children to the needs of both participants in a conversation commenced with Glucksberg, Krauss, and Higgins during the mid-1960s. Their investigations of school-age children demonstrated an improving ability to provide accurate descriptions of objects and designs so that listeners who could not see the objects and designs were still able to draw them. Younger children typically produced brief, idiosyncratic communications that did not help the listener complete the task. Furthermore, they were relatively unresponsive to feedback from the listener who said "I don't understand." Whereas older children hearing this would try to explain the task in another way, 5- and 6-year-olds tended to repeat themselves or to remain silent.

Not only were kindergarten and first-grade children egocentric communicators, they were also poor listeners. Good listeners know when the information they are being given is unclear and can ask the speaker to clarify the message, as college students often do when they ask a professor to explain a point more fully. Glucksberg, Krauss, and Higgins (1975) noted that first graders do not even seem to realize when a speaker gives them confusing or contradictory information. A similar type of study by Sonnenschein (1986a) did reveal, however, that both first- and fourth-grade children had an easier time communicating with friends than with strangers.

No one knows for certain why young children fail to monitor accurately their own comprehension, but Markman (1977) proposed that they seem to process spoken information very superficially. She based her conclusion on comparisons of the performances of first, second, and third graders in evaluating a totally inadequate set of instructions for playing a game and doing a magic trick. First graders seemed especially oblivious to the missing information and obvious misinformation recited by the experimenters. Although the tasks were simple and the children were specifically told to focus on faulty communication, the younger children appeared not to realize that they did not understand. More recently, Sonnenschein (1986b) found that young children evaluated ambiguous and inconsistent messages more accurately when the speakers were adults rather than when they were peers. Sonnenschein cautioned teachers that their pupils "may be too ready to assume that the communications of adults are clear and that therefore failures in comprehension are due to errors by the children" (p. 168).

During adolescence, language reflects both the powers of formal thought and the search for a secure identity. In the cognitive area, linguistic abilities continue to improve so that the adolescent can appreciate poetic metaphors, complex analogies, ironic statements, and literary symbolism. These improved abilities, along the with the normal expansion of vocabulary that occurs during adolescence, create a flexible speaking and listening language system. A cross-sectional study of 6-, 9-, and 13-year-olds and college students revealed that sarcastic remarks are not recognized until adolescence (Demorest, Meyer, & Phelps, 1984). Researchers imply that like children with new toys, adolescents enjoy playing with and showing off their linguistic abilities.

Not only does language reveal the adolescent's development of biological and cognitive processes; it also exposes the need for strong social

Issues in Human Development
Learning a Second Language

Acquiring fluency in a second language is a skill that has been the subject of increasing attention in recent years, for at least three reasons. First, the task is one of the most difficult for either children or adults to master (Asher, 1977). Second, a widespread belief that has been supported by empirical research suggests that bilingualism facilitates better thinking (Ben-Zeev, 1977). Finally, the process of language development—especially the notion of a critical period—might be more clearly revealed by studying the acquisition of a second language (Snow & Hoefnagel-Hohle, 1978).

Many of us have felt the frustrations of trying to learn a foreign language. Asher (1977) reported that fewer than 5 percent of students who start to learn a second language ever achieve proficiency. He speculated that three elements crucial to first-language development usually are violated in teaching a foreign language:

1. Receptive skills precede productive speech.
2. Speech is fostered in conjunction with motor skills.
3. Spontaneous readiness for language cannot be rushed.

Therefore, Asher set up an experimental format to teach Spanish that was based on delaying speech until after 12 hours of exposure to the language, getting the students actively involved when speaking, and tolerating errors with few attempts at correction. In comparison with control groups, Asher found that the experimental fifth, sixth, seventh, and eighth graders, as well as an adult group, learned to speak and write Spanish more quickly.

Even if better ways to teach a second language exist than those typically used, how does this knowledge influence cognitive development? Ben-Zeev (1977) tested children in Israel and the United States who were monolingual and those who were bilingual from about 2 or 3 years of age. All children were between 5½ and 8½ years old and from middle-class, Jewish, professional families. Although no significant IQ differences existed, Ben-Zeev found that the bilingual children were more advanced in processing verbal material and more sensitive to perceptual distinctions than the monolingual children. She contended that bilingual children are confronted by an unusual verbal environment. To deal with this complexity, "they seem to have developed special facility for seeking out rules and for determining which are required by the circumstances" (Ben-Zeev, 1977, pp. 1017–1018).

Because learning a second language is both feasible and desirable, the point at which this can be best accomplished should be identified. McLaughlin's (1982) review of second-language learning suggests that the process is both similar to and different from that of learning a first language. In part, this may be due to influences of the original language. Nevertheless, he concluded that "younger-is-better does not seem to be a good rule of thumb . . . early adolescence is the best time to learn a second language, both in terms of rate and eventual language proficiency" (McLaughlin, 1982, p. 217). Support for this is illustrated by Snow and Hoefnagel-Hohle's (1978) 1-year longitudinal research on the naturalistic acquisition of Dutch by English speakers. These researchers found that 12- to 15-year-olds and adults made faster progress than 3- to 5-year-olds and 8- to 10-year-olds. The critical period for second-language learning may not correspond to its dubious counterpart for acquiring a first language.

supports and identity formation. The slang expressions created by every generation of adolescents serve as an aid to effective communication, but their more essential purpose may be to distinguish the adolescent culture from that of the adult world (Rice, 1990). Teenagers have to make certain that their slang is current, however; users of last year's slang expressions may be viewed as hopelessly out of fashion. Expressions such as *far out* and

To express their emerging personalities, adolescents employ several forms of language, ranging from poetic to destructive. Graffiti may represent a bold attempt to proclaim an identity to the rest of the world.

right on were appropriate in the early 1970s, but an adolescent who uses them today may be regarded by peers as a refugee from the Stone Age. Finally, verbal dueling—whereby friends insult and challenge each other— is especially characteristic of adolescent boys. Adolescents use language to achieve status, claim dominance, vent anger, and avoid physical confrontation (Romaine, 1984).

COURSE OF LANGUAGE DURING ADULTHOOD AND OLD AGE

Almost all the research and theory on the development of language has emphasized the early portion of the life span. In fact, few of the major textbooks concerning adulthood or aging devote more than a few paragraphs to the subject. The underlying consensus of language experts appears to be that if developmental changes do occur beyond childhood, they have little significance. One exception to this pattern, as noted in *Issues in Human Development,* "Learning a Second Language," is the acquisition of a second or third language. However, this process may be quite different from the usual sequence of language development (and for many individuals it does not ever occur).

Phonological and grammatical changes are surely minor considerations in the language of adults. Among the elderly, a decline in communication abilities is possible, although not inevitable. Furthermore, vocabulary growth often continues throughout life. The aspects of language development that seem to be ripest for study through adulthood are semantic and pragmatic. References to some of these issues were made in discussing parent-child communications and in contrasting childhood and adult performance. Therefore, this section will highlight the nature of language development beyond adolescence and indicate the potential directions of future study.

Adult Skills and Patterns

The potential for continual development of linguistic awareness remains the hallmark of adult language. Verbal proficiency and growth in communication skills is particularly diverse during the adult years. This is seen in areas ranging from broadcasting, publishing, and public speaking to creative writing, philosophy, and comedy. Adults are also capable of expanding their receptive language. They learn to interpret the speech of infants and children, to decode the "word salads" of schizophrenics, to distinguish genuine affection from insincere romantic expressions, and to "read between the lines" of a supervisor's orders. Although the extent of an adult's education may contribute to the level of language ability, the frequency with which these skills are used determines their effectiveness. It is not likely that linguistic competence will decline during most of the adult years for the mentally active individual. Investigations of language must interact with and eventually may contribute to a greater understanding of the development of social, personality, and cognitive variations observed throughout adulthood.

Although language deficiencies are not a likely development during early and middle adulthood, strokes, or, more typically, head-related traumas, can result in aphasias—language disturbances following brain damage (Davis & Holland, 1981). Such problems may usually be traced to the anterior region of the left hemisphere of the brain. Adults with aphasia, before old age, tend to comprehend spoken or written language accurately and to know what they wish to communicate to others (Albert, 1981). However, their ability to formulate orally the actual words and phrases is seriously impaired. Aphasic adults struggle to pronounce words, omit words in a form of telegraphic speech, but generally understand written or spoken language without difficulty.

Across the early and middle adulthood years, little evidence exists of variation in language comprehension; that is, the ability to process language seems neither to improve nor to decline (Obler & Albert, 1985). Of course, researchers must take into account the decrease in hearing ability that typically begins to occur after the age of 30 in evaluating language reception. In addition, as discussed in Chapter 6, learning and memory play an important role in processing language. For example, recitation skills seem to increase somewhat across adulthood, whereas paragraph recall appears to decrease slightly. Finally, other patterns characterize different language skills, such as elaborateness of speech. Obler (1980), for instance, reported data from a cross-sectional study that indicates adults in their 30s and 70s used somewhat more complex sentences in both speech and writing than adults in their 50s.

Interpreting the small variations in language skills across the adulthood years is difficult. Because most of the available data reflect cross-sectional designs, the possibility of cohort effects influencing the results remains an issue. A more recent sequential-longitudinal study by Kemper (1987), for example, revealed an age-related decline in syntactic complexity. Obler and Albert (1985) also pointed out that some of their research has been confirmed across different cultures, increasing the likelihood that the patterns are, in fact, universal. They stress the need to examine various language skills separately because they suspect diversity in the ways such skills develop across the life span. In any event, the early and middle adulthood years should now be recognized as a period of both stability and change in language skills.

Are There Deficits Among the Elderly?

Late in life, language capacities may decline slowly. However, the problems an elderly person has with language often are related to physical and perceptual loss. For the elderly who retain reasonable health and sensory acuity, and especially for those who do not withdraw from social and cognitive experiences, language abilities should not be diminished. Unless affected by, for example, a stroke, the productive aspects of language can remain as clear and effective as ever.

The language comprehension area is more likely to become a handicap for the elderly. Aside from hearing deficiency itself, many researchers have suggested that the understanding of rapid and complex language information is more difficult in old age. Based on a series of three experiments in story comprehension, Cohen (1979) concluded that such "tasks demand concurrent processing of surface meaning and deeper level processing of underlying meaning and this dual demand appears to exceed the capacity of older subjects" (p. 427). Therefore, when communicating with the elderly, it may be helpful to keep messages short and explicit, as well as to slow the rate of speech.

There may be a fine line, however, between legitimate language simplification for the benefit of elderly adults and an exaggerated treatment of them that communicates helplessness and powerlessness. A field study by Caporael (1981) investigated the speech interactions of caretakers to nursing home residents. About 22 percent of the tape-recorded sentences were classified as baby talk or motherese. No correlation existed between listener competency and the proportion of motherese used by caretakers. In addition, college students who rated the caretaker speech evaluated the motherese sentences more positively than standard sentences and intonation. Caporael's study, however, did not address the elderly's perceptions of motherese speech. The fundamental question is whether such motherese for the elderly is appropriately nurturant, warm, and helpful, or if older people construe it as demeaning and reinforcing of diminished status.

Language disorders among the elderly are most likely to be stroke-induced aphasia or senile dementia. Unlike earlier aphasia, the stroke-induced aphasia of old age occurs in the posterior region of the left hemisphere, and the effects are predominantly on language comprehension, not production (Obler & Albert, 1985). The receptive deficits may be so severe that the affected individuals do not even realize their communication difficulties. Dementia progresses more slowly from earlier to later stages of the disease. Although simpler sentences may be comprehended at first, more subtle or humorous sentences may not be understood (Bayles, 1984). By the middle stages, conversation is impaired to the extent that basic syntax in receptive and productive speech is difficult for the afflicted person. Later stages of dementia are characterized by totally disorganized speech and a complete inability to understand language (Obler & Albert, 1985).

For the normal elderly adult who is not handicapped by aphasia, dementia, or sensory loss, deficits in areas of phonology (Goodglass, 1980) or syntax (Ulatowska, Cannito, Hayashi, & Fleming, 1985) are not significant. Furthermore, when information processing skills peripherally related to language ability are examined, declines in semantic abilities do not appear either (Ulatowska et al., 1985). Much research, as noted in the previous section, even suggests improvements in semantic aspects of language. At this time, little research on pragmatic aspects of language in the elderly has been done. Based on the socioemotional flavor of pragmatics, this appears to be a topic particularly ripe for future investigations of language development.

Later adulthood years should not necessarily be hindered by language disorders. Most elderly people are not aphasic, senile, or sensorily dysfunctional. Although some deterioration in auditory acuity and processing information does appear to be age related, the effect of such changes on language usage can be minimized. Even some of the more serious problems can often be remediated through speech therapy and electronic devices. Much of the mythology regarding language deficits among the elderly needs to be reinterpreted, both professionally and publicly, by acknowledging the context of previous research. Obler and Albert (1985) noted that language variations may be influenced by cohort effects, levels of education, native versus nonnative speakers, institutionalized versus noninstitutionalized individuals, and the physical health of the elderly persons.

THEORIES OF LANGUAGE DEVELOPMENT

Theories of language development can be most easily distinguished by noting the emphasis devoted to either innate (biological) or experiential (environmental) factors. Furthermore, each theory tends to focus on particular types of evidence that support the approach taken, while minimizing findings that contradict the position. This section will introduce the three dominant theoretical views toward language acquisition. In brief, behavioral or learning theory stresses the acquisition of speech habits; nativistic or biological theory emphasizes the maturation of brain functions;

and cognitive or interactionist theory focuses on the development of thought processes. Table 9.2 summarizes the major characteristics of the three theories of language development.

Behavioral Approach

According to learning theorists, language develops largely as a response to environmental stimulation. Aside from the vocal apparatus itself and the capacity of the human species to learn, this perspective dismisses innate factors in language acquisition. Instead, behaviorists believe that children learn to speak because they are reinforced for producing sounds, for making associations between sounds and objects, and for imitating the sounds to which they are exposed. Behaviorists do not consider language different from other skills and therefore reject acquisition explanations that reflect unobservable processes or biological readiness. Although the behavioral approach was instrumental in stimulating a systematic analysis of language development, the influence of this view declined sharply after the late 1950s until the late 1970s (de Villiers & de Villiers, 1978).

Because children learn to speak the language or dialect they hear during their early years, environmental variation would seem to be the crucial developmental variable. However, considerable research has indicated that such an explanation is quite incomplete. Certainly, the influence of a person's native language cannot be ignored, but this does not verify the role of the environment as the principal cause for learning to produce and respond to speech. For instance, why would young children raised by well-educated parents ever say "No go movie"? Such an expression is not

Table 9.2
Characteristics of Theories of Language Development

	Behavioral	Nativist	Interactionist
General orientation	Environmental	Hereditary	Interactive
Basis for development	Learning processes	Language acquisition device (LAD)	Cognitive processes
Emphasis of study	Surface structure	Deep structure	Deep and surface structure
Significance of language universals	Minimal	Maximal	Moderate
Role of parents	Simplify speech for teaching rules	Exhibit speech during critical period	Use speech in the appropriate contexts
Special features	Methods for remediation	Demonstrate creative qualities	Reciprocity of thought and language

found in the English language, is not likely to have been positively reinforced, and is not an imitation of a parental expression. The behavioral approach offers no convincing account for this phenomenon.

Even when parents make an effort to teach language directly to their children through modeling, the experience may be frustrating. The following dialogue reported by developmental linguist David McNeill (1966) illustrates this point:

> *Child:* Nobody don't like me.
> *Mother:* No, say "nobody likes me."
> *Child:* Nobody don't like me. (Eight repetitions of this correction and error)
> *Mother:* No, now listen carefully; say *"Nobody likes me."*
> *Child:* Oh! "Nobody don't likes me." (p. 69)

It would be less exasperating, if more time-consuming, for a parent to train appropriate speech patterns using a schedule of reinforcements. Aside from the fact that few parents are aware of the rules of grammar or the principles of operant conditioning, there are not enough hours in the day to reward systematically the complexities of human language that are acquired so quickly. Furthermore, parents typically express approval or disapproval of their children's speech on the basis of what the children are trying to say, not the grammatical accuracy of their utterances (Brown, Cazden, & Bellugi, 1969). The strategy of correcting infant speech, in fact, may backfire. Nelson (1973) found that language development proceeded more slowly for those 1- and 2-year-olds whose mothers imposed their own pronunciations and syntax on their children.

Nevertheless, the environment is necessary for stimulating language development (Hoff-Ginsberg, 1986). Parents will alter their sentence structure and simplify their vocabulary when speaking to infants and young children (Clark & Clark, 1977). Snow (1972) suggested that the willingness of adults to modify their speech and to repeat themselves helps give children consistent information to create the rules of grammar. For example, one of the most frequently employed language-training techniques is known as **expansion**. If the child says, "Daddy drink," the parent may respond with an elaborated type of imitation: "Yes, Daddy is having a drink." Considerable controversy has been generated about the value of expansions for improving language development. Earlier research indicated that expansions were not highly useful (Cazden, 1968; Feldman, 1971); however, a more recent investigation (Newport, Gleitman, & Gleitman, 1977) found that certain linguistic structures attained by children were significantly related to parental expansion.

The behavioral approach, then, concerns the ability of children to generalize from the speech of adults to their own use of the language. Contradictory findings in this area may be the result of such factors as the age of the children, the familiarity of the researchers with the children, the artificiality of a laboratory environment, and the differential effectiveness of

Expansion
An informal language-training technique frequently employed by parents, in which the child's simple sentences are reiterated in a more elaborate form.

parents in providing appropriate models or corrections. Therefore, behavioral explanations of natural language development may not be able to account for the full richness and rate of acquisition but may provide insights about the environmental features that build on biological foundations. Several special language situations undoubtedly are the products of specific learning processes. Teaching people to speak a foreign language, offering forms of therapy to language-disabled persons, or finely tuning the grammatical abilities of adult speakers all depend on particular learning experiences.

Nativist Approach

From the perspective of nativist theory, the impetus for language acquisition can be attributed to innate features of the brain. Noam Chomsky (1957) and Eric Lenneberg (1967) have been the major proponents of the nativist approach. In contrast to the behavioral view, these theorists focus on the biological aspects of language. Specifically, they are interested in universal patterns of language development, the basic similarities among all languages, and the relationship between nervous system maturation and linguistic ability. Although few contemporary theorists totally dismiss the effects of the learning environment, many researchers have been persuaded that such factors are less relevant than innate determiners in guiding the process of language acquisition.

Perhaps the most impressive evidence supporting the nativist approach to language is the unfolding of developmental milestones. Despite a wide range of differences in linguistic environments for infants and young children, the sequence and timing of language achievements throughout the world are surprisingly invariant. A striking degree of "prewired" preparedness is suggested in all stages from babbling sounds to constructing sentences, in the errors in formulating questions or negatives, and in the synchronization of motor and languge skills. Even among deaf children—who spontaneously vocalize during the early months of life in a manner indistinguishable from that of hearing infants—the course of sign language development and rate of acquisition are virtually identical to those of normal speech. This process is described more fully in *Applying Our Knowledge,* "Language Acquisition in the Deaf." Therefore, whether a child is Polish or Portuguese, silent or vocal, or middle- or lower-class, the path toward language competence is remarkably alike.

Another biologically based notion concerns whether people must acquire language during a critical period. Ethologists, for example, identify time intervals during which a species may be especially sensitive to certain types of change. What support do we have for the applicability of critical-period constraints on language development? Because Lenneberg (1967) proposed that exposure to language is essential between infancy and puberty, language deprivation for much or all of this period would be

Hearing-impaired persons need not be isolated linguistically or unstimulated cognitively. American Sign Language facilitates accurate, sensitive communication that follows the same developmental course as vocal language.

expected to make complete command of a language unlikely. Although the difficulties in either regaining linguistic functions following brain damage or learning a foreign language beyond puberty are clearly recognized, a more stringent evaluation of the critical-period concept demands raising a child without the usual language environment until adolescence.

Naturally, no researcher would suggest that such an unethical experiment be deliberately conducted. There have been several examples, however, of infants abandoned in remote areas or of children reared under extremely deprived conditions. Attempts subsequently were made to teach the children to communicate using language rather than simply through gestures, grunts, and facial expressions. Knowing exactly what physical and emotional traumas or possible mental retardation had influenced the development of these children was impossible; however, none has been successfully trained to demonstrate much language skill (Brown, 1958). The efforts to teach some language have been more rewarding in the case of children who were severely unstimulated due to parental insanity, sensory handicaps, or limited intelligence.

The discovery of a 14-year-old girl named Genie provided only some evidence for Lenneberg's position. Curtiss (1977) described Genie's life from the age of 20 months as one of physical neglect and abuse, darkened and roped confinement, and no linguistic stimulation. Despite years of language remediation, Genie's knowledge of phonological and syntactic rules was still impaired. However, her speech, especially the semantic aspect, had progressed well past the minimal level suggested by the critical-period hypothesis. The story of Isabelle, an equally deprived child, had a more encouraging ending (Brown, 1958). After only a year of special training, her language skills were normal for her age. At the time of Isabelle's discovery, however, she was much younger than Genie—about 6 years old.

Chomsky's (1957) analysis of the process of language acquisition originates with the position that the mind is predisposed to construct and respond to language in specific ways. Children, therefore, have a tendency to attend to the language environment, formulate rules about how language functions, and modify the rules based on feedback. The reason for such similarity in language development, according to Chomsky, is that a language acquisition device (LAD) in the brain controls language learning as strongly as our biological endowment influences physical and perceptual development. No matter what language the child first hears, an identical set of basic structural rules is available for transformation to the rules of a particular language. Psycholinguists such as Slobin (1973) have been trying to establish the universal strategies used to relate these basic and specific language rules. Thus, the language children eventually learn consists of a subset of possible language rules—the ones that the child experiences.

Nativists also recognize the importance of the environment in achieving the specific rules of a language, just as the behavioral approach to language developments admits to certain biological givens. However, nativists do not emphasize individual differences in language use. Instead, they have been fascinated by the child's capacity to generate an extraordinary variety of sentences to which they have never been exposed. Earlier in this chapter, we illustrated some of the common grammatical features often cited in support of the biological approach to language development. Although recognition of the universal acquisition elements and of the similarity in formal structure of different languages is noteworthy, the nativist approach has been criticized for covering up presently unexplainable developmental processes with a biological label. Nativists have left unanswered the question of just how children are able to create a language.

Interactionist Approach

The final theoretical perspective favors neither hereditary factors nor environmental input as the dominant contribution to language acquisition. The interactionist approach, reflecting the concepts introduced in Chapter 7, can be characterized by a somewhat different question: How does the linguistically receptive mind interpret stimulation from the world? When language development is construed in this manner, controversial issues are addressed not through instincts or habits, but as an interactive process composed of many phenomena. Similarly, describing the phonological and grammatical aspects of language is minimized, with a shift toward semantic and pragmatic components. One of the major themes pervading the interactionist approach, for example, is the extent to which language is a product of thought or thought is rigidly constrained by language. In fact, whether language and thought develop simultaneously or according to different mechanisms is still unresolved (de Villiers & de Villiers, 1978).

Perhaps the most extreme view of the link between thought and language has evolved from the work of cultural anthropologists such as Benjamin Whorf (1956), who argue against the notion of universal sequences and biological determinants of language acquisition. Instead, they regard language as a tool of the culture for shaping the thinking process. As a consequence of distinctly varied languages, according to Whorf's *linguistic relativity hypothesis,* people from different cultures perceive the world and communicate in dissimilar ways. Whorf himself believed that language actually causes thought to take a certain form. A more modest version of this approach suggests that "languages differ not so much as to what *can* be said in them, but rather as to what it is *relatively easy* to say in them" (Hockett, 1954, p. 122). In other words, although Eskimos have many different words to describe varieties of snow, English speakers could describe the same ideas using combinations of words.

Research on color naming, color memory, and color distinctions has yielded similar results that cast doubt on the extreme version of Whorf's hypothesis (Brown & Lenneberg, 1954; Gleason, 1961; Lantz & Steffire, 1964). The evidence on colors led Dale (1976) to conclude the opposite of linguistic relativity: "universal aspects of the human perceptual and cognitive apparatus lead to universal aspects of color naming" (p. 246). Slobin (1971) reminds us about the relationship between language and thought in summarizing the fate of Whorf's hypothesis:

> Cultural anthropologists are looking for ways in which the underlying structures of cultures are alike, and psychologists are moving out of Western culture to cross-cultural studies, in an attempt to understand general laws of human behavior and development. Perhaps in an age when our world has become so small, and the most diverse cultures so intimately interrelated in matters of war and peace, it is best that we come to an understanding of what all men have in common. But at the same time it would be dangerous to forget that different languages and cultures may indeed have important effects on what men will believe and what they will do. (p. 133)

An opposing view to the linguistic relativity approach was proposed by Jean Piaget (1967). Piaget believed that language depended on, at times reflected, and helped facilitate cognitive development. Language, however, is never more than a tool to aid in thinking or a vehicle to permit communication and the expression of ideas. Piaget believed that language

Linguistic relativity hypothesis
The position held by cultural anthropologist Benjamin Whorf that a language actually determines the nature of thought for the speaker of that language.

serves to mentally represent the world as a means for liberating thought from the immediacy of perception. In other words, people can talk about events and objects in the world without simultaneously having to perceive them. Language is acquired, and increasingly becomes more complex, because it follows in the footsteps of intellectual development. Therefore, although language is a valuable medium to use for gaining knowledge, it cannot be regarded as a causative agent for thought.

Creative thinkers, such as Albert Einstein, frequently suggest that words—written or spoken—are not essential for the construction of new ideas (Ghiselin, 1955). Images and symbols may provide equally significant methods for representing fantasy or reality, especially for younger children. Furth's well-known research on cognitive development in deaf children is particularly persuasive on this point. He found that many deaf children attained advanced levels of reasoning despite the lack of an aural environment or a speech system (Furth & Youniss, 1975). Investigators such as Beilin (1975) have attempted to explain how the difficulties children have in using complex grammatical structures are linked to their cognitive developmental status.

A third position, proposed by Lev Vygotsky (1986) in the Soviet Union, is less cognitively dominated than Piaget's theory. According to Vygotsky, language and thought develop separately during infancy; early speech is preintellectual and early intelligence is prelinguistic. These independent streams of development converge during early childhood so that language becomes rational and thought becomes appropriately verbalized. Vygotsky suggested that the blending of cognitive and linguistic processes leads to *inner speech,* the unarticulated use of language to create meaning for the child. Therefore, speech arises from different roots than thought—language is not controlled by cognition, nor is thinking exclusively verbal.

Reich (1986) cited a variety of supportive evidence for Vygotsky's general position (e.g., see Berk, 1986), which is less unidrectional than Piaget's approach to thought and language. Vygotsky's work does not contradict Piaget's ideas as much as it elaborates on how speech provides another source of stimulation for cognitive development. In sum, the interactionist perspective is made up of several shades of opinion that diverge on the extent to which language and cognition have mutual origins and reciprocal influences.

Inner speech

According to Lev Vygotsky, the process by which spoken language becomes a silent, private form of thinking.

VARIATIONS IN LANGUAGE DEVELOPMENT

Much of this chapter has discussed the common patterns of language use and development, regardless of the particular group or individual. Many linguistic variations could be described, in addition to the distinctions that generally accompany chronological age. This section will focus on two that are of special interest to those who study human development: the contrasts between middle and lower classes and the distinctions among language dialects. Both topics have generated controversy, yet they are intertwined with critical developmental issues. Our consideration of linguistic variations is designed not simply to illustrate the nature of individual differences in language, but also to shed light on some sensitive issues in human development.

Communication and Socioeconomic Status

The consistent observation that lower- and working-class individuals do not attain the same level of language skills as middle- and upper-class individuals has challenged linguists to explore the reasons for this socioeconomic variation. However, the idea that socioeconomic status itself actually causes differences in speech or understanding is an oversimplification (and, as will be noted later, some theorists are not even persuaded that such differences should be considered deficits). Articulate speakers and creative writers have certainly emerged from less-than-ideal social circumstances. However, the bulk of evidence indicates that particular factors associated with poor language skills are more prevalent at the lower-socioeconomic levels.

The most unambiguous aspect of language variation between socioeconomic levels concerns the acquisition of vocabulary. A careful study by Stodolsky and Lesser (1967), which controlled for ethnic background and test bias, found significant differences on picture and word vocabulary between middle- and lower-class black, Hispanic, Jewish, and Oriental first graders in the United States. Ethnic variations were minor in terms of total English vocabulary development, but all of the middle-class groups demonstrated clear verbal superiority. In his assessment of grammatical competence, however, Dale (1976) stated that equally convincing evidence for social-class differences has not been obtained.

A variety of research has examined the syntactic and morphological skills of the middle versus the lower classes. Although some investigations, such as the one by Dewart (1972) in Ireland, concluded that lower-class children have more difficulty with passive constructions and complex sentences than their middle-class peers, most research has yielded negligible differences. Furthermore, Dale (1976) argued that when socioeconomic status variations are obtained, they may frequently be a function of dialect differences, a lack of familiarity with middle-class testers and environments typically used for testing, or test biases and researcher expectations. Confusion among these extraneous variables—along with the distinct vocabulary and grammatical structures of lower-socioeconomic speakers— probably has contributed to an image of the lower-class person as communicatively handicapped.

One study, however, is especially noteworthy because the researchers minimized vocabulary problems and did not introduce ethnic complications. Pozner and Saltz (1974) taught white, middle- and lower-class fifth graders (with approximately equal IQs) how to play a simple game involving the positioning of various shapes, colors, and coins. After half the subjects had mastered the game, they were asked to teach the rules to the remaining children. No significant social-class differences were found in listening abilities, but lower-class children were less effective communicators (to both middle- and lower-class listeners). They tended to provide incomplete and inaccurate instructions while trying to use motoric demonstrations (the children were separated by a partition and could not see each other). Pozner and Saltz concluded that lower-class children have difficulty in verbal expression because of an "inability to take the perspective of their listeners in attempting to communicate information" (p. 770). However, this study does not help us with the task of specifying the origins of the presumed cognitive immaturity and linguistic egocentrism characteristic of some lower-class members.

Because social-class differences in either language or thought do not become evident until after 2 or 3 years of age, what are the components of a lower-class environment that ultimately may begin to take their toll? Bee (1978) suggested that malnutrition and generally poor health might retard brain development, resulting in inferior performance. Lower-class homes also may not provide adequate stimulation in terms of the amount or variety of exploratory experiences. These probably are important factors; however, the specific influences on language development are more controversial. At the heart of this debate is a sociopolitical dispute about the value of speaking a nonstandard version of a language. Linguists are convinced that one variation is not grammatically superior or more complex than another, but the utility of a nonstandard form for educational and vocational success is questionable. In sum, nonstandard language need not be viewed as a deficit unless it hinders the communicative effectiveness of the speaker.

Communication patterns within homes of lower-socioeconomic status differ in both style and substance from those of middle-class environments. Bernstein (1971) was the first theorist to describe social-class differences in language use. He hypothesized that middle-class speakers engage in an elaborated style of speech, including lengthy sentences, detailed and complex explanations, fluent transitions from one thought to another, and an extensive vocabulary. In contrast, Bernstein suggested that lower-class speakers use a restricted form of language that is less explicit, is more concrete, involves a limited vocabulary, and is more private. Higgins (1976), Labov (1972), and others severely criticized the notion of elaborated versus restricted language codes. They challenged Bernstein's lack of evidence and pointed out research that does not support this distinction when the social context is controlled.

Bernstein (1971) also suggested that middle-class families tend to emphasize the individuality of each member, whereas lower-class families stress clearly defined and strictly observed roles. In her review of family interaction studies, Bee (1978) indicated that middle-class parents do talk to their children more often, provide frequent praise, and use rational explanations for controlling behavior. Lower-class parents tend to be more critical of their children and use authoritarian methods of discipline. Should we be surprised, then, that the speech of lower-class people is not highly sensitive to the communicative needs of their listeners, especially those who have middle-class expectations?

Dialect Differences

An alternative position to Bernstein's is the approach of Bryen, Hartman, and Tait (1978). They regard all language variations reflecting sociocultural factors as equally effective dialects. From their perspective, language competence can be interpreted only within the framework of the dialect used by the speaker. Whether language variations are due to sex, age, race, social class, geography, or context, no dialect can be considered superior to another, nor does any particular dialect reflect linguistic immaturity or cognitive deficiency. Furthermore, Bryen, Hartman, and Tait reject the implication that impoverished environments produce language weaknesses. They believe that variant forms of a language are looked down on because of negative attitudes toward people from other regions of a country, toward minority groups and immigrants, or toward the poor. No single, standard form of any language really exists; rather, overlapping variations share more similarities than differences.

Disentangling the various sociocultural influences on language development has proved difficult. Nevertheless, the pattern of all dialect

In terms of language competence, different does not mean deficient. The use of variant dialects rarely hinders communication, and instead may contribute to the enrichment and diversification of language.

acquisitions appears to be similar, and each dialect is a complete, complex language. Dale (1976) commented that moving away from the "deficiency approach" to a "differences model" may benefit society by promoting more extensive vocabularies, expanding the meanings of language, and offering new ways to communicate. The diversity of U.S. culture can enrich our lives rather than foster snobbishness or dissension.

Unfortunately, speakers with certain dialects are made to feel ashamed of their culture or their intelligence because they use a variant form of language. Sometimes such individuals feel compelled to imitate the dialect of more prestigious groups to compensate for their perceived deficiencies. This hypercorrect speech usually results in stilted pronunciations and awkward grammar. Bryen (1974) suggested that instead of trying to modify the language of variant-dialect speakers to ensure social mobility, "the responsibility for change [should] be placed on societal institutions, rather than the individual" (p. 596).

Researchers like Bryen and Labov have been somewhat instrumental in shifting attitudes toward increasing tolerance of variant dialects, but many children and adults still must cope with the prejudices of teachers, peers, employers, and institutional representatives. There is no reason that multiple dialects cannot coexist. Dale (1976) believes that knowing two dialects offers the individual a choice of languages that may be appropriate in different settings without eradicating or demeaning cultural heritage. Simultaneously, an awareness that dialect differences are superficial variations that do not indicate intellectual ability should be promoted.

Black English, for example, one of many variant forms of our language, seems to function as a barrier to communication because it establishes negative expectations about the competence of the speaker (see Table 9.3). In fact, black English is actually several dialects that are spoken by many, but not all, black people in the United States. These dialects also are used by many white Southern people, especially those from rural, lower-class backgrounds. The confusion among ethnicity, social class, and dialect may be responsible for some of the performance variations observed on cognitive tasks. Research frequently has compared middle-class whites to lower-class blacks, leading to unfavorable racial connotations. Similar problems face Hispanic, Native American, and French-Canadian minorities today, as they did Jewish, Irish, and Italian immigrants earlier in this century.

This exploration of language has turned from a discussion of common developmental pathways to an evaluation of variations. Just as studying themes of universal language acquisition reveals our shared humanity, becoming aware of variations in use demonstrates our need to identify with a smaller group or tradition. However, an additional level of analysis is possible. Not only do we each speak a version of a specific language, but we each create a unique "idiolect." Because no two of us speak or write in precisely the same fashion, language, like a fingerprint, also acts as a vehicle for expressing individuality (Bryen et al., 1978).

Table 9.3
Variant English Forms

Linguistic Feature	Variant English	Standard English
Phonological		
Voiced *th* (initial position)	Dem	Them
ing in final position	Singin	Singing
Unstressed initial syllable	'Bout	About
Indefinite article	A apple	An apple
Morphological		
Plural marker	Feets	Feet
Reflexive pronoun	Hisse'f	Himself
Possessive marker	Boy' hat	Boy's hat
Noun-verb agreement	Mary have	Mary has
Syntactic		
Auxiliary verb	I' see you deuhe.	I'll see you there.
Direct question	Who you want?	Who do you want?
Negation (present tense)	I ain't ready.	I'm not ready.
Nominative pronoun addition	My sistuh, she' pretty.	My sister is pretty.

Source: Adapted from D. N. Bryen, C. Hartman, & P. Tait. *Variant English: An introduction to language variations.* Columbus, OH: Merrill, 1978, pp. 248–250. Used with permission of the author.

Although language is one of the primary mechanisms for bringing people closer together, it is also one of the most distinctive features about any person. Two people who speak the same dialect may be clearly distinguished by their tone of voice, rate of speech, vocabulary level, sentence style, volume and pitch, length of discourse, characteristic pauses, and numerous other factors. This adds to the complexity and variety of the communication process as it functions throughout language development.

Summary

1. Although language development is an elusive and intricate process, the expressive, regulative, and clarifying functions that language serves are invaluable.
2. The dilemmas of nature versus nurture, animal versus human communication, receptive versus productive language, and deep versus surface structure often serve as the framework for analyses of language and communication.
3. Linguists and developmentalists have defined five types of rules that capture the interacting uses of language. These include phonological, morphological, syntactical, semantic, and pragmatic rules.
4. Infants have the capacity both to produce and to attend to sound.
5. Throughout the world, the second year of life is characterized by the appearance of simple words and two-word utterances.

6. Infants use language in ways that are different from adult expectations. For the speaker or the listener, conversation with infants requires attention to the context to improve communication.

7. During early childhood, language development proceeds rapidly. Phonological rules become highly refined, and other aspects of language advance dramatically.

8. The struggle to acquire the rules of grammar follows a common, creative course for preschool children. The way to understand language acquisition is to analyze children's linguistic errors.

9. The young child's remarkable development of language is evident from the expanding vocabulary and sentence structure. No less significant is an increasing sensitivity to semantic and pragmatic rules.

10. A highlight of later childhood and adolescence is mastery of the subtleties of language in both speaking and listening.

11. The major linguistic challenges in later childhood are the process of coordinating language skills with cognitive development and the need to share knowledge of the world within social settings.

12. Adolescents refine their linguistic skills and use language to help develop an identity as well as to demonstrate cognitive development.

13. Language development beyond adolescence is characterized less by dramatic advance or decline than by the quality and the contexts of language usage.

14. The early and middle adulthood years are represented by a diversity of language skills that usually do not evidence major changes unless affected by head-related trauma.

15. During old age, sensory handicaps and brain damage may limit language use; however, aside from information processing difficulties, many elderly individuals will not experience significant declines in receptive or productive abilities.

16. Behaviorist, nativist, and interactionist theories have influenced the study of language development. The behaviorists emphasize environmental aspects of communication but neglect nonobservable language competence. Nativists are convinced that the principal determinants of language development are innate biological processes. Therefore, they examine universal aspects of language and minimize variations. Interactionist theories do not ignore either biological or environmental factors in language development. Research centers on the relationship between communication and cognition.

17. Exploring language variations provides insights about development that are as rewarding as those gained from examining universal patterns.

18. A controversial issue is whether the speech of the lower class should be regarded as deficient or merely different. This dilemma is complicated by the lesser educational achievement of lower-class individuals.

19. Recent evaluations of language variation stress the legitimacy of all sociocultural dialects. Therefore, negative attitudes must be replaced by tolerance and appreciation of language diversity.

Key Terms

deep structure (p. 343)
expansion (p. 368)
holophrases (p. 353)
implicit information
   (p. 358)
inner speech (p. 373)

linguistic relativity hypothesis (p. 372)
morphology (p. 345)
phonology (p. 344)
pragmatics (p. 347)

productive process
   (p. 342)
receptive process
   (p. 342)
semantics (p. 346)

surface structure
   (p. 343)
syntax (p. 345)
telegraphic speech
   (p. 355)

Review Questions

1. Select any of the controversial issues that arise in the study of language development (such as nature versus nurture, productive versus receptive, deep versus surface structure). Explain why integrating several perspectives can help resolve these difficulties.
2. Describe the five components of language study and indicate how they are related to one another. Provide an example of each component to demonstrate your knowledge of what it means.
3. To what extent have researchers been able to teach chimpanzees to use language for communication? What is necessary to suggest more conclusively that chimpanzees can truly use language in a manner equivalent to humans?
4. Outline the progression of language acquisition in the realms of phonological and morphological development during infancy. Include the approximate ages at which these major milestones tend to occur.
5. The linguistic explosion of early childhood is perhaps most interesting and remarkable with respect to syntactic growth. Discuss and provide examples of a few of the significant phenomena that typically emerge at this time.
6. What has been learned about the acquisition of language in deaf individuals? What implications does this research have for a more general understanding of language development?
7. Refinements of language usage that occur during later childhood and adolescence usually are focused on semantics and pragmatics. Describe and offer examples of language development for this phase of the life span.
8. How would you characterize language development during adulthood? In particular, what skills, patterns, or deficiencies are likely to occur, and how does this relate to myths about old age?
9. The process of learning a second language has often been used to illustrate the concept of a critical period in language development. Explain the meaning of this statement and indicate what research evidence supports the concept.
10. The three dominant theoretical views of language development include the behaviorist, nativist, and interactionist positions. Compare and contrast any two of them with regard to orientation, developmental basis, emphasis, language universals, role of parents, and other factors.
11. What evidence suggests that lower-socioeconomic-status individuals are deficient in language skills? How has this position been refuted by researchers who focus on dialect differences? Based on your own knowledge of language development, evaluate these arguments.

Suggested Reading

Curtiss, S. (1977). *Genie: A psycholinguistic study of a modern-day "wild child."* New York: Academic Press.
　　The fascinating story of language remediation in a young child of unidentifiable origins. This book provides a rare example of research on the critical-period hypothesis of language acquisition in humans.

Dale, P. S. (1976). *Language development: Structure and function* (2nd ed.). New York: Holt, Rinehart & Winston.
　　The finest paperback in print on language acquisition. Dale's book is clear, interesting, and filled with useful examples and charts.

de Villiers, J. G. & de Villiers, P. A. (1978). *Language acquisition.* Cambridge, MA: Harvard University Press.
　　An excellent and thorough introduction to the processes and major issues related to the child's development of language.

Miller, G. A. (1981). *Language and speech.* San Francisco: W. H. Freeman.
　　A brief but extremely well-written overview of the nature of language and speech. The biological approach provides the foundation for this paperback volume.

Reich, P. A. (1986). *Language development.* Englewood Cliffs, NJ: Prentice-Hall.

A fine paperback that is filled with examples, charts, and drawings. This book also has good chapters on bilingualism and language problems.

Rumbaugh, D. M. (Ed.). (1977). *Language learning by a chimpanzee: The Lana project.* New York: Academic Press.

A firsthand evaluation of the work with primates on language acquisition. Several members of the project team present balanced perspectives.

Chapter Ten

Personality and the Self

Freud's Psychoanalytic Revolution
Basic Principles
Personality Structures
Stages of Development
Psychoanalytic Controversy

Erikson's Psychosocial Modifications
Basic Principles
Stages of Development
Psychosocial Evaluation

Development of the Self
Maslow's Hierarchy of Needs
What Is the Self?
Development of the Self-Concept
Self-esteem and Life Satisfaction

Issues in Personal Development
Does Personality Have Biological Origins?
How Does Culture Affect Personality?
Does Personality Change Across the Life Span?
How Does Personality Development Deviate from "Normality"?

 Before exploring the development of personality and the self, let us simulate the way in which much of the research in this area is conducted—that is, through the analysis of personality inventories. Table 10.1 presents an inventory by Lee Willerman (1975) that provides a brief example of this method for assessing personality.

By examining Table 10.2, you can compare your standing on each of the three personality categories with a college-age sample tested by Willerman. Thinking about how your perceptions of yourself match these results may be instructive. According to Willerman, "If your score falls below or above these ranges, you may regard yourself as exceptionally high or low [in that disposition]" (1975, p. 35). Also note the different ranges for males versus females. In addition, you might be interested in speculating about how you would have responded to these items 10 years ago and how you think you might describe yourself 10 years from now.

A recurring dilemma in attempting to grasp the nature of human development, and one that is particularly important for the study of personality and the self, is the issue of stability versus change. We have shown that the concept of development implies certain changes beyond mere physical or quantitative growth. On the one hand, most definitions of personality include the notion of an enduring, characteristic pattern of behavior. Maddi (1980), for instance, conceptualized personality as a set of tendencies that determine thoughts, feelings, and actions over time. On the other hand, theory and research in personality development also have indicated that patterns of behavior do not remain unaltered from birth to death.

Disagreement abounds about how much change is possible and what sources may promote personality development. For example, how critical are the early years of life in establishing the foundation for later characteristics? Does an inherited disposition persist throughout development despite environmental influences? What kinds of experiences, with what regularity, are necessary to alter personality? Are developmental changes in personality relatively predictable, or do random events foster a gradual evolution of individual styles of adaptation?

Table 10.1
Personality Inventory

Item	How True Is This of You? Hardly at All ... A Lot				
1. I make friends easily.	1	2	3	4	5
2. I tend to be shy.	1	2	3	4	5
3. I like to be with others.	1	2	3	4	5
4. I like to be independent of people.	1	2	3	4	5
5. I usually prefer to do things alone.	1	2	3	4	5
6. I am always on the go.	1	2	3	4	5
7. I like to be off and running as soon as I wake up in the morning.	1	2	3	4	5
8. I like to keep busy all of the time.	1	2	3	4	5
9. I am very energetic.	1	2	3	4	5
10. I prefer quiet, inactive pastimes to more active ones.	1	2	3	4	5
11. I tend to cry easily.	1	2	3	4	5
12. I am easily frightened.	1	2	3	4	5
13. I tend to be somewhat emotional.	1	2	3	4	5
14. I get upset easily.	1	2	3	4	5
15. I tend to be easily irritated.	1	2	3	4	5

To score this inventory, reverse the numbers of items 2, 4, 5, and 10; that is, for those items only, change any selection of 1 to 5, 2 to 4, 4 to 2, and 5 to 1 (there is no need to alter selections of 3 for these items). Next, add your responses to the statements for items 1 through 6, then for 6 through 10, and finally for 11 through 15. You should now have three total scores; these pertain to the basic personality dimensions of sociability, activity level, and emotionality, respectively. Please be cautious in the interpretation of your scores since this short inventory can offer only a limited analysis of the complexity of one's personality.

Source: L. Willerman, *Individual and Group Differences,* 1975. Austin, Texas: Hogg Foundation.

Answers to these questions, which are only beginning to emerge, illustrate the difficulties of studying personality. Interactions between biological and environmental factors produce both continuity and transformations of personality. Furthermore, whereas fairly regular changes might be anticipated, dramatic events or unusual circumstances may modify more predictable patterns. Although at least a dozen widely recognized theories of

Table 10.2
Personality Inventory Score Evaluation

Personality Disposition	Statement Numbers	Typical Range for Males	Typical Range for Females
Sociability	1–6	13–19	15–20
Activity level	6–10	13–19	13–20
Emotionality	11–15	9–16	11–18

Source: L. Willerman, *Individual and group differences,* 1975. Austin, Texas: Hogg Foundation.

personality are categorized in many different ways, we will attempt a detailed analysis of only three theorists: Sigmund Freud, Erik Erikson, and Abraham Maslow. Other theorists have espoused similar approaches to personality, or their work has not been well integrated within the mainstream of developmental research. Sigmund Freud (1856–1939) and Erik Erikson (1902–   ) have provided numerous insights concerning the dynamic stages and interpersonal relationships within human development. Their efforts, characterized by the term *psychodynamics,* emphasize the flow of personality changes across time. In contrast, behavioral and trait theories of personality tend to be more situational or static and will not, therefore, be addressed in this discussion of development. Elements of these theories, however, have been incorporated into the appropriate discussions in earlier chapters on biological, information processing, and social aspects of change.

Following the presentation of Freud's and Erikson's theories, we will explore the nature of self-concept and self-esteem; that is, people's own awareness of their personalities. In particular, the phenomenological theory of Abraham Maslow (1908–70) will be discussed. Finally, we will raise issues that pervade the analysis of personality development and introduce some examples of appropriate research in the realms of biology and culture as well as for the questions of stability and normality.

FREUD'S PSYCHOANALYTIC REVOLUTION

Sigmund Freud set himself the task of analyzing the dynamic workings of the human mind. His medical training and background in literature and philosophy helped him formulate an insightful theory that linked the physical, social, and psychological aspects of development.

Basic Principles

Freud (1953) postulated several interrelated themes that contribute to the development of personality. The first is the principle of *psychic determinism,* which states that mental activity is caused by the activities or events that preceded it. Telling a joke, having a dream, saying something "by mistake," or even singing a certain song for no apparent reason, according to Freud, may be caused by influences from the past. Although we may not be able to identify the sources of our thoughts or feelings, there are few mental accidents. If we find ourselves wondering why a friend's comment angered us so much or why we are so fearful about attending a forthcoming party, Freud would suggest that the answers may be found in previous events; past events determine our reactions to the present.

A second principle of personality is the significance of *unconscious motivation.* We are often completely unaware of the processes that guide our daily lives. Because we are not conscious of the motivating factors for all that we think and feel, we tend to perceive a gap between our superficial mental activities and the reasons for their occurrence. If we could become aware of the entire psychic pattern, both conscious and unconscious, a consistency would be revealed. For example, the spouse's remark that angered us so easily may be a reminder of the criticism and tone of voice that we heard so frequently from a parent. According to Freud, the unconscious also is the source of our psychological problems, because it is the repository of forgotten early experiences and memories that may be unpleasant.

In addition, Freud (1933) believed that two instinctual energy forces are responsible for stimulating the course of personality development. The more important of these instincts is termed *eros,* or the life force. The life force includes such physiological drives as hunger, thirst, and sex. The energy of the life force, known as *libido,* generates a sense of mental excitement or tension concerning sexuality; this energy was the object of Freud's intense analysis. He maintained that the human being attempts to reduce the demands of libido and to seek gratification through sexual pleasure. Freud did not suggest that sexual intercourse is the only way to reduce erotic drives. For instance, even the pleasure that an infant may derive from sucking would be considered an appropriate means for satisfying erotic tensions. Other pleasurable activities associated with libidinal energy include touching, kissing, defecating, and displaying the body to others.

Later in his career, Freud introduced an opposing instinctual force, known as *thanatos,* which functions as a kind of perpetual, yet unconscious, death wish. This instinct becomes more powerful as the individual ages, but it is present from birth and is responsible for our hostile or

Libido

According to Sigmund Freud, the instinctual psychosexual energy force that provides the motivation for thought and behavior.

Emotions and the behaviors that emanate from them are often complex and ambiguous. An adolescent's Halloween costume may contain elements of diverse feelings—fear, anger, sensuality, joy—that reflect the developing personality.

self-destructive behaviors. In the case of suicide, for example, the aggressive energy that is usually expressed outwardly is turned inward as thanatos overwhelms eros to reach the ultimate state of reduced anxiety.

Moreover, the aggressive drive operates in a fascinating and simultaneous interplay with the life force. The infant, for example, may use the mouth to gratify opposite instincts by both sucking and biting. A toddler can deliberately urinate on the rug to anger a parent as well as to satisfy a physical urge. The genitals, which we usually associate with sexual pleasure, also can be thought of as weapons. Rapists are performing an act of hostility, not merely reducing sexual tensions.

As each of the previous examples demonstrates, separating the erotic from the hostile components of our behavior is often difficult. Freud believed that the two instincts are usually fused (although one may dominate at a particular time), which explains how we can have contradictory feelings (of love and hate, for instance) toward another person. Each of us, at least occasionally, has felt confused about motives for certain behaviors or thoughts. Freud would suggest that we need to disentangle our early sources of instinctual satisfaction to see how the intricate pieces of the personality were assembled.

Personality Structures

The instinctual forces in people will certainly bring them into conflict with society. This conflict is at the heart of Freud's theory. To resolve the clash, certain structures of the personality—the id, the ego, and the superego—must be understood (Freud, 1933).

    Present from birth, the *id* is the irrational, unconscious, and selfish component of our personalities that seeks gratification at any cost. Being pushed toward immediate tension reduction by the id, we are led to engage in what Freud called *primary process thinking,* an example of which is provided by infant behavior. In a sense, the infant personality is pure id. Infants are not interested in logical consistency, societal restrictions, or the problems of other people. When they want to be fed, changed, or held, they cry impatiently. Around-the-clock feedings are not considered unreasonable demands, because infants have yet to develop moderating personality structures.

    During the second year of life, infants become increasingly aware that things do not always work in the way they demand. Sometimes a toddler will have to wait for or even be denied the pleasure sought. To handle the restrictions imposed by reality, a new structure emerges. Freud labeled this component of personality the *ego.* By siphoning off some of the energy that the id possesses, the ego functions primarily at the conscious level to help us deal sensibly with other people and the rest of the world. Freud felt that the ego promotes the use of *secondary process thinking,* which is characterized by an ability to postpone gratification. In contrast to the id, which seeks fulfillment through any means available, the ego develops patient and rational means for alleviating demands. Ego development is not a sudden change in the child's outlook but a gradual and sometimes painful adjustment to the restrictions on immediate gratification. As the mechanism for placating the demands of both id and eventually society, the ego's purpose is to serve as the great mediator of personality.

    The last structure to emerge, beginning by the age of 3 or 4 and developing over the next few years, is known as the *superego.* Like the ego, this component of the personality arises by using energy from the id in a largely conscious or preconscious (readily brought to awareness) way so as to establish acceptable, internal standards of behavior. Through identification with parents, children learn to view themselves as members of a culture and to incorporate the society's values as their own. Thus, the id represents the needs of the self, the superego represents society's point of view, and the ego serves to moderate the demands of the id to accommodate civilization.

Id

In psychoanalytic theory, a personality structure that is present from birth and contains the irrational, unconscious, and selfish aspects of human beings.

Primary process thinking

According to Sigmund Freud, the tendency of the id to strive for immediate gratification of needs or reduction of tensions by any available means.

Ego

In psychoanalytic theory, a personality structure that develops during the second year of life to deal consciously and rationally with the restrictions that reality imposes on the infant.

Secondary process thinking

According to Sigmund Freud, the tendency of the ego to postpone instinctual gratification through the use of logic and the testing of reality.

Superego

In psychoanalytic theory, a personality structure that emerges during the preschool years as a result of identification with parents and the establishment of cultural standards for behavior. The superego includes a conscience and an ego ideal.

Freud believed that the superego is composed of two highly interconnected parts: the conscience and the ego ideal. On the one hand, the little voice inside us that warns about doing something wrong is our conscience (do not confuse this with *conscious*). The infant may refrain from a particular activity because adults will physically prohibit it, not because of the pangs of conscience. Older children who are developing a superego, however, may behave to avoid violating standards that they have adopted, not because they were literally prevented from carrying out the activity.

Our ego ideal, on the other hand, is the embodiment of what we should be doing—the perfection of parental and cultural values that create a personal, internal hero for us to imitate. Once established, this image and the rules for conduct derived from it are as rigid and demanding in their own moralistic fashion as the instinctual drives of the id. Therefore, the ego takes on a more difficult and critical role than ever before. It must check the "I want" of the id, as well as placate the "I should" or "I should not" of the superego.

Somewhere in the conflict between the other two structures, the ego attempts to maintain a functional system. If the id gains the upper hand, our selfish behaviors will lead to condemnation and rejection by society. If our superego is permitted too much control, however, we will experience so much anxiety or guilt that we will become incapable of effective and creative functioning. Freud (1930) felt that civilization could not survive unless the demands of the id are sufficiently curbed, but the individual could not maintain psychological health (relatively free of anxiety) unless tensions are released.

Stages of Development

Human development, from a psychoanalytic perspective, is the process of learning to cope with the various manifestations of instinctual energy. Libido is focused on certain areas of the body at different times in life. Thus, psychological gratification depends on a biological source of tension and excitement that defines a particular stage of development.

Freud (1953) identified five stages of development. The terms used to identify each stage—oral, anal, phallic, latency, and genital—clearly indicate Freud's greater concern with erotic, or psychosexual, drives than with other life or death instincts (see Table 10.3). All stages are generally related to chronological age, but they also overlap with preceding and subsequent stages. The following sections describe the sequence of psychosexual development and its consequences for the personality.

Oral Stage

Libidinal energy, according to Freud, is concentrated in the mouth during the first year or so of life. Infants derive much pleasure from sucking and mouthing objects in their world. Oral activities, especially the experience of

Table 10.3
Freud's Psychosexual Stages of Development

Stage of Development	Emerging Structure	Approximate Age Range	Erogenous Zone and Gratification	Characteristic Area of Tension
Oral	Id	Birth–18 months	Mouth/breast	Weaning
Anal	Ego	1½–3 years	Anus/feces	Toilet training
Phallic	Superego	3–6 years	Genitals/opposite-sex parent	Oedipal conflict
Latency	Balance of personality	6–12 years	None	None
Genital	Reintegration of personality	Puberty–death	Genitals/opposite sex	Instincts versus society

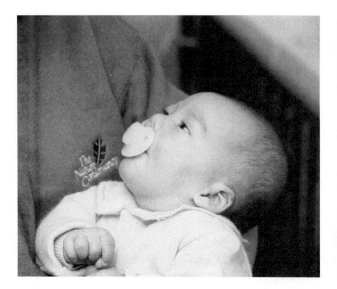 

According to Sigmund Freud, the pattern of frustration and indulgence of oral needs that the infant establishes helps to determine adult personality characteristics. Adults are especially likely to revert to early sources of satisfaction when they are under stress.

being fed, constitute the mechanism for incorporating and knowing reality. Compared with other activities, infants spend considerable time sucking, biting, chewing, teething, spitting up, vocalizing, crying, and breathing. Some of these behaviors satisfy the instinctual demands of aggression as well as infantile eroticism. Freud believed that the pattern of frustration and indulgence of oral needs, which parents help the infant to establish, determines the foundation for adult personality characteristics. However, the oral stage represents only the initial area for human gratification and conflict.

Anal Stage

A second source for psychosexual energy becomes dominant sometime during the second year and remains especially crucial for a year or two thereafter. Libidinal energy now is centered in the anal region. Therefore, the sensations accompanying retention and evacuation of feces are satisfying for the toddler. (To a lesser extent, similar gratification is associated with urination.)

At the same time that feelings of pleasure surround anal activities, the child has the opportunity to express aggressive drives. Whereas infants are not expected to delay impulses or to control their behavior, toddlers begin to be faced with explicit social demands. Freud speculated that as the child moves slightly closer toward death, the aggressive drive begins to exert a bit more influence. The ego must develop to help the young child confront the competing pressures of libido and society. Although the problems involved in weaning an infant from extensive dependence on oral activities should not be minimized, the conflicts regarding toilet training tend to be more difficult to resolve. In psychoanalytic theory, parental-toddler interactions concerning toilet training, which may range from punitive to permissive, can encourage personality characteristics that last a lifetime.

Phallic Stage

By the end of the second year or the beginning of the third year of life, the child has entered the most important stage of psychosexual development: the phallic stage. Libidinal energy now is concentrated in the genital region. Although children do not understand the reproductive nature of the genitalia, Freud believed they have an unconscious tendency to associate their phallus (erect penis) or clitoris (small penis) with some kind of activity with the parent of the opposite sex. Genital tensions lessen at approximately 5 or 6 years of age, bringing the phallic stage to a close. However, the events that occur during this period have major consequences for the development of morality, sexuality, and gender role identity (these will be described in subsequent chapters), and for the fixation of personality structures.

Latency Stage

Freud believed that from the ages of 7 or 8 until puberty, libidinal energy is diffuse; that is, it is not concentrated intensely at any one part of the body. As a result, the child moves into the latency stage. During this period, sexual interests usually diminish (*latent* means "hidden"). The attraction to the opposite-sex parent, which was not permitted to be completely fulfilled at the phallic stage, turns to an affectionate attachment. Social roles and sexual identification become increasingly solidified as the child is encouraged to emulate the same-sex parent. In other words, the increasing demands of society force the ego to reorient libidinal energy away from the id and toward a less selfish compromise with reality.

Freud never maintained that sexual feelings and experimentation do not occur during the latency stage. In fact, they can occur and are especially likely to do so in a sexually permissive environment. In cultures in which sexual play is common among children, no latency stage may occur at all. In more restrictive societies, such as our own, sexual interests are usually discouraged, leading to a curious interruption in psychosexual development.

Genital Stage

As adolescence emerges, libidinal energy returns to the genital organs, which now have a reproductive function. Psychosexual development, therefore, culminates in a genital stage that continues throughout adulthood. The young adolescent experiences a reawakening of oral, anal, and phallic conflicts. In particular, the adolescent may fall in love with, or have a crush on, older persons of the opposite sex. Movie stars, sports figures, or teachers, for example, are often the targets of adolescent infatuation. As knowledge about sexuality increases, expressions of libidinal energy may take more direct forms. In contrast, adolescents who are embarrassed or confused about their sexual feelings may seek outlets other than masturbation, necking, or intercourse itself. Instead, they may channel libidinal energy into "safe" areas such as political activism, athletics, or volunteer work.

Freud believed that the mature adult must learn to accept sexual needs and find an appropriate marriage partner to gratify them. However, love for a spouse must involve more than lust. It also concerns the strong feelings of affection that characterize relations with the opposite-sex parent during latency. In this way, adults do not have to deny or disguise sexual feelings, but may combine them with a healthy attachment for a person who allows them also to fulfill their sexual identification. The challenge for an adult, as Freud saw it, is to cope with libidinal energy in a socially responsible fashion, as well as to control inner aggressive forces.

Instinctual energy, if not channeled into mature sexuality or other constructive activities, will create intolerable levels of anxiety that result in neurotic behaviors derived from conflicts in the pregenital stages. Because early experiences were assumed to determine present personality, the residual effects of earlier stages might indicate the nature and degree of our individual patterns of satisfaction. Freud referred to the process of attaching libidinal energy to mental representations of gratifying persons or objects as a *cathexis*. During the oral stage, for example, the infant cathects the mother's breast or the bottle to reduce the tension associated with the mouth. If these sources of oral satisfaction are not available, the infant may find acceptable substitutes. Likewise, the infant who is not encouraged to

Cathexis
According to psychoanalytic theory, the process of attaching libidinal energy to mental representations of gratifying persons or objects.

move on to other forms of gratification (i.e., the later stages of development) may have difficulty directing psychosexual energy in new ways. The failure to abandon primitive libidinal attachments—whether because of frustration or indulgence—creates permanent characteristics for the adult.

Freud referred to this manifestation of stunted personality development as a *fixation*. Therefore, the heavy smoker or perpetual gum chewer would be considered orally fixated. People are especially likely to revert to early sources of satisfaction when undergoing stress in their lives. Temporary regressions, which are common to all of us, are less neurotic forms of character fixation and reflect the ego's mechanisms for defending against the self-centered and unsocialized impulses of the id (Freud, 1936).

Fixation
According to Sigmund Freud, the failure of a person—whether because of frustration or indulgence—to abandon primitive libidinal attachments, which remain as manifestations of stunted personality development.

Psychoanalytic Controversy

Even among Freud's followers, serious disagreements surfaced within a decade of the founding of the psychoanalytic movement. *Issues in Human Development,* "Neoanalytic Critiques of Freud's Theory," outlines some of the perceived inadequacies of orthodox psychoanalysis. Controversy centered on his overemphasis on sexual and unconscious motivation, his fatalistic stress on early personality formation, and his pessimistic view that all behavior is essentially defensive. Freud's followers also questioned his view that even scientific inventions and works of art are examples of *sublimation* (the release of libidinal tensions in socially desirable ways). The rejection or modification of Freud's ideas by his followers led to the establishment of interpretations of personality development that differed from his but still maintained important elements of the original position.

ERIKSON'S PSYCHOSOCIAL MODIFICATIONS

Discontent with the limitations of Freudian theory stimulated others to reassess psychoanalytic principles from new perspectives. One of the most notable attempts to preserve the spirit of psychoanalysis, while infusing it with new life, was fostered by Erik Erikson. In contrast to the relatively narrow range of opportunities experienced by Freud, Erikson brought a wealth of cultural diversity to his theory of human development.

Basic Principles

Erikson has been one of several theorists responsible for extending and transforming the psychoanalytic account of personality development. Despite his belief in basic Freudian structural and functional characteristics, Erikson shifted emphasis from the unconscious and irrational id to the aware and rational ego. Not only did he feel that the ego is present at birth rather than emerging from the id, but he also assigned to the ego its own energy and a goal beyond that of helping to satisfy the id. For Freud, the ego

Issues in Human Development
Neoanalytic Critiques of Freud's Theory

 Freud's psychoanalytic theory of personality development has long been considered an original, broad-ranging, and comprehensive approach to understanding human behavior. His writings provided an interdisciplinary and inspiring challenge to explore the irrational, unconscious forces of the mind. In addition, Freud created a compelling blend of normative developmental processes, including defense mechanisms to deal with threats to the personality, and a method of treating problems that occurred as a result of conflict between the individual's needs and the demands of civilization. Despite these important achievements, legitimate criticism of his work arose during his career and has continued in the years since. We will explore briefly some of the theorists who built on Freud's ideas, altering them in critical ways, but did not completely reject the foundations of the theory.

The first major departure, for example, within Freud's inner circle of adherents, was the resignation of Alfred Adler (1870–1937) from the Vienna Psychoanalytical Society, founded and headed by Freud. Although Adler did not dispute the significance of early childhood in the formation of personality, he proposed that the striving toward superiority, rather than the release of sexual tension, was the most important motivational factor in development. Instead of focusing on parent-child conflict over weaning or toilet training, Adler suggested looking at the total dynamics of the family system (he was an early proponent of family therapy). In particular, he felt that the child's birth order (e.g., firstborn, middle child, only child, last born) influences the interaction between parents and their children. Attempting to achieve perfection may lead to a constructive personality if the child was treated with respect and fairness. Children who were threatened, exploited, or made to feel like failures will seek ultimately to assert superiority through coercion or guile or avoidance of problems. Furthermore, Adler disputed Freud's emphasis on the dominance of unconscious factors in human development. He believed that the goals people set for themselves determine, in part, the directions their lives take. (Ansbacher & Ansbacher, 1956).

Only 2 years after Adler's resignation, Carl Jung (1875–1961) split with Freud and began to create his own complex variation of psychoanalytic theory. Like Adler, he downplayed the notion that libido is the primary motivator of behavior. Instead, he suggested that the unconscious also includes basic personality tendencies (such as introversion-extraversion), varied personal experiences (not specifically sexual), and a shared human repository of instincts and images that guide behavior. Of even greater significance to the process of development, Jung rejected Freud's insistence on the primacy of early childhood. He insisted that before 40, individuals are concerned largely with satisfying biological needs

was an arbitrator between instincts and civilization. The Eriksonian ego is a creative force for change that accounts for both the biological needs of individuals and the cultural and historical contexts of their lives.

A comparison of the conceptions of Freud and Erikson clearly shows that Erikson takes a more optimistic view of human nature. The crises of development originate in the accommodation of personal goals to social expectations, not simply in the inhibition of sexual demands. Thus, Erikson stresses psychosocial—rather than psychosexual—drives. Erikson is interested in how individuals are able to develop healthy egos that can be accepted and confirmed by those around them. Development is a continuous growth process in which the ego thrives on the challenge of resolving the potential conflicts between the self and society. Crises are not seen as pitfalls and acquiring a sense of mastery over their environment. This includes strong interest in sexuality, raising a family, achieving career recognition, and gaining material security. Beginning at middle age, people become more interested in spiritual and philosophical matters. Although this transition may be difficult to achieve, Jung felt that the second part of life offered renewed opportunities for personality transformation as well as the development of wisdom and patience (Jung, 1953).

Karen Horney (1885–1952) continued the transition of neo-Freudian theory away from biological instincts and toward more of a sociocultural emphasis on personality development. She believed that anxiety in people was derived from mistreatment within the family and other hostile social forces during childhood. The fears and alienation of early development, according to Horney, lead one to construct neurotic coping strategies for alleviating conflict. Although she agreed with Freud that behavior is often irrational and unconsciously motivated, she believed that the drive for security, not sexuality, caused personal disturbances. Whereas Freud had a fairly negative view of human personality as essentially negative and aggressive at the core, Horney felt that every individual has the potential for constructive, healthy functioning. Furthermore, Horney offered some harsh criticism of Freud's differential treatment of the personality development of

males and females (this will be discussed further in Chapter 14). In many ways, Horney promoted the humanistic approach that inspired theorists such as Erich Fromm and Abraham Maslow. Although her work relied initially on the classic psychoanalytic framework, Horney credited both Adler and Jung for influencing her eventual rejection of that theory (Horney, 1950).

Freud's theoretical constructions were grounded in the history and culture of nineteenth-century Vienna. This limited realm of human experience dominated his thinking by preventing him from recognizing the profound impact of social variations on the process of development. His methodology for understanding the personality, using the retrospective accounts of sexually repressed individuals, further slanted his view of human nature. The pessimism and fatalism that pervade Freud's account of development are not surprising, given the sample he worked with, his own troubled past, and the times in which he lived. Unfortunately, many of his key concepts are stated somewhat vaguely and are difficult, if not impossible, to verify empirically. The final evaluation of Freud's legacy is still decades away; however, the controversies he raised suggested a revolution in our notions of human development, modified by numerous corrections to the original course he charted.

to be avoided or escaped from, but as opportunities for successful maturation. Although Freud recognized the significance of social conflict—particularly parent-child relationships—he tended to stress their negative outcomes and early foundations.

Stages of Development

Another major change that Erikson brought to psychoanalytic theory was the addition of adult stages of personality development. He replaced Freud's genital stage with four phases of life ranging from adolescence to old age. Therefore, instead of five developmental stages as Freud had suggested, Erikson postulated an eight-stage sequence that paralleled Freud's theory only in the childhood aspects (see Table 10.4). More recently, in response to the increased proportion of the population to live to advanced ages, Erikson hinted at the possibility of adding a ninth stage, including a sense of immortality, to his theory (Erikson, Erikson, & Kivnick, 1986).

Psychosocial crisis
A predominant conflict associated with each of Erik Erikson's eight stages of development. Resulting from both biological and cultural demands, the crisis may be favorably or unfavorably resolved.

Each of Erikson's stages is defined by a universally determined *psychosocial crisis* that builds on and incorporates previous development, as well as cultural influences and biological change. Erikson's theory is not strictly tied to chronological age, nor are the stages always easy to separate. However, Erikson felt that each stage throughout the life span offers an important contribution to the total personality. The *epigenetic principle,* Erikson's (1968) summation of development, states that "anything that grows has a ground plan, and that out of this ground plan the parts arise, each part having its time of special ascendancy, until all parts have arisen to form a functioning whole" (p. 92). Failure to deal adequately with early

Epigenetic principle
According to Erik Erikson, the notion that development proceeds from a universal plan that continually builds upon itself at the appropriate times.

Table 10.4
Erikson's Psychosocial Stages of Development

Phase of Life	Psychosocial Crisis	Favorable Outcome	Significant Relations	Social Modality
Infancy	Basic trust versus mistrust	Hope	Mother	To get—to give in return
Toddlerhood	Autonomy versus shame or doubt	Willpower	Parents	To hold (on)—to let (go)
Early childhood	Initiative versus guilt	Purpose	Family	To make (going after)—to "make like" (playing)
School age	Industry versus inferiority	Competence	Neighborhood and school	To make things—to do together
Adolescence	Ego identity versus role confusion	Devotion	Peer groups	To be oneself—to share oneself
Young adulthood	Intimacy versus isolation	Love	Partnerships and friends	To lose and find oneself in another
Middle adulthood	Generativity versus stagnation	Care	Divided labor and shared household	To make "be" (create)—to take care of
Maturity and old age	Ego integrity versus despair	Wisdom	"Mankind"	To be through having been—to face not being

Source: Adapted from *CHILDHOOD AND SOCIETY,* 2nd Edition, by Erik H. Erikson, Copyright 1950, © (1963) by W. W. Norton & Company, Inc. Copyright renewed 1978 by Erik H. Erikson; and from *IDENTITY AND THE LIFE CYCLE* by Erik H. Erikson, Copyright © 1980 by W. W. Norton & Company, Inc. Copyright © 1959 by International Universities Press, Inc. Copyright renewed 1987. Used by permission of W. W. Norton & Company, Inc.

crises jeopardizes, but does not render impossible, the successful resolution of later crises. The same issues can and do occur throughout the life span, but are particularly salient at the stages identified. In contrast to Freud's pregenital-stage determinism, Erikson does not dismiss the capacity of the individual to again confront and reintegrate previous conflicts.

Infancy

According to Erikson, the young infant's first major crisis is whether a sense of basic trust or mistrust of the world will be established. To allow healthy ego functioning to develop, infants must learn to sleep deeply and to feed easily; they must gain a feeling of confidence that their needs will be met regularly. Because this is the most helpless period of life, infants must obtain consistent and loving care to feel secure. However, Erikson (1968) stated that

> the amount of trust derived from earliest infantile experience does not seem to depend on absolute quantities of food or demonstrations of love, but rather on the quality of the maternal relationship. Mothers create a sense of trust in their children by that kind of administration which in its quality combines sensitive care of the baby's individual needs and a firm sense of personal trustworthiness within the trusted framework of their culture's lifestyle. (p. 249)

Ultimately, the infant should tolerate parental absence without undue anxiety, gain a sense of certainty about social relations, and have hope for a positive future. Of course, an infant should also develop a certain measure of mistrust. To survive in this world, one cannot trust blindly everyone and everything. However, an infant's failure to achieve a favorable balance in the direction of trust sets the stage for later anxiety about satisfying essential needs, creates suspicion of other people's motives, and leads to feelings of depression.

Toddlerhood

Instead of centering the source of conflict in the second stage exclusively on issues of toilet training, Erikson described this stage as a crisis of autonomy and self-control versus shame or doubt. Toddlers must learn to accept the privileges and limitations that growing up entails. The task of parents is to help children become independent—literally "stand on their own feet." At the same time, the infant must learn to control muscular activity that is socially unacceptable. Obviously, the anal and urethral muscles can become a battleground for this conflict. Erikson (1963) explained how the delicate balance of this stage

> becomes decisive for the ratio of love and hate, cooperation and willfulness, freedom of self-expression and its suppression. From a sense of self-control without loss of self-esteem comes a lasting sense of good will and pride; from a sense of loss of self-control and of foreign over-control comes a lasting propensity for doubt and shame. (p. 254)

Parents should protect their toddlers from experiences leading to failure and destructiveness without curbing their desires to do .things for themselves. If Mary insists on pouring a glass of milk by herself, for example, perhaps she should be allowed to do so, even though she is apt to make a mess. In contrast, no parent should allow a toddler to play with matches. As in all of Erikson's stages, a delicate balance is required. Parental control is both realistic and necessary. Yet, if toddlers are habitually punished for their strivings toward independence, they may begin to doubt their decision-making abilities, feel ashamed of their "incompetence," and become inflexible and secretive adults.

Early Childhood

The third stage of psychosocial development builds on earlier trust and autonomy to overcome the crisis of initiative versus guilt. Children who successfully resolve this conflict learn to plan their own activities and organize the directions for channeling their energy. As a consequence, they have a feeling of purpose that is expressed by their imagination, curiosity, and experimentation. If parents resent the questions their child frequently asks (including those about sexuality and sex differences), if they are not models of responsible behavior, if they belittle the child's fantasies or ideas, and if they discourage interaction with the peer group, the child will develop a sense of resignation and guilt about initiating new tasks or pondering the mysteries of life.

For the individual who does not establish a favorable ratio of initiative to guilt during early childhood, particular personality characteristics may hinder subsequent development. Adults who are passive, impotent, or irresponsible might still fear the punishment and ridicule they received from their parents many years ago. Erikson (1964) suggests that such people lack a sense of purpose or "the courage to envisage and pursue valued goals uninhibited by the defeat of infantile fantasies, by guilt and by the foiling fear of punishment" (p. 122).

School Age

With the advent of later childhood comes a shift from family and fantasy toward a more formal introduction to the culture. Now that children are physically and intellectually stronger, as well as more emotionally stable, they are expected to demonstrate relevant forms of competence:

> Thus the inner stage seems all set for "entrance into life," except that life must first be school life, whether school is field or jungle or classroom. The child must forget past hopes and wishes, while his exuberant imagination is tamed and harnessed to the laws of impersonal things—even the three R's . . . he now learns to win recognition by producing things. (Erikson, 1963, pp. 258–259)

Virtually ignored by Freud, the latency period is a crucial conflict between industry and inferiority, according to Erikson. Children must learn to use the tools of their society, whether the tools include spears or computers, rain dances or written language, pottery or mathematics. Although young children are rarely expected to contribute much to the traditions or direct transmission of the culture, they must prepare for entrance into adulthood by showing perseverance and diligence in the completion of assigned tasks. Productive activities and the mastery of complex skills are demanded of children in diverse ways—for example, doing chores around the house, participating in religious ceremonies, earning good grades in school, and playing constructively with friends.

The danger of this crisis is the sense of inferiority that might result from failure to compete effectively with peers or from constant criticism from significant adults (mostly parents and teachers). Failure may lead not only to humiliation, but also to the possibility of becoming a conformist slave to achievement while neglecting socioemotional growth. Again, a delicate balance is required here, too. Children must learn that failure is a normal part of life; experiencing occasional failure and learning to cope with it can actually strengthen children.

Adolescence

Adolescence, the period of the life span in which Erikson has shown the greatest interest, is designated by the crisis of ego identity versus role confusion. Although the biological changes of puberty may trigger the onset of this crisis, Erikson does not view a conflict between society and sexuality as the chief source of adolescent anxiety. Instead, the ego's task is to integrate previous childhood experiences to create a commitment to a set of values, a sense of personal identity, and a direction for the future. Searching for a sense of who they are and where they are going is particularly difficult for adolescents raised in contemporary technological civilizations. In addition to coping with the dramatic physical changes of puberty that cause them great concern about their appearance to others, adolescents must negotiate a complex array of choices on the road to adulthood.

Erikson regarded the interval between the role confusion of early adolescence and the achievement of a secure identity by adulthood as a psychosocial moratorium. He felt that this is a time of delaying adult commitments. It is

> characterized by a selective permissiveness on the part of society and of provocative playfulness on the part of youth, and yet it also often leads to deep, if often transitory, commitment on the part of youth, and ends in a more or less ceremonial confirmation of commitment on the part of society. (Erikson, 1968, p. 157)

Through such free experimentation, the adolescent may find a unique and appropriate sociocultural niche. However, the turmoil and dilemmas of the period may result in perpetual role confusion, premature and unexplored identities (possibly adopted from parents), temporary overidentification with popular heroes or ideologies (e.g., rock musicians or revolutionary movements), and socially deviant identities (e.g., the attitude that being a

Adolescents face a great array of choices on the road to adulthood. Experimentation with clothing, hairstyles, music, ideas, and activities helps adolescents learn who they are and where they are going.

delinquent gang member is better than being a nobody). If self-consciousness and the protection of cliques and slogans can be overcome, fidelity— "the ability to sustain loyalties freely-pledged in spite of the inevitable contradictions of value systems" (Erikson, 1964, p. 125)—can emerge.

Early Adulthood

Having constructed the basis for an adult identity, the individual is ready to face the crisis of intimacy versus isolation. Only when people are comfortable with themselves are they capable of sharing their intimate feelings and ideas with another person in a mature, nonselfish way. Neither the dependent attachment of infants nor the blind infatuation of adolescents qualifies as genuine love. However, the young adult,

> emerging from the search for and the insistence on identity, is eager and willing to fuse his identity with that of others. He is ready for intimacy, that is, the capacity to commit himself to concrete affiliations and partnerships and to develop the ethical strength to abide by such commitments even though they may call for significant sacrifices and compromises. (Erikson, 1963, p. 263)

Achieving intimacy requires taking risks that expose weaknesses, as well as demonstrating admiration, concern, and devotion to others. The failure to attain intimacy with friends, parents, siblings, and marriage partners leads to social withdrawal. This may not take the form of literal hermitlike isolation, but it can include the emptiness and self-absorption that accompanies strictly formal and superficial relationships (e.g., those of business associates and community organizations).

In sum, Erikson (1963) has attempted to show that the psychoanalytic conception of genitality really implies more than libidinal discharge and includes "(1) mutuality of orgasm, (2) with a loved partner, (3) of the other sex, (4) with whom one is able and willing to share a mutual trust, (5) and with whom one is able and willing to regulate the cycles of work, procreation, and recreation, (6) so as to secure to the offspring, too, all the stages of a satisfactory development" (p. 266). Intimacy is the devotion to lasting friendships and ethical commitments.

Middle Adulthood

If people learn how to love and how to share in early adulthood, they will be able to care for and guide the next generation effectively. Concern for the welfare of society may be expressed through rearing children; teaching younger individuals; enhancing culture with works of art, music, or literature; maintaining social traditions and transmitting values; producing technological innovations; and creating new ideas. Erikson considered the crisis of this long, seventh stage of personality development, which may extend until the fifth or sixth decade of life, to be one of generativity versus stagnation.

The middle adulthood years should be characterized by assuming responsibility for social progress, preserving the benefits of our experience for the future, and replacing our own lives with healthy new human beings. According to Erikson (1963), the notion of generativity

> encompasses the evolutionary development which has made man the teaching and instituting as well as the learning animal. The fashionable insistence on dramatizing the dependence of children on adults often blinds us to the dependence of the older generation on the younger one. Mature man needs to be needed, and maturity needs guidance as well as encouragement from what has been produced and must be taken care of. (pp. 266–267)

The adult who does not make a contribution to children's development or to humanity is left with a sense of impoverishment and stagnation. These feelings may be reflected by excessive self-indulgence and other manifestations of a middle-age crisis.

Later Adulthood

Erikson believed that the final conflict of development focuses on how people look back over their lives and how they approach impending death. He related this later adult stage to the infant crisis of trust versus mistrust by saying that "healthy children will not fear life if their elders have integrity enough not to fear death" (Erikson, 1963, p. 269). Thus, the elderly must negotiate between ego integrity and despair. On the one hand, individuals who have achieved favorable ratios with regard to the earlier conflicts may attain wisdom—"a detached and yet active concern with life in the face of death" (Erikson, 1968, pp. 291–292). In reviewing their past, they have a sense of satisfaction rather than regret.

On the other hand, some people are filled with despair and fear of death: "despair expresses the feeling that the time is now short, too short for the attempt to start another life and to try out alternate roads to integrity" (Erikson, 1963, p. 269). Instead of fulfillment, these people long for another chance to imbue their lives with meaning. The elderly who are bitter, depressed, and hypochondriacal (simultaneously wishing for and fearful of death) may end up helpless and alone. In contrast to this gloomy portrait are those older adults who participate in life despite physical limitations, have a feeling of wholeness and accomplishment, and know "that an individual life is the accidental coincidence of but one life cycle with but one segment of history . . . in such final consolidation, death loses its sting" (Erikson, 1963, p. 268).

Psychosocial Evaluation

Erikson's theory is an impressive modification of the psychodynamic approach to personality development. In his emphasis on flexibility, optimism, and environmental factors, he created a more contemporary variation of Freudian theory. Although Erikson credited his own contributions to Freud's foundation and maintained much of the flavor of psychoanalytic theory in his writing, definite anthropological and behavioral elements in his work might have made Freud quite uncomfortable. Chapter 6 described how the processes of learning theory represent an important component of human development. The mechanisms of reinforcement and observational learning play a role in the formation of personality, just as they do in affecting cognitive activities. Erikson, by no means a behavioral theorist, supports a position that regards the nurture aspects of development in a more equal balance than the dominant nature position that Freud never relinquished.

Nevertheless, weaknesses in Erikson's theory often parallel weaknesses in Freud's approach. For instance, both psychodynamic theories fail to distinguish adequately between the personality development of males and females. Although Erikson's ideas have been somewhat less offensive than Freud's views, the section on the self in this chapter and the discussion of gender roles in Chapter 14 will elaborate on these weaknesses. A different limitation of both theories is the lack of systematic data that would either support or refute Freud's and Erikson's positions. Their theories were created on the basis of clinical sessions with patients rather than from the collection of empirical evidence. As vague and difficult to demonstrate as some of these ideas are, more and more research on the details of Erikson's theory, at least, are proving that his ideas are not only testable, but also valid. The crisis of identity versus confusion, in particular, has attracted the attention of many personality development researchers in recent years. For more details on this work, see *Research Close-up,* "James Marcia and the Identity Status Interview."

DEVELOPMENT OF THE SELF

A number of personality theorists, such as Gordon Allport (1961), Carl Rogers (1961), Charlotte Buhler (1968), and George Kelly (1955), view the study of the self as the central issue in personality and its development. Phenomenological theories evolved, in part, as a reaction to prevailing approaches to personality development that seemed to neglect the self—people's own views of their characteristics, perceptions, and relationships. For the phenomenological theorist, the key to understanding someone's personality is to see things through the eyes of that person rather than describe how that person is seen by others. Concentration on the present and the future, not on the past, is also necessary. Clearly, the determinism and the pessimism of psychoanalysis has little place in phenomenological theory.

Some phenomenologists attribute a small role to irrational, unconscious motivation; they are convinced that conscious, rational awareness is more significant. Furthermore, they reject the psychoanalytic notion of conflict as a major motivating factor. Phenomenologists view the human being as active and dynamic; energy is used for making choices and expressing the self, not for reducing tensions or resolving intrapsychic battles. Finally, phenomenologists see human beings not as passive respondents to social and circumstantial forces, but as shapers of their own destinies. These theorists do not totally ignore the environment, but they believe that much of personality development involves the expression of certain innate characteristics of the self.

The methods of phenomenological theorists tend to be clinical rather than statistical or experimental. They consider traditional research to have lesser value in understanding personality than intensive therapeutic interactions or rich personal interviews. Phenomenologists frequently are criticized on the basis that their theories are philosophical, spiritual, and ethical statements about what human beings might ideally become rather than genuine scientific formulations about how people actually behave. Consider how psychotherapist Carl Rogers (1961) responded to that criticism:

> I do not have a Pollyanna view of human nature. I am quite aware that out of defensiveness and inner fear individuals can and do behave in ways which are incredibly cruel, horribly destructive, immature, regressive, antisocial, hurtful. Yet one of the most refreshing and invigorating parts of my experience is to work with such individuals and to discover the strongly positive directional tendencies which exist in them, as in all of us, at the deepest levels (p. 27)

Research Close-Up
James Marcia and the
Identity Status Interview

 On the basis of Erikson's extensive theorizing about the adolescent's search for identity, researcher James Marcia has constructed an interview technique that probes the two critical dimensions of crisis and commitment. The crisis component refers to the exploratory period of intensive struggle and questioning among meaningful alternatives. Commitment, in contrast, is the degree of firm investment by the individual in particular beliefs and activities. Marcia's (1966) original semistructured interview consisted of a variety of questions on career plans, political attitudes, and religious ideology. More recently, Grotevant and Thorbecke (1982) have extended the interview to incorporate the realms of social relaxations, sex role orientation, and dating/sexuality. Responses to the entire set of items allow a researcher to classify a person's identity status according to a four-part scheme: identity diffusion, identity foreclosure, psychosocial moratorium, or identity achievement.

Identity diffusion is the least developmentally mature of the four status categories and most characteristic of young adolescents. Such individuals have an incomplete and disjointed sense of self, have given little thought to vocational goals, have not evolved a coherent set of political or religious values, feel personally and sexually inadequate, exhibit high levels of anxiety with stereotyped patterns of behavior, and tend to drift from one faddish and meaningless activity to another. Identity-diffused adolescents have clearly not made a commitment to a stable future, nor have they been actively engaged in the process of arriving at such a construction. These are likely to be alienated teenagers who may attempt to escape the struggle for identity through drug and alcohol abuse, reckless driving, and related thrill seeking, as well as by avoiding close friendships and academic competition.

Adolescents may emerge from diffusion status by adopting a foreclosed identity. This development is attained by avoiding any serious confrontation with the concerns of identity formation. Rather than considering alternative choices for the future and experimenting with different roles, these adolescents circumvent the exploration of self. They borrow identities from others, most often a parent or other close relative, and commit themselves prematurely and unquestioningly to a style of life and a set of values. Because identity foreclosure implies a commitment to plans endorsed by someone else, the possibilities for achieving full expression of personality and potential are short-circuited. A superficial examination of foreclosed adolescents may suggest healthy development; however, they tend to be fairly dependent on the opinions of others, relatively unadaptive, somewhat authoritarian, and emotionally inhibited.

The essence of the adolescent identity crisis is represented by the psychosocial moratorium status. As expected, these individuals are in the midst of exploring their sense of self. This crisis should not be avoided or regarded as a personality problem. Instead, the moratorium is a time for making decisions about the future and thoroughly examining different values. The moratorium is a prolonged interval when clear commitments are not made, but, unlike identity diffusion, the struggle during this status is a self-directed, largely conscious, and positive attempt to learn about and define oneself. Although such adolescents have strong feelings of anxiety and self-consciousness, they are open to new experiences, tend to be highly reflective and idealistic, and are usually comfortable dealing with other people. The moratorium status is associated with a heavy investment in role experimentation, and adolescents during this time are curious about their world and eager to argue with and criticize authority figures.

Finally, identity achievement can be considered the most developmentally advanced status of adolescence. The only route to achieving an identity is through first experiencing a psychosocial moratorium. Once an adequate search for identity has been completed, the individual is able to arrive at a set of commitments that are freely chosen. In other words, having pondered the possibilities, identity achievers look to their futures with some confidence and should be capable of resolving the intimacy crisis of Erikson's subsequent psychosocial stage. Identity achievement rarely occurs before late adolescence. In fact, even 10 or 20 years later, there is no guarantee that the crisis of identity versus role diffusion will ever be satisfactorily resolved. Nonetheless, identity achievers are characterized by emotional maturity, a harmony between individual and social needs, resistance to conformity pressures, and a generally adaptive personality style.

The four identity statuses are diagrammed in Figure A according to the absence or presence of both crisis and commitment. Many hundreds of people have been interviewed using Marcia's questions, or several variations of his technique, leading to the profiles discussed here. The dozens of studies that have investigated the topic of identity status are indebted not only to Erikson's conceptual framework but to the empirical translation provided by Marcia. The work of Marcia, his colleagues, and others in this field demonstrates the value of creatively building from a given theoretical position to a large body of fascinating and invaluable research. In addition, Marcia's technique highlights the continued significance of using interview procedures for obtaining a greater understanding of personality development.

Figure A

		Crisis	
		Presence	**Absence**
Commitment	**Absence**	Identity Achievement	Identity Foreclosure
	Presence	Psychosocial Moratorium	Identity Diffusion

Maslow's Hierarchy of Needs

Abraham Maslow, trained in behaviorist psychology, became one of the strongest advocates of the positive aspects of human nature. For example, the Freudian emphasis on biological determinism and the behaviorist claim of environmental determinism disturbed Maslow greatly. He believed that much of personality theory had ignored healthy individuals and, therefore, created a bias toward inadequate development. Maslow felt that the study of exceptionally healthy people rather than unhappy ones might restore the balance of personality development to include motivations of a higher level. At the core, according to Maslow, all people are essentially good and possess unique potentials. However, he did not think that such endowments were necessarily permanent characteristics or that development followed any prescribed course:

> This inner nature is not strong and overpowering and unmistakable like the instincts of animals. It is weak and delicate and subtle and easily overcome by habit, cultural pressure, and wrong attitudes toward it. Even though weak, it rarely disappears in the normal person—perhaps not even in the sick person. Even though denied, it persists underground forever pressing for actualization. (Maslow, 1968, p. 4)

Thus, human nature is neither evil nor totally flexible, but is inherently benign and susceptible to negative influences.

Maslow suggested that all individuals are motivated by an actualizing tendency—the need to enhance ourselves and to fulfill unique potentials. He claimed, however, that before we are able to satisfy our needs for *self-actualization,* we must meet lower-level needs. The five types of human motives that Maslow considered most essential can be arranged in a *hierarchy of needs* as depicted in Figure 10.1.

At the base of the pyramid are the physiological needs, which include air, food, water, sleep, sex, elimination, and so on. Once these needs have been met, higher-level needs become more critical. The second level consists of safety and security needs. Although the hierarchy may appear to have a chronological age basis, lower-level needs continue to require satisfaction for adults as well as for infants and children. For example, fears about loss of employment or living in a crime-ridden neighborhood might limit the capacity for achieving higher-level needs. The need for belonging and love occupies the third level of Maslow's hierarchy. These needs for affiliation and intimacy can be met in a variety of ways, including families, lovers, close friends, cult organizations, personal growth groups, and psychotherapy. At the fourth level are the needs for self-esteem. Maslow believed that the respect and recognition of others completes the lower, or deficiency, levels of the hierarchy. Only individuals who have satisfied each of the previous needs can become in touch with their true potentials. The self-actualization, or "being," level is concerned with such values as goodness, truth, beauty, unity, perfection, justice, order, playfulness, richness, simplicity, and meaningfulness.

Self-actualization

According to Abraham Maslow, the tendency of all human beings, after having satisfied lower-level needs, to enhance their lives and fulfill their unique potentials.

Hierarchy of needs

According to Abraham Maslow, the arrangement of human motives into five basic levels from the most pressing physiological needs to the least critical self-actualization.

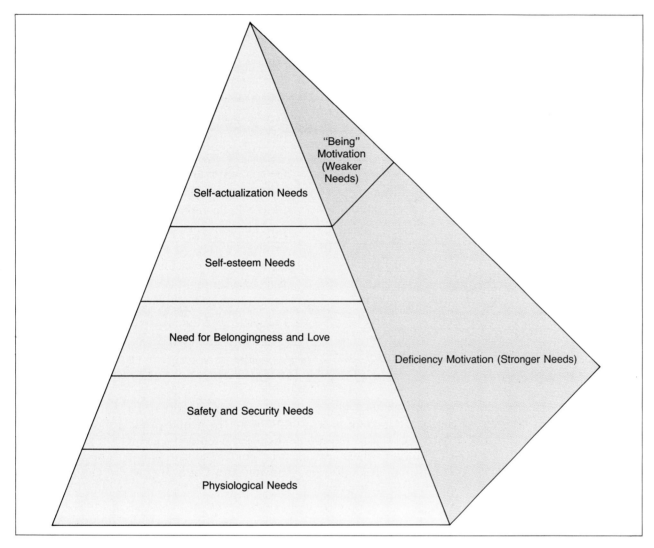

Figure 10.1
Maslow's Hierarchy of Needs

Maslow recognized that only a relative handful of people are actively engaged in the pursuit of self-actualization needs—not simply because such needs occupy the top of the hierarchy, but because self-actualization is a risky and uncertain process. Furthermore, our cultural standards often encourage conformity rather than freedom of expression, and our concern with lower-level needs may blind us to the possibilities for knowing our inner selves.

Maslow's (1970) study of contemporary and historical figures led him to develop a list of 15 characteristics that he believed all self-actualizers would

Table 10.5
Qualities of Self-Actualizers

Qualities of Self-Actualizers

1. Accurate perception of reality.
2. Acceptance of self and others.
3. Spontaneous and natural behaviors.
4. Concern with problems rather than self.
5. Need for privacy and detachment.
6. Independence of judgment.
7. Continuous freshness of appreciation.
8. Mystic or peak experiences.
9. Desire to help improve humanity.
10. Few, but deep, friendships.
11. Genuine belief in democratic values.
12. Strong sense of right and wrong.
13. Philosophical, not hostile, humor.
14. Interest in novelty and creativity.
15. Resistance to cultural conventions.

Source: Adapted from A. H. Maslow. *Motivation and personality* (2nd ed.). New York: Harper & Row, 1970.

exhibit despite the typical lack of social support for becoming a self-actualized individual (see Table 10.5). The people Maslow considered in the "probable self-actualization" category included Jane Addams, Albert Einstein, Albert Schweitzer, Baruch Spinoza, William James, Thomas Jefferson, Abraham Lincoln, Eleanor Roosevelt, and Aldous Huxley. Certainly Maslow's research in this realm is limited and informal, substantially colored by his own value system, and subject to several interpretations. In addition, testing Maslow's theory is difficult because it is imprecise; when empirical analyses have been conducted, the evidence is not consistently supportive (Ryckman, 1989). Nevertheless, his contribution toward the articulation of the positive directions in which human development can proceed should not be minimized.

What Is the Self?

A simple task, used in a number of studies on the self, can demonstrate several points about the nature of the self. Label the top of a blank sheet of paper with the question "Who am I?" Now proceed to respond to this question, taking about 15 minutes to do so; be sure to answer with the first things that come to mind. Try to list 20 answers to the question. Now try to answer again as if you were an 8-year-old, then a 14-year-old, and then a 66-year-old (or as a young adult if you are older than 50).

Answering the Twenty Statements Test (Kuhn & McPartland, 1954), as the foregoing task is called, requires *objectification* of the self. For some adults, this may not be as easy as it looks; adults may run out of answers after the fourth item. This task of objectification is especially hard for young children. As you look over the responses generated, you may find that they typically fall into a number of categories that reflect physical aspects of the self (e.g., tall, thin), social roles (e.g., student, daughter), and personality qualities (e.g., moody, conservative). Thus, people tend to think of themselves along a variety of dimensions. These dimensions may change with age, as may be seen by comparing your hypothetical responses with your actual responses. Thus, the self is a developmental phenomenon that undergoes significant change and modification.

Some of these insights are a part of psychology's heritage. William James, a professor at the turn of the century who is considered the founder of psychology in the United States, devoted a large portion of his textbook *Principles of Psychology* (1890) to the self. James divided the self into the subject, or knower (the "I"), and the object, or the known (the "me"). The study of the self as "I" (the active and engaged self) has only recently received attention in the developmental literature (Damon & Hart, 1982; Harter, 1983; Logan, 1986), but the self as "me" (the reflective and descriptive self) has been the focus of numerous theoretical and empirical studies since James's original work. James further divided the self as known into the *material me* (physical self and possessions), the *social me* (roles and interpersonal relations), and the *spiritual me* (consciousness and thoughts).

Self-concept

All the components of one's personality of which a person is aware.

Self-esteem

The evaluative component of the self-concept whereby "good" or "bad" labels are attached to aspects of the self.

The term **self-concept** refers to the aspect of the self that is objectively known. The self-concept includes all the ideas, concepts and attributes linked to the awareness of the self. **Self-esteem** is the evaluative, or subjective, aspect of the self-concept. When labels and emotions such as "good" or "bad" are related to the social, physical, and personality/spiritual aspects of the self, the level of self-esteem can be raised or lowered. Often, as James (1968) noted, comparisons are made between an "ideal" self and the current status of the self (the "real" self). When an individual rates a large discrepancy between the ideal and the real self, low levels of self-esteem may result. In contrast, a close resemblance to an individual's ideal self serves to raise self-esteem.

Finally, to reduce the complexity of the self, one can view the self-concept as influenced by three major developmental components. The first component involves cognitive development. Because the self-concept is a result of thinking, qualitative changes in thinking will significantly affect ideas about the self. Contemporary self-concept theorists have discovered a number of parallels between self-concept development and the stages of pre-operational, concrete operational, and formal operational development as presented by Piaget (Harter, 1983; Noppe, 1983).

The second component involves interpersonal development. The notion that the concept of the self arises from social interaction has a long history (Baldwin, 1897; Cooley, 1902; Mead, 1934). According to this view, as children develop they construct a "looking-glass self"; that is, the reflection of the self in the eyes of others is what forms the basis of the self-concept. People who are highly valued (significant others) are especially likely to have their appraisals and ideas incorporated into an individual's sense of self. The cast of significant others changes with development. Thus, parents and teachers are significant others during the early childhood years; their influence gradually defers to the influence of peers and best friends during adolescence and beyond (Harter, 1983).

Personality development, particularly in the Eriksonian sense of achieving unity and self-consistency, is the final major component to influence the self-concept. According to Erikson (1968), certain developmental tasks are necessary for the achievement of an integrated personality. These tasks—leading to a sense of self-trust, self-autonomy, self-initiative, and so on—have important implications for the concepts of self, self-esteem, and the "I" as the self that organizes and interprets experience.

Development of the Self-Concept

Using the previous analysis of the self as a conceptual framework, this section analyzes the developmental course of the self-concept from infancy through adulthood.

Infancy

Infants need to establish a subjective and objective sense of self. They must first learn that they can cause things to happen, such as mother's approach, the shake of a rattle, and the scratching sound of their sheets. Such a sense of self emerges from the feedback babies receive in their everyday interactions with people and objects (Lewis & Brooks-Gunn, 1979). In particular, parental imitation of the baby's actions seems to be a significant source of feedback (Harter, 1983). These experiences are important for the emergence of the "I," as well as the "me."

Theoretically, the objective sense of self may be linked to the development of object permanence (the knowledge that objects continue to exist even when they are out of view). The development of the self as object has been studied by presenting a mirror to infants and noting how they respond. One of the earliest studies to use this technique was published by Dixon (1957). He longitudinally observed five infants, from the ages of 4 months to the age of 12 months. He found a four-stage developmental sequence of visual self-recognition:

1. The baby has no interest in the reflection in the mirror.
2. The baby responds to the image in the mirror as if it were an interesting playmate.
3. The baby is able to differentiate between his or her own reflection and the mirror image of another child.
4. The baby shows definite signs of self-recognition.

Does this infant recognize himself in the mirror? According to several developmental re-searchers, a primitive concept of self begins to evolve during the second year of life.

Later studies on visual self-recognition have supported Dixon's developmental sequence, although the age at which true self-awareness becomes evident varies between 12 and 20 months.

Observing self-recognition through mirror play is difficult, because the researcher has to determine whether infants perceive their own facial features or those of "another child" in the mirror. Several studies have attempted to separate these factors. Amsterdam (1972) and Lewis and Brooks-Gunn (1975) placed rouge on the noses of infants as a point of reference for evaluating self-recognition. Infants showed obvious signs of self-recognition if they looked in the mirror, saw rouge on the nose of the image, and then touched their own noses. This occurred sometime during the latter half of the second year. Finally, Lewis and Brooks-Gunn (1979) found that infants, beginning at about 15 months of age, were able to distinguish between live television images of themselves, television images of themselves taken a week earlier, and television images of another infant.

Research on the self-concept during infancy has been limited, of course, by the infant's lack of language. Yet, the evidence seems to point out strongly—at least on a visual basis—that older infants have constructed a sense of "I" and "me," are able to tell themselves apart from others of the same age, and can distinguish between their knowledge of themselves and their knowledge of their mothers (Pipp, Fischer, & Jennings, 1987).

Childhood

During the childhood years, changes in the self-concept are related to a number of important developmental processes. First, the child can now use words to label himself or herself and can verbalize what aspects are of the self and what are "not-self" (Markus, 1977). Second, ways of conceiving the self become more diverse with increasing age (Mullener & Laird, 1971). A differentiation of the self during childhood leads older children to think of themselves using more ideas and categories than younger children. Third, children's self-concept development appears to parallel the general cognitive developmental sequence of pre-operational to concrete operational to formal operational thought. That is, children's self-descriptions begin by focusing on physical, external aspects of the self; then, as they mature, they refer to themselves more often in psychological terms.

Montemayor and Eisen (1977), for example, charted the development of the self-concept by giving the Twenty Statements Test to children aged 10 to 18 years. When the researchers classified the answers, they found that younger children described themselves in concrete ways: their sex, name, age, likes, dislikes, eye color. Older children and young adolescents described themselves more in terms of their interpersonal relationships and personality characteristics: truthful person, good cellist, old-fashioned, lose my temper. The older adolescent in this study was much more focused on psychological aspects of the self: an individual, a moody person, a liberal person, a loner. Self-conception, according to Montemayor and Eisen, becomes increasingly more abstract with development. Mature self-concepts also seem to be more differentiated, because a greater number of categories are incorporated into the self.

Many of these points also were studied by Guardo and Bohan (1971). They examined the sense of self exhibited by 6- to 9-year-olds. To do this, the researchers asked the children if they could become a pet (testing for the sense of humanity), an opposite-sex peer (testing for the sense of sexuality), or a same-sex peer (testing for the sense of individuality), and whether they were the same person in the past and future (testing for the sense of continuity). All of the children expressed a sense of their humanity, individuality, sexuality, and continuity. But, Guardo and Bohan found that the 6- and 7-year-olds emphasized their physical characteristics (e.g., not being able to assume the identity of a friend because their looks are different).

Adolescence

Many people consider adolescence the crucible of self-concept development. As previously discussed, Erikson (1968) viewed adolescence as a time of the establishment of a sense of identity. Identity involves a sense of unity across different components of the self; a sense of continuity between past, present, and future selves; and a sense of mutuality between the individual's self-concept and the views that significant others have of the self. Adolescents strive for self-consistency, which is a fundamental aspect of a mature self-concept (Lecky, 1945), at a time when the self as others view it takes on a heightened importance. They are very self-conscious about the view others may have of them (Elkind & Bowen, 1979) and anchor much of their self-concepts in social roles (Noppe, 1983). Additionally, the emergence of formal-operational reasoning opens the way for an increase in self-reflection—thinking about the self in a hypothetical plane and generally using more psychological and abstract concepts to describe the self.

Adolescence is the time for the construction of a "self-theory." A self-theory is much like a scientific theory; it has principles, serves to generate hypotheses, attempts to be internally consistent, and can be verified by experiments (Epstein, 1973). The major difference between a self-theory and a scientific theory is that a self-theory is constructed by an individual about himself or herself. Much of the self-reflection during adolescence, therefore, functions to develop a self-theory that can be used as an aid to interpret experience. Abstract thoughts, broadened and more intimate social relationships, and a newly acquired future orientation act as catalysts for the emergence of the self-theory, which maintains its importance throughout adolescence and in the years beyond.

Adulthood

One of the chief difficulties in comparing self-concepts during adulthood to earlier self-concepts is the lack of longitudinal research. Cross-sectional studies that yield differences in self-concept may be the result of cohort influences rather than genuine maturational change. In addition, the research is marked by diversity in the age ranges studied, the definitions of self-concept, the particular populations sampled, and the selection of methods for assessing the self. Nevertheless, a detailed review of the research on adult self-conceptions led Bengtson, Reedy, and Gordon (1985) to conclude that much stability endures across age ranges, that individuals' subjective perceptions of change are greater than more objective indicators show, and that whatever changes tend to occur are likely to be a function of individual life experiences instead of any universal, age-related processes.

Bengtson, Reedy, and Gordon (1985) proposed, for example, that temperamentally related components of the self—such as introversion/extroversion or security/insecurity—show fairly stable patterns over the life span whereas dimensions such as autonomy or excitability will probably vary across the years. The social roles that typically accompany aging may also foster change; that is, becoming a grandparent, retiring from a job, losing a spouse, and so on, tend to create instability at whatever age they may occur. Somewhat more predictable alterations in the self, according to McCrae (1987), are based on biological losses of strength, stamina, and youthful looks. Perhaps the most helpful perspective on aging and the self is that how people evaluate themselves should be less identified with any age stereotypes and more related to whatever positive images they wish to pursue.

Self-esteem and Life Satisfaction

Self-esteem becomes increasingly important as people learn to evaluate themselves. Research using pictorial self-esteem scales has indicated that young children (aged 4 to 7) do not have a general sense of self-esteem; rather, they evaluate themselves only on specific behaviors (Harter, 1981).

Imaginary audience

The extreme self-consciousness characterizing young adolescents, with feelings that others are as concerned with them as they are with themselves.

During the childhood and adolescent years, feedback from parents, peers, and teachers becomes an important source of self-esteem. Older elementary school children are fairly stable in their levels of self-esteem. Puberty—and the accompanying shift from elementary to junior high or middle school—seems to bring lowered levels of self-esteem, particularly for girls (Noppe, 1983). The adolescent's hypercritical interpretations of the self have been labeled by Elkind (1978) as a performance for an ***imaginary audience***. As the adolescent matures, a rise in self-esteem is observed. Enright, Lapsley, and Shukla (1979), for instance, noted a decline in imaginary audience perceptions by later adolescence. Interestingly, researchers have also found that young elementary school children are just beginning to formulate an idea of what their ideal selves may be, and, as they age, the distance between ideal and real selves increases. This discrepancy, which is a part of developmental maturation, may also tie into the lower levels of self-esteem found during the young adolescent years.

What promotes or lowers a child's self-esteem? A classic work by Coopersmith (1967) with 10- to 12-year-old boys provided important clues to this question. Coopersmith found that parents of boys with high self-esteem were more affectionate, accepting, and respectful, but that they also enforced rules consistently and held high standards for achievement. Furthermore, these parents always tried to explain the reasons underlying their disciplinary actions. Harter (1983) cited evidence that the same parenting style has a positive effect on girls' self-esteem, too. Such parenting communicates to children that they have value, are loved for who they are, and are capable of measuring up to their parents' expectations.

Another important factor related to self-esteem in children is school performance. Whether low self-esteem leads to poor academic achievement or whether poor academic achievement lowers self-esteem, the two are clearly interrelated. In all probability, low self-esteem and poor school performance form a vicious cycle that is difficult to break. Several experimental programs that have worked at maximizing school success have yielded promising results in raising self-esteem in children (Harter,

1983); teachers who communicate positive attitudes and high expectations for their low self-esteem students may also see a corresponding rise in their pupils' schoolwork. Such research findings emphasize how significant self-esteem is to developing children in both their personal and academic lives.

The self-esteem patterns of adults do not appear to be very different from those of children or adolescents. Nearly all the research comparing age groups (none of it is longitudinal) suggests that no particular period of low self-esteem occurs during the adulthood years. In fact, older adults seem to have the highest levels of self-esteem, contradicting the stereotypes of widespread unhappiness among the elderly. We can only speculate why this may be so: It could be the result of a developmental age trend, or certain

Life satisfaction among elderly people depends partly on the basic needs of adequate health and income. In addition, personality attributes, such as extroversion, may contribute signif-icantly to happiness during old age.

Applying Our Knowledge
A Positive Note on the Institutionalization of the Elderly

 The vast majority of older men and women in the United States live on their own or with friends and relatives. Many also live in nursing homes, but the occasional media exposé of substandard conditions in certain nursing homes has created a fairly negative image for these institutions. The quality of life for nursing home residents obviously is influenced by such factors as adequate nutrition and cleanliness, appropriate medical care, and a balance between privacy and social activities. Psychologists Ellen Langer and Judith Rodin felt that people's feelings of personal control within their environments might produce additional beneficial effects.

Langer and Rodin (1976), therefore, conducted an experiment in a natural setting: two floors of a high-quality-care nursing home in Connecticut. Despite the lack of complaints against the facilities or the staff of this nursing home, residents usually were not provided with the opportunity to make decisions or to have responsibilities. The researchers enlisted the aid of the nursing home administrator to present the residents of each floor with separate communications:

> On one floor, the emphasis was on the residents' responsibility for themselves, whereas on the other floor, the communication stressed the staff's responsibility for them. In addition . . . residents in the responsibility-induced group were asked to give their opinion of the means by which complaints were handled rather than just being told that any complaints would be handled by staff members; they were given the opportunity to select their own plant and to care for it themselves, rather than being given a plant to be taken care of by someone else; and they were given a choice of a movie night, rather than being assigned a particu-

lar night, as was typically the case in the old age home. However, there was no difference in the amount of attention paid to the two groups. (Langer & Rodin, 1976, p. 194)

Three weeks after the communications were presented, questionnaires were given to the nurses and the residents themselves concerning the emotions and behaviors of the elderly participants in this experiment. (One week before the communications, no differences appeared on the questionnaire results between the two floors of residents. Furthermore, the interviewers were not aware of the purposes of the research.) Langer and Rodin found that the residents from the responsibility-induced group were significantly happier, more active, and more alert in comparison to the other group. Their movie attendance was higher than that of the residents who were given the standard communication, and they participated to a greater extent in a jelly bean–guessing contest.

Langer and Rodin (1976) concluded that "inducing a greater sense of personal responsibility in people who may have virtually relinquished decision making, either by choice or necessity, produces improvement" (p. 197). Although this study was of short duration and did not demonstrate permanent changes, the implications for institutional policy are clear. Langer and Rodin even suggest that "some of the negative consequences of aging may be retarded, reversed, or possibly prevented by returning to the aged the right to make decisions and a feeling of competence" (p. 197). Consequently, the atmosphere of a nursing home does not have to be one of passivity and depression.

cohort differences may be operating, or lower self-esteem individuals may be less likely to survive to old age. At this point, no available data unequivocally support any one of these hypotheses.

Bengtson, Reedy, and Gordon (1985) also pointed out that most of the research on self-esteem in adults employs a global evaluation rather than dividing the concept into more specific components. Combining the overall lack of studies on adult self-esteem with their methodological flaws, we must wait for further results before drawing more definite conclusions. George (1987) has stated, however, that self-esteem in older adults is associated with factors similar to those at any age—personal achievement, interpersonal success, and meaningful activities—as well as with physical health and attitudes toward aging. Any crucial changes in roles (such as when the last child leaves home) or any dramatic differences from normative attributes (such as unattractive facial features) may prompt at least temporary declines in self-esteem. After a period of readjustment or reappraisal, adults are often surprised that the negative feelings have lessened.

The concept of life satisfaction typically has been applied to adult development rather than to children and adolescents. As with any aspect of the self, life satisfaction may take different forms, depending on the experiences each individual encounters. Although much dissension concerns the definition and measurement of the concept of life satisfaction (Gubrium & Lynott, 1983; Horley, 1984; Sauer & Warland, 1982), among the elderly, sufficient income and good self-rated health are excellent predictors of life satisfaction (Okun, Stock, Haring, & Witter, 1984). A study by Potash, Noppe, and Noppe (1981) found that an extroverted personality and an internal locus of control (the belief that we control our own destinies) were equally effective in distinguishing between high- and low-satisfaction groups. Even in the setting of a nursing home, positive behaviors and life satisfaction may result from greater opportunities for controlling one's own environment. (See *Applying Our Knowledge,* "A Positive Note on the Institutionalization of the Elderly.")

Additional variables such as education, gender, marital status, and friendships often interact to create different levels of satisfaction. For example, the research of Campbell, Converse, and Rodgers (1976), which will be discussed in greater detail in Chapter 11, suggests that single women were more satisfied with their lives than single men, but that married men and women felt more satisfied than all categories of unmarried (including widowed and divorced people). In fact, childless married couples in their 20s appeared to be the most satisfied group of people in the United States, especially among women. Over the course of a short longitudinal study (of 4 years), however, Palmore and Kivett (1977) found that levels of life satisfaction remained constant for adults between the ages of 46 and 70. In sum, feelings of self-esteem and life satisfaction depend on a combination of personal qualities, feedback from others, and particularly crucial experiences along the life span.

ISSUES IN PERSONALITY DEVELOPMENT

The study of personality and the self raises many questions concerning the influence of biology, cultural variations, and the stability of individual differences in human development. This section will discuss these issues, as well as the difficult question of distinguishing between normal and deviant patterns of personality. Caution is essential to avoid the mislabeling of behavior that may be temporary or does not extend beyond the typical range of healthy personality variations.

Does Personality Have Biological Origins?

Parents of difficult babies often wonder why their infant is so irritable. Why does the baby next door sit quietly in the mother's arms while their own child wiggles, squirms, and fusses when held? Such troubled parents may assume that they have made the child so fussy. Putting it another way, some people believe that an infant's personality is acquired completely from the environment. On the other hand, the parents of a difficult baby may assume that this is just the way the baby is. Their infant would act the same way no matter what they did. But is this really the case? Are certain aspects of personality "wired into" a child at birth?

Reliance on genetic influences as the major impetus for personality development is a concept that has waxed and waned in popularity for decades. Several theories of recent vintage—most notably those of Buss and Plomin (1984) and Thomas and Chess (1977)—lend some empirical support to the idea of **temperament** (inborn behavioral characteristics) as the forerunner of personality.

Temperament

A core set of inherited dispositions, which, after modification by experiences, serves as the foundation for later personality.

The temperament theory of Buss and Plomin (1975) contains three basic assumptions:

> (1) individuals begin life with a small number of broad, *inherited* dispositions to act in certain ways; (2) the environment reacts to and modifies these dispositions (within limits); and (3) temperaments are more concerned with stylistic than content aspects of personality. (p. 227)

Buss and Plomin's theory is related to Willerman's personality inventory presented at the beginning of this chapter. The temperament dimension that sets the tone for future interactions with other people is sociability, an adaptive quality manifested in friendliness and cooperation. Individual differences between infant cuddlers versus noncuddlers (Schaffer & Emerson, 1964), genetic evidence from twin research (Buss, Plomin, & Willerman, 1973), correlations between infancy and adolescence (Schaefer & Bayley, 1963), and correlations between early adolescence and adulthood (Kagan & Moss, 1962) support the notion of a sociability temperament.

Activity level, a second dimension of temperament, refers to the energy for initiating plans and contacts. Willerman and Plomin (1973) found strong relationships between the activity level of children and their parents' own activity level when they were children. Although the evidence of stability for activity level is less impressive than for sociability, Willerman (1979) remains convinced that it should be retained as a temperament dimension.

Finally, the emotionality component of temperament reflects the likelihood of arousal. Expressions of fear, joy, or anger may indicate varying degrees of the emotional reactivity dimension. A study by Rose and Ditto

(1983) on the heritability and stability of fears from adolescence to adulthood illustrates that such research is continuing and has extended beyond the early years of development. Remember though, all three biological dispositions are subject to parental and sociocultural modification.

For more than 30 years, Thomas, Chess, and their colleagues have studied the identification and development of temperament in infants and children. In their theory, nine factors make up the individual differences in infant temperament. Babies are grouped into three categories of behavioral style (easy, slow to warm up, and difficult).

In actual testing, however, more than one-third of all babies examined did not fit neatly into any of these classifications. Table 10.6 outlines the temperamental factors and behavioral categories. Note that some overlap occurs between these temperaments and those of Buss and Plomin.

Thomas, Chess, and Birch (1970) found temperamental stability across 10 years for many of the characteristics listed. The "difficult baby" category, for example, was overly represented among "problem children" years later. Infants at the age of 2 months who resisted diapering and cried when their carriages were rocked did not adjust well to new schools and cried when they could not solve a homework problem in the fourth grade. Other researchers have also found stability of these temperaments from infancy to the preschool years (Rothbart, 1986) and from early adolescence to early adulthood (Kern, 1984) as well as positive correlations between infant difficulty and later helping behaviors in preschoolers (Stanhope, Bell, & Parker-Cohen, 1987) or poor school achievement (Keough, 1985).

Although biological dispositions were important in determining the children's subsequent personalities, Thomas and his associates were careful to point out that "there can be no universally valid set of rules that will work equally well for all children everywhere" (1963, p. 85). Therefore, not only does each infant have a particular set of temperaments, but the reactions of parents to those qualities help to shape future personality. The goodness of fit between child temperament and parenting style, a reciprocal interaction, determines the vulnerability of a particular individual to developmental difficulties (Chess & Thomas, 1984).

Obviously, research and theory on temperament suffer from some of the same confusion that pervades the nature-nurture debate on intelligence. We cannot separate the inherited factors from the environmental factors that make up human personality. Few contemporary developmentalists doubt that genetic influences offer at least a moderately significant perspective on personality. Studies comparing identical with fraternal twins provide powerful support for this approach. Loehlin and Nichols (1976), for example, tested 850 pairs of twins on a wide variety of personality measures. They found greater similarities between identical than fraternal twins on virtually every dimension.

Of course, as Loehlin and Nichols acknowledged, most parents of identical twins tend to treat them more similarly than they do fraternal twins.

Table 10.6
Characteristics of Categories of Temperament

| | Type of child | | |
	Easy (40%)	Slow to Warm Up (15%)	Difficult (10%)
Activity Level Proportion of active periods to inactive ones	Varies	Low to moderate	Varies
Rhythmicity Regularity of hunger, excretion, sleep, and wakefulness	Very regular	Varies	Varies
Distractibility Degree to which extraneous stimuli alter behavior	Varies	Varies	Varies
Approach/Withdrawal The response to a new object or person	Positive approach	Initial withdrawal	Withdrawal
Adaptability The ease with which a child adapts to changes in the environment	Very adaptable	Slowly adaptable	Slowly adaptable
Attention Span and Persistence The amount of time devoted to an activity and the effect of distraction on the activity	High or low	High or low	High or low
Intensity of Reaction The energy of response, regardless of its quality or direction	Low or mild	Mild	Intense
Threshold of Responsiveness The intensity of stimulation required to evoke a discernible response	High or low	HIgh or low	High or low
Quality of Mood The amount of friendly, pleasant, joyful behavior as contrasted with unpleasant, unfriendly behavior	Positive	Slightly negative	Negative

Source: From "The Origin of Personality," by A. Thomas, S. Chess, and H. G. Birch. Copyright © 1970 by SCIENTIFIC AMERICAN, Inc. All rights reserved.

In fact, environmental influences cannot be ruled out even for the few reliable studies of separated twins because of the possible influences of prenatal and perinatal (labor and delivery) experiences. An extensive review of the literature on genetic effects on personality development did not lead Goldsmith (1983) to any firm conclusions. Nevertheless, he tentatively offered the idea that the stability of personality dispositions over time may itself be a heritable characteristic. In other words, some children may be more inclined than others to maintain consistent personality attributes.

How Does Culture Affect Personality?

It would be surprising if personality were totally unaffected by the surrounding culture (which here is defined broadly to include parental influences and expectations, gender roles, and friendship roles). Obviously, no person lives in a vacuum; leaving questions of temperament aside, we can readily observe that all of us are influenced in one way or another by the environment.

The early work on culture and personality, pioneered by Margaret Mead and others more than half a century ago, focused largely on intensive investigations of a single culture. More recent studies have employed a comparative approach in which at least two distinctly different cultures are researched on selected characteristics. Whiting and Whiting (1975), for example, compared six cultures that were organized according to either nuclear groupings or extended family groupings. In the nuclear family—where parents and their children form small, intimate units—interactions tended to be sociable and relatively democratic. In contrast, extended families consisting of several generations (often segregated by sex) tended to encourage aggressive and authoritarian behaviors.

Other research has identified more similarity than variability among cultures. Heath (1977), for example, evaluated the criteria for student maturity in Italy, Turkey, and the United States. Mature students in all cultures were labeled as realistic, purposeful, rational, and fulfilling their potential, among other descriptions. However, U.S. judges also selected energetic, enthusiastic, and aggressive as characteristics of mature students. Thus, the values to which a culture aspires will inevitably be reflected by the personalities that are, in part, molded by that society.

Of course, culture and personality interact and the differences among cultures are frequently not very dramatic. Probably more variation occurs within most cultures than would be found, on the average, from one culture to the next. Nonetheless, in the extensive work of Holtzman, Diaz-Guerrero, and Swartz (1975), over 80 percent of the more than 100 variables studied yielded significant differences between Mexican and U.S. groups. The samples were carefully matched according to age, sex, and socioeconomic status in a sequential design. The study was initiated with first, fourth, and seventh graders who were followed for 6 years. A major distinction between the two cultures emerged from the data analysis. Holtzman (1982) offers the following personality portraits:

> An active style of coping, with all of its cognitive and behavioral implications, involves perceiving problems as existing in the physical and social environment. A passive style of coping assumes that, while problems may be posed by the environment, the best way to cope with them is to change oneself to adapt to circumstances . . . American children tend to be more actively independent and to struggle for a mastery of problems and challenges in their environment, whereas Mexican children are more passively obedient and adapt to stresses in the environment rather than try to change them (pp. 245–246).

The responsibilities various cultures impose on children have a powerful influence on the development of the children's personalities.

Clearly, whatever individual differences are always present within a society, fundamental values may subtly affect the roles, perceptions, and behaviors of its members.

A surprising phenomenon is the lack of research comparing adult personality characteristics of one culture with those of another. Nearly all the recent cross-cultural work involves children and adolescents, with only occasional references to adults in the context of parent-child relationships or gender role development. Although anthropologists have long been interested in studying the personality characteristics of other cultures, the controlled comparisons needed are, with certain exceptions, conspicuously absent. A number of attempts have been made to translate personality tests into other languages, but often this research is fragmented, not carefully controlled, and rarely concerned with developmental issues. Of course, inherent difficulties are involved in equating the meaning and understanding of personality in other cultures with our own. Furthermore, the notion of personality assessment itself may appear unusual or incomprehensible from another cultural perspective. Although it is undoubtedly easier to conduct cross-cultural research with children, particularly using nonverbal methods, the full impact of social variations may be felt most acutely during adulthood. We can expect to find increased interest in studying the comparative patterns of development as concomitant advances are made both in cross-cultural research designs and in techniques for evaluating the personality.

An interesting direction for newer research will be to integrate the variations in cultural influences with individual differences in temperament. Comparisons between Caucasian-American and Chinese-American infants, for example, reveal that the Chinese-American babies show greater restraint when challenged by novel situations (Kagan, 1984), and they also seem to be more easy to quiet when distressed (Freedman, 1976) than Caucasian-American babies. Gannon and Korn (1983) have demonstrated that in Puerto Rican working-class families, preschool children with difficult temperaments do not tend to display greater behavioral problems than their temperamentally easier peers. Are these findings the result of genetic differences in temperament, or do they reflect variations in parenting styles, or some combinations of these influences? Ethnic differences in personality development do exist, but the puzzle has yet to be completed in terms of their biological versus cultural contributions.

Does Personality Change Across the Life Span?

The two preceding sections have noted the biological and cultural components of personality development. Based on the evidence available, we might draw the conclusion that personality remains relatively unchanged from infancy through adulthood. Despite strong biological foundations and the possibility of a consistent cultural background, the notion of personality *development* suggests that change can and does occur. Developmental change is a consequence of hereditary and environmental factors interacting to create unique patterns of individual growth. Therefore, the particular experiences that people have as they mature do influence the nature of personality development.

Comprehensive studies of personality stability versus change across the life span have yet to be conducted. The ideal plan for such research would be to include several cultures, several age cohorts, and evaluations of the participants from birth to death. Needless to say, this task would require the cooperation of an international group of developmentalists over multiple generations.

At present, we can identify three general positions on personality stability and change. One view, which has probably received the most empirical support, suggests that substantial continuity of a core set of temperaments exists throughout life and is only minimally affected by environmental factors or developmental changes. A second position focuses on personality change as a function of reasonably predictable life stages or crises. Erikson's theory has provided one framework for hypothesizing such changes. The third approach to stability versus change emphasizes the change position, but not in a universal or biological sense. Instead, change is regarded as resulting from particular social and cultural expectations, experiences, or marker events (Neugarten, 1977). We will discuss research that bears on each of the three perspectives.

Paul Costa and Robert McCrae (McCrae & Costa, 1984) have become leading advocates of the view that personality is stable from adulthood through old age. They have reviewed their own data and other longitudinal or sequential evidence (to rule out cohort effects) and are convinced that "we should begin to reconsider the advisability of continuing our quest for developmental changes in personality" (Costa & McCrae, 1980, p. 11). For example, Siegler, George, and Okun (1979) studied men and women between the ages of 54 and 70 for an 8-year period using the Cattell Sixteen Personality Factor Questionnaire. The results indicated consistency on virtually all factors. A similar study was done by Schaie and Parham (1976) on a larger sample over a longer span of years. They concluded that

> stability of personality traits is the rule rather than the exception, but that such stability, nevertheless cannot be attributed to lack of change after adolescence, as most traditional personality theorists might believe. Rather, in the 19 personality traits studied here much change was observed. The change, however, is a function of specific early socialization experiences, commonly shared generation-specific environmental impact, and particular sociocultural transitions that may affect individuals at all ages. (Schaie & Parham, 1976, p. 157)

Research on the stability of personality is not as convincing between infancy and adolescence as it is during the adulthood years; difficulties in using the same assessment methods across this earlier time interval may be largely responsible. In other words, the temperament of an infant or a toddler cannot be measured with the same tools used to evaluate the personality of an older child or an adolescent. Block (1971), MacFarlane (1964), and others have, nevertheless, demonstrated a number of aspects of consistency in child personality. Kagan and Moss (1962) provided similar data, while pointing out the need to look for gender differences and to note how stable aspects of personality may appear in a somewhat different form at various stages of development. These apparent changes in previous patterns are referred to as *sleeper effects.*

Sleeper effects
Stable aspects of personality that may appear in a somewhat different form at various stages of development.

One of the most detailed studies of personality development was conducted by Lois Murphy and her associates (Murphy & Moriarty, 1976). She began her longitudinal work when the subjects were infants and examined their development at the preschool level and again at early adolescence. The focus of the research was continuity or change in coping abilities. Murphy used a variety of observational and quantitative methods for assessing her subjects—home visits, parent and child interviews, psychological tests, pediatric examinations, and parent diaries. Much careful thought was devoted to analyzing the children's developmental status at each juncture of the study.

Many findings can be derived from Murphy's work. For example, the stability of physiological responses during infancy—such as heart rate or perspiration—was correlated with preschool personality characteristics. Greater physiological stability was associated with more independence from parents. On the other hand, physiological instability was related to higher levels of anxiety. More surprising, due to the longer time interval between measurements, were relations that linked infant and adolescent behaviors. For instance, the sensory reactivity of babies was associated with social perceptiveness, pleasure in tactile stimulation, and a curiosity about new experiences in adolescence. The researchers suggested an openness to the environment at infancy continues to elicit positive social and physical feedback throughout childhood, encouraging a pattern of highly aware and perceptive interactions.

At the same time as they noted consistency from infancy to adolescence, Murphy and Moriarty also suggested patterns of change. Some aspects of personality development (e.g., greater degrees of impulse control) seem to be a predictable function of maturity. However, the ability to adapt to change itself showed variations in style. The coping patterns of 57 percent of the sample remained consistent over the years, while the remainder of the sample showed a wide range of styles and effectiveness. Moriarty and Toussieng (1976), in completing the analysis of Murphy's subjects during adolescence, emphasized the significance of parenting style in contributing to the coping strategies developed. For example, extremely obedient and traditional adolescents probably had parents who were overly controlling and inflexible, whereas imaginative and risk-taking teenagers were likely to have had parents with unusual, less conservative values.

Perhaps the most popular and appealing view of personality development posits a sequence of stages that we can all expect to encounter as we grow older. The majority of research supporting a discontinuity approach to development has been completed on fairly small samples (usually males) from a single cohort. For example, the work of Levinson (1978) and Vaillant (1977) was concerned with U.S. men born during the 1920s. Levinson compared the lives of 40 males, especially between late adolescence and middle age, and arrived at a pattern of changes that characterized their progression through this part of the life span (see Figure 10.2). Gould (1978) has offered a remarkably similar stage theory involving a larger sample of men and women.

The crux of the life stage position is not that every person responds in the same way to the circumstances of chronological age, but that the insights from common patterns allow us to anticipate and accommodate to the inevitable changes. Levinson (1978) explained:

> The eras and periods are grounded in the nature of man as a biological, psychological and social organism, and in the nature of society as a complex enterprise extending over many generations. They represent the life cycle of the species. Individuals go through the periods in infinitely varied ways, but the periods themselves are universal. These eras and periods have governed human development for the past five or ten thousand years—since the beginning of more complex stable societies. (p. 322)

Figure 10.2
*Developmental Periods in Early
and Middle Adulthood*

Source: D. J. Levinson. *The seasons of a man's life.* New York:
Knopf, 1978, p. 57. Reprinted by
permission of the Sterling Lord
Agency, Inc. Copyright © 1978
by Daniel Levinson.

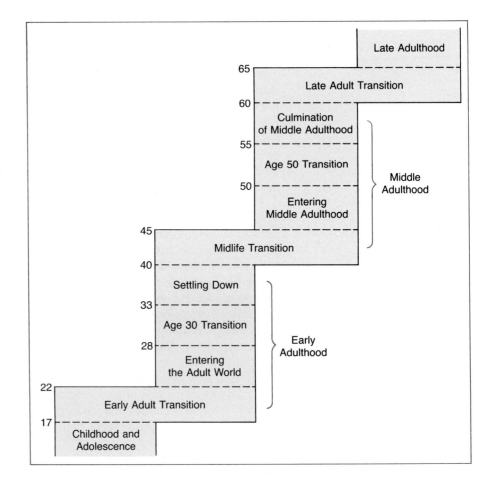

Additional studies that provide some support for the notion of adolescent
and adult developmental stages were conducted by Haan and Day (1974)
and Whitbourne and Waterman (1979). The latter suggested that the "data
presently available do provide a basis for inferring predictable change,
rather than stability" (p. 378).

Despite the continued interest in and restatement of the stage approach
to personality development beyond childhood and adolescence (Levinson,
1986), only a small percentage of theorists believe that regular periods of
adult life will be identifiable. Siegler (1987) stated strongly that "there is little
evidence supporting the hypothesis that the aging processes per se are
responsible for personality changes" (p. 520). The human tendency to
structure and sequence our own lives may be leading us to attribute more
predictability to adult personality development than is warranted. Stage
approaches, however, do offer convenient categorical benchmarks to help us

organize our understanding of complex developmental phenomena. Perhaps the scope of these theoretical blankets needs to be limited and linked more closely to both stability and random factors in personality.

Whereas the concept of typical developmental stages in personality has been taken for granted by many clinicians working with children, the view that discontinuity is unpredictable has been promoted by adulthood and gerontological researchers. Neugarten (1979) agreed that development involves personality change; however, she criticized stage theories as overly simplified. She believes that adults change in significant ways that are less regular than children's development. According to Neugarten, such changes are overlapping, follow no ordered sequence, are not related to chronological age, and do not displace previous characteristics. Instead, she postulated that various cultures and historical periods have particular age norms regarding what is appropriate for different ages.

Some societies are more rigid about age distinctions than others, but all people have internalized a timetable (or social clock) for right and wrong behaviors. These expectations refer to child development, as well as adult prescriptions. Not all cultures, for example, consider infancy and early childhood as separate stages, nor is the notion of adolescence universal. Furthermore, Neugarten and Peterson (1957) have found that self-perceptions of developmental stages are related to socioeconomic status (for example, blue-collar workers have an earlier "prime of life"). Thus, stability and change in personality may reflect consistency and variability in socially and psychologically meaningful experiences rather than in biological or developmental universals.

Developmental regularities appear to be more difficult to support beyond the adolescent years. As we noted earlier with regard to Piaget's cognitive theory, it may be similarly necessary to place less trust in stages of adult personality development. Datan, Rodeheaver, and Hughes (1987) have suggested that the debate between orderly progression and stability in adult development has been replaced "by an increasing attention to the contexts of change and continuity, and to the individual's construction of the life course" (p. 165). Continuity surely is a function of each person's attempt to maintain unity of the self, yet one of the freedoms of adulthood is a wider opportunity for making the choices and decisions that partly create our developmental paths. Research on adult personality is readily beginning to incorporate a phenomenological perspective; that is, the subjective accounts of an individual's own development are taken as seriously as the presumably objective stance of the investigator.

How Does Personality Development Deviate from "Normality"?

Since Freud's pioneering work at the turn of the century, a great deal of interest has been shown in abnormal variations of personality development. However, only since the 1970s has a genuine effort been made to create a specialty that blends the expertise of clinicians with that of developmental-ists (Cicchetti, 1984). Before then, most psychologists were either practitioners who tried to alleviate personality problems or academicans who researched normative behavior and development. The focus on pathology has now been joined with the perspective of "normal" development to create a specialty known as *developmental psychopathology*. Sroufe and Rutter (1984) proposed that developmental psychopathology be defined "as the study of the origins and course of individual patterns of behavioral maladaptation" (p. 18).

Sroufe and Rutter pointed out the difficulties of tracing the path of psychopathology across development, as well as the promise such research presents to our understanding of personality changes. Studies of developmental psychopathology will need to be expensive, demanding, and time-consuming. Longitudinal designs should be framed within the context of relevant developmental theory, although uncovering the links between earlier behavior and later pathology will not always be easy. The connections may be paradoxical and initially ambiguous. However, this exploration of abnormal development will help to clarify the issue of stability versus change in personality. A more significant effect of progress in this field is the potential to prevent serious pathology and to remediate any problems before they become rigid patterns.

Perhaps the central issue in the study of developmental psychopathology is where to draw the line between normal and abnormal behavior. In cases of extreme deviation from typical development—such as a 4-year-old child who does not use any language, a 50-year-old man who has never been able to hold a steady job, a 10-year-old boy who still sucks his thumb, a 30-year-old woman who consumes 25,000 calories daily, or a 16-year-old girl who has no friends—there is little disagreement that a problem exists. We need to recognize, however, that as behaviors, particularly social and emotional ones, become less deviant from typical patterns of development, the classification of a person as abnormal is increasingly colored by personally and culturally defined judgments. Labeling someone according to a statistical departure from "average" or from "ideal" is, nevertheless, the common yardstick for determining psychopathology.

Whereas the values of the culture, and the typical behaviors found within it, provide a standard for judging deviance, caution in designating an individual as abnormal is still warranted. For example, how far from the average does one need to be—in the ability to throw a ball, to use language, or to get along with peers—to be considered deviant? On what basis do we determine whether a person's behavior is sufficiently divergent from the ideal so that he or she requires therapeutic intervention—the guidelines of a particular theory; the context of the family, classroom, workplace, or neighborhood; or the person's own previous actions? The answer, of course, is that all these factors need to be taken into account. In addition, the longevity of a problem, its age of onset, and its impact on other children or adults must be incorporated by a professional evaluating the behaviors.

Beyond knowing whether to label a person as deviant, we may also question how the psychopathology itself should be classified. For instance, how do we distinguish mental retardation from autism or hyperactivity from learning disabilities or anxiety from depression? Overlapping symptoms, multiple abnormalities, and similar causes may be operating. This confusion is compounded by the differences between child and adult pathology and the communication difficulties therapists have with younger children, infants, or the elderly.

Although the reliability and validity of current diagnostic criteria are debatable (Garber, 1984), three broad categories of abnormality simplify the situation. First, a widely reported category of deviance is undercontrolled behavior disorders, such as hyperactivity and aggression. Substance abuse or criminal activity may also reflect a similar lack of control. Overcontrolled behavior disorders represent a second, and in many ways opposite, category of psychopathology. This category includes fears, anxiety, and depression that can have physical manifestations such as eating disorders, tics, stuttering, or sleepwalking. Finally, the rarest and most extreme disturbances are termed pervasive developmental disorders. Such individuals are highly incapacitated and may be out of touch with reality. Examples of this category range from autism to mental retardation to schizophrenia.

The debate about classification of developmental psychopathology is too extensive to be treated further here. Similarly, another textbook could be written to describe possible treatment approaches. For example, do we use medication or family counseling to help the hyperactive child? Is adult depression best treated in psychotherapy or through behavior modification? Most research on intervention in developmental psychopathology is relatively recent, and the likelihood is that serious deviations will require multifaceted treatment programs. Throughout this book, abnormal patterns

Snorting cocaine is an illegal activity, but is this adolescent simply engaging in curious experimentation and social behavior, or has he crossed the line and entered the realm of developmental psychopathology?

of development have been discussed at appropriate topical points. Integrating aspects of pathology in this manner contributes to the attitude that such developmental deviations be viewed as continuous with normative patterns of change.

One point of convergence between normal and abnormal development is the occurrence of a temporary crisis. Most human beings confront crises at various points throughout the life span. Crises, take different forms. In one sense, the time periods when they occur, such as the fabled adolescent identity crisis or the adult mid-life crisis, determine the nature of the conflicts. The degree of stress triggered by the crisis is another important factor, although the same type of crisis for one person may be much less stressful for another. Even death itself does not have to be regarded as a crisis, depending on a host of other variables (Kastenbaum, 1975).

Neugarten (1970) has suggested that events will precipitate a life crisis only when they have not been anticipated. Predictable change allows smoother adaptation, which makes the use of the term *crisis* something of a distortion. Unexpected events, however—(violations of age norms, such as a 36-year-old becoming a grandparent or a young child dying)—are often most distressing. The concept of life crisis is intimately connected to the perspectives on developmental change. We must ask, therefore, if crises are "normal" because everyone experiences them or because they are likely to occur at periodic intervals. In either case, theorists such as Riegel (1975) view most crises as the basis for developmental progression and creative innovation.

Whether or not crisis is beneficial, and regardless of how we choose to label the situation—marker event, transition or conflict—can we expect to have regular life crises? Although cross-cultural evidence has long contradicted the notion of a universal adolescent crisis, people still believe that this is a time of major turmoil, at least in Western cultures. Many researchers, however, agree with Offer and Offer (1975) that "the data lead us to hypothesize that adolescence, as a stage in life, is not a uniquely stressful period" (p. 197). This position suggests that an adolescent personality crisis would be consistent with earlier abnormality as well as predictive of future crises. In contrast, Levinson, Darrow, Klein, Levinson, and McKee (1974) believe that adolescents who have not experienced a crisis will be unprepared to cope with difficulties in adulthood.

As for the mid-life crisis, Levinson (1978) reported that for 80 percent of his sample, "this period evokes tumultuous struggles within the self and with the external world" (p. 199). However, the research of McCrae and Costa (1984) and other investigators does not support the conclusion that the period designated by Levinson (ages 40 to 45) is especially dominated by so-called mid-life issues. For example, Cooper (cited in Costa & McCrae, 1980) found no significant differences between groups of men ages 35 to 79 on job or marital dissatisfaction, disharmony with children, inner turmoil, change in time perspective, view of life as tedious, or sense of separation from parents.

Even the marker events that are not directly linked to specific chronological ages do not always justify the use of the term *crisis*. For instance, Lowenthal and Chiriboga's (1972) work on the transition to the "empty nest," which may occur in the fourth, fifth, or sixth decade of life, implies that it is not necessarily a threatening prospect. They found that many adults look forward to the imminent departure of their youngest child from home (see Chapter 11). Neugarten (1979) claims that when children fail to leave home a crisis may ensue (for both parents and children).

The perception of crisis in either unpredictable or normative form, therefore, is highly subjective. Although the belief that the age of 40 represents a major turning point in life is not without some support, this remains controversial. Similarly, the psychoanalytic notion of toilet-training trauma does not need to be considered a universal crisis. Everyone is aware of the various reactions, ranging from complete ecstasy to utter despair, that may accompany job retirement. Thus, perhaps the correlates and consequences of developmental crisis require further elaboration and clarification. Neugarten (1977) has stated that explaining the relationship between life transitions and personality would benefit

> by focusing more attention upon the issues that are of major concern to the individual—what the person selects as important in his past and his present, what he hopes to do in the future, what he predicts will occur, what strategies he elects, and what meanings he attaches to time, life, and death. In short, psychologists would do well to make greater use of the person himself as the reporting and predicting agent, and by gathering systematic and repeated self-reports along with other types of data, to combine the phenomenological and the "objective" perspectives. (pp. 639–640)

Our discussion of personality and the self has demonstrated that different theories may play a valuable role in conceptualizing the nature of development. Dynamic relationships and intrapsychic conflict relate to life crises, emotional patterns, and social behavior. Behavioral observations are necessary to confirm internal perspectives and to standardize the comparative process. Temperamental qualities remind us of our biological heritage and point the way toward human stability. Contextual factors must be considered to frame our development in cultural and societal terms. Phenomenological interpretations portray the core of personality, allowing us to understand our own well-being and our capacity to adapt to change.

There are no simple ways to describe personality development across the life span. This chapter has attempted to highlight just a small sample of the concepts, theories, and problems of contemporary interest. Some of these controversial conceptual and research issues include awareness versus the unconscious, nature versus nurture, stages versus events, stability versus change, normality versus abnormality, and the subjective versus the objective. The evidence deriving from apparently contradictory positions suggests that the self incorporates each of these ambiguities within the totality of human development.

Summary

1. Personality is a complex phenomenon involving both stability and change. Psychodynamic and phenomenological theorists have focused on how the interactions of biology and the environment lead to the development of personality.

2. Two fundamental principles of Freud's theory are psychic determinism and unconscious motivation. Two opposing energy forces, eros and thanatos, stimulate personality development.

3. Freud believed that personality is made up of three major structures: the id, the ego, and the superego. Conflict among these structures is related to mental health.

4. Early development, according to Freud, can be analyzed by the main biological feature of each stage. The oral stage of infancy and the anal stage of toddlerhood are followed by the phallic stage of early childhood. Middle childhood, called latency, lacks a strong psychosexual component.

5. The adolescent and adult years are labeled the genital stage, during which sexuality, aggression, and the experiences from previous development need to be reconciled.

6. Erikson offers a contemporary interpretation of psychoanalytic theory. His theory is more social, optimistic, ego-oriented, and life span—oriented than Freud's perspective. Erikson views development as a series of eight psychosocial crises within a cultural context: basic trust versus mistrust, autonomy versus shame or doubt, initiative versus guilt, industry versus inferiority, identity versus confusion, intimacy versus isolation, generativity versus stagnation, and ego integrity versus despair.

7. Phenomenological theories are unusual because they attempt to examine personality from the perspective of the individual rather than from an objective stance.

8. Maslow's research on exceptional individuals led him to suggest a hierarchy of needs preceding self-actualization. Personality is strongly influenced by the level of needs currently faced.

9. Investigations of self-concept and self-esteem represent a valuable, integrative way to explore personality development. The self is influenced by cognitive and social components of development, as well as a tendency toward a sense of unity.

10. In contrast to self-concept, patterns of self-esteem do not appear linked to particular ages, but rather to periods of transition or to other factors in overall life satisfaction.

11. The concept of self is quite varied among people of different ages. Research clearly suggests that infants, children, adolescents, and adults focus on very different qualities in themselves and do not construct their worlds from similar perspectives.

12. Temperamental origins may provide the basis for future personality. The theories of Buss and Plomin and of Thomas, Chess, and their associates have offered extensive evidence to support this position.

13. The environmental constraints of cultural background play a crucial part in personality development. Cross-cultural research, despite limitations, has revealed both similarities and differences among various groups.

14. Disentangling the research on stability versus change has been difficult. The evidence for personality consistency is impressive but incomplete; however, patterns of change can be attributed to both normative development and to environmental variation. Particularly beyond adolescence, the burden of proof seems to lie with those espousing a universal sequence of personality development.

15. Developmental psychopathology is a relatively new and important specialty. It combines interest in normative patterns of change with an

understanding of deviant behaviors. Neither classification nor treatment of individuals is easy because defining pathology is colored by cultural and personal values and may be mistaken for temporary crises, which are subjective and possibly beneficial.

Key Terms

cathexis (p. 392)
ego (p. 388)
epigenetic principle
  (p. 396)
fixation (p. 393)
hierarchy of needs
  (p. 406)

id (p. 388)
imaginary audience
  (p. 414)
libido (p. 386)
primary process thinking
  (p. 388)

psychosocial crisis
  (p. 396)
secondary process think-
  ing (p. 388)
self-actualization
  (p. 406)

self-concept (p. 409)
self-esteem (p. 409)
sleeper effects (p. 424)
superego (p. 388)
temperament (p. 418)

Review Questions

1. Select any one of Freud's early stages of development—oral, anal, or phallic—and describe how it may be related to adult development. Your discussion should include reference to Freud's major principles, energy forces, personality structures, and so on.
2. Why did Erikson feel the need to modify Freud's theory of personality development? Choose any two of Erikson's stages to illustrate specific differences between his view and Freud's regarding the significant qualities of those age periods.
3. The phenomenological approach to personality, exemplified by the work of Maslow, focuses on the perspective of the self. Compare and contrast aspects of his theory with the psychodynamic views of Freud or Erikson. Use the terminology appropriate to each theorist.
4. Highlight features of the development of self-concept and self-esteem from infancy through adult-

hood. Give specific examples of research on the self for each phase of the life span and indicate what it means for our understanding of developmental change.
5. The nature-nurture debate pervades research and theory in personality development. Explain how this occurs by evaluating the evidence for temperamental factors on the one hand and cultural influences on the other. Which position do you find more persuasive? Why?
6. Discuss the concept of personality crisis. How does this relate to the major questions of stability versus change and normality versus abnormality? Can we conclude that crisis is predictable or irregular? Include several examples of life-span research in your analysis.

Suggested Readings

Bengtson, V. L., Reedy, M. N., & Gordon, C. (1985). Aging and self-conceptions: Personality processes and social contexts. In J. E. Birren & K. W. Schaie (Eds.), *Handbook of the psychology of aging* (2nd ed.). New York: Van Nostrand Reinhold.

A detailed and excellent review of the research and theoretical literature, including methodological issues, on personality development during the adulthood years—but not an easy chapter to read.

Chess, S. & Thomas, A. (1984). *Origins and evolution of behavior disorders: Infancy to early adult life.* New York: Brunner/Mazel.

The most recent work of this eminent team, following up on their longitudinal studies of infant temperament as their subjects reach adulthood. This interesting and readable presentation focuses on developmental problems.

Erikson, E. H. (1963). *Childhood and society* (2nd ed.). New York: Norton.

> An illuminating collection of essays by our foremost contemporary psychoanalyst of infantile sexuality, cross-cultural patterns, play, developmental stages, and psychohistory.

Harter, S. (1983). Developmental perspective on the self-system. In P. H. Mussen (Ed.), *Handbook of child psychology* (4th ed., Vol. 4). New York: Wiley.

> An extensive and authoritative overview of the theory and research on self-concept and self-esteem. This chapter will be tough for students, but it covers the issues pertaining to childhood too thoroughly to pass up altogether.

Kegan, R. (1982). *The evolving self: Problems and processes in human development.* Cambridge, MA: Harvard University Press.

> An important book that attempts to link personality from a more phenomenological perspective with a Piagetian process approach. The result is an intriguing spiral of stages between independence and inclusion.

White, R. W. (1975). *Lives in progress: A study of the natural growth of personality* (3rd ed.). New York: Holt, Rinehart & Winston.

> An enjoyable account of how patterns of childhood lead to adult personality. This paperback, a delightfully written classic, incorporates theory in personality development with several excellent case histories.

Chapter Eleven

Family Development

The Family System

The Family Life Cycle
Marriage
Becoming a Parent: The Childbearing Years
The Childhood Years of the Family
The Adult Family

The Disrupted Family
Divorce: The Adult's Point of View
Divorce: The Child's Point of View
Stepparents and Stepchildren

Human development is an individual process, and yet none of us develops in isolation. We are all individual human beings, but we are also fathers, mothers, brothers or sisters, sons or daughters, husbands or wives. All of us are grandchildren, and some of us are grandparents. We influence and are influenced by every other person with whom we interact, and perhaps most particularly, we influence and are influenced by our families.

THE FAMILY SYSTEM

The human family is not simply a collection of individuals living in the same household; it is a *system,* and as such it has a number of features (Mattessich & Hill, 1987). The first feature of the family system is its *interdependence:* The goals, behaviors, and developmental patterns of individual family members continuously influence and are influenced by the goals, behaviors, and developmental patterns of all other members of the family. A second feature of the family system is *boundary maintenance:* Families create boundaries through which outsiders are not allowed to pass, so that each family has its own distinct culture and heritage. Third, the family system is marked by constant *adaptation to change:* The family fluctuates as new members are added, as the needs of family members change as they develop, and as members leave the family unit. Indeed, as will be discussed later in this chapter, a substantial number of American families experience major reorganization because of divorce and remarriage. Finally, the family system is characterized by *task performance:* To guarantee its survival, the family unit must perform a variety of tasks, including the physical maintenance of the home and of the people in it, the production and socialization of children, and the maintenance of morale and psychological well-being (Mattessich & Hill, 1987).

Throughout this chapter, we will highlight essential themes from the various phases of the family life cycle and focus on the *norms* of family life. The concept of family can be defined in numerous ways. Marriage is the preferred living arrangement for most men and women in the United States, yet we have witnessed recent dramatic increases in the likelihood that couples will live together without a marriage contract. The majority of U.S. marriages last until the death of one spouse, yet the divorce rate has risen markedly in the past few decades. For every nine married couples who become parents, one couple never has the experience of raising a child. Most U.S. families comprise married couples with children, yet one family in four is headed by a single parent. Finally, a family may consist of people who are not related to one another, either by law or by blood.

THE FAMILY LIFE CYCLE

Just as the life span of an individual can be divided into theoretical stages, so, too, can the life span of a family. In some sense, a family, unlike an individual, lives on indefinitely, but we are here defining the family life cycle with reference to the life span of a particular couple. Thus, the family life cycle begins when a couple first establishes a relationship, which can range from a brief sexual encounter to a lifelong association, and the cycle ends when both parties have died. In the intervening years, a variety of tasks are accomplished, which vary, of course, depending on the composition of the family.

In most U.S. families, couples initially face the challenge of adjusting to living together as partners. Most couples then choose to extend the family by bearing children, and they experience the joys and stresses caused by the arrival of their offspring. As children grow, parents are continuously challenged to provide direction and emotional support. Later in the family cycle, the now middle-aged parent must attempt to loosen the ties that were formed earlier and launch the children successfully into the adult world. Then many couples must cope with the task of rebuilding their relationship with each other when the children have gone. Some must adjust to the role of grandparents, and accept the death of their partner.

Table 11.1, based on research and theory from a variety of sources (Duvall, 1977; Hill & Rodgers, 1964; Mattessich & Hill, 1987; Rollins & Feldman, 1970), depicts the stages of the family life cycle that is most commonly found in the United States, the characteristics of husbands and wives at each stage, and the constantly changing nature of a family's goals.

Marriage

As we noted earlier, marriage is, and always has been, the living arrangement of choice for most American couples. The percentage of Americans choosing to marry has varied somewhat, but, in the twentieth century at least, it has usually remained in the vicinity of 90 percent, indicating that marriage seems to have considerable appeal. Its appeal is further illustrated by statistics pertaining to remarriage after divorce. Most divorced people, approximately 85 percent of the men and 75 percent of the women, marry again, with an average span of just 3 years between divorce and remarriage (Teachman, Polonko, & Scanzoni, 1987).

Nevertheless, despite a pattern of relative stability, changes in coupling patterns in the United States within the last three decades are worthy of note. These include changes in (1) overall marriage rate, (2) age at first marriage, (3) likelihood of cohabitation, (4) definition of marriage roles, and (5) rate of divorce. We shall discuss the rising U.S. divorce rate and its implications for family development in a later section of this chapter. Let us turn now to a discussion of the other recent trends.

Overall Marriage Rate

As noted, throughout this century, most Americans, approximately 9 out of every 10, marry at some time in their lives, and this percentage remained relatively stable until the early 1970s (Glick, 1977; Schoen, Urton, & Baj, 1985). However, the overall marriage rate in the United States has declined steadily every year since 1972. The marriage rate in 1985, for example, was particularly low compared to prior years and showed a drop of 4 percent from the year before (National Center for Health Statistics, 1988).

Table 11.1
Stages of the Family Life Cycle and Degree of Marital and Life Satisfaction at Each Stage

Stage	Age of Couple	Number of Years in Stage	Major Goal of the Family	Percent Always Satisfied With Marriage		Percent Very Satisfied With Life in General	
				H	W	H	W
Establishment (married, no children)	H 22–23 W 20–21	1	Adjusting to living as a couple	41	27	74	55
Childbearing (infants and preschool children)	H 24–30 W 22–28	6	Developing attachment between parent and child. Recognizing and adapting to the needs of infants and young children.	22–31	14–17	50–76	61–69
School-age (one or more children in elementary school)	H 30–37 W 28–35	7	Adjusting to the expanding world of school-children. Encouraging educational achievement.	11	14	35	39
Adolescence (one or more teenage children)	H 37–44 W 35–42	7	Recognizing the adolescent's need for freedom. Gradually allowing greater degrees of independence and encouraging the adolescent to behave responsibly.	14	18	17	44
Transition (children entering adulthood)	H 44–52 W 42–50	8	Launching young adults out of the home and into the world. Relinquishing the role of parent while maintaining a supportive home base.	20	27	9	9
Postparental (parents middle-aged; children no longer at home)	H 52–65 W 50–64	14	Reestablishing the husband-wife relationship. Assuming the role of grandparent.	17	27	17	24
Retirement	H 66–death W 64—death	3–13?	Adjusting to retirement and to aging. Coping with death of spouse and living alone.	38	42	82	66

Source: Adapted from "Life Cycle and Family Development" by P. Mattessich and R. Hill, in *Handbook of Marriage and the Family* (p. 447) by M. B. Sussman and S. K. Steinmetz (eds), 1987, New York: Plenum Publishing. Copyright 1987 by Plenum Publishing Corporation. Adapted by permission.

How do we interpret the decline in the overall marriage rate? Is there general disillusionment with marriage in our society? Some sociologists (e.g., Cherlin, 1988a, 1988b; Norton & Moorman, 1987) suggest that the declining marriage rate may represent only a normal falling off from the unusually high marriage rates of the late 1940s and 1950s—a return to what has been a more normal pattern in the United States. They also point out that, despite the decline, between 85 and 90 percent of U.S. women and between 90 and 95 percent of U.S. men will continue to opt for marriage as their preferred living arrangement.

Age at First Marriage

One of the most significant recent changes in U.S. marriage patterns has been an increase in the average age at first marriage by about 3 years for both women (from 20.3 to 23.6 years) and men (from 22.5 to 25.9 years) since 1960 (National Center for Health Statistics, 1988; Norton & Moorman, 1987; Rodgers & Thornton, 1985; U.S. Bureau of the Census, 1989). Dramatic declines have occurred in teenage marriages and in marriages of persons aged 20–25 years (Bumpass & Sweet, 1989).

Rate of Cohabitation

Cohabitation

A living arrangement in which two adults live together as a couple but without a marriage contract.

Since the 1960s, the incidence of **cohabitation**—a couple's living together without a marriage contract—has increased significantly (Bumpass & Sweet, 1989; Bumpass, Sweet, & Cherlin, 1989; Cherlin, 1981; Glick & Spanier, 1980; Macklin, 1978; Teachman et al., 1987). In 1978, for example, some 1.1 million households in the United States consisted of unmarried couples; this was almost double the number found in 1960 (Doherty & Jacobson, 1982). In 1970, an estimated 11 percent of U.S. married couples had lived together before marriage, while the figure for the early 1980s was 44 percent (Bumpass et al., 1989). Similar trends have been observed in other countries, such as France (Leridon & Villeneuve-Gokalp, 1988) and Australia (Bracher & Santow, 1988).

Do any characteristics appear consistently among cohabiting couples in the United States? On the basis of their national survey of over 13,000 respondents, Bumpass and Sweet (1989) concluded that cohabitants are not young, radical college students of the popular 1970s stereotype, nor are they all yuppies engaged in trial marriages. Cohabitants are found among every age group, and many—approximately 40 percent—have children; two-thirds of these children are the products of previous relationships, while one-third were born to the cohabiting couple. Far from being middle-class college students, cohabitants tend to be less well educated than the norm and are more likely to have come from poorer families and single-parent households. Regarding the stereotype that cohabitation is a trial run for marriage, 70 percent of cohabitants do expect someday to marry their partners, but one in four say they have no plans to marry anybody (Bumpass et al., 1989)!

Cohabitation is usually a temporary arrangement, lasting an average of 1½ years, with fewer than 10 percent of couples continuing to cohabitate for 5 years or longer. Most cohabitants either marry (60 percent) or break up (40 percent) within a fairly short time (Bumpass & Sweet, 1989; Macklin, 1978).

Marriage Roles

The impersonal statistics about trends in American marriage do not provide the whole story, of course. Marriage and divorce rates tell us little about how people define their relationships, and we should not assume that the experience of marriage today is the same as it is has always been. In fact, marriage roles—the behavioral expectations of husbands and wives—seem to be in a state of transition.

Three different types of marriage roles exist in our society today (Peplau, 1983). In a *traditional marriage,* the sex roles are highly specialized. The husband is the provider and the ultimate decision maker, although he delegates decision-making authority in certain areas (e.g., home management, child care) to his wife. The wife's traditional role is that of homemaker, caretaker of children, companion, confidante, sex partner, and nurse.

In a *modern marriage,* the husband is less dominant, and the marriage roles are less highly specialized. The husband often shares housekeeping responsibilities, and the wife often works outside the home. Nevertheless, the wife's outside job is considered less important than the husband's job; if their jobs conflict, his comes first. In addition, the wife must not let her outside work interfere with housekeeping responsibilities; she is expected to accomplish both. Finally, modern marriage roles emphasize emotional closeness and support, as well as shared recreational activities.

Egalitarian marriage, which rejects male dominance and the role specialization found in traditional marriage, is an ideal that some couples strive to achieve rather than a common pattern in the United States today. If traditional marriage represents our past and modern marriage represents our present, then egalitarian marriage may be the marriage of the future. In such a relationship, the partners share equally in power and responsibility, both in the home and outside it. Both husband and wife are wage earners, and both are equally involved in household responsibilities such as housekeeping and child care. The closest example of egalitarian marriage is the marriage of the dual-career couple, but even then true equality is seldom attained; the wife typically is more responsible for domestic chores, and the husband's career is seen as the more important (Peplau, 1983; Poloma & Garland, 1971; Yogev, 1981).

An examination of marriage roles suggests that U.S. marriage may be in a transitional state, moving from the traditional to the egalitarian, with modern marriage representing the middle ground. In addition, the existence of all three types of relationships at the same time illustrates the remarkable diversity of American marriage. Perhaps speaking of the characteristics of individual marriages is easier than defining the nature of marriage itself.

Traditional marriage
A marriage in which the roles of husband and wife are highly specialized, with the husband taking the role of provider and primary decision maker and the wife assuming responsibility for running of the household.

Modern marriage
A marriage in which the husband often shares housekeeping responsibilities and the wife often works outside the home, but the husband's career is of primary importance.

Egalitarian marriage
A marriage that is not characterized by elements of domination or role specialization.

Marriage and Life Satisfaction

The appeal of marriage has long been reflected in studies relating marital status to satisfaction with life. For example, in a nationwide survey (Campbell, Converse, & Rodgers, 1976) in which more than 2,000 adults were asked to rate the quality of their lives, married people of all ages, with and without children, were happier as a group than single people. Single people of both genders, whether never married, separated, divorced, or widowed, were all below the average in overall life satisfaction. Even married parents of young children, the group most likely to experience high stress levels, were happier with their lives than were every one of the unmarried groups.

The Campbell, Converse, and Rodgers data were expressed in averages, of course, and are descriptive rather than prescriptive. In other words, the group patterns may not apply to the life of any particular individual. Many single people are extremely happy with their lives, and many married people are miserable. Furthermore, these are correlational data; that married people in general are happier does not mean that marriage makes people happy. Possibly, happier people are simply more likely to get married.

A final point about marriage and life satisfaction reflects the recent trends we have discussed. Since the early 1970s, a steady decline has occurred in the degree of the positive relationship between being married and being happy, primarily because of increases in the reported happiness of never-before married men and decreases in the reported happiness of married women (Glenn & Weaver, 1988).

Becoming a Parent: The Childbearing Years

At some time in their marriages, more than 90 percent of U.S. couples increase the size of their families by becoming parents, a percentage that has remained fairly constant throughout the years (Glick, 1977). Thus the typical family, composed of a husband, a wife, and a child or children, enters a new phase of its development, which will probably last for the next 18 years, and possibly a good deal longer than that.

What motivates a couple to decide to have children? Table 11.2 lists the values of children most frequently mentioned by parents. Determining the precise reasons for childbearing is difficult, actually, because only about half of firstborn children in our society were intentionally conceived (Miller, 1978), and only 63 percent of parents report having given any serious consideration to even the possibility of parenthood (Ory, 1978).

Not all U.S. married couples have children, of course, and not all U.S. children are born to, or raised by, married couples. Much of the research discussed in this chapter, however, deals with child rearing in the traditional intact family. But because considerable diversity exists in the United States today, we shall open this section on child rearing by discussing two variations on the typical familial arrangement—the single-parent family and the family without children.

Table 11.2
Values of Children in Order of
Appearance Across Studies

1. Affectional ties. Having someone to love and be loved by, having a complete family.

2. Stimulation and fun. Enjoyment of playing with them, watching them grow up.

3. Self-expression. Fulfilling oneself, finding a purpose in life.

4. Adult status. Demonstrating maturity and worth, living up to society's expectations.

5. Achievement. Creating a new life, doing a good job.

6. Economic value. Having someone to help you and care for you in your old age.

7. Morality. Being a better person for having children.

Source: Hoffman & Manis (1982); Miller (1987).

The Single-Parent Family

Just as coupling patterns have changed in recent years, the composition of U.S. families with children has also changed. Specifically, the experiences of marriage and parenting are becoming more and more separated, in the sense that the number of families headed by single parents has increased dramatically (Cherlin, 1988a).

According to the 1980 census, approximately 10 million of the 60 million families in the United States were headed by a single parent (U.S. Bureau of the Census, 1980). By the late 1980s, estimates of single-parent families in this country ranged from 20–25 percent of all U.S. households (Cherlin, 1988a, 1988b)! This increase is partly the result of the rising divorce rate, which, as we shall discuss later, doubled from 1960 to 1980, but is also related to increases in the rate of childbearing out of wedlock. In 1965, approximately 7 percent of children born in the United States were born to unmarried women, but by the late 1980s, this percentage had increased to 23 percent (Cherlin, 1988a; Zill & Rogers, 1988)!

Approximately half of all U.S. children born during the 1970s and 1980s will live, for at least a short time, in a single-parent household (Bumpass & Sweet, 1989; Hetherington, 1979; Zill & Rogers, 1988). And most of those children, particularly those from minority groups, will spend a considerable amount of their childhood being raised by a single parent (Bumpass & Sweet, 1989).

But the single-parent household is not a phenomenon peculiar only to the 1970s and 1980s. An examination of available data on familial patterns since 1900 indicates that one-quarter to one-third of U.S. children have *always* had some exposure to disrupted families (Bane, 1979; Raschke,

1987). In the past, however, the death of a parent, rather than divorce or out-of-wedlock birth, usually created single-parent households. One in every 5 children born in 1900 could expect to see a parent die before the child was 18 years old; only 1 in 12 born in 1960 could expect a similar occurrence (Bane, 1979).

The Family Without Children

A widespread belief holds that dramatic increases have occurred in the number of voluntarily childless couples in the United States (Faux, 1984; Veevers, 1979). However, this belief is debatable, because much of the pertinent research did not distinguish between couples who were childless at the time they were questioned and couples who *never* intended to have children (Houseknecht, 1987; Mattessich, 1979). Many childless couples fully expect to become parents at some time, but since the early 1970s, the tendency to delay the beginning of childbearing has increased (Gibson, 1976). The percentage of married women who consciously decide *never* to have children has remained fairly constant at between 4 and 7 percent of the population (Houseknecht, 1987).

Why do some couples choose not to become parents? Table 11.3 lists reasons couples give for choosing to remain childless. Obviously, there is no such thing as a profile of a typical U.S. parent, but a number of typical

Table 11.3
Rationales for Voluntary Childlessness in Order of Appearance Across Studies

1. Freedom from child-care responsibility; greater opportunity for self-fulfillment and spontaneous mobility.
2. A more satisfactory relationship with one's spouse.
3. Woman's career considerations.
4. Economic benefits.
5. Concerns about population growth.
6. General dislike of children.
7. Concerns about ability to be a good parent.
8. Concerns about childbirth and recovery afterward.
9. Unwillingness to bring a child into a troubled world.

Source: Adapted from "Voluntary Childlessness" by S. K. Houseknecht, in *Handbook of Marriage and the Family* (p. 377) by M. B. Sussman and S. K. Steinmetz (eds), 1987, New York: Plenum Publishing. Copyright 1987 by Plenum Publishing Corporation. Adapted by permission.

characteristics of voluntarily childless couples have been identified. They are usually white, well-educated people who live in cities rather than rural areas. They are high achievers. Typically, both husband and wife are involved in high-status careers with incomes far above the national average (Houseknecht, 1987).

In terms of personality, voluntarily childless wives are highly independent women (Houseknecht, 1987). They do not dislike either mothers or children, but they are more likely to cultivate friendships with other childless women than with mothers, primarily because of similarity of interests (Veevers, 1979). They appear no different from women with children in terms of their overall sense of well-being and life satisfaction, personality characteristics, and general outlook on life (Callan, 1987).

Women who choose not to have children do differ from mothers, however, in some ways. They are more likely to feel satisfied with the level of freedom and creativity their lives afford them. They are more likely, for example, to report having time to do the things they want to do, to relax, and to avoid being bothered by other people. They are more satisfied than mothers, incidentally, with the amount of sleep they get at night! And childless women report that their relationships with their husbands are characterized by a greater amount of cohesion (e.g., working together, exchanging ideas), and a greater degree of consensus (e.g., agreeing on life goals, arriving at joint decisions) than is reported by wives who are also mothers (Callan, 1987).

Negative Effects of Children on Their Parents

A good deal of the research literature on parent-child relationships has emphasized the influence of parents on their children. Human relationships are interactive, however, and children can also have a profound influence on their parents. These child-to-parent influences typically occur in three areas; parental lifestyle, quality of the marriage relationship, and paternal and maternal stress (Zeits & Prince, 1982).

Lifestyle Changes.   The influences of parenthood on a couple's lifestyle may include changes in spending habits and patterns of recreation, the discovery or rediscovery of organized religion, and even changes of residence if a couple's home or apartment is no longer large enough to accommodate a growing family or is too far away from the nearest school (Harper, 1975; Mead & Newton, 1967; Zeits & Prince, 1982).

Marital Relationship Changes.   The transition to parenthood can negatively affect the quality of a couple's relationship for a number of reasons. First, the demands of children limit the amount of time a couple can devote to each other (Doherty & Jacobson, 1982; Hoffman & Manis, 1978; Zeits & Prince, 1982). A child is, in a sense, an intruder, a third party in a household—and a demanding one at that! Even the presence of occasional houseguests may put some distance between a couple, but, fortunately, houseguests eventually leave. Not only do children remain in the household for approximately 18 years, they typically require a good deal more attention than a visitor does.

Second, the presence of children has been found to affect adversely the quality of a couple's sexual interaction, and this, too, can strain their relationship (Bittman & Zalk, 1978; Zeits & Prince, 1982). Sexual contact during late pregnancy may be physically or psychologically uncomfortable for many couples, and the sexual activities of new parents may be disrupted by an infant's crying, by fatigue, or by a temporary loss of interest by one or both partners.

Third, a couple may find themselves growing apart if their expectations about child rearing are not realized (Belsky, Ward, & Rovine, 1988; Garrett, 1983; Cowan, 1988). For example, Cowan (1988) found that new mothers experienced growing dissatisfaction with their marriages if their husbands failed to take the active role in parenting that the wives had expected them to assume.

Perhaps it should not be surprising that marital satisfaction begins to decline after the birth of the first child and remains at a lowered level during the childhood stages of the family life cycle (Peterson & Rollins, 1987). However, such a trend is not inevitable. Many couples do not experience declines in marital satisfaction, and these tend to be people who were high in self-esteem and who reported high degrees of marital satisfaction before the birth of the child (Cowan, 1988; Heming, 1987).

Paternal Stress. Many expectant fathers experience some depression, and many envy the attention their pregnant wives receive (Bittman & Zalk, 1978). Later, some men whose wives are nursing may resent being excluded from the interaction (Lerner, 1979). In addition, the transition to fatherhood has been associated with depression, high degrees of stress, and the aggravation of mood disorders that may have existed previously (Cowan, 1988; Osofsky & Osofsky, 1985; Ventura & Stevenson, 1986).

Many fathers take an active role in raising young children and see the experience of fatherhood as an opportunity for personal growth (Cowan, 1988). In fact, men today are more likely than in the past to embrace the fathering role eagerly, a point we shall elaborate on in a later section of this chapter. Nevertheless, some men who are stressed by the experience of parenting simply withdraw from it, allowing their wives to assume the bulk of the responsibility for handling the new infant (Noppe, Noppe, & Hughes, in press).

Withdrawal by the father is particularly likely if he perceives little encouragement for his parenting role. On the other hand, if a new father believes that his wife thinks he is doing a good job of fathering, he is likely to become a more involved father and a happier one (Coysh, 1984; Cowan &

Cowan, 1987). In that sense, the father's role is easily affected by negative life circumstances; the father's role is less adaptable than the mother's role and depends more on the presence of social and emotional supports (Berman & Pederson, 1987).

Maternal Stress. New mothers tend to the feel the stresses of parenting more keenly than fathers do and are also more likely than fathers to report declines in marital satisfaction (Miller & Sollie, 1986; Tomlinson, 1987)—possibly because women have traditionally been expected to take the bulk of responsibility for child rearing. In fact, because of cultural expectations that motherhood is a natural role, new mothers may have difficulty admitting that they feel stressed (Barnett & Baruch, 1987).

For most new mothers, the stresses of parenting are mild to moderate (Miller & Sollie, 1986). Most readily find the resources to cope and learn to become more flexible, more patient, and more organized than they were before the child's birth. For some, however, the stresses of motherhood are more pronounced. In one major survey, for example, one in five U.S. mothers of preschoolers admitted serious concern about having a nervous breakdown (Campbell et al., 1976). Similarly, a study of nearly 500 British women indicated that mothers of young children were significantly more likely than nonmothers to experience clinical depression; middle-class mothers fared a bit better than their working-class counterparts, in part because their husbands were more likely to share the stresses of child rearing (Brown & Harris, 1978).

The stress level of a young mother, however, whether it is mild, moderate, or severe, does not seem to influence the amount of interaction she has with her infant (Noppe, Noppe, & Hughes, in press). Unlike the stressed father, the mother under stress is unlikely to turn her back on the parenting role.

Attempting to explain the stresses experienced by parents of young children, Rollins and Galligan (1978) referred to the concept of *role strain.* People come to think of themselves in terms of the particular roles they play in life and to evaluate themselves according to their success in playing those roles. Role strain occurs when the assumption of one role interferes with the performance of another. If the roles are particularly demanding, as are those of parent and spouse, those playing the roles may see neither one as satisfactory and completely successful, resulting in anxiety and even depression, especially if an individual lacks emotional support from family and friends.

Positive Effects of Children on Their Parents

Considering the stresses often associated with parenting, why do so many people have children? In a nationwide survey of more than 1,200 people, 90 percent of the parents questioned said they would still want children if they had to do it over again (Yankelovich, Skelly, & White, 1977). We can only surmise that the stresses must be offset by some pleasant consequences of parenting.

Fatherhood has been associated with an increase in self-esteem and a boost to a man's sense of masculinity (Zeits & Prince, 1982). Becoming a father is also correlated with an increase in self-awareness, emotional and social maturity, and sensitivity to the needs of other people (Heath, 1972). It can be a major growth experience for a man, as illustrated by the following comment made by a new father to psychologist Philip Cowan:

> It's the hardest thing I've ever done, but there's just nothing like having him around. He's more entertainment than the TV. And, since I've become a father, I just feel more grown up. My parents are finally letting me in on family secrets they thought I was too young to know before. And on the job I've become more serious. I've really had to get my act together. It's not just me and Barbara now. I've got a family to provide for. (Cowan, 1988, p. 14)

Raising children certainly seems to be a significant growth experience for women as well (Field & Widmayer, 1982). An effective mother can balance her children's needs for attachment with their needs to be separate from her, their needs for dependence with their needs for independence. As children develop, these needs shift in subtle ways, and the mother herself develops in her problem-solving skills as she tries to respond to her children's changing needs. Field and Widmayer (1982) suggested, therefore, that saying that children produce mothers is just as accurate as saying that mothers produce children.

Parents of both sexes say their children bring them a sense of pride, a sense of personal fulfillment, and a sense of responsibility. Parenthood is the ultimate proof of adult status in a society in which the transition from adolescence to adulthood is not clearly marked (Hoffman & Manis, 1982).

Becoming a parent requires a significant and often difficult life adjustment for many people, but it is an adjustment that can bring great satisfaction as well. Overemphasizing either the stresses or the joys of parenthood serves little purpose, because neither emphasis accurately describes the experience of the average parent. The reality is a combination of the two.

Parent-Infant Attachment

When psychologist Lillian Troll (1972) asked a group of people ranging in age from 10 to 91 to describe any person they knew, most of them—even elderly people whose parents had been dead for years—described their mother or father. Apparently, the bond between parent and child is one of the closest and most enduring of all human relationships, and attachment is the process by which the parent-child bond is initially formed.

Theories of Attachment. Two major theoretical positions address how parent-child attachments are formed. *Social learning theorists* sees parent-infant bonding as a learning process: To satisfy basic physiological needs (e.g., for food), the infant seeks attention from and contact with the caretaker and, in so doing, displays various attachment/dependency behaviors. For example, the baby cries, fusses, reaches, or clings. A caretaker who satisfies the child's need (e.g., by providing food) rewards the dependency/ attachment behaviors and, according to principles of operant conditioning, encourages future displays of such behaviors. Thus, an infant attaches to the caretaker because the infant learns to associate the caretaker with the satisfaction of basic needs.

For a number of reasons, the social learning perspective is inadequate to explain the parent-child attachment process. First, the approach ignores the two-directional nature of the parent-child relationship, by emphasizing the mechanism by which infants attach to their caretakers but not the reverse. In addition, if infants attach themselves to their caretakers only to satisfy their physiological needs, then how can one explain the following occurrences? (1) Infants attach themselves to other people, such as peers, who have never satisfied their physiological needs. (2) Infants attach themselves even to caretakers who mistreat them. (3) Infants respond socially even in situations in which physiological needs are not involved. (4) Infants apparently require much more from a caretaker than simply the satisfaction of bodily needs (Joffe & Vaughn, 1982).

According to the *ethological theory* of attachment (Bowlby, 1969, 1980), attachment is not learned but is an instinctive system that evolved as a survival mechanism in both human and nonhuman species. When infants experience the threat of separation from their parents, the attachment system is activated. The infants begin to exhibit behaviors designed to bring them closer to their parents, and these behaviors have either a signal function (e.g., calling, crying, babbling, smiling) or an executive function (e.g., reaching, grabbing, clinging, following). Consider the almost irresist-ible charm of an infant's smile! The infant's behaviors serve as elicitors to the caretaker, producing certain reactions (e.g., smiling, approaching, touching) that terminate the infant's attachment-seeking behaviors. This dynamic feature of the two-dimensional interaction is an element lacking in theories of attachment that emphasize social learning.

Bonding

The process by which the parent-offspring attachment is initially formed.

The ethological view of attachment as a survival instinct has generated a good deal of recent research on parent-infant bonding. In the literal sense of the word, **bonding** is the process by which the parent-offspring attachment is initially formed. Recently, however, the term has been used in a more restrictive sense to refer to a biologically determined attachment mechanism that must be activated within a critical period after the infant's birth. Ethologists point out that the newborn offspring of lower animal species that constantly move about in their environment (e.g., cattle, sheep, chickens) must quickly recognize and learn to follow their parents if they are to survive infancy. In such animals, a type of preprogrammed learning, called *imprinting,* occurs: The infant and parent automatically form an attachment if exposed to each other within a critical period of 1 or 2 days after birth. The infant automatically follows the parent (or other imprinted object) if such exposure occurs, and emits a species-specific call as the imprinted object moves away from it.

Might human infants also possess such a built-in predisposition toward attachment to their parents? Ethologically oriented researchers, such as pediatricians Marshall Klaus and John Kennell at Case Western Reserve University, suggested that they do. Noting that some animal parents reject their newborns if separated from them immediately after birth, but form an irreversible bond if mother-infant contact is not interfered with, Klaus and Kennell (1976; 1982; Kennell & Klaus, 1984) suggested that a critical bonding period may exist for human beings as well as for lower animals. They produced evidence to indicate that human mothers who had their infants with them immediately after delivery appeared to be more affectionate in interacting with them; they fondled their babies more, attempted to soothe them more frequently, and maintained eye contact with them more often and for longer periods of time.

Intriguing as the ethological theory of human attachment is, it has been challenged repeatedly for lack of supporting evidence (Goldberg; 1983;

Holding a newborn baby only minutes after delivery is a satisfying experience for any parent. But even if such contact is not possible, a strong bond of attachment between parent and child can still be formed.

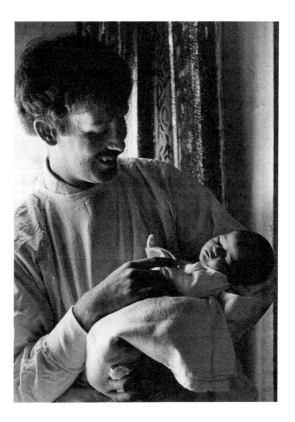

Myers, 1984a, 1984b; Reed & Leiderman, 1983). For example, Goldberg (1983) reviewed a large number of studies and concluded that no scientific evidence supports a critical period for human parent-infant attachment. She pointed out the contact between mother and newborn varies considerably in quality. It is difficult to conclude that early contact itself promotes attachment when the attitudes of new mothers engaged in such contact range from euphoria to near indifference. What is more, in most bonding studies, no efforts were made to separate *timing* of contact from actual *amount* of contact. Mothers who were given their infants immediately after birth had more overall time with them than mothers who did not have this early experience. Therefore, a closer level of attachment in the former group could have resulted from more time spent together and not from exposure to each other during a critical period after birth.

Goldberg (1983) did not suggest that early parent-infant contact has no value. Indeed, such contact may be desirable and pleasurable for both parent and child. She pointed out, however, that strong and lasting attachments can be formed between parent and child even if contact does not occur shortly after birth. Parents who for any reason may not hold their infants immediately after delivery need not fear that the parent-child relationship will be deficient in any way.

In support of Goldberg's reassuring conclusion, the bulk of the research on human attachment indicates that a strong infant-caretaker bond can be formed even under the most adverse conditions. For example, no differences exist in degree or quality of parent-infant attachment when preterm and full-term babies are compared (Frodi & Thompson, 1985; Goldberg, Perrotta, Minde, & Corter, 1986)—even though the preterm baby is unavailable for handling immediately after delivery and is often less alert, less responsive to stimulation, and less well coordinated than a full-term infant; it smiles less often in the early months and is more irritable in general (Bakeman & Brown, 1980).

One might expect that, under such conditions, the attachment process would be disrupted, because a parent would have difficulty relating to a preterm infant. In fact, parents seem to adapt their caretaking behaviors to meet the needs of the individual child; a full-term infant may be easier to warm up to, but parents of preterm infants try harder to form a bond of love by accommodating themselves to their child's limitations (Frodi & Thompson, 1985).

Research on the security of attachment between parents and adopted children also indicates that no simple bonding mechanism can fully account for the closeness of the parent-child relationship. Singer, Brodzinsky, Ramsay, Stier, and Waters (1985) compared the security of parental attachment of a group of 27 nonadopted children with a group of 46 children adopted during the first year of life. No group differences were found. Adopted children were just as securely attached as natural children.

The study of children whose early life circumstances could easily lead to attachment difficulties—but who are, in fact, closely attached to their parents—leads psychologists to the following conclusion: Some genetic predisposition toward attachment might indeed exist between human parents and child, as ethologists suggest, but the learning process seems to operate as well. Perhaps the Goldberg (1983) review pointed out the need to blend social learning and ethological perspectives to understand the attachment process in an organism as complex as a human being. Such a blending allows for the possibility that nature and nurture interact in the attachment process and emphasizes the necessity of seeing attachment in two-directional terms.

Degrees of Attachment. The attachment between parent and child has been discussed thus far with little reference to individual differences. In fact, attachment should not be viewed as an all-or-nothing phenomenon. Instead, degrees of attachment exist, with some infants and young children very securely attached to their parents and others decidedly less so.

To identify individual differences in degree of attachment, psychologist Mary Ainsworth (Ainsworth, 1977; Ainsworth, Blehar, Waters, & Wall, 1978) developed a testing procedure known as the Strange Situation: An infant and its parents are brought into a playroom containing a variety of toys and a strange adult. After a brief introductory period, the parents leave the room and then return on two occasions. The infant's reaction to their return is observed.

Secure, closely attached infants react to the return of their parents by at first seeking closeness and contact with them, but then easily returning to their independent play. A less secure group of infants, referred to as insecure-avoidant, react to their parents' return with hostility and resistance. A third group, described as insecure-ambivalent, appear angry and resist contact with the returned parents while at the same time expressing a need for such contact.

Attachment and Quality of Parenting. Why are some infants more securely attached than others to their parents, as indicated by responses in the Strange Situation? A clue might be found in the personal characteristics of the infants' mothers and their approaches to parenting. (Probably the same characteristics that affect attachment to mothers influence attachment to fathers and other caretakers, but the research in this area has focused only on the female parent.)

Mothers of securely attached infants are particularly sensitive to their babies' efforts to signal their needs; they correctly determine what their babies want at any particular time and respond quickly and consistently (Ainsworth, Bell, & Stayton, 1971). Such mothers feel good about themselves and are confident in their parenting skills. They handle their infants affectionately and seem to be both interested in and skilled at feeding and playing with them (Egeland & Farber, 1984). In short, the secure baby is the one who feels the mother is readily available to meet its needs (Main, 1981).

In marked contrast, mothers of insecure children are anxious and irritable; they lack self-confidence and react negatively to motherhood. Such mothers appear to have little interest in their infants; they feed and handle them mechanically and only when necessary (Egeland & Farber, 1984). Generally, insecure babies have limited access to their mothers (Main, 1981).

The parenting approaches that promote or prevent secure attachment show considerable stability over time (Jacobson & Wille, 1984; Main, Kaplan, & Cassidy, 1984; Thompson, Lamb, & Estes, 1982). Not surprisingly, the security of attachment is also stable. For example, Bates, Maslin, and Frankel (1985) found that the most securely attached children at 13 months of age were also the most securely attached at 24 months.

If parental availability is a key element in determining the quality of attachment, what can be said of infants who spend a considerable amount of time in nonparental care? In fact, a growing body of evidence suggests that infants who spend extensive time (20 hours a week or more) under nonmaternal care are at greater risk of being less closely attached to their mothers and less secure in their relationships with them (Barglow, Vaughn, & Molitor, 1987; Belsky, 1986, 1988; Belsky & Rovine, 1988; Jacobson & Wille, 1984; Owen & Cox, 1988).

However, these data are expressed in terms of probabilities: in fact, many infants, perhaps 50 percent of them or more, display no attachment difficulties after extensive nonmaternal care (Belsky & Rovine, 1988). Why do infants respond so differently to day care exposure? It is difficult to know at this point. The characteristics of the child's family, the child's temperament, and the nonparental child care setting must all be taken into account, and the individual contributions of each of these variables to the parent-infant attachment process have not yet been identified.

Correlates of Secure Attachment.   A number of recent studies indicate a link between parent-infant attachment and later cognitive and social behaviors. Secure, closely attached preschool-age children have been found to be more capable than less secure children of relating to their peers (Lieberman, 1977; Park & Waters, 1989; Waters, Wippman & Sroufe, 1979) and more comfortable in interacting with a strange adult (Lutkenhaus, Grossman, & Grossman, 1985). Their make-believe play is both more sustained and more complex than that of anxious children (Slade, 1987). Closely attached 6-year-olds are likely to be verbal and comfortable in exploring their thoughts and feelings (Main et al., 1985). Secure children display a greater interest and ability in exploring their environments (Cassidy, 1986; Joffe & Vaughn, 1982) and are more environmentally oriented in free play (Belsky, Garduque, & Hrncir, 1984). Perhaps as a consequence, they score higher on tests of spatial ability (Hazen & Durett, 1982). The most secure, closely attached children also appear to have advantages in solving simple problems, such as removing a desired object from a tube (Matas, Arend, & Sroufe, 1978).

In short, the most securely attached infants frequently become the most competent toddlers—close enough to adults to depend on them when necessary, but independent enough to act on their own and even to defy their caretakers. Frustrated parents of defiant toddlers may take some consolation from the conclusions drawn by Matas et al. (1978) about the competent 2-year-old problem solver:

> The competent two-year-old . . . is not the child who automatically complies with whatever the mother tells him/her. Rather, it is the child who shows a certain amount of noncompliance when requested to stop playing and clean up the toys. When, however, cooperation has clear adaptive advantage, as in the tool-using situation, these children become readily involved in the task . . . they work hard, independently at first, then request help from the mother when they get stuck. (p. 554)

The Childhood Years of the Family

We move now to that period in the span of family development in which the children are growing up. Having adjusted to a new definition of self that includes the role of mother or father, parents now begin the task of rearing their children and preparing them for the day when they reach adulthood and leave home. We shall first examine a variety of parenting styles that have been identified by psychologists, and the impact of different parenting approaches on the development of children. We shall look at the early years of what will be the longest-lasting of all family relationships—the one between siblings. Finally, we shall discuss some of the special features of the parent-child relationships during the adolescent years.

Parenting: Styles, Roles, Issues

Raising a child is one of life's most significant responsibilities, and yet most people enter parenthood with little or no preparation for the role. In this section, we focus on variations in the qualities of parents, or, more accurately, in the qualities of parent-child relationships, in the United States. First, we shall discuss the degrees of affection and control displayed by parents and the importance of both love and structure in children's lives. Then we shall examine the particular significance of the very much neglected role of the father in children's lives. Finally, we shall speak of the family with adolescent children and discuss the often misunderstood relationship between teenagers and parents in our society.

Dimensions of Affect and Control.   Research on the impact of parenting styles on children's development has focused primarily on two parental dimensions: the affective dimension, referring to the degree of parental affection and approval perceived by the child, and the dimension of restrictiveness, referring to the degree of parental control (Maccoby & Martin, 1983).

Little disagreement exists on the point that loving, accepting parents are more likely to enhance the psychological well-being of a child than hostile ones. However, the dimension of restrictiveness is far more complicated than was once imagined. To illustrate this point, a home may be characterized as restrictive because children are expected to obey many rules, but parents might be either firm or casual in implementing those rules. Furthermore, control can be psychological as well as physical; the presence or absence of rules may tell us little about the actual degree of autonomy or control in a home because some parents impose few concrete restrictions but instead control their children by instilling in them a strong sense of anxiety or guilt for misbehavior (Maccoby & Martin, 1983). Finally, other parenting dimensions, such as the degree of responsiveness to or interest in one's children, can affect the way the child interprets autonomy or control. The granting of autonomy by an involved and interested parent may communicate an attitude of trust; the uninvolved and unresponsive parent who allows children a high degree of autonomy may come across as being indifferent or even negligent.

A helpful framework for understanding the current information on the effects of parents on their children, and one that recognizes the complexity of the autonomy-control dimension, was provided by Maccoby and Martin (1983), and is illustrated in Table 11.4.

Three of the four parenting categories identified in the chart—authoritarian, authoritative, and permissive—have been investigated extensively by psychologist Diana Baumrind. Her characterizations of each style and their impacts on children are as follows:

1. *Authoritarian parenting.* Authoritarian parents attempt to shape their children's behavior to precise and absolute standards of conduct. They attempt to instill in their children such values as respect for authority, work, and tradition, and they leave little room for discussion of their standards.
2. *Authoritative parenting.* Authoritative parents are also quite willing to exercise control over their children, but they attempt to be rational in doing so. That is, they are willing to reason with their children, to explain rules, and to allow appropriate degrees of independence. These parents value obedience and conformity in their children, but they also value independence and self-direction.
3. *Permissive parenting.* Permissive parents are unwilling to exert power or control over their children. They see themselves as accepting and nonevaluative resources to which children can turn if they need help, but not as shapers of their children's behavior. They impose few regulations on their children and place a low priority on household responsibility and order.

Authoritarian parenting
Parenting designed to shape children's behavior according to precise and absolute standards of conduct, with little respect for the child and little room for discussion of parental standards.

Authoritative parenting
Parenting in which control is exercised but independence is also allowed and encouraged in the child, and discussion of parental standards is the norm.

Permissive parenting
Parenting characterized by unwillingness to exert authority or control over children, the imposition of few if any regulations, and little emphasis on responsibility and order in the household.

Table 11.4
Two-Dimensional Classification of Parenting Patterns

	Accepting, Responsive, Child-Centered	Rejecting, Unresponsive, Parent-Centered
Demanding, controlling	Authoritative	Authoritarian
Undemanding	Permissive	Indifferent, uninvolved

On the basis of a number of studies (Baumrind, 1967, 1968, 1971; Baumrind & Black, 1967), psychologist Diana Baumrind (1975) concluded that authoritative parenting is the most effective of the three approaches. Children of authoritative parents were the most independent, socially responsible, and achievement oriented. They were the most likely to be self-controlled, self-reliant, assertive, explorative, and friendly.

In contrast, children of permissive or authoritarian parents were equally likely to be anxious, dependent, lacking in self-confidence, and incapable of making decisions for themselves. Children of authoritarian parents displayed a lesser degree of internal moral control, or conscience, than children exposed to the other child-rearing patterns (Hoffman, 1970). Children of

Authoritative parents discuss family rules with their children. They exercise control but allow appropriate degrees of independence.

permissive parents tended to be more impulsive and more aggressive (Maccoby & Martin, 1983).

Baumrind suggested that the authoritative parenting style is the most beneficial of the three because it shows children that the world is orderly and rational but leaves room for challenges to the established order, and because it teaches them to be responsible for their own actions. Children need rational structure to learn independence. To stand up for themselves, they need something to stand up against. Unreasonable structure, as might be found in the authoritarian home, suppresses dissent and teaches children that they are incapable of exerting any control over their own lives. Total lack of structure, the characteristic of the permissive home, not only encourages demanding, inconsiderate behavior by the child but also fails to teach self-control. Permissively reared children often feel anxious and guilty about their own unstructured behavior.

Indifferent, uninvolved parenting communicates a desire to keep children at a distance. Such parents have little interest in their children's activities and are often unaware of their children's whereabouts. Their primary concern is for their own immediate comfort and convenience, and this emphasis is reflected in their approach to discipline: They may ignore a child's bad behaviors rather than make an effort to correct them, or they may fail to teach positive attitudes because of the time and trouble involved in doing so.

Children of uninvolved, indifferent parents lack self-confidence; have lowered self-esteem (Loeb, Horst, & Horton, 1980) and lowered achievement motivation; and are impulsive, moody, and disobedient (Block, 1971). They seem to lack a clear sense of direction in life and are the most likely to engage in antisocial behaviors, such as drug abuse, truancy, and criminal activities (Maccoby & Martin, 1983; Pulkkinen, 1982).

Considering the range and seriousness of the consequences of parental indifference, children exposed to this last pattern are the least fortunate of the four groups. As Maccoby and Martin (1983) concluded on the basis of a review of the various child-rearing patterns, active parental involvement in a child's life and decisions even into the years of adolescence serves to promote optimal child development.

The Neglected Role of the Father.   The past 15 years have seen a surge of interest in the role played by fathers in their children's development (Bronstein, 1988). Until the end of the 1960s, the father's role in the family was unappreciated, even by social scientists; the father was then "rediscovered," for the following reasons:

1. The balance of the research on parental influence was so weighted in favor of the mother-child relationship that social scientists began to wonder if fathers were totally irrelevant.
2. Rapid social changes (e.g., the rising divorce rate) caused social scientists to speculate on the future of the family—and the factor most often

Indifferent, uninvolved parenting
Parenting characterized by selfishness and by little or no interest or involvement in the lives and everyday activities of children.

associated with family disruption was father absence. In a sense, fathers became visible by their absence.

3. In recent years, fathers themselves have become increasingly interested in their part in child rearing, while mothers have begun to explore new options outside the home (Lamb, 1981).

The father's special influence on the development of his son has been investigated in three areas: gender role development, cognitive development, and socio-emotional development. In terms of gender role development, the presence in the home of a father who is affectionate, who is seen as a competent decision maker, and who is involved in family functions has a positive impact on the masculine identity of male children; the sons of such fathers are likely to feel positive about their own masculinity and to possess the competencies associated with their gender. The result is a feeling of security and self-confidence (Biller, 1981, 1982).

In the cognitive area, sons of nurturant, competent fathers earn higher scores on achievement and intelligence tests as well as higher grades in school than sons of "inadequate" fathers or boys from father-absent homes (Biller, 1981; Blanchard & Biller, 1971; Radin, 1972).

Finally, the presence of a nurturant and competent father has been associated with high self-esteem in elementary school boys (Coopersmith, 1967), personal adjustment in college-age males (Reuter & Biller, 1973), and

A father who is actively involved in family projects is likely to raise children who are self-confident and well adjusted.

Issues in Human Development
What Happens When Mother Goes to Work?

 More than half of the mothers of school-age children, and slightly less than half of the mothers of preschoolers, are employed outside the home (Hoffman, 1979). Maternal employment cannot be thought of as a temporary reaction to difficult economic times, because three out of four working women say they would continue to work even if they did not need the money (Dubnoff, Veroff, & Kulka, 1978). Hetherington (1979) attributed the increase of mothers in the U.S. work force to (1) the reduction in the size of the family, (2) a decrease in the amount of time needed to complete regular household chores, and (3) an increase in women's level of education.

Child psychologists have been particularly interested in the effects of maternal employment on children. To date research has been somewhat limited, particularly involving infants and young children, because it is difficult in research to isolate the variable of maternal employment from other variables, such as parental attitudes about children's attachment needs (Hoffman, 1989). Furthermore, the findings are mixed: Maternal employment appears to affect children both positively and negatively. Thus far, however, the positive has been found to outweigh the negative. Comparisons between children of working and nonworking mothers for the different age groups follow.

INFANCY AND EARLY CHILDHOOD

Positive. Women who work while married are best able to cope with divorce, both psychologically and economically, so some negative effects of divorce on preschoolers are diminished (Hetherington, 1979). Four-year-old children of working mothers experience better social adjustment than 4-year-olds whose mothers do not work (Gold & Andres, 1978c).

Negative. In the second year of life, children of nonworking mothers are more vocal, experience more positive social interactions, and score higher on tests of normal development (Cohen, 1978).

THE SCHOOL YEARS

Positive. School-age children of working mothers are more likely to be given greater household responsibilities and are more likely to behave independently than their age-mates with nonworking mothers (Hoffman, 1974). They are more likely to have egalitarian gender role concepts and less likely to hold rigid gender role stereotypes (Gold & Andres, 1978b). Finally, daughters of working mothers are higher in achievement motivation, set higher career goals for themselves, and are more likely to see their mothers as successful models to be emulated (Huston-Stein & Higgins-Trenk, 1978).

Negative. Sons in lower-class families experience strained relationships with their fathers, perhaps because they see maternal employment as a sign of the father's failure (Hoffman, 1979). Sons of all social classes score lower on mathematics and language achievement tests when their mothers work (Gold & Andres, 1978a).

successful heterosexual adjustment for males in early adulthood (Biller, 1974; 1982).

Girls raised in families that include a loving and respected father are most likely to become healthy, well-adjusted young women who feel a sense of pride in their femininity. This effect is observed particularly if their mothers and fathers had a warm and satisfying relationship with each other (Fish & Biller, 1973). Evidence also suggests that a warm and close father-daughter relationship is positively correlated with the daughter's later marital satisfaction (Biller, 1974). Finally, the absence of a father during his daughter's childhood has been linked to her later negative attitudes toward

ADOLESCENCE

Positive. Adolescent daughters of mothers who work outside the home are more socially outgoing, independent, achievement oriented, and personally and socially well adjusted than those of nonworking mothers (Gold & Andres, 1978a). They tend to hold more liberal gender role orientations and more egalitarian views about the division of household labor (Gardner & LeBrecque, 1986). In addition, they are more likely to expect that they will work full-time in the future in addition to being wives and mothers (Jensen & Borges, 1986).

Adolescent sons of working mothers are higher in self-esteem, social adjustment at school, and personal adjustment (Gold & Andres, 1978a). Like daughters, they, too, hold more liberal views on household labor division and on gender roles in general (Gardner & LeBrecque, 1986).

Negative. Few negative effects on adolescents related to their mothers' working have been found, although some research indicates that teenage girls whose mothers work outside the home report greater levels of familial anger and stress for reasons that have not yet been fully explored (Jensen & Borges, 1986).

At first glance, the results of studies on the effect of maternal employment may appear inconsistent. Perhaps this is because a mother's actual absence from the home may be less important in predicting a child's adjustment than other variables such as the quality of child care provided, the fa-

ther's reaction to the mother's employment status, the mother's reasons for working, and certain personality characteristics of the mother.

Consider the findings from a study by Benn (1986), who examined the quality of attachment between working mothers and their 18-month-old sons and found much variety in the relationships. Working mothers whose children were the most secure and the most closely attached were warm and loving parents and were relaxed and happy in their parenting roles. They were sensitive to their children's needs and conscientious in their choice of substitute caregivers, whom they regarded not as replacements but as extensions of themselves. They were secure, self-confident people who saw their jobs as opportunities to expand themselves rather than as means of establishing their self-worth. In contrast, working mothers of the least secure children were angry and frustrated; they took little pleasure from motherhood and saw their jobs as a means of keeping them from being depressed and of filling a void in their lives. They were careless in their choice of day care arrangements and communicated very little with their children's caretakers.

In conclusion, employment outside the home is not the only variable to consider in research on working mothers. As might be expected in an analysis of a relationship as complicated as that between mother and child, numerous other variables must also be kept in mind.

masculinity (Biller, 1982) as well as to insecurity in dealing with boys and men during the her adolescence (Hetherington, 1972).

The recent research on fatherhood is increasingly showing not only that fathers play a role in children's development, but that a man's role in child rearing may be qualitatively different in certain aspects from a woman's role. Today, we can only speculate on the full impact of fathers as parents, because research on fatherhood is still somewhat limited (Bronstein, 1988). As men take a greater interest in child rearing and as women discover options for themselves outside the home, we should continue to learn about the unique and important role of the human male parent.

The Sibling Relationship

Of all the relationships that people experience as they cross the span of life, the one that lasts the longest is the sibling relationship (Cicirelli, 1985; Pulakos, 1987; Scott, 1983). And yet, social scientists have shown relatively little interest in the interactions among siblings, particularly as compared to the vast amount of literature on parent-child relationships and marital relationships (Bank & Kahn, 1982; Goetting, 1986; Pulakos, 1987).

Some social scientists (e.g., Bank & Kahn, 1982; Gold, 1989) believe that the sibling relationship has become more and more important in recent years, for a number of reasons:

1. As families become smaller, there will be fewer siblings to relate to, and so the bond between siblings will become stronger.
2. Families today are likely to experience more major social and geographical transitions than they did in the past, and siblings represent a stability and permanence that many children will seek.
3. Because of their own life stresses, within the home and beyond it, parents may be less able to fulfill their children's emotional needs than they once did. Siblings may be seen increasingly as sources of security and emotional support.

In this section, we shall examine the increasingly important sibling relationship during the childhood years of the family. We shall also look at the experiences of children who do not have siblings and at the ways in which children's positions within the family are related to their psychological development.

Coping With a New Sibling.   The entry of a baby brother or sister into a family has a dramatic effect on the life of an older child. Four in 10 children express mixed feelings about their mother's pregnancy in the first place, 1 in 4 is ambivalent about the post-birth reunion with mother, and a striking 64 percent of firstborns display negative changes in behavior within a few weeks after a sibling's birth (Nadelman & Begun, 1982). To provide an in-depth analysis of the psychological impact of new siblings, Dunn and Kendrick (1982) observed the family situations of 40 firstborn English children coping with baby brothers and sisters. They noticed that mother-child confrontations, both verbal and nonverbal, increased considerably over prebirth levels. Naughty behaviors, involving deliberate disobedience or a direct attack on the mother, were three times more likely to occur after the sibling birth than they had before. That these outbursts were related to the presence of the new baby was suggested by the fact that naughtiness was three times more likely to occur while the mother was actually handling the newborn. What is more, even when parents made substantial efforts to prepare the first child for the baby's arrival, the child still experienced considerable adjustment difficulties to the presence of the "intruder" in the family.

Why are firstborn children so affected by the arrival of a baby brother or sister? A possible answer was suggested by Dunn and Kendrick (1982), who looked at pre- to post-birth changes in quality of the mother-child interaction. Mothers of newborns spent less time playing with their older children, showing things to them, giving them things, helping them, and initiating conversations with them. Thus, a major consequence for an older child of the arrival of a new sibling is a significant decline in mother's attention.

A number of characteristics related to the ease of post-birth adjustment have been identified in children. Gender of the child is a significant factor: boys are typically more upset by a new sibling than girls are, and more likely to withdraw. Gender of the infant has been found to influence the older sibling's reaction, in that a greater number of adjustment problems occur when the new sibling is of the same sex. Perhaps the older child is more likely to view a same-sex sibling as a possible replacement for him or her. Temperament of the older child is also related; children described as being negative in their mood are most likely to show withdrawal or sleeping difficulties after the baby arrives. Age of child is a factor as well, with younger children more likely to be disturbed by the loss of mother's

The birth of a sibling dramatically affects the life of the older child. The sibling relationship can be a stressful one that combines extremes of love and hate.

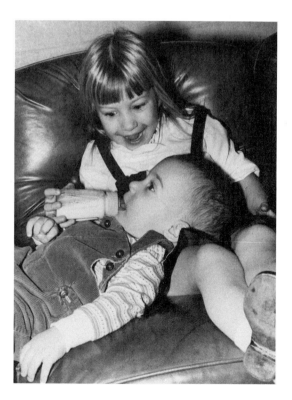

attention. Younger children are the most likely to become clingy and overly dependent and to display regressive behavior, such as toileting accidents (Dunn & Kendrick, 1982; Nadelman & Begun, 1982; Stewart, Mobley, Van Tuyl, & Salvador, 1987). Mood of mother is also a predictor of the firstborn's adjustment; if mother is overly tired or depressed after the birth of the second child, the older child is most likely to engage in negative behavior such as withdrawal. Finally, children who adjust most easily to the arrival of a new brother or sister are those who have always had close, intense involvements with their fathers (Dunn & Kendrick, 1982). Although the mother's attention to the firstborn declines after the birth of a sibling, the father's attention does not; in fact, whether or not they realize they are doing so, fathers of newborn actually increase the relative amount of time they spend with the firstborn child (Stewart, Mobley, Van Tuyl, & Salvador, 1987).

Sibling Interactions in the Preschool Years.   Because young children spend a considerable amount of time in the home, in families of two or more children an extensive amount of sibling interaction will occur. To examine the quality of that interaction, Abramovitch, Pepler, and Corter (1982) carried out home observations of nearly 120 families of two children, and they described a level of sibling interaction that was striking both in quantity and diversity.

Parents often pity the younger sibling, who seems to be the object of aggression from an older brother or sister. In fact, in the Abramovitch and associates study, older siblings initiated aggressive activity about 80 percent of the time. On the other hand, older children are usually the initiators of social activity of any sort, probably as a result of their greater social maturity. However, younger siblings initiate a third of the prosocial activities but only 20 percent of the aggressive ones. Perhaps they are simply less aggressive than older brothers or sisters or perhaps they are just realistic: They recognize that they are not likely to win if a conflict occurs. Not surprisingly, the one type of social interaction that the younger siblings displayed more frequently was imitation; thus, an older child can serve as a role model and teacher for the younger one, and, in fact, older siblings have been found to be good models for facilitating cognitive development in infants (Wishart, 1986).

Abramovitch et al. (1982) observed that girls were more prosocial than boys; boys were involved in sibling conflict more often and were more likely to display physical aggression. On the other hand, girls were just as verbally aggressive as boys and just as likely to take things from a younger sibling. Finally, older sisters seem to be kinder than are older brothers to younger siblings, particularly in same-sex pairs.

As a final note on the Abramovitch et al. (1982) study of sibling interaction among preschoolers, no differences in any aspect of the sibling relationship were attributable to the age gap between sibling pairs. This finding runs contrary to the popular belief that parents can use some ideal spacing formula to promote harmonious sibling relationships. In fact, experts on sibling interaction typically observe that the ideal age difference concept is a myth. As Dunn (1985) pointed out, play, companionship, and affection appear as frequently in siblings whether the age gap is 11 months or 4 years, and so do aggression, hostility, and teasing.

Considering the extent and variety of sibling relationships during the preschool years, one might expect that patterns acquired in the process of socializing with siblings might be carried over into other peer relationships. To investigate the degree to which social interaction patterns in the home are carried into the school, Berndt and Bulleit (1985) examined the behaviors of 34 preschoolers in both settings. A link between peer play and sibling play was found in two areas: the incidence of aggression and the incidence of onlooker play. Children who tended to be aggressive with siblings also tended to be aggressive with peers; children who were often passive watchers rather than active participants in school play often seemed to assume the same roles at home. The most passive children were girls without brothers, leading Berndt and Bulleit (1985) to suggest that the presence of a male sibling may draw a girl into the type of stereotypically masculine active play that she might refrain from in the absence of her brother's influence.

An Ambivalent Relationship. The sibling relationship beyond the preschool years is characterized by a high degree of intensity in both a positive and negative direction. The intensity is not surprising when one considers the advances in social and self-awareness that characterize the years from middle childhood through adolescence and the closeness of the physical environment that siblings share; not only do they live in the same house, but one in three U.S. siblings share a bedroom, and virtually every child shares household chores with a brother or sister (Bryant, 1982).

The sibling relationship during childhood and adolescence is thought to be one of the most stressful of all human relationships because of its ambivalence; stress might result from any relationship that combines such high degrees of love and hatred (Pfouts, 1976). As Bryant (1982) observed, even the same relationship can range from a positive extreme of psychological closeness and support to a negative extreme of the frustration, anger, and competition often referred to as sibling rivalry. The closer in age the siblings are, the greater the degree of ambivalence. That is, closely spaced siblings tend to say more positive and more negative things about one another than siblings who differ greatly in age (Bigner, 1974).

When sibling rivalry occurs during childhood and adolescence, it seems to arise from two sources: competition for parental approval and competition for status according to ground rules established by the siblings themselves (Pfouts, 1976). In other words, even if children feel their parents thoroughly approve of them, sibling rivalry can still exist as children compare themselves with their brothers and sisters.

Why would children who feel their parents love and approve of them equally still need to make comparisons and find reasons for seeing themselves as better in some way than their siblings? The answer may have to do with the fact that parents unintentionally treat siblings differently and thus set up a basis for social comparison. For example, mother may dispense equal amounts of affection to her two children (Dunn, Plomin, & Daniels, 1986), but she may provide a greater degree of attention and emotional support to the younger one (Bryant, 1982; Bryant & Crockenberg, 1980). Daniels and Plomin (1985a) discovered that 40 percent of the nearly 400 adolescents and young adults they studied reported that their parents treated them differently from their siblings. And differential parental treatment is but one aspect of environmental differences that may lead to social comparisons and sibling rivalry! Daniels and Plomin (1985a) also reported that nearly two-thirds of the participants in their study believed that they and their siblings lived in very different environments in terms of sibling interaction, peer characteristics, and specific life events. The researchers concluded that two children raised in the same family may actually be living in radically different environments.

Environmental differences in sibling experience are reflected in research findings on the effects of birth order on characteristics of sibling relationships. Firstborns are more negative toward siblings than later-borns are; they are bossier, more dominant, and likely to use power assertive techniques (e.g., hitting, bribing, referring to their status) to get what they want, whereas later-borns more often resort to pleading, crying, sulking, and appeals to parents for help (Dunn, 1985).

Children Without Siblings. Ask 100 people to describe the child without siblings, and the response will be overwhelmingly negative. In one public opinion poll, 80 percent of the respondents believed that an only child is disadvantaged (Blake, 1974). The only child has been described as maladjusted, self-centered, temperamental, anxious, unhappy, and unlikeable, among other negative traits (Thompson, 1974). On the other hand, when only children themselves and their parents are asked to describe their life experiences, the view they present is considerably more positive (Falbo, 1978a, 1978b, 1982).

What is the truth about the life of the only child in the U.S. family? In the first place, being an only child seems to be a much more positive experience than most people believe. Secondly, the life of the only child is not unique; only children and firstborn children share a considerable number of characteristics. Perhaps in keeping with their negative stereotype, only children have been found to be more egocentric and less cooperative than children with siblings (Jiao, Ji, & Ching, 1986). On the positive side, however, only children and firstborns have higher educational aspirations than later-borns and are more likely to achieve success in life as measured by conventional standards.

Only children and firstborns experience greater pressure from parents for mature behavior, and perhaps as a result are more responsible and more self-controlled. Only children and firstborns are less affiliative, have fewer friends, and typically have a less intense social life than later-borns, perhaps because the first or only child receives more parental affection and therefore requires less affection from peers. On the other hand, only children and firstborns have just as many close friends as later-borns and report being just as satisfied with their lives. No consistent differences between children with and without siblings have been found in the areas of overall popularity or self-esteem (Falbo, 1982).

Observed differences between the only child and the child with older siblings may occur for many reasons. Falbo (1982) suggested that the absence of siblings does not influence the social and personality development of the only child as much as the characteristics of the parent-child relationship in the one-child home.

The Family with Adolescents

The teenage years are often seen as the phase of life that can turn a parent's hair gray. Parents often dread these years, assuming that even the most pleasant children will turn overnight into rebellious, hostile, and disrespectful teenagers.

As a matter of fact, such concerns are unnecessary most of the time, because the adolescent-parent relationship in U.S. society is typically a healthy one (Adams & Gulotta, 1989; Montemayor, 1983; Montemayor & Hanson, 1985; Peterson, 1988; Steinberg, 1989). For example, Douvan and Adelson (1966) studied 5,000 adolescents and found that adolescents reported few serious disagreements with their parents. In another study, Larson (1975) looked at 1,500 seventh, ninth, and twelfth graders in a small Oregon city and found that nearly half the students reported a highly satisfying relationship with their parents, and three-fourths had at least a satisfying relationship. Offer, Ostrov, and Howard (1981) found that three out of four teenagers felt they could count on their parents most of the time and expected that when they became parents, their families would in some ways resemble those in which they were raised.

Despite the general good health of the adolescent-parent relationship, however, conflicts will arise. Usually, these pertain to the mundane, everyday details of life, such as doing chores, maintaining acceptable standards of grooming and dress, getting along with siblings, keeping up with schoolwork, and regulating one's use of the telephone and the television set (Adams & Gullotta, 1989; Montemayor & Hanson, 1985; Smetana, 1989). Lasting, deep-seated hostilities between parent and adolescent are the exception rather than the rule.

Parent-child conflict during the teen years is highly variable, occurring frequently in some families but rarely if ever in others (Ellis, 1986). This variability raises an interesting question: Can we identify factors that promote conflict as well as factors that promote harmonious parent-child relationships during the supposedly difficult years of adolescence? Ellis (1986) identified three specific factors that contribute to parent-adolescent conflict. The first is the *speed of social change.* Rapid social change is likely to induce intergenerational conflict. For example, in upwardly mobile families, the children may be better educated than their parents and may also be better off economically than the parents were during their own adolescence. The children may have ready access to drugs that their parents have never even heard of. They may be challenged to deal with a permissive set of sexual standards unheard of in the previous generation. In a sense, the children grow up in a world far different from the one their parents grew up in, and this difference may lead to genuine cultural conflict.

A second contributor to parent-adolescent conflict, according to Ellis (1986), is *delay of adult status.* Societies that deny adult status to older adolescents and even young adults are the most likely to experience rebelliousness among disenfranchised young people. Delay of adult status is characterized by the withholding of adult privileges and responsibilities (e.g., driving, holding a job, marrying, voting, drinking) and by attempts to keep young people "suspended" in childhood by extending the years of education.

Finally, a highly significant predictor of conflict is the *amount of control exercised by parents* in the home. The relationship between conflict and control is not a linear one, however. That is, conflict does not increase directly as amount of control increases. Instead, a curvilinear relationship exists, with the greatest intergenerational conflict at the extremes of too much or too little control and the least amount of conflict in the middle range. The authoritative approach to control, with discipline tempered by rational discussion, is associated with a lower level of conflict than is found in the authoritarian or permissive families.

Ellis (1986) noted that the strength of the conflict-control relationship is influenced by several other variables. One such variable is the degree to which adolescents adopt their parents' values. When the child shares the parent's values, control is internal rather than imposed from the outside, and the likelihood of conflict is reduced. A second variable influencing the conflict-control relationship is the timing of parental control: If control is imposed early in childhood, the child is likely to have internalized parental values by the age of adolescence, and conflict is minimized. On the other hand, if parents are permissive with young children and attempt to impose greater control when these children reach adolescence, the result will be resentment and conflict. Ellis (1986) suggested that early permissiveness and late constraint is a pattern often found in families in the United States, and thus the stage for intergenerational conflict is set. By way of contrast, parents in Denmark follow a reverse pattern of early control and later independence in raising their children, and parent-adolescent conflict in Denmark is practically nonexistent (Ellis, 1986; Kandel & Lesser, 1969).

Finally, the conflict-control relationship is influenced by the degree to which the adolescent sees parental control as legitimate (Ellis, 1986). If the control is perceived as fair, rational, and legitimate, conflict is unlikely; if the control is seen as arbitrary or unreasonable, conflict is often the result. Again, authoritative parenting is linked to conflict reduction, because authoritative parents attempt to be rational in imposing constraints on their children and indicate respect for their children by being willing to explain their rules. Often, adolescents do not rebel against the rules themselves but the ways in which the rules are imposed.

The Adult Family

The family enters the adult phase of its life cycle when the grown children leave their parents' homes. As always, the family is in continuous transition, and many adjustments are required of all its members. As their children begin the adjustment to independent living, the mother and father must give up their parental roles and often must assume the new and less clearly defined roles of grandparents. Their own parents, if still living, are now elderly and are adjusting to retirement, and perhaps to the death of a spouse. Furthermore, as longevity increases, many middle-aged couples are faced with the task of looking out for the welfare of their parents of advanced age, a situation that can strain relationships between the generations.

Whether the transitions are easy or difficult, however, the family in adulthood continues to function as a vital, dynamic unit. The modern "nuclear" family does not dissolve when the children are grown, any more than in earlier times several generations of a family chose to live together out of mutual devotion. In fact, family contacts continue to be quite extensive in the adult phase of the family life cycle, and the extended three-generation family of the past more often resulted from economic necessity than from familial devotion (Troll, 1971, 1985).

The Modified Extended Family

Modified extended family
The family in which adult children do not live with their parents but several generations remain close to one another, both socially and geographically.

The modern family in our society has been described as a *modified extended family* (Troll, 1971). That is, although several generations of adults rarely live under the same roof, as in the traditional extended family, adult generations are not separated into isolated nuclear units, either. Instead, they opt for the middle road of living in separate households but maintaining an intergenerational closeness that is both social and geographical (Troll & Bengtson, 1979, 1982).

As an illustration of this compromise pattern, most parents fully expect to see their offspring leave the nest, are psychologically prepared for their departure, and even become concerned when their children live at home longer than anticipated (Harkins, 1978; Lowenthal & Chiriboga, 1972; Pearlin & Radabaugh, 1979). And yet the bond between parent and child seems strong after the children are grown and gone. Four out of five young married people receive financial assistance of some sort from their parents, indicating that financial independence as a hallmark of maturity is more an ideal than a reality (Sussman, 1965). In fact, a good deal of intergenerational helping occurs in U.S. families. People prefer to seek help from within their families rather than from outside them, and a variety of forms of assistance between parent and child can be observed during adulthood; these include help during illness, help in child care, and advice on both business and personal concerns (Hill, Foote, Aldous, Carlson, & McDonald, 1970; Sussman, 1965).

The characteristics of the modified extended family can also be seen in the intergenerational relationships of later life. On the one hand, few elderly people want to live with their grown children, and most share their childrens' view that the adult generations should maintain separate households (Troll, Miller, & Atchley, 1979). Although a sizable percentage of elderly people who live alone would prefer to live with another person, the preferred other person is *not* one of their grown children (Beland, 1987). Those rare elderly people who do live with their children tend to be extremely old and often are incapacitated in some way; in other words, they are so dependent that they would require institutionalization if their children had not taken them in (Beland, 1984; Shapiro & Tate, 1985).

And yet, despite the preference for separate households, old people want to be close enough to their families so that they can interact regularly with them. In fact, approximately 80 percent of elderly Americans live within an hour's traveling distance from their children and manage to see them at least once a week (Kimmel, 1990; Shanas et al., 1968), and, according to a nationwide survey of elderly people (Shanas, 1979), half of the respondents had seen their children on the very day of the interview or on the day before. Furthermore, adult children usually feel a strong obligation to stay in touch with their parents. In one study, more than 90 percent of nearly 700 children of elderly parents agreed that contact with parents should be maintained through visits, calls, or letters, even when it is not convenient to do so (Finley, Roberts, & Banahan, 1988).

In summary, the family remains alive and well after the children have reached adulthood. As Troll and Bengtson (1982) concluded, virtually every survey of intergenerational relationships has resulted in similar findings: Older people in the United States are fully integrated into family structures and actively involved in the lives of their children. Adult children want to maintain contact with their parents and even feel a strong moral obligation to do so.

Combining what we know about the high degree of intergenerational involvement within the adult family with a recognition that the human life span is getting longer, we come to an inevitable conclusion: Adult children may increasingly find themselves in the roles of caretakers for their elderly parents. We turn now to an examination of the caretaking role of adult children and its relationship to the process of parent-child attachment.

Attachment and Caretaking in the Adult Family

Earlier in this chapter, we spoke of parent-infant attachment. In some sense, however, attachment within the family is a life-span process. According to *life-span attachment theory* (Bowlby, 1979, 1980; Cicirelli, 1983, 1988), attachment initially involves the infant's and young child's effort to maintain contact and communication with the parent, but as the child grows up, this effort is accompanied by an increasingly larger element of protectiveness. By the time of adulthood, the attachment behaviors designed to maintain contact with parents (visiting, writing, attending reunions) are accompanied by increasing displays of protective behavior as adults realize that their parents are now moving closer to death. Such protectiveness is illustrated by various forms of helping and caretaking and represents an effort to maintain the emotional bond initially formed during infancy. Needless to say, because death is inevitable, these protective efforts are bound to fail, and this realization can cause anxiety in the adult children of aging parents (Cicirelli, 1988).

The caretaker role of adult children, and particularly that of daughters, is actually quite extensive. Old people who need care, often referred to as frail elderly, tend to be fairly advanced in years (average age, 78 years) and are likely to be in poor health. Those who provide informal care are typically female (72 percent) and typically family members—29 percent of all caretakers are adult daughters, 23 percent are wives, and 13 percent are husbands (Stone, Cafferata, & Sangl, 1987). Consistent with the picture of continued family integration that we have been presenting, only 10 percent

Adult children typically visit, help, and even protect their elderly parents as they attempt to maintain the emotional bond first formed in infancy.

of the frail elderly rely on formal care from paid helpers. Such formal care appears to be used as a last resort in U.S. society (Soldo & Manton, 1985; Stone et al., 1987).

That the role of caring for the frail elderly is most often assumed by a family member speaks well of the integrity of the U.S. family in later life. However, the caretaker role is not without its conflicts. One major study found that one of every four adults who cares for an aging adult parent is also caring for a child under the age of 18, and approximately half (55 percent of the sons and 44 percent of the daughters) are employed outside the home. Thus, those who care for elderly relatives may be torn by competing demands on their time. In fact, 20 percent of caretakers report conflict between their jobs and their caretaking responsibilities (Stone et al., 1987).

Perhaps because they are in the category of people most often called upon to assume such responsibilities, much of the research on the caretaking role has dealt with the experiences of middle-aged women. Women caretakers typically report greater negative reactions than men (Barusch, 1988; Barusch & Spaid, 1989). One possible reason is that a woman in mid-life may be trying to fulfill a variety of marital, social, parental, and vocational responsibilities. If she is expected in addition to care for an elderly relative, she may suffer from role demand overload, a belief that she is less than adequate in all her roles (Wallace & Noelker, 1984). As a result, she may experience feelings of guilt and resentment, strains on her mental health, and dissatisfaction with the quality of her relationship with the elderly relative she is caring for (Scharlach, 1987; Scharlach & Frenzel, 1982).

Although easy solutions to the problem are not apparent, promising evidence suggests that educational and emotional support groups may lessen the strain of caring for an elderly relative (Greene & Monahan, 1989; Toseland, Rossiter & Labrecque, 1989; Zarit & Toseland, 1989). However the problem is eventually resolved, public policymakers must recognize that, although the family of adult life is still quite strong, the combination of increased longevity, the increasing proportion of old people in the population, and the increase in the numbers of roles and responsibilities confronting U.S. women may create unbearable strains for adult children who care for elderly parents (Brody, 1985; Scharlach, 1987).

The Sibling Relationship in Adulthood

We have pointed out that sibling interaction has been a neglected area of study. Relatively little is known about siblingship, as compared to the vast amount of information available about spousal relationships and relationships between parents and children. Research on siblings in adult life is particularly scarce. In fact, with a few notable exceptions, little research on adult sibling bonds was conducted before the 1980s (Bedford, 1989).

We earlier observed that childhood sibling contacts seem more important today than ever before. There is an additional reason for the growing importance of adult siblings: As the life span lengthens and as families shrink in size, fewer adult children will be available to care for the elderly in future years. As a result, brothers and sisters may be more likely to assume the caretaker roles (Bank & Kahn, 1982; Gold, 1989). Adult siblings may be needed more in the future than they have been in past years.

Two major characteristics describe the sibling relationship in adulthood. First, the sibling role is a highly diverse one, with a broad range of intimacy and involvement. Second, the sibling relationship appears to have great psychological importance for the emotional well-being of U.S. adults (Gold, 1989; Suggs, 1985).

Diversity of the Sibling Role. A broad range of intimacy is possible in the adult sibling role, depending on (1) gender, (2) marital status, and (3) childhood family experiences of the persons involved. Female siblings are usually closer than males, with the closest bond being the one between sisters, followed by the sister-brother bond, and lastly the bond between two brothers (Allan, 1977; Cicirelli, 1980, 1982, 1985; Pulakos, 1987). Marriage tends to weaken the sibling connection; single people are more likely than marrieds to rate their relationships with their siblings of both sexes as highly important to them (Bedford, 1989; Pulakos, 1987). Finally, childhood family experience comes into play; adults who had the closest, warmest families during their childhood years are the most likely to report the closest relationships with their siblings (Ross & Milgram, 1982).

Functions of Adult Siblings. What exactly are the functions of siblings in adult life? The answer depends, at least to some extent, on the phase of the life cycle the adult is going through, according to sociologist Ann Goetting (1986), who described the functions of siblings at different points in adulthood as a series of developmental tasks. During early and middle adulthood, siblings can accomplish three such tasks:

1. *Providing companionship and emotional support.* Although the relationship may be less intense than during childhood and adolescence, adult siblings continue to relate as friends and confidants. They maintain at least some degree of concern for one another and some interest in how the sibling is getting along in life.
2. *Helping to care for elderly parents and dismantling the parental home.* As their parents age and eventually die, adult siblings come together frequently to deal with various crises, to support one another emotionally, and to dismantle the parental estate.
3. *Offering aid and direct services.* Young and middle-aged siblings exchange help occasionally, as required by various life situations. For example, they may lend money, babysit, help out during illness, or share clothing or household items.

The tasks of siblings during the years of old age are somewhat different from those of earlier adulthood, although a certain amount of similarity exists as well. Goetting (1986) described the developmental tasks of siblings in later life in the following way:

1. *Providing companionship and emotional support.* As spouses and friends die, elderly adults may turn to their siblings to find the emotional support they need to cope with life changes. The bond of support between siblings seems to intensify at this time.
2. *Sharing and validating the past.* Siblings may help one another remember past events and relationships clearly, understand them better, and place them in a mature perspective.
3. *Resolving sibling rivalry.* Often, it is only late in life that many siblings put to rest their longstanding disagreements. Many people can concentrate on the more positive aspects of the sibling relationship only when they are elderly.
4. *Providing aid and direct services.* Older siblings often rely on one another for various forms of aid, including financial support; help in times of illness; and assistance with homemaking, shopping, transportation, or home repairs. Such assistance is rarely extensive, but it is essential (Suggs, 1985).

In summary, the sibling relationship continues to have considerable importance in later life, just as it did early in the life span. Siblings play a number of roles, most of which are not central in the life of an adult, but which have great meaning nonetheless.

Becoming a Grandparent

Anthropologist Margaret Mead (1972) believed that to become complete human beings, we all need to have contacts across three or more generations. "In the presence of grandparent and grandchild," she wrote, "past and future merge in the present" (p. 284). Grandparents provide a sense of continuity for their grandchildren—a link with the past. Moreover, because it is difficult to love children and to care about their development without having personal contact with specific children, contact with grandchildren elicits from grandparents a sense of caring about the future of humanity.

Studies of U.S. grandparenting (e.g., Cherlin & Furstenberg, 1985; Neugarten & Weinstein, 1964; Robertson, 1977) usually indicate that no such thing as a typical grandparent exists. Instead, the role is what the individual chooses to make of it. In fact, determining exactly what U.S. grandparents *do* in the lives of their children and grandchildren is difficult because the role varies so much across individuals and across time (Hagestad, 1985). In other words, not only can a number of grandparenting styles be identified at any given time, but an individual grandparent may continually change his or her role (Cherlin & Furstenberg, 1985). A grandparent may interact continuously with children when they are young but may become more detached as they grow up. A grandparent may take

Grandparents provide a sense of continuity for grandchildren—and grandchildren provide a link with the future for grandparents.

an active family role in a crisis but may remain passive and uninvolved in the ordinary course of events. In that sense, grandparents have been described as "family watchdogs" whose roles vary in response to family need (Troll, 1983).

And finally, to complicate the issue even further, the role of grandparent is influenced by a number of other variables such as the age of the grandparent, level of education, race, social class, gender, need for affiliation, number of extrafamilial relationships, involvement in community activities, physical proximity, personality of the grandchild, and family tradition. It is little wonder that social scientists who study the U.S. family conclude that grandparents in our country defy all stereotypes!

Typical of the research illustrating the diversity of U.S. grandparenting is the classic study by Neugarten and Weinstein (1964), who interviewed grandparents from 70 families and asked them about their perceptions of the role. The researchers identified five grandparenting styles. The *formal grandparent* espouses the traditional, authoritarian style. The formal grandparent is keenly interested in the upbringing of the grandchildren and maintains close contact with them, although the specific parenting duties are left to the parents. The formal grandparent is, in a sense, a backup parent. *Fun seekers* believe that grandparenting should be fun for them and

Research Close-Up
Behavioral Expectations of
Grandparenthood

Most studies of the roles of grandparents in the United States have examined the actual involvement of grandparents and their grandchildren. Very little is known about what Americans *expect* the experience of grandparenting to be like before it arrives. In an interesting study of grandparental expectations, Cathleen McGreal of Michigan State University asked 146 prospective grandparents what they believed the experience would be like for them and how they planned to interact with their grandchildren. She then compared their responses with the actual roles reported by grandparents in an earlier study (Robertson, 1977).

As indicated by Table A, expectant grandparents seemed to have some definite ideas about what the role would entail. But the expectations do not match the actual behaviors reported by grandparents. In general, grandparents seem to expect a greater degree of involvement with their prospective grandchildren than is actually likely to occur. Expectations for visiting, babysitting, and buying gifts appear to be realistic enough, but prospective grandparents who plan to serve as advisers to their grandchildren or as transmitters of the family history may be disappointed.

Table A

Role Behavior	Percentage of Expectant Grandparents Anticipating This Activity	Percentage of Robertson's Subjects Reporting Activity
Provide gifts	96.6	97.6
Babysit grandchild	84.2	92
Engage in home recreational activities	94.5	79.2
Drop in to visit grandchild	54.8	64.8
Relate family history	78.8	47.2
Help out with family emergencies	99.3	39.2
Take grandchild on vacations	69.9	28.4
Advise grandchild on personal problems	46.5	29.6
Advise grandchild regarding work	41.8	24
Advise grandchild regarding religion	28.8	13.6

Source: C. E. McGreal. *Grandparenthood as a symbol: Expectations for the grandparental role.* Paper presented at the annual meeting of the Gerontological Society of America, San Francisco, California, November, 1983.

their grandchildren. The fun seeker is not an authoritarian but more of a playmate for the children. The *surrogate parent* is the grandparent who takes on the actual responsibilities of a parent. This is usually a grandmother who becomes a mother to her grandchildren when their mother is unavailable because she has a job outside the home. The *reservoir of family wisdom* is usually a grandfather who has special skills or knowledge that he passes on to his grandchildren. He is clearly an authority figure. This type of grandparent is very unusual in our society today, perhaps because the skills possessed by grandparents are not as valued in our rapidly changing society as they once were. Finally, there is the *distant figure,* the grandparent who has very little contact with grandchildren and sees them only on special occasions such as birthdays or holidays.

Neugarten and Weinstein found that the fun seeker and the distant grandparent were the most common types, which was a definite turning away from the traditional authoritarian style.

Most of the research on grandparenting has dealt with the relationship between the grandparent and the young child. Little is known about young adults' perceptions of their grandparents. One of the few studies of this type was carried out by Robertson (1976), who found that young adults aged 18 to 26 expressed favorable attitudes toward their grandparents. Most felt that grandparents are not old-fashioned or out of touch with reality, do not usually spoil their grandchildren, and have much influence on the young. Another study (Matthews, 1983) found that the degree of closeness between young adults and their grandparents is related to the amount of interaction during childhood and the degree of closeness between the child's parents and grandparents. The maternal grandmother was seen as the closest of the four grandparents.

In summary, the role of grandparent in U.S. society is not a precise one but varies somewhat from family to family. However, regardless of what form it takes, the grandparent-child relationship seems to be important for most of us because it provides a sense of continuity. It helps us realize our position within the framework of the passing of generations. Finally, in a society in which age groups often are separated from one another, it provides us with a better understanding of the process of human development at various points in the life span.

THE DISRUPTED FAMILY

In the United States today, divorce is the largest single cause of marital disruption. Since 1860, the first year in which such records were kept, the rate of divorce has been rising in the United States. The increase was a slow and steady one, however, until the mid-1960s. Then, from 1960 to approximately 1980, the divorce rate per 1,000 population actually doubled as divorce seemed to gain widespread acceptance as a respectable solution to marital problems (Zill & Rogers, 1988).

The rising divorce rate seems to have hit a peak in 1980, and little change has occurred since then (Bumpass & Sweet, 1989; Cherlin, 1988a, 1988b). Nevertheless, projections indicate that nearly half the marriages entered into in any given year in the 1980s will end in divorce (Norton & Moorman, 1987; Raschke, 1987).

Let us now examine the issue of divorce, looking first at factors related to divorce, then at adults' reasons for and reactions to the break-up of their marriages, and, finally, at the impact of divorce on the children who live in disrupted families.

Divorce: The Adult's Point of View

Divorce is a reality of life for many adults in the United States today, and one that has a major impact on their lives. In this section, we look at divorce from the perspectives of the husband and wife, examining a number of factors that are correlated with divorce, the reasons couples give for seeking a divorce, and the emotional reactions that accompany and follow the dissolution of a marriage.

Factors Related to Divorce

No one knows why so many marriages in our society end in divorce. Perhaps the reasons for divorce are as varied as the divorced couples themselves. Joan Kelly (1982), one of the nation's leading experts in the study of marital breakdown, identified a number of factors related to marital stability. These factors are correlational rather than causal; they describe typical patterns instead of attempting to define reasons for divorce. The reasons, as will be seen, are more elusive. The factors outlined by Kelly are as follows:

1. *Socioeconomic status.* Lower-class Americans are more likely to divorce than middle- and upper-class couples, although class differences have been declining rapidly within the past 30 years (Norton & Glick, 1979).
2. *Age.* Men who marry before the age of 20 and women who marry before the age of 18 are twice as likely to divorce as are those who marry later (Bumpass & Sweet, 1989).
3. *Race.* The divorce rate among blacks in the United States is higher than the rate for whites, and interracial marriages have the poorest chance for success.
4. *Premarital pregnancy.* Women who are pregnant at the time of marriage are more likely to divorce than those who are not (Coombs & Zumeta, 1970). Pregnancy is thought to interfere with the necessary preparation period before marriage, and early parenthood may seriously affect a couple's earning ability (Furstenberg, 1979; Kelly, 1982).
5. *Employment.* More than the actual amount of his earnings, a husband's employment instability is related to marital failure. Women who earn high salaries are more likely to divorce, possibly because a woman with a higher income is more willing to separate from her husband than one who knows that separation will result in great financial hardship for her, and her children (Moore & Waite, 1981; Teachman et al., 1987).
6. *Parental divorce.* Children of divorced parents are more likely to see their own marriages end in divorce than children from intact families (Glenn & Kramer, 1987; Kobrin & Waite, 1984; Kulka & Weingarten, 1979; Mueller & Cooper, 1986). The reasons for such a correlation are unclear, although perhaps children of divorce may be a bit more apprehensive about marriage and may withhold some degree of commitment to their marriages (Glenn & Kramer, 1987). However, many children of divorced

parents experience stable and lasting marriages, and many children of stable marriages see their own marriages dissolve.

Reasons for Divorce

The specific reasons for a couple's decision to divorce will obviously vary from one marriage to another. However, when reasons for divorce are analyzed on a large scale, a number of interesting patterns emerge. First, as the divorce rate rose dramatically from 1960 to 1980, the likelihood increased that expressive (e.g., lack of affection, value differences) rather than instrumental (e.g., nonsupport, excessive drinking) reasons were responsible for the termination of marriage (Raschke, 1987). Second, the typical reasons given for divorce, by both husbands and wives, involve lack of communication and understanding between marriage partners, lack of appropriate attention, and feelings of being unloved (Kitson & Sussman, 1982; Wallerstein & Kelly, 1980). Third, many couples agree that gender role issues are often involved in divorce decisions. Husbands cite disagreements and confusion about the appropriate roles for men and women within the home, and wives cite their own internal conflicts about needs for independence and a life outside the family (Kitson & Sussman, 1982). In fact, the rise of feminism in the late twentieth century is often cited as a factor contributing to the rising divorce rate, in the sense that women are increasingly likely to realize that a variety of options are available other than remaining in unsatisfactory marriages (Raschke, 1987).

Finally, the reasons for divorce may vary depending on the stage of the family life cycle in which the couple is found: Middle-aged divorcing couples are less likely than young adults to report significant conflicts leading to the divorce decision. Instead, they indicate that they gradually lost interest in each other and came to find pleasure in fewer and fewer shared activities (Hayes, Stinnett, & DeFrain, 1980; Raschke, 1987).

Reactions to Divorce

Because divorce involves a major life transition, it creates stress. The emotional reactions to divorce include depression, loss of self-esteem, anger, confusion, and a feeling that a new chance at life has become available (Kelly, 1982). Of course, reactions vary greatly, depending on individual temperament, reasons for divorce, economic status, and other variables. We will examine some of the most frequently observed emotional reactions to divorce. Keep in mind that these reactions are statistically probable but certainly not inevitable.

Intense anger is a common reaction among both husbands and wives. In one major study, 20 percent of the men and 44 percent of the women said they felt extreme anger toward their separated spouses, and an additional 60 percent of the men and 46 percent of the women expressed moderate anger (Wallerstein & Kelly, 1980). Not only was the degree of anger expressed in the interviews surprisingly high, but the hostility seemed to intensify rather

Issues in Human Development
Divorce After 60: Too Old to Start Over?

 Much has been written about the tragic effects of divorce on husbands and wives and on the children of their marriages. Little has been said, however, about divorce among elderly people in the United States, which, following the general trend, has been occurring more frequently in recent years.

Barbara Cain, a supervisor at the Psychological Clinic of the University of Michigan, suggested that elderly women find divorce a particularly stressful experience and may face special problems not shared by the young. Among the special hardships of the "gray divorcée" are the following:

1. Virtually no support groups, formal or informal, are available for elderly divorcées. The young divorcée may seek the help of a national organization, such as Parents Without Partners, but there is no grandparental equivalent. Furthermore, young women may encounter and receive support from large numbers of divorced people in their age group, but elderly divorcées are unlikely to make contact with age-mates in similar circumstances.

2. The financial crisis for the elderly divorcée may be much greater than for her younger counterpart. Young and middle-aged women may have trouble finding employment in our society, but for elderly women the employment situation is virtually hopeless. Furthermore, the elderly divorcée may find herself cut off from her husband's pension and medical insurance at a time when she needs financial assistance the most.

3. Younger divorcées may lose contact with their spouses, but they still retain many of their other social contacts. They even may expand their social network if they enter the job market. Elderly women have more limited social contacts to begin with and may find themselves virtually isolated after a divorce.

4. People today who are over the age of 60 were raised in what Cain called a generation "committed to constancy" (p. 90). Thus, the elderly divorcée may feel ashamed of her circumstances. She may be overwhelmed by guilt to a much greater degree than a young divorcée.

5. Finally, the older divorcée may feel that she is too old to start over. Her younger counterpart eventually will realize that she has many active years ahead of her and will attempt to pick up the pieces and begin again. The older woman may feel that such an effort is futile.

Source: B. S. Cain. The plight of the gray divorcée. *New York Times Magazine,* December 19, 1982, pp. 89–95.

than diminish in the months after the initial separation. Kelly (1982) pointed out that the civilized and friendly divorce is quite unusual in our society, and she suggested that our legal system encourages hostility rather than friendly accommodation in a divorce settlement.

In addition to anger, another common emotional reaction to divorce is depression, which manifests itself in a variety of ways, including sleeplessness, fatigue, loss of self-esteem, or weight gains or losses (Herman, 1977; Kelly, 1982). Severe depression is most common in people who have been left by their spouses, and it seems to be equally common in men and women. In one study, one-third of the men and an equal percentage of women reported feelings of severe depression after the marital separation (Wallerstein & Kelly, 1980).

A surprising number of divorced people, particularly those who were not the initiators of the divorce proceedings, experience mental disorganization:

confusion, anxiety, fear of a complete mental breakdown, thoughts of suicide, extreme mood swings, and unpredictable emotional outbursts. One in four participants in one major study of divorce exhibited a variety of such symptoms, and in some cases brief hospitalization was required (Kelly, 1982; Wallerstein & Kelly, 1980).

Finally, not all emotional responses of divorcing couples are negative. Nearly half of such people experience a sense of relief that a difficult relationship is coming to an end (Chiriboga & Cutler, 1977; Wallerstein & Kelly, 1980). Many feel relief at having made what they long regarded as an inevitable decision. For others, separation brings relief from a constant high level of stress in their relationships. Related to the feeling of relief is a sentiment expressed by many women (but few men) that divorce brings with it a new chance—an opportunity for renewal and growth (Wallerstein & Kelly, 1980).

Divorce: The Child's Point of View

Josh, a 14-year-old boy from Massachusetts, was asked by a magazine reporter to recall his greatest worry as a child. "War," he said. "It's scary to think what could happen." Then the reporter mentioned the divorce of Josh's parents, which took place 9 years earlier, and Josh said, "Now that I think about it, war looks really small compared with that" (Morrow, 1988, p. 56).

Sad as it is, Josh's childhood memory is not at all unusual today. During every year of the 1980s, some 1 million U.S. children shared Josh's experience of divorce, and the trend is on the rise. For example, although one in four U.S. children born in 1970 lived through a divorce in the family before they were 18 years of age, estimates suggest that one in three of those born in the 1980s have already lived, or will live, through a similar experience (Bane, 1979; J. Block, J. H. Block, & Gjerde, 1988; Furstenberg, Nord, Peterson, & Zill, 1983; Zill & Rogers, 1988).

Just as marital disruption cannot be regarded as an isolated phenomenon in the 1990s, no complete discussion of U.S. parenting practices can exclude reference to the single-parent household that results from divorce. Let us now examine that household, focusing on the three areas in which marital disruption will necessitate the greatest adjustments: economic changes, emotional reactions of the custodial parent, and child's perceived loss of the parent who moves out.

Economic Changes

Perhaps the most revealing statistics about the economic circumstances of children in single-parent households are those regarding the percentage who fall below the official poverty line established by the United States government. Approximately 20 percent of *all* U.S. children were living below the poverty line in 1985, a figure that has been rising regularly since a low of about 14 percent was reached in 1969 (U.S. Bureau of the Census, 1987).

However, when the children from mother-only households are examined separately, the percentage living below the poverty line is substantially higher; it has remained for the past 20 years at somewhere between 51 percent and 56 percent (Zill & Rogers, 1988)! Households headed by single fathers fare considerably better, with incomes that are more than double those of families headed by single mothers (U.S. Bureau of the Census, 1987).

Considerable economic variation exists among single-mother households, depending on the mother's race, socioeconomic class, level of education, employment potential, and reason (divorce, separation, widowhood, never married) she is raising the children by herself. For example, divorced-mother households have incomes twice as large as the households of never-married mothers, an understandable finding when one considers that, of the two groups, divorced mothers are older, better educated, more likely to be receiving child support from the children's father, and more likely to be employed outside the home. Nevertheless, even the relatively advantaged divorced-mother household has an income that is only 40 percent of that found in the two-parent household (Zill & Rogers, 1988).

Why do female-headed families created by divorce, in which the mother is relatively advantaged compared to other single mothers, fare so poorly as compared to two-parent and single-father families? For many reasons. First, the amount of alimony and child support received by divorced mothers is low, irregular, and, in two out of three cases, nonexistent (U.S. Bureau of the Census, 1987; Zill & Rogers, 1988). One study found that most noncustodial fathers paid little or nothing for the support of their children within a few years after the divorce, and, in fact, had virtually no contact with their children (Furstenberg et al., 1983).

In addition, many single mothers may be unable to find satisfactory child care arrangements to free them to work outside the home (Bane & Jargowsky, 1988). A third reason for the economic difficulties of divorced mothers is that fewer employment opportunities exist in our society for women, many of whom lack marketable job skills, than for men. And when women do find work, it is mostly low-paying (e.g., clerical work, service work, private household work). Even when they have equivalent skills and experiences, women in the United States earn lower wages than men (Bane, 1979).

One major effect of divorce on children, therefore, is that the standard of living to which they have become accustomed may be lowered.

Emotional Reactions of the Custodial Parent

The quality of a child's home atmosphere may be affected adversely by the custodial parent's reaction to divorce. In fact, divorced and separated mothers (the typical custodial parents) have been found to suffer greater anxiety and to experience deeper depression than married mothers (Hetherington, 1972; Longfellow, 1979; Pearlin & Johnson, 1977). Divorced mothers also have reported feelings of anger and incompetence in their roles

(Hetherington, Cox, & Cox, 1978). Finally, the divorced mother may experience a substantial loss in her social contacts and consequently may lose much-needed emotional support and advice from family and friends. Such losses may adversely influence her relationship with her children (Longfellow, 1979).

If their mother is stressed, the children of divorce will feel the stress as well. Divorced mothers report having less time and emotional energy to devote to their children than they did while married (Brown, Bhrolchain, & Harris, 1975; Longfellow, 1979). Parent-child conflict is more frequent as the children become at least slightly disillusioned about the personal qualities of both of their parents (Hetherington, 1979; Tessman, 1978). In two of every three cases studied, a general overall deterioration in the mother-child relationship within the first year after the divorce has been detected (Wallerstein & Kelly, 1975).

Loss of the Noncustodial Parent

Research on parent-child separation after a divorce has focused almost exclusively on the loss of the father as a continuing source of influence. Hetherington (1979) described several effects on children of the loss of the father, a loss that can be understood best by referring to the father's functions in the intact nuclear family. Fathers participate in child rearing directly by disciplining children, teaching them, and serving as adult models. Mothers also serve as models, of course, but as Hetherington (1979) observed, two adult models expose the child to a wider range of interests, attitudes, and behaviors than only one does. A second parent in the family also can serve as a buffer of emotional support if the other parent rejects a child on a continuing basis or simply because of a difficult day. In the single-parent family, such an adult refuge is rarely available.

Fathers participate in parenting indirectly by providing economic aid to the family, sharing household chores, and providing emotional support for their wives. Such activities promote the harmonious functioning of the family unit and, as a consequence, improve the overall quality of the child rearing. The loss of the father may have a reverse effect.

Developmental Differences in Children's Reactions to Divorce

Thus far, the structural changes in the child's home life that occur as a result of marital disruption have been described. Developmental changes in children's characteristic reactions to divorce are shown in Table 11.5. As a child grows older, he or she is more likely to express freely a variety of complex feelings, to understand those feelings, and to realize that the decision to divorce cannot be attributed to any one simple cause. Self-blame virtually disappears after the age of 6; fear of abandonment diminishes after the age of 8; and confusion and fear in the young child is replaced by shame, anger, and self-reflection in the older child (Kelly & Wallerstein, 1976; Wallerstein & Kelly, 1974, 1975, 1976).

Table 11.5
Developmental Changes in Children's Reactions to Divorce

Age	Reaction
2½–6 years	Children had difficulty expressing their feelings, lacked an understanding of what the concept of divorce meant or implied in terms of parental separation or change in living arrangements, and tended to blame themselves for the situation, regardless of how carefully the parents tried to educate them to the fact that they were not responsible.
7–8 years	Children did not blame themselves for the divorce. They were aware of their feelings and easily verbalized their sadness, but not their anger. Feelings of rejection were common. They did not understand that the divorce was a mutual arrangement between the two parents; instead, the children believed that one parent simply got angry and left or told the other one to leave. The children commonly feared that they could be abandoned or thrown out as easily.
9–10 years	Children did not blame themselves for the breakup and freely expressed their feelings, including anger toward either or both parents. However, the anger was often combined with loyalty—a sense of loving and hating the parent at the same time. Unlike younger children, 9- and 10-year-olds tended to hide their sadness and present a tough exterior. Feelings of loneliness and fear of being unloved were common.
Adolescence	Strong feelings of anger, shame, sadness, and embarrassment were found in this age group. They were able to analyze carefully the nature of their parents' marriage relationship and to understand the needs and feelings of both parents. Adolescents experiencing a parental divorce often related to parents as real and complex human beings much better than they had earlier. Also, they tended to give careful consideration of the nature and requirements of marriage itself.

Source: J. B. Kelly & J. S. Wallerstein. The effects of parental divorce: Experiences of the child in early latency. *American Journal of Orthopsychiatry,* 1976, *46,* pp. 20–32; J. S. Wallerstein and J. B. Kelly. The effects of parental divorce: The adolescent experience. In J. Anthony and C. Koupernik (Eds.), *The child in his family: Children at psychiatric risk* (Vol. 3). New York: Wiley, 1974, pp. 479–505; J. S. Wallerstein and J. B. Kelly. The effects of parental divorce: Experiences of the preschool child. *Journal of the American Academy of Child Psychiatry,* 1975, *14,* pp. 600–616; J. S. Wallerstein and J. B. Kelly. The effects of parental divorce: Experience of the child in later latency. *American Journal of Orthopsychiatry,* 1976, *46,* pp. 256–269.

Gender Differences in Reaction to Divorce

The impact of divorce is initially greater on boys than on girls, as well as considerably longer lasting (Hetherington, 1979; Hetherington, Cox, & Cox, 1978). Compared with daughters of divorced parents, the sons of divorced parents tend to be more aggressive and less compliant, to have greater difficulties in interpersonal relationships, and to exhibit problem behaviors both at home and at school. Furthermore, the adjustment problems of boys are still quite noticeable even 2 years after the divorce, whereas for girls, any problems that did arise already have disappeared.

Hetherington suggested a number of possible explanations for the relatively greater impact of divorce on boys than on girls. The finding of greater male aggression and noncompliance may reflect our culture's tolerance and even encouragement of such behaviors in males. Even in two-parent families, males exceed females in the prevalence of aggressive, noncompliant behaviors (Hetherington, Cox, & Cox, 1978). Furthermore, boys may have a particular need for a strong male model of self-control, as well as for a strong disciplinarian parent. Finally, boys are more likely to be exposed to their parents' fights than girls are, and after the breakup, boys are less likely than girls to receive sympathy and support from mothers, teachers, or peers (Hetherington, 1979).

As a final point about the behavioral difficulties faced by male children of divorce, many of those difficulties may not be the result of the divorce itself, but may have been present even years before the divorce. Block, Block, and Gjerde (1986, 1988) carried out a longitudinal analysis of various families, some of whom eventually divorced and some of whom did not. The researchers were able to look back, therefore, and determine the antecedent conditions of marital disruption. They discovered that, even years before the parental decision to divorce, boys in "pre-divorce" families were more uncontrollable and impulsive than boys in families that would remain intact.

Long-Term Effects of Divorce

The experience of divorce generally entails a difficult life adjustment for children, one that can have debilitating long-term effects. Such effects have been found primarily in three areas of psychological functioning (Kalter, 1987). First, aggressive, antisocial behaviors increase after divorce (Guidibaldi & Perry, 1985; Hetherington, Cox, & Cox, 1985; Peterson & Zill, 1983)—what Kalter (1987) referred to as "externalizing" problems. Second, such "internalizing" problems as sadness, depression, and lowered self-esteem also increase (Guidibaldi & Perry, 1985; Kalter, 1984, 1987). Finally, a commonly observed reaction to divorce is later difficulty in establishing and maintaining successful heterosexual relationships (Kalter, 1984, 1987; Wallerstein, 1985; Wallerstein & Blakeslee, 1989).

All three patterns of reaction appeared in what is perhaps the most extensive investigation to date of children's long-term reactions to divorce—the California Divorce Study, conducted by Judith Wallerstein and Joan Berlin Kelly (Wallerstein, 1985, 1987; Wallerstein & Blakeslee, 1989; Wallerstein & Kelly, 1980). Sixty California families were selected for study, all of which were disrupted by divorce in 1971; a total of 131 children were involved, ranging from preschool age to young adolescence. The families were first seen shortly after the parental separation, in sessions focusing on the children's ability to cope with the impending divorce. Since then they have been interviewed on three different occasions—first at 18–24 months after the divorce, then at 5 years, and most recently at 10 years, when many of the children had grown into young adults.

Two Years Later.   The findings from the California Divorce Study demonstrate how agonizingly painful the dissolution of a marriage is for everyone concerned. At the time of the 2-year interview, for example, the vast majority of the children of divorce were still not coping well, and many were actually worse off psychologically than they had been immediately after the divorce.

Five Years Later.   At the 5-year point, one of every three children of divorce seemed to be coping well, as indicated by the absence of depression, adequate or high self-esteem, and a positive and realistic outlook on life. The researchers suggested a number of factors as predictors of successful adjustment, including (1) a continuing stable relationship with both parents; (2) a warm, nurturant relationship with the custodial parent; (3) a close relationship with the noncustodial parent; (4) the presence of good friendships outside the home; (5) the availability of other sources of emotional support, including grandparents, teachers, neighbors, and the clergy; and (6) the psychological stability of the parents.

Unfortunately, children who had adjusted successfully at the 5-year point were in the minority. Many others had adjusted adequately but unevenly, but fully 37 percent of the children in the sample were still experiencing anger, depression, inability to concentrate, and difficulty in making and maintaining friendships. A number of factors were identified as predictors of poor adjustment: (1) the failure of the divorce to resolve the conflict between the parents, (2) the presence of stress in the custodial parent, (3) inadequate parenting, which had been inadequate even before the divorce, and (4) the inability of the children to understand the reasons for the divorce in the first place.

Ten Years Later.   What happens to the children of divorce as they enter adulthood and begin to establish intimate love relationships of their own? According to Wallerstein and Blakeslee (1989), the scars of living through familial disruption are deep and lasting for many people. Four of every 10 children in the original California Divorce Study sample entered adulthood as worried, underachieving, self-deprecating, and angry young men and women.

A common experience among the daughters from the California Divorce Study as they entered young adulthood (19 to 23 years of age) was a delayed divorce reaction, which Wallerstein and Blakeslee (1989) termed a sleeper effect. That is, many children who seemed well adjusted at the time of the earlier interviews began to experience coping difficulties only later when they tried to form adult love relationships: Two-thirds of the women reported that falling in love filled them with anxiety, expressed fears about making commitments, and were overly concerned that their lovers would ultimately betray them. Such fear of relationships was less often found among the male interviewees, but 40 percent of these young men felt powerless to control their own lives and seemed unable to set meaningful goals for themselves.

Wallerstein and Blakeslee (1989) suggested that the model used by children when they form adult relationships is typically that provided by their own parents. In the aftermath of divorce, no appropriate model of a successful relationship between a man and a woman exists. In fact, young adults who grew up in disrupted families are more likely to characterize their homes as colder, less affectionate, more distant, and poorer in communication than adults remembering childhood in intact families (Fine, Moreland, & Schwebel, 1983).

Furthermore, adults from divorced families see marriage in more complex terms than those whose parents' marriages remained intact, are more aware of its limitations, and are more accepting of marriage alternatives (Amato, 1988). A final statistic in support of the view that parents provide a model of marriage for their children was presented earlier in this section: Children of divorced parents are more likely than children from intact families to see their own marriages end in divorce (Glenn & Kramer, 1987; Mueller & Cooper, 1986), although this outcome is not inevitable.

In summary, divorce can have significant long-term effects on a child's self-concept, as well as on the relationship with either or both parents. Divorce can be a painful and emotionally trying experience for children, but psychological recovery is possible if parents make great efforts to be sensitive to their children's feelings and needs. Psychologist E. Mavis Hetherington (1989), who has devoted much of her career to studying the impact of family transitions, observed that, depending on the child's characteristics, available coping resources, and subsequent life experiences, children of divorce can emerge as losers, as survivors, or as winners.

Stepparents and Stepchildren

Most people who divorce, approximately 85 percent of the men and 75 percent of the women, marry again, usually within 5 years after their divorces are final (Glick, 1984; Teachman et al., 1987). Inevitably, children in our society are affected by parental remarriage just as they are affected by divorce; 6 in 10 of the divorced people who marry again are the parents of at least one child under the age of eighteen (Bigner, 1985), and 1 in 3 children born in the United States in the early 1980s will spend at least some time in a stepfamily (Glick, 1984). Thus, there develops what is often referred to as the *reconstituted family,* members of which take on the unfamiliar roles of stepparents and stepchildren. Some 30 million adults and

Reconstituted family
A family that is formed by the marriage of a couple, one or both of whom already have children from a previous marriage.

10 million children in the United States lived in stepfamilies in the late 1980s (Cherlin & McCarthy, 1985; Fine, 1986).

In general, the effects of remarriage on the family are positive, in the sense that children in reconstituted families differ little in their psychological profiles from children living in unbroken homes (Fine, 1986; Wilson, Zurcher, McAdams, & Curtis, 1975). One exception to this general rule is found in the case of adolescent boys living with stepfathers. Perhaps because of the particular qualities of the stepfather-stepson relationship,

The reconstituted family—resulting from the marriage of people who already have children—is an increasingly familiar phenomenon in the United States today.

adolescent boys in this category more closely resemble boys in single-parent households in the frequency of their deviant behaviors than boys who live with both natural parents (Dornbusch et al., 1985).

The general observation that a parent's remarriage can relieve the stresses experienced by children in single-parent households does not imply that problems never arise when families are reconstituted. In fact, the establishment of the stepparent and stepchild relationship is sometimes a difficult process, for several reasons. New stepparents take on an unfamiliar and sometimes frightening role as they attempt to incorporate themselves into the "culture" of an existing family; they may be perceived as and may perceive themselves as outsiders (Bigner, 1985).

Stepparents may face particular difficulties in their role as disciplinarians. Their style of discipline may deviate from what the stepchildren were used to, and the disciplinary approaches of stepparent and natural parent may not be coordinated yet. Compromise is often required, and children may take advantage of the initial inconsistencies by playing the parent against the stepparent. Children may also take merciless advantage of a new stepparent who has never been a parent before (Bohannan & Erickson, 1978).

Another possible complication in the relationship between stepparent and stepchild is that children may hold a strong allegiance to the natural parent and may resent the stepparent as a poor substitute for their absent parent (Kompara, 1982). Consciously or not, children may cherish the hope that their natural parents will reunite, and may see the stepparent as an obstacle to that reunion (Bigner, 1985).

Stepmothers in particular may find themselves struggling against a negative stereotype: The wicked stepmother seems to be a stock character in many a children's fairy tale. As a result, the stepmother may try too hard to be accepted by her stepchildren and may find herself in the stressful situation of trying to make everyone in the family happy (Nelson & Nelson, 1982). Stepfathers, on the other hand, may have their own special problems. They often face the difficult prospect of trying to provide financial support for two families at once, and they may feel guilt for "abandoning" their natural children as they move into the new family.

Even though stepfamilies sometimes encounter problems in adjusting to their new living arrangements, such families also solve these problems; reconstituted families are generally quite successful in terms of the emotional well-being of the people within them (Fine, 1986). In fact, the success of reconstituted families illustrates a point about family development that we have alluded to frequently throughout this chapter. Family can be defined in many ways, but at its core it is a dynamic system, one that is capable of adapting to change. Perhaps the challenge to be adaptable is more urgent now than it has been in the past, and one can hope that the family will continue to meet that challenge.

Summary

1. The family is best thought of as a dynamic and continuously changing system rather than as a collection of individuals living in the same household.
2. Despite concerns about the rising divorce rate in the 1960s and 1970s, marriage continues to be the preferred social arrangement of the majority of adults in the United States. However, evidence suggests recent declines in the overall marriage rate.
3. Marital roles change continuously in response to varying social circumstances, and we are living in a time when several types of marriage arrangements exist simultaneously.
4. Theoretical perspectives on parent-infant attachment focus on social learning or on instinctive bonding. More than does the bonding process in lower animals, human attachment seems to involve learning.
5. The security of attachment varies from one parent-child relationship to another and is related to sociability, sense of competence, and amount of exploratory behavior in young children.
6. The major variables in research on parenting styles are the degree of child- or parent-centeredness and the degree of parental permissiveness or control.
7. Authoritative parenting, combining acceptance and understanding of children with a high degree of parental control, is most effective in promoting independence and positive self-image in children.
8. In recent years, the relatively neglected role of fathers in the parenting process has been ex-plored. The roles of male and female parents are not interchangeable but instead complement and enhance each other.
9. Despite stereotypes about intergenerational conflict, the parent-adolescent relationship is usually a close one in U.S. society. Conflict that does occur is related to several sociological variables, to parenting approaches, and to the personality of the particular adolescent.
10. Studies of sibling relationships indicate that children within the same family are often treated differently by parents and that the quality of the sibling relationship is influenced by the children's developmental level, gender, and position within the family.
11. The family unit in adulthood remains strong and close, with much evidence of intergenerational interaction and helping.
12. The divorce rate has risen rapidly in recent years, with the result that single-parent households are increasingly common in the United States.
13. Reasons for and reactions to divorce are many and varied. However, divorce is a major life transition that is usually accompanied by a high degree of stress.
14. Children are invariably stressed by their parents' divorce, but the severity of the impact depends on the child's level of development at the time, the sex of the child, the possibility of maintaining a close relationship with both parents, and the availability of outside sources of emotional support. Some children adjust poorly to divorce, but others adjust remarkably well.

Key Terms

authoritarian parenting (p. 456)
authoritative parenting (p. 456)
bonding (p. 450)
cohabitation (p. 441)

egalitarian marriage (p. 442)
indifferent, uninvolved parenting (p. 458)
modern marriage (p. 442)

modified extended family (p. 469)
permissive parenting (p. 456)

reconstituted family (p. 487)
traditional marriage (p. 442)

Review Questions

1. What have been the major changes in U.S. patterns in recent years in overall marriage rate, age at first marriage, rate of cohabitation, and marital roles? What has not changed in recent years?
2. Describe the impact of the arrival of a child on the quality of the couple's marriage relationship. What evidence suggests that the arrival of children has different effects on mothers' and fathers' perceptions of their marriage?
3. What reasons do some U.S. couples give for *not* having children? In terms of their lifestyles and their personalities, how are childless couples similar to and different from couples with children?
4. Describe the four basic parenting styles that have been identified in our society. Which of the four is thought to promote optimal child development? Why?
5. Why had relatively little research been done on the sibling relationship until recent years, as compared to research on parent-child and spousal relationships? What changes have occurred in the past two decades that lead social scientists to believe that siblings will be increasingly important in the future?
6. We suggest that the U.S. family is alive and healthy during its adult life and does not disintegrate after the children have left the nest. Discuss the evidence to indicate that the family is a dynamic, strong, intact system even when the parents have reached old age.
7. Is there such a thing as a typical American grandparent? Why or why not?
8. Describe the most often cited reasons for divorce in the United States today and the most typical reactions of adults to the dissolution of their marriages.
9. What evidence suggests that divorce can have a long-term impact on children? In what ways are the effects evident at the 2-year, 5-year, and 10-year point after the divorce? How can adults help children cope with marital disruption?
10. Describe the problems most often faced by adults as they attempt to move into the roles of stepparents. In general, are reconstituted families successful in terms of the emotional well-being of the people within them?

Suggested Readings

Bengtson, V. L., & Robertson, J. F. (1985). *Grandparenthood,* Beverly Hills, CA: Sage.

   An edited collection of readings emphasizing the diversity of the grandparenting role in U.S. society. This book contains much information about a neglected topic in human development.

Bronstein, P., & Cowan, C. P. (Eds.). (1988). *Fatherhood today: Men's changing role in the family.* New York: John Wiley.

   A compilation of articles by many of the leading experts on the subject of family development. This book represents one of the most complete treatments of the topic of fatherhood as we know it today. Included are articles on the transition to fatherhood, fatherhood among various minority groups, and approaches that might be taken to prepare men and boys for this critical life transition.

Cherlin, A. J. (Ed.). (1988b). *The changing American family and public policy.* Washington, DC: The Urban Institute Press.

   Articles by many of the better-known researchers in the area of family development. This book provides much information about changing trends in the U.S. family and the response (or sometimes the lack of it) by government agencies to these changes.

Dunn, J., & Kendrick, C. (1982). *Siblings: Love, envy, and understanding.* Cambridge, MA: Harvard University Press.

   A discussion of various topics surrounding the sibling relationship, based on an extensive study of 40 English children. Included is information about the reactions of young children to the arrival of infant siblings, the nature of sibling communication and understanding, developmental changes in the sibling relationship, and implications for parents.

Leigh, G. K., & Peterson, G. W. (1986). *Adolescents in families*. Cincinnati: South-Western.

  Many useful articles on the experiences of adolescents within the family context. Among the issues covered are intergenerational conflict, independence training, and familial influences on the self-image, vocational aspirations, and the mental health of adolescents. Included also are articles dealing with specific adolescent problems, such as delinquency and drug abuse, and with the experiences of adolescents in minority subcultures.

Chapter Twelve

Social Interaction

*Development of Social
Awareness*
Childhood and Adolescence
Social Cognition in Adulthood

Patterns of Social Interaction
Infant Peer Interactions
The Childhood Peer Group
Adolescent Groups and Dating
Characteristics of Popularity
Adulthood Socialization Patterns
*Disengagement or Continued Activity
in Later Life?*

Play and Socialization
What Is Play?
Theories of Play
Developmental Patterns in Play

Work in the Life Cycle
Early Basis for Adult Work
Occupational Choice and Personality
Women in the Work Force
Developmental Patterns in Work
Retirement from Work

 Roger and Beth were engaged in a recurring argument about the importance of playmates for Eric, their 2-year-old son. In their neighborhood, the child closest to their son's age was 8 years old, and Roger, feeling that Eric was being deprived of essential contact with age-mates, wanted to enroll the boy in a day care program. Beth disagreed. Eric would acquire playmates when he entered kindergarten, she said, and, at his young age, his parents could offer him all the socialization experience he needs.

To what extent do children need early social interaction with peers? At what age can they benefit the most from such contact, and how does their definition of friendship change with age? What roles do friends play in people's lives anyway, and do these roles change as we cross the life span? In this chapter, we shall attempt to answer these and other related questions, as we discuss the nature of peer relationships from infancy through old age.

We begin our discussion with what is a prerequisite for any type of successful social interaction—the development of an awareness of others and an understanding of the concept of friendship. We turn then to a discussion of typical patterns of social interaction throughout the life span, the benefits of such interaction, and the consequences of rejection by one's peers. Perhaps here we shall be able to provide the information that would help Roger and Beth resolve their argument.

We shall then examine play and the uses of leisure throughout the life span, because much of a child's social interaction is in the form of play, and because leisure activities facilitate social interaction among people of all ages. Finally, we shall discuss the topic of work, from the formation of career goals during childhood and adolescence to the experience of retirement, which ends the working lives of many people. With a few notable exceptions, work provides opportunities for socialization for most Americans, and, in fact, much of our adult socialization occurs not in the home but in the workplace.

DEVELOPMENT OF SOCIAL AWARENESS

Social cognition

Children's developing awareness of the needs and feelings of others, as illustrated by their changing conceptions of friendship.

In recent years, interest has grown rapidly in the study of how people's awareness of the nature of interpersonal relationships develops. Psychologists, for example, have been studying children's conceptions, expectations, and definitions of friendship (Smollar & Youniss, 1982). Considerable interest has arisen in the development of the understanding of the needs, thoughts, feelings, and intentions of others (Shantz, 1975; Damon, 1977); the development of a sense of fairness (Berndt, 1982a); and the development of a sense of compassion (Mussen & Eisenberg-Berg, 1977). Taken as a whole, the study of people's developing awareness of others and their changing conceptions of friendship is an area known as *social cognition*—the application of cognitive skills in social interactions.

Childhood and Adolescence

As children develop throughout the elementary and high school years, they mature considerably in their understanding of friendship and in their ability to relate to friends. They become increasingly skilled at role taking and thus can go beyond their self-centeredness to appreciate the world from other people's points of view. Such trends in the development of social cognition during childhood and adolescence reflect the general cognitive trends described by Jean Piaget and discussed at some length in Chapter 7. The child makes a gradual transition from an egocentric, subjective, and intuitive view of human relationships to one that is also rational and objective. In addition, the child shifts from a concrete, action-oriented concept of friendship to one based on such abstract qualities as shared psychological characteristics. Thus, a move from pre-operational to concrete operational to formal operational approaches to human relationships occurs in the social arena.

Beginnings of Friendship Selection

Even by the time they are 3 or 4 years old, children are able to provide consistent reasons for liking and disliking nursery school peers. Hayes (1978) interviewed 40 children ranging in age from 3 to 5 years, asking them questions such as "Who do you like/dislike more than anyone else?' and "Why do you like/dislike _____?" The most typical reasons given for liking another child were (1) common activities; (2) general play (e.g., "Because she plays with me"); (3) propinquity (e.g., "We live near each other"); (4) evaluation (e.g., "He is a nice boy"); and (5) physical possessions. The most typical reasons for disliking a preschool peer were (1) violation of rules, (2) aggression, and (3) deviant behavior of any sort.

In an attempt to investigate developmental changes in social awareness at the preschool level, Furman and Bierman (1983) used a variety of measures to assess young children's conceptions of friendship. A group of 4-

and 5-year-olds was found to differ significantly from a group of 6- and 7-year-olds in their reasons for describing children as friends. Responses in the categories of "affection" (liking, loving, emotional attachment) and "support" (sharing, helping, comforting) increased significantly with age; responses in the categories of "common activities," "physical characteristics," and "propinquity" did not.

The same trend was illustrated in a study by Boggiano, Klinger, and Main (1986), who looked at the types of directions that would encourage children to play with a classmate they didn't know. Five-, 7-, and 9-year-olds saw "Robby" on a TV monitor; some of the children were asked if they wanted to play with Robby "because he's real nice," while others were asked if they wanted to play with him "because he has a new Lego game." The suggestion that Robby was a nice person increased the interest of 9-year-olds in playing with him but had no impact on the 5-year-olds. On the other hand, the suggestion that Robby's new Lego set was a reason for wanting him as a playmate significantly increased interest among 5-year-olds but not among 9-year-olds.

The conclusion that might be drawn from research on children's reasons for friendship is that as children develop, they are increasingly aware of thoughts, feelings, motives, and personality characteristics as criteria for defining friendship. Perhaps as a result, the stability of friendship shows a developmental increase; the friendships of grade school children are highly stable, particularly when contrasted with the friendships of preschoolers (Berndt, Hawkins, & Hoyle, 1986).

Knowledge of Friends

As children progress through the elementary school years, knowledge of their friends' psychological characteristics increases (Berndt, 1982b). Illustrating this trend, Diaz and Berndt (1982) asked a group of fourth graders and a group of eighth graders a variety of questions about their best friends. Questions dealt with external characteristics (e.g., "What clubs or teams does your friend belong to?"), preferences (e.g., "What is your friend's favorite subject at school?"), and personality characteristics (e.g., "What does your friend worry about most?"). The friends were then asked to answer the same questions about themselves, and the two sets of answers were compared.

No age differences were observed in what might be called external knowledge about one's friends—birth date, telephone number, names of siblings, and so on. However, a significant age difference was seen in knowledge of a friend's personality and preferences: Adolescents apparently were more knowledgeable than children about their friend's internal characteristics. Diaz and Berndt (1982) concluded that adolescent friendships were therefore more "intimate" than those of children, presumably because adolescents were more likely to share intimate information with their friends.

Volpe (1976) found similar results in an investigation of age differences in the reasons that children become friends. Younger children (ages 6 to 10 felt that the way to develop a friendship is to do things together; the focus of their answers was on actions rather than personality characteristics. As one 10-year-old boy remarked, "Friends are easy to make. All you have to do is go up to a guy, say hello, and ask him if he wants to play ball; then he's a friend. If he don't want to play ball, then he's not a friend, unless you decide to play something else" (cited in Smollar & Youniss, 1982, p. 283). By contrast, 12- and 13-year-olds stressed the importance of a friend's personal qualities, the need to talk to get to know each other, to find out what the other person likes and dislikes. As in the previous study, we see the shift from external, surface characteristics to a need for in-depth knowledge in a friendship.

Obligations and Expectations of Friendship

Evidence suggests a developmental change in a child's understanding of the obligations of friendship. Ryan and Smollar (1978) found that 80 percent of the 10- and 11-year-olds they interviewed saw the major obligation of friendship as being "nice" to each other: doing things with or doing things for each other, and avoiding fights. Only 24 percent of the 13- and 14-year-olds mentioned "niceness" obligations, and by the age of 16 or 17, such action-oriented obligations were mentioned by only 1 in 10. Children showed a developmental shift from an emphasis on actions to an emphasis on the personal qualities of a friend and an increased concern for the feelings and emotional needs of the other party.

Not only does a developmental change occur in what a child feels is owed to a friend, but a change occurs in what is expected from friends as well. In studies of children ranging from first grade to eighth grade, children showed an increasing tendency to expect common interests, similarity of attitudes and values, and the potential for intimacy from a friendship and a decreasing tendency to expect a friend to give material things, to share common activities, or to enjoy the same games (Bigelow & La Gaipa, 1975; Bigelow, 1977). Again, the age trend is away from external characteristics and toward the internal qualities of friends.

Gender and Friendship Definition

When gender differences are examined in friendship research on children and adolescents, a pattern seems to emerge. If we look at the development of a child's understanding of what friendship means, we do not find gender differences (Bigelow & La Gaipa, 1975; Furman & Bierman, 1983). Similarly, no gender differences appear in children's and adolescents' intimate knowledge of their friends (Diaz & Berndt, 1982), and boys do not claim to have more friends than girls do and vice versa (Berndt, 1982b).

On the other hand, gender differences have been discovered in friendship expectations. Even among preschoolers, the expectations of friendship seem to be different for girls than for boys; in one study, 3- to 5-year-old girls were more willing to share a favorite food with a friend than with a mere acquaintance, but boys of the same age made no such distinction (Birch & Billman, 1986).

During the grade school years, girls are more likely than boys to mention the potential for intimacy and sharing of feelings (Bigelow, 1977). Girls are also more likely than boys to list emotional assistance as an obligation of friendship; when asked why emotional assistance is an obligation, girls more often give reasons related to benefiting the other person (Ryan & Smollar, 1978). Girls also seek closer attachments and greater degrees of trust and loyalty than boys do (Sharabany, Gershoni, & Hofman, 1981), and female friendships appear to be more exclusive. For example, girls are less willing to include a nonfriend in an ongoing conversation than boys are (Eder & Hallinan, 1978). Gender differences in friendship expectations apparently continue into adolescence. To illustrate, Douvan and Adelson (1966) conducted a nationwide survey of adolescents aged 14 to 16—one of the most extensive studies of adolescent friendship ever undertaken. They found that boys and girls clearly wanted different things from their friends. Boys wanted friends to help them establish their independence and to join with them in resisting adult control. They wanted friends who could meet their *instrumental needs,* giving them concrete help when needed. Girls had *expressive needs*—they wanted friends who could help them understand themselves, who could share their private thoughts and feelings, and who could offer emotional support.

No single explanation can account for gender differences in expressed friendship needs; such differences might be interpreted in more than one way. For instance, perhaps males, for whatever combination of cultural or biological reasons, simply do not need the closeness and emotional support that females do. Perhaps males do have emotional needs similar to those of females but feel less free to express them. An adolescent boy might be unwilling to admit that he seeks friends who are warm and sensitive to his needs, because such an admission might imply that he is soft, weak, or unmasculine. However we choose to interpret these data, it seems wise to follow Berndt's (1982b) suggestion to avoid such broad generalizations and value judgments as "Female friendships are closer (better?) than male friendships" and "Males are too emotionally inhibited to form close friendships." Instead, we might speak of gender-related *patterns* of friendship seeking—patterns that require greater exploration than they have thus far received and that offer a potentially rich source of information about gender role socialization in our culture.

Role-Taking Ability

A child's development in the area of peer relationships involves more than an increase in knowledge of the psychological characteristics of others and an understanding of the concept of friendship. To interact successfully with

Instrumental needs
Friendship needs that are concrete and practical as opposed to emotional.

Expressive needs
Needs for emotional closeness and support in a relationship.

peers, children must also go beyond their own self-centered perceptions and try to see the world from other people's points of view. Such role-taking ability may be a prerequisite for close interpersonal communication (Harter, 1983) and is related to altruistic, or helping, behavior among older children (Cialdini, Baumann, & Kenrick, 1981; Froming, Allen, & Jensen, 1985). the most popular children in the grade school classroom have been found to be the most sophisticated role takers (Kurdek & Krile, 1982), and role-taking skill is related to the ease of establishing intimate peer relationships in childhood (McGuire & Weisz, 1982).

The ability to take the point of view of others does not appear suddenly at some point during childhood; it develops gradually, reflecting the child's growing awareness of the world as well as the gradual transition from concrete to more abstract forms of reasoning. Psychologist Robert Selman and his associates (Selman, 1980; Selman & Byrne, 1974; Selman & Jacquette, 1978) have identified the following series of developmental stages in the progression from total self-centeredness to sophisticated role-taking ability.

> *Stage 0: Egocentrism.* Children are able to see only their own perspective and assume that what they see, feel, and want is what everybody sees, feels, and wants. This stage is typical of children from the ages of 3 to 5 or 6.

> *Stage 1: Subjective Role Taking.* Children now realize that others have different perspectives but think that the differences occur only because of differences in available information ("If you knew what I know, you would see things the correct way—my way!"). They judge the actions of others only from their own perspectives, and they cannot see themselves as others see them. The age range for this stage is 6 to 8 years.

> *Stage 2: Self-Reflective Role Taking.* By the age of 8 to 10 years, individual differences in perspectives are no longer attributed to simple information differences but to basic differences in values and purposes. Knowing what another person's values are, the child can then predict that person's reaction to a future situation. Children can now examine their own behavior as it must appear to another person.

> *Stage 3: Mutual Role Taking.* Adolescents and adults can distinguish their own perspectives from that of the "average" person in society. They can simultaneously evaluate their own point of view and that of a second person; they can even imagine how an objective third party would simultaneously evaluate their perspective and a different perspective held by the second person. To use a concrete example, a skilled role taker involved in a debate could understand the philosophical basis of an opponent's argument, predict an opponent's position on related issues, and imagine how an objective observer would evaluate arguments on both sides and understand them in the context of the differing philosophical views of the debaters.

In Selman's model, individual differences in role-taking ability appear to be related to differences in level of intellectual development. But additional reasons for individual variations may exist. For example, role-taking ability is somewhat related to performance on standard intelligence tests (Shantz, 1983). It is also related to such environmental factors as child-rearing practices and direct exposure to role-taking experiences. In regard to child rearing, children who are the most skillful role takers have parents who use a disciplinary approach known as *induction* (Hoffman, 1970; Maccoby & Martin, 1983), emphasizing the impact of the child's behavior on other people (e.g., "It makes me happy to see you sharing your toys," or "Your sister is very sad because you don't want to play with her"). By contrast, less effective role taking is found among children whose parents discipline by referring to general rules that must be followed, to status differences, or to their own positions of power (e.g., "Children should share their toys," or "You'll play with your sister because I told you to!") (Bearison & Cassel, 1975).

Induction

A disciplinary approach emphasizing the impact on other people of a child's wrong behaviors.

Because children's experience can influence the degree to which they are able to take the perspective of others, role-taking skills can be taught to children who lack them. In fact, evidence shows that role-taking training can be quite effective (Feshbach, 1979; Iannotti, 1978). For example, Iannotti (1978) trained kindergarten and third-grade boys in role taking by reading them stories and having them act out the parts of the story characters. During training, he asked the children questions about how their characters felt, why they behaved as they did, what they planned to do next, and how the other characters might have felt about them. Role-taking skills were assessed both before and after the training by having children answer questions about hypothetical social or moral dilemmas. Children who received role-taking training improved significantly in role-taking skills, while a group not receiving the training showed no such improvement.

Development of Altruism

The developing social awareness that we have been discussing thus far might be viewed as a cognitive aspect of social interaction. However, we should not neglect the affective, or feeling, dimension—the constellation of prosocial qualities that include generosity, kindness, caring, and helping. The term used to describe a variety of such prosocial behaviors is altruism, literally meaning "concern for other people," and here referring to the presence in the child of thoughts or actions concerned with the well-being of another person or persons. (*Research Close-Up,* "Concern for the Victim," describes a study dealing with the development of altruistic behavior in young children.)

Concern for other people is found early in life, and certainly appears before a child has acquired a mature social awareness. Even newborn babies cry reflexively when they hear the cries of other newborns (Simner, 1971; Sagi & Hoffman, 1976), and such reactions to the distress of peers

Research Close-Up
Concern for the Victim

 As children develop, they might be expected to become increasingly capable of displaying concern for other people, and one form of that concern is caretaking behavior toward victims in distress. Carolyn Zahn-Waxler, Sarah Friedman, and E. Mark Cummings (1983), of the National Institute of Mental Health, carried out a developmental study of children's responses to a baby's cry. The subjects in the study were five boys and five girls at each of the following levels: 4 years old, kindergarten, first grade, second grade, fifth grade, and sixth grade. These children were placed individually in a room and exposed to the sound of an infant crying in the next room. Then the infant's mother carried the baby into the room in which the child was sitting and said, "I'm looking for the baby's bottle." She searched for the bottle for 1 minute before "finding" it in a predetermined location on a nearby bench, unless the child in the room discovered it first and called it to her attention.

The experimenters were interested in finding out what types of altruistic, or prosocial, responses the children would make and whether older children would be more concerned about the baby's well-being than younger children were. Prosocial responses were expected to occur in the form of verbal help (e.g., telling the mother where to find the bottle, saying "poor baby"), gestural help (e.g., pointing to the bottle), or physical help (e.g., getting the bottle for the mother, feeding the baby).

Although the findings concerning gestural and physical help were somewhat mixed, grade school children expressed significantly more verbal concern and offered more verbal help than preschoolers and kindergartners. Furthermore, an analysis of composite overall ratings of prosocial behaviors indicated that, in general, school-age children were more altruistic than 4- and 5-year-olds. Interestingly enough, although girls are often thought of as being more prosocial than boys, no sex differences in helping were found in this study, and, in fact, most studies of this type do not find sex differences in altruistic behavior (Radke-Yarrow, Zahn-Waxler, & Chapman, 1983).

The findings of this and other studies of helping behavior in children are consistent with the pattern of findings in social cognition research in general: As a child develops, awareness of, understanding of, and concern for other persons increase. Prosocial attitudes and behaviors are increasingly sophisticated, and egocentrism declines.

have been found throughout the first and second years of life (Radke-Yarrow, Zahn-Waxler, & Chapman, 1983). Actual helping behaviors can also be found quite early. For example, Rheingold (1979) observed that nine out of ten 2-year-olds in a laboratory setting will spontaneously help their mothers with routine household chores.

As mentioned earlier in this chapter, evidence of cooperative play with peers can be found even during the second year of life (Brenner & Mueller, 1982). Finally, by the time they are 2 years old, children will indicate in a variety of ways that they feel sorry for another person in distress: They will

Infants and toddlers have a much greater interest in peer interaction than was once believed, and cooperative peer play begins to emerge in the second year of life.

verbalize sympathy, give things to a suffering person, make helpful suggestions, and try to protect a victim from harm (Radke-Yarrow, Zahn-Waxler, & Chapman, 1983).

Studies of preschool children ranging in age from 3 to 6 typically indicate that altruistic behavior is quite common in this age group (Zahn-Waxler & Radke-Yarrow, 1982; Radke-Yarrow, Zahn-Waxler, & Chapman, 1983). Cooperative play continues to increase, but beyond that, preschoolers do not seem to be any more or less altruistic than they were in the first 3 years of life. Furthermore, the motivation for altruistic behaviors in this age group is unclear; many kindly behaviors are actually motivated by fear, by a desire to control others, or by a need to gain approval from adults (Radke-Yarrow, Zahn-Waxler, & Chapman, 1983).

An examination of developmental changes in altruistic behavior during the elementary and high school years produces a complex pattern. In the first place, as social awareness improves, acts of altruism might be expected to increase. In fact, the frequency of overall prosocial behavior does not seem to change at all; some behaviors increase, others decrease, and the rest show no change. There is no support for the simple conclusion that children become kinder to one another as they advance through the years of childhood and adolescence (Radke-Yarrow, Zahn-Waxler, & Chapman, 1983).

On the other hand, if we look not at the number of altruistic behaviors but at their quality, developmental changes can be seen in reasons for prosocial behavior. The sense of caring, which was reflexive in infancy and primarily emotional in the young child, becomes increasingly linked to reasoning ability. Children progress through a series of increasingly sophisticated levels of prosocial reasoning that reflect their waning egocentrism and their improved role-taking skills (Eisenberg, Lennon, & Roth, 1983). These levels are described in Table 12.1.

To summarize the research on children's social awareness, the nature of friendship changes from early childhood to early adolescence. Intimate knowledge of friends increases, conceptions of friendship shift from an emphasis on shared activities to an emphasis on shared psychological characteristics, the sense of responsibility and commitment to friends becomes deeper, and expectations increase for reciprocal forms of commitment.

The ability to understand the needs, feelings, values, and unique perspectives of other people improves as children gradually rid themselves of their egocentric world views. Intimate communication, as opposed to surface-level social interaction, becomes the basis for mature peer relationships.

Social Cognition in Adulthood

Although the developmental patterns in childhood social cognition seem to mirror the patterns of intellectual development described by Piaget, such similarities do not emerge from the study of adult social cognition. In fact, as we suggested in Chapter 7, the formal operational model seems inadequate to explain complex social reasoning (Labouvie-Vief, 1985, 1986a, 1986b, 1986c). Formal reasoning allows a person to identify key variables in a problem, to consider all possible outcomes, and to estimate the probabilities of those outcomes (Piaget, 1983; Powell, 1984). Such reasoning is objective and dispassionate; it is not the feelings or intuitions but the reasoning skills of the knower that are important in the search for truth. And perhaps all reasonable people can agree on truths about the physical world. Relationships, on the other hand, have many different and even contradictory truths and are defined by the subjective perceptions of the people involved. Each relationship differs from all others, and any one relationship can vary from one circumstance to another. Therefore, a purely

Table 12.1
Levels of Prosocial Reasoning

Level	Orientation	Description	Group
1	Hedonistic, self-focused	The individual is concerned with self-oriented consequences rather than moral considerations. Reasons for assisting or not assisting another include consideration of direct gain to self, future reciprocity, and concern for others whom the individual needs or likes (due to the affectional tie).	Preschoolers and younger elementary school children
2	Needs of others	The individual expresses concern for the physical, material, and psychological needs of others even though the other's needs conflict with one's own needs. This concern is expressed in the simplest terms, without clear evidence of self-reflective role taking, verbal expressions of sympathy, or reference to internalized affect such as guilt.	Preschoolers and elementary school children
3	Approval and interpersonal, or stereotyped	Stereotyped images of good and bad persons and behaviors, or considerations of others' approval and acceptance are used in justifying prosocial or nonhelping behaviors.	Elementary and high school students
4	a. Empathic	The individual's judgments include evidence of sympathetic responding, self-reflective role taking, concern with the other's humanness, and guilt or positive affect related to the consequences of one's actions.	Older elementary school and high school students
	b. Transitional (empathic and internalized)	Justifications for helping or not helping involve internalized values, norms, duties, or responsibilities, or refer to the necessity of protecting the rights and dignity of other persons; these ideas, however, are not clearly stated.	Minority of people high school age
5	Strongly internalized	Justifications for helping or not helping are based on internalized values, norms, or responsibilities, the desire to maintain individual and societal contractual obligations, and the belief in the dignity, rights, and equality of all individuals. Positive or negative affect related to the maintenance of self-respect for living up to one's own values and accepted norms also characterizes this stage.	Only a small minority of high school students and virtually no elementary school children

Source: From N. Eisenberg, R. Lennon, and K. Roth (1983). Prosocial development: longitudinal study. *Developmental Psychology, 19,* pp. 846–855. Copyright 1983 by the American Psychological Association. Reprinted by permission.

logical approach may have little value in dealing with interpersonal problems.

The failure of mature formal reasoning to bring about an equally mature version of adult social reasoning has led many developmental psychologists to question the usefulness of Piaget's model (e.g., Benack, 1984; Powell, 1984: Sinnott, 1984). As Sinnott (1984) observed, a different set of operations may be needed to organize a person's understanding of complex interpersonal relationships. These are *relativistic operations,* which involve a subjective selection among logically contradictory, but internally consistent, formal operational subsystems. For example, a formal operational thinker is able to see a particular type of parent-child relationship as one of a number of possible relationships within the family unit. However, the post-formal relativistic thinker realizes that a particular parent-child relationship may actually be many relationships, even contradictory ones, depending on the particular social circumstances and prevailing moods of the persons involved. In a sense, the relationship has no existence independent of the persons within it and no existence without a given social context.

Some cognitive psychologists maintain that sophisticated peer interactions involve a component of relativism that goes beyond formal reasoning (e.g., Benack, 1984; Powell, 1984). To interact effectively with others, to develop a mature sense of empathy, a person must realize that many perspectives are possible on any particular issue. Effective social interaction requires an understanding that a search for absolutely correct courses of action is useless because reality and truth depend on the social context. What a person feels or believes in a particular social context may be different from what others think and feel; each person's thought processes may be inherently logically consistent, and yet flawlessly logical thinkers often express contradictory perspectives on any interpersonal issue.

The realization that many logically correct but inconsistent points of view characterize interpersonal relationships can improve a person's ability to interact socially. Even the adolescent who is highly skilled in formal reasoning may have a simplified view of human relationships. A mature adult who uses relativistic operations may be said to have reached a higher level of social cognition.

Relativistic operations

A set of mental operations that organize a person's understanding of complex interpersonal relationships.

PATTERNS OF SOCIAL INTERACTION

Having looked at the development of social awareness across the life span, we turn now to an examination of the actual patterns of social interaction with peers. We begin in the first year of life, when infants make efforts to communicate with their age-mates, and we continue through the years of childhood and adulthood, emphasizing the distinctive characteristics of social interaction at each phase of human development.

Infant Peer Interaction

The infant and young child have often been described as selfish and self-centered, and therefore incapable of understanding or caring about peers. As will be seen in this section, even an infant is considerably more peer oriented than many people believe. Infants are definitely interested in communicating with peers and, by the second year of life, even show glimmers of cooperative play.

Attempts to Communicate

Even during the early months of the first year of life, infants are definitely interested in one another. Fogel (1979) observed infants 5–14 weeks old in three different social settings: while alone, while looking at their mothers, and while seated on their mothers' laps facing another infant. When the babies were alone, they usually appeared relaxed and content. When mother approached, they smiled at her, made gestures with their arms and legs, and often stuck out their tongues. When they saw another infant, however, they seemed to exhibit a qualitatively different reaction, a sense of uncontrolled excitement; they stared at the other baby, leaned forward as if straining to have a closer look, and made abrupt head and arm movements.

Clearly, even young infants are capable of making social gestures to peers. However, these gestures are still somewhat limited during the first year of life. First of all, they are of very short duration; as the child develops through its first year and into its second, the time spent on individual social gestures increases (Hay, Pedersen, and Nash, 1982). A second limitation of the young infant's social gestures is that they are relatively simple,

Acts of kindness, such as sharing and helping, are fairly common among 3- to 6-year-old children.

consisting only of one or two specific behaviors at a time (e.g., smiling and vocalizing, smiling and waving the arms). The second year of life brings an increasing complexity of social overtures, in the sense that larger numbers of individual social behaviors are combined into more complex patterns; social interactions are increasingly controlled and predictable (Brownell, 1982, 1986).

Ross, Lollis, and Elliott (1982) observed a variety of communicative gestures in the play of children ranging in age from 20 to 22 months: showing toys to one's partner, offering a toy, giving a toy, requesting something, inviting a partner to play, making declarative statements protesting a partner's action, and so on. Not only were communicative overtures common among the children, they were often quite effective. In other words, even these very young children could understand and comply with the needs of peers fairly well; in the few instances when children failed to do so, they seemed to be unwilling to communicate, rather than unable to communicate.

Cooperative Play

Cooperative play between child and adult occurs even in the first half year of life, as any parent knows who has played peek-a-boo with a baby. However, true cooperative play has been observed only rarely in peer relationships in the first 2 years of life (Eckerman and Stein, 1982). Nevertheless, such play has been observed with increasing frequency in recent years. As an example, Brenner and Mueller (1982) described what they called shared meanings in the play of toddlers—themes that organize their social interactions. Such themes include "motor-copy," in which children copy each other's motor behavior, "peek-a-boo," in which one child hides and then reappears suddenly, to the delight of the other child, or "run-chase," in which the children run after each other.

The significance of these shared meanings, which increase in frequency and variety throughout the second year of life, is that they are definitely social behaviors and often quite sophisticated ones at that. The stereotype of the 1- or 2-year-old as an antisocial, totally egocentric little being with an interest only in toys and not in other children is being challenged by much of the recent research (e.g., Mueller & Lucas, 1975; Goldman & Ross, 1978; Brenner & Mueller, 1982; Hodapp & Mueller, 1982; Ross, 1982; Howes, 1983, 1988). Not all toddlers participate in social games, but some certainly do. Perhaps, as Ross (1982) suggested, those children who do not play cooperatively might do so if the social setting were conducive to cooperative play.

Effects of Early Peer Interaction

Does the experience of being with other babies affect infant's social skills or social interests? The answer appears to be no for social skills and yes for social interests. Social skills, as evidenced by the complexity of social interactions, do not seem to be affected by experience during the first 2 years of life. Age alone, and not the amount of experience with other infants, is the best predictor of an infant's social maturity. In other words, developmental limits have an impact on the quality of a child's social interactions from birth until the age of 2 (Brownell, 1986).

When we examine the infant's social interests, however, a different pattern emerges. Ricciuti (1974) noticed, for example, when he compared 12- to 19-month-olds exposed to day care with those who were not, that the children in the former group were more likely to move away from their mothers when mother and child were observed together in a playroom. The day care veterans were also more likely to play at a greater distance from mother during the observation period, more likely to look at their peers rather than at mother, and less likely to seek physical contact with her. These findings are typical in studies of the effects of day care on the young child's social development: Children exposed to the day care setting tend to be somewhat more peer-oriented than those who have not been in day care (Belsky and Steinberg, 1978). The intense peer interaction provided in a day care setting may even be related to a child's social development for many years after the actual experience. Moore (1975) reported that adolescent boys who had been placed in day care settings before the age of 5 were more interested in social activities than were home-reared boys and were more often rated as likable by their peers.

Lastly, actual day care experience is not the only predictor of later social interests. An even better predictor may be the closeness of attachment between parent and child. In a number of recent studies of children 3 years old or older, social interest and social skills (e.g., ability to take leadership roles, to interact without conflict, to display confidence in social settings) were most often found among those who had secure close attachments to a parent or parents (Jacobson & Wille, 1986; La Freniere, 1983; Lieberman, 1977). Exposure to other children at an early age is not in itself a guarantee of a child's later social success.

The Childhood Peer Group

From the ages of 6 to 10, peers become more and more important in a child's life. Family orientation decreases, while organization into peer groups increases (Minuchin, 1977). Although its composition may change from week to week, the group is, nevertheless, a close-knit society, with definite rules for membership. Occasionally, such groups even have special languages, handshakes, secret passwords, and secret clubhouses.

Not all children attach themselves to organized groups. Some prefer one-to-one relationships, while others associate with neighborhood "gangs" —loose and frequently changing confederations having no group names, secrets, or specific membership requirements (Williams & Stith, 1980).

Issues in Human Development
What are the Origins of Shyness?

 When a television program on shyness was broadcast nationwide, more than 600 people who saw themselves as shy wrote letters in response; their overriding message was that shyness is a real problem for many people, but one that is not taken seriously enough in our society (Harris, 1984).

Just how serious an obstacle to a child's normal social development is the characteristic of shyness? In the first place, the number of self-defined shy children may be greater than many of us realize. Lazarus (1982a) found that 38 percent of the approximately 400 fifth graders he surveyed labeled themselves as shy. Nearly half of those shy children felt that being shy was a personal problem, and nearly half expressed a desire to participate in a counseling group to overcome their shyness. Shyness is related to peer rejection and social isolation in childhood (Asher, Hymel, & Renshaw, 1984; Richmond, 1985), as well as to low self-esteem (Lazarus, 1982b). Among adolescents, extreme shyness has been associated with eating disorders (Segal & Figley, 1985), anxiety, and depression (Traub, 1983).

Where does shyness originate? Is it learned, or does it have a genetic basis? A growing body of evidence suggests that shyness is a stable characteristic of temperament that may have biological origins (e.g., Buss & Plomin, 1984; Jacklin, Maccoby, & Doering, 1983; Plomin & Rowe, 1979). As an illustration of research in this direction, Daniels and Plomin (1985b) examined 152 adopted infants at 12 and 24 months of age and 120 nonadopted infants at the same ages. The researchers obtained parental reports on degrees of shyness (i.e., fearfulness in strange situations) observed in the infants. The amount of shyness exhibited by both the biological and the adoptive parents was also measured, by means of standard personality tests. Results of the study indicated a high degree of similarity between children and biological parents in their tendency to be socially outgoing or socially withdrawn—and this relationship existed even when the child was being raised by someone other than the biological parent!

Before we rush to the conclusion that shyness is a genetic and not an environmentally influenced personality characteristic, we should look at another finding of the Daniels and Plomin study: A degree of similarity in sociability was seen between adoptive parents and their infants, who were obviously genetically dissimilar groups. Both genetic and environmental factors apparently have to be considered in explaining the origins of shyness. The researchers suggested that a tendency toward shyness may be inherited, but that shy mothers—by failing to expose their children to novel situations—may also set up environments that encourage shyness in their children. Exposure to novelty could be a key element in promoting a socially outgoing attitude in children. The encouraging results of programs designed to help children overcome their shyness further suggest that the environment can influence the sociability of children. Exercises in relaxation, activities to foster greater self-awareness, training in social skills, forced participation in group games and activities, and involvement in drama therapy all have been found useful in bringing shy children out of themselves (Biemer, 1983; Lowenstein, 1983).

Rules will exist in the gang, although perhaps they are not as clearly specified as in the more organized groups. Children who do not like the games their peers play, or who do not own bicycles, or who are not allowed out after dark may be excluded. Indeed, children may be excluded if they are different in any way, even if the difference is regarded as a positive one by adults. In some groups, children may be ostracized if they will not cooperate in stealing or vandalism, or if they like going to school while their peers do not.

Peer Group Functions

The peer group in middle childhood functions as a major socializing agent. In the group, children learn about the peer culture. They learn to obey rules and to follow a certain moral order. They learn to compromise. They develop a variety of physical skills, and they acquire a large supply of riddles, jokes, stories, and knowledge about games. They learn what their peers consider masculine and feminine behavior, and they will firm up sexual identities accordingly. In essence, they learn how to function in society (Williams & Stith, 1980). The peer group in middle childhood is also a source of playmates. It provides the child with a number of other children with whom to do things and is the pool from which friends are chosen.

Gender Differences in the Peer Group

Extensive peer relations
Social interactions characterized as group activities.

Intensive peer relations
One-to-one social interactions.

The middle childhood peer group, at least in our culture, may be primarily a male phenomenon. Waldrop and Halverson (1975) obtained careful records of children's weekly social interactions and found that highly sociable boys were more likely to have *extensive peer relations* (i.e., group activities), but highly sociable girls more often had *intensive peer relations* (i.e., one-to-one activities). The authors concluded that the sex difference may occur because (1) girls are more likely than boys to be kept close to home and therefore group activities are limited; (2) girls are discouraged from being noisy more often than boys, and groups tend to be noisy; or (3) girls are more likely than boys to experience close one-to-one relationships at home, with mothers and daughters often being particularly close.

Adolescent Groups and Dating

Peer groupings in the early years of adolescence usually consist of same-sex children only. In middle and late adolescence, however, the tendency toward heterosexual interaction increases. Unisex groups gradually become heterosexual groups, and heterosexual groups eventually break down into couples (Dunphy, 1963).

The process of pairing off into opposite-sex couples—the phenomenon of dating—may begin as early as 12 years of age, but today's adolescent girl usually begins dating at age 13 or 14, while boys begin to date at age 14 or 15 (Steinberg, 1989). This gender difference may be attributable to the fact that girls mature earlier than boys, both physically and emotionally. Gender differences in the timing of physical maturation were discussed in Chapter 3. The emotional advantage of the female is that she may be more experienced than a boy in forming intimate relationships, because, as was pointed out in an earlier section, she is more likely to form intimate same-sex relationships. The very experience of dating may have particular benefit to boys, therefore, in that it offers many of them their first experiences with intimate peer relationships (Buhrmester & Furman, 1987).

Dating is a sociocultural phenomenon. Its onset is triggered not so much by physical or sexual maturation as by cultural expectations. For example,

Dating usually begins in early adolescence. Reasons for dating include recreation, companionship, status, sexual experimentation, and, eventually, mate selection.

the likelihood of going on dates at a given age is largely influenced by the norms in the particular high school the adolescent attends (Steinberg, 1989). Whatever the norms of the particular social group, however, by the age of 17, virtually all adolescents have dated at least once.

A rather obvious function of dating is mate selection; but, in fact, the majority of American adolescents do not see the dating process as preparation for marriage. Rice (1990) listed a variety of reasons that adolescents date:

- *Recreation.* Dating is simply an enjoyable social experience that often becomes an end in itself rather than a means of selecting a spouse.
- *Companionship without marriage.* The need for emotional closeness expressed by adolescents is frequently met in a dating situation. In dating, adolescents may learn to share their intimate thoughts and feelings.
- *Status and achievement.* Successful dating experiences may indicate to the peer group that a boy or girl is emotionally and socially mature and sexually desirable. Nondaters may look up to the adolescent who dates and admire and envy the dater's "grown-up" heterosexual behavior.

- *Sexual experimentation.* Throughout the past 50 years, sexuality has played an increasingly greater role in adolescent interpersonal relations. Dating is an avenue for sexual experimentation and sexual satisfaction.
- *Mate selection.* Whether or not an adolescent consciously seeks a lifelong mate when dating, the process usually leads to mate selection, especially among older adolescents.

Characteristics of Popularity

In recent years, a number of psychologists (e.g., Masters & Furman, 1981; McGuire & Weisz, 1982) have emphasized the need to distinguish between friendship and popularity. Friendship refers to the degree of liking in a one-to-one relationship, whereas popularity refers to the degree to which a person is valued by the peer group as a whole. A distinction between the two concepts may be necessary, because certain characteristics (e.g., altruism, understanding, sensitivity) are related to friendship development but not to popularity (McGuire & Weisz, 1982). Other characteristics (e.g., sociability, ability to give praise and affection, social status) seem to be related to popularity but not to individual friendship selection (Masters & Furman, 1981).

Childhood

Even by the time they are 3 years old, some children are already emerging as well liked by their peers, while others clearly are not. Well-liked preschoolers engage in much cooperative play and are successful in social

Unpopular children generally lack social skills and social experiences. Training in social skills may help such children gain acceptance from their peers.

Applying Our Knowledge
Helping the Unpopular Child

 When a child is rejected or neglected by peers, a number of unfortunate consequences may result. Childhood peer rejection in particular has been associated with emotional difficulties during adolescence, dropping out of school, and juvenile delinquency (Asher, Oden, & Gottman, 1977; Hartup, 1983). Neglect by peers is a cause of childhood loneliness. Considering the possible negative impacts of social isolation, we might wonder how a caring adult might help a child who is disliked or ignored by peers. The traditional adult response has been to pressure the peer group into becoming more accepting, and this approach has usually been ineffective. Within the past 15 years, however, a new and more promising approach to dealing with children's social isolation has emerged. This involves working not with the group as a whole, but directly with the socially isolated child, and coaching that child in specific social or academic skills necessary for peer acceptance.

In one of the earliest studies illustrating this new approach, psychologists Sherri Oden and Steven Asher (1977) selected third- and fourth-grade children judged by their classmates to be socially undesirable and coached them individually for 4 weeks in strategies for participation, cooperation, and communication. Oden and Asher reported that the coaching seemed to have the desired effect. Approximately a week after the coaching sessions ended, the formerly unpopular children experienced a sig-

nificantly greater degree of acceptance from their peers. Indeed, half of the coached children were now ranked in the top half of the class in popularity. Even more encouraging was the finding that the effects of coaching were long lasting: The researchers returned a year later and found that the children they had worked with were accepted by their peers to an even greater degree than they had been a week after coaching.

Within the past 10 years, a number of other studies (e.g., Bierman, 1986; Bierman & Furman, 1984; Coie & Krehbiel, 1984; Gresham & Nagel, 1980; Ladd, 1981; La Greca & Santogrossi, 1980) have supported the view that coaching children in a variety of social skills (e.g., sharing, cooperating, initiating friendships, making conversation, playing games) can lead to a greater degree of peer acceptance. Typically, these studies included refinements and extensions of the Oden and Asher technique. For example, Ladd (1981) was concerned that some of the social success achieved by unpopular children in the earlier study could have been the result of the special attention provided by the psychologists and not the skill training itself. In his study, he provided a group of unpopular third graders with training in asking questions of peers, making suggestions to them, and offering supportive statements to them, as well as giving them opportunities to practice these skills and evaluate their own successes. A second group of children received the same amount of

conversation, making relevant and appropriate comments to other children and offering constructive suggestions. Disliked children often make inappropriate statements in conversation (i.e., remarks not related to another child's immediately preceding statement and are negative without offering constructive alternatives (Hazen & Black, 1989).

The most popular children in elementary school are friendly, intelligent, high in academic achievement, athletically skilled, and physically attractive (Hartup, 1983). They are seen as good leaders and as children who know how to cooperate and share with others (Dodge, 1983; Ladd, Price, & Hart, 1988). Not surprisingly, popular children are higher in self-esteem than the average child and have more positive self-perceptions (Boivin & Bégin, 1989).

attention from the psychologist and the same "practice" exposure to peers, but no skills training. Children trained in social skills showed significant improvement in their tendency to be accepted by peers, but those given adult attention without skills training did not. Special attention from caring adults is not enough to help a socially isolated child become more accepted by other children; skills training is needed as well.

As noted earlier, factors other than personality characteristics are related to social status in childhood. One of these is academic achievement. Rejected children tend to have problems in academic performance and are more likely to need help in the classroom (McMichael, 1980; Coie & Krehbiel, 1984; Dodge, 1983; Coie, Dodge, & Coppotelli, 1982). Why do social rejection and academic difficulties often go hand in hand? Coie and Krehbiel (1984) suggested three reasons:

1. Children with academic problems may begin to engage in antisocial activities because they are bored or anxious in the classroom.
2. Children might be looked down on by other children specifically because they are not successful academically.
3. The same immaturity that causes social problems may cause academic problems in the classroom; thus, the two sets of problems are related.

If academic failure is related to social failure, might a child's social status be improved as a result of special efforts to remedy academic problems? Coie and Krehbiel (1984) investigated this question. They worked with third graders identified as having both social and academic problems. Some of the children were provided with two sessions a week of individual tutoring in academic subjects. Others received social skills training similar to what was provided in the Ladd (1981) study mentioned earlier. A third group received training in both academic and social skills. The result was that children who were tutored in academic subjects actually showed greater improvement in social status than did those receiving only the social skills training. This does not mean, of course, that social skills training is ineffective, or that academic tutoring can help the social image of all rejected children. It does reinforce the idea, however, that adult intervention can benefit a child's standing in the peer group, and it further suggests that the intervention can be accomplished in more than one way, depending on the reasons for a particular child's unpopularity. This should provide encouragement for parents and educators and hope for children who for any reason experience the pain of isolation from their peer groups.

Grade schoolers are likely to be rejected if they are antisocial, hostile, physically unattractive, or low in achievement (Hartup, 1983). Rejected children are seen as poor leaders. They have difficulty sharing, and they often exclude other children from their play (Dodge, 1983; Dodge, Coie, & Brakke, 1982; Hartup, Glazer, & Charlesworth, 1967). Although not all rejected children are overly aggressive, aggressive behaviors are more common among rejected children than among nonrejected children (Coie, 1985). Apparently, it is not aggression itself but aggression combined with a lack of social skills that brings about social rejection (French, 1988).

A third group of children are neither liked nor actively rejected. Instead, they are virtually ignored by the peer group. This category of neglected, or socially isolated, children has received much attention in recent years

(Gottman, 1977; Dodge, Coie, & Brakke, 1982; Asher, Hymel, & Renshaw, 1984). Neglected children are not seen as hostile or aggressive, and, in fact, are often thought of as shy. They are usually more physically attractive than children who are clearly rejected. What they share with rejected children, however, is a lack of social skills or social experiences. Summarizing the differences between rejected and neglected groups, Dodge (1983) noted that the former group lacks social skills and is antisocial, while the latter group lacks social skills but is not antisocial.

Peer rejection seems to be quite consistent throughout elementary and high school, while peer neglect is variable and seems to depend on the particular social setting that the child is in (Coie & Krehbiel, 1984). A neglected child might become more popular if moved to a different classroom or a different school; a rejected child seems to be rejected everywhere.

Adolescence

Certain characteristics make adolescents popular among their peers, and Table 12.2 lists the qualities important for being a "big wheel" in one midwestern high school. Personal qualities (e.g., personality, good looks) were most frequently mentioned, followed by material possessions (e.g., cars, money, nice clothes), activities/athletics, academic achievement, and having the "right" friends.

We might expect that personal qualities would be most closely related to popularity. Wearing fashionable clothes, driving a sports car, or being a successful athlete will not help an inconsiderate, bad-tempered, dishonest, or socially withdrawn adolescent. The most popular adolescents are friendly, cheerful, easygoing, humorous, and intelligent (Hartup, 1983; Steinberg, 1989).

That material possessions rated second on the list of criteria suggests a degree of superficiality in at least some adolescent peer relationships.

Table 12.2
Criteria Necessary for Being a "Big Wheel" on Campus, as Listed by High School Students

Criteria	Percentage of Boys Listing Criterion (N = 142)	Percentage of Girls Listing Criterion (N = 178)
Personal qualities	60.6	89.3
Material possessions	49.3	55.1
Activities/athletics	35.9	23.6
Academic achievement	21.8	25.8
"Right Friends"	17.6	10.1

Source: From E. E. Snyder (1972). High school perceptions of prestige criteria. Adolescence, 6, p. 132. © 1972 Libra Publishers. Reprinted by permission.

Indeed, many adolescents seem to be so involved in developing their own identities that they are not yet ready to look beneath the surface of others and to establish intimate relationships.

An interesting and frequently observed finding is that, for boys at least, athletic success takes precedence over academic achievement. Coleman (1961) asked adolescent boys how they would like to be remembered after graduation from high school and discovered that 44 percent of them wanted to be remembered as outstanding athletes, 31 percent as brilliant scholars, and 25 percent as the most popular students. Fourteen years later, Eitzen (1975) found that the figure for athletics was 47 percent, for scholarship 23 percent, and for popularity 30 percent. Apparently, little had changed from the 1960s to the 1970s. If anything, the value of scholarship seemed to have slipped.

Adulthood Socialization Patterns

During the years from young adulthood to old age, both a similarity and a developmental difference in the nature of friendship can be seen. The definition and expectations of friendship do not change. Lowenthal, Thurnher, and Chiriboga (1975) studied friendship patterns in four groups of San Francisco residents: high school seniors, newly married young adults, middle-aged people, and elderly people. In responding to a question about the desirable characteristics of an ideal friend, the four age groups agreed that understanding, trust, and ability to confide in the person are important. Troll (1982) referred to these characteristics as *mutuality* and *reciprocity,* and Lowenthal, Thurnher, and Chiriboga (1975) suggested that needs for reciprocity and mutuality are established during adolescence and continue throughout adulthood.

The lack of age differences in the way we define friendship does not indicate, of course, that we rely on our friends in precisely the same ways at different points in the life span. As Huyck and Hoyer (1982) have noted, adolescents and young adults may have greater needs for intimacy than the elderly do, and affiliation among the elderly may be motivated more by companionship needs than by intimacy needs. The way we define friends may be constant; the way we use our friends may change with age. Definite age differences are apparent in both the stability of friendship and in the likelihood of choosing friends from within the family or outside it. However, because the studies we shall now discuss are cross-sectional rather than longitudinal, we can only speculate on whether friendship actually changes with age, particularly in the later years.

Stability in Friendship

Because young adulthood (the late teens to the middle 20s) is a time of testing in many areas of life—a time of trying out lifestyles and planning our future—it is also a period of trial and error in interpersonal relations. Troll (1975) spoke of the tendency of college students to seek intimacy with people they do not know very well. Quite often, young men and women find themselves confiding in friends they have known for only a matter of weeks and sharing their thoughts and feelings with them. These friendships may dissolve as quickly as they were formed.

By the late 20s and early 30s, such instant intimacy is unthinkable. For people in this age range, friendship takes longer to achieve but is considerably more enduring. This increasing stability of friendship patterns continues throughout life (Shulman, 1975); those who are beyond their late 20s may consider as their best friends people they have not seen in a number of years (Hess, 1972). At reunions they often remark that they are just as close as if they had never been separated. The probable reason is that they were at relatively stable points in their lives when the friendships were first developed, and they sought each other out because of genuine similarity of interests. Adolescent and young adult friendships are less stable, because they often are based on needs that are temporary. For example, if Mary befriends Susan because Susan makes Mary feel secure and positive about herself, what will happen to the friendship when Mary develops a firm identity and no longer needs Susan's assurance? It may endure, but it will have to be on a different basis. Perhaps the proportionately high rate of failure of teenage marriages could be a result of similar circumstances. A couple may marry because they satisfy each other's adolescent needs; when one or both of them mature, however, those needs may disappear, and with them the relationship.

Friends Within the Family

Whether we choose our friends from within the family or from outside it seems to depend on age and marital status. Shulman (1975) found that young adults aged 18 to 30 were less likely to name relatives as intimate friends than were adults over the age of 45. Furthermore, single people were less likely than marrieds to name relatives as their intimates. As we grow older and become more involved in the family structure, we are increasingly more likely to choose friends from within the family group. This trend, which has been referred to as *disengagement into the family* (Troll, 1971), may be characteristic of the socialization patterns only of the current elderly generation rather than of elderly people in general. Lopata (1973) suggested that we are witnessing a turning toward familial supports among today's elderly primarily because so many of them are women who have been socalized to find support within the family. Perhaps future generations of elderly will be more peer oriented and less family oriented.

Indeed, future generations of elderly may be forced to be more peer oriented if they are looking for emotional support from intimates. Kahana (1982) discussed the increasing tendency among the elderly to leave their families and long-term friends and migrate to warmer climates for their retirement years. If new friendships are not developed, elderly people may experience a sense of loneliness and uselessness, as well as a lowering of self-esteem (Gordon, 1976). The elderly who live in retirement communities cite the availability of friends or potential friends as the most positive aspect of their new locations (Christopherson, 1972; Sherman, 1971).

Importance of Intimacy

Much of the research on the value of social support systems during adulthood has focused on the elderly population, and the usual finding is that the availability of intimate contacts is positively related to the maintenance of psychological well-being (Antonucci, 1985; Beck & Leviton, 1976; Edwards & Klemmack, 1973; George, 1980; Kahana, 1982; Lowenthal & Haven, 1968; Mariwaki, 1973). For example, Lowenthal and Haven (1968) interviewed 280 people who were 60 years of age or older and found that the elderly are better able to deal with many life crises if they have someone to confide in. The death of a spouse, for example, can be a devastating experience for anyone, but particularly for a person who is unable to share feelings of grief with someone. Likewise, dealing with unwanted retirement is easier when the elderly person has a confidant.

Obviously, the accumulated losses of the elderly are more severe than the losses of people in young and middle adulthood, so the need for a confidant may be correspondingly greater in old age. Furthermore, it is difficult to generalize the findings from research on elderly populations to the lives of young and middle-aged adults. Nevertheless, friendship for all adults is a means of avoiding isolation, and early adulthood social experiences may facilitate psychological well-being in later life (Huyck & Hoyer, 1982).

Gender Differences in Friendship

At all ages across the span of adult life, women report having a larger number of friends than men do (Lowenthal, Thurnher, & Chiriboga, 1975). Moreover, consistent with the findings of much of the childhood and adolescent research, young adult women have frequently been reported to seek greater degrees of intimacy in same-sex friendships than their male counterparts (for example, Jones, 1974; Strommen, 1977; Bell, 1981). In fact, the ideal standard of friendship (trust and sharing of thoughts, feelings, and weaknesses) is almost by definition a feminine one in today's culture (Antonucci, 1985; Gibson & Mugford, 1986; Kendig, 1986).

To whom, then, does a man turn if he feels the need for intimacy in a relationship? To answer this question, Komarovsky (1976) distributed to a group of college men a self-disclosure questionnaire containing items related to a variety of life areas, including attitudes, personality characteristics, feelings about one's body, feelings about work, and issues related to money. She discovered that men were more likely to discuss most of these areas, particularly those relating to personality and body image, with a female confidant than with another male. The only exception was in the area of finances; here men were more likely to confide in their parents than in female friends. In short, men often rely on female friends to meet their needs for intimacy. As one college senior observed in explaining his preference for a female confidant, "Even your best (male) friend gets a certain amount of comfort out of your difficulty. A girl friend is ready to identify with your interests and to build you up" (Komarovsky, 1976, p. 166).

An inherent difficulty, however, is involved in expecting intimacy needs to be met primarily by a friend of the opposite sex. Perhaps because opposite-sex friendships are thought to be potentially sexual, society frowns on maintaining more than one such relationship at a time (Hess, 1972). Even though men actually have more opportunities than women to develop opposite-sex friendships (Booth, 1972; Booth & Hess, 1974; Stein, 1976), a man committed to a primary relationship with one woman will avoid becoming emotionally intimate with others. A woman emotionally involved with a man may likewise avoid emotional involvements with other men, but but she will probably have intimate contacts with other women. A woman may be intimate with her husband and with several female friends, whereas a man's intimacy needs are met primarily by his wife; he is less likely to be intimate with another woman or with other men (Huyck & Hoyer, 1982).

An overreliance on one person for a feeling of intimacy may not cause problems for the young or middle-aged man who can confide in a wife or female friend. It might be a problem, however, for the elderly man who is divorced or widowed, because in the later years of life other types of social contact may be decreasing. Certainly, both sexes experience social losses because of illness and death, but as Blau (1973) pointed out, the loss of a spouse affects the social participation of men more than that of women. Perhaps this gender difference might be explained by the difference in availability of an intimate replacement. Older men appear to be slightly more likely than older women to confide in their spouses, but women are significantly more likely to confide in a friend who is not a family member (Kendig, Coles, Pittelkow, & Wilson, 1988; Lowenthal & Haven, 1968). Therefore, the death of a spouse may rob a man of his major, or even his only, source of intimate contact, whereas a widow may still rely on an extrafamilial network of confidants. That men are more emotionally dependent on their marriages than women are may partly explain the greater difficulty men face in adjusting to widowhood (Anderson, 1984; Troll, Miller, & Atchley, 1979).

In summary, although men are not social isolates, they do not relate as freely and as intimately with same-sex friends as women do. A woman may have fewer social contacts, particularly if she does not work outside the home, but she has more friends than a man does, and her friends are apparently more meaningful to her. Finally, because men invest heavily in only one relationship to meet their needs for intimacy, they may lose more than women do when such relationships end.

Disengagement or Continued Social Activity in Old Age?

Disengagement theory
The view that aging involves a mutually agreed upon separation of the individual from other members of society.

Activity theory
The view that the happiest elderly people are those who remain active for the longest period of time.

One of the more widely circulated theories discussed in connection with interpersonal relationships among the elderly in our country is the **disengagement theory** (Cumming & Henry, 1961). Disengagement is the process whereby elderly people, as a reaction to the inevitability of the separation caused by death, gradually decrease their social contacts, and society, in turn, withdraws from them. According to this theory, the disengagement process is normal and even desirable.

In contrast to the disengagement theory is what has been described as the **activity theory** of aging (Havighurst, Neugarten, & Tobin, 1968). The activity theory suggests that, despite the biological changes associated with aging, no major psychological and social changes occur. The elderly have the same needs for social interaction that they had earlier in life. Circumstances may bring about decreased social interaction for them, but if this occurs, it is against their wishes and best interests. The happiest older people are those who maintain their typical activity patterns for as long as possible or who replace activities no longer possible with new ones (Streib, 1977).

Are elderly people happiest when allowed to slowly fade out of the social scene, give up their social roles, and decrease their social interactions—to sit, perhaps, and rock quietly on the front porch while the world withdraws from them? Or are they happiest when kept as active as possible and encouraged to overcome any physical disabilities while maintaining their former levels of physical, intellectual, and social activity? Such questions are extremely important to those who work with the elderly in institutions or recreational programs.

As might be expected, the question of disengagement versus activity has no simple answer. Havighurst, Neugarten, and Tobin (1968) found that even within the same individual there are needs for both disengagement and maintained activity. Elderly people, for example, might want to remain active to continue to feel useful and valuable, while at the same time wanting a more leisurely, less demanding, lifestyle than they had in previous years. It is a curious paradox that the elderly people who are the most socially active and who maintain the greatest diversity of social roles have been found to be the happiest (Havighurst, Neugarten, & Tobin, 1968), and yet many elderly delightedly report that retirement has allowed them the luxury of ridding themselves of unwanted relationships (Kahana, 1982).

Havighurst, Neugarten, and Tobin (1968) found that people's personalities affect their satisfaction with their activity levels. The hypothetical cases of Alice and Ellen will illustrate this finding. Alice is a woman of 73 years whose cognitive abilities are intact and who is self-confident, mature, and accepting of life changes. She is somewhat annoyed that she cannot get out of the house as often as she used to, and she has had to resign from membership in several civic organizations because she no longer has the energy to continue them. In other words, Alice has experienced at least a minor degree of social disengagement.

Alice's response to the limiting of her activities is very realistic. Because she is mature, flexible, and self-confident—what Havighurst, Neugarten, and Tobin would describe as an *integrated personality type*—she willingly limits her activities and substitutes some new ones for old ones. Her philosophy is to work with what she has rather than wasting time regretting what she has lost.

Ellen, 71 years old, has discovered, as did Alice, that her social roles have changed and her social interactions have decreased. Ellen always has been somewhat tense, controlled, ambitious, and achievement oriented— what Havighurst, Neugarten, and Tobin described as an *armored-defended personality*. She resents the physical and social restrictions placed on her. Ellen views aging as her enemy, constantly dwells on what she has lost, and structures her world so that she can reject or deny the necessity for change.

Alice and Ellen have both experienced social disengagement. Alice accepts her situation and may even come to see some positive elements in it. On the whole, she is as happy with her life as she has ever been. Ellen resents her situation and centers on her losses instead of emphasizing the positive. She is not nearly as happy with her life as she was in early and middle adulthood.

No one theory of social interaction in old age can accurately describe every situation, or even the majority of situations. Activity or lack of it cannot be used to predict life satisfaction. Even if people in the United States prefer to remain active throughout life as a general rule, we all react differently to activity restrictions.

PLAY AND SOCIALIZATION

Four-year-old Brian never complained when his mother dropped him off at nursery school. In fact, he was eager to go, and every evening would excitedly describe his day's classroom activities. However, Brian was shy around other children and, because he had few playmates in his neighborhood, was obviously inexperienced in social interaction. The teachers at the school realized that Brian needed to become more comfortable with his peers; he spent most of his free play time silently watching the other children. The teachers also knew that if they pressured him into social interaction, Brian might withdraw further into himself, so they decided to let play function as a natural socializing agent. They suggested that Brian might like to play with blocks, which he did, and they allowed him to spend the better part of his free play time in solitary block play. Within a few days, the teachers noticed that, although he still worked on his own block creations, he began to speak briefly to other children in the block corner. He would offer blocks or tell another child what he was doing. Soon he had the courage to ask to borrow other children's blocks, and within a month he was talking and laughing freely with his peers and even working cooperatively on small projects. The secure and liberating environment of play had, without adult intervention, provided a context for enhanced social interaction.

Playful or leisurely activities are central to the development of social interaction for two reasons. First, such activities frequently involve other people. Of course, solitary play takes place in childhood, and solitary recreation is often sought by adults. However, solitary play gives way eventually to more mature forms of social play among children, and social interaction/companionship is a major reason for adult recreation and one of its values. Second, as in Brian's case, play does more than just provide an opportunity for social interaction; it is actually a major socializing agent throughout childhood, and indeed throughout the entire life span. Thus, in play, children may learn how to cooperate, how to share, how to delay gratification, and how to imagine themselves in the roles of other people.

In this section of the chapter, we shall discuss play and leisure throughout the life span. We shall begin with a definition of play. Then we shall turn to a discussion of a variety of classical and modern theories of why people play. Finally, we shall look at developmental patterns of play and leisure from infancy through old age.

What Is Play?

For an activity to be thought of as play, it must exhibit a number of characteristics. First, the activity must be intrinsically motivated. That is, no external reasons exist for engaging in the activity; it is done only for its own sake. If a child plays soccer only to win a trophy or to please parents, the activity is not play—it is work. Second, to be play, an activity must be freely chosen by the child or children involved. Kindergartners regard an activity assigned by their teacher as work even though they would consider the same activity play if they initiated it themselves (Johnson, Christie, & Yawkey, 1987; King, 1979).

A third essential ingredient of play is that it must be pleasurable (Garvey, 1977). The child, or adult, must enjoy the activity. If a child riding a bicycle is in constant terror of falling off and being hurt, the activity can hardly be described as playful. A fourth characteristic of play is that it is nonliteral. That is, it involves some degree of pretense. Children in a playground may wrestle playfully, but the activity is play because it is "pretend" fighting. The children do not intend to hurt each other, at least in the beginning. Finally, play is actively engaged in. The player must be physically or psychologically involved in the activity, as opposed to being passive or indifferent while the activity is occurring (Rubin, Fein, and Vandenberg, 1983).

Theories of Play

No one simple answer explains why children play. A number of theoretical views, in combination, emphasize the value of play for a child's social, emotional, physical, and intellectual development. No single theory is complete or totally correct. Instead, each contributes pieces to a puzzle that has yet to be solved.

Early Theories

In the late 1800s and early 1900s, a number of theories of play were expressed; they shared a belief that play was natural to the human organism and fulfilled some biological function in a child's development. For example, British philosopher Herbert Spencer (1873) suggested the surplus energy theory: Every human being is supplied by nature with a certain amount of energy to be used in efforts at survival. Any surplus energy that is not used up must be discharged somehow, and children discharge it by playing.

A directly opposite interpretation of play was offered by G. T. W. Patrick (1916), who thought that play would occur only when the child was relaxed and fatigued. Thus, play was presumed to allow for the renewal of energy, avoiding idle boredom while waiting for the natural motor functions to be restored.

G. Stanley Hall offered the recapitulation theory, discussed in Chapter 1. He believed that the child's individual development parallels the evolutionary development of the human species, and so a child's play reflects our species development. For example, the hunting and chasing games of grade schoolers mirror an age in human history when people lived in caves and hunted and gathered to survive.

The German philosopher Karl Groos (1901) saw children's play as practice for adult living. In play, the child rehearses skills that will be needed later, just as the playful fighting of young animals prepares them for hunting as adults, and the play of a kitten who chases a ball prepares it to catch mice in adulthood.

Early theories of play were limited because each seemed to explain only a small aspect of the range of children's playful activities. What is more, they were all based on not very scientific views of human instincts and human evolution, and numerous exceptions could be found to challenge each of them (Johnson, Christie, and Yawkey, 1987). For example, parents often notice that their children will play to the point of total exhaustion (therefore discharging their "surplus energy") and then get up and begin to play again!

The value of these older theories is that they stimulated an interest in children's play and its adaptive significance, and in some cases, they contain elements of accuracy (Hughes, 1991). For example, although no one today would accept the view that the only function of play is to prepare children for adulthood, some play can have this function: A child playing house could learn something about family roles that might be useful later.

Contemporary Theories

Modern theories emphasize the psychological rather than the physical significance of play. The psychoanalytic theory, with its view of play as anxiety reduction, stresses the emotional and social benefits of play. Cognitive theories, on the other hand, emphasize the intellectual value of play. When examining contemporary theories, keep in mind that each looks at play in relation to a particular aspect of children's development. No one theory is completely correct, but if taken together, the combination of theories provides much information about the value of play.

Psychoanalytic Theory. The basic psychoanalytic view of play is that it is an activity the child uses to help reduce anxiety (Freud, 1966). Infants and children experience two types of anxiety: objective and instinctual.

Objective anxiety occurs because children realize that they are helpless in dealing with the huge, adult-controlled world. Play can alleviate this anxiety by giving children added strength, providing them with at least the illusion of power and control. For the infant, a rattle might become an extension of the self, allowing the child to manipulate and control the environment more effectively. Preschoolers extend themselves through play not just physically, but psychologically as well. For example, they can reduce the large and powerful world to manageable size by building with blocks or by playing with dolls or miniature toys.

Fantasy play allows children to transform the world into a less threatening environment. The child who is frightened of monsters becomes one, and frightens other children. The child who feels that parents are unfair becomes a parent to a family of toys—symbolically reversing an anxiety-producing situation. The child who is disturbed by conflicts at home role plays domestic scenes with happier endings.

The second major anxiety of early childhood is *instinctual anxiety* (Freud, 1966), children's fear of their own instincts whose expression is forbidden by society. These include anger, unreasonable fears, sexual curiosity, and the need to be messy or destructive.

Play allows children to confront and explore antisocial instincts because it offers them a chance to experience them in socially acceptable ways. For example, breaking dishes or throwing rocks through a window are unacceptable behaviors, and the feeling of destructiveness that motivated them is equally condemned. However, when a child builds towers of blocks or sand castles and then proceeds to destroy them with great enthusiasm, this destructiveness is acceptable to most adults.

Finally, the psychoanalytic view is also represented by Erik Erikson (1963). Taking a more developmental approach than Freud did, Erikson differentiated the need to master bodily and social skills from the purpose of relieving anxiety. During the first year of life, the child's behavior is referred to as *autocosmic play* because it involves exploration of the bodily self. Talking, walking, and perceptions provide the child with an exciting landscape for play.

In *microsphere play,* during the second year of life, the child's world is expanded to include an examination of toys and other objects. Such play enables the child to acquire actual mastery over the world, not simply mastery through the power of fantasy. Finally, the preschool child engages in *macrosphere play,* building on the physical manipulations of body and objects to learn about social interaction. The sharing of reality and fantasy with other children represents an important step in the child's capacity to understand the culture.

Cognitive Theories.   Cognitive theorists typically regard play as a tool that facilitates general cognitive development. For example, both Jerome Bruner (1973) and Brian Sutton-Smith (1967) believe that play allows a child to solve problems in a relatively stress-free and relaxed atmosphere and that these experiences may be useful later when the child is faced with more complex real-life problems.

Play, according to Jean Piaget (1962), is the dominance of assimilation (the incorporation of reality into one's cognitive structures) over accommodation (the changing of one's cognitive structures in response to environmental input). To understand assimilation without accommodation, consider the following example: In the mind of a child at play, an empty box becomes a boat sailing on the ocean. An accommodation to reality would involve the recognition that the box is really just a box, but the child does not conform to reality. Instead, reality is made to conform to the child's view of it, and this is "pure" assimilation.

Because intellectual development requires adaptation, and because adaptation requires both assimilation and accommodation, it follows that for Piaget, play is not the equivalent of intellectual development. In fact, Piaget wrote about the difference between play and "serious adaptation," with play involving the repetition of an activity that has already been learned, for its own sake. As an example, he cited the case of the 3-month-old child who threw his head back to look at the world from an unusual position. Initially, this behavior involved serious learning, but soon the child lost interest in the result and threw his head back time and again, laughing loudly, for the sheer enjoyment of the activity. The activity had become play.

Play in Piaget's theory has been viewed as a form of consolidation: An activity is first learned (adaptation) and is then repeated over and over again (play) as a means of incorporating the new activity into the child's previously learned activity patterns (Rubin, Fein, & Vandenberg, 1983; Sutton-Smith, 1985). As an illustration of the concept of consolidation, consider the case of the child who learns how to "pump" on a swing so that she can keep herself in motion without needing to be pushed. After the learning has taken place, the child consolidates the activity, repeating it in the same way, and also introducing variations (e.g., swinging while standing up, swinging on her stomach).

Although play is not the same as learning in Piaget's theory, play can lead to learning. This can be illustrated by an examination of Piaget's three types of play, corresponding roughly to his stages of cognitive development. Sensorimotor or *practice play* is the characteristic play of the first 18 months

Practice play

The intrinsically satisfying repetition of simple motor skills, characteristic of infants and toddlers.

of life. This is the intrinsically satisfying repetition of simple motor skills. Infants learn to master their own bodies and to manipulate the objects in their environment. Playing with balls, rattles, spoons, and cups are not only enjoyable pastimes, but activities that enable the infant to grasp the nature of physical reality.

By the second and third years of life, sensorimotor play is merged with an increasing proportion of make-believe or *symbolic play.* Symbolic play differs from real learning, but Piaget believed that the second often follows from the first. For example, in the process of symbolic play, a child might imagine that a stone or a piece of wood is a house, but the same child might then develop an interest in making the house look as realistic as possible. The child might make a serious attempt to reproduce the house faithfully with blocks or clay. Therefore, what had begun as symbolic play gradually became a "serious" learning project, a constructive game, which Piaget saw as falling on a continuum somewhere between symbolic play and adaptation.

Symbolic play
Make-believe or fantasy play, which begins in the second year of life and predominates throughout the pre-school years.

The third type of play, *games-with-rules,* emerges as the child attains the level of concrete operational thought. With the child's firmer notions about reality and decreasing egocentrism, play can become both more social and more logical. At this point, fantasy play diminishes and becomes subordinated to games-with-rules. The play of older children and adolescents begins to resemble the interactions of adults, in which shared communication, organized cooperation and competition, and more sophisticated strategies prevail. Organized sports now become popular, as do board games such as Monopoly and checkers, and games of skill such as hopscotch and video games.

Games-with-rules
The logical rule-dominated games of elementary school children.

The games of concrete operational children require skill, intelligence, and, above all, knowledge of the rules. Children who cheat, or who simply do not know the rules of the game, may find themselves quickly excluded from the organized games of their peers.

Arousal Modulation Theories. According to the arousal modulation theory of play developed by D. E. Berlyne (1969), a drive in the human central nervous system keeps our bodies at an optimal level of arousal. Extremely high or extremely low levels of stimulation create feelings of uncertainty or boredom, respectively. New or unusual stimuli in the environment can make a person feel confused or uncertain and can elevate the level of central nervous system arousal. To bring down this level of arousal, the person explores the environment and thereby reduces its uncertainty. On the other hand, when the environment lacks adequate stimulation, the person is bored and seeks a higher level of arousal. Here play enters the picture, because the child uses play to generate environmental stimulation where not enough already exists (Berlyne, 1969).

Other psychologists have suggested arousal modulation views of play that are somewhat similar to Berlyne's. For example, Ellis (1973) and Fein (1981) both argued that a major value of play is the provision of a variety of forms of physical, perceptual, and intellectual stimulation to an organism that needs it. Indeed, children at play will often appear to be intentionally stimulating themselves. They will make efforts to generate an element of risk or excitement—by climbing trees, lighting fires, scaring each other by playing monsters—that is probably lacking in their everyday activities.

Developmental Patterns in Play

The characteristics of play will differ across the span of life, and these differences reflect the players' levels of biological, social, emotional, and intellectual development. We turn now to an examination of the play of children from infancy through adolescence, and the play, or, more broadly, the leisure activities, of adults at various points in the life span.

Infancy

Even during the first year of life, a number of forms of play can be observed, including sensorimotor play, play with objects, and social play with adults. The second year is characterized by the addition of symbolic or make-believe play and social play with peers.

Sensorimotor Play.   A good deal of infant play consists of what cognitive theorist Jean Piaget (1962) referred to as sensorimotor play, which is the repetition of a sensory or motor activity for the sheer pleasure of doing so. In the beginning, such play involves the child's own body, as illustrated by the earlier example of the 3-month-old boy who tilted his head back to see the world from an unaccustomed position. At first he did this very seriously, as if learning were involved, but soon he seemed to lose interest in what might be learned and simply threw his head back again and again, laughing loudly each time.

By the middle of the second year, children focus less on their own bodies in sensorimotor play and become increasingly interest in the effects of their actions on the surrounding world.

Play with Objects.   Play with objects begins at about 4 to 5 months of age, as soon as the child has acquired eye-hand coordination in reaching and a primitive grasp. A 5-month old will play with a piece of string or a piece of paper (by crumpling it), or will playfully bang a spoon or rattle on a tabletop. However, in such early object play, the emphasis is on the action rather than the object. For example, the child may enjoy banging objects in play, and will bang a spoon, rattle, cup or anything else that is provided, with little interest in the characteristics of the objects themselves (Rubenstein, 1976). By 9 or 10 months, however, infants attend more carefully to the properties of the objects rather than just incorporating them automatically into their preferred action sequences. They notice now when something is unfamiliar and take more time with it than with a familiar toy, and they handle objects differently depending on their different physical features (Rubenstein, 1976; Ruff, 1984).

During the second year, object play matures considerably. First, children are increasingly likely to bring objects together in play; single-object play becomes quite rare by the age of 18 months (Fein & Apfel, 1979; Rubin, Fein, & Vandenberg, 1983; Zelazo & Kearsley, 1980). Second, objects are played with more and more appropriately. Children start to realize that objects have specific functions: a ball is to be thrown or rolled, for example, and blocks are to be stacked (Fenson, 1986; Rosenblatt, 1977). Third, late in the second year, the child begins to use objects in representational ways, pretending that one thing is something else (Fenson, 1986).

Social Play.   Social play with adult partners begins in the latter half of the infant's first year, as evidenced by such "games" as reciprocal smiling and peek-a-boo that are initiated by the infant's caretakers. These games involve relatively simple rules and usually contain an element of taking turns and a repetition of roles at the end of each round of activity (Ross & Lollis, 1987). For example, the parent stacks a few blocks on top of one another, the baby waits and then topples the tower, the parent builds, the baby knocks down again, and so on.

Social play with peers, which involves role playing, the taking of turns, and the engagement by partners in activities that complement one another, begins in the second year and increases in frequency throughout the preschool years (Howes, 1988; Howes, Unger, & Seidner, 1989).

Symbolic Play.   Although the first year of life is dominated by sensory and motor play, a new element appears in the second year. As we noted in discussing changes in object play, the 1-year-old begins to engage in acts of make-believe. This is known as pretend, or symbolic, play. Just as words come to represent objects, empty plates begin to represent steak dinners, mud pies represent food, or an empty box represents a boat.

Symbolic play does not emerge all at once, however. Its appearance is a gradual process characterized by several stages (Bretherton, 1984; Fenson, 1986; McCune-Nicolich & Fenson, 1984; Piaget, 1962; Watson and Jackowitz, 1984). The earliest pretend behavior, occurring even as early as 12 months of age, is usually a solitary activity and involves the performance of actions familiar to the child, such as sleeping, eating, or talking on the telephone. The element of pretense is present because the pretend activities are in no way related to the child's real needs; that is, children may pretend to sleep even when they don't feel at all tired.

A second stage of make-believe occurs when a child begins to substitute one object for another. A block becomes a boat or an empty cereal bowl serves as a hat. And, finally, the child begins to combine make-believe objects with make-believe action sequences, as when the child pretends that a toy teddy bear is eating pretend food from an empty dish (Fenson, 1986; Johnson, Christie, & Yawkey, 1987).

Although the earliest forms of symbolic play usually occur when the child is alone, more sophisticated pretend play is often a social activity. Toward the end of the second year, children become interested in watching the play of their peers (onlooker play) or in playing independently beside them (parallel play), but they do not yet engage in genuine interactive behaviors (Rubin, Maioni, & Hornung, 1976). Gradually, solitary play gives way to mature social play with peers, and this will not occur until the child is between 3 and 4 years of age.

Benefits of Infant Play. What are the values of infant play in terms of later development? Sensorimotor play may contribute to the advancement of perceptual awareness and muscular coordination (both fine motor and gross motor skills). In addition, all repetitive play of this sort serves to consolidate the infant's understanding of newly developed concepts in the social and physical environment.

Social play with adults has many benefits (Hughes, 1991). First, it keeps the infant appropriately stimulated, neither bored nor overly excited (Power & Parke, 1980). Second, it gives the infant a sense of control over the environment, and thus fosters a degree of self-confidence (Watson & Ramey, 1972). Third, because parent-infant play is such an intense and enjoyable social experience for both parties, it can facilitate parent-infant attachment (Stern, 1977). Fourth, it encourages the infant to explore surroundings. Finally, social play causes the infant to attend more closely to the social aspects of language (Ratner & Bruner, 1978).

Early Childhood

The preschool years bring a considerable number of refinements in children's play. On a physical level, the improving dexterity of preschool children makes possible such large-muscle play activities as throwing a ball, climbing a ladder, or jumping on the furniture, as well as small muscle activities such as cutting with scissors, painting with a brush, or stringing beads (Hughes, 1991).

Preschool children's social play also matures considerably. Play involving other children occurs more often and becomes more complex. The size of play groups increases, and preschoolers become increasingly choosy about their playmates. Five-year-olds prefer playmates of their own age, gender, and developmental level, while the undiscriminating 2-year-old would have played with anybody who was willing (Parten, 1933).

The solitary, onlooker, and parallel play of 1- and 2-year olds is enhanced by the addition of associative and cooperative play (Parten, 1933). Associative play involves sharing and taking turns ("I'll lend you my red paint if I can borrow your green"), and cooperative play involves working together with other children on a common activity with common goals. Dramatic play (playing house or supermarket) requires cooperation because, unless everyone agrees to play an assigned role, the game cannot proceed.

The make-believe world of early childhood contains a good deal of dramatic play, which can be classified according to four different types of roles: (1) functional, (2) relational, (3) character, and (4) peripheral (Garvey, 1977). *Functional roles* are defined by the specific behaviors of the characters involved (e.g., delivering a newspaper, climbing a mountain), but do not comprise the characters' permanent identities (Bretherton, 1986). *Relational roles* are defined as characters in a typical family relationship, such as a mommy or a daddy, and are the roles most frequently enacted by preschoolers (Garvey & Berndt, 1977). *Character roles* are assumed when children play at simply *being* somebody, rather than at doing something specific. These may be based on television characters or other stereotypical and fictional beings (e.g., Santa Claus or a cowboy or Big Bird). Finally, *peripheral roles* are roles that are incorporated within play but are never actually adopted by the child (e.g., imaginary companions, absent friends, stuffed animals).

Unlike the solitary play of younger children, the make-believe play of the preschooler typically involves friends. Johnson and Ershler (1981), for example, reported that between 70 percent and 80 percent of the pretend play of 3- to 4-year-olds occurred in groups. This pattern of highly social

Make-believe play becomes increasingly social during childhood. Such play enhances a child's self-awareness, self-confidence, and self-control.

make-believe continues to evolve throughout early childhood and does not decline until the early elementary school years (Rubin, Watson, & Jambor, 1978).

Another progression in the pretend play of preschoolers is the movement away from a literal form of object substitution. Older preschoolers are quite flexible in using their imaginations to symbolize absent objects or places (Elder & Pederson, 1978; Overton & Jackson, 1973). In fact, as playmates become more familiar with one another, their fantasy behavior becomes significantly less realistic (Matthews, 1977). Children move away from a preoccupation with familiar themes, such as playing out the roles of doctors, teachers, mommies, and daddies, to an interest in themes far removed from the child's everyday experiences—fictional characters or characters who are completely imaginary (Johnson, Christie, and Yawkey, 1987).

Additional evidence for a move toward greater flexibility in play is that the social fantasy play of preschoolers is extremely ritualized at first but becomes much less so as the children develop (Mueller & Lucas, 1975). As an illustration, young preschoolers imitate the dialogue and actions of their friends very literally. For example, Pat says, "My bunny is going down the slide," and Gerry responds with, "My Teddy is going down the slide." Older preschoolers introduce more variety into their words and their actions. Chris says "My truck is climbing over the mountain," and Leslie responds "My boat is going across the river." These trends illustrate the preschool child's maturing cognitive abilities.

What is the value of make-believe play for the preschool child? In terms of affective benefits, such play may enhance a child's self-awareness, self-confidence, and self-control (Singer, 1973). Intellectual benefits include the fact that lengthy involvement in pretense leads to improvements in concentration and reflective thought. What is more, make-believe leads children into a "what if?" mode of thinking that forms the basis for later hypothetical reasoning and problem solving (Bretherton, 1986). Dramatic play can stimulate children to think creatively and is related to creativity later on (Dansky, 1980). Finally, dramatic play has been found to have a positive influence on children's memory, language skills, and role-taking ability (Burns & Brainerd, 1979; Dansky, 1980; Saltz, Dixon, & Johnson, 1977).

Middle Childhood and Adolescence

A major change occurs in play as children develop from preschool age to the early elementary school years. Symbolic or make-believe play gradually declines and a new form of play begins to appear—the game-with-rules (Piaget, 1962). Games-with-rules, which include formal games such as baseball or basketball, informal games such as tag or red rover, or even superstitious rituals (e.g., "Step on a crack, break your mother's back"), have two essential characteristics. First, they involve at least two players who compete with each other for the purpose of winning the game. Second, the behavior of the players is regulated by a strict set of rules, which are either made up for the occasion or are handed down from one generation of children to another (Rubin, Fein, & Vandenberg, 1983).

Games-with-rules appear at the same time that logical thinking emerges—the beginning of Piaget's stage of concrete operations, which was discussed in Chapter 7. They are increasingly evident from the kindergarten year until the end of the fifth grade, after which they begin to decline in frequency (Eifermann, 1971; Rubin, Fein, & Vandenberg, 1983; Rubin & Krasnor, 1980).

What are the functions of games-with-rules? Piaget (1962) believed that, particularly when the rules are spontaneous, such games have major importance in terms of children's social and intellectual development. The process of establishing and adhering to a set of rules requires sensitivity to the viewpoints of other people, mutual understanding, willingness to delay gratification, and a high degree of cooperation. In fact, in some sense, all forms of mature socialization require adherence to a set of implicit or explicit rules for social interaction. Therefore, games-with-rules may give children practice in living in a social environment.

Many psychologists question whether games-with-rules fit the definition of play at all. For example, Garvey (1977) argued that games-with-rules do not qualify as play because they are relatively inflexible, tradition-dominated, goal-directed, competitive, formalized, and explicit. They lack the spontaneity that is a characteristic of play, and the goal of games-with-rules—winning—goes beyond the sheer enjoyment of the activity in itself.

Although games-with-rules dominate the activities of school-age children, a number of earlier forms of play continue as well. For example, children still engage in a lot of goal-free functional play (e.g., shooting baskets, throwing a ball around, riding a bicycle). Constructive play with materials such as blocks, plastic bricks, models, and clay continues throughout this period. Children also engage in a lot of aimless wandering about the neighborhood that is not specifically exploratory or goal-directed. And fantasy play continues throughout the middle childhood period, as in the case of an 8-year-old who decides to dress up like Superman and fly around the neighborhood faster than a speeding bullet!

From the age of 12 onward, the most popular play activities reflect a need for self-awareness, heterosexual socialization, and intimate communication (Hughes, 1991). For example, adolescents like going to movies, watching television, reading, going to dances and parties, and listening to music (or watching music videos). They also like to just "hang around" with friends, and much adolescent play is of this unstructured variety. Consistent with the transition from a concrete and action-oriented view of friendship to one that involves a greater degree of abstract conceptualization, socialization is defined less as *doing* something with friends and more as simply *being* with friends (Hughes, 1991).

Functional and fantasy play are incorporated during adolescence into a variety of organized activities. Games-with-rules remain important, but in increasingly complex forms—organized athletics, school clubs and organizations, video and computer games, and board games such as chess, Scrabble, and Dungeons and Dragons.

Adolescent playful behavior also exists in spontaneous and unstructured ways. Such physical activities as informal wrestling matches, skateboarding, shooting buckets, and general rough-housing are popular. In addition, a considerable amount of adolescent play is verbal in nature. Adolescents enjoy the experience of relating verbally with, showing off to, and teasing their peers—for example, "insult wars" and constant teasing games between girls and boys. As was discussed in Chapter 9, such language play appears to have social, cognitive, and linguistic benefits for the adolescent.

Adulthood

The play of adults is typically not called play at all, but is referred to as leisure, or recreational activity. Play is often seen as a childhood—and perhaps even a childish—activity, while the broader category of leisure is thought to include adult activities as well. But are play and leisure really different? All leisure activities may be seen as play, but with a more sophisticated name. Leisure is (1) the cultivation of mind and spirit; (2) a nonwork activity engaged in for relaxation, entertainment, or personal development; and (3) a relaxed state of mind (Burrus-Bammel & Bammel, 1985; Iso-Ahola, 1980; Neulinger, 1981). Many of these same elements appear in our definition of play: an activity that is freely chosen, pleasurable, intrinsically motivated, nonliteral, and actively engaged in. Perhaps the differences between play and leisure are that play is usually thought of as an activity, while leisure is also seen as a state of mind, and that play has a nonliteral, or "pretend," component that leisure may or may not have. In this vein, Gordon, Gaitz, and Scott (1976) described play, perhaps a bit too narrowly, as only one of the many forms of leisure—that which involves make-believe or fantasy and typically occurs only during childhood. Leaving aside the issue of whether play and leisure are synonymous or whether the first is a subset of the second, adult leisure activities have a broad range, all the way from total relaxation to intense physical and emotional involvement.

If we examine changes in the uses of leisure across the span of adult life, we find that age alone does not predict a person's level of leisure activity (Burrus-Bammel & Bammel, 1985; Morgan & Godbey, 1978; Nystrom, 1974). However, a number of other related variables, such as health, mobility, financial status, and available time may be responsible for the age differences in leisure that are found in cross-sectional research. What are these differences? Some leisure activities (e.g., relaxing, being alone) are found with increasing frequency in older age groups; others (e.g., dancing, drinking, sports and exercise, going to movies, reading, producing works of

Leisure—perhaps the adult form of play—affords opportunities for personal and social growth and can be an important coping mechanism during the adult life span.

art) are found less often in older age groups; finally, many leisure activities (e.g., entertaining friends, appreciating art and culture) appear just as often in all age groups (Gordon, Gaitz, & Scott, 1976; Harris, 1975). An age-related decline occurs in leisure activities that are structured and involve physical activity and intense social interaction beyond the home, and an increase occurs in activities that are sedentary, unstructured, and homebound.

The importance of leisure in adult life is demonstrated in studies of the types of activities that are most highly valued. Adults place the greatest value on leisure activities that promote social interaction with significant other people and on those that allow them to demonstrate their skills, their competence, and their worth (Kelly, 1983). Leisure can, of course, consist of being alone and doing nothing, but the leisure activities most closely related to high degrees of life satisfaction are those that promote social interaction or a feeling of personal growth (Kelly, 1987). Such activities seem to help adults cope with major life changes, as Kelly (1987) observed among the 80 percent of the adults he interviewed who used leisure activities as coping mechanisms. As an example, Margaret was divorced at age 49 and found herself with full responsibility for raising her young son. She discovered that her involvement with her church and with a woman's barbershop chorus provided the peer companionship that helped her adjust to her new role. Leisure thus become for Margaret a context for the type of supportive social interaction that was not available to her at the factory where she worked.

A similar pattern of coping was displayed by Ethel, whose husband deserted her when she was 55. Ethel's whole life and sense of worth had centered on her home and family, and she now felt devastated and useless. Then, at the suggestion of her grown children, she increased her involvement in leisure activities. She joined local clubs, volunteered to work at a local hospital, took up golf, and started to travel. These activities helped her to define herself in a new context, and soon she overcame the self-pity and despair that had absorbed her after her family role had disappeared. Leisure provided for Ethel a road to self-definition, as it had provided for Margaret a context for social interaction.

In summary, the play or leisure activities of adults are not just time fillers in what are otherwise empty lives. Leisure consists of many dimensions and affords opportunities for personal and social growth. As such, it can be a valuable coping mechanism as individuals encounter the many changes that characterize the span of adult life.

WORK IN THE LIFE CYCLE

For many adults in the United States, work is the equivalent of what play is for children, in the sense that work consumes a large portion of adult life just as play is central in children's lives. Adults in our society devote fully one-third of their waking hours to work and work-related activities and a considerable amount of time and effort before that in preparing themselves for employment (England & Misumi, 1986). The analogy between work and play can be carried just so far, however. Work, like play, may be pleasurable, but it is not necessarily so, nor is it usually a completely voluntary activity. What is more, unlike play, which has no external goals, the ultimate goal of work, whatever other needs it may serve, is usually to earn a living.

Psychologists generally agree that a person's work has much intrinsic psychological meaning, and that it is shortsighted to see work *only* in terms of earning capacity. In fact, between 65 percent and 95 percent of workers in the United States, as well as in a variety of other nations, say they would continue to work even if they were so wealthy that they did not need to do so (MOW International Research Team, 1986; Warr, 1982).

Work is clearly a dominant influence on adult life. It is rated in importance just below the family and is seen by workers as more important than leisure activities (e.g., hobbies, athletics, socialization), community involvements, and religion (England & Misumi, 1986). Why does work have such great psychological significance? Several reasons have been suggested: (1) work establishes a person's identity and peer group status in adulthood; (2) work serves as a context for competition, affiliation, and nurturance; (3) work provides adults with opportunities to develop a sense of achievement, as well as to express their inner selves (Garfinkel, 1982).

After a decade of research on the meaning of work, Kohn (1980) concluded that the psychological impact of a job derives from the *challenge* that the work itself poses, or fails to pose, and the most important of these challenges is the mastery of complex tasks. What can be said, however, of the worker who finds little or no challenge on the job? Perhaps this lack of meaning underlies much of the job dissatisfaction in our culture. Indeed, the inability of many Americans to find meaning in their jobs may be responsible for a shift from a work ethic to a self-fulfillment ethic—an unwillingness to work hard and a demand for increased leisure, pleasure, and fun out of life (Sheehy, 1981).

Early Basis for Adult Work

"And what do you want to be when you grow up?" Children in our society hear this question from the time they are preschoolers. From the age of 3 or 4, children imitate adult work roles in their play, and, as they grow up, they become increasingly likely to experiment with, fantasize about, anxiously await, and often worry about the work roles they will assume as adults. In other words, even though actual work may not begin until late adolescence, work-related questions are important in the lives of children and young teenagers as well.

Before adolescence, however, the career interests of children are neither realistic nor stable (Ginsberg, 1972). The appeal of an adult job is its perceived glamor or excitement, with little or no consideration for the child's abilities or for the likelihood that such a job will really be available. Adults smile indulgently when children say they want to be astronauts, ballerinas, cowboys, or karate instructors, realizing that in time the children will develop more realistic aspirations.

Not until the middle years of adolescence are the characteristics of anticipated careers linked to personal interests and aptitudes. Career goals then become increasingly realistic and consistent (Ginsberg, 1972). By this point in life, the teenager's growing self-awareness is combined with a realistic knowledge about various careers—sometimes as a result of actual work experience in summer and part-time jobs.

What elements influence an adolescent's occupational goals? Some influences are unpredictable, of course, such as trends in job availability or simply being in the right place at the right time. Most influences on career choice are more predictable than that, however. For example, Bachman, O'Malley, and Johnston (1978) studied more than 2,000 U.S. males from their mid-teens to their mid-20s and found a significant relationship between social class and the attainment of career goals. They also found that self-esteem was a predictor of the likelihood of attaining the career of one's choice.

The researchers concluded that adolescents from lower-class homes may be prevented from achieving high-status careers because they lack appropriate vocational models, are not encouraged to explore their occupational interests, and do not receive enough information about the value of extensive training and education. They suggested that career education should begin during childhood and should include efforts to bolster self-esteem and to help children realistically appraise their abilities and opportunities.

In support of the earlier research findings, Grotevant and Cooper (1988) recently observed that middle-class parents were more likely than lower-class parents to encourage career exploration by their children. They were also more likely to model a broader range of occupational choices.

Occupational Choice and Personality

People often complain that, despite an acceptable salary and comfortable working conditions, they feel "unfulfilled" in their jobs. They remark that their work does not allow them to express their interests and use their capabilities to the maximum. Indeed, as was pointed out earlier, work has great psychological significance because it helps people establish their identities and express their inner selves (Garfinkel, 1982). Let us now examine the need for a match between personality and occupational choice.

A pioneer in the effort to explain the dynamics of vocational choice, John L. Holland (1973, 1985) maintained that occupational preference does indeed reflect an individual's personality attributes. He believed that people look for work environments in which they can fully use their skills and abilities, express their values and attitudes, and take on roles and problems that they find agreeable. Furthermore, he argued that in the presence of a reasonable match between personality type and job environment, people are likely to be happy in their jobs and willing to remain in them for a longer period of time.

Holland (1985) described six broad personality types and six corresponding environmental themes, as outlined in Table 12.3. After completing a standard vocational inventory, people could match their profiles to the typical response patterns of people in various occupations. Although no individual's profile will perfectly fit a particular career, trained vocational counselors could help clients see that their responses roughly indicate which personality type they seem to be, and which occupations people of the same type usually enter. Someone who scored as mechanical, practical, and antisocial might realize, for example, that these traits do not resemble the profile of a typical social worker!

A number of researchers other than Holland (e.g., Lunnenborg & Lunnenborg, 1975; Meir & Ben-Yehuda, 1976; Spokane, 1985) have discovered that a knowledge of personality types does offer useful information about the prediction of job success. However, Holland's model illustrates what might be an *ideal* approach to vocational choice, rather than an accurate reflection of how most people actually choose their careers (Stevens-Long & Cobb, 1983). Many people do not have the luxury of choice, and their job selection is dictated by family or financial pressures, ethnic and racial factors, or, as we shall discuss in the section that follows, considerations related to gender (Cavanaugh, 1990).

Women in the Work Force

In the United States, the role of work in women's lives has been undergoing a profound transition in the second half of this century. Not only are child

Table 12.3
Holland's Model of Vocational Choice

Type	Personality Attributes	Representative Occupations
Realistic	Asocial, materialistic, practical, mechanical, athletic, thrifty	Machinist, game warden, mail carrier, dressmaker
Investigative	Analytical, cautious, curious, intellectual, reserved, rational	Scientist, detective, mathematician, surgeon
Artistic	Original, expressive, disorderly, impulsive, intuitive, independent	Musician, painter, writer, actor
Social	Cooperative, friendly, helpful, kind, sociable, tactful	Teacher, social worker, counselor, bartender
Enterprising	Acquisitive, ambitious, energetic, optimistic, self-confident, talkative	Salesperson, manager, politician, banker
Conventional	Conforming, efficient, orderly, inhibited, persistent, unimaginative	Secretary, accountant, data processor

Source: Adapted from J. L. Holland (1985). *Making Vocational choices: A theory of vocational personalities and work environments.* Englewood Cliffs, NJ: Prentice-Hall.

care and household maintenance increasingly being recognized as legitimate forms of labor, but employment outside the home, once thought of as an exclusively male pattern, is increasingly characteristic of women in our society as well (Greenstein, 1986; Hayghe, 1984; Waldman, 1983). In the late 1980s, more than half of all U.S. women, and more than two-thirds of those from 20 to 54 years old, were employed outside the home; 4 out of every 10 of these women was single, divorced, or widowed (U.S. Bureau of Labor Statistics, 1987).

Female employment is not a new phenomenon in our society, of course, but women in the past were either unpaid or underpaid for their work,

Women are increasingly choosing occupations that traditionally have been male dominated. But women still earn significantly less than men, even for comparable work, and still must deal with lingering gender discrimination.

limited in their career choices, and actively discouraged from attempting to compete against men for jobs (Troll, 1982). Today, however, women appear to have a greater number of employment options than ever before.

We should not paint too rosy a picture, however. The struggle for working women is still complicated by a lack of successful female role models in high-status occupations, persistently inadequate wages (between 45 percent and 75 percent of the salaries earned by men even for comparable work), and lingering forms of gender discrimination (Baron & Bielby, 1985; Cavanaugh, 1990; DiPrete & Soule, 1988; Havighurst, 1982). In addition, although certain traditional gender role patterns are rapidly changing, others seem to be changing more slowly. Working women today often must resolve conflicts between their traditional household work roles and their work roles outside the home.

The role conflicts of female workers were nicely illustrated by the findings of sociologist Arlie Hochschild (1989), who interviewed 50 married couples in which both people held jobs outside the home. Hochschild (1989) discovered, first of all, that home and family concerns occupy a larger place in the mind of a working woman than in the mind of a working man. Approximately 97 percent of the women spontaneously mentioned their homes and their children in describing a typical day, but only 54 percent of the men mentioned their homes and 69 percent mentioned their children. In addition, even though the husbands and wives both worked full-time, the wives still undertook 75 percent of the housekeeping and child-rearing responsibilities. Only 18 percent of the husbands shared equally in the housework, and 60 percent did little or none of it.

Hochschild (1989) concluded that, when household work is figured in, women employed outside the home actually worked 15 more hours a week than men and spent 15 fewer hours a week at leisure. The result was a considerable amount of psychological strain, which took its toll on both the marriages and the careers of working couples.

Despite the role conflict that may characterize their lives, employed women seem to be happy, and are particularly happy to be employed. For example, in a *New York Times* poll of women with jobs, respondents listed career and motherhood equally often when asked to describe the most enjoyable aspects of being a woman (Dowd, 1983). In addition, women who work outside the home are characterized by higher self-esteem, greater life satisfaction, and better physical and mental health than those who do not (Coleman & Antonucci, 1983; Kessler & McRae, 1982).

Findings of this nature must be interpreted cautiously, however. We should not be quick to conclude that working outside the home actually *makes* women happier than they would have been as homemakers, because much depends on the woman's definition of herself. If a woman includes an outside career as one of her life goals, her involvement in such a career will predict her psychological well-being; if she does not regard paid employment as an aspect of her self-definition, then her self-worth will not be affected by her work status (Bielby & Bielby, 1984; Pietromonaco, Manis, & Markus, 1987).

Finally, why are some women career oriented while others are not? Much seems to depend on the attitudes that parents hold when raising their daughters and the role models they provide. Career-oriented women are likely to have parents who provided encouragement, set high standards for achievement, and did not model the traditional gender role stereotypes found in our society (Barnett & Baruch, 1978; Leslie, 1986).

Developmental Patterns in Work

A person's involvement in the work force may last for 40 to 50 years, and some changes naturally occur across so long a span of time. In fact, a person's working life is typically characterized by a number of developmental changes, and, for that reason, theories of work are increasingly conceptualized within a life-span framework (Adler & Aranya, 1984; Cavanaugh, 1990; Super, 1980).

Perhaps the most elaborate "work span" theory to appear thus far is the model developed by Super (1980), who proposed five overlapping but reasonably distinct stages in a person's working life. The first stage, *implementation,* occurs during the late adolescent years. This is, in a sense, a trial period in which people may take many different short-lived jobs and may thereby discover what type of work best suits their needs and abilities (Havighurst, 1982).

Next comes the *establishment* stage in early adulthood. After selecting a specific career, workers achieve and advance at a stable rate, applying their energies to performance at this one job. In middle age (45 to 55), the *maintenance* stage occurs: Workers believe that they have already accomplished as much as they can in their jobs, or that they never will accomplish what they originally intended to. The result is a withdrawal of psychological energy, and even of actual time, devoted to work.

In the *deceleration* stage, which occurs in the late 50s and early 60s, workers begin to anticipate and plan for retirement, the process of separation of self from work begins, and interest in leisure activities increases. Finally comes the *retirement* stage.

Retirement from Work

When we look at the span of a person's working life, we discover an interesting trend in the work force participation of older Americans. Although Americans today are living longer than they did 40 years ago (Baily, 1987; Poterba & Summers, 1987), they tend to retire from their jobs at an earlier age than in the past (Ruhm, 1989). For example, in 1947, almost 90 percent of men aged 55 to 64 were still employed; in 1987, only 67 percent of those in this age group were still working. Similarly, 47.8 percent of men over the age of 65 still worked in 1947, while in 1987, only 16.6 percent of men aged 65 and over still held jobs (U.S. Department of Labor, 1987).

The trend toward living longer but retiring earlier means that elderly people will have a greater need for purposeful leisure activities. From an economic standpoint, it also means that younger workers will face a heavier tax burden as increasingly larger percentages of the population rely on tax dollars for their livelihoods. Some 90 percent of retired people depend on Social Security for at least a portion of their incomes, and between 40 percent and 53 percent of those incomes are made up of Social Security payments—a percentage that has been on the rise in recent years (Ruhm, 1989; Upp, 1983).

Retirement does not occur equally in all segments of the working population. For example, blue-collar workers, including those employed in construction, manufacturing, and transportation, are usually the first to retire. Next in terms of work longevity are those in sales and service jobs. Finally, white-collar workers and professionals tend, on the average to remain in the work force longer than other workers (Mitchell, Levine, & Pozzebon, 1988).

The decision to retire is usually a personal choice. Mandatory retirement is rare today and is found primarily in occupations that have genuine age-related performance requirements. Furthermore, even 20 years ago, when between one-third and one-half of workers faced mandatory retirement, most left their jobs voluntarily, many doing so even before the mandatory retirement age (Ruhm, 1989). There is no support, therefore, for the stereotype that older Americans are simply pushed out of the work force. This is not the case at all, and it never has been.

Why do people choose to retire? Health reasons are frequently cited, and, in fact, the retirement decision and the *perceptions* people have of their health are related (Burkhauser & Quinn, 1983; Burtless, 1986; Burtless & Moffitt, 1984). However, when objective assessments of health status are taken, the connection between physical well-being and the decision to leave work all but disappears (Ruhm, 1989). In other words, many people who say they are retiring for medical reasons are not really in poor health at all, although they may believe themselves to be. Genuinely failing health is rarely a major reason for retirement (Ruhm, 1989).

Economic factors seem to play the primary role in a person's decision to retire (Ruhm, 1989). For example, the Social Security system offers incentives to retire at age 62, because workers then first become eligible for benefits. Private pension plans are often structured so that workers can retire at age 62 without losing benefits, and in many plans the benefits are maximized if the worker retires even earlier—at the age of 60 or before (Mitchell & Fields, 1984). Finally, the magnitude of a person's wealth is a predictor of retirement age, in the sense that wealthier people are likely to retire earlier than those of modest means (Burtless & Moffitt, 1984; Ruhm, 1989). The possession of wealth allows a worker to anticipate a stress-free and enjoyable retired life; the thought of a future plagued by financial hardship is unlikely to hasten a retirement decision.

Summary

1. Infants and toddlers have a definite interest in peer relationships, as can be seen by their communicative gestures and attempts at co-operative play.

2. Extensive peer interaction during the first 2 years of life is related to later social interests but not to later social skills.

3. Even by the age of 4, children have definite preferences in friends. As children develop throughout the elementary school years, their knowledge about psychological characteristics of friends increases and they have a deepening understanding of the nature of friendship itself.

4. Role-taking skills improve from the preschool years to the years of adolescence. Decreases in egocentrism are accompanied by an increasing ability to see the world from the point of view of another person.
5. Adult social cognition requires mature formal reasoning, but also requires what have been described as relativistic operations. These involve the recognition that relationships cannot be understood without reference to the larger social context.
6. The peer group is a major socializing agent in childhood, particularly for males, who seem to be more group oriented in their friendships than females.
7. Adolescents typically begin to date at about age 14. Dating serves many functions for U.S. adolescents, including recreation, companionship, status, and opportunity for sexual experimentation.
8. In both childhood and adolescence, popularity is related to a pleasant personality, sociability, academic achievement, and physical attractiveness. Unpopular children fit into either of two categories: the rejected and the neglected.
9. Gender differences in friendship needs are apparent in U.S. society, with males seeking friends who can provide concrete forms of assistance and females more often seeking emotional closeness in a friendship.
10. Whether an elderly person continues to be socially active or withdraws from social interaction depends on physical well-being, opportunity, and individual personality characteristics. No one theory of social interaction in old age can accurately describe every person's situation.
11. Play is an activity that is intrinsically motivated, freely chosen, pleasurable, nonliteral, and actively engaged in by the player.
12. Leisure activity in adulthood varies in intensity of involvement. Leisure promotes social interaction and allows people to demonstrate their skills, their competence, and their worth.
13. Work is a dominant influence on adult life, in that it helps to establish a person's identity; serves as a context for competition, affiliation, and nurturance; and affords opportunities for the development of a sense of achievement.

Key Terms

activity theory (p. 521)
disengagement theory (p. 521)
expressive needs (p. 499)

extensive peer relations (p. 511)
games-with-rules (p. 527)
induction (p. 501)

instrumental needs (p. 499)
intensive peer relations (p. 511)
practice play (p. 526)

relativistic operations (p. 506)
social cognition (p. 496)
symbolic play (p. 527)

Review Questions

1. What is meant by social cognition? Describe how social cognition develops during childhood, adolescence, and adulthood.
2. Describe the four stages of role-taking ability and discuss how the development of this ability influences the quality of peer relations during childhood.
3. Infants and toddlers are often seen as selfish, self-centered, and unable to communicate effectively with one another. What evidence suggests that this stereotype is inaccurate?
4. What are the functions of the peer group during the elementary school years? How do boys and girls differ in the composition of their peer groups?

5. Which children are likely to be the most popular and which are likely to be the least popular among their peers? What intervention techniques have been helpful in working with the unpopular child?

6. What are three ways in which friendship changes over the span of adult life? What does research tell us about the value of having friends in later life?

7. Describe the essential characteristics of children's play. How does play differ from work?

8. Although no one knows all the reasons that children play, theoretical views on the subject vary.

What are some of the major theories, and how have theoretical perspectives changed from the nineteenth to the twentieth century?

9. Define practice play, symbolic play, and games-with-rules, and explain how each reflects the developmental level of the children who engage in them.

10. What are the psychological values of work in adult life? In what sense does occupational choice reflect an individual's personality, and what might be the result if little or no connection exists between work and personality?

Suggested Readings

Asher, S. R., Hymel, S., & Renshaw, P. D. (1984). "Loneliness in Children," *Child Development, 55,* 1456–1464.

A journal article describing the development of a loneliness questionnaire designed to be used with children. It indicates that loneliness can reliably be measured and provides information about feelings of loneliness and social dissatisfaction among grade schoolers.

Damon, W. (1983). *Social and personality development: Infancy through adolescence.* New York: Norton.

One of the most complete treatments of the topic of socialization during childhood and adolescence by a leading expert in the area. Included are chapters on prosocial behavior, adolescent social relations, and the social role of adults in transmitting cultural values to children.

Hughes, F. P. (1991). *Children, Play, and Development.* Boston: Allyn and Bacon.

An in-depth coverage of children's play from infancy through adolescence. Included are chapters on theories of play, ethological and cross-cultural comparisons, gender differences, play in special populations, and play as a form of therapy.

Rubin, K. H. & Ross, S. H. (1982). *Peer relationships and social skills in childhood.* New York: Springer-Verlag.

A collection of 16 articles dealing with theory and research on social interaction in childhood. The research trends in the rapidly expanding field of social development are well represented. Included are articles on fairness and friendship, social problem solving, social interaction during infancy, and positive effects of early socialization.

Chapter Thirteen

Morality

Theories of Moral Development
Social Learning Approach
Psychoanalytic Approach
Cognitive Approaches

Moral Judgment and Behavior
Developmental Changes
Motivation for Growth and Moral Education

Alternative Moral Perspectives
Gender Differences in Morality
Cross-cultural Research
Synthesis

 A major arena of discussion in recent years for biologists, politicians, philosophers, theologians, psychologists, lawyers, and the general public has been the abortion controversy. In a society that tries to maintain a balance among equality of opportunity, freedom of choice, quality of life, rights of survival, and ideals of justice and compassion, the abortion issue has created a national moral dilemma that refuses to fade away. Although the solution to this dilemma evades simple analysis, individuals clearly have staked out positions that are resistant to change. Where do ideas about moral issues come from? How do these notions develop over time? What factors play a role in the construction of a moral position?

Morality is a challenging and controversial aspect of human development. How do we determine if the right of a woman to control her own body should take precedence over the right of a fetus to achieve a life at all? At what point can human life be said undeniably to begin? If the mother and the father disagree, who should decide the fate of the life they have created together? Our intent is not to resolve the abortion controversy in these pages, for that is a moral dilemma we must each face. However, we hope to provide some insight into the process whereby an individual makes judgments about a variety of significant moral concerns.

We will begin this chapter with a consideration of several theories of moral development. Some of the elements of moral behavior, in particular those related to altruism, were described in the previous chapter. The rational, decision-making facets of morality will now be emphasized in contrast to the research on socially interactive considerations. Nonetheless, we must repeat that cognitive judgments about moral concerns do not occur without emotional and behavioral consequences.

In fact, in the second part of this chapter we will examine the relationship between moral behavior and moral judgment in greater detail. The connection will be elaborated in terms of developmental progression and the factors responsible for moral growth. We will conclude our discussion with some alternative perspectives on moral judgment: the influences of a masculine versus a feminine orientation and varied cultural influences on moral development.

THEORIES OF MORAL DEVELOPMENT

In its simplest terms, morality is the ability to distinguish right from wrong. In actuality, the concept of morality is considerably more complex, involving cognitive skills (e.g., role taking, reasoning, decision making), feelings (e.g., empathy, altruism, care), and behaviors (e.g., helping others, resisting temptation). In theory, the cognitive, affective, and behavioral dimensions can each be examined separately, but in practice they can never be completely separated (Rest, 1984). A person described as having high moral standards is aware of the needs and feelings of others (cognitive), concerned about others (affective), and likely to display that awareness and concern in dealing with other people (behavioral).

Deficiencies in any of the three dimensions indicate a less than perfect moral character. Thus, the ability to understand the perspectives of others will not guarantee moral behavior if a sense of care is lacking. Social awareness and social concern do not indicate a high degree of morality if they are not translated into courses of action; a vast difference often exists between what people believe is right and what they actually do when confronted with moral dilemmas! Finally, level of morality cannot be determined from an analysis of behaviors alone, but must also include reference to underlying motives. What a person does is often a less meaningful indicator of moral sophistication than why the person does it.

Several different theoretical perspectives on moral development each have their own emphasis. Social learning theory emphasizes the behavioral dimension, psychoanalytic theory focuses on the affective dimension, and cognitive developmental theory stresses the intellectual dimension. Disagreements among these theories do not focus on what is right or is wrong behavior, but on the dimensions the theorists choose to emphasize and the mechanisms by which morality is acquired.

Social Learning Approach

The social learning approach to moral development stresses the role of experience in the acquisition of a set of morally appropriate behaviors. (You may wish to review at this point the principles of learning that were presented in Chapter 6.) Right and wrong behaviors are learned in a variety of ways. In some situations, reinforcement or punishment is experienced directly: People learn that what is right is what they have been rewarded for doing, and what is wrong is what they have been punished for. Behaviors not acquired by a direct experiential learning process are often acquired through the process of *observational learning.* For example, a person sees another person being rewarded for donating to a charity or punished for cheating on an exam, and therefore learns which behavior is acceptable and which is unacceptable. In a sense, the observer also shares the consequences, but the reinforcement or punishment is *vicarious:* The observer receives it by imagining being in the place of the person who was affected directly (Liebert, 1984).

Examples of observational learning of moral behavior can be found most notably in the areas of altruism (see Chapter 12) and learned aggression (Bandura, Ross, & Ross, 1963a, 1963c; Bandura, 1965; Hicks, 1965). The typical procedure in these studies is to have young children observe aggressive behaviors, expose them to a frustrating situation—such as having toys they are playing with taken away—and then record subsequent instances of aggression in their play. Children become more aggressive if they have recently seen aggressive models, especially if the models are rewarded for their aggressive behaviors. (See *Applying Our Knowledge,* "Coping with an Aggressive Child.")

In addition, much of a child's moral development takes place through the process of "generalized imitation" (Gewirtz, 1969) or *identification* (Aronfreed, 1969): The child uses a significant adult, often a parent, as a

Identification

The process by which one person perceives himself or herself as being similar to another and, in a sense, shares in the identity of the other person. For example, a child may identify with a parent, or a person may identify with a religious or ethnic group.

Children learn right and wrong behaviors in a variety of ways. This girl may have learned about shoplifting through observation or vicarious reinforcement.

Applying Our Knowledge
Coping with an Aggressive Child

 Parents often complain that the most irritating antisocial behavior displayed by their children is aggression, and based on the high incidence of aggression observed in children of all ages, the complaint is easy to understand. One study found that approximately 80 percent of children between the ages of 3 and 17 occasionally use physical aggression against their brothers or sisters (Straus, Geller, & Steinmetz, 1980)!

Aggressive acts occur more often among younger than among older children (Hartup, 1974; Straus, Geller, & Steinmetz, 1980; Feshbach & Weiner, 1986), a fact that may provide hope to parents who feel like referees at a boxing match. However, evidence indicates that aggression may be a stable trait across the life span: Highly aggressive children at age 2 seem to grow into highly aggressive adolescents and are more likely to have a criminal record by the age of 30 (Huesmann, Eron, Lefkowitz, & Walder, 1984; Olweus, 1979; Parke & Slaby, 1983). Boys have typically been found to be more aggressive than girls, particularly when the aggressive act is specifically intended to harm another child (hostile aggression), rather than simply to achieve a goal, such as getting the toy another child is playing with (instrumental aggression) (Hartup, 1974).

We do not know the extent to which biological factors may contribute to human aggression, but we do know that some parental characteristics are closely related to aggression in children. Parents of very aggressive children tend to be permissive in dealing with their children's aggression. They make few demands for positive prosocial behavior. They are often lax in their supervision and inconsistent in their discipline. Finally, they tend to be cold or rejecting in their dealings with their children (Feshbach, 1970; Feshbach & Weiner, 1986; Parke & Slaby, 1983).

What can a parent or teacher do to help reduce aggression in children? A number of approaches have been tried, some successful and others not. Among the least successful approaches has been harsh punishment, which may inhibit aggressive behavior but actually increase the child's underlying anger and resentment. Milder forms of punishment are more effective, particularly if the punishment is given a prosocial slant (e.g., requiring that the aggressor do something nice for the victim). Also successful have been attempts to train children in social awareness and empathy—to encourage them to imagine how their victim feels ("How would you like it if someone punched you?") A third successful approach involves changing the meaning of the stimulus that produced the aggressive response. For example, Johnny is told Margie takes his toys, not because Margie is naughty but because she is too young to know better, and for this reason Johnny should not "punish" Margie by striking her. An approach that has often been successful in the classroom is for the teacher to ignore the aggressor but comfort the victim. The teacher offers the victim something interesting to do and suggests ways to be assertive and still avoid confrontations with aggressive children. In this way, the teacher models tolerance and assertiveness, and, more importantly, does not reward the aggressive child with attention (Feshbach & Weiner, 1986).

Children's aggression may not be easy for parents and teachers to tolerate, but perhaps they can ease their anxiety if they realize that some aggression is normal, that adults themselves may—without knowing it—encourage aggression in children, and that levels of children's aggression can be reduced. Adults must be especially careful not to behave aggressively themselves, even as a reaction to the child's aggression. The effectiveness of any of the preceding techniques will be severely constrained by an aggressive adult model who preaches one thing but does another.

model for behavior, and from that model the child acquires a set of behaviors that are not intentionally taught. As an illustration of the impact of models as moral teachers, Baer and Sherman (1964) had children observe a puppet who taught them a variety of simple behaviors using direct reinforcement techniques. Later, the puppet began pressing a bar, and the children imitated the behavior even though they were not specifically rewarded for doing so. Apparently, the imitation of anything the puppet did became a rewarding experience.

When children use parents as models, they learn not only the things that parents deliberately try to teach, but also their parents' attitudes toward right and wrong, their religious and moral behaviors, and other values. Because parents are the most readily available models for their children, they must do more than just teach moral principles directly; they must also practice them. It makes little sense for parents to punish a child for lying or stealing and then engage in these behaviors themselves. The child who lies may point out with embarrassing accuracy that mother lies, too, when she tells a boring caller that she is too ill to talk on the telephone. An adolescent whose father tells him not to drink beer is justifiably angered when his father pours himself a martini each evening before dinner.

Psychoanalytic Approach

Although social learning theory stresses learning in the acquisition of moral behaviors, the psychoanalytic approach emphasizes the resolution of conflict between the individual's needs and society's expectations. Conflict produces anxiety, and the establishment of a moral code helps the child reduce anxiety; thus, psychoanalytic theory focuses on internalized feelings rather than external behaviors. (Refer to Chapter 10 for a discussion of the psychoanalytic theory of personality development.)

Young infants experience little conflict with society, and little resulting anxiety, because they are indifferent to societal restrictions. Adults typically accommodate to infants' needs rather than the reverse. By the end of the first year, however, these same infants are beginning to learn that they cannot always have what they want when they want it. The conflict between what they want and what the world will allow becomes increasingly apparent.

Instinctual anxiety
In psychoanalytic theory, the fear children have of their own instincts whose expression is forbidden by society.

The toddler acquires what is referred to as *instinctual anxiety* (Freud, 1966)—a fear of those basic instincts (e.g., aggression, sexual curiosity) that society considers unacceptable. Toddlers submit to societal restrictions because they know they will be rejected if they allow their instinctual needs free expression; therefore, their very instincts cause them to suffer anxiety. For example, children may feel anxious about wanting to steal from the cookie jar because they fear the disapproval of authorities who have control over them. However, in circumstances when authorities are not in a position to supervise, they may slip and give in to temptation.

At approximately 5 years of age, children begin to assume the values and restrictions of society as their own, by the process of identification with an adult—usually the same-sex parent (see Chapter 14 for a discussion of gender role differences in psychoanalytic theory). In a sense, the values of society are internalized, and the control over the child's behavior comes not just from authority figures but from within the self. The child develops a conscience. Freud (1930) felt that conscience development is civilization's way of achieving control over the often dangerous and aggressive impulses of individuals; but, unlike the external control felt by the toddler, the conscience of an older child or adolescent is internal. The child who has internalized the values of society will still experience conflict, but the conflict will arise from opposing forces within the self. Now a child who wishes to steal a cookie before dinner will hold the impulse in check, not because of fear of authority, but because of the internal discomfort usually referred to as guilt. The depth of guilt will depend on the severity of previous fear or anxiety. Hoffman (1982) and Bettelheim (1985) have recently revived interest in the value of guilt for achieving moral behavior.

Cognitive Approaches

The cognitive developmental approach to morality emphasizes the intellectual rather than the affective dimension in the socialization process. Moral development involves a growing awareness of the needs and viewpoints of others, and, with this, a growing sensitivity. As people develop, they become increasingly capable of role taking, imagining the consequences of their actions on other people's lives, and recognizing the need for an impartial system of morality that can be applied to society as a whole.

Piaget's Theory

Piaget's (1932) work, focusing on stages of cognitive development, provides a foundation for many of our contemporary moral theorists. Although his theory of morality was not completely articulated, Piaget did contribute significantly to the understanding of the child's moral development. More than 50 years ago, Piaget rejected the view of morality as a system of controls imposed on children by adults. He argued that a mature concept of morality is based on underlying cognitive structures; the child is actively involved in the construction of personal moral values, which are based on an awareness of the perspectives of others.

Piaget distinguished between two types, or levels, of morality. The **morality of constraint** is acquired directly from adults during early childhood. Young children simply accept the definitions of right and wrong provided by their parents, who are seen as wiser and more powerful than they. Conformity to parental rules results from a combination of fear, admiration, and affection. Preschool morality is constrained in the sense that the rightness or wrongness of an act resides in the act itself and not in the intention behind it. Breaking a dish by accident is just as wrong for the

Morality of constraint
A morality characterized by the child's simple acceptance of definitions of right and wrong supplied by the parents.

young child as breaking it on purpose. Breaking two dishes, from the preschooler's perspective, is always worse than breaking one dish, even if the first act was accidental and the second act was deliberate (Wimmer, Gruber, & Peiner, 1985).

The second level or type of morality begins to appear at the age of 6 or 7 and does not reach mature status until the age of 10 or 11. This is the ***morality of cooperation,*** which children construct on the basis of their interaction with peers. Thus, for Piaget, peer relationships are extremely important in the child's moral development. When children interact with peers, a certain amount of give-and-take is required; they learn to abide by rules, and they are required to share, to cooperate, and to delay gratification of their own needs. Out of such interactions will emerge a sense of justice, the cornerstone of a mature set of moral values. In fact, Piaget believed that because peers are not authority figures in the sense of parents, they play a more crucial role than parents in the construction of rational judgments.

Moral development, according to Piaget, involves a move from egocentrism to an awareness of the perspectives of other people. It involves a move from a moral code imposed by parents to a moral code mutually agreed on as a result of peer interactions. It involves a move from a belief that moral rules are fixed and absolute to a belief that such rules are arbitrary—that morality resides not in the rules themselves but in the reasons for their establishment. Children may begin to understand, for example, that they can negotiate new curfews with their parents if they are able to demonstrate more responsibility. Finally, in moral development the child is increasingly involved in constructing a set of personal values that facilitate harmonious peer relationships.

Kohlberg's Theory

The most completely formulated cognitive developmental theory of moral development is undoubtedly that of Lawrence Kohlberg (1927–1987), who extended and refined many of the concepts discussed by Piaget. Kohlberg (1969, 1984) described moral development as a gradual progression through the six stages, divided into three broad levels, outlined in Table 13.1. As can be seen in the table, judgments at Stages 1 and 2—*preconventional morality*—are based on fear and an egocentric satisfaction of personal needs, at Stages 3 and 4—*conventional morality*—on an effort to follow social norms and obtain social approval, and at Stages 5 and 6—*postconventional morality*—on adherence to a set of personal principles standards that promote the general welfare of society. The move is from concrete self-centeredness to abstract conceptions of social responsibility.

Kohlberg developed his model of moral growth on the basis of many years of interviews with children, adolescents, and adults of different ages. This technique, derived from Piaget's approach to assessing cognitive and moral levels of reasoning, presents the subject with a dilemma to resolve.

Morality of cooperation
A morality constructed by children themselves on the basis of their interactions with peers.

Preconventional morality
The first of Kohlberg's three levels of moral judgment, based on a morality of avoiding punishments and obtaining rewards.

Conventional morality
The second of Kohlberg's three levels of moral judgment, based on a morality of social approval and the authority of law and order.

Postconventional morality
The third of Kohlberg's three levels of moral judgment, based on a morality that benefits the general welfare of society and an adherence to self-chosen principles that promote the good of humanity.

Table 13.1
Kohlberg's Classification of Moral Judgment

Level	Stage of Development	Example
I Preconventional	*Stage 1* Moral decisions are based on the desire to avoid punishment. Social norms are not violated because such actions will have unpleasant consequences.	A child decides not to steal candy from a store because the risk of detection and punishment is great.
	Stage 2 Moral decisions are based on a desire to obtain rewards. In this form of what Kohlberg called "marketplace morality" the question is "What's in it for me?"	An adolescent does not report a classmate for vandalism because the classmate may return the favor by lending a homework assignment.
II Conventional	*Stage 3* Moral decisions are based on a desire for social approval. This is the "good boy" or "good girl" orientation.	A person contributes to charity only because members of the community expect it, and peers would see the failure to make a donation as selfishness.
	Stage 4 Morality is determined by those in legitimate authority. What is legal is moral. The social order must be maintained as an end in itself.	If the leaders of a nation declare war, citizens must go to war because challenging those in command would be immoral.
III Postconventional	*Stage 5* Morality is based on the assumption of a contract among members of a society to behave in an acceptable manner. The individual submits to a moral code designed to benefit the community as a whole.	People do not commit acts of violence because they realize that if all citizens were free to commit such acts, society could not maintain itself.
	Stage 6 Moral decisions are based on self-chosen ethical principles directed toward promoting what is good for humanity as a whole.	People may believe that no human being may take the life of another; if forced to do so, they would be morally bound to refuse. Kohlberg described Jesus Christ, Mahatma Gandhi, and Martin Luther King, Jr., as Stage 6 thinkers.

Perhaps the most widely known of Kohlberg's (1969) dilemmas is the following story about Heinz:

> In Europe a woman was near death from a special kind of cancer. There was one drug that the doctors thought might save her. It was a form of radium that a druggist in the same town had recently discovered. The drug was expensive to make, but the druggist was charging ten times what the drug cost him to make. He paid $200 for the radium and charged $2,000 for a small dose of the drug. The sick woman's husband, Heinz, went to everyone he knew to borrow the money, but he could only get together $1,000, which is half of what it cost. He told the druggist that his wife was dying and asked him to sell it cheaper or let

him pay later. But the druggist said, "No, I discovered the drug, and I am going to make money from it." So Heinz got desperate and broke into the man's store to steal the drug for his wife. (p. 379)

After reading the story, the person is asked whether Heinz should have stolen the drug and why. Additional questions probe further into the reasons for Heinz's decision: Is theft a husband's obligation to save his wife's life? Does the druggist have the right to charge any price he wishes? Can a person disobey the law if he disagrees with its consequences? In other words, Kohlberg sets up a conflict between values to establish at what level of reasoning a person makes a judgment about an issue. The critical feature of this approach, however, is not *what* people believe is the best way to resolve the dilemma, but *why* they think it is correct. Table 13.2 offers both pro and con examples that Heinz's dilemma might elicit for each stage of moral reasoning.

Accurately assigning stage designations to dilemma responses is not always easy. The scoring manual last published prior to Kohlberg's death is nearly 1,000 pages long (Colby & Kohlberg, 1987). A researcher must have considerable practice with administering and scoring such interviews before becoming comfortable with the results. Although Kohlberg had been working on revising his techniques, years of criticism had produced alternative methods for assessing moral reasoning. James Rest, for instance, designed the Defining Issues Test (1979) as a self-administered and objectively scored technique that parallels the Kohlberg interviews and stage theory. Essentially, Rest's approach used three dilemmas from Kohlberg, and three other stories that are similar, and then asked a person to rate the importance of value statements that reflect the moral issues of concern for resolving the dilemmas. The overall results of research that employs the Defining Issues Test support Kohlberg's model, but Rest believed that interpretation of moral reasoning for a given individual is more consistent and accurate using this survey technique than using the more traditional Kohlberg interview (Rest, 1983). Figure 13.1 illustrates the format Rest used based on the Heinz example, in the Defining Issues Test.

In the normal course of events, Kohlberg believes a person will progress upward through the stages in sequence; skipping stages does not occur. Evidence for such a progression was obtained in a 20-year longitudinal study of adolescent boys (Colby, Kohlberg, Gibbs, & Lieberman, 1983). The same study found a degree of consistency between childhood and adulthood patterns of moral judgment. The most morally mature children seemed to become the most morally mature adults.

The stimulus for moral development in Kohlberg's model is internal disequilibrium: individuals who encounter examples of moral reasoning more sophisticated than their own will be driven to incorporate that form of reasoning into their own moral system, provided of course, that the more sophisticated reasoning is understandable to them. Blatt and Kohlberg (1975) and Colby, Kohlberg, Fenton, Speicher-Dubin, & Lieberman (1977)

Table 13.2
Examples of Kohlberg's Six Stages of Moral Development

Stage	Pro	Con
1	He should steal the drug. It is not really bad to take it. It is not like he did not ask to pay for it first. The drug he would take is only worth $200; he is not really taking a $2,000 drug.	He should not steal the drug; it is a big crime. He did not get permission; he used force and broke and entered. He did a lot of damage, stealing a very expensive drug and breaking up the store, too.
2	It is all right to steal the drug, because she needs it and he wants her to live. It is not that he wants to steal, but it is the way he has to use to get the drug to save her.	He should not steal it. The druggist is not wrong or bad; he just wants to make a profit. That is what you are in business for, to make money.
3	He should steal the drug. He was only doing something that was natural for a good husband to do. You cannot blame him for doing something out of love for his wife; you would blame him if he did not love his wife enough to save her.	He should not steal. If his wife dies he cannot be blamed. It is not because he is heartless or that he does not love her enough to do everything that he legally can. The druggist is the selfish or heartless one.
4	You should steal it. If you did nothing you would be letting your wife die; it is your responsibility if she dies. You have to take it with the idea of paying the druggist.	It is a natural thing for Heinz to want to save his wife but is still always wrong to steal. He still knows he is stealing and taking a valuable drug from the man who made it.
5	The law was not set up for these circumstances. Taking the drug in this situation is not really right, but it is justified to do it.	You cannot completely blame someone for stealing, but extreme circumstances do not really justify taking the law in your own hands. You cannot have everyone stealing whenever they get desperate. The end may be good, but the ends do not justify the means.
6	This is a situation which forces him to choose between stealing and letting his wife die. In a situation where the choice must be made, it is morally right to steal. He has to act in terms of the principle of preserving and respecting life.	Heinz is faced with the decision of whether to consider the other people who need the drug just as badly as his wife. Heinz ought to act not according to his particular feelings toward his wife, but considering the value of all the lives involved.

From Lawrence Kohlberg, "Stage and sequence: The cognitive developmental approach to socialization," in *Handbook of Socialization Theory and Research.* David A. Goslin, ed., 1969 Houghton-Mifflin Company. Reprinted by permission of the editor.

engaged junior high and high school children in regular discussions of moral issues and found that approximately one-third of the students moved from a lower- to a higher-moral stage; no noticeable change occurred in matched control groups. Kohlberg (1977) achieved similar results with college undergraduates. He concluded that exposure to more sophisticated forms of moral reasoning rather than pressure from parents or educators helps children become true moral philosophers. This research supports Piaget's earlier notions of peer influence in moral development. The progression through Kohlberg's stages of moral development appears to be related to the

Should Heinz steal the drug? (Check one)

_____ Should steal it   _____ Can't decide   _____ Should not steal it

IMPORTANCE:

Great	Much	Some	Little	No	
					1. Whether a community's laws are going to be upheld.
					2. Isn't it only natural for a loving husband to care so much for his wife that he'd steal?
					3. Is Heinz willing to risk getting shot as a burglar or going to jail for the chance that stealing the drug might help?
					4. Whether Heinz is a professional wrestler, or has considerable influence with professional wrestlers.
					5. Whether Heinz is stealing for himself or doing this solely to help someone else.
					6. Whether the druggist's rights to his invention have to be respected.
					7. Whether the essence of living is more encompassing than the termination of dying, socially and individually.
					8. What values are going to be the basis for governing how people act towards each other.
					9. Whether the druggist is going to be allowed to hide behind a worthless law which only protects the rich anyhow.
					10. Whether the law in this case is getting in the way of the most basic claim of any member of society.
					11. Whether the druggist deserves to be robbed for being so greedy and cruel.
					12. Would stealing in such a case bring about more total good for the whole society or not.

From the list of questions above, select the four most important:

Most important _____   Second most important _____

Third most important _____   Fourth most important _____

Figure 13.1

An Excerpt From the Defining Issues Test

Source: J. R. Rest, "Longitudinal Study of the Defining Issues Test: A Strategy for Analyzing Developmental Change," *Developmental Psychology*, 11, 738–748. Reprinted by permission of the author.

progression through Piaget's cognitive stages. However, the relationship is not a direct one. As Kohlberg (1976) described it, intellectual development is a necessary, but not a sufficient, condition for moral development. In other words, although a pre-operational or concrete operational child cannot reach Kohlberg's Stages 5 or 6 (because these stages require formal operational thinking), an adolescent or adult may have reach Piaget's stage of formal operations and still not be functioning at Kohlberg's highest moral stages.

In a test of the relationship between Kohlberg's moral stages and Piaget's cognitive stages, Walker and Richards (1979) studied the effects of being challenged to deal with moral dilemmas on the moral judgment of 44 adolescent girls. Half of the girls had been found to be just beginning formal operational reasoning, and half were judged to possess basic formal reasoning skills. The later group was significantly more capable of moral decision making than the former group was, leading the authors to support

The top level of moral reasoning is reached by relatively few people. Mahatma Gandhi is an example of a person guided by high ethical principles and the desire to promote the good of humanity as a whole.

Kohlberg's view that cognitive development is a necessary condition for moral development.

A non-Piagetian approach to the relationship between cognitive development and moral functioning was also attempted by Rest (1979), who studied moral comprehension. Rather than test people on formal reasoning tasks, Rest asked them merely to explain Kohlberg's moral stages described in Table 12.1 in their own words. He found that Stage 1 concepts were easiest to explain and that the concepts increase in difficulty progressing upward to Stage 6. In other words, people who could comprehend the meaning of a particular stage also could comprehend the stages below it, but not necessarily those above it. Rest also observed a definite relationship between moral comprehension and moral decision making, reinforcing the notion that a strong intellectual component influences moral judgment.

Finally, the cognitive aspects of moral development have been suggested by the consistency of the significant correlations between moral judgment tests and IQ, aptitude, and achievement tests (Rest, 1979). Clearly, intellectual development is one factor that accounts for moral development, but it is not the only one. Personality factors, experiences with role taking, and other life experiences are related to our level of moral development. As an example, Peatling (1977) suggests that the experience of being the parent of an adolescent child may be responsible for increases in authoritarianism among adults in their 40s. In general, however, moral judgment is correlated more closely with measures of intellectual functioning than with personality or emotional measures (Carroll & Rest, 1982; Colby et al., 1983; Rest, 1979).

MORAL JUDGMENT AND BEHAVIOR

Although Kohlberg's model describes the developmental progression in moral reasoning and judgment, it was not based on observations of behavior in real-life settings. Instead, it was based on analysis of how people say they would resolve hypothetical moral dilemmas. This, of course, does not imply that most actual behavior is immoral.

However, to what extent are a person's moral reasoning skills related to behavior in everyday settings? A considerable amount of evidence suggests a high degree of relationship (Blasi, 1980, 1983; Gibbs, Clark, Joseph, Green, Goodick, & Makowski, 1986; Kohlberg & Candee, 1984). Consider as an example the findings of a study by Schwartz, Feldman, Brown, & Heingartner (1969), who examined cheating among college students. Thirty-five undergraduates were given a Kohlberg moral interview and a difficult vocabulary test specifically designed to allow for the possibility of cheating. The students were carefully watched, and indications of cheating were recorded. Evidence of cheating was found to be related to a student's level of moral judgment; more than half of the Stage 3 and Stage 4 thinkers cheated, while only one in five of those at Stage 5 and Stage 6 did so! Such findings parallel those of a number of studies of cheating in the classroom, involving participants ranging from elementary school to college age; certainly one factor determining a student's willingness to cheat appears to be level of moral reasoning.

Using a slightly different approach to the question, Gibbs and his associates (1986) compared moral reasoning level with teachers' ratings of the "moral courage" of high school students. Teachers were asked questions such as: "Would this student consistently stand by his or her principles . . . support an unpopular cause if he or she believed it was right . . . defend someone who is being attacked by the group . . . support a cause only if the cause is popular with his or her friends?" Gibbs found that the degree of moral courage was significantly related to moral maturity as indicated by responses on the standard Kohlberg interview.

The findings of research on cheating, moral courage, and a variety of other morally challenging situations (e.g., helping friends in need, sharing, keeping a promise) seem to indicate a fairly consistent pattern. After reviewing 74 such studies that examined the relationship between performance on tests of moral judgment and actual behavior, Blasi (1980) concluded that the two are significantly related. In general, a correlation exists between a person's moral reasoning and behavior in real social settings.

Nevertheless, discrepancies between moral judgment and moral behavior do exist. Part of the problem undoubtedly involves the differences between espousing lofty morals when examining an imaginary dilemma compared to confronting emotional and complex situations in daily life. *Research Close-up,* "Moral Judgment and Behavior in High School and College Students," provides an example of a situation in which a lack of consistency exists. How can two people who reason at similar moral levels behave differently when dealing with a real-life situation? The pro and con examples of the Heinz dilemma in Table 13.2 illustrate this point, as do personal experiences of value conflicts with people who are cognitive equals. In fact, many people are surprised when they agree with people they believe to be either more or less cognitively mature than they are.

Knowing what to do and then actually doing it or not doing it requires a more complete discussion. Rest (1984) has proposed a four-component model of moral action that incorporates cognitive and other factors related to morality. The sequence includes (1) interpreting the situation (perceptual), (2) determining the appropriate moral ideal (reasoning), (3) choosing among the values available to meet the moral goal (decision making), and (4) implementing the intention (behavior). Although the components may not always be ordered in the sequence Rest proposes, Figure 13.2 depicts a hypothetical cycle of moral action based on this model. Unfortunately, no research to date has been designed to examine moral behavior and reasoning within this complete framework. Rest hopes that such investiga-

The discrepancy between moral judgment and behavior may be revealed when the opportunity for action, not just opinion, is present.

tions will help us "to learn more about the precise nature of the constituent processes involved in the production of morality by systematically studying which situational variations affect moral processes" (1984, p. 35).

Developmental Changes

In Kohlberg's theory, pre-operational children are not yet dealing with concepts of right and wrong. For them, what is good is what they want. At approximately age 7, the child enters Piaget's stage of concrete operations and begins to develop a concrete view of morality. Rules are fixed and unchanging, handed down by authority figures who have the power to punish for transgressions. This parallels the emergence of Kohlberg's Stage 1. Later in the concrete operational stage, when the child is 9 or 10, the rules take on a bit more flexibility, but the motive for obeying them is still a concrete one: the expectation of tangible reward. This is Kohlberg's Stage 2.

Young adolescents, who are increasingly introspective and increasingly concerned about how others evaluate them, come to view the approval of

William Sobesky was interested in examining the consistency between moral judgment and moral behavior when the consequences of the moral action are not ambiguous. Research involving moral dilemmas typically requests a solution and a rationale for it (e.g., Heinz should steal the drug to gain the approval of his friends) but does not follow up with what happens to the characters. Although this vagueness was intended to avoid complicating the analysis of moral judgments with other "realistic" factors, Sobesky believed that the resolution of moral dilemmas might be compromised by the known consequences of the presumed action for the participants in the story (for instance, Heinz and his wife). Therefore, he designed a study that would alter the traditional procedure for assessing moral reasoning by incorporating several possible resolutions to a dilemma.

Sobesky (1983) obtained a volunteer sample of 233 students from four high schools and college psychology classes; 144 were female and 83 were male. Initially, the students were given a short form of Rest's Defining Issues Test and a variety of other assessments related to another study. About a week later, the students were administered different versions of the Heinz dilemma (which was not part of the short form of the Defining Issues Test). Although the details of the procedure are too complicated to explain fully here, after reading a modified version of the original Heinz dilemma, the students were also presented with four other versions that included the following consequences:

* Severe for Heinz—he will be caught and sent to prison.
* Not severe for Heinz—the druggist will never miss the drug.
* Positive for Heinz's wife—the drug will cure her.
* Not positive for Heinz's wife—the drug will give her only a slim chance to live for a few more months.

The students were then requested to evaluate, for each of the different versions of the story, what most people would be likely to do (steal or not steal the drug) as well as what they themselves would be likely to do.

others as the motivating force behind their moral decisions. They enter Kohlberg's Stage 3. This concern parallels the typical declines in self-esteem and the imaginary audience phenomenon as noted in Chapter 10. Later, probably during their high school years, they may move on to Stage 4, basing their moral decisions on the need to maintain the social order. Adolescents' interest in the legal and political system may reflect this level of moral reasoning.

Although the emergence of formal operations does not guarantee that an individual will reason at Stage 3 or 4, formal operational thinking is a necessary, if not sufficient, condition for the appearance of these moral stages. Social approval is an abstract concept, as is the concept of the social order (Walker, 1982). Unlike children, adolescents are beginning to go beyond the surface level in their evaluation of other people; they can reason

Sobesky's (1983) results indicated that different consequences do indeed affect moral judgments. If the consequences for Heinz were severe, the students were less likely to want to save his wife's life. Based on the first testing session, when an overall level of moral reasoning for each student was obtained, Sobesky found that even if a principled level of judgment was characteristic of the person, the negative consequence still reduced the certainty about whether Heinz's wife should be saved. When the consequences for Heinz were not severe, females were more likely to approve of stealing the drug, and students generally felt that others would be more likely than themselves to steal the drug. Overall, when the consequences for Heinz were severe, the students tended to offer lower levels of moral reasoning for their actions than when no consequences were provided. On the other hand, when the consequences for Heinz's wife were positive, those students classified as principled moral reasoners were more likely to want to steal the drug, yet when the consequences for Heinz's wife were not positive, no differences appeared between students at different levels of moral judgment.

On the basis of these findings, Sobesky (1983) concluded that the consequences of moral reasoning have the potential to alter what could be described as the more purely cognitive judgments people make when confronted with moral dilemmas. He stated "that a person does not display moral thinking in the same invariant way that he or she might have blue eyes or blond hair" (p. 582). Stage designations of morality may offer an idea of the typical way in which someone would respond to a moral dilemma and could suggest a range of potential reasoning in moral situations, but the contextual features of a particular situation will certainly influence the moral action. Sobesky cautions that research on morality is likely to be inconclusive if assessment techniques of moral reasoning (i.e., the Defining Issues Test) do not take into account specific factors or consequences that are likely to cause inconsistencies between moral judgment and behavior.

about their feelings, needs, and motives, as well as their overt behaviors. Their increasing sensitivity to the feelings of others increases the likelihood that they will consider social approval as the basis for their moral decision. Not surprisingly, Berndt (1979) found that conformity to peer expectations peaks at about age 13 and then declines. Although older adolescents may be less conformist, their formal operational thinking leads them to realize that a certain amount of give and take is necessary to maintain the social order. Therefore, they may find themselves at Kohlberg's Stage 4, with its emphasis on law and order.

Stages 3 and 4 emerge during adolescence, but these stages are also characteristic of adult moral reasoning. Indeed, they are the most common bases of moral decision making among adults. These stages were labeled the conventional level of moral development because they were found to be

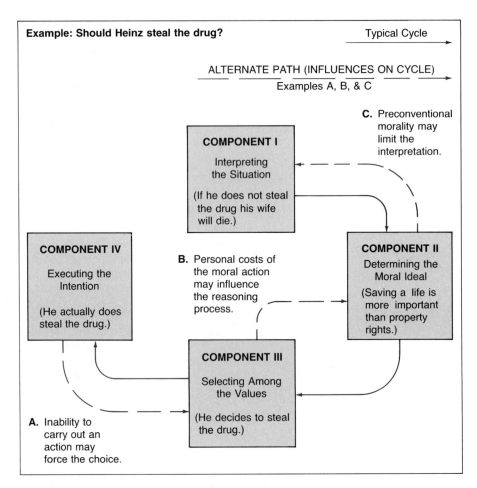

Figure 13.2
Rest's Four-Component Model of Morality

Source: Adapted from "Morality" in J. H. Flavell & E. M. Markman (Eds.), *Handbook of child psychology: Cognitive development* (Vol. 3). New York: Wiley.

so widely used. Kohlberg (1977) estimated that fewer than 20 percent of people in the United States reach the principled Stages 5 or 6.

Does any moral progress occur during the adult years, or do we fixate at the stages we reach during adolescence? Kohlberg (1973) felt that definite moral trends occur during adulthood. One surprising trend is the apparent regression to Stage 2 among many young adults, particularly college students. Haan, Smith, and Block (1968) found that students participating in the Berkeley Free Speech Movement tended to be either at the highest moral stages or at Stage 2. It was unusual to find Stage 3 or 4 individuals involved in the sit-ins. Kohlberg suggests that the return to Stage 2 is a temporary one, reflecting the confusion of the young adults in our society who are trying to resolve identity crises before committing themselves to the principled stages. The return to a "What's in it for me?" attitude may reflect the cynicism of college youth who are trying to find their places in society, but their apparent moral regression is merely a transition between conventional and postconventional levels of morality.

The young adult who has "recovered" from Stage 2 reasoning gradually progresses back toward the principled stages. Stage 5 or 6 is not usually reached—if it is reached at all—until the late 20s or early 30s. Those who are at the lower stages by the end of young adulthood will continually progress from Stage 2 to Stage 3 or from Stage 3 to Stage 4. Those who are

Exposure to the perspectives of peers and discussion of moral issues with them may be one of the most effective means of promoting the development of higher levels of moral reasoning.

at the principled stages in their early 30s will tend to stabilize at those stages. In other words, they will become more consistent in their moral reasoning.

In a longitudinal study of adolescents, Rest (1975) found that those who eventually went to college advanced from one stage to the next faster than those who did not attend college. Those who changed the most attributed the change to two factors: (1) the ideas obtained from reading and formal education and (2) the practical requirements of new responsibilities, such as those involved in choosing a job, getting married, or handling money. In a review of the literature on moral development, Rest, Davison, and Robbins (1978) concluded that an upward movement through the moral stages takes place in childhood and adolescence and a stabilization occurs in adulthood. Again, upward progress is more likely in those who attend college than in those who do not. A more recent follow-up of the original sample from Kohlberg's study indicated that the pattern of moral development from early childhood to adulthood is consistent with the theory. The basic data from the longitudinal analysis (Colby et al., 1983) are represented in Figure 13.3. Note the absence of Stage 6 reasoning and small proportion of Stage 5 morality.

Motivation for Growth and Moral Education

The similarities between Kohlberg's and Piaget's theories become more obvious if we consider the reasons for transition from one stage to the next. As will be recalled from Chapter 7, the motivation for intellectual growth according to Piaget is the resolution of the condition of disequilibrium: We must deal with perceived discrepancies between our cognitive structures and reality, and, in assimilating new material into our structures and accommodating our structures to the new material, we experience cognitive growth.

The same type of disequilibrium is the motive for moral growth. Individuals who encounter an example of moral reasoning that is more sophisticated than their own will be challenged to incorporate that form of reasoning into their own moral system—provided, of course, that they can understand the more sophisticated reasoning. This point is crucial. Piaget maintained that the cognitive structures develop only if the material presented is at the right level—slightly beyond the level of the existing structures, but not so far beyond them that the material cannot be assimilated. In terms of moral stages, Kohlberg (1977) believed that if a moral argument is too far above a person's level, it will not be understood. A Stage 2 thinker will not understand Stage 5 moral reasoning, but a Stage 4 thinker should. Not only will people at Stage 4 understand Stage 5 reasoning, but they also will be challenged by it and presumably stimulated to reevaluate their own moral position.

Progression through the stages, then, is sequential. There is no stage-skipping, because each stage builds on the stages that came before it. The ideal stimulus for moral development is a discussion of moral questions with a person who is at a more advanced stage. Kohlberg's initial suggestion

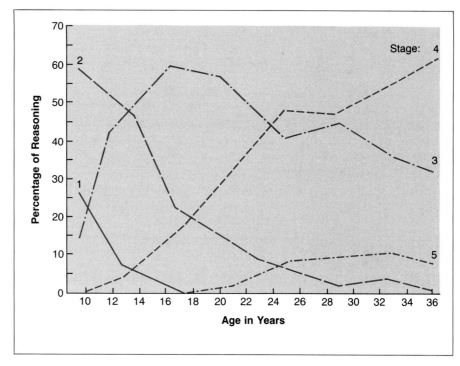

Figure 13.3

Mean Percentage of Moral Reasoning at Each Stage for Each Age Group (Colby et al., 1983)

Source: "A Longitudinal Study of Moral Developments" by A. Colby, L. Kohlberg, J. Gibbs, and M. Lieberman from SRCD monographs, 48, serial #200, p. 46. Copyright © 1983 by the Society for Research in Child Development, Inc.

was that the "stimulator" should be one stage ahead of the learner, but others (e.g., Walker, 1982) have found that even if the "teacher" is two stages ahead of the "pupil," moral advancement will take place.

Because disequilibrium provides the motivation for moral development in Kohlberg's theory, the goal of the moral educator should be to stimulate and challenge rather than to preach. Although we have pointed out that level of moral reasoning is linked to level of education, it is not entirely clear why, for example, college students seem to progress through the stages more quickly than those who do not attend college. Because intellectually capable individuals are also more likely to attend college, we cannot conclude that the college experience itself brings about advances in moral reasoning. Interestingly, however, moral progress is greatest among students who enter fields of study such as philosophy and theology, where moral decision making is discussed or even required. Apparently, a society characterized by a free exchange of ideas and a willingness to discuss moral issues is conducive to moral development, at least according to the cognitive developmental model (Colby et al., 1983; Rest, 1975; Rest, Davison, & Robbins, 1978).

Nevertheless, in encouraging moral development, a delicate balance must be maintained between avoiding both indoctrination by authority and the mere acceptance of any moral decision. The model Kohlberg introduced rejects simple right versus wrong judgments (as indicated by equally sophisticated pro and con choices) and avoids pure relativism (as indicated by a distinct hierarchy of reasoning that defines various degrees of morality). Berkowitz and Gibbs (1983) found that discussion of sensitive issues does indeed promote development through Kohlberg's hierarchy, but only when the participants are clearly communicating about their moral reasoning with each other. Efforts to establish curricula and institutional structures for fostering moral growth can be traced at least to John Dewey (1933), but more recent attempts to build on the work of Kohlberg have been constructed by Reimer, Paolitto, and Hersh (1983). Moral education, accordingly, should emphasize peer interaction, involvement in conflict situations, democratic decision making, alternative perspective taking, a positive moral climate, and the limited role of authority figures.

ALTERNATIVE MORAL PERSPECTIVES

Aside from questions pertaining to the impetus for development through sequences of moral reasoning and behavior, a broader issue involves the universality of the stages suggested by Kohlberg and other cognitive theorists. One of the basic claims of the cognitive developmental approach to morality is that the theory should apply uniformly; that is, no stages are skipped, the sequence is invariant, higher levels are more mature than lower levels in the hierarchy, stage regression does not occur, males and females are equally likely to progress through the stages, and the process of development is similar across all cultures in the world. Some of these concerns have been addressed earlier, and research has been found generally to support Kohlberg's model; however, here we will focus on the last two points to detail a couple of alternative perspectives on moral development. First, we will examine the issue of gender differences in morality, and then we will explore morality research conducted in several other cultures.

Gender Differences in Morality

All our major theories of moral development were formulated by men. In the case of Kohlberg's theory, some of the early work was based on research using only male subjects. In a widely cited book entitled *In a Different Voice,* Harvard psychologist Carol Gilligan (1982) has argued that current theories of morality, most notably Kohlberg's theory, typically describe only male behavior. To support her argument, she cited research (Haan, Smith, & Block, 1968; Holstein, 1976; Kohlberg & Kramer, 1969) to indicate that females regularly score lower than males according to Kohlberg's classifications; males are usually at Stage 4 and females at Stage 3.

Gilligan maintained that the reported gender difference can be attributed to the failure of "male" theories to recognize that moral decision making may differ along gender lines. Men are taught from infancy to separate themselves from others as they form their identities. As a result, men seek a moral code that emphasizes the rights of individuals, a *morality of justice*. Women are taught from infancy to value their relatedness to others—to identify by relating to, rather than by separating from, others. Hence, women operate with a moral code based on caring for and empathizing with others ("I would not steal from you because I don't want to hurt you" as opposed to "I would not steal from you because I respect your property rights"). A *morality of care* tends to place the value of social sensitivity above the value of abstract principles.

In Kohlberg's theory then, the "feminine" pattern of moral decision making would seem to be at a lower stage than the "masculine" one. Gilligan argued that the patterns may differ, but only a male-biased theory would interpret these gender differences as evidence of male superiority. Instead, she suggested that morality for females centers on caring and sensitivity to others, not on issues of fairness and justice. The focus for Kohlberg, claims Gilligan, is typically masculine and independent, leading to an underestimation of moral development in women. When the emphasis shifts to interdependence and concern for the self, more traditional feminine strengths are tapped.

Gilligan's thesis reminds us of the value of keeping an open mind about all developmental theory; none is so sacred that it should not be regularly questioned. She also has called attention to the importance of representative sampling in the formulation of theory. Nevertheless, the overwhelming body

Morality of justice

According to Gilligan, the moral orientation typical of males in which the rights of individuals and abstract legal principles are paramount.

Morality of care

According to Gilligan, the moral orientation typical of females in which relatedness to, concern about, and sensitivity toward others is paramount.

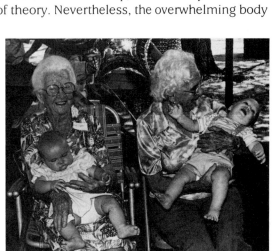

Do moral codes differ according to gender? One theorist has claimed that women tend to espouse a morality of care, putting empathy and social sensitivity above abstract principles of justice.

Issues in Human Development
Morality: Female Lawyers and Physicans

 Law and medicine are two demanding careers, laden with ethical judgments, that witnessed an increased rate of female participation in the 1980s. Physicans are presumed to possess technical proficiency and professional detachment to render the most effective patient care. Attorneys are expected to maintain an objective, analytic, and competitive stance to obtain the best outcome for their clients. Studies of first-year medical students by Gilligan and Pollak (1988) and of practicing lawyers by Jack and Jack (1988), however, implied that our approaches to the training of these professionals, as well as their actual roles, may require another look. From the perspective of the morality of care, qualities of cooperation, vulnerability, personal concern, and intimate attachment must not be overlooked in the education or the career attitudes of physicans and lawyers.

In their testing and interviewing of 236 medical students (168 men and 68 women) at Harvard and Tufts Universities, Gilligan and Pollak (1988) found some interesting differences between the responses of male and female students to the Thematic Apperception Test. This technique requires the individual to write a brief story about each of several pictures from a set of standardized drawings. The students were also interviewed about medical ideals, moral judgment, and related issues. Overall, the men and women students differed in terms of the *degree* of their moral orientations but did not evidence two clearly distinguishable orientations. In other words, much overlap was apparent between males and females in the types of stories written and in the answers to interviewer's questions. A particularly revealing indication of gender role differences, however, emerged from the analysis of stories that contained violent content. For the men, themes of violence were often associated with intimate relationships. This was never the case for the women. In contrast, violent themes for women were frequently connected to isolation, abandonment, or separation. No male student ever linked violent danger and isolation.

Interviews with the female medical students revealed that they already experienced strong tensions between personal connections with patients and high achievement in the field. The philosophy communicated in medical school apparently was to attain psychological distance and to avoid any display of emotion. With their now greater numbers in medical schools, women may provoke a series of changes that incorporate affiliative motivations in the profession. Gilligan and Pollak (1988) claim, "Like the canaries taken into mines to reveal the presence of

of research evidence does not indicate gender differences in moral functioning (Blatt & Kohlberg, 1975; Keasey, 1972; Rest, 1976, 1979, 1983). As an example, Walker (1984) reviewed 108 studies that included analyses of gender differences in morality; the studies involved thousands of children and adults. Few of these studies showed any gender differences at all in moral decision making, and in those that did, women were as likely to be superior to men as the reverse. There seems to be no reason, therefore, to support the view that women typically exhibit lower levels of morality than men, even according to Kohlberg's system.

At this point, we have little justification to assume that because Kohlberg was a man and used predominantly male subjects, his theory of moral development applies largely to men, or to conclude that moral development must proceed along different gender lines. Despite the lack of support for Gilligan's original thesis, her work has reawakened interest in the social

unseen dangers, women medical students in their heightened sensitivity to detachment and isolation often reveal the places in medical training and practice where human connection has become dangerously thin" (p. 262). If, and how, the morality of care will further manifest itself in the medical arena remains to be seen.

The interview study of Jack and Jack (1988) provided another related approach to morality in professional education and actual work. Focusing on 18 male and 18 female attorneys practicing within a particular county in the northwestern part of the United States, Jack and Jack asked the interviewees about law school, personal relationships, notions of justice and morality, and similar concerns. Although their results also suggest considerable overlap between the morality of men and women in their role of attorney, three broad patterns of female lawyers emerged with regard to a care orientation. The first pattern emulated the male model of denying the morality of care while stressing the justice orientation. A more common approach, however, was to employ a strategy in which the woman created a split between the lawyer self and the caring self; the former was maintained on the job and the latter was reserved for the home. The third pattern was to at-

tempt a professional integration of care and justice moralities. Only two of the female attorneys were able to handle this complex merger in the face of the dominant justice orientation of legal institutions.

Will the adoption of a more even balance in the moralities of justice and care effectively humanize the legal profession? This question parallels the previous work with physicans. Only if law schools and law firms endorse an alternative perspective on human morality, and only if female and male attorneys embrace a merged model for their law practice, will a genuine transformation of our legal system be attained. Jack and Jack (1988) concluded that

> the assumption that a care orientation cannot accompany the ability to be a good lawyer falls into the trap of dichotomous thinking prevalent in the legal system. Assuming a sharp division between reason and emotion, linear and associative thought, cold rationality and warm empathy reinforces the exclusion of traditionally feminine traits from the practice of law. In our research we met lawyers—women and men both—who were grappling with how to combine these attributes in their work. Just as the culture in the past has taught that these sets of traits are mutually exclusive and gender specific, in the future the message should be one of integration and compatibility. (pp. 286–287)

context of morality. In a newer collection of work, Gilligan and her associates (Gilligan, Ward, & Taylor, 1988) present theory and data that further explore the differences between a morality of justice and a morality of care (*Issues in Human Development,* "Morality: Female Lawyers and Physicans," illustrates their approach). Gilligan concludes, however, that males are also capable of a caring moral orientation. Thus, we must stimulate moral growth for both males and females in a social as well as a judicial context.

Cross-cultural Research

Just as critics have questioned the validity of gender variations in morality, consideration of cultural contexts have been similarly debated. Two of the most important claims made by Kohlberg (1969) about his stages were that they were invariant and universal. The best method for addressing these concerns is to adopt a cross-cultural design to compare moral development in other countries with moral development in the United States. To demonstrate that his stages were universal, Kohlberg (1969) presented evidence showing age trends in moral judgment for boys aged 10, 13, and 16 in the United States, Taiwan, Mexico, Turkey, and the Yucatán. Cultural differences were found in the actual percentages of statements attributed to the different stages. For example, Stage 5 responses were much more common from U.S. teenagers than from teenagers in any of the other cultures studied; Stage 1 responses were more common from adolescents from isolated villages than from urban youth. Nevertheless—and this is the critical point—the developmental changes were in the predicted direction in all cultures: Stages 1 and 2 declined with age, and Stages 3 and 4 increased.

Is morality only a set of arbitrary rules within a particular culture? Without understanding the history and beliefs of other cultures, can we make moral judgments about them? Or is morality absolute and independent of cultural considerations?

(It is difficult to say much about Stages 5 and 6, because the percentages of moral judgments in these categories were generally very low.)

Kohlberg's cross-cultural studies were later criticized, however, because he presented virtually no information about his sample size, testing or scoring procedures, or the variations in the responses in the different cultures. Furthermore, he was inferring developmental change using cross-sectional data that might be used to demonstrate that the stages themselves are universal, but not as evidence that the sequence of stages is universal.

Longitudinal comparative studies eventually were done using children and adolescents aged 8 to 17 in the Bahamas (White, Bushnell, & Regnemer, 1978) and a group of males ranging from age 10 to age 25 in a Turkish village (Turiel, Edwards, & Kohlberg, 1978). The findings showed a general age-related progression upward in the stages in both cultures. Most of the subjects in both studies advanced or stayed the same from one testing to the next. Some actually regressed between testings, but these were in the minority, and when retested a second time, those who had regressed often had begun to move forward again.

After reviewing these studies, as well as a large variety of cross-sectional studies of Kohlberg's stages using children, adolescents, and adults in England, Canada, India, Kenya, Israel, New Zealand, Honduras, and Nigeria, Edwards (1981) concluded that preliminary support exists for the universality of both the stages and the sequence of stages. She went on to say, however, that whereas the first three stages are found in most cultures, Stages 4, 5, and 6 are found only in the more complex societies. Edwards suggested that perhaps the complexity of the stages encountered in a society reflects the complexity of that society in general. A complex sociopolitical order may require more complex moral judgments than would be required in a simpler, more "primitive" society. This interpretation is in keeping with Rest's (1975) findings discussed earlier: The U.S. adults who showed the greatest moral advances attributed these advances to the demands placed on them to be responsible members of our complex society.

More recent longitudinal studies of moral development by Kohlberg and his associates in other cultures have further supported the universality of the sequence of reasoning. In Turkey, rural and city dwellers, aged 10 to 28, were interviewed individually on the traditional moral dilemmas (Nisan & Kohlberg, 1982). Although the findings revealed predictable age and sequence responses, different rates of development emerged between rural and city dwellers, with the latter moving somewhat more rapidly through the stages. In a study of Israeli adolescents being raised in a communal kibbutz, the cross-cultural validity of Kohlberg's model was again demonstrated (Snarey, Reimer, & Kohlberg, 1985). The researchers did note, however, that a relatively larger proportion of these adolescents attained principled levels of reasoning than is usually found in the United States. Therefore, moral development seems to occur in a basically similar broad pattern across cultures, but important variations specific to each culture appear to reflect particular environmental influences.

Synthesis

One danger of constructing theory and designing research on moral development is highlighted by our look at the cross-cultural work. If morality is nothing more than the standards or norms of a particular culture, what is the point of creating or debating models, such as Kohlberg's, that attempt to establish universal patterns? An orientation to morality that denies the possibility of any moral truths is known as *ethical relativism* (Kurtines & Gewirtz, 1984). From a purely relativist perspective, morality becomes an arbitrary set of rules that are almost immune to evaluation. At the other extreme, an absolutist morality is grounded in predetermined, inflexible regulations that are completely beyond cultural factors. *Moral absolutism* has been derived from purely philosophical logic or the divine faith of medieval theology (Kurtines & Gewirtz, 1984). Contemporary theory must someday bridge the gap between ethical relativism and moral absolutism.

Gibbs and Schnell (1985) have suggested the existence of two different, yet complementary, approaches to examining morality in human development. On the one hand, the earlier social learning and psychoanalytic perspectives tended to stress the cultural and emotional components of morality. This view today is largely represented by Hoffman's (1988) work and the ideas of Gilligan (1982). On the other hand, the focus of Kohlberg's theory has been on cognitive and individualistic notions of morality that are, nevertheless, based on general principles. Can some reconciliation occur between cultural relativism and cognitive absolutism? According to Gibbs and Schnell (1985), there is "no necessary dichotomy dividing the camps— only contrasting but complementary *emphases*" (p. 1078). In other words, they believe that a complete understanding of moral development will be furthered only by exploring the interdependence of the cultural-emotional and the individual-cognitive positions.

Ethical relativism

A moral orientation that denies the possibility of any absolute truths; all morality is an arbitrary set of rules.

Moral absolutism

A moral orientation in which universal truths exist that are beyond the flexibility of cultural or situational factors.

Summary

1. Moral development has been described from the perspectives of social learning, psychoanalytic, and cognitive theories. These three viewpoints differ considerably in their analyses of why human beings usually engage in morally correct behavior and tend to avoid behaviors that are morally incorrect.

2. Social learning theory stresses the acquisition of moral behaviors based on environmental influences, particularly parents as role mod-

els. Psychoanalytic theory also emphasizes the significance of parents in moral development, not so much as role models, but in terms of the resolution of moral conflict to avoid feelings of anxiety or guilt.

3. Cognitive theories of morality focus on the increasing awareness of the needs, rights, and perspectives of other people. Piaget's early work on moral development distinguished between the morality of constraint and the

morality of cooperation. He also considered the influence of peers in fostering movement toward greater moral reasoning abilities.

4. Kohlberg's cognitive approach is the most widely cited and comprehensive theory of moral development. Using Piaget's ideas, Kohlberg formulated a six-stage hierarchy of moral reasoning that was presumed to be universally applicable. In addition, Kohlberg constructed a series of standardized moral dilemma interviews to assess moral judgment.

5. Although some evidence supports the universality of moral reasoning stages, the complexity of the theory is apparently related to a variety of situational factors that go beyond normative developmental changes. The progression to higher levels of moral judgment seems to be particularly fostered by exposure to moral conflict. Educational programs to facilitate moral growth are based on this notion.

6. An underlying question concerning the validity of cognitive theories of morality is the relationship between moral reasoning and moral behavior in realistic situations. The evidence indicates some degree of inconsistency between a person's abstract judgments and actual behavior. This may be due to measurement difficulties, situational factors, or theoretical limitations.

7. Two aspects of morality that have received special attention in the search for universals in moral development are gender differences and cultural influences. Research on these topics both provides support for and shows the weaknesses of the cognitive approach of Kohlberg and other theorists.

8. Gilligan's work comparing the moral reasoning of males and females suggests that an orientation of care is more characteristic of women, while an orientation of justice is more typical of men. Although the evidence that Gilligan uses to dispute Kohlberg's universality argument is not convincing, she has clearly offered an important, complementary approach to achieving a more complete understanding of morality.

9. The cross-cultural research on the universality of Kohlberg's model generally supports the sequence he proposed. Nevertheless, variations in the rate of development, the proportions of people within different stages, and the patterns of regression did occur.

Key Terms

conventional morality (p. 553)
ethical relativism (p. 574)
identification (p. 549)
instinctual anxiety (p. 551)

moral absolutism (p. 574)
morality of care (p. 569)
morality of constraint (p. 552)

morality of cooperation (p. 553)
morality of justice (p. 569)

postconventional morality (p. 553)
preconventional morality (p. 553)

Review Questions

1. Outline the key concepts that distinguish the three major theories of moral development. Provide one or two examples highlighting how these ideas operate in daily life.

2. Briefly discuss the assumptions and stages of moral development according to Kohlberg's model. Describe how research in this tradition is conducted and evaluate the strengths and weaknesses of the evidence.

3. Explain how the process of moral development proceeds from childhood to adulthood, including cognitive and affective dimensions. To what extent is

moral judgment related to moral behavior? What
evidence supports your position?

4. Discuss how cognitive theory, particularly Kohlberg's work, might be applied to moral education.
   What are effective and ineffective ways of stimulating moral development? Does any evidence confirm
   your answer?

5. Gilligan and her associates have issued a strong
   challenge to Kohlberg's view that moral development is based largely on reasoning about justice.

Evaluate how successful the advocates of considering a morality of care have been in demonstrating
its relevance to explaining moral development.

6. Contrast the philosophical positions of ethical relativism and moral absolutism with respect to fostering moral development. Do you agree with one
   view or the other, and do you feel that the conflict
   can be resolved? What implications does this dichotomy present for creating programs of moral
   education?

Suggested Readings

Colby, A. & Kohlberg, L. (1987). *The measurement of
moral judgment.* New York: Cambridge University Press.
    A two-volume compendium of the theory, research,
    and methods of Kohlberg's approach to moral de-
    velopment. This is sometimes difficult reading, but
    it is the most recent and complete synthesis avail-
    able.

Gilligan, C. (1982). *In a different voice: Psychological
theory and women's development.* Cambridge, MA: Harvard University Press.
    The now-classic rejoinder to Kohlberg's model of
    moral development. Despite widespread criticism,
    it remains a landmark in morality theorizing. The
    author offers an important, well-written perspective
    on sex differences.

Gilligan, C., Ward, J. V., & Taylor, J. M. (Eds.). (1988).
Mapping the moral domain. Cambridge, MA: Harvard
University Press.
    A recent, edited collection by Gilligan and her asso-
    ciates, including more than a dozen chapters that
    touch on the morality of care. This book elaborates
    on a variety of ways in which the perspectives of
    gender differences may inform our understanding
    of morality.

Reimer, J., Paolitto, D. P., & Hersh, R. H. (1983).
*Promoting moral growth: From Piaget to Kohlberg (2nd
ed.).* New York: Longman.
    An excellent overview of cognitive developmental
    theory on morality. More significantly, this paper-
    back discusses moral education and contains many
    useful suggestions for classroom application.

Rest, J. R. (1979). *Development in judging moral issues.*
Minneapolis: University of Minnesota Press.
    A review of research on moral development using
    the Defining Issues Test, an objective measure
    based on Kohlberg's model and interview. The au-
    thor reviews developmental differences in moral
    reasoning and discusses various factors affecting
    moral growth.

Chapter Fourteen

Gender Roles and Gender Differences

Development of Gender Roles

Infancy

Childhood

Adolescence

Early Adulthood and Middle Age

Later Life

A Model of the Life-Span Approach

Theories of Gender Role Development

Psychoanalytic Theory

Learning Theories

Cognitive Developmental Theory

A Contemporary Cognitive View: Information Processing Theory

A Synthesis

Current Issues in Gender Development

Conducting Bias-Free Research

Androgyny

Gender Roles and Schooling

 For most people, biological sex and gender identity correspond. That is, a person's genetic makeup and internal and external reproductive organs correspond to a psychological awareness of being either male or female. However, in some cases, a discrepancy occurs between biology and psychological identity. Transsexualism, or the perception of being one sex trapped inside the body of another sex, is one such example.

An even more dramatic example is pseudohermaphroditism (or what some researchers call **hermaphroditism**), a condition in which the internal reproductive organs match the genetic sex, but the external genitalia do not. For example, a genetic female who was exposed to excessive amounts of male hormones (androgens) in utero might be born with masculine genitalia (a penis). Usually, corrective surgery is performed to feminize the external genitalia in these cases. John Money and his associates (e.g., Money & Ehrardt, 1972) have devoted their careers to investigating psychological development in male and female hermaphroditism and situations in which the child's sex is reassigned. Their findings indicate that gender identity is socially prescribed but is crystallized early in life.

Evidence from several isolated villages in the southwestern Dominican Republic has cast doubt on the definitiveness of Money and Ehrardt's conclusions. Imperato-McGinley, Guerrero, Gautier, and Peterson (1974) and Imperato-McGinley, and Peterson (1976) identified 30 male hermaphrodites born with an inherited enzyme deficiency that made them, in terms of outward appearance, females. (The relatively large number of cases resulted from genetic inbreeding.) Until puberty these individuals were reared as girls. However, at puberty a startling transformation took place: Their voices deepened, their beards grew, they increased their muscle mass, and they developed functional penises capable of intromission and ejaculation. The villagers referred to these females-turned-males as *guevedoces* ("eggs at 12") or *guevote* ("penis at 12").

The researchers of this syndrome reported that all postpubertal males except one assumed the male gender role: "Despite the sex of rearing, the affected were able to change gender identity at the time of puberty. They consider themselves as males and have a libido directed toward the opposite sex" (Imperato-McGinley, Guerrero, Gautier, & Peterson, 1974, p. 1215). Perhaps the reassignment of gender in a community that accepts such a radical morphological transformation because it is a relatively common phenomenon is not accompanied by the sort of psychological trauma that we assume would occur in the United States. However, some researchers have expressed skepticism that the transformation of Dominican children is as effortless as the original reports would have us believe. Rubin, Reinisch, & Haskett (1981) indicated, for example, that children born with this genital anomaly typically have genitalia that are not clearly one sex or the other. In addition, the Dominican villages that were studied were characterized by a notable lack of privacy. Possibly the pubertal transformation that took place might not have been shocking to either the child or the family.

This chapter will examine factors that influence gender differences and gender roles by first focusing on developmental trends and then presenting theoretical explanations for how gender develops. As we have seen, a complex interaction among biological, psychological, and sociocultural factors makes the study of gender differences and gender roles both fascinating and significant to our understanding of human development.

It would be a safe bet that in an on-the-street interview on the differences and similarities between the sexes, most interviewees would agree that men and women differ in fundamental ways. Furthermore, they would probably agree on the ways in which the sexes differ. Broverman, Vogel, Broverman, Clarkson, and Rosenkrantz (1972) conducted such a study—not on the street, but in an undergraduate psychology classroom. They asked the students to list all the characteristics, attributes, and behaviors on which they thought men and women differed. These characteristics could be listed in terms of opposing qualities (e.g., active-passive). The researchers found 41 characteristics that showed at least 75 percent agreement that one pole represented the average man and the other represented the average woman. Characteristics attributed to men (behaviors that clustered around themes of competence) were more often considered desirable than a cluster of characteristics attributed to women (warmth and expressive traits). Table 14.1 presents the stereotyped traits, including the masculine and feminine pole of each trait, found by the researchers.

In a series of investigations using this list of sex role stereotypes, the researchers found considerable agreement on what constitutes masculine and feminine behaviors from people representing a variety of backgrounds. The stereotypes seemed to cut across the sex, socioeconomic class, religion, age (17 to 56 years), educational level, and marital status of the respondents. Even male and female mental health clinicians (clinical psychologists, psychiatrists, and psychiatric social workers) responded in a stereotyped manner to the sex role questionnaire.

Such views on the differences between males and females seem to suggest simple and direct links between biological sex and behavior.

Table 14.1

Stereotypical Sex Role Items (Responses from 74 College Men and 80 College Women)

Feminine	Masculine
Competency Cluster: Masculine Pole Is More Desirable	
Not at all aggressive	Very aggressive
Not at all independent	Very independent
Very emotional	Not at all emotional
Does not hide emotions at all	Almost always hides emotions
Very subjective	Very objective
Very easily influenced	Not at all easily influenced
Very submissive	Very dominant
Dislikes math and science very much	Likes math and science very much
Very excitable in a minor crisis	Not at all excitable in a minor crisis
Very passive	Very active
Not at all competitive	Very competitive
Very illogical	Very logical
Very home oriented	Very worldly
Not at all skilled in business	Very skilled in business
Very sneaky	Very direct
Does not know the way of the world	Knows the way of the world
Feelings easily hurt	Feelings not easily hurt
Not at all adventurous	Very adventurous
Has difficulty making decisions	Can make decisions easily
Cries very easily	Never cries
Almost never acts as a leader	Almost always acts as a leader
Not at all self-confident	Very self-confident
Very uncomfortable about being aggressive	Not at all uncomfortable about being aggressive
Not at all ambitious	Very ambitious
Unable to separate feelings from ideas	Easily able to separate feelings from ideas
Very dependent	Not at all dependent
Very conceited about appearance	Never conceited about appearance
Thinks women are always superior to men	Thinks men are always superior to women
Does not talk freely about sex with men	Talks freely about sex with men

Table 14.1
Continued

Feminine	Masculine
Warmth-Expressiveness Cluster: Feminine Pole Is More Desirable	
Does not use harsh language at all	Uses very harsh language
Very talkative	Not at all talkative
Very tactful	Very blunt
Very gentle	Very rough
Very aware of feelings of others	Not at all aware of feelings of others
Very religious	Not at all religious
Very interested in own appearance	Not at all interested in own appearance
Very neat in habits	Very sloppy in habits
Very quiet	Very loud
Very strong need for security	Very little need for security
Enjoys art and literature	Does not enjoy art and literature at all
Easily expresses tender feelings	Does not express tender feelings at all easily

Source: K. Broverman Inge, Susan Raymond Vogel, Frank E. Clarkson, Donald M. Broverman, and Paul S. Rosenkrantz, "Sex Role Stereotypes: A Current Appraisal," *Journal of Social Issues,* 28, No. 2, p. 63.

However, the study of the nature of sex differences and their origins has revealed that the links between biology and behavior are quite complex. Researchers now recognize many dimensions of sex typing. It is not sufficient to refer to the sex of a child or an adult as a way of explaining possible deferences in behaviors, attitudes, and self-perceptions. Rather, within the context of biological sex, researchers recommend that activities and interests, concepts or beliefs about sex typing, values, social relationships, and personality characteristics, as well as sociocultural expectations and prohibitions also be considered (Huston, 1983).

Along these same lines, researchers use the term *gender* as opposed to *sex* because sex may refer to both biological (e.g., chromosomal or reproductive) characteristics and psychological characteristics and behaviors that differentiate male from female (Deaux, 1985). A distinction between gender and sex makes it less likely to attribute the psychological characteristics to biological factors or the other way around. Thus, sex refers to biological characteristics, and gender describes the nonphysiological aspects of sex that social convention teaches are appropriate for either males or females (Deaux, 1985; Unger 1979). Biology and psychology are intertwined, but more and more contemporary researchers are finding that the distinction between the two is helpful. Therefore, the terminology in this chapter will adhere to the distinction between sex and gender as much as possible.

Gender
The nonphysiological aspects of sex that social convention designates as appropriate for either males or females.

Sex
The term used by researchers of gender development to refer to biological characteristics and differences between males and females.

Gender identity

The personal awareness of being either male or female. It is an internalization of the characteristics, attitudes, and feelings of one sex over the other.

Gender role stereotype

Well-defined cultural prescriptions for appropriate male and female behavior. This is also referred to as gender-typed behavior.

Gender role preference

The desire to adopt the behaviors and attitudes of one sex over the other.

The term *gender identity* can take on a number of meanings. Gender identity may simply refer to the recognition that a person is a boy or a girl by noting the physical differences between males and females. Another definition of gender identity emphasizes a personal awareness of being either male or female. Gender identity may or may not parallel a person's gender role, *gender role stereotype,* or gender-typed behavior (e.g., "I like to play with trucks, *not* dolls"). These refer to the overt behaviors (as opposed to an internalized identification) that society recognizes as appropriate for men and women. Gender role stereotypes tend to be more rigidly defined and overly simplified expectations for males and females than gender roles are. *Gender role preference* refers to the desire to adopt the behaviors and attitudes of ones sex over the other (e.g., "I prefer feminine clothes"). In early childhood, such preferences may be seen in the choice of toys (trucks versus dolls) and play activities (baseball versus playing house). Later on in development, gender role preferences may manifest themselves in career and lifestyle choices. Finally, we can talk about sex differences when we compare males and females on particular traits and characteristics.

Attitudes and behaviors regarding gender may not be congruent within the same individual. For example, many women can recall their childhood as a time of climbing trees, pushing trucks across the kitchen floor, and hating frilly dresses. For these girls, behaviors and preferences for play and toys were inconsistent with social expectations of feminine behavior. Yet, playing as boys would not necessarily mean that such women thought of themselves as anything but females. Men who take paternity leaves to care for their newborn infants may not manifest gender role stereotypic behavior but may have strong gender identities. Conversely, people who are insecure about their gender identities may exhibit stereotyped versions of masculine or feminine behavior.

We have already come to the first of several questions that we will examine in this chapter on gender differences and gender role development: Aside from the biological/genetic differences between males and females, do any behavioral, social, and psychological differences exist? This chapter also will address how these sex differences develop and how concepts of masculinity and femininity change over the course of the life span. A related question concerns the origin of these differences; several intriguing theoretical explanations have been offered. This chapter also will consider a number of contemporary issues in gender development throughout the life span.

DEVELOPMENT OF GENDER ROLES

Gender is an aspect of the self that undergoes significant change and rethinking as people progress from infancy to old age. Indeed, any given adult probably has different gender identity concerns than he or she had when younger, when all that mattered was separating the pinks from the blues and the dolls from the trucks. Masculinity or femininity is a dimension of intrapsychic, or psychological, life that must be reckoned with throughout the life span. This section will examine each major developmental period in terms of the changes that occur in gender role and gender identity development.

Infancy

Few behavioral differences have been observed between girl babies and boy babies. Some evidence suggests that infant females are more sensitive to touch and that infant males are more active (Block, 1976). In terms of biological differences, boys, on the average, tend to be slightly longer and heavier at birth, but they are more neurologically immature and more irritable than females. Girls mature faster than males, and their skeletal development is more advanced.

Such differences may encourage the differential treatment shown by parents toward their young sons or daughters. For example, because females mature faster physically, parents may expect greater maturity of social skills from their daughters than from their sons (Parsons, 1980). This partly may be due differences in how male and female babies react to adults. Adults also tend to handle male babies more roughly (Maccoby & Jacklin, 1974), and, when a mother is given a baby dressed as a male, she

Adults often provide gender-stereotyped playthings to infants.

will more likely offer the child a train to play with than a doll; conversely, a baby assumed to be female will be offered a doll more frequently than a train (Will, Self, & Datan, 1976). Some evidence also suggests that men tend to stereotype their infants more than women do (Ruble, 1988; Huston, 1983).

In addition to studying the behavioral differences between male and female infants, researchers have also examined the possible effects of prenatal hormones on behavior. Returning to the issues of hermaphroditism could be instructive in clarifying these issues. Genetic male hermaphroditism (the external genitalia are female but the internal reproductive system is male) may be caused by a failure to manufacture androgens during the prenatal period or by a lack of receptivity to androgen by target tissues (androgen-insensivity syndrome).

Hermaphroditism in genetic females can be caused by an overproduction of androgen by the adrenocortical glands during fetal development, which does not affect the gonads but does cause the external genitalia to assume a masculine appearance. This problem, known as *adrenogenital syndrome* (AGS), differs from progestin-induced hermaphroditism, which occurs when the fetus is exposed to synthetic steroid hormones taken by the mother.

Adrenogenital syndrome
A form of hermaphroditism in genetic females caused by an overproduction of androgen during fetal development and resulting in masculinized external genitalia.

John Money and Anke Ehrhardt have concentrated their research efforts on assessing the psychological consequences of hermaphroditism. The logic behind the research program is as follows: If AGS females who, after corrective surgery, were raised as females manifest a relatively greater number of masculine-type behaviors than the normal (unaffected) controls, such findings would provide a powerful argument for the dominance of prenatal hormones on later behavior.

In one study, Money and Ehrhardt (1972) selected 25 fetally androgenized genetic females, aged 4 to 16 years, who had received cortisone, surgical treatment, or both and were raised as females. The researchers compared these girls with a control group of normal girls matched on age, IQ, socioeconomic background, and race. Ehrhardt and Baker (1974) compared 17 AGS females and 10 AGS males (who were exposed to higher levels of androgen than normal prenatally) to their normal male and female siblings. In yet another study, Ehrhardt and Money (1967) presented data from 10 girls whose mothers had received progesterone while pregnant. All three investigations focused on the results from IQ tests, structured doll play, and interviews with the children and their mothers.

A significant finding from this research is that girls identified themselves as female, but they were more "tomboyish" than their controls. For example, they liked to play outdoor sports and games; had a tendency to fight more often; preferred pants to dresses; were not interested in babysitting or dolls; and liked to play with cars, trucks, and blocks. Although most wanted to get married and have children of their own, they were more interested in pursuing careers than were the controls. In addition, the AGS girls exhibited a higher activity level than was typical of girls in the control group, which was also true of AGS males relative to unaffected boys (Ehrhardt & Baker, 1974). No differences in IQ were found between AGS females and normal females. Some evidence suggests that males with androgen-insensitivity syndrome manifest the typical female cognitive pattern of better verbal and poorer visual-spatial skills (Shepherd-Look, 1982).

A number of methodological problems in the design of Ehrhardt and Baker's research make it difficult to pinpoint exactly what caused the behavioral differences between AGS females and their controls. For example, parental perceptions of their AGS daughter may have been influenced by the parents' knowledge of their daughter's unique prenatal history. After all, any parent may be quick to call a daughter's activities tomboyish knowing that she looked like a little boy in the delivery room. Some of the dependent measures may not have accurately assessed gender role or gender identity. From such research, the difficulties of separating nature from nurture become clearer. Indeed, Money (1987) concluded from his work on hermaphroditism that prenatal hormones may predispose the human brain toward either masculinity or femininity, with postnatal experiential factors either facilitating or diminishing the prenatal hormonal effects.

Childhood

During the preschool years, a child's gender identity takes on a clearer focus. Children have learned to label themselves "boy" or "girl" and are aware of many of the gender role stereotypes in our culture. Most theories of gender role development—including psychoanalytic, cognitive, and learning theories—also agree that the preschool years are significant for the acquisition of a gender identity. By the time children are 3 years old, definite differences in behaviors and activities may be found between the sexes. For example, when they are given a choice either in free play or laboratory situations, preschool boys and girls choose to play with same-sex toys.

During middle childhood, the preference for gender-typed toys and activities continues for boys. However, girls become increasingly interested in masculine activities (Huston, 1983). The divergence in the male-female preferences for toys and activities could be due to the greater latitude given to girls for cross-gender play (Langlois & Downs, 1980). Another possibility is that boys' toys and activities are more fun and challenging and override the attractiveness of the dollhouse. During middle childhood, boys also become more noticeably active, particularly when other boys are around (Shepherd-Look, 1982), and both boys and girls begin to exhibit preferences for their own sex as evidenced in their doll play (Katz, 1979).

As the elementary school years go by, the preference for same-sex friends becomes increasingly pronounced (Maccoby, 1988). The term *sex cleavage* refers to the division by sex in children's friendships and group activities. "No boys allowed," or "Do not enter if you are a girl" are familiar signs on the clubhouse doors of grade school children. Segregation of children by sex also has been observed cross-culturally. Edwards and Whiting (1988) found sex cleavage in 12 communities throughout the world. As in the United States, children increasingly played with same-sex peers from early to middle childhood and did so especially when many same-aged children were available. Maccoby (1990) recently argued that such sex cleavage is based on the different interaction styles of boys and girls. Boys, when they play together, engage in more rough-and-tumble play and are more power-assertive than girls. Maccoby proposed that girls are averse to interacting with such play partners, and develop a more mutually interactive play style with their girl friends. Thus, the peer group becomes an extremely powerful agent of gender-role socialization and may account for the differing styles of interaction that persist into adulthood. Such adherence to same-sex friends almost takes on moral overtones, for children often claim that to engage in cross-sex behavior is not only deviant, but also wrong (Damon, 1977). Again, this is particularly true of boys. As children become more sophisticated about concepts of gender and confident of their own gender identities, some flexibility enters during the latter part of middle childhood (Russo, 1985).

Sources of Stereotyping

As mentioned, even young children are aware of gender role stereotyping. Another indicator may be found in the kinds of toys children acquire. Rheingold and Cook (1975) analyzed the contents of children's rooms and discovered that girls had more dolls and domestic toys; boys had more vehicles, sports equipment, and military toys. Robinson and Morris (1986) obtained a list of more than 500 toys that 86 preschool children received for Christmas. The parents of the children were asked to indicate which of these toys the children themselves had requested. By age 5, approximately 75 percent of the toys requested were gender stereotyped. Parents tended to provide more gender-neutral toys, suggesting that children are the major contributors to the stereotyped toy box.

What are some of the sources from which children learn stereotypes? The media—especially television—influence gender role development. Children under 5 years of age have been estimated to view an average of 25½ hours of television per week; by the time they reach high school, they will have viewed more than 15,000 hours of television. Analyses of the content of gender roles portrayed on television have been remarkably consistent across all sorts of programming, including cartoons and advertisements. More male than female roles are portrayed on television, and often these roles conform to gender stereotypes. Males engage in more activities and are more aggressive and constructive than females; the activities of females tend to be ignored (Sternglanz & Serbin, 1974). Males also are portrayed in professional roles, but most television females portray a nonprofessional romantic, married, or family figure. Similar trends have

Applying Our Knowledge
The Boy Scouts and Male Gender Role

 Psychologists have speculated that it is harder for a boy to identify with masculinity than for a girl to identify with femininity. This is due to the traditional pattern of the father's absence for most of the day and the boy's initial attachment to his mother. Little boys are rarely told what they should do. Rather, their behavior is defined negatively in terms of what they should not do—anything that smacks of femininity or "sissy" stuff (Hartley, 1959).

Hantover (1978) speculated that such avoidance of feminine behavior may have been one of the prime motivators behind the formation of the Boy Scouts of America in 1910. According to Hantover, the Boy Scouts was rapidly accepted among the middle class because of perceived threats to American masculinity. People feared that men could no longer flex their muscles because of the closing of the American frontier and the absence of war. More and more men entered white-collar jobs, and adolescent boys stayed at home longer to complete their educations. Scouting was portrayed as the means by which masculinity could be restored:

> The wilderness is gone, the Buckskin Man is gone, the painted Indian has hit the trail over the Great Divide, the hardships and privations of pioneer life, which did so much to develop sterling manhood are now but a legend in history, and we must depend upon the Boy Scout Movement to produce the MEN of the future. (Beard, 1914, as cited by Hantover, 1978, p. 189).

Furthermore:

> The REAL Boy Scout is not a "sissy." He is not a household plant, like little Lord Fauntleroy. There is nothing "milk and water" about him; he is not afraid of the dark. He is not hitched to his mother's apronstrings. While he adores his mother, and would do anything to save her from suffering or discomfort, he is self-reliant, sturdy and full of vim. (West, 1912, as cited by Hantover, 1978, p. 191)

In the contemporary United States, such goals of achievement and competition for the male gender role may be producing many sources of conflict. As Pleck (1976) pointed out, little boys are socialized according to the traditional male role, but adult men are expected to exhibit expressive skills in business collaboration and in their relationships with women. They are expected to show tenderness and emotional intimacy, but also to remain levelheaded and cool.

been observed for commercials: A study of stereotyping in the Canadian media found that women were twice as likely to be scantily clad, were more likely to be in a consumer role than men, and were more likely to be presented as unemployed (Makin, 1986). Significantly, puppets can influence children's gender-typed behavior (Cobb, Stevens-Long, & Goldstein, 1982). Even *Sesame Street* was once criticized as presenting gender-stereotyped characters and puppets (Action for Children's Television, 1978), a situation that has improved.

Recent concern about television and gender stereotyping has addressed the more subtle features of televised messages that convey stereotypes. Even when the content of advertisements was sex-neutral, Huston, Greer, Wright, Welch, and Ross (1984) found that children from 6 to 12 years of age recognized that fast-paced commercials with loud music, sound effects, and numerous scene changes were designed for boys. Children were also aware that soft music and many fades and dissolves were representative of commercials for girls' products. If television's portrayal of men and women has any impact on the development of gender concepts, then attention must be paid to the technical format as well as to the intended content.

Proving that television viewing has a definite impact on the gender role development of children has been difficult. However, the evidence, though mostly correlational, is beginning to mount. McGhee and Frueh (1980), for example, found a relationship between gender role stereotyping and the amount of time children spend watching television. The researchers classified first, third, fifth, and seventh graders as either heavy viewers (25 or more hours of television viewing per week) or light viewers (10 or fewer hours of television viewing per week) and then administered a children's gender stereotype questionnaire. The heavy viewers made more stereotyped responses than light viewers. Furthermore, the results showed a progressive increase in such stereotyping from grades one through five and a leveling off from grades five through seven. The researchers felt that although television may not be responsible for teaching stereotypes, it may strengthen such notions acquired elsewhere and make modifying stereotypes more difficult in the face of contrary evidence. Research studying the long-term impact of television on children's concepts of gender is needed.

Television probably has been the most visible source of gender stereotyping in the media, but others also have been identified. Children's storybooks and school readers have typically placed more male characters in the central roles; they are the doers as females passively look on. Men and women in traditional roles and occupations also are heavily represented in children's books. Although recent efforts have attempted to overcome stereotypes in children's literature, female appearances still are relatively meager, and their behaviors tend to follow the traditional lines (Huston, 1983). Furthermore, many Sunday comics also provide examples of gender stereotyping (Chavez, 1985; Brabant & Mooney, 1986). An analysis of popular comics that appear nationally (e.g., "Blondie," "Dennis the Menace," and "Peanuts") found the traditional gender roles still in fashion. Men are shown in outdoor activities and at their occupations, and women are more often found in the home, taking care of children, and rarely reading. The ultimate symbol of the female role, the apron, still abounds in comics.

Childhood organizations may also encourage gender typing. The early policies of the Boy Scouts of America were designed to turn boys into "real men" (see *Applying Our Knowledge,* "The Boy Scouts and Male Gender Role").

Gender and Aggression

A noteworthy distinction between boys and girls has been in aggressive behavior. Maccoby and Jacklin (1974), in a classic review of research on sex differences in children, found that one of the few dimensions on which boys and girls differ is aggression. The difference begins to appear at 2 to 3 years of age and continues throughout adulthood. These differences appear across many different types of aggression that have been examined—physical aggression, verbal aggression, and fantasy aggression. Maccoby and Jacklin concluded, on the basis of such pervasive evidence, that the sex differences in aggression are biological in origin.

Although such male-female differences in aggression are found in other cultures, the renowned anthropologist Margaret Mead (1935) reported gender role variation in three "primitive" tribes in New Guinea. In the Arapesh tribe, both men and women were nurturant and nonaggressive—they both manifested expressive roles. The males and females of the Mundugumor tribe, in contrast, were equally competitive and aggressive. Finally, in the Tchambuli tribe, women were independent and aggressive, while men were dependent, nurturant, and interested in arts and crafts. Although Mead's work has been subjected to misinterpretation and criticism, her conclusions are important: How the parameters of culture help define and shape the behaviors of males and females cannot be ignored.

Additionally, Tieger (1980) claimed that males are more aggressive because of their socialization. For example, parents encourage more gross-motor activity in their young sons than in their daughters and supervise their sons' play less than their daughters' play. Boys, therefore, may inadvertently be given more opportunity to engage in spontaneous aggressive behavior. Furthermore, Tieger pointed out, numerous models of male aggression exist within our culture. For example, television glorifies male aggression and often conveys the message that aggression pays off. Maccoby and Jacklin (1980) countered that male aggression has been observed in primates, cross-culturally in humans, and in very young children who have not yet had much opportunity to learn about such

The tendency for males to be more aggressive than females manifests itself in the early pre-school years.

differences. Thus, they believe that sex differences in aggression are biologically based, although modified by social interaction.

Adolescence

During adolescence, becoming a man or a woman is no longer the fantasy of childhood; it is the reality of the not-so-distant future. Contemplation of that future and its concomitant roles and activities is enhanced by the hypothetical and abstract nature of newly emerging formal operational skills (see Chapter 7).

Gender and Personality

Erikson (1968) believed a reformulation of gender identity is a crucial dimension of the normative crisis of identity versus diffusion (see Chapter 10). According to Erikson, figuring out the answer to the question *"Who am I?"* includes the "part crisis" of *sexual polarization versus bisexual confusion.* This part crisis involves the adolescent's anticipation of an intimate relationship with a person of the opposite sex and coming to grips with self-identification as a mature male or female. Thus, said Erikson, gender identity develops early in life but becomes crystallized during adolescence.

Sexual polarization versus bisexual confusion

As proposed by Erik Erikson, a part of the adolescent identity crisis. It involves accepting oneself as a physically and psychologically mature male or female.

These social and psychological changes are significant, but the biological changes make the confrontation with gender identity and gender role unavoidable. Puberty brings about dramatic changes, such as a growth spurt, the onset of menstruation or seminal ejaculation, the development of secondary sex characteristics, and a surge of sexual arousal and interest. As a result of these changes, gender identity assumes a sexual orientation that was not quite as significant during childhood. Furthermore, adolescent boys and girls become concerned with their appearance and how they present themselves to others.

According to Lamb and Urberg (1978), young adolescents become rather inflexible and rigid in playing out their gender roles. The flexibility gained in late middle childhood is lost because of the uncertainty of the young adolescent's new sexual status. A parallel exists here between young children and young adolescents in their adherence to gender role stereotypes: Both conform to tradition in their quest for a strong foothold on their gender identities. However, young children view such transgressions as altering the physical identity of the individual, whereas young adolescents see such transgressions as socially deviant behavior (Stoddart & Turiel, 1985). Ullian (1976) supported this observation in her analysis of interviews with children aged 6 to 18 years. She found, for example, that although 14-years-olds recognize that the differences between males and females are largely socially defined, they also claim that members of each sex must conform to gender role stereotypes. Such increased conformity to gender role stereotypes during adolescence has been attributed to social pressures to behave in "gender appropriate" ways (Hill & Lynch, 1983).

By the time most adolescents are 17 years old, a greater flexibility toward gender roles and gender identity develops. No longer uncomfortable with the physical changes of pubescence and more practiced in behaving as a mature male or female, the adolescent no longer bends quite so far to the pressures of gender role stereotypes. Thus, Ullian (1976) found that 18-year olds no longer believe that the differences between males and females are basic to their personal identities. Tolerance of cross-sex behavior (e.g., females calling males for dates and sharing expenses) is observed, and males feel freer to disclose their thoughts and feelings to both male and female peers. Failing to recognize the adaptive value of the temporary rigidity of their early teens, many college youths look back on the gender role conformity of their younger adolescent years with distaste and amusement.

For female adolescents, gender role socialization involves the linkage between vocational decisions and budding sexuality (Lips, 1989). The early physical maturation of the girl may lead to early pressures into the traditional female role. When the young adolescent female idealizes marriage and family as a way to assert her adulthood and maturity, she may not fully explore future vocational options, particularly in nontraditional areas. In addition, contemporary young women are becoming increasingly aware of the tensions involved in balancing career and family. Although they are encouraged to prepare for a lifetime of work, they are less than enthusiastic about their occupational goals (Weitzman, 1984).

Sex Differences in Cognition

Although differences between males and females on several characteristics (such as aggression and activity level) appear early in childhood, sex differences on certain measures of intellectual ability do not consistently appear until adolescence. The source of much of this information is a review by Eleanor Maccoby and Carol Jacklin in 1974 of more than 2,000 studies on sex differences that were published from 1966 to 1973.

Girls may be more developmentally advanced than boys in verbal ability at around ages 2 and 3, but during childhood the gender differences are not significant. Maccoby and Jacklin found that the sex difference appears during early adolescence and continues to increase throughout adolescence and early adulthood: girls score higher on both simple verbal measures and high-level verbal tasks such as reading comprehension, verbal creativity, and understanding complex logical relationships.

Another sex difference that emerges during adolescence is in the area of visual-spatial ability. Beginning in adolescence and continuing throughout the high school years, males have been found to be superior to females on nonanalytic spatial tasks that involve manipulating objects in space either mentally or physically. Such tasks usually involve finding a path through a maze, fitting shapes into their appropriate-sized holes, performing mental rotations of two-dimensional objects in three-dimensional space, and estimating the number of blocks in a two-dimensional array.

Maccoby and Jacklin found that males, again beginning at adolescence, were also superior on analytic-spatial tasks, particularly those that involve the process of "decontextualization," or the ability to separate a figure from its surrounding context. This ability, also known as *field independence,* has been linked to thinking styles, and has led to the belief that females think in a more global manner while males think in a more analytical manner. This conclusion has been questioned by a number of investigators (Caplan, MacPherson, & Tobin, 1985; Sherman, 1967) who claim that tests of cognitive styles may demonstrate that males perform better in tasks of spatial ability, but such results do not necessarily mean males are more analytical in their thinking than females.

As in the cognitive abilities already discussed, the research suggests that sex differentiation in mathematical ability does not begin until early adolescence. Before this age, the two sexes are similar in their acquisition of quantitative concepts and arithmetic skills. After puberty, males tend to perform better than females on tasks assessing quantitative skills. Maccoby and Jacklin (1974) did find evidence that males' quantitative superiority shows up in comparisons of males and females who have taken the same number of mathematics courses. In general, however, the male adolescent receives greater encouragement for active participation in mathematics-type activities than the adolescent female and is more likely to anticipate a career that involves the use of mathematics (Meece, Eccles-Parsons, 1982). Thus, interest in mathematics during the adolescent years is generally more characteristic of boys than of girls.

At present, the reason for the appearance of such sex differences in cognitive abilities during adolescence is unclear. Along with puberty may come a reorganization of brain functions related to a growth spurt of the central nervous system (Waber, 1979). Perhaps the cognitive differences between male and female adolescents are manifestations of social pressure to conform according to gender-stereotyped lines. In yet another hypothesis, Dweck (1986) suggested that girls (especially bright girls) experience different motivational patterns than boys; these patterns cause girls to avoid courses that initially may be confusing or involve new conceptional frameworks (as is found in secondary school mathematics courses). Of greater concern is the possibility that schools "track" adolescent males and females according to gender-typed vocational goals. Each of these explanations has its value, but differences in cognitive abilities do not necessarily mean *large* differences. Hyde (1981) reanalyzed the studies on verbal, spatial, and quantitative abilities reviewed by Maccoby and Jacklin. When results of the research were combined for each of the cognitive abilities, the differences between the sexes were extremely small. For example, the amount of variability in scores on verbal and quantitative tests due to gender was 1 percent; for nonanalytic visual-spatial ability, 4 percent; and for

Field independence

An analytic-spatial ability to separate an embedded figure from its surrounding context.

analytic visual-spatial ability, 2.5 percent! Furthermore, decreases in gender differences on a variety of intellectual tasks have been found over the past two decades (Linn & Hyde, 1989; Jacklin, 1989), perhaps as a result of increased efforts to use gender-neutral tests. Only on the highest end of the mathematics ability continuum do boys continue to outscore girls (Jacklin, 1989), and this may partly reflect the subject matter (e.g., sports) of some of the word problems appearing on standardized tests (Linn & Hyde, 1989).

Early Adulthood and Middle Age

Today, adults have much greater latitude in their gender role behaviors than in the past. In our culture, so many variations appear on masculine and feminine themes that deviation rather than tradition may be the norm. For many adults, the incorporation of both male and female characteristics in one individual has become the gender role ideal, as will be discussed later in this chapter. In terms of the model of flexibility and rigidity in gender roles and gender identity, then, can we assume that adulthood represents the

Mothers who work outside the home still tend to shoulder the bulk of household and child care responsibilities.

acme of flexibility? In reality, such flexibility is slow in coming, and it may be truer of the years of middle age than of young adulthood.

Freud believed that the major tasks of adulthood involve love and work. These tasks often differentiate how men and women perceive themselves. The young adult male typically crystallizes his identity around his work and career, whereas the young adult female's identity centers around her intimate relationships, particularly with her husband and children. Although more men today are becoming aware of their needs for intimacy, and more women realize their needs for fulfillment in a vocation, the gender identities of the sexes still seem to differ along the conventional lines (Hodgson & Fischer, 1979).

Of the many dimensions of adult life that affect adult gender roles and identity, probably none has as much impact as marriage and parenthood. Traditional marriage evokes images of the husband as breadwinner and the wife as tender of hearth and family. Actually, only a minority of U.S. families have such arrangements. More than half of all adult women are now in the work force (Williams, 1983). However, despite changes in marital styles over the past decade, many men and women tend to use the culturally defined roles of husband and wife as the reference point from which to gauge their own behavior.

How do the institutions of marriage and parenthood affect gender role behavior in adulthood? Two findings may serve as important clues. First of all, whether or not husbands and wives assumed traditional roles within their marriage before the birth of their first child, research examining the impact of parenthood on gender roles consistently reports that men and women shift more to the conventional roles when they become parents (Cowan, Cowan, Coie, & Coie, 1978) The wife's remaining in the work force does not seem to result in a shift back to more egalitarian roles for husband and wife. A woman who continues to work after she is married and has children still performs the majority of household chores (Athinson & Huston, 1984; Mortimer & London, 1984).

Secondly, interviews and studies of middle-aged men and women consistently reveal that men become more expressive and sensitive and that women are more outgoing and instrumental during this period of life.

To put together these two pieces of the gender role puzzle, David Gutmann (1975), a psychoanalytically trained clinical psychologist interested in charting the ways in which men and women differ during the latter part of the life span, proposed that gender roles in adulthood are guided by the ***parental imperative***. Gutmann drew on the work of Swiss psychologist Carl Jung, who believed that masculine and feminine traits are present in everyone's personality, although one modality tends to dominate over the other until mid-life. According to Gutmann, boys and girls are permitted to exhibit cross-sex behaviors during their youth, but gender role socialization prepares than for the task of suppressing the opposite-sex modality once they grow up and their children are born. This shift toward more clearly

Parental imperative

The hypothesis that emphasizes the necessity for childbearing adults to conform to gender-typed behaviors and suppress cross-sex behaviors to rear their children successfully.

defined active-mastery behaviors on the part of the father and passive-accommodative behaviors on the part of the mother is necessary for the survival of the human species.

Parents must ensure that their children are provided with two basic forms of security—emotional and physical—until they are ready to live independently. Gutmann assumed that one parent cannot provide both forms of security, because caretaking responsibilities are best suited close to home, whereas the provision for physical needs often necessitates long-distance forays. Thus, women have evolved as providers for the emotional needs, and men as providers for the material needs.

Once children have outgrown their need for emotional and physical security, men and women are free to reclaim the repressed masculine and feminine sides of their personalities. Gutmann found this change in masculinity and femininity during middle age in several different cultures: the highland and lowland Mayan Indians of Mexico, the Navaho Indians in Arizona, the Galilean and Syrian Druze of the Mideast, and residents of Kansas City. Each of his samples perceived men as more nurturant, dependent, and sensitive with age and women as more independent, aggressive, and competitive with age. Greater flexibility in gender roles, argued Gutmann, goes hand in hand with an empty nest.

Gutmann's theory has not escaped criticism (Self, 1975). His model may not be completely applicable to contemporary Western life, to single-parent families, or to childless couples. However, his claims about the changes in adult gender roles have received quite a bit of support from a variety of sources. For example, Livson (1983a, 1983b), found in her analysis of longitudinal data that as men and women approached age 50, they increasingly assumed some of the characteristics of the opposite sex while retaining their respective masculinity and feminity. Others have indicated that a middle-aged man's sense of well-being depends very much on his sense of social connectedness (Tamir, 1982). One of the dimensions of the male mid-life crisis, as discussed by Levinson et al. (1974) and Gould (1972), involves the recapturing of the feminine side of his identity. Moreland (1980) also contended that the major developmental changes in a man's life are influenced by his changing conceptions of masculinity. Furthermore, as was noted in Chapter 4, women do not necessarily experience trauma over the launching of their children. Instead, they often express delight in their newly found freedom and in their reclaiming of the talents and abilities that were seemingly lost in the years of child rearing (Lowenthal & Chiriboga, 1972; Neugarten, 1968; Black & Hill, 1984; Fausto-Sterling, 1985).

Neugarten, Wood, Kraines, and Loomis (1963) found that attitudes toward menopause among postmenopausal women also were much more positive than is commonly expected. In fact, younger women who had not experienced the *climacteric* (the cessation of menstruation) were most fearful and negative. Neugarten (1968) claimed that this finding demonstrated that women in the middle adulthood years feel a new sense of

Climacteric
The cessation of menstruation (an aspect of menopause).

opportunity as they redirect their energy from child rearing to skill development. The adulthood years, like earlier life stages, represent a progression from rigidity to flexibility in gender development. Although the differential expectations for men and women may not take on the moral, prescriptive dimension they had earlier, the male and female gender identity and gender role are constantly being challenged and changed with the progression of the years and corresponding developmental tasks.

Later Life

In contrast to the preceding developmental periods, relatively few empirical and theoretical efforts examine gender roles and gender identity in old age. To some extent, old age represents an extension of the changes in gender role development that occur during middle age. The data suggest that the acceptance of both male and female personality traits continues into old age (Turner, 1982). Grandparenthood, for example, is perceived by grandchildren as a unisex role (Turner, 1982). However, older men and women may also maintain gender-typed behaviors of their earlier years. For the current cohort of elderly, women still tend to be submissive and let men take control of conversation, and retired men do not help out significantly more with the housework than they did when they were working (Keating & Cole, 1980; McGee & Wells, 1982). Will the young adults of the 1990s carry changing attitudes toward gender roles into old age? The aging process differs for men and women on psychological, social, and biological levels, which in turn may affect attitudes toward gender identities.

Retirement is a major life event for men (and may become increasingly so for women). Because masculinity is often associated with productivity and control over material resources, men may view retirement as a threat to their traditional masculine identity (McGee & Wells, 1982). Women, in contrast, have more continuity of the gender-related tasks of middle age into old age. Household chores continue into the elderly years, and even though children may have left home, many elderly women have ample opportunity to demonstrate nurturance by watching over their husband's health.

The evidence also suggests that men and women react to the loss of a spouse in different ways (see Chapter 15). A major study on bereavement in widows and widowers suggests that men and women differentially interpret their feelings about the loss of their spouses (Parkes, 1972; Parkes & Weiss, 1983). Women often emphasized a sense of abandonment, whereas men emphasized a sense of dismemberment. Because of the disproportionate numbers of older women to older men, women tend to compensate for the loss of their husbands by developing same-sex friendships, whereas men have more opportunities for developing heterosexual relationships.

Health and sexuality may have a significant impact on the gender identity of elderly men and women. Turner (1982) suggested that poor health does not defeminize a woman, but because masculinity is typically associated with an active and vigorous body, poor health may demasculinize a man. The significance of sexuality to gender identity during adolescence and adulthood already has been discussed. During old age, obvious changes in the sexual organs do affect sexual performance. However, as we pointed out in Chapter 4, these biological changes do not necessarily mean that sexual behavior ceases during the elderly years (Masters & Johnson, 1966).

Older men and women can accommodate to the changing nature of the sexual response cycle and satisfy their intimacy and sexual needs just as in earlier years. What may inhibit sexuality in the older years, however, are a lifetime of negative and uniformed attitudes toward sexuality and aging, the lack of an available partner (particularly for women), or poor health. No one has researched the impact of sexuality on gender identities among the elderly (perhaps because of the sensitive nature of the subject), but it would not be surprising to find that sexually active older men and women have different views of their masculinity and femininity than the sexually inactive.

Finally, Sontag (1972) suggested that gender role stereotypes support a double standard of aging. Social attitudes may be more negative toward older women than older men:

> In our society, . . . aging has traditionally been for women an unenviable prospect. Her most socially valued qualities, her ability to provide sex and attractive companionship and to have children and nurture them, are expressed in the context of youth, which is endowed with physical beauty and fertility. As she ages, she is seen as less physically attractive and desirable, and her reproductive and nurturant functions are no longer relevant. (Williams, 1983 p. 396)

In addition, elderly women are at a social disadvantage because of their lack of economic power. Currently, the increased poverty of elderly women (particularly minority-group elderly women) results from a lifetime as a homemaker or a worker in a low-paying job that often does not provide a pension (Basow, 1986). The feminization of poverty is a critical issue that must be confronted as more and more women near retirement age.

However, as suggested earlier, men experience a greater discontinuity in their gender-typed behaviors when they age, and for men who value the traditional view of masculinity, aging can bring about concerns over gender identity. Our culture may not berate the old man for his wrinkles and gray hair, but it may devalue him for his lack of physical prowess and productivity in the marketplace.

Many facets of ageism and sexism are intertwined. Those elderly who can accept and incorporate both the masculine and feminine sides of their personalities and behavior—in other words, those who continue to be flexible in their gender—will fare better than those who cannot. Perhaps the double standard of aging for men and women will not be an issue for future generations of elderly, who are learning the value of such flexibility earlier in their lives (McGee & Wells, 1982).

A Model of the Life-Span Approach

The life-span approach to gender roles and gender identity can provide an appreciation of the continual process of redefinition and reformulation that takes place throughout the course of development. The general model presented in Figure 14.1 suggests that people constrict and expand their behaviors and identities in accordance with the tasks of each developmental period. For any given person, the degree and range of rigidity/flexibility in

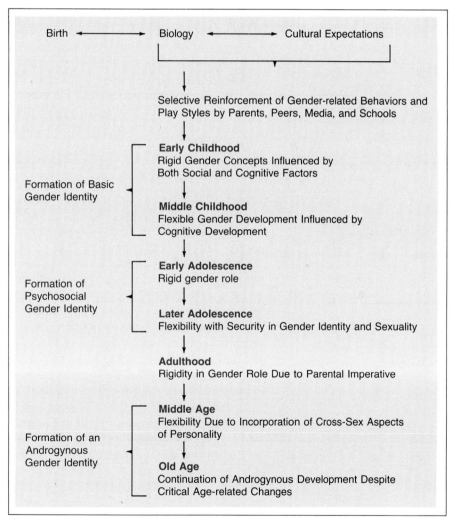

Figure 14.1
Model of Gender Role Development

gender identity and gender role will be unique. Although we refer to *individual* identities and roles, these are firmly anchored within a sociocultural framework that may differ not only across countries, but also across ethnic groups in the United States.

THEORIES OF GENDER ROLE DEVELOPMENT

The preceding discussion of gender role acquisition described "what" develops. The following discussion presents a number of theories that attempt to explain "how" gender roles develop. No one theory should be seen as the only "right" position, but rather each theory contributes a different perspective to our understanding of gender development. Thus, the psychoanalytic perspective contributes to our understanding of the emotional component of gender role development; learning theories contribute to our knowledge of how social interactions influence gender role development; and cognitive theories contribute to our knowledge of how gender role concepts are acquired.

Psychoanalytic Theory

Freud (1950b) believed that gender roles and gender identity result from the resolution of the Oedipal complex encountered during the phallic stage. Boys perceive their fathers as competitors for their mother's affections and, as a result, fear castration. To resolve the conflict, they become more like their fathers. Girls' desires for their fathers and rivalry with their mothers is properly resolved through the female aspiration of growing up to be a mother and symbolically attaining the penis (believed lost by "castration") through the birth of a child, especially a male child.

Erikson (1968) took a more positive view of female gender development than his theoretical ancestor, although his view also emphasizes the anatomical differences between males and females. His emphasis shifts from the notion of a lack of a penis to the presence of a woman's childbearing and child-rearing potential. Erikson's observations of the play construction of 10-, 11-, and 12-year-old boys and girls led him to propose that boys' identities center on active, erect, and projectile models (i.e., boys built towers and tall buildings, knocking them down when complete), whereas girls' identities center on enclosed, protected, and receptive models (i.e., girls built interior, peaceful scenes). Thus, the core of the female identity is an "inner space" that leads to a more humanitarian, compassionate, and nurturant approach toward self and society.

Nancy Chodorow (1978) used the psychoanalytic framework to explain why women mother and men do not. In her analysis, daughters and mothers experience a oneness and continuity with each other that is not disrupted by resolution of the Oedipal complex. Boys must develop a more differentiated sense of self by virtue of denying the pre-Oedipal attachment to the mother.

"Because women are themselves mothered by women, they grow up with the relational capacities and needs, and psychological definition of self-in-relationship, which commits them to mothering. Men, because they are mothered by women, do not. Women mother daughters who, when they become women, mother" (p. 209).

Many criticisms have been levied against the psychoanalytic interpretation of gender role development. The research community has faulted the lack of empirical support for the notion of the Oedipal complex. Feminist scholars have taken exception to Freud's support of the traditional female-expressive role. In Freud's theory, healthy psychosexual development for women involves no aspirations for work and achievement. However, such low-achievement motivation may be more a reflection of living within a patriarchical society than limitations of a female's biology (Horney, 1973). Freud's notion of penis envy has also upset many theorists and researchers. Clara Thompson (1974), a neo-Freudian, contended that women envy the penis because it symbolizes man's greater status and power, not because it is a coveted sexual organ. As a matter of fact, men consciously or unconsciously may envy the reproductive capabilities of women. For example, in some cultures, men go through a ritual pregnancy, childbirth, and recovery period—a practice known as *couvade* (see *Issues in Human Development,* "The Significance of the Couvade").

Erikson has not escaped criticism, either. Whereas he takes a more favorable view of women, he also reaffirms the central significance of a woman's reproductive capability and her role as mother as the major dimension of her identity. For Erikson, healthy female ego development seems to require bearing children.

Despite these criticisms, the psychoanalytic approach has made several positive contributions to the understanding of gender role acquisition. It underscores that gender identity is an early acquisition and that the process of identification is central to its development. This perspective also points out that long-term father absence can seriously hamper a young boy's socioemotional development, and calls attention to the harsher socialization practices directed toward males.

Learning Theories

Two types of learning theory are significant to the study of gender development. The first, operant conditioning theory, applies the principles of learning contingent on reinforcement to the acquisition of gender-typed behavior. The second, social learning theory, introduces the role of imitation in the development of gender roles and behavior.

Operant Conditioning

The appeal of conditioning theory (see Chapter 6) is that it explains many different behaviors by the same set of fundamental principles. Gender role acquisition, according to behaviorists, involves the shaping of children's

Issues in Human Development
The Significance of the Couvade

 Freud's analysis of female gender role development reinforced the idea that women covet the male sex organ (known as penis envy). However, does any evidence suggest that men experience a similar type of envy? Do they secretly long for the reproductive capabilities that women possess? Psychoanalyst Bruno Bettelheim (1962) claimed that the couvade, a male ritual found in preindustrial societies, exemplifies men's envy of the creative power of women. The couvade is a social ritual whereby a man whose wife is about to give birth manifests many of the signs of labor and delivery. He may experience abdominal pains, moan and groan, and follow various pregnancy-related taboos that restrict his eating and fraternizing. At the onset of his "labor," the husband may be brought to a specially prepared hut where a mock delivery takes place. After the birth of the baby, he may receive guests and rest during his "recovery period," which may be lengthier than his wife's recovery—she may shortly return to work while her husband recuperates from the whole ordeal!

Margaret Mead (1935) reported that men from the Arapesh tribe are considered childbearers along with their women. Childbirth is believed to be as physically taxing for men as for women. Mead (1935) reported that a comment that a middle-aged man is handsome may be answered with, "Good looking? Ye-e-s, but you should have seen him before he bore all those children" (p. 56).

Not everyone agrees that couvade is the male analogue to penis envy. Paige and Paige (1973) believed that couvade is a symbolic way for men of preindustrial societies to lay claim to the newborn. This is important in tribes in which paternity rights are established by social consensus. Competition over paternity is common to many societies where being the biological father may not automatically make a man the legal father. In societies in which women are not restricted by men, couvade serves as a symbolic way to help ensure paternity rights. In such societies, wealth often is not exchanged at marriage as potential compensation for sterility or other birth problems. Thus, the only way to ensure that the community will accept a man as the "legal" father is for him to claim the child symbolically through a ritualistic labor.

"Primitive" men may not be the only men who try to get as close as possible to the experience of childbirth. As Tavris & Wade (1984) pointed out, "consider the popularity of natural childbirth in this country, and the renewed participation of the father in the whole process. Is Lamaze a modern couvade?" (p. 190)

behaviors so that eventually they approximate masculine or feminine forms. Parents, peers, and teachers reward or praise gender appropriate behavior and punish, ignore, or criticize gender inappropriate behavior. The acquisition of a gender role and a gender identity, therefore, is based on socialization pressures applied to children; their gender roles are defined by the consequences of their actions.

In contrast to the psychoanalytic perspective—which uses clinical, or case-study, evidence for support—the conditioning perspective garners most of its support from research that uncovers differential treatment of boys and girls with respect to gender-typed behavior. Do the findings show that parents interact differently with their male and female children? The answer must be a qualified yes, for it really seems to depend on the sorts of behaviors and activities being observed. Parents do not seem to treat their boys or girls differently in terms of discouraging aggression and dependence (Lamb & Urberg, 1978). Parents also expect their sons and daughters to behave according to similar values, such as being helpful around the house (Lambert, Yackley, & Hein, 1971). Yet, when parents work with their sons and daughters on a task, they communicate higher expectations and a desire for more independent behavior from their sons (Block, 1978). Additionally, parents do seem to treat their sons and daughters differently in terms of play activities and toy preferences (Jacklin & Maccoby, 1983). Such differential treatment occurs as early as 6 months and continues to be observed with older children (Ruble, 1988).

Interestingly, we are now learning that children respond selectively to reinforcement on the basis of their own sex and the sex of the person giving the reinforcement (Jacklin, 1989). Thus, reinforcement does not change behavior in a rigid, automatic fashion. In Fagot's (1985) work with nursery school children, girls were observed to respond most to the reinforcements of male and female teachers and female peers, and boys were most responsive to the reinforcement given by male peers, particularly when these boys were engaged in male-typical behavior.

A unique study by Langlois and Downs (1980) directly assessed and compared the rewards and punishments that mothers, fathers, and peers administered to 3- and 5-year-olds on the basis of their gender-appropriate and gender-inappropriate play behavior. The researchers escorted a child to

Social learning theory proposes that children learn gender roles through imitating a number of individuals of their own sex, particularly those with whom they have a warm and nurturant relationship.

Issues in Human Development
The Effects of Paternal Absence

 Interest in the impact of the absence of fathers on the gender development of their children has corresponded to the rise in father-absent households. In 1988, single parents accounted for 27 percent of all family groups with children under 18 years old, and of these, 23.7 percent of all households with children were mother-headed households (U.S. Bureau of the Census, 1989).

A number of theoretical perspectives have addressed the potential harmful effects of father absence on gender development. Psychoanalytic theory emphasizes that father absence leads to an incomplete resolution of the Oedipal complex, and social learning theory highlights the lack of an important role model for boys in father-absent homes. But what findings on the effects of paternal absence appear in the empirical literature? Research on this topic began during World War II to investigate the impact of paternal absence as a result of military service. Current research generally investigates the impact of paternal absence due to death or divorce. This literature on the effects of paternal absence on gender role development has been difficult to summarize and has led to a variety of interpretations and conclusions. Stevenson & Black (1988), however, used a relatively new statistical technique, *meta-analysis,* to tease out the magnitude of the effects of paternal absence on gender role development in males and females. In meta-analysis, the results from individual studies are combined into one overall analysis. After careful consideration of which studies to include, they incorporated a total of 67 studies, beginning in 1958, in the analysis. The ages of the participants in these studies were classified into four groups: 0–6 years, 7–12 years, 13–17 years, and 18 years and older. The authors also were careful to account for the socioeconomic status and race of the participants and for the methodology of the research.

Stevenson and Black (1988) found that father absence had little impact on the gender role development of females. The only significant finding was that father-absent females were slightly less feminine than father-present females, perhaps because their single mothers behaved in a less gender-typed fashion. Even more striking was the finding that in the best controlled studies, the effects of paternal absence on boys was minimal. Significant findings were observed only when the cause of paternal absence and the developmental level of the male child were taken into account.

Research that looked at the cause of father absence found that boys whose fathers were absent due to military service were significantly less gender stereotyped than other boys. Conversely, father's death seemed to have no impact on gender role development in boys.

Stevenson and Black (1988) also found that father-absent preschool boys made less stereotyped choices of toys and activities than father-present preschool boys. Older father-absent boys, however, were more gender-typed in their overt behavior (particularly in aggression) than father-present older boys.

Noteworthy conclusions may be derived form the research of Stevenson and Black. The gender development of children seems to be less adversely affected by paternal absence than either theory or research would have us believe. Undoubtedly, many children from father-absent homes do have access to their fathers or to father substitutes. Additionally, as Stevenson and Black (1988) pointed out, the quality of fathering is more important than the presence or absence of a father in the home.

a room, where the child was given either "girl" toys (a dollhouse with furniture, a stove with pots and dishes, and women's clothing) or "boy" toys (an army set, a gas station with cars, and cowboy outfits with guns and holsters) to play with. The child was instructed to play with the toys in a gender-appropriate fashion (i.e., to play with the "boy" toys as boys do, or to

Meta-analysis

A statistical procedure that combines the results from individual studies into one overall analysis. Meta-analysis can be used to resolve conflicting findings by testing the statistical significance of the accumulated results of a group of studies.

play with the "girl" toys as girls do). While the child was playing, the child's mother, father, or same-sex peer was escorted into the room. Thus, in the event of a cross-sex situation (i.e., a boy playing with "girl" toys, or a girl playing with "boy" toys), a parent or peer could encounter a boy playing with a dollhouse or a girl setting up soldiers from the army set. Fathers, mothers, and friends did not know that their behaviors toward the child's playing with the toys were the main focus of the researchers' observations.

Langlois and Downs found that the treatment the children received for playing along gender appropriate or inappropriate lines depended both on the sex of the child and on the person observing the child's play. For example, the researchers found that when boys engaged in cross-sex play they received punishment in the form of ridicule, interference with play, or a suggested alternative from both peers and fathers. Mothers, however, tended to reward such behavior. When boys played with the masculine toys, they were ignored by their peers, received mild approval from their mothers, and were clearly rewarded by their fathers. Mothers, fathers, and peers all approved of and rewarded same-sex play of girls, and disapproved of their cross-sex play.

Several important conclusions can be drawn from these findings. First, girls are treated more consistently than boys by several different agents of socialization. Second, both peers' and fathers' responses were stronger than mothers' responses, and fathers exerted the greatest amount of pressure. These findings suggest that fathers are significant teachers of gender appropriate behavior. Indeed, Johnson's (1975) sociological analysis of the father role concludes that the father brings out masculinity in his sons and femininity in his daughters (see *Issues in Human Development,* "The Effects of Paternal Absence"). Finally, the difference in the amount of reward the fathers gave their sons for same-sex, as opposed to cross-sex, behaviors was greater than for daughters.

Langlois and Downs's study also emphasizes that gender role behavior is not learned solely from parents. That peers reinforce gender appropriate play and discourage cross-sex play has been observed in natural preschool settings (Lamb & Roopnarine, 1979), as well as in laboratory settings. Siblings also have their impact. Although more cross-gender toys are available in homes with mixed-sex siblings, boys and girls are more likely to engage in cross-sex play activities if they come from homes where all the children are of the same sex. Perhaps greater diversification of gender role behavior is permitted and necessary in all-sister or all-brother families.

Why is play so vulnerable to the lessons of gender typing? Perhaps play is an important, but fairly safe, arena for figuring out how to act in a masculine or feminine manner. In play, a boy or girl may be particularly responsive to the feedback that others provide. Thus, within certain areas of a child's life, the conditioning perspective offers valuable clues to how gender roles are acquired. Although the development of gender roles and gender identity cannot be explained totally in terms of rewards and punishments, when people important to the child reward either masculine or feminine behavior, their reactions have a significant impact on the child's development.

Social Learning Theory

The social learning, or observational, perspective (Bandura & Walters, 1963) places more responsibility for the acquisition of gender-typed behaviors on the child than conditioning theory (behavior and reinforcement/punishment) does. As you will recall from the discussion of social-learning theory in Chapter 6, new behaviors are acquired by observing and imitating the behaviors of others (models), particularly when rewards for imitation are anticipated. As applied to the development of gender roles, boys learn gender appropriate behavior from observing and imitating the masculine behaviors of their fathers; girls learn gender appropriate behavior from observing and imitating the feminine behaviors of their mothers. The social learning perspective acknowledges that anyone (teachers, siblings, grandparents, etc.) may be a model for gender typing, particularly if that person is perceived by the child as warm, nurturant, or powerful. However, parents are particularly important models because of the amount of time they spend with their children and the intensity of their relationships with their children. Such factors seem to be particularly significant for males: the degree of masculinity in sons has been found to be related to how warm and competent they perceive their fathers to be (Lamb & Urberg, 1978).

A major criticism leveled against the social learning perspective concerns research methodology used by its advocates. The typical study involves a child viewing either a male or female (usually an adult) engaged in gender neutral activity. For example, a female or male model may fashion an object out of clay or claim to prefer a balloon over a plastic horse. The child is then led to a room where a variety of objects (including those used by the model) are available and told to play with whatever he or she wishes. Observations usually are made through a one-way mirror or concealed camera to determine whether the child plays with the object used by the same-sex model or avoids the object used by the opposite-sex model. In their review of this type of research, Maccoby and Jacklin (1974) found little evidence supporting the view that a child will imitate a model on the basis of sex, and they discounted imitation as a significant determinant of gender-typed behavior.

Because the relationship between gender-typed behavior and imitation makes such intuitive sense, Maccoby and Jacklin's conclusions did not put an end to social learning theory. Instead, researchers recognized that concepts and research drew too simple a line between behavior of a model and imitation by the child. For example, Huston (1983) found in reviewing the literature on the role of observational learning in the acquisition of gender typing that children learn facets of both masculine and feminine gender typing but will behave in a gender appropriate way when the situation and situational cues demand it. And Perry and Bussey (1979)

Recent research has indicated that children are less gender-stereotyped when their fathers perform "nontraditional" chores at home.

proposed that children do not just imitate any one model. Instead, children observe the behavior of many males and females and form abstractions as to what is gender appropriate. These abstractions are based on the child's memory of relative frequencies of behaviors performed by one sex over the other. Thus, children form a composite picture of a gender role from the many models encountered over the course of their lifetimes. Perry and Bussey also found that imitation will increase when the number of same-sex models displaying a particular behavior increases. Finally, because boys and girls often seek out different types of activities, they may be exposed to different sources of gender-role socialization. Evidence shows, for example, that girls, more often than boys, seek out experiences that place them in adult-led situations (Huston, Carpenter, Atwater, & Johnson, 1986). In terms of the modeling framework, this means that girls receive more feedback and modeling from adults, and boys receive more feedback and modeling from peers.

Can modeling also encourage cross-sex behavior in children? Research on the effects of maternal employment on children's behaviors suggests that the answer is yes. In the United States, children of mothers employed outside the home tend to be less gender stereotyped (Cordua, McGraw, & Drabman, 1979). Girls of such mothers generally are more achievement oriented and have higher educational and career goals than daughters of nonworking mothers (Hoffman, 1979). Furthermore, Baruch and Barnett (1986) found evidence of reduced gender stereotyping in children whose fathers performed more traditionally feminine chores at home.

Although the social learning perspective has added much to our knowledge of gender role development, critics have contended that the social learning perspective fails to acknowledge that a child must have an initial awareness of being a boy or a girl in order to imitate. To complete the picture begun by the learning perspective, then, the cognitive component of gender identity must be addressed. Cognitive theories offer additional insight into why children actively attend to models of their sex.

Cognitive Developmental Theory

In addition to his theory of moral development, Lawrence Kohlberg (1966) discussed the role of cognition in the acquisition of gender identity and gender role. Children go through three stages in the development of a complete understanding of gender:

1. Basic gender identity, in which children recognize that they are boys or girls on the basis of physical differences between males and females.
2. *Gender stability,* in which children realize that their gender will always remain the same and that they will grow up to be men or women.
3. *Gender constancy* (conservation), in which children understand that people's gender remains the same despite such superficial changes as hairstyles, dress, or activities.

Gender stability
The child's realization that his or her gender will always remain the same and that the child will grow up to be a man or a woman.

Gender constancy
The child's understanding that his or her gender will remain the same despite such superficial changes as hairstyle, dress, or activity.

Once children use the label *boy* or *girl*—first to themselves and then to others—they begin to organize ideas and experiences actively according to the categories of maleness and femaleness. Such labeling does not depend on any one model or person but rather comes from abstractions derived from a variety of sources, such as parents, siblings, and the media. Engaging in gender-typed behavior becomes pleasurable, because it confirms the child's self-categorization system: "I am a boy, therefore, I want to do boy things; therefore, the opportunity to do boy things (and to gain approval for doing them) is rewarding" (Kohlberg, 1966, p. 89).

An understanding of the stability of gender is associated with preference for the child's own sex (Smetana & Letourneau, 1984). Just as children's knowledge of rules and obligations is rigid and inflexible when first acquired, so is their understanding of gender roles. Thus, 6- and 7-year-olds view acting in a gender appropriate manner as a moral imperative—a boy who puts on a dress, for example, is naughty (Damon, 1977).

Gender constancy is reportedly acquired at around age 6 or 7 and may be based on the concepts of conservation (see Chapter 7). This is exactly what Marcus and Overton (1978) found when they tested kindergartners, first graders, and second graders on conservation and gender constancy: The former concept was acquired before the latter. This sequence in the development of gender understanding has been observed cross-culturally in children from Belize, Kenya, Nepal, and American Samoa (Munroe, Shimmin, & Munroe, 1984).

Researchers use gender constancy tests to see if children have acquired this concept. The test in Figure 14.2 is adapted from Emmerich and his associates (1977). In this test, drawing of a boy and a girl are placed into a ring binder. The drawings are cut at the neck so that the "heads" page can

Figure 14.2
The Gender Constancy Test

Source: From W. Emmerich, K. S. Goldman, B. Kirsch, and R. Sharabany (1977). "Evidence for a transitional phase in the development of gender constancy." *Child Development, 48,* pp. 930–936. © 1977 by the Society for Research in Child Development, Inc.

be turned over. On the following page, the positions of the boy and girl heads are reversed. In this way, the boy's head can be presented with feminine clothing, and vice versa. Starting with an all-girl picture, the researcher says, "This is Janie." Then the researcher turns the page and asks the following questions (Emmerich et al., 1977):

- If Janie wants to be a boy, can she be?
- If Janie played with trucks and did boy things, what would she be? Would she be a boy or a girl?
- If Janie puts on boys' clothes (like this), what would she be? Would she be a girl or would she be a boy?
- If Janie has her hair cut short (like this), what would she be? Would she be a girl or would she be a boy?
- If Janie has her hair cut short (like this), and wears boys' clothes (like this), what would she be? Would she be a girl or would she be a boy?

The same questions are then asked with the boy's picture and a boy's name.

In contrast to Kohlberg's claims, some evidence suggests that gender constancy can be acquired as early as 2 years of age. Kuhn, Nash, and Brucken (1978) gave 2- and 3-year-olds a gender constancy test, as well as a test for gender typing and gender preference. The children were presented with two dolls, Michael and Lisa, and were asked to associate a picture of an activity with one of the dolls. Not surprisingly, children at this early age have already learned the basic fundamentals of gender stereotyping: Lisa liked to play with dolls, cook dinner, and clean house, whereas Michael liked to play with cars, build things, and help his father. More importantly, Kuhn, Nash, and Brucken found a high correlation between gender constancy and stereotyping. Children who understood the permanence of their gender were more likely to stereotype than those who did not. These same children also preferred their own gender to a significantly greater degree.

The late appearance of gender constancy in the Emmerich et al. (1977) technique may be an artifact of the type of measure used. Sandra Bem (1989) devised an interview procedure that was based on a child's knowledge of genitalia as the defining attribute of male and female. Bem presented 3-, 4-, and 5-year-olds with photos (as opposed to drawings) of nude toddlers who were then dressed in sex appropriate and sex inappropriate ways (see Figure 14.3). She found that 40 percent of the children could conserve gender, but only if they also had genital knowledge. Interestingly, girls had significantly higher genital knowledge and gender constancy scores than boys.

Why does stereotyping occur at such an early age? Perhaps when children are first learning about the permanence of their genders, their ability to process the subtleties and nuances of gender roles is limited to a few fundamental dimensions and concepts. As we shall see in the next section of this chapter, flexibility in gender roles and gender identity may only come after a child is sure of what it means to be a male or a female.

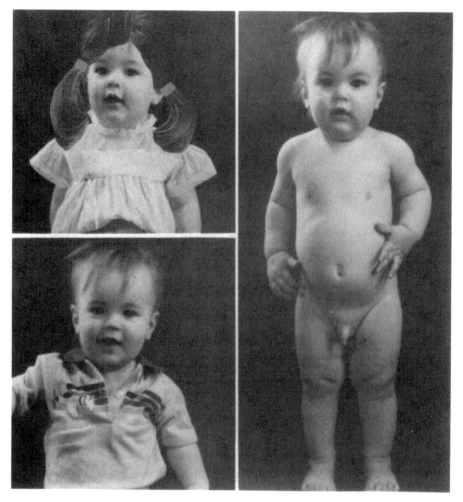

Figure 14.3
One Set of Photographs Used to Assess Gender Constancy and Genital Knowledge in Pre-schoolers. *Source:* From Sandra Lipsitz Bem (1989). "Genital Knowledge and Gender Constancy in Preschool Children." *Child Development, 60,* p. 653. Reprinted by permission of The Society for Research in Child Development, Inc., and the author.

Social learning theory considers gender identity to follow or parallel the imitation of gender-typed behaviors. Children imitate models of their own sex because they perceive a similarity between themselves and the models, and because they are rewarded for such imitation. Gender identity is then derived from such imitations. Cognitive developmental theory, in contrast, claims that imitation follows the acquisition of concepts of gender. Some evidence supports this cognitive developmental position. For example, Slaby and Frey (1975) gave 4-year-olds a gender constancy task and then showed them a film. Each half of the screen had either a man or a woman simultaneously building a fire, popping corn, playing a musical instrument, and drinking juice. The children were able to look at only half the screen at a time. Unknown to the children, Slaby and Frey observed their movie viewing through a one-way window beneath the screen, recording the amount of time spent looking at one half of the screen over the other. Boys and girls who had high gender constancy scores spent a considerably longer period of time looking at the models than children with low gender constancy scores. Thus, something about gender constancy cues children into paying particular attention to the behavior of others. Furthermore, boys high in gender constancy spent a significantly greater amount of time attending to the male actor. A similar but nonsignificant trend was noted for the girls, who attended more often to the female actor. These findings have subsequently been replicated by Ruble (as cited by Maccoby, 1980) for boys and girls 4 to 6 years old.

A Contemporary Cognitive View: Information Processing Theory

Both information processing and cognitive developmental theories of gender typing and gender role development claim that thinking serves to regulate gender-typed behavior. According to the information processing perspective, the *schema* is the main determinant of gender typing. A schema is a set of ideas (naive theories) that guide decisions and behavior (Martin & Halverson, 1981). People form schemas about many aspects of their world. We have schemas of our daily routines, our school, and ourselves. Schemas serve as cognitive frameworks that help organize information.

Schema

According to information-processing theorists of gender development, a set of ideas that help children categorize information in terms of what is appropriate and characteristic of males and females.

Schemas based on gender typing and gender roles help children categorize information in terms of what is appropriate and characteristic of males and females. Children form schemas of both masculine and feminine stereotypes. Parents who give more attention (both positive and negative) to gender-typed play in their young children encourage the early formation of such gender schemas (Fagot & Leinbach, 1989). When children encounter something they judge as appropriate for their own sex, they explore it, ask questions about it, and generally show more interest in it. In this way, an additional "own-sex" schema is formed that helps children form concepts and plans of action necessary for behaving in ways considered appropriate to their own sex. For example, a boy would learn that trucks are for boys and dolls are for girls; he also would know considerably more about trucks than about dolls. The opposite would be true for girls. In general, children would be able to recall more—and more in-depth information—about same-sex objects than about objects thought to be appropriate for the opposite sex or for both sexes (Bradbard, Martin, Endsley, & Halverson, 1986).

Whereas gender-based schemas function much like other stereotypes, children are likely to form gender schemas earlier than other schemas for characterizing people. The precedence of gender-based schemas may be due to the significance of gender and sex to the self, as well as to the

prominence of gender in our society. Martin and Halverson (1981) emphasized that gender stereotyping may be necessary for children to help them
simplify information from the environment. Such stereotypes help children
to sort actions, attributes, and preferences into the categories "things for me"
and "things not for me," although evidence suggests that preschoolers will
more readily stereotype others than the self (Cowan & Hoffman, 1986).
Research has found relationships between gender schemas and behavior.
For example, Fagot, Leinbach, and Hagan (1986) found that preschoolers
who classified pictures of men and women by gender (as opposed to other
classification schemas) spent more time playing with members of their
own sex.

Simple gender schemas may have value during childhood, but with the
more complex forms of thinking that accompany cognitive development,
gender stereotypes and concepts of gender roles become more differentiated and flexible. An older adolescent or adult who remains gender typed
may have retained the narrowly defined gender schemas of early childhood.

A Synthesis

Which theory presents the correct view on gender role and gender identity
acquisition? This question begs for an answer and continues to nag students
and researchers alike. Perhaps the resolution lies in all the theories, each of
which presents only one angle of a complex developmental process.

The psychoanalytic perspective can help to account for the affective
(emotional) dimension of gender identity. Castration anxiety and the
Oedipus complex await empirical verification, but children's desires to be
like the people with whom they experience intense relationships do not
await such verification. When identification with the same-sex parent is
coupled with the behavioral dimension of gender identity, as explained by
learning and social learning theory, we have an explanation for why children
may seek out those things that make them "just like daddy and Uncle Eddy"
or "just like mommy and Cousin Kathy." Such perceived similarities initially
are very superficial. They probably are not based on observation of genitalia
(as Freud would contend), but on similarity of hairstyle, dress, and
mannerisms. Thus, children will imitate models of the same sex even before
they have acquired principles of gender constancy.

However, once the cognitive dimension of gender identity becomes fully
articulated via a gender schema, people of the same sex become particularly
salient to children. At this point children are more interested than they were
previously in observing many models to abstract a concept of masculinity
and femininity. External reinforcement by others is no longer needed. As
Maccoby and Jacklin (1974) put it, children begin the process of self-
socialization—children now are self-motivated to follow an internal system
of rules regarding gender-typed behavior.

These different facets of gender role and gender identity therefore follow
a developmental sequence: Identification and external rewards/punish-

ments may be most significant during the early stages of gender acquisition, whereas the observation of others and the formation of an intellectual framework for gender may be more significant as children mature into their gender identity and gender role. The important point is that children become active participants in their construction of gender identity. They seek out confirmatory evidence to help bolster their growing awareness of themselves as males or females.

CURRENT ISSUES IN GENDER DEVELOPMENT

The topic of gender development easily lends itself to a number of controversial issues and debates. The final section of this chapter considers the question of conducting bias-free research, the construct of androgyny, and gender roles and schooling.

Conducting Bias-Free Research

Research on gender roles and gender differences has been the victim not only of unclear and inaccurate terminology, but also of biases and false assumptions. In particular, researchers must be wary of the self-fulfilling prophecy, or the tendency to find differences because they are expected. Research exploring the differences between men and women has been published since the mid-nineteenth century. Shields (1975) graphically demonstrated how such research was used to support the investigators' assumptions about female inferiority. For example, in the early 1800s, when Franz Joseph Gall and Johann Spurzheim popularized phrenology (the identification of specific sites of brain tissue with specific intellectual and temperamental traits), "hard" evidence was found for differences between male and female brains. The frontal lobes, considered the seat of the intellect, were found to be less developed in females. At the turn of the century, however, the parietal lobes rather than the frontal lobes came to be viewed as the repository of intellectual prowess. Not surprisingly, evidence was found that the female frontal lobes were actually larger than the male frontal lobes, but females parietal lobes were smaller.

In all probability, such blatantly biased research would not make its way into today's public forum. However, researchers and consumers of research must be attuned to more subtle biases when examining the literature. Social science research often uses only male subjects to test and develop theories or does not test for sex differences when males and females both participate in the research (Frieze, Parsons, Johnson, Ruble, & Zellman, 1978). Furthermore, sex differences, when found, are more likely be published, and failure to find sex differences will not be published (Maccoby & Jacklin, 1974). Apparently, similarities between men and women are less interesting and appealing than differences. Even when such differences are found, considerable overlap between men and women occurs despite statistically significant differences. And researchers must continually guard against assuming that whatever sex differences are found originate in biological differences between male and female.

In addition to these possible sources of biases, researchers tend to use male subjects when they wish to examine "masculine" behavior (such as aggression) and female subjects when studying "feminine" behavior. It is no small wonder that only in the past decade has research on the role of the father in child development successfully taken its place alongside research on mother-child relationships. Furthermore, the procedures used for the measurement of variables often may subtly influence the research outcomes. For example, male subjects may be tested for aggression by observation of their behavior in a frustrating or potentially abusive situation, whereas females may be given a paper-and-pencil test of aggression.

Recently, the question of the value of studying sex differences altogether has been debated. Eagly (1987) and Rothblum (1988) contended that every psychology article should report sex differences in the hope that many findings of no differences or small differences would eventually make clear how similar the sexes are. Baumeister (1988), however, believed that researchers should stop studying sex differences completely, because small differences become exaggerated in the popular literature and because the reporting and discussion of sex differences perpetuate sex discrimination.

Androgyny

Androgyny
The incorporation of masculine and feminine characteristics in one person.

Before the late 1970s, the research and theory on gender typing emphasized the acquisition of sex appropriate behavior. The literature recently has shifted to an analysis of the significance of ***androgyny,*** a term that combines the Greek words for "male" and "female." Androgyny implies the incorporation of masculine and feminine characteristics in one person. The tendency to become androgynous increases during the latter half of the life span, although it is not exclusively characteristic of older adults (Turner, 1982). According to the major proponents of androgyny theory, an androgynous person is more flexible and adaptable, because he or she is not constrained to act in accordance with gender-typed expectations (Bem, 1974; Spence & Helmreich, 1978). An androgynous person can act in a feminine manner (nurturant and expressive) in one instance, and in a masculine manner (assertive and independent) in another. Thus, behavior conforms to the situation rather than to expectations based on stereotypes.

Bem (1974) criticized personality tests that sought to measure masculine or feminine traits because they put such traits on the same continuum. In other words, a person rated "high" on masculinity would have to be rated "low" on femininity. Bem constructed her own test of gender roles, the Bem Sex Role Inventory (BSRI). The BSRI treats masculinity and femininity as two separate scales, each composed of 20 traits. The BSRI also has 20 neutral traits that serve as filler items. Subjects rate the masculine traits (e.g., "competitive," "forceful"), feminine traits (e.g., "loves children," and "tender"), and neutral traits (e.g., "happy") on a scale of 1 to 7 indicating the degree to which these traits are true for themselves.

Four types of people can be scored by this scale. The androgynous person scores high on both masculine and feminine scales, the masculine person scores high only on the masculine scale, the feminine person scores high only on the feminine scale, and the undifferentiated person scores low on both scales. A similar type of test is the Personal Attributes Questionnaire (PAQ) of Spence and Helmreich (1978). It measures instrumental and expressive characteristics and yields a categorization scheme similar to that of the BSRI.

The first publications on androgyny suggested that androgynous people were more adaptable, flexible, and creative and higher in self-esteem than people who were gender typed (Bem, 1975; Bem, 1976; Spence & Helmreich, 1978). Although gender typing was once considered a "good" thing, a new standard of mental health evolved in the 1970s suggesting that a psychologically healthy individual is androgynous (Morawski, 1987; Ruble, 1988). However, recent research has indicated that androgynous behaviors are not necessarily more advantageous than gender-typed behaviors. Hall and Halberstadt (1980), for example, extended the work on androgyny to younger children. These researchers developed a children's version of the Personal Attributes Questionnaire and administered it to third- to sixth-grade boys and girls. Hall and Halberstadt also measured the children's self-esteem and obtained teacher and maternal ratings of the children's behavior. In addition to finding that masculinity, femininity, and androgyny can be assessed in children, the researchers also learned that for girls, higher masculine scores were related to higher IQ scores; high feminine scores were negatively related to math achievement. For both girls and boys, high masculine scores were related to more positive self-concepts. Interestingly, Hall and Halberstadt found that the androgynous children had the most positive self-concept, but teachers reported that the gender-typed children were the most socially mature.

Such results correspond to Baumrind's (1982) findings that although androgynous parents were themselves more personally competent than gender-typed adults, they were not necessarily the most effective parents. For example, androgynous parents were child-centered, but not authoritative; they were responsive to their children, but less demanding. Furthermore, sons of androgynous mothers were less socially responsible than those of gender-typed mothers, and daughters of androgynous fathers were less cognitively competent that those of gender-typed fathers.

Why does androgyny seem to be an indicator of competence in some areas and not in others? The way we think of androgyny has implications for the outcomes in research. Androgyny has referred to people who possess both masculine and feminine characteristics, and it has referred to people who develop both masculine and feminine personalities (Ruble, 1988). Furthermore, the literature suggests that androgyny really is measuring masculine behavior and high self-esteem, and thus any positive outcomes as a result of "androgyny" really are due to other factors (Basow, 1986). Another concern with the construct of androgyny is that it does not eliminate sex differences (Morawski, 1987). Men and women can be "androgynous" in different ways (Basow, 1986). One androgynous male, for example, can be warm, athletic, and aggressive, and another androgynous male can be analytical, fearful, and passive. Such character typologies are obviously not equivalent to each other.

Finally, current work on androgyny needs to look more carefully at what androgyny means within the context of the life cycle. The relative advantages of masculine and feminine behavior, and the transcendence of both, may change in meaning and adaptational significance during different phases of development.

Gender Roles and Schooling

School—a most powerful agent of socialization—has been examined with respect to its differential influences on boys and girls. Sex often is used as the basis for dividing up a class in seat assignments, gym classes, classroom chores, and spelling bees. In addition, boys often have difficulty in elementary school because the norms reward "feminine" behaviors such as sitting quietly, following instructions, and turning in neat work. In countries with more male teachers, such as Germany and Japan, boys have fewer reading problems than girls (the reverse is true for the United States). Similar results on reading tests have been obtained for U.S. and English boys who have been taught by male teachers (Shepherd-Look, 1982).

Girls like elementary school more than boys do, demonstrate high levels of achievement, and receive much less attention for disruptive behavior. However, despite all their positive experiences, girls' achievement in school declines as they progress up the educational ladder, as does their motivation for achievement. Conversely, boys become more serious and studious as they enter high school. If schools are unsupportive of males, why do they excel as a group? If schools provide a comfortable environment for girls, why do they fail to achieve? Answers to this paradox may be found in the literature on differences between teacher-female and teacher-male interactions, as well as the literature on parent and teacher expectations for school achievement.

Gender and Teacher-Student Interaction
Boys and girls are treated differently by their teachers as early as nursery school. Analysis of teacher-student interactions indicates that boys receive more scoldings and discipline from their teachers than girls do (Serbin, O'Leary, Kent, & Tonick, 1973). When boys behave in an approved fashion,

they receive their teacher's attention no matter where they are in the classroom. Serbin and her associates found that girls must remain close to their teacher's side to get their teacher's attention. Thus, boys are viewed as the troublemakers, but their independence and on-task behavior are also attention getting. Girls, in contrast, are encouraged to maintain close proximity to their teachers, even to the point of seeking physical contact. Such behavior was once interpreted as evidence that girls are more dependent than boys. However, girls seek to be close to an adult most often when they are in mixed-sex groups, as if they have an implicit understanding that an adult can moderate the boisterous and somewhat overwhelming behavior of boys (Maccoby, 1990).

In elementary school, girls manifest a phenomenon that Dweck (1977) called *learned helplessness in school.* In her analysis of teacher feedback to fourth and fifth graders, Dweck found that teachers are more likely to respond to their male pupils in regard to conduct problems or to nonintellectual aspects of their work, such as lack of neatness and motivation. Thus, boys learn that teachers are generally negative toward them because they are boys and that criticism is directed toward rather superficial features of their schoolwork. Girls, in contrast, are reprimanded far less often than boys, but when they do receive negative feedback, about 90 percent of it pertains to the accuracy and intellectual quality of their work. Thus, girls attribute their school failure to lack of ability rather than to lack of effort. The implications of these findings are far-reaching. Boys learn to try harder or to discount criticism in the face of failure, whereas girls are quick to doubt themselves and to give up trying. Perhaps this is one reason that boys begin to outshine girls as they progress further up the educational ladder. The finding that boys and girls receive different types and amounts of attention from their teachers has been replicated at both the preschool and elementary school level. However, teachers usually do not *actively* seek to treat boys and girls differently. Rather, teachers' behavior may reflect the fact that boys misbehave more frequently, call out answers, and demand teacher attention whereas girls seek to comply with the teacher-determined constraints of the classroom. Thus, teachers sustain or reinforce whatever sex differences already exist (Brophy, 1985).

Gender and Expectations for Academic Achievement

In the 1970s, educational psychologists focused on how self-fulfilling prophecies influenced academic achievement. Research beginning with the work of Rosenthal and Jacobson (1968) suggested that children often perform up to the level of their teacher's expectations. Later work in this area suggested that this "Pygmalion effect" is more potent and consistent when teachers' expectations, formed on the basis of group and individual attributes of their students, affect the self-perceptions of students (Brophy & Good, 1974; Proctor, 1984). Characteristics such as race, socioeconomic status, and gender are particularly prone to expectancy effects. In general, teachers attend less to their low-expectation students, place fewer demands on them, question such students less often, and do not give as much feedback as they do give high-expectation students.

The implications for gender and academic achievement are evident: In classrooms in which teachers have differential expectations of performance for males and females, the interaction between the predispositions of the students and teacher expectations may lead to gender-related differences in academic achievement (Lindow, Marrett, & Wilkinson, 1985). Such expectations may be particularly troublesome when the students' own expectations for achievement are segregated according to gender. The differential appeal of computers to boys and girls is one such example. A computer attracts boys like moths to a flame. In the classroom, at after-school projects, in video arcades, and in computer summer camps, the ratio of boys to girls is weighted heavily in the boys' favor. The research indicates that boys and men spend more time with computers and like them more than females do

Teachers often have differing expectations for girls and boys. Girls need to be encouraged to participate in activities that involve mathematics and scientific concepts.

(Lockheed, 1985). Such sex differences are most notable in the areas of computer programming and recreation. Sex differences are smaller for word processing activities, projects involving cooperative efforts, and activities that are personally relevant. Because computers are considered on the crest of the technological wave, girls may increasingly be left behind in a technological society (Lockheed, 1985).

Several reasons may explain why boys are more drawn to computers than girls are. Hawkins (1985) argues that schools often incorporate computer instruction within science and mathematics, two areas that have a long history of male domination. In addition, girls may steer away from computers because programming is a competitive, rule-based activity, and they fail to perceive the relevance of computers for their personal lives. Placement of computer curricula in an area designated as "computer literacy," as opposed to incorporation into math and science programs, may be an important step in the reduction of a gender-based caste system in technology.

Studies of self-perceptions of mathematics achievement provide an-other example of differential treatment. Parsons, Kaczala, and Meece (1982) compared fifth- through ninth-grade classrooms in which boys and girls had equally high expectations for success in mathematics with classrooms in which boys had higher expectations than girls. Boys and girls were given equal amounts of praise and criticism in the same-expectation classrooms. However, in the sex-differentiated classes, teachers were found to rely more on public responding, to have fewer private interactions, and to make more use of student volunteers for answers. In such classrooms, boys interacted more with teachers and received more of their praise. In a related study, Parsons, Adler, and Kaczala (1982) demonstrated that parental attitudes reinforced teacher and student expectations of differential mathematics achievement for boys and girls. Even when boys and girls performed similarly, parents believed that daughters had to work harder at math than sons, and that sons needed upper-level math courses but daughters did not. Furthermore, Parsons, Adler, and Kaczala found that parental expectations had a powerful influence on their children's own expectations for math performance.

Education in Adulthood: Women Return to College

Since the 1970s, adult women have been returning to college in increasing numbers (Smallwood, 1980). These are the women who traded in their career objectives and quest for academic excellence for the traditional role of wife and mother during the early adult years because they may have been socialized into believing that performing well in school and in a career was incompatible with femininity. However, as these women approached their 30s and 40s, they became less relationship oriented, although their responsibilities at home made them relationship bound (Datan & Hughes, 1985). The adult female college student thus experiences the "release from dumbness" (Troll, 1984) that directed her younger years, but must learn to balance her academic needs with commitments made to other people. Furthermore, the degree to which she succeeds in college may depend on the emotional and household support she receives from her spouse (Datan & Hughes, 1985). Despite the obstacles and detractions that face adult women college students, many are highly motivated, do exceptionally well in school, and go on to professional careers. Lillian Troll, a renowned gerontologist at the University of California-San Francisco, finished her Ph.D. and entered academia at age 50, and serves as a good example of the accomplishments of adult women who continue their education.

The discussion of gender and education is a suitable conclusion to a survey of the development of gender roles and gender differences. This is a topic of pragmatic, theoretical, and empirical significance. To be educated in the developmental implications of gender is to support programs to reduce teacher-expectancy effects and differential treatment of children because of their gender. To be educated about the development of gender roles is also to be more understanding of how individuals forge their concepts of masculinity and femininity throughout the life span.

Summary

1. The study of gender differences requires a distinction between a personal awareness of being either male or female (gender identity) and stereotypes of suitable male and female behavior (gender role stereotypes).
2. Both biological factors, such as prenatal hormones, and experiential factors, such as whether mothers work, have important consequences for gender role development.
3. Although children learn a great deal abut gender roles from their parents, such things as toys, television, and books have been found to be powerful socialization agents of gender roles.
4. The crystallization of a sexual identity into an overall identity becomes a central issue for the adolescent.
5. Male-female differences on measures of verbal, quantitative, and visual-spatial abilities emerge most consistently in the literature on adolescence. However, the gaps between the sexes on most tests of cognitive abilities have narrowed.
6. Married couples with young children tend to develop more gender-typed patterns of behavior (Gutmann's parental imperative). During middle age, greater flexibility in gender roles is observed.
7. In old age, retirement, health, and sexuality influence men's and women's perceptions of their gender. In addition, a double standard of aging exists in which social attitudes may be more negative toward older women than toward older men.
8. According to Freud's psychoanalytic perspective, gender identity is accomplished through resolution of the Oedipal complex, whereby the child incorporates the feminine or masculine behaviors of the same-sex parent.
9. Conditioning theory claims that gender roles are acquired through the shaping of children's behavior. Gender appropriate behavior is

praised or rewarded, and gender inappropriate behavior is punished, ignored, or criticized.

10. According to the social learning perspective, boys learn gender appropriate behavior from observing and imitating the masculine behavior of men, girls from observing and imitating the feminine behavior of women.

11. According to the cognitive developmental theory of Lawrence Kohlberg, children first label themselves as either male or female, next learn that their gender remains the same despite superficial changes in appearance and behavior, and then seek out gender appropriate models to observe.

12. The acquisition of gender schemas may help young children to sort the behaviors and characteristics of people into appropriate-for-male and appropriate-for-female categories.

13. Several possible sources of bias in research on gender roles include using only males to test and develop theories; publishing only those findings that report male-female differences; and assuming that found differences are biological in origin.

14. Androgyny implies the incorporation of masculine and feminine characteristics in one person. Major proponents of androgyny theory claim that an androgynous person is more flexible and adaptable, although critics claim that androgyny is synonymous with masculinity.

15. Schools provide different socialization experiences for boys and girls. The evidence suggests that teacher-student interactions and teacher expectations may reinforce gender differences and the self-perceptions of their students.

Key Terms

adrenogenital syndrome
(p. 585)
androgyny (p. 615)
climacteric (p. 596)
field independence
(p. 593)
gender (p. 582)

gender constancy
(p. 608)
gender identity (p. 583)
gender role preference
(p. 583)
gender role stereotype
(p. 583)

gender stability (p. 608)
hermaphroditism
(p. 579)
meta-analysis
(p. 605)
parental imperative
(p. 595)

schema (p. 612)
sex (p. 582)
sexual polarization versus bisexual confusion
(p. 591)

Review Questions

1. Review the distinctions between sex, gender, gender identity, and gender stereotypes. Why should these terms be distinguished? How has the confusion between sex and gender influenced our thinking about men and women?

2. How do the male and female gender role change at each phase of the life span? What roles do parents, teachers, spouses, and social pressures (from peers, media, the workplace) play in refining and changing gender roles and gender identity throughout the life span?

3. Of all the theories of gender role development discussed in this chapter, which one do you like best?

Discuss the features of your favorite theory and critique the other theories that were presented in this chapter.

4. A review of theories of gender role development and the corresponding research shows that boys and girls undergo different socialization processes. What evidence supports this contention, and what implications does it have for both male and female gender role development?

5. Design a bias-free research project on sex differences in aggression. What factors do you need to take into account to eliminate some of the earlier bias problems in such research?

6. What is androgyny? Why is the construct appealing? What is wrong with current views of androgyny? If gender typing and androgyny no longer can be viewed as desirable developmental goals, what can take their place?

Suggested Readings

Huston, A. C. (1983). Sex-typing. In P. H. Mussen (Ed.), *Handbook of child psychology.* (4th ed., vol. 4). New York: Wiley.

> A thorough survey of the literature since 1970 on sex typing in children. Included are definitions of sex typing, the development of sex typing, socialization of sex typing within the context of the family, and clinical interventions.

Basow, S. A. (1986). *Gender stereotypes. Traditions and alternatives.* (2nd ed.). Monterey, CA: Brooks/Cole Publishing.

> An interdisciplinary overview of the study of gender and gender stereotypes. Throughout the book, the author explicitly takes the perspective that gender stereotypes are imposed by society and not by physiology.

Money, J. & Ehrhardt, A. A. (1972). *Man and woman, boy and girl: The differentiation and dimorphism of gender identity from conception to maturity.* Baltimore: Johns Hopkins University Press.

> A fine discussion of prenatal sex differentiation and the significant findings of John Money's work on hermaphroditism. This book is for those interested in the psychobiology of sex and gender.

Richardson, L., & Taylor, V. (1989). *Feminist frontiers II.* (2nd ed.). New York: Random House.

> An anthology of contemporary feminist work that has significantly contributed to our understanding of the development of gender roles. This is a diverse set of readings that includes a number of cross-cultural comparisons, discussions of the male gender role, and issues such as the relationship of gender to work and the family.

Wilkinson, L. C., & Marrett, C. B. (Eds.). (1985). *Gender influences in classroom interaction.* Orlando: Academic Press.

> Discussions of the relationships between gender and school at the preschool, elementary, and high school levels. Students who wish an in-depth treatment of the relationship between educational practice and gender stereotyping will find current research and critical evaluation of the literature in this book.

Chapter Fifteen

Death and Dying

Study of Death and Dying

Biological Definitions of Death

Social and Psychological Definitions of Death

Research on Death and Dying

Biological Perspective

Genetic Theories of Aging and Death

Error Accumulation Theories of Aging and Death

Sociological and Anthropological Perspectives

Demography of Death and Dying

Sociological Explanations of Suicide

Sociological Explanation of Death Denial

Anthropological Perspective

Psychological Perspective

Psychoanalysis

Psychological Explanation of the Process of Dying

Developmental Perspective

Infancy

Early and Middle Childhood

Adolescence and Early Adulthood

Middle Age

Old Age

Conclusions About the Life Span Approach

Special Topics in Death and Dying

Bereavement, Grief, and Mourning

The Hospice Movement

Death and Dying in the Future

 Is there life after death? Even the most rigorous social scientific methodology has not developed a robust procedure for determining the answer to this question. However, the study of life after death gained legitimacy with the publication in 1975 of Raymond Moody's *Life After Life,* and more recently with Kenneth Ring's (1984) book, *Heading Toward Omega.*

Moody's work is an account of the experiences of 150 people who have experienced a "near death experience" (NDE), defined by Moody (1977) as "an event in which a person could very easily die or be killed (and may even be so close as to be believed or pronounced clinically dead) but nonetheless survives, and continues physical life" (p. 124).

Moody reported interviews with people who have been "brought back to life" from such events as heart attacks, surgical failures, and accidents. He found that the ability to experience did not cease upon near-death; rather, the reports by NDE victims were amazingly similar. People who underwent a near-death experience reported a subjective sense of being dead (they may have heard the pronouncement by the medical staff), a sense of being removed from one's body (often reported as floating above the body), clear observations of events and objects in the situation (such as the medical procedures undertaken to revive the patient), a feeling of moving through a dark region or tunnel, a flashback of one's life, the meeting of deceased friends and relatives, a brilliant and beautiful white light, and finally, a strong pressure—sometimes unwanted—to return. Moody's subjects also reported that the experience was extremely pleasant. They felt at peace and free of pain. Once "brought back to life," the NDE victims claimed that they had lost their fear and dread of death.

Moody's work was well received by the reading public but criticized by those who felt that his method of data collection was too casual. However, more systematic investigations of NDEs, such as those by Sabom (1982) and Ring (1980, 1984) have confirmed Moody's investigations. For example, Sabom (1982), a cardiologist, interviewed individuals whose medical records indicated that they had been clinically dead and revived. He found that 43 percent of his interviewees had an NDE and recounted a tale that very nearly mirrored the experiences reported in Moody's book (the majority of the interviews took place before Moody's book hit the bookstores in the North Florida community where Sabom collected his data.)

The work on NDEs has immense emotional appeal. However, several alternative interpretations of the meaning behind the NDE are possible. Siegel (1980), for example, claimed that the NDE is rooted in neuropsychological events that precede and follow the extreme crisis of near-death. Visual experiences could be the result of neural excitation of the visual pathways. Encounters with the dead, out-of-body experiences, and brilliant lights could be hallucinations and reenacted memories that result from the stress of a profound biological crisis. Noyes (1979) felt that the NDE was a result of the psychological defense mechanism of depersonalization, of a psychological detachment from one's body in the face of a catastrophic threat to one's being.

The popularity of work on NDEs reflects a sociocultural change in attitudes toward death in the United States. "Scientific" speculations about life after death have appeared since the late 1800s (Siegel, 1980) but only recently have they been accepted by both laypersons and professionals. As death and dying become less of a taboo topic, organizations such as the International Association for Near-Death Studies have become possible.

Thanatology (from Thanatos, the mythological Greek god of death) is the study of death and dying. The topic is new to the social sciences, but this largely uncharted territory has a rich history and ancient landmarks. The thanatological landscape not only yields mythology and old legends, but also significant implications for the study of human development. What are some of the reasons for including a chapter on death and dying in a book about life?

1. *Death is an organizer of time.* Kalish (1981) pointed out that death places a boundary on life. The awareness of the inevitability of death, as well as the uncertainty of its appearance, lends a tinge of urgency to our tasks. Why finish something today if we have an infinite number of tomorrows?
2. *Death is a marker event.* Developmentalists often refer to critical events in the life span of an individual as **marker events,** or life events. Although these events vary across individuals and cultures, birth, marriage, and retirement all can be considered critical events of the life span. Personal death and the death of those significant to us also may be considered marker events because of the many transitions to our lives that such deaths bring.
3. *Death is a significant dimension of adult development and aging.* Negative social attitudes toward the elderly may partly reflect the linkage between aging and death. As we age, we become less shielded from death because of an accumulation of personal losses of family and friends. Several major theories have recognized that the study of aging and death are inevitably yoked to each other. Butler (1968) proposed that the elderly

---

Thanatology

The study of death and dying (from Thanatos, the mythological Greek god of death).

Marker events

Idiosyncratic or normative critical events in the life span of an individual.

engage in a life review, or a reminiscence of past accomplishments with the aim of setting things in order before death. Erikson (1968) wrote that the major developmental crisis of old age involves maintaining a sense of integrity instead of despairing that life is nearly at its end.

4. *Death and dying may be viewed as a process.* Most people do not make the transition from "alive" to "dead" in a single moment. Dying typically is a psychological, social, and biological process that takes time. The developmentalist's construct of *stage* also may have something to offer to the literature on death and dying. If we commit ourselves to learning about the entire life span, death must be included as a significant dimension, or perhaps stage, of human development.

These four reasons underscore the idea that death gives meaning to life. The study of death and dying is largely interdisciplinary. A large portion of this chapter will discuss the literature on death and dying from biological, sociological, anthropological, and psychological perspectives. Each of these disciplines help us understand death and dying across the human life span. We also will attempt to demonstrate that death is a socioemotional phenomenon that changes in meaning and context with age.

THE STUDY OF DEATH AND DYING

The formal study of death and dying has several major aspects. The terms *death* and *dying* can take on many different meanings, and the meanings must be clear and appropriate. Once definitions have been derived, any research endeavor must carefully transpose them into measurable concepts. For example, how do we measure death anxiety, the development of death concepts, and personal attitudes toward death? These preliminary tasks, although not unique to this area of research, can be especially demanding in the field of thanatology. Take, for example, the task of defining *death* and *dying.* Pattison (1977) distinguished among biological, sociological, and psychological death.

Biological Definitions of Death

Most people view death as a biological event. As Jeffko (1980) pointed out, defining death used to be simple when it referred to the cessation of breathing and heartbeat (the cardiopulmonary definition). With the tremendous advances made in life support systems and organ transplantation, however, a need for more inclusive criteria for the determination of death became increasingly urgent. In 1968, the Ad Hoc Committee of the Harvard Medical School published guidelines for the determination of death. Significant is the emphasis placed on the cessation of brain activity—

Brain death
The most commonly accepted definition of death, which includes total lack of responsivity, lack of movements and reflexes, and a flat electroencephalogram (a recording of brain wave patterns).

commonly referred to as **brain death** in the list. Four criteria were listed for the determination of death (Beecher, 1968):

1. Total unreceptivity and unresponsivity, even to the most painful stimuli.
2. No movements for 1 hour as observed by a physician and no breathing for 3 minutes when taken off a mechanical respirator.
3. No reflexes (e.g., fixed and dilated pupils) and no brain stem activity.
4. A flat electroencephalogram (EEG, a measure of brain wave patterns).

In cases in which the determination of death was unclear (as when a person manifested no brain wave activity but breathing could be maintained with a respirator), the committee recommended that these criteria be reapplied 24 hours later. Cases of hypothermia (body temperature at 90 degrees Fahrenheit) and cases in which nervous system depressants were present were to be excluded.

These criteria have been widely accepted over the traditional cardiopulmonary definition of death, but not without controversy. In an effort to end possible "vegetative existences" in which an irreversibly comatose person can be sustained (sometimes for years, on life supports), the absence of consciousness has been proposed as the ultimate criteria in determining the time of an individual's death (Veatch, 1972). Until the seat of consciousness can be definitively linked to the neocortex, claiming death on the basis of a flat EEG alone will be a risky endeavor.

Many legislators have recognized that the determination of death has become an ambiguous affair and have attempted to legalize the process. Thus, many states have incorporated the cessation of cortical activity into their more traditional criteria. Currently, an attempt is being undertaken to make the criteria sufficiently broad so that they could be acceptable to all states. The Uniform Determination of Death Act, proposed by the President's Commission for the Study of Ethical Problems in Medicine and Biomedical and Behavioral Research (1981) determines death as the following:

> An individual who has sustained either 1) irreversible cessation of circulatory and respiratory functions, or 2) irreversible cessation of all functions of the entire brain, including the brain stem, is dead. A determination of death must be made in accordance with accepted medical standards. (p. 73)

The commission emphasized that the absence of functioning of the entire brain (including the brain stem) would provide a reliable way of declaring death, particularly in the case of individuals whose vital functions were being maintained by a respirator. The "whole brain" definition seems to have wider acceptance than a "higher brain" definition; not only have a number of professional organizations accepted the Uniform Determination of Death Act (including the American Bar Association and the American Medical Association), but as of September 1, 1987, 30 states had adopted the statute as is or in a variant form (Currens, 1988).

Social and Psychological Definitions of Death

The next two definitions of death differ from the first in one fundamental way: Although biological death is irreversible, the potential for reversal of social and psychological death is always present. *Social death* may be independent of biological death. Social death is based on another's failure to recognize a person as being among the living. A woman who enters a nursing home and is never acknowledged again by members of her family experiences social death (Kalish, 1981). Some nurses who do not respond as often to the call lights of the terminally ill as they do to those who may recover, and who avoid touching and eye contact with terminal patients consign them to social death (Kastenbaum & Aisenberg, 1972). People suffering from AIDS may experience a form of social death when others who fear contagion avoid them. Excommunication from a church and shunning of members of a tribal group or sect also may be viewed as forms of social death (Kastenbaum, 1977).

Psychological death (or phenomenological death) actually may be viewed in two different ways. The first interpretation refers to a state in which

Social death
An individual's or group's failure to recognize a person as being among the living.

Psychological death
A state in which self-awareness is absent (i.e., there is confusion and disorientation) or in which individuals no longer consider themselves living.

Ryan White poses in his Kokomo, Indiana bedroom after being barred from attending school in 1985. White later changed schools to one in Arcadia, Indiana where he was better received by students despite his having AIDS. White, who contracted AIDS from treatment for hemophilia, went on to win hearts and better understanding of the disease across the nation, before dying in 1990 at age 18. People suffering from AIDS experience a unique form of social death.

The AIDS quilt commemorates those who have died of AIDS in an effort to partially compensate for the social stigma the disease's victims bear.

self-awareness is absent, as when people are confused, disoriented, and only dimly aware of what is going on around them (Kalish, 1981). Some psychotic states also have been characterized as a form of psychological death, although in psychopathology it may be difficult to determine just what the individual is processing.

Psychological death may also result from severe cognitive impairment (dementia), as found in advanced cases of Alzheimer's disease. More prevalent after age 65, and responsible for at least half of the admissions to nursing homes, Alzheimer's can lead to an individual's forgetting basic facts as well as names of family members (Cohen, 1988). Such intellectual impairment may render dead the person's former sense of awareness, and family members may experience an "ongoing funeral" of their loved one (Kapust, 1982).

All three forms of death—biological, social, and psychological—often interact. Consider the situation in which a person is cut off from the community—social death. If the break is significant to the person, depression, lack of appetite, and neglect of personal hygiene and care may result. This situation may lead to a lack of interest in living and experiencing (a form of psychological death), and ultimately the stresses may lead to a breakdown in physiological defenses, leading to biological death. The path is usually not as straight as described here, but it has been observed in some elderly people who have lost spouses or were forced to retire or move to nursing homes.

Thus, we must clarify whether we are discussing biological death, social death, or psychological death. Many other meanings are associated with death and dying, but the three definitions provided here at least open up the field of thanatology to systematic investigation.

Research on Death and Dying

Many research tools available to the developmentalist have been used, or can be used, to investigate death and dying. Kubler-Ross (1969), for example, used the clinical case study to derive her stage theory of dying. Kastenbaum and Briscoe (1975), in a most creative piece of naturalistic research, related how pedestrians crossed a busy intersection in Detroit (an act of some life-threatening potential) to their answers on questions concerning death-related issues. (See *Research Close-up,* "A Naturalistic Study of Death Attitudes.")

Questionnaire and interview studies on death attitudes and death anxiety appear most frequently in the literature. Shneidman (1970) developed a 75-item questionnaire concerning attitudes, beliefs, and experiences involving death, dying, and suicide, and invited the responses of readers of *Psychology Today.* More than 30,000 people responded to the survey, providing concrete evidence that the general public has significant interest in death and dying.

The interview technique was demonstrated in a study by Kalish and Reynolds (1976), who conducted 1-hour interviews with African-American, Japanese-American, Mexican-American, and Anglo-American adults broken down into three age groups (20 to 39, 40 to 59, and 60 and over). Kalish and Reynolds asked more than 150 questions, such as "How often have you visited someone's grave, other than a burial service, during the past 2 years?" and "Should your friend who is dying of cancer be told that he or she is going to die?" The researchers found that many attitudes toward death and dying varied as a function of ethnic background and age, or both. This massive study concluded, among other things, that Anglo-Americans had the fewest encounters with death and avoided death-related phenomena more than the other three groups. Younger adults, as compared with the middle-aged sample, rarely dreamed of their own deaths. And Japanese-American and Mexican-American respondents were more conservative with regard to standards of grief and mourning than African-Americans and Anglo-Americans.

Psychological autopsy

An in-depth analysis of the life and death of an individual to determine the circumstances and subtle causes of the death.

Other research procedures have studied death themes in people's picture descriptions, analyzed population demographics (for example, what percentage of married men die each year), and performed the *psychological autopsy* (Kastenbaum, 1977). This involves an in-depth analysis of the life and death of an individual to determine the circumstances and subtle

Research Close-Up
A Naturalistic Study of
Death Attitudes

Kastenbaum and Briscoe (1975) noted that pedestrians crossing a busy intersection in Detroit could be classified into one of five categories based on how cautiously they crossed the street. The Type A pedestrian was the most careful crosser, who waited for the light to change, entered the crosswalk, moved at a brisk pace, and checked traffic before and during the crossing. At the other end of the continuum, Type E pedestrians typically crossed at a location other than the corner, from between parked cars, without looking, and against the light. Types B, C, and D fell in between these two extremes.

In the study, an observer classified the pedestrian's behavior in negotiating the intersection and then approached the pedestrian for a brief on-the-spot interview. The 125 males and females who participated in the study (25 pedestrians for each category) were asked about their typical street-crossing behavior, the types of safety precautions and risks they took behind the wheel of an automobile, their characteristic mood, and questions relevant to life-threatening behavior ["How much of the time do you consider your life to be in danger, in jeopardy?" (p. 40); "Have you ever attempted or contemplated suicide?" (p. 41); "To what age do you expect to live, want to live?" (p. 41).]

Kastenbaum and Briscoe found a startling relationship between the observed street crossing and self-reported life-threatening situations. Table A contains some of the results of the interview questions. The data indicate that the people who throw caution to the wind when crossing a busy street also are greater risk takers, are more likely to be suicidal, and do not expect or wish to live as long as the more cautious pedestrian. Only 5 out of 25 Type A crossers had been in an accident while driving, whereas all 23 of the Type E crossers who operated automobiles claimed to have been in at least one accident. Thus, by using both naturalistic and interview methods, Kastenbaum and Briscoe found that the most mundane of behaviors, such as crossing the street, is linked to a person's approach to life and death. Think about that the next time you are tempted to jaywalk.

Table A
Relationship between Death Attitudes and Street-Crossing Behavior

Death Attitude	Street-crossing Behavior				
	Type A	Type B	Type C	Type D	Type E
Percentage of time life was in danger during a typical week	2.1%	3.0%	6.6%	9.0%	16.1%
Had attempted or thought of suicide	8.0%	12.0%	16.0%	24.0%	32.0%
Age expected to live	81	77	72	69	67
Age wanted to live	92	89	82	77	69

Source: R. J. Kastenbaum & L. Briscoe. (1975). The street corner: A laboratory for the study of life-threatening behavior. *Omega, 6,* pp. 33–44. Adapted with permission from Baywood Publishing Company, Inc., and the author.

causes of death; the procedure involves researching a person's intentions, feelings, and experiences, as well as what family, friends, and medical staff did, hoped, and feared before the death. The psychological autopsy has been particularly useful in unearthing clues about motive in the case of a suicide.

Some problems in the research on death and dying, as in most research in other fields, involve the need for better sampling, validation of instruments, and checking reliabilities. However, thanatology encounters some unique obstacles as well. Attitudes such as "Death is unknowable, so don't attempt to examine it" and "Don't corrupt children who are naive about death" have been deterrents to thanatological research (Kastenbaum & Costa, 1977). Some have felt that asking the elderly and dying patients about their attitudes toward death is unfair and cruel. Furthermore, when individuals claim that they are not concerned about their own deaths, are they being honest or engaging in denial? Kastenbaum and Costa (1977) are critical of the lack of longitudinal research, particularly the cross-sequential designs that could assess age changes and age differences. Cohort analysis also could provide a valuable source of information about attitudes toward death and dying. For example, will the attitudes of the elderly of 2001 toward death be similar to the attitudes of the elderly in 1990? (For a more detailed discussion of developmental research methods, see Chapter 2.)

BIOLOGICAL PERSPECTIVE

Life expectancy
The number of years the average person is expected to live.

However defined, death in the biological sense seems the most absolute, the most certain. It is the ultimate common denominator between the royal and the plebeian. For most of human history, ills such as disease, famine, and war limited *life expectancy,* or the number of years the average person is expected to live. It was considered a great advance in civilization that, by 1800, life expectancy had reached 35 years in more industrialized countries (Gruman, 1966). An individual born in 1986 can be expected to live to 71.3 years if male, 78.3 years if female (U.S. Bureau of the Census). Perhaps death and aging are caused by extrinsic factors such as the mistakes of leaders and the limitations of the medical profession. If war, famine, and disease were eradicated, could we be immortal?

Consider the data on the longevity of the oldest known living persons. The extreme limit of the human life span has been estimated to be 110 years, a number that has remained relatively constant throughout history. Reports of individuals living far beyond this upper limit (over 140 years) in the Caucasus Mountains in the southern Soviet Union or in the Ecuadorean Andes have been viewed skeptically, because careful birth records have not been kept in these areas (Moment, 1978). Data on the human life span, therefore, suggest that death is inevitable after a certain number of years.

Such inevitability of death ultimately may serve evolutionary aims. Perhaps older organisms must be removed from the population so that they do not compete with reproductively capable younger organisms or immature organisms. Another evolutionary hypothesis proposes that evolution really did not program death. Instead, organisms are programmed to remain viable until offspring are produced and reared. Those of the prolongevity camp, however, point out that an equally viable hypothesis is that evolution may still be in the process of lengthening the life span.

Contemporary biologists have proposed that death may be genetically programmed or the result of a lifetime of wear and tear and biological errors. The following sections will review some of the relevant research and theories on the biological basis of death.

Genetic Theories of Aging and Death

Does a genetic biological clock program all living organisms for eventual death? Researchers who believe in such a genetic program point to the differential life spans of a variety of species; to the finding that females (who have XX rather than XY chromosomes) of many species, such as humans, rats, mice, fleas, and dogs, live longer than the males of each of the species; and to the finding that humans with long-lived parents tend to be long-lived themselves (Shock, 1977). Also, the average difference in age at death between fraternal twins is about twice as large as the average difference in age at death for identical twins (Kallman & Sander, 1948).

The probable source for the genetic basis of death is DNA, the genetic material located in the nucleus of every cell that has the potential for duplication. RNA, which transcribes the genetic code of the DNA and relays it for eventual protein synthesis, also may be involved. Perhaps, at some fixed point in the life of a cell, DNA ceases to duplicate itself, and the cell dies.

Confluency
The point at which duplicating cells cover, in a single layer, the entire available area of a growth container.

Some of the best-known experiments along these lines have been performed by Leonard Hayflick and his colleagues (Denny, 1975). Hayflick grew human fetal cells in a tissue culture growth medium. These fetal cells settled on the bottom of the bottle and began duplicating, eventually reaching a point at which the cells covered, in a single layer, the entire available surface area, a phenomenon known as *confluency*. Once confluency was reached, the cells ceased to duplicate themselves. However, Hayflick found that if he took half of these cells and put them in a new bottle, he once again could attain a population doubling, or confluency. Hayflick found that, on the average, the cell populations maintained a constant rate of doubling for about 50 population doublings, at which point the rate of cell doublings slowed down and eventually ceased altogether. This finding became known as the *Hayflick limit* and suggested a fixed capacity of DNA renewal, perhaps programmed into the DNA itself. Arguments that cells can live forever have been disputed by Hayflick (1987), who claimed that even when normal cells are cultured *in vivo* (i.e., transferred to new, young, inbred hosts) they have a finite number of population doublings. Cell lines that seemingly duplicate on into perpetuity are either cancerous or abnormal in some other fashion (Hayflick, 1987).

Not everyone agrees that death is programmed at the cellular level. Denckla (1975), for example, believed that a more global genetic death "clock" may be located in the body's endocrinologic system. The death clock promotes the deterioration of the circulatory and immunological systems (the systems most often implicated in the deaths of the elderly), eventually leading to heightened susceptibility to disease. Denckla proposed that a pituitary hormone that he labeled DECO (for decreasing oxygen consumption hormone) gradually becomes more significant as the organism ages. This pituitary hormone, acting upon another (thyroxine), may lead to a decrease in oxygen consumption, which is an age-correlated metabolic index. Could immortality be achieved once we learn how to synthesize anti-DECO pills?

Error Accumulation Theories of Aging and Death

Somatic mutation theory
A theory that proposes that aging and death are due to a lifetime of exposure to nonlethal radiation.

For those who like a sense of order to the timing of biological events, the notion of a death clock programmed in every individual, whether on the cellular or systemic level, has tremendous appeal. However, several theories claim that aging and death are the result of a lifetime of biological mishap and mayhem. One variation of this approach, **somatic mutation theory,** says that exposure to nonlethal radiation over a lifetime breaks the DNA chain, possibly causing cellular mutation and eventual death. Another approach claims that death and aging are due to the loss of a living organism's battle against disorganization, or entropy. Perhaps we die as a result of an accumulation of toxic materials in the body, a wearing out of vital tissues and organs, or a lifetime of stress. Another plausible hypothesis is that we die after a lifetime of errors in the chain of information transfer from the DNA molecule to the formation of a protein molecule (Shock, 1977). An additional proposal claims that free radicals, or chemical compounds that become unstable as a result of oxidation or radiation, are major culprits in aging and death. Because they react with many kinds of biological molecules (e.g., they sour food and ruin automobile tires), they may alter the composition of many compounds that are significant for the effective functioning of the body.

Thus, over time, the effective functioning of the body is hampered by the accumulation of mistakes in a variety of biological compounds. The effects of this accumulation are seen in the gradual changes we all experience when we age. The faulty compounds exponentially foster the creation of additional faulty compounds until a point known as *error catastrophe* may be reached—a total collapse of the system, or death.

At present, any one of the biological approaches has both advantages and disadvantages in its explanation of the causes of aging and death. Rosenfeld (1976) believed that all these causes may be operative. In other words, nature may have provided most organisms with several backup systems to ensure their eventual destruction. However, the hopes for prolonging a youthful, active life are becoming increasingly more realistic with every research hypothesis and empirical finding.

SOCIOLOGICAL AND ANTHROPOLOGICAL PERSPECTIVES

The experience of death and dying is not uniquely a biological event. It depends on our relationships with significant people in our lives, the roles we play in the lives of others (e.g., father, teacher, or scapegoat), and the way society and its various institutions are organized. In some respects, then, we could claim that no one ever dies alone. Instead, death derives its meaning from the social context in which it occurs. Even a hermit's death will affect the lives of others—ambulance personnel, who must go way over to the other side of town to fetch the body, medical professionals who must certify the death, the county coroner and cemetery workers who are responsible for dispensing with the body, and the statistician who must compile all the data relevant to the death of the hermit (e.g., age, sex, race, income, and place and cause of death). Perhaps our hypothetical hermit had a huge sum of money concealed in the walls of his shack, which city construction workers found while tearing the shack down. Whether or not the hermit left a will, the fallout from the discovery would be immense: the inevitable story on the five o'clock news; the legal wrangling to settle the estate; and a dramatic search for next of kin. Perhaps the hermit made a greater impact on others upon his death than he did during his life! Furthermore, all this activity, involving many individuals, illuminates several dimensions of society for us. For example, how much interest would the hermit have generated had newspaper rather than dollar bills lined the walls of his shack? Perhaps the cursory treatment the hermit may have had in the emergency room of the hospital reflects social attitudes toward presumably lower socioeconomic-status individuals (Sudnow, 1967).

Obviously, this example is exaggerated to illustrate several dimensions of the sociological perspective. Kastenbaum (1986) claimed that the death of an individual involves a sociophysical network known as the **death system**. The death system involves people, places (e.g., cemeteries), times (e.g., Memorial Day), objects (e.g., the obituary section of the newspaper), and symbols (e.g., the color black as a sign of mourning). The components of the death system are fluid and depend on the circumstances. For example, the funeral director may always be part of the death system, but the florist is more sporadically involved. The death system also is inherently tied into the prevailing values and norms of a particular culture. In the United States, where a strong investment is made in the prevention of death, much effort is directed toward eradicating disease and legislating against life-threatening behavior. Kastenbaum (1986), however, noted that the death system in the United States also gives high priority to white, young, middle-class

Death system
The relationship between society and death involving people, places (e.g., cemeteries), events (e.g., Memorial Day), and symbols (e.g., the color black).

The funeral is a readily visible part of our death system. Opponents of the funeral claim that its expense exploits the recently bereaved. Supporters contend that the funeral is an essential element in the grief process.

individuals in its death-prevention efforts. Practices in the death system also change with time. Whereas the U.S. funeral at the turn of the century was a home-centered event that intimately involved the immediate and extended family, present-day funerals are primarily supervised by funeral directors and take place at funeral homes.

The sociological perspective on death and dying has several important facets. It has contributed a sophisticated methodology to the social sciences that includes analysis of population dynamics (demography) and the construction of questionnaires and interviews that have resulted in several cross-national surveys on attitudes toward death and dying. A subarea of sociology, known as *medical sociology,* has investigated the medical profession's treatment of and attitudes toward the dying. Sociologists, beginning with the pioneering work of Emile Durkheim (1951), have also made a number of important contributions toward our understanding of suicide. Finally, several sociological theories of death and dying have been formulated that attempt to analyze the relationship between the dead and living in a given society.

Demography of Death and Dying

Demography offers a good starting point for research on death and dying. For example, in the United States, infant mortality rates have declined dramatically (162.4 per 1,000 in 1900 as compared with 10.4 per 1,000 in 1986); the chances of living to a ripe old age are better than ever for a very

Issues in Human Development
Funerals

Funeral practices in the United States were rarely questioned until the appearance in 1963 of Jessica Mitford's *The American Way of Death* and Ruth Mulvey Harmer's *The High Cost of Dying.* Both Mitford and Harmer claimed that funeral practices exploited the bereaved for the profit of a well-endowed funeral industry. They contended that funerals were too expensive and that people really could not afford them. Mitford and Harmer also accused the funeral industry of using unethical practices to make money. Despite the fact that funeral directors (or "grief counselors," as they tend to call themselves these days) present themselves as a support system at the time of death, the little available evidence suggests that they are profit-minded people who have not considered death on complex and deep levels (Kastenbaum & Aisenberg, 1972). Inexpensive caskets may be displayed in sickly colors, and inexpensive funeral packages may be labeled "a pauper's funeral." Responding to perceived abuses, the Federal Trade Commission in 1984 put into effect its Trade Regulation Rule on Funeral Industry Practices. This rule mandates that detailed information about prices and legal requirements are provided to those making funeral arrangements (Office of the Federal Register, National Archives and Records Administration, 1989).

However, traditional funeral practices also may serve useful functions. Critics of U.S. funeral practices, according to their advocates, are highly insensitive to the psychological, philosophical (or religious), and social values of funerals. Raether (1971) believed that funeral and burial services give the bereaved an opportunity to face the reality of the death, to express grief over the loss of a significant other, to receive the support of family and community, and to place death within a meaningful context. In addition, funeral directors may have been presented in an unfair light. Because they are so closely associated with the dead, they may be the targets of the hostility and anger that the bereaved often feel.

Thus, although our treatment of the dead has become highly bureaucratized and subject to abuse, the socially approved patterns of behaviors surrounding the preparation and burial of the dead may bring a sense of order at a chaotic time in a person's life. In this regard, our rituals surrounding the dead have a common purpose with those of the past and of other cultures. A 1979 survey of the recently bereaved found that 96 percent were satisfied with the services provided by the funeral homes (Kalish & Goldberg, 1979–1980). Children, too, have been found to benefit from attendance at funerals, if they are not forced to go, and if a supportive adult is available to answer questions and provide information (Weller, Weller, Fristad, Cain, & Bowes, 1988).

large number of people. The United States, as well as other countries, is moving toward what has been called a *gerontocracy:* More and more elderly people will become influential as their power base grows as a function of their sheer numbers.

A major reason for the recent trends in both life and death rates is the control of the major communicable diseases that were the leading causes of death in 1900 (e.g., influenza, pneumonia, and tuberculosis). Childhood diseases such as whooping cough, measles, and scarlet fever also exacted their toll in the past. Today, the major causes of death are chronic degenerative diseases, or diseases that occur in later life and are somehow related to the aging process (e.g., diseases of the heart; malignant neoplasms, or cancer; and vascular lesions affecting the nervous system).

When Lerner (1980) divided the population of the United States into three (admittedly crude) socioeconomic levels, several interesting mortality patterns were found. Members of the poverty class (the poor in large-city ghettos and the rural poor) tended to die from communicable diseases, whereas the affluent middle and upper classes were most likely to die from degenerative diseases. The blue-collar working class (most semiskilled and unskilled workers) seemed to have the best of both worlds. They had access to good medical care that minimized the incidence of communicable diseases, and they did not experience the diseases that were associated with the stresses of maintaining "the good life."

Demographic data also provide some interesting insights into where people die. Most people would prefer to die at home (Kalish & Reynolds, 1976), but a large rise in the percentage of deaths in hospitals has been observed—from 50 percent in 1949 to 70 percent in 1970 (Baum & Baum, 1980). The increase in the number of degenerative diseases as a major cause of death has been a major factor in the shift from home to hospital deaths. This rise has had a profound impact on a medical profession that has been trained in the maintenance of life. No doubt the increasing interest in hospices (which will be discussed in greater detail later in this chapter) is a reflection of the changes in where death occurs.

Sociological Explanations of Suicide

Almost 30,000 Americans a year commit suicide (U.S. Government Printing Office, 1987). The suicide rate for any given year varies as a function of age, race, and gender. Consistently, the number of completed suicides has been highest for white males in all age categories (Kastenbaum, 1986). Although teenage suicide has been a newsworthy topic, ranking as the third cause of death for this particular age group, statistics reveal that white elderly males have the highest rate of all. They are 2 times as likely to commit suicide as elderly black males, 5 times as likely as elderly white females, and 17 times as likely as elderly black females (U.S. Government Printing Office, 1987). In all likelihood, these figures underrepresent the actual number of people who take their lives each year, and they certainly do not reflect the hundreds of thousands who are affected by someone else's suicide.

To take one's life intentionally is incomprehensible to many of us. One theoretical model that has been useful in explaining suicide derives from the hypothesis, originally presented by Durkheim (1951), that suicide is a result of an imbalance or upset in the relationship between an individual and society. For example, the potential for suicide increases when an individual's social world is destroyed by a catastrophe or trauma, or when an individual is excessively integrated within his or her social world (as when more than 900 people took their lives in Jonestown, Guyana, on November 20, 1978).

People who exist on the fringes of society in any way also are at greater risk for suicide. Recent extensions of Durkheim's perspective have focused on this notion of social or status integration to predict which groups of people may be at greatest risk for suicide (Martin, 1968).

Sociological Explanation of Death Denial

The study of the effects of social factors on the individual's perception of death and dying has made a valuable contribution to thanatology. However, this dimension of the literature on death and dying has been a mere spark compared with the bonfire of sociological theory on the denial of death. Becker (1973) has written a scathing attack on the injustice our society has done to its members in refuting the existence of death, although the fact that his *Denial of Death* was a best-seller may refute his major premise!

Perhaps all the hoopla about our denial of death has outlived its usefulness as an explanatory construct. Fresh insights can be obtained when creative thinkers take old ideas and shake them upside down. Baum and Baum (1980) are two sociologists who did just that in their analysis of the relationship between society and death (the death system). They contended that our society does not deny death as much as avoid it, primarily because of our lack of experience with death. We are unprepared to cope with our own death or the with deaths of others, because most of us have had few encounters with dying people.

Furthermore, the death of others does not have quite the same impact on our sense of self as it did during preindustrial times. In preindustrial societies, specific people played many interrelated and irreplaceable social roles and thus affected the lives of many others. For example, Mr. Smith was the town blacksmith; he also was the mayor and the organizer of community celebrations. His death would have affected more people in a personal way than it would in contemporary society, where people maintain segmented and interchangeable roles. Today an empty desk chair is quickly filled after the death of a co-worker.

Only the deaths of a few people (family and close friends) threaten both our sense of immortality and our sense of self. Because such experiences are fewer in number now than in the past, we are caught off guard when death occurs. We also do not know how to share emotions and thoughts with those who are dying or grieving. "I wish I knew what to say" is a common lament of the would-be consoler. So uneducated are we about the procedures that are necessary when someone close to us dies that we must hire a professional (the funeral director). Baum and Baum claim that unpreparedness, rather than fear of death, promotes a pulling back from those who are dying or bereaved.

Support for this **unpreparedness hypothesis** may be garnered from an examination of the training (or lack of training) received by medical professionals with regard to death and dying and in their behaviors toward

Unpreparedness hypothesis
The contention that our society does not deny death as much as avoid it because of of our lack of experiences with, and preparedness for, death.

the terminally ill. For example, Baum and Baum found that both physicians and nurses do not receive much formal classroom or clinical training in the care and treatment of the dying. The unfortunate omission of thanatology from the medical curriculum is not so much a function of death denial as a result of the emphasis placed on the curing of illness. So significant is the emphasis upon cure that death is regarded as a failure by some physicians, particularly by those who do not regularly encounter death in their specializations. Consequently, the institution of the hospital, where most people die, is not geared toward meeting the social and psychological needs of the terminally ill. Kalish (1981) aptly reported that many physicians suffer emotional anguish over the death of their patients, which may magnify their feelings of impotence and guilt. Nurses, because of their caring (as opposed to curing) role, read books about death and attend conferences and workshops on the subject (Kalish, 1981).

Baum and Baum (1980) pointed out that the blame for the social abandonment of the dying patient should be placed on institutional norms that do not provide training on death and dying for medical staff and that emphasize cure over care. Medical staff usually do attend to the physical needs of the terminally ill, but the staff members do not develop an adequate support system and satisfying social interaction pattern with the terminally ill.

Unpreparedness for death may also account for why so many of us feel inept at consoling the bereaved. How often do we avoid a friend or relative who has suffered a loss because we do not know what to say? Jensen (1980) advised: (1) say little on an early visit; (2) avoid cliches and easy answers ("He had a good life," or "You're young, you can have more children"); (3) encourage others to visit or help with practical matters; (4) accept silence; (5) be a good listener; (6) do not attempt to tell the bereaved how they feel; (7) do not probe for details about the death; (8) comfort children in the family (who often are ignored at such times of intense stress); (9) avoid talking to others about trivia in the presence of the recently bereaved; and (10) give the bereaved time to deal with personal feelings and reintegrate the loss into their lives.

Greater concern and awareness of our lack of preparedness for death has led to what is known as the *death education movement*. Professional groups in particular (e.g., nurses, physicians, psychologists, law enforcers) are beginning to realize that significant gaps in their training would be filled by courses on death and dying. Although scarcely a few university courses were offered on the topic during the 1960s, more than 1,000 such courses were available in colleges, nursing schools, and high schools at the beginning of the 1980s (Noland, Richardson, & Bray, 1980). Those involved in the death education movement also have worked on making the topic suitable for the preschool and elementary school levels using a "teachable moment" approach (Leviton & Forman, 1974). Here, the assumption is that death education should be a long-term process geared to different developmental levels and needs (Freiberg, 1975; Galen, 1972; Leviton & Forman, 1974).

At present, the research evaluating the success of death education programs has not found any clear-cut patterns. Some find no differences in the reduction of fear of death as a result of taking a death and dying course (see, e.g., Mueller, 1976), but others find that death education does promote a significantly greater cognitive awareness of and more positive attitudes toward material typically covered in thanatology courses (see, e.g., Leviton, 1975, 1977; Linn, Linn, & Stein, 1983; Noland, Richardson, & Bray, 1980).

In sum, the sociological perspective integrates many important facets of the relationship between death and society. Analysis of population dynamics, results from surveys, and observations of hospital staff and their patients fill out the skeletal outlines of sociological theory. The characterization of our death system as unprepared and ignorant is actually more theoretically and pragmatically useful than the death denial perspective. Whereas the latter perspective offers a sad commentary on the current state of affairs, the former perspective offers the hope of solving some of the current dilemmas of our death system through carefully constructed educational programs.

Anthropological Perspective

The anthropological perspective on death and dying is intimately linked with the sociological perspective. By examining the beliefs, attitudes, and behaviors of various cultures, the anthropologist attempts to tease out the universal (i.e., common to all) dimensions of death and dying, as well as that which is particular to a given culture (i.e., its death system). Anthropologists have learned that the universality of death has resulted in common beliefs and parallel attitudes between disparate societies. For example, the belief in an afterlife may be a fundamental component in all religions and cultures (Achte, 1980). In our culture, we honor our dead because somehow they "know" we are at their gravesite. The Karelians of Finland are careful not to put any metal objects in the coffin of the deceased to prevent the metal from sparking as the dead cross the river of Hades (Achte, 1980).

An interesting parallel to western notions of "appropriate death" (living the end of one's life according to the wishes of the individual) comes from the Kaliai (a Melanesian-speaking people from West New Britain, New Guinea) belief in what constitutes the "good death" (Counts, 1980). When a Kaliai is dying, an effort is made to sever social ties by slackening work activities, putting financial obligations in order, and becoming removed from social relationships. This death ideal of the Kaliai is strikingly similar to our notions of disengagement (Cumming & Henry, 1961) and acceptance of death (Kubler-Ross, 1969).

Another prevalent theme found in other cultures reflects the belief that the dead have influence on the living. In many native American groups, the soul or spirit of a recently deceased person is believed to hover near the place of death before passing on to the world of the dead. For the Yoruba of

Southwestern Nigeria, chickens are killed and their blood put in the grave of the deceased so that the soul will not bother surviving relatives (Williams, 1965).

Many times, however, the death-related beliefs found in other cultures are quite different from those found in our own. In several cultures, death is believed to result from an external agent (often magical), such as a sorcerer, evil spirit, or hostile human (Counts, 1980; Simmons, 1945). The Kaliai contend that it is possible to die from the wear and tear of an aged body. However, this ideal death can only happen to the rare individuals who have lived so careful a life that they have not run into demons or offended people. Such attributions differ from those of our own culture, where all too often we believe that we are solely responsible for our own deaths.

Death and dying are considered universal cultural categories, but the rituals and practices that various peoples have devised to cope with death and dying are amazing in their number and diversity. The deceased may be burned, buried, eaten (cooked or raw), embalmed, smoked, pickled, dismembered, abandoned, or ritually exposed (Huntington & Metcalf, 1979). The value of the anthropological perspective, claimed Huber (1980), is that it demonstrates that these behaviors and rituals are not mere manifestations of bizarre superstitions, but instead maintain important features of a society's order and continuity. Examples of death and dying in other cultures should underscore an awareness that death and dying occur within a social structure and cultural context.

Death is universal, but each culture has its own rituals and practices to deal with death. Shown here is an Indian funeral pyre.

Issues in Human Development
How the Hmong in the United States Cope with Death

 When an ethnic group migrates to another country, conflicts can arise between the burial customs of two different cultures. Such is the case of the Hmong refugees from Laos, 60,000 of whom have settled in the United States during the past decade, mostly in California, Minnesota, and Wisconsin. The Hmong lost 10 percent of their population while fighting the Pathet Lao and North Vietnamese who invaded their country in the 1960s (Sherman, 1988) and another 35 percent died in their flight to Thailand. Hayes and Kalish (1987) claimed that the experiences of surviving Hmong are akin to the emotional numbing witnessed in survivors of the Holocaust.

In the United States, the clash between Hmong burial customs and U.S. traditions and laws have been an additional source of anguish to the Hmong, and especially to the Hmong elderly. In Laos, the Hmong were able to pick their own burial spot, which did not require approval in a sparsely populated mountain area. "It is difficult to accept that I cannot have freedom to decide where I am to be buried. In Laos, the old found comfort knowing where they were to be placed" said an elder Hmong in an interview with Hayes and Kalish (1987, p. 67).

Traditional Hmong burial practices also involve the use of a sacrificial cow and the keeping of a horse in the yard of the deceased. The duration of funeral activities is 2 weeks, involving chanting, feasting, and a procession on foot to the burial spot. Many of these practices are related to the Hmong belief that for 13 days after the burial the soul undergoes a transformation from a human state to a spiritual one. It is easy to see how difficult it would be for residents in areas like southern California to accommodate to such practices.

The discordance in death-related customs are exacerbating the severe mental health problems many older Hmongs face as they try to adjust to a new life in the midst of so much loss. In U.S. cities that have a large Hmong population, several funeral homes are trying to make adjustments to meet the needs of bereaved Hmongs, if only in symbolic form.

PSYCHOLOGICAL PERSPECTIVE

The psychological perspective of death and dying examines an individual's thoughts, feelings, and behaviors with respect to death and dying. The psychoanalytic theorists (notably Sigmund Freud) were contemporary pioneers in the consideration of how death affects the psychological makeup of an individual. Much of the psychological assessment of death anxiety stems from the psychoanalytical tradition. The stage theory of dying has been a more recent development in the psychology of death and dying. This section will consider both of these unique contributions of psychology to the thanatological literature.

Psychoanalysis

Freud certainly dwelt on topics that were unpopular for his time; along with sex, Freud tried to grapple with how the inevitability of death affects the human psyche (see Chapter 10). The resulting hypothesized death instinct (thanatos) has been acknowledged by many as one of the most controversial aspects of Freud's theory (Kalish, 1981). According to Freud (1959), all living matter eventually must return to the inorganic state that is part of its evolutionary history. We all have this fundamental need to die, but our unconscious cannot accept the reality of death and behaves as though it were immortal. However, thanatos may manifest itself in daily behavior by way of smoking, reckless driving, accident proneness, and the like. Suicide would be the result of stress becoming so great that the tendency toward self-destruction overwhelms the defense mechanisms of the self. In the Freudian model, the tendency for self-preservation is overcome by the desire to destroy an internalized other. Thus, suicide represents the "murder" of a symbolic person, whereas in reality it is the killing of the self.

The unconscious also becomes the repository for death fears and anxieties. Death becomes either inadmissible or anxiety provoking when it can no longer be denied. Thus, the Freudian legacy to the psychological dimension of thanatology may be the constructs of both death denial and death anxiety.

Erikson did not refer to a death instinct in his eight-stage model of development (see Chapter 10). Instead, the issue of death became an integral dimension of the eighth crisis, integrity versus despair. Within the shadow of death, individuals attempt to assess whether their lives were lived according to value principles and whether what was done was meaningful. A negative evaluation, on the one hand, may led to a sense of disgust and despair over the lost chances of their one and only life. A sense of integrity, on the other hand, is attained by aging people who accept their lives as lived and who feel that there was value in the deeds of the past and the legacy of the future:

> Clinical and anthropological evidence suggests that the lack or loss of this accrued ego integration is signified by disgust or despair; fate is not accepted as the frame of life, death not as its finite boundary. Despair expressed the feeling that time is short, too short for the attempt to start another life, and try out alternative roads to integrity. (Erikson, 1968, p. 140)

Along a different but compatible vein, existential psychologists such as Rollo May (1953) and Viktor Frankl (1963) alluded to the fundamental need for meaning in life. Such meaning is enhanced by the acceptance and acknowledgement of death. Existential psychologists claim that this awareness structures the way in which we conduct our lives.

The psychoanalytic and existential approaches often have served as the theoretical basis for research on death fear and death anxiety. The research consistently finds that when individuals are directly questioned about death, they rarely admit that they fear it (Kalish, 1981). However, more indirect methods of questioning (such as having people fantasize about their own deaths) suggest that many people fear death (Feifel & Branscomb, 1973).

What conclusions can be drawn from the research and theory on death fear and death anxiety? The most definitive statement that can be made is that this is an area crying out for more work (Kastenbaum, 1988). We have to be careful to recognize that death fear and death anxiety are not the same and that each is probably made up of several components, such as death avoidance, death fear, death denial, and a reluctance to interact with the dying (Nelson & Nelson, 1975). We also must try to learn if the fear of death is universal, normal, and adaptive, as Becker (1973) and Kalish (1981) claimed.

Kastenbaum and Costa (1977) are frustrated by psychologists who support the hypothesis that fear of death is normal. They claim that only psychologically disturbed populations consistently manifest death anxiety:

> The more parsimonious interpretation that fear of death is an exceptional phenomenon limited to disturbed populations is rarely entertained. While defensive denial of death concerns may or may not characterize most individuals, denial of the evidence seems to characterize most researchers. (Kastenbaum & Costa, 1977, p. 235)

Psychological Explanation of the Process of Dying

Thus far, more emphasis has been placed on death (the state and event) than on dying (the process). In many ways, the study of an individual's psychological confrontation with an interval of time in which death is anticipated is a contemporary concern. As mentioned previously, more people now than in the past are dying from degenerative diseases and are told of the prognosis fairly soon after diagnosis. According to estimates, in the United States between 100,000 and 1.2 million people each year become aware of their impending death, and half of these individuals live with this knowledge for at least 3 months (Schulz & Schlarb, 1988). This period of time, labeled the *living-dying interval* (Pattison, 1977), has a profound impact on the perception of virtually all of an individual's existence.

As obvious as this may seem, the psychological impact of this living-dying interval was not systematically explored until Swiss-born psychiatrist Elisabeth Kubler-Ross published *On Death and Dying* (1969), a compassionate account of her clinical experiences with approximately 200 terminally ill patients. Kubler-Ross's (1969) work led to her formulation of a theory of five stages experienced by the dying person:

1. *Denial and isolation.* People declare, "No, not me!" upon learning that they have a terminal illness. In addition to denying impending death, they may try to isolate feelings from thoughts about death.
2. *Anger.* "Why me?" queries the dying person. Once death is admitted, everyone and everything becomes the object of fury and rage. Behavior at this stage tests the patience and sympathy of all involved with the dying person.
3. *Bargaining.* At this point, a change in strategy occurs. Usually kept as a secret between themselves and God, dying people attempt to bargain for a postponement of the death sentence.

4. *Depression.* The dying person can no longer deny the severity of the illness because of more surgery, progressive weakness, or symptoms. An overwhelming sense of loss accompanies the acknowledgment of death.
5. *Acceptance.* The dying person who has worked through mourning of the self is no longer anguished by impending death. Acceptance of death is characterized by a disengagement from people and activities, as well as periods of rest and reminiscence.

Kubler-Ross's book rapidly became the authoritative work on death and dying, for it filled the information gaps felt by clinicians working with the dying and the theoretical gaps felt by thanatologists writing and researching the area. Kubler-Ross's work has had a profound impact on the study of death and dying, but it should not be viewed as a how-to manual for dying.

On a pragmatic level, much criticism has been leveled against medical practitioners who have applied the theory in an uncritical and simplistic fashion. In some cases, dying patients have been encouraged to proceed through the stages outlined by Kubler-Ross, and patients become concerned about whether they are "dying the right way" (Kalish, 1976). Many dying people do exhibit the behaviors of each stage, but any stage may occur at any time during the dying process. Thus, denial and acceptance may alternate throughout a large proportion of the living-dying interval (Shneidman, 1980). Some question whether acceptance actually should be the final goal of dying. Rather, maintaining the integrity and personhood of the dying person should be the key element to an "appropriate" death (Feifel, 1990). Schulz and Schlarb (1988) concluded that emotions such as fear, anger, sadness, and depression are common to the dying process, and they appear in no particular order.

Kubler-Ross's theory has been criticized on empirical grounds as well. Her theory was not derived from a systematic research program and should not be accepted as proven fact (Kastenbaum, 1975; Kastenbaum & Costa, 1977). For example, Schultz and Aderman (1974) found that rather than going through a series of stages, patients adopt their own particular modal pattern of behavior that is maintained throughout the living-dying interval. Because Kubler-Ross worked primarily with cancer patients, her theory may be more applicable to their dying than to those suffering from, say, emphysema or heart disease. Along these lines, what is the response to dying of those individuals with acquired immune deficiency syndrome (AIDS), not only a life-threatening disease, but a stigmatized disease as well? Sex differences may even affect the dying process, for women report concern about the impact of their illness on others, whereas men voice concern about pain, dependence, and loss of job (Kastenbaum, 1975).

Glaser and Strauss (1968) found that the dying process may be affected by duration (e.g., sudden, slow, or erratic pacing) and shape through time (e.g., steady downhill pattern or erratic pattern). This combination of duration and shape of the dying process constitutes a *dying trajectory.* Perhaps the Kubler-Ross stages of dying interact in some significant way with the patterns of these dying trajectories. A slow lingering trajectory, for example, may provide the time necessary to work through all the death issues proposed by Kubler-Ross. A quick trajectory, however, may lead to more denial and anger than acceptance, whereas an erratic trajectory may encourage the emotional roller coasters observed by so many who have worked with the terminally ill.

Kubler-Ross emphasized that hope persists throughout the entire process of dying, even during the stage of acceptance. This is a crucial element of her theory and one that unfortunately has been overlooked too often. A lack of hope may lead the dying person to be overwhelmed by a sense of learned helplessness (Kastenbaum & Kastenbaum, 1971), a sense of having little control over fate, and little hope for recovery. Some fascinating evidence indicates that psychological attitudes may have a significant effect on the dying trajectory. Weisman and Worden (1975), using the psychological autopsy, found that cancer patients who had good interpersonal relationships until the very end and who accepted the seriousness of their illness but not the inevitability of death lived longer than those who had a poor emotional support system, had had destructive relationships in the past, and were depressed and pessimistic.

Thus, there literally may be a will to live. A survey of the literature that examined the relationship between psychological traits and either predisposition toward or cure of cancer suggests that a lonely, passive, and repressed existence may make people more prone to become cancerous and die sooner than a more emotionally open and aggressive existence (Holden, 1978). In a footnote, Holden (1978) cited a most vivid demonstration of how the psychological dimension of hope can influence death:

> One thought-provoking case history, reported by Bruno Klopfer in *Psychological Variables in Human Cancer:* A man with advanced lymphosarcoma was included in an experimental study of the since-discredited drug Krebiozen. After one administration, his tumors disappeared. When reports came out that the drug was ineffective, he again became bedridden. His physician, in a last-ditch attempt to save him, told him not to believe what he read and treated him with "double strength" Krebiozen—actually an injection of water. The man again experienced rapid remission. Then the AMA and FDA pronounced the drug worthless. The man died within a few days. (p. 1369)

DEVELOPMENTAL PERSPECTIVE

The classic study by Nagy (1948) on the development of death concepts in children will introduce the developmental perspective on death and dying. During the 1930s, Nagy asked more than 400 children from Budapest, Hungary, aged 3 to 10 years, to write, draw, and talk about death. Her analysis of the children's responses resulted in one of the first systematic studies of the child's concept of death, as well as the dubious honor of being named "Auntie Death" by the children she had interviewed. Nagy (1948) found that the child's understanding of death progressed through three stages that roughly corresponded to the age of the child:

1. The child between the ages of 3 and 5 has a rather global and unformulated notion of death. Life and consciousness are attributed to death, and death is considered a temporary state akin to sleep. Thus, T. Pintvoke, 4½ years, said, "At funerals you're not allowed to sing, just talk, because otherwise the dead person couldn't sleep peacefully. A dead person feels it if you put something on his grave" (Nagy, 1948, p. 10).
2. During the early childhood years, ages 5 to 9, Nagy found that death was personified. Death often was thought of as a skeleton, a ghost, a bad man, or the traditional reaper who more often than not worked at night. The death man could be outsmarted or outrun, so a privileged few did not die. Thus, claimed Br. Marta, who was 6½ years old, "Once I talked about it and at night the real death came. It has a key to everywhere, so it can open the doors. . . . It came over to the bed and began to pull away the covers. I covered myself up well. It couldn't take them off. Afterwards it went away" (Nagy, 1948, p. 16).
3. Nagy found that after the age of 9, children recognized that death was universal and irreversible, and represented the cessation of bodily functions. Cz. Gyula, aged 9 years and 4 months, said of death: "Death is the termination of life. Death is destiny. Then we finish our earthly life. Death is the end of life on earth" (Nagy, 1948, p. 26).

Nagy's findings were, and still are, illuminating, particularly in light of the commonly held assumption that children do not understand death and should be protected from death-related phenomena (Kastenbaum & Costa, 1977). Apparently, children do think about death, and their ideas about death change as they grow older. Developmentalists attempt to chart the changing nature of our feelings and attitudes toward death from infancy through old age. The developmental perspective considers death as a significant element in the interpersonal and intellectual development of the child and adult. This approach also poses several important questions that will serve as guides to our examination of death and dying:

1. What do children know or understand about death at a particular time in their lives? How does this understanding of death relate to their overall cognitive development?
2. What concerns about death and dying are relevant to each particular period of the life span? How do our general developmental tasks affect our perceptions of death? Could the so-called mid-life crisis, for example, be ushered in when death takes on a more vivid shade of reality?
3. Do children who experience death have a more sophisticated concept of it than those who have been sheltered from death? What individual

differences exist? What is the impact of television, with its daily portrayal of death, on children's concepts of death?

4. What impact does dying from a terminal illness have on children? Do they understand their fate? Do they differ in their death conceptions from the healthy child?

   With these questions in mind, it may be useful first to trace death conceptions through each of the major periods of development.

Infancy

Attributing a concept of death to infants may be farfetched; they certainly cannot tell us how they feel about death. However, the future course of death awareness may be laid down very early in life by the sleep-wake cycles that are the first presentation of being, and not being, and by the disappearance and reappearance of objects and people that key into the development of the object concept (see Chapter 7). Maurer (1966) has boldly hypothesized that even the infant's delight at peek-a-boo stems from vacillation between being and nonbeing states in a playful, safe situation. Perhaps the fear of separation, as described by Bowlby (1969) may be the infantile version of what we know as death anxiety. Separation by death does become a major theme in comments about death during childhood (Anthony, 1940).

Early and Middle Childhood

We know more about the child's awareness of death during early and middle childhood than during infancy and adolescence. Interview studies typically ask children such questions as: What happens when people die? Can dead people come back to life? Does everybody die? and What does *dead* mean? Research based on such interviews generally has confirmed Nagy's findings. Preschoolers tend to have a rather limited notion of death as sleep or as a temporary state when people can have feelings and thoughts like the living. Young children seem to have many contradictory notions about death (e.g., that a person could be dead but still be alive, in a physical sense, in heaven). Children in the early elementary school years (roughly from 6 to 9 years), in contrast, are more sophisticated in their death awareness. Most of the research seems to concur that by the time a child has reached the upper levels of elementary school, death is acknowledged as the fate of all living things and as the cessation of biological functioning (Childers & Wimmer, 1971; Gartley & Bernasconi, 1967; Melear, 1973). Most children of this age also claim that death is final and irreversible, although some children are still uncertain about this aspect of death (Childers & Wimmer, 1971).

   Many of these findings were confirmed in a study by Lonetto (1980), wherein children in middle childhood were asked to draw pictures about death and discuss their images. Lonetto found that children equated death with growing old (sometimes defined as age 18 or 29) and presented it most often in terms of separation. Older children were more likely to portray death as horrible and in the form of a monster (akin to Nagy's "bogeyman"), and the drawings of those entering adolescence were more abstract (e.g., using the color black as a way to depict death).

Thus, despite the best efforts of their elders, children do achieve fairly sophisticated concepts of death before adolescence. What factors may promote a change in death concepts? Television may be one major death educator for contemporary children (Kastenbaum & Costa, 1977). Several interview studies (e.g., Gartley & Bernasconi, 1967; Safier, 1964) noted the many references that children make to television. Perhaps the confusion about the irrevocability of death can be attributed to watching actors and actresses pop back to life on another program or network. In addition, Hornblum (1977) found evidence that the greater children's exposure and preference for violent television programs, the poorer their understanding of death's universality and inevitability.

Some children have experienced the death of a pet, parent, or sibling. Such events may promote an early sophistication of death understanding (Bluebond-Langner, 1977). Perhaps this is why children from lower socio-economic levels, who may have had more exposure to death than their middle-class peers, tend to be more aware of death at younger ages (Tallmer, Formaneck, & Tallmer, 1974). Entry into school also seems to play a central role in the child's developing concept of death (Lonetto & Templer, 1986). As children make the transition from home to school, they begin to question the *why* of events as opposed to the *what* of events. Such a change in perception makes children realize, perhaps for the first time, that events are not always under their own control or the control of their parents (Lonetto & Templer, 1986), and death becomes linked to uncontrollable outside forces.

In addition to experiential factors, cognitive development may underlie some of the shifts that have been observed in the way children think about death. Children's notions of the bogeyman are not cute manifestations of the innocence of their age. They are part of children's overall constructions of the world, one of the first intellectual puzzles to be encountered (Kastenbaum & Aisenberg, 1972). For example, casuality is a concept that undergoes development transformation. Young children often juxtapose and confuse cause-and-effect relationships, sometimes putting the cart before the horse (e.g., "It's raining because I put my boots on") and sometimes linking together unrelated phenomena because they coincide in time (e.g., "I did well in school because I was wearing my red socks"). Such undifferentiated notions of causality may lead a child to feel responsible for the death of a person close to him or her, especially when the child recalls past feelings of ill will toward a parent or sibling at the time of sickness and death. Anecdotal evidence indicates that children feel extreme guilt and responsibility for death, as if thinking of a thing (death) is the same as causing that thing (Kalish, 1981).

Children progress through stages toward an understanding of death. Children who experience the death of a parent may arrive at an early understanding of the finality of death.

A striking parallel exists between the types of concepts children and adolescents use to explain death and the characteristics of pre-operational, concrete operational, and formal operational thought as outlined by Piaget (see Chapter 7). That is, the higher the level of cognitive development, the fewer the immature, concrete, or egocentric responses given to questions regarding death and dying (Koocher, 1973; White, Elsom, & Prawat, 1978; Jenkins & Cavanaugh, 1985). The pre-operational child, whose thought is characterized by egocentricity and an inability to reverse mental actions, has difficulty comprehending the universal, inevitable, and irreversible nature of death (Hornblum, 1977). Appreciating these aspects of death may have to await concrete operational acquisitions such as role-taking abilities and conservation.

The concrete operational thinker may be more concerned with concrete manifestations of death, such as graves, funerals, and skeletons than the formal operational thinker (Anthony, 1940; Gartley & Bernasconi, 1967). Because children take things so literally at this stage, adults must be careful not to refer to death as "going to sleep," or "taking a trip" (Bluebond-Langner, 1977). The adolescent at the formal operational stage can think in terms of hypothetical events; possibilities become the focal point of thought. Death concepts may take on a more abstract quality at this time. The adolescent may ponder the meaning of death, as well as project into the future and think about what it would be like to be dead.

Thus, some evidence supports the hypothesis that death concepts undergo developmental changes similar to those of other concepts. However, some children will have more exposure to death and dying than their peers, and such experiences may accelerate the development of mature death concepts, with or without a corresponding acceleration of cognitive development.

This point was underscored in Bluebond-Langner's (1977) study of terminally ill children. Bluebond-Langner questioned the age-graded patterns of death concepts as described by Nagy (1948) and others. Instead, Bluebond-Langner found that the terminal illness of the children she studied (who were mostly between ages 3 and 9) forced them to view death as adults do—as an irreversible, final process. Such understanding was a result of the child's acquisition of information about the illness, which led the child to a redefinition of self-concept from healthy child, to ill child, to perpetually ill child, to dying child. Bluebond-Langner found that the death of a peer with a similar illness was the primary catalyst for recognizing one's own impending death. Time also took on a different meaning than it typically does for healthy children. The children infrequently discussed the future, attempted to rush holidays (e.g., celebrating Christmas in October), and were concerned with wasting time. On the basis of her work, Bluebond-Langner concluded that all views of death (i.e., as separation, as a person, and as an irreversible event) are present at all stages of development, but the concerns of the moment (e.g., an illness) modulate the child's beliefs.

Adolescence and Early Adulthood

The research on death conception during adolescence and adulthood is meager compared with such research about childhood. The numerous biological, social, intellectual and personal changes that are made at this time present adolescents with a unique, if sometimes conflicting, perspective of themselves in relation to life and death (Noppe and Noppe, in press). By puberty, death is certainly understood as a universal, irreversible fact. Formal operational thinking, with its emphasis on possibility, makes thinking about the future (of which death is a part) a significant activity. Identity development, one of the central tasks of adolescence, entails integrating the concept of self within the context of a personal time line (Erikson, 1968). Such concerns with time and understanding of the self must have a significant impact on the adolescent's thoughts about death. Therefore, adolescents think of death more often than they ever had before (Kalish, 1981). Although adolescent death is a relatively infrequent occurrence (mostly due to accidents and suicide), many adolescents will engage in death-defying and reckless behavior. Such behavior may appear incongruous with a mature concept of death. However, adolescents have been known to behave according to their personal fable—the belief that they are unique and immune from the laws governing the rest of humanity, particularly when the results are bad (Elkind, 1967). Such beliefs may even make death appealing in a romantic sense. The romanticization of death during the adolescent years may be manifested in the themes of death and destruction in contemporary rock music (Attig, 1986; Wass et al., 1988).

Adolescence typically is the first developmental period in which social and performance-related pressures, personality disturbances, and interpersonal conflicts may result in depression, loss of a sense of futurity, and life-threatening behavior. For example, the effect of the threat of nuclear war may partly be responsible for the "live-for-today" attitude and intensification of daredevil acts for which contemporary adolescents are known (Hesse, 1986). Even more significant is the rise in the rate of adolescent suicides, both attempted and completed. Although the frequency of attempted suicides is about 50 times greater than the frequency of completed suicides (Petti & Larson, 1987), an alarming rise has been reported in the completed suicide rate in the 15- to 24-year-old age group. Recent estimates have documented a 41 percent increase for this age group, and the rise is primarily due to the increase in suicides by white males (Petti & Larson, 1987). Many reasons have been offered to explain this alarming rise in the adolescent suicide rate, including the increased availability of lethal items such as drugs and firearms, family discord and stress, increased pressures to grow up faster, and the unpredictability of the future (Petti & Larson, 1987). A contagion effect has also been observed, wherein a particular school or community may be vulnerable to a rash of suicides once one has been committed. To date, no one particular factor has been pinpointed, and adolescent suicides most likely are due to a multitude of personality and situational factors. Researchers may wish to analyze adolescents' concepts and attitudes about death to see if adolescents who are at risk for suicide can be differentiated from those who are not.

Even less is known about the psychology of death during adulthood than during adolescence. During adulthood, the major and normative developmental events of marriage, parenthood, and career development signify a life-expanding time. However, young adults also become more vulnerable to facing the losses of adult life: loss of progeny due to abortion, miscarriage, sudden infant death syndrome (SIDS), or death in war. Although the modern day "epidemic" of AIDS has no age limitation, AIDS-related deaths are more prevalent among young adults than in any other age group.

The social and psychological consequences of AIDS have been profound. AIDS was a little-known disease until 1981, but currently about 75,000 cases of AIDS have been diagnosed in the United States, with estimates of almost 2 million Americans carrying the AIDS virus (Backer, Batchelor, Jones, & Mays, 1988). Transmitted by sexual contact or infected blood, AIDS renders the immune system helpless in warding off disease. An individual with AIDS is extremely susceptible to life-threatening illnesses, and at present no cure is available to fend off almost certain early death. Persons afflicted with AIDS must also face intense social rejection in the form of harassment, hostility, job discrimination, and isolation, just at the time when they most need social support (Herek & Glunt, 1988). Compounding the problem, AIDS initially was present in already stigmatized groups, such as drug users and male homosexuals, although the disease is spreading to the general heterosexual population as well. In addition to these social stressors, people who have been diagnosed with AIDS, or with AIDS-related complex (a pre-AIDS condition in which AIDS antibodies are found in the blood) typically know other people who have died of AIDS. Thus, the AIDS victim experiences the multiple bereavement of others, and well as an anticipatory bereavement of the self (Tross & Hirsch, 1988). Anxiety, depression, lowered self-esteem, and a sense of helplessness are common psychological experiences for those with AIDS (Tross & Hirsch, 1988). Ironically, the major life-threatening health problem of the 1980s and 1990s has been identified in an age group that traditionally has been one of the healthiest.

Middle Age

For the middle-aged person, death is significant because that final end point becomes the anchor for the personal time line—"time-left-to-live" rather than "time-since-birth" (Neugarten, 1968, p. 97). As one subject in a study on middle age said:

> There is now the realization that death is very real. Those things don't quite penetrate when you're in your twenties and you think that life is all ahead of you. Now you know that death will come to you, too. (Neugarten, 1968, p. 97)

This reorientation seems to occur during mid-life because of the convergence of several factors. During mid-life, more peers die than ever before. As parents age, adult children feel increased concern about their deaths, which eliminates "one psychological barricade protecting us from death" (Kalish, 1981, p. 127). Middle-aged adults also realize that they no longer have enough time to do all the things they planned when they were younger. These factors, coupled with undeniable physical obligations (e.g., the empty nest syndrome), may be responsible for the popularized malady of this age period, the mid-life crisis. The debate about the middle years rages on (Cytrynbaum, Blum, Patrick, Stein, Wadner, & Wild, 1980), but researchers of adult development seem to agree that a psychosocial transition is fairly common to this age period and that one of its major tasks is the recognition of one's own mortality.

Old Age

When people are asked to link a period of the life span to death, old age is typically their nominee. This is a reasonable association, although people do not first confront issues of death on the day they turn 65; recognition of personal mortality may be a more significant task at mid-life. Perhaps what differentiates the elderly from their younger counterparts is their orientation toward and preparation for death. Such preparation does not necessarily imply that they eagerly anticipate death. Instead, many elderly people try to put their houses in order by making wills, attending to funeral and burial arrangements, and formalizing arrangements for the settlement of their estates (Kalish, 1981). Butler (1968) found that aged people devote a considerable amount of time to reminiscence, a sort of introspective life review. When the process is constructive, it is not an escape from the infirmities of old age or an excessive preoccupation with the self. Instead, the life review serves as a way to order one's life, facilitating "a serene and and dignified acceptance of death" (Butler, p. 494).

Several thanatologists have been puzzled by the consistent finding that elderly persons have lower death anxiety scores on death anxiety questionnaires as compared with younger people (Kalish, 1981; Kalish & Reynolds, 1976; Kastenbaum & Aisenberg, 1972). The elderly do talk and think about death more often than younger people, but they do not seem to fear it as much (Kalish, 1976). Logic would dictate that those closest to death should be the most fearful of it. Perhaps the preparation and orientation toward death is a strategy used by the elderly to cope with an inevitable end that is rapidly approaching. Kalish (1976) proposed that the elderly become socialized to their deaths. Such "anticipatory socialization" leads to the sort of acceptance of death during old age that could not be attained at an earlier age. The deaths of family and friends also may promote such anticipation of death, although the deaths of many significant people can lead to a debilitating "bereavement overload" (Kastenbaum & Aisenberg, 1972). In general, some evidence indicates that death rates are higher for elderly who experience losses typical of their age—that is, death of a spouse, relocation of residence, and retirement from the work role (Rowland, 1977).

Conclusions About the Life Span Approach

In conclusion, death is truly a developmental phenomenon, because it is significant throughout the life span even as attitudes and feelings toward death change during each major developmental period. The childhood years reflect a time in which a realistic conception of death is constructed out of earlier fantastic notions. During adolescence and early adulthood, death becomes embedded into the crystallizing life plan that evolves from the construction of an identity. Mid-life represents a time when the future as "time-left-to-live" forces a reordering of priorities and self-reevaluation. Finally, old age is a time of preparing for death and coming to terms with the concrete reality of personal death—with or without acceptance. Throughout each developmental stage, individual experiences (e.g., terminal illness, death of significant others, and deaths publicized in the media) influence views of death.

SPECIAL TOPICS IN DEATH AND DYING

Several topics cut across all the perspectives on death and dying—biological, sociological, psychological, and developmental—and warrant mention to round out the thanatological journey presented in this chapter. This final section will introduce important ideas concerning grief and bereavement, the hospice movement, and the impact of the nuclear era on our concept of death and dying.

Bereavement, Grief, and Mourning

Obviously, the study of how people survive the deaths of others is important in thanatology. Some of us, unfortunately, will be involved with the process of dying from a terminal disease, but all of us survive the deaths of others. Many of the issues here are similar to or compatible with those in the previous discussion, but this section also will introduce some of the important concepts and findings on the impact of death on those who continue to live.

Bereavement

The loss of a significant other. The term comes from the root word meaning "shorn off" or "torn from."

Grief

The emotional expression of those who are bereaved, such as sorrow, anger, guilt, and confusion.

Mourning

The culturally prescribed means for expressing bereavement and grief.

Three Major Dimensions of Survivorship

Understanding survivorship necessitates distinguishing among bereavement, grief, and mourning. *Bereavement,* which literally means "to take away from," refers to a state of loss and encompasses both situations in which the loss is painful and situations in which it is not. *Grief* refers to the expression of those who are bereaved, such as sorrow, anger, guilt, and confusion (Kalish, 1981).

Unlike grief, which is an emotion common to all cultures, *mourning* behavior—the culturally prescribed means for expressing bereavement and grief—has yielded an impressive catalog of variations throughout the world. Mourning behavior may vary from the Hindu practice of suttee, or burning the widow of a dead man (outlawed since 1829, but evident as late as 1954); wearing a black armband for a year; celibacy for a surviving spouse; the Jewish practice of sitting Shiva for 7 days following the funeral; to having a ceremonial meal (Kalish, 1981). Mourning practices are so diverse because they are an integral and interwoven dimension of the culture from which they emanate.

Individual Differences and the Impact of Death

We must be wary of generalizing about grief and mourning, for the impact of a person's death on survivors is mediated by several factors, such as the form of the death (e.g., slow, sudden, or catastrophic), the relationship of the survivor to the dead person (e.g., parents, spouse, or child), and the age and sex of the survivors. So intense can be the reaction to bereavement that detrimental effects to physical and mental health have been well documented (Parkes, 1988).

Was the Death Slow, Sudden, or Catastrophic?   Ironically, sudden death is preferred for the self, whereas survivors desire a period of time to work out "unfinished business" with the individual who is about to die. In the case of a slow death, the survivors have the opportunity to engage in anticipatory grief. Such grieving does not seem to lessen the impact of death, although if the dying person lingers too long, the bereaved may feel relief as well as grief. Survivors of suicide experience feelings of rejection by the deceased and a fear of "catching" suicidal feelings through heredity. They may also engage in a prolonged search for the motives underlying the death and may try to conceal the cause of death from others. Despite these distinctive features of the survivor of suicide, no evidence to date shows that the grief process itself is unique or that those who survive a suicidal death experience severe complications and pathological grief reactions (van der Wal, 1989).

What Was the Relationship of the Survivor to the Dead?   Much has been written about the child who loses a parent early in life. The seriousness of this tragedy is reflected in the finding that children who lose their parents may have psychiatric problems in adult life. For example, Archibald, Bell, Miller, and Tuddenham (1962) studied more than 400 patients who were hospitalized for psychiatric problems. The researchers found a higher-than-chance rate of parental death for this group; the earlier the death of the parent, the more serious the problem. For bereaved children who are able to sustain the blow, the possibility exists that psychological distress might occur when they reach the age that their parent was when he or she died. The same may be true when the bereaved child's own children reach that age (Kalish, 1981).

Perhaps childhood bereavement is exacerbated by the way adults handle the bereaved child. Often, little information, or distorted information, is given, because the surviving parent feels the child will not understand (Becker & Margolin, 1967) or because the parent fails to take into account the developmental level of the child. The parent's own grief drains energy away from attending to the needs of the child, who may react to the loss by behaving poorly in school, acting aggressively with playmates, becoming fearful of the dark, or saying nasty things about the deceased (Kastenbaum, 1977). The loss of a parent during adulthood and middle age also can be the source of intense grief. Bereaved older children do not receive as much support as they apparently need (Kastenbaum, 1969).

Not much is known about children's reactions to the death of a sibling, but the loss of a brother or sister is severely distressing. How parents treat the surviving siblings is extremely important. Parents need guidance so that they do not alternate between neglect and overprotection of their surviving children.

The parent as survivor is the victim of an unparalleled tragedy. One of our fundamental assumptions about life and death is that children will survive their parents. When this is not the case, parents may feel as if they have been betrayed by a cosmic breach of contract. Nowhere is this more evident than in the case of sudden infant death syndrome (SIDS), or crib death, a malaise of uncertain origin responsible for approximately 10 percent of deaths in the first year of life in the United States. Parents today finally are being treated as victims, not as agents, of SIDS. However, an intense amount of guilt, as well as a feeling of being cursed or toxic, is a common dimension of such bereavement (Kalish, 1981).

Do Responses to Grief and Bereavement Follow Specific Patterns?   Parkes and his colleagues (Glick, Weiss, & Parkes, 1974; Parkes, 1972) investigated the process of grief by interviewing widows and widowers on several occasions during the first year of bereavement. Parkes outlined four phases of the grief reaction:

1. *Numbness,* during which the bereaved may give way to denial. Newly bereaved people may feel that they will never move, act, or think again. They may experience waves of intense grief lasting from a few days to two weeks.
2. *Yearning or pining,* a phase during which the bereaved engages in behavior that attempts to recover the dead person. People report dreaming of the dead person, getting fleeting glimpses of the person, or sensing the person's presence.
3. *Disorganization, despair, or depression,* which results from the acknowledgment of the reality of the death.
4. *Recovery or reorganization,* which seems to take at least a year, although some (e.g., Kalish, 1981) believe that the sadness, guilt, and anger always remain in some residual form.

Parkes chronicled feelings of anger directed toward medical profession-als, the dead spouse, and the self. Such feelings occurred throughout the course of the grief reaction. Another common emotion was guilt, most frequently found in the if-I-had-only syndrome. Many of the widowed also tended to relive the events surrounding their spouses' death over and over. Retelling the history of the death seemed to make it easier to assimilate both on a cognitive and on an affective level. In the case of a sudden, unanticipated death, survivors have been found to create their own story of the death to make it more comprehensible.

The astute reader probably has noted the striking similarities between the grief reaction and the responses to dying outlined by Kubler-Ross. This should not be surprising, for the death of self and those important to us may reflect the same intrapsychic loss. Perhaps the major difference is that for the bereaved, there can be no bargaining once a loved one has died (Kalish, 1976). It is also important to note that these stages do not represent a prescribed order for mourning; grieving is as much an individual experience as is dying (Feifel, 1990).

Our cultural norms encourage a quick recovery from grief, but adapting to loss from death involves a slow journey of a year at the very least. Even when recovery has been judged to be fairly complete, some experience an anniversary reaction. Around the anniversary of the death, grief reactions such as depression and even suicidal behavior increase (Kalish, 1981). Thus, to recover from death does not necessarily mean to forget. Another common reaction is to present the dead as an ideal person, a phenomenon that Lopata (1973) called sanctification.

Hospice Movement

During the Middle Ages, hospitality centers, or hospices, were set up along pilgrimage routes as places where the tired, destitute, hungry, or sore could find a respite from their long journey. During the 1800s, the Irish Sisters of Charity borrowed the medieval notion of the hospice to establish a center in Dublin that was dedicated to take care of the dying. This hospice was the precursor of the first modern hospice, St. Christopher's Hospice near London, which was initiated in 1967 and is directed by a charismatic British physician, Cicely Saunders.

The contemporary hospice does not attempt to cure terminally ill patients. Instead, it serves as a place and a process where the uncomfortable physical and psychological symptoms of a terminal illness are treated and, if possible, eliminated; this is known as palliative care. The hospice subscribes to the following goal: "When the quantity of life is limited, the quality of that life must be optimal" (e.g., Butterfield-Picard & Magno, 1982, p. 1255). Saunders (1977) and others (e.g., Lack, 1980) believe that the hospice can provide an alternative to hospital care, which may inflict additional psychological and physical suffering during the treatment of terminal illness. Not surprisingly, most hospice advocates claim that the hospice is a much better alternative to *euthanasia* (the illegal act of

Euthanasia
The act of painless putting to death persons suffering from incurable diseases or severe disabilities.

painlessly putting to death people suffering from incurable diseases or severe disability). They believe that when the quality of a person's remaining life is improved, the desire for a voluntary and premature ending of life is diminished.

The treatment that the dying receive in a hospice differs from hospital treatment in several fundamental ways (Butterfield-Picard & Magno, 1982; Lack, 1980):

1. A major dimension of hospice care is the control and alleviation of physical and psychological distress. Hospice workers have become experts in the field of pain control and continually administer a mixture of narcotic and nonnarcotic drugs such as the Brompton's cocktail (a mixture of dimorphine, cocaine, and gin). The aim is to find a balance such that the individual is relatively pain-free but alert.
2. The hospice actively involves the terminally ill patient's family. An effort is made to keep the dying at home as much as possible, to train the family to attend to the special needs of the ailing relation, and to provide a respite so that the family can get away once in while from the demands of caring for a terminally ill person.
3. Finally, the staff of the hospice is interdisciplinary (i.e., made up of doctors, nurses, psychologists, clergy, and social workers) and ideally is available on a 24-hour basis, 7 days a week. An important element of the hospice team is the heavy reliance on community volunteers.

In the United States, the hospice movement has quickly become popular, largely because hospitals must limit admittance to patients who require acute care. Hospices here are either established in a separate building and grounds (like St. Christopher's Hospice), as a wing of a traditional hospital, or as a roving team that conducts both hospital and home-based treatment. Whatever the locale, a desired aim is to provide a nonsterile, noninstitutionalized setting. Because of the increasing numbers of hospices in the United States, physicians, psychologists, and the federal government are trying to articulate and control the implementation, evaluation, and maintenance of hospice programs. (See the November 1982 issue of *American Psychologist* for a thorough presentation of these public policy issues.)

Death and Dying in the Future

One major theme of this chapter has been the multidisciplinary nature of the study of death and dying. As Feifel (1977) claimed, death has many faces, meanings, and perceptions that we can only begin to understand through the combined insights of people from many different fields. A second major theme underscores the need to understand the diversity of cultural and individual perspectives of death and dying. Death is a universal phenomenon, but the significance of the process and event bears different meanings according to cultural and experiential factors. An appropriate death for one person or society may not be so appropriate for another.

Applying Our Knowledge
The Living Will and Euthanasia

 The document in Figure 15.1 is designed to be filled out by an individual who is free of debilitating illness and is in a coherent frame of mind. This Living Will is a statement of people's wishes when and if they are in pain from an incurable illness, comatose, or viable only with the aid of life-sustaining equipment. Although Concern for Dying, an organization that disseminates information about recent developments in the field of death and dying, believes that the Living Will should be upheld on constitutional and common law grounds, legal sanction has been controversial, because adherence to the terms of the will is viewed as a form of euthanasia (Williamson, Evans, & Munley, 1980). Recently, however, several states have approved the legalization of the Living Will.

Proponents of the legalization of euthanasia (some may be in favor of passive euthanasia, as opposed to active euthanasia—when something is deliberately done to a patient to cause death) argue that current medical technology can lead to dehumanized treatment of a patient and prolonged agony for the patient's family. They claim that people have the right to request an end to their lives, especially in situations in which death would have been the "natural" course of events if not for medical intervention.

Opponents of euthanasia object to it on moral and religious grounds or fear that its legalization would make it easier for physicians to let people die. They say that it could open the door for passive or active death of deformed infants, the indigent elderly, or potential organ donors. Williamson, Evans, and Munley (1980) offered the insight that some people would ask for euthanasia not because of a desire to die, but because they felt burdensome to their families or that somehow they were expected to request their deaths. Finally, although those who are against euthanasia acknowledge that it is sometimes practiced anyway, they believe that its illegality accounts for the extreme caution and deliberation surrounding the practice.

Finally, our society's perspective on death and dying has changed tremendously within a few decades. We are now much more open, caring, concerned, and curious about death and dying. We also are much more aware of a number of ethical issues (such as whether to resuscitate a dying person) that correspond to advancing medical technology. Much of the thanatological landscape remains uncharted, but progress has been made on many fronts. Thanatological research, theories of death and dying, and the hospice movement are but a few of the indicators of our changing attitudes and feelings toward death.

Several explanations for our greater awareness of death and dying have been mentioned throughout the chapter. One other speculation, however, links the nuclear era to our unceasing quest for immortality. Death and immortality probably have been linked in the psyche of humanity since the beginning of conscious reflection.

According to Lifton (1977), our sense of immortality can be expressed in five symbolic modes. In the biological mode, we are immortal through our children and their children; the theological mode enables us to transcend death through spiritual attainment. We also can become immortal by

To My Family, My Physician, My Lawyer
And All Others Whom It May Concern

Death is as much a reality as birth, growth, and aging—it is the one certainty of life. In anticipation of decisions that may have to be made about my own dying and as an expression of my right to refuse treatment, I _____ , being of sound mind, make this statement of my wishes and instructions concerning treatment. _____(print name)

By means of this document, which I intend to be legally binding, I direct my physician and other care providers, my family, and any surrogate designated by me or appointed by a court, to carry out my wishes. If I become unable, by reason of physical or mental incapacity, to make decisions about my medical care, let this document provide the guidance and authority needed to make any and all such decisions.

If I am permanently unconscious or there is no reasonable expectation of my recovery from a seriously incapacitating or lethal illness or condition, I do not wish to be kept alive by artificial means. I request that I be given all care necessary to keep me comfortable and free of pain, even if pain-relieving medications may hasten my death, and I direct that no life-sustaining treatment be provided except as I or my surrogate specifically authorize.

This request may appear to place a heavy responsibility upon you, but by making this decision according to my strong convictions, I intend to ease that burden. I am acting after careful consideration and with understanding of the consequences of your carrying out my wishes. *List optional specific provisions in the space below. (See other side)*

Durable Power of Attorney for Health Care Decisions (Cross out if you do not wish to use this section)

To effect my wishes, I designate _____ ,
residing at _____ (Phone #) _____ ,
(or if he or she shall for any reason fail to act, _____ (Phone #) _____ ,
residing at _____) as my health care surrogate—
that is, my attorney-in-fact regarding any and all health care decisions to be made for me, including the decision to refuse life-sustaining treatment—if I am unable to make such decisions myself. This power shall remain effective during and not be affected by my subsequent illness, disability or incapacity. My surrogate shall have authority to interpret my Living Will, and shall make decisions about my health care as specified in my instructions or, when my wishes are not clear, as the surrogate believes to be in my best interests. I release and agree to hold harmless my health care surrogate from any and all claims whatsoever arising from decisions made in good faith in the exercise of this power.

I sign this document knowingly, voluntarily, and after careful deliberation, this ____ day of _____, 19____.

_____
(signature)

Address _____

_____

I do hereby certify that the within document was executed and acknowledged before me by the principal this_____ day of _____, 19____.

_____
Notary Public

Witness_____

Printed Name _____

Address _____

_____

Witness_____

Printed Name _____

Address _____

_____

Copies of this document have been given to:

(Optional) My Living Will is registered with Concern for Dying (No. _____)
Distributed by Concern for Dying, 250 West 57th Street, New York, NY 10107 (212) 246-6962

Figure 15.1
The Living Will

Reprinted with the permission of Concern for Dying, 250 West 57th St., New York, New York 10107.

leaving a legacy of creative works. The perpetuation of nature beyond our deaths offers a fourth symbolic mode of immortality. The fifth symbolic mode, according to Lifton, refers to a psychological spiritual transcendence—a peak experience where notions of time and death disappear.

Lifton (1982) believes that the threat of nuclear holocaust robs us of the first four of these symbolic modes of immortality. Whereas many religions have prophecies of a final judgment (e.g., Armageddon), such images are related to a worldview and belief in a higher being that would enact such a drastic measure only for a special purpose or reason. In the nuclear era, however, "the danger comes from our own hand, from man and his technology. The source is not God or nature. Our 'end' is perceived as a form of self-destruction and try as we may we are hard put to give it purpose or meaning" (Lifton, 1982, p. 58).

Perhaps one result of such a serious threat to our symbolic immortality is the worldwide grass roots movement to put an end to the nuclear arms race. Another result may be the increased need to understand how death fits within our own personal worldview. In any event, our need to know more about the thanatological landscape will have a positive outcome, for understanding death can lead to a greater appreciation of life.

Summary

1. Thanatology, the study of death and dying, is important to the study of human development because death is an organizer of time, a marker event, a significant dimension of adult development and aging, and a stage-related process.

2. The biological definition of death has attempted to pinpoint the death of the organism in terms of the cessation of vital body functions. Brain death, which is diagnosed by four criteria (total unreceptivity, no movements, no reflexes, and a flat electroencephalogram), is currently accepted by the medical profession.

3. Social death occurs when other people fail to acknowledge an individual as a member of the living. Psychological death can be defined either as the absence of self-awareness or an individual's belief that he or she is no longer alive.

4. According to the biological perspective on death and dying, life expectancy (the number of years the average person is expected to

live) is distinct from life span (the longevity of the oldest known living member of a species). Biological theories of death have proposed that genes, hormones, exposure to harmful environmental elements, and wear and tear on the body are the causes of death.

5. Many have claimed that the avoidance and fear of death in our culture are due to our denial of death, but the unpreparedness hypothesis claims that we avoid death because we do not have the experience to cope with it.

6. From the anthropological perspective, death and dying are culturally universal concepts. However, many different rituals and practices make up the death system of a particular culture.

7. The psychoanalytic approach to death and dying originated with the Freudian concept of the death instinct, which led to the concepts of death denial and death anxiety.

8. The psychological analysis of the process of dying is largely based on the work of Kubler-

Ross, who posited a five-stage model: denial and isolation, anger, bargaining, depression, and acceptance.

9. Developmentalists attempt to chart the changing nature of our feelings and attitudes toward death from infancy through old age. During early and middle childhood, children progress from believing that death is a limited form of living to understanding death's universality and irrevocability.

10. During adolescence, the concept of death is affected by the developing sense of identity and a new perspective on the future. The developmental milestones of adulthood, such as career and family building, may cause individuals to take stock of their personal time lines.

11. Death and dying take on a new significance during middle age, with a psychosocial transition that involves the acknowledgment of personal mortality. Old age, in contrast, may be characterized as a period of orientation toward, and preparation for, death.

12. The three major dimensions of surviving death are bereavement (the loss of a significant other), grief (the personal-emotional expression of those who are bereaved), and mourning (the culturally prescribed modes for the expression of grief and bereavement).

13. The hospice, designed to provide an alternative to hospitalization for the terminally ill, attempts to promote alleviation of psychological and physical distress without cure. Such aims are accomplished by the use of pain-controlling drugs and the active involvement of the family and community volunteers.

Key Terms

bereavement (p. 657)
brain death (p. 628)
confluency (p. 634)
death system (p. 636)
euthanasia (p. 660)
grief (p. 657)

life expectancy (p. 633)
marker events (p. 626)
mourning (p. 657)
psychological autopsy (p. 631)

psychological death (p. 629)
social death (p. 629)
somatic mutation theory (p. 635)

thanatology (p. 626)
unpreparedness hypothesis (p. 640)

Review Questions

1. What is a near death experience (NDE)? Why have NDEs captured the interest of contemporary U.S. society? What alternative explanations account for this phenomenon?

2. What are biological death, psychological death, and social death? Present examples in which a person may be dead by one definition but not by another What particular problems emerge from biological definitions of death?

3. Are we genetically programmed to die? What adaptational advantages would emerge from a biological death clock?

4. Discuss the concept of the death system. What aspects of the U.S. death system enable us to cope with death? What aspects of the U.S. death system perpetuate death denial?

5. Suicide was discussed from a number of perspectives. Describe the sociological and psychological explanations for suicidal behavior. Do either of these theoretical perspectives help to explain the current increase in adolescent suicide and the finding that white males have the highest suicide rate in all age categories?

6. What general phases do people with life-threatening illnesses go through as they cope with their impending deaths? What criticisms have been leveled against Kubler-Ross's stage theory of death and dying?

7. How do death concepts change over the life span?
8. How does the stigma associated with AIDS make issues of life and death particularly difficult for AIDS patients?
9. What would you have to know about the grief process to provide necessary emotional support to a recently bereaved friend? What changes would you expect in your friend's responses to the death during the course of a year?

Suggested Readings

Grollman, Earl A. (1970). *Talking about death.* Boston: Beacon Press.

    A valuable guide for explaining death to children.

Kastenbaum, R. J. (1986). *Death, society, and human experience* (3rd ed.) Columbus: Merrill Publishing Co.

    An insightful overview of thanatology. Kastenbaum lends his own personal insights and perspective to such topics as the meaning of death, bereavement, and the development of death awareness.

Kubler-Ross, E. (1969). *On death and dying.* New York: Macmillan.

    A classic in the literature on death and dying. Kubler-Ross's work with terminally ill cancer patients set the context for her stages of dying.

Rosenfeld, A. (1976). *Prolongevity.* New York: Knopf.

    Delightful descriptions of the current work of researchers who desire to learn how to greatly extend the human life span. Those interested in the quest for immortality will enjoy this volume.

Sabom, M. B. (1982). *Recollections of death: A medical investigation.* New York: Harper & Row.

    A credible investigation, conducted by a Florida physician, of people who have had a near death experience.

Shneidman, E. S. (Ed.). (1984). *Death: Current perspectives.* (3rd ed.). Palo Alto, CA: Mayfield.

    Readings on suicide, hospices, bereavement, and the determination of death.

Glossary

Accommodation. The adjusting of the cognitive structures to adapt to new information from the environment.

Activity Theory. The view that the happiest elderly people are those who remain active for the longest period of time.

Adrenogenital Syndrome. A form of hermaphroditism in genetic females caused by an overproduction of androgen during fetal development and resulting in masculinized external genitalia.

Affordances. According to differentiation theory, things that the environment provides to the perceiver that yield possibilities for action.

Afterbirth. The third and last phase of the birth process, during which the amniotic sac and placenta are expelled from the uterus by the uterine contractions.

Amniotic Sac. The fluid-filled sac in which the embryo and fetus develop throughout the pregnancy.

Androgens. Male sex hormones.

Androgyny. The incorporation of masculine and feminine characteristics in one person.

Animism. The belief of pre-operational children that, because they themselves have life, all things are alive.

Anoxia. A lack of oxygen during the birth process, which can result in brain damage or even fetal death.

Aphrodisiacs. Any substances, from bananas to dried salamanders, that have erroneously been thought to increase sexual drive.

Artificialism. The belief that everything that exists, even natural phenomena, has a psychological reason for existence.

Assimilation. The aspect of the adaptive functioning of human intelligence that involves fitting new intellectual material into already existing cognitive structures.

Attention. The screening mechanism by which an individual selects certain features of the environment to be processed while ignoring other features.

Attention-Deficit Hyperactivity Disorder. A syndrome characterized by inattention, impulsivity, and hyperactivity lasting at least 6 months and not attributable to any known specific mental disorder or to mental retardation.

Authoritarian Parenting. Parenting designed to shape children's behavior according to precise and absolute standards of conduct, with little respect for the child and little room for discussion of parental standards.

Authoritative Parenting. Parenting in which control is exercised but independence is also allowed and encouraged in the child, and discussion of parental standards is the norm.

Baby Biography. The informal and personal diary that certain educated middle-class parents keep regarding the development of their children.

Behaviorism. The theoretical view that environmental factors are largely responsible for influencing the observable changes of human development.

Bereavement. The loss of a significant other. The term comes from the root word meaning "shorn off" or "torn from."

Binocular Disparity. The tendency of each eye to view a visual display from a slightly different vantage point.

Blastocyst. A cluster of about 500 cells that the fertilized egg has become by the time it has moved from the oviduct to the uterus.

Body Image. The view people have of their bodies, which may or may not correspond to objective reality.

Bonding. The process by which the parent-offspring attachment is initially formed.

Brain Death. The most commonly accepted definition of death, which includes total lack of responsivity, lack of movements and reflexes, and a flat electroencephalogram (a recording of brain wave patterns).

Case-study Method. An individual research strategy, derived from the methods of psychoanalysis, in which the details of a person's life are carefully documented and discussed within a flexible format.

Cathexis. According to psychoanalytic theory, the process of attaching libidinal energy to mental representations of gratifying persons or objects.

Centration. A characteristic of pre-operational thought whereby a child centers on the most noticeable features of the environment while ignoring others.

Cephalocaudal Growth. Physical growth that proceeds in a pattern from the head to the trunk of the body.

Cerebral Cortex. The outer surface of the human brain, which is responsible for the sophisticated psychological functioning of the human organism.

Chromosome. A microscopic, threadlike structure, found in the nucleus of every human cell, which contains hereditary material in the form of genes.

Classical Conditioning. A basic form of learning involving reflexive behavior, in which two stimuli become associated when presented at the same point in time.

Classification. The ability to perceive logical similarity among a group of objects and to sort them according to their common features.

Climacteric. The cessation of menstruation (an aspect of menopause).

Clinical Method. An individual research strategy, popularized by Jean Piaget, in which the child is provided with certain materials and problems to solve within a flexible format and then observed closely, one on one. This strategy has more recently been termed the method of critical exploration.

Cognitive Conceit. A phenomenon whereby children new to the stage of concrete operations develop too much faith in their reasoning ability.

Cognitive Social Learning. Learning characterized by imitation of, or identification with, observed models.

Cognitive Structures. The ways in which human beings organize their knowledge, which determine their intellectual view of the world.

Cohabitation. A living arrangement in which two adults live together as a couple but without a marriage contract.

Concrete Operations. A stage of thinking, extending from the age of 6 to adolescence, in which a child can reason logically about concrete situations or events.

Confluence Theory. The theory that the intelligence of any particular family member is influenced by the average intellectual ability of other members of the family.

Confluency. The point at which duplicating cells cover, in a single layer, the entire available area of a growth container.

Conservation. A task requiring the ability to recognize that variations in the physical appearance of a substance do not alter the amount of the substance in question.

Continuous Culture. A culture in which development is a smooth and gradual process, in that children are never taught anything that they will have to relearn as adults.

Contrast Sensitivity. The sensitivity of the viewer to contrast between object and background in a visual display.

Conventional Morality. The second of Kohlberg's three levels of moral judgment, based on a morality of social approval and the authority of law and order.

Convergent Thinking. The bringing together of various pieces of information to formulate a single correct solution to a problem.

Cornea. The curved transparent outer surface at the front of the eye.

Correlational Statistics (Positive and Negative Correlations). Mathematical procedures that organize data to show the strength and direction of relationship between two or more variables. Positive correlations indicate that as scores on one variable increase, scores on a second variable also increase. Negative correlations indicate that as scores on one variable increase, scores on a second variable decrease.

Cross-sectional Design. A developmental research method that compares the data from different chronological age groups simultaneously.

Crystallized Intelligence. Intelligence that is based on previously acquired skills or information.

Death System. The relationship between society and death involving people, places (e.g., cemeteries), events (e.g., Memorial Day), and symbols (e.g., the color black).

Deep Structure. The meaning inferred from, or imparted to, the language that is heard or read (see also *Surface Structure*).

Demand Characteristics. The cues about the nature of a research project to which the subjects unknowingly may react, thereby biasing the results.

Depth Perception. The ability to perceive the world in three rather than two dimensions.

Descriptive Statistics. Mathematical procedures that simplify and succinctly summarize data (e.g., averages and percentages).

Developmental Stage. A period within the life span characterized by a cohesive cluster of physical, emotional, intellectual, or social characteristics.

Differentiation Theory. The theory of perception that states that as people develop they attend more and more closely to the distinctive features of the environment.

Discontinuous Culture. A culture characterized by age segregation and clearly defined differences in the roles and responsibilities of people at different points in the life span.

Disengagement Theory. The view that aging involves a mutually agreed upon separation of the individual from other members of society.

Divergent Thinking. An aspect of intelligence requiring the ability to branch out from a single starting point to reach a variety of possible problem solutions.

Ectoderm. The outer layer of the embryo from which develop such structures as the skin, sensory organs, brain, and spinal cord.

Egalitarian Marriage. A marriage that is not characterized by elements of domination or role specialization.

Ego. In psychoanalytic theory, a personality structure that develops during the second year of life to deal consciously and rationally with the restrictions that reality imposes on the infant.

Embryo. The developing human organism in the womb from the second to the eighth week after conception.

Empiricism. The philosophical position that the only source of knowledge is sensory information.

Endoderm. The inner layer of the embryo from which develop such structures as the digestive system, respiratory system, and the linings of the internal organs.

Enrichment Theory. The belief that, as people develop, their perception is increasingly influenced by what they themselves bring to the process of perceiving.

Environmentalism. The belief that human beings grow to be what the environments in which they find themselves make them.

Epigenetic Principle. According to Erik Erikson, the notion that development proceeds from a universal plan that continually builds upon itself at the appropriate times.

Estrogen. The major female sex hormone, secreted from a woman's ovaries and responsible for feminizing a woman's body.

Ethical Relativism. A moral orientation that denies the possibility of any absolute truths; all morality is an arbitrary set of rules (contrast with *Moral Absolutism*).

Ethology. The naturalistic study of animal behavior and its underlying mechanisms.

Euthanasia. The act of painlessly putting to death persons suffering from incurable diseases or severe disabilities.

Expansion. An informal language-training technique frequently employed by parents, in which the child's simple sentences are reiterated in a more elaborate form.

Experimental Strategy. A type of research in which one or more variables are manipulated and isolated to determine cause-and-effect relationships. The part of the sample that is given a treatment is known as the experimental group. The part of the sample that is not given the treatment, for comparative purposes, is known as the control group.

Expressive Needs. Needs for emotional closeness and support in a relationship.

Extensive Peer Relations. Social interactions characterized as group activities.

Extinction. The process by which learned responses are unlearned because stimulus-response connections cease to be made.

Fetal Alcohol Syndrome. A set of congenital problems in a child resulting from alcohol ingestion by a pregnant woman, which may include mental retardation, facial anomalies, and delayed growth.

Fetus. The human organism in the womb from 8 weeks after conception to delivery.

Field Experiment. A type of experimental strategy in which the research is conducted relatively unobtrusively in a natural setting rather than in a laboratory.

Field Independence. An analytic-spatial ability to separate an embedded figure from its surrounding context.

Fixation. According to Sigmund Freud, the failure of a person—whether because of frustration or indulgence —to abandon primitive libidinal attachments, which remain as manifestations of stunted personality development.

Fluid Intelligence. A formless, intuitive type of intelligence that is unrelated to education or experience.

Formal Operations. A stage of thinking during adolescence and adulthood in which people can deal with abstract, hypothetical, and contrary-to-fact propositions.

Frequency. A characteristic of sound waves perceived by human beings as the pitch of sound.

Games-with-rules. The logical rule-dominated games of elementary school children.

Gender. The nonphysiological aspects of sex that social convention designates as appropriate for either males or females.

Gender Constancy. The child's understanding that his or her gender will remain the same despite such superficial changes as hairstyle, dress, or activity.

Gender Identity. The personal awareness of being either male or female. It is an internalization of the characteristics, attitudes, and feelings of one sex over the other.

Gender Role Preference. The desire to adopt the behaviors and attitudes of one sex over the other.

Gender Roles. The behaviors that society recognizes as appropriate for males and females.

Gender Role Stereotype. Well-defined cultural prescriptions for appropriate male and female behavior. This is also referred to as gender-typed behavior.

Gender Stability. The child's realization that his or her gender will always remain the same and that the child will grow up to be a man or a woman.

Gene. Hereditary material in the chromosomes that carries coded information that influences the physical characteristics of the organism.

Genotype. The total genetic inheritance of a living organism.

Gerontology. The study of the human aging process from an interdisciplinary perspective.

Grief. The emotional expression of those who are bereaved, such as sorrow, anger, guilt, and confusion.

Group Differences Statistics. Mathematical procedures that organize data in a manner to permit comparisons between two or more groups within a sample.

Group Intelligence Tests. Intelligence tests that can be administered to groups of people at a time.

Gynecomastia. Temporary breast enlargement that occurs in approximately one in three boys at the onset of puberty.

Habituation. The process by which a stimulus becomes so familiar that it no longer brings about an orienting response.

Heritability. The degree to which characteristics vary within the population as a result of genetic factors.

Hermaphroditism. A condition in which the internal reproductive system matches one genetic sex, but the external genitalia do not.

Hierarchy of Needs. According to Abraham Maslow, the arrangement of human motives into five basic levels from the most pressing physiological needs to the least critical self-actualization.

Holophrases. The first words infants use, which tend to convey more meaning (i.e., the meaning of whole phrases) than the typical adult usage would imply.

Hormone. A chemical substance secreted into the bloodstream by one of the various glands in the human body, whose function is to direct the course of growth or regulate the body's metabolism.

Humanism. The philosophical perspective that maintains that freedom, subjectivity, and creativity are essential for understanding the process of development.

Hypothalamus. The area of the brain that regulates body temperature, blood pressure, and blood flow to the brain, and controls the endocrine system.

Hypothesis. The formal statement of a researcher's educated guess about how two or more variables are related.

Id. In psychoanalytic theory, a personality structure that is present from birth and contains the irrational, unconscious, and selfish aspects of human beings.

Idealism. The philosophical view that reality cannot be known independently from the mind that is perceiving it.

Identification. The process by which one person perceives himself or herself as being similar to another and, in a sense, shares in the identity of the other person. For example, a child may identify with a parent, or a person may identify with a religious or ethnic group.

Imaginary Audience. The extreme self-consciousness that characterizes young adolescents, with feelings that others are as concerned with them as they are with themselves.

Implicit Information. The skills that competent users of a language possess and take for granted in the process of having a conversation. For example, competent speakers are aware when the topic of conversation changes.

Indifferent, Uninvolved Parenting. Parenting characterized by selfishness and by little or no interest or involvement in the lives and everyday activities of children.

Individual Intelligence Tests. Intelligence tests administered by a trained psychologist to one person at a time.

Induction. A disciplinary approach emphasizing the impact on other people of a child's wrong behaviors.

Inferential Statistics. Mathematical procedures that estimate the probability of obtaining similar data with a different sample from the same population.

Inner Speech. According to Lev Vygotsky, the process by which spoken language becomes a silent, private form of thinking.

Instinctual Anxiety. In psychoanalytic theory, the fear children have of their own instincts whose expression is forbidden by society.

Instrumental Needs. Friendship needs that are concrete and practical as opposed to emotional.

Intensity. The characteristic of sound waves perceived by humans as variations in the loudness of sound.

Intensive Peer Relations. One-to-one social interactions.

Interactionist Approach. The belief that human development is a dynamic, multidirectional process in which heredity and environment continuously influence each other in such a way that determining the relative contributions of each to the developmental process is difficult.

Iris. The colored surface of the eye located behind the cornea that adjusts to control the amount of light admitted through the opening at its center.

Labor. The first and longest stage of the birth process, during which the cervix is gradually opened to permit the passage of the child through the birth canal.

Law of Contiguity. The principle that learning occurs because two stimuli presented at the same time become associated in the mind of the learner.

Law of Effect. The principle of learning that states that behaviors followed by reinforcement are likely to be maintained or increased.

Lens. The structure of the eye located behind the iris that bulges or flattens to focus a visual image on the retina.

Libido. According to Sigmund Freud, the instinctual psychosexual energy force that provides the motivation for thought and behavior.

Life Expectancy. The number of years the average person is expected to live.

Linguistic Relativity Hypothesis. The position held by cultural anthropologist Benjamin Whorf that a language actually determines the nature of thought for the speaker of that language.

Longitudinal Design. A developmental research method that compares the data from one sample at different chronological age intervals.

Long-term Memory. Memory for information that is no longer held at the level of consciousness but must be retrieved from permanent storage.

Marker Events. Idiosyncratic or normative critical events in the life span of an individual.

Maternal Sensitization. A condition that occurs when an Rh-negative mother becomes "sensitized" to the Rh factor as a result of pregnancy and produces antibodies that will attack the red blood cells of an Rh-positive child she may carry at some future time.

Maturationism. The theoretical view that hereditary mechanisms are largely responsible for influencing the path of development.

Mediation Theory. A theory that attempts to explain developmental differences in human learning by suggesting that internal "mediating" responses come between an external stimulus and an external response.

Meiosis. The process of cell division by which sex cells are produced, in which two new cells are formed, each containing half the number of chromosomes found in its parent cell.

Menarche. The first episode of menstrual bleeding, which can occur at any time from age 10 to age 16 in the developing adolescent girl (corresponds to *Spermarche* in adolescent boys).

Menopause. The cessation of the menstrual cycles, which occurs between the ages of forty-five and fifty-five. The remaining egg cells in a woman's uterus will not mature, because the follicle cells surrounding them are no longer responsive to follicle-stimulating hormone.

Mesoderm. The middle layer of the embryo, which develops into such structures as the circulatory system, the muscles, and the blood.

Meta-analysis. A statistical procedure that combines the results from individual studies into one overall analysis. Meta-analysis can be used to resolve conflicting findings by testing the statistical significance of the accumulated results of a group of studies.

Metamemory. The understanding people have of their own memory processes.

Mitosis. A process of cell division by which two identical new cells are formed from a parent cell.

Modern Marriage. A marriage in which the husband often shares housekeeping responsibilities and the wife often works outside the home, but the husband's career is of primary importance.

Modified Extended Family. The family in which adult children do not live with their parents but several generations remain close to one another, both socially and geographically.

Moral Absolutism. A moral orientation in which universal truths exist that are beyond the flexibility of cultural or situational factors (contrast with *Ethical Relativism*).

Morality of Care. According to Gilligan, the moral orientation typical of females in which relatedness to, concern about, and sensitivity toward others is paramount (see also *Morality of Justice*).

Morality of Constraint. A morality characterized by the child's simple acceptance of definitions of right and wrong supplied by the parents.

Morality of Cooperation. A morality constructed by children themselves on the basis of their interactions with peers.

Morality of Justice. According to Gilligan, the moral orientation typical of males in which the rights of individuals and abstract legal principles are paramount (see also *Morality of Care*).

Morphology. The study of the basic word units of a language, including how they are constructed and how they are modified.

Motherese. A pattern of speech, characterized by high pitch and exaggerated intonations, that is typically used by adults when speaking to infants.

Mourning. The culturally prescribed means for expressing bereavement and grief.

Müllerian-inhibiting substance. A male hormone (see androgens), secreted by the newly formed testes after 6 to 8 weeks of prenatal development, which prevents the formation of female internal organs.

Multivariate Statistics. Mathematical procedures that are used to analyze the data of multiple dependent variables simultaneously (see also Univariate Statistics).

Natural Experiment. A type of nonexperimental strategy in which the researcher is able to take advantage of a naturally occurring manipulation instead of deliberately intervening.

Naturalism. The philosophical view that nature provides the child with a plan for development, and no harm will result if the child is allowed to develop with little adult supervision.

Neuron. A nerve cell.

Normative Tradition. The research approach that attempts to establish the natural timing and sequence of developmental change through the use of developmental norms.

Observational Learning. Learning that results from the observation of the behavior of others and its consequences.

Observational Research. Data collection procedures that use checklists, rating scales, narrative methods, or behavioral samples to obtain results. Researchers or their appointees usually try to obtain the data relatively unobtrusively in natural settings.

Operant Conditioning. Learning in which the positive or negative consequences of a person's behavior influence the future occurrence of that behavior.

Operational Definition. The specific meaning, in quantitative or categorical terms, assigned to the use of a variable.

Organismic Theory. A type of theory that stresses the importance in human development of factors within the organism itself over those that are found in the environment.

Osteoporosis. A condition of middle and old age in which the bones become lighter, less dense, and more brittle.

Parental Imperative. The hypothesis that emphasizes the necessity for childbearing adults to conform to gender-typed behaviors and suppress cross-sex behaviors to rear their children successfully.

Permissive Parenting. Parenting characterized by unwillingness to exert authority or control over children, the imposition of few if any regulations, and little emphasis on responsibility and order in the household.

Phenotype. The manifestation of genetic information as evidenced in the physical appearance of the organism.

Phonology. The study of the patterns of sound in a language, including intonation, stress, pronunciation, and blending.

Pituitary Gland. A pea-sized gland connected to the hypothalamus by a stalk of nerve fibers and responsible for stimulating and controlling all other glands in the endocrine system.

Placenta. The vascular disklike membrane that serves as an exchange filter between the mother's bloodstream and that of the developing fetus.

Postconventional Morality. The third of Kohlberg's three levels of moral judgment, based on a morality that benefits the general welfare of society and an ad-

herence to self-chosen principles that promote the good of humanity.

Practice Play. The intrinsically satisfying repetition of simple motor skills, characteristic of infants and toddlers.

Pragmatics. The study of the social and contextual factors that govern conversation, as well as the nonverbal aspects of language.

Preconventional Morality. The first of Kohlberg's three levels of moral judgment, based on a morality of avoiding punishments and obtaining rewards.

Pre-operational Intelligence. The mental activity of preschool children, who are capable of mental representation but do not yet have a system to organize their thinking.

Primary Process Thinking. According to Sigmund Freud, the tendency of the id to strive for immediate gratification of needs or reduction of tensions by any available means.

Productive Process. One of the two basic aspects of communication, which involves the attempts to transmit effectively a message through speaking or writing (see also *Receptive Process*).

Progesterone. The female sex hormone that prepares the wall of the uterus to receive a fertilized egg cell.

Proximodistal Growth. The pattern of human growth that proceeds from the center of the body out to the extremities.

Psychic Determinism. The psychoanalytic principle that past events continue to influence present psychological reality.

Psychoanalytic Theory. The view that stresses the importance of unconscious mechanisms in development and sees the human organism as a creature of appetite rather than reason.

Psychological Autopsy. An in-depth analysis of the life and death of an individual to determine the circumstances and subtle causes of the death.

Psychological Death. A state in which self-awareness is absent (i.e., there is confusion and disorientation) or in which individuals no longer consider themselves living.

Psychosocial Crisis. A predominant conflict associated with each of Erik Erikson's eight stages of development. Resulting from both biological and cultural demands, the crisis may be favorably or unfavorably resolved.

Punishment. An outcome that follows a behavior and decreases the likelihood that the behavior will occur in the future.

Pupil. The opening at the center of the iris through which light enters the eye.

Realism. The philosophical position that reality has an existence independent of the perceiver's consciousness of it.

Receptive Process. One of the two basic aspects of communication, which involves the attempts to receive and make sense of a message through listening or reading (see also *Productive Process*).

Reconstituted Family. A family that is formed by the marriage of a couple, one or both of whom already have children from a previous marriage.

Reinforcement. An outcome that follows a behavior and increases the likelihood that the behavior will occur in the future.

Relativistic Operations. A set of mental operations that organize a person's understanding of complex interpersonal relationships.

Reliability. The consistency of the scores yielded by a particular psychological test.

Response Set. The tendency of either subjects or researchers to react in a constantly similar manner despite variations in stimulation, thereby biasing the results of an experiment.

Retina. The grainy inner rear surface of the eye, made up of light-sensitive nerve cells, on which visual images are projected.

Reversal Shift. A form of discrimination learning in which the learner is initially rewarded for responding to one example of a particular dimension and is later rewarded for responding to an opposite example of the same dimension.

Sample. The persons, or subjects, who participate in a research project. They are generally chosen to reflect the characteristics of larger similar group, or population, that the sample represents.

Schema. According to information-processing theorists of gender development, a set of ideas that help children categorize information in terms of what is appropriate and characteristic of males and females.

Schemes. The sensorimotor equivalent of concepts; consistent action sequences made up of classes of acts that have regular, common features.

Secondary Process Thinking. According to Sigmund Freud, the tendency of the ego to postpone instinctual gratification through the use of logic and the testing of reality.

Secular Trend. The tendency for each generation from the early 1800s to recent times to be taller and heavier, and to develop faster, than the generation that preceded it.

Self-actualization. According to Abraham Maslow, the tendency of all human beings, after having satisfied lower-level needs, to enhance their lives and fulfill their unique potentials.

Self-concept. All the components of one's personality of which a person is aware.

Self-esteem. The evaluative component of the self-concept whereby "good" or "bad" labels are attached to aspects of the self.

Semantics. The study of the meaning of the words and sentences of a language.

Sensorimotor Intelligence. The action-oriented form of intelligence and problem solving that is typically engaged in by infants.

Sequential Design. A developmental research method that blends elements of cross-sectional, longitudinal, and time lag designs to maximize the advantages and minimize the disadvantages of these simpler methods.

Seriation. A task designed to measure a child's understanding of ordinal relations.

Sex. The term used by researchers of gender development to refer to biological characteristics and differences between males and females.

Sexual Polarization Versus Bisexual Confusion. As proposed by Erik Erikson, a part of the adolescent identity crisis. It involves accepting oneself as a physically and psychologically mature male or female.

Shape Constancy. The realization that the actual shape of an object remains the same even when the object is viewed from a different angle.

Shared Meanings. Themes that organize the social interactions of children in the second and third years of life, including such games as "run and chase" and "stack and topple."

Short-term Memory. Memory for material still at the level of consciousness because it has recently been presented and is in the process of being rehearsed.

Size Constancy. The realization that the size of an object remains the same even when the actual visual image of the object changes when it is viewed from a different distance.

Sleeper Effects. Stable aspects of personality that may appear in a somewhat different form at various stages of development.

Social Clock. The tendency of people to measure their developmental progress in terms of adherence to established norms.

Social Cognition. Children's developing awareness of the needs and feelings of others, as illustrated by their changing conceptions of friendship.

Social Death. An individual's or group's failure to recognize a person as being among the living.

Social Learning. The belief that development is heavily influenced by imitation or avoidance of behavior that is modeled by other people.

Somatic Mutation Theory. A theory that proposes that aging and death are due to a lifetime of exposure to nonlethal radiation.

Spermarche. The first ejaculation of seminal fluid at orgasm, which occurs as a boy reaches puberty (corresponds to Menarche in adolescent girls).

Standard Deviation. A numerical indication of the variance of all reported scores from the statistical mean.

Standardized Tests or Tasks. Systematic methods for obtaining samples of categorical or numerical information that are inferred to represent a person's characteristics.

Stereopsis. Depth perception resulting from binocular disparity and involving the convergence of the eyes on a single target and the fusion of the different visual images perceived by each eye.

Sudden Infant Death Syndrome. The unexplained death of an apparently healthy infant.

Superego. In psychoanalytic theory, a personality structure that emerges during the preschool years as a result of identification with parents and the establishment of cultural standards for behavior. The superego includes a conscience and an ego ideal.

Surface Structure. The particular language sounds heard or spoken and their arrangement as words, phrases, or sentences (see also Deep Structure).

Survey Approach. Data collection procedures that use the direct techniques of interviewing and questionnaires to obtain results.

Symbolic Play. Make-believe or fantasy play, which begins in the second year of life and predominates throughout the preschool years.

Syntax. The way in which a language's words are arranged in terms of phrases and sentences, as well as their variations.

Telegraphic Speech. The first, abbreviated sentences that very young children create. They contain the minimum number of words needed to relate meaning but lack the auxiliary words that adults typically omit from telegram messages.

Temperament. A core set of inherited dispositions, which, after modification by experiences, serves as the foundation for later personality.

Teratogens. Environmental factors that can affect the development of the fetus.

Terminal Drop. A sharp and dramatic intellectual decline that occurs in many elderly people shortly before death.

Testosterone. The male sex hormone secreted by the testicles that masculinizes the body during and after puberty.

Thanatology. The study of death and dying (from Thanatos, the mythological Greek god of death).

Time Lag Design. A research method that compares the data from different groups at different times while keeping chronological age constant.

Traditional Marriage. A marriage in which the roles of husband and wife are highly specialized, with the husband taking the role of provider and primary decision maker and the wife assuming responsibility for running the household.

Transductive Reasoning. An illogical form of reasoning that is typical of children under the age of 6.

Trophins. Hormones secreted by the pituitary gland that stimulate one of the other glands in the endocrine system to secrete its particular hormone.

Unconscious Motivation. The psychoanalytic principle that people are usually unaware of the processes and factors that motivate their behavior and mental activity.

Univariate Statistics. Mathematical procedures that are used to analyze the data of only one dependent variable at a time (see also Multivariate Statistics).

Unpreparedness Hypothesis. The contention that our society does not deny death as much as avoid it because of our lack of experiences with, and preparedness for, death.

Validity. The accuracy with which a psychological test actually measures what it is intended to measure.

Variable. A concept with a property that varies in at least two ways. An independent variable is presumed to cause or influence a dependent variable.

Visual Acuity. The ability of the perceiver to recognize all the components in a visual display.

Visual Cliff. An apparatus used to test depth perception in the human infant.

Zygote. A newly fertilized egg cell.

References

Abramovitch, R., & Grusec, J. E. (1978). Peer imitation in a natural setting. *Child Development, 49,* 60–65.

Abramovitch, R., Pepler, D., & Corter, C. (1982). Patterns of sibling interaction among perschool-age children. In M. E. Lamb & B. Sutton-Smith (Eds.), *Sibling relationships: Their nature and significance across the lifespan.* Hillsdale, NJ: Erlbaum.

Abranavel, E., & Sigafoos, A. D. (1984). Exploring the presence of imitation during early infancy. *Child Development, 55,* 381–392.

Achenbach, T. M. (1978). *Research in developmental psychology: Concepts, strategies, methods.* New York: Free Press.

Achte, K. (1980). Death and ancient Finnish culture. In R. S. Kalish (Ed.), *Death and dying: Views from many cultures.* Farmingdale, NY: Baywood Publishing.

Ackerman, B. P. (1982). Contextual integration and utterance interpretation: The ability of children and adults to interpret sarcastic utterances. *Child Development, 53,* 1075–1083.

Acredolo, L. P., & Hake, J. L. (1982). Infant perception. In B. B. Wolman (Ed.), *Handbook of developmental psychology.* Englewood Cliffs, NJ: Prentice-Hall.

Action for Children's Television (ACT), Spring, 1978, 7(3).

Adams, G. R., & Crossman, S. M. (1978). *Physical attractiveness: A cultural imperative.* Roslyn Heights, NY: Libra.

Adams, G. R., & Gullotta, T. (1989). *Adolescent life experiences* (2nd ed.). Pacific Grove, CA: Brooks/Cole.

Adams, G. R., & Huston, T. L. (1975). Social perception of middle-aged persons varying in physical attractiveness. *Developmental Psychology, 2,* 657–658.

Adams, R. J., & Maurer, D. (1984). *The use of habituation to study newborns' color vision.* Paper presented at the 4th International Conference on Infant Studies, New York.

Adams, R. J., Maurer, D., & Davis, M. (1986). Newborns' discrimination of chromatic from achromatic stimuli. *Journal of Experimental Child Psychology, 41,* 267–281.

Adler, S., & Aranya, N. (1984). A comparison of the work needs, attitudes, and preferences of professional accountants at different career stages. *Journal of Vocational Behavior, 25,* 574–580.

Ahr, P. R., & Youniss, J. (1970). Reasons for failure on the class inclusion problem. *Child Development, 41,* 131–144.

Aiken, L. R. (1982). *Later life* (2nd. ed). New York: Holt, Rinehart, & Winston.

Ainsworth, M. D. S. (1977). Attachment theory and its utility in cross-cultural research. In P. H. Leiderman, S. R. Tulkin, & R. Rosenfeld (Eds.), *Culture and infancy* (pp. 49–67). New York: Academic Press.

Ainsworth, M. D. S., Bell, S. M., & Stayton, D. J. (1971). Individual difference in strange situation behavior in one-year-olds. In H. R. Schaffer (Ed.), *The origins of human social relations* (pp. 17–57). London: Academic Press.

Ainsworth, M. D. S., Blehar, M. C., Waters, E., & Wall, S. (1978). *Patterns of attachment: A psychological study of the strange situation.* Hillsdale, NJ: Erlbaum.

Albert, M. C. (1981). Changes in language with aging. *Seminars in Neurology, 1,* 43–46.

Alegria, J. R., & Noirot, E. (1978). Neonate orientation behavior towards the human voice. *International Journal of Behavioral Development, 1,* 291–312.

Allan, G. (1977). Sibling solidarity. *Journal of Marriage and the Family, 39,* 177–184.

Allport, G. W. (1961). *Pattern and growth in personality* (2nd ed.). New York: Holt, Rinehart, & Winston.

Alpaugh, P. K., & Birren, J. E. (1977). Variables affecting creative contributions across the adult life span. *Human Development, 20,* 240–248.

Alter-Reid, K., Gibbs, M. S., Lachenmeyer, J. R., Sigal, J., & Massoth, N. A. (1986). Sexual abuse of children: A review of the empirical findings. *Clinical Psychology Review. 6,* 249–266.

Alwitt, L., Anderson, D., Lorch, E., & Levin, S. (1980). Preschool children's visual attention to television. *Human Communication Research, 7,* 52–67.

Amato, P. R. (1988). Parental divorce and attitudes toward marriage and family life. *Journal of Marriage and the Family, 50,* 453–461.

American Psychiatric Association (1980). *Diagnostic and statistical manual of mental disorders* (3rd. ed.). Washington, DC: American Psychiatric Association.

American Psychiatric Association (1987). *Diagnostic and statistical manual of mental disorders* III-R. Washington, DC: American Psychiatric Association.

American Psychological Association. (1982). *Ethical principles in the conduct of research with human participants.* Washington, DC: Author.

Amsterdam, B. K. (1972). Mirror self-image reactions before age two. *Developmental Psychology, 5,* 297–305.

Anastasi, A. (1958). Heredity, environment and the question "How?" *Psychological Review, 65,* 197–208.

Anastasi, A. (1988). *Psychological testing* (6th ed.). New York: Macmillan.

Anderson, D. R., & Levin, S. (1976). Young children's attention to "Sesame Street." *Child Development, 47,* 806–811.

Anderson, D. R., & Lorch, E. (1983). Looking at television: Action or reaction. In J. Bryant & D. Anderson (Eds.), *Children's understanding of television: Research on attention and comprehension* (pp. 1–33). New York: Academic Press.

Anderson, D. R., Lorch, E. P., Field, D. E., Collins, P. A., & Nathan, J. G. (1986). Television viewing at home: Age trends in visual attention and time with TV. *Child Development, 57,* 1024–1033.

Anderson, H. H. (1959). Creativity in perspective. In H. H. Anderson (Ed.), *Creativity and its cultivation.* New York: Harper & Row.

Anderson, J. R. (1983). *The architecture of cognition.* Cambridge, MA: Harvard University Press.

Anderson, J. R. (1985). *Cognitive psychology and its implications* (2nd ed.). New York: W. H. Freeman.

Anderson, J. R., & Paulson, R. (1977). Representation and retention of verbatim information. *Journal of Verbal Learning and Verbal Behavior, 16,* 439–451.

Anderson, T. B. (1984). Widowhood as a life transition: Its impact on kinship ties. *Journal of Marriage and the Family, 46,* 105–114.

Ansbacher, H. L., & Ansbacher, R. R. (Eds.). (1956). *The individual psychology of Alfred Adler.* New York: Basic Books.

Anthony, S. (1940). *The child's discovery of death.* New York: Harcourt, Brace and World.

Antonak, R. F., King, S., & Lowy, J. J. (1982). Otis-Lennon Mental Ability Test, Stanford Achievement Test, and three demographic variables as predictors of achievement in grades 2 and 4. *Journal of Educational Research, 75,* 366–373.

Antonucci, T. C. (1985). Personal characteristics, social support, and social behavior. In R. H. Binstock & E. Shanas (Eds.), *Handbook of aging and the social sciences.* New York: Van Nostrand Reinhold.

Apgar, V. (1953). A proposal for a new method of evaluation of the newborn infant. *Current Researches in Anesthesia and Analgesia, 32,* 260–267.

Appelbaum, M. I., & McCall, R. B. (1983). Design and analysis in developmental psychology. In P. H. Mussen (Ed.), *Handbook of child psychology* (4th ed., Vol. 1). New York: Wiley.

Apps, J. W. (1981). *The adult learner on campus.* Chicago: Follett.

Archibald, H. C., Bell, D., Miller, C., & Tuddenham, R. D. (1962). Bereavement in childhood and adult psychiatric disturbance. *Psychosomatic Medicine, 24,* 343–351.

Arenberg, D. (1965). Anticipation interval and age differences in verbal learning. *Journal of Abnormal Psychology, 17,* 419–425.

Aries, P. (1962). *Centuries of childhood.* (R. Baldick, Trans.). New York: Vintage. (Original work published 1960.)

Arieti, S. (1976). *Creativity: The magic synthesis.* New York: Basic Books.

Arlin, P. K. (1975). Cognitive development in adulthood: A fifth stage? *Developmental Psychology, 11,* 602–606.

Arlin, P. K. (1984). Adolescent and adult thought: A structural interpretation. In M. L. Commons, F. A. Richards, & C. Armon (Eds.), *Beyond formal operations: Late adolescent and adult cognitive development.* New York: Praeger.

Aro, H., & Taipale, V. (1987). The impact of timing of puberty on psychosomatic symptoms among fourteen- to sixteen-year-old Finnish girls. *Child Development, 58,* 261–268.

Aronfreed, J. (1969). The concept of internalization. In D. Goslin (Ed.), *Handbook of socialization theory and research* (pp. 263–480). New York: Rand McNally.

Asher, J. J. (1977). Children learning another language: A developmental hypothesis. *Child Development, 48,* 1040–1048.

Asher, S. R., Hymel, S., & Renshaw, P. D. (1984). Loneliness in children. *Child Development, 55,* 1456–1464.

Asher, S. R., Oden, S. L., & Gottman, J. (1977). Children's friendships in school settings. From L. Katz, et al. (Eds.), *Current topics in early childhood education* (Vol. 1). Norwood, NJ: Ablex.

Aslin, R. N., Pisoni, D. P., & Jusczyk, P. W. (1983). Auditory development and speech perception in infancy. In M. H. Haith & J. J. Campos (Eds.), *Handbook of child psychology: Vol. 2. Infancy and developmental psychology.* New York: Wiley.

Atchley, R. C. (1977). *The social forces in later life.* Belmont, CA: Wadsworth.

Atchley, R. C. (1988). *Social forces and aging: An introduction to social gerontology* (5th ed.). Belmont, CA: Wadsworth Publishing.

Atkinson, J., & Huston, T. L. (1984). Sex role orientation and division of labor early in marriage. *Journal of Personality and Social Psychology, 46,* 330–345.

Attig, T. (1986). Death themes in adolescent music: The classic years. In C. A. Corr & J. N. McNeil (eds.), *Adolescence and death.* New York: Springer-Verlag.

Austin, J. H. (1978). *Chase, chance, and creativity.* New York: Columbia University Press.

Bacharach, V. R., & Luszcz, M. A. (1979). Communicative competence in young children: The use of implicit linguistic information. *Child Development, 50,* 260–263.

Bachman, J. G., O'Malley, P., & Johnston, J. (1978). *Youth in transition: Vol. 6. Adolescence to adulthood—change and stability in the lives of young men.* Ann Arbor, MI: University of Michigan Institute for Social Research.

Backer, T. E., Batchelor, W. F., Jones, J. M., & Mays, V. M. (1988). Introduction to the special issue: Psychology and AIDS. *American Psychologist, 43,* 835–836.

Baer, D. M., & Sherman, J. A. (1964). Reinforcement control of generalized imitation in young children. *Journal of Experimental Child Psychology, 1,* 37–49.

Baillargeon, R., Spelke, E. S., & Wasserman, S. (1985). Object permanence in five-month-old infants. *Cognition, 20,* 191–208.

Baily, M. (1987). Aging and the ability to work. In G. Burtless (Ed.), *Work, health, and income among the elderly.* Washington, DC: Brookings.

Bakeman, R., & Brown, J. (1980). Early interaction: Consequences for social and mental development at three years. *Child Development, 51,* 437–447.

Baldwin, J. M. (1897). *Social and ethical interpretations in mental development.* New York: Macmillan.

Baltes, P. B. (1982). Developmental psychology: Observations on history and theory revisited. In R. M. Lerner (Ed.), *Developmental psychology: Historical and philosophical perspectives,* Hillsdale, NJ: Erlbaum.

Baltes, P. B., & Baltes, M. M. (1980). Plasticity and variability in psychological aging: Methodological and theoretical issues. In G. Gorsk (Ed.), *Determining the effects of aging on the nervous system.* Berlin: Schering.

Baltes, P. B., Dittman-Kohli, F., & Dixon, R. A. (1984). New perspectives on the development of intelligence in adulthood: Toward a dual-process conception and a model of selective optimization with compensation. In P. B. Baltes & O. G. Brim (Eds.), *Life span development and behavior* (Vol. 6, pp. 33–76). New York: Academic Press.

Baltes, P. B., Reese, H. H., & Nesselroade, J. R. (1988). *Life span developmental psychology: Introduction to research methods.* Hillsdale, NJ: Erlbaum.

Baltes, P. B., & Willis, S. L. (1982). Plasticity and en-hancement of intellectual functioning in old age: Penn State's Adult Development and Enrichment Project (ADEPT). In F. I. M., Craik & S. Trehub (Eds.), *Aging and cognitive processes* (pp. 353–389). New York: Plenum.

Bandura, A. (1965). Influence of models' reinforcement contingencies on the acquisition of imitative responses. *Journal of Personality and Social Psychology, 1,* 589–595.

Bandura, A. (1969). Social learning theory of identifica-tory processes. In D. A. Goslin (Ed.), *Handbook of social-ization theory and research.* Chicago: Rand McNally.

Bandura, A. (1971). *Psychological modeling: Conflicting theories.* New York: Lieber-Atherton.

Bandura, A. (1977). *Social learning theory.* Englewood Cliffs, NJ: Prentice-Hall.

Bandura, A. (1986). *Social foundations of thought and action: A social cognitive theory.* Englewood Cliffs, NJ: Prentice-Hall.

Bandura, A., Ross, D., & Ross, S. A. (1963a). A compar-ative test of the status envy, social power, and second-ary reinforcement theories of identificatory learning. *Journal of Abnormal and Social Psychology, 67,* 527–534.

Bandura, A., Ross. D., & Ross, S. A. (1963b). Imitation of film-mediated aggressive models. *Journal of Abnor-mal and Social Psychology, 66,* 3–11.

Bandura, A., Ross, D., & Ross, S. A. (1963c). Vicarious reinforcement and imitative learning. *Journal of Abnor-mal and Social Psychology, 67,* 601–607

Bandura, A., & Walters, R. H. (1963). *Social learning and personality development.* New York: Holt, Rinehart & Winston.

Bane, M. J. (1979). Marital disruption and the lives of children. In G. Levinger & O. Moles (Eds.), *Divorce and separation: Context, causes and consequences.* New York: Basic Books.

Bane, M. J., & Jargowsky, P. A. (1988). The link between government policy and family structure: What matters and what doesn't. In A. J. Cherlin (Ed.), *The changing American family and public policy.* Washington, DC: The Urban Institute Press.

Bank, S., & Kahn, M. D. (1982). *The sibling bond.* New York: Basic Books.

Banks, M. S. (1980). The development of visual accom-modation during early infancy. *Child Development, 51,* 646–666.

Banks, M. S., & Salapatek, P. (1981). Infant pattern vi-sion: A new approach based on the contrast sensitivity function. *Journal of Experimental Child Psychology, 31,* 1–45.

Banks, M. S., & Salapatek, P. (1983). Infant visual per-ception. In M. M. Haith & J. J. Campos (Eds.), *Handbook of child psychology: Vol. 2. Infancy and developmental psychobiology.* New York: Wiley.

Barglow, P., Vaughan, B., & Molitor, N. (1987). Effects of maternal absence due to employment on the quality of infant-mother attachment in a low-risk sample. *Child Development, 58,* 945–954.

Barnett, R. C., & Baruch, G. K. (1987). Social roles, gen-der, and psychological distress. In R. C. Barnett, L. Biener, & G. K. Baruch (Eds.), *Gender and stress.* New York: The Free Press.

Baron, J. N., & Bielby, W. T. (1985). Organizational bar-riers to gender equality: Sex segregation of jobs and opportunities. In A. S. Rossi (Ed.), *Gender and the life course.* New York: Aldine.

Barrera, M. E., & Maurer. D. (1981). The perception of facial expressions by the three-month-old. *Child Devel-opment, 52,* 203–206.

Barron, F., & Harrington, D. M. (1981). Creativity, intel-ligence and personality. *Annual Review of Psychology, 32,* 439–476.

Bartoshuk, L. M., Rifkin, B., Marks, L. E., & Bars. P. (1986). Taste and aging. *Journal of Gerontology, 41,* 51–57.

Baruch, G. K., & Barnett, R. C. (1986). Father's partici-pation in family work and children's sex role attitudes. *Child Development, 57,* 1210–1223.

Barusch, A. S. (1988). Problems and coping strategies of elderly spouse caregivers. *The Gerontologist, 28,* 677–685.

Barusch, A. S., & Spaid, W. M. (1989). Gender differ-ences in caregiving: Why do wives report greater bur-den? *The Gerontologist, 29,* 667–676.

Bases, R. (1985). Diagnostic ultrasound. *Science, 228,* 648–649.

Basow, S. A. (1986). *Gender stereotypes: Traditions and alternatives* (2nd ed.). Monterey, CA: Brooks/Cole.

Bates, E. (1976). *Language and context: The acquisition of pragmatics.* New York: Academic Press.

Bates, J. E., Maslin, C. A., & Frankel, K. A. (1985). Attachment security, mother-child interaction, and temperment as predictors of behavior-problem rating at age three years. In I. Bretherton & E. Waters (Eds.), *Growing points of attachment theory and research. Monographs of the Society for Research in Child Development, 50* (1–2, Serial No. 209), 167–193.

Baum, A., & Nesselhoff, S. E. A. (1988). Psychological research and the prevention, etiology, and treatment of AIDS. *American Psychologist, 43,* 900–906.

Baum, M., & Baum, R. C. (1980). *Growing old.* Englewood Cliffs, NJ: Prentice-Hall.

Baumeister, R. F. (1988). Should we stop studying sex differences altogether? *American Psychologist, 43,* 1092–1095.

Baumrind, D. (1967). Child care practices anteceding three patterns of preschool behavior. *Genetic Psychology Monographs, 75,* 43–88.

Baumrind, D. (1968). Authoritarian vs. authoritative parental control. *Adolescence, 3,* 255–272.

Baumrind, D. (1971). Current patterns of parental authority. *Developmental Psychology Monograph, 4* (1, Pt. 2).

Baumrind, D. (1975). Some thoughts about childbearing. In U. Bronfenbrenner & M. A. Mahoney (Eds.), *Influences on human development* (2nd ed.). Hinsdale, IL: Dryden Press.

Baumrind, D. (1982). Are androgynous individuals more effective persons and parents? *Child Development, 53,* 44–75.

Baumrind, D. (1985). Research using intentional deception: Ethical issues revisited. *American Psychologist, 40,* 165–174.

Baumrind, D., & Black, A. E. (1967). Socialization practices associated with dimensions of competence in preschool boys and girls. *Child Development, 38,* 291–327.

Bayles, K. A. (1984). Language and dementia. In A. L. Holland (Ed.), *Language disorders in adults* (pp. 209–244). San Diego: College-Hill Press.

Bayley, N. (1949). Consistency and variability in the growth of intelligence from birth to eighteen years. *Journal of Genetic Psychology, 75,* 165–196.

Bayley, N. (1955). On the growth of intelligence. *American Psychologist, 10,* 805–818.

Bayley, N. (1957). Data on the growth of intelligence between 16 and 21 years as measured by the Wechsler-Bellevue Scale. *Journal of Genetic Psychology, 90,* 3–15.

Bayley, N. (1966). Learning in adulthood: The role of intelligence. In H. J. Klausmeier & C. W. Harris (Eds.), *Analysis of concept learning.* New York: Academic Press.

Bayley, N. (1968). Cognition in aging. In K. W. Schaie (Ed.), *Theory and methods of research on aging.* Morgantown: West Virginia University Library.

Bayley, N. (1969). *Bayley Scales of Infant Development.* New York: The Psychological Corporation.

Bayley, N., & Schaefer, E. S. (1964). Correlations of maternal and child behaviors with the development of mental abilities: Data from the Berkeley Growth Study. *Monographs of the Society for Research in Child Development, 29* (Serial No. 97).

Bearison, D. J., & Cassel, T. Z. (1975). Cognitive decentration and social codes: Communicative effectiveness in young children from differing family contexts. *Developmental Psychology, 11,* 29–36.

Beauchamp, G. K., Cowart, B. J., & Moran, M. (1986). Developmental changes in salt acceptability in human infants. *Developmental Psychobiology, 19,* 75–83.

Beauchamp, G. K., & Moran, M. (1985). Acceptance of sweet and salty tastes in 2-year-old children. *Appetite, 5,* 291–305.

Bechtoldt, H. P., & Hutz, C. S. (1979). Stereopsis in young infants and stereopsis in an infant with congenital esotropia. *Journal of Pediatric Opthalmology, 16,* 49–54.

Beck, A. A., & Leviton, B. (1976). *Social support mediating factors in widowhood and life satisfaction among the elderly.* Paper presented at the annual meeting of the Gerontological Society of America, New York.

Becker, D. (1973). *The denial of death.* New York: Free Press.

Becker, D., & Margolin, F. (1967). How surviving parents handled their young children's adaptation to the crisis of loss. *American Journal of Orthopsychiatry, 37,* 753–757.

Beckwith, L., & Parmelee, A. H. (1986). EEG patterns of preterm infants, home environments, and later IQ. *Child Development, 57,* 777–789.

Bedford, V. H. (1989). A comparison of thematic apperceptions of sibling affiliation, conflict, and separation at two periods of adulthood. *International Journal of Aging and Human Development, 28,* 53–66.

Bee, H. (1978). *Social issues in developmental psychology* (2nd ed.). New York: Harper & Row.

Beecher, H. K. (1968). A definition of irreversible coma. *Journal of the American Medical Association, 205,* 85–88.

Beilin, H. (1975). *Studies in the cognitive basis of language acquisition.* New York: Academic Press.

Belal, A. (1975). Presbycusis: Physiological or pathological? *Journal of Laryngology, 89,* 1011–1025.

Beland, F. (1984). The family and adults 65 years and older: Co-residency and availability of help. *Canadian Review of Sociology and Anthropology, 21,* 302–317.

Beland, F. (1987). Living arrangement preferences among elderly people. *The Gerontologist, 27,* 797–803.

Bell, A. P., Weinberg, M. S., & Hammersmith, S. K. (1981). *Sexual preference: Its development in men and women.* Bloomington, IN: University Press.

Bell, B., Wolf, E., & Bernholtz, C. D. (1972). Depth perception as a function of age. *Aging and Human Development, 3,* 77–88.

Bell, R. R. (1981). *Worlds of friendship.* Beverly Hills, CA: Sage.

Bell, S. M., & Ainsworth, M. D. S. (1972). Infant crying and maternal responsiveness. *Child Development, 43,* 1171–1190.

Bellugi, U., & Klima, E. (1982). From gesture to sign: Deixis in a visual-gestural language. In R. J. Jarrella & W. Klein (Eds.), *Speech, place and action: Studies in deixis and related topics.* Sussex: Wiley.

Belmont, L., & Marolla, G. A. (1973). Birth order, family size, and intelligence. *Science, 182,* 1096–1101.

Belsky, J. (1986). Infant day care: A cause for concern? *Zero to Three, 6,* 1–7.

Belsky, J. (1988). The effects of infant day care reconsidered. *Early Childhood Research Quarterly, 3,* 235–272.

Belsky, J., Garduque, L., & Hrncir, E. (1984). Assessing performance, competence and executive capacity in infant play: Relations to home environment and the security of attachment. *Developmental Psychology, 20,* 406–417.

Belsky, J., & Rovine, M. R. (1988). Nonmaternal care in the first year of life and the security of infant-parent attachment. *Child Development, 59,* 157–167.

Belsky, J., & Steinberg, L. D. (1978). The effects of day care: A critical review. *Child Development, 49,* 929–949.

Belsky, J., Ward, H., & Rovine M. (1988). Prenatal expectations, postnatal experiences, and the transition to parenthood. In R. Ashmore & D. Brodzinsky (Eds.), *Perspectives on the family.* Hillsdale, NJ: Erlbaum.

Bem, S. L. (1974). The measurement of psychological androgyny. *Journal of Consulting and Clinical Psychology, 42,* 155–162.

Bem, S. L. (1975). Sex role adaptability: One consequence of psychological androgyny. *Journal of Personality and Social Psychology, 31,* 634–643.

Bem, S. L. (1976). Probing the promise of androgyny. In A. G. Kaplan & J. P. Bean (Eds.), *Beyond sex-role stereotypes: Readings toward a psychology of androgyny.* Boston: Little, Brown.

Bem, S. L. (1989). Genital knowledge and gender constancy in preschool children. *Child Development, 60,* 649–662.

Benack, S. (1984). Postformal epistemologies and the growth of empathy. In M. L. Commons, F. A. Richards, & C. Armon (Eds.), *Beyond formal operations: Late adolescent and adult cognitive development.* New York: Praeger.

Benedict, R. (1938). Continuities and discontinuities in cultural conditioning. *Psychiatry, 1,* 161–167.

Bengtson, V. L., Reedy, M. N., & Gordon, C. (1985). Aging and self-conceptions: Personality processes and social contexts. In J. E. Birren & K. W. Schaie (Eds.), *Handbook of the psychology of aging* (2nd ed.) (pp. 544–593). New York: Van Nostrand Reinhold.

Bengston, V. L., & Robertson, J. F. (1985). *Grandparenthood.* Beverly Hills, CA: Sage.

Benn, R. K. (1986). Factors promoting secure attachment relationships between employed mothers and their sons. *Child Development, 57,* 1224–1231.

Ben-Zeev, S. (1977). The influence of bilingualism on cognitive strategy and cognitive development. *Child Development, 48,* 1009–1018.

Berger, R. M. (1982). *Gay and gray: The older homosexual man.* Chicago: University of Chicago Press.

Bergman. M. (1971). Changes in hearing with age. *The Gerontologist, 11,* 148–151.

Berk, L. E. (1986). Relationship of elementary school children's private speech to behavioral accompaniment to task, attention, and task performance. *Developmental Psychology, 22,* 671–680.

Berko, J. (1958). The child's learning of English morphology. *Word, 14,* 150–177.

Berkowitz, M. W. & Gibbs, J. C. (1983). Measuring the developmental features of moral discussion. *Merrill-Palmer Quarterly, 29,* 399–410.

Berlyne, D. E. (1969). Laughter, humor, and play. In G. Lindzey & E. Aronson (Eds.). *The handbook of social psychology* (Vol. 3). Reading, MA: Addison-Wesley.

Berman, P. W., & Pedersen, F. A. (1987). Research on men's transitions to parenthood: An integrative discussion. In P. W. Berman & F. A. Pedersen (Eds.), *Men's transitions to parenthood: Longitudinal studies of early family experience.* Hillsdale, NJ: Erlbaum.

Berndt, T. J. (1979). Developmental changes in conformity to peers and parents. *Developmental Psychology, 15,* 608–616.

Berndt, T. J. (1982a). Fairness and friendship. In K. H. Rubin & H. S. Ross (Eds.), *Peer relationships and social skills in childhood.* New York: Springer-Verlag.

Berndt, T. J. (1982b). The features and effects of friendship in early adolescence. *Child Development, 53,* 1447–1460.

Berndt, T. J., & Bulleit, T. N. (1985). Effects of sibling relationships on preschooler's behavior at home and at school. *Developmental Psychology, 21* (5), 761–767.

Berndt, T. J., Hawkins, J. A., & Hoyle, S. G. (1986). Changes in friendship during a school year: Effects on children's and adolescents' impressions of friendships and sharing with friends. *Child Development, 57,* 1284–1297.

Bernstein, B. (1971). *Classes, codes and controls.* London: Routledge and Kegan Paul.

Berscheid, E., Walster, E., & Bohrnstedt, G. (1973, November). Body image, *Psychology Today,* 119–131.

Bettelheim, B. (1962). *Symbolic wounds.* New York: Collier.

Bettelheim, B. (1985 November). Punishment versus discipline. *The Atlantic, 256* (5), 51–59.

Bettes, B. A. (1988). Maternal depression and motherese: Temporal and intonational features. *Child Development, 59,* 1089–1096.

Bielby, D. D., & Bielby, W. T. (1984). Work commitment, sex-role attitudes, and women's employment. *American Sociological Review, 49,* 234–247.

Biemer, D. J. (1983). Shyness control: A systematic approach to social anxiety management in children. *School Counselor, 31,* 53–60.

Bierman, K. L. (1986). Process of change during social skills training with preadolescents and its relation to treatment outcome. *Child Development, 57,* 230–240.

Bierman, K. L., & Furman, W. F. (1984). The effects of social skills training and peer involvement in the social development of preadolescents. *Child Development, 55,* 151–162.

Bigelow, B. J. (1977). Children's friendship expectations: A cognitive development study. *Child Development, 48,* 246–253.

Bigelow, B. J., & La Gaipa, J. J. (1975). Children's written descriptions of friendships: A multidimensional analysis. *Developmental Psychology, 11,* 857–858.

Bigner, J. J. (1974). Second born's discrimination of sibling role concept. *Developmental Psychology, 10,* 564–573.

Bigner, J. J. (1985). *Parent-child relations: An introduction to parenting.* (2nd ed.) New York: Macmillan.

Biller, H. B. (1974). *Paternal deprivation.* Lexington, MA: Lexington Books.

Biller, H. B. (1981). The father and sex role development. In M. E. Lamb (Ed.), *The role of the father in child development (2nd ed.).* New York: Wiley.

Biller, H. B. (1982). Fatherhood: Implications for child and adult development. In B. B. Wolman (Ed.), *Handbook of developmental psychology.* Englewood Cliffs, NJ: Prentice-Hall.

Birch, L. L., & Billman, J. (1986). Preschool children's food sharing with friends and acquaintances. *Child Development, 57,* 387–395.

Bischof, L. J. (1976). *Adult psychology.* New York: Harper & Row.

Bittman, S., & Zalk, S. R. (1978). *Expectant fathers.* New York: Hawthorn.

Black, S. M., & Hill, C. E. (1984). The psychological well-being of women in their middle years. *Psychology of Women Quarterly, 8,* 282–292.

Blake, J. (1974). Can we believe recent data on birth expectation in the United States? *Demography, 11,* 25–44.

Blanchard, R. W., & Biller, H. B. (1971). Father availability and academic performance among third-grade boys. *Developmental Psychology, 81,* 85–88.

Blanche, S., Rouzioux, C., Moscato, M., Veber, F., Mayaux, M.-J., Jacomet, C., Tricoire, J., Deville, A., Vial, M., Firtion, G., De Crepy, A., Douard, D., Robin, M., Courpotin, C., Ciraru-Vigneron, N., le Diest, F., & Griscelli, C. (1989). A prospective study of infants born to women seropositive for Human Immunodeficiency Virus Type 1. *New England Journal of Medicine, 320,* 1643–1648.

Blasi, A. (1980). Bridging moral cognition and moral action: A critical review of the literature. *Psychological Bulletin, 88,* 1–45.

Blasi, A. (1983). Moral cognition and moral action: A theoretical perspective. *Developmental Review, 3,* 178–210.

Blatt, M. J., & Kohlberg, L. (1975). The effects of classroom moral discussion upon children's level of moral judgment. *Journal of Moral Education, 4,* 129–161.

Blau, Z. S. (1973). *Old age in a changing society.* New York: Franklin Watts.

Block, J. (1971). *Lives through time.* Berkeley, CA: Bancroft.

Block, J. H. (1976). Issues, problems and pitfalls in assessing sex differences. *Merrill-Palmer Quarterly, 22,* 283–308.

Block, J. H. (1978). Another look at sex differentiation in the socialization behaviors of mothers and fathers. In F. Wenmark & J. Sheman (Eds.), *Psychology of women: Future direction of research.* New York: Psychological Dimensions.

Block, J., Block, J. H., & Gjerde, P. F. (1988). Parental functioning and the home environment in families of divorce: Prospective and concurrent analyses. *Journal of the American Academy of Child and Adolescent Psychiatry, 27,* 207–213.

Bloom, A., Wagner, M., Bergman, A., Altshuler, L., & Raskin, L. (1981) Relationship between intellectual status and reading skills for developmentally disabled children. *Perceptual and Motor Skills, 52,* 853–854.

Bloom, B. S. (1964). *Stability and change in human characteristics.* New York: Wiley.

Bloom, L. P., Lightbown, P., & Hood, L. (1975). Structure and variation in child language. *Monographs of the Society for Research in Child Development, 40* (Serial No. 160).

Bluebond-Langner, M. (1977). Meanings of death to children. In H. Feifel (Ed.), *New meanings of death.* New York: McGraw-Hill.

Blumstein, P. W., & Schwartz, P. (1983). *American couples.* New York: William Morrow.

Boggiano, A. K., Klinger, C. A., & Main, D. S. (1986). Enhancing interest in peer interaction: A developmental analysis. *Child Development, 57,* 852–861.

Bohannan, P. M., & Erickson, R. (1978). Stepping in. *Psychology Today, 11,* 53.

Boivin, M., & Bégin, G. (1989). Peer status and self-perception among early elementary school children: The case of the rejected children. *Child Development, 60,* 591–596.

Bonvillian, J. D., Orlansky, M. D., Novack, L. L., & Folven, F. J. (1983). Early sign language acquisition and cognitive development. In D. R. Rogers & J. A. Stoboda (Eds.), *The acquisition of symbolic skills.* New York: Plenum.

Booth, A. (1972). Sex and social participation. *American Sociological Review, 37,* 183–192.

Booth, A., & Hess, E. (1974). Cross-sex friendships. *Journal of Marriage and the Family, 36,* 38–47.

Bornstein, M. H. (1976). Infants' recognition memory for hue. *Developmental Psychology, 12,* 185–191.

Bornstein, M. H. (1978). Chromatic vision in infancy. In H. W. Reese and L. P. Lipsitt (Eds.), *Advances in child development and behavior* (Vol. 12), New York: Academic Press.

Borstelmann, L. J. (1983). Children before psychology: Ideas about children from antiquity to the late 1800s. In P. H. Mussen (Ed.), Vol. 1, *Handbook of child psychology* (4th ed.). New York: Wiley.

Bossard, M. E., & Galusha, R. (1979). The utility of the Stanford-Binet in predicting WRAT performance. *Psychology in the Schools, 16,* 488–490.

Botwinick, J. (1978). *Aging and behavior* (2nd. ed.). New York: Springer-Verlag.

Botwinick, J., & Birren, J. E. (1963). Cognitive processes: Mental abilities and psychomotor responses in healthy aged men. In J. E. Birren et al. (Eds.), *Human aging: A biological and behavioral study.* Washington, DC: U.S. Government Printing Office.

Botwinick, J., & Kornetsky, C. (1960). Age differences in the acquisition and extinction of GSR. *Journal of Gerontology, 15,* 83–84.

Bower, T. G. R. (1964). Discrimination of depth in premature infants. *Psychonomic Science, 1,* 368.

Bowerman, M. (1978). Systematizing semantic knowledge: Changes over time in the child's organization of word meaning. *Child Development, 49,* 977–987.

Bowlby, J. (1969). *Attachment and loss: Vol. 1. Attachment.* New York: Basic.

Bowlby, J. (1979). *The making and breaking of affectional bonds.* New York: Tavistock.

Bowlby, J. (1980). *Attachment and loss: Vol. III. Loss, sadness, and depression.* New York: Basic Books.

Brabant, S., & Mooney, L. (1986). Sex role stereotyping in the Sunday comics: Ten years later. *Sex Roles, 14,* 141–148.

Bracher, M., & Santow, G. (1988). *Changing family composition from Australian life-history data.* Working paper No. 6, Australian Family Project.

Brackbill, Y. (1958). Extinction of the smiling response in infants as a function of reinforcement schedule. *Child Development, 29,* 115–124.

Bradbard, M. R., Martin, C. L., Endsley, R. C., & Halverson, C. F. (1986). Influence of sex stereotypes on children's exploration and memory: A competence versus performance distinction. *Developmental Psychology, 22,* 481–486.

Bradley, R. M., & Stearn, I. B. (1967). The development of the human taste bud during the foetal period. *Journal of Anatomy, 101,* 743–752.

Brainerd, C. J. (1978). *Piaget's theory of intelligence.* Englewood Cliffs, NJ: Prentice-Hall.

Brainerd, C. J. (1979). *The origins of the number concept.* New York: Praeger.

Brainerd, C. J. (1983). Working memory systems and cognitive development. In C. J. Brainerd (Ed.) *Recent advances in cognitive-development theory: Progress in cognitive developmental research.* New York: Springer-Verlag.

Braun, H. W., & Geiselhart, R. (1959). Age differences in the acquisition and extinction of the conditioned eyelid response. *Journal of Experimental Psychology, 57,* 386–388.

Brazelton, T. B. (1984). *Neonatal behavioral assessment scale* (2nd ed.). Philadelphia: Lippincott.

Brecher, E. (1984). *Love, sex and aging.* Boston: Little Brown.

Brenner, J., & Mueller, E. (1982). Shared meaning in boy toddler's peer relations. *Child Development, 53,* 380–391.

Bretherton, I. (1984). Representing the social world in symbolic play: Reality and fantasy. In I. Bretherton (Ed.), *Symbolic play: The development of social understanding.* New York: Academic Press.

Bretherton, I. (1986). Representing the social world in symbolic play: Reality and fantasy. In A. W. Gottfried & C. C. Brown (Eds.), *Play interactions: The contributions of play materials and parental involvement to children's development* (pp. 119–148). Lexington, MA: D.C. Heath.

Brim, O. G., & Kagan, J. (1980). Constancy and change: A view of the issues. In J. Kagan & O. G. Brim (Eds.), *Constancy and change in development* (pp. 1–25). Cambridge, MA: Harvard University Press.

Broderick, C. B. (1982). Adult sexual development. In B. B. Wolman (Ed.), *Handbook of developmental psychology.* Englewood Cliffs, NJ: Prentice-Hall.

Brody, E. M. (1985). Parent care as a normative family stress. *The Gerontologist, 25,* 19–29.

Brody, E. B., & Brody, N. (1976). *Intelligence: Nature, determinants, and consequences.* New York: Academic Press.

Bronfenbrenner, U. (1977). Toward an experimental ecology of human development. *American Psychologist, 32,* 513–531.

Bronfenbrenner, U. (1979). *The ecology of human development: Experiments by nature and design.* Cambridge, MA: Harvard University Press.

Bronfenbrenner, U., & Crouter, A. C. (1983). The evolution of environmental models in developmental research. In W. Kessen (Ed.), *Handbook of child psychology: Vol. 1. History, theory and methods* (4th ed). New York: Wiley.

Bronstein, P. (1988). Marital and parenting roles in transition: An overview. In P. Bronstein & C. P. Cowan (Eds.), *Fatherhood today: Men's changing role in the family*. New York: Wiley.

Bronstein, P., & Cowan, C. P. (Eds.). (1988). *Fatherhood today: Men's changing role in the family*. New York: Wiley.

Brooks-Gunn, J. (1987). Pubertal processes: Their relevance for developmental research. In V. B. Van Hasselt & M. Hersen (Eds.), *Handbook of adolescent psychology*. New York: Pergamon Press.

Brooks-Gunn, J., Warren, M. P., Samuelson, M., & Fox, R. (1986). Physical similarity of and disclosure of menarcheal status to friends: Effects of grade and pubertal status. *Journal of Early Adolescence, 6,* 3–14.

Brophy, J. (1985). Interactions of male and female students with male and female teachers. In L. C. Wilkinson & C. B. Narrett (Eds.) *Gender influences in classroom interaction*. New York: Academic Press.

Brophy, J., & Good. T. (1974). *Teacher-student relationships: Causes and consequences*. New York: Holt, Rinehart, & Winston.

Broverman, T. K., Vogel, S. R., Broverman, D. M., Clarkson, F. F., & Rosenkrantz, P. S. (1972). Sex-role stereotypes: A current appraisal. *Journal of Social Issues, 28,* 59–79.

Brown, A. L., & Smiley, S. S. (1978). The development of strategies for studying texts. *Child Development, 49,* 1076–1088.

Brown, G. W., Bhrolchain, M. N., & Harris, T. (1975). Social class and psychiatric disturbance in an urban population. *Sociology, 9,* 225–254.

Brown, G. W., & Harris, T. (1978). *Social origins of depression: A study of psychiatric disorders in women*. New York: Free Press.

Brown, R. (1958). *Words and things*. New York: Free Press.

Brown, R. (1973). *A first language: The early stages*. Cambridge, MA: Harvard University Press.

Brown, R., Cazden, C., & Bellugi, U. (1969). The child's grammar from I to III. In J. P. Hill (Ed.), *Minnesota symposium of child psychology* (Vol. 2). Minneapolis: University of Minnesota Press.

Brown, R. & Lenneberg, E. H. (1954). A study in language and cognition. *Journal of Abnormal and Social Psychology, 49,* 454–462.

Brownell, C. A. (1982). *Effects of age and age-mix on toddler peer interaction*. Paper presented at the International Conference on Infant Studies, Austin, TX.

Brownell, C. A. (1986). Convergent developments: Cognitive-developmental correlates of growth in infant/toddler peer skills. *Child Development, 57,* 275–286.

Brownmiller, S. (1984). *Femininity*. New York: Linden Press/ Simon and Schuster.

Bruce, P. A., Coyne, A. C., & Botwinick, J. (1982). Adult age differences in metamemory. *Journal of Gerontology, 37,* 354–357.

Bruce, P. R., & Herman, J. F. (1986). Adult age differences in spatial memory: Effects of distinctiveness and repeated experience. *Journal of Gerontology, 41,* 774–777.

Bruch, H. (1978). *The golden cage*. New York: Vintage Books.

Bruch, H. (1980). Thin-fat people. In J. R. Kaplan (Ed.), *A woman's conflict: The special relationship between women and food*. Englewood Cliffs, NJ: Prentice-Hall.

Bruner, J. S. (1973). Going beyond the information given. In J. M. Anglin (Ed.), *Beyond the information given*. New York: Norton.

Bruner, J. S., & Goodman, C. C. (1947). Value and need as organizing factors in perception. *Journal of Abnormal and Social Psychology, 42,* 33–44.

Bryant, B. K. (1982). Sibling relationships in middle childhood. In M. E. Lamb & B. Sutton-Smith (Eds.), *Sibling relationships: Their nature and significance across the lifespan*. Hillsdale, NJ: Erlbaum.

Bryant, B. K., & Crockenberg, S. (1980). Correlates and dimensions of prosocial behavior: A study of female siblings with their mothers. *Child Development, 51,* 529–544.

Bryen, D. N. (1974). Special education and the linguistically different child. *Exceptional Children, 40,* 589–599.

Bryen, D. N., Hartman, C., & Tait, P. (1978). *Variant English: An introduction to language variation*. Columbus, OH: Merrill.

Buell, S. J., & Coleman, P. D. (1979). Dendritic growth in the aging human brain and failure of growth in senile dementia. *Science, 206,* 854–856.

Buhler, C. (1968). *Psychology for contemporary living*. New York: Hawthorn Books.

Buhrmester, D., & Furman, W. (1987). The development of companionship and intimacy. *Child Development, 58,* 1101–1113.

Bullock, M., & Gelman, R. (1979). Preschool children's assumptions about cause and effect: Temporal ordering. *Child Development, 50,* 89–96.

Bullock, M., Gelman, R., & Baillargeon, R. (1982). The development of causal reasoning. In W. Friedman (Ed.), *The developmental psychology of time.* New York: Academic Press.

Bumpass, L., & Sweet, J. (1989). National estimates of cohabitation: Cohort levels and union stability. *Center for Demography and Ecology,* Madison, WI: University of Wisconsin.

Bumpass, L., Sweet, J., & Cherlin, A. (1989). The role of cohabitation in declining rates of marriage. *Center for Demography and Ecology,* Madison, WI: University of Wisconsin.

Burgess, A. W. (1984). *Child pornography and sex rings.* Lexington, MA: D.C. Heath.

Burkhauser, R., & Quinn, J. (1983). Is mandatory retirement overrated?: Evidence from the 1970's. *Journal of Human Resources, 18,* 358–377.

Burns, S. M., & Brainerd, C. J. (1979). Effects of constructive and dramatic play on perspective-taking in very young children. *Developmental Psychology, 15,* 512–521.

Burrus-Bammel, L. L. & Bammel, G. (1985). Leisure and recreation. In. J. E. Birren & K. W. Schaie (Eds.), *Handbook of the psychology of aging* (pp. 848–863). New York: Van Nostrand Reinhold.

Burtless, G. (1986). Social Security, unanticipated benefit increases, and the timing of retirement. *Review of Economic Studies, 53,* 781–805.

Burtless, G., & Moffitt, R. (1984). The effects of Social Security benefits on the labor supply of the aged. In H. Aaron & G. Burtless (Eds.), *Retirement and economic behavior.* Washington, DC: Brookings.

Buss, A. H., & Plomin, R. A. (1975). *A temperament theory of personality development.* New York: Wiley.

Buss, A. H., & Plomin, R. (1984). *Temperament: Early developing personality traits.* Hillsdale, NJ: Erlbaum.

Buss, A. H., Plomin, R., & Willerman, L. (1973). The inheritance of temperament. *Journal of Personality, 41,* 513–524.

Butler, R. N. (1968). The life review: An interpretation of reminiscence in the aged. In B. L. Neugarten (Ed.), *Middle age and aging.* Chicago: University of Chicago Press.

Butterfield-Picard, H., & Magno, J. B. (1982). Hospice the adjective, not the noun: The future of a national priority. *American Psychologist, 37,* 1254–1259.

Byrne, D., Ervin, D. H., & Lamberth, J. (1970). Continuity between the experimental study of attraction and real-life computer dating. *Journal of Personality and Social Psychology, 1,* 157–165.

Byrne, J. M. & Horowitz, F. D. (1979). Rocking as a soothing intervention: The influence of direction and type of movement. *Infant Behavior and Development, 2,* 209–214.

Byrnes, D. A. (1987). The physically unattractive child. *Childhood Education, 64,* 80–85.

Cain, B. S. (1982, December 19). The plight of the gay divorcee. *New York Times Magazine,* pp. 89–95.

Cairns, R. B. (1983). The emergence of developmental psychology. In P. H. Mussen (Ed.), *Handbook of child psychology* Vol. 1, (4th ed.). New York: Wiley.

Calderone, M. (1983). Fetal erection and its message to us. *Siecus Report XI, 5/6,* 9–10.

Calfee, R. C., Venezky, R. L., & Chapman, R. S. (1969). *Pronunciation of synthetic words with predictable and unpredictable letter-sound correspondences* (Tech. Rep. No. 71). Wisconsin Research and Development Center for Cognitive Learning.

Callan, V. J. (1987). The personal and marital adjustment of mothers and of voluntary and involuntary childless wives. *Journal of Marriage and the Family, 49,* 847–856.

Campbell, A., Converse, P. E., & Rodgers, W. L. (1976). *The quality of American Life: Perceptions, evaluations, and satisfactions.* New York: Russell Sage.

Campbell, P. B. (1976). Adolescent intellectual decline. *Adolescence, 11,* 629–635.

Campos, J. J., Langer, A., & Crowitz, A. (1970). Cardiac responses on the visual cliff in prelocomotor human infants. *Science, 1790,* 196–197.

Canestrari, R. E. (1963). Paced and self-paced learning in young and elderly adults. *Journal of Gerontology, 19,* 165–168.

Canestrari, R. E. (1968). Age changes in acquisition. In G. A. Talland (Ed.), *Human aging and behavior*. New York: Academic Press.

Caplan, P. J., MacPherson, P. M., & Tobin, P. (1985). Do sex-related differences in spatial abilities exist?: A multi-level critique with new data. *American Psychologist, 7,* 786–799.

Caporael, L. R. (1981). The paralanguage of caregiving: Baby talk to the institutionalized aged. *Journal of Personality and Social Psychology, 40,* 876–884.

Caron, A. J., Caron, R. F., Caldwell, R. C., & Weiss, S. J. (1973). Infant perception of the structural properties of the face. *Developmental Psychology, 9,* 385–389.

Caron, R. F., Caron, A. J., & Carlson, V. R. (1979). Infant perception of the invariant shape of objects varying in slant. *Child Development, 50,* 716–721.

Carroll, J. J. & Gibson, E. J. (1981). *Infants' differentiation of an aperture and an obstacle.* Paper presented at the biennial meeting of the Society for Research in Child Development, Boston.

Carroll, J. L. & Rest, J. R. (1982). Moral development. In B. B. Wolman (Ed.), *Handbook of developmental psychology.* Englewood Cliffs, NJ: Prentice-Hall.

Carter, J. (1982). The effects of aging upon selected visual functions: Color vision, glare sensitivity, field of vision, and accommodation. In R. Sekuler, D. Kline, & K. Dismukes (Eds.), *Aging and human visual function* (pp. 121–130). New York: Alan R. Liss.

Cash, T. F., Winstead, B. A., & Janda, L. H. (1986, April). The great American shape-up. *Psychology Today,* pp. 30–37.

Cassidy, J. (1986). The ability to negotiate the environment: An aspect of infant competence as related to quality of attachment. *Child Development, 57,* 331–337.

Cavanaugh, J. C. (1990). *Adult development and aging.* Belmont, CA: Wadsworth.

Cavior, N., & Dokecki, P. R. (1969, April 18). *Physical attractiveness and popularity among fifth grade boys.* Paper presented at the meeting of the Southwestern Psychological Association, Austin, TX.

Cavior, N., & Dokecki, P. R. (1970, April 25). *Physical attractiveness and popularity among fifth grade boys: A replication with Mexican children.* Paper presented at the meeting of the Southwestern Psychological Association, St. Louis, MO.

Cavior, N., & Dokecki, P. R. (1973). Physical attractiveness, perceived attitude similarity, and academic achievement as contributors to interpersonal attraction among adolescents. *Developmental Psychology, 9,* 43–54.

Cazden, C. (1968). The acquisition of noun and verb inflections. *Child Development, 39,* 433–438.

Cernoch, J. M., & Porter, R. H. (1985). Recognition of maternal axillary odors by infants. *Child Development, 56,* 1593–1598.

Charlesworth, W. R. (1972). Developmental psychology: Does it offer anything distinctive? In W. R. Looft (Ed.), *Developmental psychology: A book of readings.* Hinsdale, IL: Dryden Press.

Chasnoff, I. J., Burns, W. J., Schnoll, S. H., & Burns, K. A. (1985). Cocaine use in pregnancy. *The New England Journal of Medicine, 313,* 666–669.

Chavez, D. (1985). Perpetuations of gender inequality: A content analysis of comic strips. *Sex Roles, 13,* 93–102.

Chedd, G. (1981, January-February). Who shall be born? *Science, 81,* pp. 32–41.

Cherlin, A. (1981). *Marriage, divorce, remarriage.* Cambridge: Harvard University Press.

Cherlin, A. J. (1988a). The weakening link between marriage and the care of children. *Family Planning Perspectives, 20,* 302–306.

Cherlin, A. J. (1988b). The changing American family and public policy. In A. J. Cherlin (Ed.), *The changing American family and public policy.* Washington, DC: The Urban Institute Press.

Cherlin, A., & Furstenberg, F. F. (1985). Styles and strategies of grandparenting. In. V. L. Bengtson & J. F. Robertson (Eds.), *Grandparenthood* (pp. 97–116). Beverly Hills CA: Sage

Cherlin, A., & McCarthy, J. (1985). Remarried couple households: Data from the June 1980 Current Population Survey. *Journal of Marriage and the Family, 47,* 23–30.

Cherry, K. E., & Park, D. C. (1989). Age-related differences in three-dimensional spatial memory. *Journal of Gerontology: Psychological Sciences, 44,* 16–22.

Chess, S., & Thomas, A. (1984). *Origins and evolution of behavior disorders: Infancy to early adult life.* New York: Brunner/Mazel.

Chickering, A. W. & Assoc. (1981). *The modern American college.* San Francisco: Jossey-Bass.

Childers, P., & Wimmer, M. (1971). The concept of death in early childhood. *Child Development, 42,* 1299–1301.

Chiriboga, D. A., & Cutler, L. (1977). Stress responses among divorcing men and women. *Journal of Divorce, 1,* 95–106.

Chodorow, N. (1978). *The reproduction of mothering: Psychoanalysis and the sociology of gender.* Berkeley: University of California Press.

Chomsky, N. (1957). *Syntactic structures.* The Hague: Mouton.

Chomsky, N. (1972). *Language and mind* (2nd ed.). New York: Harcourt Brace Jovanovich.

Christenson, C. V., & Gagnon, J. H. (1965). Sexual behavior in a group of older women. *Journal of Gerontology, 20,* 351–356.

Christopherson, V. A. (1972). Retirement communities: The cities of two tales. *Social Science, 47,* 82–86.

Cialdini, R. B., Baumann, D. J., & Kenrick, D. T. (1981). Insights from sadness: A three step model of the development of altruism as hedonism. *Developmental Review, 1,* 207–223.

Cicchetti, D. (1984). The emergence of developmental psychopathology. *Child Development, 55,* 1–7.

Cicirelli, V. G. (1980 Sibling relationships in adulthood: A life span perspective. In L. W. Poon (Ed.), *Aging in the 1980's: Psychological issues.* Washington, DC: American Psychological Association.

Cicirelli, V. G. (1982). Sibling influence throughout the life span. In M. E. Lamb & B. Sutton-Smith (Eds.), *Sibling relationships: Their nature and significance across the life span.* Hillsdale, NJ: Erlbaum.

Cicirelli, V. G. (1983). Adult children's attachment and helping behavior to elderly parents: A path model. *Journal of Marriage and the Family, 45,* 815–822.

Cicirelli, V. G. (1985). Sibling relationships throughout the life cycle. In L. L'Abate (Ed.), *The handbook of family psychology and therapy.* Homewood, IL: Dorsey Press.

Cicirelli, V. G. (1988). A measure of filial anxiety regarding anticipated care of elderly parents. *The Gerontologist, 28,* 478–482.

Clark, E. V., & Sengul, C. J. (1978). Strategies in the acquisition of deixis. *Journal of Child Language, 5,* 457–475.

Clark, H., & Clark, E. V. (1977). *Psychology and language: An introduction to psycholinguistics.* New York: Harcourt Brace Jovanovich.

Clark, L., & Knowles, J. (1973). Age differences in dichotic listening performance. *Journal of Gerontology, 28,* 173–178.

Clark, R., & Hatfield, E. (1982). Gender differences in receptivity to sexual offers. Reported in E. Hatfield. What do women and men want from love & sex? In E. R. Allgeior & N. B. McCormick (Eds.), *Changing boundaries: Gender roles and sexual behavior* (pp. 106–134). Palo Alto, CA: Mayfield Publishing.

Clarren, S. K., & Smith, D. W. (1978). The fetal alcohol syndrome. *New England Journal of Medicine, 298,* 1063–1067.

Clifford, M. M. (1975). Physical attractiveness and academic performance. *Child Study Journal, 5 (4),* 201–209.

Clifton, R. K. (1974a). Cardiac conditioning and orienting in the infant. In P. A. Obrist, A. H. Black, J. Brener, & L. V. DiCara (Eds.), *Cardiovascular Psychophysiology.* Chicago: Aldine.

Clifton, R. K. (1974b). Heart rate conditioning in the newborn infant. *Journal of Experimental Child Psychology, 18,* 9–21.

Clifton, R. K., & Nelson, M. N. (1976). Developmental study of habituation in infants: The importance of paradigm, response system, and state. In T. J. Tighe & R. N. Leaton (Eds.), *Habituation: Perspectives from child development, animal behavior, and neurophysiology.* Hillsdale, NJ: Erlbaum.

Cobb, N. J., Stevens-Long, J. & Goldstein, S. (1982). The influence of televised models on toy preference in children. *Sex Roles, 8,* 1075–1080.

Cohen, G. (1979). Language comprehension in old age. *Cognitive Psychology, 11,* 412–429.

Cohen, G. D. (1988). *The brain in human aging.* New York: Springer Publishing.

Cohen, S. E. (1978). Maternal employment and mother-child interaction. *Merrill-Palmer Quarterly, 24,* 189–197.

Coie, J. D., (1985). Fitting social skills intervention to the target group. In B. H. Schneider, K. H. Rubin, &

J. D. Ledingham (Eds.), *Children's peer relations* (pp. 141–156). New York: Springer-Verlag.

Coie, J. D., Dodge, K. A., & Coppotelli, H. (1982). Dimensions and types of social status: A cross-age perspective. *Developmental Psychology, 18,* 557–570.

Coie, J. D., & Krehbiel, G. (1984). Effects of academic tutoring on the social status of low-achieving, socially rejected children. *Child Development, 55,* 1465–1478.

Colby, A., & Kohlberg, L. (1987). *The measurement of moral judgement.* New York: Cambridge University Press.

Colby, A., Kohlberg, L., Fenton, E., Speicher-Dubin, B., & Lieberman, M. (1977). Secondary school moral discussion programs led by social studies teachers. *Journal of Moral Education, 6,* 2.

Colby, A., Kohlberg, L., Gibbs, J., & Lieberman, M. (1983). A longitudinal study of moral development. *Monographs of the Society for Research in Child Development, 48* (1–2, Serial No. 200).

Coleman, J. S. (1961). *The adolescent society.* New York: Free Press.

Coleman, L. M., & Antonucci, T. C. (1983). Impact of work on women at midlife. *Developmental Psychology, 19,* 290–294.

Comstock, G., Chaffee, S., Katzman, N., McCombs, M., & Roberts, D. (1978). *Television and human behavior,* New York: Columbia University Press.

Condon, W. S., & Sander, L. W. (1974). Synchrony demonstrated between movements of the neonate and adult speech. *Child Development, 65,* 456–462.

Conger, J. J., & Peterson, A. C. (1984). *Adolescence and youth* (3rd. ed.). New York: Harper and Row.

Conry, R., & Plant, W. T. (1965). WAIS and group test predictions of an academic success criterion: High school and college. *Educational and Psychological Measurement, 25,* 493–500.

Cooley, C. H. (1902). *Human nature and the social order.* New York: Charles Scribner's Sons.

Coombs, L. C., & Zumeta, Z. (1970). Correlates of marital dissolution in a prospective fertility study: A research note. *Social Problems, 18,* 92–101.

Cooney, T. M., Schaie, K. W., & Willis, S. L. (1988). The relationship between prior functioning on cognitive and personality dimensions and subject attrition in longitudinal research. *Journal of Gerontology, 43,* 12–17.

Cooper, A. J. (1986). Progesterones in the treatment of male sex offenders: A review. *Canadian Journal of Psychiatry, 31,* 73–79.

Coopersmith, S. (1967). *The antecedents of self-esteem.* San Francisco: W. H. Freeman.

Cordua, G. D., McGraw, K. O., & Drabman, K. S. (1979). Doctor or nurse: Children's perceptions of sex typed occupations. *Child Development, 50,* 590–593.

Correll, R. E., Rokosz, S., & Blanchard, B. M. (1966). Some correlates of WAIS performance in the elderly. *Journal of Gerontology, 21,* 544–549.

Corso, J. F. (1977). Auditory perception and communication. In J. E. Birren & K. W. Schaie (Eds.), *Handbook of the psychology of aging.* New York: Van Nostrand Reinhold.

Costa, P. T., & McCrae, R. R. (1980). Still stable after all these years: Personality as a key to some issues in adulthood and old age. In P. B. Baltes & O. G. Brim (Eds.), *Life span development and behavior* (Vol. 3). New York: Academic Press.

Counts, D. R. (1980). The good death in Kalia: Preparation for death in western New Britain. In R. A. Kalish (Ed.), *Death and dying: Views from many cultures.* Farmingdale, NY: Baywood Publishing.

Cowan, P., Cowan, C., Coie, J., & Coie, L. (1978). In L. Newman & W. Miller (Eds.), *The first child and family formation.* Durham: University of North Carolina Press.

Cowan, C. P., & Cowan, P. A. (1987). Men's involvement in parenthood: Identifying the antecedents and understanding the barriers. In P. W. Berman & F. A. Pedersen (Eds.), *Men's transitions to parenthood: Longitudinal studies of early family experience.* Hillsdale, NJ: Erlbaum.

Cowan, G., & Hoffman, C. D. (1986). Gender stereotyping in young children: Evidence to support a concept-learning approach. *Sex Roles, 14,* 211–224.

Cowan, P. A. (1988). Becoming a father: A time of change, an opportunity for development. In P. Bronstein & C. P. Cowan (Eds.), *Fatherhood today: Men's changing role in the family.* New York: Wiley.

Cowart, B. J., & Beauchamp, G. K. (1986). The importance of sensory context in the young children's acceptance of salty tastes. *Child Development, 57,* 1034–1039.

Coysh, W. S. (1984). *Factors influencing men's roles in caring for their children and the effects of father develop-*

ment. Doctoral dissertation, University of California, Berkeley.

Craik, F. I. M. (1968). Short-term memory and the aging process. In G. A. Talland (Ed.), *Human aging and behavior.* New York: Academic Press.

Craik, F. I. M. (1977). Age differences in human memory. In J. E. Birren & K. W. Schaie (Eds.), *Handbook of the psychology of aging.* New York: Van Nostrand Reinhold.

Craik, F. I. M., & Masani, P. A. (1967). Age differences in the temporal integration of languages. *British Journal of Psychology, 58,* 291–299.

Crassini, B., & Broerse, J. (1980). Auditory-visual integration in neonates: A signal detection analysis. *Journal of Experimental Child Psychology, 29,* 144–155.

Cratty, B. J. (1970). *Perceptual and motor development in infants and children* (1st ed.). New York: Macmillan.

Cratty, B. J., & Martin, M. M. (1969). *Perceptual-motor efficiency in children.* Philadelphia: Lea and Febiger

Crockett, L., & Dorn, L. (1987). *Young adolescents' pubertal status and reported heterosexual interaction.* Paper presented at the biennial meetings of the Society for Research in Child Development, Baltimore.

Crockett, L., Losoff, M., & Petersen, A. C. (1984). Perceptions of the peer group and friendship in early adolescence. *Journal of Early Adolescence, 4,* 155–181.

Cronbach, L. J. (1984). *Essentials of psychological testing* (4th ed.). New York: Harper & Row.

Crook, W. G. (1980). Can what a child eats make him dull, stupid, or hyperactive? *Journal of Learning Disabilities, 13,* 281–286.

Cross, K. P. (1971). *Beyond the open door: New students to higher education.* San Francisco: Jossey-Bass.

Cross, K. P. (1981). *Adults as learners.* San Francisco: Jossey-Bass.

Cross, K. P. (1985). The changing role of higher education in the learning society. *Continuum, 49,* 101–110.

Cultice, J. C., Somerville, S. C., & Wellman, H. M. (1983). Preschoolers' memory monitoring: Feeling of knowing judgements. *Child Development, 54,* 1480–1486.

Cumming, E., & Henry, W. E. (1961). *Growing old: The process of disengagement.* New York: Basic Books.

Cunningham, C. E., & Barkley, R. A. (1979). The interactions of normal and hyperactive children with their mothers in free play and structured tasks. *Child Development, 50,* 217–224.

Cunningham, L., Cadoret, R. J., Loftus, R., & Edwards, J. E. (1975). Studies of adoptees from psychiatrically disturbed biological parents: Psychiatric conditions in childhood and adolescence. *British Journal of Psychiatry, 126,* 534–549.

Cunningham, W. R., & Owens, W. A. (1983). The Iowa State Study of adult development and abilities. In K. W. Schaie (Ed.), *Longitudinal studies of adult psychological development* (pp. 20–39). New York: Guilford.

Currens, W. C. (1988). *The book of the states (1988–1989.* Lexington, KY: Council of State Governments.

Currier, R. L. (1981). Juvenile sexuality in global perspective. In L. L. Constantine & F. M. Martinson (Eds.), *Children and sex: New findings, new perspectives* (pp. 9–19). Boston: Little Brown.

Curtiss, S. (1977). *Genie: A psycholinguistic study of a modern-day "wild child."* New York: Academic Press.

Cytrynbaum, S., Blum, L., Patrick, R., Stein, J., Wadner, D., & Wild, C. (1980). Midlife development: A personality and social systems perspective. In L. W. Poon (Ed.), *Aging in the 1980's.* Washington DC: American Psychological Association.

Dale, P. S. (1976). *Language development: Structure and function* (2nd ed.). New York: Holt, Rinehart & Winston.

Damon, W. (1977). *The social world of the child.* San Francisco: Jossey-Bass.

Damon, W. (1983). *Social and personality development: Infancy through adolescence.* New York: Norton.

Damon, W., & Hart, D. (1982). The development of self-understanding from infancy through adolescence. *Child Development, 53,* 841–864.

Daniels, D., & Plomin, R. (1985a). Differential experience of siblings in the same family. *Developmental Psychology, 21,* 747–760.

Daniels, D., & Plomin, R. (1985b). Origins of individual differences in infant shyness. *Developmental Psychology, 21,* 118–121.

Dansky, J. L. (1980). Make-believe: A mediator of the relationship between play and associative fluency. *Child Development, 51,* 576–579.

Dasen, P. (1975). Concrete operational development in three cultures. *Journal of Cross-Cultural Psychology, 6,* 156–172.

Dasen, P., & Heron, A. (1981), Cross-cultural tests of Piaget's theory. In H. C. Triandis & A. Heron (Eds.), *Handbook of cross-cultural psychology: Vol. 4. Developmental psychology*. Boston: Allyn and Bacon.

Datan, N., & Hughes, F. (1985). Burning books and briefcases: Agency, communion, and the social context of learning in adulthood. *Academic Psychology Bulletin, 7,* 175–186.

Datan, N., Rodeheaver, D., & Hughes F. P. (1987). Adult development and aging. *Annual Review of Psychology, 38,* 153–180.

Davies, E., & Furnham, A. (1986). Body satisfaction in adolescent girls. *British Journal of Medical Psychology, 59,* 279–287.

Davis, G. A. (1975). Care and feeding of creative adolescents. In R. E. Grinder (Ed.), *Studies in adolescence: A book in readings in adolescent development* (3rd ed.). New York: Macmillan.

Davis, G. A., & Holland, A. L. (1981). Age in understanding and treating aphasia. In D. S. Beasley & G. A. Davis (Eds.), *Aging communication processes and disorders* (pp. 207–228). New York: Greene & Stratton.

Day, R. H., & McKenzie, B. E. (1981). Infant perception of the invariant size of approaching and receding objects. *Developmental Psychology, 17,* 670–677.

de Villiers, J. G., & de Villiers, P. A. (1978). *Language acquisition*. Cambridge, MA: Harvard University Press.

Deaux, K. V. (1985). Sex and gender. *Annual Review of Psychology, 36,* 49–81.

DeCasper, A. J., & Fifer, W. P. (1980). Human newborns' perception of male voices: Preference, discrimination and reinforcing value. *Developmental Psychology, 17,* 481–491.

DeCasper, A. J., & Prescott, P. A. (1984). Human newborns' perception of male voices: Preference, discrimination, and reinforcing value. *Developmental Psychology, 17,* 481–491.

DeLamater, J. (1987). Gender differences in sexual scenarios. In K. Kelley (Ed.), *Females, males, & sexuality: Theories & research* (pp. 127–139). Albany: SUNY Press.

DeLamater, J., & MacCorquodale, P. (1979). *Premarital sexuality: Attitudes, relationships, behaviors*. Madison: University of Wisconsin Press.

DeLicardie, E. R., & Cravioto, J. (1974). Behavioral responsiveness of survivors of clinically severe malnutrition to cognitive demands. In J. Cravioto (ed.), *Early malnutrition and mental development*. Uppsala, Sweden: Almquist and Wiksell.

DeLoache, J. S., Cassidy, D. J., & Brown, A. L. (1985). Precursors of mnemonic strategies in very young children. *Child Development, 56,* 125–137.

DeLora, J. S., & Warren, C. A. B. (1977). *Understanding sexual interaction*. Boston: Houghton-Mifflin.

D'Emilio, J., & Freedman, E. B. (1988). *Intimate matters: A history of sexuality in America*. New York: Harper & Row.

Demorest, A., Meyer, C., & Phelps, E. (1984). Words speak louder than actions: Understanding deliberately false remarks. *Child Development, 55,* 1527–1534.

Denckla, W. D. (1975). A time to die. *Life Sciences, 16,* 31–44.

Denney, N. W. (1980). Task demands and problem-solving strategies in middle-aged and older adults. *Journal of Gerontology, 35,* 559–564.

Denney, N. W. (1981). Adult cognitive development. In D. S. Beasley & G. A. Davis (Eds.), *Aging: Communications processes and disorders* (pp. 123–137). New York: Grune and Stratton.

Denney, D. R., & Denney, N. W. (1973). The use of classification for problem-solving: A comparison of middle and old age. *Developmental Psychology, 9,* 275–278.

Denney, N. W., & Palmer, A. P. (1981). Adult age differences on traditional and practical problem-solving measures. *Journal of Gerontology, 36,* 323–328.

Denney, P. (1975). Cellular biology of aging. In D. S. Woodruff & J. E. Birren (Eds.), *Aging: Scientific perspectives and social issues*. New York: Van Nostrand Reinhold.

Desor, J. A., Maller, O., & Andrews, K. (1975). Ingestive responses of human newborns to salty, sour, and bitter stimuli. *Journal of Comparative and Physiological Psychology, 89,* 966–970.

Desor, J. A., Maller, O., & Greene, L. S. (1977). Preference for sweet in humans: Infants, children, and adults. In J. Weiffenbach (Ed.), *Taste and development: The ontogeny of sweet preference*. Washington, DC: U.S. Government Printing Office.

Desor, J. A., Maller, O., & Turner, R. (1973). Taste in acceptance of sugars by human infants. *Journal of Comparative and Physiological Psychology, 84,* 496–501.

Dewart, N. H. (1972). Social class and children's understanding of deep structure sentences. *British Journal of Educational Psychology, 42,* 198–203.

Dewey, J. (1933). *How we think: A restatement of the relation of reflective thinking to the educative process.* Boston: D.C. Heath.

Di Maria, H., Courpotin, C., Rouzioux, C., Cohen, D., Rio, D. & Boussin, F. (1986). Transplacental transmission of human immunodeficiency virus. *Lancet, 11 (8500),* 215–216.

Diamond, A. M. (1986). The life-cycle research productivity of mathematicians and scientists. *Journal of Gerontology, 41,* 520–525.

Diamond, N. (1982). Cognitive theory. In B. B. Wolman (Ed.), *Handbook of developmental psychology.* Englewood Cliffs, NJ: Prentice-Hall.

Diaz, R. M. & Berndt, T. J (1982). Children's knowledge of a best friend: Fact or fancy? *Developmental Psychology, 18,* 787–794.

Dion, K. K. (1977). The incentive value of physical attractiveness for young children. *Personality and Social Psychology Bulletin, 3,* 67–70.

Dion, K. K. (1986). Stereotyping based on physical attractiveness: Issues and conceptual perspectives. In C. P. Herman, M. P. Zanna, & E. T. Higgins (Eds.), *Appearance, stigma, and social behavior: The Ontario Symposium on Personality and Social Psychology* (Vol. 3). Hillsdale, NJ: Erlbaum.

Dion, K. K., Berscheid, E., & Walster, E. (1972). What is beautiful is good. *Journal of Personality and Social Psychology, 24,* 285–290.

Dion, K. L., & Dion, K. K. (1987). Belief in a just world and physical attractiveness stereotyping. *Journal of Personality and Social Psychology, 52,* 775–780.

DiPrete, T. A. & Soule, W. T. (1988). Gender and promotion in segregated job-ladder systems. *American Sociological Review, 53,* 26–40.

Dixon, J. C. (1957). Development of self-recognition. *Journal of Genetic Psychology, 91,* 251–256.

Dixon, R. A., Simon, E. E., Nowak, C. A., & Hultsch, D. F. (1982). Text recall in adulthood as a function of level of information, input modality, and delay interval. *Journal of Gerontology, 37,* 358–364.

Dodd, D. H. (1980). Language development. In R. L. Ault (Ed.), *Developmental perspectives.* Santa Monica, CA: Goodyear.

Dodge, K. A. (1983). Behaviorial antecedents of peer social status. *Child Development, 54,* 1386–1399.

Dodge, K. A., Coie, J. D., & Brakke, N. P. (1982). Behavior patterns of socially rejected and neglected preadolescents: The roles of social approach and aggression. *Journal of Abnormal Child Psychology, 10,* 389–410.

Doherty, W. J., & Jacobson, N. S. (1982). Marriage and the family. In B. B. Wolman (Ed.), *Handbook of developmental psychology.* Englewood Cliffs, NJ: Prentice-Hall.

Dominick, J. R., & Greenberg, B. S. (1972). Attitudes toward violence: The interaction of television exposure, family attitudes and social class. In G. A. Comstock & E. A. Rubinstein (Eds.), *Television and social behavior: Vol. 3. Television and adolescent aggressiveness.* Washington, DC: U.S. Government Printing Office.

Doppelt, J., & Wallace, W. (1955). Standardization of the WAIS for older persons. *Journal of Abnormal and Social Psychology, 51,* 312–330.

Dornbusch, S. M., Carlsmith, J. M., Bushwall, S. J., Ritter, P. L., Leiderman, H., Hastorf, A. H., & Gross, R. T. (1985). Single parents, extended households, and the control of adolescents. *Child Development, 56,* 326–341.

Dornbusch, S. M., Carlsmith J. M., Gross, R. T., Martin, J. A., Jennings, D., Rosenberg, A., & Duke, P. (1981). Sexual development, age, and dating: A comparison of biological and social influences upon one set of behaviors. *Child Development, 52,* 179–185.

Douvan, E., & Adelson, J. (1966), *The adolescent experience.* New York: Wiley.

Dowd, M. (1983, December 5). Many women in poll value jobs as much as family life. *The New York Times,* pp. 1, 66.

Dreyer, P. H. (1982). Sexuality during adolescence. In B. B. Wolman (Ed.), *Handbook of developmental psychology.* Englewood Cliffs, NJ: Prentice-Hall.

Dubnoff, S. J., Veroff, J., & Kulka, R. A. (1978, August). *Adjustment to work: 1957–1976.* Paper presented at the annual meeting of the American Psychological Association, Toronto.

Dubowitz, L. M. S., Dubowitz, V., & Goldberg, C. (1970). Clinical assessment of gestational age in the newborn infant. *Journal of Pediatrics, 77,* 1.

Duncan, P. D., Ritter, P. L., Dornbusch, S. M., Gross, R. T., & Carlsmith, J. M. (1985). The effects of pubertal timing on body image, school behavior, and deviance. *Journal of Youth and Adolescence, 14,* 227–236.

Dunn, J. (1985). *Sisters and brothers.* Cambridge, MA: Harvard University Press.

Dunn, J., & Kendrick, C. (1982). *Siblings: Love, envy, and understanding.* Cambridge, MA: Harvard University Press.

Dunn, J. G., Plomin, R., & Daniels, D. (1986). Consistency and change in mothers' behavior toward young siblings. *Child Development, 57,* 348–356.

Dunphy, D. C. (1963). The social structure of urban adolescent peer groups. *Sociometry, 26,* 230–246.

Durkheim, E. (1951). *Suicide: A study in sociology* (J. A. Spaulding & G. Simpson, Trans., 1951). New York: Free Press.

Duvall, E. (1977). *Marriage and family development* (5th ed.). New York: Lippincott.

Dweck, C. S. (1977). Learned helplessness and negative evaluation. *UCLA Educator, 19,* 44–49.

Dweck, C. S. (1986). Motivational processes affecting learning. *American Psychologist, 41,* 1040–1048.

Dwyer, J., & Mayer, J. (1968–1969). Psychological effects of variations in physical appearance during adolescence. *Adolescence, 3,* 353–368.

Eagly, A. H. (1987). Reporting sex differences. *American Psychologist, 42,* 756.

Eagly, R. (1974). Contemporary profile of conventional economists. *History of political economy, 6,* 88.

Ebel, R. L., & Frisbie, D. A. (1986). *Essentials of measurement* (4th ed.). Englewood Cliffs, NJ: Prentice-Hall.

Eckerman, C. O., & Stein, M. R. (1982). The toddler's emerging interactive skills. In K. H. Rubin & H. S. Ross (Eds.), *Peer relationships and social skills in childhood.* New York: Springer-Verlag.

Eder, D., & Hallinan, M. T. (1978). Sex differences in children's friendships. *American Sociological Review, 43,* 247–250.

Edwards, C. P., & Whiting, B. B. (1988). *Children of different worlds.* Harvard University Press.

Edwards, D. P. (1981). The comparative study of the development of moral judgment and reasoning. In R. H. Munroe, R. L. Munroe, & B. B. Whiting (Eds.), *Handbook of cross-cultural human development.* New York: Garland Press.

Edwards, J. N., & Klemmack, D. L. (1973). Correlates of life satisfaction: A re-examination. *Journal of Gerontology, 28,* 497–502.

Egeland, B., & Farber, E. A. (1984). Infant-mother attachment: Factors related to its development and changes over time. *Child Development, 55,* 743–771.

Ehrhardt, A. A., & Baker, S. W. (1974). Fetal androgens, human central nervous system differentiation, and behavior sex differences. In R. C. Friedman, R. M. Richart, & R. L. Vande Wiele (Eds.), *Sex differences in behavior.* New York: Wiley.

Ehrhardt, A. A., & Money, J. (1967). Progestin-induced hermaphroditism: IQ and psychosexual identity in a study of 10 girls. *Journal of Sex Research, 3,* 83–100.

Eichorn, D. H. (1970). Physiological development. In P. H. Mussen (Ed.), *Carmichael's manual of child psychology.* New York: Wiley.

Eifermann, R. R. (1971). Social play in childhood. In R. E. Herron & B. Sutton-Smith (Eds.), *Child's play.* New York: Wiley.

Eilers, R. E., & Oller, D. (1976). The role of speech discrimination in developmental sound substitutions. *Journal of Child Language, 3,* 319–330.

Eimas, P. D. (1985, January). The perception of speech in early infancy. *Science,* 46–51.

Eimas, P. D., Siqueland, E. R., Jusczyk, P. W., & Vigorito, J. (1971). Speech perception in infants. *Science, 171,* 303–306.

Eisenberg, N., Lennon, R., & Roth, K. (1983). Prosocial development: A longitudinal study. *Developmental Psychology, 19,* 846–855.

Eitzen, D. A. (1975). Athletics in the status system of male adolescents: A replication of Coleman's *The adolescent society. Adolescence, 10,* 267–276.

Elder, J., & Pederson, D. (1978). Preschool children's use of objects in symbolic play. *Child Development, 49,* 500–504.

Elias, M. F., Elias, P. K., & Elias, J. W. (1977). *Basic processes in adult developmental psychology.* St. Louis: C. V. Mosby.

Elkind, D. (1967). Egocentrism in adolescence. *Child Development, 38,* 1025–1034.

Elkind, D. (1978). Understanding the young adolescent. *Adolescence, 13,* 127–134.

Elkind, D. (1980). *Children and adolescents*. New York: Oxford University Press.

Elkind, D. (1981a). *The hurried child: Growing up too fast too soon*. Reading, MA: Addison-Wesley.

Elkind, D. (1981b). *Childhood and adolescence: Interpretive essays on Jean Piaget*. New York: Oxford.

Elkind, D., & Bowen, R. (1979). Imaginary audience behavior in children and adolescents. *Developmental Psychology, 15,* 38–44.

Elliot, A. J. (1981). *Child language*. Cambridge: Cambridge University Press.

Ellis, G. F. (1986). Societal and parental predictors of parent-adolescent conflict. In G. K. Leigh & G. W. Peterson (Eds.), *Adolescents in families* (pp. 155–178). Cincinnati: South-Western Publishing Co.

Ellis, H. C., Bennett, T. L., Daniel, T. C., & Rickert, E. J. (1979). *Psychology of learning and memory*. Monterey, CA: Brooks/Cole.

Ellis, M. J. (1973). *Why people play*. Englewood Cliffs, NJ: Prentice-Hall.

Elvik, S., Reikowitz, D., & Greenberg, J. I. (1986). Child sexual abuse: The role of the NP. *Nurse practitioner, 11,* 15–16, 19–20, 22.

Emmerich, W., Goldman, K. S., Kirsh, B., & Sharabany, R. (1976). *Development of gender constancy in economically disadvantaged children*. Princeton, NJ: Educational Testing Service.

Engen, T. (1977). Taste and smell. In J. E. Birren & K. W. Schaie (Eds.), *Handbook of the psychology of aging*. New York: Van Nostrand Reinhold.

Engen, T., Lipsitt, L. P., & Peck, M. B. (1974). Ability of newborn infants to discriminate sapid substances. *Developmental Psychology, 10,* 741–746.

England, G. W., & Misumi, J. (1986). Work centrality in Japan and the United States. *Journal of Cross-Cultural Psychology, 17,* 339–416.

Enright, M. K., Rovee-Collier, C. K., Fagen, J. W., & Caniglia, K. 1983). The effects of distributed training on retention of operant conditioning in human infants. *Journal of Experimental Child Psychology, 36,* 209–225.

Epstein, S. (1973). The self-concept revisited, or a theory of a theory. *American Psychologist, 28,* 405–416.

Erikson, E. H. (1963). *Childhood and society* (2nd ed.). New York: Norton.

Erikson, E. H. (1964). *Insight and responsibility*. New York: Norton.

Erikson, E. H. (1968). *Identity, youth, and crisis*. New York: Norton.

Erikson, E. H., Erikson, J. M., & Kivnick, H. Q. (1986). *Vital involvement in old age: The experience of old age in our time*. New York: Norton.

Eysenck, H. J., & Kamin, L. (1981). *The intelligence controversy*. New York: Wiley.

Fagot, B. I. (1985). Beyond the reinforcement principle: Another step toward understanding sex role development. *Developmental Psychology, 21,* 1097–1104.

Fagot, B. I., & Leinbach, M. D. (1989). The young child's gender schema: Environmental input, internal organization. *Child Development, 60,* 663–672.

Fagot, B. I., Leinbach, M. D., & Hagan, R. (1986). Gender labeling and the adoption of sex-typed behaviors. *Developmental Psychology, 22,* 440–443.

Fakouri, M. E. (1976). "Cognitive development in adulthood: A fifth stage?": A critique. *Developmental Psychology, 12,* 472.

Falbo, T. (1978a). Reasons for having an only child. *Journal of Population, 1,* 181–184.

Falbo, T. (1978b). Only children and interpersonal behavior: An experimental and survey study. *Journal of Applied Social Psychology, 8,* 244–253.

Falbo, T. (1982). Only children in America. In M. E. Lamb & B. Sutton-Smith (Eds.), *Sibling relationships: Their nature and significance across the lifespan*. Hillsdale, NJ: Erlbaum.

Fallon, A. E., & Rozin, P. (1984). *Sex differences in perceptions of body shape*. Unpublished manuscript. Cited in J. Rodin, L. Silberstein, & R. Striegel-Moore (1984).

Fantz, R. L. (1958). Pattern vision in young infants. *Psychological Record, 8,* 43–47.

Fantz, R. L. (1961). The origin of form perception. *Scientific American, 204,* 66–72.

Fantz, R. L. (1963). Pattern vision in newborn infants. *Science, 140,* 296–297.

Fantz, R. L., Fagan, J. L., & Miranda, S. B. (1975). Early visual selectivity. In L. B. Cohen & P. Salapatek (Eds.), *Infant perception: From sensation to cognition*. New York: Academic Press.

Fantz, R. L., & Nevis, S. (1967). Pattern preferences and perceptual-cognitive development in early infancy. *Merrill-Palmer Quarterly, 13,* 77–108.

Faunce, P. S., & Phipps-Yonas, S. 1979). Women's liberation and human sexual relations. In J. H. Williams (Ed.), *Psychology of women.* New York: Norton.

Fausto-Sterling, A. (1985). *Myths of gender: Biological theories about women and men.* New York: Basic Books.

Faux, M. (1984). *Childless by choice.* New York: Doubleday.

Feifel, H. (1977). Epilogue. In H. Feifel (Ed.), *New meanings of death.* New York: McGraw-Hill.

Feifel, H. (1990). Psychology and death: Meaningful rediscovery. *American Psychologist, 45,* 537–543.

Feifel, H., & Branscomb, A. B. (1973). Who's afraid of death? *Journal of Abnormal Psychology, 81,* 282–286.

Fein, G. G. (1981). Pretend play in childhood: An integrative review. *Child Development, 52,* 1095–1118.

Fein, G. G. & Apfel, N. (1979). Some preliminary observations on knowing and pretending. In M. Smith & M. B. Franklin (Eds.), *Symbolic functioning in childhood.* Hillsdale, NJ: Erlbaum.

Feingold, B. F. (1975). *Why your child is hyperactive.* New York: Random House.

Feldman, C. (1971). *The effects of various types of adult responses in the syntactic acquisition of two- to three-year-olds.* Unpublished manuscript, University of Chicago.

Feldman, D. (1974). Universal to unique. In S. Rosner & L. E. Abt (Eds.), *Essays in creativity.* Croton-on-Hudson, NY: North River Press.

Fenson, L. (1986). The developmental progression of play. In A. W. Gottfried & C. C. Brown (Eds.), *Play interactions: The contribution of play materials and parental involvement to children's development.* Lexington, MA: D.C. Heath.

Ferreira, A. J. (1960). The pregnant mother's emotional attitude and its reflection upon the newborn. *American Journal of Orthopsychiatry, 30,* 553–561.

Feshbach, N. D. (1979). Empathy training: A field study of affective education. In S. Feshbach and A. Fraazeh (Eds.), *Aggression and behavior change: Biological and social processes* (pp. 234–249). New York: Praeger.

Feshbach, S. (1970). Aggression. In P. H. Mussen, (Ed.), *Carmichael's manual of child psychology* (Vol. 2, 3rd ed.). New York: Wiley.

Feshbach, S., & Weiner, B. (1986). *Personality* (2nd ed.). Lexington, MA: D. C. Heath.

Field, J., Muir, D., Pilon, R., Sinclair, M., & Dodwell, P. (1980). Infants' orientation to lateral sounds from birth to three months. *Child Development, 50,* 295–298.

Field, T. M., & Widmayer, S. M. (1982). Motherhood. In B. B. Wolman (Ed.), *Handbook of developmental psychology.* Englewood Cliffs, NJ: Prentice-Hall.

Fine, M. A. (1986). Perceptions of stepparents: Variations in stereotypes as a function of current family structure. *Journal of Marriage and the Family, 48,* 537–543.

Fine, M. A., Moreland, J. R., & Schwebel, A. I. (1983). Long-term effects of divorce on parent-child relationships. *Developmental Psychology, 19,* 703–713.

Finkelhor, D. (1984). *Child sexual abuse.* New York: Free Press.

Finkelhor, D., & Araji, S. (1986). Explanations of pedophilia: A four-factor model. *The Journal of Sex Research, 22,* 145–161.

Finley, N. J., Roberts, M. D., & Banahan, F. (1988). Motivators and inhibitors of attitudes of filial obligation toward aging parents. *The Gerontologist, 28,* 73–78.

Fish, K. D., & Biller, H. B. (1973). Perceived childhood paternal relationships and college females' personal adjustment. *Adolescence, 8,* 415–420.

Flavell, J. H. (1963). *The developmental psychology of Jean Piaget.* New York: Van Nostrand Reinhold.

Flavell, J. H. (1982). Structures, stages, and sequences in cognitive development. In W. A. Collins (Ed.), *The concept of development* (Minnesota Symposia on Child Psychology, Vol. 15). Hillsdale, NJ: Erlbaum.

Flavell, J. H. (1985). *Cognitive development* (2nd ed.). Englewood Cliffs, NJ: Prentice-Hall.

Flavell, J. H., Beach, D. R., & Chinsky, J. M. (1966). Spontaneous verbal rehearsal in a memory task as a function of age. *Child Development, 37,* 283–299.

Flavell, J. H., Friedrichs, A. G., & Hoyt, J. D. (1970). Developmental changes in memorization processes. *Cognitive Psychology, 1,* 324–340.

Flavell, J. H., & Wellman, H. M. (1977). Metamemory. In R. V. Kail & J. W. Hagen (Eds.), *Perspectives on the development of memory and cognition*. Hillsdale, NJ: Erlbaum.

Fodor, I. G., & Thal, J. (1984). Weight disorders: Overweight and anorexia. In E. A. Blechman (Ed.), *Behavior modification with women*. New York: Guilford Press.

Fogel, A. (1979). Peer vs. mother-directed behavior in 1- to 3-month old infants. *Infant Behavior and Development, 2*, 215–216.

Fogel, A. (1984). *Infancy: Infant, family, and society*. St. Paul, MN.: West Publishing Co.

Forehand, R., Faust, J., & Baum, C. G. (1985). Accuracy of weight perception among young adolescent girls: An examination of personal and interpersonal correlates. *Journal of Early Adolescence, 5*, 239–245.

Fouts, R. S., & Fouts, H. (1985, May). *Signs of conversation in chimpanzees*. Paper presented at the meeting of the American Association for the Advancement of Science, Los Angeles.

Fox, N., Kagan J., & Weiskopf, S. (1979). The growth of memory during infancy. *Genetic Psychology Monographs, 99*, 91–130.

Fozard, J. L., Wolf, E., Bell, B., McFarland, R. A., & Podolsky, S. (1977). Visual perception and communication. In J. E. Birren & K. W. Schaie (Eds.), *Handbook of the psychology of aging*. New York: Van Nostrand Reinhold.

Frankl, V. E. (1963). *Man's search for meaning: An introduction to logotherapy*. New York: Washington Square Press.

Frazier, A., & Lisonbee, L. K. (1950). Adolescent concerns with physique. *Social Review, 58*, 397–504.

Freedman, D. G. (1976). Infancy, biology, and culture. In L. P. Lipsitt (Ed.), *Developmental psychobiology: The significance of infancy* (pp. 35–54). Hillsdale, NJ: Erlbaum.

Freiberg, H. J. (1975). Teaching children to understand about death. *Death Education, 31*, 318–320.

French, D. C. (1988). Heterogeneity of peer-rejected boys: Aggressive and non-aggressive sub-types. *Child Development, 59*, 976–985.

Freud, A. (1946). *The psycho-analytical treatment of children*. (Trans. N. Procter-Gregg.) New York: International Universities Press.

Freud, S. (1930). *Civilization and its discontents*. London: Hogarth.

Freud S. (1933). *New introductory lectures in psychoanalysis*. New York: Norton.

Freud S. (1936). *The problem of anxiety*. New York: Norton.

Freud, S. (1953). *A general introduction to psychoanalysis*. New York: Permabooks.

Freud, S. (1959). Thoughts for the times on war and death. In *Collected Papers* (Vol. 4). New York: Basic. (Original work published 1915.)

Freud, S. (1962). *Three essays on the theory of sexuality*. (Edited and translated by J. Strachey.) New York: Avon.

Freud, S. (1966). Contributions to the psychology of love. In J. Strachey (Ed.), *Complete psychological works of Sigmund Freud* (Vol. 22). London: Hogarth.

Friedrich, L. K., & Stein, A. H. (1973). Aggressive and prosocial television programs and the natural behavior of preschool children. *Monographs of the Society for Research in Child Development, 38*, (4, Serial no. 151).

Frieze, I. H., Parsons, J. E., Johnson, P. B., Ruble, D. N., & Zellman, G. L. (1978). *Women and sex roles: A social psychological perspective*. New York: Norton.

Frodi, A., & Thompson, R. (1985). Infant's affective responses in the Strange Situation: Effects of prematurity and of quality of attachment. *Child Development, 56*, 1280–1290.

Fuchs, F. (1980). Genetic amniocentesis. *Scientific American, 242* (6), 47–53.

Furman, W., & Bierman, K. (1983). Developmental changes in young children's conception of friendship. *Child Development, 54*, 549–556.

Furstenberg, F. F. (1979). Premarital pregnancy and marital instability. In G. Levinger & O. Moles (Eds.), *Divorce and separation: Contexts, causes, and consequence*. New York: Basic Books.

Furstenberg, F. F., Nord, C. W., Peterson, J. L., & Zill, N. (1983). The life course of children of divorce. *American Sociological Review, 48*, 656–668.

Furth, H. G., & Wachs, M. (1974). *Thinking goes to school: Piaget's theory in practice*. New York: Oxford.

Furth, H. G., & Youniss, J. (1975). Congenital deafness and the development of thinking. In E. H. Lenneberg & E. Lenneberg (Eds.), *Foundations of language development*, (Vol. 2). New York: Academic Press.

Gaddis, A. & Brooks-Gunn. J. (1985). The male experience of pubertal change. *Journal of Youth and Adolescence, 14,* 61–69.

Galbraith R. C. (1982). Sibling spacing and intellectual development: A closer look at the confluence model. *Developmental Psychology, 18,* 151–173.

Galen, H. (1972). A matter of life and death. *Young Children, 27,* 351–356.

Galler, J. R., Ramsey, F., & Solimano, G. (1985). A follow-up study of the effects of early malnutrition on subsequent development. Eleven fine motor skills in adolescence. *Pediatric Research, 19,* 524–527.

Gannon, S., & Korn, S. J. (1983). Temperament, cultural variation, and behavior disorder in preschool children. *Child Psychiatry and Human Development, 13,* 203–212.

Ganon, E. S., & Swartz, K. B. (1980). Perception of internal elements of compound figures by one-month-old infants. *Journal of Experimental Child Psychology, 30,* 159–170.

Garber, J. (1984). Classification of childhood psychopathology: A developmental perspective. *Child Development, 55,* 30–48.

Gardner, H. (1982). *Art, mind, and brain: A cognitive approach to creativity.* New York: Basic Books.

Gardner, K. E., & LeBrecque, S. V. (1986). Effects of maternal employment on sex role orientation of adolescents. *Adolescence, 21,* 875–885.

Gardner, R. A., & Gardner, B. T. (1978). Comparative psychology and language acquisition. *Annals of the New York Academy of Science, 309,* 37–76.

Garfinkel, R. (1982). By the sweat of your brow. In T. M. Field, A. Huston, H. C. Quay, L. Troll, & G. E. Finley (Eds.), *Review of human development.* New York: Wiley.

Garrett, E. (1983). *Women's experience of early parenthood: Expectations versus reality.* Paper presented at the annual meeting of the American Psychological Association, Anaheim, CA.

Gartley, W., & Bernasconi, M. (1967). The concept of death in children. *Journal of Genetic Psychology, 110,* 71–85.

Garvey, C. (1977). *Play.* Cambridge, MA: Harvard University Press.

Garvey, C., & Berndt, R. (1977). *Organization of pretend play.* Paper presented at the meeting of the American Psychological Association, Chicago.

Gelman, R. (1972). Logical capacity of very young children: Number invariance rules. *Child Development, 43,* 75–90.

Gelman, R. (1980). What young children knew about numbers. *Educational Psychologist, 15,* 54–68.

Gelman, R. (1982). Basic numerical abilities. In R. J. Sternberg (Ed.), *Advances in the psychology of human intelligence* (Vol. 1). Hillsdale, NJ: Erlbaum.

Gelman, R., & Baillargeon, R. (1983). A review of some Piagetian concepts. In J. H. Flavell & E. M. Markman (Eds.), *Handbook of child psychology: Cognitive development* (Vol. 3). New York: Wiley.

Gelman, R. & Spelke, E. (1981). The development of thoughts about animate and inanimate objects: Implications for research on social cognition. In. J. H. Flavell & L. Ross (Eds.), *Social cognitive development: Frontiers and possible futures.* New York: Cambridge University Press.

Gentner, D. (1978). On relational meaning: The acquisition of verb meaning. *Child Development, 49,* 988–998.

George, L. K. (1980). *Role transitions in later life.* Monterey, CA: Brooks/Cole.

George, L. K. (1987). Self-esteem. In G. L. Maddox (Ed.), *The encyclopedia of aging* (p. 593). New York: Springer Publishing.

Gewirtz, J. L. (1969). Mechanisms of social learning: Some roles of stimulation and behavior in early human development. In D. Goslin (Ed.), *Handbook of socialization theory and research* (pp. 57–212). New York: Rand McNally.

Ghiselin, B. (1955). *The creative process.* New York: New American Library.

Gibbs, J. C., Clark, P. M., Joseph, J. A., Green, J. L., Goodrick, T. S., & Makowski, D. G. (1986). Relations between moral judgement, moral courage, and field independence. *Child Development, 57,* 185–193.

Gibbs, J. C., & Schnell, S. V. (1985). Moral development "versus" socialization. *American Psychologist, 40,* 1071–1080.

Gibson, C. (1976). The U.S. fertility decline. 1961–1975: The contribution of changes in marital status and marital fertility. *Family Planning Perspectives, 8,* 249–252.

Gibson, D., & Mugford, S. (1986). Expressive relations and social support. In H. L. Kendig (Ed.), *Aging and families: A social networks perspective.* Sydney: Allen and Unwin.

Gibson, E. J. (1969). *Principles of perceptual learning and development*. New York: Appleton-Century-Crofts.

Gibson, E. J., Gibson, J. J., Pick, A. D., & Osser, H. (1962). A developmental study of the discrimination of letter-like forms. *Journal of Comparative and Physiological Psychology, 55,* 897–906.

Gibson, E. J., & Levin, H. (1975). *The psychology of reading.* Cambridge, MA.: MIT Press.

Gibson, E. J., & Spelke, E. S. (1983). The development of perception. In P. H. Mussen (Ed.), *Handbook of child psychology* (4th ed., Vol. 3). New York: Wiley.

Gibson, E. J., & Walk, R. D. (1960). The "visual cliff." *Scientific American, 202* (4), 64–71.

Gibson, J. J. (1979). *The ecological approach to visual perception.* Boston: Houghton-Mifflin.

Gilbert, J. G. (1941). Memory loss in senescence. *Journal of Abnormal and Social Psychology, 36,* 73–86.

Gilligan, C. (1982). *In a different voice: Psychological theory and women's development.* Cambridge, MA: Harvard University Press.

Gilligan, C. & Pollak, S. (1988). The vulnerable and invulnerable physician. In C. Gilligan, J. V. Ward, & J. M. Taylor (Eds.), *Mapping the moral domain.* Cambridge, MA: Harvard University Press.

Gilligan, C., Ward, J. V., & Taylor, J. M. (Eds.). (1988). *Mapping the moral domain.* Cambridge, MA: Harvard University Press.

Gilman, A. G., Goodman, L. S., Rall, T. W., & Murad, F. (Eds.), (1985). *Goodman and Gilman's pharmacological basis of therapeutics* (7th. Ed.). New York: Macmillan.

Ginsberg, E. (1972). Toward a theory of occupational choice: A restatement. *Vocational Guidance Quarterly, 20,* 169–176.

Ginsburg, H., & Opper, S. (1988). *Piaget's theory of intellectual development* (3rd ed). Englewood Cliffs, NJ: Prentice-Hall.

Glaser, B. G., & Strauss, A. (1968). *Time for dying.* Chicago: Aldine Publishing.

Gleason, H. A. (1961). *An introduction to descriptive linguistics.* New York: Holt, Rinehart & Winston.

Gleitman, H. (1986). *Psychology.* New York: Norton.

Glenn, N. D. & Kramer, K. B. (1987). The marriages and divorces of the children of divorce. *Journal of Marriage and the Family, 49,* 811–825.

Glenn, N. D. & Weaver, C. N. (1988). Changing relationship of marital status to reported happiness. *Journal of Marriage and the Family, 50,* 317–324.

Glick, P. C. (1977). Updating the life cycle of the family. *Journal of Marriage and the Family, 39,* 5–13.

Glick, P. C. (1984). Marriage, divorce, and living arrangements: Prospective changes. *Journal of Family Issues, 5,* 7–26.

Glick, P., & Spanier, G. (1980). Married and unmarried cohabitation in the United States. *Journal of Marriage and the Family, 42,* 19–30.

Glick, I. O., Weiss, R. S., & Parkes, C. M. (1974). *The first year of bereavement.* New York: Wiley.

Glucksberg, S., Krauss, R. M., & Higgins, E. T. (1975). The development of referential communication skills. In F. D. Horowitz (Ed.), *Review of child development research.* Chicago: University of Chicago Press.

Goethals, G. W., & Klos, D. S. (1976). *Experiencing youth: First-person accounts.* Boston: Little, Brown.

Goetting, A. (1986). The developmental tasks of siblingship over the life cycle. *Journal of Marriage and the Family, 48,* 703–714.

Gold, D., & Andres, D. (1978a). Developmental comparisons between adolescent children with employed and nonemployed mothers. *Merrill-Palmer Quarterly, 24,* 243–254.

Gold, D., & Andres, D. (1978b). Developmental comparisons between 10-year-old children with employed and nonemployed mothers. *Child Development, 49,* 75–84.

Gold, D., & Andres, D. (1978c). Relations between maternal employment and development of nursery school children. *Canadian Journal of Behavioral Science, 10,* 116–129.

Gold, D. T. (1989). Sibling relationships in old age: A typology. *International Journal of Aging and Human Development, 28,* 37–51.

Goldberg, S. (1983). Parent-infant bonding: Another look. *Child Development, 54,* 1355–1382.

Goldberg, S., Perrotta, M., Minde, K., & Corter, C. (1986). Maternal behavior and attachment in low-birthweight twins and single twins. *Child Development, 57,* 34–46.

Goldin-Meadow, S., & Mylander, C. (1984). Gestural communication in deaf children: The effects and noneffects of parental input on early language development.

Monographs of the Society for Research in Child Development, 49, Serial No. 207.

Goldman, B. D., & Ross, H. S. (1978). Social skills in action: An analysis of early peer games. In J. Glick & K. A. Clarke-Stewart (Eds.), *Studies in social and cognitive development: Vol. 1. The development of social understanding.* New York: Gardner Press.

Goldman, R., & Goldman, J. (1982). *Children's sexual thinking: A comparative study of children aged 5 to 15 years in Australia, North America, Britain, and Sweden.* London: Routledge & Kegan Paul.

Goldman, W. & Lewis, P. (1977). Beautiful is good: Evidence that the physically attractive are more socially skillful. *Journal of Experimental and Social Psychology, 13,* 125–130.

Goldschmid, M. L., Bentler, P. M., Debus, R. L., Rawlinson, R., Kohustamm, D., Modgil, S., Nicholls, J. C., Reykowski, J., Strupczewska, B., & Warren, N. (1973). A cross-cultural investigation of conservation. *Journal of Cross-Cultural Psychology, 4,* 75–88.

Goldsmith, H. H. (1983). Genetic influences on personality from infancy to adulthood. *Child Development, 54,* 331–335.

Goldstein, M. J., Baker, B. L., & Jamison, K. R. (1986). *Abnormal psychology: Experiences, origins, and interventions* (2nd ed.). Boston: Little, Brown, & Co.

Goleman, D. (1980, February). 1528 little geniuses and how they grew. *Psychology Today,* 28–43.

Goodglass, H. (1980). Naming disorders in aphasia. In L. Obler & M. Albert (Eds.), *Language and communication in the elderly.* Lexington, MA: D.C. Heath.

Goodman, N., & Marx, G. (1982). *Society today* (4th ed.). New York: Random House.

Gordon, C., Gaitz, C. M., & Scott, J. (1976). Leisure and lives. In R. H. Binstock & E. Shanas (Eds.), *Handbook of aging and the social sciences.* New York: D. Van Nostrand.

Gordon, F. R., & Yonas, A. (1976). Sensitivity to binocular depth information in infants. *Journal of Experimental Child Psychology, 22,* 413–422.

Gordon, H. (1923). *Mental and scholastic tests among retarded children,* (Educational pamphlet, No. 44), London: Board of Education.

Gordon, S. (1976). *Lonely in America.* New York: Simon and Schuster.

Gordon, S., & Gilgun, J. F. (1987). Adolescent sexuality. In V. B. Van Hasselt & M. Herson (Eds.), *Handbook of adolescent psychology* (pp. 147–167). New York: Pergamon.

Gottman, J. M. (1977). Toward a definition of social isolation in children. *Child Development, 48,* 513–517.

Gough, H. G. (1979). A creative personality scale for the adjective check list. *Journal of Personality and Social Psychology, 37,* 1398–1405.

Gould, J. L. (1982). *Ethology.* New York: Norton.

Gould, R. L. (1972). The phases of adult life: A study in developmental psychology. *American Journal of Psychiatry, 129,* 521–531.

Gould, R. L. (1978). *Transformations.* New York: Simon and Schuster.

Gould, S. J. (1981). *The mismeasure of man.* New York: Norton.

Goulet, L. R. & Baltes, P. B. (Eds.). (1970). *Life-span developmental psychology: Research and theory.* New York: Academic Press.

Gowan, J. C. (1977). Background and history of the gifted-child movement. In J. C. Stanley, W. C. George, & G. H. Solano (Eds.), *The gifted and the creative: A fifty-year perspective.* Baltimore: Johns Hopkins University Press.

Goyert, G. L., Bottoms, S. F., Treadwell, M. C., & Nehra, P. C. (1989). The physician factor in cesarean birth rates. *The New England Journal of Medicine, 320,* 706–709.

Gray, D. S., & Gorzalka, B. B. (1980). Adrenal steroid interactions in female sexual behavior: A review. *Psychoneuroendocrinology, 15,* 157–175.

Green, R. (1974). *Sexual identity conflict in children.* New York: Basic Books.

Green, R. L. (1969). Age-intelligence relationships between ages sixteen and sixty-four: A rising trend. *Developmental Psychology, 1,* 618–627.

Green, R. L. (1971). *Age, intelligence, and learning.* Paper presented to the Industrial Gerontology Seminar, National Institute of Industrial Gerontology, Minneapolis, MN, June.

Greene, V. L., & Monahan, D. J. (1989). The effect of a support and education program on stress and burden among family caregivers to frail elderly persons. *The Gerontologist, 29,* 472–477.

Greenfield, P. M., & Smith, J. H. (1976). *The structure of communication in early language development.* New York: Academic Press.

Greenstein, T. N. (1986). Social-psychological factors in perinatal labor-force participation. *Journal of Marriage and the Family, 48,* 565–571.

Gresham, F. M., & Nagel. R. (1980). Social skills training with children: Responsiveness to modeling and coaching as a function of peer orientation. *Journal of Consulting and Clinical Psychology, 18,* 718–729.

Grollman, E. A. (1970). *Talking about death.* Boston: Beacon Press.

Groos, K. (1901). *The play of man.* New York: Appleton-Century-Crofts.

Gross, A. E., & Crafton, C. (1977). What is good is beautiful. *Sociometry, 40,* 85–90.

Grossman, H. J. (1983). *Classification in mental retardation.* Washington, DC: AAMD.

Grotevant, H. D., & Cooper, C. R. (1988). The role of family experience in career exploration: A life-span perspective. In P. B. Baltes, D. L. Featherman, & R. M. Lerner (Eds.), *Life-span development and behavior: Vol. 8.* Hillsdale, NJ: Erlbaum.

Grotevant, H., & Thorbecke, W. (1982). Sex differences in the styles of occupational identity formation in late adolescence. *Developmental Psychology, 18,* 396–405.

Groth, A. N. (1979). *Men who rape: The psychology of the offender.* (With H. J. Birnbaum.) New York: Plenum.

Gruber, H. E. (1982). On the hypothesized relation between giftedness and creativity. In D. H. Feldman (Ed.), *Developmental approaches to giftedness and creativity.* San Francisco: Jossey-Bass.

Gruendel. J. M. (1977). Referential extension in early language development. *Child Development, 48,* 1567–1576.

Gruman, G. J. (1966). A history of ideas about the prolongation of life. *Transactions of the American Philosophical Society, 56* (Pt. 9).

Grusec, J. E., & Abramovitch, R. (1982). Imitation of peers and adults in a natural setting: A functional analysis. *Child Development, 53,* 636–642.

Guardo, C. J., & Bohan, J. B. (1971). Development of the sense of self-identity in children. *Child Development, 42,* 1909–1921.

Gubrium, J. F., & Lynott, R. J. (1983). Rethinking life satisfaction. *Human Organization, 42,* 30–38.

Guidibaldi, J., & Perry, J. D. (1985). Divorce and mental health sequelae for children: A two-year follow-up of a nationwide sample. *Journal of the American Academy of Child Psychiatry, 24,* 531–537.

Guilford, J. P. (1967). *The nature of human intelligence.* New York: McGraw-Hill.

Gunderson, E. K. E. (1965). Body size, self-evaluation, and military effectiveness. *Journal of Personality and Social Psychology, 2,* 902–906.

Gutmann, D. L. (1975). Parenthood: A key to the comparative study of the life cycle? In N. Datan & L. Ginsberg (Eds.), *Life-span developmental psychology: Normative life courses.* New York: Academic Press.

Guttmacher, A. F. (1973). *Pregnancy, birth and family planning.* New York: Signet.

Haan, N., & Day, D. (1974). A longitudinal study of change and sameness in personality development: Adolescence to later adulthood. *International Journal of Aging and Human Development, 5,* 11–39.

Haan, N., Smith, M., & Block J. (1968). Moral reasoning of young adults: Political or social behaviors, family background, and personality correlates. *Journal of Personality and Social Psychology, 10,* 183–201.

Hagen, J. W. (1971). Some thoughts on how children learn to remember. *Human Development, 14,* 262–271.

Hagen, M. A., & Johnson, M. M. (1977). Hudson Pictorial Depth Perception Test: Cultural content and questions with a Western sample. *Journal of Social Psychology, 101,* 3–11.

Hagestad, G. O. (1985). Continuity and connectedness. In V. L. Bengtson & J. F. Robertson (Eds.), *Grandparenthood* (pp. 31–48). Beverly Hills, CA: Sage.

Haith, M. M. (1979). Visual cognition in early infancy. In R. B. Kearsley & I. E. Sigel (Eds.), *Infants at risk: Assessment of cognitive functioning.* Hillsdale, NJ: Erlbaum.

Haith, M. M., Bergman, T., & Moore, M. J. (1977). Eye contact and face scanning in early infancy. *Science, 198,* 853–855.

Hall, E. (1970). A conversation with Jean Piaget and Barbel Inhelder. *Psychology Today, 3* (12), 25–56.

Hall, J. A., & Halberstadt, A. G. (1980). Masculinity and femininity in children: Development of the children's personal attributes questionnaire. *Developmental Psychology, 16,* 270–280.

Hamill, P. V., Dried, T. A., Johnson, C. L., Reed, R. B., & Roche, A. F. (1977). *NCHS growth curves for children, birth to 18 years.* (Vital and Health Statistics: Series 11. National Heath Survey, No. 154.) Washington, DC: U.S. Government Printing Office.

Hamilton, G. V. (1929). *A research in marriage.* New York: Albert and Charles Boni.

Haney, W. (1981). Validity, vaudeville, and values: A short history of social concerns over psychological testing. *American Psychologist, 36,* 1021–1034.

Hanson, S. W., Streissguth, A. P., & Smith, D. W. (1978). The effects of moderate alcohol consumption during pregnancy on fetal growth and morphogenesis. *Journal of Pediatrics, 92,* 457–460.

Hantover, J. P. (1978). The Boy Scouts and the validation of masculinity. *Journal of Social Issues, 34,* 184–195.

Harkins, E. B. (1978). Effects of empty nest transition on self-report of psychological and physical well-being. *Journal of Marriage and the Family, 40,* 549–556.

Harmer, R. M. (1963). *The high cost of dying.* New York: Crowell-Collier.

Harper, L. V. (1975). The scope of offspring effects: From caregiver to culture. *Psychological Bulletin, 82,* 784–801.

Harrington, D. M., Block, J. H., & Block, J. (1983). Predicting creativity in preadolescence from divergent thinking in early childhood. *Journal of Personality and Social Psychology, 45,* 609–623.

Harris, L. (1975). *The myth and reality of aging in America.* New York: National Council on Aging.

Harris, P. (1984). The hidden face of shyness: A message from the shy for researchers and practitioners. *Human Relations, 37,* 1079–1093.

Harry, J., & DeVall, W. (1978). Age and sexual culture among homosexually-oriented males. *Archives of Sexual Behavior, 7,* 199.

Harter, S. (1982). A model of intrinsic mastery motivation in children: Individual differences and developmental change. In W. A. Collins (Ed.), *Minnesota Symposium on Child Psychology* (Vol. 14). Hillsdale, NJ: Erlbaum.

Harter, S. (1983). Developmental perspectives on the self-system. In E. M. Hetherington (Ed.), *Socialization, personality, and social development; Handbook of Child Psychology* (Vol. 4). New York: Wiley.

Hartley, A. A., & Anderson, J. W. (1983a). Task complexity and problem-solving performance in young and older adults. *Journal of Gerontology, 38,* 72–77.

Hartley, A. A., & Anderson, J. W. (1983b). Task complexity, problem representation, and problem-solving performance by younger and older adults. *Journal of Gerontology, 38,* 78–80.

Hartley, R. E. (1959). Sex role pressures in the socialization of the male child. *Psychological Reports, 5,* 457–468.

Hartup, W. W. (1974). Aggression in childhood: Developmental perspectives. *American Psychologist, 29,* 336–341.

Hartup, W. W. (1983). Peer Relations. In E. M. Hetherington (Ed.), P. H. Mussen (Series Ed.), *Handbook of child psychology (Vol. 4): Socialization, personality and social development.* New York: Wiley.

Hartup, W. W., Glazer, J. A., & Charlesworth, R. (1967). Peer reinforcement and sociometric status. *Child Development, 38,* 1017–1024.

Harvey, S. M. (1987). Female sexual behavior: Fluctuations during the menstrual cycle. *Journal of Psychosomatic Research, 31,* 101–110.

Hass, A. (1979). *Teenage sexuality: A survey of teenage sexual behavior.* New York: Macmillan.

Hatano, G., Miyake, K., & Tajima, N. (1980). Mother behavior in an unstructured situation and child's acquistion and number conservation. *Child Development, 51,* 379–385.

Havighurst, R. J. (1982). The world of work. In B. B. Wolman (Ed.), *Handbook of developmental psychology.* Englewood Cliffs, NJ: Prentice-Hall.

Havighurst, R. J., Neugarten, B., & Tobin, S. S. (1968). Disengagement and patterns of aging. In B. Neugarten (Ed.), *Middle age and aging.* Chicago: University of Chicago Press.

Hawkins, J. (1985). Computers and girls: Rethinking the issues. *Sex Roles, 13,* 165–180.

Hay, D. L., Pederson, J., & Nash, A. (1982). Dyadic interaction in the first year of life. In K. H. Rubin & H. S. Ross (Eds.), *Peer relationships and social skills in childhood.* New York: Springer-Verlag.

Hayes, C. (Ed.). (1987). *Risking the future: Adolescent sexuality, pregnancy, and childbearing.* Washington, DC: National Academy Press.

Hayes, C. L., & Kalish, R. A. (1987). Death-related experiences and funerary practices of the Hmong refugee in the United States. *Omega, 18,* 63−70.

Hayes, M. P., Stinnett, N., & DeFrain, J. (1980). Learning about marriage from the divorced. *Journal of Divorce, 4,* 23−29.

Hayflick, L. (1987). Cell aging in vivo. In G. L. Maddox (ed.). *The encyclopedia of aging.* New York: Springer.

Hayghe, H. (1984). Working mothers reach record number in 1984. *Monthly Labor Review, 99,* 31−34.

Hazen, N. L., & Black, B. (1989). Preschool peer communication skills: The role of social status and interaction context. *Child Development, 60,* 867−876.

Hazen, N. L., & Durett, M. E. (1982). Relationship of security of attachment to exploration and cognitive mapping abilities in two-year-olds. *Developmental Psychology, 18,* 751−759.

Heath, D. H. (1977). *Maturity and competence: A transactional view.* New York: Halsted Press.

Heming, G. (1987). *Predicting adaptation during the transition to parenthood.* Paper presented at the biennial meeting of The Society for Research in Child Development, Baltimore, MD.

Herek, G. M, & Glunt, E. K. (1988). An epidemic of stigma: Public reactions to AIDS. *American Psychologist, 43,* 886−891.

Herman, S. J. (1977). Women, divorce, and suicide. *Journal of Divorce, 1,* 107−117.

Herrnstein, R. J (1971). *I. Q. in the meritocracy.* Boston: Little, Brown.

Hess, B. (1972). Friendship. In M. W. Riley, M. Johnson, & A. Loner (Eds.), *Aging and society.* New York: Russell Sage.

Hesse, P. (1986). Children's and adolescents' fears of nuclear war: Is our sense of the future disappearing? *International Journal of Mental Health, 15,* 93−133.

Hetherington, E. M. (1972). Effects of father absence on personality development in adolescent daughters. *Developmental Psychology, 7,* 313−326.

Hetherington, E. M. (1979). Divorce: A child's perspective. *American Psychologist, 34,* 851−858.

Hetherington, E. M. (1989). Coping with family transitions: Winners, losers, and survivors. *Child Development, 60,* 1−14.

Hetherington, E. M., Cox M., & Cox, R. (1978). The aftermath of divorce. In J. H. Stevens and M. Matthews (Eds.), *Mother-child, Father-child-relations.* Washington, DC: National Association for the Education of Young Children.

Hetherington, E. M., Cox, M., & Cox, R. (1985). Long-term effects of divorce and remarriage on the adjustment of children. *Journal of the American Academy of Child Psychiatry, 24,* 518−530.

Hicks, D. J. (1965). Imitation and retention of film-mediated aggressive peer and adult models. *Journal of Personality and Social Psychology, 2,* 97−100.

Higgins, E. T. (1976). Social class differences in verbal communicative accuracy: A question of "which question?" *Psychological Bulletin, 83,* 695−714.

Hildebrant, K., & Fitzgerald, H. (1983). The infant's physical attractiveness: Its effect in bonding and attachment. *Infant Mental Health Journal, 4,* 3−12.

Hill, J., & Lynch, M. (1983). The intensification of gender-related role expectations during early adolescence. In J. Brooks-Gunn & A. Petersen (Eds.), *Female Puberty.* New York: Plenum Press.

Hill, R. N., Foote, J., Aldous, R., Carlson, R., & McDonald, R. (1970). *Family development in three generations.* Cambridge, MA: Schenkman.

Hill, R., & Rodgers, R. (1964). The developmental approach. In H. Christensen (Ed.), *Handbook of marriage and the family.* Chicago: Rand McNally.

Hirschman, R., Melamed, L. E., & Oliver, C. M. (1982). The psychophysiology of infancy. In B. B. Wolman (Ed.), *Handbook of developmental psychology.* Englewood Cliffs, NJ: Prentice-Hall.

Hite, S. (1976). *The Hite Report: A nationwide study of female sexuality.* New York: Dell.

Hochschild, A. (1989). *The second shift.* New York: Viking.

Hockett, C. F. (1954). Chinese vs. English: An exploration of the Whorfian thesis. In H. Hoijer (Ed.), *Language in culture.* Chicago: University of Chicago Press.

Hodapp, R. M., & Mueller, E. (1982). Early social development. In B. B. Wolman (Ed.), *Handbook of developmental psychology.* Englewood Cliffs, NJ: Prentice-Hall.

Hodgson, J. W., & Fischer, J. L. (1979). Sex differences in identity and intimacy development in college youth. *Journal of Youth and Adolescence, 8,* 37–50.

Hodson, B. (1980). *The assessment of phonological processes.* Danville, IL: Interstate.

Hofferth, S. L., Kahn, J. R., & Baldwin, W. (1987). Premarital sexual activity among U.S. teenage women over the past three decades. *Family Planning Perspectives, 19,* 46–53.

Hoff-Ginsberg, E. (1986). Function and structure in maternal speech: Their relation to the child's development of syntax. *Developmental Psychology, 22,* 155–163.

Hoffman, L. W. (1974). Effects of maternal employment on the child: A review of the research. *Developmental Psychology, 10,* 204–228.

Hoffman, L. W. (1979). Maternal exployment: (1979). *American Psychologist, 34,* 859–865.

Hoffman, L. W., & Manis, J. D. (1978). Influences of children on marital interaction and parental satisfaction and dissatisfaction. In R. M. Lerner & G. B. Spanier (Eds.), *Child influences on marriage and family interaction.* New York: Academic Press.

Hoffman, L. W. & Manis, J. D. (1982). The value of children in the United States. In L. I. Nye (Ed.), *Family relationships: Rewards and costs.* Beverly Hills, CA.: Sage.

Hoffman, M. L. (1970). Moral development. In P. H. Mussen (Ed.), *Carmichael's Manual of Child Psychology.* New York: Wiley.

Hoffman, M. L. (1982). Development of prosocial motivation: Empathy and guilt. In N. Eisenberg (Ed.), *Development of prosocial behavior.* New York: Academic Press.

Hoffman, M. L. (1988). Moral development. In M. H. Bornstein & M. E. Lamb (Eds.), *Developmental psychology: An advanced textbook* (2nd ed.). Hillsdale, NJ: Erlbaum.

Hofland, B. F., Willis, S. L., & Baltes, P. B. (1980). Fluid intelligence performance in the elderly: Intraindividual variability and conditions of assessment. *Journal of Educational Psychology, 73,* 573–586.

Hold, E. C. L. (1976). Attention structure and rank specific behavior in preschool children. In M. R. A. Chance & R. R. Larsen (Eds.), *The social structure of attention.* New York: Wiley.

Holden, C. (1978). Cancer and the mind: How are they connected? *Science, 200,* 1363–1369.

Holland, J. L. (1973). *Making vocational choices: A theory of careers.* Englewood Cliffs, NJ: Prentice-Hall.

Holland, J. L. (1985). *Making vocational choices: A theory of vocational personalities and work environments.* Englewood Cliffs, NJ: Prentice-Hall.

Holmes, D. L., Nagy, J. N., Slaymaker, F., Sosnowski, R. J., Prinz, S. M., & Pasternak, J. K. (1982). Early influences of prematurity, illness, and prolonged hospitalization on infant behavior. *Developmental Psychology, 18,* 744–750.

Holstein, C. B. (1976). Irreversible, stepwise sequence in the development of moral judgement: A longitudinal study of males and females. *Child Development, 47,* 51–61.

Holtzmann, W. H. (1982). Cross-cultural comparisons of personality development in Mexico and the United States. In D. A. Wagner & H. W. Stevenson (Eds.), *Cultural perspectives on child development.* San Francisco: W. H. Freeman.

Holtzmann, W. H., Diaz-Guerrero, R., & Swartz, J. D. (1975). *Personality development in two cultures: A cross-cultural longitudinal study of school children in Mexico and the United States.* Austin: University of Texas Press.

Honzik, M. P., Macfarlane, J. W., & Allen, L. (1948). The stability of mental test performance between two and eighteen years. *Journal of Experimental Education, 18,* 309–324.

Horley, J. (1984). Life satisfaction, happiness, and morale: Two problems with the use of subjective well-being indicators. *The Gerontologist, 24,* 124–127.

Horn, J. L. (1970). Organization of data on life-span development of human abilities. In L. R. Goulet & P. B. Baltes (Eds.), *Life-span developmental psychology.* New York: Academic Press.

Horn, J. L. (1978). Human ability systems. In P. B. Baltes (Ed.), *Life span development and behavior.* New York: Academic Press.

Horn, J. L. (1981). The theory of fluid and crystallized intelligence in relation to apprehension, memory, speediness, laterality, and physiological functioning through the "vital years" of adulthood. In F. I. M. Craik & S. E. Trehub (Eds.), *Aging and cognitive processes.* New York: Plenum.

Horn, J. L. (1982). The aging of human abilities. In B. B. Wolman (Ed.), *Handbook of developmental psychology.* Englewood Cliffs, NJ: Prentice-Hall.

Horn, J. L., & Cattell, R. B. (1966). Refinement and test of the theory of fluid and crystallized general intelligence. *Journal of Educational Psychology, 57,* 253–270.

Horn, J. L., & Cattell, R. B. (1967). Age differences in fluid and crystallized intelligence. *Acta Psychologica, 26,* 107–129.

Horn, J. L., & Donaldson, G. (1980). Cognitive development: 2. Adulthood development in human abilities. In O. G. Brim & J. Kagan (Eds.), *Constancy and change in human development.* Cambridge, MA: Harvard University Press.

Hornblum, J. N. (1977). *Cognitive-developmental level and the child's understanding of death.* Unpublished doctoral dissertation, Temple University, Philadelphia.

Horney, K. (1950). *Neurosis and human growth.* New York: Norton.

Horney, K. (1973). *Feminine psychology.* New York: Norton.

Houseknecht, S. K. (1987). Voluntary childlessness. In M. B. Sussman & S. K. Steinmetz (Eds.), *Handbook of marriage and the family* (pp. 369–396). New York: Plenum.

Howes, C. (1983). Patterns of friendship. *Child Development, 54,* 1041–1053.

Howes, C. (1988). Peer interaction of young children. *Monographs of the Society for Research in Child Development, 53* (Serial No. 17).

Howes, C., Unger, O., & Seidner, L. B. (1989). Social pretend play in toddlers: Parallels with social play and with solitary pretend. *Child Development, 60,* 77–84.

Hoyer, L. W., Hoyer, W. J., Treat, N. J., & Baltes, P. B. (1978–1979). Training response speed in young and elderly women. *International Journal of Aging and Human Development, 9,* 247–253.

Hoyer, W. J., & Plude, D. J. (1980). Attentional and perceptual processes in the study of cognitive aging. In L. W. Poon (Ed.), *Aging in the 1980's: Psychological issues* (pp. 227–238). Washington, DC: American Psychological Association.

Huang, M. S. (1983). A developmental study of children's comprehension of embedded sentences with and without semantic constraints. *Journal of Psychology, 114,* 51–56.

Huber, P. S. (1980). Death and society among the Anggor of New Guinea. In R. A. Kalish (Ed.), *Death and dy-ing: Views from many cultures.* Farmingdale, NY: Baywood Publishing.

Hudson, L. (1966). *Contrary imaginations.* London: Methuen.

Hudson, W. (1960). Pictorial depth perception in subcultural groups in Africa. *Journal of Social Psychology, 52,* 183–208.

Huesmann, L. R., Eron, L. D., Lefkowitz, M. M., & Walder, L. O. (1984). Stability of aggression over time and generations. *Developmental Psychology, 20,* 1120–1134.

Hughes, F. P. (1980, July). *Review of research in selected areas of adult cognitive development: Implications for adult education.* ERIC Clearinghouse on Adult, Career, and Vocational Education. (ERIC Document Reproduction Service No. ED 203 078).

Hughes, F. P. (1991). *Children and play.* Boston: Allyn and Bacon.

Hulicka, I. M. (1965, April). *Age group comparisons for the use of mediators.* Paper presented at the Southwestern Psychological Association Meeting, Oklahoma City, Oklahoma.

Hulicka, I. M. (1966). *Age changes and age differences in memory functioning.* Unpublished manuscript, D'Youville College, Buffalo, New York.

Hulicka, I. M. (1967). Age differences in retention as a function of interference. *Journal of Gerontology, 22,* 180–184.

Hulicka, I. M., & Grossman, J. L. (1967). Age group comparisons for the use of mediators in paired-associate learning. *Journal of Gerontology, 22,* 46–51.

Hultsch, D. L. (1969). Adult age differences in the organization of free recall. *Developmental Psychology, 4,* 673–678.

Hultsch, D. L. (1971a). Adult age differences in free classification and free recall. *Developmental Psychology, 4,* 338–342.

Hultsch, D. L. (1971b). Organization and memory in adulthood. *Human Development, 14,* 16–29.

Hultsch, D. F., & Dixon, R. A. (1983). The role of preexperimental knowledge in text processing in adulthood. *Experimental Aging Research, 9,* 17–22.

Humphrey, T. (1978). Function of the nervous system during prenatal life. In U. Stave (Ed.), *Perinatal physiology.* New York: Plenum.

Hunt, M. (1974). *Sexual behavior in the 1970's.* Chicago: Playboy.

Huntington, R., & Metcalf, P. (1979). *Celebrations of death: the anthropology of mortuary ritual.* Cambridge: Cambridge University Press.

Huston, A. (1983). Sex-typing. In P. H. Mussen (Ed.), *Handbook of Child Psychology* (Vol. 4, 4th ed.). New York: Wiley.

Huston, A., Carpenter, C. J., Atwater, J. B. & Johnson, L. M (1986). Gender, adult structuring of activities, and social behavior in middle childhood. *Child Development, 57,* 1200–1209.

Huston, A. C., Greer, D., Wright, J. C., Welch, R., & Ross, R. (1984). Child comprehension of televised formal features with masculine and feminine connotations. *Developmental Psychology, 20,* 707–716.

Huston-Stein, A., & Higgins-Trenk, A. (1978). Development of females from childhood through adulthood: Career and feminine observations. In P. B. Baltes (Ed.), *Life-span development and behavior* (Vol. 1). New York: Academic Press.

Huyck, M. H., & Hoyer, W. J. (1982). *Adult development and aging.* Belmont, CA: Wadsworth.

Hyde, J. S. (1981). How large are cognitive differences? A meta-analysis using W^2 and d. *American Psychologist, 36,* 892–901.

Iannotti, R. J. (1978). Effect of role-taking experiences on role-taking, empathy, altruism, and aggression. *Developmental Psychology, 14,* 119–124.

Imperato-McGinley, J., Guerrero, L., Gautier, T., & Peterson, R. E. (1974). Steroid 5-reductase deficiency in man: An inherited form of male pseudohermaphroditism. *Science, 186,* 1213–1215.

Imperato-McGinley, J., & Peterson, R. E. (1976). Pseudohermaphroditism: The complexities of phenotypic development. *American Journal of Medicine, 61,* 251–272.

Inglis, J., Ankus, M. N., & Sykes, D. H. (1968). Age-related differences in learning and short-term memory from childhood to the senium. *Human Development, 11,* 42–52.

Inglis, J., & Caird, W. K. (1963). Age differences in successive responses to simultaneous stimulation. *Canadian Journal of Psychology, 17,* 98–105.

Ingram, C. (1974). Phonological rules in young children. *Journal of Child Language, 1,* 49–64.

Ingram, D. (1981). *Procedures for the phonological analysis of children's language.* Baltimore: University Park Press.

Inhelder, B., & Piaget, J. (1958). *The growth of logical thinking from childhood to adolescence.* New York: Basic.

Inhelder, B., & Piaget, J. (1964). *The early growth of logic in the child.* New York: W. W. Norton.

Irwin, D. M., & Bushnell, M. M. (1980). *Observational strategies for child study.* New York: Holt, Rinehart and Winston.

Iso-Ahola, S. E. (1980). *The social psychology of leisure and recreation.* Dubuque, IA: Wm. C. Brown Co.

Jack, I., & Jack, R. (1988). Women lawyers: Archetype and alternative. In C. Gilligan, J. V. Ward, & J. M. Taylor (Eds.), *Mapping the moral domain.* Cambridge, MA: Harvard University Press.

Jacklin, C. N. (1989). Female and male: Issues of gender. *American Psychologist, 44,* 127–133.

Jacklin, C. N., & Maccoby, E. E. (1983). Issues of gender differentiation in normal development. In M. D. Levine, W. B. Corey, A. C. Crocker, & R. T. Gross (Eds.), *Developmental-Behavioral Pediatrics.* Philadelphia: E. B. Saunders.

Jacklin, C. N., Maccoby, E. E., & Doering, C. H. (1983). Neonatal sex steroid hormones and timidity in 6–18-month-old boys and girls. *Developmental Psychobiology, 16,* 163–168.

Jacobson, J. L., & Wille, D. E. (1984). Influence of attachment and separation experience on separation distress at 18 months. *Developmental Psychology, 20,* 477–484.

Jacobson, J. L., & Wille, D. E. (1986). The influence of attachment pattern on developmental changes in peer interaction from the toddler to the preschool period. *Child Development, 57,* 338–347.

Jacobson, S. W. (1979). Matching behavior in the young infant. *Child Development, 50,* 425–430.

Jacobson, S. W. Fein, G. G. Jacobson, J. L., Schwartz, P. M., & Dowler, J. K. (1985). The effect of intrauterine PCB exposure on visual recognition memory. *Child Development, 56,* 853–860.

Jacobvitz, D. & Sroufe, L. A. (1987). The early caregiver-child relationship and Attention Deficit Disorder with hyperactivity in kindergarten: A prospective study. *Child Development, 58,* 1488–1495.

Jakobson, R. (1968). *Child language, aphasia, and phonological universals.* (Trans. A. Keiler). The Hague: Mouton.

James, W. (1890). *Principles of psychology.* New York: Henry Holt.

James, W. (1968). The self. In C. Gordon & K. J. Gergen (Eds.), *The self in social interaction* (Vol. I). New York: Wiley.

Jani, S. N. (1966). The age factor in stereopsis screening. *American Journal of Optometry, 43,* 653–655.

Janos, P. M., & Robinson, N. M. (1985). Psychosocial development in intellectually gifted children. In F. D. Horowitz & M. O'Brien (Eds.). *The gifted and talented: Developmental perspectives.* Washington DC: American Psychological Association.

Jaquish, G. A., & Ripple, R. E. (1981). Cognitive creative abilities and self-esteem across the adult life span. *Human Development, 24,* 110–119.

Jeffko, W. G. (1980). Redefining death. In E. S. Shneidman (Ed.), *Death: Current Perspectives* (2nd ed.). Palo Alto, CA: Mayfield Publishing.

Jenkins, Richard A., & Cavanaugh, J. C. (1985). Examining the relationship between the development of the concept of death and overall cognitive development. *Omega,* 193–199.

Jensen, A. H. (1980). *Is there anything I can do to help?* Issaquah, WA: Medic Publishing Co.

Jensen, A. R. (1981). *Straight talk about mental tests.* New York: Free Press.

Jensen, L., & Borges, M. (1986). The effect of maternal employment on adolescent daughters. *Adolescence, 21,* 659–666.

Jiao, S., Ji, G., & Ching, C. C. (1986). Comparative study of behavioral qualities of only children and sibling children. *Child Development, 57,* 357–361.

Joffe, L. S., & Vaughn, B. E. (1982). Infant-mother attachment: Theory, assessment, and implications for development. In B. B. Wolman (Ed.), *Handbook of developmental psychology.* Englewood Cliffs, NJ: Prentice-Hall.

Johnson, D. F., & Pittenger, J. B. (1984). Attribution, the attractiveness stereotype, and the elderly. *Developmental Psychology, 20,* 1168–1172.

Johnson, J. E., Christie, J. F., & Yawkey, T. D. (1987). *Play and early childhood development.* Glenview, IL: Scott, Foresman.

Johnson, J. E., & Ershler, J. (1981). Developmental trends in preschool play as a function of classroom setting and gender. *Child Development, 52,* 995–1004.

Johnson, M. M. (1975). Fathers, mothers, and sex typing. *Sociological Inquiry, 45,* 15–26.

Jones, D. (1974). *Sex differences in the friendship patterns of young adults.* Unpublished paper. Cited in L. Troll, *Early and middle adulthood.* Monterey, CA: Brooks/Cole.

Jones, H. E. & Conrad, H. S. (1933). The growth and decline of intelligence: A study of a homogeneous group between the ages of ten and sixty. *Genetic Psychology Monographs, 13,* 223–298.

Jones, M. C. (1957). The later careers of boys who were early- or late-maturing. *Child Development, 28,* 113–128.

Jones, M. C., & Mussen, P. H. (1958). Self-conceptions, motivations and interpersonal attitudes of early and late maturing girls. *Child Development, 29,* 491–501.

Jones, R. E. (1984). *Human reproduction and sexual behavior.* Englewood Cliffs, NJ: Prentice-Hall.

Jourard, S. M., & Secord, P. L. (1955). Body cathexis and the ideal female figure. *Journal of Abnormal and Social Psychology, 50,* 243–246.

Joyce, L. K. (1977). A study of formal reasoning in elementary education majors. *Science Education, 61,* 153–158.

Jung, C. G. (1953). *Collected works.* (H. Read, M. Fordham, & G. Adler, Eds.) Princeton, NJ: Princeton University Press.

Kagan, J. (1984). *The nature of the child.* New York: Basic Books.

Kagan, J., & Moss, H. A. (1962). *Birth to maturity.* New York: Wiley.

Kahana, B. (1982). Social behavior and aging. In B. B. Wolman (Ed.), *Handbook of developmental psychology.* Englewood Cliffs, NJ: Prentice-Hall.

Kail, R., & Hagen, J. W. (1982). Memory in childhood. In B. B. Wolman (Ed.), *Handbook of developmental psychology.* Englewood Cliffs, NJ: Prentice-Hall.

Kalish, R. A. (1976). Death and dying in a social context. In R. H. Binstock & E. Shanas (Eds.), *Handbook of aging and the social sciences.* New York: Van Nostrand Reinhold.

Kalish, R. A. (1981). *Death, grief, and caring relationships.* Monterey, CA: Brooks/Cole.

Kalish, R. A., & Goldberg, H. (1979–1980). Community attitudes toward funeral directors. *Omega, 10,* 335–346.

Kalish, R. A., & Reynolds, D. K. (1976). *Death and ethnicity: A psychocultural study.* Los Angeles: University of Southern California Press.

Kallman, F. J., & Sander, G. (1948). Twin studies on aging and longevity. *Journal of Heredity, 39,* 349–357.

Kalter, H., & Warkany, J. (1983). Congenital malformations: Etiologic factors and their role in prevention. *The New England Journal of Medicine, 308,* 424–431.

Kalter, N. (1984). Conjoint mother-daughter treatment: A beginning phase of psychotherapy with adolescent daughters of divorce. *American Journal of Orthopsychiatry, 54,* 490–497.

Kalter, N. (1987). Long-term effects of divorce on children: A developmental vulnerability model. *American Journal of Orthopsychiatry, 5,* 587–600.

Kamin, L. (1974). *The science and politics of IQ.* Potomac, MD: Erlbaum.

Kandel, D., & Lesser, G. S. (1969). Parent-adolescent relationships and adolescent independence in the United States and Denmark. *Journal of Marriage and the Family, 31,* 348–358.

Kaplan, E., & Kaplan, G. (1971). The prelinguistic child. In J. Elliot (Ed.), *Human development and cognitive process.* New York: Holt, Rinehart, and Winston.

Kapust, L. R. (1982). Living with dementia: The ongoing funeral. *Social Work in Health Care, 7,* 79–91.

Kart, C. S., Metress, E. K., & Metress, S. P. (1988). *Aging, health, and society.* Boston: Jones and Bartlett.

Kastenbaum, R. J. (1969). Death and bereavement in later life. In A. H. Kutscher (Ed.), *Death and bereavement.* Springfield, IL: Charles C. Thomas.

Kastenbaum, R. J. (1975). Is death a life crisis? On the confrontation with death in theory and practice. In N. Datan & L. H. Ginsberg (Eds.), *Life-span developmental psychology: Normative life crises.* New York: Academic Press.

Kastenbaum, R. J. (1977). *Death, society, and human experience.* St. Louis: Mosby.

Kastenbaum, R. (1985). Dying and death: A life span approach. In J. E. Birren & K. W. Schaie (Eds.), *Handbook of the psychology of aging* (2nd ed., pp. 619–643). New York: Van Nostrand Reinhold.

Kastenbaum, R. J. (1986). *Death, society, and human experience* (3rd ed.). Columbus, OH: Merrill.

Kastenbaum, R. (1988). Theory, research, and application: Some critical issues for thanatology. *Omega, 18,* 397–410.

Kastenbaum, R. J., & Aisenberg, R. B. (1972). *The psychology of death.* New York: Springer-Verlag.

Kastenbaum, R. J., & Briscoe, L. (1975). The street corner: A laboratory for the study of life-threatening behavior. *Omega, 6,* 33–44.

Kastenbaum, R. J., & Costa, P. T. (1977). Psychological perspectives on death. *Annual Review of Psychology, 28,* 225–249.

Kastenbaum, R. J., & Kastenbaum, B. S. (1971). Hope, survival, and the caring environment. In E. Palmore & F. C. Jeffer (Eds.), *Prediction of life span.* Lexington, MA: Heath.

Katchadourian, H. (1989). *Fundamentals of human sexuality* (5th ed.). New York: Holt, Rinehart, and Winston.

Katz, P. A. (1979). The development of female identity. *Sex Roles, 5,* 155–178.

Katz, S. L. & Wilfert, C. M. (1989). Human Immunodeficiency Virus infection of newborns. *New England Journal of Medicine, 320,* 1687–1688.

Kauffman, J. M., Gordon, M. E., & Baker, A. (1978). Being imitated: Persistence of an effect. *Journal of Genetic Psychology, 132,* 319–320.

Kauffmann, R., Maland, J., & Yonas, A. (1981). Sensitivity of 5- and 7-month-old infants to pictorial depth information. *Journal of Experimental Child Psychology, 32,* 162–168.

Kausler, D. H. (1985). Episodic memory: Memorizing performance. In N. Charness (Ed.), *Aging and human performance* (pp. 101–141). New York: Wiley.

Kavrell, S. M., & Petersen, A. C. (1986). Patterns of achievement in early adolescence. In M. L. Maehr & M. W. Steinkamp (Eds.), *Women and Science.* Greenwich, CT: JAI Press.

Kaye, K. (1982). *The mental and social life of babies: How parents create persons.* Chicago: University of Chicago Press.

Kaye, K., & Marcus, J. (1978). Imitation over a series of trials without feedback: Age six months. *Infant Behavior and Development, 1,* 141–155.

Keasey, C. B. (1972). The lack of sex differences in moral judgements of preadolescents. *Journal of Social Psychology, 86,* 157–158.

Keating, N. C., & Cole, P. (1980). What do I do with him 24 hours a day? Changes in the housewife role after retirement. *The Gerontologist, 20,* 84–89.

Keenan, E. O. (1975). Conversational competence in children. *Journal of Child Language, 2,* 163–183.

Kegan, R. (1982). *The evolving self: Problems and processes in human development,* Cambridge, MA: Harvard University Press.

Keith, R. W. (1975). Middle ear function in neonates. *Archives of Otolaryngology, 101,* 375–379.

Kelly, G. A. (1955). *The psychology of personal constructs.* New York: Norton.

Kelly, J. (1977). The aging male homosexual: Myth and reality. *The Gerontologist, 17,* 328.

Kelly, K. (Ed.). (1987). *Females, males, and sexuality: Theories and research,* Albany, NY: State University of New York Press.

Kelly, J. B. (1982). Divorce: The adult perspective. In B. B. Wolman (Ed.), *Handbook of developmental psychology.* Englewood Cliffs, NJ: Prentice-Hall.

Kelly, J. B., & Wallerstein, J. S. (1976). The effects of parental divorce: Experiences of the child in early latency. *American Journal of Orthospsychiatry, 46(a),* 20–32.

Kelly, J. R. (1983). *Leisure identities and interactions.* London and Boston: Allen and Unwin.

Kelly, J. R. (1987). *Peoria winter: Styles and resources in later life.* Lexington, MA: D.C. Heath.

Kemper, S. (1987). Life-span changes in syntactic complexity. *Journal of Gerontology, 42,* 323–328.

Kendig, H. L. (Ed.). (1986). *Aging and families: A social networks perspective.* Sydney: Allen and Unwin.

Kendig, H. L., Coles, R., Pittelkow, Y., & Wilson, S. (1988). Confidants and family structure in old age. *Journal of Gerontology, 43,* S31–S40.

Kendler, T. S. (1963). Development of mediating responses in children. *Monographs of the Society for Research in Child Development, 28* (2, Serial No. 86), 333–348.

Kennell, J. H., & Klaus, M. H. (1984). Mother-infant bonding: Weighing the evidence. *Developmental Review, 4,* 275–282.

Kenshalo, D. R. (1977). Age changes in touch, vibration, temperature, kinesthesis, and pain sensitivity. In J. E. Birren & K. W. Schaie (Eds.), *Handbook of the psychology of aging.* New York: Van Nostrand Reinhold.

Kent, S. (1976). How do we age? *Geriatrics, 31,* 128–134.

Keough, B. (1985). Temperament and schooling: Meaning of "Goodness of fit?" In J. V. Lerner & R. M. Lerner (Eds.), *New directions for child development* (No. 31, pp. 89–108). San Francisco: Jossey-Bass.

Kerlinger, F. N. (1973). *Foundations of behavioral research* (2nd ed.). New York: Holt, Rinehart and Winston.

Kessen, W. (1960). Research design in the study of developmental problems. In P. H. Mussen (Ed.), *Handbook of Research Methods in Child Development.* New York: Wiley.

Kessen, W. (1965). *The child.* New York: Wiley.

Kessen, W., Haith, M. M., & Salapatek, P. (1970). Human infancy: A bibliography and guide. In P. H. Mussen (Ed.), *Carmichael's Manual of Child Psychology* (3rd Ed.). New York: Wiley.

Kessler, R., & McRae, J. A. (1982). The effects of wives' employment on the mental health of married men and women. *American Sociological Review, 47,* 216–227.

Kidd, J. R. (1973). *How adults learn.* New York: Associated Press.

Kilpatrick, A. C. (1986). Some correlates of women's childhood sexual experiences: A retrospective study. *The Journal of Sex Research, 22,* 221–242.

Kilpatrick, A. C. (1987). Childhood sexual experiences: Problems and issues in studying long-range effects. *The Journal of Sex Research, 23,* 173–196.

Kimble, G. A., & Pennypacker, H. S. (1963). Eyelid conditioning in young and aged subjects. *Journal of Genetic Psychology, 103,* 283–289.

Kiminyo, D. M. (1977). A cross-cultural study of the development of conservation of mass, weight, and volume among Kamba children. In P. Dasen (Ed.), *Piage-*

tian psychology: Cross-cultural contributions. New York: Gardner Press.

Kimmel, D. C. (1978). Adult development and aging: A gay perspective. *Journal of Social Issues, 34,* 113–120.

Kimmel, D. C. (1979–1980). Life-history interview of aging gay men. *International Journal of Aging and Human Development, 10,* 239–248.

Kimmel, D. C. (1990). *Adulthood and aging* (3rd ed.). New York: Wiley.

King, M. R., & Manaster, G. J. (1977). Body image, self-esteem, expectations, self-assessments, and actual success in a simulated job interview. *Journal of Applied Psychology, 62,* 589–594.

King, N. R. (1979). Play: The kindergartner's perspective. *Elementary School Journal, 80,* 81–87.

Kinsey, A., Pomeroy, W. B., & Martin, C. (1948). *Sexual behavior in the human male.* Philadelphia: Saunders.

Kirkendall, L. A. (1978). Sexuality and the life cycle: A broad concept of sexuality. In J. R. Barbour (Ed.), *Annual editions: Human sexuality 79/80.* Guilford, CT: Dushkin.

Kitson, G. C., & Sussman, M. B. (1982). Marital complaints, demographic characteristics, and symptoms of mental stress in divorce. *Journal of Marriage and the Family, 44,* 87–101.

Klaus, M. H., & Kennell, J. H. (1976). *Maternal-infant bonding: The impact of early separation or loss on family development.* St. Louis: Mosby.

Klaus, M. H., & Kennell, J. H. (1982). *Parent-infant bonding.* St. Louis: Mosby.

Klausmeier, H. J. (1985). *Educational psychology* (5th Ed.). New York: Harper and Row.

Kleck, R. E., Richardson, S. A., & Ronald, L. (1974). Physical appearance cues and interpersonal attraction in children. *Child Development, 45,* 305–310.

Klein, A. R., & Young, R. D. (1979). Hyperactive boys in their classroom: Assessment of teacher and peer perceptions, interactions, and classroom behaviors. *Journal of Abnormal Child Psychology, 7,* 425–442.

Klima, E. S., & Bellugi, U. (1973). Teaching apes to communicate. In G. Miller (Ed.), *Communications, language, and meaning.* New York: Basic.

Kline, D., & Schieber, F. (1982). Visual persistence and temporal resolution. In R. Sekuler, D. Kline, & K. Dis-

mukes (Eds.), *Aging and human visual function* (pp. 231–244). New York: Alan R. Liss.

Knowles, M. S. (1978). *The adult learner: A neglected species* (2nd ed.). Houston: Gulf.

Kobrin, F. E., & Waite, L. W. (1984). Effects of childhood family structure on the transition to marriage. *Journal of Marriage and the Family, 46,* 807–816.

Kogan, N. (1973). Creativity and cognitive style: A life-span perspective. In P. B. Baltes & K. W. Schaie (Eds.), *Life-span developmental psychology.* New York: Academic Press.

Kogan, N. (1983). Stylistic variation in childhood and adolescence: Creativity, metaphor and cognitive styles. In J. H. Flavell & E. M. Markman (Eds.), *Handbook of child psychology, Volume III: Cognitive development.* New York: Wiley.

Kohlberg, L. (1966). A cognitive-developmental analysis of children's sex-role concepts and attitudes. In E. E. Maccoby (Ed.), *The development of sex differences.* Stanford, CA: Stanford University Press.

Kohlberg, L. (1969). Stage and sequence: The cognitive-developmental approach to socialization. In D. Goslin (Ed.), *Handbook of socialization theory and research.* New York: Rand McNally.

Kohlberg, L. (1973). The claim to moral adequacy of a highest stage of moral judgment. *Journal of Philosophy, 60,* 630–646.

Kohlberg, L. (1976). Moral stages and moralization: The cognitive developmental approach. In T. Lickona (Ed.), *Moral development and behavior.* New York: Holt, Rinehart, and Winston.

Kohlberg, L. (1977). The implications and moral stages for adult education. *Religious Education, 77,* 183–201.

Kohlberg, L. (1984). Moral stages and moralization: The cognitive developmental approach. In L. Kohlberg (Ed.), *Essays on moral development. Volume II: The psychology of moral development* (pp. 170–205). San Francisco: Harper and Row.

Kohlberg, L., & Candee, D. (1984). The relationship of moral judgment to moral action. In L. Kohlberg (Ed.), *Essays on moral development. Volume II: The psychology of moral development* (pp. 498–581). San Francisco: Harper and Row.

Kohlberg, L., & Kramer, R. (1969). Continuities and discontinuities in childhood and adult moral development. *Human Development, 12,* 93–120.

Kohn, A. (1989, November). Suffer the restless children. *The Atlantic, 264,* 90–100.

Kohn, M. L. (1980). Job complexity and adult personality. In N. J. Smesler & E. H. Erikson (Eds.), *Themes of work and love in adulthood.* Cambridge, MA: Harvard University Press.

Kolody, G. (1977). Cognitive development and science teaching. *Journal of Research in Science Teaching, 14,* 21–26.

Komarovsky, M. (1976). *Dilemmas of masculinity.* New York: Norton.

Kompara, D. (1982) Difficulties in the socialization process of step-parenting. *Family Relations, 29,* 69–73.

Koocher, G. P. (1973). Childhood, death, and cognitive development. *Developmental Psychology, 9,* 369–375.

Kosnik, W., Winslow, L., Kline, D., Rasinski, K., & Sekuler, R. (1988). Visual changes in daily life throughout adulthood. *Journal of Gerontology, 43,* P63–P70.

Krantz, M. (1987). Physical attractiveness and popularity: A predictive study. *Psychological Reports, 60,* 723–726.

Kreuz, L. E., Rose, R. M., & Jennings. J. R. (1972). Suppression of plasma testosterone levels and psychological stress. *Archives of General Psychiatry, 26,* 479–482.

Krieger, L. H., & Wells, W. D. (1969). The criteria for friendship. *Journal of Social Psychology, 78,* 109–112.

Kubie, L. S. (1958). *Neurotic distortion of the creative process.* New York: Noonday.

Kubler-Ross, E. (1969). *On death and dying.* New York: Macmillan.

Kuczaj, S. A. (1978). Children's judgments of grammatical and ungrammatical irregular past-tense verbs. *Child Development, 49,* 319–326.

Kuhl, P. K. & Miller, J. D. (1982). Discrimination of auditory target dimensions in the presence or absence of variations in a second dimension by infants. *Perception and Psychophysics, 31,* 279–292.

Kuhn, D., Nash, S. C., & Brucken, L. (1978). Sex role concepts of two- and three-year-olds. *Child Development, 49,* 445–451.

Kuhn, M. H. & McPartland, T. (1954). An empirical investigation of self-attitudes. *American Sociological Review, 19,* 68–76.

Kulka, R. A. & Weingarten, H. (1979). The long-term effects of parental divorce in childhood on adult adjustment. *Journal of Social Issues, 35,* 50–78.

Kunzinger, E. L. (1985). A short-term longitudinal study of memorial development during early grade school. *Developmental Psychology, 21,* 642–646.

Kurdek, L. A., & Krile, D. (1982). A developmental analysis of the relation between peer acceptance and both interpersonal understanding and perceived social self-competence. *Child Development, 53,* 1485–1491.

Kurtines, W. M., & Gewirtz, J. L. (1984). Certainty and morality: Objectivistic versus relativistic approaches. In W. M. Kurtines & J. L. Gewirtz (Eds.), *Morality, moral behavior, and moral development* (pp. 3–23). New York: Wiley.

La Greca, A. M., & Santogrossi, D. A. (1980). Social skills training with elementary school students: A behavioral group approach. *Journal of Consulting and Clinical Psychology, 48,* 220–227.

Labouvie-Vief, G. (1977). Adult cognitive development: In search of alternative interpretations. *Merrill-Palmer Quarterly, 23,* 227–263.

Labouvie-Vief, G. (1984). Logic and self-regulation from youth to maturity. In M. L. Commons, F. A. Richards, & C. Armon (Eds.), *Beyond formal operations: Late adolescent and adult cognitive development.* New York: Praeger.

Labouvie-Vief, G. (1985). Intelligence and cognition. In J. E. Birren & K. W. Schaie (Eds.), *Handbook of the psychology of aging* (2nd ed., pp. 500–530). New York: Van Nostrand Reinhold.

Labouvie-Vief, G. (1986a). Modes of knowledge and the organization of development. In M. L. Commons, C. Armon, F. A. Richards, & J. Sinnott (Eds.), *Beyond formal operations 2: The development of adolescent and adult thinking and perception.* New York: Praeger.

Labouvie-Vief, G. (1986b). Towards adult autonomy: A theoretical sketch. In E. Langer & C. Alexander (Eds.), *Adult development.* Cambridge, MA: Oxford University Press.

Labouvie-Vief, G., Campbell, S., Weaver, S., & Tannenhaus, M. (1979, November). *Metaphoric processes in young and old adults.* Paper presented at the Annual Meeting of the The Gerontological Society of America, Washington, DC.

Labov, W. (1972). *Language in the inner city: Studies in the black English vernacular.* Philadelphia: University of Pennsylvania Press.

Lack, D. (1980). I want to die while I'm still alive. In E. S. Shneidman (Ed.)., *Death: Current perspectives* (2nd ed.). Palo Alto, CA: Mayfield Publishing.

Ladd, G. W. (1981). Effectiveness of a social learning method for enhancing children's social interaction and peer acceptance. *Child Development, 52,* 171–178.

Ladd, G. W., Price, J. M., & Hart, C. H. (1988). Predicting preschoolers' peer status from their playground behaviors. *Child Development, 59,* 986–992.

LaFreniere, P. (1983). *From attachment to peer relations: An analysis of individual differences in preschool peer competence.* Paper presented at the biennial meeting of the Society for Research in Child Development, Detroit.

Lakoff, R. T., & Scherr, R. L. (1984). *Face value: The politics of beauty.* Boston: Routledge and Kegan Paul.

Lamb, M. E. (1981). Fathers and child development: An integrative overview. In M. E. Lamb (Ed.), *The role of the father in child development* (2nd ed.). New York: Wiley.

Lamb, M. E., & Bornstein, M. H. (1987). *Development in infancy: An introduction* (2nd ed.). New York: Random House.

Lamb, M. E., & Roopnarine, J. L. (1979). Peer influences on sex-role development in preschoolers. *Child Development, 50,* 1219–1222.

Lamb, M. E., & Urberg, K. A. (1978). The development of gender role and gender identity. In M. E. Lamb (Ed.), *Social and personality development.* New York: Holt, Rinehart and Winston.

Lambert, W. E., Yackley, A., & Hein, R. N. (1971). Child training values of English Canadian and French Canadian parents. *Canadian Journal of Behavioral Science, 3,* 217–236.

Laner, M. R. (1979). Growing older female: Heterosexual and homosexual. *Journal of Homosexuality, 4,* 267.

Langer, E. J., & Rodin, J. (1976). The effects of choice and enhanced personal responsibility for the aged: A field experiment in an institutionalized setting. *Journal of Personality and Social Psychology, 34,* 191–198.

Langer, J. (1969). *Theories of development.* New York: Holt, Rinehart and Winston.

Langfeldt, T. (1981). Sexual development in children. In M. Cook & K. Howells (Eds.), *Adult sexual interest in children.* London: Academic Press.

Langlois, J. H., & Downs, A. C. (1980). Mothers, fathers, and peers as socialization agents of sex-typed play behaviors in young children. *Child Development, 51,* 1237–1247.

Langsdorf, P., Izard, C. E., Rayias, M., & Hembree, E. A. (1983). Interest expression, visual fixation, and heart rate changes in 2- to 8-month-old infants. *Developmental Psychology, 19,* 375–386.

Lantz, D., & Steffire, V. (1964). Language and cognition revisited. *Journal of Abnormal and Social Psychology, 69,* 472–481.

Lanyon, R. I. (1986). Theory and treatment in child molestation. *Journal of Consulting and Clinical Psychology, 54,* 176–182.

Larson, L. E. (1975). The relative influence of parent-adolescent affect in predicting the salience hierarchy among youth. In J. J. Conger (Ed.), *Contemporary issues in adolescent development.* New York: Harper & Row.

LaRue, A., & Waldbaum, A. (1980, February). *Aging vs. illness as predictors of Piagetian problem-solving in older adults.* Paper presented at the tenth annual Interdisciplinary International Conference on Piagetian Theory and the Helping Professions, Los Angeles.

Lazarus, P. J. (1982a). Incidence of shyness in elementary school age children. *Psychological Reports, 51,* 904–906.

Lazarus, P. J. (1982b). Correlation of shyness and self-esteem for elementary school children. *Perceptual and Motor Skills, 55,* 8–10.

Lecky, P. (1945). *Self-consistency: A theory of personality.* New York: Island Press.

Lefkowitz, M. M., Eron, L. D., Walder, L. O., & Huesmann, L. R. (1972). Television violence and child aggression: A follow-up study. In G. A. Comstock & E. A. Rubinstein (Eds.), *Television and social behavior: Vol. 3. Television and adolescent aggressiveness.* Washington, DC: U.S. Government Printing Office.

Lefkowitz, M. M., Walder, L. O., & Eron, L. D. (1963). Punishment, identification, and aggression. *Merrill-Palmer Quarterly, 9,* 159–174.

Lehman, H. C. (1953). *Age and achievement.* Princeton, NJ: Princeton University Press.

Leigh, G. K., & Peterson, G. W. (1986). *Adolescents in families*. Cincinatti: South-Western

Lenneberg, E. H. (1967). *Biological foundations of language*. New York: Wiley.

Leridon, H., & Villeneuve-Gokalp, C. (1988). Les nouveaux couples: nombres, caractéristiques, et attitudes. *Population, 43,* 331–374.

Lerner, J. W. (1981). *Children with learning disabilities*. Boston: Houghton Mifflin

Lerner, M. (1980). Why, when, and where people die. In E. S. Shneidman (Ed.), *Death: Current perspectives* (2nd ed.). Palo Alto, CA: Mayfield Publishing.

Lerner, R. M. (1986). *Concepts and theories of human development* (2nd. ed.). New York: Random House.

Lerner, R. M., & Kauffman, M. B. (1985). The concept of development in contextualism. *Developmental Review, 5,* 309–333.

Lerner, R. M., Orlos, J. B., & Knapp, J. R. (1976). Physical attractiveness, physical effectiveness, and self-concept in late adolescence. *Adolescence, 11,* 313–326.

Leslie, L. (1986). The impact of adolescent females' assessments of parenthood and employment on plans for the future. *Journal of Youth and Adolescence, 15,* 29–49.

Leung, E. H., & Rheingold, H. L. (1981). Development of pointing as a social gesture. *Developmental Psychology, 17,* 215–220.

Leventhal, A. S., & Lipsitt, L. P. (1964). Adaptation, pitch discrimination, and sound localization in the neonate. *Child Development, 35,* 759–767.

Levin, R. J., & Levin, A. (1975, September). Sexual pleasure: The surprising preferences of 100,000 women. *Redbook,* pp. 51–58.

Levinson, D. J. (1978). *The seasons of a man's life*. New York: Knopf.

Levinson, D. J. (1986). A conception of adult development. *American Psychologist, 41,* 3–13.

Levinson, D. J., Darrow, C. M., Klein, E. B., Levinson, M. H., & McKee, B. (1974). The psychosocial development of men in early adulthood and the mid-life transition. In D. F. Ricks, A. Thomas, & M. Roff (Eds.), *Life history research in psychopathology* (Vol. 3). Minneapolis: University of Minnesota Press.

Leviton, D. (1975). Education for death, or death becomes less a stranger. *Omega, 6,* 183–191.

Leviton, D. (1977). Death education. In H. Feifel (Ed.), *New meanings of death*. New York: McGraw-Hill.

Leviton, D., & Forman, E. C. (1974). Death education for children and youth. *Journal of Clinical Child Psychology, 3,* 8–10.

Lewis, M., & Brooks-Gunn, J. (1975). Infant's social perception: A constructionist view. In L. Cohen & P. Salapatek (Eds.), *Infant perception*. New York: Academic Press.

Lewis, M., & Brooks-Gunn, J. (1979). *Social cognition and the acquisition of self*. New York: Plenum.

Lieberman, A. F. (1977). Preschoolers' competence with a peer: Relations with attachment and peer experience. *Child Development, 48,* 1277–1287.

Liebert, R. M. (1984). What develops in moral development? In W. M. Kurtines & J. L. Gewirtz (Eds.). *Morality, moral behavior, and moral development* (pp. 177–192). New York: Wiley.

Lief, H. I. (1978). Homosexualities: A review. *SIECUS Report, 7*(2), 13–14.

Lifton, R. (1977). The sense of immortality: On death and the continuity of life. In H. Feifel (Ed.), *New meanings of death*. New York: McGraw-Hill.

Lifton, R. J. (1982, September 26). The psychic toll of the nuclear age. *New York Times Magazine,* 52–66.

Light, L. L., & Zelinski, E. M. (1983). Memory for spatial information in young and old adults. *Journal of Gerontology, 39,* 901–906.

Light, L. L., & Zelinski, E. M. (1988). Young and older adults' use of context in spatial memory. *Psychology and Aging, 3,* 99–101.

Lindow, J., Marrett, C. B., & Wilkinson, L. D. (1985). Overview. In L. C. Wilkinson & C. B. Marrett (Eds.), *Gender influences in classroom interaction*. Orlando: Academic Press.

Linn, P. L., & Horowitz, F. D. (1983). The relationship between infant individual differences and mother-infant interaction during the neonatal period. *Infant Behavior and Development, 6,* 415–428.

Linn, M. C., & Hyde, J. S. (1989). Gender, mathematics, and science. *Educational Researcher, 18,* 17–27.

Linn, M. W., Linn, B. S., & Stein, S. (1983). Impact on nursing home staff of training about death and dying. *Journal of the American Medical Association, 250,* 2332–2335.

Lips, H. M. (1989). Gender-role socialization: Lessons in femininity. In J. Freeman (Ed.). *Women: A feminist perspective* (4th ed.). Palo Alto, CA: Mayfield.

Lipsitt, L. P., Kaye, H., & Bosack, T. N. (1966). Enhancement of neonatal sucking through reinforcement. *Journal of Experimental Child Psychology, 4,* 163–168.

Livson, F. B. (1983). Gender identity: A life-span view of sex-role development. In R. B. Weg (Ed.), *Sexuality in the later years.* New York: Academic Press.

Livson, N., & Peskin, H. (1980). Perspectives on adolescence from longitudinal research. In J. Adelson (Ed.), *Handbook of adolescent psychology.* New York: Wiley.

Lockheed, M. E. (1985). Women, girls, and computers. *Sex Roles, 13,* 115–122.

Loeb, R. C., Horst, L., & Horton, P. J. (1980). Family interaction patterns associated with self-esteem in preadolescent girls and boys. *Merrill-Palmer Quarterly, 26,* 201–217.

Loehlin, H. C., & Nichols, R. C. (1976). *Heredity, environment, and personality: A study of 850 twins.* Austin: University of Texas Press.

Loehlin, J. C., Lindzey, G., & Spuhler, J. N. (1975). *Race differences in intelligence.* San Francisco: W. H. Freeman.

Logan, L. A. (1976). *Fundamentals of learning and motivation.* Dubuque, IA.: William C. Brown.

Logan, R. D. (1977). Sociocultural change and the emergence of children as burdens. *Child and Family, 16,* 295–304.

Logan, R. D. (1986). A reconceptualization of Erikson's theory: The repetition of existential and instrumental themes. *Human Development, 29,* 125–136.

London, S. N., & Hammond, C. B. (1986). The climacteric. In D. N. Danforth & J. R. Scott (Eds.), *Obstetrics and gynecology* (5th ed.). Philadelphia: J. P. Lippincott.

Lonetto, R. (1980). *Children's conceptions of death.* New York: Springer.

Lonetto, R., & Templer, D. I. (1986). *Death anxiety.* Washington: Hemisphere Publishing Co.

Longfellow, C. (1979). Divorce in context: Its impact on children. In G. Levinger & O. Moles (Eds.), *Divorce and separation: Context, causes, and consequences.* New York: Basic Books.

Lopata, H. (1973). *Widowhood in an American city.* Cambridge, MA: Schenkman.

Lowenstein, L. F. (1983). The treatment of extreme shyness in maladjusted children by implosive, counseling, and conditioning approaches. *Interdisciplinaria, 4,* 115–130.

Lowenthal, M., & Chiriboga, D. (1972). Transition to the empty nest: Crisis, challenge, or relief? *Archives of General Psychiatry, 26,* 8–14.

Lowenthal, M., & Haven, C. (1968). Interaction and adaptation: Intimacy as a critical variable. *American Sociological Review, 33,* 20–30.

Lowenthal, M., Thurner, M., & Chiriboga, D. (1975). *Four stages of life.* San Francisco: Jossey-Bass.

Lowrey, G. H. (1973). *Growth and development of children* (6th ed.). Chicago: Year Book Medical.

Lunnenborg, C. E. & Lunnenborg, D. W. (1975). Factor structure of the vocational interest models of Roe and Holland. *Journal of Vocational Behavior, 7,* 313–326.

Luria, Z. & Rose, M. D. (1979). *Psychology of human sexuality.* New York: Wiley.

Lutkenhaus, P., Grossman, K. E., & Grossman, K. (1985). Infant-mother attachment at twelve months and style of interaction with a stranger at the age of three years. *Child Development, 56,* 1538–1542.

Maccoby, E. E. (1969). The development of stimulus selection. In J. P. Hill (Ed.), *Minnesota symposia on child psychology* (Vol. 3). Minneapolis: University of Minnesota.

Maccoby, E. E. (1980). *Social development.* New York: Harcourt Brace Jovanovich.

Maccoby, E. E. (1988). Gender as a social category. *Developmental Psychology, 24,* 755–767.

Maccoby, E. E. (1990). Gender and relationships: A developmental account. *American Psychologist, 45,* 513–520.

Maccoby, E. E., & Jacklin, C. N. (1974). *The psychology of sex differences.* Stanford, CA: Stanford University Press.

Maccoby, E. E., & Jacklin, C. N. (1980). Sex differences in aggression: A rejoinder and reprise. *Child Development, 51,* 964–980.

Maccoby, E. E., & Martin, J. A. (1983). Socialization in the context of the family: Parent-child interaction. In E. M. Hetherington (Ed.), *Socialization, personality, and social development; Handbook of child psychology, Vol. 4.* New York: Wiley.

Maccoby, E. E., & Konrad, K. W. (1966). Age trends in selective listening. *Journal of Experimental Child Psychology, 3,* 113–122.

MacFarlane, A. (1975). Olfaction in the development of social preferences in the human neonate. In *Parent-infant interaction.* Amsterdam: CIBA Foundation.

Macfarlane, J. W. (1963). From infancy to adulthood. *Childhood Education, 39,* 336–342.

Macfarlane, J. W. (1964). Perspectives on personality consistency and change from the guidance study. *Vita Humana, 7,* 115–126.

Mackay, H. A., & Inglis, J. (1963). The effect of age on a short-term auditory storage process. *Gerontologia, 7,* 193–200.

Macken, M. A., & Barton, D. (1980). The acquisition of the voicing constrast in English: The study of voice onset time in work-initial stop consonants. *Journal of Child Language, 7,* 41–74.

Macklin, E. D. (1978). Review of research on non-marital cohabitation in the United States. In B. I. Murstein (Ed.), *Exploring intimate lifestyles.* New York: Springer.

Maddi, S. R. (1980). *Personality theories: A comparative analysis* (4th ed.). Homewood, IL: Dorsey.

Mader, S. M. (1988). *Human biology* (2nd ed.). Dubuque, IA: Wm. C. Brown.

Magnussen, D., Stattin, H., & Allen, V. (1986). Differential maturation among girls and its relationship to social adjustment in a longitudinal perspective. In P. Baltes, D. Featherman, & R. Lerner (Eds.), *Lifespan development and behavior* (Vol. 7). Hillsdale, NJ: Erlbaum.

Main, M. (1981). Avoidance in the service of attachment: A working paper. In K. Immelmann, G. Barlow, L. Petrinovich, & M. Main (Eds.), *Behavioral development: The Bielefeld Interdisciplinary Project* (pp. 651–693). New York: Cambridge University Press.

Main, M., Kaplan, N., & Cassidy, J. (1985). Security in infancy, childhood, and adulthood: A move to the level of representation. In I. Bretherton & E. Waters (Eds.), *Growing points of attachment theory and research.* Monographs of the Society for Research in Child Development, 209 (50, Serial No. 1–2), 66–106.

Mainville, F., & Friedman, R. J. (1976). Peer relations of hyperactive children. *Ontario Psychologist, 8,* 17–20.

Makin, J. W., & Porter, R. H. (1989). Attractiveness of lactating females' breast odors to neonates. *Child Development, 60,* 803–810.

Makin, K. (1986, February 1). Media image of women is under fire. In report *Globe and Mail,* (Toronto), pp. A1–A2.

Malina, R. M. (1979). Secular changes in size and maturity: Causes and effects. In A. L. Roche (Ed.), Secular trends in human growth, maturation, and development (pp. 59–102). *Monographs of the Society for Research in Child Development, 44* (3–4, Serial No. 179).

Mancini, J. A., & Orthner, D. K. (1978). Recreational sexuality preferences among middle-class husbands and wives. *The Journal of Sex Research, 14,* 96–106.

Mandler, J. M. (1983). Representation. In J. H. Flavell & E. M. Markman (Eds.), *Handbook of child psychology, Volume III: Cognitive development.* New York: Wiley.

Marcia, J. (1966). Development and validation of ego-identity status. *Journal of Personality and Social Psychology, 3,* 551–558.

Marcus, D. E., & Overton, W. F. (1978). The development of cognitive gender constancy and sex role preferences. *Child Development, 49,* 434–444.

Marion, R. W., Wiznia, A. A., Hutcheon, R. G., & Rubenstein, A. (1986). Human T-cell Lymphotrophic Virus Type III (HTLV-III) Embryopathy. *American Journal of Diseases of Children, 140,* 638–640.

Mariwaki, S. Y. (1973). Self-disclosure, significant others, and psychological well-being in old age. *Journal of Health and Social Behavior, 14,* 226–232.

Markman, E. M. (1977). Realizing that you don't understand: A preliminary investigation. *Child Development, 48,* 986–992.

Markus, H. (1977). Self-schemata and processing information about the self. *Journal of Personality and Social Psychology, 35,* 63–78.

Martin, A. D. (1982). Learning to hide: The socialization of the gay adolescent. *Adolescent Psychiatry, X,* 52–65.

Martin, C. E. (1977). Sexual activity in the aging male. In J. Money & H. Musaph (Eds.), *Handbook of sexuality* (Vol. 4). New York: Elsevier.

Martin, C. L., & Halverson, C. F. (1981). A schematic processing model of sex typing and stereotyping in children. *Child Development, 52,* 1119–1134.

Martin, J. L. (1987). The impact of AIDS on gay male sexual behavior patterns in New York City. *American Journal of Public Health, 77,* 578–581.

Martin, W. T. (1968). Theories of variation in the suicide rate. In J. P. Gibbs (Ed.), *Suicide*. New York: Harper & Row.

Mash, E. J., & Johnston, C. (1980, November). *A behavioral assessment of sibling interactions in hyperactive and normal children*. Paper presented at the meeting of the Association for the Advancement of Behavior Therapy, New York.

Maslow, A. H (1964). *Religions, values, and peak experiences*. Columbus, OH: Ohio State University Press.

Maslow, A. H. (1968). *Toward a psychology of being* (2nd ed.). Princeton: Van Nostrand.

Maslow, A. H. (1970). *Motivation and personality* (2nd ed.). New York: Harper & Row.

Masters, J. C., & Furman, W. (1981). Popularity, individual friendship selection and specific peer interaction among children. *Developmental Psychology, 17*, 344–350.

Masters, W. H., & Johnson, V. E. (1966). *Human sexual response*. Boston: Little, Brown.

Masters, W. H., & Johnson, V. E. (1970). *Human sexual inadequacy*. Boston: Little, Brown.

Masters, W. H., Johnson, V. E., & Kolodny, R. C. (1988). *Human sexuality* (3rd ed.). Glenview, IL: Scott Foresman/Little Brown.

Matarazzo, J. D. (1972). *Wechsler's measurement and appraisal of adult intelligence* (5th ed.). Baltimore: Williams and Wilkins.

Matas, L., Arend, A., & Sroufe, L. A. (1978). Continuity of adaptation in the second year: The relationship between quality of attachment and later competence. *Child Development, 49*, 547–556.

Mattessich, P. W. (1979). Childlessness and its correlates in historical perspective: A research note. *Journal of Family History, 4*, 299–307.

Mattessich P., & Hill, R. (1987). Life cycle and family development. In M. B. Sussman & S. K. Steinmetz (Eds.), *Handbook of marriage and the family* (pp. 437–470). New York: Plenum.

Matthews, S. H. (1983, November). *Adolescent grandchildren's evaluations of their relationships with their grandpparents*. Paper presented at the annual meeting of the Gerontological Society of America, San Francisco.

Matthews, W. S. (1977). Modes of transformation in the initiation of fantasy play. *Developmental Psychology, 13*, 212–216.

Mauer, D. (1975). Infant visual perception: Methods of study. In L. B. Cohen and P. Salapatek (Eds.), *Infant perception: From sensation to cognition: Basic visual processes* (Vol. 1). New York: Academic Press.

Maurer, A. (1966). Maturation of concepts of death. *British Journal of Medical Psychology, 39*, 35–51.

Maurer, D., & Barrera, M. E. (1981). Infants' perception of natural and distorted arrangements of a schematic face. *Child Development, 52*, 196–202.

May, R. (1953). *Man's search for himself*. New York: Norton & Norton Co.

McCall, R. B. (1977a). Challenges to a science of developmental psychology. *Child Development, 48*, 333–344.

McCall, R. B. (1977b). Childhood IQ's as predictors of adult educational and occupational status. *Science, 197*, 482–483.

McCall, R. B. (1981). Nature-nurture and the two realms of development: A proposed integration with respect to mental development. *Child Development, 52*, 1–12.

McCall, R. B. (1983, Winter). A developmental psychologist looks at those "other disciplines" in SRCD. *SRCD Newsletter*, pp. 7–8.

McCall, R. B. (1984). Developmental changes in mental performance: The effect of the birth of a sibling. *Child Development, 55*, 1317–1321.

McCall, R. B., Applebaum, M. I., & Hogarty, P. S. (1973). Developmental changes in mental performance. *Monographs of the Society for Research in Child Development, 38* (3, Serial No. 150).

McCall, R. B., Parke, R. D., & Kavanaugh, R. D. (1977). Imitation of live and televised models by children one to three years of age. *Monographs of the Society for Research in Child Development, 42*(5, Serial No. 173).

McCrae, R. R. (1987). Self-concept. In G. L. Maddox (Ed.), *The encyclopedia of aging* (pp. 590–591). New York: Springer Publishing.

McCrae, R. R., & Costa, P. T., Jr. (1984). *Emerging lives, enduring dispositions: Personality in adulthood*. Boston: Little, Brown.

McCune-Nicolich, L., & Fenson, L. (1984). Methodological issues in studying early pretend play. In T. D. Yawkey & A. D. Pellegrini (Eds.), *Child's play: Developmental and applied*. Hillsdale, NJ: Erlbaum.

McGee, J., & Wells, K. (1982). Gender typing and androgyny in later life: New directions for theory and research. *Human Development, 25,* 116–139.

McGhee, P. E., & Frueh, T. (1980). Television viewing and the learning of sex-role stereotypes. *Sex Roles, 6,* 179–188.

McGinnies, E. (1949). Emotional and perceptual defense. *Psychological Review, 56,* 244–251.

McGreal, C. E. (1983, November). *Grandparenthood as a symbol: Expectations for the grandparental role.* Paper presented at the annual meeting of the Gerontological Society of America, San Francisco.

McGuire, K. D., & Weisz, J. R. (1982). Social cognition and behavior correlates of preadolescent chumship. *Child Development, 53,* 1478–1484.

McKenzie, B. E., Tootell, H. E., & Day. R. H. (1980). Development of visual size constancy during the first year of human infancy. *Developmental Psychology, 16,* 163–174.

McKusick, L. (1988). The impact of AIDS on practitioner and client: Notes for the therapeutic relationship. *American Psychologist, 43,* 935–940.

McLaughlin, B. (1982). Current status of research on second-language learning in children. *Human Development, 25,* 215–222.

McLeish, J. A. B. (1976). *The Ulyssean adult: Creativity in the middle and later years.* New York: McGraw-Hill.

McMichael, P. (1980). Reading difficulties, behavior, and social status. *Journal of Educational Psychology, 72,* 76–86.

McNeill, D. (1966). Developmental psycholinguistics. In F. Smith & G. Miller (Eds.), *The genesis of language.* Cambridge, MA.: MIT press.

Mead, G. H. (1934). *Mind, self, and society.* Chicago: University of Chicago Press.

Mead, M. (1935). *Sex and temperament in three primitive societies.* New York: Morrow.

Mead, M. (1972). *Blackberry winter.* New York: Morrow.

Mead, M., & Newton, N. (1967). Cultural patterning of perinatal behavior. In S. A. Richardson & A. F. Guttmacher (Eds.), *Childbearing: Its social and psychological aspects.* Baltimore: Williams and Wilkins.

Meadors, A. C. (1984). Non-traditional education: A slowly-developing giant. *Educational Research Quarterly, 9,* 5–9.

Meece, J. L., Eccles-Parsons, J., Kaczala, C. M., Goff, S. B., Futterman, R. (1982). Sex differences in math achievement. *Psychological Bulletin, 91,* 324–448.

Mehler, J., Bertoncini, J., Barriere, M., & Jassik-Gerschenfeld, D. (1978). Infant recognition of mother's voice. *Perception, 7,* 491–497.

Meir, E. I., & Ben-Yehuda, A. (1976). Inventories based on Roe and Holland yield similar results. *Journal of Vocational Behavior, 8,* 269–274.

Melear, J. D. (1973). Children's conceptions of death. *Journal of Genetic Psychology, 123,* 359–360.

Meltzoff, A. N., & Moore, M. K. (1977). Imitation of facial and manual gestures by human neonates. *Science, 198,* 75–78.

Meltzoff, A. N., & Moore, M. K. (1983). Newborn infants imitate adult facial gestures. *Child Development, 54,* 702–709.

Mendelson, M. J., & Haith, M. M. (1976). The relation between audition and vision in the human newborn. *Monographs of the Society for Research in Child Development, 41,* (Serial No. 167).

Menez-Bautista, R., Fikrig, S. M., Pahwa, S., Sarangadharan, M. G., & Stoneburner, R. L. (1986). Monozygotic twins discordant for the acquired immunodeficiency syndrome. *American Journal of Diseases of Children, 140,* 678–679.

Menyuk, P. (1982). Language development. In C. B. Kopp & J. B. Krakow (Eds.), *The child: Development in a social context.* Reading, MA: Addison-Wesley.

Meyer, B. J. F., & Rice, G. E. (1981). Information recalled from prose by young, middle, and old adult readers. *Experimental Aging Research, 7,* 253–268.

Meyer, B. J. F., & Rice, G. (1983). Learning and memory from text across the adult life span. In J. Fine & R. O. Freedle (Eds.), *Developmental studies in discourse.* Norwood, NJ: Ablex.

Meyer, B. J. F., Rice, G. E., Knight, C. C., & Jensen, J. L. (1979). *Differences in the type of information remembered from prose by young, middle, and old adults.* (Research report No. 5, Prose Learning Series.) Tempe: Arizona State University.

Meyners, R. & Wooster, C. (1979) *Sexual style: Facing and making choices about sex.* New York: Harcourt Brace Jovanovich.

Miles, C. C., & Miles, W. R. (1932). The correlation of intelligence scores and chronological age from early to late maturity. *American Journal of Psychology, 44,* 44–78.

Milewski, A. E. (1976). Infants' discrimination of internal and external pattern elements. *Journal of Experimental Child Psychology, 22,* 229–246.

Milewski, A. E. (1978). Young infants' visual processing of internal and adjacent shapes. *Infant Behavior and Development, 1,* 359–371.

Milgram, S. (1963). Behavioral study of obedience. *Journal of Abnormal and Social Psychology, 67,* 371–378.

Miller, B. C., & Sollie, D. L. (1986). Normal stresses during the transition to parenthood. In R. H. Moos (Ed.), *Coping with life crises: An integrated approach.* New York: Plenum.

Miller, G. A. (1981). *Language and speech.* San Francisco: W. H. Freeman.

Miller, P. H. (1989). *Theories of developmental psychology* (2nd ed.). New York: W. H. Freeman.

Miller, S. A. (1987). *Developmental research methods.* Englewood Cliffs, NJ: Prentice-Hall.

Miller, W. B. (1978). The intendedness and wantedness of the first child. In W. B. Miller & L. F. Newman (Eds.), *The first child and family formation,* Chapel Hill: University of North Carolina Press.

Mills, N., & Melhuish, E. (1974). Recognition of mother's voice in early infancy. *Nature, 252,* 123–124.

Minton, H. L., & Schneider, F. W. (1980). *Differential psychology.* Monterey, CA: Brooks/Cole.

Minuchin, P. P. (1977). *The middle years of childhood.* Monterey, CA: Brooks/Cole.

Mitchell, O., & Fields, G. (1984). The economics of retirement behavior. *Journal of Labor Economics, 2,* 84–105.

Mitchell, K. R., & Orr, L. E. (1976). Heterosexual social competence, anxiety, avoidance, and self-judged physical attractiveness. *Perceptual and Motor Skills, 43,* 553–554.

Mitchell, O. S., Levine, P. B., & Pozzebon, S. (1988). Retirement differences by industry and occupation. *The Gerontologist, 28,* 545–551.

Mitford, J. (1963). *The American way of death.* New York: Simon and Schuster.

Molfese, D. L., Molfese, V. J., & Carrell, P. L. (1982). Early language development. In B. B. Wolman (Ed.), *Handbook of developmental psychology.* Englewood Cliffs, NJ: Prentice-Hall.

Moment, G. B. (1978). The Ponce de Leon Trail today. In J. A. Behnke, C. E. Finch, & G. B. Moment (Eds.), *The biology of aging.* New York: Plenum.

Money, J. (1987). Sin, sickness, or status? Homosexual gender identity and psychoneuroendocrinology. *American Psychologist, 42,* 384–399.

Money, J., & Ehrhardt, A. A. (1972). *Man and woman, boy and girl: The differentiation and dimorphism of gender identity from conception to maturity.* Baltimore: Johns Hopkins.

Monge, R. (1969). Learning in the adult years: Set or rigidity? *Human Development, 12,* 131–140.

Monge, R. H. & Gardner, E. L. (1972). *A program of research in adult differences in cognitive performance and learning: Backgrounds for education and vocational training.* U.S. Department of Health, Education, and Welfare, Final Report. Project No. 6-1963.

Monge, R., & Hultsch, D. (1971). Paired-associate learning as a function of adult age and length of anticipation and inspection intervals. *Journal of Gerontology, 26,* 157–162.

Montemayor, R. (1983). Parents and adolescents in conflict: All families some of the time and some families most of the time. *Journal of Early Adolescence, 3,* 83–103.

Montemayor, R., & Eisen, M. (1977). The development of self-perceptions from childhood to adolescence. *Development Psychology, 13,* 314–319.

Montemayor, R., & Hanson, E. (1985). A naturalistic view of conflict between adolescents and their parents and siblings. *Journal of Early Adolescence, 5,* 285–294.

Moody, R. A., Jr. (1975). *Life after life.* Atlanta: Mockingbird Books.

Moody, R. A., Jr. (1977). *Reflections on life after life.* New York: Bantam/Mockingbird Books.

Moore, K., & Waite, L. (1981). Marital dissolution, early motherhood, and early marriage. *Social Forces, 60,* 20–40.

Moore, L. M., Nielsen, C. R., & Mistretta, C. M. (1982). Sucrose taste thresholds: Age-related differences. *Journal of Gerontology, 37,* 64–69.

Moore, T. (1967). Language and intelligence: A longitudinal study of the first eight years: 1. Patterns of developments in boys and girls. *Human Development, 10,* 88–106.

Moore, T. (1975). Exclusive early mothering and its alternatives: The outcome to adolescence. *Scandinavian Journal of Psychology, 16,* 255–279.

Moore, T. E., Richards, B., & Hood, J. (1984). Aging and the coding of spatial information. *Journal of Gerontology, 39,* 210–212.

Moreland, J. (1980). Age and change in the adult male sex role. *Sex Roles, 6,* 807–818.

Morgan A., & Godbey, G. (1978). The effect of entering an age-segregated environment upon the leisure activity patterns of older adults. *Journal of Leisure Research, 10,* 177–190.

Moriarty, A. E., & Toussieng, D. W. (1976). *Adolescent coping.* New York: Grune & Stratton.

Morawski, J. G. (1987). The troubled quest for masculinity, femininity, and androgyny. In P. Shaver & C. Hendrick (Eds.), *Sex and gender.* Newberry Park, CA: Sage Publications.

Morrongiello, B. A., & Clifton, R. (1984). Effects of sound frequency on behavioral and cardiac orienting in newborn and five-month-old infants. *Journal of Experimental Child Psychology, 38,* 429–446.

Morrongiello, B. A., Clifton, R. K., & Kulig, J. W. (1982). Newborn cardiac and behavioral orienting responses to sound under varying precedence-effect conditions. *Infant Behavior and Development, 5,* 249–259.

Morrow, L. (1988). Through the eyes of children. *Time Magazine, 132,* 32–57.

Mortimer, J. T., & London, J. (1984). The varying linkages of work and family. In P. Voyaroff, (Ed.), *Work and family: Changing roles of men and women.* Palo Alto, CA: Mayfield.

MOW International Research Team (1986). *The meaning of working: An international perspective.* New York: Academic Press.

Mueller, D. P., & Cooper, P. W. (1986). Children of single-parent families: How they fare as young adults. *Family Relations, 35,* 169–176.

Mueller, E., & Lucas, T. A. (1975). A developmental analysis of peer interaction among toddlers. In M. Lewis & L. A. Rosenblum (Eds.), *Friendship and peer relations.* New York: Wiley.

Mueller, M. L. (1976). Death education and death fear education. *Education, 97,* 145–148.

Mullener, N., & Laird, J. D. (1971). Some developmental changes in the organization of self-evaluations. *Developmental Psychology, 5,* 233–236.

Muller, E., Hollien, H., & Murry, T. (1974). Perceptual responses to infant crying: Identification of cry tapes. *Journal of Child Language, 104,* 135–136.

Munroe, R. L., & Munroe, R. H. (1977). Land, labor, and the child's cognitive performance among the Logoli. *American Ethnologist, 4,* 309–320.

Munroe, R. H., & Munroe, R. L. (1978). Compliance of socialization and short-term memory in an East African society. *Journal of Social Psychology, 104,* 135–136.

Munroe, R. H., Munroe, R. L., & Whiting, B. B. (Eds.). (1981). *Handbook of cross-cultural development.* New York: Garland Publishing.

Munroe, R. H., Shimmin, H. S., & Munroe, R. L. (1984). Gender understanding and sex role preference in four cultures. *Developmental Psychology, 20,* 673–682.

Murphy, C. M. (1978). Pointing in the context of a shared activity. *Child Development, 49,* 371–380.

Murphy, L. B., & Moriarty, A. E. (1976). *Vulnerability, coping, and growth: From infancy to adolescence.* New Haven, CT: Yale University Press.

Murphy, M. D., Sanders, R. E., Gabriesheski, A. S., & Schmitt, L. A. (1981). Metamemory in the aged. *Journal of Gerontology, 36,* 185–193.

Mussen, P., & Boutourline-Young, H. (1964). Relationships between rate of physical maturing and personality among boys of Italian descent. *Vita Humana, 7,* 186–200.

Mussen, P. & Eisenberg-Berg, N. (1977). *Roots of caring, sharing, and helping.* San Francisco: W. H. Freeman.

Muus, R. E. (1988). *Theories of adolescence* (5th ed.). New York: Random House.

Myers, B. J. (1984a). Mother-infant bonding: A rejoinder to Kennell and Klaus. *Developmental Review, 4,* 283–288.

Myers, B. J. (1984b). Mother-infant bonding: The status of the critical period hypothesis. *Developmental Review, 4,* 240–274.

Nadelman, L., & Begun, A. (1982). The effect of the newborn on the older sibling: Mothers' questionnaires.

In M. E. Lamb & B. Sutton-Smith (Eds.), *Sibling relationships: Their nature and significance across the lifespan.* Hillsdale, NJ: Erlbaum.

Naeye, R. L. (1978). Relationship of cigarette smoking to congenital anomalies and perinatal death. *American Journal of Pathology, 90,* 289–294.

Naeye, R. L., Ladis, B., & Drage, J. S. (1976). Sudden infant death syndrome: A prospective study. *American Journal of Diseases of Children, 130,* 1207–1210.

Nagy, M. H. (1948). The child's theories concerning death. *Journal of Genetic Psychology, 73,* 3–27.

National Center for Health Statistics. (1988, April 29). Advance report of final marriage statistics, 1985. *37(1).*

National Institute of Child Health (1980). Cesarean childbirth. *Consensus Development Conference Summaries, 3,* 39–53.

Neisser, U. (1982). *Memory observed: Remembering in natural contexts.* San Francisco: W. H. Freeman and Company.

Nelson, C. A., & Dolgin, K. G. (1985). The generalized discrimination of facial expressions by seven-month-old infants. *Child Development, 56,* 58–61.

Nelson, K. E. (1971). Accommodation of visual tracking patterns in human infants to object movement patterns. *Journal of Experimental Child Psychology, 12,* 182–196.

Nelson, K. (1973). Structure and strategy in learning to talk. *Monographs of the Society for Research in Child Development, 38,* (1–2, Serial No. 149).

Nelson, K., Rescorla, L., Gruendel, J., & Benedict, H. (1978). Early lexicons: What do they mean? *Child Development, 49,* 960–968.

Nelson, L. D., & Nelson, C. C. (1975). A factor analytic inquiry into the multi-dimensionality of death and anxiety. *Omega, 6,* 171–178.

Nelson, M. & Nelson, G. K. (1982). Problems of equity in the reconstituted family: A social exchange analysis. *Family Relations, 31,* 223–231.

Nerlove, S. B., & Snipper, A. S. (1981). Cognitive consequences of cultural opportunity. In R. H. Munroe, R. L. Munroe, & B. B. Whiting (Eds.), *Handbook of cross-cultural human development.* New York: Garland Publishing.

Nesselroade, J. R. & Baltes, P. B. (1974). Adolescent personality development and historical change: 1970–1972. *Monographs of the Society for Research in Child Development, 39,* (1, Serial No. 154).

Nesselroade, J. R., Schaie, K. W., & Baltes, P. B. (1972). Ontogenetic and generational components of change in adult cognitive behavior. *Journal of Gerontology, 27,* 222–228.

Neugarten, B. L. (1967). A new look at menopause. *Psychology Today, 1,* 42–45, 67–69, 71.

Neugarten, B. L. (1968). The awareness of middle age. In B. L. Neugarten (Ed.), *Middle age and aging.* Chicago: University of Chicago Press.

Neugarten, B. L. (1970). Adaptation and the life cycle. *Journal of Geriatric Psychiatry, 4,* 71–87.

Neugarten B. L. (1973, August). *Transitions in adult life.* Paper presented at the biennial meeting of the International Society for the Study of Behavioral Development. Ann Arbor, MI.

Neugarten, B. L. (1977). Personality and aging. In J. E. Birren & K. W. Schaie (Eds.), *Handbook of the psychology of aging.* New York: Van Nostrand.

Neugarten, B. L. (1979). Time, age, and life cycle. *American Journal of Psychiatry, 136,* 887–894.

Neugarten, B. L., Moore, J. W., & Lowe, J. C. (1965). Age norms, age constraints, and adult socialization. *American Journal of Sociology, 70,* 710–717.

Neugarten, B. L., & Peterson, W. A. (1957). A study of the American age-grade system. *Proceedings of the International Association of Gerontology, Fourth Congress 3,* 497–502).

Neugarten, B. L., & Weinstein, K. K. (1964). The changing American grandparent. *Journal of Marriage and the Family, 26,* 199–204.

Neugarten, B. L., Wood, N., Kraines, R., & Loomis, B. (1963). Women's attitudes toward the menopause. *Vita Humana, 6,* 140–151.

Neulinger, J. (1981). *To leisure: An introduction.* Boston: Allyn and Bacon.

Newcomer S. F., & Udry, J. R. (1985). Oral sex in an adolescent population. *Archives of Sexual Behavior, 14,* 41–46.

Newport, E. L., Gleitman, H., & Gleitman, L. R. (1977). "Mother, I'd rather do it myself": Some effects and non-effects of maternal speech style. In C. E. Snow & C. A. Ferguson (Eds.), *Talking to children.* Cambridge: Cambridge University Press.

Nichols, R. (1964). Parental attitudes of mothers of intelligent adolescents and creativity of their children. *Child Development, 35,* 1041–1049.

Ninio, A., & Bruner, J. (1978). The achievement and antecedents of labeling. *Journal of Child Language, 5,* 1–15.

Nisan, M., & Kohlberg, L. (1982). Universality and variation in moral judgement: A longitudinal and cross-sectional study in Turkey. *Child Development, 53,* 865–876.

Nisbett, R., & Gurwitz, S. (1970). Weight, sex, and the eating behavior of human newborns. *Journal of Comparative and Physiological Psychology, 73,* 245–253.

Noland, M., Richardson, G. E., & Bray, R. M. (1980). The systematic development and efficacy of death education unit for ninth-grade girls. *Death Education, 4,* 43–59.

Noppe, I. C. (1983). A cognitive-developmental perspective on the adolescent self-concept. *Journal of Early Adolescence, 3,* 275–286.

Noppe, I. C., & Noppe, L. D. (1976, June 11). *Creativity from a cognitive-developmental perspective.* Paper presented at the Sixth Annual Symposium of The Jean Piaget Society, Philadelphia.

Noppe, I. C., Noppe, L. D., & Hughes, F. P. (in press). Stress as a predictor of the equality of parent-infant interactions. *Journal of Genetic Psychology.*

Noppe, L. D., & Noppe, I. C. (in press). Dialectical themes in adolescent conceptions of death. *Journal of Adolescent Research.*

Norton, A. J., & Glick, P. C. (1979). Marital instability in America: Past, present, and future. In G. Levinger & O. Moles (Eds.), *Divorce and separation: Contexts, causes, and consequences.* New York: Basic Books.

Norton, A. J., & Moorman, J. E. (1987). Current trends in marriage and divorce among American women. *Journal of Marriage and the Family, 49,* 3–14.

Notzon, F. C., Placek, P. J., & Taffel, S. M. (1987). Comparisons of national cesarean-section rates. *The New England Journal of Medicine, 316,* 386–389.

Noyes, R., Jr. (1979). Near-death experiences: Their interpretation and significance. In R. Kastenbaum (Ed.). *Between life and death.* New York: Springer-Verlag, pp. 73–78.

Nyiti, R. M. (1982). The validity of "cultural differences explanations" for cross-cultural variations in the rate of Piagetian cognitive development. In D. A. Wagner & H. W. Stevenson (Eds.), *Cultural perspectives on child development.* San Francisco: W. H. Freeman.

Nystrom, E. P. (1974). Activity patterns and leisure concepts among the elderly. *American Journal of Occupational Therapy, 28,* 337–345.

Obler, L. (1980). Narrative discourse style in the elderly. In L. Obler & M. Albert (Eds.), *Language and communication in the elderly.* Lexington, MA: D.C. Heath.

Obler, L. K. & Albert, M. L. (1985). Language skills across adulthood. In J. E. Birren & K. W. Schaie (Eds.), *Handbook of the psychology of aging* (2nd ed.) (pp. 463–473). New York: Van Nostrand Reinhold.

Oden, S., & Asher, S. R. (1977). Coaching children in social skills for friendship making. *Child Development, 48,* 495–506.

Offer, D., & Offer, J. B. (1975). *From teenage to young manhood.* New York: Basic Books.

Offer, D., Ostrov, E., & Howard, K. I. (1981). *The adolescent: A psychological self-portrait.* New York: Basic Books.

Office of the Federal Register, National Archives and Records Administration (1989). *Code of Federal Regulations: 16 CFR453.* Washington, DC: U.S. Government Printing Office.

Okun, M. A., Stock, W. A., Haring, M. J., & Witter, R. A. (1984). Health and subjective well-being: A meta-analysis. *International Journal of Aging and Human Development, 19,* 111–132.

Olds, S. W. (1985). *The eternal garden: Seasons of our sexuality.* New York: Times Books.

Olsho, L. W. (1984). Infant frequency discrimination. *Infant Behavior and Development, 7,* 27–35.

Olsho, L. W., Harkins, S. W., & Lenhardt, M. L. (1985). Aging and the auditory system. In J. E. Birren & K. W. Schaie (Eds.), *Handbook of the psychology of aging* (pp. 332–377). New York: Van Nostrand Reinhold.

Olsho, L. W., Schoon, C., Sakai, R., Turpin, R., & Sperduto, V. (1982). Preliminary data on frequency discrimination in infancy. *Journal of the Acoustical Society of America, 71,* 509–511.

Olson, G. M. (1981). The recognition of specific persons. In M. E. Lamb & L. R. Sherrod (Eds.), *Infant social cognition: Empirical and theoretical considerations.* Hillsdale, NJ: Erlbaum.

Olson, G. M. & Sherman, T. (1983). Attention, learning, and memory in infants. In M. M. Haith & J. J. Campos

(Eds.), *Handbook of child psychology: Vol. 2. Infancy and developmental psychobiology* (pp. 1001–1080). New York: Wiley.

Olweus, D. (1979). Stability and aggression reaction patterns in males: A review. *Psychological Bulletin, 86,* 852–875.

Opper, S. (1977). Concept development in Thai urban and rural children. In P. Dasen (Ed.), *Piagetian psychology: Cross-cultural contributions.* New York: Gardner Press.

Ornstein, P. A., Medlin, R. G., Stone, B. P., & Naus, M. J. (1985). Retrieving for rehearsal: An analysis of active rehearsal on children's memory. *Developmental Psychology, 21,* 633–641.

Ornstein, P. A., & Naus, M. J. (1978). Rehearsal processes in children's memory. In P. A. Ornstein (Ed.), *Memory development in children* (pp. 69–99). Hillsdale, NJ: Erlbaum.

Ornstein, P. A., & Naus, M. J. (1983). Rehearsing according to artificially generated rehearsal patterns: An analysis of active rehearsal. *Bulletin of the Psychonomic Society, 21,* 419–422.

Ory, M. G. (1978). The decision to parent or not: Normative and structural components. *Journal of Marriage and the Family, 40,* 531–539.

Ostrov, E., Offer, D., Howard, K. I., Kaufman, B., & Meyer, H. (1985). Adolescent sexual behavior. *Medical Aspects of Human Sexuality, 19,* 28, 30–31, 34–36.

Ottinger, D., & Simmons, J. (1964). Behavior of human neonates and prenatal maternal anxiety. *Psychological Reports, 14,* 391–394.

Overton, W. R., & Jackson, J. P. (1973). The representation of imagined objects in action sequences. A developmental study. *Child Development, 44,* 309–314.

Owen, M., & Cox, M. (1988). Maternal employment and the transition to parenthood. In A. E. Gottfried & A. W. Gottfried (Eds.), *Maternal employment and children's development: Longitudinal research.* New York: Plenum.

Owens, W. A. (1953). Age and mental abilities: A longitudinal study. *Genetic Psychology Monographs, 48,* 3–54.

Owsley, C., Sekuler, R., & Siemsen, D. (1983). Contrast sensitivity throughout adulthood. *Vision Research, 23,* 689–699.

Paige, K. E., & Paige, J. M. (1973). The politics of birth practices: A strategic analysis. *American Sociological Review, 38,* 663–676.

Palmore, E., & Cleveland, W. (1980). Aging, terminal decline, and terminal drop. In M. Tallmer, D. J. Cherico, A. H. Kutscher, & D. E. Sanders (Eds.), *Thanatological perspectives on aging* (pp. 1–6). New York: Highly Specialized Promotions.

Palmore, E., & Kivett, V. (1977). Change in life satisfaction: A longitudinal study of persons aged 46–70. *Journal of Gerontology, 32,* 311–316.

Papalia, D. E., & Del Vento Bielby, D. (1974). Cognitive functioning in middle- and old-age adults: A review of research based on Piaget's theory. *Human Development, 17,* 424–443.

Papousek, H. (1967). Experimental studies of appetitional behavior in human newborns and infants. In H. W. Stevenson, E. H. Hess, & H. L. Rheingold (Eds.), *Early behavior.* New York: Wiley.

Park, D. C., Puglisi, J. T., & Smith, A. D. (1986). Memory for pictures: Does an age-related decline exist? *Psychology and Aging, 1,* 11–17.

Park, K. A., & Waters, E. (1989). Security of attachment and preschool friendships. *Child Development, 60,* 1076–1081.

Parke, R. D., & Slaby, R. G. (1983). The development of aggression. In E. M. Hetherington (Ed.), & P. H. Mussen (Series Ed.), *Handbook of child psychology: Vol. 4. Socialization, personality, and social development.* New York: Wiley.

Parkes, C. M. (1972). *Bereavement.* New York: International Universities Press.

Parkes, C. M. (1988). Research: Bereavement. *Omega, 18,* 365–377.

Parkes, C. M., & Weiss, R. S. (1983). *Recovery from bereavement.* New York: Basic Books.

Parkinson, S. R., Lindholm, J. M., & Inman, V. W. (1982). An analysis of age differences in immediate recall. *Journal of Gerontology, 37,* 425–431.

Parmelee, A. H., Wenner, W. H., & Schulz, H. R. (1964). Infant sleep patterns from birth to 16 weeks of age. *Journal of Pediatrics, 65,* 576–582.

Parsons, J. E. (1980). Psychosexual neutrality: Is anatomy destiny? In J. E. Parsons (Ed.), *The psychobiology of sex differences and sex roles.* Washington: Hemisphere Publishing.

Parsons, J. E., Adler, R. F., & Kaczala, C. M. (1982). Socialization of achievement attitudes and beliefs: Parental influences. *Child Development, 53,* 310–321.

Parsons, J. E., Kaczala, C. M., & Meece, J. L. (1982). Socialization of achievement attitudes and beliefs: Classroom influences. *Child Development, 53,* 322–339.

Parten, M. E. (1933). Social play among preschool children. *Journal of Abnormal and Social Psychology, 28,* 136–147.

Paton, D., & Craig, J. A. (1974). Cataracts: Development, diagnosis, management. *CIBA Clinical Symposia, 26,* 1–32.

Pattison, E. M. (1977). *The experience of dying.* Englewood Cliffs, NJ: Prentice-Hall.

Pearlin, L. I., & Johnson, J. S. (1977). Marital status, life strains, and depression. *American Sociological Review, 42,* 704–715.

Pearlin, L. I., & Radabaugh, C. (1979). Age and stress: Perspectives and problems. In M. Fiske (Ed.), *Time and transitions.* San Francisco: Jossey-Bass.

Peatling, J. H. (1977). Research on adult moral development: Where is it? *Religious Education, 72,* 213–224.

Pelosi, N. (1988). AIDS public policy: A legislative view. *American Psychologist, 43,* 843–845.

Peplau, L. A. (1983). Roles and gender. In H. H. Kelley, E. Berscheid, A. Christensen, J. H. Harvey, T. L. Huston, G. Levinger, E. McClintock, L. A. Peplau, & D. R. Peterson (Eds.), *Close relationships.* New York: W. H. Freeman.

Perception: *Mechanisms and Models: Readings from Scientific American.* (1972). San Francisco: W. H. Freeman.

Perlmutter, M., & List, J. A. (1982). Learning in later adulthood. In T. M. Field, A. Huston, H. C. Quay, L. Troll, & G. E. Finley (Eds.), *Review of human development.* New York: Wiley.

Perry, D. G., & Bussey, K. (1979). The social learning theory of sex differences: Imitation is alive and well. *Journal of Personality and Social Psychology, 37,* 1699–1712.

Persky, H. (1983). Psychosexual effects of hormones. *Medical Aspects of Human Sexuality, 17,* (9).

Petersen, A. C. (1985). Pubertal development as a cause of disturbance: Myths, realities, and unanswered questions. *Genetic, Social, and General Psychology Monographs, 111,* 205–232.

Petersen, A. C. (1988). Adolescent development. *Annual Review of Psychology, 39,* 583–607.

Petersen, A. C., & Crockett, L. (1985). Pubertal timing and grade effects on adjustment. *Journal of Youth and Adolescence, 14,* 191–206.

Peterson, G. W. & Rollins, B. C. (1987). Parent-child socialization. In M. B. Sussman & S. K. Steinmetz (Eds.), *Handbook of marriage and the family.* New York: Plenum Press.

Peterson, J. L., & Zill, N. (1983). *Marital disruption, parent/child relationships, and behavior problems in children.* Paper presented at the biennial meeting of The Society for Research in Child Development, Detroit.

Petti, T. A., & Larson, C. N. (1987). Depression and suicide. In V. B. VanHasselt & M. Hersen (Eds.). *Handbook of adolescent psychology.* New York: Pergamon Press.

Pfeiffer, E. (1969). Geriatric sex behavior. *Medical Aspects of Human Sexuality, 3,* 19–27.

Pfouts, J. H. (1976). The sibling relationship: A forgotten dimension. *Social Work, 21,* 200–204.

Piaget, J. (1932). *The moral judgement of the child.* London: Routledge & Kegan Paul.

Piaget, J. (1962). *Play, dreams and imitation in childhood.* New York: Norton.

Piaget, J. (1963). *The origins of intelligence in children.* New York: Norton.

Piaget, J. (1964). Development and learning. In R. E. Ripple & V. N. Rockcastle (Eds.), *Piaget revisited.* Ithaca, NY: Cornell University Press.

Piaget, J. (1967). *Six psychological studies.* New York: Vintage.

Piaget, J. (1981). Creativity. In J. M. Gallagher & D. K. Reid (Eds.), *The learning theory of Piaget and Inhelder.* Monterey, CA: Brooks/Cole.

Piaget, J. (1983). Piaget's theory. In W. H. Kessen (Ed.), *Handbook of child psychology, Vol. I: History, theory, and methods* (pp. 103–128). (P. H. Mussen, Series Ed.). New York: Wiley.

Piaget, J. & Inhelder, B. (1956). *The child's conception of space.* London: Routledge and Kegan Paul.

Piaget, J., & Inhelder, B. (1969). *The psychology of the child.* New York: Basic Books.

Pietromonaco, P. R., Manis, J., & Markus, H. (1987). The relationship of employment to self-perception and well-being in women: A cognitive analysis. *Sex Roles, 17*, 467–478.

Pipp, S., Fischer, K. W., & Jennings S. (1987). Acquisition of self- and mother knowledge in infancy. *Developmental Psychology, 23*, 86–96.

Pitts, D. (1982). The effects of aging on selected visual functions: Dark adaptation, visual acuity, stereopsis, and brightness contrast. In R. Sekuler, D. Kline, & K. Dismukes (Eds.), *Aging and human visual function* (pp. 131–159). New York: Alan R. Liss.

Plech, J. H. (1976). The male sex role: Definitions, problems, and sources of change. *Journal of Social Issues, 32*, 155–164.

Plomin, R., & Rowe, D. C. (1979). Genetic and environmental etiology of social behavior in infancy. *Developmental Psychology, 15*, 62–72.

Plomp, R., & Mimpen, A. M. (1979). Speech reception threshold for sentences as a function of age and noise level. *Journal of the Acoustical Society of America, 66*, 1333–1342.

Plude, D. J., & Hoyer, W. J. (1985). Attention and performance: Identifying and localizing age deficits. In N. Charness (Ed.), *Aging and human performance* (pp. 47–99). New York: Wiley.

Polikanina, R. I. (1961). The relation between automatic and somatic components in the development of the conditioned reflex in premature infants. *Pavlov Journal of Higher Nervous Activity, 11*, 51–58.

Poloma, M. M., & Garland, T. N. (1971). The myth of the egalitarian family: Family roles and the professionally-employed wife. In A. Theodore (Ed.), *The professional woman.* Cambridge, MA: Schenkman.

Poon L. W. (1985). Differences in human memory with aging: Nature, causes, and clinical implications. In J. E. Birren & K. W. Schaie (Eds.), *Handbook of the psychology of aging* (2nd ed.). New York: Van Nostrand Reinhold.

Porter, R. H., Cernoch, J. M., & McLaughlin, J. H. (1983). Maternal recognition of neonates through olfactory cues. *Physiology and Behavior, 30*, 151–154.

Postman, L., Bruner, J. S., & McGinnies, E. (1948). Personal values as selective factors in perception. *Journal of Abnormal and Social Psychology, 43*, 142–154.

Postman, N. (1982). *The disappearance of childhood.* New York: Delacorte.

Potash, M., Noppe, I., & Noppe, L. (1981, November). *The relationship of personality factors to life satisfaction among the elderly.* Paper presented at the Annual Meeting of the Gerontological Society of America, Toronto.

Poterba, J., & Summers, L. (1987). Public policy implications of declining old-age mortality. In G. Burtless (Ed.), *Work, health, and income among the elderly.* Washington, DC: Brookings.

Powell, P. M. (1984). Stage 4A: Category operations and interactive empathy. In M. L. Commons, F. A. Richards, & C. Armon (Eds.), *Beyond formal operations: Late adolescent and adult cognitive development.* New York: Praeger.

Powell, P. H., & Dobbs, J. M. (1976). Physical attractiveness and personal space. *Journal of Social Psychology, 100*, 59–64.

Power, T. G., & Parke, R. D. (1980). Play as a context for early learning: Lab and home analyses. In I. E. Sigel & L. J. Laosa (Eds.), *The family as a learning environment.* New York: Plenum.

Pozner, J., & Saltz, E. (1974). Social class, conditional communication, and egocentric speech. *Developmental Psychology, 10*, 764–771.

Premack, D. (1976). *Intelligence in ape and man.* Hillsdale, NJ: Erlbaum.

Price, G. G., Walsh, D. J., & Vilberg, W. R. (1984). The confluence model's good predictions of mental age beg the question. *Psychological Bulletin, 96*, 195–200.

Price-Williams, D. (1981). Concrete and formal operations. In R. H. Munroe, R. L. Munroe, & B. B. Whiting (Eds.), *Handbook of cross-cultural human development.* New York: Garland Publishing.

Prinz, R. J., Roberts, W. A., & Hartman, E. (1980). Dietary correlates of hyperactive behavior in children. *Journal of Consulting and Clinical Psychology, 48*, 760–769.

Proctor, C. P. (1984). Teacher expectations: A model for school improvement. *Elementary School Journal, 84*, 469–481.

Puglisi, J. T., & Park, T. C. (1987). Perceptual elaboration and memory in older adults. *Journal of Gerontology, 42*, 160–172.

Pulakos, J. (1987). Brothers and sisters: Nature and importance of the adult bond. *The Journal of Psychology, 121*, 521–522.

Pulkkinen, L. (1982). Self-control and continuity from childhood to adolescence. In P. B. Baltes & O. G. Brim (Eds.), *Life-span development and behavior* (Vol. 4). New York: Academic Press.

Puri, R., Chawla, P., Sharma, M., & Pershad, D. (1984). Impact of an ongoing supplementary feeding programme on the mental abilities of children. *Indian Journal of Pediatrics, 51,* 653–657.

Queenan, J. T. (1988). The c-section crisis: why we must solve it ourselves. *Contemporary Obstetrics and Gynecology, 31,* 9–10.

Rabbitt, P. M. A. (1965). An age decrement in the ability to ignore irrelevant information. *Journal of Gerontology, 20,* 233–238.

Radin, N. (1972). Father-child interaction and the intellectual functioning of four-year-old boys. *Developmental Psycholgy, 6,* 353–361.

Radke-Yarrow, M., Zahn-Waxler, C., Chapman, M. (1983). Children's prosocial dispositions and behavior. In E. M. Hetherington (Ed.), *Handbook of child psychology: Vol. 4. Socialization, personality, and social development.* New York: Wiley.

Raether, H. C. (Ed.). (1971). *Successful funeral service practice.* Englewood Cliffs, NJ: Prentice-Hall.

Raschke, H. J. (1987). Divorce. In M. B. Sussman & S. K. Steinmetz (Eds.), *Handbook of marriage and the family* (pp. 597–624). New York: Plenum.

Ratner, N., & Bruner, J. (1978). Games, social exchange, and the acquisition of language. *Journal of Child Language, 5,* 391–401.

Reed, G. L., & Leiderman, P. H. (1983). Is imprinting an appropriate model for human infant attachment? *International Journal of Behavioral Development, 6,* 51–69.

Reese, H. W. (1976). *Basic learning processes in childhood.* New York: Holt, Rinehart and Winston.

Reich, P. A. (1986). *Language development.* Englewood Cliffs, NJ: Prentice-Hall.

Reimer, J., Paolitto, D. P., & Hersh, R. H. (1983). *Promoting moral growth: From Piaget to Kohlberg* (2nd ed.). New York: Longman.

Reiss, I. L. (1986). *Journey into sexuality: An exploratory voyage.* Englewood Cliffs, NJ: Prentice-Hall.

Renner, J. W. (1977). *Analysis of cognitive processes.* Washington, DC: National Science Foundation.

Renninger, K. A., & Wozniak, R. H. (1985). Effect of interest on attentional shift, recognition and recall in young children. *Developmental Psychology, 21,* 624–632.

Rest, J. R. (1975). Longitudinal study of the Defining Issues Test: A strategy for analyzing developmental change. *Developmental Psychology, 11,* 738–748.

Rest, J. R. (1976). New approaches in the assessment of moral judgement. In J. T. Lickona (Ed.), *Moral development and behavior.* New York: Holt, Rinehart & Winston.

Rest, J. R. (1979). *Revised manual for the Defining Issues Test.* Minneapolis: Minnesota Moral Research Projects.

Rest, J. R. (1983). Morality. In J. H. Flavell & E. M. Markman (Eds.), *Handbook of child psychology: Cognitive development* (Vol. 3). New York: Wiley.

Rest, J. (1984). The major components of morality. In W. M. Kurtines & J. L. Gewirtz (Eds.), *Morality, moral behavior, and moral development.* New York: Wiley.

Rest, J. R., Davison, M. L., & Robbins, S. (1978). Age trends in judging moral issues: A review of cross-sectional, longitudinal, and sequential studies of the Defining Issues test. *Child Development, 49,* 263–279.

Reuter, M. W., & Biller, H. B. (1973). Perceived paternal nurturance-availability and personality adjustment among college males. *Journal of Consulting and Clinical Psychology, 40,* 339–342.

Rheingold, H. L. (1979). *Helping by two-year-old children.* Paper presented at the biennial meeting of the Society for Research in Child Development, San Francisco.

Rheingold, H. L., & Cook, K. V. (1975). The contents of boys' and girls' rooms as an index of parents' behavior. *Child Development, 46,* 459–463.

Rheingold, H. L., Gewirtz, J. L., & Ross. H. W. (1959). Social conditioning of vocalizations in the infant. *Journal of Comparative and Physiological Psychology, 52,* 68–73.

Ricciuti, H. (1974). Fear and development of social attachments in the first year of life. In M. Lewis & L. A. Rosenblum (Eds.), *The origins of human behavior: Fear.* New York: Wiley.

Ricciuti, H. N. (1981). Developmental consequences of malnutrition in early childhood. In E. M. Hetherington &

R. D. Parke (Eds.), *Contemporary readings in child psychology* (2nd ed., pp. 21–33). New York: McGraw-Hill.

Rice, B. (1979, September). Brave new world of intelligence testing. *Psychology Today.*

Rice, F. P. (1990). *The adolescent: Development, relationships, and culture* (6th ed.). Boston: Allyn and Bacon.

Rice, G. E., & Meyer, B. J. F. (1985). Reading behavior and prose recall performance of young and older adults with high and average verbal ability. *Educational Gerontology, 11,* 57–72.

Rice, G. E., & Meyer, B. J. F. (1986). Prose recall: Effects of aging, verbal ability, and reading behavior. *Journal of Gerontology, 41,* 469–480.

Rich, J. (1975). Effects of children's physical attractiveness on teacher's evaluation. *Journal of Educational Psychology, 67,* 599–609.

Richards, M., & Petersen, A. C. (1987). Biological theoretical models of adolescent development. In V. B. Van Hasselt & M. Hersen (Eds.), *Handbook of adolescent psychology.* New York: Pergamon Press.

Richardson, D. W., & Short, R. V. (1978). Time of onset of sperm production in boys. *Journal of Biosocial Science, 5,* 15–25.

Richardson, L., & Taylor, V. (1989). *Feminist frontiers II.* (2nd ed.). New York: Random House.

Richardson, S. A. (1976). The relation of severe malnutrition in infancy to intelligence of school children with differing life histories. *Pediatric Research, 10,* 57–61.

Richmond, V. P. (1985). Shyness and popularity: Children's views. *Western Journal of Speech Communication, 49,* 116–125.

Riegel, K. F. (1975). Toward a dialectical theory of development. *Human Development, 31,* 689–700.

Riegel, K. F. (1976) The dialectics of human development. *American Psychologist, 31,* 689–700.

Riegel, K. F., & Riegel, R. M. (1972). Development, drop, and death. *Developmental Psychology, 6,* 306–319.

Riegel, K. F., Riegel, R. M., & Meyer, G. (1967). The study of drop-out rates in longitudinal research on aging and the prediction of death. *Journal of Personality and Social Psychology, 4,* 342–348.

Riekehof, L. L. (1978). *Talk to the deaf.* Springfield, MO: Gospel Publishing House.

Rierdan, J., & Koff, E. (1980). The psychological impact of menarche: Integrative versus disruptive changes. *Journal of Youth and Adolescence, 9,* 49–58.

Ring, K. (1980). *Life at death: A scientific investigation of the near-death experience.* New York: Coward, McCann, & Geoghegan.

Ring, K. (1984). *Heading toward omega.* New York: William Morrow.

Roberts, S. O., Crump, E. P., Dickerson, A. E., & Horton, C. P. (1965, September). *Longitudinal performance of Negro American children at 5 and 10 years on the Stanford-Binet.* Paper presented at the annual meeting of the American Psychological Association, Chicago.

Robertson, J. F. (1976). Significance of grandparents: Perceptions of young adult grandchildren. *The Gerontologist, 16,* 137–140.

Robertson, J. F. (1977). Grandmother: A study of role conceptions. *Journal of Marriage and the Family, 39,* 165–174.

Robinson, C. C., & Morris, J. T. (1986). The gender-stereotyped nature of Christmas toys received by 36-, 48-, and 60-month-old children: A comparison between nonrequested vs. requested toys. *Sex Roles, 15,* 21–32.

Robinson, P. K. (1983). The sociological perspective. In R. B. Weg (Ed.), *Sexuality in the later years.* New York: Academic Press.

Roche, A. F. (Ed.). (1979). Secular trends in human growth, maturation, and development. *Monographs of the Society for Research in Child Development, 44,* (3–4, Serial No. 179).

Rodgers, J. L., & Rowe, D. C. (1985). Does contiguity breed similarity? A within-family analysis of nonshared sources of IQ differences between siblings. *Developmental Psychology, 21,* 743–746.

Rodgers, W. L., & Thornton, A. (1985). Changing patterns of first marriage in the United States. *Demography, 22,* 265–279.

Rodin, J., Silberstein, L., & Striegel-Moore, R. (1984). Women and weight: A normative discontent. *Nebraska Symposium on Motivation, 32.* Lincoln: University of Nebraska Press.

Rodin, J., & Stoddard, P. (1981). *Predictors of attitudes toward weight and eating.* Unpublished manuscript. Cited in J. Rodin, L. Silberstein, & R. Striegel-Moore (1984).

Rodin, J., & Striegel-Moore, R. H. (1984, September). *Predicting attitudes toward body weight and food intake in women.* Paper presented at the 14th Congress of the European Association of Behavior Therapy, Brussels.

Rogers, C. (1961). *On becoming a person: A therapist's view of psychotherapy.* Boston: Houghton Mifflin.

Rogoff, B. (1981). Schooling and the development of cognitive skills. In H. C. Triandis & A. Heron (Eds.), *Handbook of cross-cultural psychology: Developmental psychology* (Vol. 4, pp. 233–294). Boston: Allyn and Bacon.

Rollins, B., & Feldman, H. (1970). Marital satisfaction over the family life cycle. *Journal of Marriage and the Family, 32,* 20–27.

Rollins, B. C. & Galligan, R. (1978). The developing child and marital satisfaction of parents. In R. M. Lerner & G. B. Spanier (Eds.), *Child influences on marriage and family interaction.* New York: Academic Press.

Romaine, W. (1984). *The language of children and adolescents.* Oxford: Basil Blackwell.

Romaniuk, J. G., & Romaniuk, M. (1981). Creativity across the life span: A measurement perspective. *Human Development, 24,* 336–381.

Rose, R. J., & Ditto W. B. (1983). A developmental-genetic analysis of common fears from early adolescence to early adulthood. *Child Development, 54,* 361–368.

Rosenbaum, M. (1979). The changing body image of the adolescent girl. In M. Sugar (Ed.), *Female adolescent development.* New York: Brunner/Mazel.

Rosenblatt, D. (1977). Developmental trend in infant play. In B. Tizard & D. Harvey (Eds.), *The biology of play.* Philadelphia: Lippincott.

Rosenblith, J. F., & Sims-Knight, J. E. (1985). *In the beginning: Development in the first two years of life.* Monterey, CA: Brooks/Cole.

Rosenfeld, A. (1976). *Prolongevity.* New York: Knopf.

Rosenstein, D., & Oster, H. (1988). Differential facial responses to four basic tastes in newborns. *Child Development, 59,* 1555–1568.

Rosenthal, R. & Jacobson, L. (1968). *Pygmalion in the classroom.* New York: Holt, Rinehart & Winston.

Ross, E. (1968). Effects of challenging and supportive instructions in verbal learning in older adults. *Journal of Educational Psychology, 59,* 261–266.

Ross, G. S. (1980). Categorization in 1- to 2-year-olds, *Developmental Psychology, 16,* 391–396.

Ross, H. S. (1982). Establishment of social games among toddlers. *Developmental Psychology, 18,* 509–518.

Ross, H. S., & Lollis, S. P. (1987). Communication within infant social games. *Developmental Psychology, 23,* 241–248.

Ross, H., & Milgram, J. (1982). Important variables in adult sibling relationships: A qualitative analysis. In M. E. Lamb & B. Sutton-Smith (Eds.), *Sibling relationships: Their nature and significance across the life span.* Hillsdale, NJ: Erlbaum.

Ross, H. S., Lollis, S. P., & Elliott, C. (1982). Toddler-peer communication. In K. H. Rubin & H. S. Ross (Eds.), *Peer relationships and social skills in childhood.* New York: Springer-Verlag.

Rothbart, M. K. (1986). Longitudinal observation of infant temperament. *Developmental Psychology, 22,* 356–365.

Rothblum, E. D. (1988). More on reporting sex differences. *American Psychologist, 43,* 1095.

Routh, D. K. (1986). Attention deficit disorder. In R. T. Brown & C. R. Reynolds (Eds.), *Psychological perspectives on childhood exceptionality: A handbook.* New York: Wiley.

Rovee, C. K., Cohen, R. Y, & Shlapack, W. (1975). Life-span stability in olfactory sensitivity. *Developmental Psychology, 11,* 311–318.

Rovee-Collier, C. (1984). The ontogeny of learning and memory in human infancy. In R. V. Kail, Jr., & N. E. Spear (Eds.), *Comparative perspectives on the development of memory* (pp. 103–134). Hillsdale, NJ: Erlbaum.

Rowe, E. J., & Schnore, M. M. (1971). Item concreteness and reported strategies in paired-associate learning as a function of age. *Journal of Gerontology, 26,* 470–475.

Rowland, K. F. (1977). Environmental events predicting death for the elderly. *Psychological Bulletin, 84,* 349–372.

Rubenstein, J. L. (1976). Concordance of visual and manipulative responsiveness to novel and familiar stimuli: A function of test procedures or of prior experience? *Child Development, 47,* 1197–1199.

Rubin, K. H., Fein, G. C., & Vandenberg, B. (1983). Play. In P. H. Mussen (Ed.), *Handbook of child psychology* (4th ed., Vol. 4). New York: Wiley.

Rubin, K. H., & Krasnor, L. R. (1980). Changes in the play behaviors of preschoolers: A short-term longitudinal investigation. *Canadian Journal of Behavioral Science, 12,* 278–282.

Rubin, K. H., Maioni, T. L., & Hornung, M. (1976). Free play behaviors in middle and lower class preschoolers: Parten and Piaget revisited. *Child Development, 47,* 414–419.

Rubin, K. H., & Ross, S. H. (1982). *Peer relationships and social skills in childhood.* New York: Springer-Verlag.

Rubin, K. H., Watson, K., & Jambor, T. (1978). Free play behaviors in preschool and kindergarten children. *Child Development, 49,* 534–536.

Rubin, R. T., Reinisch, J. M., & Haskett, R. F. (1981). Postnatal gonadal steroid effects on human behavior. *Science, 211,* 1318–1324.

Ruble, D. N. (1988). Sex-role development. In M. H. Bornstein & M. E. Lamb (Eds.), *Developmental psychology: An advanced textbook* (2nd ed.). Hillsdale, NJ: Erlbaum.

Ruble, D. N., & Brooks-Gunn, J. (1982). The experience of menarche. *Child Development, 53,* 1557–1566.

Ruff, H. A. (1984). Infants' manipulative exploration of objects: Effects of age and object characteristics. *Developmental Psychology, 21,* 295–305.

Ruhm, C. J. (1989). Why older Americans stop working. *The Gerontologist, 29,* 294–299.

Rumbaugh, D. M. (Ed.). (1977). *Language learning by a chimpanzee: The Lana project.* New York: Academic Press.

Runyan, D. K. (1986). Incest: The trauma of intervention: *Siecus Report, 15,* 1–14.

Russell, M. J., Mendelson T., & Peeke, H. V. S. (1983). Mother's identification of their infants' odors. *Ethology and Sociobiology, 4,* 29–31.

Russo, N. F. (1985). Sex-role stereotyping, socialization, and sexism. In A. G. Sargent (Ed.), *Beyond sex roles* (2nd ed.). St. Paul, MN: West Publishing.

Ryan, J., & Smollar, H. (1978). *A developmental analysis of obligations of parent-child and friend relations.* Unpublished manuscript. The Catholic University of America.

Rybash, J. M., Hoyer, W. J., & Roodin, P. A. (1986). *Adult cognition and aging: Developmental changes in processing, knowing, and thinking.* New York: Pergamon Press.

Ryckman, R. (1989). *Theories of personality* (4th ed.). Pacific Grove, CA: Brooks/Cole.

Rykken, D. E. (1987). Sex in the later years. In P. Silverman (Ed.), *The elderly as modern pioneers* (pp. 158–182). Bloomington: Indiana University Press.

Sabo, F., & Runfola, D. R. (Eds.) (1980). *Jock: Sports and the male identity.* Englewood Cliffs, NJ: Prentice-Hall.

Sabom, M. B. (1982). *Recollections of death: A medical investigation.* New York: Harper & Row.

Safier, G. (1964). A study in relationships between the life and death concepts in children. *Journal of Genetic Psychology, 105,* 283–294.

Sagi, A., & Hoffman, M. L. (1976). Empathic distress in the newborn. *Developmental Psychology, 12,* 175–176.

Salapatek, P. (1975). Pattern perception in early infancy. In L. B. Cohen & P. Salapatek (Eds.), *Infant perception: From sensation to cognition.* New York: Academic Press.

Saltz, E., Dixon, D., & Johnson, J. (1977). Training disadvantaged preschoolers on various fantasy activities: Effects on cognitive functioning and impulse control. *Child Development, 48,* 367–380.

Salvia, J., Algozyne, R., & Sheare, J. B. (1977). Attractiveness and school achievement. *Journal of School Psychology, 15,* 60–67.

Sameroff, A. J. (1971). Can conditioned responses be established in the newborn infant: 1971? *Developmental Psychology, 5,* 1–12.

Sameroff, A. J., & Cavanaugh, P. J. (1979). Learning in infancy: A developmental perspective. In J. Osofsky (Ed.), *Handbook of infant development.* New York: Wiley.

Sandfort, T. (1984). Sex in pedophiliac relationships: An empirical investigation among a non-representative group of boys. *Journal of Sex Research, 20,* 123–142.

Sands, L. P., & Meredith, W. (1989). Effects of sensory and motor functioning on adult intellectual performance. *Journal of Gerontology: Psychological Sciences, 44,* 56–58.

Sarnat, H. B. (1978). Olfactory reflexes in the newborn infant. *Journal of Pediatrics, 92,* 624–626.

Sarrel, L. J. & Sarrel, D. M. (1984). *Sexual turning points: The seven stages of adult sexuality.* New York: D.C. Heath.

Sattler, J. M. (1982). *Assessment of children's intelligence.* Philadelphia: Saunders.

Sauer, W. J., & Warland, R. (1982). Morale and life satisfaction: In D. J. Mangen & W. A. Peterson (Eds.), *Research instruments in social gerontology: Clinical and social psychology,* (Vol. 1, pp. 3–20). New York: Springer Publishing.

Saunders, C. (1977). Dying to live: St. Christopher's Hospice. In H. Feife (Ed.), *New Meanings of death.* New York: McGraw-Hill.

Sayre, S. A., & Ball, D. W. (1975). Piagetian cognitive development and achievement in science. *Journal of Research in Science Teaching, 12,* 165–174.

Scarr, S. (1981). *Race, social class, and individual differences in IQ.* Hillsdale, NJ: Erlbaum.

Schacter, D. L., & Moscovitch, M. (1984). Infants, amnesics, and dissociable memory systems. In M. Moscovitch (Ed.), *Infant memory* (pp. 173–215). New York: Plenum.

Schacter, D. L., Moscovitch, M., Tulving, E., McLachlan, D. R., & Freedman, M. (1986). Mnemonic precedence in amnesic patients: An analogue of the AB error in infants? *Child Development, 57,* 816–823.

Schaefer, C. E. (1985). Play therapy. *Early Child Development and Care, 19,* 95–108.

Schaefer, E. S. (1961). Converging conceptual models for maternal behavior and for child behavior. In J. C. Glidewell (Ed.), *Parental attitudes and child behavior.* Springfield, IL: Charles C. Thomas.

Schaefer, E. S., & Bayley, N. (1963). Maternal behavior, child behavior and their intercorrelations from infancy through adolescence. *Monographs of the Society for Research in Child Development, 28,* 1–27.

Schaffer, H. R. (1971). *The growth of sociability.* Harmondsworth, England: Penguin.

Schaffer, H. R., & Emerson, P. E. (1964). The development of social attachments in infancy. *Monographs of the Society for Research in Child Development, 29* (Serial No. 94).

Schaie, K. W. (1970). A reinterpretation of age-related changes in cognitive structure and functioning. In L. R. Goulet & P. B. Baltes (Eds.), *Life span developmental psychology.* New York: Academic Press.

Schaie, K. W. (1982). Toward a stage theory of adult cognitive development. In K. W. Schaie & J. Geiwitz (Eds.), *Readings in adult development and aging.* Boston: Little, Brown.

Schaie, K. W., & Labouvie-Vief, G. (1974). Generational versus ontogenetic components of change in adult cognitive behavior: A fourteen-year cross-sequential study. *Developmental Psychology, 10,* 305–320.

Schaie, K. W., & Parham, I. A. (1976). A stability of adult personality traits: Fact or fable? *Journal of Personality and Social Psychology, 34,* 146–158.

Schaie, K. W., & Parham, I. A. (1977). Cohort-sequential analysis of adult intellectual development. *Developmental Psychology, 13,* 649–653.

Schaie, K. W. & Strother, C. R. (1968). Cognitive and personality variables in college graduates of advanced age. In G. A. Talland (Ed.), *Human aging and behavior.* New York: Academic Press.

Scharlach, A. E. Role strain in mother-daughter relationships in later life. *The Gerontologist, 27,* 627–631.

Scharlach, A. E., & Frenzel, C. (1982). *Correlates of psychological stress in wives of disabled adults.* Paper presented at the 36th Annual Scientific Meeting of the Gerontological Society of America, San Francisco, CA.

Schetky, D. H. (1986). Emerging issues in child sexual abuse. *Journal of the American Academy of Child Psychiatry, 25,* 490–492.

Schiff, W., Benasich, A., & Bornstein, M. H. (1986). *Infants' audio-visual integration of information specifying approach and recession.* Unpublished manuscript, New York University (cited in Lamb and Bornstein, 1987).

Schneider, B., Trehub, S. E., & Bull, D. (1980). High frequency sensitivity in infants. *Science, 207,* 1003–1004.

Schoen, R. W., Urton, K. W., & Baj, J. (1985). Marriage and divorce in twentieth-century American cohorts. *Demography, 22,* 109–114.

Schonfield, D., & Robertson, B. A. (1966). Memory storage and aging. *Canadian Journal of Psychology, 20,* 228–236.

Schuknecht, H. L., & Igarashi, M. (1964). Pathology of slowly-progressive sensorineural deafness. *Transcripts of the American Academy of Opthalmology and Otolaryngology, 68,* 222–242.

Schultz, R., & Aderman, D. (1974). Clinical research and the stages of dying. *Omega, 5,* 137–143.

Schulz, R., & Schlarb, J. (1988). Two decades of research on dying: What do we know about the patient? *Omega, 18,* 299−317.

Schumaker, J. F., Small, L., & Wood, J. (1986). Self-concept, academic achievement, and athletic participation. *Perceptual and Motor Skills, 62,* 387−390.

Schwartz, S. H., Feldman, R., Brown, M., & Heingartmer, A. (1969). Some personality correlates of conduct in two situations of moral conflict. *Journal of Personality, 37,* 41−57.

Scott, J. P. (1983). Siblings and other kin. In T. H. Brubaker (Ed.), *Family relationships in later life.* Beverly Hills, CA: Sage.

Scribner, S., & Cole, M. (1973). Cognitive consequences of formal and informal education. *Science, 182,* 553−559.

Segal, S. A., & Figley, C. R. (1985). Bulimia: Estimate of incidence and relationship to shyness. *Journal of College Student Personnel, 26,* 240−244.

Self, P. A. (1975). The further evolution of the parental imperative. In N. Datan & L. H. Ginsberg (Eds.), *Life-span developmental psychology: Normative life crises.* New York: Academic Press.

Selman, R. L. (1980). *The growth of interpersonal understanding.* New York: Academic Press.

Selman, R. L., & Byrne, D. F. (1974). A structural-developmental analysis of levels of role-taking in middle childhood. *Child Development, 45,* 803−806.

Selman, R. L., & Jacquette, D. (1978). Stability and oscillation in interpersonal awareness: A clinical-development analysis. In C. B. Keasey (Ed.), *The XXV Nebraska Symposium on Motivation.*

Senn, M. J. E. (1975). Insights on the child development movement in the United States. *Monographs of the Society for Research in Child Development, 40* (304, Serial No. 161).

Serbin, L. A., O'Leary, K. D., Kent, R. N., & Tonick, I. J. (1973). A comparison of teacher response to the preacademic and problem behavior of boys and girls. *Child Development, 44,* 796−804.

Shaheen, S. J. (1984). Neuromaturation of behavior development: The case of childhood lead poisoning. *Developmental Psychology, 20,* 542−550.

Shanas, E., (1979). Social myth as hypothesis: The case of family relations of old people. *The Gerontologist, 19,* 3−9.

Shanas, E., Townsend, P., Wedderburn, D., Friis, H., Milkhoj, P., & Slehouwer, J. (1968). *Older people in three industrial societies.* New York: Atherton Press.

Shantz, C. U. (1975). *The development of social cognition.* Chicago: University of Chicago Press.

Shantz, C. U. (1983). Social cognition. In J. H. Flavell & E. M. Markman (Eds.), *Handbook of child psychology: Vol. 3. Cognitive development* New York: Wiley.

Shapiro, E., & Tate, R. B. (1985). Predictors of long-term care facility use among the elderly. *Canadian Journal of Aging, 4,* 11−19.

Sharabany, R., Gershoni, R., & Hofman, J. (1981). Girl-friend, boyfriend: Age and sex differences in intimate friendship. *Developmental Psychology, 17,* 800−808.

Sharps, M. J., & Gollin, E. S. (1987). Memory for object locations in young and elderly adults. *Journal of Gerontology, 42,* 336−341.

Sharps, M. J., & Gollin, E. S. (1988). Aging and free recall for objects located in space. *Journal of Gerontology, 43,* 8−11.

Shatz, M., & Gelman, R. (1973). The development of communication skills: Modifications in the speech of young children as a function of listener. *Monographs of the Society for Research in Child Development, 38* (5, Serial No. 152).

Sheehy, G. (1981). *Pathfinders.* New York: Bantam.

Shepherd-Look, D. L. (1982). Sex differentiation and the development of sex roles. In B. B. Wolman (Ed.), *Handbook of developmental psychology.* Englewood Cliffs, NJ: Prentice-Hall.

Sherman, J. A. (1967). Problems of sex differences in space perceptions and aspects of intellectual functioning. *Psychological Review, 74,* 290−299.

Sherman, M., & Key, C. B. (1932). The "intelligence" of isolated mountain children. *Child Development, 3,* 279−290.

Sherman, S. (1971). The choice of retirement housing among the well elderly. *Aging and Human Development, 2,* 118−138.

Sherman, S. (October, 1988). The Hmong in America. Laotion refugees in the "Land of the Giants." *National Geographic,* pp. 587−610.

Sherrod L. R. (1981). Issues in cognitive perceptual development: The special case of social stimuli. In M. E. Lamb & L. R. Sherrod (Eds.), *Infant social cognition.* Hillsdale, NJ: Erlbaum.

Shields, J. (1962). *Monozygotic twins.* London: Oxford University Press.

Shields, S. A. (1975). Functionalism, Darwinism, and the psychology of women: A study in social myth. *American Psychologist, 30,* 739–754.

Shipman, G. (1968). The psychodynamics of sex education. *Family Coordinator, 17,* 3–12.

Shmavonian, B. M., Miller, L. H., & Cohen, S. I. (1970). Differences among age and sex groups with respect to cardiovascular conditioning and reactivity. *Journal of Gerontology, 25,* 87–94.

Shneidman, E. S. (Ed.). (1984). *Death: Current perspectives* (3rd ed.). Palo Alto, CA: Mayfield.

Shneidman, E. S. (1980). Death work and stages of dying. In E. S. Shneidman (Ed.), *Death: Current perspectives* (2nd ed.). Palo Alto, CA: Mayfield Publishing.

Shneidman, E. S. (1970). Death questionnaire. *Psychology Today, 4,* 67–72.

Shock, N. W. (1977). Biological theories of aging. In J. E. Birren & K. W. Schaie (Eds.), *Handbook of the psychology of aging.* New York: Van Nostrand Reinhold.

Shulman, N. (1975). Life-style variations in patterns of close relationships. *Journal of Marriage and the Family, 37,* 813–821.

Shultz, T., & Pilon, R. (1973). Development of ability to detect linguistic ambiguity. *Child Development, 44,* 728–733.

Siegel, R. K. (1980). The psychology of life after death. *American Psychologist, 35,* 911–931.

Siegler, I. C. (1987). Personality. In G. L. Maddox (Ed.), *The encyclopedia of aging* (p. 520). New York: Springer-Verlag.

Siegler, I.C., George, L. K., & Okum, M. A. (1979). Cross-sequential analysis of adult personality. *Developmental Psychology, 215,* 350–351.

Siegler, R. S. (1986). *Children's thinking.* Englewood Cliffs, NJ: Prentice-Hall.

Simmons, L. W. (1945). *The role of the aged in primitive society.* New Haven, CT: Yale University Press.

Simmons, R. G., & Blyth, D. A. (1987). *Moving into adolescence: The impact of pubertal change and school context.* New York: Aldine.

Simmons, R. G., Blyth, D. A., & McKinney, K. L. (1983). The social and psychological effects of puberty on white females. In J. Brooks-Gunn & A. C. Petersen (Eds.), *Girls in puberty: Biological and psychosocial perspectives.* New York: Plenum Press.

Simner, M. L. (1971). Newborn's response to the cry of another infant. *Developmental Psychology, 5,* 136–150.

Simon, W., & Gagnon, J. H. (1969). On psychosexual development. In D. A. Goslin (Ed.), *Handbook of socialization theory and research.* Chicago: Rand McNally.

Simonton, D. K. (1984). *Genius, creativity, and leadership: Historiometric inquiries.* Cambridge, MA: Harvard University Press.

Singer, J. L. (Ed.). (1973). *The child's world of make-believe: Experimental studies of imaginative play.* New York: Academic Press.

Singer, L. M., Brodzinsky, K. M., Ramsay, D., Steir, M., & Waters, E. (1985). Mother-infant attachment in adoptive families. *Child Development, 56,* 1543–1551.

Sinnott, J. D. (1984). Postformal reasoning: The relativistic stage. In M. L. Commons, F. A. Richards, & C. Armon (Eds.), *Beyond formal operations: Late adolescent and adult cognitive development.* New York: Praeger.

Sinnott, E. W. (1959). The creativeness of life. In H. H. Anderson (Ed.), *Creativity and its cultivation.* New York: Harper & Row.

Siqueland, E. R. (1964). Operant conditioning of head-turning in four-month-old infants. *Psychonomic Science, 1,* 223–224.

Siqueland, E. R. & DeLucia, A. (1969). Visual reinforcement of nonnutritive sucking in human infants. *Science, 65,* 1144–1146.

Skeels, H. & Dye, H. B. (1939). A study of the effects of differential stimulation of mentally-retarded children. *Proceedings of the American Association of Mental Deficiency, 44,* 114–136.

Slaby, R., & Frey, K. L. (1975). Development of gender constancy and selective attention to same-sex models. *Child Development, 46,* 849–856.

Slade, A. (1987). Quality of attachment and early symbolic play. *Developmental Psychology, 23,* 78–85.

Slobin, D. I. (1971). *Psycholinguistics.* Glenview, IL: Scott, Foresman.

Slobin, D. I. (1973). Cognitive prerequisites for the acquisition of grammar. In C. A. Ferguson & D. I. Slobin (Eds.), *Studies of child language development.* New York: Holt, Rinehart and Winston.

Smallwood, K. B. (1980). What do adult women college students really need? *Journal of College Student Personnel, 21,* 65–73.

Smart, M. S., & Smart, R. C. (1982). *Children: Development and relationships* (4th ed.). New York: Macmillan.

Smetana, J. G. (1989). Adolescents' and parents' reasoning about actual family conflicts. *Child Development, 60,* 1052–1067.

Smetana, J. G., & Letourneau, K. J. (1984). Development of gender constancy and children's sex-typed free play behavior. *Developmental Psychology, 20,* 691–696.

Smiley, S. S. & Brown, A. L. (1979). Conceptual preference for thematic or taxonomic relations: A non-monotonic trend from preshool to old age. *Journal of Experimental Child Psychology, 28,* 249–257.

Smith, D. (1978). Preparation for new life. In D. W. Smith, E. L. Bierman, & N. M. Robinson (Eds.), *The biologic ages of man.* Philadelphia: W. B. Saunders.

Smith, G. J. (1985). Facial and full-length ratings of attractiveness related to the social interactions of young children. *Sex Roles, 12,* 287–293.

Smith, K. V., & Smith, W. M. (1962). *Infant control of the behavioral environment: Perception and motion.* Philadelphia: Saunders.

Smith, R. M. (1982). *Learning how to learn: Applied theory for adults.* Chicago: Follett.

Smits, G. J., & Cherhoniak, I. M. (1976). Physical attractiveness and friendliness in interpersonal attraction. *Psychological Reports, 39,* 171–174.

Smollar, J., & Youniss, J. (1982). Social development through friendship. In K. H. Rubin & H. S. Ross (Eds.), *Peer relationships and social skills in childhood.* New York: Springer-Verlag.

Snarey, J. R., Reimer, J., & Kohlberg, L. (1985). Development of social-moral reasoning among Kibbutz adolescents: A longitudinal cross-cultural study. *Developmental Psychology, 21,* 3–17.

Snow, C. E. (1972). Mothers' speech to children learning language. *Child Development, 43,* 549–565.

Snow, C. E. (1977). The development of conversation between mothers and babies. *Journal of Child Language, 4,* 1–22.

Snow, C. E., & Hoefnagel-Hohle, M. (1978). The critical period for language acquisition: Evidence from second language learning. *Child Development, 49,* 1114–1128.

Snyder, E. E. (1972). High school student perceptions of prestige criteria. *Adolescence, 6,* 129–136.

Snyder, E. E., & Kivlin, J. E. (1975). Women athletes and aspects of psychological well-being and body image. *Research Quarterly, 46,* 191–199.

Sobesky, W. E. (1983). The effect of situational factors on moral judgements. *Child Development, 54,* 575–584.

Soldo, B. J., & Manton, K. G. (1958). Health status and service needs of the oldest old: Current patterns and future trends. *Milbank Memorial Fund Quarterly/Health and Society, 63,* 286–319.

Solyom, L., & Barik, H. C. (1965). Conditioning in senescence and senility. *Journal of Gerontology, 20,* 483–488.

Sommer, B. B. (1978). *Puberty and adolescence.* New York: Oxford University Press.

Sonnenschein, S. (1986a). Development of referential communication skills: How familiarity with a listener affects a speaker's production of redundant messages. *Developmental Psychology, 22,* 549–552.

Sonnenschein, S. (1986b). Development of referential communication: Deciding that a message is uninformative. *Developmental Psychology, 22,* 164–168.

Sonnenstein, F. L., Pleck, J. H., & Ku, L. C. (1989). Sexual activity, condom rise, and AIDS awareness among adolescent males. *Family Planning Perspectives, 21,* 152–158.

Sontag, L. W., Baker, C. T., & Nelson, V. L. (1958). Mental growth and personality development: A longitudinal study. *Monographs of the Society for Research in Child Development, 23* (2, Serial No. 68).

Sontag, S. (1972). The double standard of aging. *Saturday Review, 39,* 29–38.

Sorenson, R. C. (1973). *Adolescent sexuality in contemporary America.* New York: World Publishing.

Spearman, C. (1927). *The abilities of man.* New York: Macmillan.

Spears, W. C., & Hohle, R. H. (1967). Sensory and perceptual processes in infants. In Y. Brackbill (ed.), *Infancy and early childhood.* New York: Free Press.

Spelke, E. S. (1979). Perceiving bimodally specified events in infancy. *Developmental Psychology, 15,* 623–636.

Spelke, E. S. (1981). The infant's acquisition of knowledge of bimodally specified events. *Journal of Experimental Child Psychology, 31,* 279–299.

Spelke, E. S. (1985). Perception of unity, persistence, and identity: Thoughts on infants' conceptions of objects. In J. H. Mehler & R. Fox (Eds.), *Neonate cognition: Beyond the blooming, buzzing confusion.* Hillsdale, NJ: Erlbaum.

Spence, A. P. (1989). *Biology of human aging.* Englewood Cliffs, NJ: Prentice-Hall.

Spence, J. T., & Helmreich, R. L. (1978). *Masculinity and femininity: Their psychological dimensions, correlates, and antecedents.* Austin: University of Texas Press.

Spencer, H. (1873). *Principles of psychology.* New York: Appleton-Century-Crofts.

Spitzer, M. E. (1988). Taste acuity in institutionalized and non-institutionalized elderly men. *Journal of Gerontology, 43,* 71–74.

Spokane, A. R. (1985). A review of research on person-environment congruence in Holland's theory of careers. *Journal of Vocational Behavior, 26,* 306–343.

Spoor, A. (1967). Presbycusis values in relation to noise-induced hearing loss. *International Audiology, 6,* 48–57.

Sroufe, A. (1989). Quoted in Kohn, A. (1989, November) Suffer the restless children. *The Atlantic, 264,* 90–100.

Sroufe, L. A., & Rutter, M. (1984). The domain of developmental psychopathology. *Child Development, 55,* 17–29.

Stanhope, L., Bell, R. Q., & Parker-Cohen, N. Y. (1987). Temperament and helping behavior in preschool children. *Developmental Psychology, 23,* 347–353.

Stark, R. (1982). *The book of aphrodisiacs.* New York: Stein & Day.

Starr, B. D. (1987). Sexuality. In G. L. Maddox (Ed.), *The encyclopedia of aging* (pp. 606–608). New York: Springer.

Stechler, B., & Halton, A. (1982). Prenatal influences on human development. In B. B. Wolman (Ed.), *Handbook of developmental psychology.* Englewood Cliffs, NJ: Prentice-Hall.

Stein, P. (1976, November). *On same-sex and cross-sex friendships.* Paper presented at the meeting of the National Council of Family Relations, New York.

Stein, Z. H., Susser, M. W., Saenger, G., & Marolla, F. (1975). *Famine and human development: The Dutch hunger winter of 1944–1945.* New York: Oxford University Press.

Steinberg, L. D. (1981). Transformations in family relations at puberty. *Developmental Psychology, 17,* 833–840.

Steinberg, L. D. (1989). *Adolescence* (2nd ed.). New York: Alfred A. Knopf.

Steiner, J. E. (1979). Human facial expressions in response to taste and smell stimulation. In H. E. Reese & L. Lipsitt (Eds.), *Advances in child development and behavior* (Vol. 13). New York: Academic Press.

Steinschneider, A. (1970). Obstetrical medication and infant outcome: Some summary considerations. In W. B. Bowes, Y. Brackbill, E. Conway, & A. Steinschneider (Eds.), The effects of obstetrical medication on fetus and infant. *Monographs of the Society for Research in Child Development, 36* (4, Serial No. 137).

Stern, D. M. (1977). *The first relationship.* Cambridge, MA: Harvard University Press.

Stern, D. N., Spieker, S., & MacKain, K. (1982). Intonation contours as signals in maternal speech to prelinguistic infants. *Developmental Psychology, 18,* 727–735.

Sternberg, R. J. (1985). Beyond IQ: A triarchic theory of human intelligence. New York: Cambridge University Press.

Sternberg, R. J. (1986). *Intelligence applied: Understanding and increasing your intellectual skills.* New York: Harcourt, Brace, Jovanovich.

Sternglanz, S. H., & Serbin, L. A. (1974). Sex-role stereotyping in children's television programs. *Developmental Psychology, 10,* 710–715.

Steuer, F. B., Applefield, J. M., & Smith, R. (1971). Televised aggression and the interpersonal aggression of preschool children. *Journal of Experimental Child Psychology, 11,* 442–447.

Stevens, J. C., Bartoshuk, L. M., & Cain, W. S. (1984). Chemical senses and aging: Taste versus smell. *Chemical Senses, 9,* 167–179.

Stevens, J. C., Plantinga, A., & Cain, W. S. (1982). Reduction of odor and nasal pungency associated with aging. *Neurobiology of Aging, 3,* 125–132.

Stevens, R. (1979). Maternal smoking during pregnancy: Risks to the unborn baby. Unpublished manuscript. University of Wisconsin-Green Bay.

Stevens-Long, J. & Cobb, N. (1983). *Adolescence and young adulthood.* Palo Alto, CA.: Mayfield.

Stevenson, H. W. (1970). Learning in children. In P. H. Mussen (Ed.), *Carmichael's manual of child psychology* (3rd ed.), New York: Wiley.

Stevenson, M. R., & Black, K. N. (1988). Paternal absence and sex-role development: A meta-analysis. *Child Development, 59,* 793–814.

Stewart, R. B., Mobley, L. A., Van Tuyl, S. S., & Salvador, M. A. (1987). The firstborn's adjustment to the birth of a sibling: A longitudinal assessment. *Child Development, 58,* 341–355.

Stoddart, T., & Turiel, E. (1985). Children's concepts of cross-gender activities. *Child Development, 56,* 1241–1252.

Stodolsky, S., & Lesser, G. (1967). Learning patterns in the disadvantaged. *Harvard Educational Review, 37,* 546–593.

Stone, R., Cafferata, G. L., & Sangl, J. (1987). Caregivers of the frail elderly: A national profile. *The Gerontologist, 27,* 616–626.

Stott, D. H., & Latchford, S. A. (1976). Prenatal antecedents of child health, development, and behavior: An epidemiological report of incidence and association. *Journal of the American Academy of Child Psychiatry, 15,* 161–191.

Straus, M. A., Geller, R., & Steinmetz, S. (1980). *Behind closed doors.* New York: Doubleday.

Streib, G. L. (1977). Changing roles in the later years. In R. A. Kalish (Ed.), *The later years: Social applications of gerontology.* Monterey, CA: Brooks/Cole.

Streissguth, A. P., Martin, D. D., Martin, J. C., & Barr, H. M. (1981). The Seattle longitudinal prospective study of alcohol and pregnancy. *Neurobehavioral Toxicology and Teratology, 3,* 223–233.

Streissguth, A. P., Martin, D. D. Barr, H. M., & Sandman, B. M. (1984). Intrauterine alcohol and nicotine exposure: Attention and reaction time in 4-year-old children. *Developmental Psychology, 20,* 533–541.

Strommen, E. A. (1977). Friendship. In E. Donelson & J. Gullahorn (Eds.), *Women: A psychological perspective.* New York: Wiley.

Stuart, R. B., & Jacobson, J. (1979). Cited in Richards, M. & Petersen, A. C. (1987). Biological theoretical models of adolescent development. In V. B. Van Hasselt & M. Hersen (Eds.), *Handbook of adolescent psychology.* New York: Pergamon Press.

Sudnow, D. (1967). *Passing on.* Englewood Cliffs, NJ: Prentice-Hall.

Suggs, P. K. (1985). Discriminators of mutual helping behavior among older adults and their siblings. *Journal of Applied Gerontology, 4,* 63–70.

Sulik, K. K., Johnston, M. C., & Webb, M. A. (1981). Fetal alcohol syndrome: Embryogenesis in a mouse model. *Science, 214,* 936–938.

Sunderland, A., Watts, K., Baddeley, A., & Harris, J. E. (1986). Subjective memory assessment and test performance in elderly adults. *Journal of Gerontology, 41,* 376–384.

Super, D. E. (1980). A life span, life space approach to career development. *Journal of Vocational Behavior, 16,* 282–298.

Sussman, M. B. (1965). Relationships of adult children with their parents in the United States. In E. Shanas & G. Streib (Eds.), *Social structure of the family: Generational relations.* Englewood Cliffs, NJ: Prentice-Hall.

Sutton-Smith, B. (1967). The role of play in cognitive development. *Young Children, 22,* 361–370.

Sutton-Smith, B. (1985). The child at play. *Psychology Today, 19,* 64–65.

Taft, L. T., & Cohen, H. J. (1967). Neonatal and infant reflexology. In T. Hellmuth (Ed.), *Exceptional infant* (Vol. 1). New York: Brunner/Mazel.

Tallmer, M., Formaneck, R., & Tallmer, J. (1974). Factors influencing children's conceptions of death. *Journal of Clinical Child Psychology, 3,* 17–19.

Tamir, L. M. (1982). Men at middle age: Developmental transitions. *Annals of the American Academy of Political and Social Science, 464,* 47–56.

Tamis-LeMonda, C., & Bornstein, M. H. (April 1986). *Mother-infant interaction: The selectivity of encouraging attention.* Paper presented at the International Conference on Infancy Studies, Los Angeles.

Tanner, J. M. (1962). *Growth at adolescence.* Oxford: Blackwell Scientific.

Tanner, J. M. (1970). Physical growth. In P. H. Mussen (Ed.), *Carmichael's manual of child psychology.* New York: Wiley.

Tanner, J. M. (1973). Growing up. *Scientific American, 229(3),* 34–43.

Tanner, J. M. (1978). *Fetus into man: Physical growth from conception to maturity.* Cambridge, MA: Harvard University Press.

Taub, H. A. (1979). Comprehension and memory of prose materials by young and old adults. *Experimental Aging Research, 5,* 3–13.

Tavris, C., & Wade, C. (1984) *The longest war: Sex differences in perspective* (2nd ed.). New York: Harcourt Brace Jovanovich.

Taylor, I. A. (1974). Patterns of creativity and aging. In E. Pfeiffer (Ed.), *Successful aging.* Durham, NC: Duke University Center for the Study of Aging and Human Development.

Teachman, J. D., Polonko, K. A., & Scanzoni, J. (1987). Demography of the family. In M. B. Sussman & S. K. Steinmetz (Eds.), *Handbook of marriage and the family* (pp. 3–36). New York: Plenum.

Terrace, H. S., Pettito, L. A., Sanders, R. J., & Bever, T. G. (1979). Can an ape create a sentence? *Science, 206,* 891–202.

Tessman, L. H. (1978). *Children of parting parents.* New York: Aronson.

Thevenin, D. M., Eilers, R. E., Oller, D. K., & Lavoie, L. (1985). Where's the drift in babbling drift? A cross-linguistic study. *Applied Psycholinguistics, 6,* 3–15.

Thomas, A., & Chess, S. (1977). *Temperament and development.* New York: Brunner-Mazel.

Thomas, A., Chess, S., & Birch, H. G. (1970). The origin of personality. *Scientific American, 223,* 102–109.

Thomas, A., Chess, S., Birch, H. G., Hertiz, M. E., & Korn, S. (1963). *Behavioral individuality in early childhood.* New York: New York University Press.

Thompson, R. A., Lamb, M. E., & Estes, D. (1982). Stability of infant-mother attachment and its relationships to changing life circumstances in an unselected middle-class sample. *Child Development, 53,* 144–148.

Thompson, C. (1974). The role of women in this culture. In J. Strouse (Ed.), *Women and analysis: Dialogues on psychoanalytic views of femininity.* New York: Grossman Publishers.

Thornburg, H. D. (1978). *The bubblegum years: Sticking with kids from 9–13.* Tucson, AZ: H.E.L.P. Books.

Thurstone, L. L. (1938). Primary mental abilities. *Psychometric Monographs* (No. 1).

Tieger, T. (1980). On the biological basis of sex differences in aggression. *Child Development, 51,* 943–963.

Tobian L. (1983) Salt and hypertension. In J. Genest, O. Knochel, P. Hamet, & M. Cantin (Eds.), *Hypertension,* New York: McGraw-Hill.

Tobin-Richards, M., Boxer, A., & Petersen, A. C. (1983). The psychological impact of pubertal change: Sex differences in perceptions of self during early adolescence. In J. Brooks-Gunn & A. C. Petersen (Eds.), *Girls at puberty: Biological, psychological and social perspectives.* New York: Plenum.

Tomlinson, P. S. (1987). Spousal differences in marital satisfaction during transition to parenthood. *Nursing Research, 36,* 239–243.

Torgersen, A. M., & Kringlen, E. (1978). Genetic aspects of temperamental differences in infants: A study of same-sexed twins. *Journal of the American Academy of Child Psychiatry, 17,* 433–444.

Tortora, C. J., & Anagnostakos, N. P. (1990). *Principles of anatomy and physiology* (6th ed.). New York: Harper & Row.

Toseland, R. W., Rossiter, C. M., & Labrecque, M. S. (1989). The effectiveness of peer-led and professionally led groups to support family caregivers. *The Gerontologist, 29,* 465–471.

Townsend, J. W., Klein, R. E., Irwin, M. H., Owens, W., Yarbrough, C., & Engle, P. L. (1982). Nutrition and preschool mental development. In D. A. Wagner & H. W. Stevenson (Eds.), *Cultural perspectives on child development.* San Francisco: W. H. Freeman.

Traub, G. S. (1983). Correlations of shyness with depression, anxiety, and academic performance. *Psychological Reports, 52,* 849–850.

Travin, A., Bluestone, H., Coleman, E., Cullen, K., & Melella, J. (1986). Pedophile types and treatment perspectives. *Journal of Forensics Science, 31,* 614–620.

Treat, N. J., Poon, L. W., & Fozard, J. L. (1981). Age, imagery, and practice in paired-associated learning. *Experimental Aging Research, 7,* 337–342.

Trehub, S. E. (1973). Infants' sensitivity to vowel and tonal contrasts. *Developmental Psychology, 9,* 91–96.

Trehub, S. E., & Schneider, B. (Eds.) (1985). *Auditory development in infancy.* New York: Plenum.

Trehub, S. E., Schneider, B., & Endman, M. (1980). Developmental changes in infants' sensitivity to octave ‒

+ and noises. *Journal of Experimental Child Psychology, 29,* 283–293.

Troll, L. E. (1971). The family of later life: A decade review. *Journal of Marriage and the Family, 33,* 263–290.

Troll, L. E. (1972). *The salience of members of three-generation families for one another.* Paper presented at the annual meeting of the American Psychological Association, Honolulu.

Troll, L. E. (1975). *Early and middle adulthood.* Monterey, CA: Brooks/Cole.

Troll, L. E. (1982). *Continuations: Adult development and aging.* Monterey, CA: Brooks/Cole.

Troll, L. E. (1983). Grandparents: The family watchdogs. In T. Brubaker (Ed.), *Family relationships in later life* (pp. 63–74). Beverly Hills, CA: Sage.

Troll, L. E. (1984, August). *Old women: "Poor, dumb, and ugly."* Invited address, Division 35, American Psychological Association, Toronto.

Troll, L. E. (1985). *Early and middle adulthood* (2nd ed.). Englewood Cliffs, NJ: Prentice-Hall.

Troll, L. E. & Bengtson, V. L. (1979). Generations in the family. In W. Burr, R. Hill, I. Nye, & I. Reiss (Eds.), *Contemporary theories about the family.* New York: Free Press.

Troll, L. E. & Bengston, V. L. (1982). Intergenerational relations throughout the life span. In B. B. Wolman (Ed.), *Handbook of developmental psychology.* Englewood Cliffs, NJ: Prentice-Hall.

Troll, L. E., Miller, S., & Atchley, R. (1979). *Families of later life.* Belmont, CA: Wadsworth.

Tross, S. & Hirsch, D. A. (1988). Psychological distress and neuropsychological complications of HIV infection and AIDS. *American Psychologist, 43,* 929–934.

Turiel, E., Edwards, C. P., & Kohlberg, L. (1978). Moral development in Turkish children, adolescents, and young adults. *Journal of Cross-cultural Psychology, 9,* 75–86.

Turner, B. F. (1982). Sex-related differences in aging. In B. B. Wolman (Ed.), *Handbook of developmental psychology.* Englewood Cliffs, NJ: Prentice-Hall.

U.S. Bureau of the Census (1980). *Population and housing.* Current Population Reports, Washington, DC: U.S. Government Printing Office.

U.S. Bureau of the Census. (1987). *Statistical abstracts of the United States 1988* (108th ed.). Washington, DC.

U.S. Bureau of the Census (1989). *Changes in American family life. Current Population Reports: Special Studies.* Series P-23, No. 163.

U.S. Bureau of the Census (1989). *Studies in marriage and the family.* Current Population Reports, Series P-23, No. 162. Washington, DC: U.S. Government Printing Office.

U.S. Bureau of Labor Statistics (1987). *Employment and earnings.* Washington, DC: U.S. Government Printing Office.

U.S. Department of Labor. (1987). *Handbook of labor statistics.* Washington, DC: U.S. Government Printing Office.

U.S. Government Printing Office. (1987). *Statistical Abstract of the United States 1986* (106th ed.). Washington, DC.

Udry, J. R., Billy, J. O. G., Morris, N. M., Groff, T. R., Raj, M. H. (1985). Serum androgenic hormones motivate sexual behavior in adolescent boys. *Fertility and Sterility, 43,* 90–94.

Ulatowska, H. K., Cannito, M. P., Hayashi, M. M., & Fleming, S. G. (1985). Language abilities in the elderly. In H. K. Ulatowska (Ed.), *The aging brain: Communication in the elderly* (pp. 125–139). San Diego: College-Hill Press.

Ullian, D. Z. (1976). The development of conceptions of masculinity and femininity. In B. Lloyd & J. Archer (Eds.), *Exploring sex differences.* New York: Academic Press.

Umberson, D., & Hughes, M. (1987). The impact of physical attractiveness on achievement and psychological well-being. *Social Psychology Quarterly, 50,* 227–236.

Unger, R. K. (1979). Toward a redefinition of sex and gender. *American Psychologist, 34,* 1085–1094.

Upp, M. (1983). Relative importance of various income sources of the aged. *Social Security Bulletin, 46,* 3–10.

Uzgiris, I. C. (1984). Imitation in infancy: Its interpersonal aspects. In M. Perlmutter (Ed.), *The Minnesota Symposia on Child Psychology* (Vol. 17, pp. 1–31). Hillsdale, N.J.: Erlbaum.

Vaiilant, G. E. (1977). *Adaptation to life.* Boston: Little, Brown.

Vander Linde, E., Morrongiello, B. A., & Rovee-Collier, C. (1985). Determinants of retention in 8-week-old infants. *Developmental Psychology, 21,* 602–613.

Van der Wal, J. (1989). The aftermath of suicide: A review of empirical evidence; *Omega, 20,* 149–171.

Vaughn, B. E., & Langlois, J. H. (1983). Physical attractiveness as a correlate of peer status and social competence in preschool children. *Developmental Psychology, 19,* 561–567.

Veatch, R. M. (1972). Brain death: Welcome definition . . . or dangerous judgment? *Hastings Center Report, 2.*

Veevers, J. E. (1979). Voluntary childlessness: A review of issues and evidence. *Marriage and Family Review, 2,* 3–26.

Vener, A., & Stewart, C. (1974). Adolescent sexual behavior in middle America revisited: 1970–1973. *Journal of Marriage and the Family, 36,* 728–735.

Ventura, J. N., & Stevenson, M. B. (1986). Relations of mothers' and fathers' reports of infant temperament, parents' psychological functioning, and family characteristics. *Merrill-Palmer Quarterly, 32,* 272–289.

Vernon, P. E. (1979). *Intelligence: Heredity and environment.* San Francisco: W. H. Freeman.

Volpe, J. (1976). *The development of children's conceptions of friendship.* Unpublished master's thesis. The Catholic University of America.

von Hofsten, C. (1982). Eye-hand coordination in newborns. *Developmental Psychology, 18,* 450–461.

Vurpillot, E. (1968). The development of scanning strategies and their relation to visual differentiation. *Journal of Experimental Child Psychology, 6,* 632–650.

Vygotsky, L. (1986). *Thought and language* (A. Kozulin, Trans. & Rev.). Cambridge, MA: The MIT Press.

Waber, D. P. (1979). Cognitive abilities and sex-related variations in the maturation of cerebral cortical functions. In M. A. Wittig and A. C. Petersen (Eds.), *Sex-related differences in cognitive functioning. Developmental issues.* New York: Academic Press.

Wahler, R. G., Winkel, G. H., Peterson, R. L., & Morrison, D. C. (1968). Mothers as therapists for their own children. In H. C. Quay (Ed.), *Children's behavior disorders* (pp. 92–95). New York: Van Nostrand Reinhold.

Waldman, E. (1983). Labor force statistics from a family perspective. *Monthly Labor Review, 98,* 14–18.

Waldrop, M. L., & Halverson, C. L. (1975). Intensive and extensive peer behavior: Longitudinal and cross-sectional analyses. *Child Development, 46,* 19–26.

Walk, R. D. (1981). *Perceptual development.* Monterey, CA: Brooks/Cole.

Walker, L. J. (1982). The sequentiality of Kohlberg's stages of moral development. *Child Development, 53,* 1330–1336.

Walker, L. J. (1984). Sex differences in the development of moral reasoning: A critical review. *Child Development, 55,* 677–691.

Walker, L. J., & Richards. B. S. (1979). Stimulating transitions in moral reasoning as a function of stage of cognitive development. *Developmental Psychology, 15,* 95–103.

Wallace, D. B. (1985). Giftedness and the construction of a creative life. In F. D. Horowitz & M. O'Brien (Eds.), *The gifted and talented: Developmental perspectives.* Washington, DC: American Psychological Association.

Wallace, R. W., & Noelker, L. S. (1984). *Conceptualizing family caregiving: An application of role theory.* Paper presented at the 37th Annual Scientific Meeting of the Gerontological Society of America, San Antonio, TX.

Wallach, M. A. (1985). Creativity testing and giftedness. In F. D. Horowitz & M. O'Brien (Eds.), *The gifted and talented: Developmental perspectives.* Washington, DC: American Psychological Association.

Wallerstein, J. S. (1985). Children of divorce: Preliminary report of a ten-year follow-up of older children and adolescents. *Journal of the American Academy of Child Psychiatry, 24,* 545–553.

Wallerstein, J. S. (1987). Children of divorce: Report of a ten-year follow-up of early latency-age children. *American Journal of Orthopsychiatry, 57,* 199–211.

Wallerstein, J. S., & Blakeslee, S. (1989). *Second chances: Men, women, and children a decade after divorce.* New York: Ticknor and Fields.

Wallerstein, J. S., & Kelly, J. B. (1974). The effects of parental divorce: The adolescent experience. In J. Anthony & C. Koupernik (Eds.), *The child in his family: Children at psychiatric risk* (Vol. 3). New York: Wiley.

Wallerstein, H. S., & Kelly, J. B. (1975). The effects of parental divorce: Experiences of the preschool child. *Journal of the American Academy of Child Psychiatry, 14,* 600–616.

Wallerstein, J. S., & Kelly, J. B. (1976). The effects of parental divorce: Experiences of the child in later latency. *American Journal of Orthopsychiatry, 46* (b), 256–267.

Wallerstein, J. S., & Kelly, J. B. (1980). *Surviving the break-up: How children and parents cope with divorce.* New York: Basic.

Walsh, D. (1982). The development of visual information processes in adulthood and old age. In R. Sekuler, D. Kline, & K. Dismukes (Eds.), *Aging and human visual function* (pp. 203–280). New York: Alan R. Liss.

Warr, P. B. (1982). A national study of non-financial employment commitment. *Journal of Occupational Psychology, 55,* 297–312.

Wass, H., & Olejnik, S. F. (1983). An analysis and evaluation of research in cognition and learning among older adults. *Educational Gerontology, 9,* 323–337.

Wass, H., Roup, J. L., Cerullo, K., Martel, L. G., Mingione, L. A., & Sperring, A. M. (1988). Adolescents' interest in and views of destructive themes in rock music. *Omega, 19,* 177–186.

Waters, E., Wippman, J., & Sroufe, L. A. (1979). Attachment, positive affect, and competence in the peer group: Two studies in construct validation. *Child Development, 50,* 821–829.

Watkins, J. J. (1974). Concept and measurement of primary memory. *Psychological Bulletin, 81,* 695–711.

Watson, J. B. (1925). *Behaviorism.* New York: Norton.

Watson, J. B., & Rayner, R. (1920). Conditioned emotional reactions. *Journal of Experimental Psychology, 3,* 1–14.

Watson, J. S., & Ramey, C. T. (1972). Reactions to response-contingent stimulation in early infancy. *Merrill-Palmer Quarterly, 18,* 219–227.

Watson, M. M., & Jackowitz, E. R. (1984). Agents and recipient objects in the development of early symbolic play. *Child Development, 55,* 1091–1097.

Watson, R. I. (1978). *The great psychologists* (4th ed.). Philadelphia: Lippincott.

Weatherly, D. (1964). Self-perceived rate of physical maturation and personality in late adolescence. *Child Development, 35,* 1197–1210.

Wechsler, D. (1958). *The measurement and appraisal of adult intelligence* (4th ed.). Baltimore: Williams and Wilkins.

Wechsler, D. (1974). *Manual for the Wechsler Intelligence Scale for Children—Revised.* New York: The Psychological Corporation.

Weg, R. B. (Ed.). (1983). *Sexuality in the later years.* New York: Academic Press.

Weiffenbach, J. M., Baum, B. J., & Burghauser, R. (1982) Taste thresholds: Quality specific variation with human aging. *Journal of Gerontology, 37,* 372–377.

Weill, B. C. (1930). "Are you training your child to be happy?" *Lesson material in child management, 1.* Washington, DC: U.S. Government Printing Office.

Weisberg, P. (1963). Social and non-social conditioning of infant vocalizations. *Child Development, 34,* 377–388.

Weisman, A. D., & Worden, J. W. (1975). Psychosocial analysis of cancer deaths. *Omega, 6,* 61–75.

Weiss, B., Williams, J. H., Margen, S., Abrams, B., Caan, B., Citron, L. J., Cox, C., McKibben, J., Ogar, D., & Schultz, S. (1980). Behavioral responses to artificial food colors. *Science, 207,* 1487–1489.

Weissberg, J. A., & Paris, S. G. (1986). Young children's remembering in different contexts: A reinterpretation of Istomina's study. *Child Development, 57,* 1123–1129.

Weitzman, L. J. (1984). Sex-role socialization: A focus on women. In J. Freeman (Ed.), *Women: A feminist perspective* (3rd ed.). Palo Alto, CA: Mayfield.

Wellborn, S. N. (1987, April 13). "How genes shape personality." *U.S News and World Report,* 58–66.

Weller, E. B., Weller, R. A., Fristad, M. A., Cain, S. E., & Bowes, J. M. (1988). Should children attend their parent's funeral? *Journal of the American Academy of Child and Adolescent Psychiatry, 27,* 559–562.

Wertheimer, M. (1961). Psychomotor coordination of auditory and visual space at birth. *Science, 134,* 1692.

Whalen, C. K., Henker, B., & Dotemoto, S. (1980). Methylphenidate and hyperactivity: Effects on teacher behaviors. *Science, 208,* 1280–1282.

Whitbourne, S. K. (1986). *Adult development,* (2nd. ed.). New York: Praeger.

Whitbourne, S. K., & Waterman, A. S. (1979). Psychosocial development during the adult years: Age and cohort comparisons. *Developmental Psychology, 15,* 373–378.

White, R. W. (1975). *Lives in progress: A study of the natural growth of personality* (3rd ed.). New York: Holt, Rinehart & Winston.

White, C. B., Bushnell, N., & Regnemer, J. L. (1978). Moral development in Bahamian school children: A three year examination of Kohlberg's stages of moral development. *Developmental Psychology, 14,* 58–65.

White, E., Elsom, B., & Prawat, R. (1978). Children's conceptions of death. *Child Development, 49,* 307–310.

Whitehurst, G. J. (1982). Language development. In B. B. Wolman (Ed.), *Handbook of developmental psychology.* Englewood Cliffs, NJ: Prentice-Hall.

Whiting, B. B., & Whiting, J. W. M. (1975). *Children of six cultures: A psychocultural analysis.* Cambridge, MA: Harvard University Press.

Whorf, B. L. (1956). *Language, thought, and reality.* New York: Wiley.

Wilkinson, L. C., & Marrett, C. B. (Eds.). (1985). *Gender influences in classroom interaction.* Orlando: Academic Press.

Wilkinson, R. T., & Allison, S. (1989). Age and simple reaction time: Decade differences for 5325 subjects. *Journal of Gerontology: Psychological Sciences, 44,* 29–35.

Will, J. A., Self, P. A., & Datan, N. (1976). Maternal behavior and perceived sex of infant. *American Journal of Orthopsychiatry, 46,* 135–139.

Willerman, L. (1975). *Individual and group differences.* New York: Harper's College Press.

Willerman, L. (1979). *The psychology of individual and group differences.* San Francisco: W. H. Freeman.

Willerman, L., & Plomin, R. (1973). Activity level in children and their parents. *Child Development, 44,* 854–858.

Williams, J. H. (1983). *Psychology of women: Behavior in a psychosocial context.* New York: W. W. Norton.

Williams, J. W., & Stith, M. (1980). *Middle childhood: Behavior and development* (2nd ed.). New York: Macmillan.

Williams, T. R. (1965). *The Dunsun: A North Borneo Society.* New York: Holt, Rinehart & Winston.

Williamson, J. B., Evans, L., & Munley, A. (1980). *Aging and society.* New York: Holt, Rinehart, and Winston.

Wilson, L., Zurcher, L., McAdams, L., & Curtis, R. (1975). Stepfathers and stepchildren: An exploratory analysis from two national surveys. *Journal of Marriage and the Family, 37,* 526–536.

Wilson, W. C. (1975). The distribution of selected sexual attitudes and behaviors among the adult population of the United States. *Journal of Sex Research, 11,* 46–54.

Wimmer, H., Gruber, S., & Peiner, J. (1985). Young children's conception of lying: Moral intuition and the denotation and connotation of "to be." *Developmental Psychology, 21,* 993–995.

Winer, G. A. (1980). Class inclusion reasoning in children: A review of the empirical literature. *Child Development, 51,* 309–328.

Wingfield, A., Lahar, C. J., & Stine, E. A. L. (1989). Age and decision strategies in running memory for speech: Effects of prosody and linguistic structure. *Journal of Gerontology: Psychological Sciences, 44,* 106–113.

Winick, M., Meyer, K., & Harris, R. C. (1975). Malnutrition and environmental enrichment by adoption. *Science, 190,* 1173–1175.

Winick, M., & Russo, P. (1969). Head circumferences and cellular growth of the brain in normal and marasmic children. *Journal of Pediatrics, 74,* 774–778.

Winn, R., & Newton, N. (1982). Sexuality in aging: A study of 106 cultures. *Archives of Sexual Behavior, 11,* 283–298.

Wishart, J. G. (1986). Siblings as models in early infant learning. *Child Development, 57,* 1232–1240.

Wishart, J. G., Bower, T. G. R., & Dunkeld, J. (1978). Reaching in the dark. *Perception, 7,* 507–512.

Wohlwill, J. F. (1973). *The study of behavioral development.* New York: Academic Press.

Wolf, D. C. (1978). *Close friendship patterns of older lesbians.* Paper presented at the annual meeting of the Gerontological Society of America, Dallas.

Wolf, F. M., & Larson, G. L. (1981). On why adolescent formal operators may not be creative thinkers. *Adolescence, 16,* 345–348.

Wolff, P. H. (1966). The causes, controls, and organization of behavior in the neonate. *Psychological Issues,* Vol. 5, No. 1, Monograph 17.

Wolff, P. H. (1971). Mother-infant relations at birth. In J. G. Howels (Ed.), *Modern perspectives in international child psychiatry.* New York: Brunner-Mazel.

Wolman, B. B. (Ed.) (1982). *Handbook of developmental psychology.* Englewood Cliffs, NJ: Prentice-Hall.

Wooley, S. C., & Wooley, O. W. (1980). Eating disorders: Obesity and anorexia. In A. M. Brodsky & R. Hare-

Mustin (Eds.), *Women and psychotherapy*. New York: Guilford Press.

Wormith, S. J., Pankhurst, D., & Moffitt, A. R. (1975). Frequency discrimination by young infants. *Child Development, 46,* 272–275.

Wozniak, R. H. (1986). Notes toward a co-constructive theory of the emotion/cognition relationships. In D. Bearison & H. Zimiles (Eds.), *Thought and motion: Developmental perspectives.* Hillsdale, NJ: Erlbaum.

Yankelovich, Skelly, & White, Inc. (1977). *Raising children in a changing society: The General Mills American Family Report, 1976–1977.* Minneapolis: General Mills, Inc.

Yeates, K. O., Macphee, D., Campbell, L. A., & Ramey, C. T. (1983). Maternal IQ and home environment as determinants of early childhood intellectual competence: A developmental analysis. *Developmental Psychology, 19,* 731–739.

Yogev, S. (1981). Do professional women have egalitarian marital relationships? *Journal of Marriage and the Family, 43,* 865–871.

Yonas, A., Cleaves, W., & Pettersen, L. (1978). Development of sensitivity to pictorial depth. *Science, 200,* 77–79.

Yonas, A., Pettersen, L., & Granrud, C. E. (1982). Infants' sensitivity to familiar size as information for distance. *Child Development, 53,* 1285–1290.

Yonas, A., Petterson, L., Lockman, J., & Eisenberg, P. (1980). *The perception of impending collision in three-month-old infants.* Paper presented at the International Conference of Infant Studies, New Haven, Connecticut.

Young, R. J., & Semail, A. H. (1976). Personality differences of adult men before and after a physical fitness program. *Research Quarterly, 47,* 513–519.

Yussen, S. R., & Levy, V. M. (1975). Developmental changes in predicting one's own span of short-term memory. *Journal of Experimental Child Psychology, 19,* 502–508.

Zabin, L. S., Hirsh, M. B., Smith, E. A., & Hardy, J. B. (1984). Adolescent sexual attitudes and behavior: Are they consistent? *Family Planning Perspectives, 16,* 181–186.

Zahn-Waxler, C., & Radke-Yarrow, M. (1982). The development of altruism: Alternative research strategies. In N. Eisenberg-Berg (Ed.), *The development of prosocial behavior.* New York: Academic Press.

Zahn-Waxler, C., Friedman, S. L., & Cummings, E. M. (1983). Children's emotions and behaviors in response to infants' cries. *Child Development, 54,* 1522–1528.

Zajonc, R. B., & Markus, G. (1975). Birth order and intellectual development. *Psychological Review, 82,* 74–88.

Zakin, D. F. (1983). Physical attractiveness, sociability, athletic ability, and children's preference for their peers. *Journal of Psychology, 115,* 117–122.

Zarit, S. H., & Toseland, R. W. (1989). Current and future direction in family caregiving research. *The Gerontologist, 29,* 481–483.

Zeits, C. R., & Prince, R. M. (1982). Child effects on parents. In B. B. Wolman (Ed.), *Handbook of developmental psychology.* Englewood Cliffs, NJ: Prentice-Hall.

Zelazo, P. R. & Kearsley, R. B. (1980). The emergence of functional play in infants: Evidence for a major cognitive transition. *Journal of Applied Developmental Psychology, 1,* 95–117.

Zelnick, M. & Kantner, J. L. (1977). Sexual and contraceptive experience of young unmarried women in the United States, 1976 and 1971. *Family Planning Perspectives, 9,* 55–71.

Zelnick, M., & Kantner, J. L. (1980). Sexual activity, contraceptive use, and pregnancy among metropolitan-area teenagers: 1971–1979. *Family Planning Perspectives, 12*(5), 230–237.

Zigler, E., & Lang, M. E. (1986). The "Gourmet Baby" and the "Little Wildflower." *Zero to Three, 7,* 8–12.

Zill, N., & Rogers, C. C. (1988). Recent trends in the well-being of children in the United States and their implications for public policy. In A. J. Cherlin (Ed.), *The changing American family and public policy.* Washington, DC: The Urban Institute Press

Index

Abnormal personality, 427–31
Abramovitch, R., 230, 464
Abranavel, E., 229
Accommodation function of intelligence, 258
Achenbach, T. M., 48
Achte, K., 642
Ackerman, B. P., 360
Acquired Immune Deficiency Syndrome (AIDS), 83, 152, 647, 655
Acrodolo, L. P., 184, 190, 193, 195
Activity theory of aging, 521
Adams, G. R., 110, 113, 118, 467
Adams, R. J., 180
Adelson, J., 467, 499
Aderman, D., 647
ADHD (Attention-deficit hyperactivity disorder), 212–13
Adler, Alfred, 394
Adler, R. F., 620
Adler, S., 542
Adolescence
   body development, 95–96, 97–99, 101, 102, 103, 105
   brain development, 95–96
   cognitive development, 278–81, 285
   creativity, 332–34
   death, concepts of, 653, 654–55
   divorce, reactions to, 484
   employment, 537–38, 542
   and family life cycle, 467–69
   gender roles, 591–94
   language development, 361–63
   and maternal employment, 461
   moral development, 552, 556, 558, 561–63
   personality development, 392, 396, 399–400, 404–5, 413, 414, 424, 425
   play, 533–34
   sexuality, 125, 140–45, 146–47
   social relations, 497, 498, 499, 500, 505, 511–13, 516–17, 518
   timing of, 98, 107–12

Adrenogenital syndrome, 585
Adulthood. See also Old age
   attention, 214–15
   cognitive development, 281–86
   creativity, 334–35
   death, concepts of, 654–56
   education, 237–38, 620–21
   of family, 469–77
   gender roles, 594–97
   intelligence, 311–18
   intergenerational relations, 469, 470, 471–72
   language development, 364–65
   learning, 234–39
   memory, 245–51
   moral development, 564–66
   perceptual development, 180–82, 187, 192
   personality development, 392–93, 395–96, 400–402, 413–14, 415–17, 424
   physical development, 96, 97, 99, 101, 102, 103, 105
   play, 534–36
   sexuality, 145–55
   sibling relationships, 472–74
   social relations, 500, 504, 506, 517–20
Affordances (environmental), 202
Afterbirth, 88
Age norms, 6, 7, 14, 29
Aggression, 231–34, 549, 550, 589–91
Aging. See Old age
Ahr, P. R., 273
AIDS (Acquired Immune Deficiency Syndrome), 83, 152, 647, 655
Aiken, L. R., 106
Ainsworth, M. D. S., 65, 453
Aisenberg, R. B., 629, 638, 651, 656
Albert, M. C., 364
Albert, M. L., 364, 365, 366
Aldous, R., 470
Alegria, J. R., 196
Algozyne, R., 119
Allan, G., 473

Allen, L., 500
Allen, L., 311
Allen, V., 110
Allison, S., 105
Allport, Gordon, 403
Alpaugh, P. K., 334
Alter-Reid, K., 139
Altruism, 501–4
Altshuler, L., 308
Alwitt, L., 212
Alzheimer's disease, 630
Amato, P. R., 487
American Association of Mental Deficiency (AAMD), 306
American Psychiatric Association, 212
American Psychological Association, 48
Amniotic sac, 76
Amsterdam, D. K., 411
Anagnostakos, Nicholas P., 71, 80, 97, 103
Anal stage of development, 390, 391
Anastasi, A., 12, 300, 305
Anderson, D. R., 212, 213, 214
Anderson, J. R., 207, 240, 241
Anderson, J. W., 236
Anderson, T. B., 520
Andres, D., 460, 461
Andrews, K., 191
Androgens, 127
Androgyny, 615–17
Animal behavior, 30, 341–43, 450–51
Animism, 267–68
Ankus, M. N., 246
Anthony, S., 650, 653
Anthropology, 8, 9, 24, 27–28, 642–44. See also Cross-cultural research
Antonak, R. F., 308
Antonucci, T. C., 519, 541
Apfel, N., 529
Apgar Screening Test, 88–89
Aphasia, 364, 365–66
Aphrodisiacs, 125
Appelbaum, M. I., 45, 324
Applefield, J. M., 45
Apps, J. W., 238

Araji, S., 139
Aranya, N., 542
Archibald, H. C., 658
Arenberg, D., 234
Arend, A., 455
Aries, P., 17
Arieti, S., 334
Aristotle, 11, 16–17
Arlin, Patricia K., 283, 284
Aro, H., 108
Aronfreed, J., 549
Arousal modulation theory of play, 527–28
Artificialism, 268
Asher, J. J., 362
Asher, Steven R., 510, 514, 516
Aslin, R. N., 184, 185, 186
Assimilation function of intelligence, 258
Atchley, R., 470, 520
Atchley, R. C., 22, 157
Atkinson, J., 595
Attachment, 449–55
Attention, 208–15
Attention-deficit hyperactivity disorder (ADHD), 212–13
Attig, T., 654
Attractiveness stereotype, 109, 113–16, 118–20
Atwater, J. B., 607
Audition, 182–90, 364, 366
Austin, J. H., 328
Authoritarian parenting, 456–57
Authoritative parenting, 456–57
Autocosmic play, 525

Baby biography, 19, 47
Bacharach, V. R., 358
Bachman, J. G., 537
Backer, T. E., 152, 655
Baddeley, A., 251
Baer, D. M., 551
Baillargeon, R., 256, 265, 270, 271
Baily, M., 542
Baj, J., 439
Bakeman, R., 452
Baker, A., 229
Baker, B. L., 306
Baker, C. T., 311
Baker, D. W., 282, 287
Baker, S. W., 585, 586
Baldwin, J. M., 409
Baldwin, W., 144
Ball, D. W., 282, 287
Balogh, 193
Baltes, M. M., 315
Baltes, P. B. F., 63–64, 313, 315, 318
Bammel, G., 534
Banahan, F., 470
Bandura, Albert, 24, 26, 226, 227, 229, 230, 231, 233, 549, 606

Bane, M. J., 444, 445, 481, 482
Banilivy, M., 115
Bank, S., 462, 473
Banks, M. S., 171, 172, 173, 174, 175, 177, 178, 179
Barglow, P., 454
Barik, H. C., 223
Barkley, R. A., 212
Barnett, R. C., 448, 541, 608
Baron, J. N., 540
Barr, H. M., 85
Barrera, M. E., 176
Barriere, M., 186
Barron, F., 327, 328, 329
Bars, P., 192
Barton, D., 355
Bartoshuk, L. M., 192, 195
Baruch, G. K., 448, 541, 608
Barusch, A. S., 472
Bases, R., 78
Basow, S. A., 598
Batchelor, W. F., 152, 655
Bates, E., 352
Bates, J. E., 454
Baum, A., 152
Baum, B. J., 192
Baum, C. G., 115
Baum, M., 639, 640
Baum, R. C., 639, 640
Baumann, D. J., 500
Baumeister, R. F., 615
Baumrind, Diana, 48, 457, 458, 616
Bayley, Nancy, 104, 303, 311, 312, 324, 326, 418
Bayley Scales of Infant Development, 303–4
Beach, D. R., 243
Bearison, D. J., 501
Beauchamp, G. K., 191, 192
Bechtold, H. P., 177
Beck, A. A., 519
Becker, D., 646, 659
Beckwith, L., 91
Bedford, V. H., 472, 473
Bee, H., 375
Beecher, H. K., 628
Begin, G., 514
Begun, A., 462, 464
Behavioral approach, 11, 23, 24, 25–27, 65, 216–25, 367–69. *See also* Operant conditioning
Behavior modification, 222
Beilin, H., 373
Belal, A., 187
Beland, F., 470
Bell, A. P., 138, 143, 161
Bell, B., 180, 182
Bell, D., 658
Bell, R. Q., 419
Bell, R. R., 519

Bell, S. M., 65, 453
Bellugi, Ursula, 342, 350, 368
Belmont, L., 325
Belsky, J., 447, 454, 509
Bem, Sandra, 610, 611, 615, 616
Bem Sex Role Inventory (BSRI), 615–16
Benack, S., 506
Benasich, A., 197
Benedict, H., 354
Benedict, Ruth, 24, 27
Bengtson, V. L., 413, 416, 470
Benn, R. K., 461
Bennett, T. L., 220
Ben-Yehuda, A., 538
Ben-Zeev, S., 362
Bereavement, 657–60
Berger, R. M., 160
Bergman, A., 308
Bergman, M., 189
Bergman, T., 172, 175
Berk, L. E., 373
Berkowitz, M. W., 568
Berlyne, D. E., 527
Berman, P. W., 448
Bernasconi, M., 650, 651, 652
Berndt, R., 531
Berndt, T. J., 465, 496, 497, 498, 499, 563
Bernholtz, C. D., 182
Bernstein, B., 375
Berscheid, E., 115, 116, 118
Bertoncini, J., 186
Bettelheim, Bruno, 552, 602
Bettes, K., 186
Bever, T. G., 343
Bhrolchain, M. N., 483
Biases, in research, 51, 56
Bielby, D. D., 541
Bielby, W. T., 540, 541
Biemer, D. J., 510
Bierman, K., 496, 498, 514
Bigelow, B. J., 498, 499
Bigner, J. J., 465, 487, 489
Biller, H. B., 459, 460, 461
Billman, U., 499
Billy, J. O. G., 125
Binet, Alfred, 296–97, 300
Binet intelligence tests, 296–97, 300–301
Binocular disparity, 176, 177
Biological perspective, 8, 9, 10, 30, 577–82, 585–86, 627–28, 633–36. *See also* Nature-nurture controversy; Physical development
Birch, H. G., 332, 419, 420
Birch, L. L., 499
Birren, J. E., 313, 334
Birth order, 326, 394, 466–67
Birth process, 86–88
Bischof, L. J., 97

Bisexual confusion, 591
Bittman, S., 447
Black, A. E., 457
Black, B., 514
Black, K. N., 604
Black, S. M., 596
Black English, 377
Blake, J., 466
Blakeslee, S., 485, 486, 487
Blanchard, B. M., 313
Blanchard, R. W., 459
Blanche, S., 83
Blasi, A., 559, 560
Blastocyst, 74, 75
Blatt, M. J., 570
Blau, Z. S., 520
Blehar, M. C., 453
Block, J., 332, 424, 481, 485, 564, 569
Block, J. H., 332, 458, 481, 485, 584, 603
Bloom, A., 308
Bloom, B. S., 303
Bloom, L. P., 352
Blot, W. J., 86
Bluebond-Langner, M., 651, 653
Bluestone, H., 139
Blum, L., 656
Blumstein, P. W., 135
Blyth, D. A., 108, 109
Body development, 93–106. *See also* Physical development
Body image, 109, 110, 113–20. *See also* Self-concept
Boggiano, A. K., 497
Bohan, J. B., 412
Bohannan, P. M., 489
Bohrnstedt, G., 115
Boivin, M., 514
Bonding, 449–55
Bonvillian, J. D., 350
Booth, A., 520
Borges, M., 461
Bornstein, M. H., 179, 185, 193, 197, 209
Bosack, T. N., 220, 221
Bossard, M. E., 308
Bottoms, S. F., 88
Botwinick, J., 223, 235, 251, 312, 313
Boutourline-Young, H., 116
Bowen, R., 413
Bower, T. G. R., 178, 197
Bowerman, M., 360
Bowes, J. M., 638
Bowlby, J., 24, 30, 450, 471, 650
Boxer, A., 109
Boy Scouts, 588
Brabant, S., 589
Bracher, M., 441
Brackbill, Y., 223
Bradbard, M. R., 612

Bradley, R. M., 190
Brain death, 628–31
Brain development, 94–96
Brainerd, C. J., 532
Brainerd, C. U., 270
Brakke, N. P., 515, 516
Branscomb, A. B., 645
Braun, H. W., 223
Bray, G. E., 642
Bray, R. M., 641
Brazelton, T. Barry, 89
Brazelton Neonatal Behavioral Assessment Scale (NBAS), 89
Brecher, E., 159
Brenner, J., 502, 508
Bretherton, I., 529, 531
Brim, O. G., 17, 22
Briscoe, L., 632
Broderick, C. B., 134, 145, 146, 152, 153
Brody, E. B., 308
Brody, E. M., 472
Brody, N., 308
Brodzinsky, K. M., 452
Broerse, J., 196
Bronfenbrenner, Urie, 22, 50
Bronstein, P., 458, 461
Brooks-Gunn, J., 108, 115, 129, 134, 410, 411
Brophy, J., 618
Broverman, Donald M., 580, 581
Broverman, Inge K., 581
Broverman, T. K., 580
Brown, A. L., 244, 245, 270
Brown, G. W., 448, 483
Brown, J., 452
Brown, M., 559
Brown, R., 341, 355, 368, 370, 371, 372
Brownell, C. A., 508, 509
Brownmiller, Susan, 115
Bruce, P. A., 251
Bruce, P. R., 249
Bruch, H., 115
Brucken, L., 610
Bruner, J. S., 203, 353, 526, 530
Bryant, B. K., 465, 466
Bryen, D. N., 376, 377
Buell, S. J., 96
Buhler, Charlotte, 24, 30, 403
Buhrmester, D., 511
Bull, D., 185
Bulleit, T. N., 465
Bullock, M., 271
Bumpass, L., 441, 442, 444, 477, 478
Burgess, A. W., 139
Burghauser, R., 192
Burkhauser, R., 543
Burns, K. A., 85
Burns, S. M., 532
Burns, W. J., 85

Burrus-Bammel, L. L., 534
Burtless, G., 543
Bushnell, Margaret M., 54, 55
Bushnell, N., 573
Buss, A. H., 418, 419, 510
Bussey, K., 606, 607
Butler, R. N., 626, 656
Butterfield-Picard, H., 660, 661
Byrne, D., 119, 500
Byrne, J. M., 91
Byrnes, D. A., 119, 120

Cadoret, R. J., 212
Cafferata, G. L., 471
Cain, Barbara S., 480
Cain, S. E., 638
Cain, W. S., 195
Caird, W. K., 246
Calderone, M., 135
Caldwell, R. C., 176
Calfee, R. C., 200
California Divorce Study, 480, 481, 485–87
Callan, V. J., 446
Campbell, A., 417, 443
Campbell, L. A., 325
Campbell, P. B., 448
Campbell, P. M., 326
Campbell, S., 248
Campos, J. J., 178
Candee, D., 559
Caniglia, K., 244
Cannito, M. P., 366
Canstrari, R. E., 234, 235
Caplan, P. J., 593
Caporael, L. R., 365
Carlsmith, J. M., 110, 111
Carlson, R., 470
Carlson, V. R., 179
Caron, A. J., 176, 179
Caron, R. F., 176, 179
Carpenter, C. J., 607
Carrell, P. L., 348
Carroll, J. J., 177
Carroll, J. L., 559
Carter, J., 181
Case-study method of research, 47–48. *See also* Research
Cash, T. F., 113, 114, 115
Cassel, T. Z., 501
Cassidy, D. J., 245
Cassidy, J., 454
Cathexis, 392–93
Cattell, R. B., 315, 316
Cavanaugh, J. C., 538, 540, 542, 653
Cavenaugh, P. J., 221
Cavior, N., 119
Cazden, C., 357, 368
Centration, 268
Cephalocaudal growth, 104

Cerebral cortex, 94–96
Cernoch, J. M., 193, 194
Chaffee, S., 211
Chapman, M., 502, 503, 504
Chapman, R. S., 200
Charlesworth, R., 515
Charlesworth, W. R., 8
Chasnoff, I. J., 85
Chavez, D., 589
Chawla, P., 325
Checklists, 54–55
Chedd, G., 78
Cherhoniak, I. M., 118, 119
Cherlin, A. J., 441, 444, 474, 477, 488
Cherry, K. E., 248
Chess, S., 332, 418, 419, 420
Chickering, A. W., 237
Childers, P., 650
Childhood. See also Adolescence;
    Family; Infancy; Parenting;
    Physical development
  attention, 210–14
  cognitive development, 265–81, 285,
    287
  creativity, 331–34
  and death, 648–53, 658–59
  in empirical theory, 23
  employment goals, 537
  and family life cycle, 455–67
  gender roles, 586–91
  historical attitudes toward, 17, 18–
    19, 20–21
  intelligence, 311
  language development, 354–61
  learning, 225–34
  and maternal employment, 460
  memory development, 243–45
  mental retardation, 306–7
  moral development, 549–59
  perceptual development, 172, 192
  personality development, 388, 391–
    92, 396, 397–99, 412, 414–15, 424
  physical development, 94–96, 97, 98,
    100–101, 102–3, 104
  play, 522–28, 530–33
  psychoanalysis for, 32
  research methods, 53, 54
  sexuality, 137–40
  siblings, 462–66
  social learning, 230–31
  social relations, 496–504, 505, 509–
    11, 513–16
Child sexual abuse, 138–39
Ching, C. C., 466
Chinsky, J. M., 243
Chiriboga, D., 431, 469, 481, 517, 519,
    596
Chodorow, Nancy, 600
Chomsky, Noam, 369, 371
Christenson, C. V., 159

Christie, J. F., 523, 524
Christopherson, V. A., 519
Chromosomes, 70, 71
Cialdini, R. B., 500
Cicchetti, D., 428
Cicirelli, V. G., 462, 471, 473
Clark, E. V., 356, 357, 368
Clark, H., 356, 368
Clark, L., 246
Clark, P. M., 559
Clark, R., 161
Clarkson, F. F., 580
Clarren, S. K., 84
Classical conditioning, 216–17, 220–22
Classification, 272–73
Cleaves, W., 177, 198
Cleveland, W., 313
Clifford, M. M., 119
Clifton, R. K., 185, 209, 221
Climacteric, 596
Clinical method of research, 47. See
    also Research
Cobb, N., 538, 587
Cognitive conceit, 277–78
Cognitive development, 24, 29, 255–90.
    See also Piaget, Jean
  adulthood, 281–86
  concrete operations, 272–78, 282,
    533, 653
  and death, 651, 653
  environmental influences, 286–90
  formal operations, 278–81, 282,
    283–86, 653
  and gender, 592–94, 608–13
  Kohlberg's theory, 553–59, 560, 561–
    68, 569, 570, 571, 572–73, 574,
    608
  and language development, 361, 362,
    365–66
  and moral development, 552–59
  and perceptual development, 16,
    197–203
  and play, 526–27
  pre-operational intelligence, 265–71,
    561, 653
  sensorimotor intelligence, 259–65,
    287
  and sensory impairment, 182
  and social cognition, 504, 506
Cognitive social learning, 226
Cognitive structures, 257
Cohabitation, 442–43
Cohen, G., 248, 365, 630
Cohen, H. J., 90
Cohen, R. Y., 194
Cohen, S. I., 223
Coie, J., 514, 515, 516, 595
Coie, L., 595
Colby, A., 555, 559, 566, 567, 568
Cole, M., 288

Cole, P., 597
Coleman, E., 139
Coleman, J. S., 119, 517
Coleman, L. M., 541
Coleman, P. D., 96
Coles, R., 520
Collins, P. A., 212
Color vision, 179–80
Comenius, John Amos, 17–18
Comstock, G., 211
Concrete operations, 272–78, 282, 533,
    653
Conditioning, 216–25. See also
    Behavioral approach; Operant
    conditioning
Condon, W. S., 348
Confluence theory of intelligence, 326
Confluency, 634
Conger, J. J., 98, 99, 101, 116
Conrad, H. S., 312
Conry, R., 308
Conservation, 270, 274–77
Continuous culture, 27
Contrast sensitivity, 171
Conventional morality, 553, 554, 556,
    559, 562–64, 565, 569, 572, 573
Converse, P. E., 417, 443
Cook, K. V., 587
Cooley, C. H., 409
Coombs, L. C., 478
Cooney, T. M., 62, 314
Cooper, A. J., 126, 430
Cooper, C. R., 537
Cooper, P. W., 478
Coopersmith, S., 414, 459
Coppotelli, H., 515
Cordua, G. D., 608
Cornea, 168, 180
Correlational statistics, 43, 45, 46
Correll, R. E., 313
Corso, J. F., 187, 189
Corter, C., 452, 464
Costa, P. T., 424, 633, 646, 649, 651
Counts, D. R., 642, 643
Couvade, 601, 602
Cowan, C., 595
Cowan, C. P., 447–48
Cowan, D. A., 448
Cowan, G., 613
Cowan, P., 595
Cowan, Philip A., 447, 449
Cowart, B. J., 191, 192
Cox, M., 454, 483, 484, 485
Cox, R., 483, 484, 485
Coyne, A. C., 251
Coysh, W. S., 447
Crafton, C., 118
Craig, J. A., 180
Craik, F. I. M., 246, 247, 248
Crassini, B., 196

Cratty, B. J., 104, 105
Cravioto, J., 325
Creativity, 326—35. *See also* Intelligence
Crib death, 84, 659
Critical period of language development, 370
Crockenberg, S., 466
Crockett, L., 107, 110, 111, 119
Cromer, 201
Cronbach, L. J., 248, 321
Crook, W. G., 213
Cross, K. P., 237, 238
Cross-cultural research, 9, 24, 27—28
 cognitive development, 286—88
 death and dying, 631, 642—44
 gender roles, 587, 589—90, 596
 language development, 372
 moral development, 571—74
 personality development, 421—23
Crossman, S. M., 113
Cross-sectional research, 59—60, 314, 573. *See also* Research
Crouter, A. C., 22
Crowitz, A., 178
Crump, E. P., 324
Crystallized intelligence, 315—17
Cullen, K., 139
Cultice, J. C., 250
Cultural anthropology. *See* Cross-cultural research
Cumming, E., 521, 642
Cummings, E. Mark, 502
Cunningham, C. E., 212
Cunningham, L., 212
Cunningham, W. R., 312
Currens, W. C., 628
Currier, R. L., 140
Curtis, R., 488
Curtiss, S., 371
Cutler, L., 481
Cytrynbaum, S., 656

Dale, P. S., 350, 353, 354, 372, 374, 377
Damon, W., 409, 496, 587, 609
Daniel, T. C., 220
Daniels, D., 466, 510
Dansky, J. L., 532
Darrow, C. M., 430
Darwin, Charles, 19
Dasen, P., 287, 288
Data collection methods, 52—58. *See also* Research
Datan, N., 237, 285, 326, 427, 585, 621
Dating, 511—13. *See also* Sexuality
Davies, E., 115
Davis, G. A., 334, 364
Davis, M., 180
Davison, M. L., 566, 568
Day, R. H., 178
Deafness, 349, 350—51, 369, 373

Death and dying, 625—64
 anthropology, 631, 642—44
 bereavement, 657—60
 biology, 627—28, 633—36
 development, 648—57
 near-death experiences, 525—26
 psychology, 644—48
 sociology, 636—42
Death system, 636
Deaux, K. V., 582
DeCasper, A. J., 186, 187
Deep structure of language, 343—44, 359
Defining Issues Test, 555, 562, 563
DeFrain, J., 479
DeLameter, J., 142, 160, 161
DeLicardie, E. R., 325
De Loache, J. S., 245
DeLora, J. S., 154, 155
DeLucia, A., 222
Del Vento Bielby, D., 282, 283
Demand characteristics, 51
D'Emilio, J., 162
Demorest, A., 361
Denckla, W. D., 635
Denney, D. R., 236
Denney, N. W., 235, 236, 315
Denny, 634
Depth perception, 176—77, 178, 182, 198—99, 202
Descriptive statistics, 42
Desor, J. A., 190, 191
DeVall, W., 160
Developmental designs, 58—64
Developmental psychopathology, 427—31
Developmental stages, 14—15, 18, 28
Developmental theory, 4, 15—16, 23—33, 65. *See also specific theories*
 history of, 16—23
De Villiers, J. G., 341, 360, 367, 372
De Villiers, P. A., 341, 360, 367, 372
Dewart, N. H., 374
Dewey, John, 568
Dialects, 310, 376—78
Diamond, A. M., 334
Diamond, N., 225
Diaz, R. M., 497, 498
Diaz-Guerrero, R., 421
Dickerson, A. E., 324
Differentiation theory of perception, 202—3
Di Maria, H., 83
Dion, K. K., 118, 119
Dion, K. L., 118, 119
DiPriete, T. A., 540
Discontinuous culture, 27
Disengagement theory of aging, 521
Dittman-Kohli, F., 318
Ditto, W. B., 418

Divergent thinking, 329
Divorce, 458—59, 460, 477—89
Dixon, D., 532
Dixon, J. C., 410
Dixon, R. A., 248, 318
Dobbs, J. M., 118
Dodd, D. H., 349
Dodge, K. A., 514, 515, 516
Dodwell, P., 196
Doering, C. H., 510
Doherty, W. J., 441, 446
Dokecki, P. R., 119
Dolgin, 176
Dominick, J. R., 233
Donaldson, G., 317
Doppelt, J., 313
Dorn, L., 107, 111
Dornbusch, S. M., 107, 110, 111, 489
Dotemoto, S., 212
Douvan, E., 467, 499
Dowd, M., 541
Dowler, J. K., 86
Downs, A. C., 586, 603, 605
Drabman, K. S., 608
Drage, J. S., 84
Dreyer, Philip H., 141, 142, 143
Drizd, T. A., 97
Dubnoff, S. J., 460
Dubowitz, L. M. S., 89
Dubowitz, V., 89
Dubowitz Scoring System, 89
Duncan, P. D., 110, 111
Dunkeld, J., 197
Dunn, J., 462, 463, 464, 465, 466
Dunn, J. G., 466
Dunphy, D. C., 511
Durett, M. E., 454
Durkheim, Emile, 637, 639
Duvall, E., 439
Dweck, C. S., 593, 618
Dwyer, J., 113, 115, 116
Dye, H. B., 324
Dying. *See* Death and dying

Eagly, A. H., 615
Eagly, R., 334
Ebel, R. L., 308
Eccles-Parsons, J., 593
Eckerman, C. O., 508
Ecology of Human Development, The (Bronfenbrenner), 50
Ectoderm, 76
Eder, D., 499
Education, 237—38. *See also* Learning
 and cognitive development, 284, 288—89
 and gender roles, 593, 617—21
 and intelligence, 307—8, 312—13
 and moral development, 566
 and self-esteem, 414—15

Edwards, C. P., 573, 587
Edwards, J. E., 212
Edwards, J. N., 519
Egalitarian marriage, 442
Egeland, B., 453, 454
Ego, 388, 389, 393–94
Ehrhardt, Anke A., 127, 128, 579, 585
Eichorn, D. H., 102, 103
Eilers, R. E., 354
Eimas, P. P., 186
Eisen, M., 412
Eisenberg, N., 504, 505
Eisenberg-Berg, N., 496
Eitzen, D. A., 113, 517
Elder, J., 532
Elderly people. *See* Old age
Elias, J. W., 22
Elias, M. F., 22
Elias, P. K., 22
Elkind, D., 20, 21, 278, 280, 413, 414, 654
Elliot, A. J., 357
Elliott, C., 508
Ellis, G. F., 467, 468, 469
Ellis, H. C., 220
Ellis, M. J., 527
Elsom, B., 653
Elvik, S., 139
Embryo, 75–77
Emerson, P. E., 418
Emmerich, W., 609, 610
Empiricism, 23, 24, 25
Employment, 308–9, 460–61, 478, 536–43, 597, 608
Endman, M., 185
Endoderm, 76
Endsley, R. C., 612
Engen, T., 190, 192
England, G. W., 536
Enlightenment, 18–19
Enrichment theory of perception, 16, 203
Enright, M. K., 244
Enright, R. D., 414
Environment, influence of, 23, 24, 25–28. *See also* Nature-nurture controversy
cognitive development, 286–90
Epigenetic principle, 396–97
Epstein, S., 413
Erickson, R., 489
Erikson, Erik H., 10, 24, 30, 32–33
on death, 627, 645, 654
on gender roles, 591, 600, 601
on personality development, 385, 393–403, 404, 410, 413, 423
on play, 525–26
Erikson, J. M., 396
Eron, L. D., 233, 550
Ershler, J., 531

Ervin, D. H., 119
Estes, D., 454
Estrogen, 73, 101, 125, 126, 127, 129, 130, 132, 151
Ethical Principles in the Conduct of Research with Human Participants (American Psychological Association), 48
Ethical issues in research, 45, 48–49, 78
Ethical relativism, 574
Ethology, 30, 450–53
Euthanasia, 660–61, 662
Evans, L., 662
Existential psychology, 645
Expansion, 368
Expectancy effect, 51
Experimental strategy, 45–46
Expressive needs, 499
Extensive peer relations, 511
Extinction, 217
Eysenck, H. J., 321, 322, 323

Faces, perception of, 175–76
Fagan, J. L., 174
Fagen, J. W., 244
Fagot, B. I., 603, 612, 613
Fakouri, M. E., 283
Falbo, T., 466, 467
Fallon, A. E., 116
Family, 160, 290, 394, 421, 437–89.
    See also Marriage; Parenting
adolescents in, 467–69
adult, 469–77
and divorce, 458–59, 460, 477–89
and intelligence, 325–26
sibling relationships, 462–67, 472–74
Fantz, Robert L., 174, 175
Farber, E. A., 453, 454
Fathers. *See* Parenting
Faunce, P. S., 110
Faust, J., 115
Fausto-Sterling, Ann, 596
Faux, M., 445
Feifel, H., 645, 661
Fein, G. G., 86, 523, 526, 527, 529, 533
Feingold, B. F., 213
Feldman, C., 368
Feldman, David H., 331
Feldman, H., 439
Feldman, R., 559
Feminism, 479
Fenson, L., 529, 530
Fenton, E., 555
Ferreira, A. J., 83
Feshbach, N. D., 501
Feshbach, S., 550
Fetal alcohol syndrome (FAS), 84–85
Fetus, 78–86

Field, D. E., 212
Field, G., 543
Field, J., 196
Field, T. M., 449
Field experiment, 50
Field independence, 593
Fifer, W. P., 186
Figley, C. R., 510
Fikrig, S. M., 83
Fine, M. A., 487, 488, 489
Finkelhor, D., 138, 139
Finley, N. J., 471
Fischer, J. L., 595
Fish, K. D., 460
Fitzgerald, H., 119
Fixation, 393
Flavell, J. H., 29, 199, 228, 229, 243, 244, 250, 257, 262, 263, 264, 270, 271
Fleming, S. G., 366
Fluid intelligence, 315, 316–18
Fodor, I. G., 115
Fogel, A., 78, 186, 507
Follicle-stimulating hormone (FSH), 129, 130, 132
Folven, F. J., 350
Foote, J., 470
Forehand, R., 115
Foreign language acquisition, 362, 370
Formal operations, 278–81, 282, 283–86, 653
Forman, E. C., 641, 642
Formaneck, R., 651
Form perception, 171–73
Fouts, H., 343
Fouts, R. S., 343
Fox, N. J., 265
Fox, R., 108
Fozard, J. L., 180, 181, 182, 247
Frankel, K. A., 454
Frankl, Viktor, 645
Frazier, A., 115
Freedman, D. G., 423
Freedman, E. B., 162
Freedman, M., 265
Freiberg, H. J., 642
French, D. C., 515
Frenzel, C., 472
Frequency, auditory, 185
Freud, Anna, 24, 30, 32
Freud, Sigmund, 10, 24, 30, 31–32. *See also* Psychoanalytic theory
on death, 644–45
on gender roles, 151, 595, 600, 601, 602
on morality, 551–52
on personality development, 385–93, 394–95
on play, 525
on sexuality, 32, 135, 137–38, 151

Frey, K. L., 611, 612
Friedman, R. J., 212
Friedman, Sarah, 502
Friedrich, L. K., 231, 233
Friedrichs, A. G., 244
Friendship, 496–501, 517–20, 586–87
Frieze, I. H., 614
Frisbie, D. A., 308
Fristad, M. A., 638
Frodi, A., 452
Froming, 500
Fromm, Erich, 395
Frueh, T., 588
Fuchs, F., 78
Funerals, 638
Furman, W., 496, 498, 511, 513, 514
Furnham, A., 115
Furstenberg, F. F., 474, 478, 481, 482
Furth, H. G., 373

Gabriesheski, A. S., 251
Gaddis, A., 134
Gagnon, J. H., 148, 159
Gaitz, C. M., 534, 535
Galbraith, R. C., 326
Galen, H., 642
Gall, Franz Joseph, 614
Galler, J. R., 325
Galligan, R., 448
Galusha, R., 308
Games-with-rules, 527, 533
Gannon, S., 423
Ganon, E. S., 173
Garber, J., 429
Gardner, Allen, 342
Gardner, Beatrice, 342
Gardner, E. L., 235
Gardner, H., 328
Gardner, K. E., 461
Garduque, L., 454
Garfinkel, R., 536, 538
Garland, T. N., 442
Garrett, E., 447
Gartley, W., 650, 651, 653
Garvey, C., 531, 533
Gautier, T., 579, 580
Gebhard, P. H., 149
Geiselhart, R., 223
Geller, R., 550
Gelman, R., 256, 270, 271, 358
Gender, definition of, 582
Gender constancy, 608–10
Gender differences
  aging, 112
  body image, 113, 114
  death and dying, 647
  divorce, 481, 484–85
  employment, 538–41
  moral development, 550, 568–71
  parenting stress, 447–48

physical development, 73, 88, 97, 98–99, 101, 102–3, 104, 127–34
  self-esteem, 414
  sexuality, 139, 148, 157–58, 160–61
  sibling relationships, 463, 464
  social relations, 498–99, 502, 511, 519–20
Gender identity, 583
Gender role preference, 582
Gender roles, 126, 579–621
  androgyny, 615–17
  and body image, 109, 110
  development, 583–600
  and education, 593, 617–21
  and intelligence, 326
  and marriage, 442, 479
  and maternal employment, 460, 541
  and parenting, 459, 584–85, 590, 595–96, 600–601, 602–5
  and peer groups, 511
  in psychoanalytic theory, 151, 402, 591, 595–96, 600–601, 602
  research, 614–15
  and sexuality, 110, 151, 160–62, 598
  theories, 600–614
Gender role stereotype, 583
Gender stability, 608–10
Gene, definition of, 70
Genetic abnormalities, 75–76, 78, 81
Genetics, 70–73, 634–35. *See also*
  Biological perspective;
  Nature-nurture controversy
Genital stage of development, 392–93
Genotype, 70
Gentner, D., 358
George, L. K., 416, 424, 519
Gerontology, 22. *See also* Old age
Gershoni, R., 499
Gesell, Arnold, 10, 24, 28–29
Gewirtz, J. L., 223, 549, 574
Ghiselin, B., 373
Gibbs, J., 555, 559, 560, 567, 568, 574
Gibbs, M. S., 139
Gibner, 489
Gibson, C., 445
Gibson, D., 519
Gibson, E. J., 177, 178, 196, 198, 200, 201, 202
Gibson, J. J., 202
Gilbert, J. G., 234
Gilgun, J. F., 145
Gilligan, Carol, 568–69, 570, 571, 574
Gilman, A. C., 73
Ginsberg, E., 537
Ginsburg, H., 262, 284
Gjerde, P. F., 481, 485
Glaser, B. G., 647
Glazer, J. A., 515
Gleason, H. A., 372
Gleitman, H., 9, 219, 368

Gleitman, L. R., 368
Glenn, N. D., 443, 478, 487
Glick, I. O., 659
Glick, P. C., 439, 441, 443, 478, 487
Glucksberg, S., 360, 361
Glunt, E. K., 655
Godbey, G., 534
Goethals, G. W., 142
Goetting, Ann, 462, 473, 474
Gold, D., 460, 461, 462, 473
Goldberg, C., 89
Goldberg, H., 638
Goldberg, S., 451, 452, 453
Goldman, B. D., 508
Goldman, J., 138
Goldman, K. S., 609
Goldman, R., 138
Goldman, W., 119
Goldschmid, M. L., 287
Goldsmith, H. H., 420
Goldstein, M. J., 306
Goldstein, S., 587
Goleman, D., 309
Gollin, E. S., 248, 249
Good, T., 618
Goodglass, H., 366
Goodman, C. C., 203
Goodman, L. S., 73
Goodman, N., 9
Goodrick, T. S., 559
Gordon, C., 413, 416, 534, 535
Gordon, F. R., 177
Gordon, H., 324
Gordon, M. E., 229
Gordon, S., 145, 519
Gorzalka, B. B., 126
Gottman, J., 514, 516
Gough, H. G., 327
Gould, J. L., 30
Gould, R. L., 425, 596
Gould, Stephen J., 296
Gowan, J. C., 330
Goyert, G. L., 88
Grammar, 352, 355–59, 374–75
Grandparents, 474–77, 597
Granrud, C. E., 177, 198
Gray, D. S., 126
Greek philosophers, 11, 16–17
Green, J. L., 559
Green, R., 151, 312, 313, 317
Greenberg, B. S., 233
Greenberg, J. I., 139
Greene, L. S., 190
Greene, V. L., 472
Greenfield, P. M., 353
Greenstein, T. N., 539
Greer, D., 588
Gresham, F. M., 514
Grief, 657
Groff, T. R., 125

Groos, Karl, 524
Gross, A. E., 118
Gross, R. T., 110, 111
Grossman, H. J., 306
Grossman, J. L., 235
Grossman, K., 454
Grossman, K. E., 454
Grotevant, H. D., 404, 537
Groth, A. N., 139
Group differences statistics, 43
Group intelligence tests, 305
Gruber, H. E., 330
Gruber, S., 553
Gruendel, J. M., 351, 354
Gruman, G. J., 633
Grusec, J. E., 230
Guardo, C. J., 412
Gubrium, J. F., 417
Guerrero, L., 579, 580
Guidibaldi, J., 485
Guilford, J. P., 297, 298, 328
Gullotta, T., 110, 113, 467
Gunderson, E. K. E., 113
Gurwitz, S., 191
Gutmann, David, 595, 596
Guttmacher, A. F., 82, 86, 88
Gynecomastia, 101

Haan, N., 564, 568
Habituation, 170
Hagan, R., 613
Hagen, J. W., 243, 245
Hagen, M. A., 199
Hagestad, G. O., 474
Haith, M. M., 169, 171, 172, 175, 196
Hake, J. L., 184, 190, 193, 195
Halberstadt, A. G., 616
Hall, E., 270
Hall, G. Stanley, 10, 24, 28, 524
Hall, J. A., 616
Hallinan, M. T., 499
Halo effect, 51
Halton, A., 84, 85
Halverson, C. F., 612, 613
Halverson, C. L., 511
Hamill, P. V., 97
Hamilton, G. V., 154
Hammersmith, S. K., 138, 143
Hammond, C. B., 99
Haney, W., 305
Hanson, E., 467
Hanson, S. W., 85
Hantover, J. P., 588
Hardy, J. B., 146
Haring, M. J., 417
Harkins, E. B., 469
Harkins, J. W., 187, 190
Harmer, Ruth Mulvey, 638
Harper, L. V., 446
Harrington, D. M., 327, 328, 329, 332

Harris, J. A., 93
Harris, J. E., 251
Harris, L., 535
Harris, P., 510
Harris, R. C., 325
Harris, T., 448, 483
Harry, J., 160
Hart, C. H., 514
Hart, D., 409
Harter, S., 409, 410, 414–15, 500
Hartley, A. A., 236
Hartley, R. E., 588
Hartman, C., 376
Hartman, E., 213
Hartup, W. W., 514, 515, 516, 550
Harvey, S. M., 125
Haskett, R. F., 580
Hass, A., 141, 142
Hatano, G., 289
Hatfield, E., 161
Haven, C., 519, 520
Havighurst, R. J., 521, 523, 540, 542
Hawkins, J., 497, 620
Hay, D. L., 507
Hayashi, M. M., 366
Hayes, C. L., 644
Hayes, Catherine, 342
Hayes, D. S., 496
Hayes, Keith, 342
Hayes, M. P., 479
Hayflick, Leonard, 634, 635
Hayghe, H., 539
Hazen, N. L., 454, 514
Hearing, 182–90, 364, 366
Heath, D. H., 421, 449
Hein, R. N., 603
Heingartner, A., 559
Helmreich, R. L., 615, 616
Hembree, E. A., 242
Heming, G., 447
Henker, B., 212
Henry, R. A., 521
Henry, W. E., 642
Herek, G. M., 655
Heritability, 322, 369–71, 418–20. *See also* Nature- nurture controversy
Herman, J. F., 249
Herman, S. J., 480
Hermaphroditism, 579, 585–86
Heron, A., 287, 288
Herrnstein, Richard J., 322, 323
Hersh, R. H., 568
Hess, B., 518
Hess, E., 521
Hesse, P., 654
Heterosexual activity, 139–40, 143–45, 146–47, 153–55. *See also* Sexuality
Hetherington, E. Mavis, 444, 460, 461, 482, 483, 484, 485, 487

Hicks, D. J., 231, 233, 549
Hierarchy of needs, 406–7
Higgins, E. T., 360, 361, 375
Higgins-Trenk, A., 460
Hildebrandt, K., 119
Hill, C. E., 596
Hill, J., 591
Hill, R., 438, 439, 440, 470
Hirsch, D. A., 655
Hirsch, M. B., 146
Hirschman, R., 220, 221
Hite, Shere, 148
Hochschild, Arlie, 540, 541
Hockett, C. F., 372
Hodapp, R. M., 508
Hodgson, J. W., 595
Hodson, B., 355
Hoefnagel-Hohle, M., 362
Hofferth, S. L., 144
Hoff-Ginsberg, E., 368
Hoffman, C. D., 613
Hoffman, L. W., 444, 446, 449, 460, 608
Hoffman, M. L., 457, 501, 574
Hofland, B. F., 318
Hofman, J., 499
Hogarty, P. S., 324
Holland, A. L., 364
Holland, John L., 538, 539
Hollien, H., 348
Holmes, Deborah, 39, 40–41, 42, 43, 44, 46, 59
Holophrases, 353–54
Holstein, C. B., 569
Holtzman, W. H., 421
Homosexuality, 139, 142–43, 148–53, 160. *See also* Sexuality
Honzik, M. P., 311
Hood, J., 248
Hood, L., 352
Horley, J., 417
Hormones, 71–73, 129, 130, 132, 579, 635. *See also* Estrogen; Testosterone
Horn, J. L., 315, 316, 317
Hornblum, J. N., 651, 653
Horney, Karen, 30, 395, 601
Hornung, M., 530
Horowitz, F. D., 89, 91
Horst, L., 458
Horton, C. P., 324
Horton, P. J., 458
Hospice movement, 639, 660–61
Houseknecht, S. K., 445, 446
Howard, K. I., 145, 467
Howes, C., 508, 529
Hoyer, L. W., 313

Hoyer, W. J., 96, 208, 215, 234, 313, 517, 519, 520
Hoyle, S. G., 497
Hoyt, J. D., 244
Hrncir, E., 454
Huang, M. S., 360
Huber, P. S., 643
Hudson, L., 329
Hudson, W., 198, 199
Huesmann, L. R., 233, 550
Hug-Hellmuth, Hermine, 32
Hughes, F., 237, 285, 326, 427, 447, 448, 524, 530, 533, 621
Hughes, M., 119
Hulicka, I. M., 235
Hultsch, D. F., 248
Hultsch, D. L., 234, 235, 247
Human development
  and change, 10, 12–13
  common sense beliefs, 3
  individual nature of, 4–6, 18, 107–13
  interdisciplinary approach, 8–10
  life-span approach, 6–8
  and quantitative age, 6, 10, 14–15
Humanism, 24, 29–30
Humphrey, T., 190
Hunt, M., 147, 153, 154, 155
Hunt, N., 135
Huntington, R., 643
Huston, A., 582, 585, 586, 589, 606, 607
Huston, A. C., 588
Huston, T. L., 118, 595
Huston-Stein, A., 460
Hutcheon, R. G., 83
Hutz, E. J., 177
Huyck, M. H., 96, 234, 517, 519, 520
Hyde, J. S., 593, 594
Hymel, S., 510, 516
Hyperactivity, 212–13
Hypothalamus, 71, 72, 73, 126, 127
Hypothesis, 39

Iannotti, R. J., 501
Id, 388, 389, 393
Idealism, 16
Identification, 549, 551
Identity. *See* Self; Self-concept
Identity status interview, 404–5
Igarashi, M., 187
Imaginary audience, 414
Imitation. *See* Social learning theory
Imperato-McGinley, J., 579, 580
Implicit information, 358
Imprinting, 450–51
Indifferent parenting, 458
Individual intelligence tests, 305
Induction, 501

Infancy. *See also* Childhood; Parenting
  attachment, 449–55
  attention, 209
  cognitive development, 259–65, 287
  conditioning research, 220–23
  creativity, 331–32
  crib death, 84, 659
  deafness in, 349, 350–51
  and death, 650
  gender roles, 584–86
  hearing, 184–87
  intelligence testing, 303, 305
  language development, 347–54, 368
  learning, 228–30
  and maternal employment, 460
  moral development, 551
  personality development, 388–90, 392–93, 396, 397, 418–19, 424–25
  physical development, 88–93, 94, 97, 100, 101, 102, 104
  play, 528–30
  self, 410–12
  sexuality, 135–37
  smell, sense of, 193–94
  social relations, 507–9
  taste, sense of, 190–92
  touch, sense of, 195–96
  vision, 168–77, 178–80
Inferential statistics, 42
Information processing theory, 207–8, 612–13. *See also* Attention; Cognitive development; Learning; Memory
Inglis, J., 246
Ingram, C., 355
Ingram, D., 355
Inhelder, B., 268, 270, 271, 279, 281
Inman, V. W., 247
Inner speech, 373
Instinctual anxiety, 525, 551
Instrumental needs, 499
Intelligence. *See also* Cognitive development; Creativity
  definitions, 295–99
  development, 310–18
  environmental influences, 323–26
  genetic influences, 318–23
  Piaget's theory, 256–59, 296
  and self-esteem, 295, 306
  and sensory impairment, 188
  testing, 299–310
Intensity, auditory, 184
Intensive peer relations, 511
Interactionist approach, 12, 367, 371–73
Interstitial cell-stimulating hormone (ICSH), 132
Interviews, 52–53
IQ. *See* Intelligence

Iris, 168, 180
Irwin, D. Michelle, 54, 55
Iso-Ahola, S. E., 534
Izard, C. E., 242

Jack, I., 570, 571
Jack, R., 570, 571
Jacklin, Carol N., 114, 510, 584, 589, 590, 592, 593, 594, 603, 606, 613, 614
Jackowitz, E. R., 529
Jackson, C. M., 93
Jackson, J. P., 532
Jacobson, J., 115
Jacobson, J. L., 86, 454, 509
Jacobson, L., 618
Jacobson, N. S., 441, 446
Jacobson, S. W., 86, 228, 229
Jacobvitz, 213
Jacquette, D., 500
Jakobson, R., 349
Jambor, T., 532
James, William, 409
Jamison, K. R., 306
Janda, L. H., 113, 114, 115
Jani, S. N., 182
Janos, P. M., 327
Jaquish, G. A., 334
Jargowsky, P. A., 482
Jassick-Gerschenfeld, D., 186
Jeffko, W. G., 627
Jenkins, R. A., 653
Jennings, J. R., 125
Jensen, A. H., 641
Jensen, A. R., 322, 323
Jensen, J. L., 248
Jensen, L., 461
Jensen, R., 500
Ji, G., 466
Jiao, S., 466
Joffe, L. S., 450, 454
Johnson, C. L., 97
Johnson, Douglas, 118, 120
Johnson, J., 532
Johnson, J. E., 523, 524, 530, 531, 532
Johnson, J. S., 482
Johnson, L. M., 607
Johnson, M. M., 199, 605
Johnson, P. B., 614
Johnson, V. E., 134, 138, 159, 598
Johnston, C., 212
Johnston, J., 537
Johnston, M. C., 85
Jones, D., 519
Jones, H. E., 312
Jones, J. M., 152, 655
Jones, M. C., 112
Jones, R. E., 73, 82, 85, 132, 135, 137, 139, 151
Joseph, J. A., 559

Jourard, S. M., 116
Joyce, L. K., 282, 287
Jung, Carl, 394–95, 595
Jusczyck, P. W., 184, 186

Kaczala, C. M., 620
Kagan, J., 17, 22, 265, 418, 423, 424
Kahana, B., 518, 519, 521
Kahn, J. R., 144
Kahn, M. D., 462, 473
Kail, R., 243, 245
Kalish, R. A., 626, 629, 630, 631, 638,
    639, 641, 644, 645, 646, 647, 651,
    654, 656, 657, 658, 659
Kallman, F. J., 634
Kalter, H., 81, 86
Kalter, N., 485
Kamin, L., 321, 322
Kandel, D., 468
Kantner, J. L., 144, 145
Kaplan, E., 349
Kaplan, G., 349
Kaplan, N., 454
Kapust, L. R., 630
Kart, C. S., 99, 100, 102, 103, 113
Kastenbaum, B. S., 648
Kastenbaum, R. J., 313, 430, 629, 631,
    632, 633, 636, 638, 639, 645, 646,
    647, 648, 649, 651, 656, 659
Katchadourian, H., 73, 74, 99, 105, 109,
    115, 125, 130, 132, 134
Katz, S. L., 83
Katzman, N., 211
Kauffman, J. M., 229
Kauffman, M. B., 23
Kaufman, B., 145
Kaufmann, R., 177
Kausler, D. H., 246, 247, 251
Kavanaugh, R. D., 229, 230
Kavrell, S. M., 308
Kaye, H., 220, 221, 229
Kearsley, R. B., 529
Keasey, C. B., 570
Keating, N. C., 596
Keenan, E. O., 358
Keith, R. W., 184
Kelly, George, 403
Kelly, J., 160, 535
Kelly, Joan Berlin, 478, 479, 480, 481,
    483, 484
Kelly, M., 287
Kemper, S., 364
Kendig, H. L., 519, 520
Kendler, Howard, 24, 27, 223–25
Kendler, Tracey, 24, 27
Kendrick, C., 462, 463, 464
Kennell, John, 451
Kenrick, D. T., 500
Kenshalo, D. R., 196
Kent, R. N., 617

Kent, S., 97
Keough, B., 419
Kerlinger, F. N., 53
Kern, 419
Kessen, William, 14, 18, 19, 169
Kessler, R., 541
Key, C. B., 324
Kidd, J. R., 238
Kilpatrick, A. C., 139
Kimble, G. A., 223
Kiminyo, D. M., 287
Kimmel, D. C., 160, 470
King, M. R., 117
King, N. R., 523
King, S., 308
Kinsey, A. C., 137, 148, 149
Kirkendall, L. A., 137, 139
Kirsh, B., 609
Kitson, G. C., 479
Kivett, V., 417
Kivlin, J. E., 117
Kivnick, H. Q., 396
Klaus, Marshall, 451
Klausmeier, H. J., 332
Kleck, R. E., 119
Klein, A. R., 212
Klein, E. B., 430
Klein, Melanie, 24, 32
Klemmack, D. L., 519
Klima, Edward, 342, 350
Kline, D., 182
Klinger, C. A., 497
Klos, D. S., 142
Knapp, J. R., 113
Knight, C. C., 248
Knowles, J., 246
Knowles, M. S., 238
Kobrin, F. E., 478
Koff, E., 107
Kogan, N., 327, 329
Kohlberg, Lawrence, 553–56, 558–59,
    560, 561–68, 569, 570, 571, 572–
    73, 574, 608
Kohn, A., 212, 213
Kohn, M. L., 536
Kolodny, R. C., 138
Kolody, G., 282, 287
Komarovsky, M., 519, 520
Kompara, D., 489
Konrad, K. W., 211
Koocher, G. P., 653
Korn, S. J., 423
Kornetsky, C., 223
Kosnik, W., 182
Kraines, R., 596
Kramer, K. B., 478, 487
Kramer, R., 569
Krantz, M., 119
Krauss, R. M., 360, 361
Krehbiel, G., 514, 515, 516

Kreuz, L. E., 125
Krieger, L. H., 119
Krile, D., 500
Kringlen, E., 212
Ku, L. C., 144, 145
Kubie, L. S., 327
Kübler-Ross, Elizabeth, 631, 642, 646,
    647, 648, 660
Kuczaj, S. A., 357
Kuhl, P. K., 186
Kuhn, D., 610
Kuhn, M. H., 408
Kulig, J. W., 185
Kulka, R. A., 460, 478
Kunzinger, E. L., 243
Kurdeck, L. A., 500
Kurtines, W. M., 574

Labouvie-Vief, G., 248, 285, 286, 313,
    315, 318, 504
Labor, 86–87
Labov, W., 375, 377
Labrecque, M. S., 472
Lachenmeyer, J. R., 139
Lack, D., 660, 661
LAD (Language acquisition device), 371
Ladd, G. W., 514, 515
Ladis, B., 84
LaFreniere, P., 509
La Gaipa, J. J., 498
La Greca, A. M., 514
Lahar, C. J., 248
Laird, J. D., 412
Lakoff, R. T., 120
Lamb, M. E., 185, 193, 197, 326, 454,
    459, 591, 603, 605, 606
Lambert, W. E., 603
Lamberth, J., 119
Laner, M. R., 160
Lang, M. E., 21
Langer, A., 178
Langer, Ellen J., 416
Langer, J., 23, 28, 31
Langfeldt, T., 135
Langlois, J. H., 119, 586, 603, 605
Langsdorf, P., 242
Language acquisition device (LAD), 371
Language development, 339–78
    adolescence, 361–63
    adulthood, 364–65
    childhood, 354–61
    and deafness, 349, 350–51, 369, 373
    infancy, 347–54, 368
    old age, 365–66
    and socioeconomic status, 374–76
    theories, 341, 366–73
Language structure, 343–46
Lantz, D., 372
Lanyon, R. I., 138
Lapsley, D. K., 414

Larson, C. N., 654
Larson, G. L., 333
Larson, L. E., 467
LaRue, A., 313
Latchford, S. A., 84
Latency stage of development, 391–92, 398–99
Law of contiguity, 220
Law of effect, 218
Lazarus, P. J., 510
Learning, 200–201, 215–39, 284, 364. *See also* Education; Social learning theory
LeBrecque, S. F., 461
Lecky, P., 413
Lefkowitz, M. M., 233, 550
Lehman, H. C., 334
Leiderman, P. H., 452
Leinbach, M. D., 612, 613
Leisure, 522–36
Lenhardt, M. L., 187
Lenneberg, Eric H., 369, 371, 372
Lennon, R., 504, 505
Lens, 168, 180, 181
Leridon, H., 441
Lerner, H., 447
Lerner, M., 639
Lerner, Richard M., 22–23, 29, 113
Leslie, L., 541
Lesser, G., 374, 468
Letourneau, K. J., 608
Leung, E. H., 353
Leventhal, A. J., 185
Levin, A., 135
Levin, H., 200, 201
Levin, R. J., 135
Levin, S., 212
Levine, P. B., 543
Levinson, D. J., 425, 426, 430, 596
Levinson, M. H., 430
Leviton, B., 519
Leviton, D., 641, 642
Levy, V. M., 250
Lewis, M., 410, 411
Lewis, P., 119
Libido, 386, 389, 391, 392, 394
Lieberman, A. F., 454, 509
Lieberman, M., 555, 567
Liebert, R. M., 549
Lief, H. I., 153
Life expectancy, 633
Life-span attachment theory, 471
Lifschitz, F., 115
Lifton, R. J., 662, 664
Light, L. L., 248
Lightbown, P., 352
Lindholm, J. M., 247
Lindow, J., 619
Linguistic relativity hypothesis, 372
Linn, B. S., 642

Linn, M. C., 594
Linn, M. W., 642
Linn, P. L., 89
Lips, H. M., 592
Lipsitt, L. P., 185, 190, 220, 221
Lisonbee, L. K., 115
List, J. A., 223, 234
Living will, 662, 663
Livson, F. B., 112, 596
Locke, John, 23, 24, 25
Lockheed, M. E., 620
Loeb, R. C., 458
Loehlin, H. C., 321, 419
Loftus, R., 212
Logan, L. A., 219
Logan, Richard D., 20, 21, 409
Lollis, S. P., 508, 529
London, J., 595
London, S. N., 99
Lonetto, R., 650, 651
Longfellow, C., 482, 483
Longitudinal research, 60–62, 314
Long-term memory, 241
Loomis, B., 596
Lopata, H., 518, 660
Lorch, E. P., 212, 213
Losoff, M., 119
Lowe, J. C., 6, 7
Lowenstein, L. F., 510
Lowenthal, M., 431, 469, 517, 519, 520, 596
Lowrey, G. H., 98
Lowy, J. J., 308
Lucas, T. A., 508, 532
Lunnenborg, C. E., 538
Lunnenborg, D. W., 538
Luria, Z., 125, 146, 147, 148, 149–50, 151, 152
Luszcz, M. A., 358
Lutkenhaus, P., 454
Lykken, David, 10
Lynch, M., 591
Lynott, R. J., 417

McAdams, L., 488
McCall, R. B., 45, 50, 229, 230, 308, 324, 326
McCarthy, J., 488
Maccoby, E. E., 114, 210, 211, 456, 458, 501, 510, 584, 586, 589, 590, 592, 593, 603, 606, 612, 613, 614
McCombs, M., 211
MacCorquodale, P., 142
McCrae, Robert R., 414, 424
McCune-Nicolich, L., 529
McDonald, R., 470
McFarland, R. A., 180
MacFarlane, A., 193
McFarlane, J. W., 311, 424

McGee, J., 597, 598
McGhee, P. E., 588
McGinnies, E., 203
McGraw, K. O., 608
McGreal, Cathleen, 476
McGuire, K. D., 500, 513
MacKain, K., 186
MacKay, H. A., 246
McKee, B., 430
Macken, M. A., 355
McKenzie, B. E., 178
McKinney, K. L., 108
Macklin, E. D., 441, 442
McKusick, L., 152
McLachlan, D. R., 265
McLaughlin, B., 362
McLaughlin, J. H., 194
McLeish, J. A. B., 334
McMichael, P., 515
McPartland, T., 408
MacPhee, D., 325
MacPherson, P. M., 593
McRae, J. A., 541
Macrosphere play, 526
Maddi, S. R., 383
Mader, S. M., 70, 71, 74
Magno, J. B., 661
Magnussen, D., 110
Main, D. S., 497
Main, M., 453, 454
Mainville, F., 212
Maioni, T. L., 530
Makin, J. W., 193
Makowski, D. G., 559
Maland, J., 177
Malina, R. M., 98
Malinowski, Bronislaw, 27
Maller, O., 190, 191
Malun, 587
Manaster, G. J., 117
Mancini, J. A., 153
Mandler, J. M., 270
Manis, J., 444, 446, 449, 541
Manton, K. G., 472
Marcia, James, 404–5
Marcus, D. E., 609
Marcus, G., 326
Marcus, J., 229
Margolin, F., 659
Marion, R. W., 83
Mariwaki, S. Y., 519
Marker events, 626
Markman, E. M., 361
Marks, L. E., 192
Markus, H., 412, 541
Marolla, F., 82
Marolla, G. A., 325
Marrett, C. B., 619
Marriage, 439–43, 446–47, 473
divorce, 458–59, 460, 477–87

Marriage, *continued*
  stepfamilies, 487–89
  traditional, 442
Martin, A. D., 143
Martin, C., 137
Martin, C. E., 149, 153
Martin, C. L., 612, 613
Martin, D. D., 85
Martin, J. A., 456, 458, 501
Martin, J. C., 85
Martin, J. L., 153
Martin, M. M., 105
Martin, W. T., 640
Marx, G., 9
Masani, P. A., 248
Mash, E. U., 212
Maslin, C. A., 454
Maslow, Abraham H., 24, 30, 327, 385, 395, 406–8
Massoth, N. A., 139
Masters, W. H., 134, 138, 159, 513, 598
Masturbation, 135, 137–39, 141–42, 146–48, 159–60
Matarazzo, J. D., 308, 309, 315
Matas, L., 455
Maternal employment, 460–61, 541
Maternal sensitization, 82
Mattessich, P. W., 438, 439, 440, 445
Matthews, S. H., 477
Matthews, W. S., 532
Maturationism, 11, 24, 28–29
Mauer, D., 168, 176
Maurer, A., 650
Maurer, D., 180
May, Rollo, 645
Mayer, J., 113, 115, 116
Mays, V. M., 152, 655
Mead, G. H., 409
Mead, M., 446
Mead, Margaret, 7, 24, 27, 421, 474, 589–90, 602
Meadors, A. C., 237
Mediation theory, 223–25
Medical sociology, 637
Medlin, R. G., 243
Meece, J. L., 593, 620
Mehler, J., 186
Meiosis, 71, 72
Meir, E. I., 153
Melamed, L. E., 220
Melear, J. D., 650
Melella, J., 139
Melhuish, E., 186
Meltzoff, A. N., 228
Memory, 239–51, 364
Men. *See* Gender differences; Gender roles
Menarche, 129–30
Mendelson, M. J., 196
Mendelson, T., 194

Menez-Bautista, R., 83
Menopause, 130–31, 596
Menstruation. *See* Menarche; Menopause
Mental retardation, 306–7
Menyuk, P., 343, 344
Mercer, Jane, 310
Meredith, William, 188
Merrill, Maud, 301
Mesoderm, 76
Metamemory, 250–51
Metcalf, P., 643
Metress, E. K., 99, 100
Metress, S. P., 99, 100
Meyer, B. J. F., 248
Meyer, C., 361
Meyer, G., 314
Meyer, H., 145
Meyer, K., 325
Meyners, R., 159, 160
Microsphere play, 525–26
Mikaye, K., 289
Miles, C. C., 312
Miles, W. R., 312
Milewski, A. E., 173
Milgram, J., 473
Milgram, S., 49
Miller, A. A., 444
Miller, B. C., 448
Miller, C., 658
Miller, G. A., 342
Miller, J. D., 186
Miller, L. H., 223
Miller, Patricia H., 11, 15, 16, 29, 31, 33
Miller, R. W., 86
Miller, S., 470, 520
Miller, S. A., 60, 62
Miller, W. B., 357, 443
Mills, N., 186
Mimpen, A. M., 189
Minden, K., 452
Minton, H. L., 208
Minuchin, P. P., 509
Miranda, S. B., 174
Mistretta, C. M., 192
Misumi, J., 536
Mitchell, K. R., 117
Mitchell, O., 543
Mitchell, O. S., 543
Mitford, Jessica, 638
Mitosis, 71, 72
Mobley, L. A., 464
Modern marriage, 442
Modified extended family, 469–70
Moffitt, A. R., 185
Moffitt, R., 543
Molfese, D. L., 348
Molfese, V. J., 348
Molitor, N., 454
Moment, G. B., 633

Monahan, D. J., 472
Money, John, 127, 128, 579, 585, 586
Monge, R. H., 234, 235
Montemayor, R., 412, 467
Moody, Raymond, 625
Mooney, L., 589
Moore, J. W., 6, 7
Moore, K., 478
Moore, L. M., 192
Moore, M. J., 172, 175
Moore, M. K., 228
Moore, T., 248, 311, 326, 509
Moorman, J. E., 441, 477
Moral absolutism, 574
Morality, 545–74
  behavior, 559–68
  of care, 569–71
  of constraint, 552–53
  of cooperation, 553
  cross-cultural research, 571–74
  development theories, 546–59
  gender differences, 550, 568–71
  of justice, 569–71
Moran, M., 191, 192
Morawski, J. G., 616, 617
Moreland, J., 487, 596
Moriarty, A. E., 424, 425
Morphology, 345, 358, 359–60, 374
Morris, J. T., 587
Morris, N. M., 125
Morrison, D. C., 222
Morrongiello, B. A., 185, 244
Morrow, L., 481
Mortimer, J. T., 595
Moscovitch, M., 265
Moses, N., 115
Moss, H. A., 418, 424
Motherese, 186, 365
Mothers. *See* Parenting; Prenatal development
Mourning, 657–58
MOW International Research Team, 536
Mueller, D. P., 478
Mueller, E., 502, 508, 532
Mueller, M. L., 642
Mugford, S., 519
Muir, D., 196
Mullener, N., 412
Muller, E., 348
Müllerian-inhibiting substance, 127
Multivariate statistics, 43–44, 45
Munley, A., 662
Munroe, R. H., 9, 289, 609
Munroe, R. L., 9, 289, 609
Murad, F., 73
Murphy, C. M., 353
Murphy, Lois B., 424, 425
Murphy, M. D., 251
Murry, T., 348
Mussen, P., 97, 112, 116, 496

Muuss, R. E., 17, 18, 28, 33
Myelination, 95–96
Myers, B. J., 452

Nadelman, L., 462, 464
Naeye, R. L., 84
Nagel, R., 514
Nagy, Jill, 39, 40–41, 42, 43, 44, 46, 59
Nagy, M. H., 648, 649, 650, 653
Narrative observation methods, 54
Nash, A., 507
Nash, S. C., 610
Nathan, J. G., 212
National Center for Health Statistics, 441
National Institute of Child Health, 88
Nativist approach to language development, 367, 369–71
Natural experiment, 50–51
Naturalism, 24, 28
Nature-nurture controversy, 10–12, 23, 24, 28–29, 30, 402
  intelligence, 318–26
  language development, 366–69, 371–72, 375
Naus, M. J., 243, 245
NBAS (Brazelton Neonatal Behavioral Assessment Scale), 89
Near death experiences (NDEs), 625–26
Nehra, P. C., 88
Neisser, U., 251
Nelson, 176
Nelson, G. K., 489
Nelson, K., 263, 349, 353, 368
Nelson, M., 209, 489
Nelson, V. L., 311
Neonatal development. *See* Infancy
Nerlove, S. B., 288, 289, 290
Nesselhoff, S. E. A., 152
Nesselroade, J. R., 63–64, 315
Neugarten, Bernice L., 6, 7, 131, 132, 424, 427, 430, 431, 474, 475, 477, 521, 522, 596, 655
Neulinger, J., 534
Neurons, 95
Nevis, S., 174
Newcomer, S. F., 145
Newton, N., 134, 446
Nichols, R., 321, 327, 419
Nielsen, C. R., 192
Ninio, A., 353
Nisan, M., 573
Nisbett, R., 191
Noelker, L. S., 472
Noirot, E., 196
Noland, M., 641, 642
Noppe, I. C., 331, 333, 409, 413, 414, 417, 447, 448
Noppe, L. D., 331, 333, 417, 447, 448

Nord, C. W., 481
Normative tradition, 29. *See also* Age norms
Norton, A. J., 441, 477, 478
Notzon, F. C., 88
Novack, L. L., 350
Nowak, C. A., 248
Noyes, R., Jr., 626
Nutrition, 81, 103, 290
Nyiti, Raphael, 288
Nystrom, E. P., 534

Objective anxiety, 525
Obler, L. K., 364, 365, 366
Observational learning, 226–27, 548–49
Observational research, 53–56
Oden, Sherri, 514
Offer, D., 145, 430, 467
Offer, J. B., 430
Okun, M. A., 417, 424
Old age
  attention, 215
  and attractiveness stereotype, 120
  cognitive development, 282–83
  death, concepts of, 656
  divorce, 480
  gender roles, 597–98
  intelligence, 312–15, 316–18
  intergenerational relations, 469, 470, 471–72
  language, 365–66
  learning, 234–35, 236–37, 238, 239
  memory, 246–47, 248, 249–50, 251
  personality development, 395, 396, 401–2, 413–14, 415–17
  physical development, 96, 99–100, 102, 103, 106, 112–13
  play, 535–36
  research on, 22, 62
  sensory impairment, 180–82, 187–90, 192–93
  sexuality, 155–60
  sibling relationships, 474
  social relations, 518–19, 520, 521–22
O'Leary, K. D., 617
Olejnik, S. F., 237
Oliver, C. M., 220
Oller, D., 354
Olsho, L. W., 185, 187, 189, 190
Olson, G. M., 174, 175, 176, 209, 213, 244
Olweus, D., 550
O'Malley, P., 537
Operant conditioning, 217–18, 220, 221–23, 226, 601–6
Operational definition, 39
Opper, S., 262, 284, 287
Oral stage of development, 389–90

Organismic theories, 24, 28–30
Origins of Intelligence in Children, The (Piaget), 47
Orlansky, M. D., 350
Orlos, J. B., 113
Ornstein, P. A., 243, 245
Orr, L. E., 117
Orthner, D. K., 153
Ory, M. G., 443
Osofsky, H. J., 447
Osofsky, J. D., 447
Osser, H., 200
Ossification, 98
Osteoporosis, 99
Oster, H., 191
Ostrov, E., 145, 467
Ottinger, D., 83
Overton, W. F., 609
Overton, W. R., 532
Owen, M., 454
Owens, W. A., 312
Owsley, C., 180

Pahwa, S., 83
Paige, J. M., 602
Paige, K. E., 602
Paired-associate design, 234
Paired comparisons, 170
Palmer, A. P., 235, 236
Palmore, E., 313, 417
Pankhurst, D., 185
Paolitto, D. P., 568
Papalia, D. E., 282, 283
Papousek, H., 221
Parental imperative, 595–96
Parenting, 443–69. *See also* Childhood; Family; Genetics; Prenatal development
  attachment, 449–55
  in behaviorist theory, 25, 65
  and cognitive development, 289–90
  and divorce, 481–83
  and gender roles, 459, 584–85, 590, 595–96, 600–601, 602–5
  and hyperactivity, 213
  and intelligence, 324–25
  and language development, 367
  and maternal employment, 460–61
  and moral development, 551–52
  and personality development, 391, 394, 397–98, 425
  and sexuality, 136, 151
  stress, 446–48
  styles, 455–58
Parham, I. A., 315, 424
Paris, S. G., 245, 250
Park, D. C., 248, 250
Park, K. A., 454
Parke, R. D., 229, 230, 530, 550
Parker-Cohen, N. Y., 419

Parkes, C. M., 597, 658, 659, 660
Parkinson, S. R., 247
Parmelee, A. H., 91
Parsons, J. E., 584, 614, 620
Parten, M. E., 530
Pasternak, J. K., 41
Paton, D., 180
Patrick, G. T. W., 524
Patrick, R., 656
Pattern perception, 173–75
Patterson, D. G., 93
Pattison, E. M., 627, 646
Paulson, R., 241
Pavlov, Ivan, 216
Pearlin, L. I., 469, 482
Peatling, J. H., 559
Peck, M. P., 190
Pedersen, J., 507
Pederson, D., 532
Pederson, F. A., 448
Peeke, H. V. S., 194
Peer-group relations, 134, 509–17, 605.
    See also Social relations
Peiner, J., 553
Pelosi, N., 152
Pennypacker, H. S., 223
Peplau, L. A., 442
Pepler, D., 464
Perceptual development, 167–203
    cognitive aspects, 16, 197–203
    hearing, 182–90, 364, 366
    smell, 193–95
    taste, 190–93
    touch, 195–96
    vision, 168–82
Perlmutter, M., 223, 234
Permissive parenting, 456–58
Perrotta, M., 452
Perry, D. G., 606, 607
Perry, J. D., 485
Pershad, D., 325
Personal Attributes Questionnaire
    (PAQ), 616
Personality development, 383–431
    cross-cultural research, 421–23
    developmental psychopathology,
        427–31
    heritability, 418–20
    psychoanalytic theory, 385–403, 404,
        410, 413, 423
    self, 403–17, 654
Personality inventories, 383–85
Peskin, H., 112
Pestalozzi, Heinrich, 19
Petersen, A. C., 98, 99, 101, 107, 109,
    110, 111, 115, 116, 119, 308, 467
Peterson, G. W., 447
Peterson, J. L., 481, 485
Peterson, R. E., 579, 580

Peterson, R. L., 222
Peterson, W. A., 427
Pettersen, L., 177, 198
Petti, T. A., 654
Pettito, A., 343
Pfeiffer, E., 155
Pfouts, J. H., 465
Phallic stage of development, 391
Phelps, E., 361
Phenomenological theories, 403
Phenotype, 70–71
Phipps-Yonas, S., 110
Phonology, 344–45, 354–55, 359–60
Physical attractiveness, 109, 113–16,
    118–20
Physical development, 69–120. *See
    also* Prenatal development
    birth process, 86–88
    body, 93–106
    brain, 94–96
    gender differences, 73, 88, 97, 98–
        99, 101, 102–3, 104, 127–34
    genetic influences, 70–73
    individual variations, 107–13
    infants, 88–93, 94, 97, 100, 101, 102,
        104
    old age, 96, 99–100, 102, 103, 106,
        112–13
    psychological issues, 113–20
    reproductive system, 127–34
    vision, 168–69
Piaget, Jean, 10, 24, 29, 255–56
    on adult cognitive development,
        282–83, 284
    on creativity, 331
    criticisms of, 284–86
    and education, 284, 289
    on intelligence, 257–59, 296
    on language development, 372–73
    on moral development, 552–53, 556,
        558, 566
    on play, 526–27, 528, 529, 533
    on reflexes, 90–91
    research methods, 47
    on sensory integration, 196
    on social cognition, 496, 504, 506
    on social learning, 227–28
    on stages of cognitive development,
        259–81
Pick, A. D., 200
Pietromonaco, P. R., 541
Pilon, R., 196, 359
Pisoni, D. P., 184
Pittelkow, Y., 520
Pittenger, John, 118, 120
Pitts, D., 181
Pituitary gland, 71
Placek, P. J., 88
Placenta, 76

Plant, W. T., 308
Plantinga, A., 195
Plato, 11, 16
Play, 522–36
Play therapy, 32
Pleck, J. H., 144, 145, 588
Plomin, R., 418, 419, 466, 510
Plomp, R., 189
Plude, D. J., 208, 215
Podolsky, S., 180
Polikanina, R. I., 221
Pollack, S., 570
Poloma, M. M., 442
Polonko, K. A., 439
Pomeroy, W. B., 137, 149
Poon, L. W., 190, 247, 248
Popularity, 513–17
Population, 40
Porter, R. H., 193, 194
Postconventional morality, 553, 554,
    556, 558, 560, 565, 572, 573
Postman, N., 20, 21
Potash, M., 417
Poterba, J., 542
Powell, P. H., 118
Powell, P. M., 504, 506
Power, T. G., 530
Pozner, J., 374–75
Pozzebon, S., 543
Practice play, 526–27
Pragmatics, 347, 352–53, 354, 358,
    360, 361–62, 366
Prawat, R., 653
Preconventional morality, 553, 554,
    556, 559, 561, 564–65, 572
Premack, D., 342
Prenatal development, 73–86, 94, 97,
    100
    perceptual, 168, 184, 193, 195
    reproductive system, 127–29
Pre-operational intelligence, 265–71,
    561, 653
Prescott, P. A., 187
Price, C. G., 326
Price-Williams, D., 288
Primary process thinking, 388
Prince, R. M., 446, 447, 449
Prinz, R. J., 213
Prinz, S. M., 41
Problem solving, 235–37
Proctor, C. P., 618
Productive process of language, 342–
    43, 364
Progesterone, 73
Proximodistal growth, 104
Psychic determinism, 32, 386
Psychoanalytic theory, 10, 24, 30–33,
    135, 151
    Adler's theory, 394

Psychoanalytic theory, *continued*
  criticisms of, 393, 394–95, 601
  death and dying, 627, 644–46, 654
  gender roles, 151, 402, 591, 595–96,
    600–601, 602
  Horney's theory, 30, 395, 601
  Jung's theory, 394–95, 595
  morality, 551–52
  personality development, 385–403,
    404, 410, 413, 423
  play, 525–26
  sexuality, 32, 33, 135, 137–38, 151
Psychodynamics, 385
Psychological autopsy, 631, 633
Psychological death, 629–31
Psychology in interdisciplinary studies,
    8–10, 644–48
Psychosocial crisis, 396
Puberty. *See* Adolescence
Puglisi, J. T., 250
Pulakos, J., 462, 473
Pulkkinen, L., 458
Punishment, 218–20
Pupil, 168
Puri, R., 325

Quay, H. C., 222
Queenan, J. T., 88
Questionnaires, 53
Quinn, J., 543

Rabbitt, P. M. A., 214, 215
Race, 112, 310, 478, 618, 639
Radabaugh, C., 469
Radin, N., 459
Radke-Yarrow, M., 502, 503, 504
Raether, H. C., 638
Raj, M. H., 125
Rall, T. W., 73
Ramey, C. T., 325, 530
Ramsay, D., 452
Ramsey, F., 325
Raschke, H. J., 444, 477, 479
Rasinsky, K., 182
Raskin, L., 308
Ratner, N., 530
Rayias, M., 242
Rayner, R., 217
Reading, 200–201
Realism, 17
Receptive process of language, 342–
    43, 361, 364
Reconstituted family, 487–89
Reed, G. L., 452
Reed, R. B., 97
Reedy, M. N., 416
Reese, H. W., 220, 221
Reflexes, 89–91
Regnemer, J. L., 573

Reich, P. A., 350, 373
Reikowitz, D., 139
Reimer, J., 568, 573
Reinforcement, 218
Reinisch, J. M., 580
Reiss, I. L., 143
Relativistic operations, 506
Reliability, 300
Renaissance, 17–18
Renner, J. W., 282, 287
Renninger, K. A., 242
Renshaw, P. D., 510, 516
Reproductive system, 127–34
Rescorla, L., 353
Research, 5, 9, 16, 22, 37, 62, 65. *See
    also* Cross-cultural research
  data collection methods, 52–58
  ethical considerations, 45, 48–49, 78
  gender roles, 614–15
  infant perception, 170
  intelligence, 312–15
  locations, 50–51
  personality development, 383, 402,
    424
  scientific method, 38–44
  sexuality, 134–35
  strategies, 44–51, 52
Response set, 51
Rest, James, 548, 555, 559, 560, 566,
    568, 570, 573
Retina, 168
Reuter, M. W., 459
Reversal shift, 224–25
Reynolds, D. K., 631, 639
Rheingold, H. L., 223, 353, 502, 587
Rh factor, 82
Ricciuti, H. N., 325, 509
Rice, B., 310
Rice, F. P., 362, 512
Rice, G. E., 248
Rich, J., 119
Richards, B., 248, 558
Richards, M., 115
Richardson, D. W., 132
Richardson, G. E., 641
Richardson, R. M., 642
Richardson, S. A., 119, 325
Richmond, V. P., 510
Rickert, E. J., 220
Riegel, Klaus F., 23, 62, 314, 430
Riegel, R. M., 62, 314
Rierdan, J., 107
Rifkin, B., 192
Ring, Kenneth, 625
Ripple, R. E., 334
Ritter, P. L., 110, 111
Robbins, S., 566, 568
Roberts, D., 211
Roberts, M. D., 470

Roberts, S. O., 324, 326
Roberts, W. A., 212
Robertson, J. F., 474, 476, 477
Robinson, B. A., 247
Robinson, C. C., 587
Robinson, N. M., 327
Robinson, Pauline K., 157
Roche, A. F., 97, 98
Rodeheaver, D., 237, 285, 427
Rodgers, J. L., 326
Rodgers, R., 439
Rodgers, W. L., 417, 441, 443
Rodin, Judith, 113, 114, 115, 116, 416
Rogers, C. C., 444, 477, 481, 482
Rogers, Carl, 24, 30, 403
Rogoff, B., 288, 289
Rokosz, S., 313
Role-taking, 499–501
Rollins, B., 439, 447, 448
Romaine, W., 363
Romaniuk, J. G., 331, 334
Romaniuk, M., 331, 334
Ronald, L., 119
Roodin, P. A., 208
Roopnarine, J. L., 605
Rose, M. D., 125, 146, 147, 148, 149–
    50, 151, 152
Rose, R. J., 418
Rose, R. M., 125
Rosenbaum, M., 114
Rosenblatt, D., 529
Rosenblith, J. F., 84, 170, 186
Rosenfeld, A., 635
Rosenkrantz, Paul S., 580, 581
Rosenstein, D., 191
Rosenthal, R., 618
Ross, D., 226, 549
Ross, E., 238
Ross, G. S., 271
Ross, H., 473
Ross, H. S., 508, 529
Ross, H. W., 223
Ross, R., 588
Ross, S. A., 226, 549
Rossiter, C. M., 472
Roth, K., 504, 505
Rothbart, M. K., 419
Rothblum, E. D., 615
Rousseau, Jean-Jacques, 24, 28
Routh, D. K., 212, 213
Rovee-Collier, C. K., 194, 195, 244
Rovine, M. R., 447, 454
Rowe, D. C., 326, 510
Rowland, K. F., 656
Rozin, P. 116
Rubenstein, A., 83
Rubenstein, J. L., 528
Rubin, K. H., 523, 526, 529, 530, 532,
    533

Rubin, R. T., 580
Ruble, D. N., 129, 585, 603, 612, 614, 616, 617
Ruff, H. A., 195
Ruhm, C. J., 542, 543
Rumbaugh, Duane, 343
Runfola, D. R., 113
Runyan, D. K., 139
Russell, M. J., 194
Russo, P., 81
Rutter, M., 428
Ryan, J., 498, 499
Rybash, J. M., 208
Ryckman, R., 408
Rykken, D. E., 146

Sabo, F., 113
Sabom, M. B., 625
Saenger, G., 82
Safier, G., 651
Sagi, A., 501
Sakai, R., 185
Salapatek, P., 169, 171, 172, 173, 174, 175, 177, 178, 179
Salvador, M. A., 464
Salvia, J., 119
Saltz, E., 374–75, 532
Sameroff, A. J., 220, 221
Sample, 39, 40
Samuelson, M., 108
Sander, G., 634
Sanders, L. W., 348
Sanders, R. E., 251
Sanders, R. J., 343
Sandfort, T., 138
Sandman, B. M., 85
Sands, Laura, 188
Sangl, J., 471
Santogrossi, D. A., 514
Santow, G., 441
Sarangadharan, M. G., 83
Sarnat, H. B., 193
Sattler, J. M., 297
Sauer, W. J., 417
Saunders, C., 660
Sayre, S. A., 282, 287
Scammon, R. E., 93
Scanzioni, J., 439
Scarr, S., 322
Schaal, 193
Schacter, D. L., 265
Schaefer, C. E., 32
Schaefer, E. S., 324, 327, 418
Schaie, K. Warner, 62, 239, 312, 314, 315, 424
Schaffer, H. R., 348, 418
Scharlach, A. E., 472
Schatz, M., 358
Schema, 612

Schemes, 259–60
Scherr, R. L., 120
Schetky, D. H., 138
Schieber, F., 182
Schiff, W., 197
Schlarb, J., 646, 647
Schmitt, L. A., 251
Schneider, B., 184, 185
Schneider, F. W., 308
Schnell, S. V., 574
Schnoll, S. H., 85
Schoen, R. W., 439
Schonfield, D., 247
Schools. *See* Education; Learning
Schoon, C., 185
Schuknecht, H. L., 187
Schulz, H. R., 91
Schulz, R., 644
Schumaker, J. F., 111
Schwartz, P. M., 86, 135
Schwartz, S. H., 559
Schwebel, A. I., 487
Scott, J., 462, 534, 535
Scribner, J., 288
Sears, Pauline, 309
Sears, Robert, 309
Secondary process thinking, 388
Secord, P. L., 116
Secular trend, 98
Segal, S. A., 510
Seidner, L. B., 529
Sekuler, R., 180, 182
Self, 403–17, 654
Self, P. A., 596
Self-actualization, 406–8
Self-concept, 111, 409–14. *See also* Self; Self-esteem
Self-esteem, 116–18, 295, 306, 409, 414–17. *See also* Self; Self-concept
Selman, Robert, 500
Semail, A. H., 117
Semantics, 346–47, 357–58, 359, 360, 366, 371
Sengul, C. J., 357
Senn, M. J. E., 29
Sensorimotor intelligence, 259–65, 287
Sensorimotor play, 528
Sensory development. *See* Perceptual development
Sensory impairment, 180–82, 187–90, 192–93
Sequential research, 63–64, 314–15
Serbin, L. A., 587, 617
Seriation, 273–74
Sexual abuse, child, 138–39
Sexuality, 134–62. *See also* Heterosexual activity; Homosexuality; Physical development; Psychoanalytic theory

in adolescence, 125, 140–45, 146–47
adult behavior, 145–55
biological factors, 125–26
and body image, 115–17
childhood, 137–40
and dating, 513
gender differences, 139, 148, 157–58, 160–61
gender roles, 110, 151, 160–62, 598
infancy, 135–37
and menopause, 131
old age, 155–60
and parenting, 447
in psychoanalytic theory, 32, 33, 135, 137–38, 151
Sexual polarization, 591
Shaheen, S. J., 86
Shanas, E., 470
Shantz, C. U., 496, 501
Shape constancy, 177–79
Shapiro, E., 470
Sharabany, R., 499, 609
Sharma, M., 325
Sharps, M. J., 248, 249
Sheare, J. B., 119
Sheehy, G., 537
Shepherd-Look, D. L., 586, 617
Sherman, J. A., 551, 593
Sherman, M., 324
Sherman, S., 519, 644
Sherman, T., 174, 175, 176, 209, 213, 244
Sherrod, L. R., 176
Shields, J., 321
Shields, S. A., 614
Shimmin, H. S., 609
Shipman, G., 132
Shlapack, W., 194
Shmavonian, B. M., 223
Shneidman, E. S., 631, 647
Shock, 634, 635
Short, R. V., 132
Short-term memory, 240
Shukla, D. G., 414
Shulman, N., 518
Shultz, R., 647
Shultz, T., 359
Shyness, 510
Sibling relationships, 462–67, 472–74
SIDS (Sudden Infant Death Syndrome), 84, 659
Siegel, R. K., 626
Siegler, I. C., 424, 426
Siegler, R. S., 173, 176, 179, 186, 196
Siemsen, D., 180
Sigafoos, A. D., 229
Sigal, J., 139
Sign language, 350–51
Silberstein, L., 113, 115

Simmons, J., 84
Simmons, L. W., 643
Simmons, R. G., 108
Simner, M. L., 501
Simon, E. E., 248
Simon, W., 148
Simonton, D. K., 334
Sims-Knight, J. E., 84, 170, 186
Sinclair, M., 196
Singer, J. L., 532
Singer, L. M., 452
Sinnott, Edmund, 331
Sinnott, J. D., 506
Size constancy perception, 177–79
Skeels, H., 324
Skinner, B. F., 24, 25–26
Slaby, R., 550, 611, 612
Slade, A., 454
Slaymaker, F., 41
Sleeper effects, 424
Slobin, D. I., 355, 356, 371, 372
Small, L., 111
Smallwood, K. B., 620
Smart, M. S., 98, 100, 103
Smart, R. C., 98, 100, 103
Smell, sense of, 193–95
Smetana, J. G., 467, 608
Smiley, S. S., 244, 270
Smith, A. D., 250
Smith, D., 81, 84, 85
Smith, E. A., 146
Smith, G. J., 119
Smith, J. H., 353
Smith, K. V., 223
Smith, M., 564, 568
Smith, R., 45, 238
Smith, W. M., 223
Smits, G. J., 118, 119
Smollar, H., 498, 499
Smollar, J., 496, 498
Snarey, J. R., 573
Snipper, A. S., 288, 289, 290
Snow, C. E., 353, 362, 368
Snyder, E. E., 113, 117, 516
Sobesky, William, 562, 563
Social clock, 6
Social cognition, 496–501, 504, 506
Social death, 629–31
Social learning theory, 26, 225–34,
    449–50, 453, 548–51, 606–8
Social relations, 495–543
    development, 496–506
    employment, 536–43
    patterns, 506–22, 586, 587
    play, 522–36
Socioeconomic status, 310, 374–76,
    478, 618, 639
Sociology, 8, 9, 636–42
Soldo, B. J., 472

Solimano, G., 325
Sollie, D. L., 448
Solyom, L., 223
Somatic mutation theory, 635
Somerville, S. C., 250
Sommer, B. B., 142
SOMPA (System of Multicultural
    Pluralistic Assessment), 310
Sonnenschein, S., 361
Sonnenstein, F. L., 144, 145
Sontag, L. W., 311, 326
Sontag, S., 598
Sorenson, R. C., 142, 143
Sosnowski, R. J., 41
Soule, W. T., 540
Spaid, W. M., 472
Spanier, G., 441
Spearman, C., 297
Spears, W. C., 185, 195
Specimen descriptions, 54
Speicher-Dubin, B., 555
Spelke, E. S., 196, 197, 198, 202, 265
Spence, A. P., 96, 103, 112, 134
Spence, J. T., 615, 616
Spencer, Herbert, 524
Sperduto, V., 185
Spermarche, 132, 134
Spieker, S., 186
Spina bifida, 76–77, 78
Spitzer, M. E., 192, 193
Spokane, A. R., 538
Spoor, A., 188
Spurzheim, Johann, 614
Sroufe, A., 213
Sroufe, L. A., 428, 454, 455
Stages, developmental, 14–15, 18, 28
Standardized tests or tasks, 56–58
Stanford-Binet Intelligence Scale, 296,
    301
Stanhope, T., 419
Stark, R., 125
Starr, B. D., 158
Statistics, 41–44, 45, 306–7
Stattin, H., 110
Stayton, D. J., 453
Stearn, I. B., 190
Stechler, B., 84, 85
Steffire, V., 372
Stein, A. H., 231, 233
Stein, J., 656
Stein, M. R., 508
Stein, P., 520
Stein, S., 642
Stein, Z. H., 82
Steinberg, L. D., 107, 109, 110, 111,
    112, 509, 511, 516
Steiner, J. E., 191, 194
Steinmetz, S., 550
Steinschneider, A., 85
Stepfamilies, 487–89

Stereopsis, 176, 177
Stereotypes, 157, 158, 489. See also
    Gender roles
    physical attractiveness, 109, 113–16,
    118–20
Stern, D. M., 530
Stern, D. N., 186
Sternberg, R. J., 298, 300
Sternglanz, S. H., 587
Steuer, F. B., 45, 46
Stevens, J. C., 195
Stevens, R., 84
Stevens-Long, J., 538, 587
Stevenson, H. W., 231
Stevenson, M. B., 447
Stevenson, M. R., 604
Stewart, C., 140, 141
Stewart, R. B., 464
Stier, M., 452
Stine, E. A. L., 248
Stinnett, N., 479
Stith, M., 509, 511
Stock, W. A., 417
Stoddard, P., 115
Stoddart, T., 591
Stodolsky, S., 374
Stone, B. P., 243
Stone, R., 471, 472
Stoneburner, R. L., 83
Stott, D. H., 84
Straus, M. A., 550
Strauss, A., 647
Streib, G. L., 521
Streissguth, A. P., 85
Striegel-Moore, R. H., 113, 115, 116
Strommen, E. A., 519
Strother, C. R., 312, 314
Stuart, R. B., 115
Sublimation, 393
Sudden Infant Death Syndrome (SIDS),
    84, 659
Sudnow, D., 636
Suggs, P. K., 473, 474
Suicide, 639–40, 645, 654
Sulik, K. K., 85
Summers, L., 542
Sunderland, A., 251
Super, D. E., 542
Superego, 388–89
Surface structure of language, 343–44,
    359
Survey research method, 52–53
Susser, M. W., 82
Sussman, M. B., 470, 479
Sutton-Smith, Brian, 526
Swartz, K. B., 173
Swarz, J. D., 421
Sweet, J., 441, 442, 444, 477, 478
Sykes, D. H., 246
Symbolic play, 527

Syntax, 345–46, 374. *See also* Grammar
System of Multicultural Pluralistic
    Assessment (SOMPA), 310

Taffel, S. M., 88
Taft, L. T., 90
Taipale, V., 108
Tait, P., 376
Tajima, N., 289
Tallmer, J., 651
Tallmer, M., 651
Tamis-LeMonda, C., 209
Tannenhaus, M., 248
Tanner, J. M., 71, 94, 97, 98, 99, 101,
    102, 103, 105, 107, 132
Taste, sense of, 190–93
Tate, R. B., 470
Taub, H. A., 248
Tavris, C., 602
Taylor, I. A., 330
Taylor, J. M., 571
Teachman, J. D., 439, 441, 478, 479
Telegraphic speech, 355
Television, 211–14, 230, 231–34, 587–
    89, 650, 651
Temperament, 418
Templer, D. I., 651
Teratogens, 81–86
Terman, Lewis M., 296, 301, 309
Terminal drop, 62
Terrace, H. S., 343
Tessman, L. H., 483
Test bias, 310, 374
Testosterone, 73, 98–99, 125–26, 127,
    132, 151
Thal, J., 115
Thanatology, 626
Thanatos, 386–87
Theory. *See* Developmental theory
Thevenin, D. M., 349
Thinness, female preoccupation with,
    115–16
Thomas, A., 332, 418, 419, 420
Thompson, C., 466
Thompson, Clara, 601
Thompson, R., 452
Thompson, R. A., 454
Thorbecke, C. R., 404
Thornburg, H. D., 138, 140
Thorndike, Edward L., 217–18
Thornton, A., 441
Thurnher, M., 517, 519
Thurstone, L. L., 297
Tiedemann, Dietrich, 19
Tieger, T., 590
Time lag research, 62–63
Time-sampling observation method, 54
Tobian, L., 193
Tobin, P., 593
Tobin, S. S., 521, 522

Tobin-Richards, M., 109, 111, 114
Tomick, I. J., 617
Tomlinson, P. S., 448
Tootel, H. E., 178
Torgersen, A. M., 212
Tortora, Gerard J., 71, 80, 97, 103
Toseland, R. W., 472
Touch, sense of, 195–96
Toussieng, D. W., 425
Townsend, J. W., 290
Traditional marriage, 442
Transductive reasoning, 266–67
Traub, G. S., 510
Travin, A., 139
Treadwell, M. C., 88
Treat, N. J., 247, 313
Trehub, S. E., 184, 185, 186
Troll, Lillian E., 6, 97, 100, 101, 112,
    326, 449, 469, 470, 517, 518, 520,
    540, 621
Trophins, 72
Tross, S., 655
Tuddenham, R. D., 658
Tulving, E., 265
Tumir, 596
Turiel, E., 573, 591
Turner, B. F., 597, 615
Turner, R., 190
Turpin, R., 185

Udry, J. R., 125, 145
Ulatowska, H. K., 366
Ullian, D. Z., 591, 592
Umberson, D., 119
Unconscious motivation, 32, 386, 394
Unger, O., 529
Unger, R. K., 582
Uninvolved parenting, 458
Univariate statistics, 43–44
Unpreparedness hypothesis, 640–41
Upp, M., 542
Urberg, K. A., 326, 591, 603, 606
Urton, K. W., 439
Uzgiris, I. C., 229

Validity, 300
Valliant, G. E., 425
Vandenberg, B., 523, 526, 529, 533
Vander Linde, E., 244
Van der Wal, J., 658
Van Tuyl, S. S., 464
Variables, 38, 39, 45–47, 60
Vaughn, B. E., 114, 119, 450, 454
Veatch, R. M., 628
Veevers, J. E., 445, 446
Vener, A., 140, 141
Verbal learning, 234–35
Vernon, P. E., 322
Veroff, J., 460
Vigorito, J., 186

Vilberg, W. R., 326
Villeneuve-Gokalp, C., 441
Vision, 168–82
Visual acuity, 169–71
Vocabulary, 349–51, 374
Vogel, Susan Raymond, 580, 581
Volpe, J., 498
Von Hofsten, C., 197
Vurpillot, E., 210, 211
Vygotsky, Lev, 373

Waber, D. P., 593
Wade, C., 602
Wadner, D., 656
Wagner, M., 308
Wahler, R. G., 222
Waite, L., 478
Waite, L. W., 478
Waldbaum, A., 313
Walder, L. O., 233, 550
Waldman, E., 539
Waldrop, M. L., 511
Walk, R. D., 192, 210, 211
Walker, L. J., 558, 562, 567, 570
Wall, S., 453
Wallace, D. B., 330
Wallace, R. W., 472
Wallace, W., 313
Wallach, M. A., 329
Wallerstein, Judith S., 479, 480, 481,
    483, 484, 485, 486, 487
Walsh, D., 182, 326
Walster, E., 115, 118
Walters, R. H., 606
Ward, H., 447
Ward, J. V., 571
Warkany, J., 81, 86
Warland, R., 417
Warr, P. B., 536
Warren, C. A. B., 154, 155
Warren, M. P., 108*f*
Wass, H., 237, 654
Wasserman, S., 265
Waterman, A. S., 426
Waters, E., 452, 453, 454
Watkins, J. J., 246
Watson, J. B., 23, 25, 65, 217
Watson, J. S., 530
Watson, K., 532
Watson, R. I., 17, 19
Watts, K., 251
Weatherly, D., 112, 116
Weaver, C. N., 443
Weaver, S., 248
Webb, M. A., 85
Wechsler, David, 297, 301, 302, 303
Wechsler intelligence tests, 188, 301–
    3, 310
Weg, R. B., 131, 132
Weiffenbach, J. M., 192

Weinberg, M. S., 138, 143
Weiner, B., 550
Weingarten, H., 478
Weinstein, K. K., 474, 475, 477
Weisberg, P., 223
Weiskopf, S., 265
Weisman, A. D., 648
Weiss, B., 213
Weiss, R. S., 597
Weiss, S. J., 176
Weissberg, J. A., 245, 250
Weisz, J. R., 500, 513
Weitzman, L. J., 592
Welch, R., 588
Wellborn, S. N., 10
Weller, E. B., 638
Weller, R. A., 638
Wellman, H. M., 250
Wells, K., 597, 598
Wells, W. D., 119
Wenner, W. H., 91
Wertheimer, M., 196
Whalen, C. K., 212
Whitbourne, S. K., 17, 426
White, C. B., 573
White, E., 653
Whitehurst, G. J., 347
Whiting, B. B., 9, 421, 587
Whiting, J. W .M., 421
Widmayer, S. M., 449
Wild, C., 656
Wilfert, C. M., 83
Wilkinson, L. D., 619
Wilkinson, R. T., 105

Wille, D. E., 454, 509
Willerman, Lee, 308, 309, 320, 383, 384—85, 418
Williams, J. H., 595, 598
Williams, J. W., 509, 511
Williams, T. R., 643
Williamson, J. B., 662
Willis, S. L., 62, 318
Wilson, L., 488
Wilson, S., 520
Wilson, W. C., 155, 156
Wimmer, H., 553
Wimmer, M., 650
Winer, G. A., 272
Wingfield, A., 248
Winick, M., 81, 325
Winkel, G. H., 222
Winn, R., 134
Winslow, L., 182
Winstead, B. A., 113, 114, 115
Wippman, J., 454
Wishart, J. G., 197, 464
Witter, R. A., 417
Wiznia, A. A., 83
Wohlwill, J. F., 46
Wolf, E., 180, 182
Wolf, F. M., 333
Wolff, Peter H., 91, 92, 348
Women. *See* Gender differences; Gender roles
Wood, J., 111
Wood, N., 596
Wooley, O. W., 115
Wooley, S. C., 115

Wooster, C., 159, 160
Worden, J. W., 648
Work. *See* Employment
Wormith, S. J., 185
Wozniak, R. H., 242
Wright, J. C., 588

Yackley, A., 603
Yankelovich, Skelly & White, Inc., 448
Yawkey, T. D., 523, 524
Yeates, K. O., 325
Yogev, S., 442
Yonas, A., 177, 198
Young, R. J., 117, 212
Youniss, J., 273, 496, 498
Yussen, S. R., 250

Zabin, L. S., 146, 147
Zahn-Waxler, Carolyn, 502, 503, 504
Zajonc, R. B., 326
Zakin, D. F., 119
Zalk, S. R., 447
Zarit, S. H., 472
Zeits, C. R., 446, 447, 449
Zelazo, P. R., 529
Zelinski, E. M., 248
Zellman, G. L., 614
Zelnick, M., 144, 145
Zigler, E., 21
Zill, N., 444, 477, 481, 482, 485
Zumeta, Z., 478
Zurcher, L., 488
Zygote, 74